SIXTH EDITION

# Gender in Cross-Cultural Perspective

Edited by

## Caroline B. Brettell

Southern Methodist University

and

## Carolyn F. Sargent

Washington University in St. Louis

Routledge
Taylor & Francis Group

LONDON AND NEW YORK

For Richard Brettell and David Freidel, men who have given new meaning to the gendered division of labor, with gratitude for the intellectual and emotional support that they have provided for many years.

First published 2013, 2009, 2005, 2001, 1997, 1993 by Pearson Education, Inc.

Published 2016 by Routledge

2 Park Square, Milton Park, Abingdon, Oxon OX14 4RN

711 Third Avenue, New York, NY 10017, USA

*Routledge is an imprint of the Taylor & Francis Group, an informa business*

ISBN: 9780205247288 (pbk)

Cover Designer: Suzanne Behnke

**Library of Congress Cataloging-in-Publication Data**
Gender in cross-cultural perspective / edited by Caroline B. Brettell and Carolyn F. Sargent.
   p. cm.
  ISBN-13: 978-0-205-24728-8
  ISBN-10: 0-205-24728-8
  1. Sex role–Cross-cultural studies.  I. Brettell, Caroline.  II. Sargent, Carolyn Fishel
GN479.65.G4634 2012
   305.3—dc23
                                   2012015639

# Contents

# Preface

The initial idea for this reader came from the experience of teaching undergraduate courses in gender and anthropology. In reviewing the textbooks available for an introductory course, we came to the conclusion that there was a need for a readable text that built on the classic contributions of the 1970s while incorporating the more recent and diverse literature on gender roles and ideology around the world. Although a number of sophisticated theoretical works devoted to this subject existed, we felt there was a dearth of classroom material available in one volume and appropriate for less advanced students, whether undergraduates or beginning graduate students.

We have had several goals in mind as we selected materials for the sixth edition. As in previous editions, we want to introduce students to the most significant topics in the field of the anthropology of gender. These include the study of men and women in prehistory; the relationship between biology and culture; the cultural construction of masculinity, femininity, sexuality, personhood, and the body; variations in the sexual division of labor and economic organization; women's involvement in ritual and religion; and the impact of the state and the global economy on gender relations and gender identities. In this edition, we have added some additional articles on lesbian and gay identities.

We have always considered it important to maintain the broad cross-cultural coverage evident in the first edition of this book. This breadth encourages comparative analysis of the themes under discussion and allows us to address issues of gender in industrial society as well as in developing societies. In this edition, we have added a few more articles based on research in North America as well as replaced some older articles with those based on more current field research in some of the sections. Some may find a favorite article no longer in the book. We thought hard about this and decided, based on our own experiences of teaching the class, that several of these articles no longer had an impact on twenty-first century students. We are always willing to receive feedback regarding these "classics."

In the sixth edition, we have asked several new authors to write original pieces (Covey, Gulbas, Joyce, Parikh, Matza, Bowen, Lewin, Santos, and MacDonald) or to adapt previously published pieces for use here (Hirsch, Childs, Brennan, Moodie, Osella and Osella). In this edition, we have also continued to expand the number of studies that deal with masculinity and male gender roles (Santos, Osella and Osella, Lewin).

Although we have maintained a commitment to combining theoretically and ethnographically based essays in the book, in this edition we have included more case studies, choosing to incorporate the broader theoretical questions in our section introductions. In these introductions, we continue to review as clearly as possible some of the significant issues debated in particular subject areas within the anthropology of gender. These introductions, updated for the current edition, are intended to orient students to the essays in the section and to provide a context in which readers can understand more fully each essay. Each introduction concludes with a list of references that can be used by teachers and students to examine further the questions raised in that section.

We do not expect all instructors to assign the sections in the order that they appear in the text. We have maintained the order of the fifth edition but retitled and reorganised the final section to better represent the articles contained in it. The order makes sense to us, but our ultimate goal is to provide for maximum flexibility in teaching. Indeed, there are essays in some sections that can be related to essays in other sections. We also have no intention of imposing a particular theoretical perspective, although our own predilections may be apparent to some readers. We include readings that reflect a variety of theoretical orientations to enable instructors to emphasize their own approach to the subject. We hope that we have compiled a book that can stand alone or, if the instructor so desires, can be complemented by the use of full ethnographies.

## ACKNOWLEDGMENTS

Many people have contributed substantially to the preparation and development of this book over its multiple editions. For the first edition, Andrew Webb provided invaluable clerical and organizational assistance. The undergraduate students in Professor Sargent's course "Gender and Sex Roles: A Global Perspective" have consistently offered valuable criticisms of selected essays. Their opinions continue to influence us enormously in the final selection process. John Phinney acted as an invaluable library of knowledge for obscure references; Sue Linder-Linsley offered indispensable computer advice and tirelessly scanned in text to save us time in the preparation of the second edition; and Sue Racine and Scott Langley contributed clerical assistance. Tim Benner and Louann Miller worked conscientiously to help us complete the third edition; Melissa Nibungco helped us with the fourth edition. We are also grateful to Southern Methodist University for various forms of support over the years.

We want to thank the reviewers of the original manuscript and the professors around the world who have used previous editions and offered valuable suggestions for improvements to the sixth edition. Finally, we wish to acknowledge Sharon Chambliss, formerly with Prentice Hall, who worked with us on the first four editions; Kate Ferguson, Monica Ohlinger, and Sudha Balasundaram who have worked with us on the sixth edition; and Nancy Roberts, who first recognized the importance of this project and whose confidence in our judgment and constant support are much appreciated. We have a wonderful partnership!

*Caroline B. Brettell*
*Carolyn F. Sargent*

# About the Editors

**Caroline Brettell** received her B.A. degree from Yale University and her M.A. and Ph.D. degrees from Brown University. She joined the faculty of the Department of Anthropology at Southern Methodist University in 1988, and in 2008 was named University Distinguished Professor. From 1989 to 1994, she served as Director of Women's Studies, and from 1994 to 2004 she served as Chair of the Department of Anthropology. From 2006 to 2008, she served as Interim Dean of Dedman College, the Humanities and Sciences College at Southern Methodist University. Her research interests are in the areas of immigration, gender roles, European ethnography, and anthropology and history. She is the author of *Men Who Migrate, Women Who Wait: Population and History in a Portuguese Parish* (1986), *We Have Already Cried Many Tears: The Stories of Three Portuguese Migrant Women* (1982, 1995), *Writing against the Wind: A Mother's Life History* (1999), and *Anthropology and Migration: Essays on Transnationalism, Ethnicity and Identity* (2003); coauthor with Richard Brettell of *Painters and Peasants in the 19th Century* (1983); editor of *When They Read What We Write: The Politics of Ethnography* (1993) and *Constructing Borders/Crossing Boundaries: Race, Ethnicity, and Immigration* (2007); coeditor of *International Migration: The Female Experience* (1986), *Gender in Cross-Cultural Perspective* (Prentice Hall 1993, 1997, 2001, 2005), *Gender and Health: An International Perspective* (1996), *Migration Theory: Talking Across Disciplines* (2000, 2007), *Citizenship, Political Engagement, and Belonging: Immigrants in Europe and the U.S.* (2008), and *America's Twenty-First Century Immigrant Gateways: Immigrant Incorporation in Suburbia* (2008). Her most recent book, coauthored with Deborah Reed-Danahay, is titled *Civic Engagements: The Citizenship Practices of Indian and Vietnamese Immigrants* (2012). She is also the author of numerous book chapters, and articles. Professor Brettell has served as a member of National Institutes of Health (NIH) Study Section-SNEM 3 and several selection panels for the Social Science Research Council and the National Endowment for the Humanities (NEH). She has served as President of the Society for the Anthropology of Europe and of the Social Science History Association. She has conducted field research in France, Portugal, Canada, and the United States.

**Carolyn Sargent** received her B.A. degree from Michigan State University, her M.A. degree from the University of Manchester, and her Ph.D. from Michigan State University. She is Professor of Anthropology and Professor of Women, Gender, and Sexuality Studies at Washington University in St. Louis. From 1979 to 2008, she served as Professor of Anthropology at Southern Methodist University, where she was Director of Women's Studies from 1994 through 2007. She is currently a research fellow at IRIS, an interdisciplinary social science laboratory associated with the University of Paris 13, CNRS, EHESS, and INSERM. Her research interests are in the areas of global health, gender and reproduction, and bioethics. Sargent is the author of *The Cultural Context of Therapeutic Choice: Obstetrical Decisions among the Bariba of Benin* (1982), and *Maternity, Medicine and Power: Reproductive Decisions in Urban Benin* (1989); and coeditor of *Reproduction, Globalization and the State* (Duke University Press 2011); *Medical Anthropology: A Handbook of Theory and Method, Gender in*

*Cross-Cultural Perspective* (Prentice Hall 1993, 1997, 2001, 2005), *Gender and Health: An International Perspective* (1996), *Childbirth and Authoritative Knowledge* (1997), and *Small Wars: The Cultural Politics of Childhood* (1998). In addition to several book chapters, she has also authored numerous articles, many of them published in *Medical Anthropological Quarterly* and *Social Science and Medicine.* She has conducted fieldwork in West Africa and the Caribbean and is currently engaged in a long-term study of West African immigrants in France funded by the Wenner Gren Foundation and the National Science Foundation. She has served on a Senior Advisory Panel of the National Science Foundation and on the Executive Board for the Society for Medical Anthropology. She served as President of the Society for Medical Anthropology from 2007 to 2011 and has also served on the French *Agence Nationale de la Recherche* as external reviewer for social science research.

# I

# Biology, Gender, and Human Evolution

What is the role of biology in human behavior? To what extent are differences between men and women explained by biology, by culture, or by an interaction between the two? Is there a biological basis for the sexual division of labor? These questions are hotly debated in the United States as we struggle with such issues as why men dominate the fields of math and science, whether women are equipped for war and combat, and the implications for child development of female participation in the labor force (Blum 1998; Gallagher and Kaufman 2005; Geary 1998; Udry 2000). In this chapter, we consider issues of gender in a cross-cultural context, and we explore whether women are universally subordinated to men and to what extent biological differences explain the allocation of roles and responsibilities between men and women.

The relative importance of biology, or nature, versus culture, or nurture, as these influence sex differences, is an enduring dilemma. This issue was addressed by anthropologist Margaret Mead early in the twentieth century; based on her fieldwork in Samoa and New Guinea, Mead (1928, 1935) set out to establish the significance of culture or environment in order to offer an alternative to the powerful intellectual principles of biological determinism and eugenics (biological engineering) that dominated academic circles in the 1920s. She also hoped to demonstrate to North American women that a range of possibilities was open to them and that the social roles of housework and child rearing were not their inevitable lot. In her view, anatomy was not destiny.

Mead's work was challenged in the 1980s by Derek Freeman (1983). Freeman accused Mead of cultural determinism (i.e., giving priority to culture over biology) and opened a lively debate within academic and nonacademic circles (Holmes 1987; Leacock 1993; Orans 1996; Rensberger 1983; Scheper-Hughes 1987; Schneider 1983). For some, Freeman's book was taken (erroneously) as new support for the sociobiological approach to an understanding of human behavior, an approach formulated by Edward Wilson (1975) that contends that there is a genetic basis for all social behavior.

Although few people deny the anatomical and hormonal differences between men and women, they disagree about the importance of these differences for gender roles and personality attributes. Biologists point to the considerable complexity of sex differences as these are related to genes, chromosomes, and hormones (Low 2000). Another body of research, much of it conducted by psychologists, suggests that male and female infants cannot be significantly distinguished by their degree of dependence on parents, their visual and verbal abilities, or their aggression as measured by activity level (Bleier 1984; Fausto-Sterling 1985; Renzetti and Curran 1989). These characteristics tend to emerge later in the development process, indicating the importance of environment.

Controversy also surrounds the question of how the brain is organized and to what extent brain lateralization is related to sex differences in cognition (Kimura 1999). There are scholars who argue that sex hormones affect brain organization very early in life, resulting in brains that are differently wired in boys and girls (Geary 1998). Alternatively, others argue, "there is little evidence indicating that the sexual differentiation of the brain, if it occurs in humans, consequently predisposes males

1

and females to behave in gender-specific ways" (Renzetti and Curran 1989: 33; see also Fausto-Sterling 1985, 2000). The scholarly literature often focuses on the view that women are left-brain dominant, giving them superior verbal skills, whereas men are right-brain dominant, giving them superior visual–spatial skills. This may, however, vary across cultures in relation to different modes of subsistence—for example, the varying demands of hunting and gathering activities (Berry 1976; Silverman and Phillips 1998). Based on research in Kenya, Munroe, Munroe, and Bresler (1985) have demonstrated that movement through the environment is an important foundation for the earlier acquisition of spatial abilities among boys by comparison with girls. The literature on differences in mathematical skills also indicates some cross-cultural variation, suggesting that both biological and social factors may be at play (Kimura 1999).

Cordelia Fine (in this book) takes up the debates about the "gendered brain" and cautions against equating structural differences in the brain to male/female differences in any simple way. Indeed she documents some of the contradictions in the research, stemming not only from cultural biases and flawed methodology, but also from the "theoretical U-turns that have always beset the neuroscience of sex differences." She challenges ideas that equate bigger brain or more active brain with better brain as well as claims that men and women are hardwired for distinct roles and occupations. The broader goal of the book, *Delusions of Gender*, from which these chapters are excerpted here, is to point to the various stereotypes (she calls them implicit associations) about men and women who enter into neuroscientific research. As Fine (2010: 26) suggests, "we can't understand gender differences in female and male minds—the minds that are the source of our thoughts, feelings, abilities, motivations, and behavior—without understanding how psychologically permeable is the skull that separates the mind from the sociocultural context in which it operates. When the environment makes gender salient, there is a ripple effect on the mind."

In her book, *Delusions of Gender*, Fine (2010: 176) refers to the field of evolutionary psychology and its central assumption that the gendered brain was initially developed and shaped by processes of natural selection that operated in the context of a hunting and gathering adaptation. Within some branches of anthropology, the evolutionary framework, and hence an emphasis on the role of biology in explaining differences between men and women, including social behaviors such as the division of labor and the tendency for women to be subordinated to men, has also been important. Evolutionary theories fall roughly into four categories: male strength hypotheses, male aggression hypotheses, male bonding hypotheses, and women's childbearing hypotheses. Male strength hypotheses argue that men are physically stronger than women and this gives them superiority. They are larger, and they have stronger muscles and less fat, a pelvis better adapted for sprinting, larger hearts and lungs, and so forth. These physical differences between the males and females of a species are referred to as sexual dimorphism.

Several anthropologists have studied both fossil and nonhuman primates in order to explore the evolutionary origins of sexual dimorphism (differences in morphology, such as weight and body dimensions) and, by analogy, sexual asymmetry, the sexual division of labor, and the emergence of the nuclear family (Fedigan 1992; Leigh 1995; Plavcan and van Schaik 1997a, 1997b; Zihlman 1993). This research with nonhuman primates is part of a large body of literature that uses animals as models for understanding human behavior. One of the earliest statements was Leibowitz's (1975) discussion of the evolution of sex differences. Leibowitz challenged the tendency to link sexual dimorphism to particular sex role patterns by demonstrating enormous variations among different species of primates. Rather than explaining greater male size and strength solely as an adaptation to the roles of protection and provisioning associated with hunting, Leibowitz urged consideration of the reproductive advantage to women of the cessation of growth soon after sexual maturity is reached. In the process, she asked us to reconsider what we mean by strength. She also cautioned that our stereotypes of human male attributes have been drawn from one of the most sexually dimorphic species of nonhuman primates, the plains baboon. As Sperling observed, "This use of the baboon troop as model for ancestral human populations was very influential in forming both sexist and anthropomorphic views of monkeys in popular culture" (1991: 210). Sperling, Fedigan (1986), and Leibowitz have all emphasized the inappropriateness of the "baboonization" of early human life, given the distant relationship between humans and baboons. If we are going to draw comparisons with nonhuman primates, it would be preferable to draw analogies with the great apes, particularly the chimpanzees.

In this book, biologist Marlene Zuk takes up the question of animal models in gender studies, exploring the biological roots of sex differences. She argues forcefully that we should not succumb to stereotypes that would make us pawns of our evolutionary heritage. She cites current research that supports the idea of female preference for particular types of males as a major force in evolution. But she also stresses that there is a great deal of diversity and variation in sexual selection in the animal world and that this variation should offer lessons for how we understand the biological basis of sex differences and mating practices in humans. Even the nonhuman primate world is characterized by this variation.

A second line of argument attempts to explain male dominance with reference to the biological basis of aggression. Many studies of aggression contend that men are more aggressive than women (Wilson 1975; see Fedigan 1992: 71 for a critique of this position) and often link this difference to levels of male hormones (testosterone) (see Geary 1998; Mealey 2000). According to Fausto-Sterling (1985: 126), "Many societies, including our own, have tested this belief by castrating men who have a history of violent or antisocial behavior." Scientific research has demonstrated that there is no connection between castration and aggression, and in Fausto-Sterling's (2000) view, cultural constructions of gender have influenced research that links hormones to particular behaviors.

It has also been argued that male aggressive tendencies are an adaptation to the male role in defense (Keeley 1996; Martin and Voorhies 1975) among both human and nonhuman primates. The problem with any line of argument that links male dominance or male social roles to male aggression is that it ignores the wide variation in behaviors and personalities not only between the sexes, but also within them (Renzetti and Curran 1989: 38). This is certainly true of nonhuman primates. Smuts (1986), for example, argues that both males and females in various species are capable of opportunistic alliances and defense of victims, depending on the circumstances.

Cross-cultural ethnographic data indicate that human societies also differ in culturally appropriate levels of aggression expressed by men and women (Burbank 1994; Counts, Brown, and Campbell 1992; Daly and Wilson 1990; Munroe et al. 2000). Richard Lee's (1979) classic study of conflict and violence among the !Kung San, a relatively egalitarian and peace-loving people, addresses the issue of aggression among men and women. He lends support to the argument that both men and women are aggressive in different ways. !Kung women engage in verbal abuse, but homicides are disproportionately committed by men. Lee compares trends in !Kung violence to those in several other societies. Although his statistics are from the 1950s and 1960s, more recent research indicates that the patterns remain similar. Statistics on criminal activity in the United States indicates that while violent offenses committed by women increased between the mid-1970s and the mid-1980s, they were still predominantly committed by men (Morris 1987: 35). Between 1986 and 1991, the proportion of violent offenses among female prison inmates declined from 40.7 to 32.2 percent. Corresponding figures for males were from 55.2 to 47.4 percent (U.S. Department of Justice 1991). In 2000 in the United States, 83 percent of convicted criminals were male and 17 percent were female. In the United Kingdom, the comparable figures were 82 percent and 18 percent for males and females, respectively. Although there has been some convergence between men and women in theft offenses, there is little convergence for violent offenses (Austin 1993). Today it is still true that men are more likely to be incarcerated than women, are more likely to commit murder than women, and are more likely to be the victims of violent crime by comparison with women. A comparison between the !Kung and a modern industrial society such as the United States suggests that the reasons for gender differences in aggressive behavior are complex. In addition to biological factors, access to weapons, culturally approved expressions of hostility, and the role of the state in the evolution of social control should also be considered.

Among the !Kung, the victims of violent crimes tend to be other men, a finding that supports Maccoby and Jacklin's (1974) observation that primate males in general demonstrate more aggression against one another than against females (Daly and Wilson 1990). Dominance of men over women through aggression is thereby brought into question, as is the concept of aggression itself. As Fedigan (1992: 89) suggests, aggression "is such a heterogeneous category of behaviors and interactions that 'amount of aggression' is not a very useful concept." Fausto-Sterling (1985: 129) concurs and points to the fact that no studies on hormone levels and aggression use female subjects or compare men and women. She raises fundamental questions regarding the causal relationship between testosterone levels and aggression.

A third body of evolutionary theory attempts to explain male domination in terms of their supposedly greater ability to form social bonds among themselves (Tiger 1969). This ability is presumed to be genetically programmed and associated with the evolutionary adaptation to hunting. Women, conversely, are thought to lack the genetic code for bonding and are therefore unsuited to the kinds of cooperative and political endeavors that give men power and prestige. A number of anthropologists have explored the development of the sexual division of labor among early humans and have critiqued the bias that is inherent in the emphasis on hunting, a male activity, as the distinctive human activity (Lee and DeVore 1968). Margaret Ehrenberg (1989) has in fact argued that women were often the social center of groups and fostered sociability and sharing. In her reevaluation of a discussion that essentially omitted half of humanity from the story of evolution (the "Man the Hunter" approach), Ehrenberg suggests that hunting probably evolved from the physical, technological, and social innovations associated with gathering (a female activity).

In this book, Lucinda J. Peach explores how the ideas about male strength, male bonding, and male aggression have shaped the debate in the United States about women in the military. While women in the U.S. military are now "seeing combat," U.S. policy continues to exclude them from the majority of combat roles. Peach suggests that such exclusions are based on assumptions and stereotypes about female "nature" rather than on verifiable gender differences that clearly demonstrate women's inability to perform competently specific combat duties such as operating offensive, line-of-sight weapons or participating in ground fighting. Warfare is a masculine arena; women need to be protected; women lack the necessary physical and psychological strength to perform adequately; the presence of women in combat units would undermine unit cohesion by disrupting male bonding—these are some of the arguments that are put forward to justify the banishment of women from specific military activities. One result, by extension, is that women are denied certain opportunities for promotion that are predicated on active combat service.

A fourth body of theory linking biology to gender difference and gender hierarchy explains the absence of women from cooperative and political activity in the nondomestic sphere (hence their subordination) in terms of their reproductive roles. A corollary of this argument is the idea that women possess a maternal instinct. The fact that women bear children and lactate has been the basis of assertions that women innately experience an attachment to their children that forms the foundation of effective mothering, whereas men lack a similar capacity to nurture (Peterson 1983; Rossi 1977, 1978). This attachment may be the result of such factors as hormone levels (O'Kelly 1980: 30) or the experiences of pregnancy, labor, and nursing (Whitbeck 1983: 186). In contrast, Collier and Rosaldo (1981: 315) have argued, "there are no facts about human sexual biology that, in and of themselves, have immediate social meanings or institutional consequences. Mothering is a social relation, much like fathering, judging, or ruling, whose meaning and organization must be understood with reference to a particular configuration of relationships within a complex social whole."

The chapter by Nancy Scheper-Hughes (in this book) illustrates this assertion. She examines the inevitability of maternal–infant attachment among mothers in the shantytowns of northeast Brazil. In an environment of poverty, chronic hunger, and economic exploitation, Scheper-Hughes finds that mothers adopt a strategy of delayed attachment and neglect of weaker children thought unlikely to survive. Such attitudes of resignation and fatalism toward the death of children are documented in historical studies of other cultures as well; for example, Ransel's account of child abandonment in Russia relates the passive attitude toward childhood death to child death rates in the 50 percent range (1988: 273; see also Boswell 1988). Parental attitudes are reflected in an entire category of lullabies with the motif of wishing death on babies; women sang these lullabies to infants who were sick, weak, or crippled (Ransel 1988: 273). Thus, mother love seems less a "natural and universal maternal script" than a luxury reserved for the strongest and healthiest children. In the context of frequent infant death, maternal attachment means grief, and mother love emerges as culturally and socially constructed rather than as an innate emotion.

Barry S. Hewlett (in this book) offers a somewhat different perspective on the question of maternal instinct by exploring the role of fatherhood among the Aka pygmies, a group of foragers who live in the tropical forest regions of central Africa. Aka fathers spend a significant portion of their day caring for and nurturing their children. A good father, among the Aka, is a man who stays near his children, shows them affection, and assists the mother with her work. Indeed Aka male–female relations are very egalitarian. Women and men each contribute significantly to subsistence; although Aka men hold all the named positions of status, women challenge men's authority regularly and play a decisive role in all kinds of decision making; physical violence is infrequent, and violence against women is rare (Hewlett 1991). Hewlett suggests that strong father–infant attachment among the Aka can be explained by a range of ecological, social, ideological, and demographic factors. The implications of the Aka example, especially for alternate parenting models in the United States, are clear. As Hewlett argues, "The Aka demonstrate that there are cultural systems where men can be active, intimate and nurturing caregivers" (Hewlett 1991: 171).

Research on nonhuman primates has shown that role variability and plasticity are deeply rooted in the evolutionary history of primates. Cross-cultural data suggest a similar plasticity among humans. The evidence from this section should support the argument that biology merely sets the parameters for a broad range of human behaviors. Thus, biological differences between men and women have no uniform and universal implication for social roles and relations. Biology, for humans, takes on meaning as it is interpreted in human culture and society (Rosaldo and Lamphere 1974: 4).

## REFERENCES

Austin, Roy L. 1993. "Recent Trends in Official Male and Female Crime Rates: The Convergence Controversy." *Journal of Criminal Justice* 21: 447–466.

Berry, John Widdup. 1976. *Human Ecology and Cognitive Style: Comparative Studies in Cultural and Psychological Adaptation.* New York: Wiley.

Bleier, Ruth. 1984. *Science and Gender: A Critique of Biology and Its Theories on Women.* New York: Pergamon Press.

Blum, Deborah. 1998. *Sex on the Brain: The Biological Differences Between Men and Women.* New York: Penguin Books.

Boswell, John. 1988. *The Kindness of Strangers: The Abandonment of Children in Western Europe from Late Antiquity to the Renaissance.* New York: Pantheon Books.

Burbank, Victoria Katherine. 1994. *Fighting Women. Anger and Aggression in Aboriginal Australia.* Berkeley: University of California Press.

Collier, Jane E., and Michelle Z. Rosaldo. 1981. "The Politics of Gender in Simple Societies." In Sherry S. Ortner and Harriet Whitehead (eds.). *Sexual Meanings,* pp. 275–330. Cambridge, UK: Cambridge University Press.

Counts, D., J. Brown, and J. Campbell (eds.). 1992. *Sanctions and Sanctuary: Cultural Perspectives on the Beating of Wives.* Boulder, CO: Westview Press.

Daly, M., and M. Wilson. 1990. "Killing the Competition: Female/Female and Male/Male Homicide." *Human Nature* 1: 81–107.

Ehrenberg, Margaret. 1989. *Women in Prehistory.* Norman: University of Oklahoma Press.

Fausto-Sterling, Anne. 1985. *Myths of Gender.* New York: Basic Books.

———. 2000. *Sexing the Body: Gender Politics and the Construction of Sexuality.* New York: Basic Books.

Fedigan, Linda Marie. 1986. "The Changing Role of Women in Models of Human Evolution." *Annual Review of Anthropology* 15: 25–66.

———. 1992. *Primate Paradigms: Sex Roles and Social Bonds.* Chicago: University of Chicago Press.

Fine, Cordelia. 2010. *Delusions of Gender: How Our Minds, Society, and Neurosexism Create Difference.* New York: W.W. Norton and Company.

Freeman, Derek. 1983. *Margaret Mead and Samoa: The Making and Unmaking of an Anthropological Myth.* Cambridge, MA: Harvard University Press.

Gallagher, Anne M., and James C. Kaufman (eds.). 2005. *Gender Differences in Mathematics: An Integrative Psychological Approach.* Cambridge, UK: Cambridge University Press.

Geary, David C. 1998. *Male, Female: The Evolution of Human Sex Differences.* Washington, DC: American Psychological Association.

Hewlett, Barry S. 1991. *Intimate Fathers: The Nature and Context of Aka Pygmy Paternal Infant Care.* Ann Arbor: University of Michigan Press.

Holmes, Lowell D. 1987. *Quest for the Real Samoa: The Mead/Freeman Controversy and Beyond.* South Hadley, MA: Bergin Garvey.

Keeley, L. H. 1996. *War before Civilization: The Myth of the Peaceful Savage.* New York: Oxford University Press.

Kimura, Diane. 1999. *Sex and Cognition.* Cambridge, MA: MIT Press.

Leacock, Eleanor. 1993. "Women in Samoan History: A Further Critique of Derek Freeman." In Barbara Diane Miller (ed.). *Sex and Gender Hierarchies,* pp. 351–365. Cambridge, UK: Cambridge University Press.

Lee, Richard. 1979. *The !Kung San: Men, Women, and Work in a Foraging Society.* Cambridge, UK: Cambridge University Press.

Lee, Richard S., and Irven DeVore (eds.). 1968. *Man the Hunter.* New York: Aldine.

Leibowitz, Lila. 1975. "Perspectives on the Evolution of Sex Differences." In Rayna Rapp (ed.). *Toward an Anthropology of Women,* pp. 20–35. New York: Monthly Review.

Leigh, S. R. 1995. "Socioecology and the Ontogeny of Sexual Size Dimorphism in Anthropoid Primates," *American Journal of Physical Anthropology* 97: 339–356.

Low, Bobbi. 2000. *Why Sex Matters.* Princeton: Princeton University Press.

Maccoby, E. E., and C. N. Jacklin. 1974. *The Psychology of Sex Differences.* Stanford, CA: Stanford University Press.

Martin, M. Kay, and Barbara Voorhies. 1975. *Female of the Species.* New York: Columbia University Press.

Mead, Margaret. 1928. *Coming of Age in Samoa.* New York: Dell.

———. 1935. *Sex and Temperament in Three Primitive Societies.* New York: Dell.

Mealey, Linda. 2000. *Sex Differences: Developmental and Evolutionary Strategies.* San Diego: Academic Press.

Morris, Allison. 1987. *Women, Crime and Criminal Justice.* Oxford, UK: Basil Blackwell.

Munroe, Robert L., Robert Hulefeld, James M. Rodgers, Damon L. Tomeo, and Steven K. Yamazaki. 2000. "Aggression among Children in Four Cultures." *Cross-cultural Research* 34 (1): 3–25.

Munroe, Ruth H., Robert L. Munroe, and Anne Bresler. 1985. "Precursors of Spatial Ability: A Longitudinal Study among the Logoli of Kenya." *Journal of Social Psychology* 125 (1): 23–33.

O'Kelly, Charlotte. 1980. *Women and Men in Society.* New York: D. Van Nostrand Co.

Orans, Martin. 1996. *Not Even Wrong: Margaret Mead, Derek Freeman and the Samoans.* New York: Chandler and Sharp.

Peterson, Susan Rae. 1983. "Against 'Parenting'." In Joyce Trebilcot (ed.). *Mothering: Essays in Feminist Theory,* pp. 41–62. Totowa, NJ: Rowman and Allanheld.

Plavcan, J. M., and C. P. van Schaik. 1997a. "Interpreting Hominid Behavior on the Basis of Sexual Dimorphism." *Journal of Human Evolution* 32: 345–374.

———. 1997b. "Intrasexual Competition and Body Weight Dimorphism in Anthropoid Primates." *American Journal of Physical Anthropology* 103: 37–68.

Ransel, David L. 1988. *Mothers of Misery: Child Abandonment in Russia.* Princeton, NJ: Princeton University Press.

Rensberger, Boyce. 1983. "Margaret Mead: The Nature-Nurture Debate: From Samoa to Sociobiology." *Science* 83: 28–46.

Renzetti, Clair M., and Daniel J. Curran. 1989. *Women, Men and Society: The Sociology of Gender.* Needham Heights, MA: Allyn and Bacon.

Rosaldo, Michelle Z., and Louise Lamphere (eds.). 1974. *Woman, Culture, and Society.* Stanford, CA: Stanford University Press.

Rossi, Alice. 1977. "A Biosocial Perspective on Parenting." *Daedalus* 106: 1–31.

———. 1978. "The Biosocial Side of Parenthood." *Human Nature* 1: 72–79.

Scheper-Hughes, Nancy. 1987. "The Margaret Mead Controversy: Culture, Biology and Anthropological Inquiry." In Herbert Applebaum (ed.). *Perspectives in Cultural Anthropology,* pp. 443–454. Albany: State University of New York Press.

Schneider, David. 1983. "The Coming of a Sage to Samoa." *Natural History* 92(6): 4–10.

Silverman, Irwin and Krista Phillips. 1998. "The Evolutionary Psychology of Spatial Sex Differences." In Charles Crawford and Dennis L. Krebs (eds.). *Handbook of Evolutionary Psychology: Ideas, Issues and Applications,* pp. 595–612. Hillsdale, NJ: Erlbaum.

Smuts, Barbara. 1986. "Gender, Aggression, and Influence." In Barbara Smuts, Dorothy L. Cheney, Robert Seyfarth, Richard Wrangham, and Thomas Struhsaler (eds.). *Primate Societies,* pp. 400–412. Chicago: University of Chicago Press.

Sperling, Susan. 1991. "Baboons with Briefcases vs. Langurs in Lipstick. Feminism and Functionalism in Primate Studies." In Micaela di Leonardo (ed.). *Gender at the Crossroads of Knowledge: Feminist Anthropology in the Postmodern Era,* pp. 204–234. Berkeley: University of California Press.

Tiger, Lionel. 1969. *Men in Groups.* New York: Random House.

Udry, J. Richard. 2000. "Biological Limits of Gender Construction." *American Sociological Review* 65: 443–457.

U.S. Department of Justice. 1991. *Women in Prison.* Bureau of Justice Statistics, Special Report. Washington, DC: U.S. Department of Justice.

Whitbeck, Caroline. 1983. "The Maternal Instinct." In Joyce Trebilcot (ed.). *Mothering: Essays in Feminist Theory,* pp. 185–192. Totowa, NJ: Rowman and Allenheld.

Wilson, Edward O. 1975. *Sociobiology: The New Synthesis.* Cambridge, MA: Harvard University Press.

Zihlman, Adrienne L. 1993. "Sex Differences and Gender Hierarchies among Primates: An Evolutionary Perspective." In Barbara Diane Miller (ed.). *Sex and Gender Hierarchies,* pp. 32–56. Cambridge, UK: Cambridge University Press.

# Animal Models and Gender

## Marlene Zuk

The notion that biology, particularly evolutionary biology, can explain much about gender differences in humans raises hackles in many people. The fear is that science will be used to justify sexism, so that men are "naturally" dominant and women submissive, men natural philanderers and women naturally inclined to stop them from straying. These stereotypes are often said to arise from the animal kingdom, apparently leaving us with no other choices than to accept our evolutionary heritage and resign ourselves to a life of oppression, or reject the idea that biology has any relevance to explaining gender in modern day humans.

In this chapter I hope to counter this impression, both by explaining how biologists view the evolution of sex differences in animals and by showing how understanding the connection between our sexual behavior and that of other species can be liberating rather than restrictive. It is possible to use evolution to inform us about gender without either succumbing to the old stereotypes or substituting new ones; a caricature of a nature-girl is just as damaging as one that stays barefoot and pregnant. Much of the material here is discussed in more detail in Zuk (2002). Numerous other authors have attempted to link feminism and evolutionary biology, and provide feminist critiques of biology from a scientific perspective, perhaps most notably Patricia Gowaty (1997, 2003), but also including Hrdy (1986, 1997, 1999), Keller (1985), Fausto-Sterling (1987, 2003), Liesen (1995), and many others. Here I focus on studies from animals, rather than examining the field of biology as a whole, and examine the use of animal models in studies of gender.

## SEXUAL SELECTION

Sex differences in animals are of much interest to biologists, and the body of theory commonly accepted as the explanation of how these differences evolve is called sexual selection. Like its relative natural selection, sexual selection relies on individual differences in the likelihood of leaving genes in succeeding generation, but unlike natural selection, the differential reproduction due to sexual selection occurs because of an individual's ability to acquire the best and/or most mates, not because of survival ability. Thus a bird with a long ungainly tail that attracts more females

Marlene Zuk, *Sexual Selections: What We Can and Can't Learn About Sex from Animals.* © 2003 University of California Press, Berkeley.

than his shorter-tailed counterparts is at a sexual selection advantage, even if he has a harder time flying and cannot escape predators as easily.

Also like natural selection, the theory of sexual selection has its origin in the work of Charles Darwin. When Darwin began to develop his ideas about the origin of species, he attempted to explain the evolution of traits that differ between the sexes, but are not necessary for the physical act of reproduction, such as the mane on male lions or the antlers of male deer. Darwin devoted an entire book, *The Descent of Man and Selection in Relation to Sex*, published in 1871, to explaining such traits, which he called secondary sexual characters, and noted that in many cases they simply could not seem to have arisen through natural selection because they are often costly to produce and make their bearers more conspicuous to predators.

Darwin suggested that secondary sexual characters could evolve in one of two ways. First, they could be useful to one sex, usually males, in fighting for access to members of the other sex; hence, the antlers and horns on male ungulates, such as bighorn sheep, or on the aptly named male rhinoceros beetles. These are weapons, and they are advantageous because better fighters are presumed to get more mates and have more offspring. The second way was more problematic. Darwin noted that females often pay attention to traits like long tails and elaborate plumage during courtship, and he concluded that the traits evolved because the females preferred them. Peahens find peacocks with long tails attractive, just like we do. The sexual selection process, then, consisted of two components: male–male competition, which results in weapons, and female choice, which results in ornaments.

While competition among males for the rights to mate with a female seemed reasonable enough to Darwin's Victorian contemporaries, virtually none of them could swallow the idea that females—of any species, but especially the so-called dumb animals—could possibly do anything so complex as discriminating between males with slightly different plumage colors. Alfred Russell Wallace, who also independently arrived at some of the same conclusions about evolution and natural selection that Darwin did, was particularly vehement in his objections (Wallace 1889). He, and many others, simply found it absurd that females could make the sort of complex decision required by Darwin's theory; it would require the female to possess an aesthetic sense like that of humans, an idea they were unwilling to accept. According to the thinking of his time, even among humans only those of the upper social classes could appreciate aesthetic things like art and music, so it seemed ridiculous to imagine that animals could do something many humans—particularly non Englishmen—could not.

Largely because of this opposition to the idea of female choice, sexual selection as a theory lay dormant for several decades. This time lag meant that while sexual selection and natural selection were introduced at about the same time, sexual selection has not received the same continuous scrutiny by scientists. In some ways, therefore, the study of sex differences is a younger science than the study of species origin and diversity. It was not until the late 1960s that interest in the evolution of sex differences was revived, and the most important contribution to the new theory was a 1972 paper by Robert Trivers, who argued that selection acts differently on males and females because of how they allocate resources into succeeding generations. Females are limited by the number of offspring they can successfully produce and rear. Because they are the sex that supplies the nutrient-rich egg, and often the sex that cares for the young, they have an upper limit set at a relatively low number. They leave the most genes in the next generation by having the highest quality young they can. Which male they mate with could be very important, because a mistake in the form of poor genes or no help with the young could mean that they have lost their whole breeding effort for an entire year.

Males, on the other hand, can leave the most genes in the next generation by fertilizing as many females as possible. Because each mating requires relatively little investment from him, a male who mates with many females sires many more young than a male mating with only one female. Hence, males are expected to compete among themselves for access to females, and females are expected to be choosy, and to mate with the best possible male they can. In addition, females were often referred to as "coy," with the implication that the impetus for sex came largely from males, who fought among themselves to get to the females and allow the choices to occur.

This, of course, is the same division of sexual selection that Darwin originally proposed, and Trivers had given it a new rationale. What he did, too, was bring female choice back to the forefront of sexual selection, and suggest a more modern underlying advantage to it. Furthermore, ideas about the evolution of behavior had advanced enough that scientists no longer worried about an "aesthetic sense" in animals; it didn't matter how females recognized particular males, just that if they did, and it was beneficial, the genes associated with the trait females were attracted to would become more common in the population than the genes of less-preferred traits. Evolutionary biologists, therefore, could ignore questions about motivation and get to the more testable issue of how discrimination among males might

result in the evolution of ornamental traits that did not function either in day-to-day life or in male combat.

Current work on female behavior in many species of animals has confirmed Trivers'—and Darwin's—basic idea about female preference for particular types of males being a major force in evolution (Andersson 1994). Again and again, females have been shown to be able to distinguish small differences among available mates, and to prefer to mate with those individuals bearing the most exaggerated characters. In some cases those males are also more healthy and vigorous, so that ornaments appear to indicate not just attractiveness but the ability to survive.

One of the most well-known examples can be found in peacocks, often used as the symbol of sexual selection with their huge elaborate tails. English gentry have kept peacocks (more correctly, peafowl, as the term peacock strictly speaking refers only to the male) for many years, and British biologist Marion Petrie studied the behavior of flocks that were allowed to range freely in a park in England (Petrie 1994; Petrie and Halliday 1994). She discovered that females did indeed prefer males with greater numbers of eyespots on their tail feathers, and that this preference could be manipulated by cutting the eyespots off of some males' tails and gluing them onto others; females lost interest in the dubbed peacocks, and became attracted to the augmented ones. Even more interesting, she allowed females to mate with males that had variable numbers of eyespots, and then reared all of the offspring in communal incubators to control for differences in maternal care. The chicks fathered by the more ornamented males weighed more than the other chicks, an attribute usually connected with better survival in birds. Indeed, when the individually marked chicks were then released into the park and recaptured the following year, the ones with the more attractive fathers also were more likely to evade predators and survive in the seminatural conditions.

The notion that females are "coy" has not survived so well, as it has been amply demonstrated that females frequently seek out matings with multiple males, and that they often take an active part in many kinds of sexual interactions (Andersson 1994; Jennions and Petrie 1997, 2000; Gowaty and Buschhaus 1998). The reasons behind such behaviors are the subject of intensive study by biologists, and ideas are changing all the time. Nevertheless, the concept of sexual selection, and the core ideas of reproductive competition and mate choice, appears to explain a great deal about animal sexual differences.

### The Philandering Male, the Coy Female, and Other Myths

What about humans? Does this mean that males are designed by evolution to be indiscriminate in seeking sex, and females are forever conscribed by the need to raise children alone? The answer is an emphatic no, and to understand why it is important to understand how animal models are used in biology.

First of all, even among animals a great deal of variation exists in the manifestation of the basic principles of sexual selection. For example, male elephant seals come ashore at isolated beaches along the Pacific coast during late summer. The males can weigh up to three tons, more than twice the size of females, and spend several weeks fighting among themselves for dominance. Females arrive after the males, and after they come ashore the dominant males attempt to sequester groups of females and keep them from rival males; the females themselves, although they do exert some degree of choice, are constrained in their movements by the males (Le Boeuf and Reiter 1988; Galimberti et al. 2002). The male competition aspect of sexual selection appears to prevail in this species.

In contrast, female bowerbirds have virtually total control over mating. This group of several species of birds is found in Australia and New Guinea. The males construct elaborate structures out of twigs, grass and other objects, and then decorate them with ornaments that can include plastic items as well as fruit, flowers, bones, and shells (Borgia 1995; Uy et al. 2001; Madden 2003). Each species has a characteristic bower type. After the bowers are made, males wait for females to visit; the bowers are generally rather widely separated, so males cannot hear or see each other when they are tending their bowers. A female generally visits the bowers of several males before choosing one of them. When a female arrives, the male courts her with elaborate vocal and visual displays, but he cannot prevent a female from leaving to sample additional males, something the females commonly do. Eventually a female selects a male, mates with him, and leaves to lay her eggs and rear her chicks alone. The bower is not a nest, and males take no part in rearing offspring. Female choice, rather than male competition, is paramount among bowerbirds.

These two systems illustrate completely different "solutions" to the same problem of reproduction faced by all species. Other examples, including substantial male contributions to offspring, extreme female aggression and competition, and sexual behavior outside the fertile period, could also be cited. Among bonobos, small relatives of chimpanzees, sexual activity occurs between virtually all members of a social group, including members of the same sex. This point is an important one: although male competition and female choice are the basic elements of sexual selection, even among animals tremendous diversity exists in how they are implemented. Those unfamiliar with the behavior of animals in the wild often do not realize that animal family life, or lack of it, is not a simplified

version of human existence, even human existence in an imaginary early hunter–gatherer society. It is simply incorrect to suggest that finding a link between our gender-related behavior and that of other animals would inevitably mean a link to a male-dominated social system. A single animal model for the origin of sex roles does not exist, even if we were to accept that finding such a model would make it impossible to act outside of it.

Note that this diversity also precludes claiming that women are naturally caring, verbal, peace loving, or sexually adventurous. Substituting one stereotype, of a strong Amazon, for the more traditional one of a coy stay at home mom uninterested in sex, does not solve the problem. We may like the previously unappreciated female bonobo, with her overt sexuality, more than another animal model, but it is important to remember that the animals are model systems for understanding a range of behaviors, and not role models.

How, then, can we learn from animals about gender and sex roles? Below I detail two examples of topics that are often discussed in the context of animal behavior, maternal instinct and mate fidelity. I hope to show that we can learn from biology without either succumbing to old stereotypes or substituting new ones for them.

## MATERNAL INSTINCT AND MOTHER LOVE

One of the cornerstones of popular belief in a biological basis for gender-based behavior is that females instinctively care for their young. If maternal care-giving behavior is natural, then presumably all women want to do it, know how to do it without learning how, and feel deprived if they do not. A modern version of the maternal instinct is the mother–infant bond, this mysterious connection that supposedly naturally occurs between a woman and her child soon after birth.

How fixed is this bond, and how ingrained in a female's psyche is the ability—and even the desire—to care for her young? It would seem reasonable to assume that animals should show a behavior that women are supposed to have inherited, and it is therefore instructive to look at research from the 1950s and 1960s using rhesus macaques, the monkeys used in numerous medical and behavioral studies; the "Rh" in Rh-positive or Rh-negative blood types comes from the name of this species. Two psychologists named Harry and Margaret Harlow were interested in understanding the effects of social deprivation on humans, the kind of deprivation that arises through abuse, neglect, and warfare. The Harlows wanted to know how these problems arose and thus perhaps gain insight into correcting them. They could not, of course, perform controlled experiments on human children, and so they used an animal model and manipulated the early rearing environment of groups of macaques so that deprived youngsters could be compared to more normally raised controls. The Harlows' research is expertly analyzed by Deborah Blum (2002), who also raises some of the interesting ethical issues that arise from the treatment of the monkeys.

The infant macaques were taken from their mothers at birth, and raised under one of several different sets of conditions. For example, some were allowed access to a monkey-sized, wire-covered model that had a bottle attached to it approximately where the nipple of a mother monkey might be. The bottle was filled with milk and the cages cleaned at appropriate intervals by human caretakers who had no contact with the monkeys. Other baby macaques had the wire-covered model with the food, and in addition were given another model covered with terrycloth. In some instances, the monkeys saw or contacted other equally deprived infants during their development, while in others they were kept in isolation. As the monkeys grew up, they were used in a variety of tests to examine their social behavior and eventually their ability to mate and have offspring of their own.

To the surprise of few, the socially deprived monkeys did not exhibit normal behavior. They were more fearful when new stimuli were introduced to their cages, they did not interact with other juvenile monkeys the way that babies raised with their mothers did, and they showed numerous other signs of psychological abnormality. Interestingly, however, the babies given the cloth-covered model "mother" were better adjusted than those given only the wire model, and when a novel and potentially frightening object was introduced into the cage, they ran not to the source of food but to the source of what the Harlows called "contact comfort." In other words, clinging to a soft object is more soothing than returning to the place where essential nourishment is found.

The Harlows went on from these studies to discuss a number of fascinating theories about the need for this contact comfort and its potential value in helping children with minimal resources develop more normally. Their ideas have been thoroughly dissected—and in some cases debunked—by developmental psychologists. For my purposes here, however, a more relevant finding was the discovery that females raised with the models had difficulties in mating with male monkeys once they reached sexual maturity. They simply did not know how to have sex—they didn't know the postures, the signals, the responses. Even more significant, if they were artificially inseminated and became pregnant, they were incapable of caring for the resulting young, and their infants had to be removed from their mothers lest they be seriously injured. The mothers did get better with experience, so that subsequent young fared better, but the early babies were as foreign as extra-terrestrials to their mothers.

These results seem to flatly contradict the notion of a simple maternal instinct. Even mother monkeys, animals very similar to ourselves, do not automatically feel bonded to their infants, much less know how to take care of them. The mystical mother–child relationship is shattered when the mother is raised without others of her kind. This situation is clearly unusual, of course. The monkeys are not usually raised by wire models, and under natural circumstances they can relate to their offspring perfectly well. This, however, is precisely my point: even a behavior supposedly as sacrosanct as the love a mother will have for her child depends on the environment. And therefore it is also clear that the evidence does not support assuming a particular behavior in humans is "natural," even one as supposedly biological as mothering.

The consequences of acknowledging this fact are many. If one is freed from the idea of the maternal instinct, one is also freed from equating being female to being a mother, as if no other role was possible or important. Examining female behavior, in humans or animals, is therefore enriched by abandoning the stereotype. Females can exhibit all kinds of behavior, and females, human or not, are not only defined by their relationship to their offspring. One can also start dissecting maternal behavior itself, asking questions about what kind and how much of an investment would benefit mothers under different circumstances. The "maternal-infant bond" becomes a malleable behavior rather than a fixed biological entity.

The idea of variable mothering leads to some interesting and sometimes startling predictions. For example, the eminent anthropologist Sarah Blaffer Hrdy has found that infanticide can be adaptive for monkeys and other mammals that exhibit it (Hausfater and Hrdy 1984). While I hasten to point out that this hardly justifies the behavior in humans, it does suggest that an analysis that does not focus exclusively on the stereotypical nurturing mother can be enlightening.

## ADULTERY AND PHILANDERING MALES

Infidelity, again whether in humans or animals, is a topic of great interest to those wanting to understand whether animals show us our own biologically based behaviors. The classic stereotype of male nature is of the man seeking multiple sexual partners while the woman is content to remain with a single partner for her entire life. Infidelity has also recently become a subject of interest to scientists, because the advent of genetic testing has allowed us to sample the DNA from a set of chicks in a nest and compare it to the DNA of the male and female associated with the young. As it turns out, so-called extra-pair paternity is quite common among birds; estimates of the proportion of offspring sired by males other than the one attending a female and her nest range from 0 in snow geese to a whopping 90% in a species of fairy wren, brilliantly colored tiny birds from Australia (Griffith et al. 2002; Griffith and Montgomerie 2003). Although frequently only one male and one female are seen associating, including feeding and protecting the young, it has become apparent that additional males fathered offspring in the nest. In mammals that have multiple young in a litter, the young may also have more than one father, though mammals are less likely to appear to be monogamous in the first place.

This discovery was quite a shock to scientists, because outwardly it had appeared that most birds were monogamous. If this was not the case, many questions arose. What are the advantages to females of having multiple fathers for her brood? Do males attempt to deter females from such multiple mating, since it is costly to them to help rear offspring not their own? Why, given the apparent disparity of investment of males and females in offspring, should females pursue quantity rather than quality of mates? Questions like these are currently the subject of ongoing research in a variety of species.

The occurrence of extra-pair mating is also rather surprising to non-scientists, perhaps because the birds unwittingly had served as something of a role model for human marriage. It is tempting to conclude that if warblers, robins, and other models of monogamy are doing it, we should admit that extra-pair copulation, or adultery—or whatever term you prefer—is natural, expected, and maybe we should stop making such a fuss about it and resign ourselves to our evolutionary heritage.

But the problem is that the birds are not "cheating," they are just doing what they do, and they did not invent the rules about the pair bond between a male and female, we did. It isn't cheating if there are no rules to break. Some animals are monogamous, some are not, and one mating system is no more "natural," or "biological," than the other. Certainly multiple mating appears to be favored in many species, more species than had previously been believed, but that does not argue for the death of fidelity. Instead, it suggests a reexamination of sexual selection theory, something that is already occurring among scientists. This brings up an important point about the use of animal models for human behavior. Animals are useful for showing us what kinds of solutions exist to the common biological problems involved in survival and reproduction. How does the environment influence the costs and benefits of multiple mating? This is an interesting and relevant question—whether human males are biologically destined to cheat on their wives is not. As with maternal behavior, in mating systems multiple solutions are virtually always the norm, and there is no single natural male or female role.

What about the primates, our closest relatives? Here too, the sex role stereotypes are crumbling. Male dominance was viewed as the major force in primate societies when most monkeys and apes were studied in the middle of the twentieth century (Strum and Fedigan 2000), with females viewed as relatively uninterested in sex outside the time when they were most likely to become pregnant. However, probably not coincidentally with the growing numbers of women entering primatology, as more species were studied more intensively, it soon became clear that male-female relationships were more complex and furthermore that females often sought out sex (sometimes with both males and females) outside the period of maximum fertility (Smuts 1999; Strum and Fedigan 2000). In olive baboons, some males and females became what primatologist Barbara Smuts called "friends," with bonds of association that went beyond the brief act of sex itself (Smuts 1999). This complexity argues against the caricature of sex-crazed males and demure females that people sometimes thinks constitutes our heritage from other animals.

Studying a diversity of human cultures is also of interest once we recognize this multiplicity of solutions in other animals. What patterns of courtship and marriage seem to be universal, and what patterns depend on environmental attributes such as food availability and distribution?

## Model Systems and Role Models

It is also important to remember not to substitute one stereotype for another; it would be just as fallacious to conclude that all women are sexual adventuresses as to adhere to the old model of the frigid female. Deciding that biology is relevant to understanding gender does not mean that we imitate the species we prefer; model systems like the fruit flies used in genetics are useful tools for generalizing because we understand a great deal about them, but, as I mentioned earlier, they should not be confused with role models. Animals tell us that females can be assertive, but perhaps more important they tell us that females are variable. Furthermore, like many other biologists, I urge caution in interpreting nature. The naturalistic fallacy holds that what is natural is good, but what is natural can't be inherently "good" any more than it can be inherently amusing, inherently painful, or more likely to keep your hair shiny. Finding out that some animals eat their young says no more about the ethics of infanticide than finding out that some animals are yellow says about fashion trends.

As a scientist studying animals, not humans, I am also concerned about how our verdict of cheating affects our views of the animals themselves. Some of the early papers on extra-pair paternity in birds are interestingly divided in whom is portrayed as the active party in the behavior. Initially, there seemed to be two approaches, neither one particularly favorable to females. Either the males were roaming around taking advantage of hapless females waiting innocently in their own territories for the breadwinner males to come home with the worms, or else females were brazen hussies, seducing blameless males who otherwise would not have strayed from the path of moral righteousness into turpitude. One scientist refers rather peevishly to "female promiscuity" in blackbirds. Several papers, including one published in the prestigious journal *Nature*, call young birds fathered by males not paired with the mother as "illegitimate," as if their parents had tiny avian marriage licenses and chirped their vows (Gyllensten et al. 1990; Hasselquist et al. 1995; Bjornstad and Lifjeld 1997). Scientists, of course, are subject to social influences just like other people, but we should try not to allow our prejudices to influence our interpretation of what we see the animals doing. A paper on Tasmanian native hens, birds with a rather complex set of relationships between the sexes, discussed what appears to be polyandry, multiple males associated with a single female (Maynard Smith and Ridpath 1972). The paper refers to this behavior as "wife-sharing," but I have never seen multiple females associated with a male, its mirror image, and a common mating pattern, called "husband-sharing." Making the males the active parties (they "share" the female, as if she were a six-pack of beer) may reduce the likelihood of noticing what the females do, of seeing things from their point of view. Similarly, if we only see female baboons as mothers, we are less likely to notice that in fact their relationships, not those of males, determine troop structure and movement (Smuts 1999).

## CONCLUSIONS

It is no surprise that many people get twitchy when they hear about any so-called "biological" explanations of behavior in humans. They are also nervous when scientists study behaviors in animals that seem to occur in humans, for the reasons I described above. Here I have tried to ameliorate this fear, though at least in part it should be replaced with caution and awareness. Biology has great potential for harming women, but it is through our misbehavior, not the science itself. Biology can extend the boundaries of our thinking about gender as it can for so many other ideas. Contrary to popular belief, biology does not set limits, it demolishes them.

It is also important to remember that discoveries of mate fidelity, male tenderness or female sexual violence do not argue for a human nature that includes or excludes them. Evolution is an important explanation for the origin and diversity of life on earth, including human life. It helps us understand how organisms are related to each other, how the species that occur on a coral reef got there, whether a reed warbler female is likely to have any surviving young in a given year, how the members of chimpanzee groups sometimes benefit by being kind to one another, and why diet may help determine the probability of getting heart disease. Suggesting that evolutionary biology is irrelevant to human lives is as foolish as suggesting that it is irrelevant to the lives of fruit flies. Men and women are not the same, both from the standpoint of physiology and evolution. Neither are male and female goldfish, or fruit flies, or weasels. But this does not mean that men and women inherit templates of irreversible behavior.

## REFERENCES

Andersson, M. 1994. *Sexual Selection*. Princeton University Press, Princeton.

Bjornstad, G. and Lifjeld, J. T. 1997. High frequency of extra-pair paternity in a dense and synchronous population of Willow Warblers *Phylloscopus trochilus*. *J. Avian Biol.* 28 (4): 319–324.

Blum, D. 2002. *Love at Goon Park*. Perseus Publishing, New York.

Borgia, G. 1995. Why do bowerbirds build bowers? *Amer. Sci.* 83: 542–547.

Fausto-Sterling, A. 1987. *Myths of Gender: Biological Theories about Women and Men*. Basic Books, New York.

_____. 2003. Science matters, culture matters. *Perspec. Biol. Med.* 46: 109–124.

Galimberti, F., Fabiani, A., and Sanvito, S. 2002. Measures of breeding inequality: A case study in southern elephant seals. *Can. J. Zool.* 80: 1240–1249.

Gowaty, P. A. and Buschhaus, N. 1998. Ultimate causation of aggressive and forced copulation in birds: Female resistance, the CODE hypothesis, and social monogamy. *Amer. Zool.* 38: 207–225.

Gowaty, P. A. (ed.). 1997. *Feminism and Evolutionary Biology: Boundaries, Intersections, and Frontiers*. Chapman and Hall, New York.

Gowaty, P. A. 2003. Sexual natures: How feminism changed evolutionary. *Signs* 28: 901–921.

Griffith, S. C., Owens I. P. F., and Thuman K. A. 2002. Extra pair paternity in birds: a review of interspecific variation and adaptive function. *Molec. Ecol.* 11: 2195–2212.

Griffith, S. C. and Montgomerie, R. 2003. Why do birds engage in extra-pair copulation? *Nature* 422: 833–833.

Gyllensten, U. B., Jakobsson, S., and Temrin, H. 1990. No evidence for illegitimate young in monogamous and polygynous warblers. *Nature* 343: 168–170.

Hasselquist, D., Bensch, S., and von Schantz, T. 1995. Low frequency of extrapair paternity in the polygynous great reed warbler *Acrocephalus arundinaceus. Behav. Ecol.* 6: 27–38.

Hausfater, G. and Hrdy, S. B. (eds.). 1984. *Infanticide: Comparative and Evolutionary Perspectives.* Aldine de Gruyter, New York.

Hrdy, S. B. 1986. Empathy, polyandry, and the myth of the coy female. In: *Feminist Approaches to Science*, R. Bleier, ed. Pergamon Press, New York.

_____. 1997. Raising Darwin's consciousness—Female sexuality and the prehominid origins of patriarchy. *Hum. Nature* 8: 1–49.

_____. 1999. *Mother Nature.* Pantheon, New York.

Jennions, M. D., and Petrie, M. 1997. Variation in mate choice and mating preferences: A review of causes and consequences. *Biol. Rev. Cam. Phil. Soc.* 72: 283–327.

_____. 2000. Why do females mate multiply? A review of the genetic benefits. *Biol. Rev. Cam. Phil. Soc.* 75: 21–64.

Keller, E. F. 1985. *Reflections on Gender and Science.* Yale University Press, New Haven.

Le Boeuf, B. J. and Reiter, J. 1988. Lifetime reproductive success in northern elephant seals. pp. 344–362 in *Reproductive Success: Studies of Individual Variation in Contrasting Breeding Systems*, T. H. Clutton-Brock, ed. University of Chicago Press, Chicago.

Liesen, L. T. 1995. Feminism and the politics of reproductive strategies. *Politics Life Sci.* 14: 145–162.

Madden, J. R. 2003. Male spotted bowerbirds preferentially choose, arrange and proffer objects that are good predictors of mating success. *Behav. Ecol. Sociobiol.* 53 (5): 263–268.

Maynard Smith, J. and Ridpath, M. G. 1972. Wife sharing in the Tasmanian native hen, *Tribonyx mortierii:* a case of kin selection? *Amer. Nat.* 106: 447–452.

Petrie, M. 1994. Improved growth and survival of offspring of peacocks with more elaborate trains. *Nature* 371: 598–599.

Petrie, M. and Halliday, T. 1994. Experimental and natural changes in the peacock's (*Pave cristatus*) train can affect mating success. *Behav. Ecol. Sociobiol.* 35: 213–217.

Smuts, B. B. 1999. *Sex and Friendship in Baboons.* 2nd ed. Harvard University Press, Cambridge, MA.

Strum, S. C. and Fedigan, L. M. (eds.). 2000. *Primate Encounters: Models of Science, Gender, and Society.* University of Chicago Press, Chicago.

Trivers, R. L. 1972. Parental investment and sexual selection. Pp 136–179 in *Sexual Selection and the Descent of Man, 1871–1971*, B. Campbell, ed. Heinemann, London.

Uy, J. A. C., Patricelli, G. L., and Borgia, G. 2001. Complex mate searching in the satin bowerbird *Ptilonorhynchus violaceus. Amer. Nat.* 158: 530–542.

Wallace, A. R. 1889. *Darwinism: An Exposition of the Theory of Natural Selection with Some of Its Applications.* MacMillan Press, London.

Zuk, M. 2002. *Sexual Selections: What We Can and Can't Learn about Sex from Animals.* University of California Press, Berkeley.

# Delusions of Gender: What Does It all Mean, Anyway? and Brain Scams

## Cordelia Fine

## WHAT DOES IT ALL MEAN, ANYWAY?

Seeing that the average brain weight of women is about five ounces less than that of men, on merely anatomical grounds we should be prepared to expect a marked inferiority of intellectual power in the former. Moreover, as the general physique of women is less robust than that of men—and therefore less able to sustain the fatigue of serious or prolonged brain action—we should also on physiological grounds be prepared to entertain a similar anticipation. In actual fact we find that the inferiority displays itself most conspicuously in a comparative absence

Fine, Cordelia. 2010. *Delusions of Gender: How Our Minds, Society, and Neurosexism Create Difference.* New York: W. W. Norton & Company.

of originality, and this more especially in the higher levels of intellectual work.

*George J. Romanes, evolutionary biologist and physiologist (1887)*[1]

It's always pleasant when data confirm predictions. But did George Romanes never once consider whether an African Grey parrot (with a brain weight of less than half an ounce) might outsmart a cow with a brain more than thirty times heavier? Did he really know not a single weedy intellectual, nor one muscular chump, to provoke him to wonder whether physical strength really was correlated with tenacity of "brain action"? Perhaps it was only natural that the brain scientists who meticulously measured men's and women's head dimensions, skull volume, and brain weight should try to relate their findings to psychological differences between the sexes. But with the benefit of hindsight we can see that it was not just neuroscientific understanding they lacked, but humility. "Optimistic" is the only kind word to use to describe their confident assertions that differences in the engine power of male and female *minds* were being probed by tape measures, sacks of millet grain, and sets of scales.

Today, we are no less interested in pinning our more sophisticatedly obtained sex differences in the brain onto the mind. "[H]ope springs eternal," Fausto-Sterling wryly notes. "Is it now possible that finally, with *really* new, *really* modern approaches, we can demonstrate the biological basis of sexual or racial inequality?"[2] And, as neuroendocrinologist Geert De Vries has pointed out, it is intuitive to assume that males and females have different brains so that they can behave differently. With the discovery of differences in hormone receptors, or neuronal density, or corpus callosum size, or different proportions of gray and white matter, or brain region size, the instinct is to look for a psychological difference to pin it on. But the counterintuitive possibility that always needs to be considered is that sex differences in the brain may also "just as well do the exact opposite, that is, they may prevent sex differences in overt functions and behavior by compensating for sex differences in physiology."[3] For example, a smaller number of neurons in a particular brain region can be compensated for by greater neurotransmitter production per neuron.[4]

One very striking example of the principle that brain difference can yield behavioral similarity, discussed by De Vries, comes from the prairie vole. In this species, males and females contribute equally to parenting (excepting, of course, nursing). In female prairie voles, parenting behavior is primed by the hormonal changes of pregnancy. But this leaves a mystery. How do father voles, which experience none of these hormonal changes, come to show paternal behavior? The answer turns out to lie in a part of a region of the brain called the lateral septum, which is involved in the triggering of paternal behavior. This part of the brain is very different in males and females, being much more richly endowed with receptors for the hormone vasopressin in the male, yet this striking sex difference in the brain enables male and female prairie voles to behave the same. We can't assume that even quite substantial sex differences in the brain imply sex differences in the mind. As Celia Moore has pointed out, "Some neural differences are inconsequential, because they are offset by other compensatory differences. Other neural differences are alternative pathways to the same behavioral end."[5]

In humans, one indisputable physiological difference between males and females is size—including the brain. Although there is overlap, men on average have larger brains than do women, and a large brain is not simply a smaller brain scaled up. Larger brains create different sorts of engineering problems and so—to minimize energy demands, wiring costs, and communication times—there are physical reasons for different arrangements in differently sized brains.[6] From this perspective, "men and women confront similar cognitive challenges using differently sized neural machinery."[7] The brain can get to the same outcome in more than one way. And in line with this, recent studies of brain structure have argued that it is not that *women* have larger corpora callosa, or a more generous serving of gray matter, relative to brain volume. Rather, it is people with *small brains,* male or female, who show this quality. As one group put it: "brain size matters more than sex."[8] If this principle proves to be correct—there's currently no agreed way of controlling for absolute brain size—then, unless we're happy to start comparing the spatial or empathizing skills of big-headed men and women with those of their pinheaded counterparts, we may have to abandon the idea that we will find the answers to psychological gender differences in gray matter, white matter, corpus callosum size, or any other alleged sex difference in brain structure that turns out to have more to do with size than sex.

This, one would think, would secretly be a relief. This is not just because those gender differences can wax and wane, depending on the time, place, and context. But also the very idea of trying to relate these kinds of structural differences to psychological function is fantastically ambitious, given that, as neuroscientist Jay Giedd and colleagues have put it, "most brain functions arise from distributed neural networks and that within any given region lies a daunting complexity of connections, neurotransmitter systems, and synaptic functions."[9]

Yet sometimes the temptation is too much to resist.

Twenty years ago, my mother proposed a neuroscientific model to explain why some brains have an extraordinary capacity for deeply focused thought. Her hypothesis was that "[a]ll the blood in your brain rushes to the really clever bits and there's none left over to warm up the roots."[10] My mother, by the way, is a novelist. Yet her idea, coined as an acerbic marital insult in a work of fiction, shares an important flaw with a suggestion made in a prestigious journal of science. Simon Baron-Cohen and his colleagues, as mentioned earlier, suggested in *Science* that a brain skewed toward local connectivity is "compatible with strong systemizing, because systemizing involves a narrow attentional focus to local information, in order to understand each part of a system."[11] Likewise, in the recent book *Why Aren't More Women in Science?* neuroscientists Ruben and Raquel Gur conjecture that "the greater facility of women with interhemispheric communications may attract them to disciplines that require integration rather than detailed scrutiny of narrowly characterized processes."[12]

But why, we might ask, should shorter circuits in the brain allow narrower focus in the mind? As McGill University philosopher of science Ian Gold has said, "[m]ay as well say hairier body so fuzzier thinker. Or that human beings are capable of fixing fuses because the brain uses electricity."[13] Consider what's involved in zooming in your attention on, say, a small aspect of the process of photosynthesis. Does only a little bit of the brain get involved because only a little detail is being processed? Or is there—as seems far more likely—activity all over the brain as distracting information is suppressed, the inner voice formulates ideas and poses questions, visual stimuli are processed, motion is imagined, and information is retrieved from memory?[14]

In truth, if it was the male brain that seemed to be more long range, we could easily concoct a plausible hypothesis to explain why this enhances their systemizing skills. And this is the problem: the obscurity of the relationship between brain structure and psychological function means that just-so stories can be all too easily written and rewritten. Do you find that your male participants are actually *less* lateralized on a spatial problem? Not to worry! As the contradictory data come in, researchers can draw on both the hypothesis that men are better at mental rotation because they use just one hemisphere, as well as the completely contrary hypothesis that men are better at mental rotation because they use *both* hemispheres. So flexible is the theoretical arrangement that researchers can even present these opposing hypotheses, quite without embarrassment, within the very same article.[15]

Likewise, Gur and his colleagues happily tinker with the long-standing idea that it is males' more lateralized spatial processing that underlies their superiority on mental rotation tasks. They found that performance on two spatial tasks correlated with the volume of interconnecting white matter in the brain.[16] White matter is made up of the axons, insulated for speed of travel of the electrical signal by the white fat myelin, which communicate between distant brain regions. "When we looked at the top performers for spatial tasks in our study . . . there were nine men and only one woman," Gur explained for the *Science Daily* news release. "Of these nine men, seven [actually, it was six] had greater white-matter volumes than any of the women in the study."[17] Now, we're talking about ten people here—hardly a sample size on which to base sweeping generalizations about the sexes. It's also, as psychologists

well know, dangerous to assume that correlation means causation. Further, in the scientific article itself, Gur cautions that the "correlations could be spurious and should be interpreted with extreme caution."[18] And they really could be spurious, given that 1 in 20 "significant" results occur by chance, and the researchers tested for thirty-six relationships. Of course, we don't know who decided that this caveat was not worth mentioning in the report designed for public consumption. But despite all this, Gur goes on to suggest to *Science Daily* that "in order to be a super performer in that area, one needs more white matter than exists in most female brains." Following up this line of argument in their chapter in *Why Aren't More Women in Science?* the Gurs conjecture that "[t]he requirement of large volume of WM [white matter] for complex spatial processing may be an obstacle in some branches of mathematics and physics."[19] This, they suggest, is because men's greater white-matter volumes enable better within-hemisphere processing.

But meanwhile, back in the functional neuroimaging lab, the Gurs and their colleagues have found that in some regions of the brain men show more *bilateral* activation than women while performing spatial tasks. They therefore suggest a "reformulation" of the spotlight hypothesis, namely, "that optimal performance requires both unilateral activation in primary regions, left for verbal and right for spatial tasks, and bilateral activation in associated regions."[20] Well, maybe they are right to now emphasize the importance of participation from both hemispheres. Interestingly, researchers who study people with exceptional talent in mathematics argue that enhanced interaction *between* the hemispheres—supposedly a female brain characteristic—is a special feature of the mathematically gifted brain.[21] But maybe, just until such a time as we have a somewhat firmer grasp of how the structural properties of the brain relate to complex cognition, the Gurs should stick to the lower-maintenance hypothesis that optimal performance requires whatever features of the brain happen to be observed in males.[22]

This kind of theoretical U-turn has always beset the neuroscience of sex differences. For example, in the nineteenth century, when the seat of the intellect was thought to reside in the frontal lobes, careful observation of male and female brains revealed that this region appeared both larger and more complexly structured in males, while the parietal lobes were better developed in women. Yet when scientific thought came to the opinion that it was instead the parietal lobes that furnished powers of abstract intellectual thought, subsequent observations revealed that the parietal lobes were more developed in the male, after all.[23] With startling insight, Havelock Ellis, the author of a comprehensive late–nineteenth-century review of sexual science, described these earlier erroneous observations as "inevitable":

> It was firmly believed that the frontal region is the seat of all the highest and most abstract intellectual processes, and if on examining a dozen or two brains an anatomist found himself landed in the conclusion that the frontal region is relatively larger in women, the probability is that he would feel he had reached a conclusion that was absurd. It may, indeed, be said that it is only since it has become known that the frontal region of the brain is of greater relative extent in the ape than it is in Man, and has no special connection with the higher intellectual processes, that it has become possible to recognise the fact that that region is relatively more extensive in women.[24]

Of course, there's nothing wrong with changing your mind in the light of new evidence about the sexes. But those who are tempted to play this game, by claiming that sex differences in the structure of the brain yield essentially different kinds of minds, should be aware that this sort of flipping seems to be a common part of the process. And, with the benefit of hindsight, it never looks good.

No less care is required when it comes to interpreting differences between the sexes in brain activity. No doubt about it, functional neuroimaging technologies have brought the fresh, modern zing of neuroscience to old stereotypes. Allan and Barbara Pease, for example, purport to demonstrate in their book *Why Men Don't Listen and Women Can't Read Maps* the striking sex differences in the sheer volume of brain devoted to emotion processing. A brain diagram of "Emotion in men" shows two blobs in the right hemisphere. As the text explains, emotion in men is highly compartmentalized, meaning that "a man can argue logic and words (left brain) and then switch to spatial solutions (right front brain) without becoming emotional about the issue. It's as if emotion is in a little room of its own." But in the illustration of "Emotion in women" there are more than a dozen blobs scattered across both hemispheres of the brain. What this means, according to the Peases, is that "women's emotions can switch on simultaneously with most other brain functions." Or, to call a spade a spade, emotion can cloud all and any of a woman's mental activities.[25]

These emotion maps of the male and female brain, the Peases inform readers, are based on fMRI research by neuroscientist Sandra Witelson. In order "to locate the position of emotion in the brain," she used "emotionally-charged images that were shown first to the right hemisphere via the left eye and ear and then to the left hemisphere via the right eye and ear."[26] Should readers have both the time and the resources to check out the six Witelson references in the book's

bibliography, they will find only two studies published after functional neuroimaging techniques first began to be substantively put to use by cognitive neuroscientists in the 1980s. One study did not involve brain research (it is a survey of handedness in gay men and women). The other is a comparison of corpus callosum size in right-and mixed-handed people.[27] It might also be worth mentioning that it was a postmortem study. Possibly Sandra Witelson really did present her samples of dead brain tissue with emotionally charged images—but if she did, it's not mentioned in the published report.

It may be that the Peases were referring to functional neuroimaging research published by Sandra Witelson and colleagues in 2004.[28] It's hard to know: this study used PET rather than fMRI; stimuli were presented in the normal two-eyed, two-eared fashion; and the male/female blob tallies and locations are dissimilar to those presented by the Peases. However, this study did at least look at brain activity while men and women performed one of two emotion-matching tasks. The easier task involved deciding which of two faces match the emotion of a third, target, face. The harder task involved deciding which of two faces match the emotion expressed in a voice. According to Susan Pinker's summary of Witelson's results, "[w]hen women looked at pictures of people's facial expressions, both cerebral hemispheres were activated and there was greater activity in the amygdala, the almond-shaped seat of emotion buried deep in the brain. In men, perception of emotion was usually localized in one hemisphere." Pinker then goes on to suggest that since research also shows that women have a thicker corpus callosum, allowing speedy interhemispheric transmission of information (a claim that, as you will recall from the previous chapter, is under serious scientific dispute), "the hardware for women's processing of emotion seems to take up more space and have a more efficient transportation grid than men's. Scientists infer that this allows women to process emotion with dispatch."[29]

In fact, the researchers found no differences in how quickly men and women performed the tasks. It's also worth noting that although the statement "both cerebral hemispheres were activated" in women might conjure up an image much like that presented by the Peases, with activity over a generous portion of the female brain, this is not the case. Rather—and take a deep breath before reading on—in the easy task women showed greater activation than men in left fusiform gyrus, right amygdala, and left inferior frontal gyrus. In the hard task they showed greater activity in left thalamus, right fusiform gyrus, and left anterior cingulate. Men, meanwhile, showed greater activity than women in right medial frontal gyrus and right superior occipital gyrus for the easy task, and in left inferior frontal gyrus and left inferior parietal gyrus for the hard task. Or, rather less technically, women always had two left blobs and one right blob, while men had either two right blobs or two left blobs, depending on the task—painting a rather less striking image of contrast. (Bear in mind, too, that blobs represent *differences* in brain activity, not brain activity per se. If a search for regions activated more in men yields a blob-free left hemisphere, for example, that doesn't mean that that hemisphere is switched off in men. Rather, it means that the researchers didn't find any regions in the hemisphere that were activated more in men than in women.)[30]

Does this complicated-sounding list of brain activations tell us something interesting about gender difference in emotional experience? The researchers, like Pinker, certainly think so. They conclude that their "findings suggest that men tend to modulate their reaction to stimuli, and engage in analysis and association, whereas women tend to draw more on primary emotional reference."[31] (By this they mean that only women find others' emotions innately arousing.) As you will have already realized, a simpler, and more familiar, way to put the same idea would be to say that men are thinkers and women are feelers.

So does this neuroimaging study simply confirm what everyone already suspected—that "men may take a more analytic approach" to emotion processing while "women are more emotionally centered"?[32] Or is it possible that these interpretations are, to paraphrase Fausto-Sterling, unwittingly projecting assumptions about gender onto the vast unknown that is the brain?

With the previous chapter's cautionary tale of premature speculation in mind, it's worth noting that Witelson's neuroimaging study compared just eight men with eight women on each task—a modest-sized sample. Could the sex differences in brain activation be spurious? When looking for changes in blood flow between two conditions, researchers search in thousands of tiny sections of the brain (called voxels), and many researchers are now arguing that the threshold commonly set for declaring that a difference is "significant" just isn't high enough. To illustrate this point, some researchers recently scanned an Atlantic salmon while showing it emotionally charged photographs. The salmon—which, by the way, "was not alive at the time of scanning"—was "asked to determine what emotion the individual in the photo must have been experiencing." Using standard statistical procedures, they found significant brain activity in one small region of the dead fish's brain while it performed the empathizing task, compared with brain activity during "rest." The researchers conclude not that this particular region of the brain is involved in postmortem piscine

empathizing, but that the kind of statistical thresholds commonly used in neuroimaging studies (including Witelson's emotion-matching study) are inadequate because they allow too many spurious results through the net.[33]

This of course does not mean that all reported activations are spurious. It just highlights the importance of being aware of the possibility. We might be more confident that Witelson's study genuinely identified brain regions that function differently in the two sexes during emotion recognition tasks if at least some of the brain regions that showed sex differences in activation in the easy emotion-matching tasks also turned up in the harder task.[34] However, if you look back at the list of brain activations you'll see that in neither men nor women was any brain region activated more during both the easy and difficult emotion-matching tasks.

But even if we assume that results such as these are reliable, what do they tell us about male/female differences in psychology? Does it mean that men are more analytic, if their left inferior frontal gyrus activates more, or that women are more emotional because the right amygdala is on fire? Inferring a psychological state from brain activity (like *The amygdala was activated so that means our participants were fearful*) is known as reverse inference, and as any neuroimager will tell you, it is fraught with peril.[35] Some neuroscientists have even died while making reverse inferences. Actually, I made that last bit up, but as we will see, it is extremely tricky. There are two ways that males and females can diverge in brain activation: how much activation is seen and where that activation is. Neither piece of information, unfortunately, tells us much about psychological sex differences.

Just as bigger doesn't necessarily mean better with regards to the size of brain structures, neither does more activation necessarily mean better or psychologically more. Researchers who study development, or learning, sometimes find that some patterns of activation reduce, or become more streamlined, as development or expertise proceeds.[36] Bizarrely, activation isn't even a surefire sign that the activity is doing *anything* useful. For example, Chris Bird and colleagues studied a patient who suffered extensive damage to the medial prefrontal cortex following a stroke. The scope of the damage included pretty much all of the brain regions that have been reliably activated in literally dozens of functional imaging studies of mind reading. Yet the patient was fine at mind reading! As the researchers note, "the data reported here urge caution in concluding that medial frontal cortex is critical for effecting ToM [theory of mind]."[37] Vision scientist Giedrius Buracas and colleagues had an equally surprising finding. They found that brain region V1 was activated more than region MT in a motion perception task. Yet it's well-established from neurophysiological research with primates that MT—which was activated less—is critically involved in motion detection, while V1—which was activated more—is not.[38] These two studies serve as warning flags: even though a part of the brain might light up during a task, it may not be especially or crucially involved.

The location of activation in the brain is also surprisingly uninformative. Clearly, the whole brain isn't involved in doing everything. Different parts of the brain are specialized for processing different sorts of information. But a particular cortical region or population of neurons can be specialized for different jobs in different contexts. As imaging experts Karl Friston and Cathy Price put it, specialization is dynamic and context-dependent.[39] For example, a particular population of neurons in the temporal cortex may, at different times, represent both identity (*Whose face is it?*) and expression (*Is it happy or sad?*). What those neurons are doing depends both on what sort of information is being fed in, and also what sort of information is being fed back from higher regions in the processing chain. "Specialisation is therefore not an intrinsic property of any region," argue Price and Friston, and that means that seeing a brain region in action doesn't mean you know what it's up to in your particular task. For many parts of the brain, this problem is acute. For example, the anterior cingulate is activated by so many tasks that one cognitive neuroscientist I know refers to it as the "on button."

There just isn't a simple one-to-one correspondence between brain regions and mental processes, which can make interpreting imaging data a difficult task. As Jonah Lehrer recently explained in the *Boston Globe:*

> [O]ne of the most common uses of brain scanners—taking a complex psychological phenomenon and pinning it to a particular bit of cortex—is now being criticized as a potentially serious oversimplification of how the brain works. . . . [C]ritics stress the interconnectivity of the brain, noting that virtually every thought and feeling emerges from the crosstalk of different areas spread across the cortex.[40]

If so, the familiar spots of color on brain activation maps (derided by some as "blobology"), labeled as male-female difference in activation, are going to tell a very oversimplified story, and one in which much of the important information may be lost. It's also a story that, as neuropsychologist Anelis Kaiser and colleagues point out, is geared to emphasize difference over similarity.[41]

Then, there is the sad fact that, at its most precise, functional imaging technology averages over a few seconds the activity of literally millions of neurons that can fire up to a hundred impulses a second. (For PET the timescale is even longer.) "Using fMRI to spy on neurons is something like using Cold War-era satellites to spy on people: Only large-scale activity is visible," says *Science* journalist Greg Miller.[42] This severely limits the interpretations that can be made about brief psychological events. Understandably, given all these interpretive gaps, many neuroscientists hesitate to speculate what their data might mean in terms of sex differences in thinking. Many, to their credit, have performed admirably as The Voice of Restraint in popular articles about gender and the brain, and in their academic work explicitly warn against making unwarranted inferences (pleas that, in certain quarters, fall on deaf ears).

It's not, by the way, my intention to present myself as a neuroscience skeptic. Not only are some of my best friends, as well as family members, neuroimagers, but I also think that neuroscience is an extremely exciting and promising field, and can be usefully employed in combination with other techniques. I also understand that speculation is an important part of the scientific process. Nor is the topic of gender difference by any means the only area in which overinterpretation can occur. And I certainly don't think that research into sex differences in the brain is wrong or point-less. There *are* sex differences in the brain (although, as we've seen, agreeing on what these are is harder than you might think)[43]; there are sex differences in vulnerabilities to certain psychological disorders, and hopefully greater understanding of the former might help to illuminate the latter. My point is simply this: that neither structural nor functional imaging can currently tell us much about differences between male and female minds. As Rutgers University psychologist Deena Skolnick Weisberg has recently argued, we should "remember that neuroscience, as a method for studying the mind, is still in its infancy. It shows much promise to be someday what many people want to make it into now: a powerful tool for diagnosis and research. We should remember that it has this promise, and give it the time it needs to achieve its potential—without making too much of it in the meantime."[44]

Are early twenty-first–century neuroscientific explanations of inequality—too little white matter, an unspecialized brain, too rapacious a corpus callosum—doomed to join the same garbage heap as measures of snout elongation, cephalic index, and brain fiber delicacy? Will future generations look back on early twenty-first–century interpretations of imaging data with the same shocked amusement with which we regard early twentieth-century speculations about the relevance of sex differences in spinal cord size? I suspect they will, although only time will tell. But to any scientist considering trying to relate sex differences in the brain to complex psychological functions . . . well, let's just say, "Remember Dr. Charles Dana."

And it *is* important to remember him. For as we'll see in the next chapter, the speculations of a few scientists quickly evolve into the colorful fabrications of popular neurosexism—the subspecialty within the larger discipline of neurononsense to which we now turn.

## BRAIN SCAMS

My husband would probably like you to know that, for the sake of my research for this chapter, he has had to put up with an awful lot of contemptuous snorting. For several weeks, our normally quiet hour of reading in bed before lights out became more like dinnertime in the pigsty as I worked my way through popular books about gender difference. As the result of my research, I have come up with four basic pieces of advice for anyone considering incorporating neuroscientific findings into a popular book or article about gender: (1) unless you have a time machine and have visited a future in which neuroscientists can make reverse inferences without the nagging anxieties that keep the more thoughtful of them awake at night, do not suggest that parents or teachers treat boys and girls differently because of differences observed in their brains; (2) if you don't know what a reverse inference is, read the previous chapter of this book; (3) exercise extreme caution when making the perilous leap from brain structure to psychological function; and (4) don't make stuff up.

When it comes to selecting examples from those who have failed to follow one or more of these four simple rules, one's choices abound. Possibly my favorite illustration of a self-serving projection of prejudices onto brain jargon is a section in John Gray's *Why Mars and Venus Collide* in which he discusses the inferior parietal lobe (IPL). In men, says Gray, the left IPL is more developed, while in women it is the right side that is larger. It will be no surprise to anyone, I am sure, to learn that "[t]he left side of the brain has more to do with more linear, reasonable, and rational thought, while the right side of the brain is more emotional, feeling, and intuitive." But it *is* extraordinary just how differently the IPL serves its master and its mistress. According to Gray a man's large left IPL, being involved in the "perception of time," explains why he becomes impatient with how long a woman talks. By contrast, the IPL also "allows the brain to process information from the senses, particularly in selective attention, like when women are able to respond to a baby's crying in the night."[45] Perhaps deliberately, we are left in the dark as to whether the male inferior parietal lobe enables a man to do the same.

In *Leadership and the Sexes*, Michael Gurian and Barbara Annis inform executives that "women's brains tend to link more of the emotional activity that is going on in the middle of the brain (the limbic system) with thoughts and words in the top of the brain (the cerebral cortex). Thus a man might need many hours to process a major emotion-laden experience [*I . . . just . . . got . . . fired . . . I . . . am . . . sad . . . and . . . angry.*], whereas a woman may be able to process it quite quickly [*Oh, crap!*] ."[46] A further neurophysiological disadvantage for men may be found in another of Gurian's books, *What Could He Be Thinking?* Implicitly drawing on a working metaphor of *The Brain as Pinball Machine*, he explains how in men the "signal" of an emotional feeling, having made it to the right hemisphere, "may well get stopped, disappearing into neural oblivion because the signal found no access to a receptor in a language center in the left side of the brain." This doesn't happen in the female brain because, according to Gurian, while men have just one or two language centers in the left hemisphere, women have as many as seven such centers, dotted all over the brain, as well as a 25 percent larger corpus callosum. (Despite this embarrassment of neurological riches, the contrast Gurian draws between male and female brain function leaves me speechless.) And so, in men, a feeling signal is much less likely to hit the jackpot of contact with a neuron involved in language.[47]

We also discover in *Leadership and the Sexes* that when a woman leader asks her colleagues, "What do you all think?" this is a typically female "white matter" question. It seems that white matter isn't just involved in integrating information from different parts of the brain, but also from different people in the office.[48] Brain differences may also be behind a female-leadership problem-solving style: when a female leader "knows what to do, she's not as worried as a man might be about proving it with data." Gurian and Annis suggest that "[o]ne reason for this intuitiveness may be that she has a larger *corpus callosum* connecting both hemispheres of the brain." By contrast, male leaders favor a problem-solving style that, in part, "relies on more linear data and proof."[49]

Perhaps my own corpus callosum runs to a smaller size than the standard female issue, but I find these intuitive leaps from brain structure to psychological function unconvincing, as noted in the previous chapter. Why should arriving at a solution to a problem through an analysis of data and proof require any less integration between hemispheres? As an example of just how wrong our intuitions can be in these matters, despite the popular assumption that a more lateralized brain will be worse at multitasking, neurobiologist Lesley Rogers and her colleagues found precisely the opposite to be the case in chicks.[50] Chicks with more lateralized brains were better at simultaneously pecking for food grains and looking out for predators (the established chick equivalent of frying a steak while making a salad).

While it may not be too surprising to discover self-appointed "thought-leaders" dressing up stereotypes in neuroscientific finery, it is more of a shock to see this in an alumnus of Harvard Medical School, the University of California-Berkeley, and Yale School of Medicine. Step forward Louann Brizendine, director of the University of California-San Francisco Women's Mood and Hormone Clinic. Her book, *The Female Brain*, cites literally hundreds of academic articles. To the unwary reader, both she and the book seem reliable and authoritative. And yet, as a review of the book in *Nature* comments, "despite the author's extensive academic credentials, *The Female Brain* disappointingly fails to meet even the most basic standards of scientific accuracy and balance. The book is riddled with scientific errors and is misleading about the processes of brain development, the neuroendocrine system, and the nature of sex differences in general." The reviewers later go on to say that, "[t]he text is rife with 'facts' that do not exist in the supporting references."[51] This is a common discovery made by people who take the time to fact check Brizendine's claims. Mark Liberman, a professor at the University of Pennsylvania with no special interest in gender issues, has nonetheless been provoked to provide many detailed but humorous critiques of pseudoscientific claims about gender differences on his online Language Log. His patient corrections of Brizendine's many false assertions about sex differences in communication is a chore that, as he puts it, "is starting to make me feel like the circus clown that follows the elephant around the ring with a shovel."[52]

But despite these forewarnings, when I decided to follow up Brizendine's claim that the female brain is wired to empathize, it nonetheless proved to be an exercise that turned up surprise after surprise. I tracked down every neuroscience study cited by Brizendine as evidence for feminine superiority in mind reading. (No, really, no need to thank me. I do this sort of thing for pleasure.) There were many such references, over just a few pages of text, creating the impression it was no mere opinion, but scientifically established fact, that the female brain is wired for empathy in a way that the male brain is not. Yet fact checking revealed the deployment of some rather misleading practices. For example, let's work our way through the middle of page 162 to the top of page 164 in her book. We kick off with a study of psychotherapists, which found that therapists develop a good rapport with their clients by mirroring their actions.[53] Casually, Brizendine notes, "All of the therapists who showed these responses

happened to be women."[54] For some reason, she fails to mention that this is because only female therapists, selected from phone directories, happened to be recruited for the study.

Brizendine's next claim—that girls have an advantage in understanding others' feelings—does find support in the work of Erin McClure and Judith Hall, which she cites. These researchers both conducted meta-analyses that found advantages for females in decoding nonverbal expressions of emotion.[55] The edge is, however, moderate. McClure's meta-analysis suggests that about 54 percent of girls will perform above average in facial emotion processing, compared with 46 percent of boys. Hall's review of research with tests such as the PONS nonverbal decoding task (which we encountered in Chapter 2) suggests that if you randomly chose a boy and a girl, over and over, more than a third of the time the boy would outperform the girl. Brizendine does not understate these findings, then, when she says that "[g]irls are years ahead of boys" in these abilities.[56] She then speculates that mirror neurons may lie behind these skills, enabling girls to observe, imitate, and mirror the nonverbal cues of others as a way to intuit their feelings. (Mirror neurons are neurons that respond to another animal's actions as though the animal-observer itself were acting. Some scientists think that mirror neurons may provide the neural grounding for understanding people's minds. Other scientists are dubious about the whole concept.) The study she cites here does explore the potential role of the mirror system in intuiting others' mental states—but not specifically in females.[57] Indeed, its participants (some of whom had autism-spectrum disorders) were all male.

A little later, readers are told that "brain-imaging studies show that the mere act of observing or imagining another person in a particular emotional state can automatically activate similar brain patterns in the observer—and females are especially good at this kind of emotional mirroring."[58] Cited as support for this feminine superiority in emotional mirroring is a 2004 neuroimaging study by cognitive neuroscientist Tania Singer and colleagues, who compared brain activation when someone was either receiving a painful electric shock to the hand or was aware that a loved one was receiving the same painful electric shock to the hand.[59] Singer and colleagues found that some brain regions were activated both by being shocked and watching someone else be shocked. If you think I'm going to be nitpicky about what any sex differences in activation in this study *mean*, you're wrong. Actually, the problem of interpretation is rather more basic. Only women were scanned.

Continuing the theme of women's special sensitivity to the pain of others in the next paragraph,

Brizendine informs us that when a woman, for example, responds empathically to the stubbed toe of another, she is "demonstrating an extreme form of what the female brain does naturally from childhood and even more in adulthood—experience the pain of another person."[60] Brizendine marshals two functional neuroimaging studies as support for this claim. The first is Singer's 2004 study of females' empathic responses to pain. The second is a study by Tetsuya Iidaka and colleagues, who asked participants to judge the gender of faces showing positive, negative, or neutral expressions. They compared brain activations in young versus old participants, but not in females versus males.[61] (Her third citation is a review of anxiety and depression in childhood and adolescence. It doesn't discuss responses to others' pain, or gender differences in this capacity, although the authors note that "[b]ecause females are known to be more emotionally responsive than males to the problems of *others,* a wider range of interpersonal contexts may arouse them.")[62]

In the last part of this page range, Brizendine describes Singer's 2004 study, and states that "the same pain areas of [the women's] brains that had activated when they themselves were shocked lit up when they learned their partners were being strongly shocked."[63] She references the Singer 2004 study here, naturally, but also another functional neuroimaging study by the same research team, published in 2006.[64] This study was similar, but instead of being a romantic partner who was shocked, it was a confederate who had played either fairly or unfairly in a game just before. In this study, both men and women were scanned. Again, empathy-related responses were seen in reaction to the pain of another, although in men this was only the case when the confederate had played fairly. Having referenced these two studies, Brizendine concludes that "[t]he women were feeling their partner's pain. . . . Researchers have been unable to elicit similar brain responses from men."[65] She has, however, just cited a study that *did* elicit similar brain responses from men, albeit only in response to people they liked.

By this point the reader may have a poor opinion indeed of the male neurological capacity for empathy—especially since earlier on in the chapter Brizendine suggests that females may have more of the neurons that enable mirroring. She writes that "[a]lthough most of the studies on this topic have been done on primates, scientists speculate that there may be more mirror neurons in the human female brain than in the human male brain." Look to the notes at the back of the book and no fewer than five scholarly references appear to affirm this claim.[66] The first study is in Russian. Although it did compare the sexes, from the abstract I would lay a substantial bet on it not offering much insight into gender differences in mirror

neurons, as it was a postmortem study of neuron characteristics in the frontal lobes. (One would, I imagine, have to see mirror neurons in action to be able to identify them.) Three further studies did indeed look at some aspect of what is thought to be the mirror neuron system. However, none of them compared males and females, or speculated about possible differences between the sexes. And that leaves just one remaining citation, which is "personal communication" with Harvard-based cognitive neuroscientist Lindsay Oberman, entitled "There may be a difference in male and female mirror neuron functioning." When I emailed Dr. Oberman to confirm, to my surprise, she informed me that not only had she never communicated with Brizendine, but went on to write that, "to the contrary, I have looked at many of my studies and have not found evidence for better mirror neuron functioning in females."[67] (Once you've picked your jaw up off the floor, don't forget to briefly think about the 5 percent rule I mentioned in Chapter 12, in which only sex *differences* get reported.)

What is deliciously ironic about all of this is that Brizendine presents herself as the reluctant but fearless messenger of truth:

> In writing this book I have struggled with two voices in my head—one is the scientific truth, the other is political correctness. I have chosen to emphasize scientific truth over political correctness even though scientific truths may not always be welcome.[68]

When I am in the mood to be irked, I flip through Brizendine's book. Perhaps because of the particular stage of life I happen to be in, I found myself most enraged by her claim that only when "the children leave home, the mommy brain circuits are finally free to be applied to new ambitions, new thoughts, new ideas."[69] But it's the sexism that bursts through the doors of preschools and schools, cleverly disguised in neuroscientific finery, that I find most disturbing. As neuroimaging takes its first steps on the long journey to understanding how neuronal firing yields mental abilities, you will find no shortage of so-called experts willing to explain the educational implications of differences in boy wiring and girl wiring. The medal for the most outrageous claim must surely go to an American educational speaker. According to reports sent to Mark Liberman's Language Log, this educational consultant has been informing audiences that girls see the details while boys see the big picture because the "crockus"—a region of the brain that does not exist—is four times larger in girls than in boys.[70]

I should reassure you that most people who talk about the educational implications of sex differences in the brain do limit themselves to regions recognized by the majority of the scientific community. I also have little doubt that many of them have the very best intentions behind their use of the brain science literature. They want to improve educational outcomes for children of both sexes. Those who promote single-sex schools may certainly have good reasons for their cause that have nothing to do with the brain. But promoting that cause by projecting gender stereotypes onto brain data is worse than useless.

Perhaps the most influential of this group of educational speakers is Leonard Sax of the National Association for Single Sex Public Education (NASSPE), and author of two books that argue a brain-based need for single-sex schooling. Sax has a punishing speaking schedule, that so far has included the United States, Canada, Australia, and New Zealand, as well as countries in Europe—and some schools are clearly impressed. NASSPE has been involved in about half of the 360 single-sex public school programs in the United States, and Sax has told *New York Times* journalist Elizabeth Weil that about 300 of them "are coming at this from a neuroscience basis."[71] Let's take a closer look at what that means.

Take English class, for example; In the girls' class, you will find teachers asking their students to reflect on story protagonists' feelings and motives: *how would you* feel *if*?. . . sort of questions. But not in the boys' classroom, because "[t]hat question requires boys to link *emotional* information in the amygdala with *language* information in the cerebral cortex. It's like trying to recite poetry and juggle bowling pins at the same time. You have to use two different parts of the brain that don't normally work together." The problem for boys and young children, according to Sax, is that emotion is processed in the amygdala, a primitive, basic part of the brain—"that makes few direct connections with the cerebral cortex."[72] (In fact, the amygdala appears to be richly interconnected with the cerebral cortex.)[73] This supposedly renders them incapable of talking about their feelings. But in older girls, emotion is processed in the cerebral cortex, which conveniently enables them to employ language to communicate what they're feeling. The implications for teaching are clear: *girls to the left, phylogenetically primitive ape-brains to the right!* Yet this "fact" about male brains—variants of which I have seen repeated several times in popular media—is based on a small functional neuroimaging study in which children stared passively at fearful faces.[74] It's doubtful whether any negative emotion was involved during the study (except perhaps boredom)[75]; the children were not asked to speak or talk about what they were feeling and, critically, brain activity was not even measured in most of the areas of the brain involved in processing emotion and language.[76] As Mark Liberman has

pointed out, "the disproportion between the reported facts and Sax's interpretation is spectacular."[77] Even if studies *did* show what Sax claims (questionable),[78] why on earth would we assume that the language parts of the brain wouldn't get involved if the child wished to speak? Shifting information from A to B is, after all, what axons and dendrites are *for*. Yet Sax describes with admiration a boy-brain-friendly English class in which boys study *The Lord of the Flies* by reading the text not with an eye on the plot, or characterization, but so as to be able to construct a map of the island.

And it's all happening at a school near you. At a coeducational school in my neighboring suburb, "parallel education" is provided for boys and girls in certain years. As a journalist explains, "teaching boys [math] was more about hands-on practice: drawing, doing the exercise. But in a class with girls, Davey [the middle school principal] discusses the issues for a full 10 minutes at the start of the class, while the graph is put in the context of a relationship between two people."[79] Perhaps Davey has read one of the other "neurofallacies" propagated by Sax, that because boys process math in the hippocampus (another one of those primitive parts of the brain that males so seem to favor), but girls process geometry and math "in the cerebral cortex" (a statement so unspecific as to be a bit like saying, "I'll meet you for coffee in the Northern Hemisphere"), this indicates a need for very different educational strategies. Sax claims that because the primitive hippocampus has "no direct connections to the cerebral cortex" [um, again, not quite right] boys are happy dealing with math "'for its own sake' at a much earlier age than girls are." But for the girls, because they're using their cerebral cortex, "you need to tie the math into other higher cognitive functions."[80] The goal of inspiring children to get excited about math is certainly admirable. But Sax's claim that the results of a neuroimaging study of maze navigation point to a brain-based need to teach girls and boys in these different kinds of ways is simply neurononsense.[81]

Mark Liberman has analyzed in meticulous detail many of Sax's dubious brain-based educational claims, and has described the way so-called educational experts like Sax and Gurian use scientific data as "shockingly careless, tendentious and even dishonest. Their over-interpretation and mis-interpretation of scientific research is so extreme that it becomes a form of fabrication."[82] While it might be amusing to think up romance stories involving stolid Mr. X-Axis and flighty Ms. Y to amuse the girls, or an interesting challenge to discuss a book without mentioning mental states, the danger is that self-fulfilling prophecies are being delivered alongside the new-look, single-sex curriculum.

Vicky Tuck, while president of the Girls' School Association, UK, recently argued that there are "neurological differences" between the sexes that are "pronounced in adolescence." The practical implication? "You have to teach girls differently to how you teach boys."[83] Is she right? Remember how easily spurious findings of sex differences can lead to premature speculation. Remember what Celia Moore and Geert De Vries have pointed out—sex differences in the brain can be compensation, or a different path to the same destination. Bear in mind that neuroscientists are still quarreling over the appropriate statistical analysis of highly complex data. Recall that many sex differences in the brain may have more to do with brain size than sex per se. Remember that psychology and neuroscience— and the way their findings are reported—are geared toward finding difference, not similarity. Male and female brains are of course far more similar than they are different. Not only is there generally great overlap in "male" and "female" patterns, but also, the male brain is like nothing in the world so much as a female brain. Neuroscientists can't even tell them apart at the individual level. So why focus on difference? If we focused on similarity, we'd conclude that boys and girls should be taught the same way.

You're not convinced? You feel sure these brain differences must be educationally important? Okay, fine. Separate your boys and girls. Or, if you want to be really thorough, because there is overlap with these sex differences, strictly speaking one should provide separate streaming for, say, Large Amygdalas and Small Amygdalas, or Overactivated versus Underactivated Left Frontal Lobes. And now tell me *how* you tailor your teaching to the size of the amygdala, or to patterns of brain activity to a photo of a fearful face. There is no reliable way to translate these brain differences into educational strategies. It is, as philosopher John Bruer has poetically put it, "a bridge too far": "Currently, we do not know enough about brain development and neural function to link that understanding directly, in any meaningful, defensible way to instruction and educational practice. We may never know enough to be able to do that."[84] And so, instead, we quickly find ourselves falling back on god-awful gender stereotypes.

We never seem to learn.

No discussion of the brain, sex, and education would be complete without mention of the now-notorious theory of Professor Edward Clarke of the Harvard Medical School. In his highly successful nineteenth-century book, *Sex in Education* (subtitled, somewhat ironically as it turned out, *Or, A Fair Chance for Girls*), he proposed that intellectual labor sent energy rushing dangerously from ovaries to brain, endangering fertility as well as causing other severe medical ailments.[85] As biologist Richard Lewontin dryly remarked of this hypothesis, "Testicles,

apparently, had their own sources of energy."[86] From our modern vantage point we can laugh at the prejudice that gave rise to this hypothesis. Yet we may have little cause for complacency.

Tuck says she has "a hunch that in 50 years' time, maybe only 25, people will be doubled up with laughter when they watch documentaries about the history of education and discover people once thought it was a good idea to educate adolescent boys and girls together."[87] But when I survey the popular literature, I suspect that this will not be where the people of the future will find their biggest laughs. Frankly, I think they will be too busy giggling in astonished outrage at the claims of early twenty-first-century commentators who, like their nineteenth-century predecessors, reinforced gender stereotypes with crude comparisons of male or female brains; or who, like Brizendine with her talk of "overloaded brain circuits," attempted to locate social pressures in the brain. (*Here it is, Michael! I finally found the neural circuits for organizing child care, planning the evening meal, and ensuring that everyone has clean underwear. See how they crowd out these circuits for career, ambition, and original thought?*)

I end with a plea. Although, as we'll see in the next chapter, there is something captivating about neuroscientific information, please, no more neurosexism! Follow the four simple steps I set out at the beginning of the chapter or leave the interpretations to the trained professionals. Neuroscience can be dangerous when mishandled, so if you're not sure, be safe.

As the blogger known as Neuroskeptic wisely advises those who peddle neurononsense, "Save yourself . . . put the brain down and walk away."[88]

## NOTES

1. (Romanes 1887/1987), p. 11, footnote removed.
2. (Fausto-Sterling 1985), p. 260.
3. (De Vries 2004), p. 1064.
4. An example of this, in the rat, is described by (Moore 1995), p. 53.
5. (Moore 1995), pp. 53 and 54. Similarly, Haier and colleagues have suggested that "different brain designs may manifest equivalent intellectual performance" (Haier et al. 2005), p. 320.
6. See (Im et al. 2008).
7. (Leonard et al. 2008), p. 2929.
8. (Im et al. 2008; Leonard et al. 2008). Leonard et al. quoted on p. 2929. Effects of sex were very small, or nonexistent, once effect of total brain volume was taken into account. Leonard et al.'s findings with regard to gray matter in proportion to total brain volume are consistent, too, with work by Luders and colleagues, who also conclude that "brain size is the main variable determining the proportion of gray matter" (Luders, Steinmetz, and Jäncke 2002), p. 2371. Im and colleagues also argue

that their results show "that sex effects are mostly explained by brain size effects in the cortical structure of human brains" (Im et al. 2008), p. 2188.

9. (Giedd et al. 2006), p. 159.
10. (Fine 1990), p. 133.
11. (Baron-Cohen, Knickmeyer, and Belmonte 2005), p. 821.
12. (Gur and Gur 2007), p. 196.
13. Ian Gold, personal communication, October 24, 2008.
14. I am very grateful to Ian Gold, whose insights have greatly enhanced my understanding of the problems inherent in trying to relate brain structure to brain function.
15. (Halari et al. 2006), see pp. 1 and 3.
16. (Gur et al. 1999).
17. Quoted in (University of Pennsylvania Medical Center 1999), para. 7.
18. (Gur et al. 1999), p. 4071. Regarding the point that correlation doesn't mean causation, some third factor (or complex of factors), like education, could enhance both white matter volume *and* spatial ability.
19. (Gur and Gur 2007), p. 196.
20. (Gur et al. 2000), p. 166.
21. (O'Boyle 2005; O'Boyle et al. 2005; Singh and O'Boyle 2004).
22. Again, this is an issue raised long ago by Ruth Bleier who pointed out the circularity of the reasoning that men are superior in visuospatial skills because they have right-hemisphere lateralization for visuospatial processing, and that right-hemisphere lateralization is superior for visuospatial processing because men are superior at visuospatial processing and they show right-hemisphere lateralization (Bleier 1986).
23. See (Russett 1989; Shields 1975).
24. H. Ellis, *Man and Woman: A Study of Human Secondary Sexual Characteristics* (London: Walter Scott, 1894), p. 28. Quoted in (Russett 1989), pp. 184 and 185.
25. (Pease and Pease 2008), pp. 145 and 146, respectively. Illustrations appear on p. 145.
26. (Pease and Pease 2008), p. 145.
27. The first study is C. M. McCormick, S. F. Witelson, and E. Kingstone, "Left-handedness in homosexual men and women: Neuroendocrine implications," *Psychoneuroendocrinology* 15, no. 1 (1990), pp. 69–76. The second study is S. F. Witelson, "The brain connection: The corpus callosum is larger in left-handers," *Science* 229, no. 4714 (1985), pp. 665–668.
28. (Hall et al. 2004). Although the Peases also describe the Witelson emotion study in the 1999 edition of their book, researchers often present their results before publication, which can take many years. I contacted Pease International in the hope that the Peases might be able to clarify to what research they are referring in this passage, but they were unable to assist.
29. (Pinker 2008), p. 116.
30. In discussing these results, I focus on between-group comparisons between males and females, rather than within-group contrasts, on the basis of the argument made by Kaiser and colleagues that "[o]nly by comparing women and men directly with one another within one statistical test can significance be ensured" (Kaiser et al. 2009), p. 54.

31. (Hall et al. 2004), p. 223.
32. (Hall et al. 2004), p. 223.
33. (Bennett et al. 2009), p. S125.
34. See (Ihnen et al. 2009).
35. For discussions of the role of reverse inferences in understanding cognitive mechanisms, limitations, and conditions in which they are more or less likely to be a valid form of inference, see (Poldrack 2006; Poldrack and Wagner 2004).
36. For example (Blakemore et al. 2007; Burnett et al. 2009; Haier et al. 1992).
37. (Bird et al. 2004), p. 925.
38. (Buracas, Fine, and Boynton 2005).
39. (Friston and Price 2001), p. 275.
40. (Lehrer 2008), para. 7.
41. (Kaiser et al. 2009).
42. (Miller 2008), p. 1413.
43. Men's brains are, on average, about 8 to 10 percent larger than female brains. Beyond this, as Kaiser et al. have pointed out, results demonstrating sex differences in "*a/symmetries* between the left and right hemisphere in anatomy and function, the size of the *corpus callosum*, and the *extent* of defined brain areas . . . have never been both conclusive and unchallenged" (Kaiser et al. 2009), p. 50, emphases in original, references removed. Also, as discussed in this chapter, what appear to be sex differences in brain structure may turn out to be differences between people with larger versus smaller brains. Nor does the existence of differences in the brain indicate their origins. One last point is the importance of not assuming that sex differences observed in the rat apply to humans. With these extremely important caveats in mind, a brief overview of research finding sex differences in brain anatomy, neurochemistry, and function, and discussion of their potential importance in understanding clinical disorders, is provided in (Cahill 2006).
44. (Weisberg 2008), p. 56.
45. (Gray 2008), pp. 44 and 45, respectively.
46. (Gurian and Annis 2008), p. 9.
47. (Gurian 2004), p. 88.
48. (Gurian and Annis 2008), p. 34.
49. (Gurian and Annis 2008), p. 59, emphasis in original.
50. (Rogers, Zucca, and Vallortigara 2004). Thanks to Lesley Rogers for alerting me to this study.
51. (Young and Balaban 2006), p. 634.
52. http://itre.cis.upenn.edu/~myl/languagelog/archives/003923.html, accessed on October 5, 2009.
53. The study cited is (Raingruber 2001).
54. (Brizendine 2007), p. 162.
55. (Hall 1978, 1984; McClure 2000).
56. (Brizendine 2007), p. 162.
57. The study cited is (Oberman et al. 2005).
58. (Brizendine 2007), p. 163.
59. The study cited is (Singer et al. 2004).
60. (Brizendine 2007), p. 163.
61. The study cited is T. Iidaka, "fMRI study of age related differences in the medial temporal lobe responses to emotional faces," Society for Neuroscience, New Orleans [*sic*, should be San Diego], 2001. The first author confirmed that the research presented at this conference was subsequently published in (Iidaka et al. 2002) and

that, as in the published report, gender differences were not mentioned.

62. The study cited is (Zahn-Waxler, Klimes-Dougan, and Slattery 2000), p. 458, emphasis in original.

63. (Brizendine 2007), p. 163.

64. The study cited is (Singer et al. 2006).

65. (Brizendine 2007), pp. 163 and 164. Note that the researchers actually interpret their empathy-related responses to the pain of another as being limited to the affective aspect of the pain response, rather than the sensory aspects of pain.

66. (Brizendine 2007), p. 158. The citations are, in order discussed in current text: (Orzhekhovskaia 2005; Uddin et al. 2005; Oberman et al. 2005; Ohnishi et al. 2004); and L. M. Oberman, "There may be a difference in male and female mirror neuron functioning," personal communication, 2005.

67. Lindsay M. Oberman, personal communication (with me), October 21, 2008.

68. (Brizendine 2007), p. 210.

69. (Brizendine 2007), pp. 188 and 189.

70. http://itre.cis.upenn.edu/~myl/languagelog/archives/004926.html, accessed March 3, 2010.

71. Quoted in (Weil 2008), para. 14.

72. (Sax 2006), pp. 106 and 107 and p. 106, respectively. The study Sax bases this claim on is described on pp. 29 and 30 of his book *Why Gender Matters*.

73. See (Freese and Amaral 2009).

74. The study cited is (Killgore, Oki, and Yurgelun-Todd 2001).

75. Although negative emotions conveyed in faces can be contagious, the children were not asked to try to induce a particular mood, and it was not the purpose of the experimental design to induce negative emotion in the children.

76. Brain activity was measured in two small parts of the brain bilaterally, in the amygdala and a region of the dorsolateral prefrontal cortex. For further critique of Sax's interpretation of this study, see Mark Liberman's discussion at http://itre.cis.upenn.edu/~myl/languagelog/archives/003284.html.

77. http://itre.cis.upenn.edu/~myl/languagelog/archives/003284.html, accessed September 2, 2009.

78. Sax cites one other study as support for his claim that in women brain activity associated with negative affect is "mostly up in the cerebral cortex" whereas in men it is "stuck down in the amygdala" (Sax 2006), p. 29. This study (Schneider et al. 2000), involving thirteen men and thirteen women, found increased activity in the right amygdala in males but not females during induced sadness (but similar left amygdala activity during induced sadness, and similar amygdala activation in both hemispheres during induced happiness). Gender differences in cortical activations during induced sadness and happiness are not discussed. Sax also cites two other studies as evidence that emotions are processed differently in the sexes. Although he does not claim that these studies support the hypothesis that negative emotional experience is more subcortical in males and cortical in females, for the sake of completeness it is worth noting that these studies do not offer support for this idea. The first study (Killgore and Yurgelun-Todd 2001) did not involve emotional experience but looked at amygdala activity in seven men and six women as they looked at fearful or happy faces (compared with the control condition of looking at a small circle). It did not look at brain activations in cortical regions. Amygdala response while looking at fearful faces was similar in the two sexes. When looking at happy faces, amygdala activation was lateralized to the right in men but not women—a lateralization difference, rather than a difference in the engagement of the amygdala per se. Second, Sax cites a meta-analysis of functional imaging studies of emotion (Wager et al. 2003) as evidence that emotions are processed differently in the sexes. However, the conclusions of this study are not consistent with the idea that emotional experience is more subcortical in males and more cortical in women. The authors tentatively summarize the gender differences from their analysis as follows: "Men tend to activate posterior sensory and association cortex, left inferior frontal cortex, and dorsal striatum more reliably than women, whereas women tend to activate medial frontal cortex, thalamus, and cerebellum more reliably" (p. 528). Translation: Men [cortical, cortical, cortical, subcortical] versus Women [cortical, subcortical, subcortical].

79. (Bachelard and Power 2008), para. 46.

80. (Sax 2006), p. 102 (boys) and p. 104 (girls). The term "neurofallacy" coined by (Racine, Bar-Ilan, and Illes 2005). For details of hippocampus-cortex connections, take your pick from the articles in the 2000 Special Issue of the journal *Hippocampus* entitled "The nature of hippocampal-cortical interaction: Theoretical and experimental perspectives."

81. See (Sax 2006), pp. 100–101. Perhaps the most important reason that implications for math education cannot be drawn from the cited neuroimaging study is that it did not involve math, or even numbers. Rather, the task involved navigating out of a complex three-dimensional virtual maze. The control condition involved looking at a frozen shot of the maze and making key presses in response to flickering rectangles. We can immediately see that this study will not tell us anything about the parts of the brain involved in mathematical processing. Even if the debate concerned whether single-sex classrooms are necessary for lessons in virtual maze navigation, this study would not help us much. More male activity was seen in the left hippocampus while women showed greater activation in right prefrontal and parietal areas, but this is in the context of "great overlap" between the sexes in which regions were activated (Grön et al. 2000), p. 405. It's impossible to make useful inferences from these differences. What do we make of greater male activation of the left hippocampus given that the right was activated equally in the sexes? What is the significance of greater female activation of the superior parietal lobule on one side of the brain but not the other? It does not make sense to say that only females use the cerebral cortex and only males use the hippocampus while performing spatial navigation (and even less sense to make this claim for math)! Moreover, we don't know whether more activation means "better." It could mean "less

efficient." Were the differences due to performance differences rather than sex per se? (The men were significantly faster at getting out of the maze.) What cognitive role are these regions playing in the performance of the task? We have no idea—which makes developing educational strategies on the basis of these findings impossible. Discussing a similar claim about sex differences in math processing made by a commentator on the BBC's "Today" program, the blogger known as Neuroskeptic provides a useful explanation of some of the confusion behind such claims (see http://neuroskeptic.blogspot .com/2008/11/educational-neuro-nonsense-or-return-of.html, accessed on September 10, 2009).

82. http://itre.cis.upenn.edu/~myl/languagelog/ archives/004618.html, accessed December 9, 2009.
83. Quoted in (Garner 2008), para. 7.
84. (Bruer 1997), p. 4.
85. (Clarke 1873).
86. (Lewontin 2000), p. 208.
87. Quoted in (Garner 2008), para. 3.
88. http://neuroskeptic.blogspot.com/2008/11/educational-neuro-nonsense-or-return-of.html, accessed September 2, 2009.

## REFERENCES

Bachelard, M., and L. Power. 2008. "The Class Divide." *Sunday Age* (November 9): 15.

Baron-Cohen, S., R. C. Knickmeyer, and M. K. Belmonte. 2005. "Sex Differences in the Brain: Implications for Explaining Autism." *Science* 310: 819–823.

Bennett, C. M., A. A. Baird, M. B. Miller, and G. L. Wolford. 2009. "Neural Correlates of Interspecies Perspective Taking in the Post-mortem Atlantic Salmon: An Argument for Multiple Comparisons Correction." [Paper presented at the Organization for Human Brain Mapping 2009 Annual Meeting, San Francisco, CA.] *Neuro-Image* 47(51): S125.

Bird, C. M., F. Castelli, O. Malik, U. Frith, and M. Husain. 2004. "The Impact of Extensive Medical Frontal Lobe Damage on 'Theory of Mind' and Cognition." *Brain* 127: 914–928.

Blakemore, S.-J., H. den Ouden, S. Choudhury, and C. Frith. 2007. "Adolescent Development of the Neural Circuitry for Thinking about Intentions." *Social Cognitive and Affective Neuroscience* 2: 130–139.

Bleier, R. 1986. "Sex Differences Research: Science or Belief?" In R. Bleier (ed.). *Feminist Approaches to Science*, pp. 147–164. New York: Pergamon Press.

Brizendine, L. 2007. *The Female Brain*. London: Bantam Press.

Bruer, J. T. 1997. "Education and the Brain: A Bridge too Far." *Educational Researcher* 26(8): 4–16.

Buracas, G. T., I. Fine, and G. M. Boynton. 2005. "The Relationship between Task Performance and Functional Magnetic Resonance Imaging Response." *Journal of Neuroscience* 25(12): 3023–3031.

Burnett, S., G. Bird, J. Moll, C. Frith, and S. J. Blakemore. 2009. "Development during Adolescence of the Neural Processing of Social Emotion." *Journal of Cognitive Neuroscience* 21(9): 1736–1750.

Cahill, L. 2006. "Why Sex Matters for Neuroscience." *Nature Reviews Neuroscience* 7(6): 477–484.

Clarke, E. H. 1873. *Sex in Education: Or, a Fair Chance for Girls*. Boston: James R. Osgood & Company. Released by The Project Gutenberg, June 5, 2006.

De Vries, G. J. 2004. "Sex Differences in Adult and Developing Brains: Compensation, Compensation, Compensation." *Endocrinology* 145(3): 1063–1068.

Fausto-Sterling, A. 1985. *Myths of Gender: Biological Theories about Women and Men* (2nd ed.). New York: Basic Books.

Fine, A. 1990. *Taking the Devil's Advice*. London: Viking.

Freese, J. L., and D. G. Amaral. 2009. "Neuroanatomy of the Primate Amygdala." In P. J. Whalen and E. A. Phelps (eds.). *The Human Amygdala*, pp. 3–42. New York: Guilford Press.

Friston, K. J., and C. J. Price. 2001. "Dynamic Representations and Generative Models of Brain Function." *Brain Research Bulletin* 54(3): 275–285.

Garner, R. 2008. "Single-Sex Schools 'Are the Future.'" From *The Independent* (November 18) online: http:// www.independent.co.uk/news/education/education-news/singlesex-schools-are-the-future-1023105.html, accessed May 22, 2009.

Giedd, J. N., L. S. Clasen, R. Lenroot, D. Greenstein, G. L. Wallace, and S. Ordaz. 2006. "Puberty-Related Influences on Brain Development." *Molecular and Cellular Endocrinology* 254/255: 154–162.

Gray, J. 2008. *Why Mars and Venus Collide*. London: Harper Collins.

Grön, G., A. P. Wunderlich, M. Spitzer, R. Tomczak, and M. W. Riepe. 2000. "Brain Activation during Human Navigation: Gender-Different Neural Networks as Substrate of Performance." *Nature Neuroscience* 3(4): 404–408.

Gur, R. C., and R. E. Gur. 2007. "Neural Substrates for Sex Differences in Cognition." In *Why Aren't More Women in Science? Top Researchers Debate the Evidence*, pp. 189–198. Washington, DC: American Psychological Association.

Gur, R. C., D. Alsop, D. Glahn, R. Petty, C. L. Swanson, J. A. Maldjian, et al. 2000. "An fMRI Study of Sex Differences in Regional Activation to a Verbal and a Spatial Task." *Brain and Language* 74(2): 157–170.

Gur, R. C., B. I. Turetsky, M. Matsui, M. Yan, W. Bilker, P. Hughett, and R. E. Gur. 1999. "Sex Differences in Gray and White Brain Matter in Healthy Young Adults: Correlations with Cognitive Performance." *Journal of Neuroscience* 19(10): 4065–4072.

Gurian, M. 2004. *What Could He Be Thinking? A Guide to the Mysteries of Man's Mind*. London: Elsevier.

Gurian, M., and B. Annis. 2008. *Leadership and the Sexes: Using Gender Science to Create Success in Business*. San Francisco, CA: Jossey-Bass.

Haier, R. J., R. E. Jung, R. A. Yeo, K. Head, and M. T. Alkire. 2005. "The Neuroanatomy of General Intelligence: Sex Matters." *NeuroImage* 25: 320–327.

Haier, R. J., B. V. Siegal, A. MacLachlan, E. Soderling, S. Lottenberg, and M. S. Buchsbaum. 1992. "Regional Glucose Metabolic Changes after Learning a Complex Visuospatial/Motor Task: A Positron Emission Tomographic Study." *Brain Research* 570: 134–143.

Halari, R., T. Sharma, M. Hines, C. Andrew, A. Simmons, and V. Kumari. 2006. "Comparable fMRI Activity with Differential Behavioural Performance on Mental Rotation and Overt Verbal Fluency Tasks in Healthy Men and Women." *Experimental Brain Research* 169(1): 1–14.

Hall, J. A. 1978. "Gender Effects in Decoding Nonverbal Cues." *Psychological Bulletin* 85(4): 845–857.

———. 1984. *Nonverbal Sex Differences: Communication Accuracy and Expressive Style.* Baltimore and London: The Johns Hopkins University Press.

Hall, G. B. C., S. F. Witelson, H. Szechtman, and C. Nahmias. 2004. "Sex Differences in Functional Activation Patterns Revealed by Increased Emotion Processing Demands." *NeuroReport* 15(2): 219–223.

Ihnen, S. K. Z., J. A. Church, S. E. Petersen, and B. L. Schlaggar. 2009. "Lack of Generalizability of Sex Differences in the fMRI BOLD Activity Associated with Language Processing in Adults." *NeuroImage* 45(3): 1020–1032.

Iidaka, T., T. Okada, T. Murata, M. Omori, H. Kosaka, N. Sadato, and Y. Yonekura. 2002. "Age-Related Differences in the Medial Temporal Lobe Responses to Emotional Faces as Revealed by fMRI." *Hippocampus* 12: 352–362.

Im, K., J.-M. Lee, O. Lyttelton, S. H. Kim, A. C. Evans, and S. I. Kim. 2008. "Brain Size and Cortical Structure in the Adult Human Brain." *Cerebral Cortex* 18: 2181–2191.

Kaiser, A., S. Haller, S. Schmitz, and C. Nitsch. 2009. "On Sex/Gender Related Similarities and Differences in fMRI Language Research." *Brain Research Reviews* 61(2): 49–59.

Killgore, W. D. S., M. Oki, and D. A. Yurgelun-Todd. 2001. "Sex-Specific Developmental Changes in Amygdala Responses to Affective Faces." *NeuroReport* 12(2): 427–433.

Killgore, W. D. S., and D. A. Yurgelun-Todd. 2001. "Sex Differences in Amygdala Activation During the Perception of Facial Affect." *NeuroReport* 12(11): 2543–2547.

Lehrer, J. 2008. "Of Course I Love You, and I Have the Brain Scan to Prove It—We're Looking for too Much in Brain Scans." *Boston Globe* (August 17): K1.

Leonard, C. M., S. Towler, S. Welcome, L. K. Halderman, R. Otto, M. A. Eckert, and C. Chiarello. 2008. "Size Matters: Cerebral Volume Influences Sex Differences in Neuroanatomy." *Cerebral Cortex* 18(12): 2920–2931.

Lewontin, R. 2000. *It Ain't Necessarily So: The Dream of the Human Genome and Other Illusions.* New York: New York Review of Books.

Luders, E., H. Steinmetz, and L. Jäncke. 2002. "Brain Size and Grey Matter Volume in the Healthy Human Brain." *NeuroReport* 13(17): 2371–2374.

McClure, E. B. 2000. "A Meta-analytic Review of Sex Differences in Facial Expression Processing and Their Development in Infants, Children, and Adolescents." *Psychological Bulletin* 126(3): 424–453.

Miller, G. 2008. "Growing Pains for fMRI." *Science* 320(5882): 1412–1414.

Moore, C. L. 1995. "Maternal Contributions to Mammalian Reproductive Development and the Divergence of Males and Females." *Advances in the Study of Behavior* 24: 47–118.

O'Boyle, M. W. 2005. "Some Current Findings on Brain Characteristics of the Mathematically Gifted Adolescent." *International Education Journal* 6(2): 247–251.

O'Boyle, M. W., R. Cunnington, T. J. Silk, D. Vaughn, G. Jackson, A. Syngeniotis, and G. F. Egan. 2005. "Mathematically Gifted Male Adolescents Activate a Unique Brain Network during Mental Rotation." *Cognitive Brain Research* 25(2): 583–587.

Oberman, L. M., E. M. Hubbard, J. P. McCleery, E. L. Altschuler, V. S. Ramachandran, and J. A. Pineda. 2005. "EEG Evidence for Mirror Neuron Dysfunction in Autism Spectrum Disorders." *Cognitive Brain Research* 24: 190–198.

Ohnishi, T., Y. Moriguchi, H. Matsuda, T. Mori, M. Hirakata, E. Imabayashi, et al. 2004. "The Neural Network for the Mirror System and Mentalizing in Normally Developed Children: An fMRI Study." *NeuroReport* 15(9): 1483–1487.

Orzhekhovskaia, N. S. 2005. "Sex Dimorphism of Neuron-Glia Correlations in the Frontal Areas of the Human Brain". *Morfologiia* 127(1): 7–9.

Pease, A., and B. Pease. 2008. *Why Men Don't Listen and Women Can't Read Maps.* New York: Pease International Pty Ltd.

Pinker, S. 2008. *The Sexual Paradox: Men, Women, and the Real Gender Gap.* New York: Scribner.

Poldrack, R. A. 2006. "Can Cognitive Processes Be Inferred from Neuroimaging Data?" *Trends in Cognitive Sciences* 10(2): 59–63.

Poldrack, R. A., and A. D. Wagner. 2004. "What Can Neuroimaging Tell Us about the Mind? Insights from Prefrontal Cortex." *Current Directions in Psychological Science* 13(5): 177–181.

Racine, E., O. Bar-Ilan, and J. Illes. 2005. "fMRI in the Public Eye." *Nature Reviews Neuroscience* 6(2): 159–164.

Raingruber, B. J. 2001. "Settling into and Moving in a Climate of Care: Styles and Patterns of Interaction between Nurse Psychotherapists and Clients." *Perspectives in Psychiatric Care* 37(1): 15–27.

Rogers, L. J., P. Zucca, and G. Vallortigara. 2004. "Advantages of Having a Lateralized Brain." *Proceedings of the Royal Society of London, Ser. B* 271: S420–S422.

Romanes, G. J. 1887/1987. "Mental Differences between Men and Women." In D. Spender (ed.). *Education Papers: Women's Quest for Equality in Britain, 1850–1912.* London and New York: Routledge and Kegan Paul.

Russett, C. E. 1989. *Sexual Science: The Victorian Construction of Womanhood.* Cambridge, MA: Harvard University Press.

Sax, L. 2006. *Why Gender Matters: What Parents and Teachers Need to Know About the Emerging Science of Sex Differences.* New York: Broadway Books.

Schneider, F., U. Habel, C. Kessler, J. B. Salloum, and S. Posse. 2000. "Gender Differences in Regional Cerebral Activity during Sadness." *Human Brain Mapping* 9: 226–238.

Shields, S. 1975. "Functionalism, Darwinism, and the Psychology of Women: A Study in Social Myth." *American Psychologist* 30(7): 739–754.

Singer, T., B. Seymour, J. O'Doherty, H. Kaube, R. J. Dolan, and C. D. Frith. 2004. "Empathy for Pain Involves the Affective but not Sensory Components of Pain." *Science* 303(1157): 1157–1162.

Singer, T., B. Seymour, J. P. O'Doherty, K. E. Stephan, R. J. Dolan, and C. D. Frith. 2006. "Empathic Neural Responses Are Modulated by the Perceived Fairness of Others." *Nature* 439(7075): 466–469.

Singh, H., and M. W. O'Boyle. 2004. "Interhemispheric Interaction during Global-Local Processing in Mathematically Gifted Adolescents, Average-Ability Youth, and College Students." *Neuropsychology* 18(2): 371–377.

Uddin, L. Q., J. T. Kaplan, I. Molnar-Szakacs, E. Zaidel, and M. Iacoboni. 2005. "Self-face Recognition Activates a Frontoparietal 'Mirror' Network in the Right Hemisphere: An Event-Related fMRI Study." *NeuroImage* 25: 926–935.

University of Pennsylvania Medical Center. 1999. "Sex Differences Found in Proportions of Gray and White Matter in the Brain." http://www.sciencedaily.com/releases/1999/05/990518072823.htm. Accessed November 6, 2008.

Wager, T. D., K. L. Phan, I. Liberzon, and S. F. Taylor. 2003. "Valence, Gender, and Lateralization of Functional Brain Anatomy in Emotion: A Meta-analysis of Findings from Neuroimaging." *NeuroImage* 19(3): 513–531.

Weil, E. 2008. "Teaching to the Testosterone." *New York Times Magazine* (March 2): 38.

Weisberg, D. S. 2008. "Caveat Lector: The Presentation of Neuroscience Information in the Popular Media." *Science Review of Mental Health Practice* 6(1): 51–56.

Young, R. M., and E. Balaban. 2006. "Psychoneuroindoctrinology." *Nature* 443: 634.

Zahn-Waxler, C., B. Klimes-Dougan, and M. J. Slattery. 2000. "Internalizing Problems of Childhood and Adolescence: Prospects, Pitfalls, and Progress in Understanding the Development of Anxiety and Depression." *Development and Psychopathology* 12: 443–466.

# Gender and War:
# Are Women Tough Enough for Military Combat?

## Lucinda J. Peach

## INTRODUCTION

*"Women are not supposed to be in combat. The fact of the matter is they are in combat"* (Army Captain Kevin Hanrahan, quoted in Little 2005: 1). As the traditional boundary between "the front line" and "behind the front line" vanishes in the face of the kinds of combat tactics and military technologies now being used to wage war in the twenty-first century, more soldiers, including women, are facing dangerous and life threatening situations. This fact has been made starkly evident with the current Iraq war, where guerilla tactics have put women soldiers constantly in the line of fire. They have routinely participated in convoy missions where they have been at risk of being hit. Women at times even have been assigned as "gunners," positioned at the machine gun on the top of the Humvee during such convoys, while their fellow soldiers of both sexes use their weapons when the convoy stops to "pull a perimeter" and protect the area from hostile fire. As one female Iraqi vet put it, "That may not be hand-to-hand combat, but if it isn't combat, I don't know what is" (Martineau and Wiegand 2005: 6).

In addition, whenever a unit is ambushed, any women in that unit are of necessity "in combat" (Little 2005: 1). Women soldiers in Iraq also regularly serve as military police and at checkpoints, where they are indispensable to search women because of cultural notions regarding women's modesty, but which put them at higher risk of being fired upon (see Cox 2006). Despite this indisputable evidence that women serving in the American military are "seeing combat," often on a daily basis, official US policy has been, and continues to be, that women are prohibited from serving in the majority of combat roles.[1]

Even before being highlighted because of the striking number of deaths of female soldiers during the seemingly interminable Iraq War which began in 2003 (see, e.g., Cox 2006), the issue of whether women *should* participate in military combat has been debated sporadically by military personnel, government officials, public policy makers, and members of the public since women's military service in the Persian Gulf War was given high profile media attention in the early 1990s.

A number of arguments have been made over the years to justify excluding women from what has been considered the "heart" of war-making: combat, and especially ground combat. Although certain positions in the military designated as "combat" were opened up to women by the Clinton Administration following the Persian Gulf War, especially on combat aircraft and naval vessels (except for submarines), the majority

Original material prepared for this text. Reprinted by permission of the author.

of combat positions—including all ground combat positions—remain closed to them.

The definition of "direct ground combat" that was adopted in 1993 bars women from units that engage the enemy with weapons on the ground while exposed to hostile fire and which involve substantial probability of direct physical contact with hostile forces (see Lancaster 1994: A1; Pine 1994: A5; Schmitt 1994a, 1994b: A18). Under this policy, exposure to risk, alone, is an insufficient ground for excluding women from a particular assignment. Nevertheless, women are barred from almost all assignments that involve operating offensive, line-of-sight weapons, and from all positions involving ground fighting. This includes armor, infantry, and field artillery, the three specialties that are considered the core of combat (see Schmitt 1994a; 1994b. It also has included combat support positions, such as those providing fuel, food, ammunition, etc., to units which are engaged in combat, called "collocation," which literally means "to place side by side" (see Martineau and Wiegand 2005: 5).

The combat exclusions have become an especially vexed issue in the past couple of years as the Iraq War has continued, putting increasing strain on the military to find adequate numbers of service *men* available and qualified to perform all of the combat and combat support roles. Both the Army and Marines have been using women in combat support positions since the beginning of the Iraq War (Katz 2005: 1). Yet in January 2005, President Bush reaffirmed that there would be no change of policy regarding "No women in combat" (Scarborough and Curl 2005: 1).[2]

The consequence of these combat restrictions is that servicewomen have been excluded from certain benefits and opportunities for promotion and advancement within (and outside) the military that are available only to those with combat experience. The exclusion also functions to limit the numbers of women who can participate in military service because of the relatively small percentage of positions that are available to them. (As of June 2007, over 200,000 women—about 15 percent of those recruited to active duty—are on active duty in the U.S. armed services and an additional 150,000 serve in the National Guard and Reserves. However, this comprised only approximately 19 percent of the Navy, 15 percent of the Army, 20 percent of the Air Force and 24 percent of the Army Reserve (Martineau and Wiegand 2005)). In addition, the exclusion of women from combat contributes to other forms of discrimination against women, both within and outside of the military.

In this essay, I will argue that all of these arguments have been based more on "gender ideology"—that is, on assumptions, prejudices, stereotypes and myths about male and female "natures" and "natural" or "proper" sex

roles and behaviors (see Code 1991: 196)—than on empirically verifiable gender differences that demonstrate women's inability to competently perform combat roles in the U.S. military (see also Gold and Solaro 2005: 1).

Two ideological myths about gender in particular underlie many of the arguments against according combat positions to women. First, identification of the military as masculine makes males the standard by which females are assessed. The male standard operates, sometimes explicitly, but more often implicitly, to perpetuate the stereotype that women are out of place in the military, particularly in combat. Throughout history, war has been a theater in which men could prove their masculinity, and in which masculinity has been deemed a necessary prerequisite to success. During his 1992 presidential election campaign, for example, Bill Clinton's lack of military experience received a lot of attention, some of it based on the view that Clinton's lack of exposure to war made him unfit for presidential leadership. The perception that the virtues of "manliness" are necessary for effective combat soldiering, and that women are incapable or ill-suited to the development of these virtues, has contributed to the maintenance of women's exclusion from most combat assignments.

The second myth used as a rationale to exclude women from combat duty suggests that the purpose for which men fight is to protect women (see Stiehm 1989: 6–7; Kornblum 1984). Women, according to the myth, are the weaker sex and need to be protected by strong men; they are victims dependent upon men rather than autonomous agents who are competent to defend themselves. Members of the military have expressed "a special regard for women who must be protected as the symbolic vessel of femininity and motherhood" (Karst 1991: 536). An example of this perspective is implicit in the rationale of Republican Duncan Hunter, the chairman of the House Armed Services Committee, in support of a congressional bill restricting combat roles for women (which was defeated) in 2005:

> I think one of the marks of civilization is we have not had our women in direct ground combat. In fact, we have decried the enemy when they have pushed women into the frontlines and into combat situations, and utilized women to attack combat forces. We have said that is wrong. That is not something that civilized nations do (Ho 2005: 1).

The fact of "civilization" alone was apparently a sufficient reason for the prohibition in the Congressman's mind, without the need to explain specifically what made women's participation in combat uncivilized, although he also added that the "lack of privacy," and the fact that combat is "brutal and grim" were additional reasons (Ho 2005: 1). In the absence of an underlying gender ideology that women are supposed to be protected, not do the protecting, none of these reasons, either alone or together, provides any explanation of *why* women should be excluded from combat.

Such myths are bolstered by arguments that integrating women into combat would be deleterious to combat effectiveness and the military's ability to mobilize in time of war (Hooker 1989: 36; Kelly 1984: 103; Marlowe 1983: 194; Mitchell 1989: 159; Rogan 1981: 21). Women's supposed physical, physiological, and psychological characteristics are offered as the basis for this argument. Although none of these rationales, alone or combined, provides an adequate ethical basis for maintaining the combat restrictions for women, their popularity and prominence makes it important to note how each of them is based on ideological notions of gender that frequently are inconsistent with the realities of gender difference.

The most common arguments in support of the view that the inclusion of women would diminish combat readiness and effectiveness are that: (1) women lack the necessary physical and psychological strength to perform adequately; (2) their capacity for pregnancy and childbearing makes them inappropriate combatants; and (3) women's participation in combat units would reduce unit cohesion by disrupting male bonding and promoting sexual fraternization. Let us examine each of these arguments in greater detail.

## PHYSICAL AND PSYCHOLOGICAL STRENGTH

Military effectiveness is often said to be compromised by women's lack of physical and psychological strength and stamina relative to men (D'Amico 1990: 6; Gordon and Ludvigson 1991: 20–22; Kantrowitz 1991; Mitchell 1989: 156–62). Regarding the physical strength issue, military personnel have testified before Congress that few women would meet the physical standards for combat duty (Cramsie 1983: 562; Hackworth 1991: 25; United States Senate Appropriations Hearings 1991). Women's purported inferior physical capability is voiced especially loudly by enlisted men, who deny that women have the strength necessary for fighting on the front lines (see Kantrowitz 1991: 23). For example, one of the reasons integrated basic training was ended in the Army in 1982 was because of enlisted men's complaints that women were holding them back (see Coyle 1989; Rogan 1981: 27; Stiehm 1985b: 209). A study of enlisted service personnel's attitudes toward women in the Army in 1975 indicated that only about 50 percent of men interviewed thought women had the physical strength for combat (see Mitchell 1989: 157–58; Stiehm 1989: 102).

There is no question that, in general, most men are physically stronger than most women. Military studies document that men have some advantages in upper body and leg strength, cardiovascular capacity, and lean muscle, which make men "more fitted for physically intense combat" (see Mitchell 1989: 157; Hooker 1989: 44; Kelly 1984: 100–101; Marlowe 1983: 190). However, these tests generally do not also indicate the fact that some women are capable of meeting the standards established for men. Nor do they typically take into consideration the disparities in prior physical training and physical conditioning that men and women have undergone. Army reports reveal that some women do have the requisite upper body strength to qualify for combat. In addition, some women are stronger than some men. Women have performed well in the limited number of combat-type situations in which they have been tested. However, because the combat exclusion has precluded the possibility of obtaining data about women's physical performance under actual combat conditions, gender-based assumptions and prejudices have dominated policy discussions.

The assumption that women lack the physical strength necessary for combat is ideological because it often persists in the face of direct evidence to the contrary. The nature of modern combat, with its emphasis on high-technology equipment, makes the issue of physical strength far less important than it was in an era when war involved primarily hand-to-hand combat. Physical size and strength are of minimal, if any, consideration, when weapons are being fired at the touch of a button from a location far removed from the combat theatre. As Judith Stiehm argues, the question should not be "how strong women are, but how strong they need to be" (1989: 219). The positive experiences with using women in traditionally all-male fields, such as police and fire fighting forces, which require similar skills to combat, support the conclusion that women are capable of performing satisfactorily in physical defense of self and others in situations involving the use of lethal force (see McDowell 1992; Karst 1991: 539; Kornblum 1984: 392–93; Segal 1982: 286).

Nonetheless, skeptics point out that "there is no real evidence that technology has in fact reduced the need for physical strength among military men and women. What evidence there is shows that many military jobs still require more physical strength than most women possess" (Mitchell 1989: 157). To the contrary, although there are some combat positions that most women are unable to perform satisfactorily because of inadequate physical strength, there is a considerable range of combat positions that many, if not most, women are qualified to perform. Although sheer physical strength may occasionally be an issue when technology fails to function properly, more often than not, the physical strength issue is no longer a legitimate reason for excluding women from combat duty. In addition, physical strength is only one of many factors that needs to be assessed in determining the capability of persons for military combat.

Several proposals have been forwarded, by military personnel and others, to assign combat positions on the basis of the physical strength required to perform them, as at least one of several relevant criterion, rather than exclusively on the basis of gender (Coyle 1989: 31; Nabors 1982: 51; Proxmire 1986: 110; Rogan 1981: 306; Roush 1990: 11–12; Segal 1982: 270–71, 1983: 110; United States Senate Hearings 1991: 865).[3] Such proposals would result in a fairer and more accurate measure of "fit" between persons and assignments than the current reliance on gender difference. The main rationale used by military officers for their failure to implement such a gender-neutral scheme is that it may not be "cost-effective" (see Association 1991: 54; Rogan 1981: 20). However, the military's failure to demonstrate how gender-neutral standards for assignments would be financially infeasible suggests that the maintenance of the combat exclusion is based more on the continuing force of gender ideology than on financial expense or damage to military effectiveness.

Sometimes the protection myth serves to reinforce the physical strength argument by portraying women as "the weaker sex" who need to be protected from the risks of being raped and physically violated in war. It is sometimes argued that the presence of women in combat would cause male soldiers to respond by becoming more concerned about protecting them than fighting the enemy, thus compromising combat effectiveness (see Barkalow 1990: 260 (quoting Colonel Houston's comment that men's emotional commitment to recapture POW women would be so intense and extreme as to cause fighting to escalate); Beecraft 1989: 43; Van Creveld 1993).

Such arguments are ripe for resurgence as a result of the Iraq war, where unprecedented numbers of American women soldiers are being killed, most of them in combat situations (see Martineau and Wiegand 2005: 6). Although the total number is still less than one-thirtieth of the number of male soldiers killed, it is still larger than the number of military women killed in Korea, Vietnam and the Persian Gulf War combined (Schleicher 2006).

The notion that women in the military are in need of protection is based on stereotypes of male machismo and female weakness and vulnerability. Further, the assumption that males are able to protect military women is itself a myth, since women are too integrated throughout the armed forces to be protected by their exclusion from combat. (Providing women soldiers with arms and training in self-defense would provide a measure of protection against sexual violence that

they would not otherwise have.) The rationale that women need to be protected from becoming POWs because of the risk that their torture would include sexual abuse ignores the reality that men as well as women are raped in war, and that women are already subject to such sexual violence at home or by their fellow soldiers on or near the field of combat. In addition, military women are susceptible to being captured and raped during war, regardless of whether they are themselves engaged in combat.

Regarding women's alleged psychological lack of fitness for military combat, during the Gulf War, the press raised the argument that women soldiers would be psychologically unable to handle being taken as prisoners of war, especially because of the greater possibility that they would be raped and otherwise sexually abused (see Nabors 1982: 59; Rogan 1981: 26). Here, the assumption is that women are less stable than men emotionally, and are thus less well equipped to handle the extreme psychological stresses of combat (Marlowe 1983: 195; Mitchell 1989: 7, 182–92).

There is no factual basis for the conclusion that female combatants would be any weaker or more vulnerable than men under such circumstances. To the contrary, the experience of military women such as Air Force Major Rhonda Cornum, a flight surgeon whose aircraft was shot down during the Gulf War, reveals a very matter-of-fact attitude about survival in the face of physical injury and sexual abuse at the hands of her captors. Cornum's response stands as a testament to the ability of military women to cope as POWs (see Cornum 1992).

A relatively new psychological argument has begun to emerge with the Iraq War in view of the unprecedented numbers of women soldiers who have been directly exposed to combat. Since studies have shown that *civilian* women suffer from PTSD at rates nearly twice as high as that of *civilian* men, an inference can be made that women soldiers may also suffer higher rates of post-traumatic stress disorder (PTSD) (Cox 2006). The specter of women vets flooding the health care system upon returning from their tours in Iraq have concerned some health care providers (see Martineau and Wiegand 2005: 1). However, there is little evidence from studies of the U.S. military to bear out this hypothesis. In fact, one Army study released in 2005, indicates that rates of mental health problems among returning male and female soldiers are similar (Cox 2006).

Also related to the physical and psychological strength arguments is the assumption that men are naturally more aggressive than women, and that the "natural aggressiveness" of males would be "softened" by women's participation in battle (Marlowe 1983: 191; Mitchell 1989: 7; Tuten 1982: 255).

More recently, some scholars have challenged the argument that women are innately less aggressive than men (see Marquit 1991; Rosoff 1991; Sunday 1991), while others observe the lack of evidence regarding women's psychological weakness (see Dillingham 1990: 227–28; Gordon and Ludvigson 1991; Kornblum 1984: 398–99). Many of those who conclude that men are "naturally" more aggressive than women rely on incomplete studies of primates, not humans, conducted by anthropologist Lionel Tiger. Tiger observed that male primates in the wild spend much of their time in groups organized to fight with outsiders, whereas female primates were engaged in grooming activities in pairs. Tiger's research has since been largely discredited by further research. Subsequent studies have revealed that females also engaged in collective aggressive action to protect their young, and that both males and females spend much of their time grooming (see United States Senate Hearings 1991: 981; Holm 1982: 95).

The evidence to support the claim of women's lesser aggression is very tenuous, especially after women soldiers demonstrated their competence in performing the psychologically demanding tasks required in combat duty during the Gulf War. But even assuming that women are less aggressive than men, there is still no evidence that it stems from biological causes rather than culture and socialization, which are malleable. The military has not offered empirical evidence to demonstrate that women cannot be trained to exhibit the same degree of aggressiveness that men exhibit. Nonetheless, the assumption that women are less aggressive continues to strengthen the myth of combat as a masculine institution of which only men are capable.

## PREGNANCY AND MOTHERHOOD

One specific aspect of women's physiology that some have argued disrupts unit cohesion and consequently hampers combat effectiveness is pregnancy (Nabors 1982: 56–58; see Barkalow 1990: 238–41; Rogan 1981: 256; Shields 1988: 108; Stiehm 1985b: 226). The Army has expressed concern with the effects of pregnancy on "readiness," "mission accomplishment," and "deployability" (Mitchell 1989: 6, 166–71; Rogan 1981: 26; Stiehm 1985a; see Tuten 1982: 251). Until 1975, women were automatically discharged from the military as soon as their pregnancy was discovered. This contributed to high attrition rates for women in the armed services. In 1975, the Department of Defense (DOD) made such discharge for pregnancy voluntary (see Segal 1983: 207; Treadwell 1954: 200).

Pregnancy also arguably interferes with the ability of the armed forces to rapidly mobilize troops for combat, since it cannot be predicted in advance which women will be pregnant, and thus unavailable for deployment. Pregnancy continues to be an issue of concern, both in the military and among the public. A *Newsweek* poll conducted in 1991 revealed that 76 percent of the public is concerned about military women becoming pregnant and putting the fetus at risk (Hackworth 1991: 27). Pregnancy does account for a significant percentage of women's lost time, although military women lose less service time overall than do men for illness, drug and alcohol abuse, and disability (see Coyle 1989: 39; D'Amico 1990: 8; Kornblum 1984: 417–18; Shields 1988: 109).

Because of the way military units are currently structured, pregnancy does present a genuine difficulty in the full integration of all women into combat forces. Since military policy, at least in the Army, does not provide temporary replacements for pregnant personnel, the presence of pregnant women in a unit increases everyone else's work load, and consequently brings with it the risk of breeding resentment among coworkers. In addition, although there is no certainty that women desiring to get pregnant will be successful, some opponents of women combatants contend that enlisted women will use pregnancy as a means of avoiding combat duty.

Therefore, pregnancy may be a legitimate reason to exclude women from actually engaging in some forms of combat. However, excluding all women from all positions designated as combat is far too extreme a response. Most women are not pregnant most of the time. Only about ten percent of servicewomen are pregnant at any given time (see Gordon and Ludvigson 1991: 22–23; Hackworth 1991: 27). There has been no surge of pregnancies in the military since the initiation of the Iraq war (Gold and Solaro 2005: 1). Further, the experience of pregnancy varies widely in affecting a woman's job performance. Some women are able to carry on their normal activities into the latter stages of pregnancy. Most logistical problems relating to pregnancy, such as deployment plans, etc., can be satisfactorily surmounted by careful planning.

The protection myth also operates here to call into question the propriety of risking the safety of the nation's child bearers by exposing them to the risks of combat. As with the lack of data on gender-integrated units, there have been no studies of the actual impact of pregnancy on military effectiveness because the combat exclusion has precluded the possibility of gathering data. Pregnancy is one consideration that needs to be factored into the analysis of how and whether to integrate women into certain combat roles. But it does not justify the stringency of the current restrictions.

Related to the pregnancy issue is the symbolic, if not actual, role of women as mothers. Motherhood and women's responsibilities to their families are viewed as antithetical to effective combat soldiering. The assumption underlying this view is that women's proper role is to be the center of family life. According to this perspective, women not only bear the children, but are also primarily responsible for their care and nurture (see Costin 1983: 305; Mitchell 1989: 6, 171–76; Rogan 1981: 26; Segal 1982: 274–75, 281–82). The media's promulgation of images of women soldiers kissing their infants goodbye before going off to the Gulf War, and its stories about fathers left at home to care for children emphasized the unnaturalness of female soldiers going off to combat (see Enloe 1993: 201–27).

The influence of gender ideology on this issue is evident in the view of Alexander Webster, a chaplain for the Army National Guard, who speculates about the "identity confusion that must confront any would-be woman warrior who pauses for a moment to consider her potential for motherhood." Webster also surmises that the paradigm of the citizen soldier may have been destroyed by the "social disruption and havoc among families wreaked by the mobilization and deployment of mothers of young children to the theater of operations in the Persian Gulf" (1991: 29). Webster continues: "Disturbing images on television and in the print media of mothers wrenched from their offspring may be the most enduring from the Persian Gulf War" (24–25). According to these ideological notions of gender, women need special protection because they are responsible, in turn, for protecting their children. Notably missing from this assessment is consideration of the consequences of *fathers* being "wrenched from their offspring," thus perpetuating the identification of women as the primary parent. Such testimony assumes that mothers are more responsible for family life than are fathers, so that it is women's military involvement that is questionable, not men's, whenever families are concerned.

Such ideological assumptions about the gender of parenthood are widespread. Surveys reveal that the public continues to be more willing to send young fathers into combat than young mothers. Even supporters of combat roles for women have assumed that mothers would be more reluctant to risk their lives in combat than would men (see Campbell 1992: 18; Lieberman 1990: 219). Attrition and reenlistment data for women indicate that motherhood is a primary reason why women leave the military. And surveys indicate that the large majority of service women do want to have children (see Shields 1988: 109). Former Secretary of Defense Richard Cheney argued that exempting all single parents and dual-service career couples from deployment would weaken military capability (see Campbell 1992: 18, 20). This problem impacts more heavily on women, who comprise the larger percentage of single parents in the military. Women's family obligations may thus present a practical problem for women's ability to carry out combat assignments, particularly for single mothers.

Several other factors need to be considered, however. Many military women are not mothers, and have no plans to become mothers. Most women entering the military are not (yet) mothers. The belief that women are essentially mothers is an outdated ideological assumption. It leads to the irrational result that men who are fathers can be required to participate in combat whereas women who are not mothers cannot (see Association of the Bar of the City of New York 1991: 25; Segal 1982: 283). Such beliefs underlie the former Army prohibition on the enlistment of women who had children in certain age groups (see Treadwell 1954: 496).[4]

Further, although most women traditionally *have* taken primary responsibility for protecting and providing for their children, not all mothers are primary caretakers. Many families include alternative arrangements for childcare that do not make the mother primarily responsible. Finally, tradition should not determine who *should* be responsible for national defense in time of war. Fathers have equal responsibility for protecting and providing for their children. Yet, since the Korean War, they have not been exempted from combat duty. In addition, the legislation mandating women's exclusion from combat does not exempt them from military service in time of war. Children of military parents are just as much in need of care and protection during wartime, regardless of whether their mothers are assigned to combat duty or some other position. In the absence of evidence indicating that combat jobs are more incompatible with being a wife and mother than a husband and father, families should be entitled to make their own decisions about child care in the event that the mother is called to serve in combat duty. Current military policy provides that if both parents are in the services, one can claim an exemption in the event that troops are deployed. There is no rational basis for the government to preempt the parents' right to choose based on a set of assumptions about motherhood.

## UNIT COHESION AND MALE BONDING

Unit or troop "cohesion" is a function of interpersonal relationships between military leaders and their troops, and the leader's ability to create and sustain "those interpersonal skills that allow him to build strong ties with his men" (Gabriel 1982: 172–73). The argument that male soldiers will lose the camaraderie and team spirit necessary for unit cohesion if they are required to share their duties with women has been advanced as a reason to exclude women from military combat.

For example, former Marine Corps Commandant Robert Barrows defends the notion of male bonding as a "real . . . cohesiveness," a "mutual respect and admiration," and a "team work" that would be destroyed by the inclusion of women. "If you want to make a combat unit ineffective," he said, "assign some women to it" (United States Senate Hearings 1991: 985–96).

Although the argument about the indispensability of cohesion to effectiveness is persuasive, the view that the presence of women will damage the "male bonding" linked to that cohesion is exaggerated by the influence of gender ideology. This "influence" is often supported by outdated and anecdotal evidence, such as Tiger's largely discredited research (Mitchell 1989; Golightly 1987; Hooker 1989: 45; Rogan 1981: 25). In addition, the military has not studied the impact that integration of the forces has had on "male bonding" in actual combat for the past several years, nor has it made efforts to instill male–female or female–female bonding in its soldiers (see Stiehm 1989: 236; Stiehm 1985a: 172).

There is also anecdotal evidence that there is a lack of gender integration that harms troop cohesion (and by extension, combat effectiveness). For example, after seven years in the Army and another seven in the Reserves, retired servicewoman Elizabeth Vasquez opined: "I think we have every right and capability to be on the front lines. . . . But you need that sense of unity, and I don't think it's possible in integrated units. Its hard to do your job to your fullest capability when you're thought of as less than what I wanted to be—a soldier" (Martineau and Wiegand 2005: 8). However, the experience with female soldiers in the Iraq and Persian Gulf Wars, as well as the limited studies that have been done in simulated combat and field conditions, indicate that the presence of women in combat units does not adversely affect combat effectiveness (see Gold and Solaro 2005: 1). The Army Research Institute conducted two of these studies, labeled "REFWAC" and "MAXWAC" (Johnson et al. 1978; United States Army Research Institute 1977). MAXWAC results showed that female ratios varying from 0 to 35 percent had no significant effect on unit performance. REFWAC results similarly showed that the presence of 10 percent female soldiers on a REFORGER ("Return of Forces to Germany") ten-day field exercise made no difference in the performance of combat support and combat service support units.

In addition, Navy Commander Barry Boyle, participating in Navy squadron preparations, Charles Moskos, observing an Army exercise in Honduras, and Constance Devilbliss, participating in rigorous Army exercises, reached similar conclusions that integrated units performed as effectively, if not more so, than all-male units (see Coyle 1989; Devilbliss 1985; Moskos 1985). Experience with women in combat in other nations, as well as the successful integration of women into police and other traditionally male-only professions, also provides useful analogies indicating that the participation of American military women in combat would not hamper unit or troop cohesion (Association 1991; Goldman 1982a, 1982b; United States Senate Hearings 1991).

## FRATERNIZATION

Women in uniform represent an anomaly to traditional social ordering based on traditional sex-gender distinctions, and thus to traditional sexual morality. Thus, in addition to their supposedly detrimental effect on male bonding, including women in combat roles is sometimes alleged to diminish troop effectiveness because of the inevitable sexual attraction and behavior that would follow from having mixed-gender units. Some express a fear that men will be preoccupied with winning the sexual favors of women rather than concentrating on their mission (Donnelly 2006: 2; Golightly 1987: 46; Mitchell 1989: 176–78; Rogan 1981: 27).

The fraternization argument ignores the capability of the sexes to interact with one another in nonsexual ways, particularly under the exigent circumstances of combat. The limited studies that have been conducted under simulated combat conditions indicate that fraternization does not hamper combat readiness or troop effectiveness. Studies show that gender-integrated combat units are as effective as all-male units, and that members of gender-integrated units develop brother-sister bonds rather than sexual ones.

Fraternization is most likely to be a problem where there is ineffective leadership. It is likely that unit bonding depends more on shared experiences, including sharing of risks and hardships, than on gender distinctions (see Karst 1991: 537, 543; Devilbliss 1985: 519; Opinion 1988: 138). Experience has shown that actual integration diminishes prejudice and fosters group cohesiveness more effectively than any other factor. It is thus likely that women's integration into combat forces would parallel that of black men into previously all-white forces during the 1950s and 1960s (see Moskos 1990: 74; Holm 1982: 257; Kornblum 1984: 412, 422; Segal 1983: 203–04, 206).

## CONCLUSION

It is a fact that U.S. servicewomen are involved in military combat despite the lack of official recognition they are given. As the preceding discussion reveals, none of the primary rationales that have been forwarded to exclude women from being able to "officially" serve in combat roles provides a legitimate basis for maintaining the current restrictions on women's participation in combat. The analysis of these rationales suggests that the resistance of Congress, the courts, the military, and the public to removing the combat restrictions results more from gender ideology than from demonstrated evidence of women's inability to perform combat roles effectively.

Once outdated stereotypes and myths about women's capabilities and deficiencies are eliminated from consideration of the ethics of women in military combat, the current restrictions on combat roles for women are revealed to lack persuasive foundations. Certainly, differences in physical strength and other physiological distinctions between men and women need to be taken into consideration, but these can be accommodated without the need to exclude women from combat roles. Only when the military begins assigning women to positions on the basis of gender-neutral standards for evaluating the degree of physical strength, psychological fortitude, bonding and troop cohesiveness necessary to perform combat roles can the issue of women in combat be addressed without the undue influence of ideological notions of gender.

## NOTES

1. Interestingly, this parallels the findings of a recent *USA Today*/CNN/Gallup public opinion poll, which found that "Americans overwhelmingly favor the use of female troops in Iraq, including having them serve in support jobs that often put them in or near combat. . . . A majority of those polled, however, oppose women serving as ground troops" (Moniz 2005).
2. However, a House of Representatives bill to codify the combat exclusions (which up until then had been military policy rather than congressionally mandated), as well as further limit the military positions open to women, was defeated in May 2005 (Ho 2005: 1; Moniz 2005: 1) Instead, a measure was passed instead that requires the Defense Department to notify Congress 60 days in advance of any policy change that would put women in new direct combat roles (id.).
3. A standard based on physical strength rather than gender could be waived in emergency situations where rapid mobilization is necessary and individual testing would be inefficient (see Segal 1982: 270–71).
4. This policy was reversed in *Crawford v. Cushman*, 531 F.2d 1114 (2d Cir. 1976).

## REFERENCES

Association of the Bar of the City of New York, "The Combat Exclusion Laws: An Idea Whose Time Has Gone," *Minerva*, Vol. 9, No. 4 (Winter, 1991), pp. 1–55 (Association).

Barkalow, Carol, *In the Men's House* (New York: Poseidon Press, 1990).

Beecraft, Carolyn, "Personnel Puzzle," *Proceedings (of the U.S. Naval Institute)*, Vol. 115, No. 4 (April, 1989), pp. 41–44.

Campbell, D'Ann, "Combatting the Gender Gulf," *Temple Political and Civil Rights Law Review*, Vol. 1, No. 2 (Fall, 1992), reprinted in *Minerva*, Vol. X, Nos. 3–4 (Fall/Winter 1992), pp. 13–41.

Code, Lorraine, *What Can She Know? Feminist Theory and the Construction of Knowledge* (Ithaca, NY: Cornell University Press, 1991).

Cornum, Rhonda, *She Went to War: The Rhonda Cornum Story* (Novato, CA: Presidio Press, 1992).

Costin, Lela, "Feminism, Pacifism, Nationalism, and the United Nations Decade for Women," in Judith Stiehm (ed.), *Women and Men's Wars* (Oxford: Pergamon Press, 1983), pp. 301–16.

Cox, Amy, "Women at War: Mental Health Toll Unknown," *CNN.com* (posted May 22, 2007; originally published May 2006), http://www.cnn.com/2006/US/05/26/ch.women.vets/index.html (accessed June 20, 2007).

Coyle, Commander Barry, U.S. Navy, "Women on the Front Lines," *Proceedings (of the U.S. Military Institute)*, Vol. 115, No. 4 (April, 1989), pp. 37–40.

Cramsie, Jodie, "Gender Discrimination in the Military: The Unconstitutional Exclusion of Women From Combat," *Valparaiso Law Review*, Vol. 17 (1983), pp. 547–88.

D'Amico, "Women at Arms: The Combat Controversy," *Minerva*, Vol. 8, No. 2 (1990), pp. 1–19.

Devilbliss, M. C., "Gender Integration and Unit Deployment: A Study of G.I. Jo," *Armed Forces and Society*, Vol. 11, No. 3 (1985), pp. 523–52.

Dillingham, Wayne, "The Possibility of American Military Women Becoming Prisoners of War: Justification for Combat Exclusion Rules?" *Federal Bar News and Journal*, Vol. 37, No. 4 (1990), pp. 223–30.

Donnelly, Elaine, "Rumsfeld Dithers on Women in Combat," *Center for Military Readiness* (June 16, 2006), online at http://www.cmrlink.org/WomenInCombat.asp?docID=273 (accessed June 21, 2007).

Enloe, Cynthia, *The Morning After: Sexual Politics at the End of the Cold War* (Berkeley, CA: University of California Press, 1993).

Gabriel, Richard, *To Serve With Honor: A Treatise on Military Ethics and the Way of the Soldier* (Westport, CT: Greenwood Press, 1982).

Gold, Philip and Erin Solaro, "Facts About Women in Combat Elude the Right," *Seattle Post-Intelligencer* (May 18 2005), online at http://seattlepi.nwsource.com/opinion/22465_womenincombat18.html (accessed June 21, 2007).

Goldman, Nancy Loring (ed.), *Female Soldiers—Combatants or Noncombatants? Historical and Contemporary Perspectives* (Westport, CT: Greenwood Press, 1982a).

_____. *The Utilization of Women in Combat: An Historical and Social Analysis of Twentieth-Century Wartime and Peacetime Experience* (Alexandria, VA: U.S.A.R.I., 1982b).

Golightly, Lieutenant Neil L., U.S. Navy, "No Right to Fight," *Proceedings (of the U.S. Naval Institute)*, Vol. 113, No. 12 (1987), pp. 46–49.

Gordon, Marilyn and Mary Jo Ludvigson, "A Constitutional Analysis of the Combat Exclusion for Air Force Women," *Minerva: Quarterly Report on Women and the Military*, Vol. 9, No. 2 (1991), pp. 1–34.

Hackworth, Colonel David, "War and the Second Sex," *Newsweek* (August 5, 1991), pp. 24–28.

Ho, Stephanie, "US House Debates Role of Women in Combat," *VOA News.com* (2005), http://www.voanews.com/english/archive/2005-05/2005-05-22-voa38.cfm?CFID=165219291&CFTOKEN=53222921 (accessed June 21, 2007).

Holm, Maj. Gen. Jeanne, U.S.A.F. (Ret.), Women in the Military (Novato, CA: Presidio Press, 1982).

Hooker, Richard, "Affirmative Action and Combat Exclusion: Gender Roles in the U.S. Army," *Parameters: U.S. War College Quarterly*, Vol. 19, No. 4 (1989), pp. 36–50.

Johnson, Cecil, et al., *Women Content in the Army:* REFORGER (REFWAC 77) (Alexandria, VA: U.S.A.R.I., 1978).

Kantrowitz, Barbara, "The Right to Fight," *Newsweek* (August 5, 1991), pp. 22–23.

Karst, Kenneth, "The Pursuit of Manhood and the Desegregation of the Armed Forces," *U.C.L.A. Law Review*, Vol. 38, No. 3 (1991), pp. 499–581.

Katz, Amy, "The Future of Women Serving in Combat Being Debated," *VOA News.com* (May 23, 2005), on line at http://www.voanews.com/english/archive/2005-05/2005-05-23-voa16.cfm?CFID=91000318&CFTOKEN=87046523 (accessed June 21, 2007).

Kelly, Karla, "The Exclusion of Women From Combat: Withstanding the Challenge," *Judge Advocate General Journal*, Vol. 33, No. 1 (1984), pp. 77–108.

Kornblum, Lori, "Women Warriors in a Men's World: The Combat Exclusion," *Law and Inequality*, Vol. 2 (1984), pp. 351–445.

Lancaster, John, *Washington Post* (January 13, 1994), pp. A1, A7.

Lieberman, Jeanne, "Women in Combat," *Federal Bar News and Journal*, Vol. 37, No. 4 (1990), pp. 215–22.

Little, Vince, "Debate Aside, Women in Uniform Know Combat Roles," *Stars and Stripes* (June 15, 2005), online at http://www.estripes.com/article.asp?section=104&article=26903&archive=true (accessed June 21, 2007).

Marlowe, David, "The Manning of the Force and the Structure of Battle: Part 2—Men and Women," in Robert Fullinwider (ed.), *Conscripts and Volunteers: Military Requirements, Social Justice, and the All-Volunteer Force* (Totowa, NJ: Rowman & Allanheld, 1983), pp. 189–99.

Marquit, Doris and Erwin Marquit, "Gender Differentiation, Genetic Determinism, and the Struggle for Peace," in Anne E. Hunter (ed.), *Genes and Gender VI: On Peace, War, and Gender: A Challenge to Genetic Explanations* (New York: Feminist Press, 1991), pp. 151–62.

Martineau, Pamela and Steve Wiegand, "Women at War," *Sacramento Bee* (March 6, 2005).

McDowell, Jeanne, "Are Women Better Cops?" *Time* (February 17, 1992), pp. 70–72.

Mitchell, Brian, *The Weak Link: The Feminization of the American Military* (Washington, DC: Regnery Gateway, 1989).

Moniz, Dave, "Public Backs Female Troops in Iraq, But Not in Ground Force," *USA Today* (May 25, 2005), online at http://www.usatoday.com/news/world/iraq/2005-05-25-women-combat_x.htm (accessed June 21, 2007).

Moskos, Charles, "Female GI's in the Field," *Society*, Vol. 22, No. 6 (1985), pp. 28–33.

_____. "Army Women," *Atlantic Monthly*, Vol. 266, No. 2 (August, 1990), pp. 70–78.

Nabors, Major Robert, "Women in the Army: Do They Measure Up?" *Military Review* (October, 1982), pp. 50–61.

Opinion, "No right to Fight?" *Proceedings of the U.S. Naval Institute*, Vol. 114, No. 5) (May, 1988), pp. 134–39.

Pine, Art, "Women Will Get Limited Combat Roles," *Los Angeles Times* (January 14, 1994), p. A5.

Proxmire, Senator William, "Three Myths About Women and Combat," *Minerva*, Vol. 4, No. 4 (Winter, 1986), pp. 105–19.

Rogan, Helen, *Mixed Company: Women in the Modern Army* (New York: G.P. Putnam's Sons, 1981).

Rosoff, Betty, "Genes, Hormones, and War," in Hunter (ed.), *Genes and Gender VI: On Peace, War, and Gender: A Challenge to Genetic Explanations* (New York: Feminist Press, 1991), pp. 39–49.

Roush, Paul, "Combat Exclusion: Military Necessity or Another Name For Bigotry?" *Minerva*, Vol. 13, No. 3 (Fall, 1990), pp. 1–15.

Scarborough, Rowan and Joseph Curl, "Despite Pressure, Bush Vows 'No Women in Combat'" (January 12, 2005), online at http://www.washingtontimes.com (accessed June 20, 2007).

Schleicher, Annie, "More Women Soldiers Dying in Iraq" (December 18, 2006), online at http://www.pbs.org/newshour/extra/features/july-dec06/military-women_12-18.pdf (accessed April 22, 2012).

Schmitt, Eric, "Generals Oppose Combat by Women," *Newsweek* (June 17, 1994a) pp. A1, A18.

_____, "Army Will Allow Women in 32,000 Combat Posts," *New York Times* (July 28, 1994b), p. A5.

Segal, Mady Wechsler, "The Argument for Female Combatants," in Goldman (ed.), *Female Soldiers—Combatants or Noncombatants? Historical and Contemporary Perspectives* (Westport, CT: Greenwood Press, 1982), pp. 267–90.

_____. "Women's Roles in the U.S. Armed Forces: An Evaluation of Evidence and Arguments for Policy Decisions," in Robert Fullinwider (ed.), *Conscripts and Volunteers: Military Requirements, Social Justice, and the All-Volunteer Force* (Totowa, NJ: Rowman & Allanheld, 1983), pp. 200–13 .

Shields, Patricia, "Sex Roles in the Military," in Charles Moskos and Frank Wood (eds.), *The Military—More Than Just a Job?* (Washington, DC: Pergamon Basseys, 1988), pp. 99–111.

Stiehm, Judith Hicks, "Women's Biology and the U.S. Military," in Virginia Sapiro (ed.), *Women, Biology, and Public Policy* (Beverly Hills: SAGE Publications, 1985a), pp. 205–32.

_____. "Generations of U.S. Enlisted Women," *Signs: Journal of Women in Culture and Society*, Vol. 11, No. 1 (1985b), pp. 155–75.

_____. *Arms and the Enlisted Woman* (Philadelphia: Temple University Press, 1989).

Sunday, Suzanne R., "Biological Theories of Animal Aggression," in Hunter (ed.), *Genes and Gender VI: On Peace,*

*War, and Gender: A Challenge to Genetic Explanations* (New York: Feminist Press, 1991), pp. 50–63.

Treadwell, Mattie, *The Women's Army Corps, in World War II Special Studies*, Vol. 8 (Washington, DC: Office of the Chief of Military History of the Army, 1954).

Tuten, Jeff, "The Argument Against Female Combatants," in Goldman (ed.), *Female Soldiers—Combatants or Non-combatants? Historical and Contemporary Perspectives* (Westport, CT: Greenwood Press, 1982), pp. 237–66.

United States Army Research Institute, *Women Content in Units Force Deployment Test* (MAXWAC) (Alexandria, VA: U.S.A.R.I., 1977).

United States Senate, Hearings before the Committee on Appropriations, DOD Appropriations, 102d Cong., 1st Sess., H.R. 2521, Pts. 4 & 6, *Utilization of Women in the Military Services* (Washington, DC: Government Printing Office, 1991) (Appropriations Hearings).

Van Creveld, Martin, "Why Israel Doesn't Send Women into Combat," *Parameters*, Vol. 23, No. 1 (Spring, 1993), pp. 5–9.

Webster, Alexander, "Paradigms of the Contemporary American Soldier and Women in the Military," *Strategic Review* (Summer 1991), pp. 22–30.

# Lifeboat Ethics:
## Mother Love and Child Death in Northeast Brazil

### Nancy Scheper-Hughes

I have seen death without weeping.
The destiny of the Northeast is death.
Cattle they kill.
To the people they do something worse.

*Anonymous Brazilian singer (1965)*

"Why do the church bells ring so often?" I asked Nailza de Arruda soon after I moved into a corner of her tiny mud-walled hut near the top of the shantytown called the Alto do Cru-zeiro (Crucifix Hill). I was then a Peace Corps volunteer and a community development/health worker. It was the dry and blazing hot summer of 1965, the months following the military coup in Brazil, and save for the rusty, clanging bells, of N. S. das Dores Church, an eerie quiet had settled over the market town that I call Bom Jesus da Mata. Beneath the quiet, however, there was chaos and panic. "It's nothing," replied Nailza, "just another little angel gone to heaven."

Nailza had sent more than her share of little angels to heaven, and sometimes at night I could hear her engaged in a muffled but passionate discourse with one of them, two-year-old Joana. Joana's photograph, taken as she lay propped up in her tiny cardboard coffin, her eyes open, hung on a wall next to one of Nailza and Zé Antonio taken on the day they eloped.

Nailza could barely remember the other infants and babies who came and went in close succession. Most had died unnamed and were hastily baptized in their coffins. Few lived more than a month or two. Only Joana, properly baptized in church at the close of her first year

and placed under the protection of a powerful saint, Joan of Arc, had been expected to live. And Nailza had dangerously allowed herself to love the little girl.

In addressing the dead child, Nailza's voice would range from tearful imploring to angry recrimination: "Why did you leave me? Was your patron saint so greedy that she could not allow me one child on this earth?" Zé Antonio advised me to ignore Nailza's odd behavior, which he understood as a kind of madness that, like the birth and death of children, came and went. Indeed, the premature birth of a stillborn son some months later "cured" Nailza of her "inappropriate" grief, and the day came when she removed Joana's photo and carefully packed it away.

More than fifteen years elapsed before I returned to the Alto do Cruzeiro, and it was anthropology that provided the vehicle of my return. Since 1982 I have returned several times in order to pursue a problem that first attracted my attention in the 1960s. My involvement with the people of the Alto do Cruzeiro now spans a quarter of a century and three generations of parenting in a community where mothers and daughters are often simultaneously pregnant.

The Alto do Cruzeiro is one of three shantytowns surrounding the large market town of Bom Jesus in the sugar plantation zone of Pernambuco in Northeast Brazil, one of the many zones of neglect that have emerged in the shadow of the now tarnished economic miracle of Brazil. For the women and children of the Alto do Cruzeiro the only miracle is that some of them have managed to stay alive at all.

The Northeast is a region of vast proportions (approximately twice the size of Texas) and of equally vast social and developmental problems. The nine states that make up the region are the poorest in the country and are representative of the Third World within a dynamic and rapidly industrializing nation. Despite waves of migrations from the interior to the teeming shantytowns of coastal cities, the majority still live in rural areas on farms and ranches, sugar plantations and mills.

Life expectancy in the Northeast is only forty years, largely because of the appallingly high rate of infant and child mortality. Approximately one million children in Brazil under the age of five die each year. The children of the Northeast, especially those born in shantytowns on the periphery of urban life, are at a very high risk of death. In these areas, children are born without the traditional protection of breast-feeding, subsistence gardens, stable marriages, and multiple adult caretakers that exists in the interior. In the hillside shantytowns that spring up around cities or, in this case, interior market towns, marriages are brittle, single parenting is the norm, and women are frequently forced into the shadow economy of domestic work in the homes of the rich or into unprotected and oftentimes "scab" wage labor on the surrounding sugar plantations, where they clear land for planting and weed for a pittance, sometimes less than a dollar a day. The women of the Alto may not bring their babies with them into the homes of the wealthy, where the often-sick infants are considered sources of contamination, and they cannot carry the little ones to the riverbanks where they wash clothes because the river is heavily infested with schistosomes and other deadly parasites. Nor can they carry their young children to the plantations, which are often several miles away. At wages of a dollar a day, the women of the Alto cannot hire baby sitters. Older children who are not in school will sometimes serve as somewhat indifferent caretakers. But any child not in school is also expected to find wage work. In most cases, babies are simply left at home alone, the door securely fastened. And so many also die alone and unattended.

Bom Jesus da Mata, centrally located in the plantation zone of Pernambuco, is within commuting distance of several sugar plantations and mills. Consequently, Bom Jesus has been a magnet for rural workers forced off their small subsistence plots by large landowners wanting to use every available piece of land for sugar cultivation. Initially, the rural migrants to Bom Jesus were squatters who were given tacit approval by the mayor to put up temporary straw huts on each of the three hills overlooking the town. The Alto do Cruzeiro is the oldest, the largest, and the poorest of the shantytowns. Over the past three decades many of the original migrants have become permanent residents, and the primitive and temporary straw huts have been replaced by small homes (usually of two rooms) made of wattle and daub, sometimes covered with plaster. The more affluent residents use bricks and tiles. In most Alto homes, dangerous kerosene lamps have been replaced by light bulbs. The once tattered rural garb, often fashioned from used sugar sacking, has likewise been replaced by store-bought clothes, often castoffs from a wealthy *patrão* (boss). The trappings are modern, but the hunger, sickness, and death that they conceal are traditional, deeply rooted in a history of feudalism, exploitation, and institutionalized dependency.

My research agenda never wavered. The questions I addressed first crystallized during a veritable "die-off" of Alto babies during a severe drought in 1965. The food and water shortages and the political and economic chaos occasioned by the military coup were reflected in the handwritten entries of births and deaths in the dusty, yellowed pages of the ledger books kept at the public registry office in Bom Jesus. More than 350 babies died in the Alto during 1965 alone—this from a shantytown population of little more than 5,000. But that wasn't what surprised me. There were reasons enough for the deaths in the miserable conditions of shantytown life. What puzzled me was the seeming indifference of Alto women to the death of their infants, and their willingness to attribute to their own tiny offspring an aversion to life that made their death seem wholly natural, indeed all but anticipated.

Although I found that it was possible, and hardly difficult, to rescue infants and toddlers from death by diarrhea and dehydration with a simple sugar, salt, and water solution (even bottled Coca-Cola worked fine), it was more difficult to enlist a mother herself in the rescue of a child she perceived as ill-fated for life or better off dead, or to convince her to take back into her threatened and besieged home a baby she had already come to think of as an angel rather than as a son or daughter.

I learned that the high expectancy of death, and the ability to face child death with stoicism and equanimity, produced patterns of nurturing that differentiated between those infants thought of as thrivers and survivors and those thought of as born already "wanting to die." The survivors were nurtured, while stigmatized, doomed infants were left to die, as mothers say, a mingua, "of neglect." Mothers stepped back and allowed nature to take its course. This pattern, which I call mortal selective neglect, is called passive infanticide by anthropologist Marvin Harris. The Alto situation, although culturally specific in the form that it takes, is not unique to Third World shantytown communities and may have its correlates in our own impoverished urban communities in some cases of "failure to thrive" infants.

I use as an example the story of Zezinho, the thirteen-month-old toddler of one of my neighbors,

Lourdes. I became involved with Zezinho when I was called in to help Lourdes in the delivery of another child, this one a fair and robust little tyke with a lusty cry. I noted that while Lourdes showed great interest in the newborn, she totally ignored Zezinho who, wasted and severely malnourished, was curled up in a fetal position on a piece of urine- and feces-soaked cardboard placed under his mother's hammock. Eyes open and vacant, mouth slack, the little boy seemed doomed.

When I carried Zezinho up to the community day-care center at the top of the hill, the Alto women who took turns caring for one another's children (in order to free themselves for part-time work in the cane fields or washing clothes) laughed at my efforts to save Zé, agreeing with Lourdes that here was a baby without a ghost of a chance. Leave him alone, they cautioned. It makes no sense to fight with death. But I did do battle with Zé, and after several weeks of force-feeding (malnourished babies lose their interest in food), Zé began to succumb to my ministrations. He acquired some flesh across his taut chest bones, learned to sit up, and even tried to smile. When he seemed well enough, I returned him to Lourdes in her miserable scrap-material lean-to, but not without guilt about what I had done. I wondered whether returning Zé was at all fair to Lourdes and to his little brother. But I was busy and washed my hands of the matter. And Lourdes did seem more interested in Zé now that he was looking more human.

When I returned in 1982, there was Lourdes among the women who formed my sample of Alto mothers—still struggling to put together some semblance of life for a now grown Zé and her five other surviving children. Much was made of my reunion with Zé in 1982, and everyone enjoyed retelling the story of Zé's rescue and of how his mother had given him up for dead. Zé would laugh the loudest when told how I had had to force-feed him like a fiesta turkey. There was no hint of guilt on the part of Lourdes and no resentment on the part of Zé. In fact, when questioned in private as to who was the best friend he ever had in life, Zé took a long drag on his cigarette and answered without a trace of irony, "Why my mother, of course!" "But of course," I replied.

Part of learning how to mother in the Alto do Cruzeiro is learning when to let go of a child who shows that it "wants" to die or that it has no "knack" or no "taste" for life. Another part is learning when it is safe to let oneself love a child. Frequent child death remains a powerful shaper of maternal thinking and practice. In the absence of firm expectation that a child will survive, mother love as we conceptualize it (whether in popular terms or in the psychobiological notion of maternal bonding) is attenuated and delayed

with consequences for infant survival. In an environment already precarious to young life, the emotional detachment of mothers toward some of their babies contributes even further to the spiral of high mortality—high fertility in a kind of macabre lock-step dance to death.

The average woman of the Alto experiences 9.5 pregnancies, 3.5 child deaths, and 1.5 stillbirths. Seventy percent of all child deaths in the Alto occur in the first six months of life, and 82 percent by the end of the first year. Of all deaths in the community each year, about 45 percent are of children under the age of five.

Women of the Alto distinguish between child deaths understood as natural (caused by diarrhea and communicable diseases) and those resulting from sorcery, the evil eye, or other magical or supernatural afflictions. They also recognize a large category of infant deaths seen as fated and inevitable. These hopeless cases are classified by mothers under the folk terminology "child sickness" or "child attack." Women say that there are at least fourteen different types of hopeless child sickness, but most can be subsumed under two categories—chronic and acute. The chronic cases refer to infants who are born small and wasted. They are deathly pale, mothers say, as well as weak and passive. They demonstrate no vital force, no liveliness. They do not suck vigorously; they hardly cry. Such babies can be this way at birth or they can be born sound but soon show no resistance, no "fight" against the common crises of infancy: diarrhea, respiratory infections, tropical fevers.

The acute cases are those doomed infants who die suddenly and violently. They are taken by stealth overnight, often following convulsions that bring on head banging, shaking, grimacing, and shrieking. Women say it is horrible to look at such a baby. If the infant begins to foam at the mouth or gnash its teeth or go rigid with its eyes turned back inside its head, there is absolutely no hope. The infant is "put aside"—left alone—often on the floor in a back room, and allowed to die. These symptoms (which accompany high fevers, dehydration, third-stage malnutrition, and encephalitis) are equated by Alto women with madness, epilepsy, and worst of all, rabies, which is greatly feared and highly stigmatized.

Most of the infants presented to me as suffering from chronic child sickness were tiny, wasted famine victims, while those labeled as victims of acute child attack seemed to be infants suffering from the deliriums of high fever or the convulsions that can accompany electrolyte imbalance in dehydrated babies.

Local midwives and traditional healers, praying women, as they are called, advise Alto women on when to allow a baby to die. One midwife explained: "If I can see that a baby was born unfortuitously, I tell the mother that she need not wash the infant or give it a cleansing tea. I tell her just to dust the infant with baby powder and wait for it to die." Allowing nature to take its course is not seen as sinful by these often very devout Catholic women. Rather, it is understood as cooperating with God's plan.

Often I have been asked how consciously women of the Alto behave in this regard. I would have to say that consciousness is always shifting between allowed and disallowed levels of awareness. For example, I was awakened early one morning in 1987 by two neighborhood children who had been sent to fetch me to a hastily organized wake for a two-month-old infant whose mother I had unsuccessfully urged to breast-feed. The infant was being sustained on sugar water, which the mother referred to as soro (serum), using a medical term for the infant's starvation regime in light of his chronic diarrhea. I had cautioned the mother that an infant could not live on *soro* forever.

The two girls urged me to console the young mother by telling her that it was "too bad" that her infant was so weak that Jesus had to take him. They were coaching me in proper Alto etiquette. I agreed, of course, but asked, "And what do you think?" Xoxa, the eleven-year-old, looked down at her dusty flip-flops and blurted out, "Oh, Dona Nanci, that baby never got enough to eat, but you must never say that!" And so the death of hungry babies remains one of the best-kept secrets of life in Bom Jesus da Mata.

Most victims are waked quickly and with a minimum of ceremony. No tears are shed, and the neighborhood children form a tiny procession, carrying the baby to the town graveyard where it will join a multitude of others. Although a few fresh flowers may be scattered over the tiny grave, no stone or wooden cross will mark the place, and the same spot will be reused within a few months' time. The mother will never visit the grave, which soon becomes an anonymous one.

What, then, can be said of these women? What emotions, what sentiments motivate them? How are they able to do what, in fact, must be done? What does mother love mean in this inhospitable context? Are grief, mourning, and melancholia present, although deeply repressed? If so, where shall we look for them? And if not, how are we to understand the moral visions and moral sensibilities that guide their actions?

I have been criticized more than once for presenting an unflattering portrait of poor Brazilian women, women who are, after all, themselves the victims of severe social and institutional neglect. I have described these women as allowing some of their children to die, as if this were an unnatural and inhuman act rather than, as I would assert, the way any one of us might act, reasonably and rationally, under similarly desperate

conditions. Perhaps I have not emphasized enough the real pathogens in this environment of high risk: poverty, deprivation, sexism, chronic hunger, and economic exploitation. If mother love is, as many psychologists and some feminists believe, a seemingly natural and universal maternal script, what does it mean to women for whom scarcity, loss, sickness, and deprivation have made that love frantic and robbed them of their grief, seeming to turn their hearts to stone?

Throughout much of human history—as in a great deal of the impoverished Third World today—women have had to give birth and to nurture children under ecological conditions and social arrangements hostile to child survival, as well as to their own well-being. Under circumstances of high childhood mortality, patterns of selective neglect and passive infanticide may be seen as active survival strategies.

They also seem to be fairly common practices historically and across cultures. In societies characterized by high childhood mortality and by a correspondingly high (replacement) fertility, cultural practices of infant and childcare tend to be organized primarily around survival goals. But what this means is a pragmatic recognition that not all of one's children can be expected to live. The nervousness about child survival in areas of northeast Brazil, northern India, or Bangladesh, where a 30 percent or 40 percent mortality rate in the first years of life is common, can lead to forms of delayed attachment and a casual or benign neglect that serves to weed out the worst bets so as to enhance the life chances of healthier siblings, including those yet to be born. Practices similar to those that I am describing have been recorded for parts of Africa, India, and Central America.

Life in the Alto do Cruzeiro resembles nothing so much as a battlefield or an emergency room in an overcrowded inner city public hospital. Consequently, morality is guided by a kind of "lifeboat ethics," the morality of triage. The seemingly studied indifference toward the suffering of some of their infants, conveyed in such sayings as "little critters have no feelings," is understandable in light of these women's obligation to carry on with their reproductive and nurturing lives.

In their slowness to anthropomorphize and personalize their infants, everything is mobilized so as to prevent maternal overattachment and, therefore, grief at death. The bereaved mother is told not to cry, that her tears will dampen the wings of her little angel so that she cannot fly up to her heavenly home. Grief at the death of an angel is not only inappropriate, it is a symptom of madness and of a profound lack of faith.

Infant death becomes routine in an environment in which death is anticipated and bets are hedged. While the routinization of death in the context of shantytown life is not hard to understand, and quite possible to empathize with, its routinization in the formal institutions of public life in Bom Jesus is not as easy to accept uncritically. Here the social production of indifference takes on a different, even a malevolent cast.

In a society where triplicates of every form are required for the most banal events (registering a car, for example), the registration of infant and child death is informal, incomplete, and rapid. It requires no documentation, takes less than five minutes, and demands no witnesses other than office clerks. No questions are asked concerning the circumstances of the death, and the cause of death is left blank, unquestioned and unexamined. A neighbor, grandmother, older sibling, or common-law husband may register the death. Since most infants die at home, there is no question of a medical record.

From the registry office, the parent proceeds to the town hall, where the mayor will give him or her a voucher for a free baby coffin. The full-time municipal coffinmaker cannot tell you exactly how many baby coffins are dispatched each week. It varies, he says, with the seasons. There are more needed during the drought months and during the big festivals of Carnaval and Christmas and São Joao's Day because people are too busy, he supposes, to take their babies to the clinic. Record keeping is sloppy.

Similarly, there is a failure on the part of city-employed doctors working at two free clinics to recognize the malnutrition of babies who are weighed, measured, and immunized without comment and as if they were not, in fact, anemic, stunted, fussy, and irritated starvation babies. At best the mothers are told to pick up free vitamins or a health "tonic" at the municipal chambers. At worst, clinic personnel will give tranquilizers and sleeping pills to quiet the hungry cries of "sick-to-death" Alto babies.

The church, too, contributes to the routinization of, and indifference toward, child death. Traditionally, the local Catholic church taught patience and resignation to domestic tragedies that were said to reveal the imponderable workings of God's will. If an infant died suddenly, it was because a particular saint had claimed the child. The infant would be an angel in the service of his or her heavenly patron. It would be wrong, a sign of a lack of faith, to weep for a child with such good fortune. The infant funeral was, in the past, an event celebrated with joy. Today, however, under the new regime of "liberation theology," the bells of N. S. das Dores parish church no longer peal for the death of Alto babies, and no priest accompanies the procession of angels to the cemetery where their bodies are disposed of casually and without ceremony. Children bury children in Bom Jesus da Mata. In this

most Catholic of communities, the coffin is handed to the disabled and irritable municipal gravedigger, who often chides the children for one reason or another. It may be that the coffin is larger than expected and the gravedigger can find no appropriate space. The children do not wait for the gravedigger to complete his task. No prayers are recited and no sign of the cross made as the tiny coffin goes into its shallow grave.

When I asked the local priest, Padre Marcos, about the lack of church ceremony surrounding infant and childhood death today in Bom Jesus, he replied: "In the old days, child death was richly celebrated. But those were the baroque customs of a conservative church that wallowed in death and misery. The new church is a church of hope and joy. We no longer celebrate the death of child angels. We try to tell mothers that Jesus doesn't want all the dead babies they send him." Similarly, the new church has changed its baptismal customs, now often refusing to baptize dying babies brought to the back door of a church or rectory. The mothers are scolded by the church attendants and told to go home and take care of their sick babies. Baptism, they are told, is for the living; it is not to be confused with the sacrament of extreme unction, which is the anointing of the dying. And so it appears to the women of the Alto that even the church has turned away from them, denying the traditional comfort of folk Catholicism.

The contemporary Catholic Church is caught in the clutches of a double bind. The new theology of liberation imagines a kingdom of God on earth based on justice and equality, a world without hunger, sickness, or childhood mortality. At the same time, the church has not changed its official position on sexuality and reproduction, including its sanctions against birth control, abortion, and sterilization. The padre of Bom Jesus da Mata recognizes this contradiction intuitively, although he shies away from discussions on the topic, saying that he prefers to leave questions of family planning to the discretion and the "good consciences" of his impoverished parishioners. But this, of course, sidesteps the extent to which those good consciences have been shaped by traditional church teachings in Bom Jesus, especially by his recent predecessors. Hence, we can begin to see that the seeming indifference of Alto mothers toward the death of some of their infants is but a pale reflection of the official indifference of church and state to the plight of poor women and children.

Nonetheless, the women of Bom Jesus are survivors. One woman, Biu, told me her life history, returning again and again to the themes of child death, her first husband's suicide, abandonment by her father and later by her second husband, and all the other losses and disappointments she had suffered in her long forty-five years. She concluded with great force, reflecting on the days of Carnaval '88 that were fast approaching:

> No, Dona Nanci, I won't cry, and I won't waste my life thinking about it from morning to night. . . . Can I argue with God for the state that I'm in? No! And so I'll dance and I'll jump and I'll play Carnaval! And yes, I'll laugh and people will wonder at a pobre like me who can have such a good time.

And no one did blame Biu for dancing in the streets during the four days of Carnaval—not even on Ash Wednesday, the day following Carnaval '88 when we all assembled hurriedly to assist in the burial of Mercea, Biu's beloved *casula*, her last-born daughter who had died at home of pneumonia during the festivities. The rest of the family barely had time to change out of their costumes. Severino, the child's uncle and god-father, sprinkled holy water over the little angel while he prayed: "Mercea, I don't know whether you were called, taken, or thrown out of this world. But look down at us from your heavenly home with tenderness, with pity, and with mercy." So be it.

# The Cultural Nexus of Aka Father–Infant Bonding

## Barry S. Hewlett

Despite a steady increase in the quantity and quality of studies of infants, young children and motherhood in various parts of the world (e.g., LeVine et al. 1994), we know relatively little about the nature of father–child relations outside of the U.S. and Western Europe (see Hewlett 1992 for some exceptions). In general, mother-oriented theories of infant and child development have guided cross-cultural research. The majority of these theories view the mother–infant relationship as the prototype for subsequent attachments and relationships (Ainsworth 1967; Bowlby 1969; Freud 1938; Harlow 1961). According to Freud and Bowlby, for instance, one had to have a trusting, unconditional relationship with his or her mother in order to become a socially and emotionally adjusted adult. These influential theorists generally believed that the father's role was not a factor in the child's development until the Oedipal stage (3–5 years old). The field methods to study infancy reflected this theoretical emphasis on mother. Observations were either infant or mother-focused and conducted only during daylight hours; father-focused and evening observations were not considered. Also, standardized questionnaires and psychological tests were generally administered only to the mother. One consistent result from the cross-cultural studies was that fathers provided substantially less direct care to infants than mothers. In fact, all cross-cultural studies to date indicate that a number of other female caretakers (older female siblings, aunts, grandmothers) provide more direct care to infants than do fathers. Since fathers are not as conspicuous as mothers and other females during daylight hours researchers tend to emphasize a "deficit" model of fathers (Cole and Bruner 1974); that is, fathers are not around much and therefore do not contribute much to the child's development.

Given the paucity of systematic research outside of the U.S. on father's interactions with children, it is ironic that this variable (i.e., the degree of father vs. mother involvement with children) should be so consistently invoked as an explanatory factor in the literature. It is hypothesized to be related, for example, to gender inequality (Chodorow 1974), universal sexual asymmetry (Rosaldo and Lamphere 1974), and the origin of the human family (Lancaster and Lancaster 1987).

### FATHER–INFANT BONDING

Bowlby's (1969) theory, mentioned above, suggested that an early secure attachment (or "bonding") between infant and caregiver (usually mother) was crucial for normal development. Lack of bonding between mother and infant led to the infant's protest, despair, detachment, and eventual difficulty in emotional and social development. Most studies of attachment have focused on mother–infant bonding, but an increasing number of studies in the U.S. and Europe have tried to understand if and when infants become attached to fathers. Numerous psychological studies now indicate

Adapted for this text from Barry S. Hewlett, *Intimate Fathers: The Nature and Context of Aka Pygmy Paternal-Infant Care* (Ann Arbor: University of Michigan Press, 1991). Copyright © 1991 by the University of Michigan Press.

that infants are attached to their fathers and that the infants become attached to fathers at about the same age as they do to mothers (8–10 months of age) (Lamb 1981). But how does this bonding take place if infant bonding to mother is known to develop through regular, sensitive, and responsive care? American fathers are seldom around to provide this type of care. The critical factor that has emerged in over 50 studies of primarily middle-class American fathers is vigorous play. The physical style of American fathers is distinct from that of American mothers, is evident three days after birth, and continues throughout infancy. The American data have been so consistent that some researchers have indicated a biological basis (Clarke-Stewart 1980). The idea is that mother–infant bonding develops as a consequence of the frequency and intensity of the relationship, while father–infant bonding takes place because of this highly stimulating interaction. British, German, and Israeli studies generally support this hypothesis. This chapter examines the process of father–infant bonding among the Aka, a hunter–gatherer group living in the tropical forest of central Africa.

## THE AKA

There are about 30,000 Aka hunter–gatherers in the tropical rain forests of southern Central African Republic and northern Congo-Brazzaville. They live in camps of 25–35 people and move camp every two weeks to two months. Each nuclear family has a hut, and each camp generally has 5–8 huts arranged in a circle. The circle of huts is about 12 meters in diameter and each hut is about 1.5 meters in diameter. Each hut has one bed of leaves or logs on which everyone in the family sleeps. The Aka have patriclans and many members of a camp belong to the same patriclan (generally a camp consists of brothers, their wives and children, and unrelated men who are doing bride service for the sisters of the men in camp). The Aka have high fertility and mortality rates: A woman generally has five to six children during her lifetime, and one-fifth of the infants die before reaching 12 months and 43 percent of children die before reaching 15 years.

Life in the camp is rather intimate. While the overall population density is quite low (less than one person per square kilometer), living space is quite dense. Three or four people sleep together on the same 4-feet-long by 2-feet-wide bed, and neighbors are just a few feet away. The 25–35 camp members live in an area about the size of a large American living room. The Aka home represents the "public" part of life, while time outside of camp tends to be relatively "private." This is the reverse of the American pattern (i.e., home is usually considered private). The camp is relatively

young as half of the members of the camp are under 15 and most women have a nursing child throughout their childbearing years.

The Aka use a variety of hunting techniques, but net hunting, which involves men, women, and children, is the most important and regular hunting technique. Women generally have the role of tackling the game in the net and killing the animal. Game captured is eventually shared with everyone in camp. Some parts of the game animal are smoked and eventually traded to Bantu and Sudanic farmers for manioc or other domesticated foods. The Aka have strong economic and religious ties to the tropical forest. The forest is perceived as provider and called friend, lover, mother, or father.

Sharing and cooperation are pervasive and general tenets of Aka camp life. Food items, infant care, ideas for song and dance, and material items such as pots and pans are just some of the items that are shared daily in the camp. An Ngandu farmer describes Aka sharing:

> Pygmies [the Ngandu use the derogatory term Babinga to refer to the Aka] are people who stick together. Twenty of them are able to share one single cigarette. When a pygmy comes back with only five roots she shares them all. It is the same with forest nuts; they will give them out to everybody even if there are none left for them. They are very generous.

The Aka are also fiercely egalitarian. They have a number of mechanisms to maintain individual, intergenerational, and gender equality. The Ngandu villager mentioned above describes his concerns about Aka intergenerational egalitarianism:

> Young pygmies have no respect for their parents; they regard their fathers as their friends. . . . There is no way to tell whether they are talking to their parents because they always use their first names. Once I was in a pygmy camp and several people were sitting around and a son said to his father "Etobe your balls are hanging out of your loincloth" and everyone started laughing. No respect, none, none, none. . . . It's real chaos because there is no respect between father and son, mother and son or daughter. That's why pygmies have such a bad reputation, a reputation of being backward.

Three mechanisms that promote sharing and egalitarianism are prestige avoidance, rough joking and demand sharing. The Aka try to avoid drawing attention to themselves, even if they have killed an elephant or cured someone's life-threatening illness. Individuals who boast about their abilities are likely to share less or request more from others in the belief that they are better than others. If individuals start to draw attention to themselves, others in the camp will use rough and crude jokes, often about the boastful person's genitals, in order to get the individuals to be more modest about their abilities. Demand sharing also helps to maintain egalitarianism: if individuals like or want something (cigarettes, necklace, shirt) they simply ask for it, and the person generally gives it to them. Demand sharing promotes the circulation of scarce material goods (e.g., shoes, shirt, necklaces, spear points) in the camp.

Gender egalitarianism is also important. For instance, there are male and female roles on the net hunt, but role reversals take place daily and individuals are not stigmatized for taking the roles of the opposite sex. If one does the task poorly, regardless of whether it is a masculine or feminine task, then one is open to joking and teasing by others (e.g., when the anthropologist chases the game in the wrong direction).

The rough joking mentioned above is also linked to another feature of Aka culture—playfulness. There is no clear separation between "work" and "play" time. Dances, singing, net hunting, male circumcision, sorcery accusations all include humorous mimicking, practical jokes, and exaggerated storytelling. Aka life is informal because of egalitarianism and the playful activity that occurs throughout the day by both adults and children. Play is an integral part of both adult and child life and contributes to enhanced parent–child and adult–child communication. Parents and adults have an extensive repertoire of play, and can and do communicate cultural knowledge to children through their playful repertoire.

Greater ethnographic detail on the Aka can be found in Hewlett (1991) or Bahuchet (1985).

## AKA INFANCY

The infant lives with a relatively small group of individuals related through his or her father (unless the infant is the first born in which case the family is likely to be in the camp of the wife for the purposes of bride service) and sleeps in the same bed as mother, father, and other brothers and sisters.

Cultural practices during infancy are quite distinct from those found in European and American cultures. Aka parents are indulgent as infants are held almost constantly, nursed on demand (breast-fed several times per hour), attended to immediately if they fuss, and are seldom, if ever, told "no! no!" if they misbehave (e.g., get into food pots, hit others, or take things from other children). An Aka father describes Aka parenting and contrasts it with parenting among his Ngandu farming neighbors:

We, Aka look after our children with love, from the minute they are born to when they are much older. The

villagers love their children only when they are babies. When they become children they get beaten up badly. With us, even if the child is older, if he is unhappy, I'll look after him, I will cuddle him.

Older infants are allowed to use and play with knives, machetes, and other "adult" items. They are allowed to crawl into a parent's lap while the parent is engaged in economic (e.g., butchering animal, repairing net) or leisure (e.g., playing a harp or drum) activity. While older infants are given considerable freedom to explore the house and camp, parents do watch infants to make sure they do not crawl into the fire.

Extensive multiple caregiving of 1- to 4-month-old infants (Hewlett 1989) exists, especially while the Aka are in the camp. Individuals other than mother (infant's father, brothers, sisters, aunts, uncles, grandmothers) hold the infant the majority of the time (60 percent) in this context, and the infant is moved to different people about seven times per hour. Mothers' holding increases to 85 percent and the transfer rate drops to two transfers per hour outside of the camp (i.e., on net hunt or in fields).

Infancy is very active and stimulating. Infants are taken on the hunt and are seldom laid down. They are held on the side of the caregiver rather than on the caregiver's back as in many farming communities so there are opportunities for caregiver–infant face-to-face interaction and communication. The infant can also breast feed by simply reaching for the mother's breast and can nurse while mother walks. While out on the net hunt the infant sleeps in the sling as the caregiver walks, runs, or sits.

## THE STUDY

I started working with the Aka in 1973 so by the time I started the father–infant study in 1984 I was familiar with specific Aka families and Aka culture in general. Since I wanted to test some of the psychological hypotheses regarding father–infant relations, I incorporated psychological methods into my research. The quantitative psychological methods consisted of systematically observing 15 Aka families with infants from 6 *a.m.* to 9 *p.m.* (the observations focused either on the father or the infant). This enabled me to say precisely how much time Aka versus American fathers held or were near their infants and precisely describe how American versus Aka styles of interaction were similar or different. Informal discussions while on the net hunt and in camp were also utilized to develop structured interviews. Men and women, young and old, were asked about their feelings regarding relations with their mothers, fathers, and other caregivers.

The study focused on two domains important for trying to understand father–infant bonding: the degree of father involvement and mother's versus father's parenting style. For degree of father involvement I wanted to know: How often do fathers actually interact with their infants, how often are fathers available to their infants, if fathers are not involved with infants what other activities are they involved in, how do children characterize the nature of their involvement with their father? Questions regarding paternal versus maternal parenting style included: Are there distinctions between the mother's and the father's play behavior with their infants, do mothers and fathers hold their infants for different purposes, what do mothers and fathers do while they hold the infant, do infants show different types of attachment behavior to mothers and fathers, how do children view their mother's and father's parenting styles?

## WHY ARE AKA FATHERS SO INVOLVED WITH THEIR INFANTS? THE CULTURAL NEXUS OF FATHER–INFANT BONDING

Although few cross-cultural studies of father–child relations have been conducted, Aka father involvement in infancy is exceptional, if not unique. Aka fathers are within an arm's reach (i.e., holding or within one meter) of their infant more than 50 percent of 24-hour periods. Table 1.1 demonstrates that Aka fathers hold their very young infants during the day at least five times more than fathers in other cultures, while Table 1.2 indicates Aka fathers are available to their infants at least three times more frequently than fathers in other cultures. American and European fathers hold their infants, on average, between 10 and 20 minutes per day (Lamb et al. 1987) while Aka

**Table 1.1  Comparison of Father Holding in Selected Foraging Populations**

| POPULATION | AGE OF INFANTS (MOS.) | FATHER HOLDING (PERCENT OF TIME) | SOURCE |
|---|---|---|---|
| Gidgingali | 0–6 | 3.4 | Hamilton (1981) |
| | 6–18 | 3.1 | |
| !Kung | 0–6 | 1.9 | West and Konner (1976) |
| | 6–24 | 4.0 | |
| Efe Pygmies | 1–4 | 2.6 | Winn et al. (1990) |
| Aka Pygmies | 1–4 | 22.0 | Hewlett (1991) |
| | 8–18 | 14.0 | |

NOTE: All observations were made in a camp setting (Table from Hewlett 1991).

**Table 1.2  Comparison of Father Presence with Infants or Children among Selected Foraging and Farming Populations**

| POPULATION | LOCATION | SUBSISTENCE | PERCENT TIME FATHER PRESENT/IN VIEW | PRIMARY SETTING OF OBSERVATIONS | SOURCE |
|---|---|---|---|---|---|
| *Gusii* | Kenya | farming | 10 | house/yard & garden | 1 |
| Mixteca | Mexico | farming | 9 | house/yard | 1 |
| Ilocano | Philippines | farming | 14 | house/yard | 1 |
| Okinawan | Japan | farming | 3 | public places & house/yard | 1 |
| Rajput | India | farming | 3 | house/yard | 1 |
| !Kung | Botswana | foraging | 30 | camp | 2 |
| Aka Pygmies | Central African Republic | foraging | 88 | forest camp | 3 |
| Logoli | Kenya | farming | 5 | house/yard | 4 |
| Newars | Nepal | farming | 7 | house/yard | 4 |
| Samoans | Samoa | farming | 8 | house/yard | 4 |
| Carib | Belize | farming | 3 | house/yard | 4 |
| Ifaluk | Micronesia | farm-fish | 13 | house/yard | 5 |

Sources (Table from Hewlett 1991):
1. Whiting and Whiting 1975
2. West and Konner 1976
3. Hewlett 1991
4. Munroe and Munroe 1992
5. Betzig, Harrigan, and Turke 1990

fathers, on average, hold their infants about one hour during daylight hours and about 25 percent of the time after the sun goes down. At night fathers sleep with mother and infant, whereas American fathers seldom sleep with their infants. While Aka father care is extensive, it is also highly context dependent—fathers provide at least four times as much care while they are in the camp setting than they do while out of camp (e.g., out on the net hunt or in the villagers' fields). What factors influence this high level of paternal emotional and physical involvement among the Aka?

Aka father–infant bonding is embedded within a cultural nexus—it influences and is influenced by a complex cultural system. This brief overview describes some of the cultural facets linked to Aka father–infant bonding.

Like many other foragers, the Aka have few accumulable resources that are essential for survival. "Kinship resources," the number of brothers and sisters in particular, are probably the most essential "resource" for survival, but are generally established at an early age. Food resources are not stored or accumulated, and Aka males and females contribute similar percentages of calories to the diet. Cross-cultural studies have demonstrated that in societies where resources essential to survival can be accumulated or where males are the primary contributors to subsistence, fathers invest more time competing for these resources and, consequently, spend less time with their children. In contrast, where resources are not accumulable or men are not the primary contributors to subsistence, men generally spend more time in the direct care of their children. Katz and Konner (1981: 174) found that father–infant proximity (degree of emotional warmth and physical proximity) is closest in gathering-hunting populations (gathered foods by females are principal resources, meat is secondary) and most distant in cultures where herding or advanced agriculture is practiced. In the latter cultures, cattle, camels, and land are considered the essential accumulable resources necessary for survival. These findings are consistent with Whiting and Whiting's (1975) cross-cultural study of husband–wife intimacy. They found husband–wife intimacy to be greatest in cultures without accumulated resources or capital investments. While there are other factors to consider (the protection of resources and the polygyny rate), there is a strong tendency for fathers/husbands to devote more time to their children/wives if there are no accumulable resources.

Three additional factors seem to be especially influential in understanding the extraordinarily high level of Aka paternal care. First, the nature of Aka subsistence activity is rather unique cross-culturally. Usually mens' and womens' subsistence activities take place at very different locations. The net hunt and other subsistence activities, such as caterpillar collecting, involve men, women, and children. If men are going to help with infant care on a regular basis they have to be near the infant a good part of the day. The net hunt makes this possible. The net hunt also requires that men and women walk equal distances during the day. In most foraging societies, females do not travel as far from camp as males. Older siblings are not useful for helping their mothers because of the extensive labor involved in walking long distances with an infant. If a mother is to receive help on the net hunt, it needs to come from an adult. Most of the other adult females carry baskets full of food and have their own infants or young children to carry since fertility is high. Fathers are among the few alternative caregivers regularly available on the net hunt to help mothers. While fathers do carry infants on the net hunt, especially on the return from the hunt when the mothers' baskets are full of meat, collected nuts, and fruit, father–infant caregiving is much more likely to occur in the camp.

Another influential factor is the nature of husband–wife relations. The net hunt contributes substantially to the time husband and wife spend together and patterns the nature of that time spent together. Observations in the forest and village indicate husbands and wives are within sight of each other 46.5 percent of daylight hours. This is more time together than in any other known society, and it is primarily a result of the net hunt. This percentage of course increases in the evening hours. But, husbands and wives are not only together most of the day, they are actively cooperating on the net hunt. They have to know each other well to communicate and cooperate throughout the day. They work together to set up the family net, chase game into the net, butcher and divide the game and take care of the children. Husbands and wives help each other out in a number of domains, in part because they spend so much time together. Husband–wife relations are many-stranded; that is, social, economic, ritual, parenting, and leisure activities are shared and experienced in close proximity. When they return to camp the mother has a number of tasks—she collects firewood and water, and prepares the biggest meal of the day. The father has relatively few tasks to do after returning from the hunt. He may make string or repair the net, but he is available to help with infant care. He is willing to do infant care, in part, because of the many-stranded reciprocity between husband and wife. In many societies men have fewer tasks to do at the end of the day, while women have domestic tasks and prepare a meal. Men are available to help out with childcare, but seldom provide much assistance, in part, due to the more distant husband–wife relationship.

The third important factor in understanding Aka fathers' involvement with infants is father–infant bonding. Father and infant are clearly attached to each other. Fathers seek out their infants and infants seek out their fathers. Fathers end up holding their infants frequently because the infants crawl to, reach for, or fuss for their fathers. Fathers pick up their infants because they intrinsically enjoy being close to their infants. They enjoy being with them and carry them in several different contexts (e.g., out in the fields drinking palm wine with other men).

While the factors described above are especially influential, other cultural factors also play a part. Gender egalitarianism pervades cultural beliefs and practices: Men do not have physical or institutional control over women, violence against women is rare or nonexistent, both women and men are valued for their different but complementary roles, there is flexibility in these gender roles, and holding infants is not perceived as being feminine or "women's work." Sharing, helping out, and generosity are central concepts in Aka life; this applies to subsistence and parenting spheres. Aka ideology of good and bad fathers reiterates the importance of father's proximity—a good father shows love for his children, stays near them, and assists mother with caregiving when her workload is heavy. A bad father abandons his children and does not share food with them. There is no organized warfare and male feuding is infrequent, so men are around camp and help with subsistence rather than being away at battle. Fertility is high, so most adult women have nursing infants and there are few other adult women around to help out. Finally, the Aka move their camps several times a year and consequently do not accumulate material goods that need to be defended.

The point here is that Aka father-infant relations have to be viewed in a complex cultural nexus. Some cultural factors are somewhat more influential than others—net hunting, husband–wife relations, for instance—but even these cultural features take place in a web of other cultural beliefs and practices that contribute to the intimate nature of Aka father–infant relations.

## FATHER–INFANT BONDING IN THE AKA AND UNITED STATES

Over 50 studies of European and American fathers indicate that father's interactions with infants and young children are clearly distinguished from mother's interactions in that fathers are the vigorous rough and tumble playmates of infants and young children, while mothers are sensitive caregivers. The American literature suggests that this rough and tumble play is how infants become attached to fathers ("bond") and develop social competence (Lamb et al. 1987).

The Aka father–infant study is not consistent with the American studies that emphasize the importance of father's vigorous play. Aka fathers rarely, if ever, engage in vigorous play with their infants; only one episode of vigorous play by a father was recorded during all 264 hours of systematic observation. Informal observations during more than 10 field visits over the last 20 years are also consistent with this finding. The quantitative data indicate that by comparison to mothers, Aka fathers are significantly more likely to hug, kiss, or soothe a fussy baby while they are holding the infant.

While Aka fathers do not engage in vigorous play with their infants, they are slightly more playful than mothers; fathers are somewhat more likely to engage in minor physical play (e.g., tickling) with their one- to four-month-old infants than are mothers. But characterizing the Aka father as the infant's playmate would be misleading. Other caretakers, brothers and sisters in particular, engage in play with the infant while holding much more frequently than fathers or mothers. Mothers have more episodes of play over the course of a day than fathers or other caretakers because they hold the infant most of the time. The Aka father–infant relationship might be better characterized by its intimate and affective nature. Aka fathers hold their infants more than fathers in any other human society known to anthropologists, and Aka fathers also show affection more frequently while holding than do Aka mothers.

So how can vigorous play be a significant feature in American studies of father–infant bonding, but not among the Aka? Four factors appear to be important for understanding the process of Aka father–infant bonding: familiarity with the infant; knowledge of caregiving practices (how to hold an infant, how to soothe an infant); the degree of relatedness to the infant; and cultural values and parental goals.

First, due to frequent father-holding and availability, Aka fathers know how to communicate with their infants. Fathers know the early signs of infant hunger, fatigue, and illness as well as the limits in their ability to soothe the infant. They also know how to stimulate responses from the infant without being vigorous. Unlike American fathers, Aka wait for infants to initiate interaction. Aka caregivers other than mothers and fathers are less familiar with the infants and the most physical in their play, suggesting a relationship between intimate knowledge of the infant's cues and the frequency of vigorous play while holding. Consistent with this is the finding that working mothers in the U.S. are more likely to engage in vigorous play than are stay-at-home mothers.

Second, knowledge of infant caregiving practices seems to play a role in determining how much play is exhibited in caretaker–infant interactions. Child caretakers were the most physical and the loudest (singing) in their handling of infants. Children were not restricted from holding infants, but they were closely watched by parents. While "other" caretakers were more playful than mothers or fathers, younger fathers and "other" caretakers were more physical than older ones, probably because they did not know how to handle and care for infants as well as adult caretakers.

A third factor to consider is the degree of relatedness of the caretaker to the infant. If vigorous play can assist in developing attachment, more closely related individuals may have a greater vested interest in establishing this bond than distantly related individuals. Attachment not only enhances the survival of the infant, but it can potentially increase the related caretaker's survival and fitness. Aka mothers and fathers establish attachment by their frequent caregiving; vigorous play is not necessary to establish affective saliency. Brothers and sisters, on the other hand, might establish this bond through physical play. Aka brothers and sisters, in fact, provided essentially all of the physical play the focal infants received; cousins and unrelated children were more likely to engage in face-to-face play with the infant instead of physical play.

Finally, cultural values and parental goals of infant development should be considered. American culture encourages individualistic aggressive competition; Aka culture values cooperation, nonaggression, and prestige avoidance (one does not draw attention to oneself even, for instance, if one kills an elephant). Apparently, Americans tolerate—if not actually encourage—aggressive rough-and-tumble types of play with infants. Also, due to the high infant mortality rate, the primary parental goal for Aka is the survival of their infants. The constant holding and immediate attention to fussing reflect this goal. In the United States, infant mortality rates are markedly lower and, as a result, parental concern for survival may not be as great. The Aka infant is taken away from a caretaker who plays roughly with the infant, in part because it could be seen as aggressive behavior, but also because the pervasive aim of infant care practices is survival of the infant, and rough-and-tumble play could risk the infant's safety.

These factors tentatively clarify why Aka fathers do not engage in vigorous play like American fathers, but do participate in slightly more physical play than Aka mothers (but not more than other caretakers). American fathers infrequently participate directly in infant care and consequently are not as familiar with infant cues. To stimulate interaction and (possibly) bonding, they engage in physical play. Aka brothers and sisters are also much less physical in their play with infants than American fathers (Aka never tossed infants in the air or swung them by their arms),

again suggesting that Aka children know their infant brother or sister and the necessary infant caregiving skills better than American fathers. These observations are obviously speculative and need further empirical study.

Sociologists LaRossa and LaRossa (1981) also describe stylistic differences between American mothers' and fathers' interactions with their infants. They list a number of male–female role dichotomies that reflect different parenting styles. One distinction they make is role distance versus role embracement. Fathers are more likely to distance themselves from the parenting role while mothers are more likely to embrace the parenting role. American women generally want to remain in primary control of the children, and while fathers may show interest in caregiving, they are more likely to distance themselves from caregiving while embracing their roles as the breadwinners. LaRossa and LaRossa also suggest that fathers generally have low intrinsic value and relatively high extrinsic value, while mothers have the reverse.

> The intrinsic value of something or someone is the amount of sheer pleasure or enjoyment that one gets from experiencing an object or person. The extrinsic value of something or someone is the amount of social rewards (e.g., money, power, prestige) associated with having or being with the object or person. (64)

They use this dichotomy to explain why fathers are more likely to carry or hold an infant in public than in private. Fathers receive extrinsic rewards from those in public settings, while this does not happen in the home. According to LaRossa and LaRossa,

> Fathers will roughhouse with their toddlers on the living-room floor, and will blush when hugged or kissed by the one-year-olds, but when you really get down to it, they just do not have that much fun when they are with their children. If they had their druthers, they would be working at the office or drinking at the local pub. (65)

These role dichotomies may be useful for understanding American mother–father parenting styles, but they have limited value in characterizing Aka mother–father distinctions. Aka mothers and fathers embrace the parenting role. Generally, mothers and fathers want to hold their infants, and certainly they derive pleasure from infant interactions. As indicated earlier, fathers were in fact more likely to show affection while holding than mothers. Fathers also offered their nipples to infants who wanted to nurse, cleaned mucus from their infants' noses, picked lice from their infants' hair, and cleaned their infants after they urinated or defecated (often on the father). Fathers' caregiving did not appear any more or less perfunctory than mothers'. Aka fathers are not burdened with infant care; if a father does not want to hold or care for the infant he gives the infant to another person. Overall, Aka fathers embrace their parenting role as much as they embrace their hunting role.

The intrinsic–extrinsic role dichotomy does not fit well with Aka mother–father parenting styles either. Again, both Aka mothers and fathers place great intrinsic value and little extrinsic value on parenting. The fathers' intrinsic value is demonstrated above, but the lack of extrinsic value among the Aka can best be seen by comparing Aka and Ngandu fathers (the Ngandu are the horticulturalist trading partners of the Aka). When a Ngandu father holds his infant in public he is "on stage." He goes out of his way to show his infant to those who pass by, and frequently tries to stimulate the infant while holding it. He is much more vigorous in his interactions with the infant than are Aka men. The following experience exemplifies Ngandu fathers' extrinsic value towards their infants. An Ngandu friend showed me a 25-pound fish he had just caught, and I asked to take a photograph of him with his fish. He said fine, promptly picked up his nearby infant, and proudly displayed his fish and infant for the photograph. His wife was also nearby but was not invited into the photograph. Aka fathers, on the other hand, are matter-of-fact about their holding or transporting of infants in public places. They do not draw attention to their infants. Aka fathers also hold their infants in all kinds of social and economic contexts.

## CONCLUSION

This paper has examined the cultural nexus of Aka father–infant bonding and has made some comparisons to middle-class American father–infant relations. American fathers are characterized by their vigorous play with infants, while Aka fathers are characterized by their affectionate and intimate relations with their infants. Aka infants bond with their fathers because they provide sensitive and regular care, whereas American infants bond to their fathers, in part, due to their vigorous play. The purpose of this paper is not to criticize American fathers for their style of interaction with their infants; physical play is important in middle-class American context because it is a means for fathers who are seldom around their infants to demonstrate their love and interest in the infant. Vigorous play may also be important to American mothers who work outside the home; studies indicate they are also more likely than stay-at-home mothers to engage in vigorous play with their infants. The Aka study does imply that father–infant bonding does not always take place through physical play, and it is necessary to explore a complex cultural nexus in order to understand the nature of father–infant relations.

Aka fathers are very close and affectionate with their infants, and their attachment processes, as defined in Western bonding theory, appear to be similar to that of mothers. While Aka mother– and father–infant relations are similar they are not the same. Fathers do spend substantially less time with infants than do mothers, and the nature of their interactions is different. Aka and American fathers bring something qualitatively different to their children; father's caregiving pattern is not simply a variation of mother's pattern. More research is needed on the unique features of father involvement so we can move away from a "deficit" model of fathering.

Finally, this paper identifies cultural factors that influence father–infant bonding; biological forces are not considered. This is unusual in that mother–infant bonding generally mentions or discusses the biological basis of mother's attachment to the infant. The release of prolactin and oxytocin with birth and lactation is said to increase affectionate feelings and actions toward the infant. These same hormones exist in men but endocrinologists generally believe they have no function in men. Is there a biology of fatherhood, or is motherhood more biological and fatherhood more cultural? This is a complex question as both men and women probably have evolved ("biological") psychological mechanisms that influence their parenting, but if one just focuses on endocrinology, few data exist on the endocrinology of fatherhood. For instance, Gubernick et al. (unpublished paper) found that men's testosterone levels decreased significantly two weeks after the birth of their children; the decrease was not linked to decline in sexual behavior, increased stress, or sleep deprivation. Another small study of American fathers indicated significant increases in plasma prolactin levels after fathers held their 3-month-old infants on their chest for 15 minutes (Hewlett and Alster, unpublished data). The few biological studies that do exist suggest that biology can and does influence fatherhood. More studies of the biocultural nexus of fatherhood are needed.

While biology probably influences both mothers' and fathers' parenting to some degree, this chapter has demonstrated that the cultural nexus is a powerful force that profoundly shapes the nature and context of father–infant bonding. Aka father–infant bonding takes place through regular and intimate (i.e., hugging, kissing, soothing) care while American father–infant bonding takes place through vigorous play. American fathers often do not know their infants very well and try to demonstrate their love and concern through vigorous play. American mothers that work outside the home also tend to be more vigorous with their infants. American fathers are not necessarily "bad" fathers because they do not do as much direct caregiving as the Aka fathers. Fathers around the world "provide" and enrich the lives of their children in diverse ways (e.g., physical and emotional security, economic well-being). The Aka data do suggest that there are alternative processes by which father–infant bonding can and does take place and that Americans and others might learn from this comparative approach as policy decisions about parental leave and other topics are considered.

## REFERENCES

Ainsworth, M. D. S. 1967. *Infancy in Uganda: Infant Care and the Growth of Love.* Baltimore: Johns Hopkins Press.

Bahuchet, S. 1985. *Les Pygmées Aka et la Fôret Centrafricaine.* Paris: Selaf.

Betzig, L., A. Harrigan, and P. Turke. 1990. "Childcare on Ifaluk." *Zeitscrift fur Ethnologie* 114.

Bowlby, J. 1969. *Attachment and Loss Vol. 1: Attachment.* New York: Basic Books.

Chodorow, N. 1974. "Family Structure and Feminine Personality." In *Woman, Culture, and Society*, ed. Michelle Zimbalist Rosaldo and Louise Lamphere. Stanford, CA: Stanford University Press.

Clarke-Stewart, K. A. 1980. "The Father's Contribution to Children's Cognitive and Social Development in Early Childhood." In *The Father–Infant Relationship*, ed. S.A. Pedersen. New York: Praeger.

Cole, M., and J. S. Bruner. 1974. "Cultural Differences and Inferences about Psychological Processes." In *Culture and Cognition*, ed. J. W. Berry and P. R. Dasen. London: Methuen.

Freud, S. 1938. *An Outline of Psychoanalysis.* London: Hogarth.

Gubernick, D. J., C. M. Worthman, and J. F. Stallings. "Hormonal Correlates of Fatherhood in Men." Unpublished paper.

Hamilton, A. 1981. *Nature and Nurture: Aboriginal Child-Rearing in North-Central Arnhem Land.* Canberra: Australian Institute of Aboriginal Studies.

Harlow, H. F. 1961. "The Development of Affectional Patterns in Infant Monkeys." In *Determinants of Infant Behavior*, Vol. 1, ed. B. M. Foss. London: Methuen.

Hewlett, B. S. 1989. "Multiple Caretaking among African Pygmies." *American Anthropologist* 91: 186–191.

———. 1991. *Intimate Fathers: The Nature and Context of Aka Pygmy Paternal-Infant Care.* Ann Arbor, MI: University of Michigan Press.

———, ed. 1992 *Father-Child Relations: Cultural and Biosocial Perspectives.* New York: Aldine de Gruyter.

Hewlett, B. S., and D. Alster. "Prolactin and Infant Holding among American Fathers." Unpublished manuscript.

Katz, M. M., and Melvin J. Konner. 1981. "The Role of Father: An Anthropological Perspective." In *The Role of Father in Child Development*, ed. Michael E. Lamb. New York: John Wiley and Sons.

Lamb, M. E., ed. 1981. *The Role of the Father in Child Development*, 2nd ed. New York: John Wiley& Sons.

Lamb, M. E., J. H. Pleck, E. L. Charnov, and J. A. LeVine. 1987. "A Biosocial Perspective on Paternal Behavior and Involvement." In *Parenting Across the Lifespan*, ed. J. B. Lancaster, J. Altmann, A. Rossi, and L. R. Sherrod. Hawthorne, NY: Aldine.

Lancaster, J. B., and C. S. Lancaster. 1987. "The Watershed: Change in Parental-Investment and Family Formation Strategies in the Course of Human Evolution." In *Parenting Across the Life Span*, ed. J. B. Lancaster, J. Altmann, A. S. Rossi, and L. R. Sherrod. Hawthorne, NY: Aldine.

LaRossa, R., and M. M. LaRossa. 1981. *Transition to Parenthood: How Infants Change Families.* Beverly Hills: Sage Publications.

LeVine, R. A., S. Dixon, S. LeVine, A. Richman, P. H. Leiderman, C. H. Keefer, and T. B. Brazelton. 1994. *Child Care and Culture: Lessons from Africa.* New York: Cambridge University Press.

Munroe, Ruth H., and Robert L. Munroe. 1992. "Fathers in Children's Environments: A Four Culture Study." In *Father-Child Relations: Cultural and Biosocial Contexts*, ed. Barry S. Hewlett. New York: Aldine de Gruyter.

Rosaldo, M. Z., and L. Lamphere, eds. 1974. *Woman, Culture and Society.* Stanford, CA: Stanford University Press.

West, M. M., and M. J. Konner. 1976. "The Role of Father in Anthropological Perspective." In *The Role of the Father in Child Development*, 2nd ed., ed. M. E. Lamb. New York: John Wiley & Sons.

Whiting, B. B., and J. W. M. Whiting. 1975. *Children of Six Cultures.* Cambridge, MA: Harvard University Press.

Winn, S., G. A. Morelli, and E. Z. Tronick. 1990. "The Infant in the Group: A Look at Efe Caretaking Practices." In *The Cultural Context of Infancy*, ed. J. K. Nugent, B. M. Lester, and T. B. Brazelton. Norwood, NJ: Ablex.

# II

# *Gender and Prehistory*

A popular introductory archaeology text began its career thirty-seven years ago with the title *Men of the Earth* (Fagan 1974). For the last thirteen editions (published between 1977 and 2009; see Fagan 2009), it has been called *People of the Earth*. This change is deliberate and illustrates a growing sensitivity on the part of archaeologists to the importance of considering the contribution of women, as well as men, to the history of our species (Adavasio, Soffer, and Page 2007; Ardren 2002; Claassen and Joyce 1997; Geller 2009; Gero and Conkey 1991; Hays-Gilpin and Whitley 1998; Joyce 2000, 2009; Seifert 1991; Wright 1996; Wylie 1991, 1992). An archaeological focus on gender provides a lens for reassessing modern myths about the past that single out men as the prime movers of cultural change. As some archaeologists seek to reinstate women as agents and as subjects, widely held assumptions about "mankind" and "man's past" are challenged by a focus on women's involvement in production, politics, ritual performance, and the generation of symbol systems in past societies. In contrast to earlier archaeological orientations (see Hays-Gilpin and Whitley 1998; Geller 2009; Joyce 2009 for a review of archaeological approaches), an "engendered" archaeology proposes that the process of adaptation throughout human history has of necessity involved a collaborative effort between men and women.

Beginning in the 1970s, a new generation of anthropologists questioned the universality of many assumptions about gender. They have explored such issues as women's participation in the creation of wealth (e.g., women's production of textiles or ceramics and power relations among craft producers), women's roles in the dynamics of state formation, representations of powerful women in prehistoric art in relation to gender inequality and identity, and women's roles in the development of agriculture.

Today, Joyce observes (in this book), archaeologists engaged in work on gender ask questions not only about the sexual division of labor, but about how people in the past understood the variation in sexual anatomy, diverse sexual desires and practices, and lived the experience of gender. Rather than assuming gender uniformity, archaeologists, like cultural anthropologists working in contemporary societies, have documented how class, race, and age may divide women from each other or link certain men and women in opposition to others.

Joyce notes that recent archaeological research on biology and gender has challenged us to rethink assumptions about how we recognize sexual anatomical variation and how we explain it. Even the traits of the skeleton considered most diagnostic of sex can be ambiguous. In response to this reality, some archaeologists call for increased use of DNA testing to determine the genetic sex of skeletons. But intriguingly, bone chemistry studies may show little difference between the sexes. Instead, we may find more pronounced differences between men and women of a privileged group and those less advantaged.

The engendering of archaeology, Joyce argues, began with a search for women in the past (Ehrenberg 1989). That search has now definitively resulted in rich understandings of the roles of particular women, and of women as a group, that sometimes confirm but as often contradict the assumptions archaeologists once made. Innovative archaeological explorations of gender increasingly investigate how embodied personhood, including differences in sexual anatomy and sexual practices, affected people's lives. In this way, we can hope to better understand the lives of women, men, and people of other genders across time and space.

As Margaret W. Conkey (2009) contends, in the study of gender in archaeology, we are reminded of the importance of confronting presuppositions and values that guide our work, however "scientific" we presume our methodologies to be. Eliminating gender bias from archaeology will require a major commitment to the same critical reflection that has characterized other branches of anthropology. Nelson and Kehoe (1990: 4) observe, "disentangling our culture-bound assumptions from the actual archaeological record will be a long and wrenching procedure."

Nelson's discussion of Upper Paleolithic "Venus" figurines in archaeology textbooks (1990) illustrates the potential for distortion in the archaeological record when cultural values affect archaeological analysis. She demonstrates that most textbooks convey the same ideological message in their treatment of Venus figurines—adult male humans are and have always been fascinated by women's bodies and view them as signs of fertility. The widely held assumption that Upper Paleolithic figurines possibly depicting human females are fertility fetishes is, according to Nelson, poorly founded. Feminist analysis of the figurines suggests alternative explanations regarding their production, functions, and symbolism, and serves as a warning that "reinforcing present cultural stereotypes by projecting them into the past allows whole generations of students to believe that our present gender constructs are eternal and unchanging" (Nelson 1990: 19; see also Rice 1991; Wright 1996: 9).

Similarly, J. M. Adovasio, Olga Soffer, and Jake Page (in this book) present a scenario representing the division of labor in a European village 26,000 years ago. Based on recent scholarship, they observe that it is now evident that female humans "have been the chief engine in the unprecedentedly high level of human sociability, were the inventors of the most useful of tools (called the String Revolution), have shared equally in the provision of food for human societies, almost certainly drove the human invention of language, and were the ones who created agriculture" (2007: 3). Like Nelson, they assess the meanings attributed to a famous figurine, which came to be known as the "Vestonice Venus." In contrast to the conventional views Nelson describes, Adavasio, Soffer, and Page note that it is most likely that this figurine was carved by a woman, probably the "priestess" who used it. They then turn to the important but overlooked "Fiber" or "String Revolution," referring to the gendered development of fiber arts (weaving, basketry, cordage). The String Revolution, they contend, is a technological breakthrough with profound effects on human destiny. Although ethnographic accounts of fiber arts among contemporary bands indicates that making things such as baskets, clothing, sandals, or other fiber items is not the exclusive prerogative of either sex, in such societies both men and women know the production techniques. Further, weaving is practiced primarily by women in the tribal world today. Thus they present their "default" position: most ceramics, weaving, basketry was done by women in the time frame of the Vestonice Venus, 26,000 years ago. Hence they conclude that the concept of gender, and some division of labor, was already in place at that time.

The provocative argument concerning the String Revolution reflects the dramatic changes in archaeology since the mid-1970s, as archaeologists have uncovered increasing evidence of women's work and women's roles in everyday social life. In an innovative exploration of gender, social organization, and settlement patterns, Galloway (1997) argues that ethnocentric bias has shaped archaeological interpretations of structures found in late prehistoric Southeastern Indian societies. She suggests that archaeologists have neglected the importance of menstrual houses in these societies and proposes that the search for evidence of menstrual practices is a direct route to finding women in the archaeological record. Menstrual seclusion may be an important correlate of social organization, indicating the probability of matrilineal kinship. Accordingly, investigation of menstrual structures may provide a means of testing for matriliny archaeologically. In spite of the likelihood that there are thousands of menstrual structures in the Southeast, so far none has been reliably reported from an archaeological context. Galloway argues that discomfort with the topic has produced its erasure from scientific discourse, and she urges archaeologists both to reinterpret existing data and search for new evidence to identify these "women's houses" and the artifactual evidence of ritual elements and requirements of daily life associated with them.

In an effort to better explain contemporary gender relations, archaeological evidence has offered a means of understanding the present by reconstructing our evolutionary past. Scholarly and public imaginations have been drawn to the possibility that archaeological data might document the existence of a matriarchal society in which women occupied a privileged position as rulers. If powerful women could be found in history or prehistory, this would serve as evidence that male dominance is not inevitable.

Myths of past matriarchy exist in both western and nonwestern societies. Nineteenth-century evolutionists such as J. J. Bachofen (1967) described a history of humankind that passed from a state of primitive communal marriages, through mother right, or a rule of women, to patriarchy. Similar myths of matriarchy have been recorded in several South American societies (Bamberger 1974: 266). According to Bamberger, these myths share a common theme, that of women's loss of power through moral failure. The myths describe a past society in which women held power; however, through their incompetence, the rule of women was eventually replaced by patriarchal leadership.

Rather than representing historical events, the myths of matriarchy serve as a tool to keep "woman" bound to her place. They reinforce current social relations by justifying male dominance (Bamberger 1974: 280). There is no historical or archaeological evidence of matriarchal societies in which women systematically and exclusively dominated men. In spite of the absence of such evidence the idea remains popular, precisely because it conveys the possibility of a future society characterized by female dominance that is reminiscent of the matriarchal past.

We can avoid projecting our common assumptions and wishful fantasies about gender roles in the past by paying more careful attention to a range of sources at our disposal in the archaeological record. The reconstruction of gender roles and relations in ancient societies may be facilitated by representations of women and men in burials, images, and written texts. The oldest writing tradition in the world is found in the cities of the Sumerian civilization in southern Iraq. Four-thousand-year-old literary texts pertaining to early Sumer portray women in supportive, nurturing roles, acting to further the interests of male political rulers or heroes (Pollock 1991). In some texts, women are also described as political officeholders, or queens. Pollock concludes that some women seem to have had significant political and economic power, although few of them were written about compared with the number of men in such positions whose lives were more fully recorded. Sumerian women also held offices in the temple hierarchy as priestesses; it is possible that these were the primary positions of power available to women. An informative example is that of the priestess Enheduanna, installed at Ur by her father King Sargon. Literary texts suggest that she acted to further her father's political ambitions as well as her own authority (Pollock 1991). These texts, as well as burials and images, suggest that Sumerian women were not pawns to be manipulated by men, but were able to attain positions of high status and power.

Similarly, recent access to Maya history by decipherment of glyphic texts on public monuments has shown that some royal women played politically central roles in their kingdoms. Hypogamy, or the marriage of higher-status women to lower-status men, insured the alliance of these lower-status men to higher-status men of their wives' families. Hypergamy, or the marriage of lower-status women to higher-status men, also occurred. More importantly, the women involved in marriage alliance and royal politics were anything but passive pawns in the games of men. Stanley Guenter and David Freidel (2009) examined the lives and exploits of powerful Maya women, demonstrating that Maya royal women were important political players. Guenter and Freidel present the saga of one of these women, a queen at Yaxchilan, who rose to full partnership with her king in matters of war and statecraft and saw to it that her son succeeded to the throne despite the rivalry to a younger queen's child. The queen's success resulted not only from a forceful personality, but from religious and political currents in Maya culture that thrust women into the forefront of regional struggles for imperial power.

Whether as queens, daughters of kings, mothers of kings, or political envoys, Maya royal women wielded considerable power. The various forms of power exercised by these women suggest that although there were no matriarchies in the past, women could control important resources and influence the course of public events. Breakthroughs in the translation of Maya texts correlated with archaeological findings are now yielding important information relevant to gender relations and meanings among ancient royal Maya. Little is known about the lives of commoner women, whose exploits are less visible in texts and other representations. This gap highlights the need for innovative conceptual and methodological approaches to the archaeological record that will help reconstruct gender in past societies.

One such initiative is that by Covey (in this book), who explores the construction of gender in Inca society in the early years of the Spanish conquest. He draws on chronicles of the colonial period to assess pre- and postconquest gender constructions. In contrast with more patriarchal arrangements in early modern Europe, he argues for complementary roles of Inca men and women. In addition, the powerful status of noble Andean women challenges entrenched assumptions regarding the role of women in states. Accordingly, he looks not only at the Inca family and the place of gender in the life cycle but beyond, to examine how the Inca state constructed gender in elite life and imperial administration.

Among the Inca, women were more influential in the politics of kinship than in the bureaucracy of the empire. Yet some Inca women were able to assemble a faction of their noble relatives to support a son in succession disputes to the throne. Military prowess was considered a male-gendered trait, although accounts exist of women military commanders. Thus in ordinary households and in elite contexts, both women and men followed diverse routes to power.

Covey describes the interest of the Inca state in managing sexuality, gender, and marriage among its subjects. The state objective was to limit the local power of marriage alliances and to assure a sufficient supply of households to provide labor for state projects. Colonial chronicles convey the significance of restricted housing for Inca young women selected by the state, eventually to marry approved provincial men. These women played important roles in religious rituals, cloth production, and the transformation of maize into beer for ceremonial events. Although the status of Andean women was diminished in the post-conquest period, recent re-analyses of colonial writings suggest that gender complementarity and women's power characterized pre-conquest Inca society.

Conkey and Spector discuss the general problem of the prehistoric "archaeological invisibility" of women (1984: 5), which, they contend, is more the result of a false notion of objectivity and of the gender paradigms archaeologists use than of an inherent invisibility of such data (Conkey and Spector 1984: 6). Questions that would elicit information about prehistoric gender behavior or organization are too infrequently asked, while researchers "bring to their work preconceived notions about what each sex ought to do, and these notions serve to structure the way artifacts are interpreted"—for example, the presumption of linkages between projectile points with men and pots with women (Conkey and Spector 1984: 10). In contrast, goals for feminist archaeologies would include gender-inclusive reconstructions of past human behavior, the development of a specific paradigm for the study of gender, and an explicit effort to eliminate androcentrism in the content and mode of presentation of archaeological research (Conkey and Spector 1984: 15). As Brian Fagan has observed, "an engendered archaeology ventures into new territory, using innovative approaches to present the multiple voices of the past." (2006: 23).

# REFERENCES

Adavasio, J. M., O. Soffer, and J. Page. 2007. *The Invisible Sex. Uncovering the True Roles of Women in Prehistory.* Smithsonian Books. New York: Harper Collins.

Ardren, Traci. 2002. *Ancient Maya Women.* Lanham, MD: Rowman and Littlefield.

Bachofen, Johann. 1967. *Myth, Religion and Mother Right* [Die Mutterrecht 1861 orig.]. London: Routledge and Kegan Paul.

Bamberger, Joan. 1974. "The Myth of Matriarchy: Why Men Rule in Primitive Society." In Michelle Z. Rosaldo and Louise Lamphere (eds.). *Woman, Culture, and Society*, pp. 263–281. Stanford, CA: Stanford University Press.

Claassen, Cheryl, and Rosemary A. Joyce (eds.). 1997. *Women in Prehistory.* Philadelphia: University of Pennsylvania Press.

Conkey, Margaret W. 2009. "The Archaeology of Gender Today: New Vistas, New Challenges." In C. Brettell and C. Sargent (eds.). *Gender in Cross-Cultural Perspective*, pp. 56–65. Upper Saddle River, NJ: Pearson Prentice Hall.

Conkey, Margaret W., and Janet Spector. 1984. "Archaeology and the Study of Gender." In Michael B. Schiffer (ed.). *Advances in Archaeological Method and Theory*, Vol. 7, pp. 1–29. New York: Academic Press.

Ehrenberg, Margaret. 1989. *Women in Prehistory.* Norman, OK: University of Oklahoma Press.

Fagan, Brian. 1974. *Men of the Earth.* Boston: Little, Brown and Co.

_____. 2006. *People of the Earth.* Upper Saddle River, NJ: Prentice Hall

_____. 2009. *People of the Earth.* Upper Saddle River, NJ: Prentice Hall.

Galloway, Patricia. 1997. "Where Have All the Menstrual Huts Gone? The Invisibility of Menstrual Seclusion in the Late Prehistoric Southeast." In C. Claussen and R. Joyce (eds.). *Women in Prehistory: North America and Mesoamerica*, pp. 47–62. Philadelphia: University of Pennsylvania Press.

Geller, Pamela L. 2009. "Identity and Difference: Complicating Gender in Archaeology." *Annual Review of Anthropology* 38: 64–81.

Gero, J. M., and Margaret W. Conkey (eds.). 1991. *Engendering Archaeology: Women in Prehistory.* Oxford, UK: Basil Blackwell.

Guenter, Stanley, and David Freidel. 2009. "Warriors and Rulers: Royal Women of the Classic Maya." In C. Brettell and C. Sargent (eds.). *Gender in Cross-Cultural Perspective*, pp. 76–85. Upper Saddle River, NJ: Pearson Prentice Hall.

Hays-Gilpin, K., and D. Whitley. 1998. *Reader in Gender Archaeology.* London: Routledge.

Joyce, Rosemary. 2000. *Gender and Power in Prehispanic Mesoamerica.* Austin: University of Texas Press.

_____. 2009. *Ancient Bodies, Ancient Lives: Sex, Gender, and Archaeology.* London: Thames and Hudson.

Nelson, Sarah M. 1990. "Diversity of the Upper Paleolithic Venus Figurines and Archeological Mythology." In Sarah M. Nelson and Alice B. Kehoe (eds.). *Powers of Observation: Alternative Views in Archeology*, pp. 11–23. Archeological Papers of the American Anthropological Association, Number 2.

Nelson, Sarah M., and Alice B. Kehoe. 1990. "Introduction." In Sarah M. Nelson and Alice B. Kehoe (eds.). *Powers of Observation: Alternative Views in Archeology*, pp. 1–10. Archeological Papers of the American Anthropological Association, Number 2.

Pollock, Susan. 1991. "Women in a Men's World: Images of Sumerian Women." In Joan Gero and Margaret Conkey (eds.). *Engendering Archaeology: Women and Prehistory*, pp. 366–388. Oxford: Basil Blackwell.

Rice, Patricia. 1991. "Prehistoric Venuses: Symbols of Motherhood or Womanhood?" *Journal of Anthropological Research* 37(4): 402–414.

Seifert, Donna J. (ed.). 1991. "Gender in Historical Archaeology." *Historical Archeology* (special issue) 25(4): 1–132.

Wright, Rita P. (ed.). 1996. *Gender and Archaeology.* Philadelphia: University of Pennsylvania Press.

Wylie, Alison, 1991. "Feminist Critiques and Archaeological Challenges." In D. Walde and N. Willows (eds.). *The Archaeology of Gender*, pp. 17–23. Calgary: The Archaeological Association of Calgary.

_____. 1992. "The Interplay of Evidential Constraints and Political Interests: Recent Archaeological Research on Gender." *American Antiquity* 57(1): 15–35.

# The Past Is a Foreign Country:
## Archaeology of Sex and Gender

### Rosemary A. Joyce

Archaeology may seem to be hampered in understanding gender. Only archaeologists of the very recent past have the ability to ask people about their own ideas and views, and when they do, they still have to sort through how to reconcile what people say about the past and what actually happened (Wilkie and Hayes 2006). While some archaeologists work on time periods and societies that produced contemporary written records, these have to be translated, and often the contexts that would help us relate them to lived experiences of sex and gender are poorly understood. The majority of archaeologists work on societies in the more distant past that did not use writing, and so have to rely entirely on what can be said from the physical evidence alone.

Despite these challenges, there have always been archaeological interpretations of gender, even before feminist archaeologists began to insist that gender was a

category of archaeological analysis (Conkey and Spector 1984). By the 1960s, when anthropological archaeology in North America was transformed by challenges to become more scientific, archaeologists could rely on cross-cultural surveys to support the assumptions they made about gender in the past. These allowed generalization from a sample of ethnographic studies: archaeologists could argue that if a majority of ethnographies showed that women carried out certain activities, like spinning and weaving, then that was sufficient ground to at least propose that spinning and weaving tools in the past were evidence of women's work.

Beginning in the 1970s, a new generation of anthropologists questioned the universality of many assumptions about gender. In the United States, an entire generation of budding archaeologists were exposed to studies questioning gendered assumptions. Many of these students wanted to know more about women's roles and experiences in the past and were unsatisfied with making broad assumptions that rested

Courtesy of Rosemary A. Joyce.

on arguing that the past was like the present, only a little less technologically advanced.

So began a revolution in archaeological investigation of gender that is still unfolding today (Claassen 1992; Conkey and Gero 1991). Today, archaeologists actively engaged in work on gender ask how people in the past understood variation in sexual anatomy; how people in the past understood diverse sexual desires and practices; how people in the past experienced different lives because of differences in their sexual anatomy or sexuality; and what the hard work of trying to answer those questions can tell us about how we understand the same questions about humans living in the world today (Joyce 2008; Nelson 2006).

## BIOLOGY AND GENDER

Archaeologists used to say that gender was the culturally variable ways of organizing people who differed in biological sex. Yet treating sex assignment as simply recognizing natural categories has been questioned by scholars outside and inside archaeology for a long time (Meskell 2005). While differences exist in sexual anatomy, how we recognize sexual anatomical variation, and how we explain it, is variable. If we employ two and only two categories, male and female, then everybody has to be assigned to one or the other. In the United States, gender assignment historically has relied on external anatomical differences: genitalia. These are intuited from other outwardly visible characteristics: the distribution of body hair, apparent muscularity, and height, to name three biological features.

Archaeologists, though, work for the most part with skeletal remains. These obviously no longer have sexual organs or hair. Specialists who work with skeletal remains, bioarchaeologists, categorize sexes from other characteristics: height and robusticity (bone size and thickness), for example. While popular culture is rife with forensic anthropologists easily identifying sex through relatively superficial examination, even the traits of the skeleton considered most diagnostic of sex can be ambiguous (Geller 2005). In practice, bioarchaeologists normally divide the skeletons they study into more than two simple groups. Younger people's bodies before puberty do not have easily identified sex-based variability, so it is uncommon to see children or juveniles classified as male or female. Sexually mature females show changes to the pelvic anatomy that when most pronounced are considered reliable signs that the pelvis came from a woman; but when these features are not as pronounced, the individual may be of less certain sex. So it is common for bioarchaeologists to divide their adult samples into a spectrum of categories: from clearly female to clearly male, with possible female, possible male, and indeterminate groups in between. Even this differentiation has a level of uncertainty due to the fact that as women age, their pelvic anatomy continues to be remodeled, coming to look more like that of males.

In response to the reality that skeletal determination of sex is not as simple and objective as people might assume, some archaeologists call for increased use of DNA testing to determine the genetic sex of skeletons. This is not yet widely used as a method to "sex" skeletons. If it ever does become widespread, it will still not make it possible to assign all skeletons to two categories, male and female. Modern biologists know that a small but not inconsiderable number of human beings do not just have XX or XY chromosomes, but may have a third sex chromosome (XXY, for example). Such individuals may have differences in external or internal sexual anatomy as well. While in the modern United States, surgeons were in the habit of operating to alter the bodies of infants they could not clearly assign as male or female, there is no reason to assume that such interventions were universal. Many populations in the past probably included people who were anatomically neither male nor female, meaning that assigning all skeletons to one of two categories would distort the real population we are trying to understand.

Even when bioarchaeologists arrive at a satisfactory division of adult skeletons into a spectrum from certainly female to certainly male, their analyses often indicate that the experiences of the people whose bodies they are studying were not entirely explained by sexual differences. Bioarchaeologists have used analyses of chemical elements in bone to investigate everything from where the person grew up and if they migrated, to what diet they were accustomed to eat, and whether their protein came from plants, fish, or land animals. Many bone chemistry studies began with a separation of males and females, assuming that, as is true in many recent societies, men and women might have had different diets (Ambrose, Buikstra, and Krueger 2003). Sometimes that assumption holds up, and we find, for example, that men consumed more maize than women did in their own villages (Hastorf 1991). But just as often, these bone chemistry studies show little difference between the sexes. Instead, we may find that men and women of a privileged group, perhaps rulers and nobles, enjoyed a diet that most people in their towns did not (White 2005).

This kind of outcome is explained by using the concept of "intersectionality," meaning that sex isn't always the most important factor in the kind of life people lived. Instead, intersecting forms of identity may be more important: wealth and power may group men and women together in classes; race may divide women from each other; or age may be more important in people's lives than sex, with older men and women facing similar challenges.

In recent years, bioarchaeologists have looked at human populations to ask whether things we take for granted as normal for males and females have always been the same. Osteoporosis, the loss of bone in aging accompanied by a tendency for bones to fracture easily, is understood by most people today as an inevitable consequence of women's aging. Archaeological study of medieval Britain challenges that notion (Agarwal, Dumitriu, Tomlinson, and Grynpas 2004). Here, analyses showed that in some places, tendencies of men and women toward bone loss and bone fracture were similar in old age; while men sometimes had a higher risk than women did in the same population. Examining historical populations from different settings, the bioarchaeologist was able to determine that heavy work in agricultural villages helped women's bone health, and that women's reproductive cycles of childbirth and breast-feeding improved bone remodeling in ways not available to men in the same settings, whether rural or urban.

Contemporary archaeology of sex and gender has complicated the picture we have about how it was to be female or male in the past, even if we just limit ourselves to physical bodies and their experiences. When we shift our framework to look at the culturally mediated experience of sexual desire and sexual practices, archaeology again tells us that things have historically been more complex than we used to think.

## SEXUALITY

When a group of archaeologists met to talk about sexuality in a session at the national archaeology meetings in 1998 (Schmidt and Voss 2000), few had actually ventured to write about the topic directly. Archaeology, in other words, was repressed. It would be difficult to say that now (Voss 2006). Yet how do we think we can know anything about something as personal as sexuality from the kinds of material remains we find?

A first line of evidence for ancient sexualities is imagery: whether carved in stone, modeled in clay, painted or drawn, human beings have a long history of recording sexual acts. Archaeologists have almost as long a history of explaining these as symbolic. But even symbols need living practices for people to understand what the symbol is intended to convey. Archaeologists now can talk about and illustrate masturbation, anal sex, oral sex, different sexual positions, sex between men and men, men and boys, men and women, and men and men cross-dressed as women, although mutual sexuality between women remains underrepresented in archaeological studies.

Of course, simply having an image of a sex act does not help greatly in assessing what the status of such acts was, and it leaves us a long way from understanding the subjective experience of sexualities. Here archaeologists draw on ethnographic and historical analogies, not so much to explain what sexuality *must have* been like in other times and places, but what the sexual activity seen in imagery *might have* implied for people in these societies. The main lesson we learn from comparative studies is that experiences of apparently similar sexual practices can be quite variable in different social settings.

Archaeologically, this point has been made very clearly by Classical archaeologists: those who study the ancient Greeks and Romans. This is a perfect case study for sexuality in some ways. In addition to imagery, the Greeks and Romans left us a large documentary record. Scholars have been working to translate these texts and images and place them in context for a very long time.

For example, Classical Greek art and texts both tell us that older men were expected to have sex with young boys. Yet at the same time, texts suggest that adult males were not expected to have sex with other adult males, and when young boys matured, they were not expected to continue their relations with older men. To call these cultural practices "homosexuality" would ignore the specific historical situation. First, for the ancient Greeks, men and women were not two biological sexes: they were different versions of a single sex (Laqueur 1990). Male anatomy was an externalization of what in women was anatomically interiorized. Maleness developed distinctly from femaleness, although both were based on the same organs, because males had more heat, while women were colder. Young males benefited from sex with older males because this helped develop the male state of the shared sexual anatomy. Continued sexual acts between adult males, however, would endanger sexual development.

Archaeologists have noted that all of this philosophy of sexuality comes to us from texts referring to free citizens, and cannot be applied to the large numbers of people who were not free, or to foreigners. Nor does it speak to us about women's views of these sexual practices, or the complicated lives of women married to men who engaged in these relationships. This is where archaeology has a unique role. Studies of Classical Greek houses have demonstrated that normative models in which women were secluded in separate quarters don't hold up: house plans are highly variable (Goldberg 1999, Nevett 1994). Instead of evidence of male power over women, house plans suggest that men and women formed a group that prized its privacy and separated the family quarters from those the public could enter.

When we turn to a less familiar society, the Moche of north coast Peru, the same kind of socially complicated approach is helpful. Moche pottery vessels present sexually explicit imagery, scenes showing males and females engaged in a variety of sexual acts. By drawing on historical and ethnographic analogies, recent scholars have been able to argue that the explicit sex scenes on Moche pots tell us about how the Moche understood people to be linked over generations through exchanges of body fluids (Weismantel 2004). Sexual acts of all kinds transfer fluids from one body to another, and keep the substances that gave life to people moving from ancestors to adults to children who mature to become adults and continue the cycle. This doesn't tell us whether the sex acts we see on these pots were common or uncommon; but it does tell us to be careful not to project a modern interpretation, in this case of male sexual dominance, on ancient materials.

When archaeologists began to talk openly about sexuality, they also began to talk about the life experiences of people who chose voluntarily not to express their desires in physical acts. Cross-culturally, groups of men or women living in communities based on celibacy are not uncommon. A study of medieval nunneries in Britain argued that women's cloisters were more austere than monasteries, partly as a way to discipline women's sexuality, seen in Christian theology as less controlled than men's (Gilchrist 2000). At the same time, the precincts where the nuns lived were decorated with images that recall texts about their spiritual life that were expressed in highly physical terms. Women in these communities disciplined their bodies and internalized their desires, turning them to the divine.

The histories of sexuality that archaeology is exploring today are complex. Challenges based in contemporary "queer theory" argue that ignoring the abundant evidence of sexuality offered by archaeology allowed the creation of a very narrow story that made twentieth-century sexual norms seem inevitable (Joyce 2008; Perry and Joyce 2001; Voss 2006). The independent history of the Americas testifies to a much more fluid concept of sexuality and gender identities than that of Europe. What Native American activists and scholars call "two spirits," and archaeologists often refer to as third and fourth genders, are people who occupied a separate status in their societies, neither male nor female (Hollimon 2006). Third- and fourth-gender people may sometimes have been biologically intersex, but were not necessarily so. They were individuals who in some way exceeded the definition of either male or female in their societies. Often they distinguished themselves in activities in which most people with similar sexual anatomy did not participate. They might have sexual relations with people of the same sexual anatomy or different sexual anatomy, or both. Rather than being based on a set of rigid categorical sexual or gender identities, third and fourth genders exemplified a more fluid way of responding to the individual preferences and abilities of members of these societies.

## DIFFERENCE

While archaeologists increasingly address sexuality directly, and question the security of what once was a firm separation of biological sex as nature given and cultural gender as social category, they have also continued to work on basic questions of gender difference and hierarchies in past societies. The multiplying of possible sexualities and gendered positions, and the importance of intersectionality, have been critical in moving forward what started as a search for women in the past. That search has now definitively resulted in rich understandings of the roles of particular women, and of women as a group, that sometimes confirm but as often contradict the assumptions archaeologists once made. Sensibly, contemporary archaeologists of gender no longer try to find some specific methods that can be used to "see" women or to see gender, instead they insist that all methods archaeologists use be scrutinized so that any assumptions about gender that they contain are revealed and, if necessary, amended.

Many gender analyses in archaeology start by asking about differences in labor between males and females. Originally taking for granted a history of inequality between men and women, archaeologists now investigate the specific facts to show how variable economic relations have been (Pyburn 2004). Who did what activities? Where did people of different genders carry out their tasks? What relative value was placed on the labor of people of different genders? Under what circumstances did people have the ability to claim credit for the products of their work? Archaeology, which has a long history of materialist analysis, has developed a strong set of tools to address these questions.

Many studies began, and some still begin, by examining the distributions of tools, raw materials, and partially worked products across space within settlements. When clusters of tools, raw materials, and products are found, the archaeologist can then propose that evidence of a specific industry exists. The leap from industry to gender or sex of the participants is always indirect, often based on analogies. Archaeologists are comfortable with procedures for using analogies with better documented historical or ethnographic settings, and have created clear guidelines for how to do this. We consider analogies as being of two kinds. Some are historical: if you know that a particular contemporary society or historically documented group lived in an area, you can propose that older archaeological sites may represent the ancestors of the documented group. Many archaeological studies of the Mexica (Aztec) and Classic Maya assume that spinning and weaving were carried out by women, and so identify the tools of these tasks and the places they are found as evidence of women's work (Hendon 1997; McCafferty and McCafferty 1991). This is based on historical and ethnographic studies of the Nahuatl- and Maya-speaking peoples of Mexico and Central America, where women are normally spinners and weavers.

In contrast to such local or "specific" analogies, archaeologists may draw on what are called general analogies. These do not rest on the assumption of historical identity between the inhabitants of an archaeological site and later people in the same area. Instead, a general analogy is created between a known case in a similar environment, with a similar level of technology, and a similar social scale, and the archaeological site under study. For example, understanding Palaeolithic hunters of the European Ice Age does not rely on specific, local analogy with modern French, Spanish, or Germans. It may, however, draw on studies of hunters in northern latitudes, where cold weather and similar seasonality of herd animals provide somewhat comparable conditions. Archaeologists have conducted original ethnographic or "ethnoarchaeological" studies (Weedman 2006) themselves to produce general analogies from northern hunters. Such work has demonstrated that hunting parties are not automatically segregated by sex, but may instead be organized by age, providing a mixed group with good physical abilities to travel out from base camps, hunt, process carcasses, and transport the products of the hunt back to the older and younger people waiting behind (Brumbach and Jarvenpa 2006). Drawing on this kind of analogy, archaeologists studying hunter-gatherer societies would not assume that men hunted while women gathered, and instead would explore the specific range of tasks carried out and the skills necessary to complete them.

Whether general or specific, archaeologists today assess whether an analogy is well developed by examining both how well the source of the analogy is understood, and how well the society to which it is applied has been studied. Source side critique often identifies gaps in ethnography, including gendered assumptions by ethnographers. In a study aimed at identifying the contributions of men and women to farming in Classic Maya society (Robin 2006), the modern sources of analogy were found to be problematic, ignoring changes in farming techniques since the Classic period, and underemphasizing some agricultural tasks in favor of others. This had led to a model in which men were farmers and women were not. The alternative suggested was that men and women probably cooperated in the more complex farming systems that archaeologists have documented, which would have been unlike more recent farming techniques.

Sometimes critical attention to analogy may result in questioning the very assumptions that have been used by earlier researchers to find evidence of women's lives. In the case of spinning and weaving in prehispanic Mexico and Central America, while the evidence is good for these being female tasks for the Classic Maya and Postclassic Aztec, the evidence for gendered labor of this kind in earlier periods is weak. Aztec and Maya cases provide multiple lines of evidence to support the application of the modern analogy: images showing women doing these tasks; texts talking about them as women's work; and clusters of the tools of these tasks in household settings (Hendon 1997). When we turn to earlier time periods, though, none of these patterns is found. Tools for textile production in graves at one central Mexican site predating the Classic Maya by more than 1000 years are not found with females more often than with males (Joyce 2001). In fact, most evidence from this site fails to distinguish women's burials from those of men. Instead of sex, most variation is related either to age or to the specific house or neighborhood where the person was buried.

Instead of taking associations of gender and labor as consistent and unchanging, archaeologists working on Aztec and pre-Aztec sites examined the patterns of different tools during the period in which the Aztec conquered other towns, placing new demands for tribute on them, and during the period of Spanish conquest. Expecting to see evidence of reorganization of spinning to meet increased demands for cloth, they instead found evidence of changes in cooking, from an emphasis on stews that could not be easily transported to the fields by workers, to tortillas that could be carried (Brumfiel 1991). Rather than see women only in textile production, these researchers were able to see how incorporation in empire affected daily cooking activities, also assumed to be carried out by women.

Other work inspired by the historical association of women and weaving in this region looked at patterns of distribution of spindle whorls, the tool used for producing thread, in late prehispanic Cholula, south of the Aztec capital. Here, spindle whorls were found in the burials of males as well as females (McCafferty and McCafferty 2000). Rather than questioning the strong ideological association of spinning with women, we can suggest that ideology and pragmatism went side by side. The researchers noted that the one high status woman in their sample was buried with textile tools, and that the men with spindle whorls appeared to be lower status. Women's feminity was expressed in their talents as spinners and weavers, activities that had sexual connotations in everyday speech. When men spun thread, it wouldn't have had those associations for them. Their spinning was, however, economically valuable because it contributed to the production of cloth that was critical to political life in this society.

The suggestion that men could, in situations where thread was valuable, undertake a task typical of women without being feminized is an example of an argument made by archaeologists about masculinity. Almost more than women, men in the past have been imagined to be homogeneous, usually hypermasculine creatures. Archaeologists examining masculinity suggest instead that we need to think in terms of masculinities, differences among men, as much as differences between men and women. Noting that rock art in Scandinavia shows some males with exaggerated leg muscles, often with erections, archaeologists suggest that scenes once thought to show normative males and females in fact depict varying masculinities, with other figures also males but with a less exaggerated masculine body (Yates 1993). Examination of medieval burials in Britain showed that some males buried with weapons had more robust skeletons than others buried without these objects, suggesting we think in terms of a "warrior" masculinity juxtaposed to other forms of masculinity (Gilchrist 2004). Other archaeologists proposed that a material culture of male body care might tell us that a similar "warrior" masculinity was being cultivated in Bronze Age Europe (Treherne 1995).

For some, such new approaches threaten to make women disappear as a specific subject of analysis. After so much hard work has been expended to insist that women need to be treated as actors who may have had their own agendas, and who may have caused historical change, it can seem like asking different questions about gender means abandoning the project of understanding specifically female forms of experience and agency. The solution to that is not to abandon studies of masculinity, or ignore intersectionality: it is to ensure that every archaeological study begins by asking how embodied personhood, including differences in sexual anatomy and sexual practices, affected people's lives. Such a question cannot fail to illuminate the lives of women, but it also will of necessity help us understand the lives of men, and of people of other genders, as well, from birth to death.

## REFERENCES

Agarwal, Sabrina C., Mircea Dumitriu, George A. Tomlinson, and Marc D. Grynpas. 2004. "Medieval Trabecular Bone Architecture: The Influence of Age, Sex, and Lifestyle." *American Journal of Physical Anthropology* 124: 33–44.

Ambrose, Stanley H., Jane Buikstra, and Harold W. Krueger. 2003. "Status and Gender Differences in Diet at Mound 72, Cahokia, Revealed by Isotopic Analysis of Bone." *Journal of Anthropological Archaeology* 22: 217–226.

Brumbach, Hetty Jo, and Robert Jarvenpa. 2006. "Gender Dynamics in Hunter-Gatherer Society: Archaeological Methods and Perspectives." In Sarah Nelson (ed.). *Handbook of Gender in Archaeology*, pp. 503–535. Lanham, MD: AltaMira Press.

Brumfiel, Elizabeth. 1991. "Weaving and Cooking: Women's Production in Aztec Mexico." In Joan Gero and Margaret Conkey (eds.). *Engendering Archaeology: Women and Prehistory*, pp. 224–251. Oxford: Basil Blackwell.

Claassen, Cheryl (ed.). 1992. *Exploring Gender through Archaeology*. Madison, WI: Prehistory Press.

Conkey, Margaret W., and Joan Gero (eds.). 1991. *Engendering Archaeology*. Oxford: Basil Blackwell.

Conkey, Margaret W., and Janet Spector. 1984. "Archaeology and the Study of Gender." *Advances in Archaeological Method and Theory* 7: 1–38.

Geller, Pamela L. 2005. "Skeletal Analysis and Theoretical Complications." *World Archaeology* 37: 597–609.

Gilchrist, Roberta. 2000. "Unsexing the Body: The Interior Sexuality of Medieval Religious Women." In Robert A. Schmidt and Barbara L. Voss (eds.). *Archaeologies of Sexuality*, pp. 89–103. London: Routledge Press.

———. 2004. "Archaeology and the Life Course: A Time and Age for Gender." In Lynn Meskell and Robert Preucel (eds.). *A Companion to Social Archaeology*, pp. 142–160. Oxford: Blackwell.

Goldberg, Marilyn Y. 1999. "Spatial and Behavioural Negotation in Classical Athenian City Houses." In Penelope M. Allison (ed.). *The Archaeology of Household Activities*, pp. 142–161. London: Routledge.

Hastorf, Christine. 1991. "Gender, Space and Food in Prehistory." In Margaret W. Conkey and Joan Gero (eds.). *Engendering Archaeology*, pp. 132–159. Oxford: Basil Blackwell.

Hendon, Julia A. 1997. "Women's Work, Women's Space, and Women's Status among the Classic-Period Maya Elite of the Copan Valley, Honduras." In Cheryl Claassen and Rosemary A. Joyce (eds.). *Women in Prehistory: North America and Mesoamerica*, pp. 33–46. Philadelphia: University of Pennsylvania Press.

Hollimon, Sandra. 2006. "The Archaeology of Nonbinary Genders in Native North America." In Sarah Nelson (ed.). *Handbook of Gender in Archaeology*, pp. 435–450. Lanham, MD: AltaMira Press.

Joyce, Rosemary A. 2001. "Burying the Dead at Tlatilco: Social Memory and Social Identities." In Meredith Chesson (ed.). *New Perspectives on Mortuary Analysis*, pp. 12–26. Alexandria, VA: American Anthropological Association.

———. 2008. *Ancient Bodies, Ancient Lives*. London: Thames and Hudson.

Laqueur, Thomas W. 1990. *Making Sex: Body and Gender from the Greeks to Freud*. Cambridge, MA: Harvard University Press.

McCafferty, Sharisse D., and Geoffrey G. McCafferty. 1991. "Spinning and Weaving as Female Gender Identity in Post-Classic Mexico." In Janet C. Berlo, Margot Schevill, and Edward B. Dwyer (eds.). *Textile Traditions of*

*Mesoamerica and the Andes: An Anthology*, pp. 19–44. New York: Garland.

———. 2000. "Textile Production in Postclassic Cholula, Mexico." *Ancient Mesoamerica* 11: 39–54.

Meskell, Lynn M. 2005. "De/naturalizing Gender in Prehistory." In Susan McKinnon and Sydel Silverman (eds.). *Complexities: Beyond Nature and Nurture*, pp. 157–175. Chicago: University of Chicago Press.

Nelson, Sarah M. (ed.). 2006. *Handbook of Gender in Archaeology*. Lanham, MD: AltaMira Press.

Nevett, Lisa. 1994. "Separation or Seclusion? Towards an Archaeological Approach to Investigating Women in the Greek Household in the Fifth to Third Centuries B.C." In Michael Parker Pearson and Colin Richards (eds.). *Architecture and Order: Approaches to Social Space*, pp. 98–112. London: Routledge.

Perry, Elizabeth M., and Rosemary A. Joyce. 2001. "Providing a Past for *Bodies that Matter*: Judith Butler's Impact on the Archaeology of Gender." *International Journal of Sexuality and Gender Studies* 6: 63–76.

Pyburn, K. Anne (ed.). 2004. *Ungendering Archaeology*. New York: Routledge.

Robin, Cynthia. 2006. "Gender, Farming, and Long-term Change: Maya Historical and Archaeological Perspectives." *Current Anthropology* 47: 409–434.

Schmidt, Robert A., and Barbara Voss (eds.). 2000. *Archaeologies of Sexuality*. London: Routledge Press.

Treherne, Paul. 1995. "The Warrior's Beauty: The Masculine Body and Self-identity in Bronze-Age Europe." *Journal of European Archaeology* 3: 105–144.

Voss, Barbara L. 2006. "Sexuality in Archaeology." In Sarah Nelson (ed.). *Handbook of Gender in Archaeology*, pp. 365–400. Lanham, MD: AltaMira Press.

Weedman, Kathryn. 2006. "Gender and Ethnoarchaeology." In Sarah Nelson (ed.). *Handbook of Gender in Archaeology*, pp. 247–294. Lanham, MD: AltaMira Press.

Weismantel, Mary. 2004. "Moche Sex Pots: Reproduction and Temporality in Ancient South America." *American Anthropologist* 106: 495–505.

White, Christine D. 2005. "Gendered Food Behaviour among the Maya: Time, Place, Status and Ritual." *Journal of Social American* 5: 356–382.

Wilkie, Laurie A., and Katherine Howlett Hayes. 2006. "Engendered and Feminist Archaeologies of the Recent and Documented Pasts." *Journal of Archaeological Research* 14: 243–264.

Yates, Tim. 1993. "Frameworks for an Archaeology of the Body." In Christopher Tilley (ed.). *Interpretive Archaeology*, pp. 31–72. Providence, RI: Berg.

# The Fashioning of Women

## J. M. Adovasio, Olga Soffer, and Jake Page

In which we visit a pleasant encampment full of Brooks Brothers–style weaving and other womanly creations, the first fireworks, mammoth non-hunts, and people who could be your neighbors.

**THE PLACE:** A camp on the gentle, grassy slope of a hill in today's Pavlov Hills, from which three limestone outcrops rise above the broad south Moravian plain in the eastern region of today's Czech Republic. The view to the north, south, and east stretches for miles over grassland and forest: a broad valley that served people and wildlife as a highway from the flatlands of the mighty Danube into northern Europe. The Pavlov Hills lie along the right bank of a river that flows into the Morava River, a major tributary to the Danube. To the north, a month's march away, lies the great wall of glacial ice. Equally far to the southwest, ice blankets the great mountains known today as the Alps. The village is

J. M. Adovasio, Olga Soffer and Jake Page, "The Fashioning of Women," in *The Invisible Sex: Uncovering the True Roles of Women in Prehistory*, by J. M. Adovasio, Olga Soffer and Jake Page, pp. 169–193. © 2007 by James M. Adovasio, Olga Soffer and Jake Page. Reprinted by permission of HarperCollins.

not far above a swampy area fed by the river that courses through the plains, its moisture supporting a variety of deciduous trees—alder, ash, birch, groves of willows, the occasional oak, and beyond, in drier soils, the conifers, pines, spruce, and others. Off in the distance, a few clusters of reindeer and small herds of horses head south. Beyond, a group of female mammoths and their young plod northward.

**THE TIME:** 26,000 years ago. The summer has ended, and the nightly temperatures in these early autumn weeks reach near freezing. It will get colder as the winter comes on, but for now the days are relatively warm once the sun rises above the hills.

**THE VILLAGE:** This is where several groups of people have come together to spend the long fall, winter, and early spring, just as they and their ancestors have done since longer than anyone can remember or compute. The camp is about 200 yards upslope from the river at a place where natural mineral licks attract nutrient-starved animals in the spring months, especially mammoth females and their young. There the weaker ones die, leaving their bones for the people to use. Over the eons, people have made use of their bones and tusks as raw materials to build dwellings and make tools and other objects. Now they have erected five tent like structures over depressions in the ground they have cleaned out, throwing away last year's broken flint and bone and broken tools and other household trash. Walls and roofs of skins sewed together are held up by wooden poles, their edges held down against the force of the cold winds with rocks. In the largest of these structures, sitting in the middle of the camp, five hearths have been delineated with circles of rocks. The others contain single hearths. Upslope from the camp about 80 yards sits another structure, with limestone slabs holding down walls of hide on three sides. Inside this structure are layers of ashes and ceramic fragments.

On this particular morning, just as the eastern sky is beginning to lighten, a woman emerges from one of the tents and nods to the sleepy youth who is tending the fire in the middle of the camp that burns through the night as a warning to predators. She walks slowly and painfully up the slope to this small structure. Taking sticks of wood from a pile she ordered her young grandchildren to make yesterday, she builds a fire. The flames lick hungrily at the pine sticks, reaching into the cold air. Not pausing to warm herself, she piles more sticks, larger ones, on the flames, and then retreats down the slope to her dwelling. Moments later, she reemerges, carrying a tightly woven basket filled with water and a cloth carrying bag filled with dusty brown soil. By now the fire has rendered the fuel into glowing hot coals. She nods approvingly, then sits down beside the kiln with a grunt about her complaining knee joints. Making clay by mixing the fine dusty soil with water, she fashions a tiny bear's head and body. She sets that aside, fashions legs, and presses them into the body. She intones some words and throws the bear into the fire. In minutes, the bear explodes with a sharp *Crack!* and a cascade of sparks and pieces of the bear rattle off the walls of the kiln. Thus does the old woman's day begin, rendering their world as safe as she can for the rest of the people.

By now people are stepping outside their dwellings into the cold, scratching, yawning, looking up at the sky for signs of the weather for this day. Young children begin darting here and there, yelping and shouting, parents hissing at them to be quiet. Two women, each suckling a new baby, stand together talking. Some of the group's men stand in a circle, chewing on narrow strips of rabbit jerky, glancing out to the horse herds moving across the plains far away, making plans. From up the hillside at the kiln, the sharp pops of the old woman's fireworks are reassuring sounds. As the sun rises over the hills, casting long shadows that reach down the slope, activity in the camp begins to pick up. Innumerable chores need doing. Several men are soon engaged in replacing the tiny old blades affixed to the ivory foreshafts of their wooden spears

with newly knapped flint blades, renewing the lethally sharp array. These weapons are for hunting horses and the small red deer out on the plains, a task that could take several men an entire day and night and still result in failure.

Another man grinds a piece of gray slate into a pendant to replace the one that shattered the day before when he fell onto some rocks while running. An older man, his hands now gnarled and crooked, slowly opens up a long hunting net, unrolling it on the ground. He then inspects it from one end 40 feet to the other end, seeing that the knots are still all secure. Satisfied, he rolls it back up and places it on the ground near a lone tree that stands a few feet from the dwelling where he, with his family, sleeps.

Inside, his daughter boils a mush of various wild seeds in a tightly plaited basket with hardened clay inside. The thickening gruel bubbles, some of it slopping over the edge of the basket and falling into the hearth. The young woman has been feeding this to her four-year old daughter for a week now, weaning her from the breast. Earlier, she and three other mothers sent their daughters off to collect the nettles that grow in the disturbed soil around the camp and are now ready to be processed. The girls and their mothers will set about soaking the nettles to remove the outer cover and free up the finer fibers inside. The fibers will then be twisted into string of various plies.

The Old Woman, the oldest person in camp, though she is still vigorous, will supervise the making of the string and will take the finest as warps and wefts for her own work on her loom. Last year, she taught the young girls five of the eight ways of twining, some for making baskets and floor mats, some for making the wall hangings that helped keep out the icy winds of winter, and yet others for the fine mysteries of creating loom-woven fabric to sew together into form-fitting warm-weather clothes. The Old Woman, who is a bit scary for the girls because she is so powerful, has chosen one of the girls as a special student: she will learn to sew the seams of ceremonial shirts. She will show another girl the arts of the loom, and one day perhaps this girl will become the Old Woman, the weaver who makes the finest fabric for clothing for whoever in her lifetime emerges as the leader.

As the day goes on, several of the men set out for the plains below, bristling with flint knives and spears of wood tipped with ivory and stone blades, sweating in the midday sun, their hide shirts hanging from their belts. They will be on the march most of the day, camping near a place on the river favored by horses and some of the local deer. Other men stay in camp, a few telling exaggerated tales of hunting to the boys, a few others digging up the loose dusty soil and carrying it up the hill in bags made of fiber to the old woman at the kiln. In the shade of one of the freestanding trees, three young women gossip and laugh as they grind the small tough seeds of certain prairie grasses. It is a good day for a feast to celebrate the coming together here of these related families for the season.

By late afternoon, each family's net has been unrolled and carefully inspected, and tied together to form two long nets, each some 80 feet across. Now the children, some of the women and men, and a few elders set out with the nets. The children carry sticks, which they brandish bravely as they run along behind the adults. Several of the adults carry clubs fashioned from fallen branches. Led by the oldest in the party, they pause after a half hour's walk on the slopes that are covered by underbrush. Carefully the oldsters unfurl the nets, unwinding them from the carrying poles, which are then used to anchor the nets to the ground. Several of the younger women, the men, and all the children silently circle around upslope until they reach nearly to the top of the hill. There they form into a wide arc and on a signal begin the charge down the hill, shrieking wildly, whacking trees as they go by, setting up a terrifying din. Rabbits, foxes, and other small mammals emerge from the underbrush and dart back and forth, trending downhill to escape the mayhem coming their way. Within minutes several dozen of these creatures have leaped into the nets to be quickly dispatched by people swinging their clubs. As the sun drops down to the western horizon, the people head back with more meat and fur than they will be able to use for days.

The camp bustles with activity as preparations for the feast get under way—skinning the animals, starting the hearth fires and the outdoor fire that will burn all night, and performing innumerable other chores. Meanwhile, the old woman who was first to greet the day has returned to the kiln up the slope with one of her youthful apprentices. She has kneaded into existence a few dozen small clay pellets, several animal figurines, and, most elaborate, a figurine of a woman with broad hips and buttocks and pendulous breasts, faceless, footless, with lines etched into her back that suggest ample flesh, which bespeaks a prosperous woman. Carefully, she places all these objects into her basket except for the figurine, which she hands to the older of her two apprentices. The girl grins widely at the honor and holds the figurine carefully in her hand, and they set out for the camp below. As the feasting proceeds into the night, a few couples slip off into the dark, heading for courting camps a short walk away in a copse of trees. Others dance and chant, while the old woman throws an occasional pellet or animal figure into the fire as she sings a special song to herself in a high keening voice and the clay figurines explode. Toward the end of the festivities, she instructs the sleepy apprentice to throw the figurine of the woman into the flames. Most of the people in camp stop to watch as the girl flips the figurine into the fire, and they wait silently for a minute or so until a loud crack signifies the end of the ritual, of the feast, of the day.

With that, the people settle down for the night, eyelids drooping, stomachs full, ceremonies properly done to celebrate the successful hunt—a good day indeed.

## WHAT'S RIGHT ABOUT THAT PICTURE

How much of this scenario is guesswork and how much is certain? What is the evidence that lies behind this view of a day spent at a site that would come to be known as Dolni Vestonice I? This site has been excavated and examined by numerous archaeologists over the last three quarters of a century and, over this time, has yielded up several startling discoveries. Among the first such was the figurine of the woman that we saw tossed into the central fire of the camp at the end of the feast. She was subsequently discovered on July 13, 1925, during the Moravian Museum's excavation under the leadership of Karel Absolon. The workers found her in two unequal pieces less than a foot apart. The Vestonice Venus, as she came to be known, became famous as the earliest ceramic object ever found. A picture soon emerged—indeed, an actual illustration by Zdenek Burian—showing an elderly man with disheveled white hair, wearing a sleeveless shirt of some animal skin, with a necklace of teeth and other no doubt meaningful objects around his neck, carefully sculpting the figurine with a stick of animal bone. It is more likely that the figurine was carved by a woman, probably the "priestess" who used it.

At the time of its discovery, one member of the crew noted what appeared to be a fragmentary fingerprint left on the Venus's spine before firing. Recently this fingerprint was analyzed microscopically to determine such features as the breadth of ridges, which correlate with the age of the originator of the print. It turns out that the person who held this figurine was between 7 and 15 years old, and almost surely was not the maker of the figurine, since it is unlikely that a beginner or a child could have made it.

On the other hand, it was possible to call into question the actual ceramic skill of this "first" ceramicist. The site of the kiln upslope was first looked into by archaeologists in the 1950s. It yielded fragments of a total of 707 animal figurines and 14 human figurines, all fired clay. In addition there were some 2,000 small pellets. This suggests two possibilities. One, the ceramicist(s) were extremely incompetent. Two, they knew just what they were doing and had no interest in creating objects that would remain intact but instead were making objects that would, by design, harden in the flames and explode. This can be achieved by, among other things, adjusting the wetness of the clay. The building of three walls of the kiln suggests that they knew full well that the figurines would explode, adding to the suggestion that a deliberate effort was going on—not only the first ceramic objects ever known, but also perhaps the first example of a kind of fireworks. Our description of this as embodying some sort of ritual is something of an imaginative leap, but it seems unlikely that such onerous activity would be done out of sheer frivolity at a time when survival was a full-time job.

## THE CRUCIAL ROLE OF THE FIBER ARTS

More important probably than the presumably ritual use of ceramics in Dolni Vestonice is the discovery that by 26,000 years ago, these Upper Paleolithic people of Eurasia were well along in what has been called the String Revolution, a technological breakthrough (better thought of as the Fiber Revolution) that had profound effects on human destiny—probably more profound effects than any advance in the technique of making spear points, knives, scrapers and other tools out of stone. The term String Revolution was evidently the original idea of Elizabeth Wayland Barber of Occidental College in California. She wrote a lovely book, *Women's Work*, suggesting what a remarkable invention string was, whenever it first was used. String's invention, she wrote, "opened the door to an enormous array of new ways to labor and improve the odds of survival . . . " Comparing it to the steam engine, she mentioned the need of string for weaving and said that on a far more basic level, "string can be used simply to tie things up—to catch, to hold, to carry. From these notions come snares and fishlines, tethers and leashes, carrying nets, handles, and packages, not to mention a way of binding objects together to form more complex tools." Indeed, she thought, so powerful was string "in taming the world and to human will and ingenuity" that it may well have made it possible for humans to populate virtually every niche they could reach. So the fiber artifacts found in those old Moravian sites were far more important than their humble appearance would have suggested.

Three certainties exist about fiber artifacts. Compared with things made out of stone, bone, antler, shell, and even (in some cases) wood, fiber items are highly perishable. Because of this, there simply aren't as many fiber artifacts remaining in the ground as other kinds. And there are even fewer fiber artifacts in the archaeological record than have persisted in the ground because practically all archaeologists have not been trained to see them in the ground, much less recover them (often an extremely delicate and technical task). There remain only a handful of archaeology departments here and abroad where such training is available, particularly at the graduate level. The other certain thing about fiber artifacts is that, in dry caves and other places where they do not deteriorate and disappear, they have been found to outnumber stone artifacts by a factor of 20 to 1. In several other situations (places covered with water where aerobic bacteria cannot get to the artifacts, and in permafrost), fiber and wood artifacts have been found to account for 95 percent of all artifacts recovered. That amounts to a tremendous amount of information that archaeologists have missed in most parts of the world, including Late Pleistocene Eurasia.

A third certainty about fiber artifacts such as baskets is that, unlike stone or bone artifacts or even pottery, the method by which the artifact was made is apparent in the artifact itself. Modern stone-knappers who like to replicate old spear points, for example, can do so with considerable skill, and of course they know the steps they took to get to the finished product. But the earlier steps made are not necessarily present in the point. By contrast, a practiced eye can perceive which of a finite number of logical steps the basket maker took. Indeed, no weaver of baskets and fabrics and other items makes such things exactly as anyone else does, so one can actually glimpse a bit of the living individual craftswoman. At the same time, most basket makers of prehistory operated within an identifiable cultural framework, just as one sees tribal distinctions in the baskets, say, of Apache women as distinct from Paiute women. And within such a tribal tradition, one can also see what appears to be one generation, or even one basket maker, who taught those who came along afterward.

If one takes modern ethnographic studies of hunter-gatherer societies as not wholly unrepresentative of Late Paleolithic societies, the work of most human beings—especially women—has been overlooked. One result, which we noted in Chapter One, was that this left room for the picture to emerge of Upper Paleolithic society and economics dominated by the mighty hunters setting out to slaughter mammoths and other large animals—though mammoths especially caught the imagination of those reconstructing these ancient lifeways. There was some evidence for this, but only a smidgin. Most notably, in a few places archaeologists found stone points among huge mammoth bone assemblages in Eurasia (and also North America, where we will go in a later chapter). It appeared to many that astonishingly efficient and daring hunters were taking on entire herds and killing them for food.

But there was a problem here of specialization. Paleontologists, whose interest lay in the realm of prehistoric zoology rather than in the affairs of humans and hominids, found numerous similar assemblages of mammoth bones in Eurasia (and smaller assemblages in Siberia and North America) that had no stone points. And even in those assemblages where stone points and other tools were found, butchering marks were few and far between. In other words, over thousands of years and in various places (such as mineral licks, as at Dolni Vestonice, where the remains of a hundred or so mammoths were found), proboscidians died and created boneyards from which the people made what use they could.

Ethnographic studies of modern people have turned up practically no instances of deliberate elephant hunting before the advent of the ivory trade in modern times. There is no evidence of Upper Paleolithic assemblages of enough hunters (maybe 40 or so) to take down a mammoth, much less the number needed to wipe out a herd. It is dangerous enough, in fact, to go after any animal the size of a horse or a bison if one is armed with a spear. Only the foolhardiest would attempt to kill an animal that stands 14 feet high and has a notoriously bad temper when annoyed. A statement that has been assigned to multiple originators suggests that it is more likely that every so often a Paleolithic hunter brought down an already wounded mammoth (or one slowed down a bit in the mud of a swamp) and then talked about it for the rest of his life. The picture of Man the Mighty Hunter is now fading out of the annals of prehistory. By far, most of the animal remains found strewn about places like Dolni Vestonice consists of the bones of small mammals like hares and foxes.

The finds of perishable artifacts in Dolni Vestonice I and several other sites in Moravia have done much to blow the old picture of Upper Paleolithic life out of the water, and with it the dominant figure of the mighty male hunter, and replaced it with a picture something like the one with which this chapter began. The first of these finds was made in 1993, consisting of mysterious impressions in strange clay fragments in Dolni Vestonice I, which turned out to be the imprints of basketry and textiles made from wild plants. These were the earliest forms of the fiber arts known—indeed, some 10,000 years earlier than anything found before. Just what the fragments themselves were is not clear. They might have been pieces of flooring on which items of weaving or basketry had been impressed, and turned into hard evidence when the place burned down. In any event, they and subsequent finds in these sites showed that people here were already weaving and making basketry with at least eight different styles of twining, some of which

remain common today. Some of the fabrics were as fine as a Brooks Brothers shirt. People had to have been weaving textiles on looms and making freestanding basketry for a very long time to have developed such ability and diversity and sophistication of technique.

Just exactly what those people were making from all this weaving, basketry, and cordage is impossible to say with certainty, but given the excellence of technique there is reason to think that they were making baskets of various kinds and possibly mats for sleeping and wall hangings, and clothing of various kinds such as shawls, skirts, sashes, and shirts. They used whipping stitches like those used today to sew two pieces of fabric together and that no doubt served the same end 26,000 years ago.

In addition to knots and other signs of weaving, numerous tools were turned up over the many times these sites were examined that can now be seen as tools for weaving and other steps in the production of such materials. One puzzling artifact made of mammoth ivory was shaped something like a boomerang but without the curve. It makes perfect sense as a weaving batten (and in fact is nearly identical to the battens still in use today among Navajo weavers). Another tool, basically a rod with a doughnut-shaped end, has been fairly commonly found throughout the world dating from later times, and has puzzled archaeologists, whose best idea for them is that they were used somehow to straighten spear and arrow shafts. But when they are thought about in the context of Moravian weaving, it seems that they would have been useful in the spinning of threads into string or yarn for weaving. Fairly large ivory needles were already known from such places, and the assumption was that they were used for sewing together skins and furs for clothing, but the proliferation of smaller needles found across Eurasia could not have been conveniently used for stitching such tough and unforgiving materials—except for the thinnest of leather. They are the right size, however, for stitching together pieces of woven fabric. Some of the ivory needles found are so fine that they would have permitted embroidery.

The very diversity of styles and workmanship that emerges from all these perishable artifacts and their associated tools, plus the fact that most of the stone used to make stone tools was not local, all suggests that these were people who assembled here for part of the year (perhaps a large part) and separated into smaller groups—probably near-nuclear family groups—at other times. It is reasonable to speculate that each such household might well have its (her) own favored techniques and brought them to the larger group, thus accounting for much of the remarkable diversity of products.

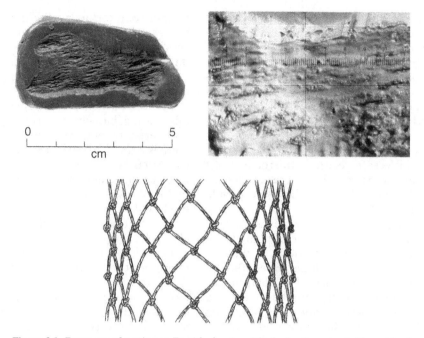

**Figure 2-1.** Fragment of netting at Zaraisk showing (clock-wise from top-left) positive impression of the cast, microphotograph of the netting structure, and schematic of the structure.
O. Soffer, J. M. Adovasio, and Stephanie Snyder

## GROUP HUNTING

Four of the fragments examined had impressions of cordage tied into sheet bends or weaver's knots and this (along with what appear to be tools for measuring the spaces between knots) strongly suggests that they were making nets for hunting relatively small mammals, as well as string bags. Earlier workers had noticed the abundance—indeed, prevalence—of bones of such small mammals as hares and foxes in Upper Paleolithic camps in eastern and central Europe, but came up with fairly weak suggestions for the means of hunting them. Anyone who has watched these animals race and dart when threatened will find it implausible in the extreme to imagine people chasing them down in the open and clubbing them, or even throwing little spears at them, both of which have been offered as serious explanations (of course by male archaeologists). The use of nets, on the other hand, as well as cordage snares, easily explains the peoples' success. They could, obviously, have made nets of wider mesh and thicker cordage for hunting larger animals as well, but no evidence of this has been found. At the same time, the large bone needles that were assumed to be used for sewing skins together would have also been handy tools for making the nets.

What then are the social implications of all this? First of all, we know from such modern hunter-gatherer societies as the Pygmies of the Ituri Forest in Africa's Congo region that net hunting is a communal affair involving women, children, and elderly people as well as adult males. It engages essentially everyone in the group as beaters, clubbers, or net holders and makes the acquisition of high-energy and high-protein food (meat) much less dangerous and more dependable. By adjusting the mesh, they could have caught even smaller forms of life—birds, even insects. This would ease the problems involved in feeding a relatively larger aggregation of people by providing a mass harvest in a short time—a surplus beyond their immediate need that in turn would make ceremonial feasts possible. Such behavior is noted ethnographically.

Making things out of fiber is not the sole prerogative of either sex in ethnographic accounts of small bands or larger tribal societies. More often than not, for example, men make sandals for themselves and their families, and it is also fairly clear that in such societies both men and women *know how* to produce sandals and other items that use basketry techniques and materials. In many cases, men probably do make things like baskets that they need for their own purposes, but throughout the tribal world, today women make most basketry. But loom or frame weaving is a craft practiced almost exclusively by women in the tribal world, as is the gathering and processing of plant products for such weaving. This is the case in virtually all tribal societies where textiles and basketry are produced for domestic and communal needs, and typically it breaks down only when such perishable products enter the domain of market exchange. One rare exception to this among American Indian tribes is the Hopi of northeastern Arizona (an agricultural society) whose men do all the weaving—restricted to ceremonial wear such as sashes and kilts and costumery of brides made by their paternal uncles. Next door to the Hopi, as it were, Navajo women do all the weaving—almost entirely rugs—though the looms are often built by the husbands, and a weaver's son-in-law is expected to supply her with some of the weaving tools.

In addition, from cross-cultural studies throughout the world, the making of ceramic items, especially pottery, in many societies that we are familiar with is chiefly the province of women. There are, to be sure, innumerable variations that people have invented over time for all such matters, but even in the face of some scholarly quibbles, it is safe to assume what could be called the default position: that most if not all of the ceramics, weaving, basketry, and clothing was made by women in the years that Dolni Vestonice and the other Moravian sites were inhabited. And from that and other evidence—notably the Venus figures—it is safe to assume that the *idea* of gender—the separate category with its associated roles and identities was now present. In other words, we see here the malleable social notion of gender, as opposed to (and in addition to) the clear biological function of sex. It is not clear from any particular archaeological evidence at these Moravian sites that the *idea* of man as opposed to male was prevalent. There is virtually no iconography that suggests otherwise, but Thurber's war of the sexes (read gender) would presumably soon begin. In any event, it is safe to say that some division of labor was in place, and with it probably a set of family relatives with whom one identified and by whom one identified oneself on a permanent intergenerational basis, a group in which every segment—children, men, women, elders—stood to gain. The population explosion that took place in this period seems to bear this out. In other words, here is one of the most vivid examples yet discovered of what we can safely call thoroughly, recognizably, behaviorally modern humans.

Does this seem to be a great deal to read into these fragments of perishable items and ceramics along with a few intact tools? In fact, it isn't, and new, closer looks at those enigmatic Venus figurines that are so fascinating a feature of this Upper Paleolithic Eurasian society tend to strengthen this hypothesis and round out our picture of life in those days.

## VENUSES

Some 200 Venus figurines and figurine fragments from across Europe are the most representational three-dimensional images made in the Gravettian period some 27,000 to 22,000 years ago, which, of course, includes the Moravian sites described above. Nothing is their equal before this period from anywhere in the world, and thousands of years go by before anything comparable appears again. As a result, they have claimed the attention of amateurs and professionals alike with almost the same continuing fascination certain scholars and most kids have for dinosaurs. As we said in Chapter Six, the Venus of Willendorf is surely the best known of all these sculptures. They remain in many ways enigmatic, mysterious, even confusing. They serve many purposes today, including as Rorschach emblems for some of today's hang-ups. They obviously mean "female," and they probably mean "woman," which suggests that they are not simply representations of the reproductive function of the female human, or gynecological and obstetrical "textbooks," as one scholar put it. At the same time, there is simply no denying that the sculptors of these figurines went to a great deal of trouble to show off the sexual and secondary sexual features of the female human, even to the point of leaving the rest of the figure—face, feet, arms, and so forth—either abstract or absent altogether. (There are exceptions to this, of course, but no exception in the entire matter is more obvious than the fact that there are only one or two examples of clearly male figurines from this region and period. There are many figurines that are androgenous, without visible sex.)

What escaped many observers, both male and female, for many years was that some of these figurines were partly clad. The Venus of Willendorf's head, for example, though faceless, did have hair, it seemed, braided and wrapped around her head. Others had little bits of decorations—body bands, bracelets, minor bits and pieces of material of some sort. But never mind—they were largely naked and had to represent fertility, menstruation, the godhead (as goddess), or (giggle) paleoporn.

Then in 1998, coming off their discovery of the many fiber artifacts from Moravian sites, which many of their colleagues considered an important rearrangement of the picture of Upper Paleolithic society in Europe, Adovasio and Soffer turned their attention to these figures. To begin with, a close inspection of the braids of the Venus of Willendorf showed that her "hair" was, on the contrary, a woven hat, a radially hand-woven item of apparel that was probably begun from a knotted center in the manner of certain coiled baskets made today by Hopi, Apache, and other American Indian tribes in which a flexible element is wrapped with stem stitches as the spiral grows. Seven circuits encircle the head, with two extra half-circuits over the nape of the neck. Indeed, so precise is the carving of all this stitchery that it is not unreasonable to think that, among the functions involved in this Upper Paleolithic masterpiece, it served as a blueprint

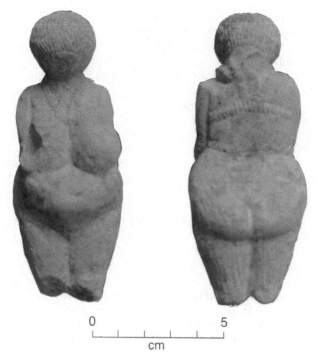

**Figure 2-2.** Front and back views of the female figurine in ivory from Kostenki I.
O. Soffer

or instruction manual showing weavers how to make such hats. Indeed, anyone who has done any sculpting in stone or wood can tell you that the fashioning of the body, while extremely closely realized, would have been easy compared with the astounding control and staying power needed to render the stitching (even a few splices) of this hat so true and precise. The carver had to have spent more time on just the hat than on the rest of the entire figurine.

Of all the scholars who have examined these figurines over the decades (and there must be hundreds), only one other, Elizabeth Barber, ever took notice of the fiber accoutrements some of them wore. One British scholar who studied the Venuses in his youth never noticed any clothing because, he recalled, he "never got past the breasts."

Several other such figurines from central and eastern Europe wear similarly detailed radial or spiral woven hats as well as some begun by interlacing grids. Western European figurines tend to be more schematic, such as the Venus of Brassempouy, whose hair may be covered, in a more abstract rendering, by some sort of hairnet

**Figure 2-3.** Close-up of the coiling start of the basket hat depicted on the head of the Venus of Willendorf.
S. Holland, Courtesy of O. Soffer

**Figure 2-4.** Left, right, and top views of the plaited start of the basket hat depicted on the marl head of the female figurine from Kostenki I.
S. Holland, Courtesy O. Soffer

or snood. One thing that seems fairly common to all the partly clad figurines is that when they wear hats or caps, the facial details are absent. This suggests a social importance to the headgear, rather than an individual statement of personal identity. In other words, these various forms of headgear may speak to a particular status or rank enjoyed by at least some women.

Other forms of clothing or cloth decorations found on Venuses of this Gravettian period include straps wrapped around the figure, often above the breasts, and sometimes held there with over-the-shoulder straps. Yet others wear belts, often low on their hips, sometimes connected to skirts of string. The Venus of Lespugue, for example—she of the truly overwhelming hips—wears a back skirt carved with a remarkable

attention to detail. It consists of eleven cords attached to a base cord that serves as a belt. The cords are secured to the belt by looping both ends of a single-ply string over the belt and twisting the ends together with a final Z twist. On several of the cords, the carver made 30 and 40 separate incisions to show the individual twists, and she took great care to depict the progressive changes in angle of twist. At the bottom of the skirt, the angle of twist is much looser, clearly suggesting that the cords were unraveling or fraying at the hem.

What is to be made of all this? An important thing to note is that, except for one sexually ambiguous fragment that has a belt, such apparel appears only on figurines that are female. Clearly, as well, the

**Figure 2-5.** The Venus of Brassempoy, carved from ivory.
S. Holland, Courtesy O. Soffer

garments so carefully portrayed are not the normal daily wear of women in these times, since they lived in climates where such clothing would be utterly insufficient against the cold—except of course for the woven hats. In the few known burials of the time, people were interred fully clothed. The body bands, belts, string skirts, and so forth could have been for ritual purposes, or they could have been signs of status, perhaps worn over one's daily clothing—or not, in the case of ceremonial use. Indeed, they might have been imagined, as with the halos depicted on icons of saints. What they do suggest is that such apparel was a woman thing, not worn by males, and that it served to immortalize at some great effort the fact that such apparel set women (or at least certain women) apart in a social category of their own. Much of the woven material from this period that was found imprinted on ceramic fragments is as finely done as anything done

later in the Bronze and Iron Ages, and equal to much of the thin cotton and linen garments worn today. Given the amount of effort involved in weaving such cloth and also in carving a replica of it in stone, one can reasonably conclude that the pieces of apparel found on so many of the Gravettian Venuses were symbols of achievement, or prestige. And it is also fair to say that, for those who were weavers or ceramicists, the workaday world was more complex, the daily round of chores, tasks, and roles more intense. Who were they?

The precision with which the carvers of the Venuses represented woven items leads almost inevitably to the conclusion that they were created by the weavers themselves, or at least under the sharp-eyed tutelage of the weavers. That it was almost surely women who did most of this fine weaving and basketry is one matter to which the ethnographic record appears to be a reliable guide.

# Inca Gender Relations, from Household to Empire

## R. Alan Covey

In 1528, a ship full of Spanish conquistadors dropped anchor off Tumbez, an Inca city on the Pacific coast of what is today northern Peru. A Greek gunner named Pedro de Candía went ashore to parlay with the lord of the place. On his return, he brought with him Inca gifts of food—and an account of a city full of gold and silver, as well as a monastery housing beautiful, amorous women who had begged their ruler to meet him. A later chronicler captured the mood of the sailors cooped up aboard the Spanish vessel: "they were crazy with pleasure to hear such things, and hoped to God to enjoy their part" (Herrera y Tordesillas 1601, *Decada* III, Book 10, Chapter 5).

Such was the situation in the early years of the Spanish conquest of the Inca empire, the greatest native civilization to develop in the Americas (Hemming 1970). As expeditions of European males penetrated the Andean world, lured by riches and adventure, they took from native communities what they needed and desired—food from storehouses, llamas from local herds, children to serve as interpreters, and women for their domestic and sexual service. These men were not careful in their actions or observations, but their accounts—and those of adventurers, priests, and administrators who came after them—serve as our key evidence for

the organization of sex and gender in the Inca empire. (It was not until about seventy years later that native Andean writers began to record detailed descriptions of life in the time of their parents and grandparents.)

This chapter explores the construction of gender in Inca society, which differed significantly from practices in early modern Spain (for a general introduction to the Incas, see D'Altroy 2002). The complementary roles of men and women contrast with more patriarchal arrangements in Christian societies of early modern Europe, and the powerful status of noble Andean women has been cited as a challenge to long-held theoretical expectations regarding the role of women in states (Silverblatt 1988). We will begin by discussing the place of gender in the Inca life cycle, and then look beyond the family to consider how the Inca state constructed gender in elite life and imperial administration. In closing, a brief look at the status of Andean women under Spanish rule provides an important contrast to Inca gender practices.

### INCA GENDER AND LIFE CYCLE

The Incas did not use writing before the Spanish conquest, but Colonial documents and dictionaries make it possible to get a sense of how they distinguished a human (*runa* in the Quechua language) from other living

Covey, R. Alan. 2013. Inca Gender Relations, from *Household to Empire*. Pearson.

**Table 2.1  Inca Age and Gende r Categories, Based on Colonial Quechua Dictionaries**

| AGE | CONNOTATION OF LIFE STAGE | FEMALE TERM | MALE TERM |
|---|---|---|---|
| <3 | Conception | Wawa | Wawa |
| 3–7 | Ignorance (not speaking) | Warma | Warma |
| 7–14 | Development | Thaski (or P'asña) | Maqt'a |
| 14–20 | Folly (sexually active) | Sipas (unmarried) | Wayna (unmarried) |
| 20+ | Maturity (body and mind) | Warmi | Qhari |
| 70 | Infirmity | Paya | Machu |
| 90 | Decrepitude | Ruku | Ruku |

things, and how they made more specific designations of sex and gender based on a person's age, physical development, social status, and personal qualities. Table 2.1 is developed from the early Colonial Quechua dictionaries of the priests Domingo de Santo Tomás (1560) and Diego González Holguín (1608), and it shows the place of gender in the Inca life cycle (chroniclers such as Santillán 1968 [1563] and Guaman Poma de Ayala 1980 [1615] offer alternative formulations of this).

### Becoming Human and Acquiring Gender

At birth, male and female infants were called *wawa*, a term also employed for newborn animals (like puppies or kittens), regardless of their sex. Babies were not considered fully human, and in a world where infant mortality was high, social investments were not made until they had survived for two or three years. At that time, the relatives of an Inca couple assembled for a ritual called *rutuchikuy*, a first haircutting in which the parents named the infant and formally introduced its extended family—the people with whom the child would eventually share life's labors, and who as kin could not be marriage partners. The family selected a day for the ceremony and notified the relatives of the child's mother and father (known as *kaka* and *masa*, respectively). Festivities began with drinking and dancing, after which members of the child's extended family stood up and made gifts of cloth, wool, and herd animals for the child. Each participant clipped a tuft of the child's hair, and the father ended the ceremony by shearing the hair that remained, inviting the assembled guests to resume their dancing (e.g., Salomon and Urioste 1991 [17th c.]: 151–153).

The *rutuchikuy* ritual probably marked the transition from *wawa* to *warma*, a gender-neutral term applied to a human child who had not fully developed language. Terms related to this stage link early childhood with ignorance, inexperience, and lack of reason, a condition that a child would overcome in time. Growing out of ignorance involved growing into gender roles and kin relationships—learning the terms of reference

for relatives and the proper behavior associated with family and other community members. For example, a boy would learn to call his brother *wawki* and his sister *pana*, while a girl would refer to her brother and sister as *tura* and *ñaña*, respectively. Gender involved learning one's social identity, and it was reinforced by giving children gender-specific tasks as they became capable of carrying them out. The assignment of gender seems to have been based not on a formal ritual, but rather on processes of individual development. By around age seven, Inca girls and boys were known by gender-specific terms (*thaski* and *maqt'a*, respectively).

### Celebrations of Maturity

Inca families marked the transition from childhood to adulthood with ceremonies where extended families gathered to celebrate the onset of sexual maturity. For boys, the annual *warachikuy* was a communal rite of passage involving fasting, feats of strength, dances, and family ceremonies in which the cohort of initiates was given new clothing and encouraged to behave properly as *wayna*, or young unmarried men (Betanzos 1996 [1550s] Part 1, Chapter 14; Molina 1989 [1575]: 111–114). Noble Inca youths had their ears pierced at this time as a symbol of their elevated social status. A girl's journey toward adulthood was more personalized based on the onset of menses, which was also marked by family celebrations (called *qikuchikuy*) as she came to be recognized as *sipas*, a young unmarried woman. A young woman went into seclusion and fasted through her first menstruation, and when she emerged, her family assembled to give her a new name, adult clothing, gifts, and advice on living appropriately as a woman (Molina 1989 [1575]: 119–120).

The Colonial dictionaries describe young adulthood as the flowering of life, a period where an individual enjoyed sexual maturity without the full responsibilities of adulthood. Dictionary entries also include terms for older men who comport themselves in the sin and folly of youth, not wishing to develop beyond this stage. This reflects the fact that sexual maturity was not the ultimate expression of gender development in Inca society—unmarried men and women in their twenties and thirties were described as "ripe" for serious thought and labor, but retained a youthful status. Only by marrying and assuming the status of husband (*qhari* or *qosa*) and wife (*warmi*) did a man and a woman truly realize their human potential. Outside of Inca mass, weddings held at imperial administrative centers (see Gender and Power among the Inca Nobility), marriages among commoners typically involved simple ceremonial acts—gifts between the families involved, or processions between houses (e.g., Cobo 1990 [1653]: Book 2, Chapter 7)—but marriage had the effect of creating a new household and articulating a new kin network that defined labor obligations and incest taboos for the next generation. Building the house itself drew on the labor and experience of a couple's relatives, just as preparing and farming agricultural land required participation in reciprocal labor networks. As Inca couples contributed their work to meet the expectations of family, community, and state, they engaged in daily practices that replicated creation and enculturation of their lands, homes, and offspring.

It is important to note that while the ideal Inca household was a male–female pair, there was much diversity across the empire. Some men were allowed to marry multiple wives, while others were not granted permission to wed. Unmarried men and women typically remained in their parents' home and provided work for the community, which probably included cultivating special fields to help widows and widowers maintain their households. It is clear that gender traits varied based on personal qualities and development, and the dictionaries list terms for those who are precocious or slow in arriving at new stages in the life cycle (e.g., *waynay sunqu warma*: "child with a young man's heart"). Terms for masculine women (*qharisunqu warmi*) and effeminate men (*warmihina*) suggest that some gendered qualities could be found among both sexes.

The Colonial documents do not deal with the issue of sexual orientation sensitively, but it appears that sexual activity—heterosexual and homosexual—was a far less important social issue than unsanctioned reproduction. Some chronicles describe adultery as a capital offense and treat the birth of illegitimate children as a serious moral lapse, but they seem less concerned with the sex act than with fidelity to one's marriage partner. Early Quechua dictionaries include a verb (*yanazay*) for female–female sexual intimacy, but references to male homosexuality are harder to identify. Spanish discussions of "sodomy" in the Andes are difficult to take at face value. Not only was homosexuality a capital offense in Spain at this time, but it was also included among a class of acts of "savagery" (along with idolatry and cannibalism) that justified enslaving indigenous peoples (Adorno 2007: 102; Kamen 1997: 267–269). Allegations of homosexuality thus served as a potent political device for justifying the Spanish conquest, while writers defending the Incas as a well-governed civilization assert intolerance toward such practices.

### Decline of Humanity and Gender

To Quechua speakers, adulthood was not seen as enduring, but rather as something that was exhausted over time. The gender terms for old age reflect this concept, and men and women surviving to old age were seen as losing their humanity and sexuality. The terms for "old man/old woman" (*machu/paya*) are gendered, but they are used not just to refer to old humans, but to old plants and animals as well. The term for extreme old age (*ruku*) is ungendered and often linked to terms of physical and mental decline. The loss of humanity and gender in these final life stages mirrors the terms used in childhood and infancy, and indigenous chronicles suggest that it was the gradual loss of sexual vitality, physical stamina, and intellectual capacity that signaled the transition from full adulthood to old age.

## GENDER RELATIONS IN ORDINARY HOUSEHOLDS

Inca creation stories often involve male–female pairs emerging onto a wild landscape and conquering it to establish houses, fields, and sacred spaces. In the villages of Andean herders and farmers, marriage reproduced the essence of creation, uniting the qualities of male and female into a single unit capable of managing the life cycles of crops, herd animals, and a household's human offspring. Male and female complemented each other, and many of the most important human activities were normally accomplished only with the participation of both genders. Work teams of men and women transformed barren land into fertile agricultural soil, and they labored together in planting and harvest activities.

While male and female cooperation was essential for domestic life, certain spaces and activities were gendered. Cloth production was generally a woman's domain, as was the transformation of food through cooking and brewing. Warfare and hunting were typically considered masculine pursuits. As we will discuss in more detail below, Inca rule influenced these gendered activities—women were required to spin and weave as a tributary activity, while men were pressed into military service, and prohibited from hunting without Inca permission. Children learned appropriate gender roles from their parents, who exercised authority over the household. Beyond the domestic realm, parental terms were also used to express hierarchical social arrangements—the terms for father (*yaya*) and mother (*mama*) could be used to mean "lord/lady" or "master/mistress," or to indicate patronage. This suggests that the Inca nobility and other Andean elites promoted themselves as parental figures responsible for the well-being of their clans and polities. These terms are distinct from those used for Inca imperial political hierarchies.

## GENDER AND POWER AMONG THE INCA NOBILITY

Every August, noble Inca men and women gathered at a place called Collcampata, a ceremonial agricultural field preserved in Cuzco, the imperial capital. Dressed in royal finery and singing songs of praise to the Sun and their royal ancestors, male–female pairs broke the earth where the founding Inca couple, Manco Capac and Mama Ocllo, had first grown maize at the end of their mythical journey to settle and civilize a homeland. Working as a team, the Inca men used a foot-plow (*chakitaqlla*) to excavate large clods of earth, while their female counterparts worked opposite them to turn the earth by hand, killing the wild vegetation and preparing an agricultural soil suitable for cultivation (Garcilaso de la Vega 1966 [1609]: Part 1, Book 5, Chapter 2).

This ceremony kicked off the maize-growing cycle in the imperial heartland, and Inca nobles played central roles that reflect the same gender balance seen in commoner households. In this and other ceremonial acts, Inca noble families also drew on mythological concepts of creation and civilization. Like their founding ancestors, royal Inca men and women created households through marriage and the establishment of the *panaqa* (from *pana*, a brother's term for his sister), or royal lineage. During their lifetimes, Inca rulers and their principal wives (*piwiwarmi*, or *quya*) received labor service through kin obligations and tribute, which they invested in improving farmlands and country estates around Cuzco, the imperial capital. After the royal couple died, their mummies remained the titular owners of the estate, which was used to support their descendants, except for the succeeding ruler and his wife, who developed their own estates. (The first Spaniards to reach Cuzco were surprised to see mummified lords and ladies brought out for public ceremonies, where their descendants offered them food and drink and consulted them on important decisions.) The Inca dynasty was thus a series of male–female founding pairs who created new resources and dwellings for their descendants, just as they claimed their ancestors had done since the time of creation.

Colonial writers record some important changes in royal Inca marriage practices and estate construction (Covey 2006). Table 2.2 lists the royal lineages as recorded in 1572, and reflects a shift from local to regional marriage alliances in the middle of the dynasty, which roughly coincides with the beginning of construction of country estates. As the Incas began to expand as an empire (traditionally in the early 1400s under Pachacutic Inca Yupanqui, the ninth ruler), a shift to sibling marriage—or at least a marriage where the principal wife was considered to be the ruler's full sister—was probably intended to clarify succession among the nobility at a time when rulers had numerous wives and consorts and hundreds of children. There are several

**Table 2.2 Inca Royal Couples, Lineages, Marriage Patterns, and Estate Development**

| INCA RULER | PRINCIPAL WIFE* | PANAQA | MARRIAGE TYPE | RURAL ESTATE |
|---|---|---|---|---|
| Manco Capac | Mama Ocllo | Chima | Sibling | No |
| Sinchi Roca | Mama Coca | Raura | Local | No |
| Lloque Yupanqui | Mama Cava | Avayni | Local | No |
| Mayta Capac | Mama Taucaray | Usca Mayta | Local | No |
| Capac Yupanqui | Curi Hilpay | Apu Mayta | Regional | No |
| Inca Rocca | Mama Micay | Vicaquirao | Regional | Yes |
| Yahuar Huaccac | Mama Chicya | Aucaylli | Regional | Yes |
| Viracocha Inca | Mama Rondocaya | Socso | Regional | Yes |
| Pachacutic Inca Yupanqui | Mama Anaguarqui | Inaca | Sibling | Yes |
| Tupa Inca Yupanqui | Mama Ocllo | Capac | Sibling | Yes |
| Huayna Capac | Araua Ocllo | Tomebamba | Sibling | Yes |

*Based on the chronicler Pedro Sarmiento de Gamboa [1572]. There is variation among writers.

writers who allude to the power that Inca women had to assemble a faction of their noble relatives to support a son as the claimant to the throne.

Elite women exercised power in local societies and noble households across the Andes. In the Inca realm, the power of kinship did not commonly translate into political power—it is clear that most offices of the imperial administrative hierarchy (*kuraka*) were staffed by men, although women were at times permitted to succeed in these positions if an able male relative was not available. Some sources mention female rulers in coastal societies, and they identify Inca wives and consorts at times as possessing *kuraka* titles corresponding to several thousand households. For example, Bernabé Cobo (1979 [1653]: Book 2, Chapter 15) recounts a story of the female ruler of the kingdom of Huarco, who refused to submit to a tributary inspection by a male Inca official. The Inca queen took charge of the situation, and instead of resorting to warfare, she relied on female ritual power to prevail. She tricked the rival queen into staging a ceremony for Mamacocha (Mother Ocean), and while the people of Huarco were on rafts in the ocean carrying out the ritual she sent inspectors and soldiers into their capital. The ruler of Huarco was captured without a fight and turned over to the Inca queen.

Such a case was not typical in imperial administration. Women were more influential in negotiating the politics of kinship among the imperial elite than they were in the bureaucratic management of the empire. Likewise, leadership in the imperial army was strongly linked to Inca men, even though there are several accounts of female warriors who might be described as military commanders. Military prowess was a male-gendered trait, and individual distinction in physical competitions and violent conflict was a key way for Inca men to set themselves apart from their peers. Having observed the masculine quality of battle, we should take note that the Incas designated both men and women for military service. Men may have done most of the fighting, but their wives often traveled with them and were undoubtedly essential for managing the logistics of the campaign (Murra 1986).

One example of this comes from an account of the first Inca imperial campaign, which does not mention women fighting, but women's work figures prominently in the celebration of victory in the field. Captives from the defeated Sora tribe were first humiliated by having red fringes woven and attached to their clothing as a mark of their conquest, and they were then drenched with maize flour and beer (*aqha*) to shame them further. When this was done, noble Inca women came forth to sing songs glorifying the Inca ruler (Betanzos 1996 [1550s]: Part 1, Chapter 19). Other colonial writers refer to such praise-songs (*taquies*), describing them as public performances of the Inca past that were strongly linked to women. Men may have won the battle, but women were essential to enshrine it in Inca memory.

## INCA IMPERIAL MANIPULATION OF MARRIAGE AND REPRODUCTION

With the household as the principal unit of tribute and a vital point of intersecting rural kin networks, it is not surprising that the Inca state took great interest in managing sexuality, gender, and marriage among its subjects. The growing empire wanted as many households as possible providing labor service for state projects, but at the same time it desired to limit the local power of marriage alliances. Several colonial writers say that Inca rulers intervened with marriage practices in provincial regions, sending officials to preside over mass marriages in the central plazas of administrative centers, and dictating which men could take multiple wives (and by extension, which men would never be permitted to create a household). The central institution aimed at the imperial restructuring of local marriage and reproduction was the *aqllawasi*, the "House of the Chosen" (see Silverblatt 1987).

The *aqllawasi* was first and foremost a repository of young women who were selected from provincial populations ("*aqllay*" means "to select or set apart"). According to several sources, girls were chosen before reaching the status of *sipas*—that is to say, they were removed from their homes after the point where they had a gender identity (*thaski* or *p'asña*) and before they were sexually mature. Selection honored provincial families and was based on a girl's beauty and nobility. Once chosen, a girl was taken into the restricted *aqllawasi* compound at the nearest Inca provincial center, where she received instruction from adult women (*mamakuna*, "matrons, mothers") who were full-time residents and instructors of the complex. Girls learned to spin wool into yarn, to weave cloth, to brew maize beer for state celebrations, and other female-gendered activities. In essence, the *mamakuna* replaced the girls' mothers and taught them to be women—following the Inca state style—while restricting their sexual activity and keeping them from marrying.

At the end of a few years' time, most of the young women were taken from the *aqllawasi* by an Inca official and married off to approved provincial men. The most noble and able of the initiates were sent to Cuzco for additional training in religious rituals and fine cloth production. In time, they became *mamakuna*, and were assigned to ritual duties, instruction in a provincial *aqllawasi*, or marriage to high-ranking men. It is important to recognize that the Incas did not have a corresponding gendered instruction for boys (although some sources state that provincial nobles sent their sons to the royal palace, where they were taught Inca ways and essentially held as hostages to guarantee their parents' cooperation). The *aqllawasi* was designed so that important ritual, economic, and stylistic knowledge was controlled by Inca women. Where men staffed the bulk of the administrative positions that managed labor across the empire, women held many of the most visible positions undergirding the ritual economy. These were complementary and necessary for imperial administration to function. While a hierarchy of male *kurakas* supervised the organization of labor to grow, transport, and store maize, female officials enacted the transformation of that maize into beer that was fundamental to the festive state reciprocation of labor service. Male priests played an important role in some aspects of Inca ritual, but the *aqllawasi* was a key imperial institution said to be off-limits to all but the Inca ruler himself.

## INCA GENDER AND THE SPANISH CONQUEST

Although Francisco Pizarro and his band of adventurers did not appreciate it at the time, their invasion and conquest of the Inca empire was made possible in part because of the gendered practices of noble families and the administrative hierarchy. In the years prior to the first Spanish expeditions, marriage alliances among the Inca nobility encouraged factionalism that ultimately boiled over into all-out civil war, fracturing imperial order and creating fissures that weakened resistance to invasion. The Spaniards exploited these divisions, finding indigenous allies eager to settle scores with rival factions or to be free from the yoke of Inca rule. As Pizarro's expedition advanced into the Andean highlands to capture the Inca ruler, the Inca imperial manipulation of household and gender in provincial regions aided the invaders in practical ways. The Spaniards and their native allies were able to take supplies from stores of food and cloth from storehouses at way stations along the Inca highway, and women from the *aqllawasi* provided them with food and drink in administrative centers.

Inca women bridged the divide between Spaniard and Andean in the 1530s and after, and the Pizarro brothers and their closest supporters robbed noble men of their wives, whom they took as mistresses until "proper" Spanish brides could be had. Leading Spaniards used these relationships to consolidate their control over lands and labor that had formerly belonged to royal Inca dynasties (Varon Gabai 1997). Noble Inca women continued to promote their children and

represent their families in the early decades of colonial rule, just as they had at the royal Inca court. For example, in the 1550s, the princess Beatriz Huayllas Ñusta coordinated diplomatic negotiations between Spanish emissaries (including her son by a Spanish conquistador) and her nephew, Sayre Tupa, who ruled an independent jungle kingdom that resisted conquest until 1572. Among the Inca families that accommodated themselves to Spanish rule, Angelina Yupanqui introduced her male relatives to her husband, Juan de Betanzos, who wrote a detailed chronicle casting the family as the legitimate heirs to the Inca dynasty. Decades after the conquest, noble Inca women still owned royal estate lands, managed the labor of Inca-era retainers (called *yanakuna*), and received incomes from the production of coca leaf on lands that had formerly belonged to royal couples.

## RE-GENDERING THE INCAS

As Spanish colonial rule developed in Inca territory during the sixteenth and seventeenth centuries, the status of Andean women was diminished (Silverblatt 1987). Spanish tribute levies (*tasas*) focused not on households, but on males aged 18–50 (Cook 1975 [1570s]), and women were excluded from legal proceedings and higher political offices. Women retained their rights to personal property, but had to rely on men to represent them. As living Andean women saw their status decline, the male writers recording Inca history imposed a similar fate on the Inca women of the past. Over time, chroniclers recast Inca gender relations into a more unequal and patriarchal model, despite written evidence of gender complementarity and women's power in earlier sources. By 1653, the Jesuit priest Bernabé Cobo (1990: Book 2, Chapter 7, p. 204) described pre-conquest Inca households this way: "[A]mong these people the women were so subjugated to their husbands and obliged to serve them that even if there were many of them [multiple wives], it made no difference, nor did they dare to do anything other than what they were ordered to do. The women performed the household duties, and in addition, they worked outdoors, in the cultivation, sowing, and caring for their *chacaras* or fields, building their houses, and carrying loads, while their husbands traveled, both in times of peace and war." Cobo probably developed this description by observing gender inequality in contemporary Andean households and assuming that indigenous practices had not changed since Inca times (Rowe 1990: ix).

The colonial stratification of Inca gender has influenced contemporary scholarship, encouraging a focus on life histories of male rulers as heroic figures who single-handedly built Inca civilization. In recent years, feminist scholars have returned to the chronicles to try and correct the modern construction of Inca gender. Archaeology has also begun to play a role in considering the way gender structured how ordinary people lived in Inca times. Excavations of Inca households show gendered differences in labor and diet, while well-preserved burials offer exciting new evidence regarding the economic, social, and religious roles of Inca men and women. As archaeologists and historians collect new evidence and work through old accounts more sensitively, new perspectives on Inca gender provide important contrasts, not just for academics, but for men and women living in contemporary nation-states.

## REFERENCES

Adorno, Rolena. 2007. *The Polemics of Possession in Spanish American Narrative.* New Haven, CT: Yale University Press.

Betanzos, Juan de. 1996 [1550s]. *Narrative of the Incas.* Translated and edited by Roland Hamilton. Austin: University of Texas Press.

Cobo, Bernabé. 1979 [1653]. *History of the Inca Empire.* Translated and edited by Roland Hamilton. Austin: University of Texas Press.

Cobo, Bernabé. 1990 [1653]. *Inca Religion and Customs.* Translated and edited by Roland Hamilton. Austin: University of Texas Press.

Cook, Noble David (ed.). 1975 [1570s]. *Tasa de la visita general de Francisco de Toledo.* Lima: Universidad Nacional Mayor San Marcos.

Covey, R. Alan. 2006. *How the Incas Built Their Heartland: State Formation and the Innovation of Imperial Strategies in the Sacred Valley, Peru.* Ann Arbor: University of Michigan Press.

D'Altroy, Terence N. 2002. *The Incas.* New York: Blackwell.

Garcilaso de la Vega, "El Inca". 1966 [1609]. *Royal Commentaries of the Incas and General History of Peru.* Translated by Harold V. Livermore.

Guaman Poma de Ayala, Felipe. 1980 [1615]. *Nueva corónica y Buen gobierno* (3 volumes). Mexico City: Fondo de Cultura Económica.

González Holguín, Diego. 1989 [1608]. *Vocabulario de la lengua general de todo el Perú, llamada lengua Qquichua o del Inca.* Lima: Universidad Nacional Mayor de San Marcos.

Hemming, John. 1970. *The Conquest of the Incas.* New York: Harvest.

Herrera y Tordesillas, Antonio de. 1601. *Historia general de los hechos de los castellanos en las islas y tierra firme del mar oceano . . .*

Kamen, Henry. 1997. *The Spanish Inquisition: A Historical Revision.* New Haven, CT: Yale University Press.

Molina, Cristóbal de. 1989 [1575]. "Relación de las fábulas y ritos de los Incas." In H. Urbano and P. Duviols (eds.). *Fábulas y ritos de los Incas,* pp. 47–134. Madrid: Historia 16.

Murra, John V. 1986. "The Expansion of the Inka State: Armies, War, and Rebellions." In J. V. Murra, N. Wachtel, and J. Revel (eds.). *Anthropological History of Andean Polities,* pp. 49–58. Cambridge: Cambridge University Press.

Rowe, John Howland. 1990. "Foreword." In Roland Hamilton (ed.). *Inca Religion and Customs, by Father Bernabé Cobo,* pp. vii–ix. Austin: University of Texas Press.

Salomon, Frank, and George L. Urioste (tr.). 1991 [17th c.]. *The Huarochirí Manuscript: A Testament of Ancient and Colonial Andean Religion.* Austin: University of Texas Press.

Santillán, Hernando de. 1968 [1563]. *Relación del orígen, descendencia, política y gobierno de los incas.* Biblioteca de Autores Españoles vol. 135, pp. 193–297. Madrid: Ediciones Atlas.

Santo Tomás, Domingo de. 1951 [1560]. *Lexicon, o vocabulario de la lengua general del Perú.* Facsimile edition of R. Porras Barrenechea. Lima: Instituto de Historia.

Sarmiento de Gamboa, Pedro. 2007 [1572]. *The History of the Incas.* Translated by Brian S. Bauer and Vania Smith. Austin: University of Texas Press.

Silverblatt, Irene. 1987. *Moon, Sun, and Witches: Gender Ideologies and Class in Inca and Colonial Peru.* Princeton, NJ: Princeton University Press.

Silverblatt, Irene. 1988. "Women in States." *Annual Review of Anthropology* 17: 427–460.

Varon Gabai, Rafael. 1997. *Francisco Pizarro and His Brothers: The Illusion of Power in Sixteenth-Century Peru.* Translated by Javier Flores Espinoza. Norman: University of Oklahoma Press.

# III

# *Domestic Worlds and Public Worlds*

In 1974, in an attempt to document a universal subordination of women, Michelle Rosaldo (1974: 18) proposed a paradigm relating "recurrent aspects of psychology and cultural and social organization to an opposition between the 'domestic' orientation of women and the extradomestic or 'public' ties, that, in most societies, are primarily available to men." As scholarship devoted to an understanding of gender issues has evolved, the influential domestic–public model has been the focus of considerable controversy, revolving around three related issues: whether male domination is universal, whether male domination is explained by the domestic–public dichotomy, and whether—and under what conditions—the concept of domestic–public has relevance.

The domestic–public model led Rosaldo to suggest that women's status is highest in societies in which the public and domestic spheres are only weakly differentiated, as among the Mbuti pygmies. In contrast, "women's status will be lowest in those societies where there is a firm differentiation between domestic and public spheres of activity and where women are isolated from one another and placed under a single man's authority, in the home. Their position is raised when they can challenge those claims to authority . . ." (Rosaldo 1974: 36). According to this argument, women may enhance their status by creating a public world of their own or by entering the men's world. In addition, the most egalitarian societies will be those in which men participate in the domestic domain.

Correspondingly, writing in the same volume (Rosaldo and Lamphere 1974), Sanday (1974) suggested that women's involvement in domains of activity such as subsistence or defense may be curtailed because of their time and energy commitment to reproduction and mothering. Men, on the other hand, are free to form broader associations in the political, economic, and military spheres that transcend the mother–child unit. While the linkage of women with the domestic and men with the public domains may imply a biological determinism based on women's reproductive roles, Rosaldo (1974: 24) argued that the opposition between domestic and public orientations is an intelligible but not a necessary arrangement.

One aspect of women's domestic responsibilities is that it is women who primarily raise children. Nancy Chodorow (1974) developed a theory linking adult sex role behavior to the fact that children's early involvement is with their female parent. Chodorow contended that girls are integrated through ties with female kin into the world of domestic work. Age, rather than achievement, may define their status, while boys must "learn" to be men. Unlike girls, boys have few responsibilities in childhood and are free to establish peer groups that create "public" ties. To become an adult male, a boy is often obliged to dissociate himself from the home and from female kin. According to Rosaldo (1974: 26), "the fact that children virtually everywhere grow up with their mothers may well account for characteristic differences in male and female psychologies" as well as set the stage for adult organization of activities.

In this book, Louise Lamphere reviews the formulation of the domestic–public model, and discusses the subsequent critiques of its validity and applicability. Rosaldo herself, rethinking her original position, said that although male dominance appears widespread, it does not "in actual behavioral terms assume a universal content or a universal shape. On the contrary, women typically have power and influence in political and economic life, display autonomy from men in their pursuits, and rarely find themselves confronted or constrained by what might seem the brute fact of male strength" (1980: 394). Although the domestic–public opposition has been compelling, Rosaldo suggested that the model assumes too much rather than helping to illuminate and explain.

As Lamphere observes, it has become increasingly clear that the domestic–public opposition is the heir to nineteenth-century social theory rooted in a dichotomy contrasting home and woman, with a public world of men, and reflecting an understanding of political rights based on sex. The domestic–public dichotomy emerged from the industrial revolution and the separation of home and workplace. Conceptualizing social life as dichotomized into domestic and public domains does not make sense in societies in which management of production occurs within the household and in which household production itself involves the management of the "public" economy (Leacock 1978: 253).

In his analysis of fatherhood in the United States, Nicholas W. Townsend (in this book) contends that in the United States, an industrialized society, it is often assumed that parenting represents a simple division of labor in which men are engaged in the public sphere of paid labor and politics, while women are involved in the domestic sphere of childcare and reproduction. His research demonstrates, however, that the domestic and public spheres interpenetrate and that arrangements made in one sphere influence behavior in another. Parenting, he argues, is deeply gendered. This means not only that fathers and mothers "do" different things, but that fatherhood has different meanings for men and women. Men interviewed in his research claimed to want greater involvement as fathers than their own fathers had experienced. They saw "marriage and children" as a package deal; for these men, a relationship with a woman was necessary for a man to see himself as a father. Correspondingly, Townsend shows that women are often influential in men's decisions about when to have children. Women are the "default parent" while men are in a more "optional" position with their role as disciplinarian or "fun dad" shaped by the interests of their children's mother. Thus women, as wives and mothers, mediate and facilitate fatherhood. Moreover, the structural division of labor placing men in the labor force and women at home has been maintained by strong cultural themes that continue to emphasize women's involvement in their children's lives, even with women's increasing labor force participation.

Townsend shows that in the United States, an ideological association of men with the public and women with the domestic does not accurately represent the interpenetration of these spheres. Similarly, in Andalusia, in southern Spain, women are ideologically associated with the home, and men with public places, yet the reality is more complex (Driessen 1983). According to widely held ideals, the woman should be virtuous, docile, and devoted to husband and children; the ideal man is the head of the household, tough, but seldom at home. However, in actuality, the involvement of men in the private sphere and women in the public sphere varies according to social class. Among agricultural laborers, women's labor is critical to the household economy. It is common for women to be employed, while their men are unemployed. This contradiction produces tensions that are reflected in men's sociability patterns. The bar offers men the opportunity to display their masculinity by heavy drinking and sexual banter. Men's sociability is best understood as a response to the vulnerability of unemployed men to women who contribute substantially to the family income through wage labor. This results in blurred idealized distinctions between male and female identities and responsibilities.

Research on the public–private distinction has implications for the interplay among gender, status, and power. Whereas traditional conceptions of power emphasized formal political behavior and authority associated with a status conferring the "right" to impose sanctions (Lamphere 1974: 99), informal power strategies such as manipulation and maneuvering are also important aspects of political activity. Cynthia Nelson (1974) examined the concept of power, focusing on images of women and power in the domestic and public domains in the societies of the Middle East. Ethnographies of this region have commonly differentiated two social worlds, a woman's private world and a man's public world. Women's concerns are domestic, men's political. Nelson argues that the assignment of private and public reflects the imposition of western cultural categories on the Middle East; the meaning of power is influenced by these categorizations, as well as by the limitations of data obtained by male ethnographers from male informants.

This is a point made forcefully by Annette Weiner (1976) in her reanalysis of Trobriand exchange. She argues that "we unquestioningly accept male statements about women as factual evidence for the way a society is structured. . . . Any study that does not include the role of women—as seen by women—as part of the way the society is structured remains only a partial study of that society. Whether women are publicly valued or privately secluded, whether they control politics, a range of economic commodities, or merely magic spells, they function within that society, not as objects, but as individuals with some measure of control" (228).

Similarly, Nelson argues that by asking such questions as "How do women influence men?" "Who controls whom about what?" "How is control exercised?" it becomes apparent that women exercise a greater degree of power in social life than is often appreciated. In addition, she challenges the idea that the social worlds of men and women are reducible to private and public domains, with power limited to the public arena. Nelson's review of ethnographies addressing the role and position of women in Middle Eastern society indicates that women play a crucial role as structural links between kinship groups in societies in which family and kinship are fundamental institutions. Women are in a position to influence men through ritual means, to channel information to male kin, and to influence decision making about alliances; consequently, women do participate in "public" activities, and women's exclusive solidarity groups exercise considerable social control and political influence. The conceptions of power as defined by the Western observer are particularly challenged by literature on women written by women who offer multiple perspectives on the experiences of Middle Eastern women, derived from the actors themselves.

Brenner (1995) also questions the value of totalizing models of gender-based power and prestige in her study of gender ideologies in Java. Her analysis critiques the stereotyped, male-centered visions of male power pervasive in Javanese cultural representations and in ethnographic accounts. The ethnographic record has emphasized male-focused gender ideologies while neglecting alternative conceptions of gender voiced by women. She shows that the home and market, both associated with women in Javanese thought, are not only sites of economic production, but also sites where conflicting understandings of male and female nature are symbolically negotiated. According to the gendered division of domestic power, the wife should defer to her husband as head of the household but in reality, women's power may far outweigh that of their husbands. Moreover, the dominance of women in the household is often linked to economic power within and outside the home. Yet in spite of their economic power, central ideologies devalue women precisely because of their commercial pursuits, which are held to detract from prestige. This analysis suggests that although women are identified with the domestic, their activities are central to the production of the family's status in the broader society.

Drawing on research that explores how gender and sexuality differ in two locations of a transnational Mexican community, Hirsch (in this book) addresses questions central to the emergence, reformulation, and lived experience of the domestic/public dichotomy. She assesses this opposition both as an analytic tool and as a cultural construct that shapes people's own understandings of their social worlds. For her research populations in Mexico and in the United States, domestic/public is a salient distinction—a foundational principle of the gendered organization of space. She argues that this distinction predates the separation of the productive and reproductive domains, and the spread of wage labor (thus providing an intriguing contrast to Lamphere's discussion).

In her chapter, she uses the domestic/public dichotomy to consider how marital ideals and practices are changing across time and space; she proposes that space itself is constitutive of gender. Accordingly, the social organization of space is central to understanding gender in any society. Discourses on gender and sexuality serve as measures of modernity, and have a clear spatial dimension. Changes in the gendered division of labor and its meanings in both contexts have contributed to a new marital ideal, that of "intimacy," or *confianza*. Comparing two generations of women in each field setting, she shows that marital sexuality has been transformed from a means to produce social relations via reproduction, to a way to produce intimate conjugal ties. Sexual intimacy is potentially a resource and a goal figuring into marital negotiations. The domestic/public construct and the concept of a gendered sexual geography illuminate the changing dynamics of marriage in this Mexican transnational community.

On the surface, the domestic/public model as initially proposed by Michelle Rosaldo (1974, 1980) provides a compelling analytic framework for understanding married women's increased risk for HIV infection in Uganda. Men's mobility in the public sphere and access to resources provide them opportunities for extramarital trysts, while wives' responsibilities that tie them to the domestic sphere impede their ability (and perhaps their desire) to detect these infidelities and to take action. However, drawing on life histories from three generational cohorts in Uganda, Parikh (in this book) chronicles the transformation of men's extramarital liaisons from private, family concerns to matters of public critique that blur the boundaries of the domestic/public. This transformation has been occasioned by shifts in the economy, gender equality campaigns, and the proliferation of discourses that have made sexuality a primary concern of public health and public morality regulation and surveillance.

Parikh's historical perspective demonstrates that while respectable middle-class women were expected to maintain the reputations of their marriages by not airing grievance publicly, in some cases women strategically disrupt the boundaries between private (marital affairs) and public (reputations of spouses) to pursue their own interests. In particular contexts, it is strategic for women to "go public" with decidedly private matters in order to gain sympathies from neighbors, shame their husbands and, importantly, present themselves as modern rational actors who protect themselves from the risk of HIV infection. This chapter brings new insight into the ongoing debates about the usefulness of the public/private model by highlighting how public health and other interventions have worked to transform male infidelity from an intimate issue relevant to spouses and families—into a matter of broader public concern with paradoxical implications.

Assuming the universality of dichotomous domestic and public spheres constrains our exploration of gendered social space and the interconnections between home and workplace, marriage and community. As numerous scholars have argued, we need to move from assumptions of the shared experience of "women" to a critical analysis of the differences among them. Yet although there is now a consensus that public and private are not universal and timeless absolutes, these concepts remain powerful signifiers of how our social worlds are ordered (Davidoff 1995; Moore 1988). We continue to confront the challenges posed by the need to critically examine the relevance of the distinctions between domestic and public in particular historical moments and diverse social and economic conditions.

## REFERENCES

Brenner, Suzanna A. 1995. "Why Women Rule the Roost: Rethinking Javanese Ideologies of Gender and Self-Control." In Aihwa Ong and Michael Peletz (eds.). *Bewitching Women, Pious Men: Gender and Body Politics in Southeast Asia.* Berkeley: University of California Press.

Chodorow, Nancy. 1974. "Family Structure and Feminine Personality." In Michelle Z. Rosaldo and Louise Lamphere (eds.). *Woman, Culture, and Society,* pp. 43–67. Stanford, CA: Stanford University Press.

Davidoff, L. 1995. "Regarding Some 'Old Husbands' tales': Public and Private in Feminist History." In *Worlds Between: Historical Perspectives on Gender and Class,* pp. 227–275. Cambridge, UK: Polity Press.

Driessen, Henk. 1983. "Male Sociability and Rituals of Masculinity in Rural Andalusia." *Anthropological Quarterly* 56(3): 125–133.

Lamphere, Louise. 1974. "Strategies, Cooperation, and Conflict among Women in Domestic Groups." In Michelle Z. Rosaldo and Louise Lamphere (eds.). *Woman, Culture, and Society,* pp. 97–113. Stanford, CA: Stanford University Press.

Leacock, Eleanor. 1978. "Women's Status in Egalitarian Society. Implications for Social Evolution." *Current Anthropology* 19(2): 247–275.

Moore, Henrietta L. 1988. *Feminism and Anthropology.* Minneapolis: University of Minnesota Press.

Nelson, Cynthia. 1974. "Public and Private Politics: Women in the Middle Eastern World." *American Ethnologist* 1(3): 551–563.

Rosaldo, Michelle Z. 1974. "Theoretical Overview." In Michelle Z. Rosaldo and Louise Lamphere (eds.). *Woman, Culture, and Society,* pp. 17–43. Stanford, CA: Stanford University Press.

———. 1980. "The Use and Abuse of Anthropology: Reflections on Feminism and Cross-Cultural Understanding." *Signs* 5(3): 389–418.

Rosaldo, Michelle Zimbalist and Louise Lamphere (eds.). 1974. *Women, Culture & Society.* Stanford, CA: Stanford University Press.

Sanday, Peggy R. 1974. "Female Status in the Public Domain." In Michelle Z. Rosaldo and Louise Lamphere (eds.). *Woman, Culture, and Society,* pp. 189–207. Stanford, CA: Stanford University Press.

Weiner, Annette B. 1976. *Women of Value, Men of Renown: New Perspectives in Trobriand Exchange.* Austin: University of Texas Press.

# The Domestic Sphere of Women and the Public World of Men: The Strengths and Limitations of an Anthropological Dichotomy

## Louise Lamphere

Since 1974 there has been a burgeoning interest within anthropology in the study of women, sex roles, and gender. Anthropology has long been a discipline that contained important women (Elsie Clews Parsons, Ruth Benedict, and Margaret Mead among the most famous) and a field in which women have been studied as well (e.g., Kaberry 1939, 1952; Landes 1938, 1947; Leith-Ross 1939; Paulme 1963; Underhill 1936). However, with the publication of *Woman, Culture, and Society* (Rosaldo and Lamphere 1974) and *Toward an Anthropology of Women* (Reiter 1975a), women scholars, many of whom were identified as feminists, began to critique the androcentric bias in anthropology, to explore women's status in a wide variety of societies, and to provide explanatory models to understand women's position cross-culturally.

One of the most powerful and influential models was proposed by Michelle Rosaldo in her introductory essay to *Woman, Culture, and Society* (1974). Her argument began by asserting that although there is a great deal of cross-cultural variability in men's and women's roles, there is a pervasive, universal asymmetry between the sexes. "But what is perhaps most striking and surprising," Rosaldo writes, "is the fact that male, as opposed to female, activities are always recognized as predominantly important, and cultural systems give authority and value to the roles and activities of men" (Rosaldo 1974: 19).

One of the quotes we chose to appear at the beginning of the book, a passage from Margaret Mead's *Male and Female*, sums up what we saw in 1974 in all the ethnographies and studies we examined. "In every known society, the male's need for achievement can be recognized. Men may cook, or weave, or dress dolls or hunt hummingbirds, but if such activities are appropriate occupations of men, then the whole society, men and women alike, votes them as important. When the same occupations are performed by women, they are regarded as less important" (Mead 1949: 125). Not only were there differential evaluations of women's activities, but, Rosaldo argues, "everywhere men have some authority over women, that [is] they have culturally legitimated right to her subordination and compliance" (1974: 21).

Having argued for a pervasive sexual asymmetry across cultures, not just in terms of cultural values, but also in terms of power and authority, Rosaldo accounted for this difference between men and women in terms of a dichotomy.[1] She argued that women are associated with a "domestic orientation," while men are primarily associated with extradomestic, political, and military spheres of activity. By "domestic" Rosaldo meant "those minimal institutions and modes of activity that are organized immediately around one or more mothers and their children." In contrast, the "public" referred to "activities, institutions, and forms of association that link, rank, organize, or subsume particular mother-child groups. Put quite simply, men have no single commitment as enduring, time-consuming, and emotionally compelling—as close to seeming necessary and natural—as the relation of a woman to her infant child; and so men are free to form those broader associations that we call 'society,' universalistic systems of order, meaning, and commitment that link particular mother–child groups."

Rosaldo, along with Sherry Ortner and Nancy Chodorow, who also wrote essays in *Woman, Culture, and Society*, insisted that the connection between women's role in reproduction (the fact that women everywhere lactate and give birth to children) and their domestic orientation is not a necessary one. In other words biology is not destiny. Women's domestic orientation was structurally and culturally constructed and "insofar as woman is universally defined in terms of a largely maternal and domestic role, we can account for her universal subordination" (Rosaldo 1974: 7).

"Although" Rosaldo writes, "I would be the last to call this a necessary arrangement or to deny that it is far too simple as an account of any particular empirical case, I suggest that the opposition between domestic and public orientations (an opposition that must, in part, derive from the nurturant capacities of women) provides the necessary framework for an examination of male and female roles in any society" (Rosaldo 1974: 24).

Original material prepared for this text. Reprinted by permission of the author.

For Rosaldo, then, women were involved in the "messiness" of daily life; they were always available for interruption by children. Men could be more distanced and may actually have separate quarters (such as men's houses) away from women's activities. Men could thus "achieve" authority and create rank, hierarchy, and a political world away from women. The confinement of women to the domestic sphere and men's ability to create and dominate the political sphere thus accounted for men's ability to hold the greater share of power and authority in all known cultures and societies.

At the time Rosaldo wrote her overview and in the introduction we both wrote, we were faced with building a framework where none existed. Despite the number of monographs on women, Margaret Mead's work and that of Simone de Beauvoir (1953) were the most provocative, and perhaps the only, theoretical works we knew.[2] The argument for universal sexual asymmetry followed in a long tradition in anthropology where scholars have sought to look for what is broadly "human" in all cultures. In addition to language, anthropologists have discussed the universality of the incest taboo, marriage, and the family. The notion that women might be universally subordinate to men thus made sense as a first attempt at theory building in this newly revived "subfield" within anthropology.

Although Rosaldo argued for universal subordination, she was careful to make clear that women are not powerless. They exercise informal influence and power, often mitigating male authority or even rendering it trivial (Rosaldo 1974: 21). In addition, there are important variations in women's roles in different cultures, and variation was discussed in most of the rest of the articles in the collection. For example, Sanday and Sacks compared women's status in a number of different societies, while Leis examined the structural reasons why women's associations are strong in one Ijaw village in Nigeria, yet absent in another. Finally, in my own article I examined the differences in women's strategies within domestic groups in a number of societies, which related to the relative integration or separation of domestic and political spheres.

Since 1974 the hypothesis of universal subordination of women and the dichotomous relationship between women in the domestic sphere and men in the public sphere have been challenged and critiqued by a number of feminist anthropologists. As appealing as this dichotomy seemed in the abstract, it turned out to be difficult to apply when actually looking at examples of women's activities in different cultures. For example, in an important article written about the same time as Rosaldo's introduction, Rayna Reiter (now Rayna Rapp) described women's and men's distinct lives in a small French village in the south of France. "They

inhabited different domains, one public, one private. While men fraternized with whomever they found to talk to in public places, women were much more enmeshed in their families and their kinship networks" (Reiter 1975b: 253). However, two categories of public space fell into women's domain: the church and three shops, including the local bakery. Men tended to avoid women's places, entering the bakery, for example, only when several men were together and joking, "Let's attack now" (Reiter 1975b: 257).

Reiter argues that men and women use public space in different ways and at different times. "The men go early to the fields, and congregate on the square or in the cafes for a social hour after work. Sometimes they also fraternize in the evenings. These are the times when women are home cooking and invisible to public view. But when the men have abandoned the village for the fields, the women come out to do their marketing in a leisurely fashion. The village is then in female hands. In the afternoon, when the men return to work, the women form gossip groups on stoops and benches or inside houses depending on the weather" (Reiter 1975b: 258). Despite the powerful imagery—women associated with the private or domestic domain and men with public space—the description also shows that the dichotomy is not neat. After all women are in public a great deal; they have taken over, in some sense, the Church and the shops and even the public square in the middle of the day.

In Margery Wolf's description of women in a Taiwanese village based on data she collected in the late 1950s, she emphasizes that because researchers have focused on the dominance of patrilineal descent in the family, they have failed to see women's presence. "We have missed not only some of the system's subtleties but also its near-fatal weaknesses" (Wolf 1972: 37). Women have different interests than men and build uterine families—strong ties to their daughters, but primarily to their sons who give their mothers loyalty and a place in the patrilineal extended family. Outside the family in the community women formed neighborhood groups—around a store, at a platform where women washed their clothes in the canal, or under a huge old tree. In a village strung out between a river and a canal, there was no central plaza dominated by men as in the South of France.

In Peihotien Wolf did not describe a cultural geography where women were in a private sphere and men in the public one; rather there was more of a functional separation—men and women had different activities and interests. They were often located in the same places but had a different relationship to the patrilineal extended family and the male-dominated community. Women's lack of power led them to different strategies, different tactics that often undermined male control of the household and even the community. As Sylvia Yanagisako (1987: 111) has pointed out, the notion of domestic–public entails both a spatial metaphor (of geographically separated or even nested spaces) and a functional metaphor (of functionally different activities or social roles) in the same conceptual dichotomy. Analysts often "mix" these different metaphors in any particular analysis—sometimes using domestic–public spatially and at other times functionally.

Even in the Middle East, the association of women with a private domain (and a lack of power) and men with a public domain (and the center of politics) was too simple, as Cynthia Nelson pointed out in her article, "Public and Private Politics: Women in the Middle Eastern World" (1974). Because they are born into one patrilineal group and marry into another, women are important structural links between social groups and often act as mediators. Because there are segregated social worlds, all-female institutions are important for enforcing social norms: Women fill powerful ritual roles as sorceresses, healers, and mediums; women are important sources of information for their male kin; and women act as "information brokers," mediating social relations within both the family and the larger society.

From Rosaldo's point of view, these aspects of women's power are primarily "informal" and very different from the public, legitimate roles of men. Nevertheless, even though Nelson affirms the separation of male and female worlds (both spatially and functionally), what is "domestic" has public ramifications (the arrangement of a marriage, the transmission of highly charged political information) and the shadow of the family and kin group (the "domestic") is present in even the most "public" of situations. What at first seemed like a simple straightforward dichotomy, in light of actual case material seems very "slippery" and complex.

Furthermore, in many cultures, particularly those with an indigenous band or tribal structure, a separation of "domestic" and "public" spheres makes no sense because household production was simultaneously public, economic, and political. Leacock pointed out the following after reviewing the literature on the Iroquois during the seventeenth and eighteenth centuries:

> Iroquois matrons preserved, stored, and dispensed the corn, meat, fish, berries, squashes, and fats that were buried in special pits or kept in the long house. Brown (1970: 162) notes that women's control over the dispensation of the foods they produced, and meat as well, gave them de facto power to veto declarations of war and to intervene to bring about peace. . . . Women also guarded the "tribal public treasure" kept in the long house, the wampum quill and feather work, and furs. . . . The point

to be stressed is that this was "household management" of an altogether different order from management of the nuclear or extended family in patriarchal societies. In the latter, women may cajole, manipulate, or browbeat men, but always behind the public facade; in the former case, "household management" was itself the management of the "public economy." (Leacock 1978: 253)

Sudarkasa has made much the same point about women in West African societies such as the Yoruba. She argues that many of the political and economic activities anthropologists discuss as public are actually embedded in households (Sudarkasa 1976, as quoted in Rapp 1979: 509). Furthermore, "in West Africa, the 'public domain' was not conceptualized as 'the world of men.' Rather, the public domain was one in which both sexes were recognized as having important roles to play" (Sudarkasa 1986: 99).

A more appropriate conception would be to recognize two domains, "one occupied by men and another by women, both of which were internally ordered in a hierarchical fashion and both of which provided 'personnel' for domestic and extradomestic (or public) activities" (Sudarkasa 1986: 94).

Furthermore, a careful examination of "domestic domain" indicates that the categories of "woman" and "mother" overlap in Western society, but the meaning of motherhood may be vastly different in another society. Women may not be exclusively defined as mothers and childrearers in terms of their status and cultural value (see Moore 1988: 20–29 for a discussion of this point).

In addition to the issue of whether the domestic–public dichotomy can provide an adequate *description* of men's and women's spatial and functional relationships in our own and other societies, the model has problems as an *explanation* of women's status. One of these problems is the inherent circularity of the model. A central point is to account for the nature of these domains, yet they are already assumed to exist widely and are treated as categories in terms of which women's activities (such as food preparing, cooking, childcare, washing) can be classified (as opposed to male hunting, warfare, political councils). Comaroff says that the model "can only affirm what has already been assumed—that is, that the distinction between the domestic and politico-jural is an intrinsic, if variable, fact of social existence" (Comaroff 1987: 59). When the model is used to explain women's positions in different societies in relation to these two orientations, the reasoning is equally circular. To put it in the words of Yanagisako and Collier, "The claim that women become absorbed in domestic activities because of their role as mothers is tautological given the definition of 'domestic' as 'those minimal institutions and modes of activity that are organized immediately around one or more mothers and their children'" (Yanagisako and Collier 1987: 19).

Finally, we have come to realize that the concepts of domestic and public were bound up in our own history and our own categories grounded particularly in a Victorian heritage. Rosaldo, in a thoughtful reevaluation of her model, came to argue this position herself.

The turn-of-the-century social theorists whose writings are the basis of most modern social thinking tended without exception to assume that women's place was in the home. In fact, the Victorian doctrine of separate male and female spheres was, I would suggest, quite central to their sociology. Some of these thinkers recognized that modern women suffered from their association with domestic life, but none questioned the pervasiveness (or necessity) of a split between the family and society. (Rosaldo 1980: 401–402)

Rosaldo traced the historical roots of domestic–public from the nineteenth-century evolutionists through twentieth-century structural functionalists to her own work. Instead of two opposed spheres (different and apart), Rosaldo suggested an analysis of gender relationships, an examination of inequality and hierarchy as they are created particularly through marriage (Rosaldo 1980: 412–413).

The dichotomy has been usefully employed in several ways since 1974. First, several authors have shown us how it works in Western societies (e.g., France and the United States, where it arose historically and still has an important ideological function) (Reiter 1975b; Collier, Rosaldo, and Yanagisako 1982). In a related way, analysts have explored the meanings surrounding domestic activities of women, putting together a much more complex picture of women's relation to men in this sphere (Chai 1987; Murcott 1983, reprinted in this book). Second, anthropological analysis has helped us to understand the historical development of domestic–public spheres in societies under colonialism. John Comaroff's analysis of the Tshidi chiefdom in South Africa during the early twentieth century is an excellent example of this approach (1987: 53–85). Finally, some analysts have used the cultural concepts of other societies to critique our own model of domestic–public orientations. Sylvia Yanagisako's essay on the clear separation of "inside–outside" domains (a spatial metaphor) and "work–family" activities (a functional dichotomy) in Japanese American culture demonstrates how the anthropological model of domestic–public mixes these metaphors, which has made analysis confusing and difficult (Yanagisako 1987).

Despite these useful attempts at examining women's lives through the lens of a domestic–public opposition, many of us would agree with Rayna Rapp's 1979 summary of the problems with this dichotomy.

We cannot write an accurate history of the West in relation to the Rest until we stop assuming that our experiences subsume everyone else's. Our public/private conflicts are not necessarily the same as those of other times and places. The specific oppression of women cannot be documented if our categories are so broad as to decontextualize what "womanness" means as we struggle to change that definition. A Tanzanian female farmer, a Mapuche woman leader, and an American working-class housewife do not live in the same domestic domain, nor will the social upheavals necessary to give them power over their lives be the same. We must simultaneously understand the differences and the similarities, but not by reducing them to one simple pattern. (Rapp 1979: 511)

Thus, many of us have tired of the domestic–public dichotomy. We feel it is constraining, a "trap," while new approaches try to get away from dichotomous thinking. These approaches do one of several things. Often they take history seriously, examining women's situation as it has evolved, often in a colonial context. Furthermore, they treat women as active agents and following Collier (1974), as people who have interests, often divergent from men, and who act on them. Third, they often focus on gender relationships, rather than only on women. Finally, they do not treat all women as part of a single universal category of "woman." Rather women are usually analyzed in terms of their social location. Age, class, race, ethnicity, and kinship are all likely to divide women, so newer analyses examine women's strategies and identities as they are differently shaped. Several examples will illustrate some of the different approaches taken in recent years.

Collier's examination of Comanche, Cheyenne, and Kiowa gender relationships (1988) illustrates the recent focus on gender and on the multiple positions that men and women hold in societies in which the domestic–public dichotomy seems inappropriate. This is because these "spheres" are integrated, and there is no firm line between domestic and public space (see Lamphere 1974; Leacock 1978).

The Comanche are an example of a bride service society in which, like many hunter–gatherer societies, men and women were relatively autonomous, the concept of femininity was not elaborated, and the greatest status differences were between unmarried and married men. Marriage established men as having something to achieve (e.g., a wife), leaving women without such a cultural goal. Young men, through providing meat for their in-laws (bride service), become equal adults, and older men, through egalitarian relations and generosity, become the repositories of wisdom and knowledge. Politics focused on the issue of sexuality and on male–male relationships, which often erupted in conflict and violence. Women celebrated their health and sexuality, and hence the roles of "woman the gatherer" or even "woman the mother" did not emerge as cultural themes.

Among the Cheyenne, an equal bride-wealth society, and among the Kiowa, an unequal bridewealth society, marriage relationships were structured in a much different way in the nineteenth century, so gender relationships had a much different content, politics were more hierarchical, and ideology played a different role. Collier's interest is not in the subordination of women in these three societies, because in all three there are several kinds of inequality: between men and women, between older women and girls, between unmarried men and married men, and between kin and affines. An interest in "spheres" and "domains" has been replaced by an emphasis on relationships and an analysis that focuses on the ways in which inequality gets reproduced through marriage transactions, claims on the labor of others, and giving and receiving of gifts. Dominance and subordination become a much more layered, contextualized phenomenon—more interesting than the simple assertion that women are universally subordinated. The processes through which women's inequality (and that of young men) is constructed are laid bare, rather than flatly asserted.

Mary Moran's study of civilized women (1990) explores the historical beginnings and present-day construction of the category "civilized," which does confine educated women among the Glebo of southeastern Liberia to a "domestic sphere." The dichotomy between "civilized" and "native" (or even tribal or country) is a result of missionization and has created a status hierarchy differentially applied to men and to women. Men, once educated and with a history of paid wage work, never lose their status as "civilized," while women, even though married to a "civilized man," may lose their status if they do not dress correctly, keep house in specific ways, and refrain from farming and marketing. Native women, who market or have farms, are more economically independent but occupy positions of lower prestige. Here we see not only the importance of historical data in examining how cultural categories evolve, but also the ways in which both civilized and native women actively manage their status positions. Civilized women, through the practice of fosterage, recruit younger women to their households to carry out the more elaborate household routines in which they must engage and to train these fostered daughters to become civilized themselves.

The civilized–native dichotomy represents the juxtaposition of two systems. One is a parallel-sex system in which native men and women are represented by their own leaders in two linked but relatively autonomous prestige hierarchies (as suggested by Sudarkasa 1986). The other is a single-sex system (based on a Western model) in which men in political positions represent both sexes, and women have little access to prestige except through their husbands. Thus, this is a much more complex system than one based on a domestic–public dichotomy. There are dichotomous categories—civilized–native, male–female—but they do not fit neatly together. Moran speaks of categories as "gender sensitive" and suggests that "the Glebo have inserted gender into the civilized/native dichotomy to the point that women's status is not only more tenuous and vulnerable than men's but also very difficult to maintain without male support." In some respects civilized women trade off dependency for prestige, but Moran provides a sympathetic picture of how both civilized and native women manage their lives.

Lila Abu-Lughod's study (1986) of Bedouin women's ritual poetry gives us further insights into the complexity of women who in 1974 we would have simply thought of as "confined to a domestic sphere." Among the Bedouin, women's marriages are arranged; wives wear black veils and red belts (symbolizing their fertility); and women must behave within a code of behavior that emphasizes family honor and female modesty and shame. When confronted with loss, poor treatment, or neglect, the public discourse is one of hostility, bitterness, and anger. In the case of lost love the discourse is of militant indifference and denial of concern. In contrast, Bedouin poetry, a highly prized and formally structured art, expresses sentiments of devastating sadness, self-pity, attachment, and deep feeling (Abu-Lughod 1986: 187). Although both men and women recite poetry for women, it may express conflicting feelings concerning an arranged marriage, a sense of loss over a divorce, or sentiments of betrayal when a husband marries a new wife. The poems are used to elicit sympathy and get help, but they also constitute a dissident and subversive discourse. Abu-Lughod sees ritual poetry as a corrective to "an obsession with morality and an overzealous adherence to the ideology of honor. . . . Poetry reminds people of another way of being and encourages, as it reflects, another side of experience. . . . And maybe the vision [offered through poetry] is cherished because people see that the costs of this system, in the limits it places on human experiences, are just too high" (Abu-Lughod 1986: 259). Bedouin women in this portrait are not simply victims of patriarchy confined to a domestic sphere; they are active individuals who use a highly valued cultural form to express their deepest sentiments, acknowledge an alternative set of values, and leave open the possibility of subverting the system in which they are embedded.

A large number of studies have been conducted in the United States that loosely focus on what used to be termed the domestic sphere and the public world of work. As in the Native American, African, and Middle Eastern cases cited previously, when one begins to examine a topic in detail, global notions like domestic–public seem too simple to deal with the complexities of women's lives. Clearly work and home are distinctly separated spheres in the United States. Women who have been employed in the paid labor force have experienced the disjunction of spending eight or more hours of the day in a place of employment where they are "female workers" and the rest of their time in the home where they are daughters, wives, and/or mothers. With this comes responsibilities for cooking, cleaning, and providing nurturance, care, and intimacy for other family members. Several recent studies have examined the contradictions women face when combining work and family, the impact of paid employment on family roles, and vice versa. I will refer to only three examples of this growing literature.

Patricia Zavella's research on Chicana cannery workers examines women's networks that link the workplace and the family (Zavella 1987). Calling these "work-related networks," Zavella describes groups of friends who saw each other outside work and who were members of a kin network employed in the same cannery. Women used work-related networks as sources of exchange for information, baby sitters, and emotional support. Networks operated in more political ways as workers organized a women's caucus and filed a complaint with the Fair Employment Practices Commission. Women's cannery work was seasonal and had relatively little impact on power relations in the family or the household division of labor. On the other hand, work-related networks of friends or kin were an important "bridging mechanism" helping women to deal with the contradictions and demands that came from two different spheres.

Karen Sacks' study of hospital workers at the Duke Medical Center examines the ways in which black and white women brought family notions of work, adulthood, and responsibility to work with them and used these values to organize a walk out and subsequent union drive (1988). Sacks focuses on the activities of "center women"—leaders in the union drive. Unlike the men who were often the public speakers at rallies and events, the center women organized support on an interpersonal, one-to-one basis. Rather than emphasizing the bridging aspect of women's networks, Sacks shows how the family is "brought to work" or in the old terminology how the "domestic" influences the "public."

In my own research I have traced the changes in the relationship between women, work, and family historically through the study of immigrant women in a small industrial community, Central Falls, Rhode Island (Lamphere 1987). Using the twin notions of productive and reproductive labor, I examined the rise of the textile industry in Rhode Island and the recruitment of working daughters and later of working mothers to the textile industry and to the other light industries that have replaced it since World War II. Rather than seeing production and reproduction as a rigid dichotomy (like public and domestic), I have used these categories to study relationships and to examine the kinds of strategies that immigrant women and their families forged in confronting an industrial system where wage work was a necessity and where working-class families had no control over the means of production. Such an approach revealed a great deal of variability both between and within ethnic groups— the Irish, English, French-Canadian, and Polish families who came to Central Falls between 1915 and 1984 and the more recent Colombian and Portuguese immigrants. Examination of strikes and walkouts in the 1920s and 1930s and my own experience as a sewer in an apparel plant in 1977 led me to emphasize the strategies of resistance the women workers used on the job, as well as the impact of women's paid labor on the family itself. When daughters were recruited as workers in textile mills, the internal division of labor within the household did not materially change because wives and mothers continued to do much of the reproductive labor necessary to maintain the household. Fathers, teenage sons, and daughters worked for wages. In the current period, in contrast, as more wives have become full-time workers, immigrant men have begun to do some reproductive labor, particularly child care. Immigrant couples often work different shifts and prefer to care for children themselves rather than trust baby sitters from their own ethnic group. In my study I argue that "the productive system as constituted in the workplaces has shaped the family more than issues of reproduction have shaped the workplace" (Lamphere 1987: 43).

More recently, Patricia Zavella, Felipe Gonzalez, and I have found that young working mothers in sunbelt industries have moved much further than Cannery women or New England industrial immigrant women in changing the nature of the household division of labor (Lamphere, Zavella, Gonzales, and Evans 1993). These new committed female workers have been employed since high school and do not drop out of the labor force for long periods of time to have children. Thus, they and their husbands construct a family life around a two-job household. Although some couples have a "traditional" division of housework (women do the cooking and the majority of the cleaning and husbands take out the garbage, do minor repairs, and fix the car), many husbands participate in "female chores" and do substantial amounts of childcare (often caring for children while the wife is at work). Here we see the impact of what we used to call the "public sphere" on the domestic one, but in our analysis we have focused more on the varied ways that Anglos and Hispanics (including single mothers) have negotiated household and childcare arrangements, viewing husbands and wives as mediating contradictions. Subtle similarities and differences among and between working class Anglo and Hispanic women have emerged from this analysis, making it clear that the impact of work in the public world is not a monolithic but a variegated process.

In summary the dichotomy between the public world of men and domestic world of women was, in 1974, an important and useful starting point for thinking about women's roles in a cross-cultural perspective. As anthropologists have written more detailed and fine-grained studies of women's lives in a wide variety of other cultures and in our own society, we have gone beyond the use of dichotomies to produce analyses of the complex and layered structure of women's lives. We now treat women more historically, viewing them as social actors and examining the variability among women's situations within one culture and in their relationship to men.

## NOTES

1. Rosaldo says that "the opposition does not *determine* cultural stereotypes or asymmetries in the evaluations of the sexism, but rather underlies them, to support a very general . . . identification of women with domestic life and of men with public life" (Rosaldo 1974: 21–22). Thus, I would argue, Rosaldo did not attempt to *explain* women's subordination through the dichotomy, but saw it as an underlying structural framework in any society that supported subordination and that would have to be reorganized to change women's position.
2. It is interesting that we did not know of Elsie Clews Parson's extensive feminist writing during 1910 to 1916, much of which is reminiscent of the kind of position we took in *Woman, Culture and Society*. In another article I have noted the similarities between Shelly's prose and that of Parsons (See Lamphere 1989; Parsons 1913, 1914, 1915).

## REFERENCES

Abu-Lughod, Lila. 1986. *Veiled Sentiments: Honor and Poetry in a Bedouin Society*. Berkeley and Los Angeles: University of California Press.

Brown, Judith. 1970. "Economic organization and the position of women among the Iroquois." *Ethnohistory* 17(3/4): 131–167.

Chai, Alice Yun. 1987. "Freed from the elders but locked into labor: Korean immigrant women in Hawaii." *Women's Studies* 13: 223–234.

Collier, Jane. 1974. "Women in politics." In Michelle Z. Rosaldo and Louise Lamphere (eds.). *Woman, Culture, and Society*. Stanford, CA: Stanford University Press.

———. 1988. *Marriage and Inequality in Classless Societies*. Stanford, CA: Stanford University Press.

Collier, Jane, Michelle Rosaldo, and Sylvia Yanagisako. 1982. "Is there a family? New anthropological views." In Barrie Thorne and Marilyn Yalom (eds.). *Rethinking the Family: Some Feminist Questions*, pp. 25–40. New York and London: Longman.

Comaroff, John L. 1987. "Sui genderis: Feminism, kinship theory, and structural 'domains'." In Jane Fishburne Collier and Sylvia Junko Yanagisako (eds.). *Gender and Kinship: Essays Toward a Unified Analysis*, pp. 53–86 Stanford, CA: Stanford University Press.

de Beauvoir, Simone. 1953. *The Second Sex*. New York: Alfred A. Knopf. Originally published in French in 1949.

Kaberry, Phyllis M. 1939. *Aboriginal Women, Sacred and Profane*. London: G. Routledge.

———. 1952. *Women of the Grassfields*. London: H. M. Stationery Office.

Lamphere, Louise. 1974. "Strategies, cooperation, and conflict among women in domestic groups." In Michelle Z. Rosaldo and Louise Lamphere (eds.). *Woman, Culture, and Society*, pp. 97–113. Stanford, CA: Stanford University Press.

———. 1987. *From Working Daughters to Working Mothers: Immigrant Women in a New England Industrial Community*. Ithaca, NY: Cornell University Press.

———. 1989. "Feminist anthropology: The legacy of Elsie Clews Parsons." *American Ethnologist* 16(3): 518–533.

Lamphere, Louise, Patricia Zavella, Felipe Gonzales, and Peter Evans. 1993. *Sunbelt Working Mothers: Reconciling Family and Factory*. Ithaca, NY: Cornell University Press.

Landes, Ruth. 1938. *The Ojibwa Woman, Part 1: Youth*. New York: Columbia University. Contributions to Anthropology, Vol. 31.

———. 1947. *The City of Women: Negro Women Cult Leaders of Bahia, Brazil*. New York: Macmillan.

Leacock, Eleanor. 1978. "Women's status in egalitarian society: Implications for social evolution." *Current Anthropology* 19(2): 247–275.

Leith-Ross, Sylvia. 1939. *African Women: Study of the Ibo of Nigeria*. London: Faber and Faber.

Mead, Margaret. 1949. *Male and Female*. New York: William Morrow and Co.

Moore, Henrietta L. 1988. *Feminism and Anthropology*. Minneapolis: University of Minnesota Press.

Moran, Mary H. 1990. *Civilized Women: Gender and Prestige in Southeastern Liberia*. Ithaca, NY: Cornell University Press.

Murcott, Anne. 1983. "'It's a pleasure to cook for him': Food, mealtimes and gender in some South Wales households." In Eva Gamarnikow, D. H. J. Morgan, June Purvis, and Daphne Taylorson (eds.). *The Public and the Private*. London: Heinemann Educational Books.

Nelson, Cynthia. 1974. "Public and private politics: Women in the Middle East." *American Ethnologist* 1: 551–563.

Parsons, Elsie Clews. 1913. *The Old Fashioned Woman*. New York: G. P. Putnam's Sons.

———. 1914. *Fear and Conventionality*. New York: G. P. Putnam's Sons.

———. 1915. *Social Freedom: A Study of the Conflicts Between Social Classifications and Personality*. New York: G. P. Putnam's Sons.

Paulme, Denise (ed.). 1963. *Women of Tropical Africa*. Berkeley: University of California Press.

Rapp, Rayna. 1979. Anthropology. *Signs* 4(3): 497–513.

Reiter, Rayna (ed.). 1975a. *Toward an Anthropology of Women*. New York: Monthly Review Press.

———. 1975b. "Men and women in the South of France: Public and private domains." In Rayna Reiter (ed.). *Toward an Anthropology of Women*, pp. 252–283. New York: Monthly ReviewPress.

Rosaldo, Michelle. 1974. "Woman, culture and society: A theoretical overview." In Michelle Z. Rosaldo and Louise Lamphere (eds.). *Woman, Culture, and Society*. pp. 17–43. Stanford, CA: Stanford University Press.

———. 1980. "The uses and abuses of anthropology." *Signs* 5(3): 389–417.

Rosaldo, Michelle Z., and Louise Lamphere (eds.). 1974. *Woman, Culture, and Society*. Stanford, CA: Stanford University Press.

Sacks, Karen. 1988. *Caring by the Hour: Women, Work, and Organizing at the Duke Medical Center*. Urbana and Chicago: University of Illinois Press.

Sudarkasa, Niara. 1976. "Female employment and family organization in West Africa." In Dorothy McGuigan (ed.). *New Research on Women and Sex Roles*. Ann Arbor, MI: Center for Continuing Education of Women.

———. 1986. "The status of women in indigenous African Societies." *Feminist Studies* 12: 91–104.

Underhill, Ruth. 1936. *Autobiography of a Papago Woman*. Supplement to *American Anthropologist* 38(3), Part II. Millwood, NY: American Anthropological Association.

Wolf, Margery. 1972. *Women and the Family in Rural Taiwan*. Stanford, CA: Stanford University Press.

Yanagisako, Sylvia Junko. 1987. "Mixed metaphors: Native and anthropological models of gender and kinship domains." In Jane Fishburne Collier and Sylvia Junko Yanagisako (eds.). *Gender and Kinship: Essays Toward a Unified Analysis*, pp. 86–119. Stanford, CA: Stanford University Press.

Yanagisako, Sylvia Junko, and Jane Fishburne Collier. 1987. "Toward a unified analysis of gender and kinship." In Jane Fishburne Collier and Sylvia Junko Yanagisako (eds.). *Gender and Kinship: Essays Toward a Unified Analysis*, pp. 14–53. Stanford, CA: Stanford University Press.

Zavella, Patricia. 1987. *Women's Work and Chicano Families: Cannery Workers of the Santa Clara Valley*. Ithaca, NY: Cornell University Press.

# From "Private" Affairs to "Public" Scandals:
## The Modern Woman's Challenge to Husband's Infidelities in Uganda

### Shanti Parikh

## INTRODUCTION

Uganda is widely touted as the HIV success story. Once considered the epicenter of the global HIV epidemic with an HIV prevalence rate of 19 percent in the early 1990s, the country experienced a remarkable decline reporting a low of 5.4 percent in 2007 (UNAIDS 2008). During this period of decline, all age and sex groups reported a decrease in infection rate except for women between the ages 30 and 39, an age group whose members are most likely married or had been married (Mbulaiteye et al. 2002). Other studies showed similar risk for married women. For instance, a study in southeast Uganda found that when both spouses were HIV negative, husbands were two times more likely than their wives to eventually bring HIV infection into marriage, suggesting that husbands' extramarital liaisons were the likely source of HIV infection (Carpenter et al. 1999). Ironically, for women around the world, the very liaison that is promoted by public health, religious, and other campaigns as the "safest" type of sex—marital sex—is precisely the one that presents women with the greatest risk for HIV infection (Hirsch et al. 2010; Mayer et al. 2004; O'Leary 2000; UNAIDS et al. 2004).

On the surface, the domestic/public model initially proposed by Michelle Rosaldo (1974, 1980, Lamphere this book), provides a compelling analytic framework for understanding married women's increased risk for HIV infection. Men's mobility in the public sphere and access to resources provide them opportunities for extramarital trysts, while wives' responsibilities that tie them to the domestic sphere impede their ability (and desire) to find out and to take action.

Research I conducted in Uganda between 2004 and 2006 supports this general explanation. However, a closer examination of ethnographic and historical data indicates that overreliance on the domestic/public divide precludes an understanding of the historic fluidity of these categories and how women strategically blur the boundaries for their marital advantage.

In this chapter, I explore three major findings that build upon and complicate the domestic/public model. My first argument demonstrates how the domestic/public model can be used to understand structural factors that underlie married women's HIV risk. My second argument is historical. It highlights how sexuality and sexual meanings, like all cultural forms, are neither static nor timeless relics, but are dynamic and responsive to wider shifts and trends. I use life histories from three generational cohorts in Uganda to chronicle how the practices of polygyny (or, a man having more than one wife) and fairly indiscreet extramarital liaisons of men have been transformed gradually into informal secondary households and more secretive trysts, respectively. This transformation has been occasioned by shifts in the economy, gender equality campaigns, and the proliferation of discourses that have made sexuality a primary concern of public health and public morality regulation and surveillance. Hence, whereas in the past men's extramarital activities were primarily considered a private family matter, today they have become a matter of great public attention, critique, and gossip.

Finally, the third argument I make in this chapter concerns married women's varied responses to their husband's infidelities. While respectable middle-class women are expected to maintain the reputations of their marriages by not airing grievances publicly, in some cases women strategically disrupt the boundaries between private (marital affairs and domestic sphere) and public (reputations of spouses and men's worlds) in an attempt to effect a desired outcome. Whereas the private/public divide may enable men's extramarital trysts and underlie women's willful silence or unawareness, in some cases it is strategic for women to "go public" with decidedly private matters in order to gain sympathies from neighbors, shame their husbands and, importantly, present themselves as modern rational actors who protect themselves. In the contemporary context in Uganda, the notion of "rational" is shaped by the highly visible messages about protecting oneself from sexual risk as espoused in public health campaigns, from gendered violations as promoted by the women's rights movement, and from moral decline as championed in religious teachings. Yet going public with their husband's affairs can also have unpleasant consequences. This chapter brings new insight to the ongoing debates about the usefulness of

the public/private model by highlighting how public health and other interventions have worked to transform male infidelity and women's responses to what had been largely a private concern—among families and close social networks—into a matter of public concern with paradoxical implications.

## ETHNOGRAPHIC SETTING AND METHODS

This chapter is based on ethnographic research in the agrarian-based, eastern central town of Iganga and its network of outlying villages, a region in which I have conducted research since 1996. I draw upon data that my research assistants and I collected during a six-month period in 2004 and three months of follow-up visits in 2005 and 2006. The research was part of a five-country comparative study on married women's HIV risk and men's extramarital sexuality.[1] Data consist of marital and life histories of seventy-four men and women, key informant interviews (including mistresses, bar owners, health officials, and religious leaders), participant observation, and discourse analysis of media and popular representations of contemporary sexuality in Uganda.

Iganga town is the rapidly growing administrative and commercial center for Iganga District (the population of the district was roughly 600,000 in 2004). The town sits along the Trans-Africa Highway, the major international road that runs from the coast of Kenya through Rwanda and into the Democratic Republic of the Congo. Once known as the "HIV corridor," the interactions between long-distance truck drivers and commercial sex workers at the rest stops along the highway were documented as being early transmitters of the virus, eventually spreading the infection to the general population. To residents in Iganga, however, this highway also represents their connection to the rest of East Africa and beyond.

The Basoga are Bantu-speaking and have exogamous and patrilocal marriages; that is, people must marry someone outside their clan, and the couple relocates to the man's residence after marriage (Radcliffe-Brown 1950). The exchange of bridewealth from the groom's family to the bride's solidifies the marriage and is considered an important sign of respect. It essentially transfers authority over a woman's productive and sexual labor from her father to her husband. Bridewealth, combined with the patrilocal residence pattern, has the effect of isolating a new bride from the protection of her natal family. This limits a wife's ability to negotiate within marriage, a point that is critical to this chapter.

Historically, residents of Iganga relied on subsistence agricultural and livestock activities as their primary source of income. To meet their needs in an increasingly monetized economy, today households must supplement farming with other income-generating activities such as small trading, shopkeeping, manual labor, driving bicycle or motorcycle taxis, repair work, selling cooked food, and working in service industries. Having a salaried position in a school, government office, bank, or a local branch of a development agency elevates a person's socioeconomic status, but such positions are few and more readily available to men, exacerbating gender inequalities. Life and marriage in Iganga is fraught with economic uncertainty, which has profound implications for marital happiness and men's extramarital behaviors. In addition to economic frustrations, this uncertainty is complicated by what I call high HIV anxiety, a by-product of Uganda's aggressive campaigns that have successfully made people aware of the possibility that they have HIV.

## THE DOMESTIC/PUBLIC DIVIDE: A STARTING POINT FOR UNDERSTANDING MEN'S EXTRAMARITAL OPPORTUNITY STRUCTURES

Despite many critiques and counterexamples, the domestic/public model provides a useful entry way into understanding gendered patterns of HIV risk. The model is compelling primarily because it moves away from a narrow focus on individuals' actions, a tendency of many conventional public health models, and instead redirects attention to wider social and economic factors that shape and constrain options from which people may choose. In other words, instead of assuming that men and women act as independent health droids who make decisions devoid of any social context, the private/domestic framework draws attention to what my collaborators and I have called "opportunity structures" that facilitate or discourage men's extramarital sexuality (see Hirsch et al. 2010). Recognizing the role of opportunity structures in facilitating men's extramarital sex is not to excuse husbands' behaviors or wives' inaction, but rather to situate both within a wider context of enabling and disenabling factors.

Findings from my research in Uganda readily support the idea that the private/public divide is both a product of and recreates the gender inequality that undergirds men's participation in extramarital sexuality and married women's increased risk for HIV. Men's migration and mobility and subsequent access to resources in the public sphere provide them opportunities for extramarital encounters away from the surveillance of "domestically" situated wives and

relatives. Physically, labor-related migration with spousal separation, which is a common feature at some point in the lives of the men in Iganga, almost inevitably leads men into sexual liaisons with women who are not their longer-term partners. Unlike their wives or girlfriends who often remain behind where mutual social and kin networks can easily provide watchful eyes on behaviors, men's absence from these connections permits them to engage in extramarital activities without similar repercussions. Conversely, instead of tarnishing a man's reputation, we found that participating in sexual liaisons sometimes has the counter-effect of bolstering his reputation within the masculine prestige structure among his migrant peer and work groups. Not only may men's peer groups directly or indirectly encourage men's extramarital activities, but men in our study also mentioned feeling lonely and desiring companionship while away from wives and children (Campbell 1997). For instance, an army man whom I interviewed frequently was assigned to posts far from Iganga for up to a year at a time. He described how it was virtually assumed that he would get an "informal wife" to take care of his domestic needs at the army camp. He also explained that army men are seen as a valuable source of money and safety to the families and young women in the conflict-ridden and often economically depressed regions where they are assigned, and hence there is a steady flow of sex-for-favors/money offers (also called transactional sex). Although possible, not participating in extramarital sexuality would seem odd to both his peers and the community.

Even men who were not participating in labor migration during the time of our study experienced greater physical mobility than their wives, which produced similar opportunity structures. As Iganga transforms from its landscape of daytime businesses into a lively nighttime outdoor bazaar, the sexual geography of town becomes visible as men and unmarried women venture to and in between a variety of commercial drinking and eating places that pepper the landscape. Similar to distant migration destinations, the semi-anonymity of town and its social distance from overseeing wives and kin serve to facilitate men's sexual networking.

Some men expressed feeling pulled to Iganga's evening activities. Ironically, although husbands are considered the "rulers" of their households, many men revealed feeling out of place and limited in the domestic arena, especially in the evening when many household chores are performed. While some men have adopted the idea of assisting with domestic chores and life, local gender convention still dictates otherwise. According to a middle-class office worker who often did assist with household chores, "If you go home, what is there for you? Your wife quarrels with you about this and that; wonders why you are not looking for money. Or, she and children have their chores so you sit alone. Nothing to do." This common sentiment essentially pulls men out of the home and into bars, pool halls or other "public" places in which drinking and socializing with single women are central to male homosocial bonding. Masculine prestige structures dominant in many of these settings are based on sexual conquests, creating a favorable atmosphere for men's extramarital liaisons.

While married men are expected to build an expanding social world in order to increase their abilities to provide for the home, married women often experience a different reality because their duties draw them to the household. Women's domestic responsibilities tie them to the home which results in a smaller social network and more limited access to resources, restricting their ability to find out about and to have an influence on their husbands' nondomestic activities. Recently married women and women with young children have particularly limited mobility not only because of breastfeeding and child raising, but also because of the need to establish themselves as competent wives and mothers in new families and communities. Women's shrinking postmarital social networks leave them dependent on husbands and nearby in-laws and less able to discuss husbands' recreational activities or to negotiate HIV preventative practices. As women matured in their marriages, we found that their social worlds expanded as they began to involve themselves more with community activities, but the earlier years were particularly precarious.

Gendered inequality in access to resources, social networks, and mobility translates into husbands' having greater authority over their wives and leaving wives dependent on their husbands. For the wives, this means that they may have a difficult time raising concerns about their husbands' suspected infidelities and negotiating HIV preventative techniques. A main reason is the fear of possible consequences such as withdrawal of a partner's support or affection, violence, counter-accusations or even that the ideal of monogamy has failed. Furthermore, two goals of many marriages—to bear children and to maintain a "happy" public reputation—may work to further women's HIV risk. The desire to reproduce discourages condom use, and the desire to maintain the appearance of a happy marriage means that women may choose to willfully ignore husband's extramarital liaisons. Thus, a woman's inability or even hesitation to negotiate HIV preventative techniques with her husband (such as condom use or the timing or frequency of sex) is influenced by her own desire, by familial pressure, or by fear of negative reactions from partners.[2]

## A HISTORICAL VIEW: THE STATE, ECONOMY, AND SHIFTS IN MEN'S EXTRAMARITAL SEXUALITY

While the domestic/public model allows us to understand marital dynamics within a specific context, it restricts our ability to understand how categories have changed over time. In this section, I use interviews with three generations of residents to examine how marital and extramarital relations were shaped by changes in the state, society, and the economy.

### The British Colonial Era: Profits, Laws, and Exacerbating Gender Inequalities

Beginning in the early 1900s, British colonial policies and ideologies interacted with the precolonial Basoga agrarian economy and patrilineal kinship system in ways that bolstered gender inequality in marriage and that provided structural incentives for men's concurrent liaisons.[3] Of particular interest to this project was the introduction of cash crops as a means of extracting wealth from the colony, which was the basis of colonial presence. Informed by prevailing British gender ideologies regarding property rights, colonial officials gave men greater control over economic resources including land and cash crops, distancing women from new forms of capitalist wealth. The workloads of ordinary women increased as they became expected to work on both their households' subsistence gardens as well as their husbands' cash crop farms, yet controlling the profits from neither. Not only did this bolster husbands' control over wives, but profits from cash crops provided men a greater incentive for polygyny. The more wives and children a man had translated into greater wealth in the form of crop production, social prestige, and subjects. Polygyny became a way for men to secure labor for cash farming.

Since the family unit became the basis for guaranteeing steady cash crop production, the colonial state had a vested interest in ensuring marital instability. In the 1940s and 1950s, British officials in Iganga became concerned about the increasing divorce rate and the negative effect it would have on farm production (Fallers 1969). In an effort to stabilize and regulate marriage, they collaborated with local male leaders to institute laws that gave husbands greater control over their "unruly" wives. One attempt to control women was greater enforcement of the 1904 Divorce Law, which required a full refund of bridewealth (by either the woman's father or new husband) upon the dissolution of a union. This had the intended effect of making divorce more difficult for women to initiate.

Another tool used to stabilize marriage was the Adultery Law which, following British law, was defined differently for husbands and wives. For a married woman, adultery was having an affair or running off with another man. For a man, adultery was defined as sexual relations with a married woman, with the offense committed against the "owner" of the woman, such as her husband. Sexual relations with an unmarried woman were not considered adultery. In other words, while a man could divorce a wife if she had extramarital sex, his own extramarital sexuality was neither legally nor socially considered grounds for divorce. The law codified a gendered double standard for extramarital sex: a man could *safely* have an extramarital liaison without any legal ramification or wider social consequence as long as it was with a woman over whom another man did not claim rights, such as a prostitute, divorcée, widow, or orphan.

In my discussions with Iganga residents about their parents' marriages, the double standard regarding the definition, meanings, and consequences of adultery clearly emerges. When asked to reflect on their parents' marriages, many older participants recounted stories of their fathers' flagrant extramarital liaisons. For instance, Tapenensi,[4] an older woman in her late sixties whose mother had come of age during the colonial period, explained that her mother had protested her husband's repeated bringing of other women into their bedroom by eventually refusing to sleep in her matrimonial bed. She chose, instead, to sleep on the floor of their bedroom. Tapenensi, as a result, was determined to never "surrender control over my bedroom as my mother did." After she had borne five children, her husband had brought a younger woman into the home as a second wife to bear more children. Remembering the fate of her mother, Tapenensi had remained steadfast about giving up neither her bedroom nor her senior position in the household. She describes how this had occurred twice, with both co-wives eventually leaving when Tapenensi's stubbornness and oversight became too much for them. After two failed attempts at polygyny, her husband did not bring another woman into the house, keeping his extramarital lovers outside the home and their marriage. Tapenensi's story shows how men's extramarital liaisons were not grounds for divorce but also women's coping strategies.

In sum, colonial policies interacted with precolonial Basoga kinship and economic systems in ways that facilitated and encouraged men's multi-partnering. While the dependence of wives on their husbands was structurally bolstered through adultery and divorce laws, women did employ varying degrees of resistance, including divorce, silent protest, and managing domestic interactions.

## The Postcolonial Era: The Emergence of the Middle Class and the Myth of Monogamy

During the postcolonial era, a visible middle class emerged. Their public dominance further shaped notions of marriage and extramarital liaisons, working in some instances to transform polygyny into a form of informal secondary households or outside wives (see Karanja 1987; Mann 1994; Musisi 1991). The marital histories of three generations reveal a pattern in which the hegemonic notion of wealth in the form of wives and children gradually was challenged as capitalist desires and Christian ideologies were further absorbed into the local landscape. In Uganda's increasingly monetized economy, wives and children not only meant more labor for farming but also more household dependents to feed, clothe, educate, and the like. The notion of "wealth in people" as a motivator for a man to marry multiple wives was displaced—in ideology if not in practice—by the ideal of marital monogamy, particularly among Uganda's emerging elite. In some cases, in order to manage multiple partnerships while not officially participating in polygyny, wealthy men took on informal "outside wives." This blurring of polygyny and extramarital sexuality is demonstrated in marital histories of Iganga's first postcolonial educated adult men, for whom professional mobility and success depended on depicting a certain type of marital image to European patrons and other elite Africans.

Take, for example, Joshua Waigona, who had been a top civil servant in Uganda's first postcolonial government. He had married Mary in 1965; he was twenty-five and she was sixteen. He described how monogamy and big church weddings were expected at that time within his social network. While he had had several lovers before marriage who were, according to him, "*ababulidho*" (common women), he had selected Mary as his wife because she was "a conservative, educated girl" from one of the female boarding schools in the area. He had thought that Mary would fit nicely into his peer network and would represent him well. He described how activities such as attending movies in the city, eating at fancy restaurants, and taking weekend trips were inaccessible to most Ugandans but had formed an important aspect of their middle-class identity. As John reflected on the prestige and the social worlds associated with Christian, monogamous marriage, he simultaneously talked about the various lovers he had maintained while away in England for training and in the Ugandan towns he had frequented for work, relationships indirectly and silently encouraged by his coworkers and supervisors.

In the late 1970s, Joshua, Mary, and their children relocated to the capital, Kampala, for his job promotion with a British bank. Joshua made frequent trips to Iganga for work and to visit his natal family. He had met and become "familiar with" the daughter of the owner of a popular pub. She got pregnant and he eventually married her. The story has an interesting twist.

Ironically, it was his angry and disappointed wife who insisted that he take his pregnant lover as a second wife. Mary's reason: she wanted to keep a watchful eye on the younger woman's behavior and hoped to have greater control over the rumors about the affair and her marriage. Joshua initially opposed turning the extramarital liaison into formal polygyny for fear that his reputation among European patrons and other African elites would be tarnished, but in the end, he gave in when the competing pressures from his wife, his mother, and the mother of his pregnant lover became too great. His second wife, however, never gained the full social status of a wife of a wealthy man. This was partly because Mary's clever planning and her position as an educated woman left no room for another wife in their social networks, and because their Christian community only recognized one formal wife. The second wife passed away in 1989, to which Mary commented, "My marriage was able to return to normal—the way it was supposed to be."

Joshua and Mary's case offers insight into how marital practices and men's management of multiple partnerships became important class markers and indexes of modernity during Uganda's recent history. Although the public appearance of marital monogamy was expected by their social networks, the wealth and mobility of many middle-class professional men gave them great access to a large pool of women—who, in turn, found them highly desirable.

Furthermore, while formal polygyny was frowned upon in elite circles, the maintenance of girlfriends was quietly accepted and facilitated by men's peer groups. Although Joshua formalized his marriage with his second wife, it was and still is more common for a long-term girlfriend relationship to turn merely into an "informal secondary" household, particularly after the birth of a child. Finally, Joshua and Mary's story also reveals the way in which a wife can participate in presenting a certain type of public appearance of her marriage in order to maintain her public reputation as well as to exert some influence over her husband's actions.

### Modern Marriage: The Economy, Love, and Secrecy

Scholars have noted that over the last fifty years around the world, there has been a rise of companionate (or love) marriage occasioned by global influences,

changes in the marketplace, and an increasing importance of individualism (Wardlow and Hirsch 2006). The same can be said of marriage in Iganga. In our study, both men and women described marriage today in terms of mutual investment in "developing the home." According to both wealthy and poor people in Iganga, this goal requires mutual economic and emotional commitment from husbands and wives to the marital project, the cornerstones of which are communication and cooperation.

As residents reflected on their parents' marriages, they were critical of their fathers' irresponsible use of income on women other than their own mothers (although this did not necessarily stop men from engaging in similar behaviors). Women commented on their mothers' passivity and seeming complacence regarding their fathers' philandering. As a result, when asked how they wanted their marriages to be different from those of their parents, most men and women said that they wanted fewer children and more equal participation in decision making and income generation. The joint economic and social investments in developing a modern household were regularly contrasted to the past in which husbands were seen as autocratic leaders who made decisions without input from or consent of their wives. Today wives can and do express their anger to husbands who misuse household funds for their own pleasures, including inquiries about suspected extramarital liaisons.

Uganda's aggressive HIV prevention campaigns have served to reinforce public ideals of monogamy and fidelity, particularly through the ABC (abstinence, be faithful, condom use) campaigns. Furthermore, Uganda's omnipresent public health campaigns have provided medical reasons and scientific support for avoiding certain types of sexual behaviors in favor of marital fidelity and partner reduction. Simultaneously, within the last couple of decades, the quickly growing Evangelical Pentecostal (or "born again") movement has had a tremendous impact on residents' ideas about the connections among marriage, monogamy, and capitalist consumption. Both men and women in our study thought that monogamy was economically and socially more desirable than polygyny. Although the ideal of monogamy was pervasive, actual practice was different. In a baseline study I conducted in a sample village in 1998, about a third of all household heads ($N = 423$ households) were in a polygynous union at the time (Parikh forthcoming).

Consumption patterns play an important role in defining a modern marriage. In reality, however, desired goods and lifestyles that mark a marriage as "modern" remain unobtainable or unsustainable for many residents in Iganga, leading to problematic outcomes.

Many women in our study said that their husbands had promised greater economic success than what their current realities are. When a husband could not meet his premarital promises of wealth and luxuries, it frequently led to frustrations and disagreements within the marriage. In order to avoid conflict and questions about their failed economic pursuits, a strategy that men employed was to stay away from home, finding solace in mistresses who seldom required the same financial investment that wives and households did. Lovers frequently demanded some material reward such as rent, money, gifts, or assistance with children, but to a much lesser degree, and did not ask questions otherwise.

Public discourses that have challenged gender inequalities within modern marriage have led to a different set of tensions within marriages. Women generally believe that the social campaigns surrounding gender reform and women's rights are positive; however, some husbands see it as threatening to their status. A man in his late sixties explains the effects of Uganda's gender equality campaigns on marriage:

> Women [in the past] had good discipline. They were not behaving like today's young wives. There was a lot of respect given to the husband. If the man said, "I want to find such a thing done," that will be final and by the time he came back, the thing will have been done. The wife would not have any complaint or anything to add. Marriage then was good, although there was a lot of wife beating.

Men repeatedly expressed the feeling that their masculine authority—once seen as both natural and a cultural given—was constantly under attack on multiple fronts, including development discourses, HIV prevention messages, women's rights campaigns and legislation, and popular songs, plays, and radio shows. Thus, one could read men's extramarital liaisons as a "protest" against the new gender regime in which men feel their power has diminished.

According to residents, another significant social factor has had tremendous impact on marriages and extramarital liaisons—the availability of young unmarried women who are no longer under the authority of their fathers. Locally, these young women are called *nakyewombekeire*, or literally "a young woman who lives on her own," which can also be understood to mean lacking steady employment. Residents view the growing supply of unmarried young women as the most immediate threat to the stability of marriages. Whereas feminist analysis portrays young and adolescent women as vulnerable victims of wealthier men's sexual advances, residents as well as the media often construct a narrative in which unmarried women are intentionally pursuing married men. Particularly

depicted as "vulnerable" are wealthy men and men of social power. Within this "men-as-victims" trope, male infidelity is construed less the result of men searching for women and more as a function of too many single women chasing after the few men with money.

The anxiety surrounding young women's sexual agency has been heightened by people's awareness of the HIV epidemic and Uganda's sizable population of young people who have come of age as orphans. This pool has contributed to the growing number of young men who find themselves searching for income opportunities, suspended in menial work, or in between jobs, and subsequently delaying marriage. As younger men postpone marriage for economic reasons, relationships with older and wealthier married men provide young women with opportunities for economic support and social networks. When asked why men cheat, one man remarked, "There are just too many unmarried beautiful young women without money and they simply tempt us [*light laughter*]."

In today's shifting moral economy, dominated by religious, public health, and popular culture discourses, a new demand for discretion has emerged—an image of discretion that privileges the appearance of sexually safe and monogamous couples. Managing social reputation requires conflicting actions from men: appearing to have sexual prowess and vitality remains an important aspect of masculine status within many male peer groups, but uncontained public knowledge of his sexual exploits can ruin a man's reputation in the wider community. Hence, a man's friends or coworkers might serve as accomplices or encouragers for his dalliances, but he may also go to great lengths to keep knowledge of his extramarital relations away from people in his home and his family's social networks. Having liaisons with women not in his wife's socioeconomic group is the socially safest type of affair from the perspective of not getting caught.

## MODERN WIVES: LOVE, GEOGRAPHIES OF BLAME, AND THE OTHER WOMAN

While doing research for this project, the album *Spare Tyre* by the popular husband and wife duo, Sam and Sophie Gombya, was wildly popular. In the album's title song, Sophie warns and ridicules mistresses or "spare tyres" who sleep with married men. The song asserts that official wives have the real power and that mistresses are simple fools who are just being (ab)used and discarded like spare tires.

The music video depicts a doting Sophie hugging and intimately touching her "husband" (played by an actor), speaking to and pointing her finger at the other woman, and looking directly at the camera to remind all "spare tyres" of their subordinate position. In response to what Sophie and other wives see as such women's unapologetic and boastful flaunting of their affairs with married men, the feisty singer reminds them:

> You have forgotten
> That you are called the *malaya* (prostitute).
> I am called the wife. . . .
> I know that you are there
> You are my helper
> You are a spare tyre
> I am his real wife. . . .
> When he comes and deceives you . . .
> He loves you in hiding
> I am the one in control
> Better wake up . . .
> You are like alcohol
> Only used to take away his boredom

The video ends with a defiantly bold Sophie pulling the wig off the head of the other woman in front of a crowd of onlookers, symbolically and publicly baring the inauthenticity of her husband's lover.

The song easily resonates with women in Iganga rebelling against its history of philandering husbands. These acts of rebellion have been gaining further validation and moral support through a variety of public movements in Uganda that forcefully denounce the historical norms that have allowed men to have multiple partners without major consequences. Furthermore, sex scandals involving Uganda's political and social elite have been constantly featured in the country's lucrative social media.

The popularity of these moral discourses reflect a wider social anxiety that surrounds the contradictions inherent in conceptions of modern marriage and persistent expectations, opportunity structures, and gender inequality that facilitate male infidelity. Christine Obbo (1987) observed that in the early 1980s in Uganda, "high status women, while striving to make their homes as comfortable as possible for the husband, [would] turn a blind eye and deaf ear to his extramarital activities" in part to spare their reputations and maintain marital harmony. Conducted twenty years after Obbo's study, my research suggests that among women in Iganga, men's infidelity is becoming increasingly intolerable, even for middle-class women who might have more at stake in terms of public reputation. In fact, during our interviews with women in Iganga, most spoke easily about their husbands' misbehaving (most commonly womanizing or overdrinking) as the source of their marital discontent. Public outcries by women were not uncommon during the research period, and there were cases in which a wife or an assigned intermediary secretly followed an adulterous husband to "catch him red-handed" with his mistress.

Wives are presented with a paradox: while the search for prestige—the appearance of modern monogamous marriage—largely motivates women's silences around their husbands' infidelities, the desire for another kind of prestige—the status of being "rational" modern women who have the knowledge and desire to protect their bodies and rights—leads some wives to go public with their complaints about their husbands' infidelities. Feigning indifference or being willfully ignorant can prove detrimental to a woman's reputation, particularly in a context in which women rights agencies, public health campaigns, and global discourses of modernity promote notions of personhood based on rational choice, individual agency, and self-efficacy. While the consequences of going public can in some cases be dire, if executed well such displays can prove to be a productive and almost necessary reaction. In airing their grievances to the wider community, women can hope to prompt three effects: to shame the husband in hopes of securing greater community surveillance, to gain sympathy from her neighbors, and to present herself as a modern woman, which in rights and public health discourses, is based on a model of rational choice in which a woman has the will to protect her self-interest and well-being.

Yet rarely did wives' outcries or public acts of rebellion lead them to initiate a divorce. As in Sophie's song and cases I saw in Iganga, a wife's anger is often not directed at the husband, but at the other woman, who is often referred to by what has turned into the derogatory term *nakyewombekeire*. No longer publicly tied to fathers, brothers, or uncles, and not yet tied to husbands, *nakyewombekeire* have been set free to compete with each other and, importantly, with older or married women. The conflict between wives and mistresses is not simply about generational tensions; it also reveals class struggles among women. While an elite man might befriend a driver or subordinate and have him collaborate in his secrets, people in Iganga speak about relationships among women in different socio-economic classes as being fraught with distrust and animosity. This vertical class animosity among women provides another opportunity structure that facilitates men's extramarital liaisons. For mistresses, relationships with the husbands of older women or women from a higher class can be read as a form of social revenge against the women who look down on them.

By breaking their silence and going public with knowledge of their husbands' infidelities, women rebel against the (not so) secret contradictions that exist between what has come to be expected of modern monogamous marriage and the realities that wider forces converge to make that expectation seemingly impossible, or what one older man called the "sexual hypocrisy" of the modern world. But like the song "Spare Tyre," in local geographies of blame, the mistress (not the husband) is constructed as the provocateur of men's infidelity. Blaming the other woman for a husband's behaviors is not only a way of articulating awareness of wider opportunity structures that propel men into extramarital liaisons; it is also a way in which a wife can make her husband's infidelities a bit more tolerable, and a way for her to protect her own reputation as a modern rational woman when she forgives him and attempts to maintain her modern marriage.

## NOTES

1. This project is part of a larger comparative study, "Love Marriage, and HIV: A Multi-Site Study of Gender and HIV Risk," funded by the National Institutes of Health (NIH) R01 41724-01A1. My four collaborators conducted the same research in different countries—Jennifer Hirsch (Mexico), Holly Wardlow (Papua New Guinea), Harriet Phinney (Vietnam), and Daniel Smith (Nigeria). Some of the ideas and concepts (particularly the notion of "opportunity structures" and the role of migration in facilitating extramarital sex) were developed jointly by our group (see Hirsch et al. 2010). I would like to thank my collaborators listed above and my research assistants in Uganda (Janet Kagoda, Isabirye Gerald, Moses Mwesigwa, John Daniel Ibembe, and Harriet Mugulusi) for the analytic insights they have provided.
2. For a fuller discussion of opportunity structures and sexual geography that facilitate men's extramarital sexuality, see Parikh (2007).
3. See Allman and Tashjian (2000) and Hunt (1991) for discussions of colonial influences in gender relations in Africa.
4. All names in this chapter are pseudonyms.

## REFERENCES

Allman, Jean, and V. Tashjian. 2000. *I Will Not Eat Stone: A Women's History of Colonial Asante, 1900–1925*. Portsmouth: Heinemann.

Campbell, Catherine. 1997. "Migrancy, Masculine Identities and Aids: The Psychosocial Context of HIV Transmission on the South African Gold Mines." *Social Science and Medicine* 45(2): 273–281.

Carpenter Lucy, A. Kamali, S. Malamba, and J. Whitworth. 1999. "Rates of HIV-1 Transmission within Marriage in Rural Uganda in Relation to the HIV Sero-Status of the Partners." *AIDS* 13:1083–1089.

Fallers, Lloyd. 1969. *Law without Precedent: Legal Ideas in Action in the Courts of Colonial Busoga*. Chicago, IL: University of Chicago Press.

Hirsch, Jennifer S., Holly Wardlow, Daniel Jordan Smith, Harriet M. Phinney, Shanti Parikh, and Constance A. Nathanson. 2010. The Secret: Love, Marriage, and HIV. Nashville, TN: Vanderbilt University Press. Hunt, Nancy Rose. 1991. "Noise over Camouflaged Polygamy, Colonial Morality Taxation, and a Woman-Naming Crisis in Belgian Africa." *Journal of African History* 32(3): 471–494.

Karanja, Wambui Wa. 1987. "'Outside Wives' and 'Inside Wives' in Nigeria: A Study of Changing Perceptions in Marriage." In David Parkin and David Nyamwaya (eds.). *Transformations of African Marriage*, pp. 247–261. Wolfeboro, NH: Manchester University Press.

Mann, Kristin. 1994. "The Historical Roots and Cultural Logic of Outside Marriage in Colonial Lagos." In Caroline Bledsoe and Gilles Pison (eds.). *Nuptiality in Sub-Saharan Africa*, pp. 167–193. Oxford: Clarendon Press.

Mayer, Kenneth, S. Newmann, S. Solomon, et al. 2004. "Marriage, Monogamy and HIV: A Profile of HIV-Infected Women in South India." *International Journal of STD & AIDS* 11: 250–253.

Mbulaiteye, Samuel, C. Mahe, J. Whitworth, A. Ruberantwari, J. Nakiyingi, A. Ojwiya, and A. Kamali. 2002. "Declining HIV-1 Incidence and Associated Prevalence over 10 Years in a Rural Population in South-West Uganda: A Cohort Study." *The Lancet* 360: 41–46.

Musisi, Nakanyike. 1991. "Women, 'Elite Polygyny,' and Buganda State Formation." *Signs* 16(4): 757–786.

Obbo, Christine. 1987. "The Old and the New in East African Elite Marriages." In David Parkin and David Nyamwaya (eds.). *Transformations of African Marriage*. Wolfeboro, NH: Manchester University Press.

O'Leary, Ann. 2000. "Women at Risk for HIV from a Primary Partner: Balancing Risk and Intimacy." *Annual Review of Sex Research* 11: 191–234.

Parikh, Shanti. 2007. "The Political Economy of Marriage and HIV: The ABC Approach, 'Safe' Infidelity, and Managing Moral Risk in Uganda." *The American Journal of Public Health* 97: 1198–1208.

Parikh, Shanti. Forthcoming. *Regulating Romance: Youth Sexual Culture, Moral Anxiety, and Love Letters in Uganda's Time of AIDS*. Nashville: Vanderbilt Press.

Radcliffe-Brown, Alfred R. 1950. "Introduction." In A. R. Radcliffe-Brown and Daryll Forde (eds.). *African Systems of Kinship and Marriage*, pp. 1–85. London: Oxford University Press.

Rosaldo, Michelle Z. 1974. "Theoretical Overview." In Michelle Z. Rosaldo and Louise Lamphere (eds.). *Women, Culture, and Society*, pp. 17–43. Stanford, CA: Stanford University Press.

———. 1980. "The Uses and Abuses of Anthropology." *Signs* 5(3): 389–417.

UNAIDS, UNFPA, and UNIFEM. 2004. *Women and HIV/AIDS: Confronting the Crisis*. Geneva: UNAIDS.

UNAIDS/WHO. 2008 Update. *Epidemiological Fact Sheets on HIV and AIDS [Uganda]*. Geneva: UNAIDS/WHO.

Wardlow, Holly, and Jennifer S. Hirsch. 2006. "Introduction." In Jennifer S. Hirsch and Holly Wardlow (eds.). *Modern Loves: The Anthropology of Romantic Courtship & Companionate Marriage*, pp. 1–31. Ann Arbor: University of Michigan Press.

# Fatherhood and the Mediating Role of Women

## Nicholas W. Townsend

In this chapter I confront an apparent paradox in men's accounts of fatherhood. Men say they want to be involved fathers, but they do not seem to be acting that way.

Nearly all the men I talked to in my research said they wanted to be more involved as fathers than their own fathers had been, and this stated desire is very common for men in the United States. But men in the United States do not put much time into domestic work or child care (Coltrane 1996), and after divorce many men in the United States pay very little or nothing in child support and frequently maintain no contact with their children (Arendell 1995; Furstenberg and Cherlin 1991). I argue that we can understand some of this paradox if we consider what men do as fathers as well as what they do not do, and if we listen to what they have to say about being fathers.

Parenting is deeply gendered. And by this I do not mean only that fathers and mothers do different things, though that is clearly the case, but also that being a parent means different things to mothers and fathers, and that being a father means different things to men and women. Parenting is also gendered in other ways, such as men's stated preference for sons and the ways they treat daughters and sons differently. I have discussed these aspects of fatherhood elsewhere (Townsend 2002). In this chapter, I am focusing on the gendered relationship between fathers and mothers. Seeing men and their accounts as gendered in this way helps us to understand how men think about being fathers and about relationships in general.

In the first section below I describe how men see "marriage and children" as elements of a "package deal" which cannot be easily separated. Conceptually, a relationship with a woman is necessary for a man to see himself as a father or "family man." In the subsequent sections, I show how women are often the "driving force" behind men's decisions about when to have children; that a structural division of labor that places men in the labor force and women at home is maintained and supported by cultural work in the face of women's increasing labor force participation; and that parenting itself is gendered, with women being the "default parents" who maintain schedules and routines, while men are in a more "optional" position, with their participation as "fun dads" or "enforcers" mediated by their children's mothers.

Courtesy of Nicholas W. Townsend

It has been easy to see the gendered division of labor in parenting as a simple division in which men are engaged in the public sphere of paid work and politics and women are involved in the domestic sphere of child care and reproduction.[1] What my description shows, however, is that these two spheres interpenetrate, and that arrangements made in one sphere influence behavior in another. For instance, we shall see that cultural ideas about the division of paid labor and about who should provide for families have an impact on ideas about who should do what for children.

My discussion in this chapter is based on talking to men who graduated from the same high school in 1972 and were in their late thirties when I interviewed them.[2] Because they all graduated from the same high school, I was able to learn a lot about the community in California in which they grew up, the events of their youth, and the opportunities they faced as adults. I can speak with confidence about the attitudes these men shared, and about the differences between them, and I would argue that these men are in many ways typical of men in the United States, but these men's experiences and meanings cannot be used to support universal or essential ideas about "male" experience or fathering as a universal pattern of behavior.[3]

What emerged from my conversations is that, for the men I talked to, the father–child relationship could not be described or thought about independent of the relationship between husband and wife. When I ask men about their parents, they talk mostly about their fathers, but when I ask them about becoming fathers they talk about their wives. Some of the paradoxes of men's relations to their children may be resolved by understanding the relative positions of men, women, and children, and specifically the crucial linking or mediating role of women.

Appreciating the linking role of women is not the same as saying that men do not care about children, or that they think that children are entirely women's business. Certainly becoming a parent is more separated from biological reproduction for men than for women. One can scarcely imagine a woman saying, as one of my male informants did: "Actually I have had a child before, although through very strange circumstances I didn't know I had a child before he was a year old and someone sent me a Christmas card saying: 'This is your baby.'" Equally certainly, men consider childbearing and child rearing to be predominantly women's responsibility. This is not to say that men are indifferent to having children. They have strong feelings about the number, timing, and kind of children they want, but at crucial points in their lives they find that their paternity depends on the cooperation of women. The men are not passively dependent on women's motivations—they actively select and try to persuade, pressure, and coerce women, but the mediating link provided by women remains crucial.

It is not just that men need, and realize that they need, a woman's physical cooperation in order to become fathers. There is also an asymmetry in the ways that men and women think about becoming parents. For instance, many women are prepared to think about single parenthood as a possible, though usually less desirable, route to motherhood; the men I talked to, on the other hand, do not even register it as a possibility. Many single, childless women are able to think and talk directly about whether they want to have children. In doing so, and in reading the advice and examples they are offered in books and magazines, it is clear that they see having a child on one's own as an option. It is an option with definite emotional, social, and financial drawbacks as well as opportunities, and it is an option that they may well reject, but it remains a possibility. That having a child on her own is a possibility to be considered means that women are able to weigh and articulate their specific desire for children outside the matrix of family and relationship with a man. The relationship between mother and child, the activity of mothering, and the transformation of self into a mother, are things women can think about directly and in isolation. The men I talked to could not talk about having children without talking about "having a family" or "being a family man." For these men, "having children" is part of "being married and having a family." They can only conceptualize the relationship between father and children within the matrix of family relationships.

Of course, the relationships between men and their wives are very important in their own right, but my interest here is in the way that marital relationships are structurally important for men's relationships with their children. Women, as wives and mothers, mediate and facilitate fatherhood. The word "mediate" describes women's role in the relationship between men and children because it captures, in its various meanings, some of the complexity of that role. Women are in the middle of this relationship, they frequently do mediate in the most literal sense of operating as go-betweens or negotiators between their husbands and their children, and their presence and activity makes possible the reproduction, both biological and social, that is at the heart of fatherhood.

For men, having children is a reproduction of fatherhood—a patrilineal process of the movement of males through the statuses of son, father, and grandfather and of child, adult, and old man (Townsend 1998). There are five moments, phases, or aspects of reproduction at which women's mediating role is most apparent: at marriage, when decisions are made about the timing and number of children, in the structural division of labor after children are born, in gendered parenting, and after divorce.

## MARRIAGE AND CHILDREN: WIFE AND MOTHER

"We always knew we wanted to get married and have a family" was a frequent comment of men who married women they had known in high school. For my informants, marriage is almost always considered to be a relationship that will involve having children. In most first marriages, husbands say they either "knew" or "assumed" that their wives would want children. For the men, marriage meant getting a "wife and family" as a sort of package deal.

As is often the case, it is when obstacles to meeting a norm arise that its existence is made most clear. Several men told me that they did not marry women with whom they had "good relationships" because those women did not want or could not have children. Conversely, men who had actually wanted to have children told me that they had ended relationships with women they did not want to marry by telling them that they did not want to have children. That this was an excuse is made clear by the rapidity with which they subsequently met, married, and had children with other women. Regardless of whether the particular men or women in any relationship or marriage really wanted children or not, the point is that the cultural idea that marriage and children go together was so clear to all that it could be used as a reason to end a relationship without rejecting the other person by saying: "I don't want to marry you." Men are making a simultaneous decision about "a wife and a mother to my children."

Greg, an earnest man with two children who worked as a programmer in a software company, had married at age twenty-nine, a fact that was very significant to him and to which he returned repeatedly. To him, twenty-nine was old to be getting married, and he did not want to be too old to be a vigorous father to his children. He felt, however, that waiting until he was twenty-nine had not been a bad thing:

I kind of got everything out of my system before I got married. And then, when I did get married I wanted it to be forever, as they say, and I was ready to have kids.

When I got married I was ready to have kids. I probably had it planned in my mind. "We'll get married and we'll have children."

Although Greg linked marriage with having children, he said that he and his wife had not talked explicitly before their marriage about having children, but that it was "Just something you kind of know."

I had seen a lot of women over a period of years. You see all kinds of women out there. I mean, there are some smart ones, but most of them are—they don't know if they're coming or going, you know. Maggie's very intelligent, which I like, very kind, and very funny. That's very important to me, a sense of humor. It is kind of hard to explain exactly why you know that that's the person, but she had all the factors that I was looking for. I remember telling myself: "I can live with this girl for the rest of my life. I mean I can actually do it through the day to day." I just had the inner feeling that I could be comfortable with her for basically the rest of my life.

Greg's choice of a wife was, however, not based simply on personal compatibility: "If I knew that she did not want to have children," he added, "I would not have married her."

Gordon, an engineer with three sons, had married his wife two years after they met, and two years later, while he was still in college, his first son was born. Gordon told me early on that: "Before we got married we had a goal of three and when we finally got three, I just said: 'I don't have enough for any more.'" Later, when I asked him if he had always wanted children, he replied, after a pause: "I never felt that I would not have children. But, you know, up until I found the person I wanted to marry and live with, I never thought 'I really want kids.' I don't think I consciously said that." And when I asked him if children are needed to complete a family, he immediately responded: "That's not the reason we had children, but I believe that's a true statement. Not to say that a couple is incomplete, but I think you're *more married* if you have children." His predisposition to have children, and his liking for children (he taught Sunday school before he was married) had not gelled into a firm plan to have children of his own until he met the person he wanted to marry. Marriage and children were inextricably linked in his thinking, as they were in another man's comment that "Getting married and not having kids at all, seems kind of incomplete. I can see you being a single person and not having kids. I can understand that more now. If you're married it would be odd not having children."

A deliberately childless marriage is definitely a thing to be negotiated beforehand. At least normatively, inability to bear children is not grounds for divorce, but one partner's unwillingness to have them might cause the other partner to hesitate or to refuse to enter into marriage in the first place. Several men said that in order to marry a woman who did not want children "you would have to love her a lot." There is an implication here that a marriage without children requires a stronger love than a marriage with children. But I think it is closer to these men's meanings that children provide structure and cohesion to a marriage, and that romantic love alone, without the cement of shared parenting and the economic partnership of working to support home and family, is a slender thread on which to hang a lifetime together.

During the 1970s and early 1980s, when the men I interviewed were aged between eighteen and thirty, the divorce rate for childless couples was higher than for couples who had children (Wienberg 1988). Divorces of childless couples also proceeded more rapidly than the divorces of couples with children (White et al. 1986). Conversely, the birth of a first child within marriage drastically reduced the divorce rate for the next year (Waite et al. 1985). Although subsequent births did not have this effect, the presence of children in a marriage did appear to slow the process of divorce (White et al. 1986).[4] Of the men I talked to, those who had been through divorces in which children had been involved reported more protracted divorces, with separations and reconciliations, whereas the divorces that did not involve children were more rapid and clear-cut. The direction of causation in these relationships between fertility and divorce is not always clear. It may be that having children makes a marriage less likely to end in divorce, but it may also be that couples who think their marriage is in trouble are less likely to embark on childbearing.

The men I talked to recognized that having a child may both strengthen and undermine the relationship between husband and wife. On the one hand, they appreciated the problems of fatigue, busy schedules, and restrictions on shared leisure that children create for marriages. On the other hand, they stressed the responsibility they felt toward maintaining an intact family and also mentioned the new connections with their wives that came from enjoying their children and from sharing activities with them. Having children certainly made divorce harder to think about. They would, they said, stay married through hard times and routine times.

The comments I heard are consistent with the statistical picture that fertility within marriage reduces the incidence and slows the process of divorce. They also indicate that childlessness within marriage is not a common goal, and would demand of a marriage something qualitatively different than is expected in a reproductive union. Several men described a couple they knew who were married soon after high school graduation but deliberately had no children. After their divorce, both partners remarried and had children. The interpretation put on this by their friends is that the marriage without children could not sustain itself, but that subsequent marriages to people with whom they were ready to have children were likely to be satisfying and successful. Childlessness, in this account, is presented as both a consequence of doubts about the marriage and a cause of its failure.

The men I spoke to depend on a marital relationship with a woman for a paternal relationship with children. In the contemporary United States, the availability of effective contraception and a relaxation of the standard of sexual chastity for brides means that a man's girlfriend, his premarital sexual partner, the woman he lives with, and his wife may all be the same person, but are not necessarily so—the roles and the individuals filling them are uncoupled. A wife, however, is unique in the formalization of her social position and in the way that she links a man to other social persons by virtue of that social position and not merely by virtue of her personal qualities and associations.

Barry, balding and hospitable, lived in a new house in a new subdivision. As we sat on his deck, watching his young children from his second marriage play in the wading pool, he told me a story that encapsulated the connection between marriage and children:

It's funny, I knew this one girl that I worked with. She was living with her boyfriend. She never took any birth control. For probably years, she never did. Never got pregnant. But they finally got married, and like their wedding night, she got pregnant. It was kind of a psychological thing, you know? Like: "Geez, I can't get pregnant, I'm not married. Well, now I'm married, it's OK."

In both his own marriages, Barry had drawn the same distinction between living together (and therefore not having children) and being married (and having or planning children).

The first time, you just get married because it was the thing to do, so to speak. The second time you're a little bit wiser and more cautious. The first time I was twenty-one and my wife had just turned nineteen. We were married for a couple of years. And what's interesting is that she was raised in a very strict Catholic background so living together was kind of taboo. So we never lived together. We basically got married and we found out that what she wanted and what I wanted were really different. We talked about children. Nothing real serious, but like: "Down the road here, we should have children." So it's a good thing that we didn't. We were using birth control. It wasn't to the point where we decided "Let's try" and we weren't successful. We weren't ready at that time.

The second time he got married, Barry proceeded very differently. Even his sentence structure and word choice when telling me about it expressed his greater deliberation:

We both had our own separate homes and lifestyles when we first met and we spent a lot of time together. We decided we had a pretty lasting relationship going and that we should live together and consolidate. That way we could really tell, by living together, whether or not we could live together forever. Because you just don't know people until you actually live with them. So we lived together for a while. And then we decided to get married and have children. In fact, that was kind of interesting. My wife—one of her comments that kind of surprised me was: "Geez, we don't need to get married to have children." And that really kind of took me by surprise because I've kind of had different morals than that. If you're going to have children, at least plan children, then you need to be married. Obviously there are times when things are not planned and you're not married. But the way I believe, if you're going to plan to have children, you should be married. She was very insistent that that didn't need to be the case. . . . She likes children, and I like children, so it was kind of a—We discussed it and decided "Let's get married and we'll have children" instead of just having children and not getting married.

Barry attributed his surprise at his wife's suggestion that they did not need to get married to have children to "different morals," but when his comments are taken as a whole, we can see that his association of children and marriage is not so much moral as conceptual. His picture of family life, his conceptual framework for social relationships, was one that included the possibility of living together and that separated sexual relations from procreation, but equated having children with being married. In this, and in the difference between him and his wife, Barry was typical. In order to be a father, he had to be married. His fatherhood, therefore, conceptually depends on his having a marital relationship with a woman. Once married, the timing of his children's births would depend on his wife's willingness and initiative.

## "THE DRIVING FORCE": WOMEN, TIMING, AND BIRTH CONTROL

In general, the men I talked to assumed that, in their own lives, conception and birth were events that could be controlled. They assumed that sexual intercourse without pregnancy was a reasonable expectation, so that premarital sex, a space of time between marriage and their first birth, a controlled space between their children's births, and a cessation of childbearing were all things to be reasonably expected and planned for.

Their confidence in their ability to plan was, to a certain extent, justified by the technological innovations of the birth control pill, the IUD, and safe and easy techniques for male and female sterilization.

Previous fertility declines and control, at the level of populations and of couples, have depended on a mix of methods, including heavy reliance on abstinence and withdrawal (Schneider and Schneider 1996). These are methods that involve at least the participation, if not the active initiation, of men. The Pill and the IUD, by contrast, are methods that are used by women and that do not require contraceptive action by men or women at the time of intercourse. They are, particularly for men, much less psychically costly than withdrawal or abstinence. For men in the United States, these methods have had the double effect of enabling a conceptual and physical separation between sexual activity and reproduction and of moving control over reproduction to women. Control over reproduction was seen as not only technically, but also morally, women's responsibility.

Barry, for example, does not say the decision about when to have children was his wife's alone, but he does put the primary responsibility on her.

> She was probably the driving force. Again, I wanted children too. So it wasn't like: "OK, I'll just give in. If you want children, we'll have children." But she was probably more the driver of that issue than myself. I could have been content to wait a couple years. But again, we both wanted children. It wasn't just because she wanted children. If she would have been very insistent against it, it would have been something we probably would have had to talk about. It's really hard to say, but I think I wanted to have children also, but not to the same degree as she did. It would have been nice to have them, but if I didn't, I could have lived without them. It wouldn't have been a decision I may have regretted.

Notice that while she is the "driving force" behind the timing, he also makes it clear that he too wanted children. But he then questions his own desire when he says "I think I wanted to have children" and "I could have lived without them." In the face of this uncertainty, he placed the initiative with his wife.

The norm expressed by all the men I talked to is that there should be a period at the beginning of married life when the couple have "time for themselves as a couple." This norm may be violated by early conception, or by a period of living together followed by marriage and rapid subsequent conception.

Marvin, a large, easygoing man, who worked in purchasing, told me that he and his wife had children sooner than he would have liked. His plan had been to graduate from college and buy a house before having children. His wife had taken the initiative and had persuaded him that they should have children while he was still in college.

> I wasn't all that hot about the idea. I was not sure I could handle all the responsibilities. I probably thought, in fact I did think, about how they develop and how you grow along with them. It's "Oh gosh, what am I gonna do when they're teenagers?" that sort of thing. So I wasn't all that hot about having kids. My wife convinced me that yeah, it's probably not all that tough. I should say now I know how tough it is. It's very hard. It's a never-ending challenge. But we finally agreed that we'd go ahead and have kids. And so we did. I wanted to make sure I had a house, which we didn't at the time. And go ahead and have college for me, which I didn't. So that was a kind of unsettling thing, to go from following this nice neat path to success. And here's the time to have kids. Here's the time to do this, to do that. I couldn't do that. So that kind of bothered me.

In the event, Marvin had not finished college, but he told me that had not been a real obstacle in his career, and he and his wife had bought a house with help from his wife's parents.

Men discuss their decisions about timing in terms of their "readiness" to become fathers.[5] Readiness is presented as a psychological state that does not necessarily coincide with the birth of the first child. Men may realize that they are "ready" when their first child is born, but they may also feel "not ready," causing personal anxiety and strain on their marriage. Several men told me that they only became ready to be fathers some time after the birth of their first child, usually at a point when they felt they could relate to their children.[6] On the other hand, other men have reported "being ready" before their wives were, and then embarking on campaigns to persuade them to become pregnant. For these men, it was not women's enthusiasm that drove the decision, but their reluctance or hesitation that put women in a position to control the realization of men's plans for fatherhood.

The men I talked to discussed the timing of births as if they were under perfect control, and difficulties getting pregnant, as well as unplanned pregnancies, were seen as surprising. From my perspective as an observer who knows something about the variability of human biology, this sense of being in perfect control was itself surprising. But being in control is a central organizing element of my informants' stories in all areas. Being out of control is an explanation for the bad things that happen, and a good deal of rhetorical effort is expended to create a life story characterized by control and the realization of intentions.[7] Men are actively involved in decisions about timing, but contraception during the childbearing years is overwhelmingly by female methods and men are dependent on the cooperation of their wives. But their dependence is not inevitable or driven simply by the use of female contraceptive methods. These men are actually *relinquishing* control and presenting the situation as if their wives were the only ones responsible.

Alfred, for instance, had wanted only one child, but he delayed his vasectomy after the birth of his first child. He reported that his wife then "surprised" him with a set of twins, but he delayed his vasectomy again. He only got around to sterilization after she "surprised" him with a second set. He is an exceptional example only because of the extreme personal and demographic consequences of his dependence on imperfect methods and his reluctance to assume responsibility for birth control. Alfred's position, however, underlines the centrality of effective birth control for the realization of these men's fertility plans and life plans in general. With five children under the age of six, he found himself living in too small a house, with bills higher than he had expected, and with no financial leeway. He worked as a skilled technician, but his skills were being made obsolete by technological change, and he was not in a position to make the expenditure, or take the cut in pay, necessary to acquire new skills or to move into a job with prospects of promotion. His high fertility, in fact, had effects on his work, his place of residence, and the division of labor in his marriage, and will continue to have effects in the future.

## MEN AT WORK, WOMEN AT HOME: THE STRUCTURAL DIVISION OF LABOR

The archetypical picture of family life in the United States has been of a nuclear household, composed of a married heterosexual couple and their children, in which the man is the breadwinner and the woman is the homemaker. This has not, of course, been an accurate picture of the family lives of many people, but it has been a cultural archetype, or hegemonic image, that shapes people's perceptions even when it does not represent their reality.[8] Even when they become very common, however, behaviors that do not conform to hegemonic cultural norms continue to be perceived as "exceptions." When people's lives diverge from cultural norms they have to do cultural work to deny, explain, or reinterpret, this divergence. Some husbands of employed women who wanted to emphasize that they were the primary providers for their families explained that their wives' incomes were used for "extras" or "luxuries." Others described their wives' work as something they did mainly for variety, social contacts, or to "get away from the kids." But in either case they were doing cultural work to interpret their arrangements as conforming to a hegemonic picture of the structural division of labor in marriage. In support of this division of labor, the men I talked to made three interlocking arguments: that they liked or chose the arrangement, that it was best for the children, and that it was natural.

Gordon, the engineer with three sons who felt "more married" once he had children, expressed very clearly the structural division of labor between parents: one parent should stay home to raise the children, and it should be the mother.

> I think it's wrong to have kids and then lock them in day-care centers while you're working. That's why I'm really grateful that my wife can stay home. And although at times we were real tight for money, and I told her she might have to start looking for a job if we were going to make ends meet, I was grateful when things worked out and she didn't have to. Because this is really the place the kids need a full-time mother, to watch them.

This arrangement works, Gordon says, because "She's not the working type." This gendered division of labor between husband and wife is a reproduction of his parents' pattern. His father had been a skilled machinist, his mother, with a college degree, had stayed home and not worked outside the home until her children were in high school. Gordon explains the arrangement he has with his wife as the result of their "choice" and in accord with his wife's personality. Although Gordon described both the division of labor and the fact that he followed his father into working on machines as "natural," this couple is an instance of a social fact: in the overwhelming number of cases where one of a couple works full time, it is the husband.

Like Gordon, Marvin attributes the division of labor in his marriage to his wife's preference. She has worked off and on, he says, selling products from the home and working as a teacher's aide for the local school district, which "gives her a lot of flexibility." When I asked him if she had ever wanted to work full-time, he said:

> She seems to have wanted more to be a good mother. And she was the type of person that when we got married, she had this view of herself as not "Super Mom," but "Nice Mom" that does the things that Moms do and takes the kids and gets involved in things. And that was a really big thing to her.

Marvin is articulating what Garey (1999) points to as a dominant cultural image of mothers as oriented either to work or to family. Garey argues that many employed mothers downplay their aspirations to "career" or to being "Super Mom" and practice "maternal visibility" by making a point of being seen as doing "the things that Moms do."

Paul went a step beyond Gordon and Marvin in his defense of a structural gendered division of labor, turning it into a timeless and natural pattern. Paul is a serious, almost intense man who talks quietly but displays a fierce protectiveness of his family. He works a night shift with lots of overtime and shift differential pay. He and his wife, who was employed full time, lived with their two sons, ages six and eight, in a townhouse near his work. The children were cared for by his wife's mother during the day, but she was about to move away and Paul's plan was for his wife to reduce her hours of employment and work part time.

> I was thinking about trying to buy a [single family] house over here, but if it's going to cause me to be away from the family, or cause [my wife] to have to work all the time, I think we're gonna back out. If I can't afford a house on my pay alone, and make it, if we can't do it on my paycheck alone, we're not gonna do it. Because that's just basic. It's just the way it's been since time began. Women stay home. I'm not trying to be chauvinist by any—but if you're gonna have a family, that's the way it works best.

The gendered division of labor, then, puts women in the home as the mothers of men's children, and this division of labor is reinforced by cultural work that emphasizes men's responsibility as providers and women's involvement in their children's lives. Such a division of labor is presented as natural and equal, but it is a product of a particular economic structure and social organization of work, and it works to the advantage of men in giving them more control over their leisure time (though less over the large amount of their lives they spend at work). The gendered division of labor at the structural level also has profound implications for the daily activity of parenting.

## DISCIPLINE, CARING, AND PROVIDING: GENDERED PARENTING

In parenting and child rearing men once again place women between themselves and their children. Their interactions with their children are controlled, arranged, or supervised by their wives. Women have most of the responsibility for arranging and enforcing children's activities, with men exerting their influence through their wives. Some men do put a lot of energy into their children's activities, especially into their athletic activities, and even more express the desire to do so, especially to do more with their children than their fathers did with them. But studies of time use continue to find differences between working husbands and wives in the total number of hours

worked when paid labor, childcare, and housework are combined.[9]

Not only is there a difference in the number of hours men and women spend in child rearing, but fathers and mothers approach parenting very differently. The men I talked to express the belief that mothers are the "default parent." They act on this belief and by their actions make it true. Being the default parent means being on terms of greater intimacy, being the one to whom a child turns first, and being the one with the responsibility for knowing what the child's needs and schedules are. The default parent, ultimately, is the one who has to be there, to whom parenting is in no sense optional (Walzer 1998). For example, fathers may go to meetings at their children's schools or take their children to sports practice, but it is usually mothers who keep track of when the meetings and practices are, and who are, therefore, the default parents. Lareau (2000a, 2000b) reports that fathers are very vague and general in their accounts of their children's daily routine, in contrast to the detailed and specific responses of mothers. In general, my informants indicated that it was their wives who kept the mental and physical calendar, and I would simply add that the person who keeps track of scheduling has a good deal of control over what is scheduled.

Even in the area of discipline and punishment, where it would seem that the father's position as ultimate authority was secure, mothers are the gatekeepers or mediators. Consider the proverbial threat of mothers to their children: "Just you wait until your father gets home!" This expression was used as an example by a number of men to express that they were deeply involved in their children's lives. It was meant to indicate that they were the source of discipline even if they were not in a position of direct supervision most of the time. On closer examination, however, the expression indicates a very different relationship, for it is the mother who decides when and what the father is told, and thus when he can act. Rather than being in an immediate disciplinary relationship with his children, he is a resource to be mobilized by his wife in her dealings with the children, and thus in a relationship mediated by his wife.

The disciplinary dynamic in families can take several forms, but two are common. While they may seem very different, in both of them the wife and mother is ultimately responsible for discipline. In the first, the husband is an authority figure and disciplinarian who sees himself as supporting or backing up his wife. In the second, the husband is allowed to be fun because his wife is the disciplinarian.

Both Ralph and Terry used the word "enforcer" to describe their role in their children's discipline. Neither of them liked this, though both accepted it as their responsibility to support their wives. Ralph had two children and was one of the most impressive men I met doing this research. He had had a troubled adolescence, but since then he had worked his way to a highly responsible job in public service and was universally admired by his former classmates. Ralph told me that there had been one disciplinarian in his family when he was growing up, and that it was the same in his marriage:

> One parent seems like the disciplinarian and the other one is not. And in my family I am. And my wife doesn't understand: "Why won't the children listen to me?" Because it's always: "I'm gonna tell your father." She had to call me here [at work]. I've had to talk to them on the phone. And they straighten right up.

Ralph felt that his wife should be more consistent in her discipline so that the children would not ignore her threats and make her lose her temper. She, on the other hand, sometimes felt overwhelmed and told him that if she were to hit the children instead of threatening: "I'd beat them to death. I'd be constantly hitting them."

Terry, the father of two boys, is also critical of his wife's treatment of the children, but he too accepts his role as enforcer.

> The thing is, you've gotta be the enforcer. The man has to be the enforcer and that's the only thing that sometimes irritates me. I come home from working a hard day and my wife right off "Terry, he's done this, he's done that." And I get mad and I go in there and yell at him. That's where a lot of times I would like to say "You're the mother. Handle it. If you want to restrict him, restrict him. If you want him to be whupped, do it." She's home every day. She knows exactly what's going on. I think she ought to handle it more herself.

For both Ralph and Terry, the structural division of labor, their position at work, and their wives' presence at home, means that their wives are the ones who determine what is expected of their children and who know what they are doing. The women then decide what to tell their husbands and so determine the kinds of interactions fathers and children will have. Terry yells at his children and Ralph spanks his, but their wives, as the default parents, mediate the flow of information and expectation between fathers and children. Women's mediation should not, however, be seen as deliberately manipulative. The gendered division of discipline is not an individual choice or decision, but part of a whole gendered system of division of labor.

Gordon's situation is a rather different manifestation of the same gendered system. In Gordon's family, he is the one who can relax and have fun with his sons because his wife is protective and strict. When it comes to parenting, he says:

> My wife does a better job. Although she is very protective of the kids. Like my eleven-year-old, she won't drop off at baseball practice. She'll stay and wait until it's over. And even though sitting in a car, she's always there. She won't leave the kids anywhere alone. . . . I think she's just worried about something happening to them. Not having an accident, like falling off of something, but with all the crazies out there, she's just worried about losing one of them. Which is—I mean, it's a real-life concern. I can't blame her for that, but it gets a little excessive sometimes. And she does discipline them better, they mind her better, she's more sensitive to their feeling and that kind of thing. It's the insensitive dad, sometimes. . . . I don't treat my kids the way [my father] treated us. He was a very heavy disciplinarian and we were afraid of him when we grew up. I don't want my kids to be afraid of me.

Partly because he does not want his children to fear him as he feared his father, and partly because his wife is watching over them, protecting them, and disciplining them, he feels he can let them run a little wild: "When they're just goofing off and it's Friday night, I'm not going to crack the whip and put them to bed." He laughs, "It wouldn't work anyway."

Edward's position as a "fun dad" to his three children is also mediated by his wife, who ran a child care business in her home when the youngest was a toddler and now teaches at the private school the children attend. She is very involved in the lives of children in general and her own children in particular, and part of her involvement is in scheduling her husband's time with his children. Edward says that: "When there are three there, it's tough. They're all vying for your attention." So his wife intervened and he now says to his children: "'Your Mom says it's your turn.' So each time I do something I take a different child with me. And it works out two ways. It's a lot cheaper for one. And also I get that one-on-one with my kids." Many of the things he does with his children are recreational activities that he enjoys, such as baseball and basketball games. While his wife is orchestrating this activity, Edward gets to be the fun father, spending quality time with his children doing something they can enjoy together. Edward also gets to be spontaneous with the whole family. Several times he told me that he would, "on the spur of the moment," sweep the family up and drive to the beach:

> Like I get them going at seven in the morning up to Santa Cruz and I'll bring my camping stuff and we'll cook breakfast and we'll just have breakfast and when other people are coming, we're leaving and coming back home. We do stuff off the wall like that. Spur-of-the-moment type things. On Friday afternoon I'll tell everyone to pack

their suitcase and we'll go to Monterey for a night and things like that. I think that's pretty neat.

Overall, Edward emphasized the fun and spontaneity of his relations with his children: "Age wise, I'm probably considered an adult, but you talk to my kids and I'm probably the biggest kid around. I'm not kidding. I'm a big kid at heart. I love sports. I love my kids." It is important to notice that Edward's ability to be spontaneous and to have fun with his children, just like his one-on-one time with his children, is dependent on the routine, day-by-day, planned, and conscientious work of his wife.

The gendered division of labor in parenting not only distributes work and fun differentially between fathers and mothers, it also distributes who gets taken for granted, and who gets the credit for what they do. Hochschild shows how couples negotiate not only a material division of labor, but also an economy of gratitude (1989): people do not just want to be appreciated, they want to be appreciated for the contributions they think are important. Psychologists Carolyn and Philip Cowan (1999) observed that, for men, paid employment "counts" as childcare—when men work they are seen as doing something for their children. In addition, wives see their husbands' attention to their children as contributions to the marriage relationship. Women's employment, on the other hand, is seen as detracting from their mothering, and their husbands do not see the care mothers give their children as couple time or as building the marriage. For the men I talked to, their fathers' employment was remembered and appreciated, while their mothers' employment was minimized or forgotten. In addition, their mothers' parenting was taken for granted, while their fathers' more occasional attention was treasured.

Even though he said his father did not spend much time with him—"Dad was working. I remember when my father worked three jobs"—Edward appreciated the hard work his father had done to build a financially stable foundation for his family: "My Dad's helped me out financially, he's helped every single one of his kids out. Financially and every other way." Edward also remembered "the few vacations we had" with his father. His fond memories of those rare occasions was one motivation for his own spontaneous family trips. But his memories of his mother are less precise and more matter-of-fact. I asked him if his mother had worked:

I know she worked off and on because she worked at [an electronics company] for the longest time. Yeah, she did work. I'm just trying to remember. There was a time when I know she didn't because I know when I was in elementary school I remember coming home at lunchtime and she would have lunch for me. So maybe when the kids were smaller she didn't work. And then she started

working. I remember her working at [the electronics company] a long time. Then went to [a computer manufacturer] and retired from there.

In fact, his mother had also worked full-time before the family moved to Orchardtown when Edward was six, but the point to notice is not so much whether she worked or not as that her son did not see her work as part of her identity, and certainly not as part of her parenting, which was represented by that daily routine of having lunch ready. On the other hand, for her husband work was central to his being a father. The financial help Edward received from his parents (both of whom were working full time when he was a young man) is reported as coming from his father, and the family activities he points to are a handful of family vacations with his father.

Mothers who are supervising and caring for their children may well know more about those children, about their hopes and insecurities, than fathers who are there to have occasional fun. They are then in a position to relay or to hold back knowledge about their children, and mothers are the ones who both fathers and children talk to about the other. Edward told me a typical story of an incident between him and his daughter about which both of them had, independently, talked to his wife. Their communication about the event, and its resolution in Edward's mind, was very directly mediated by the mother.

I just talked to my wife the other night. My oldest daughter, somehow I felt like she wasn't communicating with me lately, the last couple weeks. I was asking my wife if there was anything wrong. What particular things had happened at school. I went to pick up my son and she was gonna go somewhere else and I saw her and I know she saw me, but she didn't acknowledge me being there. So I was kind of hurt because usually they'll come up "Hi Dad!" And my wife goes "It had nothing to do with her not wanting—" What it was, I guess, her friends were wearing makeup and she knows I'm against girls at this age wearing makeup and I guess that was why she didn't come and talk to me. So that's fine. I can see why she didn't want to talk to me.

These examples illustrate that the structural division of labor, in which men are seen as providers and women as homemakers, is connected to a gendered division of parenting. Mothers not only do more child care and domestic work, they also know more about what their children are doing and feeling, they talk to them more, and they control the flow of information between fathers and children. They also schedule their children's lives and the interactions they have with their fathers. As part of this gendered system, the relationship that mothers have with their children even influences the quality of the interactions men have with their children. Mothers may invoke their husbands as disciplinarians and enforcers, so that the fathers are stricter or sterner than they might otherwise be. Or mothers may maintain the structure of family life, giving men the space to be spontaneous and fun.

Within this gendered system of parenting, men and women act out and reinforce gender stereotypes. Men are expected to play more actively with children than women do, and as a general rule they do so. Mothers, so I was told, control male exuberance, calming people down and discouraging dangerous or over-exuberant play. It is mothers, I am told, who set limits on the activity of men and children. By doing so, they constrain themselves or, rather, are constrained by an entire system of expectations from being "fun" in quite the same way that men are. Men's playfulness and men's anger, their distance and their sense of inadequacy, are reproduced in the daily interactions of family life. A crucial element of these interactions is the mediating position of women, as wives and mothers.

## CONCLUSION

The question arises of whether women jealously guard their control over the family or whether men relegate women to the less prestigious area of domestic work and childcare. At the level of family life and the lives of individual men and women, clearly both are going on (Coltrane 1989; Cowan and Cowan 1999; Hertz 1986: 64–65; Walzer 1998: 4567). The gendered division of labor in parenting is part of an "arrangement between the sexes" (Goffman 1977)—a constructed and continually reinforced division of being between men and women. Men certainly develop a learned or deliberate incompetence in certain areas. It is a joke among both men and women that after a man has once done the laundry with mixed whites and colors and turned everything pink, or fixed a meal and turned the kitchen into a disaster area, or looked after the children for a weekend during which they ate nothing but pizza and never bathed, it is easier for women to do these things themselves. But men also develop different ways of doing things—playing more aggressively, teasing, and challenging children to take risks or break out of routines. Both men and women live out and perform stereotypes, frequently performing them while acknowledging that, in some sense at least, they should not do so. So a woman who says: "I know I should learn how to check the oil in the car, but I let my husband do it," or a man who, like me, sheepishly excuses himself from making social arrangements

because "My wife keeps track of the calendar," is perpetuating a particular gendered division of labor at the same time that his words are explicitly criticizing it.

This process of negotiating gender, which is often referred to as "doing gender" (West and Zimmerman 1987) to describe gender as an activity rather than an intrinsic quality that people have, is complex and often internally contradictory. In this chapter I have shown how the cultural norm of men's public labor force participation and their role in the domestic sphere as family providers is maintained by cultural work done by men (and women) to emphasize the importance of fathers' earnings although mothers are also playing vital roles in the work force and public sphere. I have also shown that, within the domestic area, there is a gendered division of parenting, and of the meaning of being a parent, that continues to be very important even when both parents are involved in the day-to-day activities of their children. Fathering, like all human activity, is both a pattern of behavior and a set of meanings. Behavior and meaning sometimes reinforce each other, sometimes contradict each other, and sometimes work together to cover over contradictions or to make sense of changing circumstances.

In family life in the United States, as men, women, and children move back and forth between the public areas of employment and school and the domestic areas of home life and care giving, cultural ideas of what is gender-appropriate function to make sense of change and to provide meaningful continuity and coherence.

## NOTES

1. A large amount of human activity is carried on in an area that is neither strictly domestic nor public. Areas of life such as friendship, visiting, kinship, and socializing cut across the public/domestic divide. In a study of community in nineteenth-century New England, Hansen (1994) proposes the term "social" for this third sphere of action.

2. The interviews involved an interaction between my personal situation, the perceptions of the men I talked to, and my conclusions (Townsend 1999). I refer to all the men by pseudonyms. The quotations are taken from the transcripts of tape-recorded interviews. I have not changed or added to what men said, but because I do not want to distract attention from the content of what they told me, I have not presented all the "ers," "ums," and "you knows" with which real speech is studded. In the quotations, a dash (—) indicates an incomplete sentence or change of topic, ellipsis (. . .) indicates that I have omitted words or sentences from a quotation.

3. I do not mean to imply that all men, or all women, think and feel alike. Certainly, fatherhood means something different to men in the contemporary United States

than it does to men in India, in the Congo basin, or in New Guinea. Fatherhood also has different meanings to men in the United States now than it did to men in the nineteenth century or in the colonial period. Fatherhood also means different things to different groups of men in the contemporary United States. Fathers in the upper classes, for instance, have concerns about inheritance and family status that are very different from those of fathers in the middle class who are worried about their children's college education and the dangers of downward mobility, or from working class fathers whose positions in families are being transformed by declining real wages and an increasing family dependence on two incomes.

4. The birth of children before marriage is associated with a marital disruption rate 57 to 80 percent higher than for couples without premarital births for cohorts of white women married between 1970 and 1985 (Martin and Bumpass 1989: 42). This association may be because of greater strains on the early marriage, because couples who have a child before marriage have less normative commitment to marriage, or because some of the births were the biological children of men other than the husband and so do not have an "own children" effect on his behavior. My assertion of the connectedness of marriage and children is bolstered, however, by the lack of association between premarital conception and marital disruption (Billy et al. 1986).

5. Leone's (1986) discussion of the key values invoked by middle class white women in the United States to describe and explain their childbearing decisions reveals the importance of "readiness" for women as well as for men.

6. Ehrensaft (1990: 119–122) interviewed couples who had decided to share the work of parenting their children. She describes the men's reactions of "falling in love with" their children. For women, "the gap between the anticipation and the reality [of children] was smaller" and the major surprise was the absorbing day-to-day reality of parenthood. For men, the anticipation was more anxious and the realization of parenthood marked a greater break. In the terms of my discussion, the paternal relationship, the paternal sentiment, and the sense of being a father is something that is brought about, that happens, and that is not taken for granted or inevitably linked to the biological events of conception or birth. (In an absolute sense, the same is true of women. "Maternal bonding" is a cultural event also, but it is an unquestioned event of our culture in a way that "paternal bonding" is not.)

7. Langer (1983) has analyzed the psychology of "perceived control" and its importance for both a sense of well-being and the actual outcome of events.

8. The "father breadwinner, mother homemaker" family has been both historically recent and short-lived as a dominant pattern. From 1850 until the Second World War, the decline of farm families was matched by an increase in the percentage of children in "father breadwinner, mother homemaker, nonfarm families" which reached almost 60 percent by 1930 and then fluctuated around that level until 1960, when it began

a rapid drop to 27 percent by 1989. From 1950 onward, the declines in farm and father breadwinner families has been matched by a rise in the percentage of children in dual-earner and one-parent families, which was approaching 70 percent by 1990. Since 1970, less than half of the children in the United States have been in families of the father breadwinner, mother homemaker type (Hernandez 1993: 103).

9. Hochschild (1989: 3–4 and 271–273) summarized studies that concluded that there was a difference of ten to twenty hours of total work between working husbands and wives. Other studies have found that men and women spend approximately equal amounts of time on the combination of housework and paid work (Ferree 1991; Pleck 1985; Schor 1991), but certain domestic tasks continue to be overwhelmingly women's work (Coltrane 1996; Shelton 1992), and men's contribution to housework still tends to be thought of, by both husbands and wives, as helping (Coltrane 1989; Walzer 1998). When married couples have children, the division of domestic labor tends to become more traditionally gendered (Cowan and Cowan 1999) and women spend less time in the paid labor force while men spend more (Shelton 1992).

## REFERENCES

Arendell, Terry. 1995. *Men and Divorce*. Thousand Oaks, CA: Sage.

Billy, John H. G., Nancy S. Landale, and Steven D. McLaughlin. 1986. "The Effect of Marital Status at First Birth on Marital Dissolution Among Adolescent Mothers." *Demography* 23: 329–349.

Coltrane, Scott. 1989. "Household Labor and the Routine Production of Gender." *Social Problems* 36: 473–490.

———. 1996. *Family Man: Fatherhood, Housework, and Gender Equity*. New York: Oxford University Press.

Cowan, Carolyn Pape, and Philip A. Cowan. 1999. *When Partners Become Parents: The Big Life Change for Couples*. Mahwah, NJ: Lawrence Erlbaum.

Ehrensaft, Diane. 1990. *Parenting Together: Men and Women Sharing the Care of Their Children*. Urbana: University of Illinois Press.

Ferree, Myra Marx. 1991. "The Gender Division of Labor in Two-Earner Marriages: Dimensions of Variability and Change." *Journal of Family Issues* 12: 158–180.

Furstenberg, Frank F., and Andrew Cherlin. 1991. *Divided Families: What Happens to Children When Parents Part*. Cambridge, MA: Harvard University Press.

Garey, Anita Ilta. 1999. *Weaving Work and Motherhood*. Philadelphia: Temple University Press.

Goffman, Erving. 1977. "The Arrangement Between the Sexes." *Theory and Society* 4: 301–336.

Hansen, Karen V. 1994. *A Very Social Time: Crafting Community in Antebellum New England*. Berkeley: University of California Press.

Hernandez, Donald J. 1993. *America's Children: Resources from Family, Government, and the Economy*. New York: Russell Sage Foundation.

Hertz, Rosanna. 1986. *More Equal Than Others: Women and Men in Dual-Career Marriages.* Berkeley: University of California Press.

Hochschild, Arlie. 1989. *The Second Shift: Working Parents and the Revolution at Home.* New York: Viking.

Langer, Ellen J. 1983. *The Psychology of Control.* Beverly Hills: Sage.

Lareau, Annette. 2000a. "Vague Answers: Reflections on Studying Fathers' Contributions to Children's Care." Paper presented at "Work and Family, Expanding the Horizons," University of California, Berkeley.

———. 2000b. "Social Class and the Daily Lives of Children: A Study from the United States." *Childhood* 7 (2): 155–171.

Leone, Catherine L. 1986. "Fairness, Freedom, and Responsibility: The Dilemma of Fertility Choice in America," Unpublished Ph.D. dissertation in Anthropology, Washington State University.

Martin, Teresa Castro, and Larry L. Bumpass. 1989. "Recent Trends in Marital Disruption." *Demography* 26: 37–51.

Pleck, Joseph. 1985. *Working Wives/Working Husbands.* Beverly Hills, CA: Sage.

Schneider, Jane C., and Peter Schneider. 1996. *Festival of the Poor: Fertility Decline and the Ideology of Class in Sicily, 1860–1980.* Tucson: University of Arizona Press.

Schor, Juliet B. 1991. *The Overworked American: The Unexpected Decline of Leisure.* New York: Basic Books.

Shelton, B. A. 1992. *Women, Men, Time.* New York: Greenwood.

Townsend, Nicholas W. 1998. "Fathers and Sons: Men's Experience and the Reproduction of Fatherhood." In Karen V. Hansen and Anita Ilta Garey (eds.). *Families in the U.S.: Kinship and Domestic Politics,* pp. 363–376. Philadelphia: Temple University Press.

———. 1999. "Fatherhoods and Fieldwork: Intersections Between Personal and Theoretical Positions." *Men and Masculinities* 2(1): 89–99.

———. 2002. *The Package Deal: Marriage, Work, and Fatherhood in Men's Lives.* Philadelphia: Temple University Press.

Waite, Linda, Gus Haggstrom, and David Kanouse. 1985. "The Consequences of Parenthood for the Marital Stability of Young Adults." *American Sociological Review* 50: 850–857.

Walzer, Susan. 1998. *Thinking About the Baby: Gender and Transitions Into Parenthood.* Philadelphia: Temple University Press.

West, Candace, and Don H. Zimmerman. 1987. "Doing Gender." *Gender & Society* 1(2): 125–151.

White, Lynn, Alan Booth, and John Edwards. 1986. "Children and Marital Happiness: Why the Negative Relationship?" *Journal of Family Issues* 7: 131–148.

Wienberg, Howard. 1988. "Duration Between Marriage and First Birth and Marital Stability." *Social Biology* 35: 91–102.

# *Marriage, Modernity, and Migration:*
## Changing Dynamics of Intimacy in a Mexican Transnational Community

### *Jennifer S. Hirsch*

As I knitted and listened to the local gossip in the tiny yarn store and as I climbed the dusty hills to visit women in the sections of town without light or running water, I heard again and again from the younger women in Degollado: *ya no somos tan dejadas como las de antes,* we are not so easily pushed around as our mothers were. For their part, the older women told me, oh, in our day men used to kidnap their brides—but now the brides kidnap the grooms! Men too echoed these comments about historical change in gender regimes.

Adapted and revised by the author from Jennifer S. Hirsch. 2003. *A Courtship After Marriage: Sexuality and Love in Mexican Transnational Community.* Berkeley: University of California Press.

The study on which this chapter draws began as an exploration of how gender and sexuality differ in two locations of a transnational Mexican community— the sending community in Western Mexico and the US-based community in Atlanta, GA—and of the implications of those differences in gender and sexuality for reproductive health practices. During the course of the fieldwork, however, it became clear that while there were some notable differences in the social construction of gender between the two locations, a marked transformation in gender and sexuality had taken place in the sending community over the past generation. I decided, then, that my question should not be just how gender changes with migration, but more properly how the migration-related changes could be understood in the context of much broader historical changes taking place in the sending community. I saw two trajectories of change in this transnational community—generational and migration-related—and I discuss here the impact of both on ideals for marriage and intimacy.

This chapter draws on the work conducted for my doctoral dissertation, which subsequently served as the basis for *A Courtship After Marriage* (Hirsch 2003) as well as a number of other publications (Cornwall 1992; Hirsch and Nathanson 1998, 2001; Hirsch 2000, 2002, 2004, 2008; Hirsch, Higgins, et al. 2002). Here, however, I pull out threads from elements of that work to speak specifically to the questions raised in this section of the book about the emergence, reformulation, and lived experience of the public/domestic dichotomy—both as an approach to the analysis of social phenomena and as a cultural construct that shapes people's understandings of their lives and their communities.

This dual lens on the dichotomy bears underlining; as much as the assumed opposition between public and domestic underlies social science analyses of gendered social reproduction, and thus serves as one of our own sometimes unquestioned native theories, it is also a feature of the cultural landscape through which our informants navigate. Indeed, in Mexico as elsewhere in Latin American and Mediterranean societies (Da Matta 1987; Cole 1991; Gutierrez 1991; Lancaster 1992; Schneider and Schneider 1996; Collier 1997; Rebhun 1999; Carrillo 2002), the distinction between *la calle* (the street) and *la casa* (literally, the home, but more generally the domestic sphere) is a foundational principle of the gendered organization of space. This distinction predates the spread of wage labor and the separation of the productive and reproductive domains (Gonzalez 1974; Da Matta 1987; Gutierrez 1991; Parker 1991), but has been layered with new meanings as homes have increasingly become sites for class-specific forms of gendered consumption (Collier 1997; Hirsch 2003: see especially the discussion of domestic altars). In the analysis that follows, I use that distinction between *calle* and *casa* as a lens through which to consider how marital ideals and practices are changing over time and across large distances, as well as reflecting on what those changes suggest about the power of that division between domestic and public space to shape and constrain the lives of individuals in these communities. I propose here that space itself is constitutive of gender, and that rather than analyzing particular spaces (the street, the house) for their gendered properties, the overall social organization of space and access to mobility through those spaces is crucial for understanding the social organization of gender in any society.

## RESEARCH METHODS

The research was carried out in urban Atlanta and rural and semirural Western Mexico, with women all hailing from that same region of Mexico. The sampling consisted of a three-stage process: first, find a group of Mexicans in Atlanta who were all from the same place; second, select from among them 13 women to be life history informants, and third, match these women to women in the sending community. After several months of preliminary interviewing, I selected a group of women in Atlanta who were from Degollado, a town with a population of around 15,000 in Western Mexico, and El Fuerte, a small agricultural community outside of Degollado. In Atlanta, some informants lived in Chamblee, while others lived in trailer parks on the outskirts of the city. Migration from Western Mexico to the United States has deep historical roots; many of the women had grandfathers who worked on the railroads and fathers who worked in the lettuce fields in the United States. As others have discussed (Rouse 1991; Basch, Glick Schiller, et al. 1994; Goldring 1996a, 1996b), towns that are intensely tied into migrant circuits form transnational communities, characterized by social ties and identity construction across national borders, as well as by frequent back and forth movement of people and gifts and a lightning fast flow of information. Distinct locations of these transnational communities present an opportunity to explore the relative force of cultural and social influences on ideology and behavior, since first-generation migrants in the United States are quite similar culturally to their kin in Mexico but live in very different social settings.

Once I selected the sending location, I chose 13 women in Atlanta—purposely seeking out diversity in age, social class, fertility, migration history, and legal status—and then matched them to their sisters or sisters-in-law in Mexico. All of the women in Atlanta were first-generation migrants, and they all came north as adults. These 13 pairs of women between the ages of 15 and 50 served as the core of my sample, although over the course of the fieldwork I spoke with many more people. With each of these 26 key informants, I conducted six life history interviews on the following: (1) childhood and family life; (2) social networks and migration stories; (3) gender and social reproduction; (4) menstruation, reproduction, and fertility management; (5) health, reproductive health, sexually transmitted diseases and infertility; and (6) courtship and sexuality. I also formally interviewed eight of the life history informants' mothers, who ranged in age from 45 to 70, and nine of their husbands, and experimented with participatory methods, such as body-mapping[1] and life history drawing.

Overall, I spent fifteen months in this community—seven months in the Mexican field-site, and eight months doing fieldwork in Atlanta. Throughout the chapter, references to "younger women" mean the younger of the life history informants; "older women" refers to those life history informants over age 40 and to their mothers.

## GENERATIONAL DIFFERENCES IN MARITAL IDEALS

In Mexico and among the Mexican community in Atlanta, younger women and men talked about generational differences both in the emotional texture of their relationships and in more concrete aspects of marriage. The older women emphasized *respeto* as the key axis along which to evaluate a marriage, while younger women and some of their husbands spoke more about *confianza*, about emotional closeness and sharing one's problems with a spouse. Older women wished for hardworking husbands who would not drink too much, while younger women spoke of courtship as a time of looking both for a man who would respect them and for someone who would be their companion, their friend. Their mothers never would have considered leaving a man who was a good provider but a poor communicator; in contrast, several of the younger women entertained the idea.

In marriages of *confianza*, which I also refer to as companionate marriages,[2] men and women say that they make decisions together—in response to the question *"quien manda en su casa?"*, they each, separately, told me that they both do, or that neither one does. Second, women and men said that sharing *el mando*, the power, means spending time together; this contrasts strongly with the idea that men belong in the street and women in the house. Third, people talk about how the gendered division of labor is eroding, noting a trend toward "helping," *ayudando*, with the other person's job. Behind closed doors some men sweep and cook meals, and most women "help" their husbands support the family. The significant change is not in the gendered division of labor, but in its meaning; lifting a broom or heating one's own dinner—once a source of shame for a man, or a comment on his wife's inadequacy—has become of source of pride, even if something men actually do only rarely. Together, these four qualities (an emphasis on *confianza*, intimacy, in addition to respect, more room for explicit disagreement, a growing heterosociality and increased "helping") combine to form a new marital ideal.

Within these marriages of *confianza*, marital sexuality has been transformed from a way of producing social ties primarily through reproduction to a way to produce conjugal ties directly—in other words, sex makes a couple feel like a family not just because it leads to babies, but also because it creates feelings of closeness which in and of themselves strengthen the marriage. For the older women, the marital bargain entailed mutual respect and an exchange of a woman's best efforts at housekeeping for her husband's economic support. For the younger women, in contrast, the exchange included the somewhat less tangible sharing of pleasure and sentiment. The sexual relationship, they told me, creates and reinforces the *confianza*, the intimacy, on which the marriage is based. The way these younger women thought about sex is illustrated by the following conversation which I had with Victoria, a woman then in her mid-30s, in the spring of 1996.

J:   "And what do you see as the role of the sexual relationship in marriage? . . ."

V:   "Yes, it's very important, it's half [of marriage]."

J:   "And what's the other half?"

V:   "The other half is getting along well, but sex is one of the most important things. For me personally, I think that the intimacy I have with [my husband] was worth a lot, to carry us through the big problems we have had."

J:   "To strengthen the relationship?"

V:   "Yes, it was the thing that really helped the most. Perhaps it wasn't so much that we cared for each other, that we loved each other, not even the kids, as it was the sexual relationship that we have"

J:   "And why do you think it was so important, how did that work?"

V:   "I don't know, because we enjoy it. I see that both of us enjoy it a lot. I sometimes ask myself, does everyone enjoy it so much? I ask myself that, because I really do enjoy it."

Younger women may not necessarily enjoy sex more than women of their mother's generation did. The difference, rather, is in the importance they give to the shared sexual experience between husband and wife. For their mothers, the marital bond was reinforced by the fulfillment of productive and reproductive activities. If a woman also happened to have the luck to marry a man who cared that she enjoyed sex—or who would allow her to refuse sex, rather than telling her *eres mi mujer y por eso me case contigo*, you are my wife and that's why I married you, then that was icing on the cake—but if he forced her, or did not care about her pleasure, that was hardly reason to leave an otherwise perfectly good mate. The younger women, in contrast, felt that a mutually satisfying sexual relationship forms the foundation for a good and happy marriage.

This intimacy-oriented thinking about sexuality was apparent both in the US and Mexico fieldsites. When I asked a woman in her early 30s in one of the Mexican fieldsites about the role of sex in marriage, she responded: "Well, it's what keeps us going, no? If you feel good in terms of intimacy, you will feel good in [the rest of] your life. . . . because when you come—I think that when you end up happy, you get up in the morning happy, you have energy for things—I think it's what helps keep us going." She describes sex as creating a direct emotional and physical connection between the couple.

Women's word choices reflect the shift to a paradigm of mutual desire. Many of the older women—including those who seem to have shared a pleasurable intimacy with their partners—employ the word *usar*, to use, to describe vaginal intercourse (e.g., they might say *"cuando el me usa"* [when he "uses" me] to describe sexual relations). *Usar* is an instrumental word that describes the utilization of an inanimate object—one might use it to talk about an iron, or a plow. Younger women choose quite different words to describe intercourse: they talk about making love (*hacer el amor*) or being together (*estar juntos*) or having relations (*tener relaciones*). There were also generational differences in terms of other aspects of the sexual relationship, such as initiating or refusing sexual intercourse and engaging in sexual activities other than intercourse (such as oral sex).

This discourse, which uses gender and sexuality as measures of modernity, has a clear spatial component. Linda Ann Rebhun describes how in Northeast Brazil, "each city generates its own figurative temporal wheel, forming the proudly modern center of a circle that grows more old-fashioned the further out you travel from it" (Rebhun 1999: 2). This modernity was evaluated at least in part in relation to gendered notions of progress (Wardlow and Hirsch 2006), with spaces becoming inherently more traditional, the more distant they were from those urban centers. The young men I knew in Degollado went to great pains, in general, to represent themselves as engaged in marriages organized around a goal of emotional intimacy (although this frequently bore little relation to the actual gendered balance of power) (Hirsch 2007); these gendered performances were driven at least in part by their desire to show themselves as being just as modern as men whose labor migration provided better access to the material trappings of successful modern masculinity. The rise of the companionate ideal has as much to do with changes in Mexican society as it does with media- and migration-disseminated influences of Mexico's northern neighbor,[3] but the United States is perceived as inherently more egalitarian and less sexually constrained than Mexico. (As discussed below, the widely shared belief that "en el norte la mujer manda," that in the United States, women are the ones who give orders, is significantly complicated by an examination of the heterogeneity of migrant women's [and men's] lives.)

One of my favorite examples of this imagined sexual/moral geography was the time I was told by an informant—someone with whom I spent a great deal of time, and who I generally experienced as liking and respecting me—that "in the US, women go through men like kleenex." I found the comment more funny than offensive, but could read into the contrast she was drawing an important distinction between my world and her own, in which "going through men like kleenex" would be a practice that would significantly diminish one's social value. Moreover, given that it was said in a conversational, and not apparently aggressive context, I could only assume that she did not intend to offend, and therefore assumed that I would agree that women in my country behaved in a way that, were they to live in Mexico, would render them seriously damaged goods on the marriage market. The radiating spokes of the wheel indicate a continuum between an imagined tradition-bound sexual order and a liberated-by-modernity landscape of boundless sexual opportunity. In addition to potentially becoming more modern as one moves away from town and towards urban center, there are increasing opportunities, and declining social risks, associated with a variety of forms of sexual behavior that do not conform to norms of respectability. This is as true for men as it is for women, although it manifests in different ways. For young women crossing the border north, as they increasingly do, one's honor is best protected by arriving to live in a household that includes (or, ideally, traveling with) an older man who is a relative, someone whose social presence can serve as a sort of extension of the domestic moral umbrella under which an unmarried women ought to otherwise live. For men, the gendered sexual geography presents both reputational risks (it is common to hear of married or partnered men caught on video-tape by friends and relatives smooching with a girlfriend) and opportunities for new partnerships and practices, far from the moral center of gravity of home (Bronfman and Minello 1995).

Three examples illustrate the importance of seeing the spatial component, including but not limited to the distinction between the public and private, of this gender order. First, regardless of the extent to which couples practice joint decision making about priorities large and small in the privacy of their own homes, women are scrupulously careful not to contradict their husbands in public; the public challenge of a man's authority by his wife carries a very different meaning than it would at home. Second, gendered differences in men's and women's physical mobility—their *access to space*—also mark inequalities in power. Almost without exception, men are less likely to provide explanation or advance notice for trips beyond the town's limits, and the notion of a man seeking "permission" for a journey is laughable for the way in which it so clearly indicates his emasculation. (There are other, nonspatial, manifestations of inequalities in access to power, most notably in terms of even younger men's dominion over their wives' bodies [exemplified in some cases by violence, and in other cases in a gentler but no less controlling way by the shared assumption that women's husbands have the right to decide how short their skirts can be, or how revealingly tight their clothes can be]).

Third, a range of public spaces serve as a stage for the enactment of consumption-oriented modern intimacy and gendered embodiment. The diversity of these spaces help us see the ways in which gender, social class, and *mestizo* ethnicity are mutually constitutive, but they are useful beyond that for how they show gender as social rather than as a characteristic of individuals. The activities in these spaces, and sentiments and subjectivities that result from participating in these activities, are not inherent to the actors but rather a phenomenon that occurs at the intersection of the actors' access to resources that allow them to be in those spaces, the actors' socially structured desires to go to those spaces, and the broader social and economic factors that make those spaces exist at all.

Access to cars presents one example of how social class and gender intersect in the organization of space. The number of cars has increased precipitously in Degollado in the 15 years since I first began conducting fieldwork there. Older men and women still remembered a time when children could play unsupervised in the main street, but I had to rent a garage space for the car I brought with me in 2004, and the two main streets have been restricted to one-way traffic in response in the growing number of head-on accidents on those two busy streets. These cars, however, are by and large the property either of men and women with well-paying professional jobs or of the relatives of men and women working in the United States. Possession of a car enables access to Guadalajara's malls and movie theaters or to excursions to Michoacan to see the monarch butterfly nests and to experience what seems to them the exotic indigenous culture of Zinacantan and the other crafts villages surrounding Lake Patzcuaro. Closer by, the exclusive sport and tennis club in La Piedad, or the newly opened "Fun Factory" (featuring a zip line, a climbing wall, a parachute drop, and a giant bouncy castle) provide other options through which families can demonstrate both their commitment to a companionate marriage heavy on

the family-togetherness and their success as middle-class consumers.

Those who travel on foot or by bus have different options, thrilling in their own way. On Sundays, the central plaza by the town's main church fills with couples and families attending one of the many Masses, and a main focus of being in the plaza is demonstrating consumption—particularly showing off new clothes, (*estrenando*[4]), and buying ice cream, churros (fried dough filled with caramel sauce), bacon-covered hot dogs, and trinkets (balloons, plastic toys, whirligigs, giant bubble wands) for one's children. At least one water park is located immediately by the side of the main highway outside of town, and thus deliberately accessible to those reliant on public transportation, and the Sunday market is held within the town itself. Both the plaza and the water parks provide a context for gendered display of bodies as well as a space to enact companionate intimacy and a commitment to spending time as a family which is so key to this new family ideal.

These spaces, however, are not just settings in which people can act out new gendered ways of being—they actually *shape* those subjectivities. The water parks, for example, demand that young women transgress the ideals their own mothers would have held about modesty. Two generations ago, marriageable-aged women in this region hid their bodies under rebozos to keep them from being seen and visually consumed by men (as one informant, whose own children are now of courting age, told me, her mother insisted that "*santo que no es visto, no es adorado*" [a saint who is not seen cannot be worshipped]). The water parks feature picnic areas and water-attractions (slides, wading pools, waterfalls), organized with a layout that necessitates traversing fairly large spaces between picnic areas and those attractions. The wearing of street clothes, or even shorts and t-shirts, into the water is expressly forbidden, and thus participation requires a good deal of physical display. Men seemed to luxuriate in the opportunity to walk around in bathing trunks; women frequently chose to wear shorts and t-shirts over their bathing suits, although the clinging, sopping-wet clothes were more a gesture of acknowledgment of the ideal of modesty, rather than a demonstration of modesty itself. The unmarried young men and women and nuclear and extended families for whom a Sunday at a water park is such a treat use this particular terrain to experience a modern gendered subjectivity.

I found even my own practices of bodily display transformed over the course of my fieldwork. The Sunday-morning market, moved recently to the edge of town so as not to disrupt traffic on the main street, provides a space for families to stroll and shop and for young people to gather and flirt. Rather than the beautiful folk art I had so enjoyed buying during my tourist travels in Mexico, this market features almost entirely inexpensive, frequently Chinese-produced consumer goods: apparel, housewares, linens, kitchen items, CDs, and plastic toys, and so I experienced my early visits to this market as somewhat disappointing. As Wardlow describes regarding her own experience perusing the shelves of the local store in rural Papua New Guinea, after several months my own consumer desires had recalibrated to reflect local tastes, and I found myself lusting after (and actually excitedly receiving as a birthday gift) a purple and pink flowered angora cardigan with enormous purple plastic buttons. In response to critical remarks from women with whom I spent time in Degollado about my pants and skirts being too baggy, I acquired several other treasures from the *tianguis*: among them form-fitting low-rise boot-cut black stretch pants; a scoop-necked pink shirt so tight I had to buy a new bra to wear under it; red plastic high heels, and a bias-cut printed acrylic skirt which was far tighter than anything I'd wear in a professional or social context in the United States. I remember in particular how my friend Stela and I delightedly drew upon these items to plan an outfit I could wear to pick my husband up at the airport for one of his visits. I left all these clothes behind in Mexico as gifts for various friends; as I packed, my mind moving already back to the aesthetic of my "real" life as a middle-class feminist university professor, I knew that those clothes, which had elicited such complementary remarks about the success of my own gendered physicality and my improving taste in fashion, would never be worn at home.

Fourth, as I describe at great length elsewhere (Hirsch 2006; Hirsch, Wardlow, et al. 2009), this same intersection of gender, sexuality, space, and social class is manifest in the spaces that facilitate men's access to extramarital relations. Rather than being spaces for the performance of a sexuality harnessed to the strengthening of nuclear family bonds, these homosocial spaces—cantinas, strip clubs, pole-dancing bars, and local red-light districts—are crucibles for the forging of men's emotional ties with each other. Just as those who go to the Fun Factory would not be caught dead shopping in the *tianguis*, men who frequent the luxury pole-dancing venues in Guadalajara would not set foot in the dingy bars that populate the red-light district in the neighboring town, and the consumption of expensive tequila and fair-skinned women in the former setting, and cheap booze and dark-skinned women in the latter, provides opportunities for men to experience the intertwining of gender, sexuality, and social class in a most intimate way. These spaces are hardly the only contexts in which nonmarital sex occurs, but their existence is a key context for the

public production of classed and raced masculinities in Mexico.

Both within and outside the home, the spatial configuration of everyday life serves not just as a window into how women and men are constrained by gender but also as a means to mark how those constraints are changing. During my initial fieldwork in the region in 1995 to 1996, I observed how increasing neolocality, combined with growing access to migration-related wealth, was creating opportunities for newlywed couples to begin their married lives in houses that featured separate bedrooms for parents and children, electricity, and indoor plumbing, and that notably did not feature the watchful ears of a mother-in-law— circumstances propitious to the development of that companionate intimacy which was becoming such a focal indicator of marital success. Outside, however, the gendered organization of space seemed marked as much by continuity as by change. Adolescent girls with families wealthy enough to support postsecondary education were mostly limited to studying technical careers in nearby La Piedad because it was unthinkable for a nice girl to leave her father's home and reside somewhere else before marriage. I was told in no uncertain terms never to get in a car alone with a man, even on an innocent errand, because doing so would mark me as sexually available. Women rarely left town alone, instead frequently taking with them a child as a sort of moral shelter—proof that they were not going to meet a lover. And of course women themselves rarely drove. In fact the only woman I knew who drove was the other American woman in town, a working class Polish-American woman who'd married a man from Degollado, and whose gender nonconformity was marked by the way she was known: as "*la Jenys, la que maneja y fuma*" (that Jenny, the one smokes and drinks).

Ten years after that, I found changes in women's physical mobility just this side of shocking. In addition to the well-documented feminization of migration (Cerrutti and Massey 2001), women were much more mobile locally: many women, married and not, knew how to drive, and some had cars of their own; adolescent girls in cropped tops were frequently seen zooming up and down the main street on loud four-wheeled all-terrain vehicles; young women began spending newfound leisure time at the indoor soccer rink, whose popular and very aggressive local team drew large crowds for important matches; and at least on one occasion they gathered in large crowds at one of the local *terrazas* (relatively posh local cafes on the main square, serving alcoholic and nonalcoholic beverages) to drink and cheer for the Guadalajara *Chivas*, playing the rival Mexico City *Americas*, when the game was broadcast on the café's flatscreen television. It was only a decade earlier that, during one of my husband's visits to Degollado, I'd told him there was nowhere we could go for tacos and beers because nice women did not drink in public.

While it was not unknown for the women who'd been the younger generation in my first research, those born in the 1960s and 1970s, to have had pre-marital relations, the secret was jealously guarded, and a girl ran a great risk in doing so because her marital prospects were irreparably damaged if, despite promises to the contrary, that first sexual partner refused to marry her. Printed T-shirts on sale in the Sunday marketplace, such as those that read "my boyfriend is out of town"; "wanted: cute boys for personal hands on services. Must be tall and good-looking. Respond only if you are HOT!"; "Powerful brave sexy cool"; "sweet lover" underlined the intersection between women's increased mobility and a newly assertive female sexuality. What was different was not so much the implied behaviors but the public suggestion of them. Perhaps the most striking contrast to the generally recognized expectation in the mid-1990s that nice girls would be at home behind locked doors every night by ten was the moment I heard from my research assistant, Brenda, about the pole-dancing contest that took place in the make-shift disco during the town's pork-producer's festival; in that temporary disco, which also included blasts of foam spray which wet the whole assembled crowd and rendered already skin-tight clothing even more clingy and revealing, a sheet was hung, with a backlit pole behind it, and local girls competed to see who could do the sexiest faux-striptease. The pace of change seemed ever-accelerating; during a brief return visit in 2006, I saw lesbian and gay couples publicly dancing together at a new, and even more ostentatiously decorated, disco that had been built in a former agricultural building on the edge of town.

## THE GENDERED SPATIAL EFFECTS OF MIGRATION

Women's own cross-border mobility presents an additional element of these geographies of gender and sexuality. Although women in both the Mexican and Atlanta communities shared the emerging companionate ideal, the privacy, legal protections against domestic violence, and economic opportunities enabled some of the women I knew in Atlanta in the 1990s to push their husbands further toward the companionate model. While women in communities on both sides of the border may share these companionate dreams, Mexicans say that *en el norte, la mujer manda* (in the United States, women give the

orders); what they mean when they say this is that women have the social and economic resources to live without a husband, and thus the power to press for a marriage that is not just companionate but a bit more egalitarian.

Before comparing spatial aspects of gender and sexuality in the Atlanta-based migrant communities to those in the Mexican sending community, several caveats are in order. First, these gendered terrains should be thought of constraining or enabling action among men as well as women; indeed, as Rouse suggested two decades ago (1991), Mexican migrant men's relative emasculation is most clearly seen—and in some ways produced—by the social organization of space. Second, rather than begin with the underlying assumption that women are moving to communities in which their lives will be less constrained by gender, I started with the notion that the comparison should be made not with sending locations frozen in time but rather with communities (as described above) situated in complex and fluid historical processes; moreover, just as the shift to a more companionate ideal is both enabling and constraining, so too will the gendered outcomes of migration include both new opportunities and new limitations. Moreover, there is not one story to tell about gender and migration but rather many; I found that rudimentary knowledge of English, having one's own kin nearby (as opposed to a husband's family), documentation of legal residence that includes the right to work, work experience, and possession of a car were just some of the factors that led to a great deal of heterogeneity in the experiences of migrant women (Hirsch 2003: see especially chapter 6). Rather than reprise the study's broader findings about gender and migration, I focus here particularly on the ways in which the move from a Mexican provincial town to a semirural city in the American south reconfigures the division between public and private, and so the gendered social organization of marriage.

A central feature of small-town life is constant vigilance of one's movements, dress, and social interactions. It was not so much that appearances were more important than actual practice; rather, maintaining one's reputation through conforming to gendered expectations for appearance was itself a crucial element of practice. I found this true for my own behavior as well, as I was instructed by an informant not to do good things that might look like bad things (*no hagas cosas buenas que parecen cosas malas*), after she had observed me responding to a man's (what seemed to me) innocuous greeting of "*buenos días.*" Politeness dictated that women who make eye contact when passing each other on the street exchange greetings, but apparently doing so with an unknown man was in and of itself an act of moral turpitude. The plaza was a shared stage for the demonstration of respectable sexuality, and front doors with glass windows (to enable parental observation) served as critical locations for the negotiation of intimacy among dating couples.

## THE GENDERED ORGANIZATION OF SPACE IN ATLANTA

Life was laid out quite differently in the outlying suburbs of Atlanta where the Mexican women I knew settled. Domestic spaces were still locations for the development and preservation of companionate intimacy and modern practices of kinship, but they became as well safe spaces for the performance of a newly experienced ethnic identity as Mexicans. I rarely entered a home that did not display some representation of the eagle and the snake—in addition of course to the icon of the Virgin of Guadalupe found in so many Mexican homes (and cars) on both sides of the border. Calendars produced by businesses back home were proudly displayed, as was other evidence of affiliation with one's hometown community.

At the same time, however, Mexican men, women, and children experienced the inviolability of the distinction between public and private as weaker than in Mexico. A recurrent element of the discourse about women being more powerful in the United States than in Mexico was mention of the protections against domestic violence offered by being able to call 911. (People also talked about this in relation to state intervention against child abuse, noting that American [and Mexican immigrant] children were less respectful because they knew that they could call the police if a parent became violent.) Regardless of the extent to which women (or children) did actually call for police protection—and regardless as well of the extent to which that police protection would actually have been provided—the existence of this shared notion about the state's right to intervene in domestic power dynamics presented a marked contrast with experiences of the domestic sphere on the other side of the border.[5]

In addition to some changes in what separates public and domestic spaces, the public spaces themselves are radically different than those in Mexico—sites not for the preservation of a moral community but rather for the emergence of the consuming individual. Trailer parks and apartment complexes did, to be sure, feature shared spaces, but the size of the city meant that there were many more places people could go, and a much lower probability of observation by a fellow townsperson. As one married women told me, remarking upon the difference, it would be easy to have an affair in Atlanta, and no one would ever know. The Catholic church no longer looms, physically or morally, with quite the same power that it did in Mexico (Hirsch 2008); Atlanta offers many other options for entertainment on Sundays and neither priests nor other congregants have as much information about women's sexual or reproductive practices as they do in Mexico. In Degollado, the plaza is a free space, open to all, whereas access to Atlanta's recreational spaces such as the mall or the zoo depended both on disposable income and on legal status—some were much more able than others to afford both the risk and the expense of a day of leisure organized around commercialized forms of consumption. In addition to the greater options for commercially oriented leisure spaces found in Atlanta by comparison with Mexico, the social encounters that took place in work spaces— spaces that were more private than the street or the mall, yet more public than the domestic sphere— presented new possibilities for both men and women, both in terms of potential partners and through exposure to new ideas about gender and sexuality.

Public spaces in Atlanta were also locations for the expression of the economic and legal inequality that is such a core element of the Mexican immigrant experience. In Atlanta's public spaces, the specter of the state which haunts the domestic context went considerably beyond just being a specter; indeed, early in the project my ability to get to engage with the community was severely hampered by the understandable distrust engendered by the "*redadas*," immigrant raids in public spaces and workplaces, which were taking place at that time. At one point, the police set up a barricade across Buford Highway, the main thoroughfare in a neighborhood with one of the densest concentrations of Mexican immigrants, to stop drivers and demand papers. In part in response to 9/11, but also at least potentially as a reaction to the growing Mexican immigrant communities, regulations slowly came into place across the Southeastern states that made it impossible for immigrants to secure a driver's license and insure a vehicle. Particularly in cities such as Atlanta, which lack adequate public transportation infrastructure, being unable to secure a license or insurance severely hampered mobility and served as a constant reminder of one's unequal status before the law. The acrid debates about the existence of spaces for day laborers to congregate was a particularly gendered example of these spatial manifestations of inequality; the spatial organization of immigrant women's work, although not exclusively in the domestic sphere, made them much less visible as targets for the xenophobia expressed by those who so vociferously opposed the presence of these migrants in their communities.

## CONCLUSION

All of these transformations in the public and domestic space, whether with time or migration, provide concrete examples of what it means to talk about gender as changing; thinking about the political and economic forces that shape those spaces also provides some insight into the factors that produce those changes. In rural Mexico, although young women are increasingly challenging the gendered nature of public space, men's freedom in that space—whether to play dominos by the main square, to urinate in public, to drink themselves senseless, or simply to lounge in the sun with their *compadres*—goes unquestioned. In Atlanta, the distinction between private and domestic space continues to exist, but both are reconfigured. Domestic space becomes a safe haven in a context of legal insecurity, a space where both men and women feel somewhat safer from the ever-present fear of Immigration and Customs Enforcement (ICE, the reconfigured, post-9/11 version of the INS)—and yet the possibility of government intrusion, so frequently remarked upon by the idea that women or children could call 911, and demonstrated by ICE raids that separate undocumented parents from their citizen children (cites), is ever present, rendering the security of the domestic space an uncertain proposition at best. No matter how thickly adorned a home or apartment may be with Mexican flags, printed calendars from grocery stores and building supply companies back in Degollado, and icons of the Virgin of San Juan de Los Lagos and Guadalupe, the legal insecurity faced by undocumented men and women means that many never rest easy. For men, the idea that home presents a shelter from the dangers of the streets represents a powerful demonstration of how migration can curtail men's access to privileges they enjoyed in Mexico. For women, in contrast, the anonymity offered by urban environments—true not just for those who migrate to cities in the United States but also for women who travel to large cities in Mexico—presents opportunities to experiment with practices—sexual, social, and sartorial—which would have marked them quickly as fallen women back home. For us as scholars, the fluidity of this gendered patterning of space is a powerful reminder that gender is a property of societies, a phenomenon not entirely captured by a focus on ideologies of masculinity or femininity, as well as a window into tracing out the social and economic forces that are constantly recreating the gendered terrain through which people navigate.

## NOTES

1. Body-mapping is a participatory research technique (Cornwall 1992) in which women are provided with an outline of the body and asked to draw comments on it, discussing the social meanings and embodied experience of various body parts.
2. There is a vast literature on companionate marriage, exploring it in relation to the emergence of "affective individualism": (Bott 1957[1971]; Thadani 1978; Stone 1979; Skolnik 1991; Gillis, Tilly, et al. 1992) Scholars have also looked at how it varies globally (Inhorn 1996; Rebhun 1999; Hirschman and Minh 2002; Hirsch 2003; Hirsch and Wardlow 2006; Padilla, Hirsch, et al. 2007) Briefly, I use the term here to denote relations in which mutual emotional satisfaction is the most salient indicator of the quality of a marriage.
3. The vast social, economic, and demographic changes that have taken place in the rural community in which the fieldwork was carried out, which include increased access to formal education, changes in the physical structures of housing, rising neolocal residence, declining fertility, later age at first, marriage, increased access to electricity and media, are described in great detail in *Courtship*. Also worth noting conceptually here, and illustrated ethnographically in *Courtship*, is the intertwining of structure and agency exemplified by the dissemination and embrace of the companionate ideal.
4. *Estrenar*, which literally means to show off something new, was a word I learned early in my fieldwork with this community. Showing off new clothes was a much-prized activity, as indicated (at least to me) that there was a particular word for it, the equivalent of which I have not been able to find in English.
5. This contrast is likely to have waned in the years that have elapsed since that initial fieldwork took place. During the 2004 fieldwork, I noticed a widely disseminated media campaign against domestic violence, and I also heard of instances in which women in Degollado did receive police protection in response to reports of violence.

## REFERENCES

Basch, L., N. Glick Schiller, et al., Eds. (1994). *Nations Unbound : Transnational Projects, Postcolonial Predicaments, and Deterritorialized Nation-States*. Langhorne, Gordon and Breach.

Bott, E. (1957[1971]). *Family and Social Network: Roles, Norms and External Relationships in Ordinary Urban Families*. New York, The Free Press.

Bronfman, M. and N. Minello (1995). Hábitos sexuales de los migrantes temporales Mexicanos a Los Estados Unidos de América: Prácticas de riesgo para la infección por VIH. *Sida en México: Migración, Adolescencia, y Genero*. e. a. Bronfman M. Mexico City, Mexico, Información Profesional Especializada.

Carrillo, H. (2002). *The Night Is Young: Sexuality in Mexico in the Time of AIDS*. Chicago, University of Chicago Press.

Cerrutti, M. and D. S. Massey (2001). "On the Auspices of Female Migration from Mexico to the United States." *Demography* 38(2): 187–200.

Cole, S. C. (1991). *Women of the Praia: Work and Lives in a Portuguese Coastal Community.* Princeton, NJ, Princeton University Press.

Collier, J. F. (1997). *From Duty to Desire: Remaking Families in a Spanish Village.* Princeton, NJ, Princeton University Press.

Cornwall, A. (1992). "Body Mapping in Health RRA/PRA." *PRA Notes.* London, International Institute for Environment and Development. 16: 69-76.

Da Matta, R. (1987). *A Casa e a Rua.* Rio de Janeiro, Editora Guanabara.

Gillis, J. R., L. A. Tilly, et al. (1992). *The European Experience of Declining Fertility, 1850–1970: The Quiet Revolution.* Cambridge, MA, Blackwell.

Goldring, L. (1996a). "Blurring Borders: Constructing Transnational Community in the Process of U.S.-Mexico Migration." *Research in Community Sociology* 6: 69–104.

Goldring, L. (1996b). "Gendered Memory: Constructions of Rurality Among Mexican Transnational Migrants." *Creating the Countryside: The Politics of Rural and Environmental Discourse.* M. DuPuis and P. Vandergeest. Philadelphia, PA, Temple University Press: 303–329.

Gonzalez, L. (1974). *San Jose de Gracia: A Village in Transition.* Austin, University of Texas Press.

Gutierrez, R. A. (1991). *When Jesus Came, the Corn Mothers Went Away; Marriage, Sexuality and Power in New Mexico, 1500–1846.* Stanford, Stanford University Press.

Hirsch, J. S. (2000). En El Norte La Mujer Manda: Gender, Generation and Geography in a Mexican Translational Community. *Immigration Research for a New Century.* N. Foner, R. Rumbaut and S. Gold. New York, Russell Sage: 369–389.

Hirsch, J. S. (2002). "'Que, pues, con el pinche NAFTA?': Gender, Power, and Migration between Western Mexico and Atlanta." *Urban Anthropology* 31(3–4): 351–387.

Hirsch, J. S. (2003). *A Courtship after Marriage: Sexuality and Love in Mexican Transnational Families.* Berkeley, University of California Press.

Hirsch, J. S. (2004). "'Un Noviazgo Despues de Ser Casados': Companionate Marriage, Sexual Intimacy and Fertility Regulation in Modern Mexico." *Qualitative Demography: Categories and Contexts in Population Studies.* S. Szreter, A. Dharmalingam and H. Sholkamy. Oxford, Oxford University Press: 249–275.

Hirsch, J. S. (2006). "Que gusto Estar de Vuelta en Mi Tierra: Gender, Sexuality and Authenticity in las fiestas de la virgin de guadelupe." *Panel on Latin American Migration, Gender and Sexuality, Latin American Studies Association.* San Juan, Puerto Rico.

Hirsch, J. S. (2007). "'Love Makes a Family': Globalization, Companionate Marriage, and the Modernization of Gender Inequality." *Love and Globalization: Transformations of Intimacy in the Contemporary World.* M. Padilla, J. S. Hirsch, R. Sember, M. Munoz-Laboy and R. Parker. Nashville, Vanderbilt University Press.

Hirsch, J. S. (2008). "Catholics Using Contraceptives: Religion, Family Planning, and Interpretive Agency in Rural Mexico." *Studies in Family Planning* 39(2): 93–104.

Hirsch, J. S., J. Higgins, et al. (2002). "The Social Constructions of Sexuality: Marital Infidelity and Sexually Transmitted Disease—HIV Risk in a Mexican Migrant Community." *American Journal of Public Health* 92(8): 1227–1237.

Hirsch, J. S. and C. A. Nathanson (1998). "Demografia informal: como utilizar las redes sociales para construir una muestra etnografica sistematica de mujeres mexicanas en smbos lados de la frontera." *Estudios Demograficso y de Desarolio Urbano, Mexico, D.F; El Colegio de Mexico* 12(1 & 2): 177–199.

Hirsch, J. S. and C. A. Nathanson (2001). "Some Traditional Methods Are More Modern Than Others: Rhythm, Withdrawal, and the Changing Meanings of Gender and Sexual Intimacy in the Mexican Companionate Marriage." *Culture, Health & Sexuality* 3(4): 413–428.

Hirsch, J. S. and H. Wardlow, Eds. (2006). *Modern Loves: The Anthropology of Romantic Love and Companionate Marriage.* Ann Arbor, University of Michigan Press.

Hirsch, J. S., H. Wardlow, et al. (2009). *The Secret: Love, Marriage and HIV.* Nashville, Vanderbilt University Press.

Hirschman, C. and N. H. Minh (2002). "Tradition and Change in Vietnamese Family Structure in the Red River Delta." *Journal of Marriage and Family* 64: 1063–1079.

Inhorn, M. C. (1996). *Infertility and Patriarchy: The Cultural Politics of Gender and Family Life in Egypt.* Philadelphia, University of Pennsylvania Press.

Lancaster, R. N. (1992). *Life Is Hard: Machismo, Danger, and the Intimacy of Power in Nicaragua.* Berkeley, University of California Press.

Padilla, M., J. S. Hirsch, et al., Eds. (2007). *Love and Globalization: Transformations of Intimacy in the Contemporary World.* Nashville, Vanderbilt University Press.

Parker, R. G. (1991). *Bodies, Pleasures, and Passions: Sexual Culture in Contemporary Brazil.* Boston, Beacon.

Rebhun, L.-A. (1999). *The Heart Is Unknown Country: Love in the Changing Economy of Northeast Brazil.* Stanford, CA, Stanford University Press.

Rouse, R. (1991). "Mexican Migration and the Social Space of Postmodernism." *Diaspora* 1(1): 8–23.

Schneider, J. and P. Schneider (1996). *Festival of the Poor: Fertility Decline and the Ideology of Class in Sicily, 1860–1980.* Tucson, University of Arizona Press.

Skolnik, A. (1991). *Embattled Paradise: The American Family in an Age of Uncertainty.* New York, Basic Books.

Stone, L. (1979). *The Family, Sex and Marriage in England 1500–1800.* New York, Harper and Row.

Thadani, V. (1978). "'The Logic of Sentiment': The Family and Social Change." *Population and Development Review* 4(3): 457–499.

Wardlow, H. and J. S. Hirsch (2006). "Introduction." *Modern Loves: The Anthropology of Romantic Courtship and Companionate Marriage.* J. S. Hirsch and H. Wardlow. Ann Arbor, University of Michigan Press.

# IV

# *Equality and Inequality: The Sexual Division of Labor and Gender Stratification*

In most societies, certain tasks are predominantly assigned to men while others are assigned to women. In European and American cultures, it used to be considered "natural" for men to be the family breadwinners; women were expected to take care of the home and raise the children. An underlying assumption of this division of labor was that men were dominant because their contribution to the material well-being of the family was more significant than that of women. Women were dependent on men and therefore automatically subordinate to them.

The "naturalness" of this division of labor has been called into question as women increasingly enter the labor force. However, has this significantly altered the status of women within their families and in the wider society? Or has it simply meant that women are now working a double day, performing domestic tasks that are negatively valued and not considered work once they get home from their "real" day's work? If employment enhances the social position of women, why is it that women still earn less than men earn for the same work? Why is there still a high degree of occupational segregation by gender? What precisely is the relationship between the economic roles of women and gender stratification? Cross-cultural research on the sexual division of labor attempts not only to describe the range of women's productive activities in societies with different modes of subsistence, but also to assess the implications of these activities for the status of women.

In many parts of the world, women contribute significantly, if not predominantly, to subsistence. This is perhaps most apparent among hunting and gathering or foraging populations, and for this reason, such groups have been labeled the most egalitarian of human societies. Hunters and gatherers used to form the bulk of the human population, but today only a small number remain. They are found in relatively isolated regions; they possess simple technology and therefore make little effort to alter the environment in which they live. They tend to be characterized by a division of labor whereby men hunt and women gather. Friedl (1975: 18) outlines four reasons for this division: the variability in the supply of game, the different skills required for hunting and gathering, the incompatibility between carrying burdens and hunting, and the small size of seminomadic foraging populations.

Friedl (1975) further argues that in foraging societies in which gathering contributes more to the daily diet than hunting, women and men share equal status (see also Lee 1979; Martin and Voorhies 1975). Conversely, in societies in which hunting and fishing predominate (such as among the Inuit), the status of women is lower. It seems that female productive activities enhance the social position of women in society, but Sanday (1974) cautions that participation in production is a necessary but not sufficient precondition. Control over the fruits of their labor and a positive valuation of this labor are other factors to consider, as is the extent to which women are involved in at least some political activities. In addition, the absence of a sharp differentiation between public and private domains (Draper 1975) and the fact that there is no economic class structure and no well-defined male-held political offices (Leacock 1975) have been cited as explanations for the relative egalitarianism in foraging societies compared with more complex societies.

Despite the common assumption that men hunt and women gather, in some foraging societies, the division of labor is not sharply defined. This often provides the basis for the highest degree of egalitarianism. Among the Tiwi, Australian aborigines who live on Melville Island off the coast of northern Australia, both men and women hunt and gather. Goodale (1971) demonstrates that resources and technology, rather than activities, are divided into male domains and female domains. Although the big game that Tiwi men hunt provides most of the meat to the group and therefore gives them a dominant position in the society, Tiwi women, who hunt and gather, provide more than half of the food consumed; they share in both the comradery and the spoils of their endeavors. As major provisioners, women are economic assets and a source of wealth and prestige for men in this polygynous society. Despite the fact that their opportunities for self-expression may be more limited than those of men, with age women acquire social status and can be politically influential. In general, Goodale suggests that Tiwi culture emphasizes the equality of men and women in society.

Among the Agta Negritos of northeastern Luzon, the Philippines, women enjoy even greater social equality with their men than among the Tiwi. This is a society in which the division of labor and the battle of the sexes appear to be virtually absent. Agta women hunt game animals and fish just as men do. Not only do they make significant contributions to the daily food supply, but they also control the distribution of the foods they acquire, sharing them with their families and trading them in the broader community. Agnes Estioko-Griffin and P. Bion Griffin (in this book) argue that these roles are clearly the basis for female authority in decision making within families and residential groups.

The Agta case challenges the widely held notion that pregnancy and childcare are incompatible with hunting in foraging societies (Friedl 1978: 72). Agta women have developed methods of contraception and abortion to aid them in spacing their children. After becoming pregnant, they continue hunting until late in the pregnancy and resume hunting for several months after the birth of the child. There are always some women available to hunt, during which time children may be cared for by older siblings, grandparents, or other relatives. Reproduction is clearly not a constraint on women's economic roles in this society.

In horticultural societies, in which cultivation is carried out with simple hand-tool technology and slash-and-burn methods of farming, women also play important roles in production (Boserup 1970; Bossen 1989). One theory argues that the economic importance of female production in horticultural societies emerged from women's gathering activities in foraging groups. Horticultural societies vary in the degree to which men participate in crop cultivation as well as whether this cultivation is supplemented by hunting, fishing, and raising livestock. In addition, many horticultural societies are matrilineal (reckoning descent through the female line), and in these societies, women tend to have higher status than in patrilineal societies. Maria Lepowsky (in this book) points to gender egalitarianism among the horticultural and matrilineal people of the Pacific island of Vanatinai. In this society, men are not dominant over women either in practice or ideologically. Like men, women on this island can gain both prestige and power through engaging in exchange activities and the sponsorship of feasts where valuable goods are distributed. As a result of these activities, they can become "big women" as men can become "big men." Thus, Lepowsky argues that "the prominent positions of women in Vanatinai exchange and other activities outside of household and subsistence indicate as well as reinforce generally egalitarian relations between women and men. Vanatinai women have access to power both through their control of the economic capital of land and the subsistence and surplus production of yams and through their accumulation of symbolic capital in exchange and mortuary ritual" (1993: 38).

Despite descent systems and economic roles that enhance the status and power of women among horticulturalists such as the people of Vanatinai, Friedl (1975) cautions that women's status is not universally high in such societies. Male control of valued property and male involvement in warfare (an endemic feature in many of these societies) can be mitigating factors that provide the basis for male dominance over women. For example, among horticulturalists in highland New Guinea, women raise staple crops but men raise prestige crops that are the focus of social exchange. This cultural valuation is the foundation for gender stratification that is then reinforced by gender ideologies of male superiority and a high degree of sexual antagonism between men and women (Brown and Buchbinder 1976; Herdt and Poole 1982; Strathern 1988). For example, the Hua of New Guinea display a "chauvinistic" ideology that is rooted in men's roles as warriors (Meigs 1990).

Among the Mundurucú, an Amazonian horticultural society who were also once involved in fierce warfare (Murphy and Murphy 1985), the division is such that men hunt, fish, and fell the forest area for gardens while women plant, harvest, and process manioc. In their daily tasks, women form cooperative work groups, have authority, and are the equals of men. To the extent that their work "draws women together and isolates them from the immediate supervision and control of the men, it is also a badge of their independence" (Murphy and Murphy 1985: 237). However, according to a male-dominated ideology, women are subservient to men. Despite the contributions that Mundurucú women make to subsistence, what men do is assigned more value. As Murphy and Murphy state, "Male ascendancy does not wholly derive from masculine activities but is to a considerable degree prior to them" (234). Male domination among the traditional Mundurucú is symbolic. As the Mundurucú become increasingly drawn into a commercial economy based on the rubber trade, men, with their rights to rubber trees and to trading, may gain a more complete upper hand. "The women may well discover that they have traded the symbolic domination of the men, as a group, over the women, as a group, for the very real domination of husbands over wives" (238).

Although women's labor is clearly important in horticultural societies, it has been argued that it becomes increasingly insignificant relative to that of men with the development of intensive agriculture. Intensive agriculture is based on the use of the plow, draft animals, fertilizers, and irrigation systems. In a survey of ninety-three agricultural societies, Martin and Voorhies (1975: 283) demonstrate that 81 percent delegate farming to men who then achieve primacy in productive activities. One explanation for the decline in female participation in agriculture is that the female domestic workload tends to increase when root crops are replaced by cereal crops and when animal labor replaces manual labor (Martin and Voorhies 1975). Cereal crops require more extensive processing, and field animals must be cared for. Both these activities fall to women. In addition, the kin-based units of production and consumption become smaller, and this too adds to the burden on individual women.

Concomitant with the presumably declining importance of women in agricultural activities is a supposed decline in social status (Boserup 1970). Women's value is defined by their reproductive abilities rather than by their productive activities. It has been suggested that the lesser status of women in some agricultural societies, particularly those of Eurasia, compared with some horticultural societies, as in sub-Saharan Africa, is reflected in the contrast between systems of bridewealth and systems of dowry (Goody 1976). Bridewealth is a compensation to the bride's parents or her kin for the productive and reproductive rights of the bride; dowry, as a form of inheritance, provides a bride with land and other wealth and helps her to attract a husband.

Despite arguments describing a decline in women's status and their relegation to the domestic sphere in association with the emergence of intensive agriculture, cross-cultural data indicate that women in agricultural societies lead much more diverse and complex lives than some theories suggest (Bossen 1989). In northwestern Portugal, women do most of the agricultural activity, inherit property equally, and are often the recipients of a major inheritance that generally includes the parental household (Brettell 1986). This division of labor has emerged because men have been assigned the role of emigrants. Another exception is rural Taiwan, where, despite the patriarchal and patrilineal character of Chinese society, women construct a familial network that gives them a good deal of power and influence in later life (Wolf 1972). Finally, in rural Ireland today, women have become active partners in the farm business (O'Hara 1998).

Another economic adaptation is that of pastoralism or herding. Some pastoralists are fully nomadic, moving their entire communities in accordance with the demands of the herd. Others are involved in cultivation and are therefore transhumant. They engage in seasonal migration. Among pastoralists the ownership, care, and management of herds are generally in the hands of men. Although there are exceptions, male domination of herding tends to be reflected in other aspects of social organization—the near universality of patrilineal descent and widespread patrilocal residence. Pastoral societies are also generally characterized by patriarchy and a dichotomization of the sexes, both symbolically and socially. Segregation of the sexes and gender stratification, in other words, are fundamental attributes of many pastoral societies.

The symbolic opposition between men and women is apparent among the Sarakatsani, a group of transhumant shepherds who live in the mountainous regions of the province of Epirus in Greece. According to Campbell (1964), the life of pastoral Sarakatsani revolves around three things: sheep, children (particularly sons), and honor. "The sheep support the life and prestige of the family, the sons serve the flocks and protect the honour of their parents and sisters, and the notion of honour presupposes physical and moral capacities that fit the shepherds for the hard and sometimes dangerous work of following and protecting their animals" (18). Gender ideology is embedded in these three valued items, especially in the parallel oppositions between sheep and goats on the one hand and men and women on the other. The practical division of labor parallels this symbolic opposition. Women give assistance in the care of animals and make major contributions to their families. The economic roles of husband and wife are complementary. Nevertheless, Sarakatsani husbands have ultimate authority over their wives; obedience to a husband is a moral imperative for a wife. As among the Mundurucú, ideology assigns women to a lesser status, in spite of their economic complementarity.

Susan Rasmussen (in this book) reviews many of these aspects of men's and women's roles among pastoralists, but her essay focuses most closely on the Tuareg, a seminomadic, Islamic, socially stratified people who live in Niger, Mali, Burkina Faso, and Algeria. The Tuareg, in her view, offer variations to standard interpretations of gender in pastoral nomadic societies. For example, the frequent absence of Tuareg men from home (in raiding activities in the past and in separatist warfare against the central state governments of Mali and Niger more recently), as well as men's peaceful trading activities, have necessitated women's independence in work and the education of children. Tuareg women are not sequestered, they do not veil their faces (although Tuareg men do), and they do not engage in gestures of subservience to their husbands such as kneeling or bowing their heads. Men and women regularly meet and socialize in public and women regularly entertain male visitors (although not necessarily lovers) when their husbands are absent. Although Tuareg women are generally consulted by men about matters that affect the life of the camp or village, there are contexts in which women defer to men—before Islamic scholars, important chiefs, and elders on the patrilineal side. Much of the status of Tuareg women is sustained by their rights of ownership in livestock.

Rasmussen concludes with a discussion of the impact of increasing sedentarization on the roles of Tuareg men and women. Sedentarization has increased women's workloads and altered their bases of property. A shift to virilocal patterns of residence (living with the husband and his kin) has increasingly isolated women from the support of their own kin networks. And, for all Tuareg, sedentarization has reduced autonomy as it has opened new opportunities for work in cooperative agencies.

In more recent years, anthropologists have begun to exam the roles of poor urban men and women in a variety of developing countries (Nelson 1979; Smith 1989). Bossen (1989: 348) points out that most of this research shows "that men have a distinct advantage in obtaining a variety of formal, higher paying jobs, while women are concentrated in the less profitable informal service sectors, where the competition is intense." Often these women are involved in small-scale trading and marketing activities (Babb 1989). In parts of West Africa, there is a deep tradition of marketing women and these activities have given them not only economic power but also other forms of power. Falola (in this book) describes Yoruba women who, through their predominance in market activities, have become part of the political landscape in various ways. Further, their control of market space also gives them control over market rituals and hence a role in religious life. Indeed, within the Yoruba pantheon a female goddess, Yemonja, is central.

The involvement of Yoruba women in trade, both regional and long distance, dates to the precolonial period and has endured into the present. Trading activities allow women to build wealth and hence enjoy a high social status. Further, the marketplace has its own guild structure and everything that accompanies that structure in terms of the power to set rules and regulations as well as interface with and occasionally challenge the state. Falola illustrates these important connections between economic, social, and political power through a series of case studies of market women of the precolonial and contemporary period.

Generalizations are often made about the status of women according to different modes of adaptation. However, the readings in this section demonstrate that there is a great deal of diversity within each subsistence strategy. For example, in foraging societies, women may hunt as well as gather; in intensive agricultural and pastoral societies, not all women are powerless, dependent, and relegated to the domestic sphere. Although women's contributions to subsistence are important to gender stratification, a number of other factors need to be considered. These include leadership roles in family and kinship units and in the wider community; inheritance of property; control of the distribution and exchange of valued goods; authority in childrearing; and participation in ritual activities. In addition, the ideological definitions of women's roles and valuations of their economic activities are often powerful determinants of status.

To fully understand gender stratification, both ideology and participation in production must be taken into account. As Atkinson (1982: 248) states, "It is too facile to deny the significance of sexual stereotypes or to presume that women's influence in one context cancels out their degradation in another. Just as we know that women's status is not a unitary phenomenon across cultures, we need to be reminded that the intracultural picture is equally complex."

## REFERENCES

Atkinson, Jane. 1982. "Review: Anthropology." *Signs* 8: 236–258.

Babb, Florence E. 1989. *Between Field and cooking Pot: the Political Economy of Market Women in Peru.* Austin: University of Texas Press.

Boserup, Esther. 1970. *Women's Role in Economic Development.* London: G. Allen and Unwin.

Bossen, Laurel. 1989. "Women and Economic Institutions." In Stuart Plattner (ed.). *Economic Anthropology,* pp. 318–350. Stanford, CA: Stanford University Press.

Brettell, Caroline B. 1986. *Men Who Migrate, Women Who Wait: Population and History in a Portuguese Parish.* Princeton, NJ: Princeton University Press.

Brown, Paula, and Georgeda Buchbinder (eds.). 1976. *Man and Woman in the New Guinea Highlands.* Washington, DC: American Anthropological Association.

Campbell, John K. 1964. *Honour, Family and Patronage.* Oxford, UK: Oxford University Press.

Draper, Patricia. 1975. "!Kung Women: Contrasts in Sexual Egalitarianism in Foraging and Sedentary Contexts." In Rayna Reiter (ed.). *Toward an Anthropology of Women,* pp. 77–109. New York: Monthly Review Press.

Friedl, Ernestine. 1975. *Women and Men: An Anthropologist's View.* New York: Holt, Rinehart and Winston.

———. 1978. "Society and Sex Roles." *Human Nature* (April): 68–75.

Goodale, Jane C. 1971. *Tiwi Wives: A Study of the Women of Melville Island, North Australia.* Seattle: University of Washington Press.

Goody, Jack. 1976. *Production and Reproduction.* Cambridge: Cambridge University Press.

Herdt, Gilbert, and Fitz Poole (eds.). 1982. *Sexual Antagonism, Gender, and Social Change in Papua New Guinea.* Social Analysis (special issue), Volume 12. Adelaide: University of Adelaide.

Leacock, Eleanor. 1975. "Class, Commodity, and the Status of Women." In Ruby Rohrlich-Leavitt (ed.). *Women Cross-Culturally: Change and Challenge,* pp. 601–616. The Hague: Mouton.

Lee, Richard. 1979. *The !Kung San.* Cambridge: Cambridge University Press.

Lepowsky, Maria. 1993. *Fruit of the Motherland: Gender in an Egalitarian Society.* New York: Columbia University Press.

Martin, M. Kay, and Barbara Voorhies. 1975. *Female of the Species.* New York: Columbia University Press.

Meigs, Anna. 1990. "Multiple Gender Ideologies and Statuses." In Peggy Sanday and Ruth Goodenough (eds.). *Beyond the Second Sex: New Directions in the Anthropology of Gender,* pp. 99–112. Philadelphia: University of Pennsylvania Press.

Murphy, Yolanda, and Robert F. Murphy. 1985. *Women of the Forest.* New York: Columbia University Press.

Nelson, Nici. 1979. "How Women and Men Get By: The Sexual Division of Labour in the Informal Sector of a Nairobi Squatter Settlement." In Ray Bromley and Chris Gerry (eds.). *Casual Work and Poverty in Third World Cities,* pp. 283–302. New York: John Wiley & Sons.

O'Hara, Patricia. 1998. *Partners in Production? Women, Farm and Family in Ireland.* New York: Berghahn Books.

Sanday, Peggy Reeves. 1974. "Female Status in the Public Domain." In Michelle Z. Rosaldo and Louise Lamphere (eds.). *Woman, Culture, and Society,* pp. 189–206. Stanford, CA: Stanford University Press.

Smith, M. Estellie. 1989. "The Informal Economy." In Stuart Plattner (ed.). *Economic Anthropology,* pp. 292–317. Stanford, CA: Stanford University Press.

Strathern, Marilyn. 1988. *The Gender of the Gift: Problems with Women and Problems with Society in Melanesia.* Berkeley: University of California Press.

Wolf, Margery. 1972. *Women and the Family in Rural Taiwan.* Stanford, CA: Stanford University Press.

# Woman the Hunter:
## The Agta

### Agnes Estioko-Griffin and P. Bion Griffin

Among Agta Negritos of northeastern Luzon, the Philippines, women are of special interest to anthropology because of their position in the organization of subsistence. They are substantial contributors to the daily subsistence of their families and have considerable authority in decision making in the family and in residential groups. In addition, and in contradiction to one of the sacred canons of anthropology, women in one area frequently hunt game animals. They also fish in the rivers with men and barter with lowland Filipinos for goods and services.[1]

In this chapter, we describe women's roles in Agta subsistence economy and discuss the relationship of subsistence activities, authority allocation, and egalitarianism. With this may come an indication of the importance of the Agta research to the anthropology of women and of hunter–gatherers in general. . . . Women, especially women in hunting-gathering societies, have been a neglected domain of anthropological research. The recent volume edited by Richard Lee and Irven DeVore (1976) and *The !Kung of Nyae Nyae* (Marshall 1976) begin to remedy the lack but focus solely on the !Kung San of southern Africa. Other works are either general or synthetic (Friedl 1975; Martin and Voorhies 1975), or report narrowly bounded topics (Rosaldo and Lamphere 1974). Sally Slocum, writing in *Toward an Anthropology of Women* (Reiter 1975), has provided impetus for the Agta study. Slocum points out a male bias in studying hunter–gatherers, showing how approaching subsistence from a female view gives a new picture. From the insights of Slocum we have sought to focus on Agta women, to compare the several dialect groups, and to begin investigating the nature and implications of women as not "merely" gatherers but also hunters.

## THE AGTA

The Agta are Negrito peoples found throughout eastern Luzon, generally along the Pacific coast and up rivers into the Sierra Madre interior. . . . Although perhaps

fewer in numbers, they are also located on the western side of the mountains, especially on the tributary rivers feeding the Cagayan. In general terms, the Agta of Isabela and Cagayan provinces are not dissimilar to other present and past Philippine Negritos. (See Vanoverbergh 1925, 1929–30 Fox 1952; Garvan 1964; and Maceda 1964 for information on Negritos outside the present study area.) In the more remote locales, hunting forest game, especially wild pig, deer, and monkey, is still important. Everywhere, collection of forest plant foods has been eclipsed by exchange of meat for corn, rice, and cultivated root crops. Fishing is usually important throughout the dry season, while collection of the starch of the caryota palm (*Caryota cumingii*) is common in the rainy season. An earlier paper (Estioko and Griffin 1975) gives some detail concerning the less settled Agta; both Bennagen (1976) and Peterson (1974, 1978*a, b*, n.d.) closely examine aspects of subsistence among Agta in the municipality of Palanan.

A brief review of Agta economic organization will be sufficient for later discussion of women's activities. Centuries ago all Agta may have been strictly hunter-gatherers. Since at least A.D. 1900 the groups near the towns of Casiguran (Headland and Headland 1974) and Palanan have been sporadic, part-time horticulturalists, supplementing wild plant foods with sweet potatoes, corn, cassava, and rice. The more remote, interior Agta, sometimes referred to as *ebuked* (Estioko and Griffin 1975), plant small plots of roots, a few square meters of corn, and a banana stalk or two. They usually plant only in the wet season, harvesting an almost immature crop when staples are difficult to obtain by trade. *Ebuked* neglect crop production, preferring to trade meat for grains and roots.

Lee and DeVore (1968: 7) argue that women produce much of the typical hunter–gatherers' diet and that in the tropics vegetable foods far outweigh meat in reliability and frequency of consumption. The Dipagsanghang and Dianggu-Malibu Agta strikingly contradict this idea. They are superb hunters, eat animal protein almost daily, and, as noted above, may have both men and women hunting. (The Tasaday, to the south in Mindanao, may represent an extreme nonhunting adaptation, one in which plant food collection is very dominant [Yen 1976].) Hunting varies seasonally and by techniques used among various groups, but is basically a bow and arrow technology for killing wild pig and deer, the only large game in the Luzon dipterocarp forests. Monkey, although not large, is a reliable rainy season prey. Among Agta close to Palanan and Casiguran, hunting is a male domain. Many hunters pride themselves on skill with bow and arrow; less able hunters may use traps. Dogs to drive game are very desirable in the dry season when the forest is too noisy for daylight stalking of animals.

The collecting of wild plant food is not a daily task. Most Agta prefer to eat corn, cassava, and sweet potatoes, and neglect the several varieties of roots, palm hearts, and greens procurable in the forest. . . . Forest foods are difficult to collect, necessitate residence moves over long distances, and do not taste as good as cultivated foods. Emphasis of trade networks with lowland farmers favors de-emphasis of forest exploitation of plants. Only in the rainy season do Agta actively process a traditional resource, the sago-like caryota palm. Fruits are often picked on the spur of the moment; seldom do parties leave camp solely for their collection.

Trade with farmers is practiced by all Agta known to us. Rumors of Agta "farther into the mountains" who never trade (or cultivate) seem to be without substance. In the report of the Philippine Commission (1908: 334), evidence of lowland-Agta trade around 1900 indicates the *ibay* trade partner relationship to have some antiquity. As the lowlander population has increased since World War II, trade has also increased. Agta are more and more dependent on goods and foodstuffs gained from farmers; adjustments of Agta economic behavior continue to be made, with labor on farms being one aspect of change. Agta formerly simply traded meat for carbohydrates. Around Palanan they may now work for cash or kind when residing close to farmers' settlements. Hunting decreases as the demands of cultivation are met. A cycle is created, and further withdrawal from forest subsistence occurs. Farmers live in areas once solely owned by Agta. Debts to farmers increase with economic dependence; freedom of mobility and choice of activity decrease; and Agta in farming areas become landless laborers.

At the same time, Agta seek to get out of the cycle by emulating the farmers. Many Agta within ten kilometers of Palanan Centro are attempting to become farmers themselves. While the success rate is slow, the attempt is real. Again, when questioned by an early American anthropologist, Agta close to Palanan Centro claimed to be planting small rainy season plots with corn, roots, and upland rice (Worcester 1912: 841). Living informants confirm the long practice of cultivation, but suggest a recent expansion of Agta fields and commitment to abandoning forest nomadism (especially over the last fifteen years). Around the areas of Disuked-Dilaknadinum and Kahanayan-Diabut in Palanan, Agta

are well known for their interest in swidden cultivation. Even the most unsettled Agta farther upriver claim small fields and sporadically plant along the rivers well upstream of lowland farmsteads.

The horticultural efforts of the Agta appear less than is the case, since the social organization and settlement patterns are very different from those of the farmers. Agta throughout Isabela and Cagayan are loosely organized into extended family residential groups. A group, called a *pisan*, is seldom less than two nuclear families and very rarely more than five (in the dry season—perhaps slightly higher average during the wet season). The nuclear family is the basic unit of Agta society, being potentially self-sufficient under usual circumstances. The residential group is organized as a cluster of nuclear families united either through a common parent or by sibling ties. Non-kin friends may be visitors for several weeks, and any nuclear family is able to leave and join another group of relatives at will.

As is typical of hunting–gathering societies, no formal, institutionalized authority base exists. The nuclear family is the decision maker concerning residence, work, and relations with other people. Older, respected individuals, often parents and grandparents of group members, may be consulted, but their opinions are not binding. Often group consensus is desired; people who disagree are free to grumble or to leave.

The settlement pattern is determined, in part, by the seasonal cycle of rains and sunny weather, and by these influences on the flora and fauna exploited for food. Rainy season flooding restricts forest travel, brings hardships in exchange, but is compensated by good condition of the game animals. The dry season permits travel over greater distances and into the remote mountains. Predictable fish resources enhance the advantages of human dispersal; only the need to carry trade meats to farmers inhibits distant residence placement.

## WOMEN'S ACTIVITIES

Women participate in all the subsistence activities that men do. Women trade with farmers, fish in the rivers, collect forest plant foods, and may even hunt game animals. Tasks are not identical, however; a modest sexual division of labor does exist. Furthermore, considerable variation is found among the groups of Agta of Isabella and Cagayan provinces. These differences may possibly be ascribed to the degree of adjustment of Agta to lowland Filipino culture. Some differences may be due to unique culture histories and to little contact.

Although in Isabela most Agta women do not hunt with bow and arrows, with machetes, or by use of traps, most are willing to assist men in the hunt. Not uncommonly, women help carry game out of the forest. Since mature pig and deer are heavy and the terrain is difficult, this is no small accomplishment. Even in areas around Palanan and Casiguran, women are known to accompany men and dogs into the forest and to guide the dogs in the game drive. Some women are famous for their abilities to handle dogs; one informant, a girl about fifteen years of age, was especially skilled. In Palanan and Casiguran, women and men laugh at the idea of women hunting. Such a practice would be a custom of wild, uncivilized Agta (*ebuked*) far in the mountains, they say. Many of the attributes of ebuked seem to be old-fashioned customs still practiced by interior groups.

Two groups studied as part of the present research do have women who hunt. Among the Dipagsanghang Agta, several mature women claim to have hunting skills; they learned these in their unmarried teen years. They only hunt under extreme circumstances, such as low food supplies or great distances from farmers and a supply of corn. All these Agta are found in southern Isabela between Dipagsanghang and Dinapiqui.

In the northernmost section of Isabela and well into Cagayan province, women are active and proficient hunters. While we have termed the Agta here as the Dianggu-Malibu group, we are actually referring to speakers of the southeast Cagayan dialect who live on the river drainage areas of the Dianggu and Malibu rivers.[2] Both the dialect and women who hunt are found over a considerably greater territory, according to informants, reaching north to Baggao, Cagayan, and at least to the Taboan River.

Among the Dianggu-Malibu women some variation, perhaps localized, perhaps personal, is found. On the Dianggu, some of the women questioned, and observed hunting, carried machetes and were accompanied by dogs. They claim to prefer the machete to the bow and arrow, allowing dogs to corner and hold pigs for sticking with the knife. Our sample of actual observations is too small to argue that only immature pigs are killed, but we do know that in the dry season adult male pigs are dangerous in the extreme. Dogs may be killed during hunts. Since Agta dogs are seldom strong animals, we wonder if mature pigs are acquired only occasionally. On the other hand, so many dogs are owned by these Agta that sheer numbers may favor large kills. We have observed two Agta women with as many as fifteen dogs. Other Dianggu women prefer the bow.

On the Malibu River, Agta women are expert bow and arrow hunters. On both of our brief visits to this group, women were observed hunting. They claim to use bows always, and they seek the full range of prey animals. Wild pig is most desired, while deer are often killed. Future work must quantify the hunting details, but women seem to vary slightly from men in their hunting strategies. Informants say they hunt only with dogs. On closer questioning they admit to knowing techniques that do not involve dogs—for example, they may climb trees and lie in wait for an animal to approach to feed on fallen fruit. Among all Agta, hunting practices vary considerably between the rainy and dry seasons. Our fieldwork in Malibu has been confined to the dry season, when dogs are important. In the rainy season solitary stalking is practiced. Field observations should eventually provide quantitative data on women hunting in this season; we must stress that our data are primarily from interview and brief observation. We have not resided among Cagayan Agta long enough to advance quantitatively based generalizations.

Women not only hunt but appear to hunt frequently. Like men, some enjoy hunting more than others. The more remotely located Agta seem most to favor hunting. Even among Agta certain males and females are considered lacking in initiative, a fault that may not be confined to hunting.

Informant data indicate that while women may make their own arrows, the actual blacksmithing of the metal projectile points is a male activity. More field research is necessary to confirm the universality of this detail. Other items of interest pertain to the composition of hunting parties. Most people in any one residence group are consanguineally or affinely related. We have observed several combinations of hunting parties. Men and women hunt together or among themselves. Often sisters, or mother and daughter, or aunt and niece hunt together. At Malibu, two sisters, co-wives of one male, hunt together, and either or both sisters join the husband to hunt. When young children exist, one of the two wives may stay at the residence while the husband and the other wife hunt and fish. Also, sisters and brothers cooperate on the hunt. A woman would not hunt with, for example, a cousin's husband unless the cousin were along.

The only real argument, in our opinion, that has been advanced to support the contention that women must gather and men hunt relates to childbearing and nurture. Among the Agta, during late pregnancy and for the first few months of nursing, a woman will not hunt. In spite of the small size of each residential group, however, some females seem always to be around to hunt, although one or more may be temporarily withdrawn from the activity. Women with young children hunt less than teenagers and older women. On the occasion of brief hunts—part of one day—children are cared for by older siblings, by grandparents, and by other relatives. Occasionally a father will tend a child. Only infants are closely tied to mothers.

Girls start hunting shortly after puberty. Before then they are gaining forest knowledge but are not strong. Boys are no different. We have no menopause data, but at least one woman known to us as a hunter must have passed childbearing age. She is considered an older woman, but since she is strong, she hunts. The pattern is typical of men also. As long as strength to travel and to carry game is retained, people hunt. Our best inform- ant, a young grandmother, hunts several times a week.

Both Agta men and women fish. In fact, from early childhood until the infirmity of old age all Agta fish. If most adults are gone on a hunting trip for several days, the remaining adults and children must obtain animal protein by themselves. Only women in late pregnancy, with young infants, or into old age, withdraw from fish- ing, which makes considerable demands of endurance as well as skill. Some men excel at working in rough, deep, and cold waters. The everyday techniques for fish- ing are limited to underwater spear fishing. Glass-lensed wooden goggles, a heavy wire spear or rod varying acc- ording to size of fish sought, and an inner-tube rubber band complete the equipment. To fish, people simply swim underwater, seeking fish in the various aquatic envi- ronments known for each species. Girls in their teens are very capable at fishing. When fishing individually, women may be major contributors to the daily catch.

When group fishing is undertaken, a drive is con- ducted. In this operation, a long vine is prepared by attaching stones and banners of wild banana stalks. Two people drag the vine, one on each end and on opposite sides of the river, while the people in the water spear fish startled by the stones and stalks. Women join men in the drives, with older men and women dragging the vine while all able-bodied youths and adults work in the water.

Difficulty of fishing may be characterized as a gra- dient upon which men and women become less and less able as age and debilities increase. The elderly, when mobile, may still be productive, but instead of true fishing, their activities may be termed collecting. Both the coastal reef areas and freshwater rivers and streams have abundant shellfish, shrimp, and amphib- ians that may be caught by hand. Elderly women and grandchildren are especially eager to harvest these resources. Older men are not ashamed to follow suit, although the enthusiasm of others for the task seldom gives old men incentive. Men are much less eager to give up riverine fishing after middle age than are women. Clearly some emphasis on males securing protein is found among Agta. Women, however, seem to have traditionally been active in fishing. Interest- ingly, as a few Agta adopt lowland fishing technology, especially nets, women seldom participate. Like their female counterparts in lowland society, women are deemed not appropriate in net fishing.

One might expect that, on the basis of worldwide comparison, tropic hunters would really be gatherers, and that women would be the steady and substantial providers. Agta do not fit the generalizations now accepted. Few Agta women regularly dig roots, gather palm hearts, seek fruit, or pick greens. Most Agta daily consume domesticated staples grown by the farmers. Women are, however, very knowledgeable concern- ing flora and its use, and among the less settled Agta, young girls are still taught all traditional forest lore. Brides-to-be among these Agta are partially evaluated on the basis of their knowledge, skill, and endurance in collecting jungle plant foods.

Roots are collected by women whenever more desir- able food is unobtainable, when several wild pigs have been killed and the men want to eat "forest food" with pig fat, or when a visit to relatives or friends calls for a special treat. The interior groups may actually com- bine meat and wild roots for weeks when camped so far from farmers that exchange for corn is impossible. Downriver Agta consider such a practice a real hard- ship, not to be willingly endured. Men are known to dig roots, even though they say it is women's work. On long-distance hunts men do not as a rule carry food, and they may occasionally dig roots to alleviate the all meat-fish diet.

As hunting is thought of as a "sort of" male activity among many Agta (in Isabela), processing the starch of the caryota palm is a female activity. Women cruise the forest searching for trees containing masses of the starch; they also chop down the trees, split the trunks, adze out the pith, and extract the flour. Often parties of women and girls work together, speeding up the laborious task. On occasion, men will assist. Extracting the flour starch is moderately heavy work, and tir- ing. Husbands may help when wives have a pressing need to complete a task quickly. Since much of the final product is given in gift form, the need for haste occurs frequently. Perhaps most important to note is the male participation. Sexual division of labor is tenu- ously bounded among all Agta. Emphases may exist, but a man can even build a house (i.e., tie the fronds to the frame—a female task).

As noted at the beginning, trade, exchange, and horticulture are not new to Agta. Informants, early photographs, and writings indicate that all but the most remote Agta were not "pure" hunter-gatherers after about A.D. 1900. Since the mountains have been a final retreat—from the earliest Spanish attempts to conquer the Cagayan Valley until the present—Agta must have been in contact with former farmers/ revolutionaries in hiding. Keesing (1962), summariz- ing the peoples of northern Luzon, documents several societies of pagan swiddeners adjacent to or in Negrito territory. The Palanan River drainage area was inhab- ited by farmers before Spanish contact in the sixteenth century. Doubtless, Agta have participated in eco- nomic exchange and social intercourse for centuries. Agta now have institutionalized trade partnerships, at least in Palanan and Casiguran municipalities. Trade partners are called ibay (Peterson [1978a, b] discussed the *ibay* relationship in detail), and partnerships may last between two families over two or more generations. *Ibay* exchange meat for grains and roots, or meat for cloth, metal, tobacco, beads, and other goods. Services may be exchanged, especially in downriver areas. Fields may be worked by Agta, who then borrow a carabao, receive corn or rice, and satisfy any of a number of needs. What is important in relation to this chapter is that Agta women may engage in *ibay* partnerships. Among the lowland farmers almost all *ibay* are males. An Agta woman may be an *ibay* with a lowland man. According to our data, an Agta husband often is not also *ibay* with his wife's *ibay*, but he must treat the farmer as he would his own *ibay*. Of course Agta men and women trade with any farmer they choose, but such exchange is without the consideration given to an *ibay*. (Considerations include credit, acts of friendship, and first choice/best deal on goods.) Not only do women have *ibay*, but they very frequently are the most active agents of exchange. In areas where the trade rests mostly on meat and where men do most of the hunting, women are likely to carry out the dried meat and bring back the staple. They therefore gain experience in dealing with the farmers. We should note that many farmers attempt to cheat the Agta by shortchanging them on counts or weights, but they do so on the basis of gullibility or naiveté of the Agta, not on the basis of sex. Agta women are actually more aggressive traders than are men, who do not like confrontation.

Among the Dipagsanghang Agta, women seldom hunt today, and infrequently dig roots. They do carry out meat to trade. They seem to have an easier life, with emphasis on corn, rice, and roots instead of gathering wild foods. However, downriver, close to farmers, Agta women have reversed this trend, and are working harder and longer hours.[3] Intensification of the ibay relationship and need to own and cultivate land has forced women to become horticulturalists and wage laborers for farmers. On their own family plots (family-owned, not male- or female-owned) they, together with adult males and youths, clear land, break soil, plant, weed, and harvest. When clearing virgin forest of large trees, women do not participate. They do clear secondary growth in fallowed fields.

In the families that reside close to Palanan . . . men and women work almost daily in the fields of farmers. Women go to the forest to collect the lighter raw materials for house construction, mats, betel chews, medicines, and so on. Men follow a similar pattern, giving up hunting for field labor and a corn and sweet potato diet supplemented by small fish. Again we see a remarkable parallel in the activities of males and females.

Looking more closely at specialized women's activities, one may suggest increasing importance in downriver areas. Women have several domains that they use to gain cash or kind income. As just stated, income from labor in fields adds to the economic power of women. A small-scale traditional pursuit, shared by men and women, is the gathering of copal, a tree resin common to trees (*Agathis philippinensis*) found scattered in the Sierra Madre. Women often collect and carry the resin out to lowland "middlemen," who sell it to the depot in town. While corn and cash may be sought in exchange, cloth is desired in order to make skirts. Medicine and medical treatments for ailing children may be paid for by copal collection. Another example of entrepreneurship by females is a small-scale mobile variety store effort. After working in fields for cash and building a surplus, families may cross the Sierra Madre to the towns of San Mariano, Cauayan, and Ilagan. There Agta, often women, purchase in markets and stores goods for use and resale in Palanan. Palanan Centro itself has no real market, only several small general stores selling goods at highly marked up prices. Since no road reaches Palanan, all manufactured supplies must enter town by airplane from Cauayan or boat from Baler. Freight costs are high. Some Agta women are very eager to hike outside to get tobacco, which always commands a high price and a ready market.

## DISCUSSION

The role of women in Agta economic activities has been reviewed. Assessment of an hypothesized egalitarian position of women may be more difficult, and rests on assertions and interpretations drawn from the economic roles. First, drawing in part from Friedl (1975), an argument can be made that women in Agta society have equality with men because they have similar authority in decision making. The authority could be based on the equal contribution to the subsistence resources. Working back, we see that among many Agta, women do contribute heavily to the daily food supply, do perform maintenance tasks with men, and may initiate food acquisition efforts through their own skills. They do control the distribution of their acquired food, sharing first with their own nuclear family and extended family, then trading as they see fit. They may procure nonfood goods as they desire. Men may do the same; generally spouses discuss what work to do, what needs should be satisfied, and who will do what. Whole residential groups frequently together decide courses of action. Women are as vocal and as critical in reaching decisions as are men. Further examples could strongly validate the hypothesis that women do supply a substantial portion of foods, and the assertion that women have authority in major decision making. Two questions arise. May we accept a causal relationship between percentage of food production and equality? Certainly there are cases to the contrary. According to Richard A. Gould (personal communication), Australian Aboriginal women in various areas collected the bulk of the food, yet remained less than equal (as we will define equality). Second, we may ask if Agta males and females are actually "equal."

Two avenues may suffice in answering this question. First, one might explore a definition of equality, surely a culturally loaded concept. Since Agta women have authority or control of the economic gain of their own labor, they may be equal in this critical domain. Equality must surely be equated with decision-making power and control of one's own production. The second avenue of equality validation by the scientist may be to examine the female's control over herself in noneconomic matters. These could include selection of marriage partner, lack of premarital sexual intercourse proscription, spacing of children, ease of divorce, and polygyny rules.

In marriage, two forms are typical of Agta. One, the less common, is elopement by young lovers. While such marriages admittedly are fragile, elopement is not uncommon. In this case both partners must be willing. Rape and abduction are rare. Rape by Agta men is not known to the authors. Abduction must involve a slightly willing female, and is not done by young people. A mature man might abduct a married woman, crossing the mountains to a safe locale. To abduct a young girl would be difficult. Parents of eloping couples may be enraged, but usually reconcile themselves to the marriage. If the newlyweds stay together, no more is made of it.

The proper form of marriage is one arranged by customary meetings and discussions, as well as exchange of goods between two families. Often neither the bride nor the groom has had much say in the matter, although serious dislike by either would probably kill the negotiations before the marriage. Mothers are the most important in choosing who will marry whom. Even when their children are young, they are looking about for good partners. Word filters around when a young girl is marriageable, and efforts are made to get the appropriate young man and his family into negotiations before an undesirable family appears. Once any family with a prospective groom formally asks, a rejection is given only for strong and good reasons, since the denied family loses considerable face and may be angry enough to seek revenge.[4]

Criteria for choice of a marriage partner are varied. Often a young man in his early twenties marries a girl about fifteen. Girls entering marriage before puberty are not uncommon. In such cases the husband may help raise the girl until the time the marriage is consummated and full wifehood is recognized. Other combinations are seen. One much discussed case was the marriage of a woman in her forties to a man in his mid-twenties. The couple seemed very happy, with the wife paying rather special attention to her husband. The man's mother, a friend of the wife's, decided that the marriage was peculiar but acceptable.

Premarital female chastity is not an idea of much currency. Agta close to farmers will pay lip service to the idea, but should a girl become pregnant she will take a husband. There are no illegitimate Agta children, although an occasional rape of an Agta by a lowland male may produce a child. Since by the time a girl is fertile she likely will be married, illegitimacy is not the issue. Although some data are difficult to collect concerning sex, almost certainly girls are able to engage in sexual activity with relative ease; promiscuity is not favored in any circumstance. Males may have as little or great difficulty in engaging in sex as females. The Agta are widely dispersed in extended family groups; hence appropriate sexual partners are seldom seen. No homosexuality is known to exist.

Agta gossip suggests that many Agta, male and female, married and unmarried, constantly carry on extramarital sexual relations. This may be a function of gossip and a gross exaggeration. Whatever reality, neither males nor females seem to be especially singled out for criticism.

Women say they space their children. The practice certainly varies hugely from person to person, as does fecundity and luck in keeping children alive. The Agta use various herbal concoctions that supposedly prevent conception, cause abortions shortly after conception, and have several functions related to menstruation. These medicines are known to all Agta and are frequently used. Our census data indicate that some women seem to be successful in spacing births. Other cases note high infant mortality yet no infanticide, female or male. All Agta abhor the idea.

Divorce is infrequent among Agta, with elopement being more prone to failure than are arranged marriages. Divorce does happen often enough, however, for us to look at the causes and relate them to an inquiry into female equality. First, either sex may divorce the other with equal ease. Agta have no possessions. Some gift giving between the two families establishes the marriage, but most of the gifts are food. Cloth, kettles, and minor items make up the rest. Return of marriage gifts is unlikely. Spouses simply take their personal possessions and return to the residential group of close relatives.

Causes for divorce are mainly laziness or improvidence, excessive adultery, or personality clashes and incompatibility, usually caused by a combination of the first two conditions. Skill and success in subsistence activities is of primary importance to marriage. While some Agta are less industrious and less skilled than others, all Agta expect a mate to work hard at all appropriate tasks. Should a male fail, divorce is likely. Occasionally, very young couples experience extra difficulties. These may be accentuated by displeased parents of either party.

Polygamy is not found in most of Isabela. Census data collected to date reveal only monogamy or serial monogamy. That is, spouses may be divorced or widow(er)ed several times in a lifetime. In Cagayan the data are incomplete but startling. Probably some of the strongest support for the equality of women hypothesis, when added to the facts of women as hunters, comes from a study of Agta polygamy. We noted earlier that two co-wives, sisters, hunted together in Malibu. South of Malibu at Blos, another husband and two sisters/co-wives arrangement was found. In the same residential unit we recorded a woman residing with her two co-husbands. They were not brothers; one was older than the wife, one younger. The other women considered this arrangement as humorous, but acceptable. An insight into the male sexual jealousy found in many societies worldwide is the comment of a Palanan Agta man. This old man, when told of the polyandrous marriage to the north, thought for a moment and commented, "Well, perhaps one man with two wives is OK, but a woman with two husbands? I find that totally bad." The women laughed at him.

## NOTES

1. Although the authors have worked among the Agta about fourteen months, visits to the northerly group in the Dianggu-Malibu area have been brief. The practice of women hunting was first observed during a survey trip in 1972. We again visited the Dianggu group in 1975. In August 1978 we returned for one week to Dianggu and Malibu, where we verified in greater detail the subsistence activities of women. Data were collected using the Palanan Agta dialect and Ilokano.
2. Dianggu and Malibu are river names used by Agta and nearby Malay Filipinos. On the Board of Technical Surveys and Maps (Lobod Point, Philippines), the Dianggu is named the Lobod and the Malibu is named the Ilang.
3. Peterson (n.d.) argues that "downriver" Agta women are highly variable in their devotion to labor, older women being hardworking and young mothers not at all industrious.
4. Thomas Headland tells us that rejection of a prospective spouse may be a less serious matter among Casiguran Agta than among those we know.

## REFERENCES

Bennagen, Ponciano. 1976. Kultura at Kapaligiran: Pangkulturang Pagbabago at Kapanatagan ng mga Agta sa Palanan, Isabela. M.A. thesis, Department of Anthropology, University of the Philippines, Diliman, Quezon City.

Estioko, Agnes A., and P. Bion Griffin. 1975. The Ebuked Agta of northeastern Luzon. *Philippines Quarterly of Culture and Society* 3(4):237–44.

Fox, Robert B. 1952. The Pinatubo Negritos, their useful plants and material culture. *Philippine Journal of Science* 81:113–414.

Friedl, Ernestine. 1975. *Women and men: an anthropologist's view.* New York: Holt, Rinehart and Winston.

Garvan, John M. 1964. *The Negritos of the Philippines,* ed. Hermann Hochegger, Weiner beitrage zur kulturgeschichte und linguistik, vol. 14. Horn: F. Berger.

Headland, Thomas, and Janet D. Headland. 1974. *A Dumagat (Casiguran)–English dictionary.* Pacific Linguistics Series C. No. 28. Australian National University, Canberra: Linguistics Circle of Canberra.

Keesing, Felix. 1962. *The ethnohistory of northern Luzon.* Stanford, Calif.: Stanford University Press.

Lee, Richard B., and Irven DeVore. 1968. Problems in the study of hunters and gatherers. In *Man the Hunter,* ed. Lee and DeVore. Chicago: Aldine.

———. 1976. *Kalahari hunter-gatherers: studies of the !Kung San and their neighbors.* Cambridge, Mass.: Harvard University Press.

Maceda, Marcelino M. 1964. *The culture of the mamanuas (northeast Mindanao) as compared with that of the other Negritos of Southeast Asia.* Manila: Catholic Trade School.

Marshall, Lorna. 1976. *The !Kung of Nyae Nyae.* Cambridge, Mass.: Harvard University Press.

Martin, M. Kay, and Barbara Voorhies. 1975. *Female of the species.* New York: Columbia University Press.

Peterson, Jean Treloggen. 1974. An ecological perspective on the economic and social behavior of Agta hunter-gatherers, northeastern Luzon, Philippines. Ph.D. dissertation, University of Hawaii at Manoa.

———. 1978a. Hunter-gatherer farmer exchange. *American Anthropologist* 80:335–51.

———. 1978b. The ecology of social boundaries: Agta foragers of the Philippines. *Illinois Studies in Anthropology No. 11.* University of Illinois, Urbana–Champaign, Ill.

———. n.d. Hunter mobility, family organization and change. In *Circulation in the Third World,* ed. Murray Chapman and Ralph Mansell Prothero. London: Routledge & Kegan Paul.

Philippine Commission. 1908. *8th Annual Report of the Philippine Commission: 1907.* Bureau of Insular Affairs, War Department. Washington, D.C.: Government Printing Office.

Reiter, Rayna R., ed. 1975. *Toward an anthropology of women.* New York: Monthly Review Press.

Rosaldo, Michelle Zimbalist, and Louise Lamphere, eds. 1974. *Woman, culture, and society.* Stanford, Calif.: Stanford University Press.

Vanoverbergh, Maurice. 1925. Negritos of northern Luzon. *Anthropos* 20:148–99.

———. 1929–30. Negritos of northern Luzon again. *Anthropos* 24:1–75, 897–911; 25:25–71, 527–656.

Worcester, Dean C. 1912. Head-hunters of northern Luzon. *National Geographic* 23(9):833–930.

Yen, D. E. 1976. The ethnobotany of the Tasaday: III. Note on the subsistence system. In *Further studies on the Tasaday,* ed. D. E. Yen and John Nance. Makati, Rizal: PANAMIN Foundation Research Series No. 2.

# Gender, Horticulture, and the Division of Labor on Vanatinai

## Maria Lepowsky

### GENDER AND HORTICULTURE

"Women are the owners of the garden," Koita said, early one morning. I probably looked startled, because she added, emphatically, "That is our custom; it's the way of the ancestors." Koita was my neighbor, a respected female elder on the small Pacific island of Vanatinai. She was stating, with no prompting from me, a fundamental principle of island gender ideologies, part of their overall worldview, their outlook on life.

I was studying relations between women and men in what I suspected would be at least a fairly egalitarian society. I chose the island for my research in part because I had read that cultures in this region of small islands had matrilineal kinship systems. People belonged to their mothers' clans. Matrilineality meant, I reasoned, that women were central to kinship systems, control of communally held lands, and inheritance patterns. This might translate, on Vanatinai, into egalitarian relations between the sexes.

The people of Vanatinai and their neighbors are primarily horticulturalists, practicing a nonintensive form of agriculture, which anthropologists sometimes refer to as gardening. The islanders actually have a mixed economy, fishing, hunting, and gathering wild plant foods as well as planting and harvesting crops. Horticulturalists rely especially on root and tree crops. They use simple tools, such as digging sticks, rather than spending time and caloric energies on intensive, plow-based farming that uses draft animals (horses, mules, water buffalo) or machinery.

Social relations in horticultural societies vary, but they tend to be more gender egalitarian than in other agricultural societies or in large-scale industrial societies. Horticultural societies are often smaller in scale, with fewer people dependent on the resources of a particular territory. This leads to more possibilities for face-to-face negotiation, personal influence, consensus formation, and conflict resolution. All of these factors can make for more egalitarian social relations overall: less hierarchy, fewer specialized roles and positions based on age, sex, rank, and/or training; and a greater overlap between the kinship system and the political system. Leaders or influential

persons within an extended family or clan tend to be the political leaders as well, the most influential people in the community or region. Gender relations, the interactions between men and women and the ideologies that shape them, are a key aspect of the potentially more egalitarian social relations found in many small-scale societies, where people make their living by horticulture, foraging, or a mixture of the two.

Vanatinai (whose European name is Sudest Island) is the largest island of an archipelago, a chain of islands, in a remote part of the Southwest Pacific, southeast of the great island of New Guinea by 200 miles, and 700 miles northeast of Australia. The island had never previously been studied by an anthropologist. I had hypothesized that the roles of women and men, and cultural ideologies of gender, were largely egalitarian. If so, women and men would have reasonably equal rights, privileges, personal autonomy, and influence over the actions of others. Women as well as men would be involved in prestige-generating activities. Here, that would mean exchanging ceremonial valuables and hosting elaborate feasts in honor of the dead. The region has been famous to anthropologists since the pioneering research of Bronislaw Malinowski (1922) on Trobriand Island kula. Kula is a remarkable system for the ceremonial exchange of shell valuables and stone axeblades. These prized objects circulate hundreds of miles among islanders who speak a dozen different languages and travel by sailing canoe to visit their exchange partners. They trade yams, pigs, clay pots, and other, more obviously practical goods at the same time. But in the Trobriands, kula is almost entirely a male prestige activity. Trobrianders also have chiefs, and they too are almost always male. Years later, anthropologist Annette Weiner (1976) showed that Trobriand women have their own system of wealth exchange, based on banana-leaf skirts and the hosting of memorial feasts, and that it was closely articulated with kula.

On Vanatinai, 300 miles southeast, I found that there were no chiefs and no commoners. Women as well as men gained regional fame in the same way as men, by successfully exchanging the ceremonial valuables that circulate in kula as far as the Trobriands. Vanatinai women as well as men could, and did, host large-scale feasts commemorating the dead that drew hundreds of visitors from a half dozen islands.

Original manuscript prepared for this text. Reprinted by permission of the author.

Both Vanatinai women and men, it turned out, describe island women as *ghuma tanuwagai*, owners, or bosses, of gardens. This is a philosophical statement. In actuality, men and women, sisters, brothers, mothers, maternal grandmothers, mother's brothers, held land in common as matrilineal property. But it was a senior woman, or women, who tended to get everyone organized. Married men usually made gardens on their wives' matrilineal land, not that of their mothers, even though they retained the right to do so.

To a remarkable extent, the tasks considered appropriate for males and females, and for people of varying ages, were much the same. In other words, the sexual division of labor (sometimes called the gendered division of labor) was largely overlapping. This kind of overlap is a characteristic that anthropological theorists have long suggested is characteristic of a gender egalitarian society.[1] On Vanatinai, women and men alike plant weed, and harvest the large, white tropical yams that are one of the islanders' staple foods. Yams are the only annual crop, harvested just before the bright, tightly clustered stars of the Pleiades are visible once more on the eastern horizon. This marks the start of the new year. Both sexes also tend taro and banana patches, and plant and harvest the easy-to-grow, drought-resistant sweet potatoes and manioc that were introduced in the colonial era. Every stage of the process of yam gardening is hedged with garden magic and ritual. I found that only a few people had the magical knowledge, derived from ancestor spirits and handed down from elders, to officiate at communal garden rituals. But these few people included both women and men.

Women and men, sisters and brothers, wives and husbands have to agree on which clan lands they are going to use for a garden. Sometimes this is a challenge. A big woman or big man, either for powerful emotional reasons or to enlarge a regional reputation, may want to host a feast the following year to commemorate someone who has died. That means clearing an especially big garden—cutting and then burning a clearing in the rainforest canopy—so as to have plenty of high-quality yams to feed off-island visitors, who may end up camped out in the hamlet for weeks.

It is the men, young and middle-aged, who do the work of cutting old-growth hardwood trees, while women cut understory trees and shrubs. A senior woman usually supervises the burning, which takes place about a month later when the slash has had a chance to dry out. The ashes then fertilize the soil of the new garden. (This technique, characteristic of tropical horticulture, is called swidden, or slash and burn.) The population density on Vanatinai is quite low, only about four persons per square miles. In many parts of the island, land lies fallow for up to forty years before it is again made into a garden. By then it resembles mature, closed-canopy rainforest.

Men are the ones, I was told, who use eight-foot long wooden poles to loosen and aerate the soil of the new garden, forming it into mounds ready to receive yam seed. It is true that men do it most of the time. But women perform this hard labor as well. I saw a couple of my women neighbors hard at it, and took their photo. The other villagers, men and women, commented admiringly that they were *ivurigheghe*, strong. They meant both physically and socially, a reference to their good reputations and influence over others.

Women do much of the preparation and planting of seed yams, removing them from storage in small, stilted houses adjacent to the gardens, slicing off their growing tips, and stockpiling them in woven, coconut-leaf garden baskets. The rest of each seed yam is boiled with coconut cream in a clay cooking pot and served for lunch to the communal working group. Women also tend to take primary responsibility for maintaining gardens. But this is only a general rule. Some men take great pride in their gardens. And some women are less ambitious gardeners, making more of their subsistence contribution by gathering shellfish or forest fruits rather than weeding under the tropical sun.

Women do much of the harvesting of garden produce, often several times a week. There is no refrigeration, and thin-skinned tubers will go rotten in a few days. The best way to store them is by keeping them under the soil, digging them up as needed for daily subsistence, feeding visiting in-laws, or contributing food to feasts. Yams are the only annual crop. Because of their tough, thick skins, these tropical yam varieties are the only root crop it is possible to store for many months, in baskets on high shelves in house rafters, or in a small yam house. Harvesting is an individual affair, private and secret. The gardener offers prayers to ancestor spirits as she or he digs loose the tubers from the tropical soil with a long digging stick, piling them into a garden basket. Inviting acquaintances and neighbors to observe could be unwise: it might arouse envy if the garden was especially prolific. Some islanders are said to know a special kind of magic that persuades tubers growing in a neighboring garden to travel underground to the garden of the magician. People know not to appear uninvited in someone's garden for another reason as well. A garden house or shelter (a wall-less, palm-thatch roofed structure on wooden stilts) is where islanders take a work break, get out of the midday sun, and cook lunch, but also the only place where a married couple have enough privacy during the daytime for sexual relations, after lunch while it is too hot to work.

Men are strongly identified in island ideology with the production of sago, the almost pure starch extracted from the trunk of a mature female palm. Sago is the other principal food in the island diet. Extensive sago palm groves grow wild in the swamps, dim, almost primeval-looking places that are home as well to voracious clouds of mosquitoes. Islanders throughout the region count the sago swamps of Vanatinai as a source of great wealth. This is an enormous reservoir of potential food, not planted (although the occasional palm is transplanted closer to a village) but wild. The sago groves, and the tracts of swamp, are communally owned by island matrilineages.

Sago processing is not horticulture but a form of plant management. It is hard, concentrated work over the course of two or three days. But it requires far less time, caloric energy, and risk than planting a yam garden, guarding it from wild boars, dealing with drought or flooding by using weather magic to petition ancestors and place spirits, then digging up unknown numbers and sizes of tubers nine months later.

Men do most of the pounding of sago pith—the fibrous insides of the split-open palm—and the sluicing out the starch in a wooden trough, but the work party is usually mixed. Women supervise the drying of cakes of sago starch over a low fire, the cutting of long green sago leaves to use for wrapping the fresh bricks of starch, and the actual wrapping. The bundles are hung in pairs over long poles, then each is carried by two men or youths back to the village. Everyone who has joined the work party gets a share, and lines of sago bundles hang in pairs from the rafters in each house. They are ready for use at a moment's notice: to throw a chunk in a boiling pot of vegetables, prepare a sago and grated coconut dumplings or pancakes, grilled on a broken shard of clay pot over the fire, or a sago and green coconut pudding. Bundles of sago are major items to barter to people who sail to Vanatinai from the smaller coral islands to obtain sago or yams for clay cooking pots or the smoked meat of giant clams.

Vanatinai women, men, and children are all diligent foragers, studying the growth patterns, seasons, and locations of a wide array of wild nuts, legumes, tubers, fruits, ferns, and edible leaves. The large grubs that live in decaying sago palms are a special treat, usually eaten on the spot. They are also a fine source of protein. In general, I observed that women spent more time foraging than men. Foraging, and being in the forest more generally, is something that men and women alike enjoy more than the tedious, sweaty work of weeding gardens.

Shellfish collecting is another subsistence activity practiced equally by men, women, and older children. It too is something people enjoy: going down to the shore, alone or with friends or relatives, to gather the small, tasty oysters that cling to aerial roots of mangroves; hunting for blue mangrove crabs (taking care to avoid getting pinched by their giant front claws), or prying clams loose from the reef at low tide. Anyone who feels like it may fish in the lagoon, from a canoe, from shore, or by wading in the shallows. Men sometimes use metal-tipped spears to fish in the shallows, either from a canoe or on foot at low tide. The metal is often scavenged, washing ashore after a storm from some distant place.

Whole hamlets full of people troop down to the lagoon at neap tide, the lowest tides of the year. They use derris root, from a forest plant that contains a potent neurotoxin, to temporarily stun the fish that have collected in shallow pools in the coral, left behind by the falling sea. The fish are scooped up by hand, strung on a piece of cord made from a forest vine, and carried home. (Fortunately, stunning fish this way does not affect the human diner, although eating derris root directly would be fatal.) The islanders nowadays use monofilament for line fishing. But both men and women use to fish collectively, using nets woven by men from the fibrous aerial root of pandanus, a wild palm that grows in the rainforest.

Occasionally young men, and less often young women, dive in the lagoon for blacklip pearlshell, or the larger, glowing goldlip pearl that is used in other countries to make mother of pearl buttons. Shell can, in theory, be sold at the tradestore at the end of the island, but the commodity price for it, set on the London market, has been extremely low for several decades now, a result of competition from the plastic button industry. Goldlip pearlshell is rarer and harder to obtain, as it lives on reefs in deeper lagoon waters. Goldlip shell is used by islanders themselves to make the translucent pendants that are attached to ceremonial shell-disc necklaces. Young or vigorous men and women sometimes take a canoe to certain reefs where they dive for bagi, the red-rimmed shells used to make the discs for shell necklaces. The shells can be bartered or given to relatives. Discs to string into necklaces are manufactured, using pump drills with a metal bit, by island men and women, often middle-aged, who have chosen to specialize in this form of labor. Necklaces are strung together on bush cord, with mother of pearl pendants added to the larger ones. The deep reddish color of the shell discs should be set off pleasingly by the glossy black of wild banana seeds. These are bartered by visitors arriving by sailing canoe from larger islands near the mainland of New Guinea, 200 miles away; wild banana does not grow on or near Vanatinai. Newly made shell necklaces circulate through sets of exchange partners from island to island for hundreds of miles, as far as the Trobriand Islands, joining necklaces and other valuables that are 100 years and more old in the kula system of interisland exchange that Malinowski made famous.

Sometimes islanders successfully land a sea turtle by wrestling it into a canoe. Or they find a lonely beach where the female is laying eggs in the sand, turn her over, and drag her off. The eggs are scooped up as well. Once in a while, men spear a dugong, a sea mammal, cousin to the manatee of Florida and tropical South America, that grazes on the sea grasses of the lagoon. (Luckily for the dugong, they swim remarkably fast and often elude the hunters.) The islanders fish the inland streams for little silvery fish, sweet reddish prawns, and giant black eels. Every so often, parties of men, accompanied by the occasional young woman, hunt crocodiles late at night, using coconut-leaf torches and black palm, metal-tipped spears.

It is up to the individual to decide how much time she or he wishes to spend fishing or collecting shellfish versus other kinds of subsistence activities such as gardening, gathering, or hunting. The variation in time and effort expended varies based on personal preference, not by sex.

Almost every adult, and some older children and adolescents, is the proud owner of at least one pig. Big women and big men own whole herds of them, and they snuffle around the hamlet scavenging scraps of food. More dedicated owners cook their pigs a meal of sago pith (the part that is inedible to humans) at dusk, after the family dinner has been taken care of. Pigs go unfenced on Vanatinai, wandering into the forest to forage on their own during the day. They not infrequently find their way to someone's garden, where they enthusiastically dig up the sweet potatoes or yams the gardener has been carefully cultivating. Gardens too are unfenced. Islanders are always complaining about the serious damage done to gardens by both wild and domestic pigs. But it would be too much work, they say, to fence off a whole garden. They have a point. Fences have to be made from tree limbs, laboriously cut in the forest, carried to the garden, then roped together with cord made from forest vines to form a sort of corral. Since wild and domestic pigs routinely commingle in one giant, island-wide herd, the wild boars are the ones that sire the piglets. In the hamlet, juvenile males are castrated. Domestic pigs often show affection for their owners. They also serve as watchpigs, growling menacingly and sometimes charging at strangers and visitors, who shout in alarm, on entering a hamlet, "Call off your pigs!"

There is one dramatic restriction on Vanatinai subsistence activities that is based on sex. It is taboo for women to hunt using spears. In earlier times it was taboo for women to make war using spears, or using greenstone axeblades as hatchets. Young, unmarried women did go into battle, elders told me, handing spears to their brothers and dragging them to safety if they were wounded. Mature women knew

the special magic—petitions to powerful ancestor and place spirits—that was used to make war and to make peace. Senior women negotiated truces as experts in diplomacy.

Whenever I asked someone, of either sex, why women were not supposed to hunt with spears, or use weapons of war, the answer was always the same.

"Women are the life givers, and men are the death givers."

"And," the speaker usually added, "life giving is more important."

"But women hunt on Vanatinai," I would argue. "And some women are witches, or even sorcerers." In the supernatural domain of the island division of labor, most but not all witches are women, and most but not all sorcerers are men.

At this point, though, the elder I was talking would add emphatically,

"Ighabubu." It is taboo.

That always ended the conversation.

I learned first-hand from this conundrum that Vanatinai gender ideologies are multi-layered and occasionally contradictory. As is the case in all cultures, ideological statements of how people are supposed to behave are sometimes contradicted by individual actions.

Women do hunt on Vanatinai; they just don't hunt with spears.[2] They climb tall tropical hardwoods and coconut palms to capture opussum, flying foxes, and fruit bats. Young women are supposed to be the best at catching the slow-moving, four-foot-long monitor lizards that resemble miniature Komodo dragons and frequent the tall mangroves lining the estuaries. Girls and women either climb the trees or set traps for them. The rough skins of monitor lizards, stretched by men and used for drum heads, are dark gray and whitish, abstractly patterned in a way that resembles the geometric designs of the fine coconut-leaf baskets that island women weave, whose traditional colors are also gray (from being dipped in swamp water overnight) and off-white.

The climbing of trees by Vanatinai women and girls is telling in itself. In many Pacific societies, it is taboo for women to climb, or for her genitals to be higher than a man's head. Here, island women not only climb to hunt, but agile younger women and girls routinely climb areca and tall coconut palms to cut betel nuts (used daily as a stimulant and exported to other islands), brown ripe coconuts, and green drinking nuts. (The only issue, women told me jokingly, is to make sure there are no men or boys standing directly below a palm tree looking up their skirts.)

This is another aspect of Vanatinai women's physical mobility, their freedom to roam around as they wish, just as men do. Island women are manifesting their freedom of movement when they disappear of their own accord, unchaperoned, into the forest or down the shore on some vague errand. Women also paddle and pole canoes, on subsistence tasks or to visit other coastal hamlets, and some are expert sailors. A few women know how to navigate a sailing canoe between islands single-handed, although navigating and crewing sailing canoes are mostly done by men and male youths.

Woodworking is a male specialization: chopping down hardwoods in the tropical forest to clear a garden, cutting down a mature sago palm, hauling a dense log of false mahogany out of the forest to carve out a canoe hull, or cutting and hauling timbers for housebuilding. The island houses are perched on tall hardwood stilts to catch cooling sea breezes, help defeat mosquitoes, and keep the pigs from wandering in the door. The walls, flooring, and roof come from the bark and leaves of the nipa and sago palms. Women gather sago leaves and weave them into panels that will overlap on the roof, and weave sago leaves together for a particular kind of wall. They also prepare cooked yams and other food to the male housebuilders.

Vanatinai men's woodworking specialty continues with the carving of large wooden, mushroom-shaped ceremonial spatulas, decorated with shell discs, another form of ceremonial valuable used in exchange and feasting. This kind of carving is done by only a few men, middle-aged or older, as is carving narrow ebony lime spatulas incised with representations of bird's heads. These master carvers also produce large, 7-shaped ceremonial axe handles from tropical hardwoods, featuring a stylized bird's head at the apex and abstract designs at the handle. These are valuable items in interisland exchange. Vanatinai men also carve tortoise-shell into the rows of earrings worn by both sexes, as well as into smaller, mushroom-shaped lime spatulas, whose intricate curvilinear designs are outlined in the brilliant white of powdered coral lime.

Vanatinai island women are admired regionally for their fine, soft, tightly woven coconut-leaf baskets, whose zigzag and chevron patterns are picked out in contrasting colors. These small, round open baskets are used daily as purses by men and women. They are also essential objects at memorial feasts, circulating in interisland exchange. Women weave wild pandanus-leaf sleeping mats and larger, coarse garden baskets of coconut leaf, and make skirts out of dried, shredded coconut fronds. The skirts too play a key role in the ceremonial exchanges of feasts honoring the dead.

The tasks of daily household maintenance are ideologically considered by islanders to be the domain of women: cooking, washing, fetching water from spring or creek, fetching salt water from the lagoon for seasoning food, gathering firewood, and sweeping the hamlet clean of debris and pig excrement each morning with a coconut-rib broom. The house itself is considered to be a woman's house, and the pigs are usually her pigs. It is a common sight every day, though, to see a man or boy performing one or more of these tasks, with the exception of sweeping the hamlet grounds.

Childcare is the primary responsibility of women, who customarily breastfeed on demand for up to three years. (A baby's diet is supplemented with other foods starting at around six months.) But it is common to see fathers, uncles, grandfathers, and older brothers carrying babies and toddlers around. Vanatinai women also make full use of that ancient institution, the babysitter, calling on older siblings—boys as well as girls—grandparents, and neighbors to watch a child while they are weeding a garden, collecting nuts in the forest, or gathering shellfish. Both fathers and mothers are loving and indulgent parents; island childrearing is remarkably permissive. If a small child is frustrated and crying, that is, denied its desires, it may become angry and leave us, people say, meaning it might die and rejoin the ancestors. Fathers as well as mothers often take an older girl or boy to the garden, gathering, or even on a long exchange voyage.

## EXCHANGE AND THE LIFE COURSE

In Vanatinai ideologies of gender, I learned, there is no principle of male superiority or female weakness or inferiority, no idea that women are supposed to defer to men. In fact, in customary and daily life, leaving aside colonial and postcolonial government and legal systems, no adult has the right to tell another adult what to do. The only options are to persuade, influence, shame, or work magic or witchcraft or sorcery on someone to get them to behave in a certain way: join a work party planting a large yam garden, agree to have sexual relations, offer a fine red shell-disc necklace to an exchange partner, or attend a feast, bringing a giant, tusked boar as a contribution.

Vanatinai women and men are valued for the same qualities. The most admired individuals of both sexes were described to me as strong, wise, and generous. By strong, people mean hard working, morally powerful, and successful in producing large gardens, obtaining valuables from their many exchange partners, hosting feasts, and persuading kinspeople and neighbors to work with them. Wise means practical knowledge, insight, and judgment, but also good relations with powerful ancestor spirits and place spirits, who are petitioned through magic and ritual learned over a lifetime from one's elders. Generous refers directly to giving things away—shell-disc necklaces, greenstone axeblades, pigs, yams—especially as contributions offered at the sequence of three to four feasts, increasingly large and elaborate, that honor the dead. These generous people, men and women alike, were called the *giagia*, a gender-neutral term which literally means the givers. In other societies of the Southwest Pacific, this kind of influential and respected person is referred to by anthropologists as a big man. On Vanatinai, there are both big women and big men.

Neither every man nor every woman, aspires to become known as a *gia*. But each person, from youth to elder, is expected to honor kinship obligations and respect the dead—who become powerful ancestor spirits—by contributing labor, valuables, or both at the increasingly elaborate feasts that mark a person's death. Death is an all too familiar visitor to every family: women die in childbirth, babies die suddenly, toddlers are carried off in a day by cerebral malaria, and strong, healthy adults are stricken with pneumonia or tuberculosis (Lepowsky 1990). This means each person learns first-hand from youth about mortuary obligations of the matrilineal kin group. The ceremonial rules are complex; there are different expectations depending on whether the deceased is a member of one's own matrilineage, an in-law's, or the father's. Some of the heaviest responsibilities come at the death of the father himself, who in a matrilineal society is not a kinsman, but a member of another matrilineage. His heirs need to be compensated—given valuables—by the deceased man's own children and widow. The father's kin bear the heaviest ceremonial burden at the death of the mother, his wife.

To document whether Vanatinai society is gender egalitarian, in ideology and practice, we have to compare experiences, ideological principles, and expectations for each life stage, for girls and boys, men and women. Given islanders' cultural emphasis on ceremonial exchange, our comparison should highlight the ceremonial division of labor and access to the most important island domains of prestige and influence.

The life course on Vanatinai is not strongly marked by age categories. A person is referred to as child (*gama*) from birth to around puberty. There are no rituals of initiation for either males or females. A girl begins to be known as *gamaina* (literally, child woman) when her breasts start to show. She begins to menstruate a couple of years later, at around age 15 or 16, and to observe the taboo of not going to the garden during her period. Otherwise, people say, birds and animals, attracted by the blood, will eat the growing food plants (she is not considered unclean or polluting, and she may prepare and share food with others). An adolescent boy, around the time of his growth spurt and voice change, becomes known as *zeva*, or youth.

The period of youth, for both sexes, extends into the late twenties, well into what Westerners consider adulthood. (This cultural pattern of extended youth is traditional in many Pacific Island societies; see Lepowsky 1998). A person on Vanatinai is generally considered an adult (*wevo*, or woman; *ghomoli*, or man) when she or he is in a stable marriage and has a child. This is a gradual transition, as many early marriages end in divorce. Respected adults can soon earn the title of female or male elder (*laisali* for females and *amalaisali* for males), even as young as their mid-thirties. But most individuals addressed as female or male elder range in age from their fifties to their eighties. The rights, privileges, constraints, and degrees of personal autonomy of both sexes are largely congruent throughout the life course, even though they are not perfectly symmetrical. This is a hallmark of a gender egalitarian society, a society that tends toward equality (Lepowsky 1993).

Girls or boys as young as ten or so may get their start in the interisland ceremonial exchange system with a parent's gift of a piglet to care for. When it is a portly, swaying adult, it is valuable enough to be exchanged for an impressive quantity of shell-disc necklaces, greenstone axeblades, or other shell valuables. The owner of the pig, regardless of age or sex, is the one who decides whether or not to accept a request for it from a kinsperson, or new or existing exchange partner. She or he alone decides whether to contribute the pig at a feast commemorating a deceased relative or in-law. People sometimes cry over the death of the beloved pig they have offered, sacrificed, to honor the deceased and the feast host. The owner never eats the meat from her or his own pig, but instead eats pork from someone else's animal, a form of ritual sharing that emphasizes the close identity among human owner, deceased, and valued pig.

Youths of both sexes also earn a name as a hard worker and respected young person by producing yams, bundles of sago, skirts, baskets, and other goods to contribute to an upcoming feast. Some young adults go to kin, or a parent's exchange partner, to request a valuable to contribute. Eventually, they will have to replace it with another wealth object. Young people are expected to devote much of their energy to courtship and sexual intrigue: this is the stage of life for them to enjoy the cultural expectation of full premarital sexual freedom. But a young person who becomes known as lazy will be gossiped about, shamed by older kin, and spurned as a potential marriage partner.

Young people are enthusiastic attendees at feasts, working hard at the labor of provisioning hundreds of guests as directed by the host and food magician. They are sometimes gifted with a valuable, such as a greenstone axeblade, by the appreciative host. The last and largest feast, the *zagaya*, features at least one, and sometimes many, all-night sessions of drumming, singing, and traditional dancing. It is the perfect time for unmarried youths from small hamlets on far-flung islands to meet. They are expected to slip away discreetly and meet a lover in some dark corner of beach or forest. The final feast celebrates the lifting of the final mourning taboos, and the renewal and regeneration of life, the mending of ties of kinship and exchange after a death. Youthful sexuality is part of this celebration. Many marriages begin with flirtations and romances at feasts.

At feasts or occasions of communal labor such as planting a new yam garden, or raising or re-roofing a house, men and women, girls and boys work diligently at the many tasks necessary to provide food and shelter for up to several hundred people for days or weeks, fetching huge quantities of firewood and water, grating mounds of coconut, cooking, and cleaning. Women are in charge of roasting vegetable food in the earth ovens, using superheated round river rocks wrapped in soft forest leaves. Men are responsible for preparing the ritual sago and coconut pudding, stirred with a special, eight foot long carved wooden paddle. Men also take charge of spearing, butchering, and boiling the pigs that visitors and exchange partners have brought to add to those of the feast host. There is generally one man who knows the secret magical spell for making the meat multiply itself to feed the multitudes. Women and men alike know some kinds of food magic, but a few individuals are experts. A senior female or male expert is selected by the feast host to say magical spells over piles of donated yams and bundles of sago—hidden in, or underneath, the host's house—so that they will extend far enough to feed the visitors and still have food left over. The food magician is simultaneously an experienced "kitchen" manager, directing all the food workers of both sexes for the duration of the feast.

Mature adults, male and female, are equally expected to honor ceremonial obligations. Rarely, individuals, scorned and feared as anti-social sorcerers or witches, refuse to participate. Some adults, of both sexes, contribute the bare minimum of labor or ceremonial valuables. The most common path is to work especially hard at ritual obligations when a spouse's parent, or one's own parent or matrilineal aunt or uncle, dies.

A minority of adult men and women whose children are already youths or adults (or who are childless), strive to exceed others in ceremonial exchange. They accumulate valuables, garden produce, sago, and other goods; host feasts, and contribute lavishly and publicly, in acts of ritual generosity, at the numerous feasts of exchange partners, kin, or in-laws. These people seek regional fame, prestige, and influence over others; striving to be admired as *giagia*, givers, big men or big women. This is a matter of individual personality and desire. It is also related to life stage. Along with the obvious childcare issues, children are placed at risk of death or illness by the destructive magic of a parent's envious rival, so it is unwise to strive for the status of *gia* when one has young children. Mature adults also have more supernatural and practical knowledge, and greater stores of social capital through personal ties and exchange partners.

Established or aspiring *giagia* set off, on foot or by canoe, accompanied by kin or spouse, to request valuables from exchange partners. They attend and contribute to all the feasts in the region. They are admired but also feared, for their supernatural knowledge: without the power of ancestor and place spirits, exercised through magic, witchcraft, or sorcery, a person cannot be successful in ceremonial exchange.

Vanatinai women as well as men can build personal fame and renown through active participation in the prestige and ritual economy of exchange and feasting. But they may also choose to gain respect in other ways: by nurturing families and gardens, practicing food magic or weather magic, or helping kin and neighbors through the spirit-directed practices of healing. Women and men have equivalent access to supernatural powers: to apprentice with an elder knowledgeable about certain kinds of magic and ritual. Choosing to do so is up to the seeker, not limited by sex or inherited position.

Vanatinai ideologies validate powerful beliefs in personal autonomy, control of one's own actions, and wide tolerance of personal idiosyncrasies. When I asked why a person behaved a certain way, people said, "We can't know their *renuanga*, their thoughts, emotions. It's up to them." This principle applies to both sexes. Yet, in this small-scale subsistence society, people must be persuaded to cooperate, to share food, wealth, and knowledge, in order that all, or at least many, will survive and thrive. This ideological and practical tension underlies island life. Still, island ideologies grant all adults, female and male, equal opportunities to manage their own lives, and to influence others. The same personal qualities, strength, wisdom, and generosity, are valued in women and men.

## NOTES

1. In a now classic set of writings, Peggy Sanday (1974, 1981) hypothesized that if both sexes contributed equally to subsistence in a particular society, women's

status would be higher. She was the first to suggest that when the sexes commingle in the labor of everyday life, this worked against the rise of male dominance. Albert Bacdayan (1977) suggests that what he labels "task interchangeability" between men and women is a key indicator of egalitarian gender relations. See Lepowsky (1993) for further discussion of characteristics that scholars have hypothesized are associated with gender egalitarian societies. After research with the Lahu, matrilineal horticulturalists living in Yunnan, China, Shanshan Du (2002) has proposed that there are several different types, or cultural "schemas," of gender egalitarian societies worldwide. She argues, for example, that the cultural emphasis in Lahu is "dyadic," organized around the wife and husband in subsistence and divine sister-brother twins in mythology. On Vanatinai, she continues (relying on my ethnographic reports), the cultural "schema," is, in contrast, based on "individual autonomy" and "collective cooperation." In other words, there are different, viable ways to organize a gender egalitarian society.

2. Female hunting is relatively rare worldwide, compared to hunting by males, but it has been documented in many societies. Examples include foragers such as Australian aborigines (Goodale 1971; Kaberry 1939), the horticultural Agta of the Philippines (Estioko-Griffin and Griffin 1981, 1985), and the Ojibwa, Montagnais-Naskapi, and Rock Cree, who hunt large game such as moose and caribou in the eastern woodlands and boreal forests of Canada (Brightman 1996; Landes 1938; Leacock 1978). In some, but not all, cases cross-culturally, women are ideologically restricted from hunting certain animals, using particular killing technologies (such as spears and greenstone axeblades in the Vanatinai example), or hunting when they are menstruating. See Brightman (1996) for a detailed discussion.

The existence of contradictions between levels of gender ideology, the ideological positions of each sex, or between the ideal and the real, has long been pointed out by gender theorists (for example Lederman 1990; Murphy and Murphy 1974; Ortner 1996; Sanday 2002; Schlegel 1990). The strands of gender ideology on Vanatinai are more congruent than those of most societies. I found no categorical difference between what men and women stated about gender philosophies, and not much individual or situational variation. This degree of congruence, I suggest, and the lack of a major gap between gender ideologies and social life as experienced, is characteristic of societies that tend toward gender egalitarian (Lepowsky 1993: 34–35).

## REFERENCES

Bacdayan, Albert. 1977. "Mechanistic Cooperation and Sexual Equality Among the Western Bontoc." In Alice Schlegel (ed.). *Sexual Stratification: A Cross-Cultural View*, pp. 271–291. New York: Columbia University Press.

Brightman, Robert. 1996. "Biology, Taboo, and Gender Politics in the Sexual Division of Foraging Labor." *Comparative Studies in Society and History* 38(4): 687–729.

Du, Shanshan. 2002. *Chopsticks Only Work in Pairs: Gender Unity and Gender Equality Among the Lahu of Southwest China*. New York: Columbia University Press.

Estioko-Griffin, Agnes, and P. Bion Griffin. 1981. "Woman the Hunter." In Frances Dahlberg (ed.). *Woman the Gatherer*, pp. 121–140. New Haven, CT: Yale University Press.

Estioko-Griffin, Agnes, and P. Bion Griffin. 1985. "Women Hunters: The Implications for Pleistocene Prehistory and Contemporary Ethnography." In Madeleine Goodman (ed.). *Women in Asia and the Pacific: Towards an East-West Dialogue*, pp. 61–81. Honolulu: Women's Studies Program, University of Hawaii.

Goodale, Jane. 1971. *Tiwi Wives*. Seattle: University of Washington Press.

Kaberry, Phyllis. 1939. *Aboriginal Woman: Sacred and Profane*. London: Routledge.

Landes, Ruth. 1938. *The Ojibwa Woman*. New York: Columbia University Press.

Leacock, Eleanor. 1978. "Women's Status in Egalitarian Society: Implications for Social Evolution." *Current Anthropology* 19: 247–276.

Lederman, Rena. 1990. "Contested Order: Gender and Society in the Southern New Guinea Highlands." In Peggy Reeves Sanday (ed.). *Beyond the Second Sex: New Directions in the Anthropology of Gender*, pp 43–74. Philadelphia: University of Pennsylvania Press.

Lepowsky, Maria. 1990. "Sorcery and Penicillin: Treating Illness on Papua New Guinea Island." *Social Science and Medicine* 30(10): 1049–1063.

Lepowsky, Maria. 1993. *Fruit of the Motherland: Gender in an Egalitarian Society*. New York: Columbia University Press.

Lepowsky, Maria. 1998. "Coming of Age on Vanatinai: Gender, Sexuality, and Power." In Gilbert Herdt and Stephen Leavitt (eds.). *Adolescence in Pacific Island Societies*, pp. 123–147. ASAO Monograph 18. Pittsburgh: University of Pittsburgh Press.

Malinowski, Bronislaw. 1922. *Argonauts of the Western Pacific*. New York: Dutton.

Murphy, Yolanda, and Robert Murphy. 1974. *Women of the Forest*. New York: Columbia University Press.

Ortner, Sherry. 1996. "Gender Hegemonies." In *Making Gender: The Politics and Erotics of Culture*, pp. 139–172. Boston: Beacon Press.

Sanday, Peggy. 1974. "Female Status in the Public Domain." In Michelle Rosaldo and Louise Lamphere (eds.). *Woman, Culture and Society*, pp. 189–206. Stanford, CA: Stanford University Press.

Sanday, Peggy. 1981. *Female Power and Male Dominance: On the Origins of Sexual Inequality*. Cambridge: Cambridge University Press.

Sanday, Peggy. 2002. *Women at the Center: Life in a Modern Matriarchy*. Ithaca, NY: Cornell University Press.

Schlegel, Alice. 1990. "Gender Meanings, General and Specific." In *Beyond the Second Sex: New Directions in the Anthropology of Gender*, pp. 21–42. Philadelphia: University of Pennsylvania Press.

Weiner, Annette. 1976. *Women of Value, Men of Renown: New Perspectives on Trobriand Exchange*. Austin: University of Texas Press.

# Do Tents and Herds Still Matter?
## Pastoral Nomadism and Gender among the Tuareg in Niger and Mali

### Susan Rasmussen

**INTRODUCTION: TUAREG GENDER CONSTRUCTS IN ANTHROPOLOGICAL PERSPECTIVE**

*After the divorce of Aghaly and Mariama (pseudonyms), Aghaly retained his male-owned adobe mud house, and Mariama retained her female-owned tent, both of which stood inside the same courtyard surrounded by its compound walls, on the same land, in their rural Tuareg village in northern Niger. At first, the ex-husband adamantly refused to leave his house inside this compound. The couple took their case to the secular courts in the nearby town of Agadez, which ruled a compromise: each party changed the door on his or her respective residential structure, so that the buildings faced away from, rather than toward the interior courtyard of their compound. Aghaly ate his meals at his mother's home. This solution divided the property, and also saved the divorced couple from daily contentious interaction. Eventually, Aghaly moved back into his older house adjacent to his parents' compound in a neighboring village, where he worked in an oasis garden. Mariama retained her tent, near her own parents' compound, and continued to herd goats and donkeys with her mother.*

There are multiple forces impinging upon gender and pastoralism among the Tuareg, a seminomadic, Islamic, socially stratified people. This is a discussion of women's perceived economic contributions in relation to property ownership, status, prestige, and division of labor in a traditionally pastoral nomadic, stockbreeding society, the Tuareg, also known as Kel Tamajaq ("People who speak Tamajaq"), after their language, who live in Niger, Mali, Burkina Faso, and Algeria. I also offer a critique of some interpretations of gender and pastoralism in predominantly seminomadic communities. I draw upon data from my research among the Kel Ewey Tuareg in the Air Mountains near the town of Agadez in northern Niger, and more recently, among the Ifoghas and Iwllemeden Tuareg in and around the Adragh-n-Ifoghas Mountains and the town of Kidal in northern Mali.[1]

Seminomadism and agropastoralism are widely practiced by many Tuareg today, and this process brings challenges, but also offers opportunities for women, who enjoy traditionally-high social prestige and, along with men, independent property ownership of livestock: In seminomadic Tuareg communities, the presence of men's houses competes with women's tents. Men's houses, which have sprung up in many Tuareg Saharan communities and along its Sahelian fringes, complicate property disputes upon divorce, particularly in more settled agropastoral communities where predominantly men own houses and oasis gardens. By contrast, in more nomadic camps, men are guests in their wives' tents, and may be left homeless when their wives eject them from that residence upon quarrels or divorce.

The issue arising here is, to what extent do livestock herds and tents still empower women? Some, though not all Tuareg communities are moving toward sedentarization, oasis gardening, and migrant labor. Many also face wider global processes: neoliberal economic policies of structural adjustment and privatization, and national policies, in Niger and Mali, of de-centralization and semiautonomy for some northern regions following the peace accords ending the 1990–1996 Tuareg Rebellion against the central governments of these countries.

Gender is socially and culturally constructed, and can usefully be understood as a comparative, relational concept (Butler 1990: 6; Di Leonardo 1990; Davison 1997; Wood 1999). Critical to gender structuring are intertwined modalities: social variables such as ethnicity, class, religion, and age, among many (Ortner and Whitehead 1981; Di Leonardo 1990). Regional and rural–urban variations may also impinge on inter- and intragender identities and relationships (Gaidzanwa 1985; Mannathoko 1992; Meena 1992; Davison 1997). Constructions of gender therefore depend heavily upon positionality.[2]

In recent years, a number of scholars have called for studies that treat gender dynamically, as occurring in processes generated by discrete locales and through particular histories; they assert that gender is not fixed either across time or in location (di Lauretis 1984; Scott 1988, 1992; Butler 1990; Kondo 1990; Probyn

Original material prepared for this text. Reprinted by permission of the author.

1990; Flax 1993; Barlow 1996). Thus although I use the term "women," I also try to make clear that the Tuareg women about whom I write do not constitute an undifferentiated category of "essentialized woman." They interact with men, and are defined by their age, social origins, occupations, kinship roles, and other locations in Tuareg society. Gender and pastoral arrangements must be understood against the backdrop of seminomadism, sedentary oasis gardening, migrant labor, and some residence in towns, albeit with continuing rural social and economic ties, and interaction with larger, multiethnic nation-states experiencing ecological disaster, economic crisis, and political tensions.

## THE TUAREG CASE

### Tuareg Gender Constructs and Relations between the Sexes: Women's Status and Prestige

Tuareg pastoral nomads today are predominantly seminomadic and practice, to varying degrees, mixed subsistence patterns. Most Tuareg live in the central Sahara and along its borders, in the Sahel. More nomadic Tuareg herd camels, sheep, goats, cattle, and donkeys. Although Tuareg converted to Islam between the eighth and eleventh centuries C.E., different groups vary in their degree of adherence to Qur'anic law and extent of Arabic cultural influences (Norris 1972, 1975, 1990). Some Tuareg trace their origins to the Fezzan region of Libya; others trace this to Yemen. Allied descent groups comprise a drum group or confederation under the power of a drum chief called *ettebel*, a legitimate male successor from the dominant noble group within it. In each region, the large political unit, the confederation, is socially stratified into noble and vassal named groups. Eight politically distinct descent groups (drum groups) all speak mutually intelligible dialects of their Berber-derived language, Tamajaq, and are designated by geographic region. Two of these, Kel Ajjer and Kel Ahaggar, are the northern Tuareg in Algeria. The other six—Kel Adar, Kel Air, and Kel Geres, Iwllemmeden Kel Dennek, and Iwllemmeden Kel Ataram, and Kel Tademaket—live on the southern fringes of desert in Mali, Niger, and Burkina Faso, and are the southern Tuareg. Within the Kel Adar is the political confederation of Ifoghas, who live in and around the Adragh-n-Ifoghas mountains and the town of Kidal in northern Mali. Within the Kel Air are the political confederations of Kel Ewey, Kel Ferwan, and Kel Fadey, who live in and around the Air Mountains and the town of Agadez in northern Niger. Precolonial social organization was divided into nobles, Islamic religious scholars, tributaries, smiths/artisans, and

servile peoples. In most regions, slavery was abolished by the mid-twentieth century.

In general, many Tuareg women enjoy considerable rights and privileges. They are not sequestered, do not veil their faces (although Tuareg men do), and have much social and economic independence and freedom of movement. Separation of the sexes is relatively minimal. Men and women regularly meet and socialize in public. Women are singers and musicians, and organizers of many social events, such as drum playing and dance gatherings, which feature much flirting and courtship. Throughout their lives, many Tuareg women enjoy freedom of choice in sexual involvement and actively pursue romantic preferences (King 1903: 280; Rodd 1926: 174–175). They may regularly have male visitors, though not always lovers, when their husbands are absent (Rodd 1926: 174–175; Nicolas 1946: 225; Lhote 1955: 335; Murphy 1964; Claudot-Hawad 1993).

Although many of these gender constructs and relationships apply to most Tuareg, there is the need to refine and specify, rather than generalize, interpretation of some aspects of Tuareg women's status. Many Tuareg groups display variation in gender arrangements according to relative degrees of nomadism and sedentarization, religious devotion, regional and confederational, and rural–urban differences, as well as age, kinship roles, and social stratum origins. The Kel Ewey *ineslemen* clans of maraboutique Islamic scholars, for example, attempt to control their women slightly more by placing greater emphasis upon virginity and application of Qur'anic inheritance laws. Even among these clans, however, women own property, are not secluded, and go about unveiled and relatively freely visit and receive male visitors, and although extramarital affairs are less tolerated, men, not women, are fined or punished in reprisals (Rasmussen 1994, 1998a, 1998b). In some Iwllemeden Tuareg maraboutique clans in the Azawagh region in Niger, Walentowitz (2002; see also Claudot-Hawad 1993: 47-48) reports unusual restrictions: contrary to most Tuareg women who go unveiled, these women hide the face before men of equal or higher status, particularly potential marriage partners, and conceal their bodies by wrapping large mats around themselves while traveling on foot. Yet as their travel and visiting suggest, these women are not strictly secluded, and they own property independently.

There are also gender transformations over the life course. Older women enjoy security as mothers-in-law and grandmothers. Many specialize in herbal medicine, divination, and bone-setting healing specialties. A widow or divorcee may become a household head in advanced age; if younger, she usually returns to her parental household.

In rural seminomadic Kel Ewey caravanning villages in the Air Mountains, men are often gone from five to seven months a year on caravan trade and migrant labor. Young, unmarried girls and older post-childbearing-age women often go out and establish temporary camps with their herds, intermittently for four months during the dry season; elderly women in the rainy season leave for several weeks to gather leaves and roots and grasses for sauces and medicines from trees on Mount Bagzan (Rasmussen 2006).

During the cold, dry caravanning season, women construct their tent doors to face outward, toward the compounds of their female relatives, the more matrifocal or matricentric space reflecting these women's greater cooperation and sharing at this time. In contrast, in the hot and rainy seasons while many men are at home, the women close these doors and construct doors opening onto the interior courtyard of the nuclear-household compound; the emphasis here is more patrifocal, and patricentric, reflecting greater focus within the nuclear household.

Most women prefer monogamous unions, and polygyny is a rare occurrence, except among some prominent chiefs, Islamic scholars, and prosperous, more sedentarized gardeners and merchants. Polygynous men try to minimize co-wives' jealousy by installing wives in separate compounds and even distant villages. Co-wives never share cooking facilities or sleep in the same compound.

Tuareg women do not engage in any extreme gestures of subservience to their husbands. Husbands and wives may eat together in private, though not usually at public rites of passage. Name avoidance does not entail wife-to-husband deference among the Tuareg as Schlegel (1975: 167–168) inferred from the data available on Tuareg through the HRAF (Human Relations Area Files). The use of teknonymy and sobriquets is symmetric, applying to both sexes. Direct expression of anger on the part of a man toward his wife is considered shameful, and in rural areas, at least, rape and wife beating are extremely rare. Since the end of the Tuareg rebellion, however, some men returning from refugee flight and political exile have brought back alien ideas concerning gender and relations between the sexes: in order to restore their damaged masculine pride from economic unemployment and military defeat, some men value virgins upon marriage, heretofore not an important local cultural value.

Tuareg women receive their nuptial tent (*ehan*) as part of their dowry. It is constructed communally on the evening of the wedding by elderly female relatives of the bride, and torn down and reconstructed to be larger on each successive evening of the seven-day wedding ritual (Rasmussen 1997). In many dialects of Tamajaq, "to make a tent" idiomatically denotes "to marry." The nuptial tent, which after the wedding will be the married couple's residence, is erected near the compound of the bride's parents. Later, the couple may decide to remain there or move with this tent to the husband's family's camp or village. Because descent is bilateral and the tent is matrilineally defined and transmitted, the tent also becomes a metaphor for matriliny and an allegory for maternity (Prussin 1995: 92). The married woman owns the tent.

The nuptial tent is therefore women's property, but also much more: it symbolizes the traditional ideal of monogamy. Recently, however, many men have been constructing adobe mud houses that the married man owns. These houses now often stand next to the tent owned by a married woman within the married couple's household compound (Rasmussen 1994, 1996, 1997). The more nomadic Tuareg groups still count women as owners of compounds, as well as tents, in identifying the household compounds. But the semi-isedentarized Kel Ewey in the Air region of Niger have begun to identify compounds by the names of husbands, as belonging to men, as they do the men's adobe mud houses in many of these compounds, standing next to the women's tents. These processes indicate some important changes in gender roles, status, and power upon sedentarization, which disrupts the property balance between the sexes. To what extent, then, does the tent confer women's control? The key issue, as Moore (1988: 52–53) points out, is the relationship between women's productive and reproductive roles, in the descent and inheritance system.

## LEGAL/JURAL RIGHTS, PROPERTY, DESCENT, AND INHERITANCE

The Tuareg official political structure is male-dominated. Among the more nomadic groups, the camping group (*eghiwan*) is an extended family headed by a male elder (*amghar*). In more sedentarized, seminomadic groups this term *eghiwan* refers to the village or hamlet, which may include a number of families, many of whom are related, and today often also includes households whose members vary in occupation and degree of nomadism, sometimes combining or alternating between several different subsistence forms (for example, a man of diverse social stratum origins might practice caravan trade, herding, oasis gardening, and migrant labor within a single lifetime, in different seasons).

Most Tuareg descent groups are bilateral, combining influences from Arabic and Qur'anic patriliny with local matriliny. Many descent groups trace their origins matrilineally to female ancestresses or culture heroines, although some more devoutly Muslim groups and men in general tend to downplay these ancestresses and emphasize patrilineal descent and male ancestors or culture heroes. For example, many Kel Ewey Tuareg men and marabouts in rural Air communities where I conducted research mentioned Boulkhou, a patrilineal ancestor of the current *ettebel*, as their important founder (Rasmussen 1997). He had sunk the first well, built a mosque, and resisted enemies in battles in that region. By contrast, many women tended to emphasize Tagurmat, the female ancestor of the Kel Igurmaden descent group within the Kel Ewey confederation, who in a myth gave birth to twin daughters who founded the professions of herbalism and Islamic/Qur'anic healing (Rasmussen 2006). The Kel Fadey say their people descend from two sisters who came from the east, bringing with them livestock, herds, and a large wooden drum (the drum, kept by the chief's wife, is used to call the tribal sections together for political or military action) (Worley 1992: 56).

A recurring question in Tuareg ethnography has been the extent to which Tuareg practice matrilineal inheritance and descent and succession. In matriliny, theoretically, mothers and sisters of heirs enjoy status. A problem here is the use of the term to mean certain institutions, or "society" and "culture" in general (Oxby 1978, 1990). Also often ignored are variations and changes among the different Tuareg groups and according to social context. Thus the issue becomes, which kin links are most important and what factors other than kinship are important in determining relationships between the generations and the sexes? Descent group (*tawsit*) allegiance is, in practice, through the mother. Ideally, however, political office passes from father to son in all groups but the Kel Geres, where it goes from maternal uncle to sister's son. Hence both matrilateral and patrilateral kin ties are important. There are also important criteria apart from kinship in political leadership: for example, wealth and personal qualities of leadership.

Women's property is passed down mainly from mother to daughter; men's, from father to son. Objects acquired by women before marriage include jewelry, blankets, a bed, other household items, and sometimes cloth and sandals. In the past, noble women brought a slave to their married household; today, some rural noble women still inherit an attached smith/artisan client family. But this client–patron relationship is increasingly flexible. Inheritance of livestock is predominantly Qur'anic: daughters receive one-third to one-half of sons' shares. Children are considered, among most Air Tuareg, more important heirs than spouses and siblings. If there are only daughters, a brother receives the son's share. The mother's brother is a more significant figure in some

groups than in others, but everywhere the mother's brother/sister's son tie features, at minimum, affection, and frequent gifts, and security in assistance. The sibling tie sometimes competes with the husband-wife tie. Each spouse, regardless of postmarital residence, if possible spends much time during the day (for example, eating meals) at the residence of his/her own kin. Individuals often try to return to maternal kin in later years of life. Brothers often look out for sisters' legal and other interests, support sisters upon the divorce, and contribute to the support of widowed sisters' children. The father's sibling group is equated with the father, as a source of authority and possible conflict; the mother's sibling group, by contrast, is a source of love and aid, generosity, and support (Nicolaisen and Nicolaisen 1997).

Some Tuareg say, "It is the stomach that colors the child." Among the Ifoghas Tuareg in northern Mali where I conducted research, matrilineally related "children of the stomach" can be depended upon more than other relatives for future care in illness and old age. Women therefore attempt to remain close to, and surround themselves with, "children of the stomach" for affection and security. By contrast, some other Tuareg tend to place less emphasis upon these maternally-based kin ties; the Kel Ewey Tuareg in northern Niger, for example, often go into business with those they call "children of men," persons—usually men—who share a common father. Significantly, Kel Ewey also tend to be more sedentarized and also practice polygyny to a greater extent than the Ifoghas. Kel Ewey men explain that additional wives and more children are advantageous in the work of oasis gardening. Many Tuareg believe that the maternal nephew inherits intelligence from his maternal uncle. But Kel Ewey do not use separate kinship terms for a maternal versus paternal nephew; they refer to both as *tegazay*.

In some legal contexts, the concept of maternal kinship identity tends to be submerged in Qur'anic and patrilineal influence: for example, in naming, ideas about children's affiliation and identity, and marriage. Some more sedentarized Kel Ewey Tuareg men in Niger tend to disparage an older form of naming a girl "daughter of" (*welet* or *oult*), still actively practiced by the Ifoghas Tuareg in Mali, as "only done with an illegitimate child." Many urban women are now called Madame plus the name of husband's father as surname, in postal addresses, clinic rosters, and school registration. Illegitimacy is considered shameful, antisocial, and greatly stigmatizing to the mother. Some men insist that the secret, Tamajaq name which older female relatives bestow on the child in the unofficial naming ritual the evening before the official Islamic naming by the father and marabout at the mosque, is "not important, it means nothing," but women dispute this, saying the latter name is as important to the child's identity as the Arabic, Qur'anic name. Women's property is sometimes subject to dispute and challenge in Qur'anic-based rulings by marabouts. For example, although a woman has the right to eject her husband from her tent, a woman's bridewealth is only reimbursed to the person the marabout rules is not at fault in divorce; many marabouts rule the woman at fault if she requests divorce to protest polygyny.

Nonetheless women's opinions are highly valued, and they are normally consulted by men on decisions that affect the life of the camp or village (Bernus 1981: 146–147). Yet there are some contexts in which women defer to some men: namely, before Islamic scholars and important chiefs, and toward elders in general, particularly those on the patrilineal side. Female herbal medicine women, for example, referred patients to marabouts for diagnosis of illness, more often than vice versa (Rasmussen 2006).

A number of authors (Lhote 1955; Murphy 1964; Keenan 1977; Bernus 1981; Casajus 1987; Claudot-Hawad 1993) have described a Tuareg endowment known as *akh hudderan*, which allows an individual to make a pre-inheritance gift of livestock to female relatives, usually daughters, sisters, and nieces, which they then own and control corporately. This property cannot be sold or otherwise disposed of. Additionally, Tuareg women accumulate livestock through important gifts (*alkhalal*) from both parents and other relatives after birth, which form the basis of their own herds. Women may receive outright gifts of livestock from consanguine kin throughout their lives, and in all marriages after the first, it is usually the wife herself who accepts the bridewealth (*taggalt*). Women's livestock herds therefore constitute their traditional source of wealth. There has been much property loss in droughts and wars since the mid-twentieth century. Women in particular suffer here; for although these losses affect both sexes, gardens are easier than herds to reconstitute after disasters. Some non-governmental organization (NGO) and United Nations (UN) agencies are trying to compensate women and men for lost herds, in some cases by replacing them, or in other cases, by encouraging Tuareg to settle down and practice oasis gardening and other newer occupations, such as tailoring and artisan work, more extensively. There is evidence that women's bases of property are increasingly altered by all these processes. For example, much property in the Saharan town of Agadez is not independently owned by the married woman, but merged together with that of her husband in civic records. In semisedentarized communities, men's houses complicate property disputes on divorce. Some married women residing virilocally (with the husband's

family near his oasis garden) are more isolated from their own kin and more dependent upon the husband and his family.

## SEXUAL DIVISION OF LABOR

Domestic work varies according to region, nomadic/sedentarized, and rural/urban differences. In more nomadic groups, this takes a minimum of women's time. In some regions, for example in northern Mali where the water-table is too low for oasis gardening, many rural Tuareg there still practice nomadic stock-breeding, and women are discouraged from performing heavy physical labor, reflecting past noble disdain for household, herding, and gardening labor formerly performed by servile and client peoples. There, women are encouraged to limit their bodily motility and perform tasks locally defined as "light," such as tent-repair and light herding. In other regions, for example, in northern Niger on gardening oases, women do much more arduous tasks: going to the well, crushing grains, and increasingly, assisting with crop harvesting—the latter encouraged by NGO and aid agencies in that region. In these more sedentarized communities, women's time is taken up more extensively with food-processing work within the compound.

In semisedentarized and urban communities, some women are now described as "housewives" (called by the French term *menageres*) in response to this researcher's query concerning their work. These women have given up herding (though not always herd ownership), or have relegated this task to kinspersons. A few gardeners' wives have even given up their tents. Very few women individually own gardens, which are traditionally inherited and owned mostly by men, though a few women have date-palms through matrilineal *akh huderan* endowments. Until the recent establishment of women's gardening cooperatives in the rural Air region by NGO and aid agencies, planting was traditionally done by men, and harvesting was done only by elderly women. By 1998, a development agency had established a women's garden cooperative in an Air Mountain region Kel Ewey community, and some women had begun enclosing and gardening in this designated space, known as the "women's garden (enclosure)" (*afarag n tchidoden*), and traded millet on the market in Agadez. In order to prevent erosion, a fence was being constructed: each woman is paid an amount to participate in the work party, provide wood, and construct the fence. A female "president" supervises this project, in which the women take up a collection (250 CFA or approximately 50 cents each) from each household to build a well (cost: 25,000 CFA, approximately $50). When the well was completed, the project organization gave the group an animal. Alternative occupations to gardening are increasingly available: some women own small shops and restaurants, and some belong to women's sewing and leatherwork cooperatives.

Smith/artisan men and women derive much income from arts and crafts. Metal and woodworking are smith men's work; most leatherworking is smith women's work. Women of diverse social origins tan hides, but mostly smith/artisan women cut and embroider them. Smith/artisan women in rural areas obtain cash and food gifts through leatherworking and rites-of-passage services for nobles. In Saharan towns, women smiths continue to do leatherwork, but with fewer raw materials, which cost more in the sedentarized setting, and also fewer customers; for there is less demand for leatherwork than in rural communities. Recently, some aid organizations in France have assisted by bringing art objects made in workshops (by both men and women specialists) to sell in France.

## COMPARATIVE AND THEORETICAL DISCUSSION: WOMEN AND MEN IN PASTORAL NOMADISM

Some researchers (Barth 1961; Martin and Voorhies 1975: 332–366) view pastoralism as one extreme on a continuum of dependence upon herd animals and cultivation for subsistence, in which segments of sedentary tilling communities may, during periods of scarce resources (i.e., droughts, overpopulation) come to depend increasingly on the products of their herd animals for subsistence. Many Tuareg have been pressured during difficulties of drought to become more sedentary, and to depend increasingly on products of their oasis gardens rather than herd animals for subsistence. Despite this, however, a pastoralist ideology persists. Many Tuareg yearn to return to pastoral nomadism, but realize the necessity today for mixing subsistence modes of herding, oasis gardening, caravan and other itinerant trading, and migrant labor, and among the more specialized artisan social strata, arts/crafts production (Rasmussen 1992, 1994, 1996; Claudot-Hawad 1993). Martin and Voorhies also observe that during periods of plenty, when the size of herds becomes cumbersome or provides the wherewithal for purchase of arable land, pastoral segments may be repatriated to villages. Most Tuareg remain predominantly rural, but often alternate between nomadic camps, sedentarized oasis villages, and large towns according to seasonal needs and more long-term stresses, such as ecological disaster of drought and political violence of war. In the 1960s, the central government of Mali pressured many Tuareg in the

northern region to come to the towns for food relief distribution. Many migrated south during droughts of 1969–1971, 1984, and 2001. In the 1990s, there was massive refugee flight of many Tuareg from northern Niger and Mali during the armed rebellion. In more peaceful times, during the rainy season, nomads often congregate at wells and other water-points for special festivals. During the cold dry season, some men travel on caravan trading expeditions. Many Tuareg families are also dispersed in both town and countryside at different times of the year; for example, some children board with relatives in town to attend school, and return to the countryside to assist with herding and gardening tasks during the rainy season.

Tuareg patterns therefore suggest the need to modify or refine some prevalent representations of the cyclical pattern of pastoralism (Martin and Voorhies 1975: 334). They offer contradictions, or at least variations, of some previous interpretations of gender in pastoral nomadic societies, and show the need to deconstruct concepts in both pastoralist and gender studies. In a classic study, Martin and Voorhies (1975: 351) make several tentative generalizations. They note that the sexual division of labor seems related to the degree and nature of mobility required for the successful execution of subsistence activities (Martin and Voorhies 1975: 352). They argue that gender variations among pastoralists are influenced by at least three factors: (1) their specific adaptation to a given environment (settlement pattern, interaction of herding and cultivation); (2) cultural history of society (common culture areas such as sedentary community origins in Africa south of the Sahara correlate with economic independence, the hoe, polygyny, and sexual freedom; those in the Middle East and of agricultural origins display the opposite pattern); and (3) recent diffusion of ideas rather than cultural origins (Islam, for example—although the Tuareg are an exception to other Muslim pastoralists, in demonstrating less emphasis on the patriarchal family and on gender inequalities) (Martin and Voorhies 1975: 365–366).

From their study of forty-four pastoral societies, Martin and Voorhies conclude that the female contribution to the diet of herders is small. Men do almost all herding and women dairy in only about one-third of societies. Men also do most of the cultivation in half of their sample, however, where cultivation is based on horticultural techniques, women are either the exclusive cultivators, or men and women share equally in cultivation (Martin and Voorhies 1975: 339–343; O'Kelly and Carney 1986: 66). O'Kelly and Carney (1986: 66) argue that gender division of labor within many pastoral societies is "tipped toward male dominance" of economically productive tasks. These authors explain this in terms of the strength required to handle large animals. Males tend to be exclusive herders of large animals. Females may, however, herd smaller animals and serve as dairy maids for large and small species. Women and children contribute by gathering food, carrying water, and processing byproducts such as milk, wool, hides, and dung. But the lack of firm differentiation between domestic and public spheres encourages gender egalitarianism. Where women have some economic control, women's status may be raised. Tuareg women make important contributions to subsistence; most of the rural diet derives from products of small animals, and Tuareg women, unlike women in some other pastoralist societies, own herds, milk them, and control their products.

Boulding (1976: 288–299) argues that women participate more fully in the total life of these societies than they do in settled agricultural communities. But Martin and Voorhies (1975) argue that male dominance of economic production gives rise to male dominance in the wider culture and social structure of pastoral societies. Lois Beck, on the other hand, found a flexible division of labor, economic interdependence between genders, and a low degree of gender segregation among the Qashqai of Iran (Beck in Beck and Keddie 1978: 365–367). Furthermore, because of the small size of independent households of these pastoralists, males and females were partners in economically independent units, and neither males nor females formed strong separate solidarity groups.

Many authors agree that, however diverse the forms it takes, the division of labor among herders does not create a sharp dichotomy between domestic and public spheres. Women's tasks are more likely to take place in camp than men's tasks, but they do not isolate women in the household (Wood 1999). Much women's work is done in cooperation with other women. Both men and women participate in collective work patterns with other members of the same gender. Camps are typically divided into women's spaces and men's spaces, but almost all activities are carried out in the open, avoiding development of private domestic spheres for women versus public spheres for men (O'Kelly and Carney 1986: 67). Women's work may be household work, but it is public household work; public/domestic domains thus emerge as overly rigid and bound to western cultures.[3]

In many pastoral nomadic societies, ownership and control over the disposition of livestock appear to be predominantly in male hands. However, females are sometimes at least nominal owners of some livestock through inheritance, dowries, or purchase (O'Kelly and Carney 1986: 68; Hutchinson 1996). But even owners of livestock cannot usually dispose freely of their animals: they are bound by an intricate web of kinship-based exchanges, which requires giving periodically large numbers of animals to close kin, as bridewealth to the bride's family, dowries to the groom, and as compensation for violation of certain rules, for example, homicide (Evans-Pritchard 1956; Hutchinson 1996) and adultery (Rasmussen 1998a). Males who control large herds thus do not necessarily derive significant economic power from these herds; rather, use rights are important considerations. But large herds bring prestige and influence to owners.

Other factors influencing gender are the defense needs and warfare practices of herders and patricentric kinship systems. In terms of Peggy Sanday's (1981: 181) typology, many pastoralists, such as the Gabra of the Chalbi Desert on the Kenyan-Somalian border (Wood 1999), appear to fall under the rubric of "real male dominance," because in most cases the environment is sufficiently dangerous for the society to depend on the strength and aggressiveness of their men for survival. Sanday argues that under such conditions of stress, for the sake of social and cultural survival, women "accept real male dominance." The Tuareg data suggest modifications of this hypothesis. Tuareg men's frequent absence from home in past raiding and more recent separatist warfare against the central state governments of Mali and Niger, and also men's peaceful trading, have encouraged, indeed necessitated women's independence in some domains of activity (education of children and work). However, some high-status men remain at home and control official political decisions. Thus a warrior aristocracy does not produce gender inequality in all respects; rather, there is a mixed bag here. In fact, some authors report legends of "warrior queens" in Tuareg and other pastoralist nomadic cultures (Rodd 1926: 170; Boulding 1976: 303–312; Worley 1988, 1992; Brett and Fentress 1997).[4] While difficult to verify, they suggest that women's elevated position in the class structure may modify their gender roles; thus class cross-cuts gender (Ortner and Whitehead 1981; di Leonardo 1990). The pastoral-nomadic/gender relationship is therefore complex, and defies facile generalizations or typologies.

## CONCLUSIONS: DO TENTS AND HERDS STILL MATTER?

### Summary of Socioeconomic and Political Changes; Implications

One of the key changes affecting the organization of nomadic pastoralism is the nomads' loss of autonomy after incorporation into sedentary nation-states, in the wake of the military advantage of sedentary states and revolutions in transportation technology during the past century (Barfield 1993: 207). Upon sedentarization, there is disruption of traditional ties and undermining of important sources of defense and security. As men are increasingly obliged to travel as migrant laborers and children are sent to school, the workload of women extends from their traditional routines to a heavier involvement in supplementary tasks. In Niger and Mali, colonial and postcolonial eras saw pastoralist border zones farmed, depleting the soil and disrupting ecological and socio-economic balance and relations between groups and lands. Mobility has been curtailed, censuses, schools and taxes imposed by colonial and postcolonial central state governments. Sometimes these have imposed a patrilineal bias. Tuareg are unique among pastoralists in the enduring significance their matrilineal institutions have for gender and relations between the sexes. But there is evidence that matriliny is under duress. This is shown by the transformations in property balance described in this article and elsewhere (Oxby 1990; Rasmussen 1994, 1996, 1997, 1998a, 2006; Figuereido in Claudot-Hawad 1996: 113–137). It is also shown in Gast's (1992: 151–172) description of Tuareg cultural encounters with more powerful neighbors: nation-state policies toward Tuareg nomads brought many workers, functionaries, soldiers, and tourists into rural Tuareg communities. Often, they were ignorant of and disrespectful toward traditional beliefs and practices; for example, they misunderstood evening festival and courtship customs as opportunities to seduce women, whereas traditionally, Tuareg cultural values emphasize music, poetry, flirting, visits, and conversation without necessarily including sexual intercourse. In some respects, then, Tuareg women appear to have become the wards of men in encounters with outside males, and in national systems of registration/naming, food relief and medical distribution programs, taxation and census counts. However, as shown, there are also new opportunities—in new cooperative agencies and projects offering some benefits for women, as well as men.

The question raised is how nomadic pastoral Tuareg women actively respond to forces of sedentization, urbanization, and nationalism. Do they gain or lose? How? Women can use the urban setting to escape from an extended household ruled over by a mother-in-law. They can also gain access, in more sedentarized centers, to new jobs, thereby benefiting from emerging economic opportunities not available in more remote rural areas. Finally, they often alternate back and forth between locations and occupations over long-term, and/or combine different strategies at the same time. It is therefore hazardous to generalize too sweepingly about pastoralism, women, and gender—some urban Tuareg women still

own livestock, but keep them in the countryside with relatives, and some rural Tuareg women have given up herding. Hence the importance of not solely structural, but also situational meanings and practices. Rather than building models and typologies, anthropologists need to deconstruct and refine pastoral and gender-related categories and processes.

## NOTES

1. In these projects—on spirit possession, aging and the life course, herbal healers, divination, rural and urban smith/artisans, gender, and verbal art performance, I gratefully acknowledge assistance from Fulbright Hays (1983, 1998, 2001); Wenner Gren Foundation for Anthropological Research (1991, 1995, 1998, 2006); Social Science Research Council (1995); National Geographic Society for Research and Exploration (1995, 1998); Indiana University (1983), and University of Houston (1991).

2. For example, Mohanty (1992) criticizes Western feminists for essentializing women's experience regardless of race, class, or nationality. Mohanty faults Western feminists for universalizing women's oppression, as well. She argues that western feminists psychologize complex and often contradictory historical and cultural realities that mark differences among women. Differences among women need to be engaged rather than transcended. She also warns against globalizing women as victims; there is the need to acknowledge women's active agency. Yet feminists in these areas are diverse; they come from various schools of thought depending on their national and cultural orientations.

3. Pastoralist societies therefore break down the assumed dichotomy of private/public or domestic/public domains, a tenacious concept in some early feminist anthropology (Rosaldo and Lamphere 1974) later critiqued in more recent anthropology of gender studies (Ong 1987).

4. These observations of female battle warriors in mythico-history raise interesting issues. There is a paucity of data on women's roles in the recent armed rebellion. Traditionally, most women have participated indirectly in fighting because men's honor depended upon women's praise music upon their victorious return from battles; thus women control men's reputations. Women's praise songs of men often welcomed them after successful raids or migrant labor or caravan trade, but women could also mock and scorn men who returned less victorious or without money. Women still hold power over men's reputations, but many men have not returned victorious or wealthy in recent years. Some men have attempted to find social recognition through participation in the 1990–1995 nationalist/separatist military conflict. Much new music of the Tuareg rebellion composed by both sexes, as well as women's traditional songs, perhaps is responding to these new predicaments and in effect, conveys men's and women's efforts to reconstruct social prestige and independent socioeconomic status in Tuareg gender-role relationships.

## REFERENCES

Barfield, Thomas J. 1993. *The Nomadic Alternative.* Upper Saddle River, NJ: Prentice Hall.

Barlow, Tani. 1996. "Theorizing Women: Funu, Guojia, Jiating (Chinese Women, Chinese State, Chinese Family)." In Joan W. Scott (ed.). *Feminism and History*, pp. 48–59. Oxford: Oxford University Press.

Barth, Fredrik. 1961. *Nomads of South Persia: The Basseri Tribe of the Khamseh Confederacy.* Oslo, Norway: Oslo University Press.

Beck, Lois. 1978. "Women among Qashqai Nomadic Pastoralist in Iran." In Lois Beck and Nikki Keddie (eds.). *Women in the Muslim World*, pp. 351–374. Cambridge, MA: Harvard University Press.

Bernus, Edmond. 1981. *Touaregs Nigeriens: Unité Culturelle et Diversité Regionale d'un Peuple Pasteur.* Paris: Office de la Recherche Scientifique et Technique Outre-Mer.

Boulding, Elise. 1976. *The Underside of History.* Boulder, CO: Westview Press.

Brett, Michael and Elizabeth Fentress. 1997. *The Berbers.* Oxford, UK: Blackwell.

Butler, Judith. 1990. *Gender Trouble.* New York: Routledge.

Casajus, Dominique. 1987. *La Tente dans l'Essuf.* London and Paris: Cambridge.

Claudot-Hawad, Hélène. 1993. *Les Touaregs: Portrait en Fragments.* Aix-en-Provence, France: Edisud.

Davison, Jean. 1997. *Gender, Lineage, and Ethnicity in Southern Africa.* Boulder, CO: Westview Press.

Di Lauretis, Teresa. 1984. *Alice Doesn't: Feminism, Semiotics, Cinema.* Bloomington: Indiana University Press.

Di Leonardo, Michaela. 1990. *Gender at the Crossroads of Knowledge.* Berkeley: University of California Press.

Evans-Pritchard, E. E. 1956. *Nuer Religion.* Oxford, UK: Oxford University Press.

Figuereido, Christina. 1996. "Identite et concitoyennete: La reelaboration des relations entre homes et femmes aux marges de la societe Kel Adagh (Mali)." In Helene Claudot-Hawad (ed.). *Tuaregs et autres Sahariens entre plusieurs mondes*, pp. 113–137. Aix-en-Provence, France: Edisud.

Flax, Jane. 1993. *Disputed Subjects: Essays on Psychoanalysis, Politics, and Philosophy.* New York: Routledge.

Gaidzanwa, R. B. 1985. *Images of Women in Zimbabwean Literature.* Harare, Zimbabwe: College Press.

Gast, Marcel. 1992. "Relations Amoureuses chez les Kel Ahaggar." In Tassadit Yacine (ed.). *Amour, Phantasmes, et Sociétés en Afrique du Nord et au Sahara*, pp. 151–173. Paris: L'Harmattan-Awal.

Hutchinson, Sharon. 1996. *Nuer Dilemmas.* Berkeley: University of California Press.

Keenan, Jeremy. 1977. *Tuareg: People of Ahaggar.* New York: St. Martin's Press.

King, William J. Harding. 1903. *A Search for the Masked Tawaraks.* London: Smith, Elder and Co.

Kondo, Dorinne. 1990. *Crafting Selves.* Chicago: University of Chicago Press.

Lhote, Henri. 1955. *Les Touaregs du Hoggar.* Paris: Payot.

Mannathoko, C. 1992. "Feminist Theories and the Study of Gender in Southern Africa." In R. Meena (ed.). *Gender in Southern Africa.* Harare, Zimbabwe: SAPES Books.

Martin, M. Kay, and Barbara Voorhies. 1975. *Female of the Species.* New York: Columbia University Press.

Meena, R. 1992. "Gender Research/Studies in Southern Africa: An Overview." In R. Meena (ed.). *Gender in Southern Africa: Conceptual and Theoretical Issues.* Harare, Zimbabwe: SAPES Books.

Mohanty, C. T. 1992. "Feminist Encounter: Locating the Politics of Experience." In M. Barrett and A. Phillips (eds.). *Destabilizing Theory: Contemporary Feminist Debates*, pp 74–93. Palo Alto, CA: Stanford University Press.

Moore, Henrietta. 1988. *Feminism and Anthropology.* Minneapolis: University of Minnesota Press.

Murphy, Robert. 1964. "Social Distance and the Veil." *American Anthropologist* 66: 1257–1274.

Nicolaisen, Ida and Johannes Nicolaisen. 1997. *The Pastoral Tuareg.* Copenhagen: Rhodos.

Nicolas, Francis. 1946. *Tamesna: Les Ioullemmeden de l'Est, ou Tuareg Kel Dinnik, Cercle de T'awa—Colonie du Niger.* Paris: Imprimerie Nationale.

Norris, H. T. 1972. *Saharan Myth and Saga.* Oxford, UK: Clarendon Press.

———. 1975. *The Tuaregs: Their Islamic Legacy and Its Diffusion in the Sahel.* Warminster, UK: Aris and Phillips.

———. 1990. *Sufi Mystics of the Niger Desert.* Oxford, UK: Clarendon.

O'Kelly, Charlotte G., and Larry S. Carney. 1986. *Women and Men in Society: Cross-Cultural Perspectives on Gender Stratification.* Belmont, CA: Wadsworth Publishing Company.

Ong, Aihwa. 1987. *Spirits of Resistance and Capitalist Discipline: Factory Women in Malaysia.* Albany: State University of New York Press.

Ortner, Sherry, and Harriet Whitehead (eds.). 1981. *Sexual Meanings.* Cambridge, UK: Cambridge University Press.

Oxby, Clare. 1978. *Sexual Division and Slavery in a Tuareg Community.* Ph.D. dissertation, London School of Economics.

———. 1990. "The 'Living Milk' Runs Dry: The Decline of a Form of Joint Ownership and Matrilineal Inheritance among the Twareg (Niger)." In P. T. W. Baxter and R. Hogg (eds.). *Property, Poverty, and People: Changing Rights in Property and Problems of Pastoral Development*, pp. 222–228. Manchester, UK: Manchester University Press.

Probyn, Elspeth. 1990. "Travels in the Postmodern: Making Sense of the Local." In Linda J. Nicholson (ed.). *Feminism/Postmodernism*, pp. 176–190. New York: Routledge.

Prussin, LaBelle. 1995. *African Nomadic Architecture: Space, Place, and Gender.* Washington, DC: Smithsonian Institution Press.

Rasmussen, Susan. 1992. "Disputed Boundaries: Tuareg Discourse on Class and Ethnicity." *Eth-nology* 31: 351–366.

———. 1994. "Female Sexuality, Social Reproduction, and Medical Intervention: Kel Ewey Tuareg Perspectives." *Culture, Medicine, and Psychiatry* 18: 433–462.

———. 1996. "Tuareg Tent as Field Space and Cultural Symbol." *Anthropological Quarterly* 69: 14–27.

———. 1997. *The Poetics and Politics of Tuareg Aging: Life Course and Personal Destiny in Niger.* DeKalb, IL: Northern Illinois University Press.

———. 1998a. "Within the Tent and at the Crossroads: Travel and Gender Identity among the Tuareg of Niger." *Ethos* 26: 153–182.

———. 1998b. "Only Women Know Trees: Medicine Women and the Role of Herbal Healing in Tuareg Culture." *Journal of Anthropological Research* 54: 147–171.

———. 2006. *Those Who Touch: Tuareg Medicine Women in Anthropological Perspective.* DeKalb: Northern Illinois University Press.

Rodd, Francis, Lord of Rennell. 1926. *People of the Veil.* London: MacMillan and Co.

Rosaldo, Michele, and Louise Lamphere (eds.). 1974. *Women, Culture, and Society.* Stanford, CA: Stanford University Press.

Sanday, Peggy. 1981. *Female Power and Male Dominance: On the Origins of Sexual Inequality.* Cambridge, UK: Cambridge University Press.

Schlegel, Alice. 1975. "Three Styles of Domestic Authority: A Cross-Cultural Study." In Dana Raphael (ed.). *Being Female: Reproduction, Power, and Change.* The Hague, Paris: Mouton Publishers.

Scott, Joan W. 1988. *Gender and the Politics of History.* New York: Columbia University Press.

———. 1992. "Experience." In Judith Butler and Joan W. Scott (eds.). *Feminists Theorize the Political,* pp. 22–41. New York: Routledge.

Walentowitz, Saskia. 2002. "Partir sand quitter: Rites et gestes autour des deplacements feminines chez les Ineslimen de l'Azawagh." In Helene Claudot-Hawad (ed.). *Voyager d'un point de vue nomade,* pp. 37–53. Helene Hawad, Paris: Editions Paris-Mediterranee de l'IREMAM.

Wood, John. 1999. *When Men Are Women.* Madison: University of Wisconsin Press.

Worley, Barbara. 1988. "Bed Posts and Broad Swords: Tuareg Women's Work Parties and the Dialectics of Sexual Conflict." In Richard R. Randolph, David M. Schneider, and May N. Diaz (eds.). *Dialectics and Gender: Anthropological Approaches,* pp. 273–288. Boulder, CO: Westview Press.

———. 1992. "Where All the Women Are Strong." *Natural History* 101(11): 54–64.

# Gender, Business, and Space Control:
## Yoruba Market Women and Power

### Toyin Falola

This chapter sets out to show a linkage between an economic activity (trade) and power, as it relates to a segment of the population (women) and one subset (traders). Such a linkage is possible, as it is indeed of any two other aspects of the structure and institution of society. In this specific case, the assumption is that wealth translates into power. This is true, but there are limitations that must be borne in mind from the beginning. Wealth is only one criterion of power or indeed of upward mobility. There are ascriptive factors as well, like the membership in ruling families, age, and sex, to mention but a few. In addition, in a male-dominated society, gender is built into the construction of power. No matter how wealthy a woman is, she cannot become an *oba* (king) or *balogun* (war commander) in most towns or wield the highest title in many lineages. Power and reward are in general distributed by a male hierarchy, concerned with articulating its own interest.

Nevertheless, as this chapter makes clear, women constitute part of the *political landscape* in a number

of ways. Their predominance in market transactions, as sellers and buyers, enables the acquisition of control over an important sector of the economy. This control—of a space that is so central to production and exchange—provides considerable spinoff values and influence. One spinoff value is the ritual control of space in a society operating within a framework of a nonmechanical worldview that seeks spiritual balance with the universe. The marketplace is part of the *religious environment* that is integrated into the *religious pantheon.* Since women in Yorubaland control the market space, they also control the market rituals. Cases have been reported of powerful women heads of market who double as priestesses. One nineteenth-century example makes the linkage between such control and power so clear that is deserves to be quoted:

> The Eni-Oja[1] is at the head of all the devil worshippers[2] in town. She also has charge of the King's market, and enjoys the perquisites accruing therefrom. She wears a gown like a man, on her arms the King leans on the day he goes to worship at the market, i.e., to propitiate the deity that presides over the markets. She has under her (1) the Olosi who has joint responsibility with her for the market, and (2) the Aroja or market keeper, an officer whose duty it is to keep order, and arrange the management of the market, and who actually resides there (Johnson 1921: 66).

This material has been reformatted for use in this text by the authors.

In *African Market Women and Economic Power,* Bessie House-Midamba and Felix K. Ekechi, eds., pp. 23–40. Westport, CT: Greenwood Press, 1995.

As we point out below, the rituals cannot be ignored; they must be discussed as part of the makeup of the *political configurations*. Productivity and prosperity underline the concern for rituals by the power elite. Power is threatened without prosperity and productivity, and women become part of the means of maintaining both and, of course, of the spiritual balance. Thus, goddesses of wealth, productivity, and fertility must be seen as part of the process of explaining this intricate relationship between gender and power. Control of ritual power is crucial to the control of space and to the way interpersonal and intergroup relations are intricately constructed to distribute power and resources in a society.

Still on the control of the marketplace, the bulk of the financial transactions take place here, bringing together people, goods, and money in a single setting. The very nature of the interaction in this space is useful in such ways as information exchange, social interactions, social control, influence building, and networking. Women are able to participate in all the privileges conferred by this space. It is because of the *relevance* of the market to the articulation of gender image and influence that I have chosen to underscore *space control* as part of the title of this chapter. In the more formalized power structure, women are marginalized and tend to operate within a clientele framework—serving as clients and agents to a male power elite—to tap opportunities. Gender and clientelism are also beyond the scope of this chapter, but it is important to point out that women flourish more within the framework of space control than anywhere else.

One dimension the specific concern of this project does not address is that of power acquisition through other means. For instance, there were several female leaders of substance in precolonial formations, including Queen Kambassa of Bonny and Queen Amina of Zaria. In both contemporary colonial and postcolonial settings, resistance to British rule and a new political process toward democracy have thrust a number of women leaders into the limelight. Studies of women have been more concerned with these high-profile political women—the queens of African history, for want of a more appropriate description[3]—than with market women, in order to demonstrate more glorified aspects of the political worth of women and their contributions—a justifiable reaction to male-dominated historical accounts. No one should dismiss this emergency rescue operation to construct the history of women of political substance, a part of creating a balance in historiography and of correcting a generation-old lapse in methodology. Nevertheless, an *archeology* of the queens limits the range and possibility of social and political history.[4] As the case of market women demonstrates, the less structured, informal sector produces its own "queens," its own mythology, and its own conception of order and values: it may be less dramatic, but it is more revealing of the dynamics of power interplay and social institutions.

The strength of this chapter lies in the elaboration of the linkage identified above. The data are limited to the domestic, informal arena of trade and politics from the precolonial period through the colonial to the present. One limitation is that the case studies to illuminate general points are rather limited, a function of the state of gender historiography. Studies are few and far between, and their rationale is uncoordinated.[5] As I have pointed out elsewhere, the weakness in gender studies may result, among other factors, from the paucity of information in both oral and written sources on the contribution of women to the emergence and development of Yoruba kingdoms, the patrilineal nature of the Yoruba family, which emphasizes the supremacy of men over women, and the low position occupied by women in the policy and decision-making machinery (Falola 1978).

## WOMEN AND TRADE

Like members of most other societies, the Yoruba believe that everyone must work, irrespective of gender, as a means to avoid starvation and poverty, and to earn respect, fame, and prowess. While a number of activities associated with women are designed to help their husbands and raise their children, the society does not frown on women creating the opportunity to make money for themselves. Women spend money on household maintenance, social functions, and chieftaincy titles. In the process of achieving a variety of ambitions and fulfilling mutually related roles, women appear to have devoted more time to work than men, in a variety of activities ranging from the domestic to the high-profile ones of public administration and the priesthood of important cults.[6]

In precolonial formations, there was a sexual division of labor: men were farmers and craftsmen and women engaged in food processing and trading.[7] In general, women's entry into many occupations was unrestricted, although they avoided the military and certain crafts. They were not excluded from the new occupations created during the colonial rule and beyond, even if they were marginalized by the very fact that a colonial society was male dominated.[8] In the precolonial domestic economy, farming was the leading occupation, although Yoruba women were less involved in farming, compared to, say, the Ijo and Igbo of eastern Nigeria, the Akan of Ghana, or the Tio of the Middle Congo.[9] Yoruba women contributed to harvesting, processing for final consumption and storage, livestock keeping, and the selling of farm products.[10] Women of means were able to plough their profits into large-scale farming, as in the case of the nineteenth-century celebrity, Efunsetan Aniwura of Ibadan, who had more than a thousand slaves on her farms (Johnson 1921: 393). Women were active in the manufacture of a variety of goods like oil, dye, ceramics, and textiles.

By far the most important precolonial activity of women was trade, a professional occupation. The emphasis was on selling what they or their husbands produced from their farms, what they manufactured on their own, and the goods they bought from others for the purpose of reselling them. One of the earliest students of Yoruba markets, W. Hodder (1962: 110), was fascinated with the prominent role of women and dated this domination to the nineteenth century, "to the conditions of internal insecurity in which it was unsafe for men to move away from their farms, while women enjoyed relative immunity from attacks." That there was turbulence in the nineteenth century and women received better protection than men, there can be no doubt (Falola and Oguntomisin 1984). However, there is no strong evidence to associate the wars of the nineteenth century with women's dominance in trade. Earlier records reveal this domination as well (Marshall 1964: 73–78).

Two studies by Gloria Marshall (now Niara Sudarkasa) have established a close correlation among the roles of women as wives, mothers, and traders. There was the expectation that a man would assist his wife by providing some capital to start a small trade. As the relationship between the husband and wife developed and the woman had borne a certain number of children, she increased her trading business, unhindered by occasional or regular separation from the husband, who could then take another wife. The woman could assist her husband with money; but more important, she had to take care of her children in the context of competition with the children of rival wives.

With the introduction of formal Western education, the need to sponsor children was to further justify trading, especially in cases when the husband refused to pay for female children or had to limit the number of sons he could train (Belasco 1980; Sudarkasa 1973). Women also paid for the upkeep of their children and supplemented domestic expenses on food. The common pattern appears to be that a younger wife stayed closer to home to bear children and assist her husband with limited farm work. When the children grew up, she had more time for herself, and the husband could fulfill the aspiration of taking another wife. Thus, Yoruba marriages matured in such a way that women were able to acquire

their independence and men were able to divert their sexual exploits elsewhere.

The process of capital accumulation in the precolonial setting is best described by N. A. Fadipe, the first to write a sociology of his own people. A husband and network of relations furnished the necessary capital for a woman to start a trade:

> A percentage of the payment made as bride price by her husband was passed on to her before her marriage. A few days before marriage her own relatives made her, in addition to clothing and other articles of personal wear, presents of cash . . . A few days after her marriage . . . she has an opportunity of receiving presents of money not only from the various households in her husband's compound, but also from some members of the neighborhood, and from principal members of her husband's kindred group . . . Out of it she buys an animal (goat or sheep) or two and some fowls for rearing. If a wife was not brought in any trade, these animals and fowls would remain her principal investment. If she was skilled in some trade, part of it would be used for starting it (Fadipe 1970: 156).

Here is perhaps the best description of the "sentiments of kinship and social solidarity" in creating mobility for a woman who had to start from scratch, sentiments devoid of "mercenary motives" or expectations of interest. A new wife benefited from more "sentiments" in the form of gifts and other support until the birth of her first child. Thanks also to Fadipe, the continuation of the practice of accumulation is reported for the colonial period as well:

> With regard to a woman who is not married in the customary sense of the word—i.e., who lives with a man as his wife without the consent of her parents—a more generous amount for trading purposes is usually granted. Women of this type are usually of the town-dwelling class, and are generally sophisticated Muslims or Christians. They usually have not learnt any craft. But when in their husband's house, they usually ask for and receive a sum of money with which to start trading in one line of goods or another—generally cheap articles of European manufacture. These women must get all they want for the purpose from their husbands, since they cannot rely upon the sources which are open to women married in the socially approved way (Fadipe 1970: 156).

Starting in such small ways, the enterprising woman expanded by plowing capital back in, raising more capital, obtaining credit, and manipulating market opportunities.

Still on the precolonial society, women traders could be found everywhere hawking cooked food. Many women held their trading activities in their homes where they sold a variety of items like foodstuffs, cosmetics, and tobacco. Such traders were patronized by those who could not attend the market. The practice of staying home for the purpose of trading was common among older women and new brides who might not be permitted to begin full-time trading until they had spent a few years at home. There were women commissioned agents, obtaining supplies from craftsmen to sell.

Women traders were predominant in the village and town markets, the daily and periodic ones. Their activities were many, from preparations to actual selling and buying. Other trading activities took place outside the marketplace, with women hawking their wares, scouting around for goods from producers and farmers, intercepting other traders in order to buy cheap, and so on.[11] Women took part in the regional and long-distance trade, carrying their businesses to areas far away from home. Like men, they withstood the physical hardship of long journeys and the risk traveling involved, especially in periods of political instability. Those married to highly placed men like the *oba* and chiefs were also able to participate, either as independent operators or through proxies.[12]

Colonial and postcolonial rule has not diminished the role of women in trade. Throughout this century, the complex web of marketing that links villages with cities and one region with the rest of the country is dominated by women. Trade expanded considerably, thanks to the growth of cocoa, a major cash crop, improvements in transport systems, urbanization and, since the 1960s, substantial revenue from petroleum. Surveys on the division of labor conducted in the 1960s and 1970s show that higher percentages of women worked as traders—for instance in the case of Oje, a neighborhood in Ibadan where 84 percent of the women were traders, and in Lagos, where women made up 70 percent of traders (Barnes 1986: 160; Lloyd 1967: 71; Marris 1961: 68). Certainly, older institutions of the market and trade continued until the recent period, as the study by Hodder and Ukwu (1969) clearly demonstrates.[13]

## WOMEN AND POWER: POLITICAL SYSTEMS AND MYTHOLOGIES

One fact must be recognized: the Yoruba political systems create titles specific to women and recognize the need to incorporate successful women into the system. Opportunities are not many, compared to those offered men, and the distribution of principal functions and roles are no doubt male dominated. Within the avenues created for women, however, and the opportunities open to them can be found all the successful cases of women who exploit and benefit from them. In the precolonial polities, women wielded political influence that varied in degree from one community

to the other. Although the validity is yet to be ascertained, a few women are reputed to have reached the apex of authority as *oba*. Ile-Ife tradition mentioned, for instance, the reign of the tyrannical *Ooni* Luwo (Fabunmi 1969: 23–24), and there were similar cases in Akure and Ilesa.[14] There was no town without a woman chief of some kind, although the power attached to such offices varied. For instance, in Ondo the *lobun* was a powerful woman chief, excluded from farming and secluded to her palace like the male *oba*. She took part in the selection of a new king, settled quarrels among the male chiefs, and officiated in the opening of new markets. In addition, she was also regarded as the priestess of *Aje*, the god of money.[15] In Ilesa, another kingdom, the head of the women chiefs was the *arise* supported by the *Risa Arise, Odofin Arise,* and *Yeye-Soloro.* Each ward had a female head, as well (Falola 1976: 69). Other towns and villages had their *Iyalode* as heads of women chiefs.[16] A few women chiefs constituted part of the membership of secret societies responsible for executive and judicial functions in a number of communities.[17]

As an integral part of the palace system, the oba's wives (*aya oba* or *olori*) occupied a strategic position to hear and spread news and to influence major policies of state, especially in matters relating to their own lineages or communities. Many quarters in a town tried to be represented in the palace not only through the palace servants but also through marriage ties. There were marriage ties, too, with the neighboring states in order to use women to cement existing friendships or create new ones. Women were also employed to monitor and influence foreign-policy decisions.[18] The *olori,* together with other palace officials, were assigned duties of much social and political significance.[19] Women of rank, royal wives, and princesses often formed organizations to protect their own interests, as in the case of Akure.[20]

## WOMEN AND POWER: THE RITUAL AND MARKET DOMAINS

Fertility, productivity, and wealth are some of the key elements associated with female power. Goddesses of wealth and productivity are many, dominated by female worshippers. Several goddesses were associated with market protection. The goddess of the river, *Yemonja,* derives her relevance from the power to give children and general prosperity. Some traditions call *Yemonja* the mother of all gods and the "mother earth," the fountain of life and productivity. For combining life with water, Yemonja personifies greatness, which perhaps explains the widespread nature of her worship.[21]

Many localized studies have revealed the centrality of the female goddess in the Yoruba pantheon (Drewal 1983). One recent example is on Ondo where Jacob Olupona shows how the *Obitun* and the *Odun Aje* demonstrate the significance of women in the economy and politics (Olupona 1991). The *Odun Aje* in particular is more focused on wealth, as a celebration and worship of the goddess *Aje*, usually by the majority of adult females. According to Olupona, the *Aje* rituals bring out the dimensions of human reproduction and economy, symbolizing success in trade and prosperity. He provides the English version of an important lyric:

> Aje excreted on my head;
> Whoever Aje touches is made human.
> Aje slept on my head;
> Whoever Aje touches acts like a child.
> Aje elevates me like a king;
> I shall forever rejoice.
> Aje is happy, so am I.
> Aje is happy, so am I.
>
> *(Olupona 1991: 156)*

This lyric and others sing the gains of trade, gains attributable to this goddess.

By participating in various trading activities, women had the opportunity to become wealthy and could therefore enjoy the high sociopolitical status associated with people of wealth, such as collecting titles, building a following, and acquiring symbols of status like clothes and horses. The connection between the market and power is, however, much broader than the one-to-one relation of wealth and power.

To start with, there is the influential one of the control and management of the marketplace. The marketplace is an important aspect of local and national politics not only for its influence but also for its communication and social functions. It is the place where the bulk of community wealth circulates. To the political class, the market is a place to collect revenues (such as taxes, tolls, fees, dues, levies, gifts), benefit from corruption (by way of stall allocation), and exercise power (by making laws to establish control or using physical coercion or violence). In all these facets, the target is the market women. In the modern era, political parties have extended the building of machine solidarity and opposition mechanisms to the marketplace, urging women to collaborate or resist. In periods of military rule, the marketplace is a venue of propaganda to announce and spread reforms; and the target is again the market women. Building a political constituency or a sphere of influence has always been one criterion to attain prominence, seek office, or wield and retain power. The incorporation of market women into such a sphere has been recognized since the 1930s by the early political parties like the Nigerian Youth Movement, and virtually all subsequent political parties have adopted a similar strategy. In the process, power seekers pursue the means to penetrate market women. In so many instances, competition for control of the marketplace by prominent women traders becomes part of the complications of local politics itself: one recent case study of the Mushin district in Lagos has explained very convincingly how the market, with its "large bloc of support," occupies a prominent part of power struggle and political factionalism (Barnes 1986).

Invisible to buyers and other visitors to the marketplace are the powerful associations and guilds that try to dominate the space in order to maximize economic gains, create order, and wade through the muddy terrain of politics. Traders dealing in a similar commodity organize into a guild. A guild has an executive that admits new members and discusses issues relating to pricing and market administration. In recent times, organizations of women traders control and discipline their members and oversee the recruitment to the marketplace. In major urban markets, the right to participate has to be negotiated cleverly, and it is difficult to bypass women's organizations. Expulsion from the market, enforcement of discipline, checks on the activities of illegal traders, improvement of market facilities, all are part of the activities and duties of market women associations. Because the unions are powerful, they are able to police the market, and they set up microadministrations respected and recognized by the state.

Presiding over the association is the *iyalode* or *iyaloja*, a woman of means and influence. An *iyalode* wields a lot of power derived from her individual capacity and charm, her personal resources, and the role of the association that she represents. She is the link between the market, market women, and the political authorities, both formal and informal. She implements the wish of the association with regard to all allocations and the admission of members, she knows all the traders with stalls, and she keeps an eye on a floating population of street traders and hawkers. She supervises the internal administration of the market, settles disputes, and interacts with external suppliers to ensure fairness.

The market political paraphernalia is more elaborate than the office of the *iyalode*. The *iyalode* herself has a long list of lieutenants, in some cases elected by the women's association and in some others appointed by the town's traditional political authority. In Ibadan for instance, there are such subordinate titles as *otun, osi, balogun, asipa, ekarun, abese, maye, are alasa,* and *ikolaba*. There are honorary titles, too, to reward successful and prominent women. As if to create a forest of titles, each guild runs a parallel order, headed by an *iya egbe* with subcommittees presided over by chairwomen known as the *alaga*. For those who could mobilize adequate capital to expand the scale of their operations, considerable scope exists to benefit socially and politically from their business acumen.

If the established political order dominated by men assumes that it can freely manipulate the marketplace and women traders through women's association and leadership, it is wrong. These women also manipulate prominent men and political order, seeking the extension of their influence. The subject of female manipulation requires more treatment than is possible here, but its mechanisms can be highlighted briefly. Prominent male members are incorporated into market organizations through offices and honorary titles. Men are appointed as honorary consuls and to functional positions such as secretary or treasurer. These appointments are no indication that women could not perform these tasks or manage their affairs, but they are clever ways of forging alliances with men. Incorporated male members and others are expected to deliver crucial linkages with power, authority, resources, and groups external to the market in ways defined or suggested by the women.

## COPING WITH STATE POWER

What looms large in the discussion has been the role of the state. The state has always been interested in drawing women into its revenue network by collecting market levies, dues, and tolls from them. In trying to attain legitimacy and to govern, the state also makes use of the marketplace for propaganda and for building a constituency. In other words, the state understands the relevance of women. There was an argument in the 1950s that women did not understand the state and that market women are, in general, politically passive and are not "alive to demand their rights" (Mabogunje 1961: 16).

Akin Mabogunje, a geographer of international renown, responded to this position by saying that political response is a function of the interpretation of one's rights. He cited the Aba women's riot of the 1920s which arose when women were asked to pay tax. As long as women's trade is not interfered with, Mabogunje contends, they are politically quiet. However, whenever there is an economic injustice, they tend to join in male-led protest against the state. He is ambivalent in his conclusion: while on the one hand there is the assumption of passivity, on the other hand, there is an acknowledgment of the market women's political role as objects of manipulation. Whenever politics have been studied as a *social phenomenon*, beyond the highbrow boardroom negotiations and cutthroat competitions, women have been seen to play an active role. This is made clear in the study by

Cheryl Johnson-Odim (1978), to mention one important case study. Mabogunje (1961), too, underscores this point when he refers to the protest in the 1950s by women against the badly run Free Education Scheme of the Eastern region and a Yoruba oba who was using his power to control commerce to his advantage. In spite of his example of women's protest, Mabogunje still sees gender-based weakness: he concludes that women are more interested in deriving profits from their trade than participating in politics.

We cannot undermine women's understanding of politics as Mabogunje does, an error born of a limited conception of politics and trade. The marketplace itself is a *political space* dominated by women. We can move the discussion in yet another direction to show the limitation of Mabogunje's understanding and broaden the conception of women and politics. This direction is to see how women, by means that can be described only as political, confront the state.

Politics is about interest. To search for market women's role in the male-dominated arena is to abandon the substance in pursuit of a shadow. We must understand their interest: the pursuit of trade and the benefits arising therefrom. It is this interest that determines their political role, which explains why they fight the state over the allocation of market stalls, price control, regulation of street trading, and the location of new markets, to mention some of the important issues. These conflicts are many, as reading any of Nigeria's newspapers and magazines will reveal. Conflict is an expression of politics: it is public, challenging, and result oriented.

There is also resistance; a common, almost daily, occurrence is to ignore the state and disregard laws that are considered stupid or injurious to their interests. For example, most price-control measures have failed simply because the market women refused to cooperate.[22] So also is commodity rationing in moments of scarcity (Falola 1992). Rather than succumb to pressure, market women are known to close down their shops, thus bringing economic activities to a halt. Resistance is politics, a most intense manifestation of a hostile social and political intercourse between the market women and the agents of the state. To repeat an important point: in seeking data to validate assumptions about market women and politics, let us look in the right place, which is the space they dominate and manipulate better than men.

## PRECOLONIAL CASE STUDIES

So far, I have exposed the contours of the linkage. Now I turn to a few cases to illustrate the theme, drawing from four experiences of women who use the marketplace to obtain power. There are two cases of *iyalode* of the nineteenth century who attained their positions because of their trading connections and wealth. In the turbulent history of the nineteenth century, women took part in the decision to go to war, financed military expeditions, saw to the efficient organizations of markets, and competed with their male counterparts.

The first case is that of Tinubu, the famous Egba woman who achieved fame because of her trade. She left her town of Owu and settled in Badagry where she traded in salt and tobacco and acted as a middleman to Brazilian traders. The trade brought her an immense wealth; and Akitoye, the exiled king of Lagos, met her in Badagry in 1846 as one of the most influential citizens of the town. In 1851, Tinubu followed Akitoye to Lagos where she decided to settle. The change did not affect her fortune, and she was able to increase the number of her slaves.[23] She became very influential in Lagos politics and participated actively in the attacks both on the Lagos government and on the foreign merchants whom she saw as monopolists denying the indigenes of their economic rights. By 1856, this lady, now known to her opponents as "the terror of Lagos,"[24] could no longer be tolerated. She was forcibly expelled from Lagos by Consul Campbell who breathed a sigh of relief after her departure. The move was not without local protest against the British by hundreds of Tinubu's supporters. She resettled in Abeokuta where in a short while she reestablished herself as an astute politician and a patriot who supplied the town with weapons during warfare. Her contribution to trade and Egba politics fetched her the highest title of *iyalode* in 1864.

The second case is that of Efunsetan Aniwura of Ibadan who, through trade and large-scale farming, was able to rise to the leading position of *iyalode*. Her wealth was such that she could afford to build a private army of personal guards. She was active in local trade and built an extensive network of regional trade, which included the profitable articles of salt, guns, and gunpowder.[25] Her success generated considerable resentment among the male chiefs. Such resentment took a turn for the worse in the 1870s when the political head of the city-state, *Are Latosa*, instigated her brutal murder on May 1, 1874. The official reasons for this murder were all tied with her political influence and wealth: a male leader of the town accused her of political insubordination and arrogance (Johnson 1921: 391). Her death almost led to civil war, and the authorities had to use a face-saving device of executing the slaves who carried out the assignment.[26]

There were perhaps many more examples of rich and powerful women contemporaries of Tinubu and Efunsetan, although records of their careers did not survive. For instance, Aniwura's predecessor as *iyalode*

is described as a rich woman who "lost her wealth" (Johnson 1921: 392). Another lady, Adu of Ijanna, a town under Ijaye, is also mentioned in the tradition as "a rich lady" of influence (Johnson 1921: 331).

## CONTEMPORARY CASE STUDIES

A few biographies and case studies are emerging, indicating a positive shift to the recent period. As was to be expected, the biographies have focused more on those active in political life (Johnson-Odim 1978; Adeniyi 1993). To keep our concern, we take two examples of traders. One prominent example in the colonial period is Alimotu Pelewura of Lagos, whose concern was to protest colonial policies that threatened the interest of Lagos market women.[27] Her leadership of a market association 8,000 strong lasted four decades and derived from a recognition by other traders of the need to unite for a common cause. An illiterate fish trader, Pelewura emerged as a stronger leader in 1923, in alliance with the newly formed Nigerian National Democratic party led by Herbert Macaulay, the "father of Nigerian nationalism." Pelewura became a member of the Ilu Committee, the traditional executive of the town. There was a row in the mid-1930s over the attempt by the government to relocate Eleko market, a decision that met with popular protest led by her. She also successfully opposed the move to ask women to pay tax in the 1930s and 1940s, and she vigorously protested the price-control measures introduced during the Second World War. She participated in party campaigns; on one occasion at Abeokuta, she reminded the audience that there was nothing men could undertake without the support of women. She mobilized market women to accord a decent burial to Herbert Macaulay in March 1946, hosted receptions for party dignitaries, and was picked to be part of a team in 1947 to travel to London to protest the Richards Constitution although illness prevented her from traveling. She became the *erelu* of Lagos in 1947, a traditional chieftaincy that conferred upon her the right to represent women's interests. When she died in 1951, a crowd estimated at 25,000 people attended her burial.

My final example is a living legend, Humoani Alade, the current *iyalode* of Ibadan.[28] Born in the late nineteenth century, Humoani did not have the privilege of Western education but received apprenticeship as a trader in textiles. With little capital, she gradually built up her trade until she became wealthy and influential. She is the president of the Oyo State Market Traders' Association (*iyaloja*) and the *iyalode* of Ibadan. In a noncombative manner, she has contributed to a number of women's causes, ranging from market palaver to conflicts with the government. The general perception of her is that of a leader who wants peace, mediating between the government and market women. In the 1980s, she assisted the state government in seeking and building a new market and preventing a clash over street trading. She has also participated in party politics since the 1940s, identifying with the Obafemi Awolowo-led party of the Action Group (AG) and the Unity Party of Nigeria (UPN). She provided support for the AG and the UPN, mobilizing people to support the party and its programs. She never sought any party elective office, nor was she ever appointed to any political position in the government; but she is a moderating influence on the party and a mediator in intraparty rivalry. In addition, she is a member of the *Egbe Ilosiwaju Yoruba* (Yoruba Progressive Union), seeking the progress of the Yoruba people. She is a philanthropist. As the *iyalode*, she receives dignitaries to the town on behalf of women, and attends the meeting of the Olubadan-in-council, where issues relating to the town are discussed. She is the link between the women and the traditional chieftaincy. Many of her contemporaries, including political rivals, are full of praise for her. In the words of Lam Adesina, a prominent educator:

> She has been a true leader of women and a lover of the less fortunate . . . Iyalode is a very successful trader. She is also a first-class manager of human beings. Since the old Western Region, Iyalode Alade has been leading the Market Women and Traders Association. The association likes her and respects her. She commands them and they obey her. She is able to do this because her leadership is acceptable and respected (Layonu 1990: 32).

And to take a second testimony, this time from Archibong Nkana, a former commissioner of police in Oyo state:

> She is a dynamic traditional chief in Ibadan, Oyo State. She is diligent, patriotic and very honest. This respectable woman is ever willing to assist the police for the common good of the people. She has used her position as President of Oyo State Market Traders Association to foster peaceful co-existence and mutual understanding between the police and the market traders in the state. I also want to emphasize that this special mother was a serving catalyst to my glorious tenure as commissioner of police in Oyo State. I wish her well in life (Layonu 1990: 35).

## CONCLUSION

Yoruba women have plenty of scope and opportunity to trade, and they dominate the marketplace. Since the colonial period, complex factors of migration, urbanization, and Western influence have brought a number of changes to women's lives and roles, but

without diminishing their domination of the marketplace. The linkage between the marketplace and power takes several forms. First, there is the power and influence that accrue to those who grow wealthy. Second, the control of the marketplace confers ritual and symbolic power. Third, domination of the marketplace and of business provides opportunities to relate and negotiate with the political authorities, traditional and modern.

The case studies have revealed women who were able to actualize power in traditional and modern settings. Some dominated national politics, and others influenced local politics. A number of other interpretations can be drawn from these case studies. The women were able to mobilize capital to enlarge trading opportunities. They were enterprising, calculating, and shrewd. They faced considerable risk: Tinubu was expelled from Lagos, and Efunsetan was assassinated, to mention two examples. In general, they faced considerable resentment and antagonism from the male power elite. The women were independent, rejecting the stifling conditionalities of marriage, or at least overcoming the barriers that marriage and child rearing posed. They demonstrated courage in breaking from traditions that constrained their activities; and in the case of Tinubu, of fighting powerful political authority and vested interest. Once they acquired economic power, they were astute and wise enough to add political power unto it. Economic power also changed the conduct of social relations: a rich woman would certainly reject undue subordination. In general, as many studies have pointed out, Yoruba women enjoyed economic independence and limited constraints on their movement, thus enabling not a few to exercise freedom and associate with a constituency of their own choice and creation.

In spending their wealth, they behaved in ways similar to those of the male chiefs by acquiring followers, showing generosity to a large number of people, and obtaining titles for themselves and their supporters. They received *oriki*, great eulogies that captured their lives in grandiose ways and beautiful language. Part of the *oriki* of Efunsetan will suffice for our purpose, but it needs to be emphasized that *oriki* is not a peculiar trademark of this lady.[29]

> Efunsetan, Iyalode
> One who has horses and rides them not.
> The child who walks in a graceful fashion.
> Adekemi Ogunrin!
> The great hefty woman who adorns her legs with beads
> Whose possessions surpass those of the Aare
> Owner of several puny slaves in the farm.
> Owner of many giant slaves in the market.
> One who has bullets and gunpowder,
> Who has the gunpowder as well as guns,

And spends money like a conjurer,
The Iyalode who instills fear into her equals.
The rich never give their money to the poor;
The Iyalode never gives her wrappers to the lazy.[30]

Localized within its Yoruba setting and idioms, this is a brilliant rendition, made more powerful by the drumming and dancing that would accompany it. It encapsulates a message, with all the metaphors of greatness. The abundant slaves, the horses, the "graceful fashion," the guns, and gunpowder are all evidence of wealth and success. Power is adequately reflected in the references to slaves, the poor, access to weapons of violence, and warfare. There is rivalry, too: "The Iyalode who instills fear into her equals." And there is the bold comparison with the male political head of this city-state, with the *iyalode's* possessions surpassing that of the *Aare*. Grace resonates beautifully: the horses in the compound, the "great hefty" woman, "the child who walks in a graceful fashion." And here is a woman so rich in money that she spent like someone who was conjuring (i.e., minting) her own currency.

From this *oriki* and other evidence, we see how aspirations centered on the "good things of life": money, long life, power, children, and good health. In this focus on aspirations, there is no difference from how men too defined what they wanted.

The case studies should not obscure the problems women faced. Access to large amounts of capital was always a problem, and men tended to have more opportunities. Not every woman grew wealthy or powerful from trade; indeed, for the majority, trade did not translate to wealth or power. Trade was competitive, losses were recorded, and some high-profit-yielding commodities like cocoa and cattle were in the hands of male dealers. Women experienced other constraints, such as domestic responsibility, which curtailed activities in the early years of marriage; many lost a lot of time to social and religious events and to illness (Fadipe 1970: 166). Since the colonial period, obstacles to mobility and ingrained prejudices linger. Contemporary concerns of women are focused on the penetration of the more formal, public sector by better access to school, jobs, and promotion[31]; and current studies tend to ignore the informal sector, including the dynamic marketplace that has played such a significant role for so long.

## NOTES

1. This is the same as the *iyaloja* (head of market).
2. This is a reference to the god *Esu*, misunderstood by Christian writers of the nineteenth century who adopted his name for the biblical devil. Now variously interpreted, *Esu* can also be described as the god of order.
3. See, for instance, Mba (1982), Johnson (1982), Sweetman (1984), Coker (1987) and Awe (1992).
4. For the celebration and limitation of gender historiography in Africa (with little stress on the Yoruba, however) among others, see Strobel (1982), Hay (1988), Wipper (1988), and Staudt (1988).
5. Among others, see Ward (1938), Ross (1939), Harris (1940), Kaberry (1952), and Southall (1961).
6. See, for instance, Johnson (1921), pp. 64–65 and Idowu (1962), Chap 8.
7. Several works have described the sexual division of labor among the Yoruba. See, for instance, Beier (1955), Izzett (1961), and Sudarkasa (1973), Chap. 2.
8. See, for instance, UNESCO (1956).
9. A more intense role is described for women elsewhere, as in the case of the Ijo. See Leis (1964), p. 55.
10. For a gender-based discussion of farming, see Fadipe (1970), Chap. 5.
11. See, for instance, the remark by Dr. Irving, who traveled in Ibadan, Egba, and the Ijebu territories between December 1854 and January 1855, in *C. M. S. Intelligencer*, 1859, p. 259.
12. A number of nineteenth-century sources specifically mentioned encounters with these women. See, for instance, *C. M. S. Intelligencer*, January 1856, p. 20; and Lander and Lander (1833), p. 122.
13. See also William Bascom (1984), Chap. 3.
14. The thirteenth *deji* of Akure is said to be a woman who did not wear a crown. Nigerian National Archives, Ibadan (N.A.I.), "Intelligence Report on Akure" compiled by N. A. C. Weir, 1935, p. 10. See also Falola (1976).
15. N. A. I., "Intelligence Report on Ondo," by A. F. Bridges, 1934/5, p. 10. There were other women chiefs to assist the *lobun*: these included the *lisa lobun* who settles quarrels among the women, the *ogese lobun*, and *sara lobun*, both of whom were "remembrances" to the *lobun*. These offices were duplicated in the Ondo nonmetropolitan area, where the *oloja* (*baale* or village head), together with his chiefs, appointed a *lobun*. In villages such as Ajua and Aiyesan, women chiefs were called *iyalode*, not *lobun*.
16. N. A. I., "Intelligence Report on Abeokuta," by John Blair, 1937, p. 48; N. A. I., "Intelligence Report on Ijebu Ife," by E. A. Hawkersworth, 1935, p. 9. For an overview on this institution, see Awe (1977).
17. For instance, in Ago, an Ijebu village, "female members, known as *Erelu*, were allowed in the society (i.e., Osugbo society). The *Erelu* were consulted in all matters that concerned the female community, though they did not sit with the other members in judicial matters." See "Intelligence Report on Ago," by A. F. Abell, 1934, p. iii. Women membership of secret societies was, however, uncommon.
18. One interesting and mythical example of this is that of Moremi of Ile-Ife. The Igbo people are said to have repeatedly attacked Ile-Ife with success until the beautiful Moremi married the king of Igbo from whom she was able to learn the secrets of Igbo's military success. She returned to Ile-Ife and exposed the secrets. This enabled Ile-Ife to resist and defeat the Igbo.

19. For instance, Samuel Johnson (1921: 63) mentions eight women of "the highest rank" whose roles could not be dispensed within the Oyo palace (*Iya Kekere, Iya Oba, Iya Naso, Iya Monari, Iyalagbon, Orun Kumefun,* and *Are Orite*). On *Iyakekere,* Johnson writes: "She has the charge of the king's treasures. The royal insignia are in her keeping, and all the paraphernalia used on state occasions, she has the power of withholding them, and thus preventing the holding of any state reception to mark her displeasure with the king's head at the coronation." Other women holding important offices were mentioned besides those eight, and their roles within and outside the palace reveals the political influences they could wield on state matters (pp. 64–66).

20. In Akure, there was an Apate club, with a membership restricted to fifty people at a time. They were "not expected to carry loads on their heads." Other clubs included the *Ukoji,* comprising daughters of titled men, and *Esari,* daughters and granddaughters of all late obas (Weir, "Intelligence Report on Akure," p. 21).

21. On this goddess, among others, see Lucas (1948), pp. 218–219; and Gleason (1971), p. 137.

22. See, for instance, Oyemakinde (1973).

23. Public Record Office (P.R.O.), London, Foreign Office (F.O.) 84/950, Campbell to Clarendon, 11 Aug. 1854.

24. P.R.O., F.O. 84/920, Fraser to Malmesbury, 20 Feb. 1853.

25. For one interesting account of this lady, see Bolanle Awe, "Iyalode Efunsetan Aniwura (Owner of Gold)," in Awe (1992: 55–72).

26. For the political background to the crisis, see Falola (1984).

27. The account of Pelewura is based on the evidence of C. Johnson (1981).

28. This reconstruction is based on a pamphlet by T. A. Layonu (1990).

29. On this genre, see Barber (1991).

30. Translation by Awe (1992: 57).

31. See, for instance, Sola-Onifade (n.d.). and Adeyemo (1991), Chap. 3.

## REFERENCES

Adeniyi, Tola. 1993. *The Jewel: A Biography of Chief (Mrs.) H. I. D. Awolowo.* Ibadan: Gemni Press Ltd.

Adeyemo, O. A. (ed.). 1991. *Women in Development.* Ibadan: National Center for Economic Management and Administration.

Awe, Bolanle. 1977. "The Iyalode in the Traditional Political System." In Alice Schlegel (ed.). *Sexual Stratification.* New York: Columbia University Press.

———. 1992. *Nigerian Women in Historical Perspective.* Lagos and Ibadan: Sankore and Bookcraft.

Barber, K. 1991. *I Could Speak until Tomorrow: Oriki, Women, and the Past in a Yoruba Town.* Edinburgh: Edinburgh University Press.

Barnes, Sandra T. 1986. *Patrons and Power: Creating a Political Community in Metropolitan Lagos.* Manchester: Manchester University Press.

Bascom, William. 1984. *The Yoruba of Southwestern Nigeria.* Prospect Heights: Waveland Press [reprint].

Beier, N. U. 1955. "The Position of Yoruba Women." *Presence Africaine* 1/2: 39–46.

Belasco, B. 1980. *The Entrepreneur as Cultural Hero.* New York: Praeger.

Coker, F. 1987. *A Lady: A Biography of Lady Oyinkan Abayomi.* Ibadan: Evans Brothers.

Drewal, Henry John. 1983. *Gelede: Art and Female Power among the Yoruba.* Bloomington: Indiana University Press.

Fabunmi, M. A. 1969. *Ife Shrines.* Ile-Ife: University of Ife Press.

Fadipe, N. A. 1970. *The Sociology of the Yoruba.* Ibadan: Ibadan University Press.

Falola, Toyin. 1976. "A Descriptive Analysis of Ilesa Palace Organization." *The African Historian* 8: 69–79.

———. 1978. "The Place of Women in the Yoruba Pre-colonial Domestic Economy." In *Seminar Proceedings.* Ile-Ife: University of Ife Press.

———. 1984. *The Political Economy of a Pre-colonial African State, Ibadan, ca. 1830–1893.* Ile-Ife: University of Ife Press.

———. 1992. "Salt Is Gold: The Management of Salt Scarcity in Nigeria during World War II." *Canadian Journal of African Studies* 26(3): 412–436.

Falola, Toyin, and Dare Oguntomisin. 1984. *The Military in 19th Century Yoruba Political Systems.* Ile-Ife: University of Ife Press.

Gleason, J. 1971. *Orisha: The Gods of Yorubaland.* New York: Atheneum.

Harris, J. 1940. "The Position of Women in a Nigerian Society." *Transactions of the New York Academy of Sciences* 2(5): 141–148.

Hay, Margaret Jean. 1988. "Queens, Prostitutes, and Peasants: Historical Perspectives on African Women." *Canadian Journal of African Studies* 22(3): 431–447.

Hodder, B. W. 1962. "The Yoruba Market." In Paul Bohannan and George Dalton (eds.). *Markets in Africa.* Evanston, IL: Northwestern University Press.

Hodder, B. W., and U. I. Ukwu. 1969. *Markets in West Africa.* Ibadan: Ibadan University Press.

Idowu, E. B. 1962. *Olodumare, God in Yoruba Belief.* London: Longman.

Izzett, A. 1961. "Family Life among the Yorubas in Lagos, Nigeria." In Aidan Southall (ed.). *Social Change in Modern Africa.* London: International African Institute and Oxford University Press.

Johnson, Samuel. 1921. *The History of the Yorubas.* Lagos: Church Missionary Society.

Johnson, Cheryl. 1981. "Madam Pelewura and the Lagos Market Women." *Tarikh* 7(1): 1–10.

———. 1982. "Grassroots Organizing Women in Anti-colonial Activity in Southwestern Nigeria." *African Studies Review* 25(2 & 3): 137–157.

Johnson-Odim, Cheryl. 1978. *Nigerian Women and British Colonialism: The Yoruba Example with Selected Biographies.* Ph.D. dissertation, Northwestern University, Evanston, IL.

Kaberry, Phyllis Mary. 1952. *Women of the Grassfields.* London: Her Majesty's Stationery Office.

Lander, John, and Richard Lander. 1833. *Journal of an Expedition to Explore the Course and Termination of the Niger,* Vol. 1. New York: J. and J. Harper.

Layonu, T. A. 1990. *Iyalode Hunmoani Alade (The Embodiment of Truth).* Ibadan: Famlod Books.

Leis, Nancy Borric. 1964. *Economic Independence and Ijaw Woman: A Comparative Study of Two Communities in the Niger Delta.* Ph.D. dissertation, Northwestern University, Evanston, IL.

Lloyd, B. 1967. "Indigenous Ibadan." In Peter Cutt Lloyd, Akin L. Mobogunje, and B. Awe (eds.). *The City of Ibadan.* Cambridge: Cambridge University Press.

Lucas, Jonathan Olumide. 1948. *The Religion of the Yorubas.* Lagos: C.M.S. Bookshop.

Mabogunje, Akin. 1961. "The Market-Woman." *Ibadan* 11(February): 16–17.

Marris, Peter. 1961. *Family and Social Change in an African City.* London: Routledge and Kegan Paul.

Marshall, G. 1964. *Women, Trade and the Yoruba Family.* Ph.D. dissertation, New York: Columbia University.

Mba, Nina Emma.1982. *Nigerian Women Mobilized: Women's Political Activity in Southern Nigeria, 1900–1965.* Berkeley: Institute of International Studies, University of California

Olupona, Jacob Obafemi Kehinde. 1991. *Kingship, Religion, and Rituals in a Nigerian Community: A Phenomenological Study of Ondo Yoruba Festivals.* Stockholm: Almqvist & Wiksell International.

Oyemakinde, Wale. 1973. "The Pullen Marketing Scheme: Trial in Food Price Control, 1941–47." *Journal of the Historical Society of Nigeria* 4: 413–423.

Ross, S. Leith. 1939. *African Women.* London: Faber and Faber Ltd.

Sola-Onifade, Bosede. n.d. [1980s?]. *The Nigerian Woman.* Lagos: Julia Virgo Enterprises.

Southall, Aidan (ed.). 1961. *Social Change in Modern Africa.* London: International African Institute and Oxford University Press.

Staudt, Kathleen. 1988. "Women Farmers in Africa: Research and Institutional Action, 1972–1987." *Canadian Journal of African Studies* 22(3): 567–582.

Strobel, Margaret. 1982. "African Women." *Signs: Journal of Women in Culture and Society* 8(1): 109–131.

Sudarkasa, Niara. 1973. *Where Women Work: A Study of Yoruba Women in the Marketplace and in the Home.* Ann Arbor: University of Michigan Press.

Sweetman, David. 1984. *Women Leaders in African History.* London: Heinemann.

UNESCO. 1956. "The Rise of the New Elite amongst the Women of Nigeria." *International Social Science Bulletin* 8(3): 481–488.

Ward, E. 1938. "The Yoruba Husband-Wife Code." In *Catholic University of America Anthropological Studies,* No. 6. Washington, DC: Catholic University of America.

Wipper, Audrey. 1988, "Reflections on the Past Sixteen Years, 1972–1988, and Future Challenges." *Canadian Journal of African Studies* 22(3): 409–421.

# V

# *The Cultural Construction of Gender and Personhood*

We all live in a world of symbols that assign meaning and value to the categories of male and female. Despite several decades of consciousness-raising in the United States, advertising on television and in the print media perpetuates sexual stereotypes. Although "house beautiful" ads are less prominent as women are increasingly shown in workplace contexts, "body beautiful" messages continue to be transmitted. In children's cartoons, women are still the helpless victims that the fearless male hero must rescue. Toys are targeted either for little boys or little girls and are packaged appropriately in colors and materials culturally defined as either masculine or feminine.

To what extent are these stereotypes of men and women and the symbols with which they are associated universal? If they are universal, to what extent are they rooted in observed differences in the biological nature of men and women that are made culturally significant? These questions have interested scholars as they have attempted to account for both similarity and difference among the people of the world. Making the assumption that the subordination of women exists in all societies—a "true universal"—Ortner (1974: 67) sought to explain the pervasiveness of this idea not in the assignation of women to a domestic sphere of activity, but in the symbolic constructions by which women's roles are evaluated. Ortner argues that women, because of their reproductive roles, are universally viewed as being closer to nature while men are linked with culture. She defines culture as "the notion of human consciousness, or . . . the products of human consciousness (i.e., systems of thought and technology), by means of which humanity attempts to assert control over nature" (72). That which is cultural and subject to human manipulation is assigned more worth than that which is natural; hence, women and women's roles are denigrated or devalued, whether explicitly or implicitly.

The nature–culture dichotomy is a useful explanatory model in the United States where, according to Martin (1987: 17), "Women are intrinsically closely involved with the family where so many 'natural,' 'bodily' (and therefore lower) functions occur, whereas men are intrinsically closely involved with the world of work where (at least for some) 'cultural,' 'mental,' and therefore higher functions occur. It is no accident that 'natural' facts about women, in the form of claims about biology, are often used to justify social stratification based on gender."

Although this model may be applicable in some cultures, its universality has been challenged not only by those who point out that nature–culture is a dichotomy of western thought in particular (Bloch and Bloch 1980; Jordanova 1980; Moore 1988), but also by those who provide ethnographic data to indicate its lack of salience in other cultures around the world (Strathern 1980). Similarly, the assumption that women are universally subordinated while men are dominant (Ortner 1974: 70) appears questionable when viewed through the lens of recent ethnographic analysis. The critique of the concepts of universal subordination and of the nature–culture dichotomy has stimulated significant research on how gender

159

identity and gender roles are constructed in particular cultural contexts (Errington and Gewertz 1987; Ortner and Whitehead 1981; Weiner 1976). Whether and under what conditions social asymmetry between men and women emerges in the process of this construction is open to empirical investigation.

The cultural construction of gender in a particular society involves definitions of what it means to be masculine or feminine, and these definitions vary cross culturally. In this book, David D. Gilmore takes up the question of how masculinity is culturally constructed by describing his encounter with machismo in the southern Spanish region of Andalusia. He outlines three components of Andalusian "manhood"—virility, valor, and virtue. Men must live up to the anatomical equipment with which they are born—to enact their virility. There are certain rites of passage—including the activity of *abuchear*—associated with this enactment. Real manhood implies seduction. But it also requires bravery, heroism, and hard work—the elements of valor or *hombria*. Finally, being honorable, a person of rectitude, decency, and generosity, is essential to Andalusian manhood. The behavior of Spanish men in bars (Driessen 1983) must be viewed in this light. As Gilmore argues, to stay away from the bars and to hold back one's purse is considered unmanly and effeminate.

Gilbert H. Herdt (in this book) also focuses on manhood, examining how it is constructed in the context of ritual among the Sambia of New Guinea. The Sambia, like many other societies in New Guinea (Biersack 2001; Brown and Buchbinder 1976; Herdt 1982; Meigs 1984; Roscoe 2001), are characterized by a high degree of segregation and sexual antagonism between men and women, both of which are reinforced by powerful taboos. These taboos, and other facets of Sambian male identity including that of the warrior, are inculcated during a series of initiation rituals whereby boys are "grown" into men. As Herdt observes, the Sambia "perceive no imminent, naturally driven fit between one's birthright sex and one's gender identity or role" (1982: 54). Indeed, Sambian boys and men engage in what some societies would label homosexual activity, yet they do it to create masculinity. It is precisely for this reason that an analytical distinction is often made between "sex" as a biological classification and "gender" as a set of learned social roles.

Through the rituals of manhood, Sambian boys are progressively detached from the world of women, a world they occupied for the first six or seven years of their lives and which they must now learn to both fear and devalue. This process of detachment has been identified by Chodorow (1974) as a major phase of human male development. If it is unmarked and therefore ambiguous in most western cultures, it is marked in many nonwestern cultures and often associated with male circumcision. Among the Mende of Sierra Leone (Little 1951), for example, boy initiates are seized from their homes by the force of spirits—men wearing masks and long raffia skirts. In this act, they are dramatically and suddenly separated from their childhood, and carried into the bush, where they will spend several weeks in seclusion and transition before they reemerge as men.

Gilmore (1990: 11) sums up the importance of these rituals to construct manhood by identifying a recurring cross-cultural notion: that "real manhood is different from simple anatomical maleness, that it is not a natural condition that comes about spontaneously through biological maturation but rather is a precarious or artificial state that boys must win against powerful odds" (1990: 11). He examines a post-Freudian understanding of masculinity as a category of self-identity, showing how boys face special problems in separating from their mothers. A boy's separation and individuation is more perilous and difficult than a girl's, whose femininity is reinforced by the original unity with her mother. Thus, to become separate, the boy must pass a test, breaking the chain to his mother.

Initiation rituals that prepare girls for their roles as women and instruct them in what it means to be a woman in a particular cultural context can also be found in various societies around the world (Brown 1963; Lincoln 1991; Richards 1956). However, the transition to womanhood is often part of a more subtle and continuous process of enculturation and socialization. In a description of Hausa socialization, Callaway (1987) demonstrates how girls in this society learn how to behave in culturally appropriate ways. The Hausa are an Islamic people who live in northern Nigeria. Historically, ruling-class Hausa women had significant authority and social standing, but with the expansion of Islam, this position was eroded and a sexually segregated society characterized by female subordination emerged. Hausa girls marry young, generally upon reaching puberty. At that time they enter kulle, or seclusion. In seclusion, the social roles of women are specifically defined and their sexual activities are limited. Although a Hausa woman becomes part of her husband's family, her place is secured only by bearing sons, and all her children belong to her husband. Hausa women are taught the expected life course from early childhood. In Hausa society, Callaway (1987: 22) claims, "the reproduction of 'masculine' and 'feminine' personalities generation after generation has produced psychological and value commitments to sex differences that are tenaciously maintained and so deeply ingrained as to become central to a consistent sense of self." This self is defined by reproductive roles and by deference to men; thus a good daughter-in-law gives her first-born child to her husband's mother, an act that strengthens family ties.

Conceptions of the self or personhood are, as Henrietta Moore (1988: 39; see also Moore 1994) has observed, "cross-culturally as variable as the concepts of 'woman' and 'man.'" Personhood is constituted by a variety of attributes. In addition to gender, it may comprise age, status in the family and in the community, and physical appearance or impairment. In many cultures, naming is also an important mechanism for constructing personhood. In the United States, for instance, the use of Ms. to replace Mrs. and Miss is an acceptable option. It is now quite common for married women to retain the name that they were born with rather than replace it with one that only gives them an identity in relation to someone else—their husband.

Among the Chambri of New Guinea, initial identity or personhood is gained through a totemic name given by a child's patrilineal and matrilateral relatives. According to Errington and Gewertz (1987: 32, 47), "these names both reflect and affect the transactions which constitute a person's fundamental social relationships and identity. . . . Totemic names allow both men and women to pursue respectively their culturally defined preoccupations of political competition and the bearing of children. The totemic names available to men, however, convey different sorts of power and resources than do those available to women. . . . Men seek to augment their own power through gaining control of the names of others. . . . The power conveyed by [women's] names cannot shape social relationships as does the power of names men hold, but, instead, ensures reproduction."

Women's names among the Chambri work in different ways from those of men, but they nonetheless enable women to claim personhood in Chambri society. The married Chinese women described by Rubie S. Watson (in this book) have an entirely different experience. They are denied individuating names, and through this denial, their personhood is in question. They remain, says Watson, "suspended between the anonymous world of anybodies and the more sharply defined world of somebodies." In contrast with the namelessness of Chinese women, men in Chinese culture acquire numerous names as they pass through the life cycle. Nowhere is the difference more apparent than at marriage—a time when a man acquires a name that symbolizes his new status and public roles and a woman loses her girlhood name and becomes the "inner person." Like the Hausa women who assume an identity with respect to their husbands, Chinese women begin newly married life by learning the names and kinship terms for all their husbands' ancestors and relatives. Namelessness follows them to the grave—anybodies in life, they become nobodies at death.

Personhood is also encoded in the language that men and women use. Indeed anthropologists and others have focused on the relationship between language and gender, building on the pioneering work of Lakoff (1975) and, more recently, Deborah Tannen (1990). In many cultures around the world, speech styles differ between men and women, whereas in others there are no distinctions (Keenan 1974; Sherzer 1987). Sometimes these differences are associated with the relative equality/inequality between the sexes, and hence with power. As Susan Gal (1991: 177) has written, "some linguistic strategies and genres are more highly valued and carry more authority than others." Bonnie McElhinny (in this book) takes up the topic of gendered language and its relation to authority and personhood in her research on the Pittsburgh police department. She links gender to race and class, offering a complex analysis of how police officers talk about the use of physical force and how this has affected the integration of women into the police profession, a traditionally male occupation. Equally at issue is the extent to which women police officers use "tough talk" and whether this usage results in them being described as more masculine or less feminine, as well as more or less competent as police officers.

In an essay exploring embodiment and the anthropological imagination, Rosemary Joyce (2006: 48) notes that the field has long "challenged the assumption of a natural correspondence between a body and an individual person, historicizing and contextualizing both." In many societies, personhood is associated with gendered conceptions of the body (Conklin 2001; Diemberger 1993; Lambek and Strathern 1998; Strathern 1996). Sarah Lamb (2000) addresses the gendered nature of the body and how it makes and unmakes the social ties of Bengali Indian women over the life course. Purity among Bengalis is associated with touching and the controlled exchange of bodily fluids. Women are considered more impure than men and hence must bathe more often and must observe cultural practices that discipline their bodies—spatial seclusion, cloth covering, and so on. Their bodies are more open and hence more vulnerable; menstruation marks the beginning of openness—a sign of readiness for marriage and reproduction. At her wedding, a time when her personal identity is changing, a Bengali woman must absorb substances originating from her husband's body and household. This also represents a severing of ties with her natal family and a forging of ties with her husband's family. Similarly later in life, and as a widow, women begin to unmake ties. When a woman loses her husband, she becomes half a person and if young, Lamb tells us, "not merely a sexual hazard, but also a repulsive anomaly." In old age, when they are past reproduction, their bodies close and cool and they regain purity. Postmenopausal women become "like men" and enjoy many of the freedoms that men enjoy.

In some societies, men and women engage in or experience transformations of their bodies. These may occur as part of initiation rituals (see Gruenbaum later in this volume), through body art (tattoos, piercing, etc.), through dieting or skin lightening, or through cosmetic surgery. In many cases, such transformations are related to issues of gender identity. In this book, Lauren Gulbas explores the high rates of cosmetic surgery in Venezuela, a country known for producing stunning competitors for the Miss Universe and Miss World competitions. Gulbas tries to find an explanation for why men and women, especially those from poor families, allocate scarce resources to the pursuit of an ideal feminine or masculine body. She links these body ideals with notions of self and with the psychological significance of looking good and feeling good within gendered frames of reference.

The readings in this section of the book all emphasize that the biological categories of male and female are foundations upon which culturally defined and culturally appropriate gender roles, gender identities, and gendered personhood are constructed by both men and women in any society. What it means to be masculine or feminine varies across cultures, across social locations defined by such factors as class, ethnicity, or employment sector, and over the life course.

## REFERENCES

Biersack, Aletta. 2001. "Reproducing Inequality; The Gender Politics of Male Cults in the Papua New Guinea Highlands and Amazonia." In Thomas A. Gregor and Donald Tuzin (eds.). *Gender in Amazonia and Melanesia*, pp. 69–90. Berkeley: University of California Press.

Bloch, Maurice, and Jean Bloch. 1980. "Women and the Dialectics of Nature in Eighteenth-Century French Thought." In Carol MacCormack and Marilyn Strathern (eds.). *Nature, Culture and Gender*, pp. 25–41. Cambridge: Cambridge University Press.

Brown, Judith K. 1963. "A Cross-Cultural Study of Female Initiation Rites among Pre-Literate Peoples." *American Anthropologist* 65(4): 837–853.

Brown, Paula, and Georgeda Buchbinder. 1976. *Man and Woman in the New Guinea Highlands*. Washington, DC: American Anthropological Association, Special Publication, number 8.

Callaway, Barbara J. 1987. *Muslim Hausa Women in Nigeria: Tradition and Change*. Syracuse, NY: Syracuse University Press.

Chodorow, Nancy. 1974. "Family Structure and Feminine Personality." In Michele Z. Rosaldo and Louise Lamphere (eds.). *Woman, Culture, and Society*, pp. 43–67. Stanford, CA: Stanford University Press.

Conklin, Beth. 2001. "Women's Blood, Warriors' Blood, and the Conquest of Vitality in Amazonia." In Thomas A. Gregor and Donald Tuzin (eds.). *Gender in Amazonia and Melanesia*, pp. 141–174. Berkeley: University of California Press.

Diemberger, Hildegard. 1993. "Blood, Sperm, Soul and the Mountain. Gender Relations, Kinship and Cosmovision among the Khumbo (NE Nepal)." In Teresa del Valle (ed.). *Gendered Anthropology*, pp. 88–127. London and New York: Routledge.

Driessen, Henk. 1983. "Male Sociability and Rituals of Masculinity in Andalusia." *Anthropological Quarterly* 56: 125–133.

Errington, Frederick, and Deborah Gewertz. 1987. *Cultural Alternatives and a Feminist Anthropology: An Analysis of Culturally Constructed Gender Interests in Papua New Guinea*. Cambridge: Cambridge University Press.

Gal, Susan. 1991. "Between Speech and Silence: The Problematics of Research on Language and Gender." In Micaela di Leonardo (ed.). *Gender at the Crossroads of Knowledge*. Berkeley: University of California Press, 175-203.

Gilmore, David. 1990. *Manhood in the Making*. New Haven, CT: Yale University Press.

Herdt, Gilbert. 1982. *Rituals of Manhood: Male Initiation in Papua New Guinea*. Berkeley and Los Angeles: University of California Press.

Jordanova, L. J. 1980. "Natural Facts: A Historical Perspective on Science and Sexuality." In Carol MacCormack and Marilyn Strathern (eds.). *Nature, Culture and Gender*, pp. 42–69. Cambridge: Cambridge University Press.

Joyce, Rosemary A. 2006. "Feminist Theories of Embodiment and Anthropological Imagination: Making Bodies Matter." In Pamela L. Geller and Miranda K. Stockett (eds.). *Feminist Anthropology: Past, Present, and Future*, pp. 43–54. Philadelphia: University of Pennsylvania Press.

Keenan, Elinor Ochs. 1974. "Norm-Makers and Norm-Breakers: Uses of Speech by Men and Women in a Malagasy Community." In Richard Bauman and Joel Sherzer (eds.). *Explorations in the Ethnography of Speaking*, pp. 125–143. Cambridge: Cambridge University Press.

Lakoff, Robin. 1975. *Language and Women's Place*. New York: Harper and Row.

Lamb, Sarah. 2000. *White Saris and Sweet Mangoes: Aging, Gender, and Body in North India*. Berkeley: University of California Press.

Lambek, Michael, and Andrew Strathern (eds.). 1998. *Bodies and Persons: Comparative Perspectives from Africa and Melanesia*. Cambridge: Cambridge University Press.

Lincoln, Bruce. 1991. *Emerging from the Chrysalis: Rituals of Women's Initiation*. New York: Oxford University Press.

Little, Kenneth L. 1951. *The Mende of Sierra Leone: A West African People in Transition*. London: Routledge and Kegan Paul.

Martin, Emily. 1987. *The Woman in the Body: A Cultural Analysis of Reproduction*. Boston: Beacon Press.

Meigs, Anna S. 1984. *Food, Sex, and Pollution: A New Guinea Religion*. New Brunswick, NJ: Rutgers University Press.

Moore, Henrietta. 1988. *Feminism and Anthropology*. Minneapolis: University of Minnesota Press.

———. 1994. *A Passion for Difference: Essays in Anthropology and Gender*. Bloomington: Indiana University Press.

Ortner, Sherry. 1974. "Is Female to Male as Nature to Culture?" In Michelle Z. Rosaldo and Louise Lamphere (eds.). *Woman, Culture, and Society*, pp. 66–87. Stanford, CA: Stanford University Press.

Ortner, Sherry, and Harriet Whitehead. 1981. *Sexual Meanings: The Cultural Construction of Gender and Sexuality*. Cambridge, UK: Cambridge University Press.

Richards, Audrey I. 1956. *Chisungu: A Girls' Initiation Ceremony among the Bemba of Northern Rhodesia*. London: Faber and Faber.

Roscoe, Paul. 2001. "Strength and Sexuality: Sexual Avoidance and Masculinity in New Guinea and Amazonia." In Thomas A. Gregor and Donald Tuzin (eds.). *Gender in Amazonia and Melanesia*, pp. 279–308. Berkeley: University of California Press.

Sherzer, Joel. 1987. "A Diversity of Voices: Men's and Women's Speech in Ethnographic Perspective." In S. Philips, S. Steel, and C. Tanz (eds.). *Language, Gender and Sex in Comparative Perspective*, pp. 95–120. Cambridge: Cambridge University Press.

Strathern, Andrew. 1996. *Body Thoughts*. Ann Arbor: University of Michigan Press.

Strathern, Marilyn. 1980. "No Nature, No Culture: The Hagen Case." In Carol MacCormack and Marilyn Strathern (eds.). *Nature, Culture and Gender*, pp. 174–222. Cambridge: Cambridge University Press.

Tannen, Deborah. 1990. *You Just don't Understand. Women and Men in Conversation*. New York: William Morrow.

Weiner, Annette. 1976. *Women of Value, Men of Renown*. Austin: University of Texas Press.

# My Encounter with Machismo in Spain

## David D. Gilmore

Let me begin with a disclaimer. When I first went to Spain as a novice anthropologist in 1972, I did not choose machismo to study. On the contrary, machismo chose me: I had no choice. This happened during my dissertation fieldwork in the southern region of Andalusia. Being a child of the 60s and influenced by the then-fashionable mix of Marxism and do-goodism, I originally went to Spain with the intention of studying (and possibly ameliorating) the "objective realities" of what I saw as oppression under the Franco dictatorship. I envisioned a scholarly thesis on weighty matters like class consciousness and workers' rights, with an emphasis on the clandestine labor organizations that were springing up as Franco breathed his

Original material prepared for this text. Reprinted by permission of the author.

last (he died in 1975 and the dictatorship fell soon afterwards). However, while collecting data, I soon ran into a practical problem. While conducting informal discussions and interviews, I was constantly bombarded by verbal static emanating from my subjects. By "static" I mean background noise, chatter—talk about tangential topics. Since this noise struck me as irrelevant, rather like radio interference, I largely ignored it. As I soon learned this was a mistake.[1]

One's person's noise can be another's symphony. When interviewed, people would get bored talking about politics, and to liven things up would launch into gratuitous pronouncements about more interesting subjects. The most common detour was the subject of sex, perhaps not surprisingly since most of my informants were unmarried youths. Usually these impromptu digressions would lead to colorful accounts about the nature of male and female, about what a "real man" should be, "being macho" and so on. Often the talk would segue into mild boasting about how they, the Andalusians, were superior to other Spaniards in matters romantic, and certainly better than benighted foreigners such as myself. As often happens to tyro anthropologists—and despite my intentions—I became sidetracked by the "subjective reality" of sex talk and eventually the static took on a life of its own. After returning to the U.S., and for years afterwards I tried to avoid thinking too hard about it, dismissing it all as youthful braggadocio. But after having written some dull treatises on politics, I retuned to what had imposed itself upon me so urgently in the field. In what follows I will explain how—and what—I learned about Andalusian "machismo."

Of course I learned other things. For example, I learned to appreciate the good old anthropological "culture concept," about which I had been indoctrinated in graduate school. While this hoary tenet has been questioned recently by some postmodernists (see Abu-Lughod 1993), it has withstood the test of time. As anthropologists have said, culture consists of shared understandings and standards held by a group: a body of mutually-agreed upon values, norms and beliefs that work as a nonverbal grammar and also as a source of identity, of ethnic pride, and of group unity. As I quickly learned in Andalusia, people's notions of manhood (and of its converse, femininity, too, of course), were very different from my own, and indeed contrasted starkly with what I had read about other cultures elsewhere. Moreover, these ideas about gender were not only widespread, but they were enthusiastically shared by both sexes, were consensual among all ages, and were repeated by different people in different settings. Ideas about what a "real man" was, especially, were cherished by virtually all the men I knew and by many women as well. These ideas made up a very substantial part of Andalusian culture.

It is also important to point out that whatever discrepancies might exist between these ideas and my own cannot be ascribed to differences in social-class between me and my informants, as a critic has meretriciously alleged (Pina-Cabral 1989). Nor are these differences due to a deficient understanding about working-class culture in my own native America. I can say this because most of my informants in Spain were not in fact working class at all. Rather, they were similar to me in status, being mainly middle-class professionals, and they possessed an impressive vocabulary to articulate their ideas. Some were college graduates; one or two, like me, were in graduate school. Among them was a sprinkling of high-school teachers, menial workers and farmers. A few were peasants, and one or two were illiterate landless laborers who joined our almost nightly talk sessions. So I was dealing with a decidedly cross-sectional sample, with an emphasis, if anything, on the middle classes—a social setting rather analogous to my own in America.

As these nightly gabfests would gather steam, many of these friends and acquaintances would join in until we were often twenty or more guys chewing the rag, or "cutting the cloth," as they say in Spain. The conversations took place during long walks in the village park or in the bars where village men relax for hours, sipping wine or coffee, playing cards or dominoes and of course chatting. Sometimes, the men who were absent at one occasion would confirm my written notes later. All this continual affirmation led me to conclude I was dealing with a "cultural fact," because when one encounters a point of view so widely and repetitively expressed, it constitutes something objectively real, a fact. There was of course some variation of opinion as there is in any society, but such variations were of degree, not of kind. Agreement on the main principles of a proper manhood was virtually unanimous.

## VIRILITY, VALOR, VIRTUE

Let me provide some ethnographic context. The largest region of Spain, Andalusia makes up most of the southern part of the country. In many ways it is similar to America's "Deep South" or the Mezzogiorno of Italy, being a largely agrarian region, socially and culturally conservative compared to the rest of the country, and having its own distinctive accent, a "southern drawl," and well known for cultural peculiarities, in this case peculiarities from which other Spaniards often disassociate themselves as being backward or dubious. In the northern regions of Castile or Catalonia for example, many people say that Andalusians are lazy, carefree, given over to wine, song and sloth—the usual prejudices about "southerners" one encounters in Europe and America. Andalusia is also the region most closely identified with the stereotypical Spain of the travel posters: bullfights, flamenco music, raven-haired maidens with roses in their teeth, perfumed gardens, mantillas, and, of course, don Juanism. Remember that the original don Juan story was set by Tirso de Molina (1571–1648), in Seville—the unofficial capital of Andalusia.

First, before recounting my experiences, let me emphasize my main point: *machismo* and *manliness* are not synonymous in Andalusia. Although this region has been identified in some accounts as the epicenter of so-called "Hispanic machismo," and supposedly transported thence throughout the Spanish-speaking world by Andalusian emigrants (see Gonzalez-Lopez and Gutmann 2005), nevertheless the manhood code here is complex and cannot be reduced to a single factor. What I propose to do here is to explain how the bundle of manhood traits imposed itself on my ethnographic radar in Spain, then to describe the components of the manhood code, "machismo" being just one, and, finally, to compare this package briefly with such codes elsewhere. The reader will immediately gather that the so-called "machismo" so tirelessly invoked in social science in actuality represents a wide diversity of forms all of which have something in common and are therefore amenable to comparative analysis. What is needed here is what Ward Goodenough, borrowing from descriptive linguistics, has called the method of "componential analysis." This method involves breaking down a semantic category into its constituent parts and analyzing each independently before putting the whole together again as an over-all pattern, a Gestalt. Goodenough explains (1970: 72):

> . . . a linguistic expression may be said to *designate* a class of concepts or images. It may be said to *denote* a specific image or subclass. . . . And it may be said to *signify* the criteria by which specific images or concepts are to be included or excluded from the class of images or concepts that the expression designates. What is signified consist of the definitive attributes of the class, the ideational components from which the class is conceptually formed. Componential analysis is a method for forming and testing hypotheses about what words signify.

Briefly put: the main components of Andalusian "manhood" (that is, the subclasses constituting native ideas) are three, which I will here gloss as: *virility, valor,* and *virtue.* Each has its own linguistic label in standard Castilian, which will discussed in turn as we proceed. I begin by describing some eye-opening experiences from my first few months in the rural town of Fuentes de Andalucía—my research site in Spain since 1972. Fuentes is small farming pueblo (population 7,500) located in Seville Province, about equidistant between the provincial capitals of Seville and Cordoba. The ethnographic present used here is the decade between 1972 and 1982. Since then, of course, it has all changed with modernization—but that is a subject for another study.

## VIRILITY: THE MACHO

Attending to my original research program, I made friends with a number of young men (and a few women), usually seeking them out in their favorite bars or taverns. When one meets regulars in any bar in Spain, one very soon is introduced to a large coterie of friends and friends-of-friends—a kind of spontaneous expanding network that makes fieldwork in Spain both easy and pleasurable. I found that very often my queries about subjects of concern to me would be sidetracked by more immediate interests of my friends, as

I suppose is true in any social setting. But I found this to be true especially where a comparison or analogy, often invidious, could be drawn between what their own self-image and what they attributed to "*forasteros,*" (outsiders). The latter term included not only strangers from other parts of Spain, but also foreigners from what they referred to as "the north," meaning northern Europe and North America. Such exotics were referred to as "*nórdicos*" (Nordics) in what anthropologists nowadays call an invocation of "the other," that is, the formulation of a stereotype as a straw man. Although not a *nórdico* by ethnic persuasion, I became their resident representative from this mysterious world, which was to them an unofficial sounding board to their native Andalusian habits and customs.

One evening I was sitting in a bar with about ten friends, talking as usual about why Spain "is different" as the travel posters say, when the conversation turned to the influx of European tourists on the Costa del Sol, that is, the Spanish beach resorts—a hot topic and one that gave grist to the mill for judgmental comparison. The ensuing conversation turned on the point of supposed characterological differences between the nórdicos and the Andalusians. Something they had noticed keenly was the behavior of the foreign men on the crowded resort beaches. The nórdicos, they observed, would sit quietly amongst scantily-dressed tourist women and "do nothing"—an egregious act of omission which proved the inherent superiority of the Andalusians. The logic went as follows.

My friends noted that the northerners who visit the Costa del Sol beach resorts (mainly British, Germans and Scandinavians) go out to take the sun and swim in the company of beautiful blonde women who wear virtually nothing. "Those men," he scoffed, "do nothing. Are they men?" This lack of any reaction at all to the unclothed female he found both notable and bizarre. An Andalusian man would not let such an opportunity pass. A real man must "do something," a real man answers the call of his manhood. My friend repeated: some remark must be said, some sort of pass made, "something, anything" must be done to acknowledge the opportunity for a *lio,* or romantic connection.

Now, occasionally, the Spanish men observing all this at the beach resorts would converse in broken English with the foreigners in some bar and this subject would come up. My friends said that the nórdicos would explain that they were "just friends" with these naked girls, a concept that incited incredulity and scorn from the Andalusians. To get the point across my friends would recite one of their favorite aphorisms. "A man and a woman," they would say, "cannot be friends, unless the woman is very, very ugly and the man very, very foolish (*tonto*)." Explanation: to neglect one's manhood not only qualifies a man for contempt as inert, but also, as my comrades emphasized stupid, "foolish." A shy man is not only unmanly but also brainless and unnatural. Another term they used in this context is significant: weak men are called *flojo*. In Spanish *flojo* means inadequate, flaccid, weak, or soft. Literal dictionary definitions also include flabby, lax, loose, slack and sluggish. Andalusians of both sexes use *flojo* liberally to describe a flat tire, a broken tool, or anything that does not work, often with derisory connotations of debility and perversity. The analogy to sexual impotence is of course obvious: a man who "can't get it up," like a dead battery or a punctured tire, is *flojo*. But more, such a man is said to neglect his natural duty to inspire romance and make a *lio*. So even more than merely signifying inadequacy or inutility, *flojo* carries with it a strong whiff of moral disapproval and opprobrium. I detected in all this not only contempt for the moribund nórdicos, but also an invidious judgment and a not-so-hidden self-congratulation. There were nationalistic overtones to all this. This piqued my curiosity and naturally provoked further discussions.

I learned that the quality being adjudged here is "being macho" (*ser macho*). Although *machismo* is a perfectly good Spanish word (Castilian nouns take an *-ismo* ending as with the cognate *-ism* in English) it is never used in everyday speech in Spain, except nowadays as an epithet by university feminists. As elsewhere in Hispanic countries "macho" simply means "male" (Gonzalez-Lopez and Gutmann 2005). It connotes explicitly anatomical maleness, the possession of a penis and testicles. When a child is born, or a farm animal calved, for example, the first thing people ask is, "Macho o hembra?" (male or female?). "Hembra" means both female and, literally, womb; so the sexes here are initially distinguished by reproductive physiology, as is the case in many societies. But for a postpubescent male in Andalusia to "be macho" (*ser macho*) has a special the connotation of living up to the qualities attributed to the male physiology. In Andalusia, being macho means using your anatomical equipment in the expected ways; or at least giving the impression of doing so. Further concrete examples and some colorful illustrations flowed from my friends. Telling the poor deluded nórdico anthropologist about "being macho" was becoming a cottage industry in Fuentes.

A few days later, I was out walking at dusk with a few friends. We came upon a group of about twelve boys, 13 or 14 years old, milling about in one of the central squares of the pueblo. These youth packs are called *pandillas* (cliques or gangs). While nothing unusual in that male *pandillas* are often seen lurking outdoors at any time of day or night, my ethnographic alarm bell went off and told me this group was poised for some mischief which might be of interest. So I made inquiry to my companions. They told me the following. What I was witnessing was the first stage of a traditional adolescent activity called the "*abuchear*," a word I later found translated loosely as shouting, jeering, or hooting. My informants immediately understood what was going on because they had participated in such rituals themselves in their teens. The boys were in fact lying in wait for some unsuspecting and, more importantly, unaccompanied, young girl to pass by. When one did, they would rush after her, hollering obscenities, jeering and grasping at her clothing, driving her crying to her home, at which point they would relent and reorganize to repeat the process with another victim. The boys did not physically molest the girls (physical abuse is against the rules), but their victims were usually shaken up and frightened. In one famous case of abuchear, I was told, a girl ran home in tears, her clothes in tatters, and told her father that she recognized the persecutors. Angry and insulted, her father then went to the boy's house to extract an apology from the boy's father; some words were exchanged. But the response of the hooting boy's father remains a classic piece of folklore in the pueblo. Rather than being chagrined or apologetic, the father coolly replied, "Why thank you for telling about this: that means my boy must be a real macho." He took it as a compliment.

Obviously, the central theme in "ser macho" is the erotic element: by *virility* here I mean pure sexual potency, sexual assertiveness. Ser macho implies an adventurous, probing, phallic sexuality that is both predatory and peremptory. My friends consistently defined "macho" in terms of a quantifiable energy stemming from the *cojones*, testicles. When I asked a friend what macho meant in a fly-specked bar (he was a university-educated youth) he pointed to two copulating flies on the counter and said, "You see that fly, the one on top? That's what we mean by *macho*." A refrain I heard often touted in these discussions was this: we Andalusians are more highly sexed than forasteros—this was offered often as a scientific fact. Andalusians are more potent, more irrepressibly sexual than others; they have larger penises and heftier balls (a legacy some said proudly of the Moorish occupation of Andalusia). Indeed, this was the only instance I heard anything complementary said about "los moros," the generic term Andalusians use for Arabs and Muslims. One of my friends added, "You know, don David, that's how we Spaniards conquered the Americas: one hand waving the sword, the other the penis!" (I learned later this was a common saying in Spain). So macho, then, means being a sexual conquistador.

## THE PIROPO

Further conversations ensued as my friends continued amplifying on what they meant by *macho*. I heard many other local sayings, for example: "Dress a shovel in a dress and we *fontaniegos* [male residents of Fuentes] will gladly make love to it: that's macho." Then there is the venerable tradition called "*el piropo*," which remained strong in both rural and urban Andalusia until very recently (Pitt-Rivers 1971: 92). This requires a brief digression. The word *piropo* means a complement or an offering given by a man to a passing woman in public (literally it means a ruby). It can mean a gift or a gallantry of any sort, but in modern-day usage it refers to a linguistic tradition of cavalier flirtatiousness. In Andalusia, the piropo is a verbal "something," "a spoken gift" or symbolic acknowledgement that a man offers to a comely woman passing by. If a good-looking girl walks by unaccompanied by a man (piropos are off-limits when the girl has a man with her for obvious reasons of prudence), her sexual allure must be commented upon, even in some abstract sense, "something, anything," as my informants repeated, "must be done." To fail to do something is to be egregiously *flojo*, to be deficient in masculinity. Piropos are expected especially when men are in groups, as each outdoes the other in expressing appropriate lust. I recorded some of these piropos from Fuentes and some from other pueblos; they range from the chivalrous and polite to the ugly and vulgar. For example, a youth, bowing slightly or raising his cap, will say to a passing girl: "I salute your mother, to create such a beauty as you." He may then pucker up and offer a kiss, make lurid lip-smacking noises, or pantomime a dance step. Or, if less courtly, he may shout "Hooray for the brunette (or blonde, or whatever), let me hold you in my arms, let me make passionate love to you." The girl always ignores the comment and walks on. If the boy feels he has been insufficiently forceful, he may pursue the girl down the street issuing further pronouncements, and these can get aggressive and lewd (see Suarez-Orozco and Dundes 1984 for some crude Latin American examples).

Sometimes, when boys from Fuentes traveled to the next town or to a big city where they were less known, their terminology would indeed degenerate into aggressive witticisms and obscenities. However, whatever the words, the symbolic communication of the piropo was always the same. The men told me that the verbal dart was not directed so much at the woman, who, unless an actual prostitute, was always immune and never reacted, as to the general *male* audience: its purpose was to "show that you are a man," to demonstrate virility. A man, they said, needs to show his manhood constantly, to show that he never fails to appreciate feminine pulchritude and that he has no hesitations about it. Otherwise there may be doubt.

Another American anthropologist, Irwin Press, who was working in the city of Seville at about the same time I was in Fuentes, found much the same thing among relatively sophisticated urbanites. Press notes that a man in Seville feels it necessary to make a piropo in order to express his masculinity publicly, to show "his nature verbally" (1979: 133). Other anthropologists in Spain have collected hundreds of these pronouncements once again from the poetic to the uncouth. Press collected some colorful examples in his entertaining book on Seville (1979: 133–134). His remarks on this subject are worth repeating at some length:

> Traditionally, the piropo was a statement of admiration to a woman as she walked by. Piropos ranged from the elegant ("The stars and moon are at your feet, along with I, your slave, my pretty!") to the ludicrous ("I worship the mushroom that grows in the shade of the tree which you grace with your presence, beautiful!"), from the simple ("I salute your mother, my beauty!") to the complex. Today's [1979] piropos are more direct. . . .
>
> Jose Maria the painter, thirty-seven years old, married but a year, stands with his buddies at the bar when two shapely but very heavy young women walk by, arm in arm. "Wow! Look at this!" he cries to his friends. "Real juicy!" They run to the door of the bar and José Maria calls out to the girls, "Oh, how sweet this meat is, fitting sepulcher in which to bury myself!" The girls continue on, pretending to hear nothing. "Ooooooo, but I'd like to suck your cunts," he hisses loudly after them, and returns to the bar stool with his approving friends, whereupon the conversation shifts to the vulval virtues of fat versus thin women.

The corollary to such lechery is recognized outside Spain as don Juanism, personified in the image of Latin Lover, a deathless stereotype which figures prominently in folklore about all the Mediterranean peoples (for vicissitudes of the Italian variant, see Reich 2004). Stereotype it may be, but it nevertheless reflects a real, self-appointed and certainly unapologetic aspect of the masculine self-image in Andalusia. My friends insisted that a real man takes advantage of sexual opportunities regardless of context, and he does so because this is his god-given nature as a man, which he has a sacred duty to heed. So it is often said that one is not a real man who does not at least attempt to seduce an available (unattached) woman, and thus, in consequence, a man and a woman cannot be Platonic friends, unless, as they say, the girl is very ugly or the boy is very foolish. My friends adhered to these sexist sentiments without any self-doubt or squeamishness.

While in Fuentes, my friends would often resort to the abundant local poetry to get certain points across when I was being obstinate or dense. There is an old tradition in Andalusia of reciting oral poetry to hammer home a point, especially those that reflect community themes and concerns. In Fuentes, for example, many local bards (all the poets are men) composed raunchy ditties every year to be sung during February carnival, and they would march around the village with accompanists and shout their lyrics in exchange for drinks. So, in keeping with this tradition, my friends decided it would help illustrate local attitudes by reciting salacious carnival songs. I repeat one such exemplary poem below, composed in the 1960s by a most famous carnival poet. In it, a nameless everyman encounters an unchaperoned young girl, called Isabel, out at dusk seeking to buy milk. Confronted by such a rare opportunity, and being too wily to settle for a mere piropo and too mature for the abuchear, the hero of the piece performs what is expected, maneuvering the maiden into sex in a dark doorway:

Y en la Alameda me preguntó una criada,
Me dijo que si vendía
La leche merengada,
Y yo le dije: 'eso no lo vendo yo,
Pero aquí tengo un tubito
Que apretándole un poquito
Echa leche pa' los' dos.
Vamos ligero que aquí no estamo' mojando;
Vamos a una cada puerta y me la sigues topando.
Y ella me dijo, dice la niña Isabel:
"¡¿Porque me siento un chorrito
Que me coje del ombligo
Hasta la punta de los pies!?"

Once in the park I happened upon
A serving girl, who asked me
If I sold fresh milk.
I answered no, this I do not sell,
But better still, I have little spigot here
Which when squeezed a little bit,
Will make "milk" enough for both of us.
So let's not tarry here, we might get wet.
Let's go to some doorway
So I can give you what you need.
And then she cries out, does the maiden Isabel:
"Oh why do I feel a gushing that
Shakes me from the navel to the toes?!"

—*Composed by Juanillo El Gato*

The song repeats a common analogy made between male "milk" (semen) and breast milk. Perhaps it also reflects the universal male fantasy of the willing rape victim; but despite the crude metaphors the ditty evoked amusement and approval among my male friends. The innocent young maiden Isabel, not knowing what she wants, must be seduced by the cunning, tricky male.

His high-voltage sexuality is uncontainable—a life force that gushes and spurts. It is no coincidence that the original Don Juan story is entitled "the Trickster of Seville" ("El Burlador de Sevilla"). For the macho, any means, fair or foul, are acceptable to make a conquest.

A final anecdote will conclude this account; then we will look at other ingredients in Andalusian manhood. When I first went to Spain I was with my wife, and she frequently accompanied me during fieldwork. One week early in our stay in Fuentes, she returned briefly to the States. She was gone only for about a week. During this time I was conspicuously alone in the pueblo. My friends regarded this as a trial, for it is thought that without a woman to take care of him, a man is helpless and pathetic. Soon my friends became concerned for my wellbeing. They conferred among themselves, debated and finally sent a delegation to my house one evening. "Don David," they said, "now that your wife has been away all this time [three days], you must need a woman. So we have agreed to take you to Carmona [the nearest big town] and to get you a nice clean whore." When I told them this was unnecessary, they professed disbelief: "No grown man can last for more than one day without a woman. Come on, we'll take you in your car, you drive." They were being merry of course, but not facetious.

This erotic fixation is the phallic component of manhood, and for simplicity's sake, I call it *virility*. It constitutes the first and most flamboyant symbol of manliness. As well as providing a unitary and global theme to the subject in Andalusia—a shared understanding—it deviates somewhat from other instances of "machismo" such as the North American, so far as I understand it. For most Andalusians, physical power, feats of strength and bravery are not considered part of "being macho." Indeed, pugilistic prowess, fighting, issuing challenges, or taking silly risks with life and limb, and so on are highly devalued. In Andalusia, men cherish a deep culture of civility which preludes displays of bravado or belligerence. Similarly, toughness and athleticism, which seem to loom large in America, are scorned as childish and vulgar. Rarely does one see physical confrontations among Andalusians—a fact that other ethnographers working in the area have noticed. In the pueblo of Almonaster (Huelva Province), there exists "a total proscription on all expression of overt hostility. There are no angry shouts, scuffles, offenses to property, or even stumbling drunks on the streets" (Aguilera 1990: 13). In Santaella (in neighboring Cordoba Province), "the actual use of fighting is rare and people strongly devalue fighting" (Driessen 1983: 129). The same is true in Fuentes. In twenty years of working there I never witnessed a single physical fight or even a brief scrap among men. The idea of a "barroom brawl" is anathema to these genteel, courteous folk.

## OTHER "MACHISMOS"

Given the above, we should perhaps pause here to take note of the very salient discontinuities between Spanish machismo and the so-called machismos of other places and times. First of all we have a semantic problem. In my opinion, the ethno-label "machismo," like other sociological words such as "unilinear" or "matrilocal" is in danger of becoming reified aprioristically into a pigeonhole, an example of lexical "butterfly collecting." There are many variants of hyper-masculinity codes throughout the world. All of them have something in common, perhaps (because men have to "do something" to prove themselves; there are tests of manliness, etc.); but all have widely different emphases and nuances. It is true that cognate forms have been reported throughout the Spanish-speaking world, especially in Mexico, and so a supposedly monolithic "Hispanic machismo" has been held up as a kind of classic model for comparative purposes (see, for example, Lewis 1961; Ingham 1964: 96). One must point out, however, that even the model of Mexican machismo has been subject to its own critical scrutiny lately and come in for a drubbing as being ethnocentric (Gutmann 1996, 1997). There is also, for example, the Sicilian *maschio* or manliness code (Giovannini 1987: 66) and the *rajula* complex of swaggering Moroccan youths (Mernissi 1975; Geertz 1979), the violent *wand-nat* concept of Ethiopian tribesmen, and the bellicose *pwara* masculinity cult of the Trukese islanders in the South Pacific (Marshall 1979; for more examples, see Gilmore 1990; Gutmann 1997). Most of these male codes have been explicitly likened to "Mexican machismo" by their observers; and indeed the ubiquitous use of the Spanish term tends to conflate variants under that vague rubric (for a review, see Gilmore and Uhl 1987).

In most of these variants of machismo, of course, fighting and violence play a big role. For example in the Truk case, the youths demonstrate their manly *pwara* by Kung Fu combat and in weekend fistfights, and some Ethiopians show their *wand-nat* in whipping battles and by beating each other up (Levine 1966; Reminick 1982). In Sicily, Sardinia, and Greece, men may engage in violent vendettas and feuds, and may they steal each other's sheep or compete in singing and dancing contests, or engage in verbal duels, and so on (Campbell 1964; Herzfeld 1985; Sorge 2007). But in the Andalusian variety, for whatever historical reasons, violence is specifically excluded from the ideal, and as we have seen "ser macho" is fixated purely upon erotic prowess and is directed only at women (possibly the same historical actors have militated also against the violent mafias that one finds, for example in southern Italy). In other words, an Andalusian man cannot act "macho" with *only* other men present. To be macho in Andalusia needs a woman as sexual object, a *tertium*

*pro quid.* All this brings us to the second component in manliness, which I call "valor." Here, physical bravery, and in some extreme cases, even fighting, may play a role. But such behaviors are not part of the Andalusian meaning of "macho."[2]

## VALOR: BRAVERY

An emphasis on civility limits belligerence in Andalusia to a degree unknown among men in many places. But, civility notwithstanding, men in Andalusia are expected to stand up for what they believe in and to show determination in the face of danger, even if this means a fight. But this is a different matter from machismo. It constitutes a totally distinct semantic subclass of manliness, one analogous to what we might call "heroism." In Spain, in casual conversation they call a man "strong" (*un hombre fuerte*), if he stands up for himself and specifically, protects his dependents. When a man shows moral courage, they call it "valiant" (*valiente*). Valor constitutes our second component of masculinity. The qualities connoted add up to charisma. Together these criteria have their own name: *hombría*, or simply, "manhood." A man can be valorous and thus have hombría and not be a "macho" and vice versa. *Hombría* was a subject that men were somewhat less enthusiastic to talk about, but it came up in discussions later in my fieldwork; some of which are described below.

First, when my friends and I began conversations relating to courage as opposed to machismo, many resorted to a concrete example of the bullfighter (matador). One must note the matador does not fight other men, but shows—as Hemingway put it in his Spanish stories—grace under pressure. Perhaps the difference between North American machismo, as I understand it, is that for most Andalusians, bravery is not played out in contests with rivals, but rather against the inimical forces of nature, against injustice, or against adversity in the workplace. An important ingredient here is the sense of duty or obligation. This theme is often conveyed when my friends (male and female) would say that a "real man" was one who worked hard under harsh or perilous conditions and who never complained, never ran away, who was "a hard worker" and who made "sacrifices" for his family. When I spoke to women about masculinity, they often referred to this abstract quality: a real man works hard, they said, never complains, and brings home the bacon. We hear such sentiments in working-class cultures in America also, and in many other places around the world where men are expected to do their duty (a man's gotta do what a man's gotta do). The word "dignity" (*dignidad*) is often invoked in this context.

Men sometimes compete about *hombría*; so it can indeed involve contests between men. As a form of heroism, hombría is shown off in multitudinous ways. For instance, in Fuentes, a group of young men, usually after a few late drinks at a bar, will meander down to the municipal cemetery to exhibit their disdain for ghosts and goblins. On their way the boys will acquire a hammer and a nail or a metal spike pinched from some garbage heap or borrowed from someone's toolbox. After arriving at the cemetery and climbing over the five-foot high wall, they posture drunkenly for a while, then one of them pounds the spike into the cemetery's stucco wall, while reciting the following formula:

| | |
|---|---|
| Aqui hinco clavo | Here I drive in a spike |
| Del tio monero | Before goblin or sprite |
| Venga quien venga, | And whoever appear, |
| Aqui lo espero! | I remain without fear! |

The last man to flee wins the laurels as the bravest. Occasionally, I was told, young men may challenge one another to spend the night in the cemetery, but otherwise hombría is non-confrontational, as in the above instance in which the threat is displaced onto a supernatural object. Men and boys do not fight each other in shows of athletic prowess or even compete much in aggressive sports or games, although young boys do play soccer. One-on-one competition among older men is confined largely to dominoes, cards, competitive drinking and, ironically, generous barroom "inviting," as we saw above. The Hollywood "tough-guy" had little resonance in Andalusia. "Only Americans and Germans shove each other around like that," the men told me dryly. Of course, Spaniards slaughtered each other during the Civil War, but a line is drawn between the unavoidable violence of war and the civility of peacetime.

## HOMBRÍA AND "HONOR"

Julian Pitt-Rivers, who worked in Andalusia in the 1940s and 1950s, has perhaps depicted this quality of valor/hombría best: "The quintessence of manliness is fearlessness," he writes, "a readiness to defend one's own pride and that of one's family" (1971: 89). Perhaps the best way to get the idea across is to quote an old Andalusian saying which conveys the image both metaphorically and ironically in a typical Andalusian inversion: "El hombre como el oso, lo mas feo, lo mas hermoso." A rough translation: "Men are like bears, the uglier they are, the handsomer." What this means is that, unlike women, men are not supposed to be pretty or charming. Rather, a man should be strong, resolute, and determined, and even perhaps a little feisty (I call this "The beauty of the beast").[3] Masculine "beauty" is a moral, not an aesthetic, value, consisting of a man's ability to inspire respect—even fear—in the observer, rather than sympathy or love.

Unfortunately, the emphasis on valor has sometimes been, mistakenly I believe, conflated with the obsolete notion of a belligerent "honor." For Pitt-Rivers for example, honor in Andalusia as elsewhere in the Mediterranean World is a gender-bound quality, or "sex-linked." Only men have honor. The most important attribute of honor, in this traditional view, is that it forms the main public arena for a competitive masculinity based upon the sexual modesty of one's kinswomen. As Pitt-Rivers (1977: 45) remarks, "The honor of a man is involved . . . in the sexual purity of his mother, wife, and sisters." Another expert on Andalusian male norms and the author of *Metaphors of Masculinity* (1980), Stanley Brandes seems to concur in his study of a pueblo in nearby Jaen Province. He points out (1980: 75) that "a woman's sexual purity must be maintained lest her entire family's image be tainted. It is the husband's prime responsibility to control the conduct of his wife and daughter. If the females should go astray, their behavior reflects as much on him as on them." I found that in Fuentes, it was the mother, not the father, who policed the sexual morality of her daughter, but no matter. One finds similar statements in virtually all the works on Andalusia, rural and urban. Men are like bears in this regard: fierce in defense of self and kin. Most important in all this is the defense of ones' women. This is the one arena in which violence may be acceptable. One recent and well-reported incident will perhaps illustrate this.

In February of 2000, hundreds of men in and around the Andalusian pueblo of El Ejido (Almería Province) went on a violent rampage, attacking immigrant north Africans who had come to their district to take low-paying jobs in agriculture that the newly affluent Spaniards had rejected. This riot was not altogether spontaneous. The men had organized their attack days before, and armed with sticks and clubs chased, beat and pummeled Africans throughout the region. The depredations went on savagely for three days: one Moroccan man was beaten to death and many others injured before the national police intervened to stop the riot. What triggered the incident, according to local accounts, was the rape and murder of Spanish woman a few days earlier, after which a Moroccan immigrant had been arrested and charged with the crime. Interestingly enough, tensions had been running high between the Spaniards and the north Africans for months, even years, before the riot, but these had never erupted into a full-scale lynch mob attack. Interviewed later, some of the rioters spoke openly about their motives, saying that economic competition played no role in their anger, but that it was the violation of a local woman by the outsiders that caused them to react. "They can't abuse our women and get away with it," one of the men said with heat, "we're men: we have to do something." Apparently, such motives still play a role in Andalusian male culture.[4]

I finish this section with a final comment about manliness-as-valor. In Andalusia, hombría has one additional element, which is probably a political legacy of the Franco dictatorship. In the waning years of Franco, hombría could be demonstrated by active defiance of the regime, by standing up to the secret police or the paramilitary Civil Guard. It was often shown among workers who organized the clandestine unions and who refused to back down in labor disputes— these acts were praised not only as politically correct, but also as manly. Heroes of the labor movement (of whatever class) were called *valiente* and were said to be *muy hombre* (very manly). Charismatic labor leaders, especially those jailed and tortured under Franco, like Marcelino Camacho, the head of the underground Communist Party, were highly praised in this regard, almost as icons of hombría. I found it of interest that, no matter what a man's political viewpoint, most would admit the manliness of an opponent who showed courage in the face of overwhelming odds.

One concrete instance from Fuentes may help. During the years after the Civil War (1936–1939) a famous ex-Republican lived in Fuentes, and was known throughout the village by his nickname "El Robustiano" (his real name was never used as far as I knew). Literally this moniker means "the Robust One," but can best be rendered as "Hero" or perhaps more colloquially as "The Big Guy." He was so called for his height (he was almost six feet tall in a land of smallish people), and known his for political savvy and physical courage. After serving in the Loyalist Army and serving a prison term afterwards, Robustiano returned to Fuentes and began the militant labor agitation that made him famous ever since. Even while he suffered fierce persecution during the Franco dictatorship, he continued to defy the police again and again, serving numerous prison terms, undergoing torture both physical and mental. But all the beatings, threats and blackballing had no effect on him. After each jail term he returned martyr-like to the struggle. He was also known never to have betrayed a comrade, to have taken beatings with equanimity, and indeed he won admiration from all sides, including his jailors, one of who I actually met, who effused about his erstwhile victim. Robustiano developed a huge and active following in the town until his death in 1969 and is remembered to this day (2007) as a "man among men." My friends told me he represented the ideal of hombría and it was great pity that I never

got to meet him (I arrived in Fuentes three years after his death). It also helped his reputation that his wife and three daughters were beyond reproach—chaste and virginal respectively. Also in his favor was that he had fathered nine children in all, and most importantly, six sons—a sure sign of virility, because having many sons is—for reasons always unclear to me—a crowning glory of manhood. So here, the man personified both attributes of Andalusian masculinity discussed so far: the sexual and the moral, a paragon of both the machismo and valor components of manhood.

## VIRTUE: MANHOOD AND COURTESY

Finally we come to the third and last ingredient in the Andalusian masculinity ideal, which I will call for simplicity's sake *virtue.* As I mentioned above, the notion of a classical "honor" has little resonance with men in Andalusia today. Nevertheless, townsmen do speak of an analogous criterion, a moral formality, which they reckon to be as important to a man's status as being virile and valiant. This final quality is what they call being "honrado," which literally means honorable, but having the connotation in Fuentes of rectitude and personal probity; that is, it means taking one's obligations seriously and paying back one's debts, and doing so with promptness and dignity. It relates to character and also what we might call "attitude." For example, early in my fieldwork, when I asked my friends if a certain man I knew in town was "honorable" (using the term that Pitt-Rivers made so much of), I was informed that if I meant "honest," then yes, this man measured up. They said as far as they knew, he paid his debts and he returned favors reliably and courteously. Going further, they noted that, for example, in his regular bar, this man would routinely enter into exchanges of drinks and do his fair share of what they call "*invitas*" (invitations); that is, if someone bought him a drink, he would reciprocate ("invite") them back sooner or later. Honesty of this sort is crucially important to man's standing and especially in his circle of peers, wherein lies community judgment. The true measure of virtue in this sense is communicated in what Brandes calls "the estimates of personal decency" (1980: 48). In this sense it differs little from the standard English "honest" or "creditable." It has little to do with one's sexual prowess and nothing to do with bravery. Nevertheless it is intimately bound up with manliness and forms a third, independent variable of the Andalusian manhood jigsaw puzzle. The negative pole of honorability is *vergüenza,* or "shame." If a man has the requisite quality of shame, that is, has a decent respect for the opinion of others, he complies with expectations and is therefore honorable. The unethical, dishonest, man has no shame and callously ignores obligations, thumbing his nose at public opinion. He has a "hard face" (*cara dura*), they say. In this regard, Andalusian notions of decency can be elaborated further as an integral aspect of character. Its internal mechanism and social (thus measurable) manifestation is a punctilious reciprocity, which is usually balanced and predictable. Whether monetary or not, repayments of goods and services are often calculated to an amazing degree of exactitude, but just as often they are vague and approximate. In any event, returns of favors are carried out on the community public stage, in public places like streets and bars, conspicuously, but always in the spirit of nonchalance, without ostentation, as though the matter were but a trifle. Obviously reference should be made here to what Michael Herzfeld and others have called "Mediterranean hospitality" (Herzfeld 1989), a common denominator around the Mediterranean and known to the ancient Greeks and modern Arabs. These rituals of generosity are exclusively male. Women never enter the bars except for holidays and are always accompanied by a man. Women do not "invite" in bars or anywhere else; given the conservative sexual code in rural villages like Fuentes, women are not "invited" by unrelated men. Bar invitations are thus entirely male, and an integral part of a man's "connectedness" to society and his public face.

Having observed these exchanges and begun to participate in them, I soon became aware that there were many contexts in which men were expected to get involved, and in so doing to publicly demonstrate trustworthiness. The main context is the arena of the public house (bars, taverns, coffee houses, casinos, and clubs). Every man in Fuentes has a neighborhood dive where he hangs out for at least three or four hours a day, meets with cronies, palavers incessantly, and does business. Thus comfortably ensconced, he participates in the requisite rituals of exchange. These exchanges look and "feel" casual to the first-time observer, yet are deadly earnest. Always accompanying bar conviviality are serious rounds of what anthropologists call "tournaments of value," (Appadurai 1986). In Spain, these tournaments of value consist of offerings of drinks and cigarettes, usually accompanied by much backslapping and glad-handing. Although seemingly disinterested, barroom exchanges are governed by a subtle, but ironclad etiquette. While no one would ever say so openly, it is a crass transgression to accept more than a drink or two without reciprocating. As the evening proceeds, everyone makes out more or less evenly in the long run. In the circular movement of commodities, what counts most is the display of disinterested generosity and "playing the game," that is, not holding back. For a man to withhold, to hesitate, to stint, or to respond grudgingly, is to court opprobrium as a cheat and a rogue. If a man continually fails to play his part, he is quickly labeled a *sinvergüenza*, a shameless guy. Worse is the *sinvergüenzón* (a big flagrant shameless), someone who is notorious for toadying, no better than a thief. Considering the pervasiveness of bar gossip, such labeling quickly leads to general censure, and this can sometimes result in social ostracism. Hence, most men voluntarily abjure a calculus of personal aggrandizement in bar society for it can lead to economic paralysis, since no one wants to cooperate with a *sinvergüenzón*. If a man is niggardly in bars, the logic goes, he will be equally if not more untrustworthy in business deals. How all this relates to judgments about manliness is explained below.

When I inquired about what motivated all these little offerings, I was told that the point was not the object given to another, but the generosity so evidenced, and that indeed generosity was the gold standard by which character was judged. The operative principle involved is "personality." The *fontaniegos* evaluate a man's personality once again on a binary scale as either *abierto* ("open") or *cerrado* ("closed"). Although there can be degrees, I quickly noticed that most men considered the open/closed measure in absolute and oppositional terms, either/or. So when speaking of an absent party, people would usually say that he was either of an "open" or "closed" personality. Such judgments were, again, often consensual, rigid, and immutable. One of course could be "very open" or "very closed," but not slightly open or closed. (Incidentally, women were never judged by this idiom, as these words would have devastating sexual connotations for a woman in a pueblo). An "open fellow" (*un tio abierto*) is generous to a fault, convivial, gregarious, rapidly reciprocating a favor. A closed guy is sour, stingy, evasive, furtive, louche. Decisions were based largely on simple degree of *social participation*. A man who "gets involved" in the raucous conviviality of the bars and who pays back debts was open; one who kept himself apart, refused to engage, or failed to reciprocate was closed.

All of this may seem axiomatic: one finds similar judgments in most societies where men cooperate. However, it soon became clear to me that such evaluations went deeper than character assessment and touched upon a man's reputation as manly or not. A man who stayed away from the bars, or who held back his purse, or who spent "too much time" indoors avoiding male society, was regarded not only as closed and delinquent, a *sinvergüenza*, squalid, but also as unmanly, as effeminate. One unhappy example will demonstrate this connection between personality and manliness.

There lived an odd fellow in Fuentes named Alfredo Tissot, a commercial broker. I got to know him rather well, since he lived on my street, but he was scorned by my other friends as a recluse and a miser (the Catalan-sounding name did not help). What made him really repugnant was his avoidance of the bars and of men's circles in general. Alfredo was that rarity in Andalusia: an uxorious homebody, a sit-by-the-fire. In consequence he was a virtually friendless man. Although aware of men's expectations, he resisted them, because, as he confided to me, such goings-on were not only a waste of time, but also expensive: he watched his pennies and hated the profligacy of the barroom. So he preferred staying at home with his family—a wife and two adolescent daughters—reading books, watching television, or going over his accounts. I should add that he was a relatively successful businessman, indeed quite affluent by local standards, and therefore all the more susceptible to demands and expectations for generosity.

Walking past his house one day with a coterie of my friends, I was treated to a rare tirade that intensified into a crescendo of abuse. "What kind of man is he anyway," said one, nodding at his sealed and cloistered home, "Spending every second at home like that?" The others took up the cue, savaging the loner for his defects, likening him to a "brooding hen" and to a "mother cow" and other female animals. They insinuated a number of character flaws, most egregiously stinginess and furtiveness, misanthropy and avarice; but beyond these surface defects they alluded to something worse: a failure at man-acting. Intensifying the character assassination, my friends left the domain of the observable and ventured into the realm of speculation, which is common when a man is judged faulty. We proceeded up the street and the men offered their suspicions about this pathetic scapegoat. It all boiled down, they said, to his failure to be a man. This was demonstrated by his shadowy introversion, his hermit-like, withdrawn lifestyle. When I asked if his self-removal could be attributable to business requirements, I was hooted down with denunciations of "a guy who will not invite, who never goes to the bars!" "He's the worst closed," they continued, "hoarding, never participating; selfish, petty." The others seconded this and began scurrilous speculations as to the deviant's sexual preferences, some insinuating homosexuality or some sordid clandestine perversion which might explain his evasion of manliness. In all this, Tissot was paying the price for his withdrawal from the man's world. Being "closed," he must also be self-protective, introverted, guarded—traits associated with women, who must protect their chastity by social withdrawal and evasion; hence the comparison to hens and cows. One may, of course, appreciate the Freudian symbolism here of the open-closed metaphors with their anatomical suggestiveness without being psychologically reductive about it.

## SUMMARY AND CONCLUSIONS

When I first went to Spain, like many foreigners, I was duly impressed by displays of machismo. I soon noted however that Andalusian machismo differed from notions of masculinity in my culture (middle-class America) and in many others in its erotic intensity. But the main lesson I learned is not that machismo defines manhood in Spain, but, ironically, that one cannot speak of "manhood" in Andalusia by reference just to machismo. Machismo is a necessary but not sufficient ingredient in the Andalusian code of the real man. As I have tried to show, being a real man signifies (in Goodenough's term) a complex bundle of behavioral subclasses, the interplay of which results in a carefully cultivated dynamic—a multi-layered system of checks and balances. As I came to understand it, the measure of manliness in Andalusia is a three-fold package, a triumvirate of do's and don't's.

The first component is *virility* (this is what the Andalusians themselves mean when they speak of macho). It connotes sexual potency—a sexual fire in the belly. Although Americans might call this "machismo" and leave it at that, in Spain it has none of the American overtones of belligerence and risk taking. The second component is what I have called *valor*. Valor implies intestinal fortitude and tenacity—doggedness in the face of adversity. The final piece in the jigsaw puzzle is a more ambiguous concept which I call *virtue*. In Andalusia, this is measured by a man's enthusiasm in public dealings: his generosity, his honesty, his courtesy and his participation in masculine pursuits. If a man wants to be truly manly, seducing women is not enough. He must adhere strictly to rules of civility and must engage in lavish public generosity. These rules tend to prohibit or at least limit confrontations among men and they put a damper on sexual competitions and misdeeds, and so there are built-in inhibitors against antisocial behavior. Each of the three components, virility, valor, and virtue, plays its own necessary role in the evaluation a "manly man." Each component operates alongside, and in tandem with, the others.

What all this complexity shows, perhaps, is the obvious conclusion that gender evaluations in places like Spain are part of a broader moral calculus which men negotiate on an everyday basis and in a variety of contexts. From this we can conclude that in many societies, Hispanic or otherwise, anyone who wants to understand gender codes must be aware of the context in which judgments are made, and must also understand the rules governing personality assessment. Even in a famously macho land like Spain, men do not live by machismo alone.

## NOTES

1. My fieldwork in Spain, conducted intermittently between 1971 and 2003, was supported by grants and fellowships from the following institutions: the National Science Foundation, the National Endowment for the Humanities, the H. F. Guggenheim Foundation, the J. S. Guggenheim Foundation, the American Philosophical Society, the Council for Exchange of Scholars, and the Program for Cultural Cooperation between Spain's Ministry of Culture and U.S. universities. I thank these agencies for their generosity.

2. The best monograph on Andalusian machismo is that of Stanley Brandes (1980). For a comparative view from neighboring southern Portugal, see the interesting book by Vale de Almeida (1992). Matthew Gutmann attempts to debunk "Hispanic machismo" as an ethnocentric fantasy or a sexist conspiracy with varying degrees of success (1996, 1997).

3. For more on the notion of masculine "beauty" and its relationship to concepts of manliness in various cultures, see Gilmore (1994).

4. The riots were reported in all local papers, in the Malaga paper *Correos de Andalucia*, in the Madrid daily *El Pais*, and in the *New York Times*. The quotation is excerpted from interviews taken by the author in October 2006 in El Ejido.

## REFERENCES

Abu-Lughod, Lila. 1993. *Writing Women's Worlds*. Berkeley CA: University of California Press.

Aguilera, Francisco. 1990. *Santa Eulalia's People: Ritual, Structure and Process in an Andalusian Multicommunity*, 2nd edition. Prospect Heights, IL: West Publishing Co.

Appadurai, Arjun. 1986. "Introduction: Commodities and the Politics of Value." In Arjun Appadurai (ed.). *The Social Life of Things*, pp. 3–63. Cambridge, UK: Cambridge University Press.

Brandes, Stanley. 1980. *Metaphors of Masculinity: Sex and Status in Andalusian Folklore*. Philadelphia: University of Pennsylvania Press.

Campbell, John. 1964. *Honour, Family and Patronage*. Oxford, UK: Clarendon Press.

Driessen, Henk. 1983. "Male Sociability and Rituals of Masculinity in Andalusia." *Anthropological Quarterly* 56: 125–133.

Geertz, Hildred. 1979. "The Meanings of Family Ties." In Clifford Goertz et al. (eds.). *Meaning and Order in Moroccan Society*, pp. 315–386. New York: Cambridge University Press.

Gilmore, David. 1990. *Manhood in the Making*. New Haven, CT: Yale University Press.

_____. 1994. "The Beauty of the Beast: Male Body Imagery in Anthropological Perspective." In M. G. Winkler and L. B. Cole (eds.). *The Good Body: Asceticism in Contemporary Culture*, pp. 191–214. New Haven, CT: Yale University Press.

Gilmore, David, and Sarah Uhl. 1987. "Further Notes on Andalusian Machismo." *Journal of Psychoanalytic Anthropology* 10: 341–360.

Giovannini, Maureen. 1987. "Female Chastity Codes in the Circum-Mediterranean: Comparative Perspectives." In David Gilmore (ed.). *Honor and Shame and Unity of the Mediterranean*, pp. 60–73. Washington, DC: American Anthropological Association, special publication no. 22.

Gonzalez-Lopez, Gloria, and Matthew C. Gutmann. 2005. "Machismo." In M. C. Horowitz (ed.). *New Dictionary of Ideas*, Volume 4, pp. 1328–1330. New York: Thomson Gale.

Goodenough, Ward. 1970. *Description and Comparison in Cultural Anthropology*. Chicago: Aldine.

Gutmann, Matthew. 1996. *The Meanings of Macho: Being a Man in Mexico City*. Berkeley: University of California Press.

_____. 1997. "Trafficking in Men: The Anthropology of Masculinity." *Annual Reviews in Anthropology* 26: 385–409.

Herzfeld, Michael. 1985. *The Poetics of Manhood*. Princeton, NJ: Princeton University Press.

_____. 1989. *Anthropology Through the Looking Glass*. Cambridge, UK: Cambridge University Press.

Ingham, John. 1964. "The Bullfighters." *American Imago* 21: 85–102.

Levine, Donald. 1966. "The Concept of Masculinity in Ethiopian Culture." *International Journal of Social Psychiatry* 12: 17–23.

Lewis, Oscar. 1961. *The Children of Sanchez*. New York: Random House.

Marshall, Mac. 1979. *Weekend Warriors*. Palo Alto, CA: Mayfield.

Mernissi, Fatima. 1975. *Beyond the Veil: Male-Female Dynamics in a Modern Muslim Society*. New York: Schenkman.

Pina-Cabral, João. 1989. "Mediterranean Studies." *Current Anthropology* 30: 399–406.

Pitt-Rivers, Julian. 1971. *The People of the Sierra*. Chicago: University of Chicago Press.

_____. 1977. *The Fate of Shechem, or the Politics of Sex: Essays in the Anthropology of the Mediterranean*. Cambridge, UK: Cambridge University Press.

Press, Irwin. 1979. *The City as Context: Urbanism and Behavioral Constraints in Seville*. Urbana: University of Illinois Press.

Reich, Jackie. 2004. *Beyond the Latin Lover*. Bloomington: Indiana University Press.

Reminick, Ronald. 1982. "The Sport of Warriors on the Wane." In William Morgan (ed.). *Sport and the Humanities*, pp. 31–36. Knoxville, TN: Bureau of Educational Research.

Sorge, Antonio. 2007. *The Free Highlands: Honour, Identity, and Change in Central Sardinia*. Calgary: Department of Anthropology, University of Calgary. Unpublished Ph.D. Dissertation.

Suarez-Orozco, Marcelo, and A. Dundes. 1984. "The Piropo and the Dual Image of Women in the Spanish-Speaking World." *Journal of Latin Lore* 10: 111–133.

Vale de Almeida, Miguel. 1992. *The Hegemonic Male: Masculinity in a Portuguese Town*. Providence, RI: Berghahn.

# *Rituals of Manhood:*
## Male Initiation in Papua New Guinea

### *Gilbert H. Herdt*

Sambia are a mountain-dwelling hunting and horticultural people who number some 2,000 persons and inhabit one of New Guinea's most rugged terrains. The population is dispersed through narrow river valleys over a widespread, thinly populated rain forest; rainfall is heavy; and even today the surrounding mountain ranges keep the area isolated. Sambia live on the fringes of the Highlands, but they trace their origins to the Papua hinterlands; their culture and economy thus reflect a mixture of influences from both of those areas. Hunting still predominates as a masculine activity through which most meat protein is acquired. As in the Highlands, though, sweet potatoes and taro are the staple crops, and their cultivation is for the most part women's work. Pigs are few, and they have no ceremonial or exchange significance; indigenous marsupials, such as possum and tree kangaroo, provide necessary meat prestations for all initiations and ceremonial feasts (cf. Meigs 1976).

Sambia settlements are small, well-defended, mountain clan hamlets. These communities comprise locally based descent groups organized through a strong agnatic idiom. Residence is patrivirilocal, and most men actually reside in their father's hamlets. Clans are exogamous, and one or more of them together constitute a hamlet's landowning corporate agnatic body. These men also form a localized warriorhood that is sometimes allied with other hamlets in matters of fighting, marriage, and ritual. Each hamlet contains one or two men's clubhouses, in addition to women's houses, and the men's ritual life centers on their clubhouse. Marriage is usually by sister exchange or infant betrothal, although the latter form of prearranged marriage is culturally preferred. Intrahamlet marriage is occasionally more frequent (up to 50 percent of all marriages in my own hamlet field site) than one would expect in such small segmentary groupings, an involutional pattern weakened since pacification.

Sambia male and female residential patterns differ somewhat from those of other Highlands peoples. The nuclear family is an important subunit of the hamlet-based extended family of interrelated clans. A man, his

wife, and their children usually cohabit within a single, small, round hut. Children are thus reared together by their parents during the early years of life, so the nuclear family is a residential unit, an institution virtually unknown to the Highlands (Meggitt 1964; Read 1954). Sometimes this unit is expanded through polygyny, in which case a man, his cowives, and their children may occupy the single dwelling. Girls continue to reside with their parents until marriage (usually near the menarche, around fifteen to seventeen years of age). Boys, however, are removed to the men's clubhouse at seven to ten years of age, following their first-stage initiation. There they reside exclusively until marriage and cohabitation years later. Despite familial cohabitation in early childhood, strict taboos based on beliefs about menstrual pollution still separate men and women in their sleeping and eating arrangements.

Warfare used to be constant and nagging among Sambia, and it conditioned the values and masculine stereotypes surrounding the male initiatory cult. Ritualized bow fights occurred among neighboring hamlets, whose members still intermarried and usually initiated their sons together. At the same time, though, hamlets also united against enemy tribes and in staging war parties against them. Hence, warfare, marriage, and initiation were interlocking institutions; the effect of this political instability was to reinforce tough, strident masculine performance in most arenas of social life. "Strength" (*jerundu*) was—and is—a pivotal idea in this male ethos. Indeed, strength, which has both ethnobiological and behavioral aspects, could be aptly translated as "maleness" and "manliness." Strength has come to be virtually synonymous with idealized conformity to male ritual routine. Before conquest and pacification by the Australians, though, strength had its chief performative significance in one's conduct on the battlefield. Even today bitter reminders of war linger on among the Sambia; and we should not forget that it is against the harsh background of the warrior's existence that Sambia initiate their boys, whose only perceived protection against the inconstant world is their own unbending masculinity.

Initiation rests solely in the hands of the men's secret society. It is this organization that brings the collective initiatory cycle into being as jointly performed by neighboring hamlets (and as constrained by their own chronic bow fighting). The necessary feast-crop

Reprinted with permission from Gilbert H. Herdt, *Rituals of Manhood: Male Initiation in Papua New Guinea* (Berkeley, University of California Press, 1982), pp. 50–57. Copyright © 1982 The Regents of the University of California.

gardens, ritual leadership, and knowledge dictate that a handful of elders, war leaders, and ritual experts be in full command of the actual staging of the event. Everyone and all else are secondary.

There are six intermittent initiations from the ages of seven to ten and onward. They are, however, constituted and conceptualized as two distinct cultural systems within the male life cycle. First-stage (*moku*, at seven to ten years of age), second-stage (*imbutu*, at ten to thirteen years), and third-stage (*ipmangwi*, at thirteen to sixteen years) initiations—bachelorhood rites—are collectively performed for regional groups of boys as age-mates. The initiations are held in sequence, as age-graded advancements; the entire sequel takes months to perform. The focus of all these initiations is the construction and habitation of a great cult house (*moo-angu*) on a traditional dance ground; its ceremonialized building inaugurates the whole cycle. Fourth-stage (*nuposha:* sixteen years and onward), fifth-stage (*taiketnyi*), and sixth-stage (*moondangu*) initiations are, conversely, individually centered events not associated with the confederacy of interrelated hamlets, cult house, or dance ground. Each of these initiations, like the preceding ones, does have its own ritual status, social role, and title, as noted. The triggering event for the latter three initiations, unlike that for the bachelorhood rites, is not the building of a cult house or a political agreement of hamlets to act collectively but is rather the maturing femininity and life-crisis events of the women assigned in marriage to youths (who become the initiated novices). Therefore, fourth-stage initiation is only a semipublic activity organized by the youths' clansmen (and some male affines). Its secret purificatory and other rites are followed by the formal marriage ceremony in the hamlet. Fifth-stage initiation comes at a woman's menarche, when her husband is secretly introduced to additional purification and sexual techniques. Sixth-stage initiation issues from the birth of a man's wife's first child. This event is, de jure, the attainment of manhood. (The first birth is elaborately ritualized and celebrated; the next three births are also celebrated, but in more truncated fashion.) Two children bring full adulthood (*aatmwunu*) for husband and wife alike. Birth ceremonies are suspended after the fourth birth, since there is no reason to belabor what is by now obvious: a man has proved himself competent in reproduction. This sequence of male initiations forms the basis for male development, and it underlies the antagonistic tenor of relationships between the sexes.

It needs stating only once that men's secular rhetoric and ritual practices depict women as dangerous and polluting inferiors whom men are to distrust throughout their lives. In this regard, Sambia values and relationships pit men against women even more markedly, I think, than occurs in other Highlands communities

(cf. Brown and Buchbinder 1976; Meggitt 1964; Read 1954). Men hold themselves as the superiors of women in physique, personality, and social position. And this dogma of male supremacy permeates all social relationships and institutions, likewise coloring domestic behavior among the sexes (cf. Tuzin 1980 for an important contrast). Men fear not only pollution from contact with women's vaginal fluids and menstrual blood but also the depletion of their semen, the vital spark of maleness, which women (and boys, too) inevitably extract, sapping a man's substance. These are among the main themes of male belief underlying initiation.

The ritualized simulation of maleness is the result of initiation, and men believe the process to be vital for the nature and nurture of manly growth and well-being. First-stage initiation begins the process in small boys. Over the ensuing ten to fifteen years, until marriage, cumulative initiations and residence in the men's house are said to promote biological changes that firmly cement the growth from childhood to manhood. Nature provides male genitals, it is true; but nature alone does not bestow the vital spark biologically necessary for stimulating masculine growth or demonstrating cold-blooded self-preservation.

New Guinea specialists will recognize in the Sambia belief system a theme that links it to the comparative ethnography of male initiation and masculine development: the use of ritual procedures for sparking, fostering, and maintaining manliness in males (see Berndt 1962; Meigs 1976; Newman 1964, 1965; Poole 1981; Read 1965; Salisbury 1965; Strathern 1969, 1970). Sambia themselves refer to the results of first-stage collective initiation—our main interest—as a means of "growing a boy"; and this trend of ritual belief is particularly emphatic.

Unlike ourselves, Sambia perceive no imminent, naturally driven fit between one's birthright sex and one's gender identity or role.[1] Indeed, the problem (and it is approached as a situation wanting a solution) is implicitly and explicitly understood in quite different terms. The solution is also different for the two sexes: men believe that a girl is born with all of the vital organs and fluids necessary for her to attain reproductive competence through "natural" maturation. This conviction is embodied in cultural perceptions of the girl's development beginning with the sex assignment at birth. What distinguishes a girl (*tai*) from a boy (*kwulai'u*) is obvious: "A boy has a penis, and a girl does not," men say. Underlying men's communications is a conviction that maleness, unlike femaleness, is not a biological given. It must be artificially induced through secret ritual; and that is a personal achievement.

The visible manifestations of girls' fast-growing reproductive competence, noticed first in early motor coordination and speech and then later in the rapid attainment of height and secondary sex traits (e.g., breast development), are attributed to inner biological properties. Girls possess a menstrual-blood organ, or *tingu*, said to precipitate all those events and the menarche. Boys, on the other hand, are thought to possess an inactive *tingu*. They do possess, however, another organ— the *kere-ku-kereku*, or semen organ—that is thought to be the repository of semen, the very essence of maleness and masculinity; but this organ is not functional at birth, since it contains no semen naturally and can only store, never produce, any. Only oral insemination, men believe, can activate the boy's semen organ, thereby precipitating his push into adult reproductive competence. In short, femininity unfolds naturally, whereas masculinity must be achieved; and here is where the male ritual cult steps in.

Men also perceive the early socialization risks of boys and girls in quite different terms. All infants are closely bonded to their mothers. Out of a woman's contaminating, life-giving womb pours the baby, who thereafter remains tied to the woman's body, breast milk, and many ministrations. This latter contact only reinforces the femininity and female contamination in which birth involves the infant. Then, too, the father, both because of postpartum taboos and by personal choice, tends to avoid being present at the breast-feedings. Mother thus becomes the unalterable primary influence; father is a weak second. Sambia say this does not place girls at a "risk"—they simply succumb to the drives of their "natural" biology. This maternal attachment and paternal distance clearly jeopardize the boys' growth, however, since nothing innate within male maturation seems to resist the inhibiting effects of mothers' femininity. Hence boys must be traumatically separated—wiped clean of their female contaminants—so that their masculinity may develop.

Homosexual fellatio inseminations can follow this separation but cannot precede it, for otherwise they would go for naught. The accumulating semen, injected time and again for years, is believed crucial for the formation of biological maleness and masculine comportment. This native perspective is sufficiently novel to justify our using a special concept for aiding description and analysis of the data: masculinization (Herdt 1981: 255294). Hence I shall refer to the overall process that involves separating a boy from his mother, initiating him, ritually treating his body, administering homosexual inseminations, his biological attainment of puberty, and his eventual reproductive competence, as *masculinization*. (Precisely what role personal and cultural fantasy plays in the negotiation of this ritual process I have considered elsewhere: see Herdt 1981: chaps. 6, 7, and 8.)

A boy has female contaminants inside of him which not only retard physical development but, if not removed, debilitate him and eventually bring death. His body is male: his tingu contains no blood and will not

activate. The achievement of puberty for boys requires semen. Breast milk "nurtures the boy," and sweet potatoes or other "female" foods provide "stomach nourishment," but these substances become only feces, not semen. Women's own bodies internally produce the menarche, the hallmark of reproductive maturity. There is no comparable mechanism active in a boy, nothing that can stimulate his secondary sex traits. Only semen can do that; only men have semen; boys have none. What is left to do, then, except initiate and masculinize boys into adulthood?

## NOTES

1. I follow Stoller (1968) in adhering to the following distinctions: the term *sex traits* refers to purely biological phenomena (anatomy, hormones, genetic structure, etc.), whereas *gender* refers to those psychological and cultural attributes that compel a person (consciously or unconsciously) to sense him or herself, and other persons, as belonging to either the male or female sex. It follows that the term gender role (Sears 1965), rather than the imprecise term sex role, refers to the normative set of expectations associated with masculine and feminine social positions.

## REFERENCES

Berndt, R. M. 1962. *Excess and Restraint: Social Control among a New Guinea Mountain People.* Chicago: University of Chicago Press.

Brown, P., and G. Buchbinder (eds.). 1976. *Man and Woman in the New Guinea Highlands.* Washington, DC: American Anthropological Association.

Herdt, G. H. 1981. *Guardians of the Flutes: Idioms of Masculinity.* New York: McGraw-Hill.

Meggitt, M. J. 1964. Male-female relationships in the Highlands of Australian New Guinea. In *New Guinea: The Central Highlands*, ed. J. B. Watson, *American Anthropologist* 66, pt. 2 (4): 204–224.

Meigs, A. S. 1976. Male pregnancy and the reduction of sexual opposition in a New Guinea Highlands society. *Ethnology* 15 (4): 393–407.

Newman, P. L. 1964. Religious belief and ritual in a New Guinea society. In *New Guinea: The Central Highlands*, ed. J. B. Watson, *American Anthropologist* 66, pt. 2 (4): 257–272.

_____. 1965. *Knowing the Gururumba.* New York: Holt, Rinehart, and Winston.

Poole, F. J. P. 1981. Transforming "natural" woman: female ritual leaders and gender ideology among Bimin-Kuskumin. In *Sexual Meanings*, ed. S. B. Ortner and H. Whitehead, pp. 116–165. New York: Cambridge University Press.

Read, K. E. 1954. Cultures of the Central Highlands, New Guinea. *Southwestern Journal of Anthropology* 10 (1): 1–43.

_____. 1965. *The High Valley.* London: George Allen and Unwin.

Salisbury, R. F. 1965. The Siane of the Eastern Highlands. In *Gods, Ghosts, and Men in Melanesia*, ed. P. Lawrence and M. J. Meggitt, pp. 50–77. Melbourne: Melbourne University Press.

Sears, R. R. 1965. Development of gender role. In *Sex and Behavior*, ed. F. A. Beach, pp. 133–163. New York: John Wiley and Sons.

Stoller, R. J. 1968. *Sex and Gender.* New York: Science House.

Strathern, A. J. 1969. Descent and alliance in the New Guinea Highlands: some problems of comparison. Royal Anthropological Institute, *Proceedings*, pp. 37–52.

_____. 1970. Male initiation in the New Guinea Highlands societies. *Ethnology* 9 (4): 373–379.

Tuzin, D. F. 1980. *The Voice of the Tambaran: Truth and Illusion in Ilahita Arapesh Religion.* Berkeley, Los Angeles, and London: University of California Press.

# The Named and the Nameless:
## Gender and Person in Chinese Society

### Rubie S. Watson

In Chinese society names classify and individuate, they have transformative powers, and they are an important form of self-expression. Some names are private, some are chosen for their public effect. Many people have a confusing array of names while others are nameless. The theory and practice of personal naming in Chinese society is extremely complex and unfortunately little studied.

For the male villagers of rural Hong Kong, naming marks important social transitions: the more names a man has the more "socialized" and also, in a sense, the more "individuated" he becomes. To attain social adulthood a man must have at least two names, but most have more. By the time a male reaches middle age, he may be known by four or five names. Village women, by contrast, are essentially nameless. Like boys, infant girls are named when they are one month old, but unlike boys they lose this name when they marry. Adult women are known (in reference and address) by kinship terms, teknonyms, or category terms such as "old woman."

In Chinese society personal names constitute an integral part of the language of joking, of boasting, and of exhibiting one's education and erudition. The Chinese themselves are fascinated by personal names: village men enjoy recounting stories about humorous or clumsy names, educated men appreciate the elegance of an auspicious name, and all males worry about the quality of their own names and those of their sons. To a large extent women are excluded from this discourse. They cannot participate because in adulthood they are not named, nor do they name others. Until very recently the majority of village women were illiterate

and so could not engage in the intellectual games that men play with written names. Women were not even the subjects of these conversations.

The namelessness of adult women and their inability to participate in the naming of others highlights in a dramatic way the vast gender distinctions that characterize traditional Chinese culture. The study of names gives us considerable insight into the ways in which gender and person are constructed in Chinese society. Judged against the standard of men, the evidence presented here suggests that village women do not, indeed cannot, attain full personhood. The lives of men are punctuated by the acquisition of new names, new roles, new responsibilities and new privileges; women's lives, in comparison, remain indistinct and indeterminate.

In his essay "Person, Time, and Conduct in Bali," Clifford Geertz argues that our social world "is populated not by anybodies . . . but by somebodies, concrete classes of determinate persons positively characterized and appropriately labeled" (1973:363). It is this process by which anybodies are converted into somebodies that concerns me here. Do men and women become "somebodies" in the same way? Are they made equally determinate, positively characterized and labeled?

Although this discussion is based primarily on field research carried out in the Hong Kong New Territories, examples of naming practices have been drawn from other areas of Chinese culture as well. It is difficult to determine the extent to which the patterns described in this paper are indicative of rural China in general.[1] Available evidence suggests that there is considerable overlap between Hong Kong patterns of male naming and those of preliberation Chinese society and present-day rural Taiwan (see for example Eberhard 1970; Kehl 1971; Sung 1981; Wu 1927). Unfortunately, there have been no studies that specifically examine the differences between men's and women's naming, although brief references in Martin Yang's study of a Shantung village (1945: 124) and in Judith Stacey's account of women in the People's Republic (1983:43, 131) suggest that the gender differences discussed here are not unique to Hong Kong. In making these statements I do not wish to suggest that there are no substantial differences in personal naming between rural Hong Kong and other parts of China. A general survey of personal naming in China, especially one that takes the postrevolution era into account, has yet to be done.

This paper draws heavily on ethnographic evidence gathered in the village of Ha Tsuen, a single-lineage village located in the northwest corner of the New Territories. All males in Ha Tsuen share the surname Teng and trace descent to a common ancestor who settled in this region during the 12th century (see R. S. Watson 1985). For most villagers postmarital residence is virilocal/patrilocal. The Ha Tsuen Teng practice surname exogamy, which in the case of a single-lineage village means that all wives come from outside the community. These women arrive in Ha Tsuen as strangers and their early years of marriage are spent accommodating to a new family and new community. The Teng find this completely natural; "daughters," they say, "are born looking out; they belong to others."

Patrilineal values dominate social life in Ha Tsuen. Women are suspect because they are outsiders. As Margery Wolf points out, Chinese women are both marginal and essential to the families into which they marry (1972:35). They are necessary because they produce the next generation, yet as outsiders their integration is never complete. Women are economically dependent on the family estate, but they do not have shareholding rights in that estate. Half the village land in Ha Tsuen is owned by the lineage (see R. S. Watson 1985:61–72), and the other half is owned by private (male) landlords. Women have no share in this land; they do not own immovable property nor do they have rights to inherit it. Few married women are employed in wage labor, and since the villagers gave up serious agriculture in the 1960s, most women are dependent on their husbands' paychecks for family income. At the time I conducted my research (1977–78) Ha Tsuen had a population of approximately 2500—all of whom are Cantonese speakers.

## NAMING AN INFANT

Among the Cantonese a child's soul is not thought to be firmly attached until at least 30 days after its birth. During the first month of life the child and mother are secluded from all but the immediate family.

After a month has passed, the child is considered less susceptible to soul loss and is introduced into village life. The infant is given a name by his or her father or grandfather at a ceremony called "full month" (*man yueh*). If the child is a son, the "full month" festivities will be as elaborate as the family can afford; if, on the other hand, a girl is born, there may be little or no celebration (except, perhaps, a special meal for family members). The naming ceremony for a boy normally involves a banquet for neighbors and village elders, along with the distribution of red eggs to members of the community. The first name a child is given is referred to as his or her *ming*.[2]

This name (*ming*) may be based on literary or classical allusions. It may express a wish for the child's or family's future, or it may enshrine some simple event that took place at or near the time of the child's birth. Examples of this kind of naming are found not only in Ha Tsuen but in other areas of China as well. Arlington, in an early paper on Chinese naming, describes how the name "sleeve" was given to a girl of his acquaintance who at the time of her birth had been wrapped in a sleeve (1923:319). In the People's Republic of China, people born during the Korean War might be called "Resist the United States" (Fan-mei) or "Aid Korea" (Pang-ch'ao). Alternatively, children may be given the name of their birthplace, for example, "Born in Anhwei" (Hui-sheng) or "Thinking of Yunnan" (Hsiang-yun). In the past girl babies might be named Nai ("To Endure"). This name was given to infant girls who survived an attempted infanticide. One way of killing an infant was to expose it to the elements. If a girl survived this ordeal, she might be allowed to live. In these cases the name Nai commemorated the child's feat of survival.[3]

A child's name may express the parents' desire for no more children. For instance, in Taiwan a fifth or sixth child may be named Beui, a Hokkien term meaning "Last Child." Alternatively, a father may try to ensure that his next child will be a son by naming a newborn daughter "Joined to Brother" (Lien-ti). There are several girls with this name in Ha Tsuen. A father or grandfather might express his disappointment or disgust by naming a second or third daughter "Too Many" (A-to)[4] or "Little Mistake" (Hsiao-t'so) or "Reluctant to Feed" (Wang-shih). A sickly child might be given the name of a healthy child. My informants told me that a long-awaited son may be given a girl's name to trick the wandering ghosts into thinking the child had no value and therefore could be ignored (see also Sung 1981:81–82). For example, a Ha Tsuen villager, who was the only son of a wealthy family (born to his father's third concubine), was known by everyone as "Little Slave Girl" (in Cantonese, Mui-jai).

In most cases the infant receives a ming during the full month ceremony but this name is little used. For the first year or two most children are called by a family nickname ("milk name" or *nai ming*). Babies are sometimes given milk names like "Precious" (A-pao), or A-buh (mimicking the sounds infants make) or "Eldest Luck," or "Second Luck," indicating sibling order.

Some care and consideration is given to a child's *ming*, especially if it is a boy. By referring to the Confucian classics or by alluding to a famous poem, the name may express the learning and sophistication of the infant's father or grandfather. The name, as we will see, may also save the child from an inauspicious fate. Commonly girls' names (*ming*) are less distinctive and less considered than are boys' names. And, as we have seen, girls' names may also be less flattering: "Too Many" or "Little Mistake." Often a general, classificatory name is given to an infant girl; Martin Yang reports from rural Shantung that Hsiao-mei ("Little Maiden") was a "generic" girls' name in his village (1945:124).

Most Chinese personal names are composed of two characters, which follow the one character surname (for example, Mao Tse-tung or Teng Hsiao-ping). One of the characters of the *ming* may be repeated for all the children of the same sex in the family or perhaps all sons born into the lineage during one generation (for example, a generation or sibling set might have personal names like Hung-hui, Hung-chi, Hung-sheng, and so on). Birth order may also be indicated in the child's name. In these cases part of the name indicates group affiliation and sibling order. However, one of the characters is unique to the individual and so the child is distinguished from his siblings. A variation on this theme occurs when a parent or grandparent selects a name for all sons or grandsons from a group of characters that share a single element (known as the radical—a structured component found in every Chinese character). For example, Margaret Sung (1981:80) in her survey of Chinese naming practices on Taiwan notes that in some families all son's names may be selected from characters that contain the "man" radical (for example, names like "Kind" [Jen], "Handsome" [Chun], or "Protect" [Pao]).

Individuation of the name, Sung points out, is very strong in Chinese society (1981:88). There is no category of words reserved specifically for personal names and care is taken to make names (particularly boys' names) distinct. The Chinese find the idea of sharing one's given name with millions of other people extraordinary.[5] In Taiwan, Sung notes that individuation of one's name is so important that the government has established a set of rules for name changes (1981:88). According to these regulations a name can be changed when two people with exactly the same

name live in the same city or county or have the same place of work. "Inelegant" names or names shared with wanted criminals can also be changed.

In Ha Tsuen a boy might be named, in Cantonese, Teng Tim-sing, which translates Teng "To Increase Victories"; another person could be called Teng Hou-sing, "Reliably Accomplish" (Teng being the shared surname). Parents, neighbors, and older siblings will address the child or young unmarried adult (male or female) by his or her *ming* or by a nickname. Younger siblings are expected to use kin terms in addressing older siblings. It should be noted that, in contrast to personal names, Chinese surnames do not convey individual meaning. When used in a sentence or poem, the character *mao* (the same character used in Mao Tse-tung) means hair, fur, feathers, but when it is used as a surname it does not carry any of these connotations.

## THE POWER OF NAMES: NAMES THAT CHANGE ONE'S LUCK

Names classify people into families, generational sets, and kin groups. Ideally, Chinese personal names also have a unique quality. Personal names carry meanings; they express wishes (for more sons or no more daughters), mark past events ("Sleeve" or "Endure"), and convey a family's learning and status. Beyond this rather restricted sense there is, however, another level of meaning. According to Chinese folk concepts each person has a unique constitution—a different balance of the five elements (fire, water, metal, earth, and wood). When the child is about one month old a family will usually have a diviner cast the child's horoscope. The horoscope consists of eight characters (*pa tzu*)—two each for the hour, day, month, and year of birth. The combination of these characters determines in part what kind of person one is (what kind of characteristics one has) and what will happen in future years. However, the *pa tzu* do not represent destiny; one is not bound to act out this fate.

By means of esoteric knowledge a person's fate can be changed. Perhaps the most common method of accomplishing such a change is through naming. For example, if one of the five elements is missing from a person's constitution or is not properly balanced with other elements, the name (*ming*) may then include a character with the radical for that element. In the event of illness the diviner may suggest that the patient suffers from an imbalance of wood and that the radical for this element be added to the child's name. In such a case the character *mei* (plum), for example, may replace one of the original characters of the ming and thus save the child from a bad fate, illness, or perhaps death. *Mei* achieves this astounding feat not because there is anything intrinsically wood-like about *mei* but because the written character *mei* has two major components: *mu*, the radical for wood and another symbol that is largely phonetic. It is the written form of the character that is important here; in spoken Chinese there is nothing that suggests that *mei* has within it the element wood. I will return to this point later.

Significantly, it is not only one's own horoscope that matters; one must also be in balance with the horoscopes of parents, spouses, and offspring. It is particularly important that the five elements of mother and child be properly matched to ensure mutual health.[6] If conditions of conflict arise and nothing is done to resolve this conflict, the child may become ill and even die. A name change, however, can rectify the situation. It is obvious that Chinese personal names *do* things: they not only classify and distinguish but also have an efficacy in their own right.

## GENDER DIFFERENCES AND THE WRITTEN NAME

As noted above, even in childhood there are important gender distinctions in naming. Girls nearly always have less elaborate full month rituals than their brothers, and less care is taken in choosing girls' names. The greatest difference between the sexes, however, pertains not to the aesthetics of naming but to the written form of the name.

Until the 1960s in Ha Tsuen and in rural Hong Kong generally births were seldom registered with government agencies. Except in cases of a bad fate, there was no compelling reason for girls' names ever to appear in written form. There was rarely any need to attach their names to legal documents. Girls did not inherit land, they had no rights in property, and their given names were not entered in genealogies (on this point see also Hazelton 1986) or on ancestral tablets (see below). Until the 1960s girls rarely attended primary schools. Consequently, nearly all village women born prior to 1945 cannot write or recognize their own names.

Commenting on the role of nicknames, Wolfram Eberhard makes the point that in spoken Chinese with its many homonyms, a two-word combination may fail to express clearly what the speaker wants to convey. The intended meaning of a name (that is, the two-character *ming*) is only apparent when it is written. Nicknames, Eberhard notes, are not normally meant to be written and, hence, are usually longer (often three or four characters) than a person's *ming* (1970:219). Given the ambiguities, a great deal of play is possible with the spoken form of names. For example, Hsin-mei can mean "New Plum" or "Faithful Beauty" depending on the tones that one uses in pronouncing

the characters. In the written form the meaning of this name is perfectly clear, but in the spoken form it can be misunderstood or misconstrued, sometimes with disastrous consequences. The Manchu (Ch'ing) authorities played the naming game when they changed the written form of one of Sun Yat-sen's many names. During Sun's long political career, he used a variety of names and aliases (see Sharman 1934), one being Sun Wen (*wen* translates as "elegant," "civil," "culture"). In Manchu attacks on Sun the character *wen* pronounced with a rising tone (elegant, culture) was replaced by another character *wen* pronounced with a falling tone (which translates as "defile"). The change was effected simply by adding the water radical to the term for elegant. *Wen* (defile), it should be noted, was also the name of a famous criminal in southern China during the last years of Manchu rule.

Upon seeing a person's written name, the beholder may comment on the beauty, the refinement, the auspicious connotations of the characters. As long as it is simply spoken, however, it is in a sense "just a name." Although women have names, these do not convey as much information as do men's names, for the obvious reason that the former were rarely written. Until recently New Territories women were not given names with a view to their written effect. The written form of "Too Many" may be offensive or unpleasant in a way that the spoken form is not.

Given that it is the written form of names that has force, that informs, that can be used to change a bad fate, there is justification for thinking that those whose names are rarely or never written are at some disadvantage. Girls, it would appear, did not have names in the same way that boys did.[7] It is also clear that girls' names are less expressive, less individuating than their brothers' names are. Fathers strove to make son's names distinctive, unique—whereas girls' names tended to classify (for example, Endure, Little Maiden) or to be used as a vehicle for changing circumstances external to the girl herself (for example, Joined to Brother). Many girls of course had names like Splendid Orchid, Morning Flower, Resembling Jade, but in general they were more likely than were their brothers to be given negative names, stereotypic names, or goal-oriented names. These gender distinctions are significant, but the contrast between men and women becomes even more dramatic when we consider adult naming practices.

## MEN'S NAMING

When a Ha Tsuen man marries, he is given or takes (often he chooses the name himself) a marriage name, or *tzu*. Considering the importance of the written name it is significant that *tzu* is the same character that is commonly used for "word" or "ideograph." The marriage name is given in a ceremony called *sung tzu*, which literally means "to deliver written characters." This ceremony is an integral part of the marriage rites and is held after the main banquet on the first day of wedding festivities.

In Ha Tsuen, the marriage name (always two characters) is written on a small rectangular piece of red paper and is displayed in the main reception hall of the groom's house (alternatively, it may be hung in the groom's branch ancestral hall). This name is chosen with regard to its effect in the written form. Great care is taken in choosing the characters; they often have origins in the Confucian classics. In Ha Tsuen one of the two characters of this marriage name is usually shared by a lineage generational set. In some kin groups a respected scholar may be asked to choose a poem or aphorism to be used in generational naming. Each generation will then take in turn one character of the poem as part of their (*tzu*) name. Of course, this makes the selection of an auspicious, learned name more difficult and also more intellectually challenging. Naming at this level can become a highly complicated game.

In choosing a marriage name (*tzu*) the groom demonstrates his sophistication, learning, and goals. Among the people I studied, the possession of a marriage name is essential for the attainment of male adulthood, which gives a man the right to participate in important lineage and community rituals. In Ha Tsuen the correct way to ask whether a man has full ritual rights in the lineage is to inquire, "Does X have a *tzu*?" not "Is X married?" Marriage names are not used as terms of address; they may, however, appear in lineage genealogies and in formal documents.

By the time a man is married he will have acquired a public nickname (*wai hao*, literally an "outside name"). This is usually different from the family nickname he had in infancy or the "school name" given to him by a teacher.[8] Nicknames are widely used as terms of address and reference for males in the village; in fact, a man's birth and marriage names may be largely unknown.

In a discussion of naming among the Ilongot, Renato Rosaldo emphasizes the process by which names come into being (1984:13). Rosaldo argues that names are negotiated, and that naming, like other aspects of Ilongot social life, is a matter of give and take, challenge and response (1984:22). Rosaldo's approach is particularly useful for understanding Chinese nicknaming. *Ming* (birth names) are formally bestowed by one's seniors, one chooses the *tzu* (marriage name) and, as we will see, the *hao* (courtesy name) oneself.

Nicknames (*wai hao*), however, are negotiated; both the namer and the named play the game. By setting up this dichotomy between nicknames and other given names, I do not mean to suggest that these two categories have no common features or that *ming*, marriage names, and courtesy names are simply the consequence of a set of rigidly applied rules and structures. It is clear, however, that nicknames fit into the transactional world of local politics, friendship, and informal groups more comfortably than do formal names.

In Chinese society, one can gain a reputation for cleverness by giving nicknames that are particularly apt or make witty literary allusions. Chinese nicknames are highly personalized and often refer to idiosyncratic characteristics. They may also be derogatory or critical, whereas one's formal names would never be intentionally unflattering (especially for a man). Nicknames may refer to a physical quality (for example, "Fatty") or a personal quality ("Stares at the Sky" for someone who is a snob). Nicknames may also protect ("Little Slave Girl") or they may equalize, at least temporarily, unequal relationships. The richest and most powerful man in one New Territories village was nicknamed "Little Dog." In one respect this was a useful nickname for an extremely wealthy man whose political career depended on being accepted by everyone in the community. Rather than rejecting his derogatory nickname he embraced it.

In Ha Tsuen when a man reaches middle age or when he starts a business career, he usually takes a *hao*—"style" or "courtesy" name. A man chooses this name himself. Sung notes that such names are "usually disyllabic or polysyllabic, and [are] selected by oneself bas[ed] upon whatever one would like to be" (1981:86). Some people have more than one courtesy name. The *hao* is a public name par excellence. Such names, Eberhard points out, are often used on occasions when a man wants "to make his personal identity clear without revealing his personal name (*ming*)" (1970:219). In the past, and to some extent today,[9] the *ming* was considered to be too intimate, too personal to be used outside a circle of close friends and kin (Eberhard 1970:218). "The Chinese I know hide their names," writes Maxine Hong Kingston in *Woman Warrior;* "sojourners take new names when their lives change and guard their real names with silence" (1977:6).

Sung notes that *hao* names are no longer popular in present-day Taiwan except among high government officials (1981:86). However, in Hong Kong *hao* are still widely used; they are commonly found, for example, on business cards, and of course many painters or writers sign their work with a *hao*.

In one sense courtesy names are different from birth and marriage names. One achieves a courtesy name. They are a mark of social and economic status, and a poor man who gives himself such a name may be accused of putting on airs. Any man may take a *hao* but if he is not a "man of substance," the *hao* is likely to remain unknown and unused. With poor men or politically insignificant men these names, if they have them at all, may appear only in genealogies or on tombstones.

Some Ha Tsuen men have posthumous names (*shih-hao*) that they take themselves or have conferred upon them by others. Among the imperial elite posthumous names or titles were given to honor special deeds. In the village, however, taking or giving a *shih-hao* is left to individual taste. The practice has declined in recent years.

The preceding discussion suggests that names mark stages in a man's social life. The possession of a birth name, school name, nickname, marriage name, courtesy name, and posthumous name attest to the fact that a man has passed through the major stages of social adulthood. By the time a man reaches middle age he has considerable control over his names and naming. He names others (his children or grandchildren, for example) and he chooses his own marriage, courtesy, and posthumous names. He also has some control over the use of these names. This is especially true of a successful businessman or politician whose business associates may only know his courtesy name, his drinking friends one of his nicknames, his lineage-mates his birth name, and so on. The use of names is situational and involves some calculation both on the part of the named and those with whom he interacts.

Beidelman, in an article on naming among the Kaguru of Tanzania, emphasizes the point that the choice of name reflects the relation between the speaker and the person to whom he speaks (1974:282; see also Willis 1982). The choice of one name or another, or the use of a kin term rather than a personal name, is a tactical decision. In Ha Tsuen the use of nicknames, pet names, birth names, courtesy names is, like the use of kin terms, highly contextual. Intimates may address each other by a nickname when they are among friends but not when strangers are present; family nicknames may be used in the household but not outside of it; birth names and surnames with titles may be used in formal introductions but not in other settings. A man might be addressed by a kin term or a nickname depending on the speaker's goals. One can give respect by using a courtesy name or claim intimacy by using a nickname. In a single lineage village like Ha Tsuen, where all males are agnatic kinsmen, the strategic use of kin terms and personal names provides a fascinating glimpse into social relationships.

Surprisingly, however, this flexibility does not continue into old age. When a man reaches elderhood at age 61, his ability to control his names diminishes just as his control over his family and corporate resources weakens. In Ha Tsuen and in China generally men often hand over headship of the family when they become elders. The village code of respect requires that male elders be addressed by a kin term (for example, in Cantonese *ah baak*, FeB, or a combination of the given name and kin term, for example, *ah Tso baak*). Only an exceptional man, a scholar or wealthy businessman, will continue to be called by one of his personal names after his 60th birthday. For example, no villager would dare refer to or address the 93-year-old patriarch of the wealthiest family in Ha Tsuen as *ah baak*. In general, however, with advancing age the playful aspects of names and naming are taken away as is a man's power to transact his name. In old age a man has little control over what he is called, and in this respect his situation is similar to that of a married woman. As with wives, old men have left (or are leaving) the world of public and financial affairs to become immersed in the world of family and kinship where they are defined not by a set of distinctive names but by their relationship to others.

## "NO NAME" WOMEN

At one month a Ha Tsuen girl is given a name (*ming*); when she marries this name ceases to be used. Marriage is a critical rite of passage for both men and women, but the effect of this rite on the two sexes is very different. Just as a man's distinctiveness and public role are enhanced by his marriage and his acquisition of a marriage name, the marriage rites relegate the woman to the inner world of household, neighborhood, and family. On the one hand, the marriage rites seek to enhance the young bride's fertility, but on the other hand, and in a more negative vein, they also dramatize the bride's separation from her previous life and emphasize the prohibitions and restrictions that now confine her. When the young bride crosses her husband's threshold, what distinctiveness she had as a girl is thrust aside. It is at this point that she loses her name and becomes the "inner person" (*nei jen*), a term Chinese husbands use to refer to their wives.

While the groom is receiving his marriage name on the first day of marriage rites, his bride is being given an intensive course in kinship terminology by the elderly women of Ha Tsuen. Marriage ritual provides a number of occasions for the formal, ritualized exchange of kin terms (for a description of marriage rites in Ha Tsuen see R. S. Watson 1981). These exchanges, which always feature the bride, instruct the new wife and daughter-in-law in the vast array of kin terms she must use for her husband's relatives. The prevalence of virilocal/patrilocal residence means that the groom remains among the kin with whom he has always lived. It is the bride who must grasp a whole new set of kin terms and learn to attach these terms to what must seem a bewildering array of people. Two women residents in the groom's village (called in Cantonese *choi gaa,* "bride callers") act as the bride's guides and supporters during the three days of marriage rites, and it is their responsibility to instruct the bride in the kin terminology she will need in order to survive in her new environment.

These ritualized exchanges of kin terms do more, however, than serve as a pedagogic exercise; they also locate and anchor the bride in a new relational system. As the groom acquires his new marriage name—a name, it should be noted, that denotes both group or category membership *and* individual distinctiveness— the bride enters a world in which she exists only in relation to others. She is no longer "grounded" by her own special name (*ming*), however prosaic that name might have been; after marriage she exists only as someone's eBW or yBW or as Sing's mother, and so on. Eventually even these terms will be used with decreasing frequency; as she approaches old age, she will be addressed simply as "old woman" (*ah po*) by all but her close kin.

When I first moved into Ha Tsuen, I quickly learned the names of the male residents (mostly nicknames). But for the women I, like other villagers, relied on kin terms or category terms. Significantly, the rules that govern the use of these terms are not dependent on the age of the women themselves, but rather are a function of the lineage generation of their husbands. Women married to men of an ascending generation to the speaker (or the speaker's husband) may be addressed as *ah suk po* (a local expression meaning FyBW) or by the more formal *ah sam* (also meaning FyBW). For women married to men of one's own generation (male ego) the terms *ah sou* (eBW) or, if one wanted to give added respect, *ah sam* (FyBW) may be used.

A woman may also be referred to by the nickname of her husband plus "leung" (for example, ah Keung leung), or by a teknonym. For their part married women ordinarily use kin terms for their husbands' agnates and for other women in the village. I was told that a woman must use kin terms for men older in age or generation than her husband. Between husband and wife teknonyms are often used so that the father of Tim-sing might address his wife as *ah Sing nai* (ah is

a prefix denoting familiarity, *Sing* is part of the son's *ming,* nai is "mother" or, literally, "milk"). In addressing their husbands, women might use nicknames; my neighbor always called her husband "Little Servant."[10]

Although there is some flexibility in deciding what to call a woman, the reference and address terms used for women in Ha Tsuen are very rigid compared to those employed for men. Furthermore, among women there is no possibility of self-naming. Men name themselves, women are named by others. Similarly, Ha Tsuen women are more restricted than their husbands in the tactical use they can make of names and kin terms. Whereas a man may refer to or address his neighbor by his nickname ("Fatty"), his *ming* (*ah Tim*), or by a kin term, decorum dictates that his wife use either a kin term appropriate to her husband's generation or one appropriate to her children. In Cantonese society, and presumably in China generally, adults often address and refer to each other by a version of the kin term their children would use for that person. I suspect, but at this point cannot document, that women are far more likely to do this than are men.

While it is true that a man has little choice in the reference or address terms he uses for women, he does have considerable freedom in distinguishing among his male acquaintances, friends, and kin. Women, as outlined previously, have a restricted repertoire for both sexes. In this sense adult women may be said to carry a particularly heavy burden for guarding the kinship and sexual order. No adult woman is free to act alone or to be treated as if she were independent. The terms by which she is addressed and the terms she uses to address others serve as constant reminders of the hierarchical relations of gender, age, and generation.

As men grow older, as they become students, marry, start careers, take jobs, and eventually prepare for ancestorhood, their new names anchor them to new roles and privileges. These names are not, however, only role markers or classifiers. Ideally, they assign people to categories and at the same time declare their uniqueness. The pattern of naming in Chinese society presents an ever-changing image of men. Viewed from this perspective Chinese males are always growing, becoming, accumulating new responsibilities and new rights.

Peasant women, on the other hand, experience few publicly validated life changes, and those that they do undergo link them ever more securely to stereotyped roles. Women's naming leaves little room for individuation or self-expression. Unlike males, whose changes are marked by both ascribed (for example, elderhood) *and* achieved criteria (such as student, scholar, businessman, writer, politician), a woman's changes (from unmarried virgin to married woman, from nonmother to mother, from reproducer to nonreproducer) are not related to achievement outside the home. Instead of acquiring a new name at marriage or the birth of a first child, women's changes are marked by kin terminology or category shifts. At marriage the bride loses her *ming* and becomes known by a series of kin terms. At the birth of a child she may add a teknonym ("Sing's mother"), and as she approaches and enters old age more and more people will address her simply as "old woman" (*ah po*).

The most dramatic changes that women make are the shift from named to unnamed at marriage and the gradual shift from kin term to category term as their children mature and marry.[11] It would appear that as a woman's reproductive capacity declines, she becomes less grounded in the relational system. She becomes, quite simply, an "old woman" much like any other old woman. Of course, family members continue to use kin terms for these elderly women, especially in reference and address, but gradually their anonymity increases. Unlike men, women do not become elders. There is no ceremony marking their entry into respected old age. They move from reproductively active mother to sexually inactive grandmother with no fanfare and with little public recognition of their changed status.

Even in death a woman has no personal name. On the red flag that leads the spirit of the deceased from the village to the grave is written the woman's father's surname (for example, *Lin shih*, translated "Family of Lin"); no personal name is added. For men, the deceased's surname plus his courtesy and/or posthumous name is written on the soul flag. Neither do women's personal names appear on the tombstone where, here again, only the surname of the woman's father is given ("Family of Lin"). In Ha Tsuen women do not have separate ancestral tablets; if they are commemorated at all, they appear as minor appendages on their husbands' tablets. And, once more, they are listed only under the surnames of their fathers. In subsequent generations whatever individuating characteristics a woman might have had are lost—not even a name survives as testimony of her existence as a person.

## CONCLUSIONS

If one were to categorize Ha Tsuen villagers on a social continuum according to the number and quality of their names, married peasant women would stand at the extreme negative pole.[12] To my knowledge they share this dubious distinction with no other group. In the past even male slaves (*hsi min*) and household servants had nicknames (see J. L. Watson 1976:365). They may not have had *ming* or surnames as such but they did possess names that distinguished them from others. It is important to note that it is not only the possession of multiple names that matters but also the fact that, at one end of the continuum, people have no control over their own names while, at the other end, they name themselves and others.

At marriage women find themselves enmeshed in the world of family and kinship. It is a world, as noted in the introduction, that they belong to but do not control. In Ha Tsuen brides arrive as outsiders but quickly, one might even say brutally, they become firmly entrenched in their new environment. Village women can only be identified within the constellation of male names or within the limits of kinship terminology. Unlike their husbands and brothers, women—having no public identity outside the relational system—are defined by and through others.

In Ha Tsuen women are excluded from participation in most of the formal aspects of lineage or community life and they are not involved in decision making outside the home. Ha Tsuen women do not inherit productive resources; they are also restricted in the uses to which they can put their dowries (R. S. Watson 1984). Furthermore, women in Ha Tsuen cannot become household heads and, even today, they do not vote in local elections. They do not worship in ancestral halls nor do they join the cult of lineage ancestors after death. Although individual peasant women may attain considerable power within their households, they are said to have gained this power by manipulation and stealth. Women by definition cannot hold positions of authority.

In a discussion of male and female naming among the Omaha Sioux, Robert Barnes writes: "The names of Omaha males provide men with distinctive individuality, while also linking each unmistakably to a recognized collectivity. The possibility of acquiring multiple names in adulthood enhances individual prominence for men" (1982:220). Barnes goes on to say that women's names "barely rescue them from a general anonymity, neither conferring uniqueness nor indicating group membership" (1982:22). As among the Sioux, personal naming among Chinese men is a sign of both individual distinctiveness and group membership, while naming practices among village women simply confirm their marginality.

In Ha Tsuen the practice of personal naming reflects and facilitates the passage from one social level to another. Names establish people in social groups and give them certain rights within those groups. With each additional name, a man acquires new attributes. Maybury-Lewis has argued that among many Central Brazilian societies names give humans their "social persona and link [them] to other people" (1984:5;

see also Bamberger 1974). Names, Maybury-Lewis writes, "transform individuals into persons" (1984:7). Naming may not be as central to Chinese social organization and ideology as it is among the societies of Central Brazil, yet there is no doubt that, for Chinese men, names have a transformative power that binds them as individuals to society.

In Ha Tsuen the ultimate goal of all males is to produce an heir, to have a grandson at one's funeral, to leave property that guarantees the performance of one's ancestral rites. The possession of many names testifies to the fact that a man has completed the cycle of life. Full personhood is not acquired at birth, at marriage, or even at the death of one's father. It is a process that continues throughout life and is punctuated by the taking and bestowing of names. One might argue that it is a process that extends even beyond death as the named ancestor interacts with the living. If, as Grace Harris suggests, personhood involves a process of social growth "in the course of which changes [are] wrought by ceremony and ritual" (1978:49), then Chinese women never approximate the full cycle of development that their menfolk experience.[13] In stark contrast to men, women become less distinct as they age. The changes they undergo remain largely unrecognized and unnoticed.

In Chinese society, as in other societies, there is a tension between the notion of the unique individual (the individual as value) and the notion of the person tied to society.[14] In some sense the great philosophical systems of Taoism and Confucianism represent these two poles. Among men, naming involves a dual process through which they achieve personhood by being bound to society, while at the same time they acquire an enhanced sense of individuality and distinctiveness. The peasant women described in this paper seem to have been largely excluded from the individuating, individualizing world of personal naming. The situation with regard to personhood is, however, another matter. It would be wrong to say that peasant wives are nonpersons; rather, they are not persons in the same sense or to the same degree as are husbands and sons. Viewed from the perspective of names, peasant women are neither fully individuated nor "personed." In life as in death they remain suspended between the anonymous world of anybodies and the more sharply defined world of somebodies.

## ACKNOWLEDGMENTS

The research for this study was conducted in 1977–78 and was made possible by a grant from the Social Science Research Council (Great Britain) and by the University of London Central Research Fund. An earlier version of this paper was presented at the 1984 American Anthropological Association Annual Meetings. Versions of this paper were also presented at the University of London Intercollegiate Anthropology Seminar and at the University of Rochester's Anthropology Colloquium. I thank the members of those seminars for their suggestions and criticisms. I owe a special debt to Jack Dull, Hsu Cho-yun, Sun Man-li, Roderick MacFarquhar, and James Watson, all of whom have helped in this project. Deborah Kwolek, Judy Tredway, and Martha Terry of the Asian Studies Program at the University of Pittsburgh helped in the preparation of the manuscript and I thank them for their assistance.

Cantonese terms are in Yale romanization and Mandarin terms follow the Wade-Giles system.

This paper is dedicated to the memory of my friend and fellow anthropologist Judith Strauch (1942–85).

## NOTES

1. There are bound to be regional, temporal, urban-rural, and class differences in Chinese naming practices. A general discussion of Chinese naming awaits further research.
2. In Taiwan the *ming* is the legal name (it appears in the official household register) and is sometimes called the *cheng ming* (correct name) (Sung 1981:70). In Hong Kong this name may or may not be the name used on legal documents.
3. I am grateful to Professor Jack Dull for pointing out to me the significance and frequency of the personal name Nai among Chinese women.
4. In a similar vein a fifth or sixth child might be named "To End" or "To Finish." One can find such names in the Hong Kong and Taipei telephone directories (see also Sung 1981:81).
5. In China there are no given names like John that are shared by millions of people; on this point see Sung 1981:85.
6. In a discussion of the cosmic relationship between mother and child Marjorie Topley writes of her Cantonese informants:

    The constitutional imbalance of a child with a queer fate may also involve other parties. First, the child may be polarized in the same direction as someone with whom it has a continuous relationship. Then both parties may suffer from continual illness. This may be corrected by adding an element to the child's name so it is compatible with that of the other party. (1974:240)
7. This is changing now that girls go to school and their births are registered.
8. In the past when village boys started school at age five or six (girls did not attend school until the 1960s), the schoolmaster gave each student a school or "study

name" (*hsueh-ming*). School names are no longer very important in the New Territories.

9. In the past officials' *ming* could not be used except by intimates (see Eberhard 1970; Sung 1981).

10. After I gained some insight into the micropolitics of my neighbor's household, the name seemed well chosen.

11. Once a son marries reproduction becomes a matter for the younger generation, and in Ha Tsuen it was considered shameful for the mother of a married son to become pregnant.

12. It should be noted here that men do not constitute a uniform category in this regard. Highly literate men make up one extreme but many poorly educated or uneducated men fall somewhere between the two extremes. Like the names of their sisters, their names may be inelegant and rarely seen in written form, but unlike adult women, they do retain their names after marriage.

13. On this point see also La Fontaine (1985:131).

14. For discussions of the concept of the individual as value and the self in Chinese society see for example de Bary (1970); Shiga (1978:122); and more recently Elvin (1985); Munro (1985) (especially essays by Hansen, Yu, Munro, and de Bary).

## REFERENCES

Arlington, L. C. 1923. The Chinese Female Names. *China Journal of Science and Arts* 1(4):316–325.

Bamberger, Joan. 1974. Naming and the Transmission of Status in a Central Brazilian Society. *Ethnology* 13:363–378.

Barnes, Robert B. 1982. Personal Names and Social Classification. In *Semantic Anthropology*. David Parkin, ed., pp. 211–226. London: Academic Press.

Beidelman, T. O. 1974. Kaguru Names and Naming. *Journal of Anthropological Research* 30:281–293.

de Bary, William Theodore. 1970. Individualism and Humanitarianism in Late Ming Thought. In *Self and Society in Ming Thought*. W. Theodore de Bary, ed., pp. 145–247. New York: Columbia University Press.

Eberhard, Wolfram. 1970. A Note on Modern Chinese Nicknames. In *Studies in Chinese Folklore and Related Essays*. Wolfram Eberhard, ed., pp. 217–222. Indiana University Folklore Institute Monograph Series, Vol. 23. The Hague: Mouton.

Elvin, Mark. 1985. Between the Earth and Heaven: Conceptions of the Self in China. In *The Category of the Person*. Michael Carrithers, Steven Collins, and Steven Lukes, eds., pp. 156–189. Cambridge: Cambridge University Press.

Geertz, Clifford. 1973. Person, Time, and Conduct in Bali. In *The Interpretation of Cultures*. pp. 360–411. New York: Basic Books.

Harris, Grace. 1978. *Casting Out Anger: Religion among the Taita of Kenya*. Cambridge: Cambridge University Press.

Hazelton, Keith. 1986. Patrilines and the Development of Localized Lineages: The Wu of Hsiuming City, Hui-chou, to 1528. In *Kinship Organization in Late Imperial China*.

Patricia B. Ebrey and James L. Watson, eds., pp. 137–169. Berkeley: University of California Press.

Kehl, Frank. 1971. Chinese Nicknaming Behavior: A Sociolinguistic Pilot Study. *Journal of Oriental Studies* 9:149–172.

Kingston, Maxine Hong. 1977. *The Woman Warrior: Memories of a Girlhood among Ghosts*. New York: Vintage Books. (Originally published in hardcover by Alfred Knopf, 1976.)

La Fontaine, Jean. 1985. Person and Individual: Some Anthropological Reflections. In *The Category of the Person*. Michael Carrithers, Steven Collins, and Steven Lukes, eds., pp. 123–140. Cambridge: Cambridge University Press.

Maybury-Lewis, David. 1984. Name, Person, and Ideology in Central Brazil. In *Naming Systems*. Elisabeth Tooker, ed., pp. 1–10. 1980 Proceedings of the American Ethnological Society. Washington, DC: American Ethnological Society.

Munro, Donald (ed.). 1985. *Individualism and Holism: Studies in Confucian and Taoist Values*. Ann Arbor: University of Michigan Press.

Rosaldo, Renato. 1984. Ilongot Naming: The Play of Associations. In *Naming Systems*. Elisabeth Tooker, ed., pp. 11–24. 1980 Proceedings of the American Ethnological Society. Washington, DC: American Ethnological Society.

Sharman, Lyon. 1934. *Sun Yat-sen, His life and its Meaning: a Critical Biography*. New York: John Day.

Shiga, Shuzo. 1978. Family Property and the Law of Inheritance in Traditional China. In *Chinese Family Law and Social Change*. David Buxbaum, ed., pp. 109–150. Seattle: University of Washington Press.

Stacey, Judith. 1983. *Patriarchy and Socialist Revolution in China*. Berkeley: University of California Press.

Sung, Margaret M. Y. 1981. Chinese Personal Naming. *Journal of the Chinese Language Teachers Association* 16(2):67–90.

Topley, Marjorie. 1974. Cosmic Antagonisms: A Mother-Child Syndrome. In *Religion and Ritual in Chinese Society*. Arthur Wolf, ed., pp. 233–249. Stanford, CA: Stanford University Press.

Watson, James L. 1976. Chattel Slavery in Chinese Peasant Society: A Comparative Analysis. *Ethnology* 15:361–375.

Watson, Rubie S. 1981. Class Differences and Affinal Relations in South China. *Man* 16:593–615.

_____. 1984. Women's Property in Republican China: Rights and Practice. *Republican China* 10(12):1–12.

_____. 1985. *Inequality among Brothers: Class and Kinship in South China*. Cambridge: Cambridge University Press.

Willis, Roy. 1982. On a Mental Sausage Machine and other Nominal Problems. In *Semantic Anthropology*. David Parkin, ed., pp. 227–240. London: Academic Press.

Wolf, Margery. 1972. *Women and the Family in Rural Taiwan*. Stanford, CA: Stanford University Press.

Wu, Ching-Chao. 1927. The Chinese Family: Organization, Names, and Kinship Terms. *American Anthropologist* 29:316–325.

Yang, Martin C. 1945. *A Chinese Village: Taitou, Shantung Province*. New York: Columbia University Press.

# Gender and the Stories Pittsburgh Police Officers Tell about Using Physical Force

## Bonnie McElhinny

When most people think of work on language and gender, they probably think of works like linguist Deborah Tannen's *You Just Don't Understand* or perhaps even psychologist John Gray's *Men are From Mars, Women are from Venus,* studies of "miscommunications" between women and men in heterosexual couples. Despite an increasing number of different approaches, in studies of language and gender in North America the focus on cross-sex miscommunication remains influential and, at its best, insightful.[1] There are, however, a number of increasingly controversial theoretical assumptions about gender often implicitly embedded in this approach, including the notions that the study of gender is closely wedded to the study of heterosexual relations, that gender is an attribute rather than a practice, and that the study of gender is the study of individuals (McElhinny 2003). Studying gender in heterosexual dyads can suggest that "gendered talk is mainly a personal characteristic or limited to the institution of the family" (Gal 1991:185). It also draws attention away from the importance of studying the ways that gender is a structural principle organizing social institutions such as workplaces, schools, courts, and the state and the patterns they display in the recruitment, treatment, and mobility of different men and women (Gal 1991). Gender, like class and racialized ethnicity, nationality, age and sexuality, is an axis for the organization of inequality, a principle for allocating access to resources, though the way each of these axes work may have their own distinctive features (Scott 1986:1054). In this chapter, I talk about how gender structures policing, a type of work that has been traditionally reserved in the United States for men, especially working-class White men. In 1991–1992 I spent twelve months patrolling with the Pittsburgh police department, and recorded 182 hours of police officer interaction. This department was, at the time of my research, one of the most racially and sexually diverse big-city police departments in the United States, with 25% female officers

and 25% Black officers. This was largely due to a court-enforced affirmative action program in place from 1975–1991 which mandated the hiring of gender and ethnic quotas: each time the department hired a class of recruits, the class was 25% Black women, 25% White women, 25% Black men and 25% White men. The Pittsburgh police force, like many other public sector jobs, was also shaped by a veterans' hiring preference program. Each veteran who took the civil service exam for policing had ten percent added to the score achieved. This practice tended to benefit men, perhaps especially White men (see McElhinny 2000). Even though this workplace was increasingly diverse, it was still perceived as "men's work." The gender of a workplace is determined not only by the presence, or even predominance, of women or men in it but also by cultural norms and interpretations of gender that dictate who is best suited for different sorts of employment. Female police officers routinely found themselves addressed as "sir." My research investigates what the dominant kind of masculinity was in this workplace, and the ways that different officers adopted, adapted or rejected this way of defining policing.

In this chapter, I examine narratives told by male and female, Black and White police officers in Pittsburgh about moments when they found it necessary to use physical force. Policing is a job predominantly staffed by men, and the dominant style of policing is understood as masculine. Nonetheless, in this study I do not assume that men and women are different. Rather, I ask what advantages and disadvantages accrue to men and women embracing different interactional strategies at different moments, when these are associated with gender, and the ways they are associated with dominant institutional norms and practices. I believe that, "interpretations of maleness, manhood, or masculinity are not neutral, but rather all such attributions have political entailments. In any given situation, they may align men against women, some men against other men, some women against other women, or some men and some women against others. In short, the processes of gendering produce difference and inequality" (Cornwall and Lindisfarne 1994:10).

Adapted from Bonnie McElhinny, "Fearful, Forceful Agents of the Law: Ideologies about Language and Gender in Police Officers' Narratives about the Use of Physical Force," *Pragmatics* 13 (2003): 253–284. Reprinted with permission of publisher.

## "ACTING CRAZY" AS A THEORY
## OF AGENCY AND MODEL
## OF PERSONHOOD

Many male and some female police officers in Pittsburgh understand themselves as fighting a "war" on crime. These police officers believe that the only way to earn respect from citizens is by "acting crazy," a phrase they use to describe their efforts to instill fear in others so that they will not try to push them around. Acting crazy is also a useful strategy for gaining control over an interactional situation since it entails a refusal to negotiate. The construction of authority by using displays of anger raises certain dilemmas that "acting crazy," as a theory of agency and model of personhood, is meant to solve. First, police officers find it important to distinguish between acting crazy and being crazy.

> **You're not really a hard person, but you have to act that way**, because they'll brick you. [PO 30A, Black male, 30, 2 years on the job]

(For details on the transcription conventions used for these recordings, please see Appendix A.) Certain officers, often portrayed as male and older, are seen as "going off," or "blowing their tops" that is, breaking out into unexpected rages that they are not in control of. Though the suddenness of their anger is similar to "acting crazy," other officers distinguish their actions by suggesting that some of these older male officers ARE crazy, rather than ACTING crazy. The difference, then, is that police officers portray other officers as out of control even when they are in control, while understanding themselves as in control even when out of control. Second, in order to justify fear-inspiring actions which they fully realize are controversial, police officers describe the wild, dirty, terrifying world of "the streets" which they must react to. Some officers themselves come to seem inordinately fearful as they tell these stories. As a result, at the very moments when police officers exercise the most force they portray themselves as most helpless: "What else could I do?" "Acting crazy" is thus a way of simultaneously claiming and denying responsibility for action.

Although the necessity for "acting crazy" is not extensively challenged by police officers in Pittsburgh, not all police officers support or value this style of interaction. Some officers perceive themselves more like bureaucrats or social workers than street fighters, and these beliefs lead to different models of agency and personhood (McElhinny 1995). Nonetheless a focus on fighting crime, often called the *crime control* model of policing (Walker 1977) predominates. The *crime-control* model, also known as the crime fighter or militarized model, "characterizes the typical police officer as a crime fighter extraordinaire, a seasoned, well-armed, professional soldier in an unending and savage war on crime" (Appier 1998:160). Between World War II and the early 1970s, women were not seen as appropriate for policing jobs because they were thought incapable of being combat soldiers. The ideal police officer was aggressive and tough, authoritative and male. However, with the advent of affirmative action hiring programs in police departments in the early 1970s (McElhinny n.d.), the gendered ideal shifted a bit. For this reason, not all proponents of a crime-fighting ideology are men: we will look at the narratives of several women below too. A far greater percentage of men, however, embraced such a model, for a variety of complex historical and institutional reasons. At the end of this chapter, I consider what the implications of how police officers talk about the use of physical force are. I am particularly interested in understanding whether and how the integration of women into a traditionally masculine occupation like policing leads to the reinscription or transformation of certain ideologies about how interaction should proceed.

## USING NARRATIVES TO STUDY
## GENDER AND IDEOLOGY

Analyzing narratives is particularly helpful for elucidating how police officers' make sense of their experiences in particular. First, narratives are *event-centered*, that is, they focus on human action and interaction. Second, narratives are *experience-centered*, and thus allow us to infer something about what it feels like to be in the story world. Third, narratives are *performative, seductive, and evocative*. That is, narratives do not merely refer to past experience but create experiences for their audience, and they try to persuade listeners by seducing them into the world portrayed. Narratives make an argument about what happened as part of describing what happened (Mattingly 1998:31). Analyses of narratives helps us to understand how stories are given shape by their tellers but also how stories shape the way tellers see and experience themselves, how people become the stories they tell about their lives. Police officers who embrace a crime control model frequently rehearse how they will behave in certain situations if confronted with a recalcitrant husband, or drunken prisoner, or fleeing burglar. They also frequently review the moments in which they have found themselves embroiled in such situations. Narratives allow officers to simultaneously present their own views on past conflicts, shape the on-going interaction (here, with an anthropologist), and rehearse how they would, ideally, talk in the future. The very reiteration of these stories serves to keep alive for these officers the need to be prepared, always, to use force. Stories thus can provide crucial insights into how ideologies around certain styles of policing are forged or reinforced on the ground by police officers.

## ALL OF A SUDDEN: RAPID ACTION, REASONABLENESS, AND ROBOCOP

Rapid, perhaps unpredictable, behavior is a central feature of most police officers' stories about the use of force. In the following narrative, a White female officer is describing the actions of a towering young Black officer ("David") who has come to be called "Robocop" by some of the people in the neighborhood, in part because of his weight-lifter's physique, in part because he's six foot three inches tall, and in part because of his policing style.[2]

I was working behind a desk last um, last SPRING. . . . David's brought these two people in, a guy and a girl and the guy he had handcuffed to a chair and the girl he had handcuffed to the other chair and the guy's . . . was talking and ta::lking and talking and talking and David's like "SHUT UP." He told him like twenty times and Zellini's sitting behind me . . . singing these little songs like <<in song-song voice>> "You better shut u:::p, David's gonna get ma::::d." (LAUGHS) and like right when he says that **all of a sudden** David PICKED this guy up, chair and all and just like **slammed** him down to the ground. He's like "I told you to SHUT THE FUCK UP. NOW SHUT UP." (LAUGHS) and then he comes over to me afterwards he goes <<she mimics him mumbling under his breath>>, "I'm sorry. I lost my temper." He goes "I can't—I can't stand when I do that you know." (LAUGHS) I'm like, "That's cool David y::—you don't have to apologize." He's like "I didn't mean to swear that much in front of you." He's like real polite and stuff too you know but- They call him Robocop. [PO 25A, White female, 28, 3 years on the job]

Although the narrator concludes by suggesting that David's size and strength alone are enough to intimidate the public, the story suggests otherwise. He (even he) needs to construct a police persona. This female officer portrays him as being unpredictable, crazy, wild. "All of a sudden" is an adverbial phrase which marks Robocop's transition from one condition to another, and which describes him as being out of control. "Slammed," with its connotations of violence, noise and unexpectedness, is used to similar effect, as are the profanity and shouting in David's reported speech. Although David's action is portrayed as perhaps being sudden from the handcuffed man's point of view, it is also portrayed as intelligible and even predictable from a police officer's point of view. The narrator manages this by portraying the actions of the

handcuffed man as unreasonable (*"he was talking and ta::lking and talking and talking"*).

What, however, is the point of this story? Skillful narratives often include an evaluation that indicates why a story was told and what the narrator was getting at. Evaluations may be external (in which the point is made explicitly) or internal (in which the narrative dramatizes this information). Here the narrator's laughter throughout the story draws our attention to the hilarious juxtaposition of the fearsome giant with the pussycat who then apologizes to the young female officer. The juxtaposition itself implicitly suggests that David's actions are not an intrinsic part of his character, but part of a display. Indeed the narrator, here relying on the U.S. folk ideology which associates people's real selves with those they display to family and friends, may even be suggesting that the real man is the "real polite" man and not the real angry man. Such a story thus minimizes the actions that "Robocop" takes while acting out his violent role.

## ARMED ROBBERS AND AGENCY

If this story begins to illustrate the theory of personhood associated with acting crazy, the stories of Jay, a White officer in his mid-20s from a policing family (his Dad and his wife are also officers) elucidate the interactional and professional dilemmas for which "acting crazy" is a solution. One of Jay's principal fears—and it was a fear he articulated repeatedly even in the few days I rode with him—was that his firearm would be wrestled from him in a fight, or that the firearm of another officer would be taken and used against him. Even if most policing doesn't require guns or physical force, Jay repeatedly pointed out that it only takes one incident to get him killed. Jay justifies police force by describing it entirely in terms of self-defense, as a reaction to other actions. Portraying the use of force as self-defense contributes to a siege mentality. Any struggle between a police officer and another person is seen merely as a fight between individuals rather than one between an individual and an institution. Jay offers one example of series of events which were, he says, distorted by the "liberal media."

I caught an armed robber on Polka Street. Guy runs out. "Hey some black guy—" had a big knife, runs at the car. I say, "Hey, what the fuck are you doing?" Andy sees <the robber> hiding between these homes, crouched down. I hear Andy yell. Guy was supposed to be armed so Andy had his gun on him. Guy could have gone straight up on this porch. Andy couldn't see his hands—he said, "Show me your hands, real slow, or you're gonna get whacked." **Now we're in a fist fight, he got his ass beat,** <community members> saw this brutal act, by a police man, was a bunch of shit. This brutal police man. Man falsely accused. He was the guy that robbed the place. He wouldn't show Andy his hands. Community leaders saw it, and they said it's wrong. "You police man are wrong." [PO 114B, White male, 26, 5 years on the job]

In the part of the narrative where Jay is catching the robber, he regularly uses historic present tense ("*I say,*" "*Andy sees,*" "*I hear*") and leaves "guy" unmodified by a definite or indefinite article. This iconically captures and conjures up the breathless rapidity with which events happen and with which officers must make decisions about appropriate actions. The suddenness of the movement from threat to force ("*Now we're in a fist fight*") emphasizes the danger of police work, and justifies the rapidity with which he too must make a transition from one emotional state to another. Most surprising here is the vagueness at a crucial moment: Who exactly initiated the fist fight? Although police officers have a kind of discretionary power over others' freedom that would justify a portrayal of themselves as super agents, they often downplay their own agency. "Now we're in a fist fight" and "He got his ass beat" leave unmarked the agent or agents of the acts. Jay consistently blames the other person for escalating interactions from a polite to an impolite one, from a verbal interaction to one which is physically threatening, from an interaction in which a physical threat is implicit to one in which it is explicit.

If Jay accounts for his actions in terms of the activities he must respond to, Frank, a burly man who looks like Hollywood's stereotype of an Irish policeman, justifies his actions in terms of the character of the people he must deal with. He half-jokes, "Anymore when someone asks me what I do for a living, I say garbageman" [9A]. He uses other metaphors for criminals ("vermin" and "maggots") which serve to downplay the agency and humanity of those he interacts with. He portrays his actions as inevitable, as entirely determined by the situation rather than his own agency.

> I don't usually confess up to too many things, but the one time I did beat a man I didn't really have to, whereas we get a call for child molestation. We could look in the window we could see this little girl about four years old bleeding from the vagina-area. This maggot's in the corner, crying. I hit him. More than once. **What am I supposed to do.** [PO 9B, White male, 39/40, 13 years on the job]

Frank offers no apologies for actions that he sees as natural, in the circumstances. Like Jay, he sees his role as reaction, not action.

Even in seemingly frank descriptions of the emotional distress the job causes him, Frank uses agency-masking grammatical devices. After he described this child abuse call, I ask if it was difficult not to take the job home.

> Not to sound like a wimp, but more than once I've gone home and cried. I don't see myself as a wimp but . . . **it catches up to you**. One time I had to take little girls, I didn't actually take them, I helped carry them out of the

fire, they'd died. That bothered me. Thinking of those girls—nobody gets a break on a fire hydrant. [PO 9B, White male, 39/40, 13 years on the job]

Though he does say "I've cried," "it catches up to you" doesn't even give him the relative passive role of experiencer (compare "I felt"). Frank also moves quickly away from a discussion of how the job affects him to describing the sort of tough professional action he takes as a result (writing tickets for people illegally parked near fire hydrants).

## "BETWEEN A ROCK AND A HARD PLACE": THE DILEMMAS OF BEING A BLACK POLICE OFFICER

So far the stories considered here have been stories told by White officers, but a crime fighter ideology is not limited to these officers. Doug, a young African-American officer, came on the job with a college degree but no street experience. He notes that when he first became a police officer, he tried to be polite and nice (a strategy he calls being "Officer Friendly"), but these strategies did not work. He says that police officers cannot simply let others tell them what to do. Instead, he says, police officers need to take control of situations:

> **If you more or less yell at them**, tell them "Get the hell outta here, we're not gonna have this," they'll get real quiet, they'll get real soft, and everything else [PO 30A, Black male, 30, 2 years on the job]

"If you more or less yell at them" uses a hedge to downplay the police officer's action. The use of impersonal "you" ("*If you more or less yell . . .*") rather than "I" has a similar effect.

Doug uses many military metaphors to describe his work. He describes the drug trade in Pittsburgh as a "drug war," and says that the job of policing sometimes becomes so overwhelming that police men become "just like Vietnam vets—they need to get away." He describes his own style of policing as aggressive. In the accounts of officers like Doug, there often seems to be a surprisingly thin edge between displays of anger and aggression and accounts of fear. Doug himself is most aware of this when discussing other officers. As part of his training period, he worked with a White officer who was tense every time he found himself around a group of Blacks. Though Doug is critical of such White officers' actions, he also excuses them to some extent by suggesting that they're not "mean," just "scared." He reserves his harshest critique for the supervisors who deploy their officers without sensitivity to what they can and cannot do.

Like Jay, Doug argues that people's critiques of cops arise because they do not fully understand what it is like "out here," not because people might have different moral or legal views about force. Doug's comments arose when we were talking about his reaction to the beating of African-American motorist Rodney King by white police officers in Los Angeles. He quickly noted that he believed the L.A. police officers were wrong, but followed that with comments on the ways that people tend to misinterpret police actions. His comments condense a number of the strategies discussed thus far in this paper.

> Say for instance you would like be in a window and you would see me run up on some kids you seen right across the street. And you—they don't look like they're doing anything to you. But I go up and choke one of them, just running out of my car and and I go up and choke one of them. It seems like for no reason at all. It would be hard for me to explain that I told them to get off the street, I knew they were dealing drugs, I wouldn't have it, I told them if I came back, you know. Now if they would have pulled him out of the car and somebody would have shot that saying that "Oh they just beat him." Now how do they know he didn't have a gun or whatever? Now like I said, that <<the beating of Rodney King>> was excessive force, and that was ridiculous, to beat a guy like that. But I mean if they would have beat him a couple times or whatever and that was filmed, it would look kinda one-sided. See as a police officer, you have enough problems worrying about yourself (pause) being all—getting, you know, being shot, being—existing out on the street. But to worry about if you're gonna get sued, if your family's gonna, you know if you're gonna lose your house and all that stuff. Every time you question something, or move you make, it could cost you your life. If you're afraid that someone is watching you, you're afraid you don't want to hit this guy or snatch him up, and then he turns around and stabs you, and kills you. You're between a rock and a hard place. [PO 30A, Black male, 30, 2 years on the job]

Doug is torn. He wants to critique what happened in L.A., but reserve the right to use force for himself. He wants to critique outsiders' views of policing at the same time that he is an outsider to what happened in L.A. In this brief passage a cluster of grammatical features mark anxious preoccupation and serve to heighten the officer's message about his double bind, how immobilized he feels by needing to balance a need for self-defense with a concern for citizens' rights. There is a cluster of verbs and adjectives that describes worry and fear, though note that here again the officer does not construct himself as the agent or actor or even the experiencer ("*to worry about if you're gonna get sued, if you're afraid*"). The author also piles up the potential consequences of any act, with a series of "if" clauses that together imagine the worse that could happen: *if you're gonna get sued, if your family's gonna, if you're afraid.* Finally, impersonal "you" serves to distance these concerns from him in the second half of his account: "*if you're afraid,*" "*you're between a rock and a hard place.*" If Jay largely emphasizes the physical dangers of policing, Doug adds to these concerns a preoccupation with the moral and legal hazards of the job. This spiral of panic may reflect the particular dilemmas that being Black and being a police officer pose.

### Girls Who Freak: Turning Rapport Talk on Its Head

After having repeatedly heard how masculine Cissy was, I was eager to meet her. I was startled to find she was a short, plump White woman with long, curly black hair. Though following department regulations would have meant pulling her hair up into a bun, she wore it loose down on her shoulders. It was the week before Halloween and she was wearing a pumpkin tie pin. Though regulation socks are dark blue, her socks had pumpkins on them. She looked like a PTA mother. My surprise at the fact that she was perceived as masculine reflects some dominant gender ideologies that link femininity and masculinity to appearance. For police officers, however, it is interaction which is a more salient characteristic, in part because interactions are so carefully scrutinized by the public and by supervisors, but also because interactions shape the work environment for other officers. Cissy's enthusiasm for "acting crazy" led to her being perceived as masculine, and is evidence that the crime control ideology is gendered as masculine, regardless of who embraces it. There was, however, a stronger negative connotation in labelling her as masculine than in labelling male officers as such. Other officers saw Cissy as an impatient, impetuous officer who did not treat people right. More than any of the other officers I rode with, Cissy's image of the kind of police officer she was differed from my observations and from the perceptions of other officers. Cissy repeatedly painted herself as an active officer who was interested in helping people, and who had a knack for establishing rapport with the public. She describes the way people in a racially-mixed, lower-to-middle income neighborhood reacted to her and her female partner.

> [I]t was funny cause they would see two females come down in the car and it was like, "We're not afraid of you" so you kinda had to get real hard-nosed with them at first, but it was funny cause after you like really got out of the car and you show them this is the way it's gonna be, they kinda like you. **You got a rapport going** with them, where when they would see your car, they would just leave. We have worked out **such a good rapport** with those people down there. I've NE:VER had no problems. Those other officers they go down there and they give them a real hard time. . . . I had one problem and after that. "I'm not moving, you're not nothing." I'm like, "Oh yeah. We're something. Let's go." And we were out of the car. And it was like, "**Those girls are CRA:zy.** They'll actually make you move." [PO 11A, White female, mid-30s, 2 years on the job]

In the literature on language and gender, seeking rapport has been largely associated with women's talk. Tannen (1990:77) defines rapport-talk as a way of establishing connections and negotiating relations in which emphasis is placed on displaying similarities and matching experiences. She contrasts this with report-talk, in which she maintains many men display knowledge or skills as a way to preserve independence and status in a hierarchical social order. Cissy's definition of rapport is much more like Tannen's definition of report-talk. For her, rapport seems to be understood as everyone recognizing her right and ability to use verbal and physical force, and fearing that possibility.

The extent to which women officers are licensed to use physical force and tough talk is at least partly linked to the class and ethnic persona they present, and to stereotypes about White and Black femininity in the U.S. Though Cissy was seen in a negative light, as "too masculine," Ayanna, a young Black woman who was seen as ready, willing, and able to use force, did not receive similar sanctions. Ayanna was one of the few young female police officers who received the accolade of "knows her way around out there" from older White male officers. She was in her mid-20s and had been on the force for 2 years. She was a slight African-American woman (weighing about 100 pounds, she confessed, and trying to gain more), with tightly cropped hair. Though many smaller women were ignored or babied by male officers, Ayanna was, at the time I rode with her, being actively recruited by the City's Drug Task Force, which at the time of my fieldwork had no female officers. She tells stories about fights with relish.

> We had to chase this guy . . . when I first came on. We had to chase him cause they were going on a drug bust . . . and they wanted him and Jimmy Baker. . . . We got a tip right, we had to chase these boys, they were supposed to be armed. . . . We really didn't know if they were armed or not. Police officers been chasing them for months and they been lying to them, blowing them off. Me and my partner caught these guys. . . . When I finally caught them I had these fake nails on. I used to go and get my nails done every week. Broke my nail. Fifty dollars. When I seen he broke my nail, I **freaked**. I said, "You broke my nail!" I **pounded** him in his head, **acting like I was crazy.** "I can't believe you broke my nail!" I'm **tripping** over my nail right. I'm still huffing and puffing from the run. Was fun. We had a great time that day. [PO 58A, Black female, early 20s, 2 years on the job]

In a curious reversal of feminine stereotypes, here a broken fingernail does not reduce a woman to ineffectiveness, but rather leads to the use of physical force. Though a fake fingernail is a symbol of femininity, perhaps especially a symbol of a certain kind of Black femininity, her physical reaction is precisely that of other officers whose authority is questioned in any way. Again verbs mark a sudden change of state ("*was tripping*," "*freaked*," "*pounded*"). Like the male officers above, she describes her actions as a masquerade ("*acting like I was crazy*"). Ayanna also invoked the necessity for "acting crazy" in other, rather different circumstances. She was on her way to a call that had been described by the dispatcher as "complainant says her boyfriend's on the way over to her house and she expects trouble." As Ayanna drove to the largely White working-class area she said that this was an area where people were known for fighting police officers, and for their dislike of Black officers. She described the strategy she would try to adopt to handle the call ("*First I'll try to start off nice*"), but points out that sometimes "you gotta act crazy" to be recognized as an authority in such a neighborhood.

It is clear from these descriptions that women, too, can embrace a crime control ideology, and that younger women in particular are likely to do so. They are not trying to establish a distinctively feminine or womanly style of policing as a way of creating space for themselves in this predominantly masculine workplace, as women did at the turn of the century when they saw policing as an extension of social work (Appier 1998). Instead, these younger women choose to assimilate to, and reinscribe the power of, the dominant ideology of how to act, and interact, as a police officer, in ways that end up allying them with certain male officers, and against older female officers who often adopt a more critical stance towards the crime control model. Indeed, younger women argue that older women may have been qualified for the job, but they took it for the wrong reasons: "they only do it for the money." Many of the older women did enter policing at times of financial hardship (e.g. a divorce, a husband's loss of a job in a steel mill), and they do not describe policing as a job they had always dreamed of doing. Because they "only took the job for the money" they are not seen as professional. Younger women distance themselves from the problems faced by the first female officers, many of whom are still on the job, understanding them as difficulties faced by particular individuals rather than challenges linked to breaking down the barriers to women working on this job. They tend to see measures such as affirmative action as unnecessary. Young women therefore tend to over-estimate the extent to which simply being a "good" police officer allows them to succeed on the job, and to under-estimate the ways that their presence on the job was and is supported by certain institutional measures (like affirmative action). Their views do not allow them to see the ways that gender remains linked to the definition of what being a good police officer is, albeit in a less marked way that when women were seen as incapable of becoming police officers.

## CONCLUSIONS

The wide distribution of the ideology of police officer as crime fighter among Pittsburgh police officers is partial evidence for its dominant status among Pittsburgh police officers. Police officers who espouse it may be White or Black, men or women. Some have college educations and others have high school educations, some are veterans and some are not, some are rookies and some have been on the force for close to fifteen years. Among those who espouse the ideology there is, perhaps, an unusually high cluster of people who come from policing families. And yet the crime fighter ideology remains associated with a certain kind of masculinity, irrespective of the people who hold it. This makes it difficult for women, and men who have not traditionally been police officers, to be perceived as competent, and thus gives them a tenuous foothold within the job. In addition, those who challenge the dominant ideology may not be judged as policing effectively. Rather than "acting crazy" some officers focus on constructing another persona, that of the rational, calm, cool bureaucrat. Officers who orient towards this way of thinking about policing tend to be women (especially older women), or Black men, or White men with college educations. These officers may be portrayed by others as unwilling or unable to do "real" police work. Still, those who fall in with dominant norms may not be seen as effective police officers either. As affirmative action hiring plans have been rolled back in police departments in recent years, hirings of women and (to a lesser extent) minority men have immediately dropped because they still are not seen by administrators as fully capable of doing the job. Recent redefinitions of policing as community policing, or as "social work in combat boots" do offer a significant challenge to the crime-fighter ideology, and may create more permanent niches for women and minority men in policing. In Pittsburgh, however, community policing has not been embraced by either administrators or police officers.

When the police officers tell stories, to themselves or to the public or to me, about moments when the use of force was necessary, they are not merely describing those experiences, but recreating them, seducing themselves and others into believing that the sequence of events that they describe was not only justified, but inevitable. Given the emotional power of these stories, simply instructing officers to behave in other ways, where their actions are perceived as inappropriate, seems unlikely to be a productive strategy for changing the way they approach these scenarios. Activists have repeatedly found that in numerous settings presenting research which suggests to people that their beliefs are "false" is not sufficient for engendering support for change, or even agreement that the activists are right. One needs, instead, to find a way of restructuring these ways of feeling.

The discursive strategies which accompany these officers' descriptions of and justifications for their use of force focus on the ways they elicit respect and fear by acting crazy, and by acting in abrupt and unpredictable ways. These narrators also (with attentiveness to public perceptions of the use of force) often de-emphasize their own role as agents of the law. This denial of agency may be one of the defining features of legal and medical institutional talk in many settings, and one of the key ways that authority and power not only justified but disguised (see also Briggs 1997). Many of these officers' stories about the use of force are accompanied by sheer fear about the potential crumbling of their police power. By emphasizing the danger they face "out here", they justify the use of force in self-defense. Other working class jobs—mining, construction, agriculture—are, in fact, more dangerous than police work but police officers' constant sense of fear distinguishes them from these workers (Reuss-Ianni 1983:19–20). The discourse on fear here shares with studies of colonial violence, where talk about fear of the dominated was used to justify suppression, as well as a way of bargaining with other elites for resources and support needed to face down the purported threat (see Abu-Lughod and Lutz 1990:14). It does not seem inconsequential for understanding the particular stances towards violence expressed here that veterans of the U.S. military receive preference in hiring as police officers (McElhinny 2000), or that my fieldwork was conducted during a period when the U.S. government saw itself as waging a "war on drugs" both in the U.S. and in Latin and South America. Perhaps what is most striking about the worldview of police officers is precisely the ways in which they assume that social interactions are built around conflict and mayhem. They repeatedly insist that the world is violent and that no one is trustworthy. Though some may lament the loss of innocence and trust that comes with repeatedly dealing with violence, most police officers were convinced that the Hobbesian view of human nature which this led them to have was much more accurate than the blinkered and rosier view of others. The stories they tell about instances in which they use physical force, and the justifications which they offer for it, are built around this linguistic and social ideology. For them, instances of lying, conflict and violence are not extraordinary, but ordinary, everyday occurrences.

Indeed, for many police officers, violence and deception define humanity.

## ACKNOWLEDGMENTS

Research and writing were supported by the National Science Foundation (NSF Graduate Fellowship and NSF Dissertation Improvement Grant), the Mellon Foundation, the Wenner Gren Foundation for Anthropological Research (Pre-Doctoral Grant, and Richard Carley Hunt Post-doctoral Grant), the Stanford Humanities Center, the University of Pittsburgh Women's Studies Program, the Stanford Center for the Study of Conflict and Negotiation, and the Department of Anthropology at the University of Toronto.

## APPENDIX A. TRANSCRIPTION CONVENTIONS

Each transcribed example is followed by information about the tape that the example can be found on, as well as the police officer's sex (male or female), ethnicity (Black, White, Mixed ethnicity) and years of work on the Pittsburgh police force (where available). For example, [PO 11A, White female, mid-30s, 2 years on the job] indicates that the transcribed example is on side A of PO 11. The officer is White, female, and in her mid-30s. She has worked as a police officer for two years. This paper also draws on the following transcription conventions:

| (pause) | All pauses are marked between parentheses. |
|---|---|
| We were walk— | A dash marks a word or phrase broken off before it is finished. |
| LOUD | Capital letters indicate increased volume. |
| eve::ry | Semi-colon marks lengthened sound. |
| (laughs) | Laughter is marked between single parentheses. |
| "quote " | Indicates quoted speech. |
| <text> | Parentheses surround barely audible speech for which the transcription is uncertain. |
| .... | Three or four dots indicate that some material from the original transcript has been omitted. |
| <<comment>> | Double brackets enclose transcriber comments. |
| **bold** | Part of transcript highlighted for analyst's purposes. |

## NOTES

1. It is perhaps significant that Deborah Tannen's later work, focusing on men and women at work, did not receive the same public attention as her work on men and women in couples. This suggests that work which matches certain prevailing assumptions about how gender works is amplified and widely circulated, while other kinds of research are not.
2. I have chosen to use the terms *Black* and *White* throughout this paper because they are the terms which police officers usually use. Female officers tend to use *policeman* or *police officer* to describe their own role; male officers tend to use *policeman*. I have opted to use *police officer* as the default term throughout, adding a description of gender where it seems relevant.

## REFERENCES

Abu-Lughod, Lila and Catherine Lutz. 1990. Introduction: Emotion, discourse and the politics of everyday life. In Catherine Lutz and Lila Abu-Lughod (eds.), *Language and the politics of emotion*. Cambridge: Cambridge University Press, 1–23.

Appier, Janis. 1998. *Policing women: The sexual politics of law enforcement and the LAPD*. Philadelphia: Temple University Press.

Briggs, Charles. (1997). Introduction: From the ideal, the ordinary, and the orderly to conflict and violence in pragmatic research. Special issue of *Pragmatics* on "Conflict and violence in pragmatic research." 7(4): 451–459.

Cornwall, Andrea and Nancy Lindisfarne. 1994. Dislocating masculinity: Gender, power, and anthropology. In Andrea Cornwall and Nancy Lindisfarne (eds.), *Dislocating masculinities: Comparative ethnographies*. New York: Routledge, 11–47.

Gal, Susan. 1991. Between speech and silence: The problematics of research on language and gender. In Micaela di Leonardo (ed.), *Gender at the crossroads of knowledge*. Berkeley: University of California Press, 175–203.

Mattingly, Cheryl. 1998. *Healing dramas and clinical plots: The narrative structure of experience*. Cambridge: Cambridge University Press.

McElhinny, Bonnie. 1995. Challenging hegemonic masculinities: Female and male police officers handling domestic violence. In Kira Hall and Mary Bucholtz (eds.), *Gender articulated: Language and the socially constructed self*. New York: Routledge, 217–243.

McElhinny, Bonnie. 2000. Affirmative action and veterans' hiring preferences: Two quota systems. *Voices: Newsletter of the association for feminist anthropology*. July, 4(1): 1–6.

McElhinny, Bonnie. 2003. Theorizing gender in sociolinguistics and linguistic anthropology. In Janet Holmes and Miriam Meyerhof (eds.), *Handbook of language and gender*. Oxford: Basil Blackwell, pp. 21–42.

McElhinny, Bonnie. n.d. *Policing language and gender*. Unpublished ms.

Reuss-Ianni, E. 1983. *The two cultures of policing: Street cops and management cops*. New Brunswick, NJ: Transaction Books.

Scott, Joan. 1986. Gender: A useful category of historical analysis. *American Historical Review*. 91(5): 1053–1075.

Tannen, Deborah. 1990. *You just don't understand: Women and men in conversation*. New York: William Morrow.

Walker, Samuel. 1977. *A critical history of police reform: The emergence of professionalism*. Lexington, MA: Lexington Books.

# Surgical Transformations in the Pursuit of Gender

## Lauren E. Gulbas

In May 2005, I found myself sitting in my neighbor Paola's living room, talking with her about the lengths that she was willing to go to in order to replace her breast implants.[1] I was living in Caracas at the time, starting a research project on the cosmetic surgery industry in Venezuela. My work focused on exploring the high rates of cosmetic surgery in a place with marked economic inequality and with rates of illness and death that are comparable with other developing nations. In a city whose residents had to confront high poverty, food shortages, and spiraling rates of violence and homicide as a part of everyday life, I was surprised by Paola's strong preoccupation with finding a way to undergo an aesthetic procedure, but she described her predicament—and her solution to it—as a common one. She did not have the money to purchase new implants, but explained, "I am not going to buy new school uniforms for my children, and this way I can save up some more money. You know, this is how women are in Venezuela. There are women who do not feed their kids so that they can have cosmetic surgery. It is just the way things are here."

Throughout my anthropological fieldwork in Caracas, Venezuela between 2005 and 2007, I found that numerous individuals echoed sentiments similar to that of Paola. These anecdotes convey a powerful cultural stereotype about Venezuela women: in their pursuit of "feminine" bodies, they prioritize cosmetic surgery as an important, if not necessary, practice, sometimes taking drastic measures to have their bodies surgically modified. Rationing food to save money, risking surgery with a cheap back-alley quack, or electing to have surgery without general anesthesia to avoid a long wait-list in public hospitals, women—and to a more limited extent, men—hazard their bodies and lives to have cosmetic surgery. But why?

This chapter endeavors to uncover some of the reasons why women and men allocate resources in particular ways to have cosmetic surgery, specifically cosmetic breast surgery.[2] Although individuals offer many different explanations for their behavior, I argue that the construction of gendered personhood figures prominently. This chapter will begin with an exploration of the body-as-self paradigm, which encourages individuals to formulate an understanding of self, or the subjective interpretation of one's personhood (Meyer 1987), as based on appearance. I suggest that the body-as-self paradigm enables cosmetic surgeons to justify the importance of aesthetic procedures to their patients by laying claim to the psychological benefits of surgery. Then, I will contextualize the cosmetic surgery industry in Venezuela, both locally and historically. From this discussion, I will illustrate how cosmetic breast surgery is interpreted by patients as the only solution for correcting an ambiguously gendered body, allowing men and women to attain a normalized masculine or feminine self.

## SELLING THE BODY-AS-SELF

Throughout history, the cultivation of appearance has been a widespread practice in many societies. From make-up to corsets and cosmetic surgery, individuals use the body as a site for modification, actively crafting it to fit personal and social ideals of beauty. The practices individuals engage in to alter the body and its appearance vary across time and space, pointing to the importance of examining bodily practices as a means to uncover cultural meaning (Scheper-Hughes and Lock 1987).

Over the past decades, the meaning and purpose of bodywork has changed dramatically. Once a site to realize cultural ideals for beauty, the body has now become a vehicle through which individuals display the self (Becker 1994; Shilling 1993). This body-as-self paradigm both shapes and is shaped by an ever-increasing consumer-oriented society. Appearance-driven consumer markets promote the purchase of specific

Original material prepared for this text. Reprinted by permission of the author.

identities by encouraging individuals to buy products intended to transform the body (Mascia-Lees 2010). The cultivation of appearance requires that individuals become embedded within capitalist markets aimed at the manufacture and sale of face and hair products, body lotions, dieting supplements, and fashion (Malson 1998).

Consumption of these products is motivated by a global consumer industry that uses images of bodies to suggest how a given product enhances physical appearance. These images are constructed for a specific purpose: to enable an individual to develop a sense of what counts as "looking good" (Fraser and Greco 2005). In these images, the display of bodies—bodies that are retouched, airbrushed, and unlikely to exist in a natural state—creates an ideal against which individuals measure themselves and are measured by others (Rubin et al. 2003). The ability to lock people into these consumer markets is predicated on an ideological collapse of the outer body and inner self—if one *looks* good, then one *feels* good (Featherstone 1991).

Cosmetic surgery has capitalized on this perceived link between looking good and feeling good. In part, this reflects cosmetic surgery's relation to commercialism. It has, after all, turned the process of "looking good" into a multibillion-dollar industry. Yet for cosmetic surgery to be regarded as a legitimate medical practice, the field has had to demonstrate that modifying physical appearance can lead to improvements in overall patient health. Surgeons justify the practice of invasive surgery for aesthetic reasons by asserting the importance of the body-as-self paradigm: cosmetic surgery can improve a patient's image of self, promoting an enhanced sense of emotional and psychological well-being (Sullivan 2004).

In Venezuela, discourses of selfhood and psychological healing resonate deeply with cosmetic surgeons. The Venezuelan Society of Plastic Surgery describes cosmetic surgery as "absolutely necessary to maintain mental equilibrium and improve one's self-esteem" (Engel 2005:3). The eager promotion of the body-as-self paradigm among Venezuelan surgeons provides a unique opportunity to explore the intersections of body, selfhood, and gender. As I will demonstrate below, cosmetic surgery has been central to the construction of contemporary beauty standards in Venezuela, so that the industry contributes to the very problems in self-esteem that it claims to alleviate. This has not always been the case, and the local practice of cosmetic surgery in Venezuela can best be understood by considering the history of a growing symbiosis between cosmetic surgery and the ultimate symbol of female beauty: the beauty pageant contestant.

## THE EVOLUTION OF AN IDEAL: PLASTIC MISSES AND COSMETIC SURGERY IN VENEZUELA

The Miss Venezuela pageant and the national cosmetic surgery industry share a parallel, yet inexorably linked, history. Both were established in the 1950s, in Venezuela's last years as a country dominated by more than a century of dictatorial regimes. The government of General Marcos Pérez Jiménez sought to build a modern nation and demonstrate to the developed world that Venezuela was its civilized equal (Coronil 1997). The Miss Venezuela pageant, initiated in 1952, operated as a symbol of this modernizing discourse. Venezuela would export the world's most beautiful women, evidence of its fulfillment of the qualities of an educated, cultured, and enlightened nation (Raidi 2005).

At the same time the pageant was beginning to export Venezuelan beauty, surgeons were importing Western aesthetic standards and medical techniques into an incipient professional cosmetic surgery industry. In 1956, Venezuela's first plastic surgery department was established, and the Venezuelan Society for Plastic and Reconstructive Surgery was founded later that year (García de Moral and Subero 2002). Even with these developments, physicians continued to travel to Europe and the United States, returning to their native country after completing their education to share the knowledge they gained in the hopes of modernizing Venezuelan medicine (Cisneros 1978).

The field of cosmetic surgery grew quickly after Venezuela became a democratic nation in 1958. No longer constrained by the educational mandates of dictatorial regimes, numerous public hospitals established residency programs in the 1960s. Cosmetic surgeons could be trained in Venezuela for the first time, but this medical instruction continued to be shaped by the global medical practices of Europe and North America as Venezuelan medical schools continued to import English medical textbooks and teaching philosophies (SVCPREM 2005).

By 1975, cosmetic surgery began to creep into the Miss Venezuela pageant, marking the first year during which Misses are known to have undergone cosmetic surgery to enhance their chances of winning the crown (Rodríguez 2005: 143). In a matter of decades, the links between the Miss Venezuela pageant and the cosmetic surgery industry became so entrenched that the Miss Venezuela Organization, already staffed with numerous cosmetic surgeons, was dubbed "the house of dolls" and "a factory for the production of Misses" (Ortega 2005: 11). By 1992, every participant in the Miss Venezuela pageant had undergone at least one cosmetic procedure, and the winner that year, Milka Chulina, was proclaimed in the newspapers as the "most reconstructed Miss" in pageant history (Rodríguez 2005: 19).

The construction of "plastic" Misses through cosmetic surgery has produced a fundamental shift in cultural ideals of beauty: tall, extremely thin, with delicately curvaceous chest-waist-hip measurements. Although the average weight for Miss Venezuela has hovered around 123 pounds since the competition's inception, the height of contestant winners has increased dramatically over time. Prior to 1980, the median height of Miss Venezuela was 5 feet 5 inches, whereas the median height of contestants over the past three decades has been about 5 feet 9 inches. This has led to a shift in body shape, from one that "was fuller with wide hips" (Rodríguez 2005: 55), to a more emaciated physique. In fact, the average Body Mass Index, a calculation used to measure body weight to height, is below 17.5 kg/m$^2$, making a typical Miss Venezuela from recent years categorically underweight.

The extreme thinness of Miss Venezuela makes the natural accomplishment of a lean, yet curvy, body more difficult, if not impossible. As contestant BMI has dropped, the aesthetic expectations for pageant winners have continued to focus on a curvy form that is unlikely to occur naturally on a body that has been stripped of its fat. According to the Miss Venezuela Organization, the ideal feminine body should possess chest-waist-hip measurements that approximate 90-60-90 cm (36-24-36 inches) (Rodríguez 2005). Cosmetic surgery resolves the paradox of a declared preference for curvy bodies and the documented decline in BMI: successful pageant contestants strip their body of its natural curves through diet and exercise and then turn to cosmetic surgery to resculpt a body with 90-60-90 cm measurements. In this way, the ideal feminine body portrayed within the Miss Venezuela pageant has become, quite literally, a constructed one.

## THE OPENING OF ACCESS: THE PRACTICE OF COSMETIC SURGERY TODAY

Today, cosmetic surgery is pervasive in the public view. Huge billboards line Caracas' congested highways, on which cosmetic surgeons promote their myriad services. These advertisements often feature a former Miss Venezuela, suggesting that although no one is born to look like a Miss, any woman can achieve the same transformation through surgery. In magazines, banks describe credit and loan options that enable customers to finance their aesthetic procedures. The profusion of print media operates to lure potential clients into the private, shiny, modern clinics of cosmetic surgeons. Yet the ubiquity of plastic culture is not without its critics. Newspaper comic strips often play

on the excessive abundance of cosmetic surgery in cultural thought. For example, a comic published in a Caracas newspaper in December 2006 featured two little girls walking to school: one girl says that she is going to ask the baby Jesus to give her breast implants for Christmas; her friend responds that she will ask for liposuction (Estampas 2006). The underlying point of this satire is clear: how much further will the desire for cosmetic surgery among many Venezuelans go?

Ironically, a dramatic restructuring of the public health-care system in 1999 has only helped to fuel the demand for cosmetic surgery in Venezuela. In an effort to challenge immense inequalities in the distribution of wealth, President Hugo Chávez prohibited the collection of fees for all services rendered in public institutions, including the public health-care system (PAHO 2006). These reforms effectively made cosmetic surgery free in all public hospitals and clinics. In theory, this mandate makes access to cosmetic surgery equitable to all Venezuelans regardless of means. In practice, however, many patients are denied access to an idealized body because resources and surgeons for carrying out aesthetic procedures are in short supply. Public hospitals are often unable to meet the high demand for cosmetic surgery, and access depends on how physicians prioritize the treatment of patients, as well as the training of residents—which is essential for a national program of medical training to thrive. Problems with capacity are compounded by the crumbling infrastructure at many public hospitals. For example, one public hospital once touted as a symbol for medical advancement is now plagued by budget deficits and deterioration of its facilities. In weighing their options for having cosmetic surgery as quickly and cheaply as possible, patients often navigate public and private facilities as they seek procedures that will bring them closer to a body that conforms to their sense of self.

The majority of individuals who make this transformative journey are women. Although the President of the Venezuelan Society for Plastic Surgery told me that men are slowly making up a greater proportion of the population surgically modifying their bodies for aesthetic reasons, my own compilation of hospital data reveals that differences between rates of cosmetic surgery between men and women are still great. Women requesting cosmetic surgery outnumber men by twenty-two to one (see Table 5.1). Clearly, cosmetic surgery is an overwhelmingly gendered practice, and this is most evident in the case of cosmetic breast surgery.[3] Whereas women's requests for consultation for breast surgery far outnumber requests for any other procedure, men's consultations for breast surgery represent less than 1 percent of all consultations. Cosmetic breast surgery, then, is perhaps the most gendered procedure that patients seek. On the surface,

**Table 5.1 Patient Consultations for Cosmetic Surgery, July 2006 to July 2007**

| PROCEDURE | WOMEN | MEN |
|---|---|---|
| Cosmetic breast surgery | 924 | 9 |
| Liposuction | 267 | 8 |
| Tummy tuck | 170 | 3 |
| Face lift | 62 | 7 |
| Eye lift | 220 | 6 |
| Nose job | 265 | 57 |
| Total | 1908 | 90 |

the explanation for this difference seems quite simple: only women have breasts, and therefore, it is only women who have breast surgery. I assert that the diverse physical forms of male bodies, and their own narratives of surgery, defy cultural assumptions that breasts are an anatomical feature belonging solely to women. An examination of both women's and men's explanations for undergoing breast surgery reveals the powerful ways in which the breast operates as a symbol of a gendered subjectivity and how cosmetic surgery allows patients to overcome a "naturally" deficient body in order to reconstruct their sense of self.

## MEASURING UP: WOMEN, BREASTS, AND SELFHOOD

In private clinics, approximately 60 percent of women who consult for breast surgery request breast implants. This is not the case in public hospitals, where departments of plastic surgery have suspended consultations for breast implants because hospitals are not structurally equipped to meet patient demand. Every morning, dozens of women line up outside the waiting room, hoping to have a consultation with a cosmetic surgeon for breast implants; and every morning, almost all of these women are turned away. Only a fortunate few will be accepted for a consultation, usually because a resident in the program needs training in the surgical techniques.

Breast enlargement surgery may cost anywhere from $700 to $3,000 in a private clinic. In public hospitals, the cost of surgery is free, with one caveat: patients must purchase their implants from a local pharmacy. Depending on the type of implant, a patient may pay up to $560. Women carefully weigh the overall cost of surgical procedures, yet for many, the ability to purchase "the best" shapes decisions about which surgeons and breast implants to choose. Breast enlargement has

become a symbol of consumer culture in Venezuela, wherein "what you buy is a major measure of your worth" (Young 1992: 224). By purchasing a specific body through cosmetic surgery, many women feel they can change how they feel about their bodies and themselves, constructing a self that is worthy of a feminine subjectivity.

Not surprisingly, metaphors of self-worth permeate narratives of decisions to undergo breast surgery. In a consumer culture where breasts become a symbol of womanhood, many women express feeling consistently judged about the size and shape of their breasts. Most women with whom I conversed were able to recall a specific moment in time when they realized that they did not like their breasts. For some, this occurred during secondary school, when they were bullied by male and female classmates for having a chest "flat like a wall." These verbal torments were interpreted as a public rejection of individual womanhood. As one woman stated, the bullying at school left her feeling inadequate. She explained that she no longer felt "comfortable because having breasts is part of being a woman. I felt like I was missing something, that I was incomplete."

Among older women, the change in breast shape over time is perceived as a symbol of inevitable old age and decline. One 46-year-old woman described her sagging breasts as making her feel "impotent." She recalled a period when she was younger and had many admirers, who would call after her in the street and remark on the beauty of her youthful womanhood. But "now I am old," she explained, "no one tells me anything anymore." Her breasts signify powerlessness and weakness as she approaches an age where she feels she is no longer useful for sex, reproduction, or work.

And for other women, it is not necessarily about attaining or recapturing womanhood, but about restoring it, usually after pregnancy and childbirth. Although motherhood is perceived by many as the cornerstone of femininity, it is often this very process that makes some individuals feel they are less womanly. A subtle irony exists in that the achievement of womanhood through reproduction becomes a factor that weakens a mother's gendered selfhood. Paola's narrative provides an illustrative example in the ways that motherhood and womanhood intersect in contradictory ways.

When I first visited Caracas in May 2005, I lived in the same building as Paola. At that time, she was in her late thirties and married with two children. My landlady had told me that Paola had breast implants, and one afternoon I decided to ask her about her cosmetic surgery experience. I asked Paola if it was true, and she said yes. Lighting a Belmont cigarette, Paola began to tell me her experience of having breast enlargement surgery:

I got my breast implants eight years ago, after the birth of my second child. Children change your body so much, so I decided to have breast implants. My breasts were gone because I gave milk to both my children. They sucked all my breasts away! The doctor told me after the surgery that I should not move my arms. I was not supposed to do any housework, or carry my children. But I was a mother. What was I going to do? I had to take care of my children. And who was going to cook dinner and clean clothes if I was not going to. My husband? No! I had to work. And one day, maybe a week after the surgery, the wounds opened up. I had to go back to the doctor to have them sewn up again. Now I have big scars.

Paola construes her femininity as being subverted by motherhood. She constructs breastfeeding as a parasitic activity: her children literally sucked away her womanhood. Paola blames her children for her lack of breasts. Breast implants provide Paola with the means to reassert a feminine subjectivity: by making her body appear to be more feminine, Paola will *become* more feminine. It is interesting to note that having surgery poses a limitation on her ability to do what she perceives as "women's work," and because she must carry out her domestic responsibilities as a mother, she experiences complications after surgery. So strong is her desire to recreate a lost womanhood that in her determination to correct the scars and replace her implants, Paola expresses a willingness to withhold resources from her children, such as new uniforms for school.

My interpretation of women's decisions to have breast surgery reveals that breasts operate not only as a symbol of womanhood, but become part of a woman's experience of herself. The perceived failure to have "normal" breasts contributes to feelings of inadequacy, incompleteness, and many times, deterioration. The field of cosmetic surgery is complicit in the production of a normalized breast to which women feel they do not measure up: breasts that are too small (hypomastia), too big (hypermastia), or not perky enough after pregnancy (postpartum atrophy) are diagnosed as disordered, contributing to women's gendered experiences in terms of failure.

## MEN HAVE BREASTS TOO

Cosmetic breast surgery is primarily conceived of as something requested by and performed on women. Men are rarely considered to be a part of this discourse, but in actuality, men have breasts, too. The condition of "man-breasts" is referred to as *gynecomastia*, literally meaning "women-like breasts." It is a surprisingly common among most men: an estimated 40 percent of men have breasts (Carlson 1980). But where women tend to seek surgery to create or restore their breasts, accentuating them to more closely approximate a cultural and medical standard, men elect breast reduction surgery in order to remove what is considered to be a shameful femininity that is not natural to the male body.

Guillermo's narrative reflects how experiences of a deficient masculinity become intertwined with perceptions of breasts and the normal male body. I met Guillermo in February of 2007 in one of Caracas' large public hospitals. He was waiting for an appointment with a cosmetic surgeon to discuss his options for breast surgery. He arrived at the hospital with his wife, but prior to entering the examination room, he asked his wife to stay behind in the waiting room. I found this to be curious given that most of the women that I had observed and interviewed permitted their male partners to accompany them during the consultation. When I asked Guillermo why he asked his wife to stay outside, he whispered to me that his wife had never seen him with his shirt off. Not once—not even during sex.

During Guillermo's consultation, the cosmetic surgeon, a second-year male resident, provided Guillermo with an official diagnosis of gynecomastia. He explained to Guillermo that surgery would entail suctioning the subcutaneous fat that accumulated over his pectoral muscles, which created the appearance of having small breasts. The good news that surgery could treat this condition came with bad news for Guillermo—the surgical staff would not be able to perform the surgery because the hospital operating room was closed due to a bacterial contamination. The resident mentioned a possible solution: he could perform liposuction on Guillermo using local anesthesia. Guillermo replied with an emphatic yes, and his surgery was scheduled the following week.

After his consultation, Guillermo agreed to talk with me about his decision to have the procedure. He exclaimed that the risk of pain would be worth the opportunity to have surgery. He described the immense shame that he felt about his body, which forced him to feel as if he was not "truly a man." As he explained, a man is not supposed to have breasts. To disguise his chest, he often wore loose clothing and sometimes bandaged his chest when he felt that his shirt fit tightly. Whereas clothing provided a way to hide his ambiguously gendered body, his daily performance of masculinity allowed him to publicly display his manhood. Guillermo described acting like a "real" man: being dominant and assertive in the workplace, providing a substantial income so that his wife did not have to work, and going out with his friends in the evening to drink. Each of these behaviors corresponds to stereotypical notions of the Venezuelan man, where the ideology of machismo continues to retain significant cultural capital. Yet his public performance of masculinity was ultimately challenged by a biological body that was coded as feminine. This inhibited what he described as the most important aspect of a masculine identity: the ability to engage in heterosexual intercourse without risking further shame about his body. His breasts, which prevented him from displaying his naked body, made it difficult for him to perform as a man in the bedroom.

For the few men who elect to have breast reduction, surgery offers the potential to recraft the male body into a more culturally acceptable form (Atkinson 2006). Yet given the prevalence of gynecomastia among men, and the association of breasts with femininity, why is male breast reduction surgery not more popular? In part, this may be due to the fact that cosmetic surgery continues to be regarded as distinctly feminine. The increasing visibility of cosmetic surgery in Caracas, particularly in popular media, has contributed to widespread perceptions that aesthetic procedures are the domain of women.

Moreover, participation in practices designed to enhance appearance seem to contradict the dominant gender ideology of machismo in Venezuela. The ethos of machismo stems from a fear of being indistinguishable from the feminine, and manliness becomes that which contrasts with womanliness (Chant 2003). This includes attention to appearance, communicated through the expectation that a woman should take actions to pursue an accentuated femininity. Although many Venezuelans acknowledge that, in practice, both men and women pay attention to their physical appearance, for a man to do so risks attacks on his manhood. And thus, many men may shy away from the pursuit of an appropriately gendered male body through breast cosmetic surgery.[4]

## CONCLUSION

Patients turn to cosmetic surgery for a variety of reasons. The choice to submit one's body to the knife may be perceived as desirable or necessary, as a way to improve self-esteem or as a vain expense. Many patients will construct the process of having surgery as a positive experience, allowing them to transform not only how they look, but how they feel about themselves. Yet this process of transformation reveals that decisions to have surgery are shaped within a specific context, wherein ideas about attractiveness and the culturally ideal body contribute to a growing consumerism of

plastic bodies. The cosmetic surgery industry has been able to profit on individual desires to recraft the body according to cultural notions of what constitutes the ideal body precisely because such notions contribute to low self-esteem.

This chapter has focused predominantly on how cosmetic breast surgery is offered to, and interpreted by, patients as a way to craft a gendered self by modifying insufficiently or ambiguously gendered body attributes. While this draws attention to the myriad ways individuals actively choose cosmetic surgery to overcome situations which are not of their own making (Davis 1995), we must also be mindful of how women and men become locked into consumer ideologies that reduce selfhood to physical appearance. In a global consumer culture that dictates that only certain bodies are available for consumption, the potential to experience one's body and self in terms of deficiency is great. As it pronounces its role in sculpting gendered bodies and promoting healthy minds, cosmetic surgery simultaneously promotes gendered differences in how individuals interpret their bodies and their potential to transform them through surgery.

## NOTES

1. All names of individuals have been replaced with pseudonyms.
2. This chapter is based on conversations with a number of women and men living in Caracas, Venezuela. Altogether, I interviewed 499 individuals, in addition to having a number of informal conversations with people I met during the course of my fieldwork. I spoke with cosmetic surgeons, psychologists, pageant directors, employees in beauty salons and gyms, patients with cosmetic surgery or seeking consultation for surgery, and individuals without cosmetic surgery in order to gather their perspectives. I also spent hours observing cosmetic surgeons and residents in four private clinics and two public hospitals. I watched as patients interacted with their doctors and nurses during consultations and pre- and postoperative procedures, and I observed interactions among physicians and nurses during surgery. Additionally, I gathered clinic and hospital data on the prevalence of cosmetic procedures.
3. Cosmetic breast surgery includes surgical procedures aimed at the aesthetic modification of the breast and its underlying tissue and can include the enlargement, reduction, or lifting of the breast. This excludes reconstructive procedures, such as breast reconstruction after mastectomy.
4. This contrasts with other kinds of cosmetic surgery, such as rhinoplasty. Among men who have nose jobs, the procedure is described as reconstructive even when the benefits of surgery are purely aesthetic. By emphasizing the necessity of cosmetic surgery, men recast bodywork

in a way that sublimates the aesthetic focus. Thus, the male pursuit of aesthetic surgery (excluding breast cosmetic surgery) is perceived as acceptable only insofar as it recapitulates the masculine trope of machismo: it is not viewed as *macho* to change one's appearances for aesthetic reasons. Rather, the necessity of the change is articulated as a way to correct a functional defect of the physical organ.

## REFERENCES

Atkinson, Michael. 2006. "Masks of Masculinity: (Sur)passing Narrative and Cosmetic Surgery." In Dennis Waskul and Phillip Vannini (eds.). *Body/Embodiment: Symbolic Interaction and the Sociology of the Body*, pp. 247–261. Aldershot: Ashgate Publishing Limited.

Becker, Anne B. 1994. "Nurturing and Negligence: Working on Other's Bodies in Fiji." In Thomas J. Csordas (ed.). *Embodiment and Experience: The Existential Ground of Culture and Self*, pp. 100–115. Cambridge: Cambridge University Press.

Carlson, Harold E. 1980. "Gynecomastia." *New England Journal of Medicine* 303: 795–799.

Chant, Sylvia H. 2003. "Gender and Sexuality." In Sylvia H. Chant and Nikki Craski (eds.). *Gender in Latin America*, pp. 126–160. New Brunswick: Rutgers University Press.

Cisneros, M. Zuñiga. 1978. *Historia de la Medicina, Toma III: La Medicina de los Tiempos Modernos y de la Epoca Contemporanea*. Caracas: Ediciones Edime.

Coronil, Fernando. 1997. *The Magical State: Nature, Money, and Modernity in Venezuela*. Chicago: The University of Chicago Press.

Davis, Kathy. 1995. *Reshaping the Female Body: The Dilemma of Cosmetic Surgery*. New York: Routledge.

Engel, Andrés Maroti. 2005. "La Cirugía Plática no es una Frivolidad." *Boletín Informativo de la Sociedad Venezolana de Cirugía Plástica, Reconstructive, Estética y Maxilofacial* 4: 3–4.

*Estampas*. 2006. "Humor de Rayma." *Estampas*, December 17.

Featherstone, Mike. 1991. "The Body in Consumer Culture." In Mike Featherstone, Mike Hepworth, and Bryan S. Turner (eds.). *The Body: Social Process and Cultural Theory*, pp. 170–196. London: Sage Publications.

Fraser, Mariam, and Monica Greco. 2005. "Introduction." In Mariam Fraser and Monica Greco (eds.). *The Body: A Reader*, pp. 1–42. New York: Routledge.

García de Moral, Margarita, and David Yaselli Subero. 2002. "El Servicio de Cirugía Plástica del Hospital Vargas: En sus 45 Años de Aniversario." *Archivos del Hospital Vargas* 44(1–2): 88–99.

Malson, Helen. 1998. *The Thin Woman: Feminism, Post-Structuralism, and the Social Psychology of Anorexia Nervosa*. London: Routledge.

Mascia-Lees, Frances E. 2010. *Gender and Difference in a Globalizing World*. Long Grove, IL: Waveland Press, Inc.

Meyer, John W. 1987. "Self and the Life Course: Institutionalization and Its Effects." In George M. Thomas, John W. Meyer, Francisco O. Ramirez, and John Boli (eds.). *Institutional Structure: Constituting the State, Society, and the Individual*, pp. 242–260. Newbury Park, CA: Sage.

Ortega, Nelson Hippolyte. 2005. "Casa de Muñecas: Así Fabricaron a Las Misses." In Albor Rodríguez (ed.). *Misses de Venezuela: Reinas que Cautivaron a un País: Crónicas, Reportajes y Testimonios del Concurso Miss Venezuela*, pp. 11–13. Caracas: Los Libros de El Nacional.

Pan American Health Organization (PAHO). 2006. *Mission Barrio Adentro: The Right to Health and Social Inclusion in Venezuela*. Caracas: PAHO/Venezuela.

Raidi, Aberlardo. 2005. "Venezuela País de Mujeres Bellas." In Labor Rodríguez (ed.). *Misses de Venezuela: Reinas que Cautivaron a un País: Crónicas, Reportajes y Testimonios del Concurso Miss Venezuela*, pp. 25–26. Caracas: Los Libros de El Nacional.

Rodríguez, Albor (ed.). 2005. *Misses de Venezuela: Reinas que Cautivaron a un País: Crónicas, Reportajes y Testimonios del Concurso Miss Venezuela*. Caracas: Los Libros de El Nacional.

Rubin, Lisa R., Mako L. Fitts, and Anne E. Becker. 2003. "Whatever Feels Good in my Soul: Body Ethics and Aesthetics among African American and Latina Women." *Culture, Medicine and Psychiatry* 27: 49–75.

Scheper-Hughes, Nancy, and Margaret M. Lock. 1987. "The Mindful Body: A Prolegomenon to Future Work in Medical Anthropology." *Medical Anthropology Quarterly* 1: 6–41.

Shilling, Chris. 1993. *The Body and Social Theory*. London: Sage.

Sociedad Venezolana de Cirugía Plástica, Reconstructiva, Estética, y Maxilofacial (SVCPREM). 2005. "Historia y Remembranzas de Nuestra Sociedad." *Boletín Informativo de la Sociedad Venezolana de Cirugía Plástica, Reconstructive, Estética y Maxilofacial* 4: 2–3.

Sullivan, Deborah A. 2004. *Cosmetic Surgery: The Cutting Edge of Commercial Medicine in America*. New Brunswick: Rutgers University Press.

Young, Iris Marion. 1992. "Breasted Experience: The Look and the Feeling." In Drew Leder (ed.). *The Body in Medical Thought and Practice*, pp. 215–231. Norwell, MA: Kluwer Academic Publishers.

# VI

# Culture, Sexuality, and the Body

Ethnographic, theoretical, and policy-related research on sexuality is now central to anthropological scholarship and significant in its contributions to our understandings of gender, health, and the body (Browner and Sargent 2007; Day 2007; Farmer 1992; Kulick 1998; Lewin 2006; Padilla 2007; Sargent and Brettell 1996; Weeks et al. 1996). Ethnographies of sexuality address questions such as, How is sexuality a social and economic product, variable across time, within and across cultures, fluid and shifting? How are we to understand sexual agency in relation to the potential for coercion, in particular political and economic conditions? Sexual forms, practices, and desires, although locally diverse, are increasingly shaped by global products such as mass media which produce sexual meanings, sexual practices, and experiences of pleasure. As Curtis observes "sexuality is a domain of multiple contradictions: a locus of both power and powerlessness, of self-determination and cultural control" (2009: 5).

Early anthropological research on sexuality contributed to our current understanding of sexuality as culturally constructed and learned in specific historical contexts. In contrast to contemporary studies that take sexuality as their core focus, classic anthropological monographs reported exotic sexual practices in the course of "holistic" ethnographic description. For example, we learn in Malinowski's *The Sexual Life of Savages in Northwestern Melanesia* (1929) that the Trobriand islanders may bite each other's eyelashes in the heat of passion, but other than occasional esoterica, the naturalistic, biological bias dominated the study of sexuality.

However, as Vance observed in her classic volume *Pleasure and Danger: Exploring Female Sexuality* (1984: 8), "although sexuality, like all human cultural activity, is grounded in the body, the body's structure, physiology, and functioning do not directly or simply determine the configuration or meaning of sexuality." Rather, sexuality is in large part culturally constructed. Feminist theorists have argued that historical, social, and political influences "produce" the body. Just as we may inquire into the culturally variable meanings of masculinity and femininity, we may examine the ways in which sexuality and the body are invested with meanings in particular societies (Ortner and Whitehead 1981: 2).

Sexuality, as a topic of analysis, links the personal and the social, the individual and society, the local and the global. To Americans sex may imply the body, medical facts, Freud, and erotic techniques, but all of these aspects of sexuality are socially shaped and sexual activity is inevitably regulated. Within every culture, there are measures for the management of sexuality and gender expression (Ortner and Whitehead 1981: 24–25) and sanctions for those who break the rules.

These sanctions may be imposed at the level of the family, the lineage, the community, or the state. Indeed, Foucault (1981) has suggested that a feature of the recent past is the increasing intervention of the state in the domain of sexuality. In this regard, Ross and Rapp (1981: 71) conclude that it is not accidental that contemporary Western culture conceptualizes sex as a thing in itself, isolated from social, political, and economic context: "The separation with industrial capitalism of family life from work, of consumption from production, of leisure from labor, of personal life from political life, has completely reorganized the context in which we experience sexuality. . . . Modern consciousness permits, as earlier systems of thought did not, the positing of 'sex' for perhaps the first time as having an 'independent' existence." warns that while western culture may have a concept of sexuality divorced from reproduction, marriage, or other social domains, the analysis of sexuality is partial without reference to the economic, political, and cultural matrix in which it is embedded (Caplan 1987; Curtis 2009).

A comparative perspective informs us that the attributes of the body seen as sexual and erotic vary cross-culturally. For example, scarification, the corseted waist, bound feet, and the subincised penis are admired and provocative in particular cultures. Such attributes as these are not only physical symbols of sexuality, but indicators of status. Similarly, Sudanese women practice infibulation, a form of female genital cutting, causing serious pain and health risks to young women, for the honor of the family and as a sign of virtue. In the name of power, young men applied as recruits to the palace eunuch staff in Imperial China carrying their genitals in jars (Ortner and Whitehead 1981: 24). These examples are reminders of the impact of social concerns and cultural meanings in the domain of sexuality. A more challenging assertion is that the very experience of desire and the erotic are also cultural products.

Lila Abu-Lughod (in this book) explores the cultural construction of sexuality and local meanings of Islam through an analysis of wedding rituals in a Bedouin community in Egypt's Western Desert. Weddings produce and transform people's experiences of sexuality and gender relations and serve as a marker of cultural identity. Whereas sexuality in North America is considered something essentially private, separate from society and social power, to these Bedouin the wedding involves sexuality that has a public and participatory element. The defloration of the bride is a ritualized encounter between the bride and groom and including the women and men who congregate around them. Central to the ritual is the bride's virginity, which represents her family's honor; her body and the emphasis on opening the bride's vagina thus become a matter of public interest. Connections to kin and control of the kinship group are symbolized in these wedding rites. The sexual politics of gender relations were formerly portrayed in women's wedding songs and dances that represented the encounter between male and female as a contest of wills. Changing power relations have led to a de-emphasis of this mechanism for challenging male power. As Bedouins are drawn into the wider Egyptian state and economy, weddings increasingly are seen as entertainment and spectacle rather than as the ritual reproduction of the social and political dynamics of the community, symbolized in the sexual contest surrounding the bride's virginity.

Research in hunting and gathering societies also shows that sexual intercourse, while personal, can be a political act. In such societies, claims to women are central to men's efforts to achieve equal status with others (Collier and Rosaldo 1981: 291). Through sexual relations with women, men forge relationships with one another and symbolically express claims to particular women. Shostak (1981) presents the perspective of a !Kung woman, Nisa, on sex, marriage, and fertility in the broader context of a hunting and gathering society in which women have high status.

The !Kung believe that without sex, people can die, just as without food, one would starve. Shostak observes that "talk about sex seems to be of almost equal importance [to eating]. When women are in the village or out gathering, or when men and women are together, they spend hours recounting details of sexual exploits. Joking about all aspects of sexual experience is commonplace" (1981: 265). According to Nisa, "If a woman doesn't have sex . . . her thoughts get ruined and she is always angry" (Shostak 1981: 31). Nisa's characterization of sexuality among the !Kung suggests that for both men and women, engaging in sex is necessary to maintaining good health and is an important aspect of being human.

In contrast, for the past 150 years, Anglo-American culture has defined women as less sexual than men. This represents a major shift from the widespread view prior to the seventeenth century that women were especially sexual creatures. By the end of the nineteenth century, the increasingly authoritative voice of male medical specialists argued that women's bodies were characterized by sexual anesthesia (Caplan 1987: 3). Victorian ideas about male sexuality emphasized the highly sexed and baser nature of men. In contrast, Muslim concepts of female sexuality (Mernissi 1987: 33) cast the woman as aggressor and the man as victim. Imam Ghazali, writing in the eleventh century, describes an active female sexuality in which the sexual demands of women appear overwhelming, and the need for men to satisfy them is a social duty (Mernissi 1987: 39). Women symbolize disorder and are representative of the dangers of sexuality and its disruptive potential.

The example of the Kaulong of New Guinea further illustrates the extent to which understandings of male and female bodies and sexual desires are cultural products (Goodale 1980). Both sexes aspire to immortality through the reproduction of identity achieved through parenting. Sexual intercourse, which is considered animallike, is sanctioned for married people. Animals are part of the forest and nature, so the gardens of married couples are in the forest. The only sanctioned purpose of sex and marriage is reproduction; sex without childbearing is viewed as shameful. Suicide was formerly considered an acceptable recourse for a childless couple. Sexual activity is thought to be dangerous to men and women in different ways: polluting for men and leading to dangers of birth for women. Goodale notes that girls are encouraged to behave aggressively toward men, to initiate sex, and to choose a husband. In contrast, men are reluctant to engage in sex, are literally "scared to death of marriage," and rarely take the dominant role in courtship (1980: 135). Thus, the Kaulong view seems to reverse the Western idea of the passive woman and the active man (Moore 1988: 17).

For the Kaulong, as among numerous groups in New Guinea, men's anxiety about contact with the body of a woman is heightened by the understanding that menstrual blood is dangerously polluting. A man who had sexual contact with a menstruating woman would risk serious physical and mental harm. Men engage in a range of symbolic behaviors—for example, tongue scraping and smokehouse purification—to cleanse themselves of what they believe are the harmful effects of contact with women's bodies. The Mae Enga, for instance, believe that "contact with [menstrual blood] or a menstruating woman will, in the absence of appropriate countermagic, sicken a man and cause persistent vomiting, turn his blood black, corrupt his vital juices so that his skin darkens and wrinkles as his flesh wastes, permanently dull his wits, and eventually lead to a slow decline and death" (Meggitt 1964: 207).

Concern about the symbolic dangers of women's bodies is not limited to New Guinea, but rather, has been documented in diverse cultures (Buckley and Gottlieb 1988). Research on such symbolic dangers and the body as ritually polluting has often focused on menstruation. Buckley (1982) has addressed male bias and the female perspective on menstruation in his discussion of menstrual beliefs and practices among the Yurok Indians of North America. In his reanalysis of Yurok data, Buckley found that while precontact Yurok men considered women, through their menstrual blood, to be dangerous, Yurok women viewed menstruation as a positive source of power. Rather than looking on the forced monthly seclusion as isolating and oppressive, women viewed it as a source of strength and sanctuary.

In her essay in this book, Alma Gottlieb notes that most early anthropological writings on menstruation were overly simplistic in assuming that menstrual blood was necessarily a source of mystical contamination. Works such as Buckley's study of Yurok menstruation and Buckley and Gottlieb's 1988 classic collection on menstrual practices cross-culturally were groundbreaking in furthering our understanding of the diversity of women's bodily experiences and how body practices are shaped by culture and history. Gottlieb describes the growing feminist literature that focuses on menstruation and on the body in general. Recent scholarship includes accounts by anthropologists who gained firsthand knowledge of women's menstrual houses by means of participant observation. In addition, scholars have emphasized the agency of menstruating women—for example, their use of menstrual blood to engage in magical procedures to deceive their husbands or to attract sexual advances, the use of herbal and other methods to regulate menstruation, or the use of diverse techniques to induce abortions. Gottlieb's analysis reminds us that women shape their own menstrual experiences and are not bound to a solely biological or cultural script.

Such biological or cultural scripts are equally influential in whether a society defines two (and only two) gender identities, the masculine and the feminine, leaving little room for culturally defined variance. This is true in popular thought in the United States, but other cultures provide for alternative gender constructs as well as acknowledgement of physical variation. Some research suggests at least three phenotypic sexes in human cultures: female, male, and androgynous or hermaphroditic individuals. This classification refers to characteristics observable to the naked eye rather than to medical classifications of sex types based on chromosomal evidence (Jacobs and Roberts 1989: 440). Linguistic markers for gender reveal culturally specific epistemological categories (Jacobs and Roberts 1989: 439). Accordingly, in English, one may distinguish woman, lesbian, man, or gay male. The Chuckchee counted seven genders—three female and four male—while the Mohave reportedly recognize four genders—a woman, a woman who assumes the roles of men, a man, or a male who assumes the roles of women (Jacobs and Roberts 1989: 439–440). Thus, cross-cultural research suggests that we need to use categories of sex and gender that reflect the evidence of diversity rather than rigid classification systems.

In any culture gender, sex, and body are recognized, named, and given meaning in accordance with the culture's rules or customs (Jacobs and Roberts 1989: 446). When a baby is born, people generally rely on the appearance of the infant's external genitalia to determine whether that child will be treated as female or male. As a child grows, more criteria come into play, such as the phenotypic expression of sex—facial hair, voice, and breast development. In some societies, social and sexual identities may be created by means of modifying the physical body. One such example is the *hijras* of Indian society. The *hijra* role attracts people who in the West might be called eunuchs, homosexuals, transsexuals, transvestites, or hermaphrodites. *Hijras* are primarily phenotypic men who have chosen to sacrifice their genitalia in return for the power to bless or curse others with fertility or infertility.

The *hijra* role is deeply rooted in Indian culture, and it accommodates a variety of sexual needs, gender behaviors and identities, and personalities. Gayatri Reddy and Serena Nanda (in this book) show that Hinduism encompasses ambiguities and contradictions in gender categories without trying to resolve them. *Hijras,* have been identified as a "third sex" or "intersexed" identity—in Nanda's terms, "neither men nor women" (1990), situated within a larger continuum of sexual and gender configurations. In Hindu myths, rituals, and art, the theme of the powerful man–woman is significant; mythical figures who are androgynous figure in popular Indian culture. Islam also reinforces the construct of alternative genders by means of the historical role of the eunuch in the Muslim court culture of India. Although the popular understanding of *hijras* is as an alternative sex and gender, their identities are also constructed through spirituality, religious affiliation, and political action. As political candidates, some *hijras* have used their sexual and physical ambiguities as a symbolic asset in their campaign platforms.

Additional examples of cultures that tolerate gender ambiguity are found in Native American societies, in which a male who felt an affinity for female occupation, dress, and attributes could choose to become classified as a two-spirit, sometimes known as a berdache. Williams (1986) discusses alternative gender identities for Native American women. One is a woman who has manifested an "unfeminine" character from infancy, has shown no interest in heterosexual relations, and might have expressed a wish to become a man. Such women were known for their bravery and skill as warriors. For example, Kaska Indians would select a daughter to be a son if they had none; after a transformation ritual, the daughter would dress like a man and be trained for male tasks. Ingalik Indians also recognize such a status, and the two-spirit person even participated in male-only sweat baths. The woman was accepted as a man on the basis of her gendered behavior (Williams 1986).

The assignment of this changed gender "operates independently of a person's morphological sex and can determine both gender status and erotic behavior" (Williams 1986: 235). In some societies, a woman could choose to be a man, as among the Kutenai Indians. The "manlike woman" was greatly respected, although the Kutenai did not recognize a similar status for men. A tribe with an alternative gender role for one sex did not necessarily have one for the other, and the roles were not seen as equivalent. The Mohave also recognized this alternative, subjecting these women to a ritual that authorized them to assume the clothing, sexual activity, and occupation of the opposite, self-chosen sex. It is sometimes believed that such women do not menstruate because menstruation is a crucial part of the definition of a woman. Some Native American cultures thus demonstrate a flexible recognition of gender variance and fluidity in their worldview.

In North America, sexuality is an integral part of identity on a personal and a social level. Sexuality not only classifies one as male or female but also is an aspect of adult identity. In the United States, where heterosexual relations are the norm, the dominant ideology suggests that heterosexuality is innate and natural.

Matza's chapter on constructing the lesbian body describes an environment in which heteronormativity is not the default assumption. In her ethnography of the Michigan Womyn's Music Festival (Michfest), an annual celebration of women's music in the Midwestern United States, the several thousand participants experience this event as an arena for communicating identity through embodied markers such as haircuts, clothing, lesbian symbols, and other semiotic markers. Much feminist scholarship has examined the "body as text," and the ways in which individuals may use their bodies to perform and signify identities. Correspondingly, Matza contends that Michfest workers strategically use dress (or undress) and physical adornment to construct their identity in ways that display their sexuality, and other relevant social identity categories. The body becomes an expressive medium that can be crafted and recrafted to perform situated identities (see, for comparison, Gulbas' discussion of surgically transforming the body in Section V). This autoethnography offers an experiential perspective on how sexuality may be "written" on the body. Matza illustrates how music festival participants emphasize shared identity in this community environment by prioritizing certain modes of body adornment, clothing, and appearance. By means of intentional fashion and beauty practices, individuals at Michfest wear their identities on the surface of the body, whether clothed, or nude. As Matza observes, the presence of nudity is empowering for many, generating feelings of shared gender identity and honoring the diversity of female bodies. Similarly, she shows that Michfest is a "sex positive" locale for its participants, who embody their sexualization with indicators such as hickeys. These "love bites" may ritually mark women's bodies as lascivious in the broader society, but Michfest, offers a safe space for the public display of lesbian sexuality.

The articles in this section reveal that there are multiple culturally acceptable gendered and sexual identities, practices, and experiences of the body. Although Western categorizations impose a particular rigidity on concepts of gender, sex, and sexuality, cross-cultural data demonstrate that these identities are not fixed and unchangeable. This realization necessitates a critique of these Western classifications and provokes a number of challenging questions: Are heterosexuality and homosexuality equally socially constructed? Should we think in terms of a gender/sexual continuum, rather than male/female dichotomies? Is there cross-cultural variation in the extent to which sexuality represents a core feature of human identity?

## REFERENCES

Browner, C., and C. Sargent. 2007. "Engendering Medical Anthropology." In Francine Saillant and Serge Genest (eds.). *Medical Anthropology: Regional Perspectives and Shared Concerns*, pp. 233–252. London: Blackwell.

Buckley, Thomas. 1982. "Menstruation and the Power of Yurok Women: Methods in Cultural Reconstruction." *American Ethnologist* 9: 47–60.

Buckley, Thomas, and Alma Gottlieb (eds.). 1988. *Blood Magic: The Anthropology of Menstruation*. Berkeley: University of California Press.

Caplan, Pat. 1987. "Introduction." In Pat Caplan (ed.). *The Cultural Construction of Sexuality*, pp. 1–31. London: Tavistock.

Collier, Jane E., and Michelle Z. Rosaldo. 1981. "Politics and Gender in Simple Societies." In Sherry Ortner and Harriet Whitehead (eds.). *Sexual Meanings: The Cultural Construction of Gender and Sexuality*, pp. 275–330. Cambridge: Cambridge University Press.

Curtis, Debra. 2009. *Pleasures and Perils. Girls' Sexuality in a Caribbean Consumer Culture*. New Brunswick, NJ: Rutgers University Press.

Day, Sophie. 2007. *On the Game. Women and Sex Work*. London: Pluto Press.

Farmer, Paul. 1992. *AIDS and Accusation. Haiti and the Geography of Blame*. Berkeley: University of California Press.

Foucault, Michel. 1981. *The History of Sexuality*. Harmondsworth, UK: Penguin.

Goodale, Jane C. 1980. "Gender, Sexuality and Marriage: A Kaulong Model of Nature and Culture." In Carol P. MacCormack (ed.). *Nature, Culture and Gender*, pp. 119–143. Cambridge: Cambridge University Press.

Jacobs, Sue-Ellen, and Christine Roberts. 1989. "Sex, Sexuality, Gender, and Gender Variance." In Sandra Morgen (ed.). *Gender and Anthropology: Critical Reviews for Research and Teaching*, pp. 438–462. Washington, DC: American Anthropological Association.

Kulick, Don. 1998. *Travesti. Sex, Gender and Culture among Brazilian Transgendered Prostitutes*. Chicago: University of Chicago Press.

Lewin, Ellen (ed.). 2006. *Feminist Anthropology: A Reader*. London: Blackwell.

Malinowski, Bronislaw. 1929. *The Sexual Life of Savages in Northwestern Melanesia*. New York: Harvest Books.

Meggitt, M. J. 1964. "Male–Female Relationships in the Highlands of Australian New Guinea." *American Anthropologist* 66(4, Part 2): 204–227.

Mernissi, Fatima. 1987. *Beyond the Veil: Male–Female Dynamics in Modern Muslim Society*. Bloomington and Indianapolis: Indiana University Press.

Moore, Henrietta L. 1988. *Feminism and Anthropology*. Minneapolis: University of Minnesota Press.

Nanda, Serena. 1990. *Neither Man nor Woman: The Hijras of India*. Belmont, CA: Wadsworth, Inc.

Ortner, Sherry B., and Harriet Whitehead. 1981. "Introduction: Accounting for Sexual Meanings." In Sherry Ortner and Harriet Whitehead (eds.). *Sexual Meanings: The Cultural Construction of Gender and Sexuality*, pp. 1–29. Cambridge, UK: Cambridge University Press.

Padilla, Mark. 2007. *Caribbean Pleasure Industry: Tourism, Sexuality, and AIDS in the Dominican Republic*. Chicago and London: University of Chicago Press.

Ross, E., and R. Rapp. 1981. "Sex and Society: A Research Note from Social History and Anthropology," *Comparative Studies in Society and History* 20: 51–72.

Sargent, Carolyn, and Caroline Brettell. 1996. *Gender and Health*. Upper Saddle River, NJ: Prentice Hall.

Shostak, Marjorie. 1981. *Nisa: The Life and Words of a !Kung Woman.* Cambridge, MA: Harvard University Press.

Vance, Carole S. 1984. "Pleasure and Danger: Toward a Politics of Sexuality." In Carole S. Vance (ed.). *Pleasure and Danger: Exploring Female Sexuality*, pp. 1–29. Boston: Routledge and Kegan Paul.

Weeks, Margaret, Merrill Singer, Maryland Grier, and Jean Schensul. 1996. "Gender Relations, Sexuality, and AIDS Risk among African American and Latina Women." In C. Sargent and C. Brettell (eds.). *Gender and Health*, pp. 338–370. Upper Saddle River, NJ: Prentice Hall.

Williams, Walter L. 1986. *The Spirit and the Flesh.* Boston: Beacon Press.

# Is There a Muslim Sexuality?
## Changing Constructions of Sexuality in Egyptian Bedouin Weddings

### Lila Abu-Lughod

The project of defining the nature of Muslim Arab sexuality—what it is or what it should be—has engaged many people with different stakes and interests. Western discourses have tended to contrast the negative sexuality of "the East" with the positive sexuality of the West. French colonial settlers in Algeria depicted Algerian women in pornographic postcards that suggested a fantastic Oriental world of perverse and excessive sexuality (Alloula 1986). Western feminists concerned with global issues dwell on veiling and other practices like clitoridectomy found in the Muslim Arab world as signs of the repressive control over or exploitation of women's sexuality (e.g., Daly 1978).

From the Muslim world itself come other discourses on Arab Muslim sexuality. These include religious and legal texts and pronouncements, but also, more recently, some critical studies by intellectuals and scholars. How different the understandings can be is clear from two important books. One, by a Tunisian scholar with a background in psychoanalytic thought, argues that the misogynist practices of sexuality in the Muslim world are corruptions of the ideals of the Quran and other religious texts (Bouhdiba 1985). The second, by a Moroccan sociologist, argues from a feminist perspective that the legal and sacred texts themselves, like the erotic texts that flourished in the medieval period, carry negative messages about and perpetuate certain consistent attitudes toward the bodies and behavior of Muslim women (Sabbah 1984).

What these various discourses on Arab Muslim sexuality, by outsiders and insiders, defenders and critics,

share is the presumption that there is such a thing as a "Muslim sexuality." An anthropologist like myself, familiar with the tremendous variety of communities to be found in the regions composing the Muslim Arab world, would have to question this presumption. Neither Islam nor sexuality should be essentialized—taken as things with intrinsic and transhistorical meanings. Rather, both the meaning of Islam and the constructions of sexuality must be understood in their specific historical and local contexts.[1]

To show why I argue this, I will analyze wedding rituals in a community of Awlad 'Ali Bedouin in Egypt's Western Desert—a community I worked in over a period of twelve years. Weddings are the highlight of social life, awaited with anticipation and participated in with enthusiasm. Each wedding is different. And each wedding is a personal affair of great moment for the bride and groom, even if only one dramatic event in what will be their marriage, lasting for years. Yet public rituals in face-to-face societies are also arenas where people play out their social and political relations. There are other discourses and practices related to sexuality in this Bedouin community but none so powerfully seek to produce, and are now transforming, people's experiences of sexuality and gender relations as weddings do. Without pretending that a symbolic analysis exhausts the meaning of weddings for the individuals involved, I would still insist that such an analysis of Awlad 'Ali weddings is useful: It reveals both how sexuality is constructed by the symbols and practices of members of particular communities and how these symbols and practices themselves are open to change and political contestation. Islam, it will be seen, figures not so much as a blueprint for sexuality as a weapon in changing relations of power.

Original material prepared for this text. Reprinted by permission of the author.

## SEXUALITY AND CULTURAL IDENTITY

In the twelve years between 1978 and 1990 that I had been regularly returning to this community of Arab Muslim sedentarized herders in Egypt, the same questions had been asked of me, sometimes even by the same people, as were asked in the first month of my stay. Usually in the context of a gathering of older women, one old woman would lean toward me and ask if I were married. After a short discussion of the fact that I was not, she or another older woman would ask me the next intense question: "Where you come from, does the bridegroom do it with the finger or with 'it'?" The first time they asked me this, I did not know what they meant by "it" and they had a good laugh. The question that followed inevitably in such conversations was, "And do they do it during the daytime or at night?" They were asking about weddings and particularly about the defloration of the virgin bride, which is for them the central moment of a wedding.[2]

In the obsessive concern with whether they do it with the finger or "it," at night or during the daytime, is a clue to one of the things the discourse on this aspect of sexuality has become as the Awlad 'Ali Bedouins have greater contact and interaction with outsiders, primarily their Egyptian peasant and urban neighbors. Whatever its former or current meaning within the community, meanings I will analyze in the following section, the central rite of weddings has now also become a marker of cultural identity—essential to the Awlad Ali's self-defining discourse on what makes them distinctive.

Individuals vary in how they evaluate their differences from their compatriots. When I met the Bedouin representative to the Egyptian Parliament, a sophisticated man in sunglasses whose long contact with other Egyptians showed in his dialect, he assured me that there were a few Bedouin practices that were wrong: One was that they used the finger in the daytime. But he defended the practice by saying that it reminded girls to be careful. Another respected man of the community explained to me that "entering" with the finger was wrong. "We're the only ones who do it this way," he noted. Then he added, "Nothing in our religion says you should." By way of excuse, though, he said, "But the faster the groom does it, the better—the more admired he is because it means he wasn't timid or cowardly." Even women occasionally complained that it was stupid how the female wedding guests waited and waited, just to see that drop of blood. But they too defended the ceremony, saying that the defloration had to take place in the afternoon so that everyone could see and there would be no doubts about the reputation of the girl. Their horror at the idea that the groom would use "it" came from their fear that it would be more painful for the bride.

Besides asking whether they do it with the finger or "it," day or night, the women I knew often asked whether, where I came from, there was anyone with the bride to hold her down. They were surprised to hear that she needed no one and marveled that she wasn't afraid to be alone with the man. Among themselves, they almost always had a few older women, usually aunts or close neighbors of the groom and bride, in the room with the bride when the groom came to her. There in theory to hold the bride, these women also end up giving advice to the groom and making sure that he knew what to do so that everything—the display of the blood on the cloth—would turn out right.

For their part, somewhat like most Europeans and Americans, non-Bedouin Egyptians and assimilated Awlad 'Ali from the agricultural areas find Bedouin weddings scandalous and distasteful. Bedouin women are not unaware of these views and the men discussed previously were probably reacting defensively to them. These outsiders may laugh at some customs but they are embarrassed by others. After one wedding in the community in which I was living, the bride's aunt, who had spent most of her life in a non-Bedouin provincial town, talked about the wedding and some of the customs she had witnessed that made her laugh "until her stomach hurt." She obviously considered her new in-laws backward.[3]

What seemed to disturb her most was the public nature of what she felt should be private. She thought it humiliating, for example, that at night, the young men from the community (peers of the bridegroom) hung around the room, listening, shining a flashlight under the door and through the window, and generally being disruptive. More horrible to her was the public display of the blood-stained cloth. "It was incredible," she exclaimed. "After the defloration didn't you hear my son saying to his aunt when she went to hang the cloth on the tent ropes, 'It's shameful, my aunt, it's shameful to put the cloth out for people to see.'" Like other urban and rural Egyptians, she thought that the bride and groom should be brought together at night and left alone.

Although other Egyptians and Americans might feel that such privacy is more civilized, the Awlad 'Ali women I knew did not see it that way. Bedouin women were scandalized by the secrecy of night deflorations, the immediate and explicit link such weddings make between marriage and sexual intercourse, and what they view as either the total vulnerability of the poor bride forced to be alone with a man or, even worse, the bride's immodest desire for a man. They knew that instead of struggling, the Egyptian bride has her photo taken with her husband-to-be, she sits with him at weddings where the sexes mix, and she dresses in make-up and fancy clothes for all to see. Because poorer Bedouin men sometimes marry young women from peasant areas, whether they are of Egyptian stock or long-sedentarized Bedouin involved in agriculture, the Bedouin women also knew that unmarried sisters accompanied the bride. They interpreted this practice as a shameful attempt to display and "sell" marriageable daughters. They also knew that such brides sometimes arrived bringing a cooked duck or goose to feed a new husband; they took this as a sign of the bride's unseemly eagerness to please the groom.

Egyptian weddings, much like American ones, construct the couple as a separate unit, distinct from families or ties to members of the same gender group. At their center is a sexual joining that is private and intimate. For the Awlad 'Ali, this is a strange thing. The secrecy of private sex, in the dark, behind closed doors, and preferably in the foreign or anonymous setting (for the honeymoon) produces sexuality as something personal, intensely individual, apparently separate from society and social power. It produces sexuality as something belonging in an inviolable private sphere—the bedroom—a sphere in which others cannot interfere with whatever pleasure or violence and coercion accompanies it. One of the consequences of this construction of sexuality is that we, and perhaps Egyptians, come to think there is a part of oneself that is not social or affected by the prevailing power relations in society.[4]

The three crucial elements in the Bedouin discourse on differences between their weddings and those of other groups are (1) whether the defloration is public and participatory, (2) whether it involves sexual intercourse, and (3) whether it is seen as a contest, especially between bride and groom. These elements also had meaning within the local context. In Bedouin weddings the ways in which sexuality is related to power relations and the social order were clear. Marriages have been the occasion for people to collectively enact and reproduce this social order and the individual's place in it. And the individual's place was, until recently, very much a part of the group—whether the kin group or the group defined by gender.

## WEDDINGS AS PUBLIC RITES: THE POWER OF KINSHIP AND GENDER

The participants in Awlad 'Ali Bedouin weddings instantiate, by means of a bride and groom, the relations between families or kin groups on the one hand, and the relations between men and women on the other. A symbolic analysis of the central rite, the defloration, enacted in a homologous fashion on the bodies of the bride and groom and on the collective bodies of the gathered kin and friends, reveals that it produces an understanding of sexuality as something public and focused on crossing thresholds, opening passages, and

moving in and out. There are no strong messages of mingling or joining or even interchange in a private sexual act. The emphasis is on opening the bride's vagina by breaking the hymen and bringing out or making visible what was in there. And although people say that deflorations should be done during the daytime so everyone can see the cloth, the fact that in the rhythm of daily life morning and daytime generally are times of opening and going out from home or camp, while evening is a time of returning inward, cannot but reinforce the auspiciousness of this time for opening and taking outward.[5]

That this opening is a prelude to the insemination which should eventuate in childbirth is suggested by some practices associated with the blood-stained virginity cloth. It is taken out of the room by the groom and thrown to the women gathered just outside. It is said that if the cloth is then brought back into the room without the bride having exited first—if, as they say, the cloth enters upon her—it will block her from conceiving.[6] Young women are told to save their virginity cloths; if they have trouble conceiving, they must bathe in water in which they have soaked the cloth.

Everything in the rites and the songs that accompany them suggests that the individuals engaged in this opening and being opened, taking out and showing, and having something taken out and shown, embody both their kin groups and their gender groups. The connection to kin, and control by the kin group, is clear in the key role they have in arranging and negotiating marriages and is reflected in the songs the groom's female relatives sing as they go to fetch the bride from her father's household. It is also reinforced in the songs the bride's female kin sing to greet these people. Most of the songs compliment the social standing of the families of the bride and groom.

Even the practices and movements of the wedding itself perpetuate the identifications with kin groups. Most brides, even today, are brought from their fathers' households completely covered by a white woolen woven cloak (*jard*) that is the essential item of men's dress. The cloak must belong to the girl's father or some other male kinsman. So, protected and hidden by her father's cloak, she is brought out of her father's protected domain and carried to her husband's kin group's domain. There she is rushed, still hidden, into the room (or in the past, the tent) which she will share with her husband. Although nowadays the woven cloak is usually removed once she enters the room, in the past the bride remained under her father's cloak and was not revealed even to the women gathered around her until after the defloration.

The virginity of the bride is also constructed as something inseparable from her family's honor. Although one unmarried girl explained the importance of the blood-stained cloth in terms of her own reputation, she stressed the effect it would have on others.

> For us Bedouins, this is the most important moment in a girl's life. No matter what anyone says afterward, no one will pay attention as long as there was blood on the cloth. They are suspicious of her before. People talk. "She went here, she went there." "She looked at So-and-so." "She said hello to So-and-so." "She went to the orchard." But when they see this blood the talk is cut off. . . . When they see the cloth, she can come and go as she pleases. They love her and everything is fine.

The best way to get a sense of who has a stake in the girl's virginity and why is to listen to the conventional songs sung wildly outside the door of the bride's room as the defloration is underway. Unmarried girls and some young married women clap and sing rhyming songs that refer to the effect of the proof of the bride's virginity on various members of her family and community.

> Make her dear Mom happy, Lord
> Hanging up her cloth on the tent ropes
> O Saint 'Awwaam on high
> Don't let anyone among us be shamed

Older women sing more serious songs that take up similar themes:

> When the people have gathered
> O Generous One favor us with a happy ending . . .
> Behind us are important men
> who ask about what we are doing . . .

Relatives of the bride show their support and faith in the bride in songs like this:

> I'm confident in the loved one
> you'll find it there intact . . .

Even the groom's behavior during the defloration reflects on his relatives. One song a relative of his might sing as he arrives or is inside with the bride is the following:

> Son, be like your menfolk
> strong willed and unafraid . . .

After the virginity cloth is brought out by the groom and thrown to the women, a different set of songs is sung. These praise the cloth and the honor of the girl who had remained a virgin. The songs reflect on who is affected by her purity and who is proud. At one wedding a female relative of the bride sang to a nephew nearby:

> Go tell your father, Said
> the banner of her honor is flying high . . .

About the bride a woman might sing:

> Bravo! She was excellent
> she who didn't force down her father's
> eyelashes . . .

Given this group investment in the bride's virginity, the central rite of the wedding becomes a drama of suspense and relief that must powerfully shape people's experiences of sexuality as something that belongs to the many, and especially to one's family. The wedding is also, importantly, an occasion when families find themselves in some rivalry, the honor of each at stake. This was more apparent in the past when the young men celebrated all night on the eve of the wedding and expressed the rivalry through singing contests that sometimes broke out into actual fights between lineages.

Kinship is not the only power-laden aspect of social life that finds itself reflected and reinforced in the wedding. The second set of power relations weddings play with are those of gender. The bride and groom in the wedding rite enact the charged relations between men and women as distinct genders in a kind of battle of the sexes. Although most activities in the community are informally segregated by gender, at weddings—in part because there are non-family members present—the sexual segregation is more obvious and fixed, women and men forming highly separate collectivities for nearly all events.

Given this separation of the sexes, the defloration, taking place in the middle of the day when all are gathered in their distinct places, becomes a ritualized and extreme form of encounter between both the bride and groom and the women and men who surround each of them. The movements of the groom and his age-mates as they penetrate the crowd of women surrounding the bride mirror the groom's penetration of his bride, who forms a unit with the women in the room with her. The young men stand just outside the door, sometimes dancing and singing, ready to fire off guns in celebration when the groom emerges. They rush him back away from the women. This mirroring is expressed in the ambiguity of the term used for both moments of this event: the entrance (*khashsha*) refers both to the entry with the finger and the whole defloration process when the groom enters the bride's room, which can be thought of as his kin group's womb.

The encounter between male and female takes the form of a contest. The groom is encouraged to be fearless. He is expected to finish the deed in as short a time as possible. The bride is expected to try valiantly to fight him off. Taking the virginity she has been so careful to guard and thus opening the way for his progeny is the groom's victory; the bride doesn't give it up without a struggle. Calling this, as the literature often does, a virginity test is a misnomer in that it misses this combative dimension of the ritualized act. The way people describe what happens even on the wedding night suggests again that the groom and bride are involved in a contest. The rowdy young men who listen outside the marital chamber want to know "who won." They know this, some adolescent girls informed me, not just by whether the groom succeeds in having intercourse with his bride (a rare event), but by whether the groom succeeds in making his bride talk to him and answer his questions. This is, perhaps, another kind of opening up.

There is other evidence that weddings provoke a heightened attention to issues of gender and sexual mixing. One of the most revealing and intriguing is the spontaneous cross-dressing that sometimes happens at weddings. At several weddings I attended one woman in our community actually put on men's clothes, a fake mustache and beard, and covered her head in a man's headcloth. Amidst much hilarity she came out to dance in front of the bride. Others expressed some disapproval and called this woman a bit mad. But they laughed riotously anyway. One woman who thought it excessive described someone else who she thought was quite funny: All she did was dance in front of the bride with a shawl bunched up in front like male genitalia. Sometimes it was reported that the unmarried men and young boys had celebrated the night before the wedding by dressing up a boy with women's bracelets and a veil and dancing in front of him as if he were a bride.

## SEXUAL TRANSFORMATIONS

Many Awlad 'Ali claim that their rituals are changing. In this final section, I want to explore how in these changed wedding practices we can begin to track changes in the nature of power and social relations. This is further support for my initial argument that constructions of sexuality cannot be understood apart from understandings of particular forms of social power. Most people talked about changes in weddings over the last twenty years or so in terms of what had been lost. Many said weddings were not fun any more. As far as I could determine, the main element that seems to have been lost is the celebration the night before the wedding (saamir). Not only do the young men no longer sing back and forth, but no longer is it even thinkable that a young woman from the community would come out to dance in front of them. This is what used to happen and the change is crucial for Bedouin gender relations.

What happened in the past was that an unmarried sister or cousin of the groom would be brought out from among the women by a young boy. She would dance amidst a semi-circle of young men. Her face veiled and her waist girded with a man's white woven cloak, like the one the bride would come covered in the following

day, she danced with a stick or baton in her hands. According to one man who described this to me, the young men tried to "beg" the stick from her, sometimes using subterfuges like pretending to be ill; she would often bestow the stick, he said, on someone she fancied. But according to the women I spoke with, the young men would sometimes try to grab the stick from her and she would, if they were too aggressive, get angry with them and leave. The young men took turns singing songs that welcomed the dancer and then described her every feature in flattering terms. The standard parts praised in such songs were her braids, her eyes, her eyebrows, her cheeks, her lips, her tattoos, her neck, her breasts, her arms, her hands, and her waist—most of which, it should be remembered, because of the way she was dressed were not actually visible. Thus in a sense the dancer was, through men's songs, made into the ideal woman, attractive object of men's desires.

The dancer must be seen as the bride's double or stand-in, an interpretation supported by the other occasion on which a young woman danced in front of men. In the days before cars, brides were carried from their fathers' households to their husbands' on camel-back, completely cloaked and sitting hidden inside a wooden litter (karmuud) covered in red woven blankets. Another woman always preceded her on foot, dancing as young men sang to her and shot off guns near her.

In both cases, the dancer as bride and as ideal womanhood went out before men who complimented and sought her. What is crucial to notice is how the women described the dancer. They attributed to her a special bravery and described her actions as a challenge to the young men. One wedding in which a young woman was accidentally wounded by a poorly aimed gun was legendary. The wedding went on, the story went, as a second dancer who had been near her merely wiped the blood from her forehead and continued to dance. More telling is the ritualized struggle over the stick, which one anthropologist who worked with a group in Libya has argued is associated with virginity (Mason 1975). A woman explained to me, "If the dancer is sharp they can't take the stick from her. They'll be coming at her from all sides but she keeps it."

But perhaps some of the short songs traditionally exchanged between the women (gathered in a tent some distance away from the young men standing in a line near the dancer) and the young men, make clearest the ways in which a challenge between the sexes was central to weddings. One especially memorable competitive exchange was the following. As her sister danced a woman sang of her:

A bird in the hot winds glides
and no rifle scope can capture it . . .
A man responded with the song:

The heart would be no hunter
if it didn't play in their feathers . . .

In the loss and delegitimation of this whole section of the wedding ritual, an important piece of the construction of Bedouin sexual relations has disappeared. Today, all that is left in a ritual that was a highly charged and evenly matched challenge between the sexes is the enactment of the men's hunt. The groom is the hunter, the bride his prey. Decked out in her make-up and white satin dress, she is brought from her father's house and her "virginity" taken by her groom in a bloody display.

Wedding songs, only sung by women now, reinforce this construction of the bride as vulnerable prey. They liken the bride to a gazelle. This is a compliment to her beauty but also suggests her innocence and defenselessness. Other songs liken the groom to a falcon or hunter. This is no longer balanced by women's former powers to create desire but elude capture.

The disappearance of the female dancer can thus be seen to have shifted the balance such that women's capacities to successfully challenge men have been de-emphasized. Although the sexes are still pitted against each other, the contest is no longer represented as even.

There is a second important point to be made about the dancer that relates to some transformations in constructions of power and sexuality. For it is not completely true that women no longer dance in front of men at Awlad 'Ali weddings. It has become unacceptable for respectable young kinswomen to dance, but there are now some professional dancers. They accompany musical troupes hired to entertain at weddings of the Bedouin nouveau riche. These women may or may not be prostitutes but they are certainly not considered respectable.[7] In that sense, and in the fact that ordinary women go nowhere near the areas where these musicians and dancers perform, one cannot any longer claim that the dancer represents Woman or enacts women's challenge of men. The opposite may be true. This new kind of wedding may be introducing a new view of women, one quite familiar to us in the United States but quite strange to the Awlad 'Ali: women as sexual commodities stripped of their embeddedness in their kin groups or the homosocial world of women.

The professionalization of weddings as entertainment and spectacle (spectacles that retain vestiges of the participatory in that young men seize the microphone to sing songs) may also be signaling a fundamental shift in the relationship of the construction of sexuality and the construction of the social order. What seems to be disappearing is the participation of the whole community in the responsibility of ritually reproducing the fundamental social and political dynamics of the community. Does this indicate the emergence of a new kind of power? One that works differently? One whose nexus is perhaps the individual rather than the kin group or gender group? This new form of wedding is not being adopted universally in the Bedouin region since the poor cannot afford it and the respectable condemn it as undignified and inappropriate for pious Muslims. Nevertheless, as a public discourse it must enter and shape the field of sexuality for all.

The third and final historical shift I will discuss comes out in the comments women made about what had happened to weddings. One old woman reminisced about weddings of the past. She shook her head and laughed, "No, the things they did before you can't do anymore. Nowadays weddings are small, like a shrunken old man. People used to really celebrate, staying up all night, for days! But they have become like the Muslim Brothers now." The younger woman she was talking to had explained for me. "They say it is wrong. Now everything is forbidden. People before didn't know. They were ignorant." She used a term with connotations of the pre-Islamic era.

These women's invocations of Islam and the proper behavior of the pious in the contexts of weddings mark some significant changes in power relations. It has always been important to the Awlad 'Ali that they are Muslims and that they are good Muslims. And these two women themselves were devout. They prayed regularly and the old one had been on the pilgrimage to Mecca. Yet when they and other women brought up the religious wrongness of their traditional wedding practices, it was with some ambivalence since they were also nostalgic for the richer days of the past. After one wedding there was a hint of disapproval in women's gossip about one aunt in the community. Someone with a good voice who usually sang at weddings, she had just returned from the pilgrimage to Mecca and had refused this time. "It is wrong," she told them. They thought she was being self-righteous—and selfish.

What is really at stake comes out clearly from women's discussions of a happy wedding that had taken place in my absence. I was told that, as usual, for days before the wedding the women and girls had been celebrating by themselves every evening, drumming and singing. The older men of the community wanted them to stop and instructed them that at least once the guests (non-relatives) had begun to arrive, they would have to stop. It was shameful to sing in front of people, the men insisted. On the eve of the wedding as the women and girls gathered and began to sing and dance in celebration, the groom's father came in to greet his visiting female relatives. He also wanted to try to silence the group of women. When he entered the tent, he saw his own older sister, a dignified woman in her sixties, dancing. "Hey, what's this?" he said. "Rottenest of days, even you, Hajja?" He called her by the respectful title reserved for those who have performed the pilgrimage to Mecca. "That's right," she answered definitely, "even me!" Everyone laughed then and each time they retold the story.

Women still refuse to be stopped from celebrating weddings. But the older men, armed with religious righteousness, are clearly trying to assert authority over them in domains that were previously inviolable. Weddings, like the discontinued sheep-shearing festivities to which they are often likened, were always before classified as occasions where young men and young women could express desires. Elder men were not to interfere. At sheep-shearing festivities young men used to sing with impunity oblique sexual songs to flirt with the women present. The songs often insulted the patriarch whose herds the young men were shearing. Similarly, at weddings young men sang to women, not just the dancer. Even more important, women sang back—songs of love and desire. Older men made sure they were not in the vicinity.[8]

Now, not only have the exchanges between young men and women stopped but older men seem to be trying to assert control over the separate women's festivities. Their motives for this intervention are irrelevant. They may genuinely believe they are encouraging their families to live up to an interpretation of Islam that denounces such frivolity as impious. The effect, however, on women and young men, is that by means of this discourse of Islamic propriety wielded by older men, they are being displaced as the prime actors in the rites that produced and reproduced Bedouin constructions of sexuality and desire.

If, as I have tried to show, in a small Bedouin community in Egypt, sexuality can come to be a crucial marker of cultural identity, and if the construction of sexuality is so closely tied to the organization of kinship and gender and changes as the community is transformed by such broad processes as its incorporation into the wider Egyptian nation and economy, then it seems impossible to assert the existence of a Muslim sexuality that can be read off texts or shared across communities with very different histories and ways of life. Instead, we need to think about specific constructions of sexuality and, in the case of the Muslim Arab world, about the variable role discourses on religion can play in those constructions.

## AUTHOR'S NOTE

Most of the research in Egypt on which this article is based was supported by an NEH Fellowship for College Teachers and a Fulbright Award under the Islamic Civilization Program. I am grateful to Samia Mehrez for inviting me to present an early version at Cornell University. I am more grateful to the women and men in the Awlad 'Ali community who shared their lives, including their weddings, with me.

## NOTES

1. The literature, especially the feminist literature, on sexuality has become vast in the last decade or two. A helpful early text is Vance (1984). Anthropologists have recently begun to pay more attention to constructions of sexuality and their cross-cultural perspective should contribute to our understanding of the way that sexuality is constructed. For a good introduction to some of that work, see Caplan (1987).
2. For this reason the weddings of divorcees or widows are not celebrated with as much enthusiasm and are considered somewhat ordinary affairs.
3. For example, she described what is known as the *dayra* (the circling). On the evening of the wedding day, they had seated the bride and groom on a pillow, back to back. A neighbor carrying a lamb on his back, holding one foreleg in each of his hands, had walked around and around them—seven times. She mimicked the audience counting: "Hey, did you count that one? One, two, three, four." "Thank God," she said at one point, "there were no outsiders (non-relatives) from back home with us. How embarrassing it would have been."
4. The theorist who has most developed this notion of the effects on subjectivity and sense of individuality of the Western discourses on sexuality is Michel Foucault (1978, 1985).
5. For an analysis of similar kinds of symbolic constructions of gender and sexuality, see Bourdieu's (1977) work on Algerian Kabyles. My analysis of the meaning of this rite differs significantly from that of Combs-Schilling (1989), who worked in Morocco.
6. For more on rituals related to fertility and infertility, see my *Writing Women's Worlds* (1993). Boddy (1989) has analyzed for Muslim Sudanese villagers the extraordinary symbolic stress on women's fertility over their sexuality.
7. As Van Nieuwkerk (1995) has documented, this is generally true about professional dancers in Egypt.
8. Peters (1990) describes a similar avoidance by elders of wedding celebrations among the Bedouin of Cyrenaica in the 1950s.

## REFERENCES

Abu-Lughod, Lila. 1993. *Writing Women's Worlds: Bedouin Stories.* Berkeley and Los Angeles: University of California Press.

Alloula, Malek. 1986. *The Colonial Harem.* Myran and Wlad Godzich, trans. Minneapolis: University of Minnesota Press.

Boddy, Janice. 1989. *Wombs and Alien Spirits: Women, Men, and the Zar Cult in Northern Sudan.* Madison, WI: University of Wisconsin Press.

Bouhdiba, Abdelwahab. 1985. *Sexuality in Islam.* London and Boston: Routledge & Kegan Paul.

Bourdieu, Pierre. 1977. *Outline of a Theory of Practice.* Cambridge: Cambridge University Press.

Caplan, Patricia, ed. 1987. *The Cultural Construction of Sexuality.* London and New York: Tavistock Publications.

Combs-Schilling, M. E. 1989. *Sacred Performances: Islam, Sexuality and Sacrifice.* New York: Columbia University Press.

Daly, Mary. 1978. *Gyn/ecology, the Metaethics of Radical Feminism.* Boston: Beacon Press.

Foucault, Michel. 1978. *The History of Sexuality: Volume 1: An Introduction.* New York: Random House.

_____. 1985. *The Use of Pleasure.* Vol. 2 of *The History of Sexuality.* New York: Pantheon.

Mason, John. 1975. "Sex and Symbol in the Treatment of Women: The Wedding Rite in a Libyan Oasis Community." *American Ethnologist* 2: 649–61.

Peters, Emrys. 1990. *The Bedouin of Cyrenaica.* Edited by Jack Goody and Emanuel Marx. Cambridge: Cambridge University Press.

Sabbah, Fatna A. 1984. *Woman in the Muslim Unconscious.* New York and Oxford: Pergamon Press.

Vance, Carole. 1984. *Pleasure and Danger: Exploring Female Sexuality.* Boston and London: Routledge & Kegan Paul.

Van Nieuwkerk, Karin. 1995. *"A Trade Like Any Other": Female Singers and Dancers in Egypt.* Austin, TX: University of Texas Press.

# *From Pollution to Love Magic:*
## The New Anthropology of Menstruation

### *Alma Gottlieb*

Consider this story: A college student—we'll call him Eddie—is having difficulty in his love life. Girls are so keyed into feminism these days, Eddie's concluded, that they rarely consider boys worthy of their affection. How to seduce a girl of this feminist generation? One day, our frustrated student is inspired: Even the staunchest feminist might be excited at the thought of a prospective boyfriend who himself professes an interest in feminist theory, he ventures. Eddie decides to make use of campus resources and scours the bookstores for the most unabashedly, even outrageously feminist book he can find. He chooses a scholarly tome called *Blood Magic: The Anthropology of Menstruation,* a collection of essays about the ways that women around the world experience their periods (Buckley and Gottlieb 1988a). Eddie buys the volume, brings it home, and places the unread prop strategically on his coffee table before inviting his next date to his apartment, then hopes for the book to have its anticipated effect.[1]

In planning his strategy, the model Eddie used was an old one, although he was undoubtedly unaware of its pedigree: he was relying on menstrual blood—or its textual representation—as a seduction technique, a form of "love magic." This use of menstrual blood to secure sexual favors (or fidelity) is well documented in other cultural contexts (Hoskins 2002a, 2002b); in fact, a (semi-fictionalized) folk example from southen Illinois is even mentioned in the introduction to the very book Eddie was displaying on his coffee table.

However, most previously documented forms of menstrual-blood-as-love-magic involve women manipulating the substance either to seduce men, or to bind straying husbands or lovers to them; Eddie had reversed the more usual gender pattern. Using cunning and deceit, he had acted as the initiator of the sexual relationship. In his plan, he upheld the usual patriarchal structure of Western gender relations of men taking advantage of women by exercising differential access to power of one sort or another. Thus if Eddie's unexpected use of a feminist book about menstrual experiences spoke to a documented ethnographic practice, it also represented a violation of the feminist intention of the analytic project of understanding those practices. Eddie's story signals how far scholars still have to go in furthering the widespread understanding of feminism and how it can lead us to understand women's lives and bodily-based experiences.

When the book Eddie was using as a quasi-fetish in his flirtation repertoire was first published (Buckley and Gottlieb 1988b), anthropological works about menstruation were few and far between. Moreover, most early anthropological writings on menstruation tended to confirm a simplistic agenda suggesting that menstrual blood is generally taken as a source of what anthropologists call symbolic pollution (Douglas 1966). In other words, menstrual blood was assumed to be seen as mystically contaminating, hence something to be avoided at all costs by anyone who is not menstruating—and especially by men.[2] Feminism had not yet made serious inroads into the comparative, cultural study of women's bodies in general. And systematic cross-cultural fieldwork with consultants concerning the topic

"Bloody Mess, Blood Magic, or Just Plain Blood? Anthropological Perspectives on the Menstrual Experience" (adaptation/elaboration of "Afterword," *Ethnology* 41 (4): 381–390).

of menstruation, let alone with menstruating women themselves about their own perspectives on their somatic lives, was still a rarity. In assembling our collection of anthropological essays about menstrual practices cross-culturally, Buckley and I hoped to be followed by a new generation of writings that would both add new data to our existing knowledge of women's experiences of their bodies, and that would pose a range of new models inspired in one way or another by feminist theory. These future works would, we thought, investigate how women's experiences of the menstrual cycle—as with other body practices—are profoundly shaped by culture and history. For this to occur, we needed to be followed by a new generation of ethnographers committed to conducting fieldwork-based studies on somatic processes such as menstruation that seemed to belong exclusively to the domain of biology but that were nevertheless deeply defined by systems of cultural values and historical factors alike.

During the fifteen years that have elapsed since *Blood Magic* appeared, feminism has indeed made exciting inroads into the comparative, cultural study of women's bodies in general. Accordingly, systematic cross-cultural fieldwork with consultants concerning the topic of menstruation in particular, and with menstruating women themselves about their own perspectives on their somatic lives, is no longer such a rarity. Indeed, in the past decade-and-a-half, there has been a groundswell of published work, both within and outside anthropology, that focuses on menstruation as well as other aspects of reproduction in particular and the body in general. Originally, these writings emphasized *women's* bodily experiences. In many ways launched by Emily Martin's award-winning work, *The Woman in the Body* (1987), a host of books and articles have brilliantly explored the culturally and historically produced nature of a wide gamut of reproduction experiences previously assumed to be regulated by biology alone.[3] Increasingly, scholars have begun to explore cultural and historical constructions of *men's* bodily experiences as well (e.g., Gardiner 2002, Gutmann 1996, Kimmel 1987, Lugo and Maurer 2000). Contemporary authors now writing about the menstrual experience cross-culturally are thus in conversation with a larger cohort of colleagues bringing fresh perspectives to the dynamic interface between body, person, gender identity, and society.

In this chapter, I will especially focus on one recent collection of essays that offers an especially rich selection of practices, beliefs and values concerning menstrual cycle cross-culturally (Hoskins 2002a). Some important themes run through the essays in that collection. For example, the in/famous *menstrual hut* is drastically revisioned in this new writing. Long conceived as an architectural instantiation of female oppression, the "menstrual hut" in much classic anthropological

literature was usually described as a lonely and flimsy structure in which women were consigned to spend their menstruating days alone—bored, self-loathing (allowed only to scratch an itch on their contaminated bodies using the infamous "scratching sticks" to avoid auto-pollution), and in virtual (if temporary) exile. This anthropologically vaunted, somewhat mystical space was surrounded by decades of disciplinary speculation that was, however, rarely based on relevant fieldwork. The menstrual buildings described in current anthropological writings inhabit an entirely different universe.

Janet Hoskins (2002b) occupies an especially privileged position from which to understand the experiences of women while inside a menstrual residence. While living among the Huaulu people in eastern Indonesia, Hoskins herself was expected to spend time in the menstrual hut every month while she had her period. Her account runs parallel to that of another ethnographer, Wynne Maggi, who has recently conducted participant observation research in menstrual houses every month over the course of fieldwork with the (largely non-Muslim) Kalasha community in Pakistan and has written a first-person account of her experiences (Maggi 2001: 125–133). Having conducted fieldwork in societies with active menstrual shelters and a number of explicit menstrual expectations, both Hoskins and Maggi were afforded rare opportunities to gain firsthand knowledge of the occupants' activities and the general atmosphere inside the houses, and thus to demystify women's actual experiences.

Perhaps the greatest challenge posed by both the Huaulu and the Kalasha to the infamous image of the menstrual-hut-as-prison concerns the personnel. Due to the now fairly well documented but still-little-understood phenomenon of menstrual synchrony—the likelihood of co-resident women starting their periods on the same day each month (often at the new moon or full moon)[4]—there is usually a lively gathering of several simultaneously menstruating women inside both Huaulu and Kalasha menstrual huts, rather than the stereotyped single, lonely woman. Moreover, among the Huaulu, beyond the menstruating women themselves, one is also likely to find some of their young children—both boys and girls—and on occasion some visiting women friends as well. Hoskins intrigues us with her account of all manner of pleasurable female activity occurring inside the collectivity temporarily inhabiting the hut. Singing and playing instruments, telling stories, doing craftwork, relaxing, breastfeeding, caring for young children—all these occur each month inside the menstrual residence. Indeed, the sociable nature of the chamber lends itself to charismatic personalities: one Huaulu woman even turned the hut into a performance space in which she recounted lively stories, building up political reputations village-wide from her narrative skills.

Elsewhere, women do not maintain a complete monopoly over the menstrual residence. Among the Pangia of the New Guinea highlands, such buildings may also legitimately shelter *men* (Stewart and Strathern 2002). This occurs on the rare occasion that a man is said by members of the local community to be pregnant because he inadvertently ingested menstrual blood. In such a disastrous situation, the unfortunate man is said to be cured by a ritual that he undergoes inside the menstrual hut shelter—now empty of women. Writing of less legitimate cases elsewhere in New Guinea, Stewart and Strathern (ibid.) also mention in passing the possibility of *menstrual adultery* occurring in the private space of the menstrual hut. This is an under-discussed but surely fruitful topic for comparative inquiry, especially where menstrual seclusion is practiced. Both these Melanesian cases serve as a powerful reminder to the outsider that, as anthropology so often teaches us about nearly every other aspect of social life, nothing may be assumed: in this case, in any given menstrual residence, even the gender of the occupants may be variable.

In Indonesia, Hoskins (2002b) further notes that the Huaulu menstrual building shelters women not only when they are menstruating but also while they are in labor. Such dual-use structures—for both menstruation and childbirth—are reported elsewhere as well (e.g., Maggi 2001). In such cases where the menstrual shelter also serves as the birth clinic, perhaps even the term "menstrual hut" (or "house") is misleading and ought to be replaced by a more culturally inclusive term—"women's reproduction house" or even just "women's house," echoing the "men's houses" that are documented among many groups in Melanesia, Africa and South America. Such a semantic shift would be in keeping with the fact that menstruation may not always be singled out for special treatment in complete contrast to all other bodily fluids and processes.

The emphasis on *agency* in contemporary works about menstruation extends beyond the menstrual shelter to the experience of menstruating women, whether or not they inhabit a special building reserved for the occasion. Thus, the agency of the individual woman-as-menstruator is stressed in several recent essays. From Hoskins (2002b), for example, we learn of Kodi women on Sumba in eastern Indonesia who deploy menstrual blood to deceive their husbands in a variety of disempowering ways, effectively manipulating the secret powers of menstrual blood at the expense of their men. The flip side to such actions is exercised by Huaulu women, who manage the more public powers of menstruation for the *protection* of their men.

Elsewhere in Indonesia, Balinese women may make use of menstrual blood in manufacturing more friendly forms of "love magic." At the same time, in a provocative narrative, Pedersen (2002) illustrates how the individual

menstruator's own perceptions of her state can complicate seemingly simple ideologies of menstruation-as-pollution when she cites a Balinese consultant who claims that sitting on a garbage heap while menstruating makes her feel royal. Other Balinese women knowingly violate menstrual taboos by illicitly entering a temple while menstruating but apparently feel no remorse or guilt. As analyzed by Pedersen, such women employ psychological techniques to counterbalance the spiritual pollution they should in theory cause by their violation. Here we see how ideologies of pollution, where they exist, should be the beginning—not the end—of ethnographic analysis. Women's own views of a patriarchal ideology can strikingly offer an alternative reading of that ideology, sometimes affording women a form of personal resistance to a degrading cultural script, or allowing them to reinterpret it entirely.

The agency of the individual is explicitly stressed by Phyllis Morrow writing about the native American Yupik of central Alaska. Morrow (2002) explores how the Yupik generally emphasize individual responsibility in maintaining cultural expectations. Thus the Yupik allow latitude for individuals to find their own comfort level in adhering to rules, or "teachings" (as Morrow sometimes translates the Yupik word), for personal behavior—including those that pertain to menstruation. This is an apt case of an indigenous or "folk" model of social life pointing productively to an appropriate analytic model. The conjunction between indigenous and analytic models serves as a humble reminder that local systems of knowledge exist on the same level as do "scientific" ones, and each can speak productively to the other (cf. Rosaldo 1989).

Another means to deploy agency in the menstrual experience involves the use of *emenagogues:* herbal and other practical methods that women throughout the world and throughout history have devised to regulate the timing of their periods. Sometimes these techniques have been used to promote fertility, at other times, they have been used (usually furtively) to induce abortions. In either case, using such techniques may constitute a more secular effort by women to regulate their menstrual flow, thereby allowing them to exercise general control over their bodies.

Writing of Bali, for example, Pedersen (2002) mentions that women may prepare a dish with uncooked pig's blood to hasten the onset of their menstrual periods. This observation echoes abundant information contained in a new collection of essays (Renne and van der Walle 2001) reporting an impressive variety of emenagogues cross-culturally and historically. Once again, we encounter the theme of agency, as women deliberately shape their own menstrual experience rather than seeing themselves as scripted actors reading from either a biologically *or* culturally mandated text.

All these cases demonstrate how close attention to individual perspectives deconstructs the classic, monolithic view of menstrual taboos and cultural expectations as preprogrammed models from which actual subjects may never diverge. Such testimonies are theoretically critical insofar as they challenge the image that anthropologists have long held of menstrual culture—perhaps as an extension of a more general model inherited from such early scholars as Lucien Lévy-Bruhl (1985) and others, that cultural traditions in general exert a certain deadening, conservative force. This is a perspective that is very much challenged in the recent work on menstruation.

The individual manipulation of menstrual taboos and expectations speaks at another level to intracultural variation via subgroups with structurally divergent agendas or even ambiguity or ambivalence among members of a given society regarding women's menstrual activities. When Buckley (1988) first suggested that among the native North American Yurok of California, men and women, as well as aristocrats and commoners, may perceive menstruation differently from one another, it was a somewhat novel proposal. Several recent essays provide extended studies of situations that are likewise complex in their own ways. Menstruation emerges from these societies as a process that is perceived differentially according to multiple subject positions.

Writing of Bali, for example, Pedersen charts how the deeply structured system of rank adapted from the Hindu caste system has a significant impact on how girls and women experience their periods. Whereas high-ranking Balinese women may find menstrual taboos to be empowering, low-ranking girls and women may experience menstrual taboos as simply one more painful sign of their inferior status. Social change adds further layers to the entanglements of rank. Pederson notes that "'modern' working women are more prone than any to 'take advantage' of the leverage provided by the exempting options." If such options are more available to higher-ranked women than to lower-ranked ones, this would perpetuate, and perhaps even magnify, the divide between women at different ends of the system of social hierarchy. Here we see the complexity of class and gender as they work against each other. Ironically, women's bodies—which might (seemingly) serve as a foundation for female solidarity—can be culturally manipulated in such a way as to divide rather than unite women of diverse class and prestige backgrounds. The menstrual experience speaks here to broader feminist concerns: sadly, the empowerment of some women often comes at the expense of the oppression of others.

Ironically, the opposite effects of the relationship between class and menstrual symbolism are found in Bengal. In this region of Hindu India, as analyzed by Hanssen (2002), the Brahmanic view is that menstrual blood is polluting. However, when men and women of the low-ranked leatherworker caste become "renouncers" through a particular religious sect—the Vaishnava Baul group—they embrace a major precept of the sect: that menstrual blood contains a life force or "seed" within it—as with other bodily fluids in the Baul scheme of life, but even more so. Taking into account such symbolic potency, some of the "renouncers" with whom Hanssen conducted research may on occasion ingest menstrual blood so as to regain spiritual strength. Here we see the symbolic potency to menstrual fluid being harnessed not for nefarious goals, as is reported in much of the classic literature, but for regenerative purposes. Again, the menstrual pollution model is effectively challenged.

Another subgroup meriting particular attention is that of *unmarried girls*. The menstrual blood of this group—defined variously as virgins and/or unmarried—is held up for special ritual treatment in several societies that are the focus of the articles I have been discussing. For example, Stewart and Strathern (2002) report that the Duna people of Melanesia addressed societal disruptions that were said to be caused by a mischievous spirit by offering the spirit the menstrual blood of a virginal girl. The consequences to the girl chosen to supply this critical ritual ingredient were drastic: as an adult, she was not allowed ever to bear children. In exploring the individual nuances of such cases here and elsewhere, there may be a subject ripe for new, comparative analysis.

Indeed, the experiences of girls undergoing menarche in general are still under-reported by anthropologists. Scholars in history, cultural studies, nursing, journalism, and other disciplines are embarrassingly ahead of anthropologists here, inasmuch as the menarcheal histories of girls in the U.S. are now well documented by scholars in adjacent fields (e.g., Golub 1992, Houppert 1999, Lee and Sasser-Coen 1996). A few current works by anthropologists do address the issue, however. Thus Pedersen (2002) recounts intriguing menarcheal histories of Balinese women that are at great variance from those reported for contemporary North American girls. Whereas in the U.S., many women and girls still feel great shame concerning their first periods (and regarding menstruation in general), and they attest to the continuing existence of a virtual taboo against discussion of the subject in most contexts, this is not the case in Bali. Intriguingly, Pederson reports that Balinese of all ages and both genders feel comfortable in discussing menstruation quite casually, and all females with whom Pederson conversed about the subject recalled that they enjoyed their first periods, even when they were surprised by or afraid of their first flow. Such discussions of the menarcheal experiences of non-Western girls reminds us that the more negative experiences of contemporary North American and other Western girls, while now well reported, cannot be taken as universal.

Surely it is time for more anthropologists to conduct systematic fieldwork with menstruating—as well as pre-menarcheal—girls to hear their own perspectives on this crucial life passage. At a more structural level, such discussions may enable us to think about *deconstructing* the category of "menstrual blood" itself. Are we talking about a unified semantic field when we analyze the blood flow of young girls and that of married women in the same way, if a given society singles out the menstrual blood of unmarried/virginal girls as harboring special capacities that the menstrual blood of adult women does not bear?

In short, from recent work it is clearer than ever that we can no longer talk of "the" (single or hegemonic) view or model of menstruation in a particular society. Rather, it is now clear that before assuming generality, we must interrogate the *range* of views and experiences that menstruation may produce across the social divides that structure women's lives.

Related to the previous points, one notices in the essays I have been discussing an insistence that the meanings of menstrual blood and menstruating women are decidedly *plural* in a given locale depending on the particular context. The classic menstrual-blood-as-pollution model that permeated so much early writing by anthropologists is definitively discarded here in favor of much more situationally nuanced understandings. In particular, the symbolically constituted relation of menstrual blood to both *fertility and infertility*, as well as to other cultural matrices, emerges as an especially critical theme in these papers (for an earlier example, see Gottlieb 1988).

Thus Stewart and Strathern (2002) propose a dramatic re-visioning of the hegemonic, disciplinary model of menstruation-as-pollution as it was foundationally conceptualized. Taking us to the heartland of classical anthropological thinking about menstruation—the highlands of Papua New Guinea—they draw on A. Strathern's recent, stimulating book, *Body Thoughts* (1996) to ground their discussion of menstruation in broader issues relating the body and society. Their description (from Sainsbury) of the menarcheal Siane girl who is celebrated and courted for her induction into life as a menstruator is at striking odds with the classic pollution model that permeated much early anthropological writing about gender relations in New Guinea. Stewart and Strathern then produce in effect a counterfactual model, imagining what regional ethnography might have been like over the past three decades had Sainsbury's ethnography—rather than that of other Melanesianists such as Mervyn Meggitt—prevailed as the orienting study.[5]

But Stewart and Strathern's *What if . . . ?* line of thinking is not purely conjectural: they argue that the Siane would indeed serve as a more appropriate model for the New Guinea highlands. Drawing on additional Melanesian ethnography, Stewart and Strathern (2002) propose that a complementary rather than antagonistic model of gender relations is more relevant to much of Melanesia than previous ethnography suggested. Stewart and Strathern's disarmingly reorienting survey should serve to reinscribe the anthropological imagining of that cultural region with new models steeped in subtlety well beyond the classic statements. Moreover, their proposed model of complementary gender relations resonates with contemporary discussions of complementary and egalitarian models of gender being developed for a variety of independent, non-Western groups elsewhere before state conquest (e.g., Du 2002). Here we see how menstruation theory can speak to, and even inform, gender theory more broadly. This is the case insofar as menstruation is deeply implicated in a wide array of social matrices, from religion (most obviously) to such disparate spheres as architecture, political economy and beyond.

Indeed, the necessity for a contextual approach highlighting what anthropologist Victor Turner might have called *positionality*—an approach that would produce a wide-ranging analysis of how menstrual practices relate to other ritual and social forces at play in a given society—becomes quite pressing from all the work I have been discussing. Most of the societies that are the subject of the articles I have discussed—the Yupik of Alaska, several Melanesian groups, the eastern Indonesian Huaulu, and the Balinese—expect women to adhere carefully to culturally delimited menstrual restrictions; at the same time, the members of these societies orient these practices around conceptual models that are far from a simple pollution framework. Thus all the authors of the works I have discussed remind us that menstrual restrictions are best seen as one of many types of ritual and/or somatic restrictions in the lives of all who practice them. Depending on the society, the proper context for understanding menstrual restrictions may necessitate understanding comparable restrictions in the lives of both males and females, old and young, laypersons and ritual specialists alike. The language of pollution misleads here, these authors all observe; as Morrow (2002) points out, Mary Douglas' early hypothesis that menstrual pollution indexes underlying sociological ambiguity concerning women does not necessarily apply.

At the same time, writing of the Kodi, Hoskins (2002b) points out that the *absence* of menstrual taboos belies a deep-seated conviction that menstrual blood is exceedingly *potent*. Her insight signals that a lack of explicitly religious *taboos* concerning menstrual practice does not necessarily signal a lack of culturally shaped thinking about menstruation. The current outpouring of ethnographies of modern urban life speaks powerfully to this point: secular culture is still culture, these ethnographies remind us—even science is grounded in a set of cultural assumptions that appeal to deeply held but unverifiable beliefs about the nature of reality.[6] As Clifford Geertz cautioned some time ago (1983), what passes for "common sense" is not necessarily common, as peoples everywhere forge their own distinctive notion of common sense as the basis for reality. A contextual approach to social life borrowed from Turner, highlighting positionality, offers a fruitful method for teasing out local nuances that seeming similarities across cultures might otherwise conceal.

As with other taboos, the longstanding anthropological and popular images alike of menstrual taboos is that they have somehow existed since time immemorial and that their origins are untraceable. In the recent writings I have been discussing, we learn otherwise. In taking into account the press of *history and social change*, it becomes clear that menstrual practices engage with a variety of modernities. Earlier studies tended to treat the body either as an artifact of biology—i.e., more or less immutable, hence anthropologically boring—or, more recently, as cultural constructions that were nevertheless conceived as static. More recent discussions have taken up the insistence—persuasively argued by the French scholar, Michel Foucault, and others—that bodily regimes are as much subject to historical shifts as are political regimes. In keeping with this productive direction for scholarly research, in the essays I have been considering, the authors offer discussions of how menstrual practices have—or in some surprising instances have not—transformed within the recent past. Indeed, in some places, rather than insistent continuity, radical changes in menstrual practices have been documented.

Not only may their histories be knowable, but menstrual practices have weakened in some places whereas—in contrast to what modernization theory would have predicted—they have intensified in other regions. Among the Pangia in Melanesia, for example, Stewart and Strathern (2002) inform us that menstrual huts, far from having existed since some primeval *ur*-time, were first introduced to the group along with performances dedicated to a regional female spirit cult. This spirit is widely respected as promoting fertility; Stewart and Strathern treat it as an index of a more general model of gender complementarity. The traceable co-introduction of female spirit cult performances and the practice of menstrual seclusion raises fascinating questions about changing gender roles during an earlier era of Pangia history. The case suggests that we might question the seemingly unchanging history of

other menstrual practices elsewhere. Assuming that contemporary menstrual practices are a permanent feature of a given social landscape makes no more sense than assuming that any other aspect of a society—say, its political structure, or its economic base—has existed unchanged for millennia.

Moreover, in those cases where cultural continuity *is* demonstrable, its meanings are not necessarily transparent. On Bali, Pedersen (2002) tells us, menstrual taboos continue in strong force even in the face of available new menstrual technologies (industrially produced sanitary pads and tampons). However, the continuity of menstrual restrictions does not imply a thoroughgoing neglect of, or resistance to, modernity; the practices of menstrual culture can also acknowledge and even adapt to changing medical science. Thus nowadays, some Balinese women take birth control pills in order to delay the onset of their periods; precisely timing the menstrual cycle in this way can allow women to participate in traditional temple rituals from which menstruating women are still actively banned. In this menstrual culture that persists in the face of active engagement with the Western world, even tourists are subject to regulations . . . as the English-language signs at Balinese temples forbidding entrance by menstruating women remind foreign visitors. The Balinese case teaches us that apparent cultural conservatism may be maintained self-consciously for reasons engaging with modernity. Contemporary factors such as ethnic pride and nationalism in the face of international pressure to Westernize may become as relevant as insistent maintenance of tradition might have been in a previous era.

In short, tracing menstrual histories can serve to remind us that, as with other current social practices, what we observe at any given moment in the field *may* represent continuity—but it may also be an aberration, a variation, or a rejection of what has occurred in the recent or distant past. In the colonized world in particular, the ravages brought by the triple invasion of soldiers, traders and missionaries likely produced upheavals in the way that the body is culturally read and produced. *Precolonial* somatic regimes will of course be much more of a challenge to reconstruct, but oral histories, and in some cases colonial records, should help us to understand pivotal moments in history when the gendered body may have been re-thought and re-experienced. Through such records, can we begin to account for *why* menstrual taboos have relaxed in some areas whereas they have rigidified in others under varying colonial and post-colonial regimes, as indigenous populations endeavor to forge their own futures in the face of an increasingly engulfing modernity? This question contains a promising set of issues for researchers to continue to pursue.

## THE FUTURE OF MENSTRUAL STUDIES

For over fifteen years, a pedagogical engagement with menstruation has allowed me to construct a classroom-based ethnographic portrait that affords some insight into contemporary U.S. college students' perceptions and experiences of the menstrual cycle. At my home university, I have regularly taught an undergraduate course on "Cultural Images of Women" which always includes a section on menstrual practices in cross-cultural perspective. Learning of the obfuscatory terms by which American female students (who are largely but not exclusively female) still refer to their periods ("the curse," "Aunt Flo," "on the rag," and so on)—which are typically identical to terms that have been documented for the U.S. for much of the twentieth century—is a depressing exercise. For the striking continuity in such terms speaks to the continuing existence of strong menstrual taboos and a polluting image of menstruation at the heart of the supposedly rationalized and secular (and, dare one hope, decreasingly patriarchal) mainstream North American society.

However, another student exercise in this course often reveals a different, and more hopeful, portrait of the current generation of American students' attitudes toward toward menstruation. In choosing among several options for final exam essays, the most popular choice is often the essay question that invites students to design a new menstrual ritual for an imagined future daughter or niece, based on what students know from the menstrual experiences of their friends, relatives, and themselves, as well as what they have learned about women's menstrual experiences elsewhere from class readings. In writing their final essays, students year after year have proposed empowering rituals that harness the menstrual cycle to inspire menarcheal girls to feel pride rather than shame at their new somatically acquired status. One student, for example, envisioned a long ritual process of educating her not-yet-conceived daughter into the wonders of the menstrual cycle. During one portion of the imagined ritual, the author and her future husband would, she planned, "throw confetti into the air in celebration" (Schroeder 2001:2). This and other festive acts would serve to teach their future daughter to feel comfortable with her menstrual identity: "She would never once feel she had to hide the box of tampons in her bathroom or avoid the clerk's gaze while purchasing pads at the local grocery store" (ibid.:6–7).

Year after year, imagined rituals such as these have testified to a hunger by my students to revision menstruation in general, and menarche in particular, from a stigmatized to a celebrated event in contemporary North America. If my students' responses are typical, menstrual experiences offer a rich site from which to understand the embodied subject as a place in which gender, power and representation intersect in personally forceful ways. In particular, my students' writings suggest that at least some of the contemporary generation of young women is motivated to rethink their own menstrual histories and enjoys imagining menstrual futures offering ritualized revelry rather than secrecy and shame.

Meanwhile, current anthropological writings offer a range of models of menstrual practices that some of the world's women have forged. Together, these work constitute an exceedingly provocative set of writings that point to the exciting state that characterizes current comparative research into menstruation and that signal the fresh, *multiple* intellectual roads down which the anthropology of menstruation—as an exemplar of the embodied subject—is now traveling.

## ACKNOWLEDGMENTS

A short version of this chapter was first presented at the 99th Annual Meeting of the American Anthropological Association (San Francisco, 2000), and a somewhat different version was published in *Ethnology* 41(4) (2002) (special issue: "Blood Mysteries: Beyond Menstruation as Pollution," ed. Janet Hoskins). Many thanks to Janet Hoskins for comments on the earlier version.

## NOTES

1. The story was shared with me by my husband, writer Philip Graham, who heard it from a writing student of his who was "Eddie's" roommate. The writing student was visiting our home for a class party and, after noticing a copy of *Blood Magic* on my bookshelf, relayed the above narrative to his amused professor.
2. For a critical review of earlier works informed by this and other problematic perspectives, see Buckley and Gottlieb (1988a).
3. For an excellent review of earlier work, see Ginsburg and Rapp (1991). More recent works include: Bledsoe and Banja (2002), Davis-Floyd (1992), Davis-Floyd and Sargent (1997), Davis-Floyd, Cosminsky and Pigg (2002), Davis-Floyd and Dumit (1997), Feldman-Savelsberg (1999), Franklin and Ragoné (1998), Ginsburg and Rapp (1995), Handwerker (1990), Héritier (1994, 1996), Inhorn (1994, 1995), Jordan (1993), Morgan (1999), Nourse (1999), Owen (1993), Ragoné (1994), Rapp (1999), Roth (2002), Sargent (1989), and M. Strathern (1992).
4. For ethnographic and historic examples of menstrual synchrony, see Buckley (1988), Knight (1988, 1991), and Lamp (1988).
5. Their fantasy reminds one of Mary Douglas' long-ago published wondering what Africanist ethnography would look like had the British scholar, Sir E. Evans-Pritchard, studied the Dogon of francophone West Africa and the

French scholar, Marcel Griaule, studied the Nuer of anglophone northeast Africa (Douglas 1975).

6. For some examples of ethnographic accounts of contemporary scientific culture, see Gusterson (1996), Haraway (1990), Martin (1994), and Toumey (1996).

## REFERENCES

Bledsoe, Caroline with Fatoumatta Banja
2002    *The Contingent Life Course: Reproduction, Time and Aging in West Africa*. Chicago: University of Chicago Press.
Buckley, Thomas
1988    "Menstruation and the Power of Yurok Women." In *Blood Magic: The Anthropology of Menstruation*, ed. Thomas Buckley and Alma Gottlieb. Berkeley: University of California Press, pp. 187–209.
Buckley, Thomas and Alma Gottlieb
1988a   "A Critical Appraisal of Theories of Menstrual Symbolism." In *Blood Magic: The Anthropology of Menstruation*, ed. Thomas Buckley and Alma Gottlieb. Berkeley: University of California Press, pp. 1–53.
_____, eds.
1988b   *Blood Magic: The Anthropology of Menstruation*. Berkeley: University of California Press.
Davis-Floyd, Robbie E.
1992    *Birth as an American Rite of Passage*. Berkeley: University of California Press.
Davis-Floyd, Robbie E., Sheila Cosminsky and Stacy Leigh Pigg, eds.
2002    "Daughters of Time: The Shifting Identities of Contemporary Midwives." Special issue of *Medical Anthropology* 20 (3).
Davis-Floyd, Robbie E. and Joe Dumit, eds.
1997    *Cyborg Babies: From Techno Tots to Techno Toys*. New York: Routledge.
Davis-Floyd, Robbie E. and Carolyn F. Sargent, eds.
1997    *Childbirth and Authoritative Knowledge: Cross-Cultural Perspectives*. Berkeley: University of California Press.
Douglas, Mary
1966    *Purity and Danger: An Analysis of Concepts of Pollution and Taboo*. New York: Praeger.
1975 [1967]   "If the Dogon . . . ?" In *Mary Douglas, Self-Evidence: Essays in Anthropology*. London: Routledge & Kegan Paul, pp. 124–141.
Du, Shanshan
2002    *"Chopsticks Always Work in Pairs": Gender Unity and Gender Equality among the Lahu of Southwest China*. New York: Columbia University Press.
Feldman-Savelsberg, Pamela
1999    *Plundered Kitchens, Empty Wombs: Threatened Reproduction and Identity in the Cameroon*. Ann Arbor: University of Michigan Press.
Franklin, Sarah and Helena Ragoné, eds.
1998    *Reproducing Reproduction: Kinship, Power, and Technological Innovation*. Philadelphia: University of Pennsylvania Press.
Gardiner, Judith Kegan, ed.
2002    *Masculinity Studies and Feminist Theory: New Directions*. New York: Columbia University Press.

Geertz, Clifford
1983 [1975]   "Common Sense as a Cultural System." In *Local Knowledge: Further Essays in Interpretive Anthropology*, ed. Clifford Geertz. New York: Basic Books, pp. 73–93.
Ginsburg, Faye and Rayna Rapp
1991    "The Politics of Reproduction." *Annual Review of Anthropology* 20: 311–343.
Ginsburg, Faye and Rayna Rapp, eds.
1995    *Conceiving the New World Order: The Global Politics of Reproduction*. Berkeley: University of California Press.
Golub, Sharon
1992    *Periods: From Menarche to Menopause*. London: Sage.
Gottlieb, Alma
1988    "Menstrual Cosmology among the Beng of Ivory Coast." In *Blood Magic: The Anthropology of Menstruation*, ed. Thomas Buckley and Alma Gottlieb. Berkeley: University of California Press, pp. 55–74.
Gusterson, Hugh
1996    *Nuclear Rites: A Weapons Laboratory at the End of the Cold War*. Berkeley: University of California Press.
Gutmann, Matthew C.
1996    *The Meanings of Macho: Being a Man in Mexico City*. Berkeley: University of California Press.
Handwerker, W. P., ed.
1990    *Births and Power: Social Change and the Politics of Reproduction*. Boulder: Westview Press.
Hanssen, Kristen
2002    "Ingesting Menstrual Blood: Notions of Health and Bodily Fluids in Bengal." *Ethnology* 41(4): 365–380.
Haraway, Donna
1990    *Primate Visions: Gender, Race and Nature in the World of Modern Science*. New York: Routledge.
Héritier, Françoise
1994    *Les deux soeurs et leur mère*. Paris: Editions Odile Jacob.
1996    *Masculin/féminin: La pensée de la différence*. Paris: Editions Odile Jacob.
Hoskins, Janet
2002a   "Blood Mysteries: Beyond Menstruation as Pollution." *Ethnology*, special issue, Volume 41, No. 4.
Hoskins, Janet
2002b   "The Menstrual Hut and the Witch's Lair in Two Indonesian Societies." *Ethnology* 41(4), 317–334.
Houppert, Karen
1999    *The Curse—Confronting the Last Unmentionable Taboo: Menstruation*. New York: Farrar, Straus, Giroux.
Inhorn, Marcia
1994    *Quest for Conception: Gender, Infertility, and Egyptian Medical Traditions*. Philadelphia: University of Pennsylvania Press.
1995    *Missing Motherhood: Infertility, Patriarchy and the Politics of Gender in Egypt*. Philadelphia: University of Pennsylvania Press.
Jordan, Brigitte
1993 [1978]   *Birth in Four Cultures: A Cross-Cultural Investigation of Childbirth in Yucatan, Holland, Sweden and the United States*. Robbie Davis-Floyd, ed. 4th ed. Prospect Heights, IL: Waveland Press.
Kimmel, Michael S., ed.
1987    *Changing Men: New Directions in Research on Men and Masculinity*. Beverly Hills, CA: Sage.

Knight, Chris
1988 "Menstrual Synchrony and the Australian Rainbow Snake." In *Blood Magic: The Anthropology of Menstruation*, ed. Thomas Buckley and Alma Gottlieb. Berkeley: University of California Press, pp. 232–255.
1991 *Blood Relations: Menstruation and the Origins of Culture.* New Haven: Yale University Press.

Lamp, Frederick
1988 "Heavenly Bodies: Menses, Moon, and Rituals of License among the Temne of Sierra Leone." In *Blood Magic: The Anthropology of Menstruation*, ed. Thomas Buckley and Alma Gottlieb. Berkeley: University of California Press, pp. 210–231.

Lee, Janet and Jennifer Sasser-Coen
1996 *Blood Stories: Menarche and the Politics of the Female Body in Contemporary U.S. Society.* New York: Routledge.

Lévy-Bruhl, Lucien
1985 [1922] *How Natives Think.* Lilian A. Clare, transl. Princeton: Princeton University Press.

Lugo, Alejandro and Bill Maurer, eds.
2000 *Gender Matters: Rereading Michelle Z. Rosaldo.* Ann Arbor: University of Michigan Press.

Maggi, Wynne
2001 *Our Women Are Free: Gender and Ethnicity in the Hindukush.* Ann Arbor: University of Michigan Press.

Martin, Emily
1987 *The Woman in the Body: A Cultural Analysis of Reproduction.* Boston: Beacon Press.
1994 *Flexible Bodies: Tracking Immunity in American Culture—From the Days of Polio to the Age of AIDS.* Boston: Beacon Press.

Morgan, Lynne, ed.
1999 *Fetal Subjects, Feminist Positions.* Philadelphia: University of Pennsylvania Press.

Morrow Phyllis
2002 "The Woman's Vapor: Yupik Bodily Powers in Southwest Alaska." *Ethnology* 41(4): 335–348.

Nourse, Jennifer W.
1999 *Conceiving Spirits: Birth Rituals and Contested Identities among Laujé of Indonesia.* Washington, DC: Smithsonian Institution Press.

Owen, Lara
1993 *Her Blood Is Gold: Celebrating the Power of Menstruation.* San Francisco: Harper San Francisco.

Pedersen, Lene
2002 "Ambiguous Bleeding: Purily and Sacrifice in Bali." *Ethnology* 41(4): 303–316.

Ragoné, Helena
1994 *Surrogate Motherhood: Conception in the Heart.* Boulder: Westview Press.

Rapp, Rayna
1999 *Testing Women, Testing the Fetus: The Social Impact of Amniocentesis in America.* New York: Routledge.

Renne, Elisha and Etienne van der Walle, eds.
2001 *Regulating Menstruation: Beliefs, Practice, Interpretations.* Chicago: University of Chicago Press.

Rosaldo, Renato
1989 *Culture and Truth: The Remaking of Social Analysis.* Boston: Beacon Press.

Roth, Denise.
2002 *Managing Motherhood, Managing Risk: Fertility and Danger in West Central Tanzania.* Ann Arbor: University of Michigan Press.

Sargent, Garolyn
1989 *Maternity, Medicine, and Power: Reproductive Decisions in Urban Benin.* Berkeley: University of California Press.

Schroeder, Annica
2001 A "Rite" ful Passage into Womanhood for Little Gabriella. Paper for ANTH 262, University of Illinois at Urbana-Champaign, December 6, 2001. Unpublished manuscript.

Stewart, Pamela J. and Andrew Strathern
2002 "Power and Placement in Blood Practices." *Ethnology* 41(4): 349–367.

Strathern, Andrew
1996 *Body Thoughts.* Ann Arbor: University of Michigan Press.

Strathern, Marilyn
1992 *Reproducing the Future: Anthropology, Kinship, and the New Reproductive Technologies.* New York: Routledge.

Toumey, Christopher P.
1996 *Conjuring Science: Scientific Symbols and Cultural Meanings in American Life.* New Brunswick, NJ: Rutgers University Press.

# Hijras:
## An "Alternative" Sex/Gender in India

### Gayatri Reddy and Serena Nanda

In much of the current literature on sexual difference, hijras are represented as the principal "alternative" sex/gender identity in India—the so-called

"third sex," "eunuch-transvestite," or "intersexed" identity—a cultural definition that emphasizes hijras' status as "neither men nor women," as the title of Serena Nanda's (1999) book indicates. For the most part, hijras are phenotypic men who wear female clothing, and ideally renounce sexual desire and practice by undergoing a physical emasculation known as the

"The Evolution of Third-Sex Constructs in Ancient India: A Study in Ambiguity" In *Invented Identities: The Interplay of Gender, Religion and Politics in India*. Julia Leslie and Mary McGee, eds., New Delhi: Oxford University Press; pp. 99–132.

*nirvan* or rebirth operation. This operation entails the sacrifice of male genitalia to the goddess Bahuchara or Bedhraj Mata, one of the many incarnations of Devi [Goddess] worshipped throughout India, in return for the divine power to bless or curse with fertility/infertility. As vehicles of this divine power, hijras engage in their "traditional" occupations of performing at the birth of a child, at marriages, and as servants of the goddess at Bedhraj Mata's temple (Vyas and Shingala 1987; Sharma 1989; Hall, 1995, 1997; Nanda 1999; Reddy 2001, 2003).

In addition to this idealized asexual role and in apparent contradiction to it, hijras also engage in prostitution or sex work with men. Those who engage in this activity, however, legitimize it through a life-cycle trajectory; according to them, all hijras start out as sex workers and it is only when their bodies and/or desires change that they become sexual renouncers and ritual performers. Whatever their occupation, unlike the commonly understood ascetic ideal, hijras lead their daily lives as a social group, inexorably tied to the [person]-in-the-world, to paraphrase Louis Dumont (1960). Hijras' position in Indian society thus shares features of both a caste within society, complete with rules of comportment, exchange, and hierarchies of moral value, as well as of (marginal) renouncers outside it. As individuals however, it is important to note that hijras represent a wide variety of desires, abilities, identities, and gender characteristics, and also vary widely in their constructions of self in relation to their culturally defined identity.

Since Serena Nanda's work, first published in 1990, much has been written about hijras in the context of sexual difference. Drawing on the anthropological fieldwork of both authors among hijras in South India, this article traces the construction of this category through three different lenses—sex/gender, religion, and politics. It challenges existing accounts of hijras that see them solely as a "traditional" sexual category, rather than a contemporary, politically engaged identity that is crosscut by a range of axes that shape their lives. As such, this article introduces readers to hijras with a descriptive account of them as the so-called "third" sex of India, as well as provides an introduction to the theoretical and methodological issues in the analysis of gender, sexuality, and identity construction in India.

## HIJRAS AS A "THIRD" SEX AND GENDER

The popular understanding of hijras as an alternative sex and gender is predicated on a model of intersexuality—most typically, a *male* model of physical or functional anomaly of the reproductive and sexual system, although theoretically, women who do not menstruate can also become hijras. The word "hijra" is a masculine noun, widely translated into English as either "eunuch" or "hermaphrodite" (intersexed). Both these terms emphasize sexual impotence and are commonly understood in India to mean a physical defect impairing sexual function, both in the act of intercourse and in reproductive ability.

In much of the predominant literature, hijras are represented as sexually anomalous or impotent men who lack desire for women, an attribute often ascribed to their impaired reproductive capacity, or more specifically, their sexual organ. If a hijra is not born with a "defective" organ (and most are not), s/he must ideally make it so by emasculation, an act that is interpreted as a "rebirth"—from male to hijra. Whether hijras are "born" or "made," their identity is primarily envisioned in terms of a loss of virility, or as Wendy O'Flaherty (1973) puts it, they are "men minus men." But importantly, they are "men minus men" who perform many aspects of a female-gendered identity: they wear women's clothes, embody "feminine" gestures, movements and performative attributes, and adopt women's names. Importantly, this understanding is accompanied by the significant corollary that hijras are also "not women," their inability to bear children being the most significant marker of this construct. Hijras, in this scenario are therefore both "not-women" and "not-men," often, though not always, identifying as an identity outside of the binary frame of gender (see Cohen (1995) for an alternative view that troubles the desire to locate hijras as an undeniably "third" category).

## HIJRAS AND OTHER "NOT-MEN"

While hijras are clearly the most visible "alternative" sex/gender, they locate themselves within a larger spectrum of sexual and gender configurations in India. This spectrum, with its own social categories, lexicon, and criteria of membership, is indexed at the broadest level by the labels *kothi, panthi* and *naran* (cf. Hall, 1995; see Reddy, 2005, for an elaboration of this complex spectrum). In this conceptualization of sex/gender, *narans* are an undifferentiated category based primarily on gendered practice and the patriarchal naturalization of femaleness as reproductive capacity—that is, *all* women, in other words; *kothis* are those men who "like to do women's work" and desire the receptive position in same-sex encounters with other men; and *panthis* (or *giriyas* as they are referred to in north India) are the partners of *kothis* and/or *narans*, bounded both by their desire for penetrative sexuality, as well as their lack of desire for the constellation of "female" practices typically embodied by *kothis* and *narans*. In other words, the gender system in India appears to be divided on the basis of practice rather than anatomy, into "men" [*panthis*] and to use Don Kulick's phrase, "not-men" [*kothis* and *narans*] (Kulick 1998; Reddy 2005).

Within this sex/gender system, hijras identify themselves as one "category" or branch of a broader spectrum of identities they refer to as their *kothi* "family." Hijras rank themselves as the most authentic of *kothis*, deserving of the most respect (*izzat*) in the community. They base this ranking on their formal kinship affiliation with hijra lineages and houses, their absence of sexual desire, their modes of self-presentation including the kind of dress they wear, and their religious practice (Reddy 2001).

Perhaps one of the most important of these authenticating criteria for hijras is kinship. In this context, kinship is the affiliation and social obligation to one of the hijra houses or lineages in the community.[1] By engaging in a specific hijra kinship ritual, individuals not only acquire a *guru* or teacher within the community, but also signify their membership in the particular house/lineage to which the teacher belongs. This ritual not only denotes formal membership in the community, but also hierarchizes *kothis* along this axis of kinship. There are *kothis* (such as hijras) who are "official" kin—those who have engaged in this ritual kinship act—and those *kothis* who have not undertaken this formal ritual and therefore are only informally or unofficially related. While this does not prevent the latter from identifying/being identified as *kothis*, it places them lower in the *kothi* prestige hierarchy, according to hijras.

In addition to kinship, hijras' claim to asexuality—lacking sexual desire for either women or men—is another key element in their definition of themselves in relation to other *kothis* and *gandus* (a pejorative label applied to men who enjoy anal [*gand*] sex, a category which includes self-identified "gay" men). Such *gandus* are defined not only by the *form* of their sexual desire, but more importantly, by its *excess*. Excessive sexual desire is a marker of inauthenticity that apparently defines *gandus* and by that token, separates them from the supposedly asexual hijras. An active symbol of hijras' essential *a*sexuality that is deployed for this purpose is the physical excision of their reproductive organs or the nirvan operation. One becomes resolutely and irrevocably a "real hijra" following this operation, serving by this token to separate hijras from their libidinous fellow—*kothis*.

As mentioned earlier, hijras serve as the most strikingly visible dimension of *kothi* identity. For the most part, they are identifiable as "men" who grow their hair long, are clean-shaven, often adopt exaggerated "feminine" gestures and styles of self-presentation, and most importantly, wear saris, the most common dress worn by women in India. So important is this criteria that some hijras refer to themselves, in their own

terminology, as sari-wearing *kothis* (*chatla kothi*) as opposed to other, non-sari-wearing (or *kada-chatla*) *kothis*.

Finally, in addition to sexual desire, kinship and sartorial presentation, religious practice is also a key dimension of hijras' self-image as the *kothis* most deserving of respect. Whether they identify as Hindu or Muslim (see below), most hijras claim to be blessed by (Hindu) gods/goddesses. Thereby, as vehicles of divine authority, hijras see themselves as having more respect (or *izzat*) than some of the other *kothi* identities, who they see as motivated solely by sexual desire rather than religious authenticity.

## HIJRA RELIGIOUS AFFILIATION/PRACTICE

In addition to constructing identity through sex/gender difference, hijras also emphasize religious mythology and practice as an integral aspect of their identity-formation. Contrary to popular opinion, which identifies hijras as devotees of Bedhraj Mata and therefore as Hindus, many hijras in India also identify as Muslim. They do not see these identities as necessarily mutually contradictory, each identification in their eyes, providing different, contextually specific referents.

### Hinduism and Hijra Mythology

In Hinduism, the complementary opposition of male and female, man and woman, represents a key symbolic referent. The interchange of male and female qualities, transformations of sex and gender, and alternative sex and gender roles, both among deities and humans, are meaningful and positive themes in Hindu mythology, ritual and art, and are often drawn on in everyday constructions of self in India.

Hijras also draw on these mythological and divine themes and images to construct and present themselves, identifying with various gods and goddesses in this process. As "eunuch-transvestites" (Vyas and Shingala 1987), hijras identify most closely with Arjun, hero of the epic Mahabharata, who lives for a year in the guise of a "eunuch," wearing bangles, braiding [his] hair like a woman, dressing in female attire, and teaching the women of the King's court singing and dancing. In this gendered performance as a "eunuch-transvestite," Arjun participates in weddings and births, providing legitimacy for the ritual contexts in which hijras perform (Hiltebeitel 1980). The portrayal of Arjun in popular enactments of the Mahabharata in a vertically divided half-man/half-woman form highlights this identification.

This representation of Arjun resonates with the "creative ascetic" Shiva, another key mythological/divine figurehijras identify with, especially in his appearance as Ardhanarisvara, a vertically divided half-man/half-woman (representing Shiva united with his female power or shakti). Shiva is one of the most important sexual/asexual figures in Hinduism, incorporating both male and female characteristics. He is an ascetic—one who renounces sex—and yet he appears in many erotic and procreative roles (O'Flaherty 1973). His most powerful symbol and object of worship is the *linga*, or phallus, but the phallus is almost always set in the *yoni*, the symbol of the female genitals. The generative power of the phallus severed from the body is another important point of identification between Shiva and hijras, highlighting the latters' self-identification as ascetics or *sannyasis;* those who renounce sexuality and yet have the power to confer fertility.

Other Hindu deities, such as Vishnu, also have dual gender representations that are drawn on in public enactments of (hijra) self. In one myth, the basis of a festival in South India attended by thousands of hijras, Vishnu comes to earth as a woman to marry a prince, who is, by this marriage, granted success in battle by the gods. However, although the prince is destined to win the battle against his enemies, it is also well known that he will be martyred in this process, rendering marriage to the prince undesirable for would-be brides, thereby necessitating Vishnu's performance of this role. During the festival, hijras enact the role of women who marry, and later, as widows, mourn the death of their husband, represented by the prince/god Koothandavur. Similarly, an important ceremony at the Jagannatha temple in Orissa involves a ritual in which Balabhadra, the ascetic older brother of the deity Jagannatha (commonly identified with Shiva), is seduced by a young man dressed as a female temple dancer (Marglin 1985). Ancient Hindu texts and origin myths likewise refer to androgynous, intersexed or "alternative" sexes and genders both among humans as well as deities (Bullough 1976; O'Flaherty 1980). The Kama Sutra, the classic Hindu "treatise on love," also specifically refers to those of a "third nature" and the particular sexual practices prescribed for them. In fact, as some authors contend, Hinduism is sometimes characterized as having a "propensity towards androygynous thinking" (Zwilling and Sweet 2000).

### Islam and Hijra Practice

The Hindu religious context of alternative genders that provides a positive meaning for hijras is reinforced by the historical role of the "eunuch" in the five hundred year history of Muslim court culture in India. This historical role has merged with those described in Hindu texts as a source of contemporary hijra identification. Indeed, while identifying with religious figures in Hinduism, hijras also identify as Muslims. The apparent paradox of hijras identifying with Hindu religious figures while also identifying as Muslim, is partly resolved by context, with claims to Muslim religious identity being constructed mainly through practice: through the acts that hijras employ, the proscriptions they are subject to, and the festivals that they celebrate. Although some hijras maintain that "religion does not matter for us, all can join," many of them also say that when hijras join the community they "become Muslims." In many regions of India, hijras approximate the Islamic ideal in their custom of praying, using prescriptive Muslim greetings such as "salam aleikhum," undertaking the pilgrimage to Mecca, celebrating Muslim festivals, as well as engaging in certain commensal practices, sartorial prescriptions, circumcision rites, and (Muslim) burial practices. Clearly, however, hijras are not strictly "orthodox" religious practitioners. Apart from their worship of a Hindu goddess, hijras also blur the gender boundary in their practice of Islam, following rules of comportment specified by the shari'at for *both* men *and* women. Sometimes, in addition to the female names they choose at initiation, they may also choose male Muslim names. Hijra leaders (or *nayaks*) almost invariably are called by their Muslim names. Further, although not all hijras go on the Haj or pilgrimage to Mecca, those who do, go unescorted by male relatives, a prescription for post-pubescent and pre-menopausal women. In addition to these so-called "male" practices, hijras also follow Islamic practices enjoined on women, such as wearing the *burqa* on occasion (a garment that covers the entire body except for parts of the face), though they never wear this item of clothing when performing or entertaining. Though hijras also wear saris like all Indian women, for special occasions they wear green saris, as green is the color of Islam. Also, like some orthodox Muslim women, hijras are not permitted to wear *bindis* (the dot Hindu women wear on their foreheads).

Hijra practice reveals a pluralistic form of religion, which is arguably typical rather than unusual in Indian religious practice. Both Hindus and Muslims in India are characterized by an enormous diversity of communities, traditions, and customs, and religious pluralism has a long history in India. This pluralistic tradition, along with the ability to "compartmentalize" potentially conflictual beliefs and practices (Ramanujam 1990; Shweder and Bourne 1984), allows for a continuum rather than a dichotomy of religious thought, empowering hijras, amongst others, to practice their religion(s) without experiencing significant cognitive dissonance.

## HIJRAS AND CONTEMPORARY POLITICS

The association of hijras with the power of (dis)embodied generativity is clearly related to their cultural identity as ritual performers at marriages and the birth of a child. It is these "traditional" roles for which they gain their respect or *izzat* in society. But recently, hijras have also gained visibility in another role, one that on the surface would seem to be in contrast to their marginalization in Indian society and culture.

This "new" role for hijras is in contemporary Indian politics. As one hijra stated during recent fieldwork, "Within this *kaliyug* (current cosmic period), hijras will become kings and rule the world. That is what [the god] Rama decreed thousands of years ago when he blessed us." Although hijras have not become kings, they have achieved notable political success. In recent years, hijras have been standing for and winning public election to local, state and even national office, and have been actively courted by mainstream political parties for these positions. Significantly, they are entering these new spheres as hijras, explicitly highlighting their identity as gender-neutral, asexual figures.

In the past few years, at least six hijras have been elected to public office at the local and state level, defeating more prominent candidates from national political parties such as Congress (I) and the Bharatiya Janata Party, and it is their transcendant morality *as* hijras that has been central to their success at the polls. Explicitly constructing themselves as individuals without the encumbrances of a family, gender, or caste affiliation, hijras emphasize that they are free from the impetus for nepotism, and therefore are the perfect antidotes to the rampant corruption and immorality of Indian politics. And indeed, the election of hijras can be viewed, at the most obvious level, as a revolt against upper-caste privilege, nepotism and corruption. In one of these elections, the hijra candidate was enthusiastically supported by an emerging political party formed to protect lower-caste and Dalit (formerly untouchable caste) interests, with her victory being hailed by the lower castes and Dalits as a victory over the corrupt and exploitative upper castes. Hijras are also viewed as being more sensitive to issues of poverty and social stigma, and the electorate does seem to perceive hijras as more approachable and effective than other politicians. However, in the past year, the election of at least one hijra has been overturned by the lower courts in the north Indian state of Madhya Pradesh, on the grounds that hijras are in fact *men* (masquerading as women), and therefore cannot stand for election from seats reserved for women. This case is currently being appealed in the Supreme Court.

In their political campaigns, hijras selectively highlighted their resonance with the traditional *sannyasi* or ascetic identity, emphasizing religious and sexual renunciation as the source of their authenticity and *izzat* (Reddy 2003), even as this image marginalizes them in Indian society. This emphasis—on the connection between sexual renunciation and politics—has a long history in India, most prominently expressed by early Indian nationalists, Swami Vivekananda, and Mahatma Gandhi, but also by many contemporary Hindu politicians (cf. Basu 1995). The hijra political candidates also remained conspicuously silent in public on their Muslim identity, a seemingly paradoxical silence, given their articulated embrace of Islam.

An important question raised by the success of hijras in contemporary politics is what it heralds for the transformation of hijras from a culturally and socially marginalized community to a new position in Indian society (Reddy 2003). Indeed, we may look at this as part of the larger question of whether—or to what extent—gender ambiguous roles in all societies are a form of resistance that disrupts the gender and cultural status quo (Nanda 2000). Does this new role for hijras herald a "new chapter of enfranchisement in the history of India's eunuchs" as one news columnist claimed (Jacinto 2000)? Will it reformulate not only hijras' place in Indian society, but also prevailing constructions of Indian citizenship, sexuality, gender, and politics?

The answers are perhaps more ambiguous than the initial media enthusiasm suggests. Not only has the recent legal verdict located hijras as inexorably *male*, a position that precludes the possibility of a more fluid identity and presentation of self, but a closer analysis suggests that rather than remaking normative institutions, hijra political campaigns and their subsequent election appear to have subtly played with "traditional" cultural values, thereby re-inscribing the dominant status quo. Indeed, contrary to popular representations, it seems to us that hijras were elected precisely because they did not disrupt the status quo, and in fact reinforced the prevailing politics of Hindu nationalism. This not only questions the emancipatory and subversive potential of the hijras, but in fact might actually reinforce the majoritarian (Hindu) view of politics and society. If, as one hijra campaign slogan contends, "you don't need genitals for politics," incorporating those without genitals in the "new" political order might not necessarily herald a radically new or liberal social and moral order in India (Reddy 2003).

Certainly at the most basic level, the initial mandate of the hijras did not emphasize their radical potential, but rather the public's denigration of their sexual ambiguity, viewing them as symbols of politicians' impotence and the publics' disillusionment with existing (male) politicians (who are often referred to as "eunuchs"). Their election therefore might have highlighted precisely the hijras' marginality—as a caricature of virile masculinity and the lack of political capability that this apparently symbolizes. By emphasizing the renunciate aspect of their identity, hijras are complicit in this construction—a construction that equates virile (hetero) masculinity with political competence—ultimately reinforcing rather than undercutting their marginalization in society (Reddy 2003).

## HIJRAS AND CULTURAL CHANGE

Despite their marginalization, hijras have demonstrated a remarkable ability to survive throughout their long history in India. With the advent of British rule, the position of the hijras not only began to lose its traditional royal patronage, with the British ultimately removing this community from any state protection (Preston 1987), but hijras were also classified in the colonial hierarchy along with other "criminal castes," resulting in the confiscation of much of their property and the vilification of their status in society (Ayres 1992; Reddy 2005). Building on this colonial history, laws criminalizing sodomy and emasculation, specifically targeting hijras, were incorporated into the criminal code of independent India. While these state policies appear to have had little deterrent effect, combined with the declining opportunities and cultural interest in traditional performances of many kinds, hijras have had to creatively adapt to new situations to maintain their visibility and legitimacy in Indian society. Their entry into contemporary politics is perhaps one such creative re-crafting of themselves in response to changing historical and political circumstances. Despite the ambivalent feelings toward hijras, and the stigma, fear and ridicule that continues to surround them, their survival and vibrant identity is perhaps yet another powerful recognition of the *multiplicity* of differences and the complex history that goes to construct humanity, including, and perhaps especially, hijra identity.

## NOTES

1. Hijras are organized into formal groupings or lineages, each with its own leader (or Nayak). Kinship obligations within these lineages are built on hierarchical principles of seniority, similar in some respects to that of Indian joint families (see Nanda 1999; Reddy forthcoming for elaborations on hijra kinship rules and obligations).

## REFERENCES

Ayres, Alyssa C.
1992.    A Scandalous Breach of Public Decency: Defining the Decent—Indian Hijras in the 19th and 20th Centuries. B.A. Honor's thesis. Harvard University.

Basu, Amrita
1995.    "Feminism Inverted: The Gender Imagery and Real Women of Hindu Nationalism." In T. Sarkar and U. Butalia (eds.), *Women and the Hindu Right*, pp. 158–180. New Delhi: Kali for Women.

Bullough, Vern
1976.    *Sexual Variance in Society and History.* Chicago: University of Chicago Press.

Cohen, Lawrence
1995.    "The Pleasures of Castration: The Postoperative Status of Hijras, Jankhas and Academics." In P. Abramson and S. Pinkerton (eds.), *Sexual Nature, Sexual Culture.* Chicago: University of Chicago Press.

Dumont, Louis
1960.    "World Renunciation in Indian Religions." *Contributions to Indian Sociology* 4: 33–62.

Hall, Kira
1995.    Hijra/Hijrin: Language and Gender Identity. Ph.D diss., University of California, Berkeley.
1997.    "Go Suck Your Husband's Sugarcane!" Hijras and the Use of Sexual Insult. In Anna Livia and Kira Hall (eds.), *Queerly Phrased: Language, Gender, and Sexuality*, pp. 430–460. New York: Oxford University Press.

Hiltebeitel, Alf
1980.    "Siva, the Goddess, and the Disguises of the Pandavas and Draupadi." *History of Religions* 20: 147–174.

Jacinto, Leela
2000.    "Political Outing: Once Ostracized, India's Secretive Eunuchs Get Enfranchized." ABC-News.com, 30 November. http://abcnews.go.com/sections/world/dailynews/india_eunuch001129.html

Kulick, Don
1998.    *Travesti: Sex, Gender, and Culture among Brazilian Transgendered Prostitutes.* Chicago: University of Chicago Press.

Marglin, Frederique A.
1985.    *Wives of the God-King: The Rituals of the Devadasis of Puri.* Delhi: Oxford University Press.

Nanda, Serena
1999.    *Neither Man nor Woman: The Hijras of India.* Belmont, CA: Wadsworth Press.
2000.    *Gender Diversity: Cross-Cultural Variation.* Prospect Heights, IL: Waveland Press.

O'Flaherty, Wendy Doniger
1973.    *Asceticism and Eroticism in the Mythology of Siva.* London: Oxford University Press.
1980.    *Women, Androgynes, and Other Mythical Beasts.* Chicago: University of Chicago Press.

Preston, Laurence W.
1987.    "A Right to Exist: Eunuchs and the State in Nineteenth-Century India." *Modern Asian Studies* 21(2): 371–387.

Ramanujam, A. K.
1990.    "Is There an Indian Way of Thinking? An Informal Essay." In M. Marriott (ed.), *India Through Hindu Categories.* Delhi: Sage Publications.

Reddy, Gayatri
2001.    "Crossing 'Lines' of Subjectivity: The Negotiation of Sexual Identity in Hyderabad, India," Special Issue "Sexual Sites, Seminal Attitudes: Sexualities, Masculinities and Culture in South Asia," *South Asia* vol. XXIV: 91–101.
2003.    "'Men' Who Would Be Kings: Celibacy, Emasculation and the Re-Production of Hijras in Contemporary Indian Politics." *Social Research* 70(1): 163–200.

2005. *With Respect to Sex: Charting Hijra Identity in Hyderabad, India.* Chicago: University of Chicago Press.

Sharma, Satish. K.
1989. *Hijras: The Labelled Deviants.* New Delhi: Gian Publishing House.

Shweder, R. and E. J. Bourne
1984. "Does the Concept of a Person Vary Cross-Culturally?" In *Culture Theory: Essays of Mind, Self, and Emotion.* Cambridge: Cambridge University Press.

Vyas, S. and D. Shingala
1987. *The Life Style of the Eunuchs.* New Delhi: Anmol Publications.

Zwilling, Leonard and Michael J. Sweet
2000. "The Evolution of Third-Sex Constructs in Ancient India: A Study in Ambiguity." In Julia Leslie and Mary McGee (eds.), *Invented Identities: The Interplay of Gender, Religion and Politics in India*, pp. 99–132. New Delhi: Oxford University Press.

# Constructing the Lesbian Body:
## The Worker Community of the Michigan Womyn's Music Festival

### *Alexis Matza*

Thirty-six years ago, a group of women established the We Want the Music Company in order to support and highlight the production and performance of women's music in the Midwestern United States. Desiring the creation of a venue that would facilitate the exposure and dissemination of women's music and women's music culture, they started the Michigan Womyn's[1] Music Festival (Michfest). Simultaneously a place and an event, Michfest quickly transformed into what many view as a temporary utopia—a community entirely built by womyn, for womyn. Michfest, located in rural Michigan, is an annual event which attracts between three thousand and seven thousand womyn from around the globe who participate in a weeklong womyn-centered retreat. The festival provides three stages of comedy, dance, and musical performances; a movie festival; community-run educational and political workshops; a robust crafts area; holistic health care; child care, if needed; and three hot vegetarian meals a day. Michfest is both physically and ideologically constructed by a crew of workers. My research focuses on the separate and longer-term worker community, a group living in a bounded area referred to as Workerville. Depending on the day, this community included between one hundred and seven hundred members living, working, and socializing together. Workers are categorized as either "short crew" or "long crew" depending on their length of stay, which ranges from ten to thirty days before and after the festival. The workers perform all of the duties of building and supporting

this community, ranging from physical and psychological care to providing for the needs of this community (e.g., sustenance, plumbing, stage construction, security, etc.). Although the positions are unpaid, working at Michfest is regarded as a richly satisfying experience, due to the value placed by workers on constructing and maintaining a feminist community.

In the space of a few short weeks, workers coalesce and transform from a grouping of strangers into a community. While many womyn return year after year, approximately 20 percent of the worker community is comprised of first time workers. Although there is an aura of goodwill and amicability throughout the community, workers generally associate out of work with a small circle of individuals whom they know well. The rest of the community remains strangers, primarily interacting during communal activities such as a meal or shower. With coworkers or other individuals with whom one interacts on a daily basis, identity could be expressed through a myriad of traditional communication mediums, such as speech; for the rest of the community, the body became a location marking relevant social identity categories. The body developed into an expressive medium, communicating identity through the adoption and removal of semiotic affiliation markers.

In this paper, I draw upon my fieldwork experiences at Michfest to highlight embodied identity as a form of communication to the community at large. I explore and analyze how some individuals use this space to embody and perform their situated identities. I provide evidence of workers using clothing, nudity, and temporary affiliation markers including haircuts, hickeys, and lesbian symbols, as semiotically rich markers of identity. Through management of such signs, the chosen

Matza, Alexis. 2005. "Constructing the Lesbian Body: The Worker Community of the Michigan Womyn's Music Festival." in *Gender in Cross-Cultural Perspective*, edited by Caroline B. Brettell and Carolyn F. Sargent. Prentice Hall, 2005.

identity is then broadcast on the surface of the body. I argue that the Michfest workers actively utilize dress and physical adornment to construct their identity with shared metaphors (e.g., as womyn, or certain iconic types of womyn). In a related way, I argue that Michfest workers actively craft their self-representation with semiotic markers in order to display and perform their sexuality. In the pages that follow, I offer evidence of workers using clothing and nudity to mark their bodies as attractive, and therefore sexual, and using hickeys to literally mark their bodies as carnal. In addition, I provide illustrative examples of workers using their bodies to perform and embody physical signifiers of lesbianism and therefore a lesbian identity. In other words, sexuality in this environment is "written" on the body.

During the summer of 2002, I was a participant/observer/worker at the Michfest for four weeks. Much of my ethnographic data come from the perspective and interactions I had while helping build and sustain this community. However, since 2002, I have returned as a long crew worker every year, and my analysis builds on these 9 years of experience. In 2002, I informally interviewed 13 workers including bisexual, lesbian, and queer-identified womyn ranging in age from 18 to 48 years. Although my informants were primarily white, many were from outside the United States, and from many different cultural as well as geographic backgrounds. All individuals quoted were interviewed by me and are referred to by pseudonyms. In addition, I enlist my experiential data to clarify the material. Such autoethnography allows for the "layering and use of experience as a critical point of departure for both the production of the text and the interpretation of ethnographic data" (McClarin 2001: 28).

My choice of a research site for this project was motivated by my desire to do work within some of my own communities, here glossed as feminist and queer. Feminist and queer communities are both critical of the norms that bind men and women to discrete cultural roles, including rigid gender expectations and the assumption of heterosexuality. As a white, queer-identified female in my mid-thirties, I had access to a certain level of depth within this community, and I would be taken as an ally by those whom I wished to study. This initial comprehension would allow me to spend my time refining concepts rather than trying to grasp them outright. Additionally, as Lewin and Leap write, "doing ethnographic research among one's own may not only be beneficial because it frees the anthropologist from engaging in exploitation or offers the intellectual advantages of existing knowledge, but also because it enables the researcher to learn something about herself or himself" (1996: 8). However, in this community, I was perhaps more truly a "halfie," similar to Kirin Narayan (1993) and Lila Abu-Lughod (1991), meaning that I was as much an outsider as an insider.

Not only had I never slept in a tent before or attended a similar music festival, but my role as an anthropologist made me a permanent outsider.

## CONCEPTUAL SPACE

The Michigan Womyn's Music Festival was born from the lesbian-feminist movement of the 1970s. Michfest is conceptualized as a feminist utopia, an "Eden Built by Eves" (Morris 1999). Over the years, Michfest has maintained its political edge, and feminist politics are interwoven throughout the community structure (including egalitarianism, anti-racism, anti-ageism, anti-ableism, etc.). Michfest is a temporary intentional community, focused on creating a purposively womyn-centered and feminist collective. An intentional community is one in which the members are engaged in the construction of the community as an intentional pursuit. Rather than a randomized grouping of individuals, members of intentional communities seek strength in their shared purposes. This paper is broadly informed by sociological investigations of group solidarity and collective identity, defined as, "an individual's cognitive, moral, and emotional connection with a broader community, category, practice, or institution. It is a perception of a shared status or relation, which may be imagined rather than experienced directly" (Polletta and Jasper 2001: 285). In collective environments, shared identity is often given primacy over individualized concerns, and difference is often downplayed rather than celebrated (Goffman 1959, 1963; Krieger 1983). In order to demonstrate a collectivity, members are often expected to privilege one aspect of their identity over others.

At Michfest the participants are expected to privilege a shared identity as womyn.[2] A few examples of the geographic vocabulary demonstrate that location itself is seen as female; for example, the general store open during festival is called the Cunt-Tree store, and the health care area is called the Womb. In addition, workers regularly refer to each other as "sister," a linguistic strategy which foregrounds similarities between womyn. Interestingly, the advertising materials for Michfest do not directly label this community as a lesbian space, but instead focus on this community as world built and maintained by womyn (e.g., "Festival is living evidence of what womyn are capable of creating" [www.michfest.com]). However, Michfest is widely regarded a lesbian festival, which, while open to heterosexual womyn, intends to celebrate lesbian culture.

Accordingly, many assume that the majority of workers, organizers, and festival participants are lesbian-identified.[3] As a result, nonlesbian identified workers often gave primacy to identity characteristics that they share with other workers. For instance, Sofy, a bisexual-identified woman in her forties, explains that she prefers to highlight her "lesbian side" in this environment. She consistently refers to her male off-land significant other as her "partner," never specifying a name or a gendered pronoun. When I ask her about this choice of language in an interview, she says, "It's not something that I run around ringing my bell about. Hey, I'm bisexual! Hey isn't that fun! But I think they [the rest of the worker community] relate to the part of me that is more lesbian than not." Sofy indicates that she doesn't mind, saying, "I think that [the lesbian community] is who is putting on this festival and that is to be respected."

For many queer womyn, who are forced to live out aspects of their nonfestival lives closeted in some way, Michfest exists as one location where womyn feel that they can publically celebrate their sexuality. Womyn reveled in their ability to publically display their affections for one another, and openly kissed, hugged, and snuggled with both their romantic partners and close friends. At the No-Talent Show, workers perform burlesque acts and ribald comedy routines for one another. Significantly, for the workers of Michfest, flirting is a form of currency. Womyn flirted in order to facilitate the give and take of living in a community of strangers. For instance, whenever I worked a shift at the front gate, my team would openly flirt with those who were heading off the land into town in order to receive a treat, such as a soda or candy, upon their return. This flirting was playful and did not require an individual to engage in an actual sexual exchange. However, this flirting did add to the understanding that all exchanges had the potential to be sexual. During the festival, the sexually charged nature of this community intensified. There were many sexuality-themed workshops, attended by both workers and festival participants, ranging from a hands-on workshop exploring "How to Kiss" to one entitled "Tantra with Trees." In addition, one parcel of the land was designated as the "Twilight Zone" and was known as the appropriate location for alternative sexual activities. In this section, I've roughly sketched some of the dominant principles that structure the Michfest community, showing the ways in which Michfest is a womyn-centered, lesbian focused, sex-positive atmosphere. In the next section, I analyze the significance of clothing and appearance for workers in this environment.

## CLOTHING AND APPEARANCE

Scholars grappling with the connections between dress and identity argue that all understandings of dress must occur in a particular cultural system. Feminist theory asserts that the body is a "text," which must be read by others (Butler 1993). Alison Eves, in her work on lesbian sexuality and gender identities, argues that, "fashion, style and beauty practices are key sites in the construction of gendered identities since the body becomes part of a system of signification through these cultural practices" (2004: 492). She explores how the physical signifiers of lesbianism function to make lesbians visible to other lesbians. Similarly, Elizabeth Kennedy and Madeline Davis's ethnohistory of working class lesbian bar culture in Buffalo, New York, explores how individuals were expected to participate in specific social roles (1993). In this work, Kennedy and Davis argue that these individuals signaled lesbian identity by performative and ideological markers of identity, such as a choice of clothing or adoption of gendered mannerisms. Following their lead, in this section, I provide data on the significance of clothing and appearance at Michfest.

Clothing choices are very central in this environment, and this is visible in many different ways. In my ignorance, in 2002 I packed stereotypically outdoorsy clothes, including four plain white t-shirts and no hair styling products. This, I learned immediately, was a cultural mistake. In a land where so much of identity is worn on the surface of the body, mine felt dreadfully plain. This was proven to me the following year, when I returned to Michfest and was asked multiple times if this was my first year; my plain exterior the year before contributed to my invisibility during the previous year. Workers often bring a separate tent just for their clothing, referred to as "closet tents," and many hang up full-length mirrors on trees near their campsite. Clothing choices ranged from boys' and girls' accessories (such as little boy sized clip-on ties and girls' barrettes) to sporty clothing choices such as running shorts and sports bras; from sarongs, linen, and other flowing garments to dressy, western snap shirts paired with suit pants and tough-looking leather belts; from short skirts paired with vintage aprons to a simple pair of cotton underwear; from flannel shirts and work boots to animal print dresses paired with high heeled boots. Some workers would shower and dress with care every morning before work to make sure they looked as attractive as possible. Most workers would shower and change after their work shift, giving considerable consideration to how they looked. In addition, many workers bring clothing items to wear for particular occasions, such as for dances, for opening ceremony, or for themed dress-up parties which occur throughout the month. Every year, about two weeks after long crew starts (no doubt, coordinated with the arrival of the second large influx of people, the short-crew workers), there is a considerable buzz about haircuts, and a few womyn set up makeshift haircutting stations. Whether womyn were doing their hair and putting on their best thrift-store clothing, or knotting a clean sarong around their waist, there was an intense focus on attractiveness, which mandated adorning and accentuating their body.

Sofy indicated during her interview that one of the things that brought her to Michfest was being able to "dress freely," and so to prepare for the festival, she tie-dyed a bunch of cloth so she could drape it on herself. Talking about the worker community as putting on a daily fashion show with their clothing choices, Sasha says, "A lot of creativity pours into how we clothe ourselves. When we remove the social boundaries about what is appropriate where, it is really fun. . . . I think it's fantastic, really. Where else in the world can you wear saran wrap with two daisies covering your nipples?" As Drew exclaims, "Other people's clothes are *so* appreciated." This mutual appreciation inspires individuals to dress to be seen. Speaking of the outside world, the performer Leona says in her interview, "Insecurity is a serious subtext of womyn's lives . . . There is this serious 'am I ok?', 'do I look ok?', 'do I sound ok?', 'am I funny?', 'am I smart?', 'am I cute?', thing going on," which she contrasts with Workerville, where, she says, there is an, "aura of confidence back here where people strut around." One illustrative comment was expressed on my first day at a new-worker orientation where one self-identified fat worker stated that she kept coming back to Michfest because she felt sexier there than anywhere else in the world (at the time of this declaration, she was wearing a t-shirt emblazoned with her weight in glitter). In these statements, we can see both the focus on appearance and the pleasure that individuals take in such performances.

Significantly, while for some workers such as Sasha and Sofy, who believe in an "anything goes" ethos toward dress, there can be at times a surprisingly narrow range of options for workers. I experienced this tension during one morning in the summer of 2010, when my crew assignment was to help another crew on garbage duty. As it was raining, I threw on a pair of bright yellow waterproof overalls and a black raincoat, and climbed into the back of the work truck. I introduced myself to Antonia, who was also wearing bright yellow waterproof overalls and a black raincoat. After a little while, it stopped raining, and we both took off our rain gear, only to see that we were both wearing navy blue knee length shorts, bright blue T-shirts with cut off sleeves, and leather belts. Similarly, the next day as I stood at the confluence of two paths, I saw Robin walking towards me, wearing a red tank top and royal blue hot pants. At the same time, from the other direction, on the other path, I saw Evan walking towards me, wearing the same thing. How did it come to pass that two strangers who believed that they were dressing creatively were dressed alike? Every culture and subculture has standards of appropriate conduct. While individual workers had choices regarding how they wanted to display their body to gain appreciation, these choices are read

against a particular cultural system, which sometimes constrains or limits individual choice. In addition, this is increasingly complex when individuals desire to look attractive, as they must be *seen* as attractive.

David Halperin, drawing from Foucault, argues that, "gay life has generated its own disciplinary regimes, its own techniques of normalization, in the form of obligatory haircuts, t-shirts, dietary practices, body piercing, leather accoutrements, and physical exercise" (1995: 32). Compared with the conformity of style referenced here by Halperin, Michfest workers are much more unruly than disciplined. I remember the first time I saw a coworker wearing a little boy's tie; I had never imagined a woman wearing such a thing. She was simultaneously tough and cute, pretty and handsome, crafting her own identity category out of various gendered norms. Surveying any gathering of workers will confirm that there is no one way to be a lesbian, or to look like, a lesbian. While certain codes do function to inscribe the body with ideological symbols, I want to stress the multiplicity of womyn's relationships to these codes. For instance, while some womyn adopt and proudly display rainbows as a celebratory symbol of gay identity, other womyn view such icons with ironic detachment. At Michfest, such heterogeneity is valued, rather than adherence to strict norms. However, while experimentation with fashion in this environment is celebrated, it must be done in culturally intelligible ways. In the above example, I had adopted such comfort with these codes that they had become invisible.

## NUDITY

Although some individuals chose to highlight aspects of their identity through adoption of clothing and other semiotic markers, others felt most comfortable displaying their identity with their naked, unfettered body. I was not prepared for the amount of nudity that I was exposed to (and participated in) as a worker. The open air showers do not have shower curtains and are located directly on one of the main thoroughfares; it therefore became common to see both strangers and peers naked. In addition, many people feel extremely comfortable on the land and walk around at all times in various stages of undress (most commonly, topless).

The ubiquitous presence of naked womyn is empowering for many womyn, both in terms of feeling connected to a shared identity as womyn, and celebrating the diversity of womyn's bodies. When I first drove onto the land, I was greeted by bare-chested Tucker, with breasts adorned with chest hair and goatee. Since the assumption was that Tucker and every other worker was female, her chest and facial hair did not interfere with her being seen as a woman. Her naked body both confirmed her sexed identity, and connected us both to a shared identity as womyn. In addition, in my interview with Sasha, she details how when she first came to the festival as a worker twenty-eight years ago, she was very uncomfortable with all forms of nudity. One of the first womyn she encountered was a burn victim who was naked. She says, "If that woman could go around butt-ass naked, maybe so could I," and claims that for the following year she, "didn't pack a thing, because the most reliable raincoat is skin." Implicit in this statement is a celebration of womyn's bodies that provided Sasha courage to accept and display her body. This honoring of the variety of womyn's bodies stands in direct contrast to the shame and secrecy that surround womyn's bodies in the mainstream culture of the United States. As a result, for many womyn, nudity at Michfest becomes a feminist act.

Eventually, nudity became normal to me, and I even consented to interview Tova and Tonya while they were topless, though clipping the lapel microphone was a unique challenge. Seeing Megan, a twenty-something working topless every day or eating alongside Montana, a naked and bronzed septuagenarian, normalized and desexualized their nudity. Paradoxically, since nudity at Michfest was desexualized, when people wanted to appear attractive, they adorned their bodies. During the first dance in Workerville, I noted that nobody was topless, which I assume is because the prevalence and dailiness of nudity served to desexualize these unclothed bodies. In addition, many womyn had large sections of their bodies covered in multiple tattoos and/or piercings. These permanent bodily adornments created a contradictory situation where some bodies remained embellished even while naked. In the next section, I explore how identity is constructed through shared metaphors in this unique environment, giving special attention to the tensions that inform and obscure this production.

## IDENTITY WRITTEN ON THE BODY

When I first arrived and registered as a worker, my wrist was encircled with green plastic, a wrist ticket which coded green to visibly display my status as a worker (compared with red for festival attendees and blue for performers). I was now officially, ritually, and physically marked as part of the worker community. The green wristband which conferred my admission to the festival land also served to ritually mark me as an outsider the few times that I left the festival land. The presence of the wristband immediately communicated to the local townspeople my purpose, and in

some respects, they could assume aspects of my identity based on my participation in this festival. This example illustrates how identity can be conveyed by adopting temporary makers of cultural membership.

When identity is signified on the body, all choices about clothing and nudity are symbolically significant. At Michfest, although many forms of dress may be acceptable, stylized fashions give rise to associations of a shared identity. One postcard sold by Michfest is entitled "Michigan Fashion Sense," and pictures seven womyn wearing outfits that range from a topless woman wearing only a necklace and a sarong; a woman in a bikini, high heeled shoes, and a large hat; another woman wearing a t-shirt, ball cap, and exercise pants; and, finally a heavily tattooed woman wearing jeans, chaps, and a leather vest. The womyn each have thought bubbles above their heads, the majority of which indicate their derision at each other's clothing choices, calling each other out as "fashion victims," "male identified," or as a "pawn of the patriarchy." One woman is wholly unconcerned with the other womyn's appearances, and another woman eagerly gazes at the woman to her right, thinking that she looks "Cool!" This image is meant to be humorous, and should not in any way be taken as an indication that womyn in this community are that contemptuous. However, it can be taken as evidence that clothing choices at Michfest are both significant and signifying of an underlying ideology. In other words, individuals not only cared about their appearances and projected identity markers while working, but workers use stylized referents to draw conclusions about other womyn's identities.

Accordingly, many workers present more lesbian appearance at Michfest than they cultivate at home. For instance, Virginia, a 30-year-old first time worker came to Michfest with chin length curly hair. Bothered by external claims that she had "soccer mom hair," Virginia shaved off most of her hair, adopting a more stereotypically "lesbian" haircut. She also wrote her mother, requesting clothing. When I ask her about these changes during her interview, she says that she, in comparison with the other workers, "felt very underdressed." Her transition was also motivated by a desire to look attractive to facilitate romantic entanglements.

It is difficult for me to convey adequately the diversity of appearances and choices of clothing, but the consistent, butch/femme subcommunity of the Michfest worker community offers a good example of how identity can be signified on the body through attire. Butch and femme are widely regarded as specifically lesbian genders that are represented by clothing choices; roughly speaking, butch womyn often don stereotypically "masculine" clothing, and femme womyn often adorn themselves in stereotypically "feminine" clothing (Kennedy and Davis 1993). Unfortunately, there isn't room in this chapter to elaborate the many varied lesbian genders and their corresponding attire that have been enacted in historically and regionally specific ways, including stud, kiki, fluffs, bluffs, fish, etc. (cf., Faderman 1991). Every year during the festival there is a Femme Parade, a procession that conveys a range of aesthetics subsumed under the title femme (in recent years, there has also been a corresponding Butch Strut). This performance not only ritually inscribes each of the disparate participants as femme, at least in that moment, but also serves to expand and complicate our notions of femme gender identity. When Sita wore a pink ball gown and tiara and drove a tractor in the parade, she challenged both the utilitarian concepts of appropriate clothing and the relationship between femme identity and assumed hyper-feminine frailty. In addition, because individuals can slip into the parade, and therefore slip into this gender identity, the femme parade demonstrates that the worker community accepted as legitimate either claiming a static or more fluid gender identity.

## TEMPORARY AFFILIATION MARKERS

### Hickeys

As I wrote earlier, Michfest is a sex-positive locale for queer womyn. One particular embodiment of that sexualization is the ubiquity of hickeys. Toward the end of my month stay in 2002, there were more and more hickeys visible on the bodies of individuals in Workerville. I first realized the prominence of hickeys while in the showers one day, surrounded by middle-aged womyn who each had "love bites." This caused me to note the prevalence of these marks throughout the larger worker community, which then led me to question the significance of these marks. From my vantage point, age did not appear to be consequential, nor did hickey placement. Whether workers were walking around naked, or their skin was only observable in the public showers, individuals often had very visible hickeys, marking their bodies as both sexual and hedonistic. Hickeys can signify many things to many people, such as associations with youth or sexual experimentation, but within the contemporary United States, hickeys suggest excessive sexual activity. Womyn workers were ritually marking their bodies as lascivious in a forum in which they knew they would not be punished, and in fact might even be praised for their sexual bravado. The workers of Michfest knew that in these environs, lesbian sexuality was something that womyn could be proud of, and the safety of the festival space enabled them to play around with these otherwise taboo marks. In addition, a hickey typically comes from sexual acts, and these marks signified these womyn's bodies as visibly sexual. Instead of attempting to closet themselves to appear appropriately respectable, workers felt able to flaunt their active and queer sexuality.

### Labrys

Finally, I want to briefly mention a new trend at Michfest which provides evidence of increasing numbers of womyn symbolically marking their bodies as lesbian. In 2009, a middle-aged lesbian friend who knew that I love vintage neckties gifted me one of her old ties from the 1980s. This tie was shiny satin and emblazoned with a small labrys. The labrys is a double-headed axe which was used as a symbol of lesbian culture beginning in the 1970s. The labrys references Amazonian mythology, and is meant to symbolize womyn's strength and self-sufficiency. Unfortunately, I saw the labrys as a symbol of a bygone lesbian-feminism that I was too fashionable for (an attitude that now embarrasses me). Like many of my generation, I saw myself as queer, not lesbian. Lesbian signified that I was a woman who sought out relationships with other women, whereas queer was a politicized sexual identity that attempted to destabilize culturally accepted gender and sexual identities. I unconsciously held lesbiophobic attitudes that being queer was a better, more transgressive identity. I now see that I was restigmatizing lesbians, "into an old-fashioned, essentialized, rigidly defined, specifically sexual (namely, *lesbian* or *gay*) identity," by claiming that I was a member of a group of, "trendy and glamorously unspecified sexual outlaws who call themselves 'queer' and who can claim the radical chic attached to a sexually transgressive identity" (Halperin 1995: 65). Yet in 2010, at Michfest, the labrys became fashionable again, so much so that many womyn referred to 2010 as the "The Year of the Labrys." This was not mere hyperbole: there was a significant intensification of dialog about the labrys and a rapid increase in the number (and type) of womyn wearing labrys jewelry, clothing, and permanent marker "tattoos." Other evidence include so many workers (including myself) purchased labrys jewelry from the crafts area that the crafts womyn sold out these items within a few days (according to one crafts worker, the first time this has ever happened to her); many womyn crafted labrys-shaped items from found objects from the land; there was a "curated" exhibit of labryses on display in the worker kitchen; and, lastly, womyn who had worn labrys jewelry or tattoos over the years were celebrated as "herstorians." One worker that I spoke with attributed the rapid surge in labrys iconography to a general trend of reclaiming lesbianism as an identity.[4] Whether or not lesbianism as an identity category is reemerging, the sudden resurgence of the popularity of this specifically lesbian cultural artifact, which I (and others) had very recently thought to be anachronistic, is yet another example of how the workers of Michfest marked their bodies with a particular symbol of their sexuality. In all of these examples, the labrys is a temporary marker, and can be removed when womyn leave the land. Yet, in direct contrast to Halperin, the embracing by workers of markers of a specifically *sexual* identity (as opposed to "post-gay" or "queer") is an example of womyn literally inscribing their bodies with their sexuality.

## IMPLICATIONS

In this chapter, I have provided information about my experiences with the worker community of the Michigan Womyn's Music Festival. I have explained how the blend of intimacy and alienation in this environment creates a situation where individuals craft the presentation of their identity as a strategy of communication. In the absence of ordinary concerns, participants experiment with different strategies of self-presentation and focus on their bodies—both naked and clothed—as ways to convey particular messages to the community at large. I have demonstrated that identity in this environment is interactively constructed, maintained, and relationally performed on the surface of the body, with the adoption and removal of temporary affiliation markers. In particular, I have demonstrated how workers in this community utilize shared norms to mark their bodies with their sexuality, in three separate but interrelated ways. Physical attractiveness becomes paramount in this environment by offering womyn new scripts of attractiveness and beauty. As a result, womyn feel more attractive, more erotic, and by extension, more confident in this environment, which emboldens them to decorate their bodies with clothing and accessories. In addition, womyn adorn their bodies with literal marks of their active sexuality by giving and receiving hickeys. Hickeys also have symbolic dimensionality, which represent womyn's delighted celebration of lesbian sexuality, rather than shame, embarrassment, or caution. Finally, womyn utilize clothing and accessories to mark their bodies to be read as certain genders and sexualities.

As I emphasized throughout, each individual in this community has the ability to highlight aspects of her identity by actively manipulating her dress and temporary affiliation markers. By actively employing symbols, each woman is in control of who she is understood to be. As I have shown, workers needn't feel bound to any one identity or role, and in this community, multiple framings of gender and identity are encouraged and displayed. Intriguingly, this all happens with a biological essentialist backdrop; since we are all assumed to be womyn, there is an increased allowance for this kind of gender play. This liminal space isn't a complete break from daily life, but can

function as a place to try out new and old identities, performances, and affiliation markers. However, identity is always dependent on shared norms, and I have shown how both visible and invisible rules delimit "appropriate" methods of marking identities.

Michfest is part utopia, part vacation destination, part intentional community; it allows both for the performance of group identity and for the articulation of individuality; it facilitates both rebellion and conformity. All in all, the workers at the Michigan Womyn's Music Festival construct the lesbian body along with building and maintaining the festival itself.

## NOTES

1. "Womyn" is a neologism popularized by lesbian feminists during the 1970s that signifies "women" yet calls attention to the patriarchal semantic structure of the word "wo(men)." I continue to use "woman" for the singular.
2. Michfest does not allow men and boys over ten years old.
3. Not all womyn who engage in relationships with womyn identify as lesbian, preferring instead a multitude of other reclaimed terms, including dyke, queer, or gay. In this chapter, I use the term lesbian as an umbrella term to signify womyn whose primary romantic and erotic relationships are with womyn.
4. For example, see Allyson Mitchell's Deep Lez social experiment, which she describes as "rescuing lesbianism and radical feminism from being forgotten or discarded" (Lichtman 2004: 22).

## REFERENCES

Abu-Lughod, Lila. 1991. "Writing against Culture." In R. Fox (ed.). *Recapturing Anthropology*, pp. 137–162. Santa Fe, NM: School of American Research.

Butler, Judith. 1993. *Bodies that Matter: On the Discursive Limits of Sex.* New York: Routledge.

Eves, Alison. 2004. "Queer Theory, Butch/Femme Identities, and Lesbian Space." *Sexualities* 7(4): 480–496.

Faderman, Lillian. 1991. *Odd Girls and Twilight Lovers: A History of Lesbian Life in Twentieth-Century America.* Ithaca: Columbia University Press.

Goffman, Erving. 1959. *The Presentation of Self in Everyday Life.* New York: Doubleday Anchor Books.

———. 1963. *Behavior in Public Places: Notes on the Social Organization of Gatherings.* New York: The Free Press.

Halperin, David. 1995. *Saint Foucault: Towards a Gay Hagiography.* Oxford: Oxford University Press.

Kennedy, Elizabeth, and Madeline Davis. 1993. *Boots of Leather, Slippers of Gold: The History of a Lesbian Community.* New York: Penguin Books.

Krieger, Susan. 1983. *The Mirror Dance: Identity in a Women's Community.* Philadelphia: Temple University Press.

Lewin, Ellen, and William Leap (eds.). 1996. "Introduction." In Ellen Lewin and William Leap (eds.). *Out in the Field: Reflections of Lesbian and Gay Anthropologists,* pp. 1–31. Urbana: University of Illinois Press.

Lichtman, Chelsey. 2004. *Deeply Lez: An Interview with Allyson Mitchell.* Electronic document. http://www.allysonmitchell .com/action/docs/deeplez.pdf.

McClarin, Irma. 2001. "Theorizing a Black Feminist Self in Anthropology. Toward an Autoethnographic Approach." In Irma McClaurin (ed.). *Black Feminist Anthropology,* pp. 49–76. New Brunswick, NJ: Rutgers University Press.

Morris, Bonnie J. 1999. *Eden Built by Eves: The Culture of Women's Music Festivals.* New York: Alyson Books.

Narayan, Kirin. 1993. "How Native Is a 'Native' Anthropologist?" *American Anthropologist* 95(3): 671–686.

Polletta, Francesca, and James Jasper. 2001. "Collective Identity and Social Movements." *Annual Review of Sociology* 27: 283–305.

www.michfest.com. n.d. Electronic document. http://www .michfest.com/festival/index.htm.

# VII

# *Gender, Property, and the State*

Anthropological analyses of gender profit from attention to the ways in which the state works to monitor and control the bodies of its subjects. State politics and policies shape gendered meanings and practices. Individuals, in turn, strategize to negotiate, accommodate, and resist these broader state agendas. The concept of "the state," however, is complex, and the term refers to diverse types of central governments, operating at different scales and with different capacities to exercise power in the realm of gender relations. In addition, in the context of globalization (see Section XI), local, state, and global dynamics mutually intersect. Global/state/local tensions play out in the everyday lives of individual women and men, as the chapters in this section demonstrate. Two themes dominate this section: (1) the role of state institutions such as the educational and judicial systems in regulating women's bodies and managing particular populations (e.g., immigrants); (2) the means by which the state is integral to the production and reproduction of gender inequalities, viewed in historical perspective. These two themes have been central to theorizing gender since the nineteenth century.

The relationship among sexual inequality, the emergence of class structures, and the rise of the state has been an enduring interest in anthropological studies of gender. The subordination of women appears to emerge as an aspect of state formation. According to Gailey (1987: 6), "Institutionalized gender hierarchy . . . is created historically with class relations and state formative processes, whether these emerge independently, through colonization, or indirectly through capital penetration." We are led to ask what relationship class and state formation have with the oppression of women and, when gender hierarchy occurs, why women are the dominated gender. How does the state have power to penetrate and reorganize the lives of its members, whether in Sumerian legal codes decreeing monogamy for women or in welfare laws in the United States that influence household composition?

Much discussion of this subject has derived inspiration from Engels's book *The Origin of the Family, Private Property, and the State*, a nineteenth-century text in which Engels argues that the emergence of the concept of private property and its ownership by men, as well as the development of a monogamous family, led to the subordination of women. In Engels's scheme, prior to this, gender relations were egalitarian and complementary. All production was for use, and people worked together for the communal household. Thus, changes in gender relations were linked to changes in material conditions because the ownership of productive property (initially domestic animals) was concentrated in the hands of men. This thesis has been influential in many Marxist and feminist analyses of women's subordination. For example, Leacock notes, "There is sufficient evidence at hand to support in its broad outlines Engels' argument that the position of women relative to men deteriorated with the advent of class society" (1973: 30).

Following Engels, Leacock observes that in early communal society, the division of labor between the sexes was reciprocal, and a wife and her children were not dependent on the husband. Further,

"The distinction did not exist between a public world of men's work and a private world of women's household service. The large collective household was the community, and within it both sexes worked to produce the goods necessary for livelihood" (1973: 33). In this view, the oppression of women was built on the transformation of goods for use into commodities for exchange; the exploitation of workers and of women was generated by this process, which involved the emergence of the individual family as an isolated unit, economically responsible for its members, and of women's labor as a private service in the context of the family. This led to the "world historical defeat of the female sex" (Engels 1973: 120; Silverblatt 1988: 430).

In a reanalysis of Engels, Sacks agrees that women's position declined in conjunction with social classes but disputes Engels's emphasis on the role of private property in this process (Sacks 1982). Rather, Sacks links state formation and the decline in the centrality of kinship groups to the deterioration in women's status. She delineates two relationships defining women in noncapitalist societies: sisterhood and wifehood. "Sister" refers to women's access to resources based on membership in a kin group. This relation implies autonomy, adulthood, and possible gender symmetry. "Wife," on the other hand, refers to a relationship of dependency on the husband and his kin. Sacks suggests that state power undermined women's status by dismantling the kin group corporations that formed the basis for sister relations (Sacks 1982).

However, critics of Sacks's position have argued that the process of state formation may involve uneven and contradictory developments. For example, elite women in the Kingdom of Dahomey, West Africa, challenged state imperatives by means of control of marketing associations. Thus, Silverblatt (1988) rebuts Sacks's evolutionary paradigm suggesting the inevitability of the decline in women's status with state formation. Instead, she suggests that we acknowledge the complex history of the emergence of elite privilege in the rise of the state. In addition, elite women such as the royalty of Dahomey may or may not share the goals of peasant women. They may instead join with the male elite in suppressing the authority and power of peasant market women. This illustrates the potential contradictions of gender affiliation, on one hand, and class position on the other (see Joyce, Section II).

Ortner examines the process of state formation, with particular regard to its effect on gender ideology (1978; see also Goddard 2000b). She analyzes the widespread ideology that associates the purity of women with the honor and status of their families. This pattern is evident in Latin America and the Mediterranean, and in societies of the Middle East, India, and China. Broad similarities exist in these varied societies. Ortner questions why the control of female sexual purity is such a ubiquitous and important phenomenon. She notes that all modern cases of societies concerned with female purity occur in states or systems with highly developed stratification, and they bear the cultural ideologies and religions that were part of the emergence of these states. Concern with the purity of women was, in Ortner's view, structurally, functionally, and symbolically linked to the historical emergence of state structures.

One of the central questions in the analysis of the impact of state formation is the role of hypergamy (up-status marriage, usually between higher-status men and lower-status women). Ortner (1978) suggests that a significant development in stratified society involves the transformation of marriage from an essentially equal transaction to a potentially vertical one, where one's sister or daughter could presumably marry into a higher social milieu. Hypergamy may help explain the ideal of female purity because concepts of purity and virginity may symbolize the value of a girl for a higher-status spouse. Thus, "a virgin is an elite female among females, withheld, untouched, exclusive" (Ortner 1981: 32).

Hypergamous marriages often involve the exchange of significant amounts of property, particularly in the form of dowry. The relationship between dowry, inheritance, and female status has been explored in a number of societies with varying marriage patterns. Dowry has been described as a form of premortem inheritance, parallel to men's rights in property accrued through inheritance after death of parents or other legators. However, considering dowry as a form of inheritance prior to death and as part of a woman's property complex obscures an important difference between the clear legal inheritance rights that men possess and the dowry that women may or may not receive (McCreery 1976). Women obtain dowry at the discretion of their parents or brothers, and dowry is not based on the same rights as other forms of inheritance to which men have access. Responding to reported abuses, the Indian government (in part influenced by feminist activism) has sought to outlaw dowry, thus far without notable success.

In her cross-cultural exploration of the political experiences of contemporary women, Josephine Caldwell Ryan (in this book) illustrates the ways in which women engage, respond to, or resist the state. She notes that women's interaction with the state may take the shape of voting, seeking political office, participating in women's movements or other forms of collective action, or acting individually in response to state policies. A global perspective on women's encounters with the state suggests that although some women have experienced an increase in formal political rights and "real" power, others have seen their gains eroded by such forces as religious fundamentalism and global economic crises. Major world religions, including Christianity, Hinduism, and Islam, have experienced an increase in religious fundamentalism in the last thirty years. Accordingly, Caldwell Ryan traces the impact of religious fundamentalism in Iran, Afghanistan, and India on the status of women in those countries. She shows that it is useful to consider the specific circumstances of national histories and identities rather than focusing solely on religious doctrine to analyze the impact of religious fundamentalism on women in particular states.

Similarly, global economic upheavals have negatively affected women's everyday lives as well as demonstrating their limited political power. Structural adjustment policies initiated by the World Bank and the International Monetary Fund, for example, have led to higher prices for food and a decline in public spending on health and social services, all leading to increased burdens for women, who have been forced to take on a greater responsibility for providing for their families in response to economic austerity measures. Caldwell Ryan's discussion underscores the links between women's political empowerment and economic autonomy. Ultimately, one catalyst for global gender equity is the emergent international feminist movement, which has succeeded in putting gender on the agenda of nearly every state. Thus such issues as girls' education, female labor, child custody, and women's inheritance and property rights have emerged as matters for national debate and political action.

The vexing issue of acceptable dress for Muslim women in France offers another example of state interests in gendered bodies. Bowen (in this book) traces the historical trajectory of French public anxieties and state intervention in the realm of Muslim women's clothing, from the colonial period to the present. He notes that from 1989 through 2011, a recurring justification for state regulation of Muslim women's bodies has been their putative lack of autonomy. Insofar as Muslim girls and women claim to "choose" to wear a headscarf or a "veil," they are assumed to be victims of Islamist ideology and male oppression. Given the important state values of Republicanism and secularism, and longstanding government efforts to negate "cultural difference," those who choose to wear a face veil represent a threat to core constructs of French citizenship and identity. Wearing a headscarf in France today, Bowen argues, involves negotiations, anticipations, and weighing of benefits and costs. It is not simply an "obligation" or a "choice," but a subtle dance among convictions and constraints. Many young French Muslim women have made clothing choices precisely to negotiate space for their autonomy but confront widespread assumptions that head and face coverings violate the most minimal conditions of civic life. The headscarf comes to represent a profound affront to human rights upheld by the state.

French feminists have tackled the apparent contradiction between women's rights and opposition to certain items of clothing associated with Islam. They begin by acknowledging that women or girls who wear the "Islamic veil" do so in the name of their freedom to practice their religion. Yet at the same time, the veil symbolizes the subordination of women in Islam. Challenged by the fact that some women "choose" the veil, they contend that the oppressed may be among the most fervent supporters of their own domination. In this position, they are echoed by the highest institutions of French government, which has enacted legislation prohibiting the veil. State intervention and regulation of Islamic women's bodies is therefore formalized in this "dress code," a metaphor for appropriate assimilation to the values of "French" society.

Globally, the state and its judicial institutions have been identified as key players in regulating intimate gendered violence against women. Gender violence has emerged as a pervasive public policy issue, as Parsons (in this book) demonstrates in Chile. In the context of a regional move to legislate democratic reform, Chilean women's rights groups have sought to make attention to domestic violence a cornerstone of state policies. Her research reveals the state "control over the body" in the realm of gender violence, as well as in other domains, has implications for women's emotional experiences. Long entrenched gender ideals, innovative legal interventions, and women's experiences of violence and help-seeking are intertwined in complex ways. The Chilean state is a significant site for reproducing idealized constructs of womanhood. These gender ideals remain influential in shaping state judicial policies concerning domestic violence. Values associated with marriage and respectability weigh heavily on women who are in violent intimate relationships. Parsons' research illustrates the ways in which state institutions reproduce gender role expectations that then constrain women to remain in abusive relationships. In spite of formal policies designed to address problems of domestic violence, state actions and failures to take action may well enhance women's emotional and physical suffering.

If the state can shape family and gender relations directly through legislation determining rights to property, publicly acceptable dress, or regulating gendered violence, it may also have more indirect impact. Anne Allison (in this book) argues that in Japan, boxed lunches (*obentō*), prepared by mothers for their children, are invested with a gendered state ideology. The state manipulates the ideological and gendered meanings associated with the box lunch as an important component of nursery school culture. Nursery schools, under state supervision, not only socialize children and mothers into the gendered roles they are expected to assume but also introduce small children to the attitudes and structures of Japanese education. The *obentō*, elaborately and artistically arranged, is intended to allow the mother to produce something of home and family to accompany the child into this new and threatening outside world. Embedded in the school's close scrutiny of *obentō* production and consumption is a message to obey rules and accept the authority of the school and, by extension, of the state. The *obentōs* message is also that mothers sustain their children through food and support state ideology as well.

In all the works included in this chapter, we see the enduring influence of the issues raised by Engels with regard to the relationship among gender, property rights, and state structures. However, cross-cultural data demonstrate that this relationship is much more complex and varied than Engels's original formulation. Equally, universal evolutionary paradigms that posit a uniform impact of the rise of the state on gender roles cannot do justice to the myriad ways in which specific cultural histories, diverse social hierarchies, and systems of stratification affect gender relations and ideology. Thus, Silverblatt (1988: 448) asks, "What of the challenges that women and men, caught in their society's contradictions, bring to the dominant order of chiefs and castes, an order they contour and subvert, even as they are contained by it? And what of the other voices, the voices that chiefs and rulers do not (or cannot or will not) express?" (Silverblatt 1988: 452). The complex histories of the relationship between gender and the state show that government agendas are by no means inexorable; they both shape and reflect the gendered interests of particular populations.

## REFERENCES

Engels, Frederick. 1973. *The Origin of the Family, Private Property and the State.* New York: International Publishers.
Gailey, Christine Ward. 1987. *Kinship to Kingship: Gender Hierarchy and State Formation in the Tongan Islands.* Austin: University of Texas Press.
_____. 2000b. "'The Virgin and the State.' Gender and Politics in Argentina." In Victoria Ana Goddard (ed.). *Gender, Agency and Change*, pp. 221–250. London: Routledge.
Leacock, Eleanor Burke. 1973. "Introduction." In Frederick Engels (ed.). *The Origin of the Family, Private Property and the State*, pp. 7–57. New York: International Publishers.
McCreery, John L. 1976. "Women's Property Rights and Dowry in China and South Asia." *Ethnology* 15: 163–174.
Ortner, Sherry. 1978. "The Virgin and the State." *Feminist Studies* 4(3): 19–35.
_____. 1981. "Gender and Sexuality in Hierarchical Societies: The Case of Polynesia and Some Comparative Implications." In Sherry B. Ortner and Harriet Whitehead (eds.). *Sexual Meanings: The Cultural Construction of Gender and Sexuality*, pp. 359–410. Cambridge: Cambridge University Press.
Sacks, Karen. 1982. *Sisters and Wives: The Past and Future of Sexual Equality.* Urbana: University of Illinois Press.
Silverblatt, Irene. 1988. "Women in States." *Annual Review of Anthropology* 17: 427–461.

# *Encountering the State:*
## Cross-Cultural Perspectives
## on Women's Political Experience

### *Josephine Caldwell Ryan*

In 1987, a Kenyan woman named Wambui Otieno became involved in a protracted legal battle that pitted her against her husband's family (Nzomo 1997; Nzomo and Staudt 1994). Otieno, a Christian Kikuyu, had married a Luo man who, suspecting that his family might attempt to dispossess his wife after his death, had asked to be buried on his farm near Nairobi. The case was decided in favor of Otieno's husband's relatives, and he was buried in his natal village instead. The case had clear implications for women's rights in customary law, a fact that was not lost on Otieno. According to the *Washington Post*, she "warned Kenyan women that if she did not have the right to bury her husband, then they may not have the right to inherit their husband's property" (May 25, 1987, cited in Nzomo 1997: 242).

In Wambui Otieno's case, she did retain control over property rights, but this is not always the outcome. In sub-Saharan African countries with plural legal systems, disputes may be settled in courts of statutory law, customary law, and in some cases, Islamic law. Zambia, for example, has a dual legal system in which both customary law and statutory laws apply to inheritance. Statutory law, which gives more consideration to women's inheritance rights, is frequently ignored in favor of customary law that privileges male kinship ties over conjugal ties should the husband die intestate. The specifics of applicable customary law vary between ethnic groups, but in general, widows may be "inherited" as part of the estate or may be left destitute as a result of "property-grabbing" by the husband's family. New laws have attempted to address the problem by allowing men to designate women as heirs in their wills, but the problem persists. The Intestate Succession Act of 1989, for example, allows a woman to contest property-grabbing, yet a study by the Women in Southern Africa Research Trust found that most women do not take advantage of the law because of fear of witchcraft being worked against them by the husband's relatives (Munalula and Mwenda 1995: 99).

The first case provides an example of a woman choosing to use a legal system to fight for her rights, while the second shows the failure of law to ensure

Original material prepared for this text. Reprinted by permission of the author

that women's rights are protected even when that is the intent. This essay draws upon data from a variety of cultural contexts to illustrate ways in which women engage, respond to, or resist the state. Depending on their circumstances, women's interaction with the state may take the shape of formal participation (i.e., electoral politics), participation in women's movements or other forms of collective action with a political intent or effect, or individual responses to state policies that directly or indirectly affect quality of life for themselves and their families.

It is understood that the term "state" is not being considered as an impersonal, homogeneous force exclusively for evil or good but rather, as Waylen has observed, "a differentiated set of institutions, agencies, and discourses, and the product of a particular historical and political conjuncture" (1998: 7). The term "political engagement" is also used in a broad sense. Since the 1970s Western feminist scholars have mounted a critique of male-dominated mainstream political practice and "politics" as an area of intellectual investigation. Deconstructing the androcentric biases inherent in the language and basic concepts of political science, they have argued for a broader definition of politics, one that would include activities of women not usually considered to be within the parameters of "conventional politics" (Paxton and Hughes 2007; Phillips 1998; Randall and Waylen 1998; Silverblatt 1988; Waylen 1996). It is not the intention here to present a comprehensive survey of women's political activities or power; Silverblatt (1988: 452) is correct in her observation that "no uniform history of women in the state can account for the complex, often contradictory, histories of how women have engaged their particular political worlds."

## CURRENT TRENDS AFFECTING WOMEN'S POLITICAL STATUS

In the last twenty years there has been a dramatic increase in the number of women officeholders globally, most notably as legislators. According to figures from the Inter-parliamentary Union, the world average percentage of women in national parliaments had reached 17.5 percent in 2007, but this aggregate figure masked the real disparity between regions such as the Arab states, where 9 percent of members of parliaments in that year were women and the Nordic countries, where the figure was nearly 42 percent. With a few exceptions, women in contemporary states have the legal right to vote, but this does not mean it can always be exercised.[1] For example, Patience Ndetei, an elected member the Kenyan Parliament, made the following comments regarding the 1988 elections:

My experience in the field was that a lot of women do not have the final say, especially at home as to whom they should vote for. I had a woman who was badly beaten by her husband and she had to run away from him simply because she was going to vote for me. I confronted many other cases where women were not free. (*Daily Nation*, April 30, 1988, cited in Nzomo 1997: 237)

Contemporary feminist political theorists have suggested that formal representation (legal rights) is only the first step to political gender equality. Descriptive representation addresses the question of whether legislative and executive bodies actually represent the demographic, ethnic and other characteristics of their constituents. Paxton and Hughes (2007) identify five historical pathways to increase or decline in women's descriptive representation: flat rates, consistent increases in representation, rapid and significant increases ("big jumps"), small gains, and plateaus or falling rates. In Rwanda, female representation leaped from 4.3 to 17.1 percent in 1997, and in 2003, changes in the Rwandan constitution resulted in even more women being elected; currently Rwanda has the highest percentage of female legislators (48.8 percent) of any nation in the world (Paxton and Hughes 2007: 75). In contrast to the "big jump" Rwanda experienced, many of the former Soviet bloc nations saw steep declines in women's representation in the 1990s.

Jane Jaquette (1997) observed that women's political participation and representation does not automatically result from having the right to vote, cannot be explained solely by cultural factors such as the degree of gender equality, and cannot be predicted by the level of economic development. For example, women's representation in the Japanese parliament was about two percent until 1986 when a wave of women's activism known as the "Madonna Boom" led to more women winning parliament seats (Iwamoto 2001). A combination of factors, including the effects of persistent attitudes regarding proper feminine behavior and strict campaign regulations, have been suggested to explain Japan's relatively low levels of political representation for women (Paxton and Hughes 2007: 249). Jaquette (1997: 27) attributed the global increase in female officeholders to three interconnected factors:

the rise of a worldwide women's movement, a new willingness by parties and states to ease the constraints on women's access to politics through electoral reforms such as quotas, and a changed post–Cold War political environment, in which social issues supplanted security concerns, which in turn created opportunities for new styles of leadership.

In the first decade of the millennium significant changes in the international political landscape, especially concerns about terrorism and civil war, demand a new analysis, and increasingly powerful tools to evaluate women's political progress are permitting new insights. Using quantitative data from a cross-national survey of gender attitudes in forty six countries, Paxton and Kunovich (2003) demonstrated that gender ideology does affect the number of women in national legislatures; negative gender attitudes were a more powerful predictor of differences in women's political representation than labor force participation, education, industrialization and other social-structural variables. In the United States gender stereotyping in the political arena continues even as the number of female politicians has increased. The terrorist attacks of September 11, 2001, stimulated a national discussion about leadership in the "war against terrorism." Lawless (2004) reports compelling evidence that citizens in the United States prefer male leadership in a war time environment, believe that men are more competent at dealing with issues surrounding terrorism, and are less willing to vote for a qualified woman presidential candidate than they were in previous decades.

Electoral reforms have resulted in meaningful increases in women's political participation in many countries. Today about forty countries have introduced gender quotas for parliamentary elections through constitutional amendment or changes in electoral law, and in more than fifty countries political parties have included gender quotas in their statutes (Dahlerup and Freidenvall 2005). Quotas can be a "fast track" to equal representation; in Costa Rica, for example, a 40 percent quota and strong implementation resulted in an increase from 19 to 35 percent in 2002 (Dahlerup and Freidenvall 2005: 28). As noted above, quotas were also instrumental in vaulting Rwanda to the top of the gender equality rankings. Quotas are more frequently found in proportional representation systems than plurality/majority systems such as the United States and are strongly associated with higher levels of women's political representation (Paxton and Hughes 2007). In 1992 India passed legislation reforming the structure of local government, instituting a requirement that every village council (*panchayat*) have at least 33 percent women in its membership and leadership, and mandating the inclusion of lower castes and other marginalized groups. Although more women are active in local government than before, many face resistance and even physical violence as a consequence of their participation (Staudt et al. 2001). For quota systems to be effective, they must be enforced and as in the case of India, they must also eliminate other barriers to political participation such as illiteracy and poverty.

Writing in 1994, the editors of a detailed comparative study of women's political engagement in forty-three countries concluded that "in no country do women have political status, access, or influence equal to men's" (Chowdhury et al. 1994: 3). Although there have been positive changes since then, more recent work affirms the enduring truth of the statement (Burn 2005: 225). Drawing on the findings from the individual case studies, they pointed to four major trends influencing the political participation of women at the national and subnational level: the rise of religious fundamentalism, the changing nature of nationalism, international economic forces, and the growth of international feminism (1994: 4–10).

## RELIGIOUS FUNDAMENTALISM

Chowdhury et al. acknowledge an increase in religious fundamentalism in major world religions such as Christianity and Hinduism during the last three decades, but emphasize that Muslim fundamentalism has had the most significant impact (1994: 8). Two relevant examples of Muslim fundamentalism linked to political power are the 1977–1979 Revolution in Iran, led by the party of the Ayatollah Khomeini, and the fall of the modernist People's Democratic Party of Afghanistan to fundamentalist Mujahideen revolutionaries in 1992. Both events resulted in immediate and dramatic shifts in the status of women in those countries.

In Iran, women's roles were dramatically restructured through a process of Islamization after the 1979 Revolution, but as Parvin Paidar's study of gender and the political process in twentieth-century Iran shows, women were granted legal and social rights "because they were mothers or potential mothers" (1995: 260). Ayatollah Khomeini adopted a policy of women's formal participation in national processes because he believed that the new Islamic Republic would only survive if both men and women were active in society. Contrary to many expectations, the establishment of a theocratic state did not result in outright prohibition of women from social activities (Paidar 1995: 303). Policies requiring veiling and sex segregation allowed many religious women access to education and employment (Povey 2001: 46). The case of Iran continues to provoke academic debate regarding impact of Islamization on feminist consciousness and women's involvement in social change.

Valentine Moghadam's (1994) analysis shows that in Afghanistan, reform measures were introduced by the Marxist People's Democratic Party of Afghanistan (PDPA), which came to power in the Saur Revolution of 1978. These included campaigns to improve literacy rates and educational attainment for women, stop payment of bride price, the levirate, and coerced marriages, and end the exploitation of female labor. These measures met resistance because they posed a direct challenge to patriarchal values, economic practice, and the control of land. In the face of armed resistance and outside interference, the PDPA backed away from some of their original goals, and in the end the drive to raise the status of women failed. The Islamic opposition groups, known as the Mujahideen, received support from Pakistan, Saudi Arabia, Iran, and several other nations, including the United States, and the result was a protracted period of internal conflict. In 1992 the Mujahideen assumed power; this signaled the beginning of a period of reversal of gains for women. In 1996 a group of religious students, now known as the Taliban, formed an opposition army and captured the capital, Kabul, after a bloody two year campaign. Raised in refugee camps in the 1980s, the men of the Taliban espoused a particularly conservative doctrine of Islam, and according to Moghadam, had "no conception of modern governance, democratic or participatory rule, or women's rights" (1999: 180). The oppression of women in Afghanistan became a matter of world attention, partly due to efforts such the Feminist Majority Foundation's "Stop Gender Apartheid in Afghanistan" campaign (Hirschkind and Mahmood 2002).[2] In response to the September 11 terrorist attack on the United States, the United States and international allies launched Operation Enduring Freedom in Afghanistan, which resulted in the removal of the Taliban. Unfortunately, women and girls in Afghanistan still experience significant discrimination and hardship and, partly due to long-entrenched gender role expectations, are "unable to take advantage of the theoretical freedoms that are now available to them" (Coursen-Neff 2003: 10).

These examples suggest that the specific circumstances of national histories and identities must be considered in comprehending the political status of women in any particular context, rather than using Islam or Islamization as the sole explanatory factor. Deniz Kandiyoti's (1988) concept of the "patriarchal bargain" is also useful in understanding why women may act in ways that maintain the status quo of patriarchy; women pay the price of a patriarchal bargain, and in return get some degree of protection. According to Kandiyoti, different systems offer different sorts of "patriarchal bargains" to women, each with different "rules of the game and different strategies for maximizing security and optimizing their life options" (1988: 277). Gerami and Lehnerer (2001) build on Kandiyoti's work by describing how women in Iran adopted various strategies in their response to Islamization, including collaboration, acquiescence, co-optation, and subversion.

Swarup et al. (1994: 375–376) provide two singular examples of growing religious fundamentalism in India. In contrast to decades of legislative action that outlawed sati (the immolation of widows), ended child marriage, and prohibited dowry, in 1986 the Indian government introduced the Muslim Women's (Protection of Rights in Divorce) Act. This law was intended to pacify leaders of conservative factions of the Muslim community who were outraged by the outcome of the Shah Bano case, in which the Indian Supreme Court awarded alimony to the wife of a Muslim lawyer who had already married a much younger woman. The husband claimed that the Indian government was meddling in matters of Islam set forth in the Sharia. The 1986 Act affirmed the primacy of Sharia law for Muslim women and was opposed by women's rights groups and many educated Muslims. In the following year, a young widow was burned on her husband's funeral pyre. The act was condemned by women's rights organizations and intellectuals, but thousands of Hindu men and women marched in support of sati as a matter of cultural and family right. The Indian government responded by enacting the Sati Prevention Measure of 1987, but pro-Sati attitudes persist. Swarup et al. conclude:

> Thus, in the name of supporting traditional law and custom, Muslim and Hindu fundamentalists have tried to reinforce the loosening shackles of medieval paternalistic morality and preserve male supremacy. Although fundamentalists have so far been only somewhat successful, their power is increasing. This resurgence, coupled with the desire of the central government to maintain political stability at all costs, means that the influence of progressive and secular women is likely to be less powerful on this issue than on others. (1994: 377)

Historically, religion has often been a contentious issue for global feminists. For example, untangling the relationship between patriarchy and religion and refuting stereotypic depictions of Muslim women is a central theme in the writings of Nawal El Saadawi. Trained as a physician and a gifted writer, El Saadawi's activism on behalf of women's rights and other political issues in Egypt resulted in her being fired from her post as Director of Public Health and jailed by the government of Anwar Sadat. In 1982 she founded the Arab Woman's Solidarity Foundation, whose motto is "Power of Women-Solidarity-Unveiling of the Mind" (El Saadawi 1997). A controversial figure at home and

abroad, El Saadawi consistently affirms her identity as an Arab woman and a Muslim while simultaneously denouncing religious fundamentalism and its subordinating effects on women.

## THE CHANGING NATURE OF NATIONALISM

Modern nationalism is complex and variable in terms of fundamental concepts and practices, and the resulting configurations have different effects on women's status and political options. Chowdhury et al. (1994: 6–8) note that the dominant themes during the period of decolonizing and rebuilding following World War II were achieving and strengthening the political power of the nation-state. In the process of state building most women in the world achieved formal (though not actual) legal equality. In addition, state secularism resulted in more opportunities for women as it weakened the power of gender hierarchy associated with religious denominations. In recent decades, however, state-focused nationalism has been challenged by the growth of ethnic, regional, and communal forces. The expansion of the European Economic Community, on the one hand, and the disintegration of the former Soviet Union, on the other, are recent examples of the trends of universalism and particularism at work.

Nations formed through revolution, such as the former Soviet Union, or decolonization, such as many countries in sub-Saharan Africa, have had to deal with serious internal ethnic and communal conflicts, and "often with only a thin veneer of representative government to find solutions" (Chowdhury et al. 1994: 7). Another dimension of nationalism in African states is the effect of the colonial heritage on women's status. Colonialism affected women in two ways: first, colonial policies rendered women invisible and ignored any political authority they had possessed; second, the form of nationalist movements and the position of women within them and the new governments themselves reflected the colonial overlay (Staudt 1981). The new socialist governments, such as those of Angola, Ethiopia, Guinea, Mozambique, and Tanzania, were more likely to incorporate "emancipation ideology" in the state structures, explicitly mandating access to education and political participation for women, many of whom had participated in protests and guerilla movements in the nationalist cause. However, most failed to address women's roles in the domestic and subsistence spheres, which produced glaring contradictions; for example the inability of women in Tanzanian villages to access control over important resources, such as the control of land or money from crops they had farmed (Staudt 1981: 8–10). In the late 1980s and early 1990s, women's movements played an important role in the wave of electoral reform and democratization that has reconfigured the political map of Africa today. In 2006, Ellen Johnson-Sirleaf of Liberia became Africa's first democratically elected female president, signaling a permanent change in the gender dynamics of African politics (Zeleza 2006: 20).

Africa is not the only continent to be changed by democraticization, a process that has significantly altered the political map of the world. The process has varied from region to region; in Latin America, dictatorships were replaced by popular sovereignty, while many European nations shook off the mantle of Soviet control. Women were participants in the transition in both cases, but there were differences too, as described by Jaquette and Wolchik:

> In Latin America, women organized to protest economic conditions and undermined the claims of authoritarian regimes that they were creating the necessary conditions for economic growth. In Central and Eastern Europe, women contributed to undermining support for the Communist regimes by fostering values in the home which were not approved by the Communist leadership. In Latin America these strategies of resistance resulted in the mobilization of women around gender issues, whereas the reverse was true in Central and Eastern Europe, where women's movements have been slow to organize after the transitions. There some women expressed their desire to return to the home; others voiced open skepticism about the value of equality in labor force participation and politics, the core goals of Western feminism. (1998: 4)

In summary, women's political engagement is shaped partially by the form of any particular nation-state as well as the historical circumstances that produced it. It thus both reflects and creates particular forms of gender relations and inequity (Waylen 1998: 7).

## INTERNATIONAL ECONOMIC FORCES

The relationship between economic status and political power is extremely complex. Writing about the history of women and development in Africa, Snyder and Tadesse (1995) identified educational opportunities and economic empowerment as the two most pressing areas that must be addressed in Africa to improve women's status. While acknowledging the importance of women's machinery within the government to insure women's voices are heard and ultimately to transform the institution, they emphasized the idea that economic autonomy is a prerequisite for political empowerment (1995: 182–184).

It is beyond the scope of this essay to review the large body of literature on gender and economic development. Development theories have shifted several times since World War II, both with respect to economic development in general and with respect to women in particular (Burn 2005; Kabeer 1994; Marchand and Parpart 1995; Snyder and Tadesse 1995; Staudt 1990). By the mid-1970s it was clear that both planned and unplanned economic development was not benefiting women and men equally and that in some cases women were actually losing ground (Boserup 1970; Tinker 1990). Trends and crises in the global economy in the 1970s exacerbated flawed development strategies, resulting in mounting debt, run-away inflation, and declining standards of living. These problems and others were addressed by policies introduced by the World Bank and the International Monetary Fund to promote macroeconomic stabilization and force internal structural transformation beginning in 1979. Loans were granted with conditions attached to them, which frequently created major economic upheavals as a result of mandatory devaluation of currency and belt-tightening of national budgets. Although the results varied from country to country, the overall pattern was that "structural adjustment" policies decreased public spending on education, health, and food subsidies and had the result of increasing the burden on women, who frequently had to work longer hours to absorb the cost of basic necessities, frequently in the informal sector of the economy.

In Ghana, for example, high male unemployment forced women to take on greater responsibility for providing for their families' needs. Work in the informal sector provides an important survival strategy for poor women, who gain income from subsistence farming, petty trading, food processing, and soap making, but it is complicated by social and infrastructural obstacles. Women work up to sixteen hours a day in economic activities. Whereas men are more likely to be involved in cash-cropping activities, 90 percent of women are subsistence farmers, meaning that they engage in small-scale hoe cultivation for survival needs. Women also work their husbands' farms and are responsible for transporting and marketing the farm produce of their husbands' farms. Women in rural Ghana have access to communal land through their male relatives but have low levels of production because of heavy demands on their own labor and lack of capital to invest in production. They may cooperate with other women to share labor, or join a local credit pool to obtain capital but throughout the 1980s were largely bypassed by extension agents and state resources (Okine 1993).

Okine carried out research in Ghana during the regime of Flight Lieutenant Jerry Rawlings, who came to power in 1981 via a political coup. Market women, targeted as corrupt enemies of the state, were blamed for the high price of commodities (Fallon 2003). Vending or trading without a license was illegal, and petty traders had to be wary of the police in order to avoid having their goods confiscated. Okine noted that the economic activities of Ghanaian working women could hardly be described as liberating, in contrast to the way that economic productivity has been framed in Western Europe. In fact, women's economic contributions were not recognized by policy makers or given any sort of meaningful state support. From this she concluded that the cause of the "persistent impoverishment" of Ghanaian women was not a male-dominated society, but rather "a lack of political power" (Okine 1993: 191). A decade later, Ghanaian women were actively mobilizing to improve gender rights in a democratizing state. Before democratization, women had emphasized social rights and the need to generate income to support their families, but after 1992 used the rights they had obtained as a result of political changes to lobby for more social and civil rights (Fallon 2003).

Daines and Seddon (1993) also explored the responses of women to austerity measures associated with the economic reforms of the 1980s, borrowing Scott's (1985) concept of "everyday forms of resistance" to emphasize the agency that exists even in mundane, unorganized action with clearly defined, short-term objectives. They suggest that "even defensive struggles can, in the right circumstances, develop into more extensive forms of struggle with a greater capacity for expanding the room for maneuver and for changing the conditions within which struggle takes place" (Daines and Seddon 1993: 11). They also discuss ways in which women use networks, associations, and diverse forms of protest to respond to austerity measures. One dramatic form of collective action is illustrated by "bread riots," which often develop from street protests over concerns about cost of living and increases in staple commodities. The fact that such protests are spontaneous and based on immediate short-term objectives (economic relief) does not change the fact that they are political actions with the potential to change state policies.

Linked with democratization is a trend toward neoliberal economic reforms, not all of which have been positive for women. With reference to Africa, Zeleza writes:

> There is overwhelming evidence that the costs of privatization of services engendered by economic liberalization and deregulation have been disproportionately borne by women. The case for addressing the gender implications of macroeconomic policy and incorporating gender in any national project of sustainable development is imperative indeed. (2006: 21)

## WOMEN AND COLLECTIVE ACTION IN INTERNATIONAL FEMINISM

Maxine Molyneux distinguished women's movements that are based on "practical" gender interests and address short-term, immediate concerns from those based on "strategic" interests; the latter derive "deductively from an analysis of women's subordination and from the formulation of a more satisfactory set of arrangements" (1985, cited in Waylen 1996: 20–22). Activities motivated by practical gender interests are diverse and take many forms, including bread riots, communal kitchens, human rights campaigns, urban women's centers, and the like. Feminist movements involve women coming together self-consciously as women to press gender issues and are thus based on "strategic" gender interests. There is overlap between the two categories, but the scheme assists in understanding why women's movements do not necessarily involve a feminist consciousness.

The political participation of women in Argentina provides examples of both kinds of women's movements (Feijoo 1998). Although they were not enfranchised until 1947, Argentinean women were active in trade unions, anarchist and socialist movements, and other organizations. Before the 1976 military takeover, the women in various class and ethnic categories had been exposed to and had interacted with a variety of political ideologies, including international feminism in the 1970s, which resulted in the establishment of explicitly feminist organizations. The 1976 takeover introduced a period of state terrorism aimed at eliminating all dissident forces. Students, activists, and other "leftist" elements who posed a threat of popular mobilization were kidnapped and tortured, resulting in the "disappearance" of over 30,000 people (Feijoo 1998: 31–33). In response, women, generally mothers in their forties and fifties, engaged in large public demonstrations in the Plaza de Mayo, the main government square in Buenos Aires. Because they were acting in the role of mothers looking for their children, the military did not apply the usual punishments for subversion (Waylen 1996: 109). After the transition to democracy, however, the Madres distanced themselves from active political participation. Still, their example was a model for similar movements in other Latin American dictatorships as well as for groups within Argentina seeking to cope with the difficult economic times that accompanied the transition. In the process of constitutional reorganization, a quota law was passed requiring that 30 percent of upper level positions on party tickets be filled with women candidates, dramatically increasing the formal participation of women.

Further evidence of the overlap between practical and strategic gender interests in women's organizing is provided by Scarpaci's (1993) study of poor Chilean women under the Pinochet dictatorship (1973–1990). He interviewed members of a sewing cooperative formed to provide income from sewing tapestries and appliqués to offset the costs of filing appeals on behalf of family members who had been detained by the state security forces. One finding was that the collective expanded to include literacy campaigns as well as discussion of women's issues. According to one member:

> When I began working I realized that I contribute to my household. I contribute economically and therefore I don't find it fair that my husband should get upset because I participate in the [cooperative] and that he tells me I should do the wash and other things. I get upset, damn it, because I don't think only women should do these household chores. (Scarpaci 1993: 41)

In this case, it appears that a feminist consciousness was being produced through interaction in an organization that began as a response to a "practical" gender issue.

The technological advances in information processing, storage, and communications that helped fuel democratization and a new world economic order have also contributed to the emergence of a transnational women's movement. In September 1995, some 36,000 women from 189 nations met in Beijing, China, for a United Nations Conference on Women, the fourth such conference to be held since 1975. Previous conferences had been held in Mexico City, Copenhagen, and Nairobi as part of the United Nations Decade on Women (1975–1985). In the two decades between the designation of 1975 as the Year of the Woman by the United Nations and the Beijing conference, a global institutional framework for empowering women was established, a complex process involving national governments, international agencies, nongovernmental organizations, activists, and scholars. In addition to creating the institutional structures for addressing gender issues at a global level, the process also involved reconciling a myriad of diverse national and regional identities and agendas, as well as exploring diverging conceptions of feminism.

One result of the Beijing conference was the *Declaration and Platform for Action*, a sophisticated and comprehensive document that unequivocally situated gender inequality as a matter of human rights and social justice. It outlined a plan of action to create the conditions that will result in empowered girls and women achieving gender equity in all areas of life. It called for national governments, the international community, and all segments of civil society to implement proposals and instruments from earlier conferences,

such as the Convention on the Elimination of All Forms of Discrimination Against Women (CEDAW), and to take immediate action in twelve "critical areas of concern."[3] The increasing burden of poverty on women, inequality in access to equal and adequate education and training, inequality in economic structures and policies, and inequality between women and men in the sharing of power and decision making were among those so identified. In addition to putting gender issues on the global agenda, the Beijing conference was a turning point in the development of the international women's movement partly because of the political implications of the Plan of Action (Lycklama a Nijeholt et al. 1998).

The impact of the Beijing conference can be measured by the events that followed. Gender mainstreaming, an approach that requires a gender analysis to ensure that gender concerns are addressed in all types of development, was embraced by development agencies by 2000 (Burn 2005; Elson 2004). In the same year, world leaders met at the Millennium Summit and formulated a list of eight specific development goals to use as a framework for coordinated action. The third Millennium Development Goal is the promotion of gender equality and the empowerment of women, with a specific target of eliminating all gender disparity in primary and secondary education by 2015 (United Nations 2007).

The Internet, then relatively new, was extensively used in the preplanning phase of the Beijing conference, and now plays an important role for local, regional, and international non-governmental organizations and activist groups (Travers 2003). Five years before the 2001 invasion of Afghanistan, the Feminist Majority Foundation had been using the Internet to promote awareness of gender inequality under the Taliban. Today the Internet disseminates the views of organizations such as the Women's Environment and Development Organization (WEDO), which advocates for women's equality in global policy. Founded in 2000, WEDO is best known for its 50/50 campaign, which seeks to increase the percentage of women in local and national politics worldwide to 50% (Paxton and Hughes 2007: 179). However, the Internet is of little use to those who lack access, such as the lower-caste women challenging the political agenda in India (Staudt et al. 2001: 1256).

## CONCLUSION: IS IT RHETORIC OR REALITY?

As the foregoing discussion indicates, there are no easy generalizations about the nature or degree of political power of women. The last 30 years have been characterized by unprecedented global social, economic, and political change. Given that many of the obstacles to women's formal political participation have been removed (on paper at least) in most of the world's nations, does it mean that real political equality is in the near future for women?

A comprehensive evaluation of the progress in gender equality since the Beijing conference concluded that while there has been some improvement, social and economic disparities will make it hard to achieve the global gender equality goals set out in 1995 (United Nations 2005). Elson (2004) points out that even as gender awareness grows in developing nations, the ability to "engender" government budgets is often hampered by the requirements of market-led globalization, and in some less developed countries, the requirements that public international financial institutions such as the World Bank and the International Monetary Fund impose constraints on decision making.

Where women are disadvantaged educationally or struggle under entrenched patriarchal world views, political empowerment has not come easily. In Zimbabwe, for example, legislation was passed in the last two decades that permitted women to vote and made both men and women legally of age at 18. It also reformed divorce law for civil marriage, although marriage under customary law, which includes traditions of succession and inheritance, is also recognized. Before the years of structural adjustment, women also benefited from literacy campaigns and public health initiatives. Some state policies are less positive, such as the "clean up" campaigns that ostensibly target prostitutes. According to Jacobs, a 1983 campaign was directed against "younger, better-off-than-average women who appeared to be beyond 'traditional' patriarchal controls; that is, women for whom some employment opportunities have opened up recently" (1989: 168). Land tenure reforms in Zimbabwe were less beneficial for women than men due to discriminatory regulations that made it more difficult for women to gain title to land (Jacobs 1998).

In Rwanda, 800,000 people died in the genocide of 1994, leaving a population that was 70 percent female. In the subsequent social reconstruction, women gained a political toe-hold through constitutionally mandated parliamentary gender quotas. Yet, according to organizations such as Women for Women International, men's resistance to women in politics is strong. Many perceive recent achievements as attempts to deprive them of authority over women. Some women are also dissatisfied with the performance of some new members of parliament, viewing them as ineffective or disconnected from the concerns of their constituents.

This overview of trends affecting women's political engagement shows that the goals and strategies of women's political struggles are diverse and that the results of their efforts show uneven progress. It is also clear that the growth of an international feminist movement, a measurable trend to include "women's rights machinery" in national governments, and even increased numbers of female officeholders, will not bring women political power by themselves.

The international attention focused on the case of Mukhtaran Bibi, a young woman living in Pakistan, reveals both the challenge and the potential of the future. In 2002, Mukhtaran Bibi, living in a remote village in Pakistan, was raped by four men acting on order of the village council to compensate for an alleged crime her 12-year-old brother had committed. (In the investigation that followed, the accusation was found to be false.) After the legally sanctioned rape, Mukhtaran Bibi walked home nearly naked in front of several hundred people. It was assumed that she would commit suicide, the typical course of action for a dishonored woman. Instead, she took advantage of new political freedoms to testify against her accusers, and she prevailed in court. She used compensation she received from the government to start two new schools, one for boys and one for girls (Kristof 2004). In the last few years her story has been widely disseminated on the Internet, spawning petitions in her support and bringing embarrassing attention to the government of Pakistan, which has attempted to restrict her international travel (Kristof 2005). The well-publicized struggle of Mukhtaran Bibi to claim gender justice has become iconic of the need for women worldwide to be assured of civil rights and an effective political voice. At this point, it is reasonable to assume that although there is a long way to go ahead, political equality for women is not an unachievable goal.

## NOTES

1. After a long struggle, Kuwait passed women's suffrage in 2005.
2. The Feminist Majority Foundation mounted a large-scale education and petition drive to raise global awareness of the situation in Afghanistan. See the Foundation's homepage at www.feminist.org.
3. CEDAW was adopted in 1979 by the U.N. General Assembly and is an international bill of rights for women. It defines what constitutes discrimination against women and sets up an agenda for national action to end it. An Optional Protocol to the Convention sets up procedures to make claims and to investigate cases of grave or systematic violations of women's rights is in process. (See the Web site for United Nations Division for the Advancement of Women, www.un.or/womenwatch/daw.)

# REFERENCES

Boserup, Esther. 1970. *Women's Role in Economic Development*. New York: St. Martin's Press.

Burn, Megan Shawn. 2005. *Women Across Cultures: A Global Perspective* (2nd edition). New York: McGraw-Hill.

Chowdhury, Najma, and Barbara J. Nelson, with Kathryn A. Carver, Nancy J. Johnson, and Paula L. O'Loughlin. 1994. "Redefining Politics: Patterns of Women's Political Engagement from a Global Perspective." In Barbara J. Nelson and Najma Chowdhury (eds.). *Women and Politics Worldwide*, pp. 3–24. New Haven, CT: Yale University Press.

Coursen-Neff, Zama. 2003. "Afghan Women and Girls Still Held Hostage." *Middle East Report* 228: 8–11.

Dahlerup, Drude, and Lenita Freidenvall. 2005. "Quotas as a 'Fast Track' to Equal Representation for Women." *International Feminist Journal of Politics* 7 (1): 26–48.

Daines, Victoria, and David Seddon. 1993. "Confronting Austerity: Women's Responses to Economic Reform." In Meredith Turshen and Briavel Holcomb (eds.). *Women's Lives and Public Policy: The International Experience*, pp. 3–32. Westport, CT: Praeger Publishers.

El Saadawi, Nawal. 1997. *The Nawal El Saadawi Reader*. London: Zed Books.

Elson, Diane. 2004. "Engendering Government Budgets in the Context of Globalization." *International Feminist Journal of Politics* 6 (4): 623–642.

Fallon, Kathleen M. "Transforming Citizenship Rights within an Emerging Democratic State." *Gender and Society* 17 (4): 525-543.

Feijoo, Maria del Carmen. 1998. "Democratic Participation and Women in Argentina." In Jane S. Jaquette and Sharon L. Wolchik (eds.). *Women and Democracy: Latin America and Central and Eastern Europe*, pp. 29–46. Baltimore, MD: Johns Hopkins University Press.

Gerami, Shahin, and Melodye Lehnerer. 2001. "Women's Agency and Household Diplomacy: Negotiating Fundamentalism." *Gender and Society* 15 (4): 556–573.

Hirschkind, Charles, and Saba Mahmood. 2002. "Feminism, the Taliban, and Politics of Counter-Insurgency." *Anthropological Quarterly* 75 (2): 339–354.

Iwamoto, Misako. 2001. "The Madonna Boom: The Progress of Japanese Women into Politics in the 1980's." *PS: Political Science* 34 (2): 225–226.

Jacobs, Susan. 1989. "Zimbabwe: State, Class, and Gendered Models." In Jane L. Parpart and Kathleen A. Staudt (eds.). *Women and the State in Africa*, pp. 161–184. Boulder, CO: Lynne Rienner Publishers.

_____. 1998. "The Gendered Politics of Land Reform: Three Comparative Studies." In Vicky Randall and Georgina Waylen (eds.). *Gender, Politics, and the State*, pp. 121–142. London: Routledge.

Jaquette, Jane S. 1997. "Women in Power: From Tokenism to Critical Mass." *Foreign Policy*, Fall 1997: 23–37.

Jaquette, Jane S., and Sharon L. Wolchik. 1998. "Women and Democratization in Latin America and Central and Eastern Europe: A Comparative Introduction." In Jane S. Jaquette and Sharon L. Wolchik (eds.). *Women and Democracy: Latin America and Central and Eastern Europe*, pp. 1–28. Baltimore, MD: John Hopkins University Press.

Kabeer, Nalia. 1994. *Reversed Realities: Gender Hierarchies in Development Thought*. London: Verso.

Kandiyoti, Deniz. 1988. "Bargaining with Patriarchy." *Gender and Society* 2 (3): 274–290.

Kristof, Nicholas. 2004. "Sentenced to Be Raped." *New York Times*, September 29, p. A25. _____. 2005. "Raped, Kidnapped, and Silenced." *New York Times*, June 14, p. A23.

Lawless, Jennifer L. 2004. "Women, War, and Winning Elections: Gender Stereotyping in the Post-September 11th Era." *Political Research Quarterly* 57 (3): 479–490.

Lycklama a Nijeholt, Geertje, Joke Sweibel, and Virginia Vargas. 1998. "The Global Institutional Framework: The Long March to Beijing." In Geertje Lycklama a Nijeholt, Virginia Vargas, and Saskia Wieringa (eds.). *Women's Movements and Public Policy in Europe, Latin America, and the Caribbean*, pp. 25–48. New York: Garland Publishing, Inc.

Marchand, Marianne H., and Jane L. Parpart (eds.). 1995. *Feminism/Postmodernism/Development*. London: Routledge.

Moghadam, Valentine M. 1994. "Revolution, Islamist Reaction, and Women in Afghanistan." In Mary Ann Tétrault (ed.). *Women and Revolution in Africa, Asia, and the New World*, pp. 211–235. Columbia: University of South Carolina Press.

_____. 1999. "Revolution, Religion, and Gender Politics: Iran and Afghanistan Compared." *Journal of Women's History* 10 (4): 172–195.

Molyneux, M. 1985. "Mobilization Without Emancipation? Women's Interest, the State and Revolution in Nicaragua." *Feminist Studies* 11 (2): 227–254.

Munalula, Margaret Mulela, and Winnie Sithole Mwenda. 1995. "Case Study: Women and Inheritance Law in Zambia." In Margaret Jean Hay and Sharon Stichter (eds.). *African Women South of the Sahara*, pp. 93–100. New York: Longman.

Nzomo, Maria. 1997. "Kenyan Women in Politics and Public Decision-Making." In Gwendolyn Mikell (ed.). *African Feminism: The Politics of Survival in Sub-Saharan Africa*, pp. 232–254. Philadelphia: University of Pennsylvania Press.

Nzomo, Maria, and Kathleen Staudt. 1994. "Man-Made Political Machinery in Kenya: Political Space for Women?" In Barbara J. Nelson and Najma Chowdhurry (eds.). *Women and Politics Worldwide*, pp. 416–433. New Haven, CT: Yale University Press.

Okine, Vicky. 1993. "The Survival Strategies of Poor Families in Ghana and the Role of Women Therein." In Joycelin Massiah (ed.). *Women in Developing Economies: Making Visible the Invisible*, pp. 167–194. Providence, RI: Berg Publishers.

Paidar, Parvin. 1995. *Women and the Political Process in Twentieth-Century Iran*. Cambridge, UK: Cambridge University Press.

Paxton, Pamela, and Melanie M. Hughes. 2007. *Women, Politics, and Power: A Global Perspective*. Los Angeles, CA: Pine Forge Press.

Paxton, Pamela, and Sheri Kunovich. 2003. "Women's Political Representation: The Importance of Ideology." *Social Forces* 82 (1): 87–113.

Phillips, Anne (ed.). 1998. *Feminism and Politics*. New York: Oxford University Press.

Povey, Elaheh Rostami. 2001. "Feminist Contestations of Institutional Domains in Iran." *Feminist Review* 69: 44–72.

Randall, Vicky, and Georgina Waylen (eds.). 1998. *Gender, Politics and the State*. London: Routledge.

Scarpaci, Joseph L. 1993. "Empowerment Strategies of Poor Urban Women under the Chilean Dictatorship." In Meredith Turshen and Brian Holcomb (eds.). *Women's Lives and Public Policy*, pp. 33–50. Westport, CT: Greenwood Press.

Scott, J. C. 1985. *Weapons of the Weak: Everyday Forms of Peasant Resistance*. New York and London: Yale University Press.

Silverblatt, Irene. 1988. "Women in States." *Annual Review of Anthropology* 17: 427–461.

Snyder, Margaret C., and Mary Tadesse. 1995. *African Women and Development: A History*. London: Zed Books.

Staudt, Kathleen. 1981. "Women's Politics in Africa." *Studies in Third World Societies* 16: 1–28.

_____ (ed.). 1990. *Women, International Development, and Politics*. Philadelphia: Temple University Press.

Staudt, Kathleen, Shirin M. Rai, and Jane L. Parpart. 2001. "Protesting World Trade Rules: Can We Talk about Empowerment?" *Signs* 26 (4): 1251–1257.

Swarup, Hem Lata, Niroj Sinha, Chitra Ghosh, and Pam Rajput. 1994. "Women's Political Engagement in India: Some Critical Issues." In Barbara Nelson and Najma Chowdhury (eds.). *Women and Politics Worldwide*, pp. 363–379. New Haven, CT: Yale University Press.

Tinker, Irene (ed.). 1990. *Persistent Inequalities: Women and World Development*. New York: Oxford University Press.

Travers, Ann. 2003. "Parallel Subaltern Feminist Counterpublics in Cyberspace." *Sociological Perspectives* 46 (2): 223–237.

United Nations. 1995. Report of the Fourth World Conference on Women, Beijing, 4–15 September 1995. A/CONF./177/20.

_____. 2005. *Gender Equality: Striving for Justice in an Unequal World*. Geneva: United Nations Research Institute for Social Development.

_____. 2007. *Millenium Development Goals*. http://www.un.org/millenniumgoals/goals.html. Accessed on August 1, 2007.

Waylen, Georgina. 1996. *Gender in Third World Politics*. Boulder, CO: Lynne Rienner Publishers, Inc.

_____. 1998. "Gender, Feminism, and the State: An Overview." In Vicky Randall and Georgina Waylen (eds.). *Gender, Politics and the State*, pp. 1–16. London: Routledge.

Zeleza, Paul Tiyambe. 2006. "Madam President: The Changing Gender Dynamics of African Politics." *CODESRIA Bulletin* 1–2: 20–22.

# *Japanese Mothers and Obentōs:*
## The Lunch-Box as Ideological State Apparatus

### Anne Allison

## INTRODUCTION

Japanese nursery school children, going off to school for the first time, carry with them a boxed lunch (*obentō*) prepared by their mothers at home. Customarily these *obentōs* are highly crafted elaborations of food: a multitude of miniature portions, artistically designed and precisely arranged, in a container that is sturdy and cute. Mothers tend to expend inordinate time and attention on these *obentōs* in efforts both to please their children and to affirm that they are good mothers. Children at nursery school are taught in turn that they must consume their entire meal according to school rituals.

Food in an *obentō* is an everyday practice of Japanese life. While its adoption at the nursery school level may seem only natural to Japanese and unremarkable to outsiders, I will argue in this article that the *obentō* is invested with a gendered state ideology. Overseen by the authorities of the nursery school, an institution which is linked to, if not directly monitored by, the state, the practice of the *obentō* situates the producer as a woman and mother, and the consumer, as a child of a mother and a student of a school. Food in this context is neither casual nor arbitrary. Eaten quickly in its entirety by the student, the *obentō* must be fashioned by the mother so as to expedite this chore for the child. Both mother and child are being watched, judged, and constructed; and it is only through their joint effort that the goal can be accomplished.

I use Althusser's concept of the Ideological State Apparatus (1971) to frame my argument. I will briefly describe how food is coded as a cultural and aesthetic apparatus in Japan, and what authority the state holds over school in Japanese society. Thus situating the parameters within which the *obentō* is regulated and structured in the nursery school setting, I will examine the practice both of making and eating *obentō* within the context of one nursery school in Tokyo. As an anthropologist and mother of a child who attended this school for fifteen months, my analysis is based on my observations, on discussions with other mothers, daily conversations and an interview with my son's teacher, examination of *obentō* magazines and cookbooks, participation in school rituals, outings,

Reprinted with permission from *Anthropological Quarterly* 64: 195–208, 1991. Copyright © The Catholic University of America.

and Mothers' Association meetings, and the multifarious experiences of my son and myself as we faced the *obentō* process every day.

I conclude that *obentō* as a routine, task, and art form of nursery school culture are endowed with ideological and gendered meanings that the state indirectly manipulates. The manipulation is neither total nor totally coercive, however, and I argue that pleasure and creativity for both mother and child are also products of the *obentō*.

## CULTURAL RITUAL
## AND STATE IDEOLOGY

As anthropologists have long understood, not only are the worlds we inhabit symbolically constructed, but also the constructions of our cultural symbols are endowed with, or have the potential for, power. How we see reality, in other words, is also how we live it. So the conventions by which we recognize our universe are also those by which each of us assumes our place and behavior within that universe. Culture is, in this sense, doubly constructive: constructing both the world for people and people for specific worlds.

The fact that culture is not necessarily innocent, and power not necessarily transparent, has been revealed by much theoretical work conducted both inside and outside the discipline of anthropology. The scholarship of the neo-Marxist Louis Althusser (1971), for example, has encouraged the conceptualization of power as a force which operates in ways that are subtle, disguised, and accepted as everyday social practice. Althusser differentiated between two major structures of power in modern capitalist societies. The first, he called (Repressive) State Apparatus (SA), which is power that the state wields and manages primarily through the threat of force. Here the state sanctions the usage of power and repression through such legitimized mechanisms as the law and police (1971: 143–5).

Contrasted with this is a second structure of power—Ideological State Apparatus(es) (ISA). These are institutions which have some overt function other than a political and/or administrative one: mass media, education, health and welfare, for example. More numerous, disparate, and functionally polymorphous than the SA, the ISA exert power not primarily through repression but through ideology. Designed and accepted as practices with another purpose—to educate (the school system), entertain (film industry), inform (news media), the ISA serve not only their stated objective but also an unstated one—that of indoctrinating people into seeing the world a certain way and of accepting certain identities as their own within that world (1971: 143–7).

While both structures of power operate simultaneously and complementarily, it is the ISA, according to Althusser, which in capitalist societies is the more influential of the two. Disguised and screened by another operation, the power of ideology in ISA can be both more far-reaching and insidious than the SA's power of coercion. Hidden in the movies we watch, the music we hear, the liquor we drink, the textbooks we read, it is overlooked because it is protected and its protection— or its alibi (Barthes 1957: 109–111)—allows the terms and relations of ideology to spill into and infiltrate our everyday lives.

A world of commodities, gender inequalities, and power differentials is seen not therefore in these terms but as a naturalized environment, one that makes sense because it has become our experience to live it and accept it in precisely this way. This common-sense acceptance of a particular world is the work of ideology, and it works by concealing the coercive and repressive elements of our everyday routines but also by making those routines of the everyday familiar, desirable, and simply our own. This is the critical element of Althusser's notion of ideological power: ideology is so potent because it becomes not only ours but us—the terms and machinery by which we structure ourselves and identify who we are.

## JAPANESE FOOD AS CULTURAL MYTH

An author in one *obentō* magazine, the type of medium-sized publication that, filled with glossy pictures of *obentōs* and ideas and recipes for successfully recreating them, sold in the bookstores across Japan, declares, ". . . the making of the *obentō* is the one most worrisome concern facing the mother of a child going off to school for the first time" (*Shufunotomo* 1980: inside cover). Another *obentō* journal, this one heftier and packaged in the encyclopedic series of the prolific women's publishing firm, *Shufunotomo*, articulates the same social fact: "First-time *obentōs* are a strain on both parent and child" ("*hajimete no obentō wa, oya mo ko mo kinch ō shimasu*") (*Shufunotomo* 1981: 55).

An outside observer might ask: What is the real source of worry over *obentō*? Is it the food itself or the entrance of the young child into school for the first time? Yet, as one look at a typical child's *obentō*—a small box packaged with a five or six-course miniaturized meal whose pieces and parts are artistically arranged, perfectly cut, and neatly arranged—would immediately reveal, no food is "just" food in Japan. What is not so immediately apparent, however, is why a small child with limited appetite and perhaps scant interest in food is the recipient of a meal as elaborate and as elaborately prepared as any made for an entire family or invited guests.

Certainly, in Japan much attention is focused on the *obentō*, investing it with a significance far beyond that of the merely pragmatic, functional one of sustaining a child with nutritional foodstuffs. Since this investment beyond the pragmatic is true of any food prepared in Japan, it is helpful to examine culinary codes for food preparation that operate generally in the society before focusing on children's *obentōs*.

As has been remarked often about Japanese food, the key element is appearance. Food must be organized, re-organized, arranged, re-arranged, stylized, and re-stylized to appear in a design that is visually attractive. Presentation is critical: not to the extent that taste and nutrition are displaced, as has been sometimes attributed to Japanese food, but to the degree that how food looks is at least as important as how it tastes and how good and sustaining it is for one's body.

As Donald Richie has pointed out in his eloquent and informative book *A Taste of Japan* (1985), presentational style is the guiding principle by which food is prepared in Japan, and the style is conditioned by a number of codes. One code is for smallness, separation, and fragmentation. Nothing large is allowed, so portions are all cut to be bite-sized, served in small amounts on tiny individual dishes, and are arranged on a table (or on a tray, or in an *obentō* box) in an array of small, separate containers.[1] There is no one big dinner plate with three large portions of vegetable, starch, and meat as in American cuisine. Consequently the eye is pulled not toward one totalizing center but away to a multiplicity of de-centered parts.[2]

Visually, food substances are presented according to a structural principle not only of segmentation but also of opposition. Foods are broken or cut to make contrasts of color, texture, and shape. Foods are meant to oppose one another and clash: pink against green, roundish foods against angular ones, smooth substances next to rough ones. This oppositional code operates not only within and between the foodstuffs themselves, but also between the attributes of the food and those of the containers in or on which they are placed: a circular mound in a square dish, a bland colored food set against a bright plate, a translucent sweet in a heavily textured bowl (Richie 1985: 40–41).

The container is as important as what is contained in Japanese cuisine, but it is really the containment that is stressed, that is, how food has been (re)constructed and (re)arranged from nature to appear, in both beauty and freshness, perfectly natural. This stylizing of nature is a third code by which presentation is directed; the injunction is not only to retain, as much as possible, the innate naturalness of ingredients— shopping daily so food is fresh and leaving much of it either raw or only minimally cooked—but also to recreate in prepared food the promise and appearance of

being "natural." As Richie writes, ". . . the emphasis is on presentation of the natural rather than the natural itself. It is not what nature has wrought that excites admiration but what man has wrought with what nature has wrought" (1985: 11).

This naturalization of food is rendered through two main devices. One is by constantly hinting at and appropriating the nature that comes from outside— decorating food with seasonal reminders, such as a maple leaf in the fall or a flower in the spring, serving in-season fruits and vegetables, and using season-coordinated dishes such as glassware in the summer and heavy pottery in the winter. The other device, to some degree the inverse of the first, is to accentuate and perfect the preparation process to such an extent that the food appears not only to be natural, but more nearly perfect than nature without human intervention ever could be. This is nature made artificial. Thus, by naturalization, nature is not only taken in by Japanese cuisine, but taken over.

It is this ability both to appropriate "real" nature (the maple leaf on the tray) and to stamp the human reconstruction of that nature as "natural" that lends Japanese food its potential for cultural and ideological manipulation. It is what Barthes calls a second order myth (1957: 114–7): a language which has a function people accept as only pragmatic—the sending of roses to lovers, the consumption of wine with one's dinner, the cleaning up a mother does for her child—which is taken over by some interest or agenda to serve a different end—florists who can sell roses, liquor companies who can market wine, conservative politicians who campaign for a gendered division of labor with women kept at home. The first order of language ("language-object"), thus emptied of its original meaning, is converted into an empty form by which it can assume a new, additional, second order of signification ("meta-language" or "second-order semiological system"). As Barthes points out however, the primary meaning is never lost. Rather, it remains and stands as an alibi, the cover under which the second, politicized meaning can hide. Roses sell better, for example, when lovers view them as a vehicle to express love rather than the means by which a company stays in business.

At one level, food is just food in Japan—the medium by which humans sustain their nature and health. Yet under and through this code of pragmatics, Japanese cuisine carries other meanings that in Barthes' terms are mythological. One of these is national identity: food being appropriated as a sign of the culture. To be Japanese is to eat Japanese food, as so many Japanese confirm when they travel to other countries and cite the greatest problem they encounter to be the absence of "real" Japanese food. Stated the other way around, rice is so symbolically central to Japanese culture (meals and *obentōs* often being assembled with rice as the core and all other dishes, multifarious as they may be, as mere compliments or side dishes) that Japanese say they can never feel full until they have consumed their rice at a particular meal or at least once during the day.[3]

Embedded within this insistence on eating Japanese food, thereby reconfirming one as a member of the culture, are the principles by which Japanese food is customarily prepared: perfection, labor, small distinguishable parts, opposing segments, beauty, and the stamp of nature. Overarching all these more detailed codings are two that guide the making and ideological appropriation of the nursery school *obentōs* most directly: (1) there is an order to the food: a right way to do things, with everything in its place and each place coordinated with every other, and (2) the one who prepares the food takes on the responsibility of producing food to the standards of perfection and exactness that Japanese cuisine demands. Food may not be casual, in other words, nor the producer casual in her production. In these two rules is a message both about social order and the role gender plays in sustaining and nourishing that order.

## SCHOOL, STATE, AND SUBJECTIVITY

In addition to language and second order meanings I suggest that the rituals and routines surrounding *obentōs* in Japanese nursery schools present, as it were, a third order, manipulation. This order is a use of a currency already established—one that has already appropriated a language of utility (food feeds hunger) to express and implant cultural behaviors. State-guided schools borrow this coded apparatus: using the natural convenience and cover of food not only to code a cultural order, but also to socialize children and mothers into the gendered roles and subjectivities they are expected to assume in a political order desired and directed by the state.

In modern capitalist societies such as Japan, it is the school, according to Althusser, which assumes the primary role of ideological state apparatus. A greater segment of the population spends longer hours and more years here than in previous historical periods. Also education has not taken over from other institutions, such as religion, the pedagogical function of being the major shaper and inculcator of knowledge for the society. Concurrently, as Althusser has pointed out for capitalist modernism (1971: 152, 156), there is the gradual replacement of repression by ideology as the prime mechanism for behavior enforcement. Influenced less by the threat of force and more by the devices that present and inform us of the world

we live in and the subjectivities that world demands, knowledge and ideology become fused, and education emerges as the apparatus for pedagogical and ideological indoctrination.

In practice, as school teaches children how and what to think, it also shapes them for the roles and positions they will later assume as adult members of the society. How the social order is organized through vectors of gender, power, labor, and/or class, in other words, is not only as important a lesson as the basics of reading and writing, but is transmitted through and embedded in those classroom lessons. Knowledge thus is not only socially constructed, but also differentially acquired according to who one is or will be in the political society one will enter in later years. What precisely society requires in the way of workers, citizens, and parents will be the condition determining or influencing instruction in the schools.

This latter equation, of course, depends on two factors: (1) the convergence or divergence of different interests in what is desired as subjectivities, and (2) the power any particular interest, including that of the state, has in exerting its desires for subjects on or through the system of education. In the case of Japan, the state wields enormous control over the systematization of education. Through its Ministry of Education (Monbusho), one of the most powerful and influential ministries in the government, education is centralized and managed by a state bureaucracy that regulates almost every aspect of the educational process. On any given day, for example, what is taught in every public school follows the same curriculum, adheres to the same structure, and is informed by textbooks from the prescribed list. Teachers are nationally screened, school boards uniformly appointed (rather than elected), and students institutionally exhorted to obey teachers given their legal authority, for example, to write secret reports (*naishinsho*), that may obstruct a student's entrance into high school.[4]

The role of the state in Japanese education is not limited, however, to such extensive but codified authorities granted to the Ministry of Education. Even more powerful is the principle of the "*gakureki shakkai*" (lit. academic pedigree society) by which careers of adults are determined by the schools they attend as youths. A reflection and construction of the new economic order of post-war Japan,[5] school attendance has become the single most important determinant of who will achieve the most desirable positions in industry, government, and the professions. School attendance is itself based on a single criterion: a system of entrance exams which determines entrance selection and it is to this end—preparation for exams—that school, even at the nursery school level, is increasingly oriented. Learning to follow directions, do as one is told, and "*ganbaru*" (Asanuma 1987) are social imperatives, sanctioned by the state, and taught in the schools.

## NURSERY SCHOOL AND IDEOLOGICAL APPROPRIATION OF THE *OBENTŌ*

The nursery school stands outside the structure of compulsory education in Japan. Most nursery schools are private; and, though not compelled by the state, a greater proportion of the three- to six-year-old population of Japan attends preschool than in any other industrialized nation (Boocock 1989; Hendry 1986; Tobin et al. 1989).

Differentiated from the *hoikuen*, another pre-school institution with longer hours which is more like day-care than school,[6] the *yochien* (nursery school) is widely perceived as instructional, not necessarily in a formal curriculum but more in indoctrination to attitudes and structure of Japanese schooling. Children learn less about reading and writing than they do about how to become a Japanese student, and both parts of this formula—Japanese and student—are equally stressed. As Rohlen has written, "social order is generated" in the nursery school, first and foremost, by a system of routines (1989: 10, 21). Educational routines and rituals are therefore of heightened importance in *yochien*, for whereas these routines and rituals may be the format through which subjects are taught in higher grades, they are both form and subject in the *yochien*.

While the state (through its agency, the Ministry of Education) has no direct mandate over nursery school attendance, its influence is nevertheless significant. First, authority over how the *yochien* is run is in the hands of the Ministry of Education. Second, most parents and teachers see the *yochien* as the first step to the system of compulsory education that starts in the first grade and is closely controlled by Monbusho. The principal of the *yochien* my son attended, for example, stated that he saw his main duty to be preparing children to enter more easily the rigors of public education soon to come. Third, the rules and patterns of "group living" (shudanseikatsu), a Japanese social ideal that is reiterated nationwide by political leaders, corporate management, and marriage counselors, is first introduced to the child in nursery school.[7]

The entry into nursery school marks a transition both away from home and into the "real world," which is generally judged to be difficult, even traumatic, for the Japanese child (Peak 1989). The *obentō* is intended to ease a child's discomfiture and to allow a child's mother to manufacture something of herself and the home to accompany the child as s/he moves into the potentially threatening outside world. Japanese use the cultural categories of *soto* and *uchi*; *soto* connotes the outside, which in being distanced and other, is dirty and hostile; and *uchi* identifies as clean and comfortable what is inside and familiar. The school falls initially and, to some degree, perpetually, into a category of *soto*. What is ultimately the definition and location of *uchi*, by contrast, is the home, where family and mother reside.[8] By producing something from the home, a mother both girds and goads her child to face what is inevitable in the world that lies beyond. This is the mother's role and her gift; by giving of herself and the home (which she both symbolically represents and in reality manages).[9] The *soto* of the school is, if not transformed into the *uchi* of home, made more bearable by this sign of domestic and maternal hearth a child can bring to it.

The *obentō* is filled with the meaning of mother and home in a number of ways. The first is by sheer labor. Women spend what seems to be an inordinate amount of time on the production of this one item. As an experienced *obentō* maker, I can attest to the intense attention and energy devoted to this one chore. On the average, mothers spend 20–45 minutes every morning cooking, preparing, and assembling the contents of one *obentō* for one nursery school–aged child. In addition, the previous day they have planned, shopped, and often organized a supper meal with left-overs in mind for the next day's *obentō*. Frequently women[10] discuss *obentō* ideas with other mothers, scan *obentō* cookbooks or magazines for recipes, buy or make objects with which to decorate or contain (part of) the *obentō*, and perhaps make small food portions to freeze and retrieve for future *obentō*.[11]

Of course, effort alone does not necessarily produce a successful *obentō*. Casualness was never indulged, I observed, and even mothers with children who would eat anything prepared *obentō* as elaborate as anyone else's. Such labor is intended for the child but also the mother: it is a sign of a woman's commitment as a mother and her inspiring her child to being similarly committed as a student. The *obentō* is thus a representation of what the mother is and what the child should become. A model for school is added to what is a gift and a reminder from home.

This equation is spelled out more precisely in a nursery school rule—all of the *obentō* must be eaten. Though on the face of it this is petty and mundane, the injunction is taken very seriously by nursery school teachers and is one not easily realized by very small children. The logic is that it is time for the child to meet certain expectations. One of the main agendas of the nursery school, after all, is to introduce and indoctrinate children into the patterns and rigors of Japanese education (Lewis 1989; Rohlen 1989; Sano 1989). And Japanese education, by all accounts, is not about fun (Duke 1986).

Learning is hard work with few choices or pleasures. Even *obentōs* from home stop once the child enters first grade.[12] The meals there are institutional: largely bland, unappealing, and prepared with only nutrition in mind. To ease a youngster into these upcoming (educational, social, disciplinary, culinary) routines, *yochien obentōs* are designed to be pleasing and personal. The *obentō* is also designed, however, as a test for the child. And the double meaning is not unintentional. A structure already filled with a signification of mother and home is then emptied to provide a new form: one now also written with the ideological demands of being a member of Japanese culture as well as a viable and successful Japanese in the realms of school and later work.

The exhortation to consume one's entire *obentō*[13] is articulated and enforced by the nursery school teacher. Making high drama out of eating by, for example, singing a song; collectively thanking Buddha (in the case of Buddhist nursery schools), one's mother for making the *obentō*, and one's father for providing the means to make the *obentō*; having two assigned class helpers pour the tea, the class eats together until everyone has finished. The teacher examines the children's *obentōs*, making sure the food is all consumed, and encouraging, sometimes scolding, children who are taking too long. Slow eaters do not fare well in this ritual, because they hold up the other students, who as a peer group also monitor a child's eating. My son often complained about a child whose slowness over food meant that the others were kept inside (rather than being allowed to play on the playground) for much of the lunch period.

Ultimately and officially, it is the teacher, however, whose role and authority it is to watch over food consumption and to judge the person consuming food. Her surveillance covers both the student and the mother, who in the matter of the *obentō*, must work together. The child's job is to eat the food and the mother's to prepare it. Hence, the responsibility and execution of one's task is not only shared but conditioned by the other. My son's teacher would talk with me daily about the progress he was making finishing his *obentōs*. Although the overt subject of discussion was my child, most of what was said was directed to me; what I could do in order to get David to consume his lunch more easily.

The intensity of these talks struck me at the time as curious. We had just settled in Japan and David, a highly verbal child, was attending a foreign school in a foreign language he had not yet mastered; he was the only non-Japanese child in the school. Many of his behaviors during this time were disruptive: for example, he went up and down the line of children during morning exercises hitting each child on the head. Hamada-sensei (the teacher), however, chose to discuss the *obentōs*. I thought surely David's survival in and adjustment to this environment depended much more on other factors, such as learning Japanese. Yet it was the *obentō* that was discussed with such recall of detail ("David ate all his peas today, but not a single carrot until I asked him to do so three times") and seriousness that I assumed her attention was being misplaced. The manifest reference was to box-lunches, but was not the latent reference to something else?[14]

Of course, there was another message, for me and my child. It was an injunction to follow directions, obey rules, and accept the authority of the school system. All of the latter were embedded in and inculcated through certain rituals: the nursery school, as any school (except such non-conventional ones as Waldorf and Montessori) and practically any social or institutional practice in Japan, was so heavily ritualized and ritualistic that the very form of ritual took on a meaning and value in and of itself (Rohlen 1989: 21, 27–8). Both the school day and school year of the nursery school were organized by these rituals. The day, apart from two free periods, for example, was broken by discrete routines—morning exercises, arts and crafts, gym instruction, singing—most of which were named and scheduled. The school year was also segmented into and marked by three annual events—sports day (*und ō kai*) in the fall, winter assembly (*seikatsu happy ō kai*) in December, and dance festival (*bon odori*) in the summer. Energy was galvanized by these rituals, which demanded a degree of order as well as a discipline and self-control that non-Japanese would find remarkable.

Significantly, David's teacher marked his successful integration into the school system by his mastery not of the language or other cultural skills, but of the school's daily routines—walking in line, brushing his teeth after eating, arriving at school early, eagerly participating in greeting and departure ceremonies, and completing all of his *obentō* on time. Not only had he adjusted to the school structure, but he had also become assimilated to the other children. Or restated, what once had been externally enforced now became ideologically desirable; the everyday practices had moved from being alien (*soto*) to familiar (*uchi*) to him, from, that is, being someone else's to his own. My American child had to become, in some sense, Japanese, and where his teacher recognized this Japaneseness was in the daily routines such as finishing his *obentō*. The lesson learned early, which David learned as well, is that not adhering to routines such as completing one's *obent ō* on time leads to not only admonishment from the teacher, but rejection from the other students.

The nursery school system differentiates between the child who does and the child who does not manage the multifarious and constant rituals of nursery school.

And for those who do not manage there is a penalty which the child learns either to avoid or wish to avoid. Seeking the acceptance of his peers, the student develops the aptitude, willingness, and in the case of my son—whose outspokenness and individuality were the characteristics most noted in this culture—even the desire to conform to the highly ordered and structured practices of nursery school life. As Althusser (1971) wrote about ideology: the mechanism works when and because ideas about the world and particular roles in that world that serve other (social, political, economic, state) agendas become familiar and one's own.

Rohlen makes a similar point: that what is taught and learned in nursery school is social order. Called *shudanseikatsu* or group life, it means organization into a group where a person's subjectivity is determined by a group membership and not "the assumption of choice and rational self-interest" (1989: 30). A child learns in nursery school to be with others, think like others, and act in tandem with others. This lesson is taught primarily through the precision and constancy of basic routines: "Order is shaped gradually by repeated practice of selected daily tasks . . . that socialize the children to high degrees of neatness and uniformity" (p. 21). Yet a feeling of coerciveness is rarely experienced by the child when three principles of nursery school instruction are in place: (1) school routines are made "desirable and pleasant" (p. 30), (2) the teacher disguises her authority by trying to make the group the voice and unit of authority, and (3) the regimentation of the school is administered by an attitude of "intimacy" on the part of the teachers and administrators (p. 30). In short, when the desires and routines of the school are made into the desires and routines of the child, they are made acceptable.

## MOTHERING AS GENDERED IDEOLOGICAL STATE APPARATUS

The rituals surrounding the *obentō* consumption in the school situate what ideological meanings the *obentō* transmits to the child. The process of production within the home, by contrast, organizes its somewhat different ideological package for the mother. While the two sets of meanings are intertwined, the mother is faced with different expectations in the preparation of the *obentō* than the child is in its consumption. At a pragmatic level the child must simply eat everything in the lunch box, whereas the mother's job is far more complicated. The onus for her is getting the child to consume what she has made, and the general attitude is that this is far more the mother's responsibility (at this nursery school, transitional stage) than the child's. And this is no simple or easy task.

Much of what is written, advised, and discussed about the *obentō* has this aim explicitly in mind: that is, making food in such a way as to facilitate the child's duty to eat it. One magazine advises:

> The first day of taking *obentō* is a worrisome thing for mother and "*boku*" (child)[15] too. Put in easy-to-eat foods that your child likes and is already used to and prepare this food in small portions. (*Shufunotomo* 1980: 28)

Filled with pages of recipes, hints, pictures, and ideas, the magazine codes each page with "helpful" headings:

- First off, easy-to-eat is step one.
- Next is being able to consume the *obentō* without leaving anything behind.
- Make it in such a way for the child to become proficient in the use of chopsticks.
- Decorate and fill it with cute dreams (*kawairashi yume*).
- For older classes (*nencho*), make *obentō* filled with variety.
- Once he's become used to it, balance foods your child likes with those he dislikes.
- For kids who hate vegetables. . . .
- For kids who hate fish. . . .
- For kids who hate meat. . . . (pp. 28–53)

Laced throughout cookbooks and other magazines devoted to *obentō*, the *obentō* guidelines issued by the school and sent home in the school flier every two weeks, and the words of Japanese mothers and teachers discussing *obentō*, are a number of principles: (1) food should be made easy to eat: portions cut or made small and manipulable with fingers or chopsticks, (child-size) spoons and forks, skewers, toothpicks, muffin tins, containers, (2) portions should be kept small so the *obentō* can be consumed quickly and without any left-overs, (3) food that a child does not yet like should be eventually added so as to remove fussiness (*sukikirai*) in food habits, (4) make the *obentō* pretty, cute, and visually changeable by presenting the food attractively and by adding non-food objects such as silver paper, foil, toothpick flags, paper napkins, cute handkerchiefs, and variously shaped containers for soy sauce and ketchup, and (5) design *obentō*-related items as much as possible by the mother's own hands including the *obentō* bag (*obentō fukuro*) in which the *obentō* is carried.

The strictures propounded by publications seem to be endless. In practice I found that visual appearance and appeal were stressed by the mothers. By contrast, the directive to use *obentō* as a training process—adding new foods and getting older children to use chopsticks and learn to tie the *furoshiki*[16]—was emphasized by those judging the *obentō* at the school. Where these two sets of concerns met was, of course, in the child's success or failure completing the *obentō*. Ultimately this outcome and the mother's role in it, was how the *obentō* was judged in my experience.

The aestheticization of the *obentō* is by far its most intriguing aspect for a cultural anthropologist. Aesthetic categories and codes that operate generally for Japanese cuisine are applied, though adjusted, to the nursery school format. Substances are many but petite, kept segmented and opposed, and manipulated intensively to achieve an appearance that often changes or disguises the food. As a mother insisted to me, the creation of a bear out of miniature hamburgers and rice, or a flower from an apple or peach, is meant to sustain a child's interest in the underlying food. Yet my child, at least, rarely noticed or appreciated the art I had so laboriously contrived. As for other children, I observed that even for those who ate with no obvious "fussiness," mothers' efforts to create food as style continued all year long.

Thus much of a woman's labor over *obentō* stems from some agenda other than that of getting the child to eat an entire lunch-box. The latter is certainly a consideration and it is the rationale as well as cover for women being scrutinized by the school's authority figure—the teacher. Yet two other factors are important. One is that the *obentō* is but one aspect of the far more expansive and continuous commitment a mother is expected to make for and to her child. "*Kyō iku mama*" (education mother) is the term given to a mother who executes her responsibility to oversee and manage the education of her children with excessive vigor. And yet this excess is not only demanded by the state even at the level of the nursery school; it is conventionally given by mothers. Mothers who manage the home and children, often in virtual absence of a husband/father, are considered the factor that may make or break a child as s/he advances towards that pivotal point of the entrance examinations.[17]

In this sense, just as the *obentō* is meant as a device to assist a child in the struggles of first adjusting to school, the mother's role generally is perceived as being the support, goad, and cushion for the child. She will perform endless tasks to assist in her child's study: sharpen pencils and make midnight snacks as the child studies, attend cram schools to verse herself in subjects her child is weak in, make inquiries as to what school is most appropriate for her child, and consult with her child's teachers. If the child succeeds, a mother is complimented; if the child fails, a mother is blamed.

Thus at the nursery school level, the mother starts her own preparation for this upcoming role. Yet the jobs and energies demanded of a nursery school mother are, in themselves, surprisingly consuming. Just as the mother of an entering student is given a book listing all the pre-entry tasks she must complete, for example, making various bags and containers, affixing labels to all clothes in precisely the right place and with the size exactly right, she will be continually expected thereafter to attend Mothers' Association meetings, accompany children on fieldtrips, wash the clothes and indoor shoes of her child every week, add required items to a child's bag on a day's notice, and generally be available. Few mothers at the school my son attended could afford to work in even part-time or temporary jobs. Those women who did tended either to keep their outside work a secret or be reprimanded by a teacher for insufficient devotion to their child. Motherhood, in other words, is institutionalized through the child's school and such routines as making the *obentō* as a full-time, kept-at-home job.[18]

The second factor in a woman's devotion to overelaborating her child's lunch-box is that her experience doing this becomes a part of her and a statement, in some sense, of who she is. Marx writes that labor is the most "essential" aspect to our species-being and that the products we produce are the encapsulation of us and therefore our productivity (Marx and Engels 1970: 71–6). Likewise, women are what they are through the products they produce. An *obentō* therefore is not only a gift or test for a child, but a representation and product of the woman herself. Of course, the two ideologically converge, as has been stated already, but I would also suggest that there is a potential disjoining. I sensed that the women were laboring for themselves apart from the agenda the *obentō* was expected to fill at school. Or stated alternatively, in the role that females in Japan are highly pressured and encouraged to assume as domestic manager, mother, and wife, there is, besides the endless and onerous responsibilities, also an opportunity for play. Significantly, women find play and creativity not outside their social roles but within them.

Saying this is not to deny the constraints and surveillance under which Japanese women labor at their *obentō*. Like their children at school, they are watched by not only the teacher but each other, and perfect what they create, partially at least, so as to be confirmed as a good and dutiful mother in the eyes of other mothers. The enthusiasm with which they absorb this task then is like my son's acceptance and internalization of the nursery school routines; no longer enforced from outside it becomes adopted as one's own.

The making of the *obentō* is, I would thus argue, a double-edged sword for women. By relishing its creation (for all the intense labor expended, only once or twice did I hear a mother voice any complaint about this task), a woman is ensconcing herself in the ritualization and subjectivity (subjection) of being a mother in Japan. She is alienated in the sense that others will dictate, inspect, and manage her work. On the reverse side, however, it is precisely through this work that the woman expresses, identifies, and constitutes herself. As Althusser pointed out, ideology can never be totally abolished (1971: 170); the elaborations that women work on "natural" food produce an *obentō* which is creative and, to some degree, a fulfilling and personal statement of themselves.

Minami, an informant, revealed how both restrictive and pleasurable the daily rituals of motherhood can be. The mother of two children—one, aged three and one, a nursery school student, Minami had been a professional opera singer before marrying at the relatively late age of 32. Now, her daily schedule was organized by routines associated with her child's nursery school: for example, making the *obentō*, taking her daughter to school and picking her up, attending Mothers' Association meetings, arranging daily play dates, and keeping the school uniform clean. While Minami wished to return to singing, if only on a part-time basis, she said that the demands of motherhood, particularly those imposed by her child's attendance at nursery school, frustrated this desire. Secretly snatching only minutes out of any day to practice, Minami missed singing and told me that being a mother in Japan means the exclusion of almost anything else.[19]

Despite this frustration, however, Minami did not behave like a frustrated woman. Rather she devoted to her mothering an energy, creativity, and intelligence I found to be standard in the Japanese mothers I knew. She planned special outings for her children at least two or three times a week, organized games that she knew they would like and would teach them cognitive skills, created her own stories and designed costumes for afternoon play, and shopped daily for the meals she prepared with her children's favorite foods in mind. Minami told me often that she wished she could sing more, but never once did she complain about her children, the chores of child-raising, or being a mother. The attentiveness displayed otherwise in her mothering was exemplified most fully in Minami's *obentōs*. No two were ever alike, each had at least four or five parts, and she kept trying out new ideas for both new foods and new designs. She took pride as well as pleasure in her *obentō* handicraft; but while Minami's *obentō* creativity was impressive, it was not unusual.

Examples of such extraordinary *obentō* creations from an *obentō* magazine include: (1) ("donut *obentō*"): two donuts, two wieners cut to look like a worm, two cut pieces of apple, two small cheese rolls, one hard-boiled egg made to look like a rabbit with leaf ears and pickle eyes and set in an aluminum muffin tin, cute paper napkin added, (2) (wiener doll *obentō*): a bed of rice with two doll creations made out of wiener parts (each consists of eight pieces comprising hat, hair, head, arms, body, legs), a line of pink ginger, a line

of green parsley, paper flag of France added, (3) (vegetable flower and tulip *obentō*): a bed of rice laced with chopped hard-boiled egg, three tulip flowers made out of cut wieners with spinach precisely arranged as stem and leaves, a fruit salad with two raisins, three cooked peaches, three pieces of cooked apple, (4) (sweetheart doll *obentō—abekku ningyō no obentō*): in a two-section *obentō* box there are four rice balls on one side, each with a different center, on the other side are two dolls made of quail's eggs for heads, eyes and mouth added, bodies of cucumber, arranged as if lying down with two raw carrots for the pillow, covers made of one flower—cut cooked carrot, two pieces of ham, pieces of cooked spinach, and with different colored plastic skewers holding the dolls together (*Shufunotomo* 1980: 27, 30).

The impulse to work and re-work nature in these *obentōs* is most obvious perhaps in the strategies used to transform, shape, and/or disguise foods. Every mother I knew came up with her own repertoire of such techniques, and every *obentō* magazine or cookbook I examined offered a special section on these devices. It is important to keep in mind that these are treated as only flourishes: embellishments added to parts of an *obentō* composed of many parts. The following is a list from one magazine: lemon pieces made into butterflies, hard boiled eggs into *daruma* (popular Japanese legendary figure of a monk without his eyes), sausage cut into flowers, a hard-boiled egg decorated as a baby, an apple piece cut into a leaf, a radish flaked into a flower, a cucumber cut like a flower, a *mikan* (nectarine orange) piece arranged into a basket, a boat with a sail made from a cucumber, skewered sausage, radish shaped like a mushroom, a quail egg flaked into a cherry, twisted *mikan* piece, sausage cut to become a crab, a patterned cucumber, a ribboned carrot, a flowered tomato, cabbage leaf flower, a potato cut to be a worm, a carrot designed as a red shoe, an apple cut to simulate a pineapple (*Shufunotomo* 1980: 57–60).

Nature is not only transformed but also supplemented by store-bought or mother-made objects which are precisely arranged in the *obentō*. The former come from an entire industry and commodification of the *obentō* process: complete racks or sections in stores selling *obentō* boxes, additional small containers, *obentō* bags, cups, chopstick and utensil containers (all these with various cute characters or designs on the front), cloth and paper napkins, foil, aluminum tins, colored ribbon or string, plastic skewers, toothpicks with paper flags, and paper dividers. The latter are the objects mothers are encouraged and praised for making themselves: *obentō* bags, napkins, and handkerchiefs with appliquéd designs or the child's name embroidered. These supplements to the food, the arrangement of the food, and the *obentō* box's dividing walls (removable and adjustable) furnish the order of the *obentō*. Everything appears crisp and neat with each part kept in its own place: two tiny hamburgers set firmly atop a bed of rice; vegetables in a separate compartment in the box; fruit arranged in a muffin tin.

How the specific forms of *obentō* artistry—for example, a wiener cut to look like a worm and set within a muffin tin—are encoded symbolically is a fascinating subject. Limited here by space, however, I will only offer initial suggestions. Arranging food into a scene recognizable by the child was an ideal mentioned by many mothers and cookbooks. Why those of animals, human beings, and other food forms (making a pineapple out of an apple, for example) predominate may have no other rationale than being familiar to children and easily reproduced by mothers. Yet it is also true that this tendency to use a trope of realism—casting food into realistic figures—is most prevalent in the meals Japanese prepare for their children. Mothers I knew created animals and faces in supper meals and/ or *obentōs* made for other outings, yet their impulse to do this seemed not only heightened in the *obentō* that were sent to school but also played down in food prepared for other age groups.

What is consistent in Japanese cooking generally, as stated earlier, are the dual principles of manipulation and order. Food is manipulated into some other form than it assumes either naturally or upon being cooked: lines are put into mashed potatoes, carrots are flaked, wieners are twisted and sliced. Also, food is ordered by some human rather than natural principle; everything must have neat boundaries and be placed precisely so those boundaries do not merge. These two structures are the ones most important in shaping the nursery school *obentō* as well, and the inclination to design realistic imagery is primarily a means by which these other culinary codes are learned by and made pleasurable for the child. The simulacrum of a pineapple recreated from an apple therefore is less about seeing the pineapple in an apple (a particular form) and more about reconstructing the apple into something else (the process of transformation).

The intense labor, management, commodification, and attentiveness that go into the making of an *obentō* laces it, however, with many and various meanings. Overarching all is the potential to aestheticize a certain social order, a social order which is coded (in cultural and culinary terms) as Japanese. Not only is a mother making food more palatable to her nursery school child, but she is creating food as a more aesthetic and pleasing social structure. The *obentō's* message is that the world is constructed very precisely and that the role of any single Japanese in that world must be carried out with the same degree of precision. Production is demanding; and the producer must both keep within the borders of her/his role and work hard.

The message is also that it is women, not men, who are not only sustaining a child through food but carrying the ideological support of the culture that this food embeds. No Japanese man I spoke with had or desired the experience of making a nursery school *obentō* even once, and few were more than peripherally engaged in their children's education. The male is assigned a position in the outside world where he labors at a job for money and is expected to be primarily identified by and committed to his place of work.[20] Helping in the management of home and raising of children has not become an obvious male concern or interest in Japan, even as more and more women enter what was previously the male domain of work. Females have remained at and as the center of home in Japan and this message too is explicitly transmitted in both the production and consumption of entirely female-produced *obentō*.

The state accrues benefits from this arrangement. With children depending on the labor women devote to their mothering to such a degree, and women being pressured as well as pleasurized in such routine maternal productions as making the *obentō*—both effects encouraged and promoted by institutional features of the educational system heavily state-run and at least ideologically guided at even the nursery school level—a gendered division of labor is firmly set in place. Labor from males, socialized to be compliant and hard-working, is more extractable when they have wives to rely on for almost all domestic and familial management. And females become a source of cheap labor, as they are increasingly forced to enter the labor market to pay domestic costs (including those vast debts incurred in educating children) yet are increasingly constrained to low-paying part-time jobs because of the domestic duties they must also bear almost totally as mothers.

Hence, not only do females, as mothers, operate within the ideological state apparatus of Japan's school system that starts semi-officially, with the nursery school, they also operate as an ideological state apparatus unto themselves. Motherhood is state ideology, working through children at home and at school and through such mother-imprinted labor that a child carries from home to school as with the *obentō*. Hence the post–World War II conception of Japanese education as being egalitarian, democratic, and with no agenda of or for gender differentiation, does not in practice stand up. Concealed within such cultural practices as culinary style and child-focused mothering, is a worldview in which the position and behavior an adult will assume has everything to do with the anatomy she/he was born with.

At the end, however, I am left with one question. If motherhood is not only watched and manipulated by the state but made by it into a conduit for ideological indoctrination, could not women subvert the political order by redesigning *obentō*? Asking this question, a Japanese friend, upon reading this paper, recalled her own experiences. Though her mother had been conventional in most other respects, she made her children *obentōs* that did not conform to the prevailing conventions. Basic, simple, and rarely artistic, Sawa also noted, in this connection, that the lines of these *obentōs* resembled those by which she was generally raised: as gender-neutral, treated as a person not "just as a girl," and being allowed a margin to think for herself. Today she is an exceptionally independent woman who has created a life for herself in America, away from homeland and parents, almost entirely on her own. She loves Japanese food, but the plain *obentōs* her mother made for her as a child, she is newly appreciative of now, as an adult. The *obentōs* fed her, but did not keep her culturally or ideologically attached. For this, Sawa says today, she is glad.

## ACKNOWLEDGMENTS

The fieldwork on which this article is based was supported by a Japan Foundation Postdoctoral Fellowship. I am grateful to Charles Piot for a thoughtful reading and useful suggestions for revision and to Jennifer Robertson for inviting my contribution to this issue. I would also like to thank Sawa Kurotani for her many ethnographic stories and input, and Phyllis Chock and two anonymous readers for the valuable contributions they made to revision of the manuscript.

## NOTES

1. As Dorinne Kondo has pointed out, however, these cuisinal principles may be conditioned by factors of both class and circumstance. Her *shitamachi* (more traditional area of Tokyo) informants, for example, adhered only casually to this coding and other Japanese she knew followed them more carefully when preparing food for guests rather than family and when eating outside rather than inside the home (Kondo 1990: 61–2).
2. Rice is often, if not always, included in a meal: and it may substantially as well as symbolically constitute the core of the meal. When served at a table it is put in a large pot or electric rice maker and will be spooned into a bowl, still no bigger or predominant than the many other containers from which a person eats. In an *obentō* rice may be in one, perhaps the largest, section of a multi-sectioned *obentō* box, yet it will be arranged with a variety of other foods. In a sense rice provides the syntactic and substantial center to a meal yet the presentation of the food rarely emphasizes this core. The rice bowl is refilled rather than heaped as in the preformed *obentō* box, and in the *obentō* rice is often embroidered, supplemented, and/or covered with other foodstuffs.
3. Japanese will both endure a high price for rice at home and resist American attempts to export rice to Japan in order to stay domestically self-sufficient in this national food *qua* cultural symbol. Rice is the only foodstuff in which the Japanese have retained self-sufficient production.
4. The primary sources on education used are Horio (1988); Duke (1986); Rohlen (1983); Cummings (1980).
5. Neither the state's role in overseeing education nor a system of standardized tests is a new development in post–World War II Japan. What is new is the national standardization of tests and, in this sense, the intensified role the state has thus assumed in overseeing them. See Dore (1965) and Horio (1988).
6. Boocock (1989) differs from Tobin et al. (1989) on this point and asserts that the institutional differences are insignificant. She describes extensively how both *yochien* and *hoikuen* are administered (*yochien* are under the authority of Monbusho and *hoikuen* are under the authority of the Koseisho, the Ministry of Health and Welfare) and how both feed into the larger system of education. She emphasizes diversity: though certain trends are common amongst preschools, differences in teaching styles and philosophies are plentiful as well.
7. According to Rohlen (1989), families are incapable of indoctrinating the child into this social pattern of *shō ndanseikatsu* by their very structure and particularly by the relationship (of indulgence and dependence) between mother and child. For this reason and the importance placed on group structures in Japan, the nursery school's primary objective, argues Rohlen, is teaching children how to assimilate into groups. For further discussion of this point, see also Peak (1989); Lewis (1989); Sano (1989); and the *Journal of Japanese Studies* issue [15(1)] devoted to Japanese preschool education in which these articles, including Boocock's, are published.
8. For a succinct anthropological discussion of these concepts, see Hendry (1987: 39–41). For an architectural study of Japan's management and organization of space in terms of such cultural categories as *uchi* and *soto*, see Greenbie (1988).
9. Endless studies, reports, surveys, and narratives document the close tie between women and home; domesticity and femininity in Japan. A recent international survey conducted for a Japanese housing construction firm, for example, polled couples with working wives in three cities, finding that 97% (of those polled) in Tokyo prepared breakfast for their families almost daily (compared with 43% in New York and 34% in London); 70% shopped for groceries on a daily basis (3% in New York, 14% in London), and that only 22% of them had husbands who assisted or were willing to assist with housework (62% in New York, 77% in London) (quoted in *Chicago Tribune* 1991). For a recent anthropological study of Japanese housewives in English, see Imamura (1987). Japanese

sources include *Juristo zōkan sōgō tokushu* (1985); *Mirai shakan* (1979); *Ohirasori no Seifu kenkyūkai* (1980).

10. My comments pertain directly, of course, to only the women I observed, interviewed, and interacted with at the one private nursery school serving middle-class families in urban Tokyo. The profusion of *obentō*-related materials in the press plus the revelations made to me by Japanese and observations made by other researchers in Japan (for example, Tobin et al. 1989; Fallows 1990), however, substantiate this as a more general phenomenon.

11. To illustrate this preoccupation and consciousness: during the time my son was not eating all his *obentō* many fellow mothers gave me suggestions, one mother lent me a magazine, his teacher gave me a full set of *obentō* cookbooks (one per season), and another mother gave me a set of small frozen food portions she had made in advance for future *obentōs*.

12. My son's teacher, Hamada-sensei, cited this explicitly as one of the reasons why the *obentō* was such an important training device for nursery school children. "Once they become *ichinensei* (first-graders) they'll be faced with a variety of food, prepared without elaboration or much spice, and will need to eat it within a delimited time period."

13. An anonymous reviewer questioned whether such emphasis placed on consumption of food in nursery school leads to food problems and anxieties in later years. Although I have heard that anorexia is a phenomenon now in Japan, I question its connection to nursery school *obentōs*. Much of the meaning of the latter practice, as I interpret it, has to do with the interface between production and consumption, and its gender linkage comes from the production end (mothers making it) rather than the consumption end (children eating it). Hence while control is taught through food, it is not a control linked primarily to females or bodily appearance, as anorexia may tend to be in this culture.

14. Fujita argues, from her experience as a working mother of a daycare (*hoikuen*) child, that the substance of these daily talks between teacher and mother is intentionally insignificant. Her interpretation is that the mother is not to be overly involved in, nor too informed about, matters of the school (1989).

15. "*Boku*" is a personal pronoun that males in Japan use as a familiar reference to themselves. Those in close relationships with males—mothers and wives, for example—can use *boku* to refer to their sons or husbands. Its use in this context is telling.

16. In the upper third grade of the nursery school (*nenchō* class; children aged five to six) my son attended, children were ordered to bring their *obentō* with chopsticks and not forks and spoons (considered easier to use) and in the traditional *furoshiki* (piece of cloth which enwraps items and is double tied to close it) instead of the easier-to-manage *obentō* bags with drawstrings. Both furoshiki and chopsticks (*o-hashi*) are considered traditionally Japanese and their usage marks not only greater effort and skills on the part of the children but their enculturation into being Japanese.

17. For the mother's role in the education of her child, see, for example, White (1987). For an analysis, by a Japanese of the intense dependence on the mother that is created and cultivated in a child, see Doi (1971). For Japanese sources on the mother-child relationship and ideology (some say pathology) of Japanese motherhood, see Yamamura (1971); Kawai (1976); Kyūtoku (1981); *Sōrifu seihonen taisaku honbuhen* (1981); *Kadeshobo shinsha* (1981). Fujita's account of the ideology of motherhood at the nursery school level is particularly interesting in this connection (1989).

18. Women are entering the labor market in increasing numbers yet the proportion to do so in the capacity of part-time workers (legally constituting as much as thirty-five hours per week but without the benefits accorded to full-time workers) has also increased. The choice of part-time over full-time employment has much to do with a woman's simultaneous and almost total responsibility for the domestic realm (*Juristo* 1985; see also Kondo 1990).

19. As Fujita (1989: 72–9) points out, its mothers are treated as a separate category of mothers, and non-working mothers are expected, by definition, to be mothers full time.

20. Nakane's much quoted text on Japanese society states this male position in structuralist terms (1970). Though dated, see also Vogel (1963) and Rohlen (1974) for descriptions of the social roles for middle-class, urban Japanese males. For a succinct recent discussion of gender roles within the family, see Lock (1990).

## REFERENCES

Althusser, Louis. 1971. *Ideology and Ideological State Apparatuses (Notes toward an investigation in Lenin and philosophy and other essays)*. New York: Monthly Review.

Asanuma, Kaoru. 1987. *"Ganbari" no Kozo (Structure of "Ganbari")*. Tokyo: Kikkawa Kobunkan.

Barthes, Roland. 1957. *Mythologies*. Trans. by Annette Lavers. New York: Noonday Press.

Boocock, Sarane Spence. 1989. "Controlled Diversity: An Overview of the Japanese Preschool System." *The Journal of Japanese Studies* 15(1): 41–65.

*Chicago Tribune*. 1991. "Burdens of Working Wives Weigh Heavily in Japan." January 27, Section 6, p. 7.

Cummings, William K. 1980. *Education and Equality in Japan*. Princeton, NJ: Princeton University Press.

Doi, Takeo. 1971. *The Anatomy of Dependence: The Key Analysis of Japanese Behavior*. Trans. by John Becker. Tokyo: Kodansha Int'l. Ltd.

Dore, Ronald P. 1965. *Education in Tokugawa Japan*. London: Routledge and Kegan Paul.

Duke, Benjamin. 1986. *The Japanese School: Lessons for Industrial America*. New York: Praeger.

Fallows, Deborah. 1990. "Japanese Women." *National Geographic* 177(4): 52–83.

Fujita, Mariko. 1989. "'It's All Mother's Fault': Childcare and the Socialization of Working Mothers in Japan." *The Journal of Japanese Studies* 15(1): 67–91.

Greenbie, Barrie B. 1988. *Space and Spirit in Modern Japan*. New Haven, CT: Yale University Press.

Hendry, Joy. 1986. *Becoming Japanese: The World of the Pre-School Child.* Honolulu: University of Hawaii Press.

_____. 1987. *Understanding Japanese Society.* London: Croom Helm.

Horio, Teruhisa. 1988. *Educational Thought and Ideology in Modern Japan: State Authority and Intellectual Freedom.* Trans. by Steven Platzer. Tokyo: University of Tokyo Press.

Imamura, Anne E. 1987. *Urban Japanese Housewives: At Home and in the Community.* Honolulu: University of Hawaii Press.

*Juristo zōkan Sōgōtokushu.* 1985. Josei no Gensai to Mirai (The present and future of women). 39.

*Kadeshobo shinsha.* 1981. *Hahaoya (Mother).* Tokyo: Kadeshobo shinsha.

Kawai, Hayao. 1976. *Bosei shakai nihon no Byōri (The Pathology of the Mother Society—Japan).* Tokyo: Chuo Koronsha.

Kondo, Dorinne K. 1990. *Crafting Selves: Power, Gender, and Discourses of Identity in a Japanese Workplace.* Chicago, IL: University of Chicago Press.

Kyūtoku, Shigemori. 1981. *Bogenbyo (Disease Rooted in Motherhood).* Vol. II. Tokyo: Sanma Kushuppan.

Lewis, Catherine C. 1989. "From Indulgence to Internalization: Social Control in the Early School Years." *Journal of Japanese Studies* 15(1): 139–157.

Lock, Margaret. 1990. "Restoring Order to the House of Japan." *The Wilson Quarterly* 14(4): 42–49.

Marx, Karl, and Frederick Engels. 1970 [1947]. *Economic and Philosophic Manuscripts,* ed. C. J. Arthur. New York: International Publishers.

*Mirai shakan.* 1979. Shufu to onna (Housewives and Women). Kunitachishi Komininkan Shimindai-gaku Semina-no Kiroku. Tokyo: Miraisha.

Nakane, Chie. 1970. *Japanese Society.* Berkeley: University of California Press.

*Ohirasori no Seifu kenkyūkai.* 1980. Katei Kiban no Jujitsu (The Fullness of Family Foundations). (Ohirasōri no Seifu Kenkyūkai-3). Tokyo: Okurashō Insatsukyōku.

Peak, Lois. 1989. "Learning to Become Part of the Group: The Japanese Child's Transition to Preschool Life." *The Journal of Japanese Studies* 15(1): 93–123.

Richie, Donald. 1985. *A Taste of Japan: Food Fact and Fable, Customs and Etiquette, What the People Eat.* Tokyo: Kodansha International Ltd.

Rohlen, Thomas P. 1974. *The Harmony and Strength: Japanese White-Collar Organization in Anthropological Perspective.* Berkeley: University of California Press.

_____. 1983. *Japan's High Schools.* Berkeley: University of California Press.

_____. 1989. "Order in Japanese Society: Attachment, Authority and Routine." *The Journal of Japanese Studies* 15(1): 5–40.

Sano, Toshiyuki. 1989. "Methods of Social Control and Socialization in Japanese Day-Care Centers." *The Journal of Japanese Studies* 15(1): 125–138.

*Shufunotomo Besutoserekushon shiri-zu.* 1980. Obentō 500 sen. Tokyo: Shufunotomo Co., Ltd.

*Shufunotomohyakka shiri-zu.* 1981. 365 nichi no *obentō* hyakka. Tokyo: Shufunotomo Co.

*Sōrifu Seihonen Taisaku Honbuhen.* 1981. *Nihon no kodomo to hahaoya (Japanese mothers and children): Kokusaihikaku (international comparisons).* Tokyo: Sōrifu Seishonen Taisaku Honbuhen.

Tobin, Joseph J., David Y. H. Wu, and Dana H. Davidson. 1989. *Preschool in Three Cultures: Japan, China, and the United States.* New Haven, CT: Yale University Press.

Vogel, Erza. 1963. *Japan's New Middle Class: The Salary Man and His Family in a Tokyo Suburb.* Berkeley: University of California Press.

White, Merry. 1987. *The Japanese Educational Challenge: A Commitment to Children.* New York: Free Press.

Yamamura, Yoshiaki. 1971. *Nihonjin to Haha: Bunka Toshite No Haha no Kannen Ni Tsuite no Kenkyu (The Japanese and Mother: Research on the Conceptualization of Mother as Culture).* Tokyo: Toyo-shuppansha.

# *"Single Women Are Bitter"*:
## The Gendered Production of Affective States in Chile

### Nia C. Parson

During the past two decades, a "global feminist consensus" has emerged around the pervasive nature and unacceptability of gender violence against women (Johnson 2009). Forms of gender violence have been addressed as pressing public health and public policy issues by the United Nations, the World Health Organization, and the International Criminal Court, among other international bodies. In conjunction with this historically

Nia C. Parson, Nia C. 2001. "Single Women Are Bitter": The Gendered Production of Affective States in Chile. in *Gender in Cross-Cultural Perspective,* Caroline B. Brettell, Carolyn F. Sargent, eds., Upper Saddle River, NJ: Prentice-Hall.

novel global attention to gender violence against women, women's equality emerged in the 1990s as an important concern for many Latin American states recovering from recent histories of dictatorship (Alcalde 2010; Htun 2003; Jelin and Hershberg 1996). Chile, the focus of this chapter, emerged at the forefront of this region-wide move toward legislation of gender equality as an official cornerstone of the state's modernization project and the effort to recuperate a democratic government in the wake of the authoritarian regime of Pinochet from 1973 to 1990 (on Pinochet's regime see: Collier and Sater 2004; Loveman and Lira 2002; Salazar and Pinto 1999).

In the late 1980s, Chilean women's rights groups linked the broader struggle against the dictatorship and for democratic reform to women's citizenship rights under their slogan "Democracy in the Home and in the Country" (Baldez 2002; Gaviola et al. 1994; Kaplan 2004). Since 1990, women's legal rights have steadily improved and the National Women's Service (*Servicio Nacional de la Mujer*-SERNAM) has been charged with integrating gender equality throughout the state's policies (Franceschet 2003; SERNAM 2000). The first quantitative study of domestic violence was published in 1994, and documented the gravity of the problem; 60% of women reported having experienced some form of domestic violence during their lifetimes (Larrain 1994: 52). This stunning finding was upheld in a 2001 SERNAM survey where 50.3% of women reported having experienced some form of domestic violence, 34% reported physical and/or sexual violence, and 16.3% reported psychological violence only (SERNAM 2002: 17, 19).

The first Family Violence Law was passed in 1994, and state-funded agencies for women who suffered domestic violence emerged in the 1990s, including Family Care, one of the agencies where I conducted fieldwork in the 2000s. Due to these changes, women who suffered domestic violence were able to access novel legal, psychotherapeutic, social service, and narrative structures to describe and protest domestic violence. Since the early 1990s, women's rights advocates have continued to push for and achieve state-level reforms. Most notably, divorce became legal in 2004 and in 2005 Congress passed a reformed version of the Family Violence Law. My research in Santiago, Chile, which also grew out of these local and global contexts, spanned over nineteen months between 2000 and 2009. During this time, I engaged in various participant observation activities and interviews at two institutions that offered services for women who had suffered domestic violence, which I call Safe Space (a nongovernmental organization) and Family Care (a governmental agency). I conducted life history narrative interviews with 18 women who had suffered domestic violence and sought help at one of these institutions, and several group interviews with these women (see Parson 2010a, 2010b, n.d.).

Anthropologists have begun to identify the roles of the state and in particular, judicial systems, in shaping intimate, gendered violence against women cross-culturally (Adelman 2004; Haldane 2008; Hautzinger 2007; Lazarus-Black 2007; Merry 2006; Van Vleet 2002). As Sally Engle Merry (2000: 257) in her ground-breaking work on domestic violence and the law in Hilo, Hawai'i, noted:

> there are deep connections between control over the body and control over the state . . . These spheres that

generally seem separate and separable are in historical practice intimately joined.

My research on domestic violence in Chile reveals some of the implications of this intertwining of "control over the body and control over the state" in terms of women's affective states, drawing from an understanding of individuals as shaped by intersubjective engagements with others (Jackson 1998). Intersubjectivity is a concept that points to how a person's subjective experience, her lived experiences of herself and the world, is inextricably and constantly reshaped by and through her interactions with others. A focus on intersubjectivity highlights how over the life course, what in Western modes is thought of as a fixed, individual "self," is in fact constantly shifting and changing. My analysis in this chapter shows how new legal mechanisms for women who suffer domestic violence produce novel intersubjective experiences with officials of the state for these women, thereby shaping their affective states—that is, their emotional experiences—in new ways through their novel relationships to the state.

In particular, this chapter shows the relationships of deeply engrained gender ideals, novel judicial interventions, and affect in women's experiences of domestic violence and help-seeking. To do so, the first part of the chapter details the binding nature of the various gendered ideals of women's roles as bearers of respectability and morality in the family. The second part of the chapter reveals how women's experiences in the judicial system often acted to reinforce these gender expectations that women felt contributed to their suffering. This analysis shows how the state is an important site for the reproduction of gendered notions of womanhood so strongly rooted in Chilean society and is therefore also an important site for reproducing gender violence against women and the emotional suffering this violence produces. It demonstrates how state, violence, and affect are entangled in gendered ways.

## "RESPECTABILITY" AND GENDERED MORALITIES

In many women's narratives that emerged during my interviews with them, the binding nature of the cultural ideals of women's "respectability" became apparent. As Hodgson and McCurdy (2001: 6) have noted in African contexts, "gendered norms of 'respectability' often become the basis for local and even national moral and social orders." Since women are the bearers of morality, the moral fabric of society itself is threatened when women do not perform their gender roles that make them "respectable." "Respectability" in the Chilean context includes women's upholding of dominant gender roles in the home, a major part of which includes maintaining a unified family and projecting an idealized image of that family (see also Hirsch 2003).

Many of the women I interviewed expressed that they had felt pressured to marry and/or to remain in abusive marriages, in order to maintain their respectability. They felt that they had to protect their family's image, even at the expense of their own suffering. In a group interview at Family Care, women discussed a variety of common sayings that they had heard since childhood, which they felt reflected broader cultural pressures for women to remain in abusive relationships. These included, "A woman who is not married cannot be happy," "Single women are bitter," "A happy, stable woman has a [male] partner at her side," and "He who loves you beats you." The pressures that these common sayings produced comprise an important part of what Pierre Bourdieu calls the *habitus* (Bourdieu 1990). For Bourdieu, the habitus consists of the "principles which organize and generate practices," but which are not regulated by formal laws, rules, and norms, and are instead, "collectively orchestrated without being the product of the organizing action of a conductor" (Bourdieu 1990: 53).

Many women expressed to me that they felt that the "honor" of the family was at stake in their decisions to marry and/or remain with an abusive husband. During a group interview at Family Care, Celia, for example, talked about how her mother had warned her that if she did not get married to the father of her unborn child (the man who abused her) she would shame the whole family. Celia said:

> I think that it also influenced [my decision to marry] when my mother told me, "You have to marry." I was going to be a single mother . . . So she said, "I really do not want one of my daughters to have a child as a single woman because that would be a dishonor for my family." My mother pressured me [asking], "When are you going to marry? When? . . . " Without saying that it was my mother's fault what I chose, one feels pressured.

In this instance, her mother patrolled the boundaries of respectability for her daughter and deemed marriage necessary to protect her family's "honor" (see also Abu-Lughod 2002; Wikan 2008). Another woman participating in the group interview responded to Celia's narration of the pressures she experienced to get married, saying:

> And I bet that, even when you were girlfriend/boyfriend, you saw that it was already problematic [i.e., that he was violent], because the same thing happened to me, the same. My mother pressured me.

Someone else in the group noted that even after she told her parents about the violence she suffered, they pressured her to stay with her husband because they were married. She suffered, "abuse, beatings, insults." She explained:

> He didn't let me eat, all of those things; he took me by force to have sex. And it was so much that I didn't talk to anyone, that I started [to have] headaches, physical body problems. My heart was accelerated. I thought that something was wrong with my heart . . . With time, I [decided] to separate, and my father, along with my mother, wouldn't accept that from me . . . They told me that since I was married, I had to [stay with him]. So I continued living like that [i.e., married to her abusive husband].

Iris, who sought help at Safe Space also explained to me that

> Mothers always tell you—my mother did it on many occasions—that one has to . . . talk through it [the violent relationship] and keep him there. My mother-in-law [did] the same, [saying] that I had to have patience . . . They weren't the best people [to talk to about my problem].

In all of these instances, the woman's parents pressured her into marrying or staying in a marriage even when she was experiencing domestic violence. This speaks to the importance of marriage, especially for women, in Chilean society.

During the group interview at Family Care, the consensus was that negative cultural ideas about single women abounded in their life worlds. Several women noted the tendency of neighbors to talk negatively about single women in the neighborhood behind their backs, which women I interviewed individually also told me. They expressed that single women, but more specifically, separated women, are often considered "dangerous." Single women, they said, represent a threat to happy marriages and especially a threat to married *women*, as single women may "steal" a husband. Several of the women discussed this during the group interview:

> – I think that . . . at least here, in Chilean society, a separated woman isn't well looked upon, because being married gives one status.
>
> – Respect.
>
> – Exactly, and moreover . . . there are a lot of married women who see a threat in the separated woman. Women will say, "This is a danger for the neighborhood."
>
> – I have a friend who has been separated for a long time . . . and she lives on a street, and all of the married women in the other houses hate her, *hate* her, only because she is separated, because they say that when she passes by she looks at their husbands or flirts . . .
>
> – The thing is that the married woman sees a danger in the separated woman.
>
> – It's that for men we separated women are more interesting. We are an easy prey for them. That's the thing,

for a man the separated woman is easy, because she is already separated, has children . . . If he wants to go to bed with her, he knows he will be able to. I mean, for men, men think they [i.e., separated women] are easy.

- In fact for women they are a danger, because of what you said. Her husband [referring to another woman in the group], if I'm not mistaken, told her, "You have a friend who is separated. Don't get together with her."

- [The other woman responded] Of course, he didn't let me [see friends]. Friends weren't useful. One shouldn't have separated female friends. And well, [other] friends either, because they were like a bad example and weren't good for anything.

- It's that you know . . .

- . . . It's because seeing a separated woman, there is always going to be the commentary, "For *some* reason he left her."

When I asked the women in the group interview the follow-up question, "For a man who is separated, is it the same as for women who are separated?," they resoundingly agreed that it is not. Men who are separated are not looked down upon, they agreed, and are often instead objects of pity. Here is the conversation in response to my question about how separated or single men are perceived:

- He is a free being.
- Neither a married nor single man has been looked at badly because of the things he does . . .
- *Machismo* exists.
- It's like a separated man is calmer.
- I don't have a negative concept of a separated man.
- You know what happens? Here the society sees a guy who's separated and looks at him with pity. "Poor thing, he's separated." She left him.
- And especially if he is left with the children.
- Exactly.

Another woman noted that

Those of us who are here have all been abused, but still . . . if we separate [from our abusive partners], the man will look like the victim, even though it's the other way around [people would say]: "You [the woman] must have done something [to cause this situation]."

This reflects the cultural notion that a breakup in the family is the responsibility of the woman, as it implies that she has not fulfilled her role as guardian of family unity and family image. This is a very powerful way that women are often constrained by dominant gender roles and encouraged to stay in a violent relationship. To leave a relationship, even if it is violent, implies that a woman has somehow brought this misfortune on herself by failing in her primary role as mother and

moral caretaker of the family. Women often have this idea internalized, as Luz explained: "This feeling of being like the base of the family is very pronounced in women."

In protesting a violent intimate relationship, women often felt that they were not only breaking with expectations about their responsibility for maintaining family unity, but also that they were subverting the gendered expectations of women as guardians of their families' *images*. The imperative for women to remain married is a gendered facet of what Chilean anthropologist Sonia Montecino (1996) has named "*Culto a la apariencia*" or "Cult of Appearance," which points to a cultural emphasis on "keeping up appearances." When a woman leaves an abusive partner, she therefore also subverts a more generalized cultural imperative to "keep up appearances." Women's subversion of such gender roles by breaking the silence of domestic abuse can be threatening to the accepted, normative power structures that undergird society. It may threaten their identities as "respectable" women and as legitimate actors within family and society, and the social abandonment is an implicit threat (see Biehl 2005).

Maca, whom I interviewed at Family Care in 2003 spoke poignantly to the ways in which silences about domestic violence can be related to women's gendered concerns over protecting family image. Maca suffered violence in her family as a child and witnessed her father's constant abuse of her mother. At 14-years-old, she was raped and as a result became pregnant with her first child. From then on, she had several boyfriends, and she explained that all of her relationships with them were filled with violence, which she accepted as normal because of her experiences as a child. She married her current, abusive husband when she was 26, about 20 years before our conversation in 2003. Maca explained that she had fallen in love with him because he fulfilled, "a paternal role," and, "He was like my leader. Just the fact of him being military personnel meant that he had power, and he also had power over me." He had worked for 29 years in the Chilean Army, throughout the dictatorship, until around 2002. He first beat Maca when she was four months pregnant with their first child, and he became very jealous and controlling. He constantly accused her of adultery, about which she told me: "I can't explain how it feels to be accused of something you didn't do . . . Never have I been able to feel the sensation, that, 'Ahhh [sigh of relief], today I am free. No one is going to tell me anything [that I have to do].'" She felt like she was treated as a servant in her own home. "I have always carried the weight of the household [the kids, housework, etc.]. He was the provider, nothing else," she told me, adding, "I always kept my problems inside . . . for image . . . always to project a good marriage, good children." She sought help at Family Care, and she said, "Even now I feel watched and patrolled . . . It's exhausting . . . There are moments when I fall and don't know how to get back up again." Indeed, as we spoke, she continuously and anxiously looked out the window of the therapist's office where we were sitting to check for her husband's car. Her fear was palpable.

For twenty years of their relationship, Maca avoided talking about the abuse with others. She feared that speaking the truth about the violence that shaped her life in so many ways would shatter the image of her family, which was of the utmost importance to maintain. It was more detrimental to speak the truth than to hold it inside, projecting for others the image that she supposed they wanted to see. Perhaps speaking the truth in this case was made more difficult by the authority conferred on her husband through his long-term service in the military. His service spanned the entire dictatorship, and the authoritarian ethic of the military and Pinochet's nationalism left no room for those who might raise their voices in opposition. The situation in the home mirrored this at least to some extent in Maca's mind, evidenced by her statement that, "Just the fact of him being military personnel meant that he had power, and he also had power over me." Echoing Maca's concerns with maintaining family image, in a group interview at Family Care, another woman noted:

> One, sometimes, doesn't do things [i.e., seek help for the violence] because of, "What they will say?" . . . the neighbors, because they give you a hard time . . . I should have separated right away, but you know what I thought: "What will people think?," the neighbors, my mother's friends, my friends . . . I think that for [fear of] "What they will say?" I stayed [in the violent relationship].

There were other powerful reasons women sought to maintain their families intact. In a group interview Sara, her voice filled with emotions of sadness, pain and regret, brought up religion as another dimension of the imperative to maintain "respectability" by staying in a marriage, even when it was abusive. In a group interview, she explained why for her the anguish over this expectation did not end with her separation from her abuser:

> I am Catholic, and for me a religious marriage was very important because I swore in front of God a promise, so when I left my house [i.e., when she left her abusive husband], I questioned myself a lot about all of these things because sometimes I feel that I didn't come through on my promise to God. Because I swore in the good times and bad, in the adverse and favorable. I sometimes feel

guilty and like a sinner because I didn't keep my promise until the end.

She also expressed great sadness about this during an individual interview with me, when she remembered that she used to think, "I wanted to marry him. I'm going to have to take the responsibility [and stay in the marriage]. That's that." She clearly had vestiges of this thinking deeply rooted within her.

## STATE INTERVENTIONS IN INTIMATE RELATIONSHIPS

Women's narratives make clear that gender role expectations and imperatives revolve around women's responsibilities to maintain family unity and family image as part of their performance of a respectable femininity. How, then, do these gendered facets of women's social lives interact with the state's novel attention to domestic violence as an object of public policy? In particular, how has the Family Violence Law of 1994, the first ever in Chile, interacted with the dominant gendered ideals that women discussed so notably in their interviews with me in 2003? My research revealed that while this law intervened in new ways in family lives on behalf of women, in its enactment by institutions and officials of the state, it also reinstated and reproduced many of the binding gender role expectations that women felt constrained them.

For example, the state encouraged women's reconciliation with their abusive partners as *the* solution when women recurred to the legal system to use the Family Violence Law to protest the abuses they suffered. The court's main goal with the 1994 Family Violence Law was the unity of the family. As the Chilean Constitution of 1980 states, "The family is the fundamental nucleus of society" (Gobierno de Chile 1980). Therefore, the state's patriarchal protection of women from their abusive partners was deemed important in order to preserve the good of the family and therefore the good of the nation. A Chilean police manual excerpt reflects this ethic:

> [With the Family Violence Law] the legislature has attempted to bring the necessary protection to the family . . . *The family is the fundamental nucleus of society* . . . Therefore, the material in analysis is of the greatest importance for the development of the family and national well-being, and because of this, demands that the employees charged with receiving reports of family violence, specifically the Chilean Police, [give] opportune and efficient attention to those affected. (Carabineros de Chile 1999: 22463, Author's emphasis)

Officially, domestic violence deserved the state's attention because it threatened the family and therefore the nation. Put another way, judicial interventions forced women to take on a "victim role," a subordinate gender role performance commensurate with women's subordinate positions in family and society, in order to claim the new form of gendered citizenship made available to them.[1]

Overwhelmingly, in interviews in 2003 and 2009, women expressed to me their profound distress over the treatment they had received under this new law and the mechanisms it provided them to protest the intimate abuses they suffered. Many of their complaints were related to critiques of how the judicial system maintained the kinds of cultural assumptions about male dominance that I discussed previously. In their narratives of their distress some of what Das has identified as, "the structures of legitimacy through which suffering is imposed on the powerless" became visible (Das 1995: 139). The involvement of the Chilean state, in the form of the judicial system, was a major force at work in the processes of individualizing suffering and embodied distress for these women, in gendered ways.[2] In so doing, the state played a role in maintaining the gendered power inequalities between men and women in society and the cultural imperatives to perform a "respectable" femininity by maintaining family unity and image at the cost of their own suffering or even death.

Women I spoke with often launched complaints about the treatment they received in the judicial system. They noted that *machista* (sexist) judges were not attentive to their real needs, and that clerks of court often did not respond appropriately. For example, Luz told me about how she had encountered a court clerk who did not bother to write down her statement and who tried to dissuade her from filing a complaint. Marisol too described to me how a court clerk failed to take her testimony seriously and instead was friendly to her abusive husband, and in another instance, the court clerk gave her misinformation about her rights to obtain her own court records. Women also experienced inordinately long delays in judicial responses, what Lazarus-Black (2007) has identified in Trinidad as *time lags*. Such time lags are especially detrimental in such cases, since it is so difficult for women to report in the first place and then to maintain action against the violence. Often, negative interactions with the justice system in fact served to exacerbate mental and physical health complaints. These represent some of the limitations of the "cultural power of law" (Merry 2000). Put another way, this can be conceptualized as the power of the law to impact emotional states.[3]

## WOMEN'S NARRATIVES OF STATE AND AFFECT

We turn now to Dalia's narrative, which exemplifies clearly how the state's actions and inactions interacted with gendered ideologies around respectability to produce intense emotional suffering for her. Dalia felt she had been steeped in the deeply entrenched cultural ideologies of gender expectations for women. She explained to me that in her family she was taught *machismo*, which influenced her to stay in the abusive relationship. She said:

> Here [in Chile] from the time one starts out, from the time one is a girl, they are always teaching that, at least in my family it was like that, the woman has to follow the man in whatever he does. Because he is her husband she has to obey him. I was raised by my aunts. These aunts in one moment of my marriage, when I told them that I was having problems . . . once it went so far that one of my aunts told me "Jesus Christ bore the cross for us, and the sentence for all of us was that we had to bear our personal crosses. This [the violent relationship] is the cross that befell you, and you have to bear it." This is what they're teaching one from youth.

She continued:

> I told another aunt that he was jealous, [and she said], "Then you better not wear those short skirts. You better put on a longer skirt." I mean, she was always on his side, doing things so that he wouldn't get upset. That's something that one drags with her from what's taught from generation to generation, that one has to be submissive, has to obey, has to lower her head. It's difficult to struggle against that, because it comes from teachings from the past, to be, in this way, legitimizing machismo.

In order to fulfill her most basic role as a person in relationship with other people, Dalia was taught that she had to perform the dominant gender roles appropriate for women, including being "submissive," having "to obey" and "lowering one's head." She was to submit to whatever punishments her husband saw fit to subject her, and to refrain from complaining about such abuse to family and friends. She was to "deal with it" without considering the costs to herself. Jennifer Hirsch (2003) describes a similar ethic for women of this generation in Mexico. The costs of breaking with these norms, in fact, were billed as being far too great for Dalia to risk.

Even so, Dalia struggled from within her ongoing abusive relationship to improve her quality of life, and sought help from Safe Space in 2000.[4] In 2002, about a year after she completed therapy at Safe Space, she decided to make another bold move and go to the courts to file a case against her husband. After ten months, she had heard nothing. She became extremely frustrated when the court psychologist "misplaced" her report needed by the court in order to give Dalia an answer to her case and made her feel that they did not find it important enough to garner their attention. She was exasperated with contacting the courts since she never received an answer. She told me, angrily:

> They make the laws, but there the laws stay, stored away . . . I even regret having done it [gone to court]. It's that simple, because I haven't achieved anything. Judicially I didn't succeed in removing him from the house to do therapy as I wanted, which is what I asked that time in the hearing. I didn't succeed in that because he simply said that he wouldn't leave the house, period . . . They asked him, "Are you willing to leave the house?" [And he said] "No, because this is my house."

She felt that she had actually lost by bringing the court case, as she believed this prompted her abusive husband to take "revenge" against her by disinheriting their children from a house he owned prior to the marriage. She expressed with resentment and fatigue in her voice that, "with the famous court case, the only thing I achieved was to leave my children with less for the future."

All of this contributed to perpetuating and aggravating Dalia's negative emotional state. She explained to me that her depression at the time of the interviews was linked to her exasperation with the failure of the legal system to address her case. She described her emotional state in the following way:

> that feeling of being diminished intellectually, I think that is a product of all of this. And these last few days, I haven't been sleeping, 2–3 hours without being able to sleep, tossing and turning, thinking about the same thing. That is also triggered by the same. It's not voluntary . . . What I would like most would be to sleep all night, but I can't. So, that must be a product of the same thing. Nervousness and everything, it manifests in this way. For that reason, I would like to . . . see if I can continue [with therapy]. They say that here there's no therapy anymore.

Dalia had conceptualized solutions and sought help to realize her vision for her life outside of the gender expectations that she felt largely bound her, but instead experienced negation of her suffering from the state.

Similarly, Sonia was buoyed by her experiences at Safe Space and generated some "transformative ties" (Parson 2010b) there, but she was undermined by her interactions with a government-run legal assistance institution and the courts themselves. In addition to incompetent officials and the time lags she experienced, she felt that her femininity and her very personhood as a mother were attacked. She said with frustration:

> [They] didn't help me . . . I went twice. The first was to demand child support . . . I talked with a social worker . . . From there we went three times, and then they passed us off to a lawyer . . . Up to the present day, the lawyer never did the document the way she was supposed to. Because what happened was that I asked for a petition for child support, and she put in a petition for visitation. I was not asking for visitation, I was asking for child support, and the only thing that happened was that they gave him a lot visitations for the almost nothing of money he wanted to give me. So, in the end, nothing happened . . . In the end it was all red tape. I lost two years.

In addition to the lawyer's negligence in this case, she treated Sonia abusively, calling her a "bad mother." Sonia told me, "from then on I didn't want to go again. I didn't want to do any of the procedures." Sonia's history of help-seeking in the courts was marked by intertwined emotional distress and humiliation and the practical failure of the system. She told me the outcome of her attempts to seek protection through the novel state law:

> In the end what happened was . . . the lawyer didn't send the documents to the court . . . and I went to see what had happened with the documentation. They told me no [nothing had happened], because the lawyer did not [submit them] . . . Another lawyer was designated, and they told me then that, "The papers are worthless. You have to do everything over again." So that is a loss of money, loss of time. So, I preferred not to do anything more. So what happens a lot of times is that, these foundations here . . . instead of helping a woman, they intimidate her more. They further destroy her . . . One is in pain, and the only thing one wants is help with a problem. Instead of helping her, they humiliate her more and [create] more problems in the end . . . The lawyer humiliated me a lot that time that I talked with her . . . I believe that nobody, nobody has the right to call a person a bad mother if she doesn't know her . . . From then on I didn't want to do anything, going to the foundations.

Sonia was enduring the weight of almost unbearable emotional pain and reaching outside of herself for help in easing that burden. Instead of finding relief, the mechanisms of the state compounded her anguish. Her difficulties in the justice system led to her sense that it was useless to look to the state to help lessen the violence that engendered her emotional pain and torment. Again, for Sonia, like others, the state was intimately involved in her suffering, which shaped her life and possibilities in gendered ways.

Similarly, court officials treated Iris, another woman who suffered domestic violence and sought help at Safe Space, in a sexist and negating manner, often enacting versions of an authoritarian masculinity promoted by the state during the dictatorship. Meanwhile, the court insisted on a solution that included reconciliation, though Iris made clear that this was not her goal. The judicial process dictated that Iris and her abusive husband be in the same room to make their respective cases to the judge, whose state mandate was to encourage the couple to reconcile and to maintain the family's unity. This configuration in the courtroom ignored the power dynamics of abusive relationships, gender inequality in the wider society, and social pressure for the woman to acquiesce in the face of "authority," and generated a diversity of problems for women I interviewed.[5] Iris explained her experiences in the court: "We had a clerk of the court who was not on my side . . . In a civil court, the idea is always to come to a reconciliation, because [otherwise] the family violence court case is very long."

She continued:

The clerk asked if there was some possibility of reconciliation . . . I told him no, because I was living with my mother at that time, and I had a lot of money problems. I wasn't working. He didn't give me anything, because in that way he was punishing me for all that was happening [taking him to court, separating, etc.] . . . I didn't see any sign from him that he wanted to resolve our problems. Then [the court clerk] said to [the abuser]: "Look, gentleman [*caballero*], what do you think? Are you thinking of getting back together with your Mrs. [*su Señora*]?"

At this moment, the court clerk ignored Iris's wish *not* to reconcile, and she felt that he treated her as though she were a child meanwhile he engaged her abusive husband in a conversation about how to resolve the situation, effectively ignoring her presence and petitions. Iris described the scenario:

[The court clerk said] "You're going to have to give her money" . . . And he [the abuser] promised that he would find help for his alcohol problem . . . But none of this was a judge's order . . . So it ended there, the reconciliation . . . It was very little that I achieved.

In many cases, women reported similarly patronizing attitudes of judges and court officials, which often contributed to a sense of limited possibilities and difficulties within the justice system. In these instances, the judicial system and therefore the state acted to perpetuate the same gendered ideals of womanhood and femininity based on expectations about women's roles in their families.

## CONCLUSIONS

The Chilean state over the past two decades has intervened in novel though still gendered ways in intimate relationships and within families, with the express goal of gender equality. The Family Violence Law of 1994 was a major step toward this goal, since it represented the very first time the authority of the state was used to explicitly name domestic violence against women as socially unacceptable. This law and other state-level allocations of resources gave women some legal and therapeutic mechanisms to protest their situations and challenge the abuse they suffered. The state has made these women's attempts at escape and reform of violent relationships possible in a variety of ways. New laws, agencies, and other resources enable women to come to new terms with intimate abuses they have suffered—and in the process—new ways of being in the world have been made possible.

It is important to note that the women whose narratives inform this chapter constitute a very unique population. They all managed to seek help at institutions where they were offered support for the effects of the domestic violence they suffered. They learned a language to speak about their suffering of intimate gender-based violence and thereby challenge some of the power structures that undergird gender inequality within their intimate relationships and in society more generally. Their ability to come forward to name the violence is a novel form of sociality constituted through their use of language to take control over pain and fear. Elaine Scarry (1985) in *The Body in Pain* notes that pain has the power to erase language, and similarly, once pain is made expressible then it can be addressed and its power minimized. The 1994 Family Violence Law made it possible for the first time for Chilean women who suffered domestic violence to speak to the state in a way that made their pain and suffering legible. However, as women's frustrations with the judicial system's practices make clear, a language for *speaking* to the state did not necessarily mean that their suffering was fully *heard* nor *acted upon* in ways they deemed adequate.

The matter of domestic violence grows out of, in part, gendered assumptions about women's "respectability" as defined by their roles in their families. While such cultural notions are never completely fixed, certainly they emerged strongly in women's narratives as crucial aspects of what bound them in the abusive intimate relationships in which they found themselves. Women's narratives voiced concerns about how in the practice of carrying out the new Family Violence Law, the state acted to reproduce gendered ideals of women's crucial roles as guardians of their families' unity and image. The 1994 Family Violence Law explicitly encouraged reconciliation and the maintenance of the nuclear family unit—for the good of the family, the children, and thereby, the nation. In this way, the state opened up possibilities for reworking affective and filial ties but failed to address the underlying gendered cultural assumptions and expectations around women's roles and the family, ideals that women themselves expressed constitute part of what bound them into abusive relationships. The state acted to uphold gendered ideals about women's roles in maintaining family unity, which provide fertile ground for domestic violence. Many women expressed feelings of depression, sadness, and frustration linked to their interactions with the judicial system. That is, the state in its policies and practices, as they are carried out by the individuals who are its agents, is still intimately tied to and regulates women and women's bodies, albeit in new ways.

## NOTES

1. I expand on this argument about gendered citizenship and the victim role in *Curing Inequalities: Gendered Violence, Affect and the State in Chile* (Parson, 2013). Here I draw from crucial anthropological insights into how official, technological categorizations of affliction constitute important routes to make claims on structures of biopolitical authority such as the state and international organizations (Fassin and Rechtman 2009; Petryna 2002).

2. Becker, Beyene, and Ken's (2000) phenomenological analysis of traumatic memories of Cambodian refugees who were survivors of the Khmer Rouge regime points to how violent memories are embodied and cannot be undone. Traumatic memories are intertwined in the refugees' narratives with their accounts of various forms of illness experience and bodily complaints. Becker et al. (2000) therefore point to how traumatic memories cannot be disarmed but are relived at the subjective level of the body and self. The distress of traumatic memory is embodied. Becker et al. (2000) draw here from, among others, Thomas Csordas' (1990) argument for embodiment as a key framework for anthropological analysis.

3. In her analysis of the relationships of emotional distress and *la violencia* in El Salvador during the 1980s, Janis Jenkins (1991), building in part on Delvecchio Good and Good's (1988) work in Iran, has proposed a conceptual bridge to think about the relationships of a state constructed "political ethos" and subjective emotional states—to which she referred as the "state construction of affect."

4. Alcalde (2010) has observed that women in Peru in similar situations of captivity have a variety of ways of resisting intimate, gendered abuse they suffer and asserting their agency.

5. Srimati Basu (2012) analyzes similar constraints on women's agency in Family Violence courts in Kolkata, India through her ethnographic examination of mediation proceedings there.

## REFERENCES

Abu-Lughod, Lila. 2002. "Do Muslim Women Really Need Saving?: Anthropological Reflections on Cultural Relativism and Its Others." *American Anthropologist* 104(3): 783–790.

Adelman, Madelaine. 2004. "The Battering State: Towards a Political Economy of Domestic Violence." *Journal of Poverty* 8(3): 45–64.

Alcalde, M. Cristina. 2010. *The Woman in the Violence: Gender, Poverty, and Resistance in Peru*. Nashville: Vanderbilt University Press.

Baldez, Lisa. 2002. *Why Women Protest: Women's Movements in Chile*. New York: Cambridge University Press.

Basu, Srimati. 2012. "Judges of Normality: Mediating Marriage in the Family Courts of Kolkata, India." *Signs: Journal of Women in Culture and Society* 37 (2): 469-492.

Becker, Gay, Yewoubdar Beyene, and Pauline Ken. 2000. "Memory, Trauma and Embodied Distress: The Management of Disruption in the Stories of Cambodian Exiles." *Ethos* 28(3): 320–345.

Biehl, João Guilherme. 2005. *Vita: Life in a Zone of Social Abandonment*. Berkeley: University of California Press.

Bourdieu, Pierre. 1990. *The Logic of Practice*. Cambridge: Polity.

Carabineros de Chile. 1999. Boletín De Instrucciones De Carabineros De Chile No. 478. Santiago, Chile.

Collier, Simon, and William F. Sater. 2004. *A History of Chile, 1808–2002*. 2nd ed. New York: Cambridge University Press.

Csordas, Thomas J. 1990. "Embodiment as a Paradigm for Anthropology." *Ethos* 18(1): 5–47.

Das, Veena. 1995. *Critical Events: An Anthropological Perspective on Contemporary India*. Delhi: Oxford University Press.

Delvecchio Good, Mary-Jo, and Byron J. Good. 1988. "Ritual, the State, and the Transformation of Emotional Discourse in Iranian Society." *Culture, Medicine and Psychiatry* 12(1): 43–63.

Fassin, Didier, and Richard Rechtman. 2009. *The Empire of Trauma: An Inquiry into the Condition of Victimhood*. Princeton: Princeton University Press.

Franceschet, Susan. 2003. "'State Feminism' and Women's Movements: The Impact of Chile's Servicio Nacional de la Mujer on Women's activism." *Latin American Research Review* 38(1): 9–40.

Gaviola, Edda, Eliana Largo, and Sandra Palestro. 1994. *Una historia necesaria: Mujeres en Chile 1973–1990*. Santiago, Chile: Akí & Aora Ltda.

Gobierno de Chile. 1980. *Constitución Política de la República de Chile*. Valparaiso, Chile: Gobierno de Chile.

Haldane, Hilary. 2008. "Varying Perspectives on the Treatment of Domestic Violence in New Zealand." *Practicing Anthropology* 30(3): 50–53.

Hautzinger, Sarah. 2007. *Violence in the City of Women: Police and Batterers in Bahia, Brazil*. Berkeley: University of California Press.

Hirsch, Jennifer. 2003. *A Courtship after Marriage: Sexuality and Love in Mexican Transnational Families.* Berkeley: University of California Press.

Hodgson, Dorothy Louise, and Sheryl McCurdy. 2001. *"Wicked" Women and the Reconfiguration of Gender in Africa.* Portsmouth, NH: Heinemann.

Htun, Mala. 2003. *Sex and the State: Abortion, Divorce, and the Family under Latin American Dictatorships and Democracies.* New York: Cambridge University Press.

Jackson, Michael. 1998. *Minima Ethnographica: Intersubjectivity and the Anthropological Project.* Chicago: University of Chicago Press.

Jelin, Elizabeth, and Eric Hershberg. 1996. *Constructing Democracy: Human Rights, Citizenship, and Society in Latin America.* Boulder, CO: Westview Press.

Jenkins, Janis Hunter. 1991. "The State Construction of Affect: Political Ethos and Mental Health among Salvadoran Refugees." *Culture, Medicine and Psychiatry* 15(2): 139–165.

Johnson, Janet Elise. 2009. *Gender Violence in Russia: The Politics of Feminist Intervention.* Bloomington: Indiana University Press.

Kaplan, Temma. 2004. *Taking Back the Streets: Women, Youth, and Direct Democracy.* Berkeley: University of California Press.

Larrain, Soledad. 1994. *Violence Behind Doors: The Battered Woman.* Santiago, Chile: Editorial Universitaria.

Lazarus-Black, Mindie. 2007. *Everyday Harm: Domestic Violence, Court Rites, and Cultures of Reconciliation.* Urbana: University of Illinois Press.

Loveman, Brian, and Elizabeth Lira. 2002. *El espejismo de la reconciliación política: Chile 1990–2002.* Santiago, Chile: LOM.

Merry, Sally Engle. 2000. *Colonizing Hawai'i: The Cultural Power of Law.* Princeton, NJ: Princeton University Press.

———. 2006. *Human Rights and Gender Violence: Translating International Law into Local Justice.* Chicago: University of Chicago Press.

Montecino, Sonia. 1996. *Madres y huachos: Alegorías del mestizaje chileno.* Santiago, Chile: Editorial Sudamericana.

Parson, Nia. 2010a. "'I Am Not [Just] a Rabbit Who Has a Bunch of Children!': Agency in the Midst of Suffering at the Intersections of Global Inequalities, Gendered Violence, and Migration." *Violence Against Women: An International and Interdisciplinary Journal* 16(8): 881–901.

———. 2010b. "Transformative Ties: Gendered Violence, Forms of Recovery, and Shifting Subjectivities in Chile." *Medical Anthropology Quarterly* 24(1): 64–84.

———. 2013. *Traumatic States: Gendered Violence, Suffering and Care in Chile.* Nashville: Vanderbilt University Press.

Petryna, Adriana. 2002. *Life Exposed: Biological Citizens after Chernobyl.* Princeton, NJ: Princeton University Press.

Salazar, Gabriel, and Julio Pinto. 1999. *Historia Contemporánia de Chile I: Estado, Legitimidad, Ciudadanía.* Santiago, Chile: LOM.

Scarry, Elaine. 1985. *The Body in Pain: The Making and Unmaking of the World.* New York: Oxford University Press.

SERNAM. 2000. *Plan de Igualdad de Oportunidades entre Mujeres y Hombres: Lineamientos Generales.* Santiago, Chile: Servicio Nacional de la Mujer, Gobierno de Chile.

Van Vleet, Krista A. 2002. "The Intimacies of Power: Rethinking Violence and Affinity in the Bolivian Andes." *American Ethnologist* 29(3): 567–601.

Wikan, Unni. 2008. *In Honor of Fadime: Murder and Shame.* Chicago: University of Chicago Press.

# Women's Autonomy, Islam, and the French State

## John R. Bowen

In a nation where some think that assimilation means looking the same, the appearance in the late 1980s of an increasing number of women wearing Islamic scarves troubled many French public figures. The overblown reaction in the French media comparing the presence of three girls in scarves to the Munich capitulations of the 1930s started off two decades of hyperbole and anxiety. Feminists took the lead, recalling their historic struggle with the Catholic Church for control of their reproductive rights. But they faced a dilemma: feminism in France, as elsewhere, had championed a woman's right to choose how to treat her own body, so what could be said to Muslim women

who claimed to choose to wear Islamic headscarves (*foulard* or *hijâb*) or, later, a veil covering all but the eyes (*niqab* or, in France, *burqa*)? Feminists and others seeking to limit these choices of dress had to discount the very possibility of choice, by claiming that radical Islam undermined women's autonomy and thus made choice meaningless. I consider here the uses made of the scarves by Muslim women and changing critical responses to these practices in public and legal arenas.[1]

### VEILING AND THE REPUBLIC

Although French theories and anxieties about Islamic headscarves date back to colonial days, they took on added force in the late 1980s, when fears about international political Islam combined with the greater

Bowen, John R. 2001. Women's Autonomy, Islam, and the French State in *Gender in Cross-Cultural Perspective*, Caroline B. Brettell, Carolyn F. Sargent, eds., Upper Saddle River, NJ: Prentice-Hall.

domestic visibility of Islam to produce new cries of alarm. Objections to public wearing of Islamic scarves were based on multiple claims: some expressed concern that boys would place pressure on girls to don scarves; others argued that the scarves had become signs of political Islam; still others claimed that the scarf stood for the oppression of women. The debate centered on the presence of such scarves in schools, and produced a 2004 law banning conspicuous signs of religious affiliation from public schools (Bowen 2007). No longer were scarves (*foulards*) at issue, but rather the inexact term "the veil" (*le voile*).

"The veil" evokes memories of colonial rule, when women's dress became salient signs of affiliation to indigenous or to Western modes of life. In metropolitan France, however, for the first half of the twentieth century, Islam was largely present in the form of North African male workers, cycling between their birthplaces and France to work in factories. But during the postwar recovery period, the Algerian War, and especially after the 1970s, Algerians and other Muslims from northern and western Africa increasingly settled in France with their wives and children. Labor migration as such ended, and was replaced by immigration based on family reunification, which usually meant that a man or woman came to join her or his lawfully resident spouse in France. The presence of Islam now included settled women and men.

By the 1980s, the sons and daughters of those resident Muslim families began to come of age and to search for their identities. Many found it difficult to find acceptance as French, despite their status as French-born citizens. Prejudice against Muslims and against people of color, coupled with bitter memories of the recent conflict, made their acceptance difficult, and the economic downturn of the 1970s exacerbated tensions. But the new generation did not find themselves at ease "back home" either: they were French in some way, and not Algerian or Senegalese.

For some of these young Muslims, their search led them to study Islam as a formal religion rather than to inherit it as a tradition. They began to attend lectures by charismatic young preachers, read books that taught them "true Islam," and frequented mosques. They were joined by new immigrants from Muslim countries, and some members of the new generation of younger Muslims, French- and foreign-born, began to "look Muslim." Some younger women wore scarves that were pulled tightly over their heads, concealing their hair and ears. This contrasted with their mothers' scarves, worn more loosely and casually. They might wear a simple scarf, or a combination of two head coverings, one covering the forehead and the other the top of the head and the shoulders, or a more unified garment including head covering, blouse, and skirt.

The many elements that make up markedly Islamic dress—head coverings, blouses and tunics, skirts and trousers, and perhaps gloves—tended to be reduced by critical French observers to the matter of how, and how much of, the head was covered, as an index of radicalism. Did the particular scarf cover the ears, leave the roots of the hair exposed or not, come down over the forehead? For many non-Muslims in France, these differences in degree of covering came to signify differences in the degree of religiosity or of moral difference being signaled by a Muslim woman.

Then, in September 1989, three girls showed up for the first day at their middle school wearing Islamic dress. At another moment, the girls' appearance would likely have passed unnoticed. Girls had been showing up at school with scarves for years, and either attended the school with their scarves or agreed to remove them during class. But now international "political Islam" appeared on magazine covers in the form of Iranian women in Islamic dress, adding a new dimension to scarves in French schools. The conjuncture of domestic and foreign threats made scarf-wearing into a national "affaire." After initial negotiations, the local dispute became a national incident, on which everyone eventually had to take a position. The mass media jumped on the incident. The Right was relatively silent on the issue but the Left was sharply split. Antiracism groups associated with the Socialist Party emphasized the Revolution's legacy of equality and laïcité (secularity), and resisted allowing religion into the schools.

## WHY WEAR HEADSCARVES?

When two sociologists, Françoise Gaspard and Farhad Khosrokhavar (1995), set out to interview girls and young women who wore headscarves, they found two major motives. Some wore a headscarf as a way to satisfy their parents and ease their transition across the line of puberty and into late adolescence. Many of these girls adopted it during middle school years but then abandoned it during high school. They were not necessarily regular practitioners of their religion. But other, usually older girls began to wear a headscarf as part of a conscious effort to create a new identity as they entered or left high school. For them, wearing a scarf was part of two simultaneous processes: defining themselves in Islamic terms and entering the world of postsecondary education and work. These women tended to be educated and successful, and to regularly pray, fast, and observe dietary rules.

Subsequent studies, most carried out toward the end of the 1990s, confirmed Gaspard and Khosrokhavar's findings that young women chose to adopt Islamic dress, including a headscarf, as part of efforts to negotiate a sphere of social freedom and authority and to construct an identity as a Muslim, and that the relative weight of these two reasons depended on her age and social situation. Many of the women also drew explicit contrasts between, on the one hand, their own efforts to become better Muslims through study and regular prayer and, on the other, the ways in which their parents merely followed tradition, by, for example, fasting and sacrificing but rarely praying. Some distinguished between two ways of wearing a headscarf: "as in the old country" (letting some hair show), and wearing it in an Islamic manner (covering the hair). In other words, donning the scarves was part of a quest for autonomy.

When in 2004 I interviewed three young women of Algerian Kabyle background living in Paris, I found that they had thought long and hard about how to meet their sense of their faith requirements and how to present themselves to the outside world (Bowen 2007: 72–81). One had begun wearing a hijâb (the term she used) at fifteen, and had kept it ever since. Highly educated in Algeria and in France, she was a cosmopolitan intellectual and cultural actor, working for various foreign cultural services over the years while she completed a thesis on U.S. history.

A second had not been brought up to obey religious commandments, and had learned about Islam during her high school years by reading books suggested to her by friends. She began to wear a small hair band with her friends "so that people would get used to it" before eventually putting on a scarf when "one day I decided to become a woman, not a boy." She began by responding to God's call to her while adapting myself to her society "and I succeed at this, for, when I am at work I wear the scarf not like I have it now [tightly covering her head] but on top, swirled around like the Africans; that seems to work. I began wearing it as an intern and it worked. This shows that there are still people who are very tolerant. They knew me before and after the scarf and their attitude did not change. They saw that my work did not change, even got better."

The third young woman did not wear a headscarf. She observed Ramadan and avoided pork but no longer performed the prayer, insisting that her dress and her religious practices were entirely a matter of personal choice.

These three women have fashioned their public behavior both by their personal religious trajectories and by their sensibilities as to how others do and will see them. Each describes a long history of reflecting on religion and on her ability to adequately carry out religious obligations. And each also makes decisions about dress and behavior that take into account others' reactions. They reject the idea that headscarves are "religious signs" because they see the decision to wear hijâb as the result of a personal commitment rather than an intention to signal something to others. But they also acknowledge that making that decision does and should take into account the responses of others and the importance of schooling, work, and family; they see the effects that such a decision has (on attractiveness as a potential spouse, for example) as part of the entire picture. Wearing a headscarf in France today involves negotiations, anticipations, and weighing of benefits and costs. It is not simply an "obligation" or a "choice," but a subtle dance among convictions and constraints.

## CHARGING SEXUAL OPPRESSION

But this autonomy has been dismissed by many who have supported laws restricting women's clothing. Some claim that the headscarf has the objective meaning of oppression. On the Stasi Commission, advocates of a law were able to frame the question in those terms; Bernard Stasi himself declared that "the voile is objectively a sign of women's alienation" (*Ouest France*, October 31, 2003). Proponents of a law made at least three distinct claims: schoolgirls were pressured by men and boys to wear the voile; the voile intrinsically attacked the dignity and the equal status of women; and, because it did so, it encouraged violence against women living in the poor suburbs. These claims strengthened the antiscarf movement in two major ways. First, they strongly appealed to French principles and emotions concerning the equality and dignity of women. Who could defend oppression of women? Secondly, they shifted the debate from the constitutionally sensitive area of religious freedom and onto the legally safer ground of protecting rights and dignity. But what precisely was the argument? Teachers and principals testifying to the Stasi Commission mentioned the voile unfavorably, but the practices that they most strongly denounced were anti-Semitic remarks, proselytizing, praying in school, arguing over history lessons, and general incivility. What was the scarf's role in encouraging these practices? Did wearing a scarf contribute to anti-Semitism? How was that the case?

The most successful answer went as follows. The voile stands for the oppression of women and also acts as a direct mechanism for their oppression in France. Boys terrorize girls, and the voile normalizes this state of affairs. Girls who refuse to wear the voile are told they should wear it and thus are oppressed even within the school. Foreign Islamists are manipulating girls, making them think they need to wear the voile. Do away with the voile and you would do these girls a big favor. At last, a clear, causal argument! And, in the end, it won the day.

With few exceptions, feminists who were active during the 1970s in the *Mouvement de la libération des femmes*

(MLF, Women's Liberation Movement) opposed wearing the voile. Their opposition was clear early on, when, during the first "affaire" of 1989, most major feminist leaders and organizations denounced the scarves. The leading feminist politician at the time, Yvette Roudy of the Socialist Party, claimed that "the foulard is the sign of subservience, whether consensual or imposed, in fundamentalist Muslim society. . . . To accept wearing the voile is tantamount to saying 'yes' to women's inequality in French Muslim society." The Family Planning Movement (*le Mouvement pour le planning familial*, one of the MLF's pillars) agreed: "Women wearing the voile are a sign of sexist discrimination incompatible with a secularist and egalitarian education" (*Le Monde*, October 25, 1989).

Two long-standing feminists intervened in the 2003 debates over the law, in an article whose title proclaims their position: "Laïcistes because feminists" (*Le Monde*, May 30, 2003). Although the term *laïciste* is usually employed to refer negatively to people carried away by their enthusiasm for *laïcité* (secularity), the two authors here embrace it in order to attack the wearing of the voile. They begin by acknowledging that women or girls who wear the "Islamic veil" do so in the name of their freedom to practice their religion. However, they add, "wearing the voile is not only a sign of belonging to a religion. It symbolizes the place of women in Islam as Islamism understands it. That place is in the shadow, downgraded, and submitting to men. The fact that some women demand it does not change its meaning. We know that dominated people are the most fervent supporters of their domination."

They argue that laïcité presupposes a "neutral public space, free of any religious belief, where citizens develop under the same treatment, sharing common rights and duties, and a common good, all of which places them beyond discriminating differences." They call, in the end, for prohibiting the voile "in all places of teaching and of life together (*vie commune*) (school, university, business, government offices), and if attacks on women continue, forbidding the voile in the street."

Their article confronts two critical questions that arise once the debate has been reframed around women's rights rather than around the laïcité of the schoolroom: how broad should be the scope of a headscarf ban? And should one place any weight on the testimony of the girls in scarves themselves? The two questions are related. If the issue is keeping the schools free from outside pressures in order to allow pupils to learn in an atmosphere free of ideological pressures, then it makes sense to limit the ban on the scarves to the school grounds, or perhaps, as was the case in a number of schools, to the classroom. In class, all identities other than that of pupil in France are to be suppressed; in the rest of life, they may flourish, and freedom of religion requires that expressions of faith be permitted. Even if schoolgirls choose to wear the scarves, they still prevent the classroom from functioning as it should.

Now, however, the claim is that the voile is the symbol and instrument of broad, global forces that oppose French values, and that in particular oppress women. It no longer matters where the voile appears; it is equally noxious and dangerous in any public place—and why only in public places? It should be abolished everywhere that French people try to develop a life together, a *vie commune*. Such is Vigerie and Zelensky's argument, and their sentiments were shared by others. It was about this time, in May 2003, that one began to see banks, doctors' offices, and municipal offices refusing entry to women in headscarves, as well as cases where an ordinary person would ask a woman in a scarf to "leave this public place" on a bus or subway. The ambiguity of the French "public," which means sometimes "having to do with the State" and sometimes "out in public view," was at work here, generating or reinforcing a variety of norms about what such women should or should not do. For Zelensky and Vigerie, and I suspect for many French feminists, the relevant meaning of public is that of *la vie commune*, a notion which includes the workplace as well as the government office.

In this broader view of the problem, how to treat the girls' own views becomes more difficult. In the narrower argument concerning the school, one that starts from the legal and perhaps the philosophical requirements of laïcité, the claim that scarf-wearing girls have freely chosen their garments need not be refuted, because good pedagogy requires a scarf-less classroom whatever the pupils might think. In the broader argument that starts from the voile's socially corrosive force, however, statements by girls and women that they chose to wear headscarves must be addressed. What if they do not find the voile corrosive or oppressive at all?

## TELEVISION STRATEGIES

If giving voice to young women in headscarves might lead viewers to see things from their point of view, one can perhaps better understand why French television viewers seldom had to trouble themselves over such a possibility. During the critical period for shaping public opinion, from approximately April 2003 through February 2004, one seldom heard young Muslim women in headscarves setting out their positions on French television. An exception was the Lévy sisters, Alma and Lila, expelled from their *lycée* in fall of 2003, who appeared as foils for those who would defend the Republic.

The sisters appeared on February 19, 2004, on *Campus, le magazine de l'écrit,* a book-oriented talk show moderated by Guillaume Durand and shown regularly on France 2. Three of the evening's guests were the "moderate" Muslim author Malik Chebel, the strongly anti-Islamist author Martin Gozlane, and the very media-friendly Carmen bin Ladin, the ex-wife of Osama's brother.

That evening, moderator Duran let the sisters begin by explaining their decision to wear the voile; they state that the decision came from studying religious books, and not from any outside pressure. Lila: "We read the verse and then decided to wear the voile; but the four main scholars of Islam agree that it is required. . . . When we started to wear the voile, I knew no one who wore it, I did not know how it was considered." Moderator: "Do you plan to keep it for your life?" Lila: "Yes." Moderator: "Why? Good Lord! . . . and why 'good lord?'"! Alma: "Because it is our freedom of conscience, and I agree that what happens in the projects with girls who choose not to wear the foulard is terrible, but the solution is not to deny us our right to choose, but to guarantee everyone their rights."

Carmen bin Ladin picked up the questioning: "You consider that when women wear skirts men automatically think of sex and that you wear the voile to keep men from having impure thoughts, so you are in a state of submission." Bin Ladin then describes her life in Saudi Arabia as a life of submission to men, "it is in the very nature of the voile." She then turns to Alma and Lila and questions them: "You are very young and do not understand what the voile means for you as women. You are not like the others even though you say you are. Do you do sports?" Alma: "Yes, my best grades were in sports." BL: "Do you take off the voile for sports?" Alma: "No." "And you wear shorts?" "No one wears shorts, boys or girls." "My daughter wears team uniforms when she plays sports." "No one wears shorts." Bin Ladin, trying another tack: "Now women who come to Europe and refuse to be treated by a male doctor, that's the problem!"

The Lévys' efforts to focus on their real motives and choices in the specific French context are parried at each instance by claims about the voile's objectively sexist and Islamist meaning, best seen through the struggle of "sisters" in Muslim-majority countries, and the doubtless naiveté of the girls, objects of manipulation. Gozlan: "Every time there is an advance for women, Islamists react against it, as in Egypt in the 1920s, when feminists took off their voiles—yes it happened that way, Mesdemoiselles, and now in France les 'beurettes' are showing signs of a wonderful

integration, and so you see reaction, a new visibility of radical Islam, they bring out the voile. You say '[it is] your choice' but it is your choice in the context of a huge apparatus that encompasses you."

The most striking aspect of this and many other programs that appeared during this period, roughly late 2003 to early 2004, is the asymmetry of roles played by guests. Of course, hosts and commentators are expected to provoke and pose questions. But the guests, all of them invited on grounds that they had recently published books, were not all positioned in the same way. The journalist Sylvain Attal appeared as an expert, who informed us about anti-Semitism through his book and on the program. The authors Malik Chebel, Martine Gozlan, and Carmen bin Laden were asked about their books, but much less than they were asked to comment on (or simply intervened on their own to comment on) the persons and acts of the Lévy sisters. Alma and Lila, and secondarily their book, were the main object of discussion. Their claims, their choices, and their headscarves were the real text for the evening. They were only allowed to speak as examples of the problem, the real understanding of which was provided by the "experts." They do not have real autonomy; they have been duped into thinking they do, but their garments show otherwise.

## RAISING THE ANTE AGAINST AUTONOMY

By 2008, some officials had moved from condemning scarves in public spaces to condemning certain putative values shared by some Muslims, sometimes signaled by their choice of dress. Major roles were played by two of France's highest tribunals: the State Council, which rules on decisions from administrative bodies, and the Constitutional Council, which is asked to give opinions about the constitutionality of proposed or enacted laws. These decisions pushed further forward the argument that not all Muslim women can be presumed to be in a position to make their own decisions concerning their bodies, and that the decisions they have made are *ipso facto* signals of their unsuitability as autonomous citizens.

In June 2008, for example, the French State Council refused to grant French nationality to a woman from Morocco on the grounds that her religious practices had led her to hold values that ran counter to the equality of men and women and caused her to suffer from insufficient assimilation to become a French citizen: she had an "assimilation defect" (*défaut d'assimilation*) (Conseil d'État 2008). The woman had married a French convert to Islam who had requested that she wear a full-face covering (called a *burqa* by the court). She was reported to stay at home and to have insufficient knowledge of the right to vote and the basics of laïcité. She had met the formal conditions for citizenship, having waited the required period of time after marriage before requesting naturalization. However, at the government's request, the Council ruled that her failure to accept the values of women's equality made her unfit for French citizenship. They were careful not to make the couple's religion the explicit grounds for rejecting her request, in order to avoid a subsequent finding of unconstitutionality.

This decision had quick results. In July 2008, a housing authority in Vénissieux, a suburb of Lyon with a large Muslim population, refused to allow a family to occupy the apartment officially allotted to them because the wife wore a burqa. The letter of refusal repeated the words of the State Council's decision: "Madame wears the burqa, which characterizes a radical religious practice that is incompatible with the essential values of the French community and with the principle of the equality of the sexes" (*Le Monde* 2009).

Just over a year later, France was debating whether to ban the wearing of a face veil in public. Called the burqa in France but generally known as the niqab, the face veil generally leaves the eyes uncovered, sufficiently so that women have been allowed to drive while wearing the garment. In October 2010, Parliament passed such a law, notwithstanding an opinion by the State Council that such a law would unduly restrict religious freedom (Conseil d'État 2010). Because of uncertainty about whether the law would stand an eventual challenge, Parliament asked the Constitutional Council to rule on whether it was in accord with the Constitution. In upholding the law, the Council cited two principles. They argued, first, that covering the face "misrecognizes the minimal requirements of living in society" and, second, that those women who decide to wear a face veil "find themselves placed in a situation of exclusion and inferiority clearly incompatible with the constitutional principles of freedom and equality" (Conseil Constitutionnel 2010). Burqa-wearing violates minimal conditions for civic life, and it objectively reduces the autonomy of the wearer, regardless of her knowledge, capacities, or intentions, argued the Council.

These ideas have strong appeal for many in France. The decision evokes the idea that normal citizens are civil; they interact in the "shared life" of civic France. As Dominique Schnapper put it in a public forum in July 2010, giving a justification for banning burqas: "France is the country where everyone says 'bonjour'" (presentation, Université d'été d'Irrisarry, July 6, 2010). Implicitly, one cannot really greet one another from behind a veil. Here we have essentially the same claim about communication made by British minister Jack Straw a few years earlier, but whereas Straw made

it on personal grounds—he would not speak with someone whose face was covered—Schnapper made it on grounds of a theory of civic life.

This argument draws on scares about "communalism" most commonly heard in the 2001–2003 period, scares that draw from the fundamental French ambivalence concerning intermediate groups. Communalism (*communautarisme*) is used in French to evoke a sense that a group defined in ethnic or religious terms has closed itself off to others in the society; "intermediate groups" include guilds, unions, and ethnic associations.

Similar concerns were evinced then about refusals to shake hands: France is the country where one says bonjour and then shakes hands. Issues intersect here: a distaste for "communalism," an embrace of "mixité," which tends to mean in particular mixing of men and women, and gender equality. This set of concerns appears time and again in French public discussions. In the unusually hot summer of 2003, a debate erupted over the existence of women-only hours at some municipal swimming pools in several French cities. In southern Lille, one of the four municipal pools had offered such hours for two years when reporters finally stumbled on the practice in June 2003. The mayor, Martine Aubry, who later became Socialist Party leader, had authorized the special hours upon request from a number of women of North African background. In other parts of France, Jewish associations had successfully petitioned to have sex-segregated hours at municipal pools, with no media attention. But in 2003, the existence of the "Arab" women-only hours shocked certain commentators. The president of the association Europe and Laïcité, Etienne Pion, considered the arguments for women-only hours—modesty, ease with babies—to be but "alibis to force the acceptance of communalist principles" (Bowen 2007: 109–110).

A more striking instance where modesty is declared to take the back seat to mixité comes from the well-known 2002 book, *The Lost Territories of the Republic* (Brenner 2002: 194–195). One (female) lycée teacher describes how she and others felt challenged on a deeper level by Islamic attire.

"The striking fact here is that girls and boys cover themselves with a kind of violence that makes one ill at ease. It seems that prior to the religious meaning of head coverings is the notion that the head ought to be covered because the body itself presents a problem. That is what one finds again and again, in pupils' refusal to attend swimming class, in their challenges to mixité, in the problems they raise on account of modesty [*pudeur*]. We even had to refuse their demand for separate toilets for girls and boys, so as to avoid an anti-Republican politics, even though the poor treatment suffered by girls justified it for their sexual protection."

In this striking account, the field of combat is no longer the school but the girls' attitudes toward their own bodies. A measure that might strike an outsider as normal (building separate toilets), and that in this school would have protected girls from aggressions by boys, was considered to send the wrong message about Republican norms. Providing separate toilets would have meant accepting, even promoting, shame about one's body. It is this shame that lies behind wearing a headscarf and refusing to play sports with boys. It must be fought even at the cost of the girls' well-being. Gender mixing fights bad Islamic values and affirms both sociability and gender equality.

## CONCLUSION

From 1989 through 2011, a recurring justification for state regulation of Muslim women's bodies has been their putative lack of autonomy. In the classroom, boys tell girls how to dress; the solution is to forbid girls to wear Islamic scarves. Lest they accept archaic Islamic ideas about sexuality, they should not be permitted to absent themselves from swim classes, or, when grown, from swimming in mixed company. Claims of modesty conceal oppression by Muslim men. Those who choose to wear a face veil show their inability or unwillingness to function as French citizens, so objectively contrary to French Republican values is that garment. Women who protest, those who say "it's my choice," are presumed to be dupes of Islamist ideology.

And yet, many young French Muslim women have made clothing choices precisely to negotiate space for their autonomy. For some, this has involved adopting Islamic dress as a way of convincing their parents that they can be trusted to success in French schools and careers. For others, it has been a way to make clear to the wider world who they are and how they choose to live their lives. Many younger women are trying out various ways of being in the French social world as religiously practicing people. Some of those ways involve clothing; others involve ways of speaking, shaking hands (or not) with men, carving out women's space, or finding Muslim space in cultural associations or mosque events. Much as Catholics and Jews have found ways of preserving religiosity in Republican France through the path of associational life—private schools, clubs, religious events—Muslims are only beginning to develop their social forms of a religious life. The challenge is perhaps greater for Muslim women, who must overcome presumptions of submission and oppression. For men and women, however, the issue remains the classic one of creating ways to, if one so chooses, fashion oneself as deeply Republican and deeply religious.

## NOTES

1. In this article, I draw on analyses already set out in Bowen (2007, 2011); see these works for the fuller arguments.

## REFERENCES

Bowen, John R. 2007. *Why the French Don't Like Headscarves: Islam, the State, and Public Space.* Princeton: Princeton University Press.

———. 2011. "How the French State Justifies Controlling Muslim Bodies: From Harm-based to Values-based Reasoning." *Social Research,* Summer 78(2): 1–24.

Brenner, Emmanuel (ed.). 2002. *Les territoires perdus de la République: Antisémitisme, racisme et sexisme en milieu scolaire.* Paris: Mille et une nuits.

Conseil Constitutionnel. 2010. Décision no, 2010-613 DC, October, par. 4. http://www.conseil-constitutionnel.fr/conseil-constitutionnel/francais/les-decisions/acces-par-date/decisions-depuis-1959/2010/2010-613-dc/decision-n-2010-613-dc-du-07-octobre-2010.49711.html.

Conseil d'État. 2008. *Mabchour,* req. n. 286798, juin 27.

Conseil d'État. 2010. *Étude relative aux possibilités juridiques d'interdiction du port du voile intégral.* mars 25.

Gaspard, Françoise, and Farhad Khosrokhavar. 1995. *Le foulard et la République.* Paris: La Découverte.

# VIII

# Gender, Household, and Kinship

The study of kinship has been central to cross-cultural research. Marriage customs, systems of descent, and patterns of residence have been described and compared in a range of societies around the world. At the heart of traditional studies of kinship is the opposition between the domestic domain, on the one hand, and the public, political, and jural domain on the other. Anthropologists, particularly those working in Africa, studied kinship in this latter domain. They delineated large corporate descent groups called lineages that managed property and resources and that were the basic building blocks of political organization (Fortes 1949, 1953). Marriage, for some kinship theorists, is a political transaction, involving the exchange of women between men who wish to form alliances (Levi-Strauss 1969; see also Ortner 1978). A woman, from this perspective, is a passive pawn with little influence over kinship transactions. She is viewed "in terms of the rights her kin have to her domestic labor, to the property she might acquire, to her children, and to her sexuality" (Lamphere 1974: 98). The dynamic, affective, and even interest-oriented aspects of women's kinship are essentially ignored in an approach that is rooted in androcentric principles: women have the children; men impregnate the women; and men usually exercise control (Fox 1967).

Recent critiques of the traditional study of kinship have pointed out that it is "no longer adequate to view women as bringing to kinship primarily a capacity for bearing children while men bring primarily a capacity for participation in public life" (Collier and Yanagisako 1987: 7). A gendered approach to kinship takes a number of different directions but focuses on the status of men and women in different kinship systems and on the power (defined as the ability to make others conform to one's desires and wishes) that accrues to women through their manipulation of social relations (Abu-Lughod 1993; Maynes et al. 1996). Cross-cultural variations in the status of men and women have been examined in relation to rules of descent and postmarital residence (Friedl 1975; Martin and Voorhies 1975). Among horticulturalists, for example, women have higher status in societies characterized by matrilineal descent (descent through the female line from a common female ancestor) and matrilocal residence (living with the wife and her kin after marriage) than in societies characterized by patrilineal descent (descent through the male line from a common male ancestor) and patrilocal residence (living with the husband and his kin after marriage). In matrilineal systems, descent group membership, social identity, rights to land, and succession to political office are all inherited through one's mother and in some cases constitute women's "webs of power" (Blackwood 2000).

When matrilineality is combined with matrilocal residence, a husband marries into a household in which a long-standing domestic coalition exists between his wife and her mother, sisters, and broader kin relations (Friedl 1975). These women cooperate with one another in work endeavors and provide mutual support. Although in a matrilineal system a man often retains authority over his sisters and her children, the coalitions formed by kin-related women can provide them with power and influence both within and beyond the household (Brown 1970; Lamphere 1974; Menon 1996) and also with a degree of sexual freedom. The important issue for women's status, as Schlegel (1972: 96) has argued, is not the descent system per se but the organization of the domestic group.

In contrast to matrilineal and matrilocal systems, in patrilineal and patrilocal societies, women marry in to their husband's household and family and hence do not have their own kin nearby. One of the classic examples of such a family has been the patrilineal extended Han Chinese family (Hinsch 2002; see also Rubie Watson in Section V of this book). A woman entered her husband's household as a stranger. She had to pay homage to her husband's ancestors, obey her husband and mother-in-law, and bear children for her husband's patrilineage. According to Margery Wolf (1972: 32), who carried out research in Taiwan, "a woman can and, if she is ever to have any economic security, must provide the links in the male chain of descent, but she will never appear in anyone's genealogy as that all-important name connecting the past to the future." Separated from her own kin, she could not forge lateral alliances easily. However, other opportunities were open to women that enhanced their power and status in patrilineal and patrilocal societies. After a Taiwanese wife gave birth to a son, her status in the household began to change, and it improved during her life course as she forged what Wolf has called a uterine family—a family based on the powerful relationship between mothers and sons. The subordination of conjugal to intergenerational relationships that is exemplified by the Taiwanese or classic Han Chinese case, as well as the opportune ways in which women take advantage of filial ties to achieve political power within and beyond the household, are apparent in other societies around the world—for example, in sub-Saharan Africa (Potash 1986).

The introduction of the one-child policy in China has had a significant impact on the traditional patrilineal Chinese family. In a single generation, the birth rate in China declined to 1.9 children per mother. Children are being brought up without siblings, and there are some scholars who have observed the emergence of more uxorilocal marriages where a husband takes up residence with his wife and her family (Hong 1987) as well as neolocal (an independent residence for a newly married couple) and nuclear families in urban areas. Perhaps most interesting is the impact on gender equality. Fong (2002), for example, has demonstrated that urban daughters who are only children have benefited from the one-child policy since they can garner parental attention and investment that they did not have when they were part of a family with brothers. She suggests that in this context daughters have the power to defy disadvantageous gender norms. The one-child policy has also opened up educational opportunities and new career paths to young women (Veeck, Flurry, and Jiang 2003).

China is also home to numerous ethnic minority populations (Harrell 1995) and among these populations are the matrilineal Mosuo or Na of the Himalayan region of southwest China. Mosuo households are composed of brothers and sisters who reside together throughout their lives sharing household tasks and raising the children of the women. The sexual partners of the women are neither present nor responsible for their biological offspring (Hua 2008; Shih 2010). Some scholars (Johnson and Zhang 1991) have used the term polyandry (where a woman has multiple husbands) to describe this marriage/family system while others have simply labeled it a "walking marriage" or "walking back and forth" (Shih 2010).

Whether or not polyandry is the right term to use to describe the practices of the Mosuo, it is one that has been applied to other Himalayan populations. In this book, Childs, Goldstein, and Wangdui discuss the practice of fraternal polyandry (a group of brothers who marry the same woman) among rural Tibetans. This system has created a surplus population of unmarried daughters who are viewed as a form of social capital by elderly parents who may not be treated well by an in-marrying daughter-in-law. These daughters provide various forms of social support (financial, emotional, nursing, etc.) to parents and are much appreciated. This chapter also raises the important issue of how the responsibilities for eldercare are gendered and vary cross culturally. In India, for example, such responsibilities often fall to the eldest son rather than to a daughter. In the Tibetan case, although there is a cultural preference for sons, parents have come to appreciate their daughters.

As discussed above, the early work on the traditional Chinese family suggested that even within a patriarchal and patrilineal system, women could manipulate kinship to their own advantage, something that Lamphere (1974: 99) has suggested gives them a measure of power. The strategic use of kinship by women has been identified in several other cultural contexts. Pioneering work by Carol Stack (1974) demonstrated how African-American families in a Midwestern town drew on kinship networks as a mechanism for economic survival. Through their domestic networks, women exchange a range of goods and services including childcare. They rely on one another and through collective efforts keep one another afloat. When one member of the network achieves a degree of economic success, she can choose to withdraw from kin cooperation to conserve resources. However, by reinitiating gift-giving and exchange, at some point she can easily reenter the system.

Sharon Hicks-Bartlett (in this book) offers a more recent portrait of poor African-American families in the United States who are coping with urban poverty. Her research population resides in a small black suburb outside a major Midwestern city, but they too call on family-based, helping networks to minimize risk and fulfill immediate needs. Hicks-Bartlett describes the emotionally draining and labor-intensive work of parenting in a neighborhood filled with drugs and violence. The necessity of hypervigilance means that women often call on kin to help them with their children so that they can work. Adult children also put aside self-interest to assist one parent in the care of the other. In the absence of public programs and facilities, it is the kinship networks that become the lifelines of the urban poor. It is kin who provide transportation, housing, food, and employment leads, in addition to childcare service. But, given the extent of poverty and hardship, the kin networks are often stressed and overwhelmed.

Afro-Caribbean families also confront conditions of economic uncertainty and stress. Research in the Caribbean region has generated a vigorous debate about a complex of characteristics, including female-headed households, women's control of household earnings and decision making, kinship networks linked through women, and the absence of resident men. This complex of characteristics has been referred to as matrifocality, a concept first introduced by Raymond Smith (1956) to describe the central position and power of the mother within the household. Rather than viewing these households as disorganized or pathological results of slavery and colonialism, anthropologists recently have stressed their adaptive advantages (Bolles and Samuels 1989) for women who are both mothers and economic providers.

Chamberlain (in this book) offers a somewhat different portrait of Caribbean families by focusing her attention on the role of kin, especially grandmothers and elderly aunts, in childrearing, particularly when mothers are absent from the country as a result of migration. This chapter offers some interesting comparisons with the Tibetan case because both essays address the relationships of the elderly to the households of their children; however, in the Tibetan case, the emphasis is placed on the social support flowing from children to their parents, whereas in the Caribbean case, it is the reverse—although at the end of their lives grandmothers and aunts discover that what goes around comes around as social support is then returned to them when they most need it. Through two rich case studies, Chamberlain demonstrates how these family forms and gendered responsibilities result not just from economic conditions but are also deeply embedded in the cultural context and characteristics of middle class as well as poor families.

Women-centered families like those of African-Americans and Afro-Caribbeans have been described for other parts of the world (Blackwood 2000; Tanner 1974). Both Brettell (1986) and Cole (1991) find such families among populations in northern Portugal and link them to a long history of male emigration. Whether in agriculture or in fishing, many women in northern Portugal must fulfill both male and female roles within the household. In this region, women often inherit significant property, and there is a tendency for matrilocal residence or neolocal residence near the wife's kin. This matrilateral bias is also apparent among Japanese-American immigrants in the urban United States (Yanagisako 1977). Manifested in women-centered kin networks, this bias influences patterns of coresidence, residential proximity, mutual aid, and affective ties. Rather than stressing the economic reasons for the maintenance of kinship ties, Yanagisako draws attention to the role of women as kin keepers who foster and perpetuate channels of communication and who plan and stage elaborate family rituals (Lomnitz and Perez-Lizaur 1987). Di Leonardo (1987) has in fact labeled the role of women in family rituals and holidays as "kin-work."

Families in the West and by extension marriage and parenting practices, as well as broader patterns of kinship, have been undergoing significant change. New reproductive technologies (see Ragoné in Section X) are redefining concepts of motherhood and new families are being created by lesbian and gay couples (Weston 1991), as well as by processes of divorce and remarriage (Simpson 1998) or transnational adoption (Dorow 2006). In this book, Lewin takes up the issues of gay fatherhood and Lesbian motherhood. She briefly traces the journey of gays and lesbians to greater acceptance, as well as their strategies of family formation, whether by bringing children born to a prior heterosexual marriage in to a gay or lesbian relationship, through adoption, or through some form of artificial insemination or surrogacy. She then turns to an exploration of the moral discourses of lesbian and gay parents as these pertain to ideas about motherhood and fatherhood. For lesbians, motherhood and womanhood are conflated and being a mother "trumps" other sources of identity, including sexual identity. This "natural" connection is less salient for gay father, but becoming fathers involves a significant change in a previous gay lifestyle. A sense of social responsibility appears to be particularly salient for these gay fathers. Lewin's discussion offers intriguing comparisons with Scheper-Hughes' discussion of motherhood (in Section I) and Townsend's discussion of fatherhood (in Section III).

Collier and Yanagisako (1987) have argued that gender and kinship are mutually constructed and should be brought together into one analytic field (see also Stone 1997). Kinship and gender are closely allied because they are both based in, but not exclusively determined by, biology and because what it means to be a man or a woman is directly linked to the rules of marriage and sexuality that a culture constructs. As Lindenbaum (1987: 221) has observed, "Relations of kinship are in certain societies, relations of production. If kinship is understood as a system that organizes the liens we hold on the emotions and labors of others, then it must be studied in relation to gender ideologies that enmesh men and women in diverse relations of productive and reproductive work. The variable constructions of male and female that emerge in different times and places are central to an understanding of the character of kinship."

## REFERENCES

Abu-Lughod, Lila. 1993. *Writing Women's Worlds: Bedouin Stories.* Berkeley: University of California Press.
Blackwood, Evelyn. 2000. *Webs of Power: Women, Kin and Community in a Sumatran Village.* Lanham, MD: Rowman and Littlefield.
Bolles, A. Lynn, and Deborah d'Amico Samuels. 1989. "Anthropological Scholarship on Gender in the English-Speaking Caribbean." In Sandra Morgen (ed.). *Gender and Anthropology,* pp. 171–188. Washington, DC: American Anthropological Association.
Brettell, Caroline B. 1986. *Men Who Migrate, Women Who Wait: Population and History in a Portuguese Parish.* Princeton, NJ: Princeton University Press.
Brown, Judith K. 1970. "Economic Organization and the Position of Women among the Iroquois." *Ethnohistory* 17: 151–167.
Cole, Sally. 1991. *Women of the Praia: Work and Lives in a Portuguese Coastal Community.* Princeton, NJ: Princeton University Press.
Collier, Jane Fishburne, and Sylvia Junko Yanagisako. 1987. *Gender and Kinship: Essays toward a Unified Analysis.* Stanford, CA: Stanford University Press.
Di Leonardo, Michaela. 1987. "The Female World of Cards and Holidays: Women, Family and the Work of Kinship." *Signs* 12(3): 440–453.
Dorow, Sara. 2006. *Transnational Adoption: A Cultural Economy of Race, Gender, and Kinship.* New York: New York University Press
Fong, Vanessa. 2002. "China's One-Child Policy and the Empowerment of Urban Daughters." *American Anthropologist* 104: 1098–1109.
Fortes, Meyer. 1949. *The Web of Kinship among the Tallensi.* London: Oxford University Press (for International African Institute).
_____. 1953. "The Structure of Unilineal Descent Groups." *American Anthropologist* 55: 25–39.
Fox, Robin. 1967. *Kinship and Marriage: An Anthropological Perspective.* Harmondsworth, UK: Penguin.
Friedl, Ernestine. 1975. *Women and Men: An Anthropologist's View.* New York: Holt, Rinehart and Winston.
Harrell, Stevan. 1995. *Cultural Encounters on China's Ethnic Frontiers.* Seattle: University of Washington Press.
Hinsch, Bret. 2002. *Women in Imperial China.* Lanham, MD: Rowman and Littlefield.
Hong, Lawrence K. 1987. "Potential Effects of the One-Child Policy on Gender Equality in the People's Republic of China." *Gender and Society* 1: 317–326.
Hua, Cai. 2008. *A Society without Fathers or Husbands: The Na of China.* Cambridge: The MIT Press.
Johnson, Nan E., and Kai-Ti Zhang. 1991. "Matriarchy, Polyandry and Fertility among the Mosuos in China." *Journal of Biosocial Science* 23: 499–505.
Lamphere, Louise. 1974. "Strategies, Cooperation, and Conflict among Women in Domestic Groups." In Michelle Z. Rosaldo and Louise Lamphere (eds.). *Woman, Culture, and Society,* pp. 97–112. Stanford, CA: Stanford University Press.

Levi-Strauss, Claude. 1969. *The Elementary Structures of Kinship.* Boston: Beacon Press.

Lindenbaum, Shirley. 1987. "The Mystification of Female Labors." In Jane Fishburne Collier and Sylvia Junko Yanagisako (eds.). *Gender and Kinship: Essays toward a Unified Analysis,* pp. 221–244. Stanford, CA: Stanford University Press.

Lomnitz, Larissa, and Marisol Perez-Lizaur. 1987. *A Mexican Elite Family, 1820–1980.* Princeton, NJ: Princeton University Press.

Martin, M. Kay, and Barbara Voorhies. 1975. *Female of the Species.* New York: Columbia University Press.

Maynes, Mary Jo, Ann Waltner, Birgitte Soland, and Ulrike Strasser. 1996. *Gender, Kinship, Power: A Comparative and Interdisciplinary History.* New York: Routledge.

Menon, Shanti. 1996. "Male Authority and Female Authority: A Study of the Matrilineal Nayars of Keral, South India." In Mary Jo Maynes, Ann Waltner, Birgitte Soland, and Ulrike Strasser (eds.). *Gender, Kinship, Power: A Comparative and Interdisciplinary History,* pp. 131–148. New York: Routledge.

Ortner, Sherry. 1978. "The Virgin and the State." *Feminist Studies* 4 (3): 19–35.

Potash, Betty (ed.). 1986. *Widows in African Societies.* Stanford, CA: Stanford University Press.

Schlegel, Alice. 1972. *Male Dominance and Female Autonomy: Domestic Authority in Matrilineal Societies.* New Haven, CT: Human Relations Area Files.

Shih, Chuan-Kang. 2010. *Quest for Harmony: The Moso Tradition of Sexual Union and Family Life.* Stanford, CA: Stanford University Press.

Simpson, Bob. 1998. *Changing Families; An Ethnographic Approach to Divorce and Separation.* Oxford: Berg Publishers.

Smith, Raymond. 1956. *The Negro Family in British Guiana: Family Structure and Social Status in the Villages.* London: Routledge and Kegan Paul.

Stack, Carol. 1974. *All Our Kin.* New York: HarperCollins.

Stone, Linda. 1997. *Kinship and Gender: An Introduction.* Boulder, CO: Westview Press.

Tanner, Nancy. 1974. "Matrifocality in Indonesia and Africa and among Black Americans." In Michelle Z. Rosaldo and Louise Lamphere (eds.). *Woman, Culture, and Society,* pp. 129–156. Stanford, CA: Stanford University Press.

Veeck, Ann, Laura Flurry, and Haihua Jiang. 2003. "Equal Dreams: The One Child Policy and the Consumption of Education in Urban China." *Consumption Markets & Culture* 6: 81–94.

Weston, Kath. 1991. *Families We Choose: Lesbians, Gays, Kinship.* New York: Columbia University Press.

Wolf, Margery. 1972. *Women and the Family in Rural Taiwan.* Stanford, CA: Stanford University Press.

Yanagisako, Sylvia Junko. 1977. "Women-Centered Kin Networks in Urban Bilateral Kinship." *American Ethnologist* 2: 207–226.

# *What to do with Unmarried Daughters?*
# Modern Solutions to a Traditional Dilemma in a Polyandrous Tibetan Society

## Geoff Childs, Melvyn C. Goldstein, and Puchung Wangdui

Similar to other societies that lack formal social security systems, the elderly in rural Tibet[1] depend on adult children to care for them in old age. Any changes in the ties that bind adult children to their parents can therefore affect the health and welfare of the elderly. Tibet is currently undergoing major social and economic transformations that are affecting domestic

Childs, Geoff, Melvyn C. Goldstein, and Puchung Wangdui. What to Do with Unmarried Daughters? Modern Solutions to a Traditional Dilemma in a Polyandrous Tibetan Society. *Journal of Cross Cultural Gerontology* 26 (1): 1-22.

relationships, gender ideologies, and gender roles. In the last decade, China has dedicated enormous resources toward improving the standard of living in Tibet. Policies aimed at achieving modernization are increasing opportunities for secular education, non-farm employment, and rural to urban migration (Goldstein, Childs, and Wangdui 2008, 2010). According to the seminal theory on aging and modernization (Cowgill 1974; Cowgill and Holmes 1972), the very forces of modernization that are now transforming Tibet can negatively impact the elderly by producing intergenerational competition, residential segregation, social distance, and an inversion of status.[2] The social, economic, and spatial mobility of children engendered by modernization is seen as a threat to the ability of families to provide care for aging members.

In this chapter, we use data collected in three Tibetan villages to demonstrate ways that externally-resident daughters can positively impact the lives of their aging parents. Deciding which children to keep as caretakers, and which to send out of the household, has always been an important decision for parents. In traditional Tibetan societies, daughters who moved out through arranged marriages were considered a net loss to the household, as epitomized by the proverb, "The hen eats at home and lays its eggs outside" (Pemba 1996: 81). Fraternal polyandry, a type of marriage in which two or more brothers share a wife, complicated matters by generated a surplus of potential brides. Simply put, there were more women than households into which they could marry. Retaining an unmarried daughter within the household was considered problematic due to potential conflicts that could erupt between her and her brothers' in-marrying bride, yet options for removing her from the household were limited and often left her vulnerable and impoverished. Nowadays, however, social and economic changes associated with modernization are creating new opportunities for parents to send daughters out in ways whereby they can gain financial independence and continue to provide support for their parents in old age.

To explore the evolving nature of relationships between parents and externally-resident daughters, we deploy the concept of social capital. Social capital refers to connections within and between social networks that facilitate action and promote cooperation between individuals. It is rooted in interpersonal relations that involve reciprocity over the life course, and functions as a resource that people can draw upon to solve problems or achieve objectives (Bourdieu 2001; Coleman 1988; Putnam 2000). Research in social gerontology has focused on filial norms as a dimension of social capital. Silverstein and colleagues (2006) argue that the resources parents invest in their children from birth to adulthood generate a reserve of social capital, and hypothesize that the social capital imbued in the relationship with adult children may lie dormant for many years, but can be activated during a time of need such as a health crisis. The key is to determine when certain members of a latent kinship matrix (the sum of family members who vary from potential to actual providers of support) become active in providing support for the elderly, and why.

In this chapter, we view some externally-resident daughters of Tibet's rural households—namely, beneficiaries of parental investments that facilitated financial independence and urban residence—as a novel form of social capital from which the elderly can solicit social support. Social support refers to various types of assistance a person can receive from others, and herein is divided into three categories: emotional support, caretaking assistance, and financial assistance. A fundamental point of this paper is that, compared with daughters who were sent as brides to other rural households, daughters who move out of their households through education or employment represent an important form of social capital because they possess a unique combination of income, urban residence, and greater freedom to assist aging parents. This combination enhances their ability to positively impact the lives of elderly parents by providing (1) leverage against coresident children who do not treat them well, (2) temporary places of refuge from ill-treatment at home, (3) caretaking services and financial support when they require hospitalization, and (4) financial resources which they can use whenever they want, for example, to pursue age-appropriate activities like pilgrimage.

Data presented in this chapter come from surveys and interviews conducted in three Tibetan villages between 2006 and 2009. The three villages, while not representing all of Tibet, were selected to meet a research design comparing a continuum of villages from relatively wealthy to relatively poor in a study of the impacts that modernization has on rural families. Sogang, the least affected by development, is in the upper part of a tributary river valley. Norgyong, the intermediate site, is situated below Sogang on the main river and is located immediately beside the rapidly growing town of Panam. Betsag, the third site, is located 10 kilometers from Shigatse, Tibet's second largest city, and represents a wealthy farming village that is heavily affected by modernization. Despite economic differences, the three villages are geographically close and are part of the same Tibetan sub-ethnic cultural and linguistic zone.

## MOVING CHILDREN OUT OF THE HOUSEHOLD

From the 1960s until the early 1980s, rural Tibet was organized into collectives. When that system was dismantled, the commune's land was divided equally, and the household resumed its role as the primary unit of landholding and farm production. This occurred in the context of an economic paradigm shift in China from an emphasis on common property and wealth equality during the Cultural Revolution, to an emphasis on individual initiative in Deng Xiaoping's market economy with socialist characteristics.

People in our fieldwork area responded by renewing the traditional corporate family system and reviving one of most salient strategies for advancing a family's economic interests—the practice of fraternal polyandry. This type of marriage creates a kind of stem family that is the functional equivalent of primogeniture in the sense that, with only one wife per generation, only one set of offspring (heirs) was produced thereby facilitating family land being passed along intact to the next generation. Also, fraternal polyandry concentrated male labor within the family, enabling it to pursue a broad range of economic activities. For example, one brother could herd the sheep in a mountain pasture, a second could manage the farm, and a third could concentrate on trading (Goldstein 1987). Consequently, after decollectivization, there was a major revival of fraternal polyandrous marriages throughout our study area (Goldstein et al. 2002, 2003; Jiao 2001).[3]

Filial piety is a deeply held value in Tibetan society: children are expected to express gratitude to their parents and provide care for them in old age. The question is who is best suited to care for aging parents? Because the Tibetan marriage system is patrilocal, a bride moves to her husband's home at marriage. A daughter who marries out is in no position to provide support for her own parents, and in fact, a married woman who diverts resources to her natal household breaches a protocol that can compromise her status with in-laws. One household in our research area split apart after the daughter-in-law was accused of secretly sending butter and other items to her parents. The ensuing arguments prompted the family to build a wall through the center of their house; the elderly parents now live on one side of the wall, while their son, daughter-in-law, and grandchildren live on the other side.

The majority of the elderly in our study live in a family with adult sons and a daughter-in-law. They are the ones ideally tasked with providing care for elderly household members. Yet despite the cultural norms of patrilocal marriage and coresidence with sons, we found a widespread sentiment among the elderly that their own daughters are the people best suited to be primary caretakers, as elegantly expressed in a proverb one man recited when discussing the topic of elderly care: "On the morning of birth, [one prefers to have] a son. On the morning of death, [one prefers to have] a daughter," and explained,

It means we are happy when a son is born, but when we die we are happy to have a daughter present. Parents try to keep sons in the home, but the sons have to work outside so they cannot provide nursing care. When parents become invalids or are dying, then daughters

are important because they can care for the elderly. Parents are happier if a daughter is nearby during their dying days.

Typically, old folks phrase their preference in terms of receiving "food from the hands of my own daughter." For example, one woman said,

Our family decided to keep two sons at home and get a bride for them. That is the custom of the area. We sent our daughters out. Now I regret that decision. If I chose to keep a daughter and get her an in-marrying husband, then I would get food from the hands of my own daughter and life would be easier right now.

Although sending daughters out as brides to other families remains the norm, the widespread practice of fraternal polyandry leaves many women unable to marry. In fact, a salient feature of fraternal polyandry is that it produces an abundance of unmarried females—27 percent of women aged twenty-five to thirty-nine in our fieldwork villages. What to do with them becomes a major issue.

Given the preference for having one's own daughter as the primary caregiver in old age, an obvious answer for parents would be to keep one or more unmarried daughters at home. However, many feel strongly that this should not happen because the overriding goal is to maintain the family and its land intact across generations by having brothers jointly take one wife. Tibetans consider allowing an unmarried daughter to remain in the household after her brother(s)' bride has arrived almost as detrimental as allowing two brothers to each have their own wife under the same roof—the two women are likely to have conflicts over authority and control. Moving unmarried daughters out of the family, therefore, is considered an important strategy for safeguarding the integrity of the family.

What happens with a woman who is unable to marry into another rural household? Traditionally, parents could ordain her as a nun, or help her build a small house in the village where she would live separately. Unmarried daughters living separately could not only contribute labor to their natal households, but often provided caretaking services as well as places of refuge for parents when relationships within the main household broke down. As for nuns, the combined forces of a gender ideology that devalues female celibacy and the underfunding of convents (Havnevik 1989; Klein 1995) meant that they were often expected to help care for aging parents and contribute to the welfare of their natal households (Gutschow 2004). A Tibetan proverb encapsulates the value of a nun to her parents: "If you want to be a servant, make your son a monk. If you want a servant, make your daughter a nun" (Lopez 1998: 211).

Today, many women still leave their natal households through arranged marriage, or are split into independent residences once their brothers bring home a bride. The monastic option, on the other hand, is limited. During the 1980s, Sogang's residents petitioned the government to reestablish a local nunnery that had been destroyed during China's Cultural Revolution. The government granted permission but—similar to Tibetan areas throughout China—imposed a strict limit on the number of residents. The eight designated slots for Sogang's nunnery were filled immediately. Since then no other woman has been able to gain admission.

Meanwhile, new options have emerged for sending a daughter outside the natal household in ways that allow her to achieve financial independence. These include establishing a small business in a city or town, finding her a low-level salaried job, or investing in her education in the hope that she attains a higher-level salaried position. However, we found that the strategies vary by village. Close to half of the women born to households in Betsag and Norgyong currently reside in a city or town, indicating an urban-oriented strategy. In contrast, almost three out of four women who left Sogang did so through the traditional means of arranged marriage.

Norgyong's residents are taking advantage of new economic opportunities in Panam, a rapidly growing town situated a short walking distance from the village. Many parents raise capital to establish a small business for a daughter, such as a small restaurant or shop. We asked one of them to describe the process of splitting out from her natal household. She received monetary assistance from two brothers, and recalled,

I was the eldest child of my parents, I helped raise my siblings and manage the household. All of my brothers' kids call me "*ani*" (aunt), we have good relations. I stayed in the home for 13 years with the nama (bride). After she had more kids her power increased. She started to complain that I was not doing well. Our relationship became bad, we argued. I said to her, "In this village the custom is that sons stay in the household and daughters move out. So if you take good care of my parents I will split out." The nama and I did not have open arguments, but our relationship caused unhappy feelings within the family.

The restaurant/shop strategy not only gives a woman the chance to achieve economic independence, but also to marry a partner of her choice and establish a neolocal household. Importantly, town-dwelling women are not beholden to in-laws and therefore remain in a position to assist their elderly parents. One elderly man in Norgyong helped his daughter establish a business in Panam with this purpose in mind. He said,

I planned and took action to keep my daughter near. At the time my wife was already old and really needed a caretaker. We kept our daughter at home to do that. Then she fell in love with an electrician. They married, so we opened a restaurant for her [in Panam]. Last year her husband got a job offer in Shigatse. It's in a bigger city and a higher salary. He wanted my daughter to move with him to Shigatse. I said to him, "Please don't go, I really need my daughter. After I die you can take her as far away as you want. But while I'm alive, please stay nearby." Shigatse is not far away, but I still wanted her in the town. Therefore, he didn't change jobs.

Although some parents in Betsag have tried to help a daughter open a shop in the village or Shigatse, their preferred strategy is to invest in her education so she can secure employment with a regular salary. Our survey data reveals a connection between education and mobility. Women who have moved out of a Betsag household have attained an average of 7.4 years of education—nearly five years more than women of similar age living in a village household. They even have an average of 3.3 more years of education than their male siblings who still reside within natal households.

These days many parents in Betsag devalue the traditional option of sending a daughter as a bride to another household. One elderly woman explained,

Parents are more likely to send girls to school in the hope that they get a life through education. For one, you can't keep daughters in the home; you must send them out as brides which is costly [the household must provide her with sets of clothing, grain, and gifts for her marital household]. Secondly, if you send a daughter as a bride to another household then she must serve people of another family. Most parents don't want their daughters living under such circumstances. They try to make a better life for them. Education is the best way, so parents try to send their daughters to school.

When we asked another elderly person in Betsag whether parents hope to gain benefits from an educated daughter, she responded,

Yes, that is one reason to send daughters to school. Elders here are getting money from children who get jobs. Some parents are getting money, while others are hoping to receive it in the future.

In summary, parents in the three villages are using different strategies to move daughters out of the household. Sogang, the relatively poor and remote village, exhibits the most traditional pattern: most daughters continue to move out through arranged marriages. Meanwhile many parents in Norgyong are taking advantage of opportunities provided by the burgeoning town of Panam to establish commercial enterprises for daughters. The fact that they are not beholden to in-laws in a marital household leaves these women in a position to provide continuing assistance to their parents. Finally, parents in the wealthier village Betsag are using education as an opportunity to provide daughters with the means to attain financial independence. Similar to daughters in Norgyong, many of these women live neolocally and are not constrained by the obligations of living in a husband's natal household with elderly in-laws, and are thereby free to assist their own aging parents.

## SUPPORT FROM EXTERNALLY-RESIDENT DAUGHTERS

The way a daughter is moved out of her household affects the potential social support she can provide for aging parents. Although there is much variation in the support that individuals can give, in general we find that daughters who were sent as brides to other rural households have the least potential to assist elderly parents because they are beholden to their marital families whereas daughters who are educated and have secured salaried employment can provide the most support.

### Emotional Support

Parents sometimes seek solace from an externally-resident daughter after receiving bad treatment from household members. For example, Kyipa[4] complains that the nama of her household serves her black tea rather than butter tea and locks food away, both of which are serious affronts in this village. When the situation becomes intolerable—a frequent occurrence—Kyipa makes the short walk to her daughter's restaurant in Panam. Often she stays all day and only returns in the evening after eating dinner. Kyipa's daughter thereby mitigates the situation, but beyond food and emotional support there is not much she can do to improve her mother's plight.

In contrast, Butri has two educated daughters who now live in cities. Often Butri is treated disrespectfully at home by her son and daughter-in-law. When we asked how she felt about this, she responded, "Even if I can't get kindness from my son I still have my daughters in Shigatse and Lhasa. I can receive much love from them." She then told us, "My son and daughter-in-law listen to my daughters because they are more powerful. My daughters come home to scold them

about once a year." More important, Butri's daughters exert leverage by threatening to cut off financial aid to the household if their mother is not treated kindly.

### Nursing Care

Sending a daughter to another family as a bride practically guarantees the loss of her support as a caretaker. Externally-resident daughters who can potentially provide assistance include those who live independently or in urban, neolocal households. For example, Dorje from Norgyong intentionally kept his only daughter nearby by opening a restaurant for her in Panam. He explained,

> If I get sick I can stay with my daughter. At the end of life, when I'm about to die, I'll have them send me home and my daughter can stay a short time to provide nursing care with my son. I always openly say to my daughter that, because of the [bad] family relationships, I'll face difficulties at the end of life. My daughter says, "There is no need to worry. I'm nearby. When you are sick I won't let you stay with others who argue with you. I will take care of you." . . . Everybody in my household has to farm. If they were busy I'd be home alone. I don't want that. If I am with my daughter she can stay home all day. It is a better choice.

The improved transportation system in Tibet reduces the importance of close proximity as a precondition for children to provide nursing care. When we asked Migmar who would care for him if he becomes incapacitated, he responded,

> It should mainly be done by my daughter-in-law. She is in a position to serve food and provide nursing care. But of course if I'm incapacitated then my family will ask my daughter to help. It would be difficult for my other daughters to provide care because they married out. But my youngest daughter is in Lhasa. She doesn't have a regular job. Her husband also doesn't have a secure job. For both of them it is easy to ask for a 15-day leave, so she could come here to care for me.

We then asked whether it is better to receive care from one's own daughter or a daughter-in-law. He said, "Of course from your own daughter, if possible. There is more trust with her. We two love each other very much, that is the reason."

### Financial Assistance for Health Care

Externally-resident children often provide money to help parents access health care. For example, Purbu, an elderly man in Betsag, depends more on his government-employed daughter than any other family member when he is ill. When we inquired why he depends so heavily on this particular child, he responded, "Tsamchö has an office job. The others are farmers, so even if they wanted to help they couldn't." Purbu credits Tsamchö's assistance with saving his live during a recent illness. He explained,

> Last summer I had a serious illness. My son told me to go to the county clinic. I said, "We don't have the money, so we'd have to borrow it. How would we repay it?" I refused to go. Tsamchö came later to see me and we discussed the situation. She asked if I was getting better, and I replied that I wasn't. She asked, "Should we go to the hospital in Shigatse?" I relied, "That is not possible. I understand it is very costly, and the household doesn't have the money to cover the expense." She said, "We should go to the doctor immediately. I'll pay." She then took me to the hospital. . . . I stayed for one month in the hospital. I worried about not having money for the hospital. My grandchildren are in school, which is very expensive. . . . If Tsamchö had not paid my hospital expenses, I may have died. Our household doesn't have much money for health care.

Although the health care and insurance systems in rural Tibet are rapidly improving, the cost of health-care remains a serious concern for many elderly people who fear the financial burdens they may impose on their families due to illness. In general, we find that the elderly who have externally-resident children with reliable salaries feel more confident that they can obtain health care services when needed.

## Pocket Money, Pilgrimage, and Non-kin Social Networks

Going on pilgrimage and visiting temples are important age-appropriate activities that have both spiritual and social benefits. Similarly, having one's own pocket money for buying sweets and other treats for themselves and their grandchildren is also an important component of a satisfying old age.

From a religious perspective, pilgrimage allows a person to positively influence future lives by cleaning negative karma accrued over a lifetime. During the pilgrimage the elderly accomplish this goal through prayer, ritual actions like prostration and circumambulation, making offerings of butter and cash to deities, and giving alms to beggars.

The ability to go on a pilgrimage is contingent on access to cash. In the rural Tibetan corporate household, all income generated by family members should be handed over to the household head. Typically, when a man reaches his midsixties, he relinquishes the household head position to a son including control of the household's cash, after which he is expected to withdraw from economic activities and concentrate on endeavors such as prayers and pilgrimages to monasteries that prepare one for death and rebirth. Thus, most elderly people who have given up the role of household head, depend on others to provide spending money. Some coresident sons who are the head of the household readily give cash to parents. Others are more reluctant to do so, necessitating that the elderly obtain money from sources outside the household, namely their externally-resident sons and daughters. In Betsag, the richer village where educating "excess" daughters is common so that they can live and work in the city, our research revealed that more than half of the elderly who received funds from outside the household got money from a daughter.

Pilgrimage and temple visits are some of the most important social activities for the elderly in rural Tibet; they are typically undertaken with a group consisting of friends and neighbors. The elderly commented that socializing during pilgrimage gives them pleasure, makes them more relaxed, and helps them forget about anxieties at home. Between visiting temples, making offerings, and performing circumambulations, they gather in parks or restaurants to share food and drink. One man explained,

> We do a large circumambulation [around the temple complex], then sit together and eat and drink, then go do another large circumambulation, then sit together again and eat and drink. If we have more chang [fermented barley beverage], or are having a good time, then we sit together longer after lunch and forget to do the third circumambulation in the afternoon.

Three circumambulations of a sacred site are considered the most auspicious performance of a pilgrimage ritual. Admitting that he sometimes neglects the third circumambulation therefore highlights the relative importance of the social dimension of pilgrimage.

To further highlight the social and emotional benefits of pilgrimage, consider the situation of those elderly whose lack of cash hinders their ability to participate in group activities. For example, one elderly woman told us,

> My whole life has been difficult. I've been poor, so I don't have a friendship group. If you have such a group, then you must gather together and buy food [while visiting a monastery]. I don't have money for the expenses. Women say, "You should join us when we go there," or, "Come sit and join us." I say I will, but usually I don't.

Another impoverished woman stated,

> Even though I could hitch a ride and therefore not have to pay [for transportation], it would still be embarrassing because, after visiting the temples the elderly like to have food in a restaurant. If I went together with others, I would have no money to pay for it. If I remained alone, without a partner, that would be shameful. So I tell my adoptive daughter, "Nowadays it is better for me to stay

in the village, drink tea, and do circumambulations." It is better for me.

The importance of group pilgrimage activities should not be underestimated given the consistent finding that there exists a positive relationship between engagement with non-kin social networks and well-being.[5] For example, Litwin (2001) finds that the morale of the elderly is highest among those who engage in social networks that extend beyond close kin, while Giles and colleagues (2005) find that discretionary relationships (those one can choose) have a more positive effect on morale in old age and longevity than relationships over which the individual exerts little choice (i.e., one's own children).

Although our data do not allow us to test for relationships between engagement with non-kin social networks and health or well-being, at the very least we can observe that (1) pilgrimage is an important undertaking in the lives of these Buddhist villagers, (2) pilgrimage provides solace for those approaching the end of life because it allows people to feel as if they are proactively preparing for future lives, (3) the elderly derive pleasure from social activities with non-kin peers during pilgrimage, (4) those who cannot go on pilgrimage due to financial constraints feel sad or embarrassed about their inability to participate in non-kin social networks, and (5) Externally-residing children, sons and daughters, provided the elderly a highly valued resource—cash, and daughters—especially those from Betsag who are educated and earn steady incomes—have become important facilitators of their elderly parents' pilgrimage activities.

a small business. Daughters living in neolocal households who have financial independence can, and often do, provide considerable social support for their elderly parents. Tangible benefits range from caretaking during a time of illness to gifts of cash that allow the elderly to engage in pilgrimage activities and interact more intensively with non-kin networks. Contrary to many predictions associated with aging and modernization theory, the effect of rapid socioeconomic changes on the well-being of the elderly are not invariably negative. Rather than being silent victims of changes, the elderly in rural Tibet are taking proactive measures that actually increase the capacity for externally-resident daughters to provide them with various forms of support. Parents are thereby creating novel forms of social capital that they can draw upon to improve the quality of their lives in culturally relevant ways, and to help sustain them during a health crisis or a breakdown of relationships within the household.

An important shift is underway in the composition of social support networks in rural Tibet. Most elderly still reside with a son (or multiple sons) and a daughter-in-law. Nevertheless, they are increasing their reliance for support on those nonresident daughters who have attained a degree of independence. Such women have more power, influence, and financial means to positively impact the lives of their parents compared with women who were sent as brides to other rural households. Based on the common sentiment that it is best to receive care from one's own daughter, externally-resident daughters' increasing capacity to provide support is seen by many elderly in rural Tibet as a positive social development.

## CONCLUSIONS

As Bourdieu (2001) points out, children living outside of a household remain connected to parents through durable kinship relationships that normatively entail exchanges at various levels. In rural Tibet, the practice of fraternal polyandry produces a large cohort of women who never marry and have difficult lives eking out a livelihood mainly by working for others. In recent years, parents in the richest two villages have sought to improve the situation of their unmarried daughters by investing in their education or business opportunities and at the same time thereby enhancing their own old age security and quality of life. In these villages, the nature of expectations and exchanges differs depending on the circumstances under which a daughter left the household. Simply put, the social capital vested in a daughter who was sent to another rural household as a bride pales in comparison with that of a daughter who was moved out through education or by establishing

## NOTES

1. In this paper, Tibet refers exclusively to China's Tibet Autonomous Region.
2. Cowgill and Holmes theoretical framework, arguing that the status and material well-being of the elderly declines with the advent of modernization, engendered a lively debate due to conflicting research findings. Since the 1970s, a body of research has been produced by gerontologists, historians, anthropologists, and other social scientists who both support and contradict this theory. For example, see Aboderin (2004), Albert and Cattell (1994), Bengtson et al. (1995), Goldstein and Beall (1981), Rhoads (1984), and Sokolovsky (1997).
3. Not all households practice polyandry. Those that do not include (1) households with only one son, (2) households lacking male heirs so that a daughter and her husband coreside with her parents, (3) households where parents send sons out in marriage and keep a daughter home instead, and (4) households consisting of infertile couples or spinsters who live alone or with an adopted child.

4. All personal names used in this paper are pseudonyms.
5. Research across the globe shows that strong social networks have a positive correlation with longevity (Giles et al. 2005; Hanson et al. 1989; Penninx, van Tilburg, and Kriegsman 1997; Sugisawa, Liang, and Liu 1994), health among the elderly (House, Landis, and Umberson 1988; Seeman 1996), functional abilities (Michael et al. 1999), morale (Litwin 2001; Wilson, Calsyn, and Orlofsky 1994), ability to resist the onset of dementia (Fratiglioni et al. 2000), and access to health services (Logan and Spitze 1994).

## REFERENCES

Aboderin, I. 2004. "Modernisation and Ageing Theory Revisited: Current Explanations of Recent Developing World and Historical Western Shifts in Material Family Support for Older People." *Ageing & Society* 24: 29–50.

Albert, S.-M., and M.-G. Cattell. 1994. *Old Age in Global Perspective: Cross-Cultural and Cross-National Views.* New York: G.K. Hall & Co.

Bengtson, V.-L., K. W. Schaie, and L. Burton (eds.). 1995. *Adult Intergenerational Relations: Effects of Societal Change.* New York: Springer.

Bourdieu, P. 2001 [1983]. "The Forms of Capital." In M. Granovetter and R. Swedberg (eds.). *The Sociology of Economic Life*, pp. 96–111. Boulder, CO: Westview Press.

Coleman, J.-S. 1988. "Social Capital in the Creation of Human Capital." *The American Journal of Sociology* 94(suppl.): S95–S120.

Cowgill, D. 1974. "Aging and Modernization: A Revision of the Theory." In J. F. Gubrium (ed.). *Late Life*, pp. 123– 145. Springfield, IL: Thomas.

Cowgill, D., and L. Holmes. 1972. *Aging and Modernization.* New York: Appleton-Century Crofts.

Fratiglioni, L., H.-X. Wang, K. Ericsson, M. Maytan, and B. Winblad. 2000. "Influence of Social Network on Occurrence of Dementia: A Community-based Longitudinal Study." *The Lancet* 355: 1315–1319.

Giles, L.-C., G.-F.-V. Glonek, M.-A. Luszcz, and G.-R. Andrews. 2005. "Effect of Social Networks on 10 Year Survival in Very Old Australians: The Australian Longitudinal Study of Aging." *Journal of Epidemiological Community Health* 59: 574–579.

Goldstein, M.-C. 1987. "When Brothers Share A Wife." *Natural History* 96(3): 109–112.

Goldstein, M.-C., and C.-M. Beall. 1981. "Modernization and Aging in the Third and Fourth World: Views from the Rural Hinterland in Nepal." *Human Organization* 40(1): 48–55.

Goldstein, M.-C., G. Childs, and P. Wangdui. 2008. "'Going for Income': A Longitudinal Analysis of Change in Farming Tibet, 1997–98 to 2006–07." *Asian Survey* 48(3): 514–534.

———. 2010. "Beijing's 'People First' Development Initiative for the Tibet Autonomous Region's Rural Sector— A Case Study from the Shigatse Area." *The China Journal* 63: 58–75.

Goldstein, M.-C., B. Jiao, C.-M. Beall, and P. Tsering. 2002. "Fertility and Family Planning in Rural Tibet." *The China Journal* 47: 19–39.

———. 2003. "Development and Change in Rural Tibet: Problems and Adaptations." *Asian Survey* 43(5): 758–779.

Gutschow, K. 2004. *Being a Buddhist Nun: The Struggle for Enlightenment in the Himalayas.* Cambridge, MA: Harvard University Press.

Hanson, B.-S., S.-D. Isacsson, L. Janzen, and S.-E. Lindell. 1989. "Social Network and Social Support Influence Mortality in Older Men." *American Journal of Epidemiology* 128: 370–380.

Havnevik, H. 1989. *Tibetan Buddhist Nuns.* Oslo: Norwegian University Press.

House, J.-S., K. R. Landis, and D. Umberson. 1988. "Social Relationships and Health." *Science* 241: 540–545.

Jiao, B. 2001. "Socio-Economic and Cultural Factors Underlying the Contemporary Revival of Fraternal Polyandry in Tibet." Unpublished Ph.D. dissertation, Department of Anthropology, Case Western Reserve University.

Klein, A.-C. 1995. *Meeting the Great Bliss Queen.* Boston: Beacon Press.

Litwin, H. 2001. "Social Network Type and Morale in Old Age." *The Gerontologist* 41(4): 516–524.

Logan, J.-R., and G. Spitze. 1994. "Informal Support and the Use of Formal Services by Older Americans." *Journal of Gerontology: Social Sciences* 49: S25–S34.

Lopez, D.-S. 1998. *Prisoners of Shangri-La: Tibetan Buddhism and the West.* Chicago: University of Chicago Press.

Michael, Y.-L., G.-A. Colditz, E. Coakley, and I. Kawachi. 1999. "Health Behaviors, Social Networks, and Healthy Aging: Cross-Sectional Evidence from the Nurse's Health Study." *Quality of Life Research* 8: 711–722.

Pemba, L. 1996. *Tibetan Proverbs.* Dharamsala: Library of Tibetan Works and Archives.

Penninx, B., T. van Tilburg, and D. Kriegsman. 1997. "Effects of Social Support and Personal Coping Resources on Mortality in Older Age: The Longitudinal Aging Study Amsterdam." *American Journal of Epidemiology* 146: 510–519.

Putnam, R.-D. 2000. *Bowling Alone: The Collapse and Revival of American Community.* New York: Simon and Schuster.

Rhoads, E.-C. 1984. "Reevaluation of the Aging and Modernization Theory." *The Gerontologist* 24(3): 243–250.

Seeman, T.-E. 1996. "Social Ties and Health: The Benefits of Social Integration." *Annals of Epidemiology* 6(5): 442–451.

Silverstein, M., D. Gans, and F.-M. Yang. 2006. "Intergenerational Support to Aging Parents: The Role of Norms and Needs." *Journal of Family Issues* 27(8): 1068–1084.

Sokolovsky, J. 1997. "Aging, Family, and Community Development in a Mexican Peasant Village." In J. Sokolovsky (ed.). *The Cultural Context of Aging*, pp. 191–217. Westport, CT: Bergin and Garvey.

Sugisawa, H., J. Liang, and X. Liu. 1994. "Social Networks, Social Support and Mortality among Older People in Japan." *Journal of Gerontology* 49: 3–13.

Wilson, J.-G., R.-J. Calsyn, and J.-L. Orlofsky. 1994. "Impact of Sibling Relationships on Social Support and Morale in the Elderly." *Journal of Gerontological Social Work* 22: 157–170.

# Between a Rock and a Hard Place:
## The Labyrinth of Working and Parenting in a Poor Community

### *Sharon Hicks-Bartlett*

It was a quiet summer night in Meadow View. The crisp air and blue-black sky were tranquil. Suddenly the night's stillness was pierced by screams and yells of chilling distress. Shots rang out. No one could recall how many. At times like this, people move away from windows. Someone surely summoned the police. Although the station is only two minutes from any point in the community, the police take their time showing up. Events inside Lillie's apartment stunned the occupants and made it difficult later to remember exactly what transpired that terrible night. Things happened quickly. Everyone agreed, however, that men with guns broke into the apartment, yelling, cussing, and looking for Lillie's teenage son. When the boy refused to step forward, the gunmen threatened to kill everyone. Lillie's son finally identified himself. At this point, things spun out of control.

All the gunmen wanted was Lillie's only son. But this was more than Lillie was willing to give. A slight woman, barely five feet, three inches, Lillie leapt in front of him, shielding him, flailing her arms, screaming and pleading for them not to hurt her child. They didn't. In split-second pandemonium, they killed Lillie instead. Dead at the age of forty-two, leaving five children and one grandchild.

Few people were able to maintain their equanimity during Lillie's funeral. Many wept openly as versions of what transpired that night circulated through the large, crowded church. A self-described, longtime family friend sang a mournful rendition of Lillie's "favorite" song, "*It's So Hard to Say Goodbye to Yesterday.*" The minister railed at the unsaved souls, insisting that only those who had not accepted the Lord should experience difficulty saying good-bye. His words were less a eulogy than a stern lecture to those who were "living by the sword." As sounds of sobbing filled the church, the minister bellowed at those who refused to identify Lillie's killers. The woman with whom I attended the funeral pointed out Lillie's ex-husband, who evidently

had come up north to pay his respects and to retrieve his son. The community denounced the father for his son's refusal to cooperate with police. But silence, the father believed, was the only way to save his son's life. Following the funeral, father and son would be heading south to live.

At the funeral people whispered about the shame of it all, how things here had gone from bad to worse, how people couldn't even be safe at home, and how they feared for the future. They talked about the possible fallout from the killing. Might there be a retaliation murder like the one that occurred years before, when one young man shot another, only to be killed later by the brother of the man he had murdered days before? Back then, the community's lone undertaker prepared the bodies of both men. For the community's viewing convenience, the bodies were placed in adjacent parlors at the same time. Even then, many years before Lillie's murder, people were horrified by what was happening to Meadow View. Today, people continue to shake their heads in dismay, declaring that "people have simply gone mad."

In Meadow View families struggle to survive. Few do so unscathed. Even for those a step or two above the poorest, living in Meadow View is a merciless challenge. As residents often remark, "stuff is always happening here." The strain of rebounding from one crisis before the next occurs depletes the body and mind. Lillie's story captures the violence that can transpire here.

In discussing how we experience place, Tony Hiss explains that whether we realize it or not, we all react "consciously and unconsciously" to where we reside and work. "[P]laces have an impact on our sense of self, our sense of safety, the kind of work we get done, the ways we interact with other people, even our ability to function as citizens in a democracy . . . the places where we spend our time affect the people we are and can become" (Hiss 1990: xi). Meadow View is one of the nation's poorest suburbs; it is isolated from jobs, quality schools, and adequate community resources. In Meadow View, for the greatest numbers of family members to survive, space must be strategically and carefully managed, which requires a level of vigilance that burdens families and reinforces their interdependency. But despite the gloomy state of

Sharon Hicks-Bartlett, "Between a Rock and a Hard Place: The Labyrinth of Working and Parenting in a Poor Community," in *Coping with Poverty The Social Contexts of Neighborhood, Work, and Family in the African American Community*. Sheldon Danziger and Ann Chih Lin, eds., pp. 27–51. Ann Arbor: University of Michigan Press, 2000.

affairs here, residents are tied to this terrain and to each other in real and symbolic ways. Despite all its problems, people call this place home. The stigma attached to coming from this place engenders in many a defensive bond that strengthens intergroup relations at the same time that it threatens to rip them apart. Affective bonds are always at risk because material, social, and financial need is unremitting. Already vulnerable families struggle to fulfill each other's needs, and this very exertion reinforces a "collective ethos" that binds people together (Jones 1986: 229).

Here, people manage working and parenting by relying on loose, family-based networks that minimize risk and center on meeting immediate needs. These networks provide the only security available to families in the face of recurrent threats to their physical well-being, isolation from jobs both within and outside their neighborhoods, and meager finances. Personal sacrifices, made for the good of the family unit, strain already limited family resources. Not surprisingly, the help of relatives who are themselves poor is never enough to change one's life situation. But when "self-sufficiency" is promoted as a policy objective without attention to the central role that family members play for one another, it is easy to overlook the fact that family and community sufficiency is required for the problems of the poor to be fully addressed.

Meadow View is a small black suburb outside a major midwestern city. This chapter is based on more than nine years of fieldwork in Meadow View. The daily lives of ten women were explored with an emphasis on family, community, and work. Four of the ten women were first interviewed during an earlier project; the others were added during research for this project, which took place during an eighteen-month period beginning in the summer of 1995 and ending in December 1996. The women, all of whom are mothers, were engaged in conversations of both a general and specific nature. Most of the interviews were tape-recorded and transcribed verbatim. Formal interviews ranged from two to more than five per person. In addition, my impromptu visits to homes produced many opportunities to talk, woman to woman, about a variety of topics.

These mothers were located through old contacts in the community, a worker at a community center, and one or two key informants. I explained to all the participants that I was interested in learning about family and community life. Consent forms that proffered more information about the study were disseminated to everyone. Participation was unanimous. Initially, no mention of money was made. Upon completion of the first interview, ten dollars was given to each informant. No mention of money was made or offered thereafter.

Interviews transpired in one of two places, with the vast majority occurring in private homes. A small number of first interviews were conducted in a vacant office at the community center. Subsequent interviews took place in the mothers' homes at their convenience. In addition, I often dropped by for informal "interviews."

All of the mothers are African-American. They represent a cross section of the women I have interviewed over my many years of involvement in the community. Each mother has had work experience, which tends to be part-time and low wage. Welfare use has ranged from a few months to more than ten years. All the women acquired their first job as teens in a federally funded summer youth employment program. Two of the women later secured either part-time or full-time work as adults in the same program. The other women typically hold jobs in service, retail, or manufacturing. With the exception of Sissy, the mother with the most education and work experience in the group, the mothers often talk of desiring jobs in the care-giving fields.

## A SUBURB IN NAME ONLY

Although Meadow View is a suburb situated near a once-booming industrial region, it looks like the rural south, with its unpaved roads, two outhouses, and a creek set deep in the woods. Most of its nearly forty-five hundred residents, whether employed or not, are low income and black. By 1990, 49.2 percent of the population was below poverty level. Per capita income is just over $4,500. A large stamping plant sits outside the community, but few Meadow View residents hold these skilled and semiskilled jobs. By any measure, unemployment and underemployment are pervasive, creating a community dependent on government assistance. For those sixteen and over, Meadow View's unemployment rate is 26 percent. Local officials set the "real" unemployment rate higher than 50 percent. One glance around the community on any summer day gives credence to a community perception that "almost everybody is out of work."

Meadow View has always been a poor community. But not until it became poor *and* black did it develop such intractable problems. In the shift from a poor white community to a poor black community, Meadow View became a choice locale for low-income public housing projects. Now, 65 percent of housing is government projects. Their construction in this particular suburb, as opposed to other nearby middle-class suburbs, is a prime example of the collusion among local, state, and federal agencies to perpetuate racial and class segregation within Meadow View. This small community was particularly attractive to those who preferred suburban living but could only afford it where rock-bottom housing prices and regional housing discrimination allowed them to live.

Rajah, who is married and the mother of seven boys and an infant daughter, voices her trepidation about Meadow View; she routinely checks for opportunities to move to other suburbs.

> I've been looking and looking for a house for my kids. Looking forever! I got to get away from here before I go crazy or something happens to my boys. I'm sick of the water, I'm sick of the drugs, I'm sick of living here. This is insane! Too much stuff is happening all the time, something is always going on.

Theoretically, Rajah's income and housing subsidy would permit her to leave Meadow View. But if she succeeds, she will most likely relocate to another overwhelmingly poor, black suburb. Her subsidy was once a ticket into a safer, more economically viable suburb in the area. Now, those who want to leave often find themselves blocked as a result of a political battle between county and local housing authorities that restricts the mobility of the Section 8 certificates in this region (Hicks-Bartlett forthcoming). Leaving the community is even more difficult for those with little income and no housing subsidy.

Economic stability, adequate community resources, healthy infrastructure, strong institutions, a robust tax base, fiscal viability, and effective local government are some indicators of community well-being. Meadow View falls short on every single one. Like other old black suburbs, Meadow View's local government strains to keep afloat financially (Logan 1983/1988). Ironically, although Meadow View provides fewer services to its residents than its nearby suburban neighbors, its per capita expenditures are higher than theirs. This is because the local government's weak property tax base is insufficient to provide adequate services or maintain its deteriorating infrastructure. Delaying needed repairs to save money often costs more in the long run. Several times, the local government has teetered on the brink of bankruptcy. On more than one occasion both the police and fire department have gone on strike, imperiling the safety of residents. Except for church, few institutional supports are available to supplement and reinforce parental efforts. Community-sanctioned outlets for youth do not exist. Local services are so inadequate (e.g., years ago the local library had to be closed due to its unsafe structure and lack of operating funds) that people must go outside the community for most things.

In the summer of 1996, more than one hundred fifty people were arrested in a series of drug busts conducted by undercover sting operations. Previous raids had done little to clean up the community's drug trade. The latest round of sweeps came on the heels of the arrest of the police chief for allegedly permitting the drug trade to flourish with impunity, which had been rumored for years. More than a decade of police "passes" have brought down not only the police chief but also six current and former police officers, all of whom now face serious charges and lengthy prison sentences. Such corruption and graft lead many parents to believe that the job of protecting children from the fallout of this destitute place is their responsibility alone.

Surviving a summer requires considerable vigilance and management of one's space. Hot homes drive people outdoors to enjoy the camaraderie on the street. At the same time, an unremitting flow of out-of-state cars scouting for drug dealers stir feelings of besiegement and spark endless discussions of safety, drugs, and violence. Drugs control certain streets, making them difficult to maneuver. Late-model, expensive automobiles, with white people at the wheel, block traffic along some streets. These outsiders are the topic of considerable community discussion, distrust, suspicion, and anger. The mother of two young children summed up her feelings regarding these invasions:

> We can't even drive through their neighborhoods. But they can come here and do whatever they want. They don't care about nothing but getting drugs, but we the one's suppose to be so bad. We the ones *they* don't want to live by.

Often communities like this become a market for all sorts of spillover vice. Women and young girls are propositioned by strangers hunting for drugs and sexual thrills. Although men of all types scout the community for willing females, white males, perhaps because of their high visibility, evoke the greatest ire.

The fear of getting caught in the crossfire of a drug shoot-out and the concern that one's child will either use, deal drugs, or be caught up in spillover crime as a victim or participant preoccupy parents. Parents assert that "you've got to watch out for your own." Meadow View has become a place where children must learn the community's alarm call: "hit the deck" or simply, "get down." Watching children here is endless, exacting work. As one mother comments:

> We ain't been doing nothing but staying inside. They been shooting the last two nights. Girl, I'm scared to look out the window. My nerves is already bad, now they really messed up. Seems like every time I try to fall asleep, racing cars or shooting wakes me up. You gotta keep yours inside—if you want 'em safe.

During interviews, mothers habitually peek out the window. This seemingly small gesture is repeated in households throughout the community. Parents survey the landscape, tirelessly scanning the environment, monitoring slow-moving cars, scrutinizing suspicious gatherings—behavior all rooted in indisputable facts of daily life. Before venturing out, people caution each other to "be careful." Some avoid going out at night altogether for fear of getting "caught" out after dark.

Young boys risk being seduced into illegal work. A fieldnote entry describes the challenges a parent can face. Mabel, mother of eight, expressed considerable angst about her sons. Her daughters worried her less because she had more success keeping them at home. One son, a particularly quiet youth of fifteen named Mark, was approached to work as a "lookout" for a local drug dealer. Fearing his mother's wrath, the boy rebuffed the offers. Later, a rather persistent drug dealer invited himself to Mabel's house to ask permission for the youth to work for him. Mabel listened patiently to the dealer's request. When he finished, she said, "Leave my son alone. . . . He can't work for you. Just leave him alone!" She was dead serious and hoped her steely glare transmitted that spirit.

Fearing that Mark would eventually turn to drug work, Mabel first thought of sending him south to live with his father's family. When this proved not to be a viable option, she tried to get him into a special program where he would leave the community to work on an out-of-state farm, safe from Meadow View streets. "For three years I wouldn't have to worry about him getting killed or something," she sighed. The program seemed a perfect solution. One problem remained, however. Because her son had never been in serious trouble, he was not eligible to enter the program through normal channels. Only if she abdicated her parental rights, formally declaring herself unfit, could he be admitted. The logic that required her son to be in trouble before he could receive help seemed inane to Mabel. She weighed her options and declared that if giving up her rights was the only way to save her son, so be it. As she explains it:

I don't care too much about giving up my rights, if it can help him. He knows I'm his momma and I know I'm his momma. No piece of paper can change that. When he gets out, I'm quite sure he'll look me up and quite naturally he'll be grown and can understand what I had to do.

Mabel escaped having to surrender her parental rights. Her son managed to avoid drug work on his own. To Mabel, what happened seemed worse in some ways. A young cousin, while showing Mark his gun, accidentally shot and seriously wounded Mark in the head. Now, for the rest of his life, he will ingest medicines to control his seizures.

To separate working and parenting from this situational context is to fail to appreciate how bound the two are. Parents in nonpoor areas expect certain community qualities and services that support parenting. There is a vast difference, however, between the communities in which the poor and nonpoor reside, particularly those in which poor minority and poor non-minority live (Wilson 1987, 1996). While protecting children is a universal parental behavior, in Meadow View it can require extreme measures; it is labor-intensive, emotionally draining work. The need to protect children and the vigilance this requires create major barriers to working and parenting, especially when the two are attempted simultaneously. The mother of four young boys reveals what transpired one day.

Girl, a boy got shot the other day. Right out here in front of my apartment. He couldn't have been no more than fifteen. They killed him right out in broad day light. I was so glad my kids wasn't outside 'cause usually they would be right out there playing. But I had just made them come in a few minutes before. It took the ambulance a long time to get here. I was so scared . . . Blood, all in the street—it's still there. I just think about my kids. Girl what if they were out there. They coulda' got kill, too.

Frightened by her experience, she immediately requested, to no avail, that the project housing authority relocate her family to a safer area. Mothers like this woman cannot but think that if they were not at home to make their children come in, their children might be the next victims. Meadow View lacks before and afterschool programs that could engage children in constructive activities while parents work. Ironically, the luxury of such programs belongs to parents who live in neighborhoods where tax dollars can support such services or to parents who can purchase whatever care they desire for their children. But in Meadow View, where the need for such programs is so much greater, parents have neither the income nor the institutional supports to establish them.

Adults and children feel the effects of this stressful environment. Meadow View mothers often complain of "nerve problems." Some children become fearful and edgy. Others obsess about danger or being shot. Like Meadow View adults, children become extremely preoccupied with the environment and its inherent dangers. "Hypervigilance" is striking, seen in the ". . . scan[ning] [of] their surroundings for danger and over-interpret[ing] the actions of others . . . " (Brownlee 1996: 72). Nightmares about being chased, hurt, or killed are common. In one family, the stress on a mother and her two children, ages six and ten, is palpable. In discussing her children's fears, the mother laments:

I can't get them out of my bed. You know, they are too big to be sleeping with me. But they too scared to be in the room by themselves. They got good beds to sleep in, but I can't get them in them for nothing. They sleep in here real good, but now I don't get any sleep. And my back stay hurt with one on each side kicking me, and I can't get comfortable. I really don't sleep at night. I catnap in the day, when they in school.

This sleep-deprived mother frequently complains of physical ailments. The only time she rests is when her children are at school. The many implications this would have on working outside the home are obvious.

The constancy of trauma and fear in their environment causes other problems in children. One report found that children who experience early trauma (e.g., witnessing or fearing violence) show measurable physiological and chemical changes in the body and brain (Brownlee 1996: 72). When frightened, they react in a "fight-or-flight" response. The body attempts to compensate by releasing certain stress hormones. In affected children, normal physiological and chemical reactions jump track, producing abnormal levels and imbalances in the body. The impact on learning for children in these environments has been well documented (Garbarino et al. 1992; Prothrow-Stith and Weissman 1993). Affected children have a shorter attention span; language and critical thinking suffers. High levels of these harmful chemical changes create children who are ripe for a host of learning difficulties. Children in these environments may also misconstrue normal play as aggressive and get into physical altercations.

All of these challenges influence parental decisions about work and family. This does not mean that those who face such barriers should be exempt from paid labor. When faced with objective situations that require hypervigilance (e.g., children who require extraordinary nurturing, fear management, patience, and care of chronic health problems), most mothers concentrate on performing their maternal role above all else. Those lucky enough to find others they trust to care for their children are able to work—at least on and off—because of it. Without such support, employed work is difficult and sometimes impossible to sustain. Yet money for survival is as necessary as care for children and families. The support networks that spring up to meet these challenges address this dilemma, but in ways that lessen the significance of individual achievement and self-sufficiency.

## KIN MATTERS

Meadow View families depend heavily on each other. Individuals and families expect to share with others. In addition to financial support, families provide an array of essential services, without which most would not be able to work, attend school, or enroll in training programs. All of the families discussed here are involved in extensive helping networks that can buckle under the weight of a widening circle of needy members. Just how critical to survival these networks are is exemplified by one mother's family.

Wanda once lived in a two-bedroom project apartment with her two children. It also provided temporary quarters for her two brothers and two cousins, whom her parents raised after their mother died. Although she now works as a teacher's aide, Wanda received welfare for more than ten years. Throughout much of this time, she cared for her invalid mother. On occasion, Wanda received money from her parents but this was neither regular nor expected. To avoid placing the mother in a nursing home, Wanda's father, who worked full-time at a factory in a neighboring state, sought his children's help in caring for their mother. Since Wanda had a small child to care for, she was the designated sibling to help her mother and her employed siblings who might need occasional help. Two sisters, one employed in clerical work, the other in factory work, sometimes called on Wanda for child care. Providing care to those who need it is highly valued, particularly over low-wage work that may only slightly improve the individual's life while potentially burdening and making matters worse for the extended kin network.

Known for being able to stretch her welfare check, Wanda was often called on for a loan or a meal or a place to stay for a few days. She earned extra income by operating an in-house "store," a table set up in her kitchen from which she sold soda, potato chips, and candy to neighborhood youth; at best, her efforts rarely generated more than $30 a month. Although Wanda had her own share of money worries, she rarely refused anyone in need. For unexpected emergencies, she kept twenty dollars stashed away. Wanda's only complaint was that she did not have anyone as generous on whom *she* could rely. Although she felt she gave more than she ever received, Wanda did benefit from some invaluable help from this arrangement.

During her second pregnancy, Wanda moved from her parents' home into a subsidized apartment. Soon afterward, an assortment of relatives moved in and out. Until they found jobs, they were neither asked nor expected to help financially. When two relatives acquired jobs at a rehabilitation center, through another relative, they began giving Wanda money, helping with groceries and continuing to baby-sit. Whether working or not, they baby-sat whenever needed. Not only did this allow Wanda respite from her children, it also relieved the ennui of being housebound. Wanda benefited, too, from the protection and security of having men present.

I don't mind having them here, they are good company. Plus, I know that no one is going to come in here on me when they know that a man lives here. . . . They help out just by being here. Plus it's good for my kids to be around their uncles and cousins.

Years later, while living alone with her two children, Wanda suffered a near fatal brain aneurysm. Her family sprang into action. During her nearly six-month rehabilitation, the extended family focused on Wanda's health. At the time, Wanda's brother Donnie had been planning to go to Mississippi for a long-awaited job. Unemployed for years, he looked forward to finally getting work—even though it required a major relocation. Because the other siblings were engaged in full- or part-time work, they were less available to attend to Wanda's needs. Together, the family decided that Donnie should move into Wanda's apartment and assume primary care of her children and her personal affairs. Other relatives helped out on weekends. When asked how he felt about having to give up his job, Donnie remarked, "You can always get another job, but you can't get another sister" (see also Stack 1990).

Wanda and her family viewed her miraculous recovery as a sign from God that she should improve her life. With the help of her caseworker, she enrolled in a community college and eventually became a teacher's aide. During Wanda's course work, Donnie, still unemployed, continued to live with her and help out, without pressure from his family to get a job. Caring for Wanda was a job that everyone in the family valued. Donnie never mentioned going South again. Until she finished school and found a job, Donnie selflessly contributed his unpaid labor to the family and Wanda's dreams. Now and then, Wanda gave him money, but he did not receive regular pay. Without his help, her recovery would have been difficult; her schooling would have been impossible. His child care and household work allowed Wanda to recover fully, reach a goal sparked by her illness, and obtain a job.

Most families will respond supportively to each other in times of crisis. In this sense, Wanda and her family are not unique. What is truly notable in Meadow View families is the degree to which individuals are summoned to meet the needs of others and to suppress personal goals to do so (see also Rank 1994). A great deal of working and schooling is made possible only because of the willingness of others to set aside self-interest. Many who manage to hold jobs have kin willing to defer individual pursuits for the sake of others. Because poor families cannot purchase the care their families need, they must supply it to each other.

Exploring the complicated arrangements mothers must make to work and parent simultaneously reveals how tenuous these arrangements are and how even a slight error can trigger a full-blown, snowballing crisis in families. Children's illness is a universal barrier to working that all parents face, particularly parents of young children. According to Heymann, Earle, and Egleston (1996), fully one-fourth of all parents reported that they had no sick leave available to take care of sick relatives, including their children. But children's ailments often require them to miss school. An estimated ten million children have some sort of chronic disorder. Not surprisingly, poor children have poorer health. They have a higher incidence of chronic ailments, while their working parents have the least amount of sick leave to tend to them. Sissy, a young mother who worked in retail, tells how she finally had to quit her job because of her infant's chronic respiratory condition.

> My sister was watching him but he just kept a cold. He'd have one a couple of weeks. Then he'd be okay a couple of weeks. Then he'd get sick again. I had to keep taking off to take him back and forth to the doctor. He wasn't eating right at all. My baby was so sick! They wanted to put tubes in his ears. When he couldn't breathe, my sister would call me at work and I had to rush home to take him to the hospital. She couldn't take him because she had to watch her own baby. So I had to quit because I was taking off a lot. I wasn't making no money. They were going to fire me because I had so many problems with the baby. I don't know if they believed me. My mother said I need to think about my baby and stay at home to take care of him myself. So I quit.

A preference for family/friend child care over other types of care derives from the conviction that only family can be depended on to deal flexibly with frequent emergencies.

In Meadow View the importance of caregiving can compete with a work ethic that values paid labor over nonpaid caring work. Anyone trying to combine simultaneous working and parenting can identify with Darla, an unemployed mother. Darla has four sons who attend school with her sister's three daughters. Her sister, a pregnant, single mother, works as a file clerk. By 7:30 A.M. the girls arrive at Darla's apartment. When it is time, they walk to school with Darla's two school-aged sons. After school, the five children return to Dalra's, where the girls remain until their mother arrives. When the mother is late, the girls stay over or are retrieved by another family member. Before and after school, Darla is in charge of seven children under the age of eleven. She prepares snacks and sometimes entire meals for the children.

During the time we were meeting, Darla was battling cervical cancer. While often in severe physical discomfort and under medication that made her somnolent and temperamental, she took care of these children. She received little money from her sister but often was rewarded with free weekends while her boys slept at their cousin's house, a respite Darla enjoyed. Occasionally, the boys received gifts of clothing or other small items. On payday, Darla's sister brought over groceries for the children. The arrangement helped both women. As Darla explained:

> I help out my sister, she's got her hands full with the girls. And she's pregnant, too! Since I got to be here anyway, I might as well take care of hers, too. You can't just leave your kids with anybody. She knows I'll do right by my nieces—I wanted girls, she was the one wanted boys. She's not going to leave her kids with just anybody.

When Darla recovered from the cancer, she found a job at a department store. Immediately, her job altered her sister's child-care arrangements and created new child-care needs for Darla. Now her nieces spend their before-school time in the care of another aunt, who just happened to quit her job because of doctor-ordered bed rest due to pregnancy complications. The girls continue to go to Darla's after school; until she arrives home from work, the children are now in the care of Darla's new boyfriend.[1]

The strain that such child-care arrangements can place on families is also evident from Vicki's story. Vicki, mother of two teenage daughters, once worked nights at a local bar, in part so that she could take care of her young nephew during the day. Her child-care work began soon after she got home from work in the early mornings, forcing her to get by on little sleep. Although she did receive pay for caring for Tony, whose mother, Kelly, worked on a cleanup crew at a local animal shelter,[2] the pay was sporadic due to Kelly's variable work hours. But as Vicki explained, this far-from-ideal situation was still the best option that the family, as a whole, had.

> I took care of Tony' cause Kelly really didn't have anyone to watch him. She was going to get him in Head Start but someone had to get him there and go get him later. I didn't want to have to walk there and back [twice]. It was just easier to bring him over here in the morning. That way he'd be in one place all day. . . . That's why I wasn't really looking for a full-time day job then. She'd really have a hard time finding someone if I worked full-time, days.

When Vicki was unable to keep Tony because of foot surgery, another sister reluctantly used a week of her vacation time to fill in. This help was offered more out of duty to the larger family than respect for her sister. As she tells it:

> You know my sister and I don't get along at all! But that don't have nothing to do with Tony. I sure don't want to spend my vacation watching him. But somebody's got to watch him 'til Vicki gets back on her feet. My mother don't need to be bothered with this boy, she's too old. So I just took off to take care of him.

In a community without child-care programs for young and school-age children, someone willing and able to provide such care is highly valued. Child care, essential to all working parents with dependent children, is especially critical here. Mothers all want their children to receive the best care, to develop preschool skills, and to be involved in constructive activities with other children. Middle-class parents can purchase this care with greater assurance that it will be reliable and responsive to their needs.[3] Being able to purchase child care allows parents to exercise some control over the quality of that care. Quality is desired by poor mothers also. But few are fortunate enough to be able to take advantage of a program like Head Start because it fails to serve all those who want it or need it. Moreover, such programs are typically structured around a clock that conflicts with the working schedules of full-time mothers. Thus, poor mothers take what they can get. It is important to keep this point in mind when trying to understand why significant numbers of poor families' children are cared for by relatives.

Relatives can be intrinsically good caretakers and many are. But the preference for relatives must also be understood as part of an economic reality: mothers can trust and negotiate with family and friends in ways they could not with institutions. Given a choice, it is not clear that Kelly would have chosen one sleep-deprived sister and another disapproving one to care for her son. The help they offered was better than nothing. Even if her sisters were ideal caretakers, Kelly might simply wish to avoid reliance on custodial care done out of obligation. But it is unlikely that Kelly could have found a quality child-care provider who would have allowed her to pay erratically, or one who would take her son even when doing so violated the provider's self-interest. As another mother makes clear:

> . . . Beggars can't be too choosy. I'm grateful I got family that will help out. It's better than nothing. I don't particularly like them over there, but right now I can't do no better. And for what I'm paying, I can't be telling people how to run their house. I'm just grateful I have someone that can help me. It's better than nothing.

While limited options make one grateful for what one gets, they can place children at risk. Custodial care performed by caregivers with limited skills, poor health, little knowledge of normal child development, and unsafe homes creates anxiety for working mothers.[4] But out of a desperate need for care, mothers may pardon poor quality and disregard potentially hazardous situations. They make do, forever ready to establish new plans if absolutely necessary. High standards for the quality of child care one will accept is a luxury few Meadow View mothers can afford if they also want to work.

The symbiosis between working poor mothers and "nonworking" "welfare-taking" mothers makes it impossible to draw moral and ethical distinctions between the two. These mothers serve as lifelines to each other. A work ethic that always defines workers as more deserving than nonworkers misses this connection (Katz 1989). Given limited education, lack of job prospects, child-care needs, and inadequate transportation, these mothers recognize their dependence on others. They realize their ability to endure on low wages is possible, in large part, because of the misfortunes of other poor women whose labor helps them with their child-care needs. Those "lucky" enough to get a job realize that keeping it most often is directly related to someone else's current unemployment. And one frequently hears, "There but for the grace of God go I."

Reliance on the family can actually intensify after a job is obtained. One suddenly needs to find regular child care, to borrow money "til pay-day," to scrounge clothes to wear to work, to borrow bus fare or endlessly pursue other transportation means; these needs can ultimately weigh on everyone. Mabel, a mother who recently secured factory work, depends exclusively on her family's services. Just as the children are leaving for school, the mother is arriving home from work. When they return home, Mabel is often sleeping before departing for her graveyard shift. An older daughter who is a student at a local community college prepares the children for school in the morning and arranges her schedule to be home when the children return from school.[5] Without this help Mabel would not be able to keep her job. A parent working nights must maintain a schedule that is not conducive to rearing young children. Things are difficult, leading Mabel to wonder at times if she really is better off working. She comments on her ongoing struggles:

> You know, if it wasn't for [my family] I wouldn't make it. I'd be in the hole a lot. When I finish paying my bills, ain't much left. I like my job, especially getting paid every Friday, but it's hard to make it. I try to give a little to [her

daughter] for helping with the kids. [Referring to the used car she recently purchased to get to her job]; I'm deep in the hole now 'cause of that piece of car. Seems like soon as I got it, it needed some of everything done to it and that ate up my little money. And the car still ain't right. It's bad when you work and still can't do no better. Girl, sometimes my brother has to get up out of his sleep and take me to work.

Life can be as tough for employed poor mothers as it is for welfare-receiving mothers who work within the home. Having a job may *feel* worse in some ways for employed poor mothers who see that working has made their lives more complicated and unmanageable than before. One mother comments on her attempts to make it:

> I don't expect nothing on welfare so I make do with nothing. But when I was working, I expected to make it and seem like I was worse. I couldn't really stay up on it. I needed things to wear more, I needed money to pay for getting back and forth to work, the kids needed snacks when they went over to [a relative's house] and I had to send enough for her kids too, I wasn't really paid much. . . . And I could never get regular hours and that made it hard if I had to be there before they went to school. When [youngest child] is in school full-time, I can probably work more.

Alluding to the help she requires, another "self-sufficient" working mother states:

> I'm squeezing by. This has been a good month . . . knock on wood! I'm just gonna keep my fingers crossed—that's all I can do. You know, as soon as you think you doing all right, something happens to remind you, you not. I ain't had to ask my family for nothing this month, and I hope it stays that way. I know my family gets tired of me begging, 'cause I get tired of me begging, too.

Rarely does this mother get through a month without the help of relatives and close friends. Her mother "keeps a freezer full of meat," allowing her to borrow food when money is tight. Such borrowing, in turn, exacts a cost from those who may have a little more than their poorest relatives but are also living close to the financial edge themselves. In fact, a tension exists between the pursuit of individual goals and the needs of the family. One woman explains the pressures she felt at college:

> You know I knew my family needed me. I knew they were depending on my stipend. I'd call, and they would be having problems. I felt bad being here, having all this and they were having a hard time. I decided to come home after my first year and get a job to help out my family. I can always go to college at home.

This woman never finished her four-year business degree. She did, however, manage to complete two years of junior college. Until she was twenty-seven, she lived with her mother and siblings in a crowded project apartment. When she left home, she moved to an apartment a few blocks away.

Even young women with the opportunity to make a better life for themselves relinquish it to meet pressing family obligations. The assumption that working makes one better off is not always true. For whom are things better off? In this context, it is questionable that children are better off. Without reliable, affordable, quality child care for multi-aged children, it is doubtful that these mothers, who worry incessantly about the safety of their children, feel that they are better off. It makes sense to value their children's health and safety above low-wage work. When low-wage work wins out, it is in part because these mothers want to work badly and have managed to secure the support they need from others in hopes of making work pay. Many learn that work does not always pay, and that when it does, it does so primarily because of the current non-labor-force participation of others.

Some of the problems mothers face would be more easily resolved if Meadow View residents were able to work in their neighborhood. But Meadow View suffers from a lack of jobs and little transportation to where the jobs are. Family-based networks often refer workers to jobs and provide transportation alternatives. But when nearly everyone in one's network is poor, isolated from good opportunities, or dependent upon unreliable transportation, the network can provide only minimal assistance.

## FINDING WORK, REACHING WORK

One of the ironies of employment in Meadow View is that when poor mothers exchange their informal, family caretaking roles for paid, outside employment, the employment they find often involves caring for other people. In this region the demand for home health-care work is high, corresponding with a Department of Labor prediction that home health care will have the largest job growth of any industry between 1994 and 2005 (Eisler 1997). But while people everywhere must rely increasingly on purchased care, care-giving work is low paying and receives little credit for being important and necessary work (Abel and Nelson 1990; DeVault 1991; Stack 1974; Tronto 1994). These positions tend to be low wage, labor intensive, and little more than a "ghetto" for women, minorities and illegal immigrants (Eisler 1997; Statham, Miller, and Mauksch 1988). But the "soft" skills these mothers possess from

years of traditional female work are usually enough to secure a job in these female-dominated fields. At least five of the ten mothers in my study have worked in nursing homes or in home health care. When asked what type of work they felt qualified for, all but one felt they could get a job in caregiving because as one mother put it, "that's mostly what I've been doing all along."

Home health care has advantages that other low-wage work does not; it allows for some flexibility in work schedules, which is especially important for single mothers (Schein 1995). Because of high demand for these workers, mothers can enter and exit the field at will, depending on the availability of help at home. Home health care also allows for more autonomy than other types of service work. Working in private homes, women can be their own bosses. Workers also develop strong relationships with their charges and often develop a sense of loyalty to the patient. They feel positive about providing a much-needed service to those less fortunate.

Even these advantages, however, are often insufficient to compensate for the job stress and low pay. Full-time pay at some agencies is $7 per hour, a pittance for a breadwinner. Home health care remains a poorly regulated industry, whose profits depend on unskilled, poorly trained, and uncertified workers. Currently the supply of workers is high, giving agencies little incentive to invest in better training for better-qualified workers, or to share with workers the industry's considerable profits. Without better training and industry regulations, the psychological stress and backbreaking physical demands of the job ultimately take their toll. Vicki, who has worked more than once in home health care, explains:

> I stayed with old man Jones for three years. Broke my heart when he died. I told them I didn't wanna work for no one for a while. I just couldn't take it. I needed a break. I had to leave.

Maggie is married, in her fifties, and mother of two adult children. She has worked as a nurse's aide and as a home health-care worker. When asked what she does for a living, she responds, "I'm a nurse." Due to health problems, she is currently on disability. She appears clinically depressed about not being able to work and is worried about her health. She is trying to will herself back to health because she "can't afford to be sick" much longer. She comments:

> I worked in a home for years before I quit. I left 'cause it was too hard and you get so attached to those old people. I remember coming in the room and this lady I'd taken care of had died. They'd already stripped her bed and

cleaned the room. Nobody told me nothing. I just didn't want to be around all that death—took me a long time to get over that. . . . No, I will not work in the old folks homes again.

Many women suffer from the physical demands of the work:

> After awhile, moving people gets hard. That's dead weight you're trying to move, 'cause a lot of them can't move by themselves. You change diapers on grown people, clean up after them, bathe them, dress them. After awhile you just can't do it. You go home sore and hurting when you get through. I like the people and helping, but I was killing myself.

Like people everywhere, many people in Meadow View get jobs through family and friend networks. Those seeking work regularly interrogate others about job leads. But workers who sponsor relatives run the risk of damaging their own reputation if the relatives do not succeed. For instance, Wanda's brother, John, who held a respected position at a residential rehabilitation center, sponsored two cousins, a brother, and a sister for jobs. On his recommendation, all were hired, and eventually everyone quit. One resigned because he feared being fired. Because he worked a different shift than his relatives, he had to "bum" rides to and from work. Without reliable transportation, he was habitually late. The sister, who worked in the laundry, hated the drudgery of the work and claimed her supervisor was unfair and mistreated her. She left and eventually found other employment. A third quit after a disagreement with another co-worker. Of the four who terminated, one remained unemployed for more than a year. John, embarrassed, vowed never to sponsor anyone again. His sister explains why she believes things did not work out:

> They didn't really like the work. See, John has a good job there, he don't get messed over. But the rest of them . . . they caught it coming and going. And the whites kept on John about his relatives, what they did and didn't do.

On the other hand, if an employee works out well, an employer may come to view the sponsor as a reliable source for bringing responsible workers into the workplace. In Mabel's family, job sponsoring has worked out for two siblings in their early twenties.

> Both of them work at Brown's Chicken now. Ron got the job first and when his boss asked him if he knew some good workers, he told him about Juanda. Now they both are there. They're doing good, they like it. They get called in to do extra work all the time when somebody doesn't show up.

Many of the mothers I interviewed have acquired jobs through similar networks; they recognize their personal and skill limitations. They know that "good" jobs (i.e., full-time jobs that pay above minimum wage, with benefits) are not the jobs they will secure. For the most part they find jobs that are temporary, part-time, devoid of benefits, and always low paying.

The unavailability of good jobs is not the only obstacle that these mothers in Meadow View confront when they try to obtain employment. Simply getting to one's place of employment is difficult. It is widely accepted that urban communities are usually removed from suburban jobs, housing, quality schools, and other amenities. But the same isolation plagues old black suburbs. The significance of race is an indisputable fact in suburban development (Logan 1983/1988; see also Farley 1976). Decisions regarding transportation, suburban zoning codes, restrictive racial covenants in real estate investment and lending practices, redlining, and other discriminatory practices have historically been racially influenced (Massey and Denton 1993). Meadow View is not only a community that lacks industry, it is also situated in a region that is geographically isolated. Workers need to travel well beyond its borders to find work. Even though hordes of suburban workers access a highly developed transportation system that brings them to city jobs each day, traveling between suburbs in this region is much more difficult. And when Meadow View workers find jobs in the city that can be reached by public transportation, they may not be able to afford the commute. A round trip from Meadow View to the city costs almost ten dollars. To take advantage of travel discounts offered to frequent riders, one must purchase a monthly ticket, requiring a considerable outlay of money up front.

Amy, the mother of four young boys, is in her late twenties. At the age of nineteen she won custody of her five siblings after her mother died and her father abandoned them. Until recently and for ten years, she received welfare. She then got a job in a suburb not far from Meadow View and hoped that she would be able to walk the two miles from the bus to her job. The only problem she anticipated was inclement weather. When asked about arranging a daily taxi pickup from the bus, she reminded me that such luxuries were beyond her means and that the region does not have a dependable taxi service. Instead, Amy created an elaborate strategy for getting herself and her current boyfriend to and from work, which involved a carefully managed arrangement with a former boyfriend. This man, who was considerably older than Amy, considered her four children his responsibility—although he was the biological father of only the third child. Initially he agreed to drive Amy and her new boyfriend to work; if he was in a generous mood and did not have to work himself, he would even loan his car to her. But this arrangement was inherently unstable. When friends and other intimates are repeatedly called on for transportation, there is a good chance that personal mood and disposition will eventually get in the way. Amy tells of her experience calling on her former boyfriend:

> We were paying my ex-boyfriend to take Curtis (her new boyfriend) to work. No problems. Then he started getting an attitude and saying he couldn't take him. Now he knew there was no other way for him to get there. But because he was mad at me, he wanted to pull out.

Her new boyfriend worked part-time at a fast-food establishment. No bus routes went near his job and a cab was out of the question. Finally, the couple agreed to pay the ex-boyfriend more money until they could find another means of transportation. Because her plan was highly unreliable and filled with tension, Amy experienced considerable anxiety each day about getting to work.

Meadow View mothers unanimously desire work. They attempt it whenever they can. But they fail often, and not because they lack motivation or a work ethic. They fall short because the demands of simultaneous parenting and working eventually spin out of control, even with family support. They fail because the jobs for which they qualify turn out to be awful in the long run and eventually clash with family demands. They fail also because they work in job markets that discriminate against female bread-winners. In response, mothers quit. They hope to return at a more opportune time. Settings like Meadow View place considerable burdens on families, making it difficult, and often impossible, to parent and work successfully.

## SUMMARY

Barriers of space and place are not unique to Meadow View. Poverty and racial segregation, conjoined with spatial isolation and disconnection from the city that it lies near, prevent this suburb from receiving many basic services. The inability to afford a quality police and fire department, for example, exacerbate many problems here. Crime and fear of random violence force parents to become hypervigilant about their children, especially because the suburb has no institutional supports—afterschool programs, day care providers—to help parents keep their children safely occupied. Parents must rely on family networks, but such networks are often strained by the demands placed on them. For people here, options are extremely limited.

Keeping children safe consumes parents and influences decisions about looking for work outside the home. Mothers, who assume much of the parenting, easily become overwhelmed by the unrelenting demands of this environment. The community is devoid of adequate resources such as a public library, youth services, and recreation programs. Poor pay tempts some police officers and firefighters to partner with the drug economy, leaving residents unprotected and vulnerable to random violence. Consequently, considerable effort is devoted to watching and protecting children. One must be forever vigilant about keeping children near and troublemakers far, a task that is not easy.

In Meadow View, the family is key to survival. Families provide transportation, housing, food, job leads, and emotional succor. Child care, a service that every working mother with dependent children requires, is provided by relatives and friends who are outside the labor force. Because of this, mothers' work is inextricably linked to the nonwork or misfortunes of other women who may or may not be employed. Since few can afford to actually purchase the care they need, child care provided by industry chains is out of reach for these families, both financially and geographically. Although mothers appreciate the custodial care the family provides, they have limited alternatives. Head Start fails to reach all those who need it, and those who use it must make elaborate plans to retrieve children, whose school schedules do not correspond with a regular, full-time workday. Child care here is prone to disruptions and is unreliable. Unexpected illnesses interrupt work, making mothers more likely to be tardy, absent, and distracted on the job.

These family networks are not without tensions. As more and more families experience hardships, the networks become increasingly stressed. It is difficult to meet everyone's needs. In some families, substance abuse has created a need to provide shelter for children and the substance abuser. Eventually the core group of givers becomes overwhelmed, forced to make tragic choices as to who can and who cannot be salvaged.

The emphasis from both the political right and left focuses on reducing welfare dependency rather than on eliminating poverty (Schram 1995). The right, with its emphasis on the individual as the key to achievement, sees the problem as a lack of good character, behavior, and sound morals. The liberal left, with its stress on developing one's human capital (Gans 1995; Handler 1995) argues that with the proper schooling, job preparation, and skills, the poor can assimilate into the world of work and perform like other Americans. But neither understands the multiple effects of poverty on poor mothers (single or married) who live in a community context that manufactures major barriers to simultaneous working and parenting. Work does not exist in isolation from family and community (see McKnight 1995). What is missing from both camps is an understanding of the daily demands on families trapped in an economically depressed and racially segregated community that is also geographically isolated and lacks the most basic resources.

Over time, such conditions create deep and multiple needs in both people and institutions. Parenting in an impoverished, unsafe community forces parents to make decisions about employment and self-sufficiency based on how they can best protect their children and hold on to the coping strategies that have worked in the past. Being thrust into low-wage work, without substitute supports and services or a method for maintaining what has already been carved out, puts already vulnerable families and children at great risk. Parents need the security of knowing that the most vulnerable among them, their children and the elderly, will be safe, cared for, and protected.

Successful work programs will need to go beyond teaching job skills to consider community issues that program participants confront regularly. At the very least, work programs should address issues of community space, family obligation, local institutional support, and how these forces, alone and together, affect parents' ability to be productive workers and effective parents. For poor people to be simultaneously good workers and good parents, they need access to the same supports and resources that other working citizens have. Policymakers must develop a perspective that incorporates the full array of forces that go into work and parenting decisions (Dickerson 1995; McKnight 1995). Lacking this, policymakers will create policies and programs that have little relevance to the real, day-to-day world in which the poor struggle to survive.

## NOTES

1. Although few talked about leaving children with boyfriends for this chapter previous fieldwork suggests that this is often done out of desperation and rarely considered an ideal situation. The risk to children left with unskilled and unwilling care-givers needs to be examined from a child safety perspective.
2. This animal shelter worker has held several nursing home jobs but found them emotionally stressful, unpleasant, and difficult to manage without a car.
3. As more middle-class families experience problems with abusive child-care workers and poorly managed child-care chains, this is less true.
4. Living conditions in Meadow View are often unsafe. Over 34 percent of Meadow View's housing is considered "substandard."

5. The daughter's need to adjust her college schedule to accommodate the child-care needs of her family could be a barrier for completing her education. The potential exists that she will leave school due to unexpressed pressures to help her family, that family needs supersede her own. An afterschool program could ease this type of child-care issue. For now, the daughter's school schedule is secondary to her family's needs.

## REFERENCES

Abel, E. K., and M. K. Nelson, eds. 1990. *Circles of Care: Work and Identity in Women's Lives.* Albany: State University of New York Press.

Brownlee, S. 1996. "The Biology of Soul Murder." *U.S. News & World Report,* 11 November, 121:71–73.

DeVault, M. L. 1991. *Feeding the Family: The Social Organization of Caring as Gendered Work.* Chicago: University of Chicago Press.

Dickerson, B. J., ed. 1995. *African American Single Mothers: Understanding Their Lives and Families.* Thousand Oaks, CA: Sage.

Eisler, P. 1997. "Home Health Care: 'All the Components for Disaster.'" *USA Today,* Special Home Health Care Report 4D:Life, 18 March.

Farley, R. 1976. "Components of Suburban Population Growth." In *The Changing Face of the Suburbs,* ed. B. Schwartz. Chicago: University of Chicago Press.

Gans, H. J. 1995. *The War against the Poor. The Underclass and Antipoverty Policy.* New York: Basic Books.

Garbarino, J., N. Dubrow, K. Kostelny, and C. Pardo, eds. 1992. *Children in Danger: Coping with the Consequences of Community Violence.* San Francisco: Jossey-Bass.

Handler, J. F. 1995. *The Poverty of Welfare Reform.* New Haven: Yale University Press.

Heymann, S. J., A. Earle, and B. Egleston. 1996. "Parental Availability for the Care of Sick Children." *Pediatrics: The Journal of the American Academy of Pediatrics* 98:226–230.

Hicks-Bartlett, S. T. Forthcoming. *Kin of Mine: Community and Family Life in a Low Income Suburb.*

Hiss, T. 1990. *The Experience of Place.* New York: Vintage Books.

Jones, J. 1986. *Labor of Love, Labor of Sorrow: Black Women, Work and the Family, From Slavery to the Present.* New York: Basic Books.

Katz, M. B. 1989. *The Underserving Poor. From the War on Poverty to the War on Welfare.* New York: Pantheon Books.

Logan, J. R. 1983/1988. "Realities of Black Suburbanization." In *New Perspectives on the American Community,* compiled by Roland L. Warren and Larry Lyon, 231–40. Homewood, IL: Dorsey Press.

Massey, D. S., and N. A. Denton. 1993. *American Apartheid: Segregation and the Making of the Underclass.* Cambridge: Harvard University Press.

McKnight, J. 1995. *The Careless Society: Community and Its Counterfeits.* New York: Basic Books.

Prothrow-Stith, D., and M. Weissman. 1993. *Deadly Consequences.* New York: HarperCollins.

Rank, M. R. 1994. *Living on the Edge: The Realities of Welfare in America.* New York: Columbia University Press.

Schein, V. E. 1995. *Working from the Margins: Voices of Mothers in Poverty.* Ithaca and London: ILR Press.

Schram, S. F. 1995. *Words of Welfare: The Poverty of Social Science and the Social Science of Poverty.* Minneapolis: University of Minnesota Press.

Stack, C. B. 1974. *All Our Kin: Strategies for Survival in a Black Community.* New York: Harper & Row.

Stack, C. B. 1990. "Different Voices, Different Visions: Gender, Culture and Moral Reasoning." In *Uncertain Terms: Negotiating Gender in American Culture,* eds. F. Ginsburg and A. L. Tsing, 19–27. Boston: Beacon Press.

Statham, A., E. M. Miller, and H. O. Mauksch, eds. 1988. *The Worth of Women's Work: A Qualitative Synthesis.* New York: State University of New York Press.

Tronto, J. C. 1994. *Moral Boundaries: A Political Argument for an Ethic of Care.* New York: Routledge.

Wilson, W. J. 1987. *The Truly Disadvantaged: The Inner City, the Underclass, and Public Policy.* Chicago: University of Chicago Press.

———. 1996. *When Work Disappears: The World of the New Urban Poor.* New York: Knopf.

# Rethinking Caribbean Families:
## Extending the Links

### *Mary Chamberlain*

## INTRODUCTION

Amongst all the 270 families . . . studied in Jamaica, not a single one consisted only of parents and their children. Every family included additional children and adults variously described as nephews, grandsons, stepsons, cousins, "aunties" and "grannies."

*(Simey, 1946, p. 84)*

Despite the prevalence of "aunties" and, in particular, "grannies" in our knowledge of (and in the literature on) the Caribbean family, and despite the descriptions and observations relating to the widespread practice of child-shifting (the temporary or permanent fostering of the child by kin folk, usually a grandmother, aunt or a close family friend), there has been surprisingly little focus on the role of grandparents except in relation to their function as surrogate parents, a function interpreted variously as a standby position resulting from the absence of the biological parent(s), and/or as a dependency feature characteristic of what Henriques (1953) described as "lower class families." In this, the grandmother or maternal family is

so-called because the grandmother or some female relative, perhaps a sister, usurps the function of the father and at times that of the mother. Such a family

can originate through the girl becoming pregnant while still living at home. The household may consist of her mother, her mother's sister, and the girl's siblings. The girl may remain at home and look after her child, but in many cases she leaves and the child is brought up by its grandmother. The girl's child is treated in the same way as the other children in the household, no distinctions are made. If the girl's father lives in the house he will act towards his grandchild as if it were his own child.

(Henriques, 1953, p. 110)

And, as Henriques observed in this type of family, "the usual period of maternal dependence is enlarged from that of childhood to include the greater part of adult life . . . A daughter can look for protection and care for herself and her children to the latter group" (Henriques, 1953, p. 163).

For Henriques, as for other scholars, the primary explanation for both the prevalence of grandparents in the upbringing of children, and for what appears to be an extended period of dependency, lay in economics. Poverty was the overriding imperative which drove the sharing of childrearing activities, initiated by the mother as a response to the need for childcare to support her extradomestic activities in the absence of a husband or male breadwinner and willingly condoned by the grandmother. Indeed, in Henriques' view, the introduction of the grandmother or other relative into the care of the child emerges as a casual consequence of the daughter's fecklessness. Once there, however, the daughter has an obligation to support not only her child but the household in which she lives. What

All interview quotations are from the following interview transcripts from *Living arrangements, family structure and social change of Caribbeans in Britain*: JK030, JK031, JH141, JP061, and JP052.

seems to be lacking in such a perspective is a human and a cultural response: the desire of all parties to be engaged in the rearing of children, regardless of economic demands.

This article explores the role of wider kin in childrearing, using two case studies drawn from a wider sample of life stories from 60 three-generation families who originated in Jamaica, Barbados, and Trinidad. These life stories emerge from the research undertaken by Harry Goulbourne and myself on *Living arrangements, family structure and social change of Caribbeans in Britain,*[1] funded by the ESRC within their research program on Population and Household Change.

## THE RESEARCH CONTEXT

In the context of our research into Caribbean migrant families, the role of grandparents in the rearing of the children of parents absent through migration was brought into profile. Their willingness to care for grandchildren enabled their own children to migrate and may thus be seen as a necessary prerequisite for migration. It could be argued that they were central to the formation of diasporic families, such as those which have emerged in the Caribbean. Interviewing across the generations, however, reveals that the role and importance of grandparents in contributing to the upbringing of grandchildren is not solely dependent on an absent parent but is evident, to a greater or lesser degree, in many families regardless of economic circumstance, and regardless of the generation or period. Thus while many of the children of the migrants who came to Britain between 1948 and 1966 were brought up by their grandparents for part or all of their lives, their parents recounted similar family profiles. While this profile has revealed the importance of an older generation in the care and rearing of children, the narratives employed in these descriptions raise issues which extend beyond a base definition of financial or social convenience. That grandparents—and grandmothers in particular—could be relied upon to provide practical support in childcare and fostering suggests at minimum an accepted and agreed—what we may call a cultural—disposition toward assuming this role. But the role itself is multifaceted, embracing a broader disposition toward childcare as a family, even a neighborhood, responsibility. This, in turn, raises issues on the nature, purpose, and practice of networks, and extends interpretation beyond the physical nature of support into metaphysical concerns over the nature and meaning of family and lineage, and within that on the nature and meaning of the mother and the child. Equally, the presumption that the grandmother role is occupied solely with

childcare obscures not only the complex meanings behind such roles, but obscures the role which grandfathers may play in family and kinship relations—in much the same way as a concern with mother-headed households has obscured the role of fathers within the household and family. Thus, the multifaceted nature and gender-differentiated aspects of these roles may be seen not only through the practical help in childcare/fostering and support, but equally in the communicative role in linking family members and retaining (and extending) kinship networks within and between families, the symbolic role in providing continuity through the generations (including ancestors) and a socializing role. Conversely, grandchildren often have a close relationship with, and responsibility toward, grandparents, extending what Brodber (1986, p. 25) described as their "perceptual" field of family and generating a sense of "emotional expansiveness" although, in her view, while this may create a greater sense of independence, it may also lead to feelings of dislocation and anomie.

Let me now tease out some of those ideas through exploring the role of surrogate parents in two, very different, case studies.

### Case Study 1

My grandmother . . . she was, she is, a blessing, she's sweet, she is so sweet.[2]

Two images of grandmothers recur throughout the narratives. Grandmothers are invariably described in terms of endearment, frequently couched in spiritual metaphors (Chamberlain, 2000). In parallel with these images are notions of strength. Grandmothers are as frequently described in terms of being a "strong woman," and a "hard worker."

Claudine, whose description is cited above, was born in 1956. She and her two (Jamaican born) younger siblings were brought up by their maternal grandmother, Beth, when their mother migrated to Britain in 1960. Claudine's parents were not married, and each of her Jamaican-born siblings had a different father. Claudine's mother subsequently married in England, and had two more British-born children by this husband. Beth had 10 children, six of whom died in infancy. Although she was married, this occurred late in her life, to the father of her two youngest children. Beth lived on family land in Jamaica, close to her parents (Claudine's great grandparents).

Claudine's description of her grandmother is bound up with the image of strength and hard work, her contribution measured as much by the number of hours expended as by the qualitative nature of, and fruits of, her labors. Children rarely differentiated between the housework and homework performed by their grandmothers, seeing the two as an integrated whole. Indeed, many informants, when asked whether their grandmothers worked, replied in the negative, only later to explain in some detail how their grandmothers made ends meet through a variety of strategies which could generate either income or goods for home consumption. In this case, Beth worked some 10 acres of farmland, and travelled to market each week to sell the produce.

While the notion of "blessing" may be seen as an epithet of endearment, it also contained a recognition of a wider role within that community. Beth was also a "blessed person," taking in, and bringing up in addition to her three grandchildren, nine nephews and nieces, and six other non-kin children such as Tyrone who "came from a different parish, and he was like, in the area, and his dad was . . . doing little bits and pieces for her, following her to get . . . oranges when she was going to market and then, all of a sudden, he was living there!"[3]

The occurrence of child fostering or child-shifting is a feature recognized in many Caribbean households (Clarke, 1957; Herskovits, 1941; Senior, 1991; Soto, 1994) with varying degrees of stability and success and with a variety of explanations for its cultural origins and social causes, whether out of benevolence, duty, or as a form of exchange. In Beth's case, it appears to be a combination of motives. Her grandchildren were living with her when their mother migrated. Claudine's mother had never set up home independently, nor cohabited with any of the fathers of her children. Beth's nine nephews and nieces lived in the house opposite when their parents migrated. Beth took the youngest two to live with her, while the remaining seven slept in their own home, under Beth's vigilant eye. Beth was requested to care for the other, non-kin, children. Three features are significant about Beth's role. Her willingness to rear the next generation enabled her own children and her siblings to migrate to Britain and to the United States. Indeed, in this family, as in many Caribbean families, there was a long and continuing tradition of migration. Beth's father and her husband had both migrated for periods to North America. In her father's absence, Beth lived with her mother in her grandmother's house. The family model was one which implicated the grandmother in the rearing of children and featured as an unquestioned dynamic in family organization. It is commonly argued that such practices were the result of male absence, serving as an explanation of the high incidence of single-mother-headed households and the subsequent heightened authority and power of women—what Constance Sutton (1997, p. ix) calls the power by "default" thesis—and as evidence of the

singular adaptability of the Caribbean family to adverse circumstances. The corollary, however, may suggest that this family formation preceded the migration movements of the nineteenth and twentieth centuries (Higman, 1976) (in which, incidentally, women as well as men migrated [Chamberlain, 1997]) and was the enabling factor in, rather than the consequence of, migration.

Second, while child-shifting has been a regular feature of Caribbean families, Beth was a figure in the community to whom parents—and children— could turn for help. Such a status could not arise in a vacuum, but from a reputation transmitted through networks of contact and support and through an acceptance that children could be as adequately reared by another as by their own kin or mother. Tyrone, after all, came from another parish. The other children came as a result of requests: one, for instance, "his mum had three of them and she was only young and she couldn't take care of them"[4] and asked Beth to take care of one. Finally, the result for Beth was an incorporation into her family of other members who brought with them, as children, a share of and contribution to the human capital of the household. One child, for instance, a boy called Clifton, "helped her to run the house, she sent him to school, and he was there for about six or seven years".[5] Clifton would act as baby-sitter during Beth's visits to the market, taking care of the children and the house.[6]

Her "investment" reaped dividends as the children grew to adulthood. The son of one of the nephews she raised now lives with Beth in her advanced years. All the children she brought up—including those like Clifton who were not kin—continue to help support her, financially, materially and so

> she's always happy, because . . . every now and then she'll get a letter from someone who she actually brought up and if . . . they're still in Jamaica, they'll drive up and give her little bits and pieces and stay for the day and what have you. So she's well loved in the district.[7]

Indeed, as Claudine observed, "She has got everything she wants now".[8]

The element of instrumentality inherent in this behavior may be seen as a form of exchange, perhaps akin to (but by no means the equivalent of) that in works of art, "a trade in things which have no price [which] belongs to the class of practices in which the logic of pre-capitalist economy lives on (as it does, in another sphere, in the economy of exchanges between the generations)" (Bourdieu, 1993, p. 74). What generates value is the accumulation of what Bourdieu (1993, p. 75) calls symbolic capital: "'Symbolic capital' is to be understood as economic or political capital that is disavowed, misrecognized and thereby recognized, hence legitimate, a 'credit' which, under certain conditions, and always in the long run, guarantees 'economic' profits." At the same time, value—through reputation—is accrued. Thus, caring for children may in later years produce rewards which can be measured in economic terms, through direct financial support in the supply of material goods, and indirect in the supply of care and other services.

Beth's role as a surrogate parent clearly involved a degree of instrumentality and exchange which may have been one motive behind the actions which she, and many other grandmothers or women (particularly those who had been childless) in our sample, followed. This was within a context which expected and approved such activity, and which thereby extended kinship and surrogate kinship bonds and networks. As an ancillary, the value in the return extends beyond the children into the neighborhood. Beth, for instance, regularly fed passersby and acted host to a range of visitors. As a result, in her old age, Beth has the support of kin, adoptive kin, and the neighborhood.

Part of the explanation for this active incorporation into parenting must lie in the "open" structures of kin membership (Rodman, 1971; Smith, 1956), and one of the recurring features in this research has been the strength of kinship and the importance of kinship networks in sustaining the emotional and the material support of its members. Yet none of this arises in a vacuum. The "adaptive" arguments as explanation of Caribbean family formation and kinship may have a compelling rationale in terms of maximizing scarce economic resources and as responses to poverty, and may be corroborated by other studies which appear to demonstrate that the formation of powerful mother figures and extended kinship links is a modern response to poverty with parallels among the Irish community (Bott, 1957), or in London's East End (Young & Willmott, 1957). Such explanations do not, however, take into account the importance of both history and culture in the shaping of contemporary behavior. Indeed, as recent revisionist studies have shown, such patterns can also be discerned among middle-class Caribbean families (Black, 1995; Smith, 1988; Young, 1990) and among Caribbean migrant communities abroad (Sutton & Chaney, 1994), suggesting that culture may be a more enduring ingredient in family formation than (unstable) economic constraints.

There remains, however, another important consideration relating to wealth. While the symbolic capital accumulated by a woman may in the long term be translated into crude dollars, the symbolism itself has not been dissipated. While "making" a child

"for" its father may be seen as a ritualistic entry into adulthood, children themselves are regarded as the inheritors of a lineage, as evidence of continuity and, in turn, conduits of that continuity. As the distinguished anthropologist Constance Sutton has pointed out, there are important parallels between these beliefs and those held by the Yoruba who

> Consider children their most important form of wealth . . . a woman's ability to produce this form of wealth, that is, her procreative power, was regarded as a critical immanent power that women—referred to frequently as "our mothers" possessed . . . continuity was inscribed in the culturally constructed meanings of life, death, and rebirth of genealogically connected humans. New born children represented reborn ancestors, recent and distant. They in turn give birth to the future, and after their death become ancestors waiting to be reborn. This was the missing key in my earlier understanding of the power attributed to mothers in Barbados. (Sutton, 1998, p. 143)

The repetitions and commonality in the language used by women to describe their mothers and grandmothers suggest the existence of widely held beliefs relating to lineage and continuity (Chamberlain, 2000). Lineage becomes the logic which conveys the meaning of family, the "pull" of the ancestors is reflected in a strong sense of "carrying" previous generations, in a belief that ancestors have the power to "take" a child into their thrall, and an equally powerful language suggesting a reconstitution if not a rebirth through the generations: "I am a nice woman," another informant said, "I am *from* my mother" (emphasis added).[9] Lineage is both actual and symbolic, and carries responsibilities as well as privileges. Mothers and mother substitutes, such as grandmothers, have to be sufficiently strong to carry out the physical labor of childrearing (and bearing), as well as bear the spiritual or symbolic responsibilities as carriers of lineage. Part of those responsibilities is to ensure that the children in the line can mature to respect and continue it, and, as women mature into old age and grandparenthood, those responsibilities increase and extend over their grandchildren, and those of others who cannot shoulder the responsibility. It is, therefore, significant that such women are described both as "blessed," for their symbolic capital has been extended, and as "strong," "hardworking" women.

While such behavior may generate what Brodber described as an "emotional expansiveness," it is not without risks. Claudine, for instance, failed to establish a close relationship with her mother. She was 4 years old when her mother migrated to Britain, regular contact was not created until Claudine herself came to England in 1989, and the subsequent relationship has been stormy and spasmodic. Other informants also recount difficulties in reestablishing (or establishing) relationships with mothers after periods of absence. Yet the symbolic link remains, for Claudine refuses to deny her mother or ignore her existence.

The emphasis on the maternal grandmother should not obscure the role of the father's family in the sense and meaning of family. Claudine's father had migrated to Britain shortly after she was born. She did not meet him until she herself migrated to Britain, although she was aware that he took an interest in her progress, and maintained contact with her family and, to a lesser extent, her mother. Claudine knew her father's mother, although she never knew his father. Her mother's father (her grandfather) lived close to her grandmother and, although married to another woman, visited weekly, and was part of the cohort of neighbors who could be called upon to help her grandmother on the land. Indeed, Claudine included in her concept of close family her mother's (half) brothers and sisters, recalling how "we used to, like, on our way home from school, we used to go round there and get . . . [at] my uncle's, lunch . . . and my uncles . . . we had good relations with all of them."[10] The grandfather she was closest to, however, was her grandmother's husband, and it was for him that she reserved the familial endearment of "a very hard-working man," he co-farmed the land with her grandmother, and "he was so nice," acting on occasions as mediator between her grandmother and herself. He died when Claudine was 19.

Although none of her grandfathers featured as significant figures in Claudine's account of her childhood, they and their families were nevertheless actively present, and included within the broader definition of family and kin. Indeed, it was through them that her own kinship network was extended. They clearly assumed a paternal and grand-paternal role toward all children brought within the umbrella of Beth's household. Relatedly, and significantly, Claudine's maternal uncle played an equally active role in her upbringing, contributing help in cash and kind, and fostering her when she went to secondary school in Kingston. "My whole life," she said, "revolved around them."[11] It would, therefore, be mistaken to assume that the male members of the family—from all sides—were marginal figures. Indeed, when her son Gregor was born, it was to Gregor's father's family that she turned for support. Gregor lived as a young child with his father and stepmother who, in turn, lived with his parents, until Gregor's father migrated to the United States. It was at that point that his paternal aunt took over his care, and "taught me everything I knew. And when it wasn't her, it was my grandfather."[12] The arrangement permitted Claudine to work and, ultimately, to migrate to Britain. It also helped redistribute the wealth inherited in and through children, to divest some of the symbolic capital into a branch of the family where it was lacking and to return the child, a son, to the paternal line.

Indeed, Gregor's aunt lived close to his paternal grandparents, and they played an active part in his upbringing "I grew up with them," he says, "and now I've been apart from them . . . it's just your family man, they're just not here, so you miss them."[13] This grandmother travels to North America, to visit and help out her children there, with such frequency that, as Gregor joked, "I think she's got her own [aeroplane] seat!."[14] He did not meet his maternal grandparents until he came to Britain to join his mother as a teenager and, largely as a result, is not close to either of them.

It would, equally, be mistaken to equate the expansive family exclusively with lower-class values and life styles. Although Beth was a small farmer and higgler, all the children in her care—including Claudine—received secondary, and in many cases tertiary, education. Claudine herself is a professional, as is her uncle. Gregor's paternal grandfather was a businessman, and his maternal grandmother a teacher before working in the family business. Nevertheless, across both sides of the family, there was a normative assumption that childcare was, when necessary, a family affair and an equally powerful assumption that all blood kin, regardless of which side of the conjugal bed they originated, and which line of the family they most favored, shared an equality of family membership. These were values which Claudine clearly recognized in her grandparents, Gregor in his and which became an integral feature of both of their socialization. "The family," as Gregor concluded,

is the greatest thing on earth. It can also be the most troublesome, but the family is, I don't know how to put it better than blood over water. It's part of you. There's no way you can escape from it. Absolutely no way. You're tied to them for life, and beyond.[15]

### Case Study 2

I never meet a husband. I'm still a single person. I never have any children, but I grow my niece.

If the role of grandparents, and other female kin, in "growing" children is as much a product of culture as it is of economic necessity, then it is reasonable to assume that such patterns would continue in a diverse range of circumstances. Not all families are, however, as expansive as Claudine's, and the lack of a kinship network can be an issue. Miss McLeod left school at the age of 15, and at 17 migrated to Kingston from

St Anne to learn dressmaking. The wages, however, were low and she found a job in a sweet factory in 1948, where she stayed until migrating to Britain in 1960. Once in England, she sent for her niece to join her: "I used to love her, from she was a baby at home, and I used to send things for her, you know. And as I didn't have any children."[16]

The choice to "grow" this child is significant. Miss McLeod was born in 1926 in Jamaica. She was raised initially by her father, a stevedore, who "loved me so much, you know, that he wanted me." He died when she was 4, and was cared for by her paternal grandparents, who "loved me so much that they wanted me and then, you know, in the West Indies, them days, people don't fight against . . . you can't have the child . . . you just go to them."[17] Her grandfather (also a stevedore) died when she was 6, and her grandmother when she was 8 years old. Then, "my mother take me over."[18] Miss McLeod was the eldest of her mother's three children. Her mother was not married to her father. Miss McLeod's two siblings (one of whom died) were from a subsequent relationship. Their father, however, acted as a father to her: "he was kind," she recalled, "he look after the two of us. Christmas time, whatever he got, I get it. There was no difference. You know, there was no difference."[19] Miss McLeod's own childhood had been punctuated by a series of child-shifting arrangements.

The niece she "grew" was her brother's child, whom she looked after from birth. Her status as a single, childless aunt, and her love of the child, was sufficient to enable her to claim the baby as her own, in much the same way that her own grandparents had claimed her. In Miss McLeod's case, she wanted to give, as much as she received, a slightly different rendition of the symbolic capital of the first case study. Miss McLeod migrated to Britain in 1960, sending for this brother in 1962 and, in 1965, his daughter, her niece, Marvetta. Miss McLeod's brother was not married to Marvetta's mother, and they had never lived together. Marvetta's mother worked as a child attendant for a "higher status" family in Kingston, and while Marvetta's memories of her mother are "warm," they are "limited":

> I then came to England . . . I kept in touch with her through post but . . . I wouldn't say she was illiterate, but she wasn't good at writing letters . . . Over the years it dwindled, but we kept in touch . . . There wasn't much that my mum was able to do for me, really.[20]

In this case, Marvetta did not know her mother's parents, nor her mother's two sons, nor her father's other son. She was brought up by Miss McLeod, who lived in what she describes as the "tenement yard," with her paternal grandmother (she never knew her paternal grandfather, who died before she was born) and other kin in close proximity: "it was warm, it was like a big family really."[21] Her grandmother, like others, was "a hard worker" but it was to her aunt, who had no children of her own, and never married, that she reserved the notion of "strong":

> Looking back, really, I suppose she's been a mother and aunt! She was there for me before I was born, and she's always been there. She's a very independent woman . . . taking on the role as a mother, my aunt has helped stabilize . . . the family unit, because she looked after me when she herself was in Jamaica. When she left and went to England . . . she then helped send for my Dad which, in turn, both of them sent for me . . . she was the one who basically was the order of the day . . . And she's very dominant . . . just being a strong black woman has helped keep the family together and has helped put me on the right road, so to speak. She's given me all the things, really, that my mum and dad should have.[22]

Unlike many families, this family is small. Marvetta's siblings are strangers to her. Marvetta's mother had one brother who survived to adulthood. Marvetta did not know him as a child. Her father had only one sister, her aunt. Her grandmother, however, had a number of brothers so great uncles featured in her childhood, although many of them, and their children, had migrated. The family, as she described it, while "not really small [was] distant, very far apart . . . there's no strong link between anyone,"[23] a circumstance which Marvetta attributes to slavery (*sic*) and migration "so over the years you find that communication breaks down. So I put my family down to that."[24] After her aunt migrated to Britain, Marvetta (like her aunt) was "shifted" between her mother, her paternal grandmother, and "going back to that kinship thing then, you'll find that within the tenement yard, you'll find other people able to look after kids . . . knitting together as a family."[25] In 1965, when she was 9, she was sent for by her aunt to join her and her father in England. She lived with her aunt until she left home at the age of 18. At 21, Marvetta had her first child. She now has three children, by the same man, from whom she lives apart. She supports her children alone. "I'm basically back into that circle again, as my mother, my aunt, you know. With my mother, there was no support from the male. I'm now in that position."[26] Indeed, she sees herself as a replica of her aunt, "I'm a bit in her shadow . . . a lot of her has been instilled in me."[27] Marvetta works as a clerk and, despite attempts to improve her education and skills through evening classes, "what's held me back in life is that I've had my children, and *I haven't got family support*" (emphasis added).[28]

The limited circumference of the kinship circle has left Marvetta bereft of family help, and the experience of two generations of child-shifting has created a determination not to replicate the patterns with her own children. Nevertheless, despite her experiences, she argues:

I am a black West Indian woman, living in England, trying very hard to achieve certain goals, for the benefit of myself and my family, and to one day return back to my homeland ... the links in the Caribbean for my children are not very strong ... [but] I hope, by the end of the year or next year, that I can take all three boys out to meet what family I do have out there ... and through meeting ... to keep that link.[29]

## CONCLUSION

The origins of the role of grandmothers and of older women in participating in the "growing" of children remain both tantalizing and speculative. Yet, as our two case studies show, such practices and beliefs in the importance of this role, even when the kinship circle is thin, have endured across the generations and through the migration process. These are not exceptional women, operating in exceptional circumstances, for the stories of grandmothers and their role in childrearing, with or without the absence of parents, is replicated widely throughout the Caribbean. Other families describe how, in Britain, grandmothers continue to contribute to the upbringing of their grandchildren, and act as a beacon in relaying and unifying the family network. Social necessity or utility provides one explanation for its continuing practice, and, as with many useful social practices, it adapts to meet changing circumstances.

Practicality may not be the sole explanation, however, for such practices are accompanied by an elaborate system of values, and a compelling and abiding logic of kinship and descent which recognizes the role of kin in "growing" children. Indeed, the language of childbearing, childrearing, and childhood is proactive and self-conscious. Children are not "had by," but "made for" their respective fathers, language which suggests deliberation, awareness, and purpose. It suggests that children become emblems of their parents' adulthood, of their parents' relationship and sexuality and, importantly, of membership of their parents' families. Children are, similarly, "grown." Childhood memories begin when an individual "first knew himself/herself," while the family memory extends across the generations. In this, the oldest participant in the family may be the one who harbors the family memory, and is closest to the

family ancestors—a grandparent's memory of their grandparents is a direct link, for the grandchild, with his or her ancestor.

While the maternal line may be the most familiar, the paternal line, as we have seen in our two case studies, is far from excluded in the distribution of ancestors and in the sharing of children and childcare. Much of the emphasis in the literature on Caribbean families has been on the centrality of women and the subsequent marginalization of men (see Barrow, 1996). This, as Barrow (1998) points out, has reflected the ethnographic and ethnocentric focus of much of the social science research in the field. However, a "revised approach" as she argues, "which listens to people's images and experiences of family and restores culture and history, clears the way for the re-entry of men and the reconstruction of Caribbean masculinity" (Barrow, 1998, p. 357). It would be easy, in our case studies, to emphasize the role of the women—Beth, Miss McLeod—as the major nurturers and to obscure the role that the fathers, grandfathers, and male kin played in this process. Gregor was brought up by his father and subsequently by his father's mother and sister. Miss McLeod had been brought up, initially, by her father's grandparents; Marvetta was brought up by her father's sister. Equally, we should not lose sight in this of the sibling relationships, for Marvetta's father turned to his sister for support, and Gregor's father to his. Nor should we lose sight of the role that uncles played in the care of children. Claudine, as a schoolgirl, was fostered by a maternal uncle. Finally, we should remember that one of Beth's constant visitors, and neighbor upon whom she could rely for help and support, was Claudine's biological grandfather who—married to someone else—nevertheless continued to play a role in the domestic life of the mother of one of his children.

The stress which our informants put on the inclusiveness of family membership and the role this performed for them as children, as indicated by the frequency and apparent ease with which children moved between family carers, suggests an ideology, or culture, of family which plays a communal role in childcare and which, in adulthood, is confirmed through strong, and extensive, kinship bonds. In all of this, it is the family history, and its past, which shapes contemporary responses. The grandparents of today may have experienced their childhood in the Caribbean, but they are willing conduits for these memories to pass to their grandchildren, and with that, to the values which surround and support the importance of kin as both a practical element of family life and of a symbolic element of belonging. Furthermore, the centrifugal tendencies of Caribbean kinship formation increase, rather than diminish, the importance of lineage. "Blood over water," as Gregor argued ". . . you're tied to them for life, *and beyond.*"[30]

## NOTES

1. This article is based on Harry Goulbourne and Mary Chamberlain's *Living arrangements, family structure and social change of Caribbeans in Britain,* funded by the ESRC (award No. L315253009) within their research program on Population and Household Change. This study utilized life story interviews across three generations of 60 families originating in Jamaica, Barbados and Trinidad and Tobago.
2. JK030/2/1/1/9.
3. JK030/2/1/2/15.
4. JK030/2/1/2/11.
5. JK030/2/1/2/11.
6. JK0302/1/2/19.
7. JK030/2/1/2/11.
8. JK030/2/1/2/17–18.
9. JH141/1/1/1.
10. JK030/2/1/1/11.
11. JK030/2/2/2/34.
12. JK031/3/1/1/8.
13. JK031/3/1/2/18.
14. JK031/3/1/2/17.
15. JK031/3/2/1/45.
16. JP061/2/1/1/8.
17. JP061/2/1/1/11.
18. JP061/2/1/1/2.
19. JP061/2/1/1/10.
20. JP052/3/1/1/3.
21. JP052/3/1/1/4. See also Pulsipher (1993).
22. JP052/3/1/1/7.
23. JP052/3/1/1/9.
24. JP052/3/1/1/10.
25. JP052/3/1/1/10.
26. JP052/3/1/2/17.
27. JP052/3/1/2/21.
28. JP052/3/1/2/17.
29. JP052/3/1/25.
30. JK031/3/2/1/45.

## REFERENCES

Barrow, C. (1996). *Family in the Caribbean. Themes and perspectives.* Kingston: Ian Randle and Oxford: James Currey.

Barrow, C. (1998). Caribbean masculinity and family: Revisiting "marginality" and "reputation." In C. Barrow (Ed.), *Caribbean portraits. Essays on gender ideologies and identities* (pp. 339–360). Kingston: Ian Randle and the Centre for Gender and Development Studies, University of the West Indies.

Black, L.M. (1995). My mother never fathered me: Rethinking kinship and the governing of families. *Social and Economic Studies, 44*(1), 49–71.

Bott, E. (1957). *Family and social network: Roles, norms and external relationships in ordinary urban families.* London: Tavistock.

Bourdieu, P. (1993). The production of belief: Contribution to an economy of symbolic goods. In *The field of cultural production.* London: Polity Press.

Brodber, E. (1986). Afro-Jamaican women at the turn of the century. *Social and Economic Studies, 35*(3), 23–50.

Chamberlain, M. (1997). *Narratives of exile and return.* London: Macmillan, Warwick University Caribbean Studies.

Chamberlain, M. (2000). Praise songs of the family: Lineage and kinship in the Caribbean diaspora. *History Workshop Journal, 50,* 114–128.

Clarke, E. (1999 [1957]). *My mother who fathered me: A study of the families in three selected communities of Jamaica.* Barbados, Jamaica, Trinidad & Tobago: University Press of the West Indies.

Henriques, F. (1953). *Family and colour in Jamaica.* London: Eyre & Spottiswoode.

Herskovits, M. (1990 [1941]). *The myth of the Negro past.* Boston: Beacon Press.

Higman, B. (1976). *Slave population and economy in Jamaica 1807–1834.* Cambridge: Cambridge University Press.

Pulsipher, L.M. (1993). Changing roles in the life cycles of women in traditional West Indian houseyards. In J.H. Momsen (Ed.), *Women and change in the Caribbean.* London: James Currey and Kingston: Ian Randle.

Rodman, H. (1971). *Lower class families: The culture of poverty in Negro Trinidad.* London: Oxford University Press.

Senior, O. (1991). *Working miracles. Women's lives in the English speaking Caribbean.* London: James Currey and Bloomington: Indianapolis University Press.

Simey, T. (1946). *Welfare and planning in the West Indies.* Oxford: Clarendon Press.

Smith, R.T. (1956). *The Negro family in British Guiana: Family structure and social status in the villages.* London: Routledge & Kegan Paul.

Smith, R.T. (1988). *Kinship and class in the West Indies.* Cambridge: Cambridge University Press.

Soto, I.M. (1994). West Indian child fostering: Its role in migrant exchanges. In C. Sutton & E.M. Chaney (Eds.), *Caribbean life in New York City: Sociocultural dimensions* (pp. 121–137). New York: Center for Migration Studies of New York.

Sutton, C. (1997). *Introduction to Virginia Kerns, Women and the ancestors. Black Carib kinship and ritual.* Urbana and Chicago: University of Illinois Press.

Sutton, C. (1998). "Motherhood is powerful": Embodied knowledge from evolving field-based experiences. *Anthropology and Humanism, 23*(2), 143–144.

Sutton, C. & Chaney, E.M. (Eds.) (1994). *Caribbean Life in New York City: Sociocultural dimensions.* New York: Center for Migration Studies of New York.

Young, M. & Willmott, P. (1957). *Family and kinship in East London.* London: Routledge & Kegan Paul.

Young, V. (1990). Household structure in a West Indian society. *Social and Economic Studies, 39*(3), 147–179.

# Resignation and Refusal:
## The Moral Calculus of Lesbian and Gay Parenthood in the US

### *Ellen Lewin*

The early twenty-first century is an interesting time to be a lesbian or gay parent in the United States. Over the past three decades, same-sex identified parents—lesbian mothers and gay fathers—have slowly emerged from the shadows, gaining visibility in a manner that is far more positive than even recent history could have predicted. These parents first began to enter the popular imagination in connection with child-custody disputes, as formerly married mothers, and later fathers, struggled to be awarded custody or visitation rights for the children they had borne in heterosexual marriages. The outcome of the 1976 Mary Jo Risher case, for example, hinged on her ex-husband's discovery that she had become a lesbian sometime after their divorce. In a rare custody case involving a jury, the Texas mother lost her bid for custody of her younger son (her older son had already chosen to live with his father and testified against his mother). While most such cases did not get public attention, largely because lesbian mothers were careful to avoid the court system, in this instance the story was written up in book form (Gibson 1977) and was later adapted as the made-for-TV movie, "A Question of Love," starring Gena Rowlands and Jane Alexander. Lesbian motherhood had made its debut—in prime time. And lesbianism and motherhood, despite the sympathetic portrayal of the mother and her partner, were determined by the court to be two conditions that were culturally incompatible.

For both lesbian mothers and gay fathers, the journey to acceptance has been uneven. While lesbians were routinely suspected of being sexually profligate and therefore lacking in the self-sacrificial temperament demanded of good mothers, gay fathers were suspected not only of inappropriate sexual behavior, but of putting their children at risk for contracting AIDS—whether or not the fathers even had the condition (Benkov 1994; Cain 2000; Cooper 1992; Mahon 1988; Zaslow 1994). More recent media representations have challenged these stereotypes, as films like "The Kids Are Alright" and TV shows like "Modern Family" situate lesbian/gay families as perhaps entertaining but

Lewin, Ellen. Resignation and Refusal: The Moral Calculus of Lesbian and Gay Parenthood in the US. in *Gender in Cross-Cultural Perspective*, Caroline B. Brettell, Carolyn F. Sargent, eds., Upper Saddle River, NJ: Prentice-Hall.

also markedly ordinary. Still, a variety of legal impediments to family entitlements, intensified by federal laws that (as of this writing) prohibit recognition of same-sex marriages, have compounded the cultural barriers lesbian and gay families may face in their communities.

The story of lesbian and gay family formation has become more complex, however, as assisted reproduction—both low-tech and high-tech—has entered the scene and as lesbians and gay men have availed themselves of some of the various adoption pathways also used by others who desire parenthood. Beyond these developments has come the recent recognition that raising children is far more common for lesbians and gay men of color, most of whom become parents through heterosexual unions, but some of whom also take part in more informal custodial arrangements within extended families (Gates and Ost 2004). Such family arrangements are also more widespread in the southern United States. This information puts a new spin on expectations that substantial gay/lesbian populations are only to be found in major metropolitan areas, as well as to perceptions that gay men and lesbians as so economically and socially privileged that their civil rights are actually "special rights" unavailable to ordinary citizens (Sender 2004).

Finally, issues affecting lesbian/gay family formation and stability have emerged as more insistent in public dialogs as demands for equal access to marriage and for the right to serve openly in the military have sparked vigorous public debate. The response has been uneven, to say the least. In line with legal developments in much of Western Europe, Canada, and South Africa, some states have made marriage available to same-sex couples. Others have devised compromise measures like domestic partnership or civil unions; even as still others have passed measures, including constitutional amendments, that bar the recognition of such family arrangements. Even as these discussions go on, however, many employers and local jurisdictions have put some sort of legal recognition, however limited its advantages, in place. Closely related to this patchwork of rights and hindrances have been debates over the rights of gay men and lesbians to adopt or foster children, with regulations varying from state to state. All of these rights or legal barriers are enacted in a context in which federal recognition remains out of reach due to the provisions of the 1996 Defense of Marriage Act (DOMA). At the same time, the recent repeal of the "don't ask, don't tell" policy for US military service members may hasten the collapse of these impediments by highlighting the exclusion of same-sex families from the plethora of military family benefits accessible to all other service members.

The diverse stories of demographic patterns, struggles over civil rights, and the medicalization of familial desire have all been approached evocatively by anthropologists and other scholars (Lewin 1993, 1998, 2009; Mallon 2004, 2006; Mamo 2007; Sullivan 2004). The experience of lesbian and gay parents in the United States and their struggles to achieve recognition for insignia of family legitimacy form a key part of the evolving story of kinship in Western cultures. But they also very importantly reveal a particular moral calculus, a narrative that swirls around questions of how a good life ought to be crafted. These are particularly pressing issues for people whose moral standing has been assailed over generations, and who both battle against and assimilate the stigma that is associated with their sexual identities. I will speak to the moral discourse that lesbian mothers and gay fathers articulate, drawing on the narratives I have gathered from both kinds of parents over three decades of research (Lewin 1993, 2009).

## LESBIAN MOTHERS

As discussed earlier, lesbian mothers first became publicly visible in the context of disputes following the dissolution of the marriages in which their children were born. While it is likely that most lesbian mothers still have their children during heterosexual unions, it is the women who decide to form families as lesbians who have attracted more attention in recent years. The so-called gay-baby boom that accelerated beginning in the 1980s has reflected the increasing conviction among lesbians that they can choose motherhood without the participation of biological fathers.[1] Sperm banks across the country have been willing to sell sperm to lesbians (and other single women) (Sullivan 2004), and increasing access to and routinization of more high-tech forms of assisted reproduction, such as in-vitro fertilization (IVF) (Mamo 2007) has made biological reproduction a possibility for women who once would have been stymied by the attendant difficulties.

But what does motherhood *mean* to lesbians and why do some lesbians pursue it so ardently? How does being a mother help a lesbian understand her place in the wider culture?[2] The stories told by lesbian mothers reveal that being a mother emerges as the central way that these women think about themselves and understand

the moral significance of their lives (Lewin 1993). I emphasize the accounts or narratives offered by lesbian (and other) mothers, understanding that such statements may not always correspond exactly to objective reality. Mothers' (and later fathers') narratives are cultural accounts, representations of how the world ought to be; they reveal normative and sometimes socially desirable expectations and give voice to the meanings mothers wish to convey to others. As many other anthropologists have shown, speakers organize their accounts into patterns that reveal meanings with broader cultural applicability (Kleinman 1989). Linda Garro and Cheryl Mattingly observe that narratives provide useful sites for teasing out the relationship between the individual and the culture, and thus, for representing culture without doing violence to the particularity of individual experience (Garro and Mattingly 2000). Gay Becker suggests that in the United States, where "verbal self-expression is highly valued," narrative becomes the most accessible means of understanding our experience. This is a profoundly cultural experience, as cultural processes enable "people to take in and reformulate the external world" (Becker 1997). I understand the stories mothers told me as having occurred in a singular social context, and thus to be influenced by my status as a non-mother—and probably by other elements of my identity that they perceived or assumed to be present. My interlocutors were determined, I believe, to show me what was good and rewarding about their lives. More ambivalent feelings surely exist, too, and sometimes surfaced in the interviews, but even when mothers spoke at length about the sorrows they had endured, their emphasis was firmly on the "natural achievement" they saw motherhood to constitute.

What some achieved by becoming a mother is not just adulthood and a sense of responsibility, but an identity as a "good" woman. Childhood is a time of innocence and discovery, and a woman can gain spiritual benefits by being close to a child and by her contribution to the child's growth and development. One lesbian mother said:

> You get to have a lot of input into another human being's very formative years. That's real special to have that privilege of doing that, and you get to see them growing and developing, and it's sort of like you put in the fertile soil and . . . . hopefully what will happen is that they grow and blossom and become wonderful . . . . I think it's definitely the most important thing that people do . . . . to build the next generation.

Some mothers emphasized the spiritual lessons that can be learned from close association with children. Regina Carter, whose daughter is six, spoke of motherhood this way:

> My kid has given me more knowledge than any other experience in my life. She's taught me more than all the

teachings I've ever learned as far as education, and I mean that as far as academic, spiritual education [is concerned]. Taught me things that no other person, place, or thing could possibly teach me. And those are, you know, those things are without words.

Bonnie Pereira explained that motherhood is closely associated with honesty and worthiness.

I've become more at peace with me [since having my daughter]. She's given me added strength; she's made me—it's like looking in the mirror in many ways—she's made me see myself for who I am. She definitely given me self-worth. I've become, I think, a more honest person.

Camille Walsh emphasized that the basic honesty of children allows the adult to let go of the corruption that comes from life in the world.

Somehow [having a child] freed me. I don't really know how to explain it but it was like a freeing process for me. The stuff that everybody bottles up, you can let go of around kids . . . It was like a reeducation . . . It helps me a lot, I mean it helps me in everything I do. It helps me see the world better. It helps me feel other people better. It helps me, you know, understand what's happening with the people I work around and all these different things . . . I'm not sure how I figured out that having kids was going to do that for me. Obviously it is a selfish motive, but my life felt really icy without them. I mean inside of me felt kind of devoid of emotion.

These accounts make clear that the value of motherhood in American culture goes beyond conventional expectations that children are or should be reared in two-parent heterosexual homes (Coontz 1992; Smith 1993). Motherhood confers a unique moral status, one that allows women to achieve a kind of goodness not readily available to others. Motherhood, in the views of both lesbians and heterosexual single mothers I interviewed, proceeds *naturally* from being a woman—that is, womanhood and motherhood are conflated—but it also counts as an achievement because so many obstacles present themselves, especially to single mothers, regardless of their sexual identity. For lesbians, the realization of maternal status is particularly marked, as they must overcome what they perceive as sharper challenges to their success as mothers, including pervasive biases about their ability to raise children successfully, hostility from teachers and other public figures, and the threat of harm being directed to their children.

Being a mother generally "trumps" other sources of identity, no less for lesbians than for other mothers. Tanya Petroff, who lives alone with her daughter, explained that although she is on friendly terms with some people who don't have children, these relationships are inherently limited because these non-mothers are, in her words, "single." Her most important friendships are with other single mothers, regardless of whether they are straight or gay. She believes that the values of childless people are so different from her own that they offer virtually no basis for interaction or trust, but that a difference in sexual orientation is a trivial matter among mothers. She is convinced that no one who is not a parent could be a consistently supportive friend to her.

There's a difference between people who have children and people who don't have children. People who don't have children, to my way of thinking, are very selfish. . . . They needn't consider anyone other than themselves. They can do exactly what they want to do at any given time. And though I admire that, it's not possible for me to do that and I guess for that reason most of my friends are single mothers, because it's hard for me to coordinate my needs and my time with someone who's in a completely different head set. "Why can't you get a sitter for the kid?"—that kind of thing . . . . And I don't want to get into all that resentment all the time or educating other women . . . . I've spent years doing that and now I just prefer being with people who have some sense of what's it's like to be me, and I understand where they are too.

On one level, this focus is simply the result of the way mothers must organize their time. Maternal obligations make other responsibilities recede in importance; caring for one's children takes precedence over other pursuits or loyalties, including the possibility of forming new intimate relationships. This is not to say that lesbian mothers never allow themselves to fall in love or pursue intimacy with other women, but that they understand such connections normatively as taking second place to the duties of motherhood, and sometimes having to be sacrificed to assure good care of their children. The centrality of motherhood also emerges in accounts of lesbian mothers' key friendships. They tend to view non-mothers as so different from themselves that close bonds are unlikely to form or persist. Peggy Lawrence, who lives with her partner and their children in San Francisco, has chosen to stay there, rather than returning to her home in the Midwest (as she would like to do), because she sees San Francisco as a more tolerant environment for their children.

Being a mother, to me—being a mother is more consuming than any other way that I could possibly imagine identifying myself. . . . Any other way that I identify myself is an identification of some part of my being a mother. I am a lesbian mother, I am a working mother—"mother" hardly ever modifies any other thing. "Mother" is always the primary—it's always some kind of mother, but it's never a mother-anything. "Mother" is—"mother," for mothers, is always the thing that is more consuming. Because being a mother is so big, I have much more in common with all mothers than I have in common with all lesbians. It's so big. It starts out as a twenty-four-hour-day job, and it just goes on and on and on.

In like fashion, ties with blood relatives may intensify after a lesbian becomes a mother. Strains with families of orientation over the mother's lesbianism may be at least partially resolved or softened; both mothers and other family members understand the new generation as more important than even longstanding grievances. The compromises mothers may have to craft with relatives may be partial—an agreement perhaps to conduct all visits in the grandparents' home, to exclude the mother's partner, or to forgo conversations about sexuality—but the shared commitment to maintaining bonds of kinship even under difficult circumstances is understood as desirable by most mothers who shared their stories.

Deborah Cohen, who comes from an Orthodox Jewish family, described the strains that characterize her relationship with her parents. They avoid visiting her home, for fear of somehow condoning her "lifestyle," but her parents provide regular childcare and help financially with costs like summer camp fees. But the mother and her daughter attend an Orthodox synagogue with her parents, and there is a tacit agreement in place that difficult topics, like homosexuality and the Middle East, are off limits.

> It's real painful for them. They don't want to hear it. So most of the time I don't talk about it. . . . But it's a very tight family and my mother says we can't disown you. We can be can be really sad and unhappy about what you're doing, and [feel] you are making a big mistake, but we love you and that's that.

These difficulties pertain only to what Deborah calls "the normal everyday living." When a crisis erupts, the family comes to her aid, with her mother being her primary source of comfort and solace. This is how families are supposed to be, according to Deborah.

> As much as they don't approve of what I'm doing, as much as they think it's a mistake, I have been real down and out, like with my past lover, my mother called one time and I was just crying. . . . She asked me what was happening, and I could really let loose and let her see all my feelings. She was right there. When I'm really down, my mother is there. She does not judge me. . . . I know they're there, if I ever really need anything, they're there. And that's good.

Deborah's expectations for family solidarity and her experience of its reliability are echoed in the comments of many other lesbian mothers. The birth of a grandchild seems to allay parents' concerns; as one woman described her mother: "She is in love with her grandchild and [my lesbianism] just doesn't make any difference anymore." For many of the mothers, family

ties are—or should be—indestructible, both as they emerge in the unconditional love they expect from their parents and other blood relatives, and as they can be predicted to develop with their children. Bonds with kin set patterns for future relationships with children, as they attest to the durability of eternal ties.

Motherhood offers lesbians a context for asserting a number of fundamental values, some of which they draw from cultural ideals which they share with other members of the society. They understand motherhood to be a deeply moral enterprise, largely because of its demands for selflessness and empathy, but also because they view their association with children as an opportunity for exposure to purity and honesty. In that their relationships with blood kin are likely to intensify after they bring a child into the fold, they also experience motherhood as solidifying deeply reliable sources of support that are grounded in the biological universals they take to be the foundation of all kinship bonds.

## GAY FATHERS

Many gay fathers who seek out parenthood after they identify as gay also draw on moral discourses to understand their desire for parenthood and the meaning of having children as they seek to make sense of their lives.[3] But unlike lesbian mothers, who can exploit readily-available assumptions about the congruity of motherhood and moral stature, fathers face different ethical dilemmas. Even more than insistently than stereotypes of lesbians in the wider culture, gay men have been portrayed as selfish, self-indulgent, and deeply immersed in extravagant consumption. The image of the Dual-Income-No-Kids (DINKS), drawn from popular evocations of affluent couples who can indulge their every commodity-related whim because they have no family obligations, has not only been applied to gay people, but it takes on especially toxic meanings when invoked in this way (Badgett 2001; Maskovsky 2002; Sender 2004).

Unfortunately, as Jeff Maskovsky (2002) has pointed out, the image of gay men with more disposable income than other citizens has had malignant effects on struggles for gay civil rights, with demands for basic entitlements being caricatured as "special rights." The propensity of some queer theorists to embrace images of gay shopping and spending, spurred on as well by the agendas of gay commerce, leaves little room for recognition of the economic realities of gay life: that gay men are *less* affluent than others with comparable education and occupation, and that the population of low-income gay people is far from insignificant (Badgett 2001). Given this environment, it is perhaps ironic that gay fathers I interviewed were not adverse to invoking images of wanton gay spending typical of gay men's lives. These men had two kinds of reactions to these representations—*resignation* and *refusal.* Those who I would describe as resigned explained that having children presented them with a host of new economic challenges. Children are expensive to acquire (through adoption or assisted reproduction) and to care for. The costs of providing day care or nannies, schooling, and enrichment activities, such as sports and music, plus the need to save for future exigencies such as college, all mean that money that used to be available for pastimes now categorized as "frivolous" or "not really necessary" has to be reallocated. Time constraints enter into these calculations as well. Small children need attention, may interrupt their parents' sleep, and simply become central to family schedules. This means, as one couple jokingly suggested, that fathers "aren't gay anymore," because they choose their friends by the time when their children take naps.

Len Olson, who lives in a Chicago suburb with his partner, Richard Parsons, and their three-year-old son, explained the ways that parenthood imposes temporal, spatial, and material constraints that limit their ability to engage in indexical "gay" activities. In this view, gayness comes to be understood as a set of daily practices that is replaced with new activities that are more child-centered and domestic. He frames this account in terms of the impact parenthood has had on opera attendance, a pastime Len clearly sees as closely associated with gay identity. They used to purchase a subscription for the entire season at Lyric Opera, but since becoming parents going to the opera has become a difficult chore, requiring substantial outlays for tickets, dinner, parking, and babysitting, costs that compete with the many other expenses they face as a family. It also means going to bed late, problematic for the chronically sleep-deprived parents of a toddler. Beyond this, now that he has adult, that is, parental, responsibilities, going to the opera just doesn't seem as important as it once did. At the same time, however, he recalls opera attendance almost nostalgically as a memento of a past life.

Similar themes emerge in conversations with Chris O'Neill and John Stone, who live in a Chicago suburb with their three-year-old twin girls. Chris sees parenthood as having altered his sense of himself as a gay man, and in many ways that has come to pass. The two men moved to their suburban home not long after the girls were born, leaving the largely gay neighborhood of Lakeview because it has so few resources for children. Their new community has lots of gay and lesbian parents, but they've actually found friendships with straight parents whom they've met through their daughters. They've become close friends with neighbors whose kids are the same age as theirs, and now attend a theater series with the other couple, with whom they share babysitting. Children loom large in their conversations, and Chris finds himself wondering how it is that gay identity is established. Chris noted that as many of the quintessentially gay pastimes have disappeared from their daily life, "I guess I feel like we've joined another club and this club is the club of parents of three-year-old girls." While they know that they are still gay men, parenthood has introduced ambiguities into their formerly clear sense of being gay. How exactly does one know one is gay? Is it hanging out with other gay men? Is it engaging in camp repartee? How central does "gayness" have to be on a daily basis for it to be legible to others and to oneself?

Fathers I call refusers are guided by some of the same assumptions about the essential attributes of gay life. They cite frequent patronage of bars and restaurants, going to the theater and other cultural events, being well-dressed and having one's home elegantly decorated as things that gay men "do." They sometimes invoke further examples, such as circuit parties[4] and travel to gay vacation oases like Key West, Palm Springs, and Provincetown as examples of wanton consumption. These activities might be fun, these fathers explain, but they are ultimately shallow and unsatisfying.

Dennis Caruso and Harvey Wood live in Rogers Park, a middle-class neighborhood of modest Victorian houses on the Far North Side of Chicago. When I visited them, they were preparing for the arrival of the daughter they would soon be adopting from Guatemala. The lengthy process of deciding to become parents and arranging for the adoption had given the two men quite a lot of time to think about their expectations for parenthood. Both men linked their desire to be parents to a shared commitment to "social responsibility," a mandate that they share the good fortune life has brought them with a child. Dennis explained:

> At the end of our lives, do I want to say, "Wow, we had some great trips to Key West, and wasn't the Pottery Barn fabulous when we furnished our house, and wasn't my garden cute?" I mean, is that what I want the essence of my life to be? Yes, there was career and friends, and all that stuff that was important, but then there's also that bigger legacy that's important. When you think about importance, it ties to social responsibility and making a difference and growing and raising this hopefully happy, and well-adjusted, and productive, and caring human being.

Both men spoke at length about their experiences trying to balance gay identity with an understanding of the full breadth of who they are. This has meant seeing life in the gay community as both partial and morally limited. In Harvey's words,

> I think as we've both matured as gay men, finding authenticity and real down-to-earth people has been a huge

thing to us. We have this joke where we're like, it's why do we have so many lesbian friends? We find [in them] so [much] more of what we consider, like [an] authentic down-to-earth quality that we value in friends. . . . Part of this is about authenticity. Back to your point about what is really important in our lives. And this becomes one of those ways that both of us want to measure our importance in the world. And this is part of a life well-lived for us, that we would have this connection.

For many other fathers, becoming parents is connected to deeply held values about moral responsibility and justice. Randall Johnson and Trent Williams, African-American professional men who live in Chicago, share strong religious commitments. Once they agreed that they wanted to be parents, a move they linked to their desire to be legible as a "family," they quickly decided that the only possible way to achieve parenthood would be through the public foster-care system. As black men, they knew that many children languish in the system and are unlikely to be adopted. These are the children who are considered "hard to place"[5] with prospective adoptive parents, most of whom are white and who overwhelmingly prefer to adopt infants or very young children who are either white or Hispanic.[6] Black boys who are no longer infants are at particular risk for never finding adoptive homes, and thus face futures that are uncertain and often compromised by exposure to crime, drugs, and meager educational opportunities. Randall and Trent were inspired by their religious faith to take action. Having a child would allow them to form a family, for both men the nexus where faith and duty are enacted. Randall spoke of the importance to him of having a "spiritual center."

It kind of brings me back in focus. What I'm really here for. What life is really about. You could miss that for a while when you work in corporate America. It's all about the dollar. . . . I have to realize this isn't all my life. Let's really remember what I'm really here on this earth for and how I'm here on this earth.

When I ask Randall to tell me more about what he's on this earth for, he continues,

At this point, I think I'm on this earth to create justice . . . To celebrate life. To celebrate God. To make the world a better place. And that's not always through what I do for a living. That piece of it comes from your house and home and to raise [our son] the way I'd like to raise him.

Trent's answer to this question is more concise: "I'm a serving kind of person. I'm a servant," he said. In line with this moral focus, the two men went through

various stages in the process of deciding to adopt an older black child. "It was more selfish of us," Randall explains, "that we want a child to fulfill our lives, to round us out—and after going through the process. . . . it really became a matter of helping a child out of what sounded like a really awful situation."

Javier Vélez and Nate Sherman adopted two Latino children through the foster-care system. Javier's ethnic background made them favored placements for such children. The two men agreed about what parenthood should be about.

Sharing the wealth—and I mean that in the broadest sense, sharing a home, sharing the material things and the knowledge. . . . Our job as parents is to provides the environment so they can learn and they can be successful human beings.

Javier stayed home with the children until they were both in school, giving up his former career as an interior designer. His time at home made him redefine himself as a "mom," who was called upon to actualize his feminine traits, but also demanded a special commitment to absolute honesty, a shift he describes as "burning the closet."

I always feel that being gay is a special gift and that by being this way, my job is really to help other people understand that we're actually human beings . . . . The first day that I went to the supermarket with my kid, the cashier said to me, "Oh, your wife left you with your kids today." And I just thought, gosh, there's a whole lot of assumptions in that one sentence . . . and I really had to think, really quick, like what am I going to say and how am I going to say it? Because here is my kid listening to what I'm saying, and my response was, "No, I'm not married and my children have two dads." . . . That was a very crucial point for me because, it was like from this moment on, I can never go back into the closet, and I know that as gay people we often find it very convenient to do that. So by not saying anything or by answering in the way that we know people want us to answer, like not telling the whole truth. And we've been made experts at this over the years. But with my children, I realize I can't do this anymore—they're listening to me and they're going to know that I'm lying and not telling the truth, that I'm covering. And I just can't do that anymore, from now on I have to be completely out. And today I refer to that as the day I burned the closet, or actually, my children burned it for me.

Once Javier did return to work, he no longer had any desire to climb the corporate ladder in design, but decided to become a professional activist. At the time of our interview, he worked for a community organization that assists immigrants, many of whom are members of sexual minorities and face issues of HIV and AIDS. "Having children, being gay is a gift, that's another way of being different that brings about social change, just by interaction and living your life and moving through the world."

While fatherhood allows gay men to gain access to moral stature in many of the same ways that motherhood affects lesbian mothers, discourses of goodness emerge somewhat differently in the narratives of gay dads. Some gay dads see rejection of the consumption-oriented existence they associate with male homosexuality to be more readily accessible to them when they become parents. Ironically, these men draw on many of the same stereotypes of gay men as privileged and self-indulgent that circulate in the wider (homophobic) culture. Parenthood allows them to craft lives that are "down to earth" and focused on social responsibility. In some instances, fatherhood itself appears to undermine claims to being a gay man, prompting questions about what, indeed, defines gay identity. For some other men, discourses of goodness are deeply influenced by spirituality, by the moral imperatives learned in religious traditions.

## CONCLUSION: THE MORAL CALCULUS OF PARENTHOOD

What makes parenthood desirable and satisfying to lesbians and gay men? It is perhaps not surprising that many of the motivations that also drive the formation of families elsewhere in the culture influence lesbian and gay reproduction. Claiming that one is fully adult and capable of citizenship is difficult for all who don't have children; indeed, popular definitions of "family" hinge on the presence of children. "Do you have a family?" is a question that asks whether one has children, and not having children consigns individuals to a kind of permanent adolescence. And just as not having children is read as evidence of immaturity, so does it imply a lack of moral completeness. Having children demands self-sacrifice and nurturance; association with children allows adults access to reservoirs of moral goodness not available in any other way.

The stories told by gay fathers echo but also reconfigure many of the themes that emerge in lesbian mothers' account of what parenthood means. The greater levels of planning and intentionality required to become a gay father, along with the distance between popular views of masculinity and parental desires, inhibit associations of parental goodness with the natural attributes of gender, even as fatherhood is steeped in the same ethic of altruism that attaches to motherhood. Both lesbian mothers and gay fathers find their social worlds moving away from exclusively gay/lesbian associations, toward more connections based on parenthood and toward kin-based relationships. While they find that they resemble other parents more than other lesbian/gay people, they also learn that parenthood brings particular opportunities to assert their identities and to educate people they encounter about the complexities and diversities of lesbian/gay life.

### NOTES

1. Similar understandings may also help us to understand the increasing salience of out-of-wedlock births in the United States. Marriage is no longer seen as the necessary foundation for reproduction, although many single parents may eventually marry (Cherlin 2004; Coontz 1992).

2. Decades of psychological research have revealed no meaningful differences between the children of lesbian mothers and children raised by heterosexual single mothers, though studies do show that having two parents—of whatever gender—confers some advantages on children, possibly because family incomes tend to be higher and because they may get more attention from two parents, but children whose mothers are lesbians are no more likely to display emotional distress, unconventional gender and/or sexual behavior, learning difficulties, or other indicators of inadequate parenting (see, e.g., Patterson 1995).

3. Men who became fathers before coming out as gay are not generally unlike other kinds of divorced fathers. They may be intensely involved with their children; perhaps sharing custody with their former wives, or like many men, their interaction with their children may be part-time, confined to weekends, holidays, and summers. Many divorced fathers fail to maintain steady connections with their children, and gay fathers are probably neither more nor less likely to fall into such patterns. Some fathers who do wish to maintain contact with their children may feel it necessary to keep their sexuality a secret, thus avoiding conflict with their former wives. Others may find themselves marginalized from the lives of their children by ex-wives or other relatives who view their homosexuality with suspicion or hostility. And like other divorced men, some may maintain amiable relationships with their children's mothers that allow them to be open about their identities (Lewin 2009).

4. See Carrington (2006).

5. Pertman (2000) reports that this term has come to refer to any attribute that might impede adoption, including being part of a sibling set, being non-white or mixed race, or having had several foster placements, as well as referring to children who have mental or physical disabilities, are victims of violence or neglect.

6. Barbara Katz Rothman reports hearing Asian and Latin-American children "called a discreet shade of off-white, not white perhaps, but most assuredly not black" (Rothman 2005: 49). See also Gailey (1999, 2000).

## REFERENCES

Badgett, M. V. Lee. 2001. *Money, Myths, and Change: The Economic Lives of Lesbians and Gay Men.* Chicago: University of Chicago Press.

Becker, Gay. 1997. *Disrupted Lives: How People Create Meaning in a Chaotic World.* Berkeley: University of California Press.

Benkov, Laura. 1994. *Reinventing the Family: Lesbian and Gay Parents.* New York: Crown.

Cain, Patricia A. 2000. *Rainbow Rights: The Role of Lawyers and Courts in the Lesbian and Gay Civil Rights Movement.* Boulder: Westview.

Carrington, Christopher. 2006. "Circuit Culture: Ethnographic Reflections on Inequality, Sexuality, and Life on the Gay Party Circuit." In N. Teunis and G. Herdt (eds.). *Sexual Inequalities and Social Justice*, pp. 123–149. Berkeley: University of California Press.

Cherlin, Andrew J. 2004. "The Deinstitutionalization of Marriage." *Journal of Marriage and Family* 66(4): 848–861.

Coontz, Stephanie. 1992. *The Way We Never Were: American Families and the Nostalgia Trap.* New York: Basic Books.

Cooper, Elizabeth B. 1992. "HIV-Infected Parents and the Law: Issues of Custody, Visitation and Guardianship." In N.D. Hunter and W.B. Rubenstein (eds.). *AIDS Agenda: Emerging Issues in Civil Rights*, pp. 69–122. New York: The New Press.

Gailey, Christine Ward. 1999. "'Seeking Baby Right': Race, Class, and Gender in US International Adoption." In A.-L. Rygvold, M. Dalen, and B. Saetersdal (eds.). *Mine—Yours—Ours—and Theirs: Adoption, Changing Kinship, and Family Patterns*, pp. 52–81. Oslo: University of Oslo.

_____. 2000. "Race, Class, and Gender in Intercountry Adoption in the USA." In P. Selman, (ed.). *Intercountry Adoption: Developments, Trends, and Perspectives*, pp. 295–313. London: British Agencies for Adoption and Fostering.

Garro, Linda C., and Cheryl Mattingly. 2000. "Narrative as Construct and Construction." In C. Mattingly and L. C. Garro (eds.). *Narrative and the Cultural Construction of Illness and Healing*, pp. 1–49. Berkeley: University of California Press.

Gates, Gary J., and Jason Ost. 2004. *The Gay and Lesbian Atlas.* Washington, DC: Urban Institute Press.

Gibson, Gifford Guy. 1977. *By Her Own Admission: A Lesbian Mother's Fight to Keep Her Son.* Garden City, NY: Doubleday.

Kleinman, Arthur. 1989. *The Illness Narratives: Suffering, Healing, and the Human Condition.* New York: Basic Books.

Lewin, Ellen. 1993. *Lesbian Mothers: Accounts of Gender in American Culture.* Ithaca, NY: Cornell University Press.

_____. 1998. *Recognizing Ourselves: Ceremonies of Lesbian and Gay Commitment.* New York: Columbia University Press.

_____. 2009. *Gay Fatherhood: Narratives of Family and Citizenship in America.* Chicago: University of Chicago Press.

Mahon, Nancy B. 1988. "Public Hysteria, Private Conflict: Child Custody and Visitation Disputes Involving an HIV Infected Parent." *New York University Law Review* 63: 1092–1141.

Mallon, Gerald P. 2004. *Gay Men Choosing Parenthood.* New York: Columbia University Press.

_____. 2006. *Lesbian and Gay Foster and Adoptive Parents: Recruiting, Assessing, and Supporting an Untapped Resource for Children and Youth.* Washington, DC: Child Welfare League of America.

Mamo, Laura. 2007. *Queering Reproduction: Achieving Pregnancy in the Age of Technoscience.* Durham, NC: Duke University Press.

Maskovsky, Jeff. 2002. "Do We All 'Reek of the Commodity'? Consumption and the Erasure of Poverty in Lesbian and Gay Studies." In E. Lewin and W. L. Leap (eds.). *Out in Theory: The Emergence of Lesbian and Gay Anthropology*, pp. 264–286. Champaign-Urbana, IL: University of Illinois Press.

Patterson, Charlotte J. 1995. "Lesbian Mothers, Gay Fathers, and Their Children." In A. R. D'Augelli and C.J. Patterson (eds.). *Lesbian, Gay, and Bisexual Identities Over the Lifespan*, pp. 262–290. New York: Oxford University Press.

Pertman, Adam. 2000. *Adoption Nation: How the Adoption Revolution Is Transforming America.* New York: Basic Books.

Rothman, Barbara Katz. 2005. *Weaving a Family: Untangling Race and Adoption.* Boston: Beacon Press.

Sender, Katherine. 2004. *Business, Not Politics: The Making of the Gay Market.* New York: Columbia University Press.

Smith, Dorothy E. 1993. "The Standard North American Family: SNAF as an Ideological Code." *Journal of Family Issues* 14: 50–65.

Sullivan, Maureen. 2004. *The Family of Woman: Lesbian Mothers, Their Children, and the Undoing of Gender.* Berkeley: University of California Press.

Zaslow, Robert D. 1994. "Child Custody, Visitation, and the HIV Virus: Revisiting the Best Interests Doctrine to Ensure Imparital Parental Rights Determinations for HIV-Infected Parents." *Journal of Pharmacy and Law* 3: 61–84.

# IX

# Gender, Ritual, and Religion

In many non-Western societies, women's ritual roles are central and indispensable to community cohesion and well-being. In contrast, in Anglo-European cultures, women's religious activities tend to be secondary and marginal because of the preeminence of men in both organizational hierarchies and doctrine. Anthropological research has long recognized that religious systems reflect, support, and carry forward patterns of social organization and central values of a society. What has not been sufficiently recognized is the interrelationships of men and women in the perpetuation of social life through religious activities and the relationship between gender stratification and gendered religious symbolism.

The study of the ritual activities of women has often been embedded in analyses of life cycle events, such as the Nkang'a girl's puberty ritual among the Ndembu of Central Africa (Turner 1968: 198) or pregnancy and childbirth rituals in Asia (Jacobson 1989; Laderman 1983). With the exception of these areas of research, the study of women and religion has often been neglected, despite the fact that women are prominent in religious activities. As a result of a renewed interest in the study of gender in various cultures, scholars have begun to explore how the religious experience of women is different from that of men; whether and how women become ritual specialists; what religious functions they perform and the degree to which these are private or public; and, finally, what implications these ritual activities have for women's prestige, status, and empowerment (see, e.g., Griffith and Savage 2006).

This has led, in some cultural contexts, to an attempt to formulate a more complete ethnographic picture. For example, in the literature on Australian aborigines, where there is a good deal of debate about gender roles, a number of ethnologists have asserted that the dominance of senior men is sustained by their control of sacred knowledge and that their position is recognized by both men and women in the culture (Bern 1979; Warner 1937; White 1975). This viewpoint has been challenged by Diane Bell (1981, 1983), who notes that male anthropologists have underestimated and underreported the religious life of Australian aboriginal women. She argues that "both men and women have rituals that are closed to the other, both men and women allow the other limited attendance at certain of their rituals, and, finally, there are ceremonies in which both men and women exchange knowledge and together celebrate their membership in one society and their duty to maintain the law of their ancestors" (1981: 319).

Bell focuses in particular on the love rituals of women, rituals that originally were viewed by ethnologists as magic and therefore deviant, unimportant, and marginal to the central decision-making realm of men. In contrast, Bell suggests that in the celebration of these rituals, used by women to establish and maintain marriages of their own choosing, "women clearly perceived themselves as independent operators in a domain where they exercised power and autonomy based on their dreaming affiliations with certain tracts of land. These rights are recognized and respected by the whole society" (1981: 322). The love rituals of Australian aboriginal women are, in short, by no means peripheral to the society. They are underwritten by Dreamtime Law and feared by men who are often unaware that they are being performed and unable to negate their power. Through their rituals some Australian aboriginal women have, as Hamilton (1981) suggests, a mechanism with which to challenge the ideology of male superiority that is expressed in male ritual.

Mathews (1985) provides us with another example of an important arena of religious activity—the civil–religious hierarchy or cargo system in Mesoamerica—that has long been considered a public and exclusively male arena. If women were mentioned at all in studies of the cargo system, it was for their peripheral roles in food preparation. Based on her research in the state of Oaxaca in Mexico, Mathews begins by pointing out that an application of the domestic–public model (see Section III) to an understanding of these religious ceremonies obscures the significant ritual roles of women because it places the cargo system in the public sphere of activity and fails to acknowledge the importance of the household unit. Rather than oppose men and women within a rigid domestic–public model, Mathews emphasizes the parallel and interdependent roles of men and women in the execution of cargo. Male cargo holders (mayordomos) organize and coordinate the activities of men, and female cargo holders (mayordomas) organize and coordinate the activities of women. At the end of their year of responsibility, both share in the prestige gained from service.

If Oaxacan women have an important and prestige-conferring role within the religious sphere of cargo activity, similar opportunities are denied them within the civil sphere. Thus, Mathews explores the impact of the penetration of the state (see Section VII) on the lives of women. A sexual divide-and-rule state policy, she argues, makes men into social adults and women into domestic wards whose dealings with the public sphere become restricted. Prestige in local institutions is undermined by its absence in extracommunity institutions, and as civil offices assume increasing importance at the expense of cargo offices, the position of women is eroded.

In contrast to the underestimation of women's religious roles in the literature on Australian aborigines and the Mesoamerican cargo system, studies of sub-Saharan Africa have long recognized that the ritual life of women is both significant and highly elaborated. In this region, women are involved in complex ceremonies of initiation; they are engaged in witchcraft and divination (Mendonsa 1979; Ngubane 1977); they act as spirit mediums and healers (Green 1989; Sargent 1989); they lead and participate in possession cults (Berger 1976); and they form their own secret societies (MacCormack 1979).

Janice Boddy (in this book) discusses the role of women in the *zâr* spirit possession cult of northern Sudan. In particular, she emphasizes how *zâr* serves as a cultural resource mobilized by individuals, particularly women, under certain conditions. Boddy argues that the Sudanese women in the village of Hofiriyat, where she conducted her research, view themselves in a complementary rather than inferior or subordinate position vis-à-vis men. This complementarity in gender relations is reflected in the dialectical relationship between *zâr* and Islam. "If women are constrained by their gender from full participation in Islam, men are constrained by theirs from full participation in the *zâr*" (Boddy 1989: 60). *Zâr* is not, in Boddy's view, a "peripheral cult" (Lewis 1971).

In a range of cultural contexts, anthropologists have argued that women use spirit possession and trance as an outlet for the stress that results from their social and material deprivation and subordination (Broch 1985; Hamer and Hamer 1966; Lewis 1966, 1986; Morsy 1979; Pressel 1973). As Danforth (1989: 99) argues with regard to firewalking (Anastenaria) in northern Greece, "Through these rituals women seek to address the discrepancies that characterize the relationship between an official ideology of male dominance and a social reality in which women actually exercise a significant degree of power. Spirit possession . . . provides a context for the resolution of conflict often associated with gender roles and gender identity." Boddy views the *zâr* cult in more nuanced terms. Although she acknowledges that some of her informants use *zâr* to improve their subordinate status, she emphasizes that women are more susceptible to spirit attack (as illness episode) "as a function of their femininity." *Zâr* is a form of feminist discourse for women with marital or fertility problems. Close to 50 percent of Hofriyati women who were ever or are married have succumbed to possession. "Spirits, villagers assert, rarely trouble themselves with the unwed" (Boddy 1989: 166).

Discourse, in the form of sexually explicit funerary songs and dances performed by women, is also the subject of Janet McIntosh's analysis (in this book) of death rituals among the Giriama of Kenya. McIntosh begins by noting that many ritual forms, particularly in sub-Saharan Africa, lend themselves to unruliness, turning the normative social world upside down (see also Davis 1971, 1975). But, she asks, does such ritual behavior really pose a threat to patriarchal orders and how can it be understood from an insider's perspective? Have these perceptions changed in conjunction with the arrival of Western lifestyles and tourism? McIntosh argues that in a gender-neutral sense, the sexual license of funerary songs is a mechanism by which the Giriama can confront the power of death. Grief and sexual expression are assimilated such that a funeral becomes like a wedding: "the last wedding of the deceased." However, the persistence of this "tradition" occurs in a society where women's sexuality is still controlled by a set of popular expectations about female modesty and yet simultaneously challenged by the growth of a "sex safari" industry. The obscenities expressed by women in the funerary rituals are thus viewed with ambivalence—innocuous tradition on the one hand and a training ground for real sexual promiscuity and misconduct on the other. Today women are frequently derided for, if not prohibited, by their husbands from participating in these unruly rituals.

The relationship between women's religion and sexuality is equally central to Laurel Kendall's discussion (in this book) of Korean shamans, but in this case she wonders whether this is an appropriate interpretation of what is going on and suggests that it is an interpretation rooted in Western culture. While she acknowledges that the belief that shamanic experience implies a sexual union between the female shaman and her guardian god "lurks in some corners of the Korean popular imagination," she emphasizes that Korean shamanistic rituals are less about repressed sexuality than they are about expressive bodily play and challenges to gender oppression.

Kendall's essay also introduces us to the concept of female religious practitioners (healers and shamans) more generally. Such women frequently transcend local cultural definitions of womanhood and are recognized as having extraordinary characteristics. Korean women who become *mansin* (shamans) stand above the social and economic constraints generally imposed on a proper Korean wife and mother. The *mansin* occupies an ambiguous status similar to that of other "glamorous but morally dubious female marginals, the actress, the female entertainer, and the prostitute" (Kendall 1985). Although not always accorded respect, the *mansin* wears the costumes and speaks with the authority of the gods. *Mansin* and their rituals are, in Kendall's view, "integral components of Korean family and village religion. Within this religious system, women and shamans perform essential ritual tasks that complement men's ritual tasks" (1985: 25). Korean housewives come to the *mansin* for therapeutic answers to a range of personal and household problems; for divinations about the future and prospects for the coming year; and for female solidarity and a "venting of the spleen" (Kendall 1985: 25). Women's rituals in Korea, like those in some other parts of the world, are both practical and expressive.

Another important area of research addresses how forces of social, political, and economic change impact the religious lives of men and women. For a long time, scholars believed that modernization would result in secularization. Of course, this is far from true, and research has illustrated the diverse ways in which globalization impacts localized religious beliefs and practices without eradicating them (Henfer 1998; Moore and Sanders 2001; Schiller 1997). Gender is not often considered in relation to this question (Bayes and Tohidi 2001), but this is precisely the issue that Susan Starr Sered (1990) explores in her study of how modernization has affected the religious lives of elderly Jewish women of Asian origin who are now living in Israel. In their home countries, women's and men's religious lives were highly segregated, and women's religious roles focused largely on protecting the well-being of their families. Sered finds that the move to Israel has opened new religious opportunities for women. Similar processes have been found in other parts of the world and in other times (see, e.g., Espiritu 2003; Forman 1984; Kurien 2003).

A gendered approach to religious change has also identified contexts where the lives of men are also impacted. This is precisely the problem that Santos (in this book) addresses in his study of the Evangelical movement in El Salvador and its impact on masculine identities. As he suggests, scholars have observed a "reformation of machismo" that accompanies conversion to Evangelicalism. Santos offers rich ethnographic data to explain why men in El Salvador willingly abandon traditional masculine behaviors to construct a different masculine ideal rooted in God, faith, and family. He describes both the religious conversion and spiritual awakening of El Salvadoran men and in the process reminds us of how important religious values are to gender ideology.

In this book, we have taken the approach that what it means to be male and female (i.e., gender) is learned and shaped within a cultural context. Religious symbols are a powerful mechanism by which culturally appropriate gender messages are transmitted. As Bynum observes, "It is no longer possible to study religious practice or religious symbols without taking gender—that is, the cultural experience of being male or female—into account" (1986: 1–2). Very often, in fact, the diverse roles of women are projected into the religious sphere. This is as characteristic of Haitian Vodou (Brown 1991) as it is of Catholic culture where the values about ideal womanhood are sanctified by the image of the Virgin Mary, who represents submission, humility, serenity, and long suffering (Stevens 1973). In Mexico, for example, Eve and the Virgin Mary are contrasting images that "encode the cycle of reproduction within the domestic group. When a woman is nursing and sexually continent she resembles the Virgin. When she submits to sex, she is more like Eve" (Ingham 1986: 76). Hindu goddesses are also multifaceted; they are mothers, mediators, and protectresses. According to Preston (1985: 13), there is a connection "between the role of women in Indian life and the special position of female deities in the Hindu pantheon. Though Indian women are supposed to be absolutely devoted to their husbands who are respected as embodiments of the deity, women may also reign supreme in their own domains as mothers of their children."

Through participation and leadership in ritual, women may enhance or challenge their socially- or culturally defined position. Involvement in religious activities may also generate a sense of female or community solidarity through membership in a congregation or participation in ritual functions. And in many cultures, there are parallel religious traditions. If possession is more characteristic of women than it is of men, it is precisely because it provides an outlet for ritual expression. This is as true in the simpler societies as it is in state societies with masculinist or patriarchal religions. Thus, Michael Lambek (1993) has described a symbiotic relationship between Islam on the one hand and the spirit possession rituals of women on the other on the island of Mayotte off the coast of Tanzania in Africa. While men are "expected and enabled to display their moral concerns in the universalistic arena provided by Islam," women, through mediumship, "can exercise their authority and play a significant role in the *mraba* (their family) and the community. This can protect or further their own interests, for example, enabling sisters to continue to lay immoral claims upon their brothers after their parents' death" (Lambek 1993: 335, 334). These symbiotic relationships are certainly worthy of further exploration.

## REFERENCES

Bayes, Jane H., and Nayeren Tohidi (eds.). 2001. *Globalization, Gender and Religion.* New York: Palgrave McMillan.
Bell, Diane. 1981. "Women's Business Is Hard Work: Central Australian Aboriginal Women's Love Rituals." *Signs* 7: 314–337.
_____ 1983. *Daughters of the Dreaming.* London: George Allen and Unwin.
Berger, Iris. 1976. "Rebels or Status-Seekers? Women as Spirit Mediums in East Africa." In Nancy J. Hafkin and Edna G. Bay (eds.). *Women in Africa*, pp. 157–182. Stanford, CA: Stanford University Press.
Bern, J. 1979. "Ideology and Domination: Toward a Reconstruction of Australian Aboriginal Social Formation." *Oceania* 50: 118–132.
Boddy, Janice. 1989. *Wombs and Alien Spirits: Women, Men, and the Zar Cult in Northern Sudan.* Madison: University of Wisconsin Press.
Broch, Harald Meyer. 1985. "'Crazy Women Are Performing in Sombali': A Possession-Trance Ritual on Bonerate, Indonesia." *Ethos* 13: 262–282.
Brown, Karen McCarthy. 1991. *Mama Lola: A Vodou Priestess in Brooklyn.* Berkeley: University of California Press.
Bynum, Caroline Walker. 1986. "Introduction: The Complexity of Symbols." In Caroline Walker Bynum, Steven Harrell, and Paula Richman (eds.). *Gender and Religion: On the Complexity of Symbols*, pp. 1–20. Boston: Beacon.
Danforth, Loring M. 1989. *Firewalking and Religious Healing: The Anastenaria of Greece and the American Firewalking Movement.* Princeton: Princeton University Press.
Davis, Natalie Zemon. 1971. "The Reasons of Misrule: Youth Groups and Charivaris in Sixteenth-Century France." *Past and Present* 50: 41–75.
_____. 1975. "Women on Top." In Natalie Zemon Davis (ed.). *Society and Culture in Early Modern France*, pp. 124–151. Stanford, CA: Stanford University Press.
Espiritu, Yen Le. 2003. "We Don't Sleep Around Like White Girls Do: Family, Culture, and Gender in Filipina American Lives." In Pierette Hondagneu-Sotelo (ed.). *Gender and U.S. Immigration*, pp. 263–284. Berkeley: University of California Press.

Forman, Charles W. 1984. "'Sing to the Lord a New Song': Women in the Churches of Oceania." In Denise O'Brien and Sharon Tiffany (eds.). *Rethinking Women's Roles, Perspectives from the Pacific*, pp. 153–172. Berkeley: University of California Press.

Green, Edward C. 1989. "Mystical Black Power: The Calling to Diviner-Mediumship in Southern Africa." In Carole Shepherd McClain (ed.). *Women as Healers: Cross-Cultural Perspectives*, pp. 186–200. New Brunswick, NJ: Rutgers University Press.

Griffith, Ruth Marie, and Barbara Dianne Savage. 2006. *Women and Religion in the African Diaspora: Knowledge, Power and Performance*. Baltimore: The Johns Hopkins Press.

Hamer, J., and I. Hamer. 1966. "Spirit Possession and Its Socio-Psychological Implications among the Sidamo of Southwest Ethiopia." *Ethnology* 5: 392–408.

Hamilton, Annette. 1981. "A Complex Strategical Situation: Gender and Power in Aboriginal Australia." In N. Grieve and P. Grimshaw (eds.). *Australian Women: Feminist Perspectives*, pp. 69–85. Melbourne: Oxford University Press.

Henfer, Robert W. 1998. "Multiple Modernities: Christianity, Islam and Hinduism in a Globalizing Age." *Annual Review of Anthropology* 27: 83–104.

Ingham, John. 1986. *Mary, Michael and Lucifer*. Austin: University of Texas Press.

Jacobson, Doranne. 1989. "Golden Handprints and Red-Painted Feet: Hindu Childbirth Rituals in Central India." In Nancy Auer Falk and Rita M. Gross (eds.). *Unspoken Worlds: Women's Religious Lives*, pp. 59–71. Belmont, CA: Wadsworth Publishing Co.

Kendall, Laurel. 1985. *Shamans, Housewives, and Other Restless Spirits: Women in Korean Ritual Life*. Honolulu: University of Hawaii Press.

Kurien, Prema. 2003. "Gendered Ethnicity: Creating a Hindu Indian Identity in the United States." In Pierette Hondagneu-Sotelo (ed.). *Gender and U.S. Immigration*, pp. 151–173. Berkeley: University of California Press.

Laderman, Carol. 1983. *Wives and Midwives: Childbirth and Nutrition in Rural Malaysia*. Berkeley: University of California Press.

Lambek, Michael. 1993. *Knowledge and Practice in Mayotte: Local Discourses of Islam, Sorcery and Spirit Possession*. Toronto: University of Toronto Press.

Lewis, L. M. 1966. "Spirit Possession and Deprivation Cults." *Man* 1: 307–329.

_____. 1971. *Ecstatic Religion: An Anthropological Study of Spirit Possession and Shamanism*. Baltimore, MD: Penguin Books.

_____. 1986. *Religion in Context: Cults and Charisma*. Cambridge, UK: Cambridge University Press.

MacCormack, Carol P. 1979. "Sande: The Public Face of a Secret Society." In Bennetta Jules-Rosette (ed.). *New Religions of Africa*, pp. 27–39. Norwood, NJ: Ablex.

Mathews, Holly F. 1985. "'We are Mayordomo': A Reinterpretation of Women's Roles in the Mexican Cargo System." *American Ethnologist* 12(2): 285–301.

Mendonsa, Eugene L. 1979. "The Position of Women in the Sisala Divination Cult." In Bennetta Jules-Rosette (ed.). *The New Religions of Africa*, pp. 57–67. Norwood, NJ: Ablex.

Moore, Henrietta, and Todd Sanders. 2001. *Magical Interpretations, Material Realities: Modernity, Witchcraft and the Occult in Post Colonial Africa*. London and New York: Routledge.

Morsy, Soheir. 1979. "Sex Roles, Power, and Illness." *American Ethnologist* 5: 137–150.

Ngubane, H. 1977. *Body and Mind in Zulu Medicine: An Ethnography of Health and Disease in Nyuswa-Zulu Thought and Practice*. New York: Academic Press.

Pressel, Ester. 1973. "Umbanda in Sao Paulo: Religious Innovations in a Developing Society." In Erika Bourguignon (ed.). *Religion, Altered States of Consciousness and Social Change*, pp. 264–318. Columbus: Ohio State University Press.

Preston, James J. 1985. *Cult of the Goddess: Social and Religious Change in a Hindu Temple*. Prospect Heights, IL: Waveland. (Orig. pub. 1980.)

Sargent, Carolyn. 1989. "Women's Roles and Women Healers in Contemporary Rural and Urban Benin." In Carole Shepherd McClain (ed.). *Women as Healers: Cross-Cultural Perspectives*, pp. 204–218. New Brunswick, NJ: Rutgers University Press.

Schiller, Anne. 1997. *Small Sacrifices: Religious Change and Cultural Identity among the Ngaju of Indonesia*. Oxford, UK: Oxford University Press.

Sered, Susan Starr. 1990. "Women, Religion and Modernization: Tradition and Transformation among Elderly Jews in Israel." *American Anthropologist* 92(2): 306–318.

Stevens, Evelyn. 1973. "Marianismo: The Other Face of Machismo in Latin America." In Ann Pescatello (ed.). *Female and Male in Latin America*, pp. 89–101. Pittsburgh: University of Pittsburgh Press.

Turner, Victor. 1968. *Drums of Affliction*. Oxford, UK: Clarendon Press.

Warner, William Lloyd. 1937. *A Black Civilization: A Study of an Australian Tribe*. New York: Harper & Row.

White, I. 1975. "Sexual Conquest and Submission in the Myths of Central Australia." In L. Hiatt (ed.). *Australian Aboriginal Mythology*, pp. 123–142. Canberra: Australian Institute of Aboriginal Studies.

# Spirit Possession and Gender Complementarity:
## Zâr in Rural Northern Sudan

### Janice Boddy

*July 20, 1976, 4:00 P.M. The door to my hôsh bangs open. Asia ducks beneath the lintel, lifts the water container from her head, and pours its contents into my zîr. Her face is seamed with sweat. "Allaaah!" she exclaims, "The land is hot today! Shufti, ya Janice, I've heard they are drumming in Goz. Do you want to go?"*

*Of course!—a zâr is on. But the walk in this heat is a long one, and my leg has been badly swollen for several days.*

*"Sadig is borrowing camels from his cousin. You must ride."*

*Moments later I am teetering sidesaddle, following the equally inexpert Sadig along a trail that hems some withered fields of maize. My camel munches lazily at each low acacia, and I am soon covered in scratches from their thorns. Prodding seems only to anger the beast, and I fear a painful bite; it would have been faster to walk. Still beyond sight of Goz we are reached by the deep bass of drumming, fitful through the sultry air. The camels perk, raise their heads, start trotting toward the sound.*

*Goz is a newish settlement, an odd assortment of square thatched huts, thorn corrals, and a couple of half-completed mud-brick hôshs. The drumming comes from one of these. Ho-friyati[1] arriving by foot have preceded my arrival; the zâr has just begun. Ideally a zâr should take place in the room of a house, if capacious, but because of the heat, today's has been mounted in the yard.*

*A litany of greetings over, I am seated near the dancing grounds an open area (mîdân) bounded on three sides by palm-fiber ground mats. Here sit several dozen chanting women: the spirit-possessed. Now and then one rises to her knees and begins to move her upper body in time with the sonorous beat. In the center of the mîdân stands the shaykha—zâr practitioner or "priestess"—a forceful, brawny woman in an electric-pink pullover, tôb[2] tied loosely at her waist. She is arguing with a woman just as brash as she, who, between expletives, puffs furiously on a cigarette. I learn that the shaykha speaks not to the woman but to her spirit, in an effort to diagnose the source of the woman's complaint. Observing from the side is a tall, very black, incongruously muscled figure clad in a tôb, large wristwatch, and hairnet—the shaykha's reputedly transvestite assistant from south of Shendi. In contrast, the ayâna—"sick woman" and focus of the ceremony—is frail, elderly. She rests quietly on a pillow next to the musicians, facing the front of the hôsh, arms and legs curled tight against her white-tôbed body.*

This essay is excerpted from Janice Boddy, *Women, Men and the Zâr Cult in Northern Sudan* (University of Wisconsin Press, 1989) and adapted for this book.

*The shaykha concludes her discussion, sits down, and starts to drum. Using only the tips of her fingers, she beats a large earthen dallûka stretched with goat hide, its whitened flanks boldly adorned with mauve geometric designs. Another dallûka responds in shifted accents, joined half a second later by the nugarishan, a tall brass mortar that rings, when struck, like a cowbell, only deeper. A fourth woman beats a complementary rhythm on an inverted aluminum washtub or tisht. The result is a complicated syncopation, its underlying pattern one long beat, three short. The sound is less soothing than cacophonous, yet endlessly repeated and accompanied by reiterative chants, the effect is indeed soporific. The chants, I learn, are called "threads"—khuyût (singular is khayt)—and when sung they are said to be "pulled."*

*The rhythm intensifies; the ayâna rises to dance. Now visible over her tôb is a red sash attached to a reddish waist cloth in the style of a Sam Browne belt. She is possessed, my companions say, by Khawâja (Westerner) spirits: a doctor, lawyer, and military officer—all of these at once. Yet it is the lattermost she appears to manifest in dance. Her tôb is folded cowl-like over her head, obscuring her face; she flourishes a cane—hooked, as in vaudevillian burlesque. Her dance is a slow, rhythmic walk crisscrossing a chimeric square, feet first moving side to side, then forward and back. With a leap of the imagination she is an officer of the desert corps conducting drill. Every so often she bends rigidly at the hip and, cane pressed to her forehead, bobs her torso up and down. I am told that her spirits have requested the white tôb, cane, cigarettes, "European" belt, and yet to be purchased, a radio.*

*The band takes up the chant of another zâr. The ayâna sits; the shaykha leaves her drum and starts to dance, tôb covering her head. Suddenly, the tôb is thrown off. She turns on her heel, goose-steps the length of the mîdân, stops before me, abruptly pulls herself to attention. She salutes me three or four times, stiffly, eyes glazed and staring, a grin playing wildly on her face. Her left hand grips a sword within its sheath; with her right she grasps my own with unusual strength and pumps it "Western style" in time to the drums. I am shaken by this treatment and by thoughts of her sword. The chant sounds like a military march: I recognize the British Pasha spirit, Abu Rîsh Ya Amîr ad-Daysh ("Owner of Feathers, O Commander of the Army"). The drums desist. At once my hand is released. The shaykha's features assume a more dignified composure and she returns to the center of the mîdân.*

*Evening falls. Women rise to dance—or "descend" (nazal), as the zâr step is called—throughout the night. Others respond to the spirits' chants from a kneeling position, bobbing* up and down from the waist, tôbs covering their heads like so many Halloween ghosts. One who stands has mounted a zâr in the past: she has "slaughtered" (dabahat, for dhabahat) for the spirits, thus confirming relations with those by which she is possessed. A woman who remains sitting or kneeling has yet to sacrifice; though acknowledged to be possessed, and perhaps even aware of the types of zayran that bother her, she remains somewhat uncertain of her spirits and limited to kneeling at their ceremonies until she undertakes a cure. Yet she is no less an adept for this.

In the waning, eerie light I see a woman—spirit—performing a strange pantomime with a sword, crouching low, sweeping the flat of the weapon back and forth along the ground. She dashes through these postures with skill and grace; I am reminded of a hunter flushing game, or a soldier wary of enemies lying hidden in dense vegetation.

At the start of another chant a tall older woman dressed in red lights a cigarette. She struts down the mîdân, smoking, walking stick held perpendicular to the ground at the end of an outstretched arm, pompous, indifferent, mandarinlike. Some chants later she reappears, transmogrified. Now she and the transvestite stage a sword fight closely resembling the men's dance of a nearby desert people. The combatants leap at each other with apparent abandon, landing within inches of the audience, their sharp unsheathed blades swooping dangerously from aloft. Spectators shrink in terror at their bravado. The two are possessed, I learn, by zâyran of the Arab (Nomad) species.

Occasionally during the evening's drumming, the shaykha dances around the ayâna, encircling her with her arms, coaxing a seemingly reluctant spirit to enter its host and fully reveal itself before the assembly. But the ayâna has not risen since her foray into the mîdân at the start. She sits, silently watching.

I notice at the end of each chant that several who have "descended"—standing or kneeling—begin to scratch themselves, and hiccup and burp indiscriminately. Zaineb tells me these reactions signify the spirit's departure from the body of its host, of a woman's leaving trance.

July 24, 5:30 P.M. Last day of the ceremony. The sacrificial ram is led into the mîdân, and a red and gold cloth—a garmosîs or bridal shawl—is placed over its back and head. The musicians play a chant. Incense is freshly lit, and the brazier thrust beneath the shawl. The animal is forced to inhale the smoke, then led from the mîdân and slaughtered by the ayâna's son. Blood spurting from its throat is collected in a bowl and placed before the drums. The ayâna crosses seven times over the carcass before it is dragged off to be butchered. With the others I now step forward to deposit a few piasters in the victim's congealing blood. Someone whispers an invitation to drink araki (liquor) . . . being khawâja (a westerner) I am expected to imbibe. The possessed anoint themselves with blood, some also take a sip; the shaykha daubs it on herself and the ayâna's feet and arms. Drumming and chanting recommence. Still wearing her stigmata of the zâr the ayâna rises to dance.

A woman "descends" with a prayer shawl round her neck, holding its fringed ends in her hands, rocking to and fro as she paces the mîdân. The gesture echoes that of men at a zikr, a "remembrance" ceremony of the Islamic (sûfî) fraternities from whose membership women are excluded.

Later another woman (Zaineb's cousin and sister-in-law) dances briskly wearing trousers of a European cut; she is possessed, I learn, by the Airplane Captain zâr.

Later still, an older lady performs the local "pigeon dance," concluding with a shabâl[3] to the dancer in the Mediterranean head scarf. She has been seized by Muna, Sitt ash-Shabâl, a southern prostitute zâr given to mimicking village women when appearing in their midst.

An unwed girl now rises, snatches up the bridal shawl, and flings it over her head. She shuffles forward, out of time with the chant. Onlookers gasp. This is the costume of Lulîya, the Ethiopian prostitute fond of Hofriyati weddings whose thread was sung some time ago; it is unlikely that She[4] would return so soon, and uninvited. The audience tries to dissuade the girl without success. It is not right, they say, for an unmarried girl to dance so like a bride, in public. Has she no shame? Beside me a woman snaps, "That virgin is not possessed (mazûr). She just wants a husband!"

Night falls; a pressure lamp is placed on a low table near the musicians. The mîdân is a pond of light shallowing to darkness at its sides. Dancers cast weird shadows on the sand, eyes in faces lit from below appear enormous, wild. Drums throb without flagging; redolent smoke of incense clouds the evening. The atmosphere is tense, intoxicating, eerie.

A piercing cry—a uniformed schoolgirl nine or ten years old has sprawled forward into the mîdân, upheld on all four limbs, body jerking rapidly up and down from the shoulders. Immediately, she is led off by some older women, told it is not proper for a child to behave this way at a zâr. But she does not stop. Outside the mîdân the women try to calm her. Now she is sobbing and has gone quite limp. When efforts to revive her fail she is dragged, resisting, back into the center. She balks at attempts to bring her to the shaykha and is deposited before the drums. The shaykha approaches; the girl cringes. The shaykha censes her, covers her with a white tôb, and asks, "What do you want? Who are you?" No response.

Onlookers taunt the intrusive zâr, trying vainly to garner its sympathy: "Ah, her father is poor! Her mother is blind! Her brother is ill!" The shaykha sends for the girl's father. He is brought into the mîdân and made to give his daughter's spirit ten piasters (about twenty-five cents). Still there is no word from the zâr; the girl remains limp, appearing deeply entranced.

It is getting late. Smells of cooking waft through the mîdân, and laughter from the kitchen. More drumming and dancing are called for. The shaykha requests certain threads to test for various species of zayran, hoping the presumptuous spirit will be drawn to identify itself. She blows into the schoolgirl's ears and behind her neck, she pulls at her limbs, whips her softly with a length of rope, beats her lightly with an iron spear. She censes her, rolls her head along the girl's body. She takes the girl in her arms and dances to and fro, blowing a whistle to *the incessant beat. She leads the girl around the mîdân and is twice successful in getting her to move briefly of her own accord. At last the girl jogs back and forth through the open space, one arm pumping like the wheel of a locomotive, the other, raised and crooked at elbow, sounding an imagined alarm. The shaykha blows her pipe whistle in accompaniment. The troublesome spirit is identified: Basha-t-Adil the Khawâja railway engineer.*

*Still the episode continues. For over an hour the shaykha tries every technique in her repertoire, aiming to convince the implacable zâr to abandon his newfound host and refrain from bothering her again until she is a woman and married. Finally the shaykha guides the girl out of the mîdân and out of the hôsh. They cross the threshold, the khashm al-bayt,[5] backwards, facing the assembly; they remain in the path for several minutes, then return as they had left facing the mîdân. The girl, now calmed and weeping softly, is brought to sit near me—a human khawâja—but placed with her back to the ritual.*

*Soon the sacrificial meal is served and proceedings brought to a close. It is almost 2:00 A.M. The ayâna is now formally well, though tomorrow she must eat the head meat of the ram in a private ceremony followed by a procession to the Nile. Several people approach the ayâna, touch her right shoulder and say "Insha 'allâh byinf'ik," "God willing, it is benefiting you." In the company of my neighbors I return, exhausted, to Hofriyat.*

## ZÂR AND ZAYRAN

Smoking, wanton dancing, flailing about, burping and hiccuping, drinking blood and alcohol, wearing male clothing, publicly threatening men with swords, speaking loudly lacking due regard for etiquette: these are hardly the behaviors of Hofriyati women for whom dignity and propriety are leading concerns. But in the context of a zâr they are common and expected. The ceremony is rich in complex imagery and movement. Yet it has none of the solemn pageantry of a Mass, nor the predictable, repetitive manipulation of symbols which I, raised as a Catholic, might have found familiar. The tone of a zâr resembles neither the subdued formality of a Muslim Friday prayer, nor the unorchestrated ceremoniousness of life cycle rites in Hofriyat. It is closer in character to zikrs of the Qadriya and Khatmiya sûfî orders in Sudan, but lacks their cohesion and transcendent focus. What is singular about a zâr is its spontaneity, its imagination, whose basis nonetheless is a comprehensive repertoire of symbols and spirit roles—a resource on which participants draw for inspiration. Moves are lightly choreographed— improvisations on well-known themes; "players" are interchangeable, costumes readily borrowed and exchanged. But during the performance, neither players'

bodies nor their costumes belong to village women— they belong, instead, to *zayran*. *Zâr* rituals are always fraught with tension and surprise, for at any moment a woman might be "seized" by a spirit that Hofriyati did not before know existed, or she did not know she had.

How is all of this to be understood? What is this phenomenon; who or what are these spirits that so dramatically appear in women's bodies?

## THE POSSESSION CONCEPT

*Zâr* refers to a type of spirit, the illness such spirits can cause by possessing humans, and the rituals necessary to their pacification. The cult[6] is found throughout the northern Sudan and variations of the same name appear in Egypt, Ethiopia, Somalia (where it is called *sâr*), Arabia, and southern Iran.[7]

In writing of spirit "possession" in Hofriyat, I am using indigenous terms. When someone is considered to be affected by a *zâr*, people say of her, *inda rih, inda zâr*, or *inda dastûr*[8]—"she has a spirit." Alternatively, they say she is *mazûr* or *madastîr*—"with spirit," possessed. *Zâr* influence, being possessed of and by a spirit, is considered an affliction and expressed as illness. A spirit causes its novice host to suffer; however initial misery should be surpassed by a more positive concern on the part of the spirit for its host's well-being as their relationship progresses. Once possessed, always possessed: zayran never wholly abandon those they have chosen as their hosts.

Someone diagnosed as *zâr* possessed is liable to be affected by her spirit(s) at any time. *Zayran* are able to infiltrate the bodies of their hosts at will, a move which villagers say always coincides with the latter's entrancement. According to Hofriyati, possession trance (*ghaybîya* or *ghaybûba*) is a state induced by the spirit's forceful entry into the body, which displaces or shifts the person's human self to another perceptual plane. It is, as Bourguignon (1973: 12–13) suggests, "a radical discontinuity of personal identity"; yet in contrast to her model, the distortion of perception this entails pertains not only to the self but to other entities as well.

Still, trance is only one manifestation of possession in Hoftiyat, for *zayran* affect their hosts in countless additional ways (see also Constantinides 1972, 1977; Cloudsley 1983: 81). They are always near, or in local parlance "above" (*fôg*), their human hosts, whence they might influence people's perceptions and behaviors in the course of daily life. Further, despite the acknowledged powers of *zayran*, possession trance rarely occurs unpremeditatedly, outside of ritual contexts. Here one is not diagnosed as possessed because she becomes entranced; rather, she becomes entranced because she is possessed. Schoolgirl mishaps notwithstanding, the possessed rarely enter trance spontaneously; this is something one must learn to do in the course of a curing ceremony in order to negotiate an appropriate relationship with instrusive *zayran*. As adepts put it, one must learn how not to resist a spirit's attempts to enter the human world through the medium of her body. The implicit link to ideas about sexual intercourse in Hoftiyat is striking and reiterated in the fact that a woman should be married before she becomes possessed.

Thus trance is in no way aberrant; it is a practiced behavior which the possessed are expected to display under certain conditions. Although an integral part of possession therapy and relapse prophylaxis, it is not consistently evinced by the possessed during ceremonies, and when evinced, it is variable in apparent depth and duration from one episode or individual to the next. Since it is considered inappropriate to be entered by a spirit (or a husband) while menstruating, a woman at a *zâr* signals *zayran* of her condition by tying a knot in her braids, so constraining the spirits' activity. Moreover, because it must conform to prescribed patterns of "spiritness," trance performance requires skill and considerable control. Thus it is not, as some would assert, a spontaneous neurological manifestation of nutritional deficiency which (at least originally) is accounted for after the fact as possession (e.g., Kehoe and Giletti 1981). Such models betray their foundation in a Western rationalism which derogates any mode of consciousness other than that of critical self-awareness. In the search for reductive biological explanations as to why trance should occur, trance itself is misconstrued, parted from its cultural context. Here an essential point is missed. For villagers the system of meaning—possession—is both logically and contextually prior to the behavior—trance—through which it finds expression (cf. Lambek 1981: 7).

This is not to deny that biological factors might affect the proclivity to enter trance or the ease with which the behavior is learned. Some of the possessed initially experience difficulty in becoming lost from themselves and allowing their spirits to assume control; others do not. Here perhaps one's nutritional status plays a role. Still, it must be stressed that Hofriyati generally enter trance after having been diagnosed as possessed or, if undiagnosed, when attending a spirit ritual. And in either case, an individual's trance behavior is learned (cf. Bourguignon 1973: 4–15, 1976: 37–41), shaped by her knowledge of *zayran* and their provenance. It may be novel and unexpected, but must be consistent with villagers' understanding of spirits to be accepted as legitimate possession and not considered dissimulation or idiosyncratic madness. The few women who do enter trance spontaneously—apparently uninduced,

in nonceremonial situations—are hardly neophytes. Rather, they are long-term adepts of the *zâr* who, in the course of their possession careers, have become progressively more skilled at alternating modes of consciousness and allowing the spirits to exhibit themselves through their bodies (see also Besmer 1983: 24).

According to Hofriyati, the fact that possession trance typically must be induced and is rare apart from public ritual has less to do with human ability or volition than with spirit caprice. Humans convoke *zayran* through ritual drumming and singing, and normally the spirits—for whom access to the human world is a principal motive for possession—are willing to oblige. Indeed, they regard such invitations as their due, in partial fulfillment of bargains struck with humans, and are likely to become disgruntled and dangerous when neglected or put off. If the possessed take care to mollify them, spirits ought to respond by confining their appearance to ritual contexts where they can frolic and be entertained. Yet none of this is certain. Spirits are willful, and for sport or revenge might "descend" into their hosts without benefit of prior summons. So despite the controlled nature of possession trance and spirit display, the startling possibility exists that at any moment a woman might not be who she usually is.

In Hofriyat possession is a matter of fact. Here the reality of spirits and their powers goes unchallenged, even by villagers who have no firsthand experience of them and regardless of how hotly they dispute the proper therapy for possession affliction, discussed later. Clearly, Hofriyati, like the rest of us, face doubts concerning their beliefs from time to time. But cosmological mavericks they are not. Doubts, like beliefs, are grounded in a social context. Zayran are immanent in the world of Hofriyat; sceptic and zealot, both, are canopied by their existence.

## THE POSSESSED

In Hofriyat, as elsewhere in Sudan, possession activity is mainly, but not exclusively, the province of women.[9] Somewhat more than 40 percent of Hofriyati women ever married and over the age of fifteen ($N$ = 129 [1977] and 135 [1984]) claim a *zâr* affliction. Marital status is a significant factor in possession illness: spirits, villagers assert, rarely trouble themselves with the unwed—with women whose fertility has yet to be activated.[10] Most affected are those between the ages of thirty-five and fifty-five, two-thirds of whom have spirits. This proportion is due to a cumulative effect: once possessed a woman is always possessed thereafter.

By contrast, only a handful of men from the entire village area are publicly acknowledged to be possessed.

In Hofriyat itself only four men (about 5 percent of the resident adult male population) are considered adepts of the *zâr*; three have undergone the requisite ceremonies, one when only thirteen years of age. Two men born in the village but now living elsewhere are known to have spirits, and I obtained information concerning ten others from the vicinity, five of whom were deceased prior to fieldwork. During my six-year absence from the village, only one man had become possessed, in contrast to sixteen women. In 1984, several male acquaintances privately declared themselves to be possessed and confessed admiration for the *zâr*, but would not publicly seek to confirm their afflictions for fear of losing face.

Why is this the case? Why, assuming that possession is a public idiom for the articulation and interpretation of experience,[11] should there exist sexual disproportion among those who acknowledge having spirits? An obvious approach is to ask whether the range of experience that possession constructs is more common to Hofriyati women than to men. This I think to be the case, mainly because possession is closely linked to fertility with which women are identified and for which they bear responsibility. I do not agree with I. M. Lewis (1971, 1986) on this issue, who, arguing from a sociological perspective, suggests that *zâr* possession is a strategy which women use in an oblique attempt to redress the effects of their subordinate social status. Lewis holds that since spirits demand desiderata which husbands must provide if their wives are to regain well-being, possession can be seen as a measure of gender conflict: it is a strategic evocation of shared beliefs by women wishing to mitigate their subordination to men.

The perspective is illuminating, but presents a number of difficulties. First, it places unwarranted emphasis on the assumed intentionality of women and thus insidiously underestimates the factuality of spirits in the Sudanese world. Words like strategy imply volition, which may certainly be present and, if so, motivated by status considerations in some cases of possession but certainly not in all. Moreover, Lewis's deprivation hypothesis appears to presume that women seek the same status held by men, which, since men have deprived them of it, was originally within their purview. Such assumptions fail to bear scrutiny in Hofriyat, where the social worlds of men and women are largely separate and distinct, a condition due not to happenstance or the prevailing wills of men, but to cultural design. Wilson's (1967) critique of the model tries to address this problem by shifting the locus of proposed status competition from intersex to intrasex relations and, in so doing, is sympathetic to the Sudanese context. However, it shares with Lewis's theory the drawback of

a conflict orientation to social interaction that is firmly rooted in Western premises of individualism,[12] whose validity in non-Western cultures must be open to debate (cf. Morsy 1978; Boddy 1988). Even granting that status may be a consideration in certain episodes of possession illness, the sociological argument cannot account for the *zâr* in its entirety. It glosses over the issue of belief and is therefore unable to explain or interpret possession forms (for example, the characteristics of spirits, the nature and variety of possession symptoms) and processes (such as the reevaluation of one's past that acquiring a spirit entails). Such factors, however important to the possessed, are implicitly deemed incidental when the investigator's focus is competition.[13] The social status model is unidimensional, at once too general in application and too narrow in concern to deal adequately with the complexities of *zâr*.

It is imperative to ask why so many scholars—among them Kehoe and Giletti (1981)—are committed to viewing possession as a consequence of women's deprivation rather than their privilege, or perhaps their inclination. Such explanations consistently mislocate the question of why women should be more susceptible to possession than men. Especially in his early work, Lewis (1971: 77), for example, suggests that joining a *zâr* coterie enables women to express solidarity vis-à-vis men, who are seen as their oppressors. Men have Islam, which excludes women from active participation; hence women, who are socially peripheral, must resort to the equally peripheral cult of *zâr* both to mitigate their subordination and to express religious fervor (Lewis 1971: 66–99; see also Lewis 1986: 23–50, 102–5). This is a classic but unhappily androcentric portrayal of women, who are forever seen as reacting to men rather than acting for themselves within a specific cultural context.

To avoid such pitfalls, we need to examine closely how the sexes in Hofriyat conceive of their interrelations both collectively and individually. Judging from my informants, some women—by no means all or only those who are possessed—clearly feel subordinate to men, resent their positions, and are not consistently above vituperation. However, their feelings seem to derive less from their status as women than from the specific actions of individual men, notably husbands. And the problem these men pose is not that they deny women, as a class, an elevated social position, but that they sometimes—often inadvertently—thwart individual women's legitimate attempts to achieve it. The reverse can also be said for women, who may frustrate the status aspirations of men. Both sexes are active participants in the social life of Hofriyat, bisected as it is into gender-distinct yet partially overlapping spheres.

If men are central and women peripheral with respect to Islam and external relations, women are central and men peripheral when it comes to physical, social, and cultural reproduction: the worldliness of village life. Although men and women are subject to different constraints, the actions of each bear consequence for those of the other.

Indeed, whatever consciousness women have of themselves as a group is hardly one of inferiority and wholescale subordination to men, but of complementarity. As villagers see it, the sexes are engaged—not in a war—but in a dialectical relationship of qualitatively disparate yet socially equivalent parts, each commanding certain resources but reliant on the other for fulfillment. They do not conceive of themselves as locked in a struggle between classes, hierarchically understood. Although a Marxist critique might legitimately consider this to be a mystification of political realities, it cannot be ignored if we are truly concerned with the meaning of *zâr* to women and men in Hofriyat. Political relations are mystified for both within the Hofriyati universe of meaning.

When properly situated in the framework of sexual complementarity, the question of why women as a category should be more likely than men to interpret certain experiences as possession expands to two: Why women? Why not men? As Kapferer (1983: 98) astutely argues with respect to women's preponderance in Sri Lankan exorcisms, such questions cannot be resolved by focusing on the possessed's motives and intentions alone, independent of the cultural constructs that inform them. We need to consider the qualities that define the sexes in Hofriyat, the typifications each sex holds of the other, the components of gender identity (see also Nelson 1971). Only then might we have a basis for deciding whether a particular incidence of possession constitutes attempted cross-sex or intrasex status manipulation, or something else—an expression of psychological or social disturbance (cf. Crapanzano 1973, 1977b, 1980; Obeyesekere 1970, 1981; Kapferer 1983, 1986), cross-sex communication (cf. Lambek 1980, 1981), religious experience (cf. Constantinides 1972, 1977; Lewis 1986), a form of play, dramatic allegory, or all of these and more. Its cultural underpinnings— idioms of the everyday world, prosaic conceptualizations of gender—empower possession as a form of social discourse.

Thus put, a focus on the articulatory potential of possession instead of on the status aspirations of individuals possessed changes the tenor of the analytic enterprise. It widens the interpretive net and does not attempt to simplify matters where simplicity belies the facts. Rather, it makes possible a variety of explanations at different levels of analysis and experience, all of them immanent in the *zâr* as a system of meaning, all of them potentially relevant to any specific episode of possession.

Returning to Hofriyati gender constructs and the *zâr*, both sexes allege that women are naturally more vulnerable to spirit attack as a function of their femininity.[14] Spirits are attracted to women—and married women in particular—for it is they who use henna, perfumes, soaps, and scented oils; wear gold jewelry and diaphanous wraps, all human finery which spirits are known to covet. The proclivities of *zayran* are symmetrical to those of Hofriyati women: both are regarded as consumers of goods provided by men.

Although many questions remain to be addressed, this goes some way toward explaining why women interpret certain experiences and illness episodes as possession. It also suggests why, in this sexually polarized community, men do not. But here more remains to be said. A common characterization of women that they do not completely share is that because they are wanting in *'agl* (reason or social sense), they lack sufficient moral strength to uphold the tenets and ideals of Islam. According to local religious authorities it is reprehensible and abhorrent—though not, strictly speaking, *haram* (forbidden)—for Muslims to traffic with spirits. They say that each individual has the responsibility to steer a proper course of spirit avoidance, something women find more difficult to do than men. Women's perceived inability to resist and so deny *zayran* access to earthly pleasures is put down to their inherent moral frailty, notwithstanding that they are more likely to encounter jinn than men. Just as the public identity of women accounts for their greater participation in the *zâr* so the public identity of men as pious Muslims accounts, in part, for their forbearance (see also Lambek 1981: 62–64).

The last is solely a masculine perspective. Women see no incompatibility between the *zâr* and Islam: to them possession ritual is part of a general religious enterprise (cf. Constantinides 1972: 98). Hofriyati culture therefore contains conflicting interpretations of the relationship between possession and Islam. These, in turn, have divergent implications for the handling of troublesome spirits.

## EXORCISM VERSUS ACCOMMODATION

Where men hold the reputedly orthodox view that intrusive spirits can and must be dislodged from the body by force, women maintain that *zayran* cannot be got rid of at all.[15] Adepts insist that if one's illness is caused by a *zâr*, no amount of Islamic or even Western medicine will effect a cure. Attempts to exorcise the spirit serve merely to exacerbate the patient's condition. Symptom remission alone can be achieved, and only if the afflicted agrees to hold a propitiatory ceremony on behalf of the as yet unnamed *zâr*. During this ceremony, often held long after her initial illness has dissipated, the possessed enters into a contractual relationship with the spirit(s) responsible for her lapse from health. There, in response to drumming and singing chants associated with the various named *zayran*, she ideally enters trance: a spirit's chant is an invitation to "descend" (*nazal*) and enter the body of its host, where its identity can be affirmed and its demands revealed.[16] In return for certain offerings, acquisitions, and observances, the invasive spirit agrees to restore, and refrain from further jeopardizing, its host's well-being.

Henceforward, human host and possessive *zâr* are joined in continuous but unequal partnership. The spirit remains above her, able to exert its influence or infiltrate her body at will. To some extent the possessed can rely on the spirit's compliance in maintaining her health, but only so long as she regularly attends the ceremonies of others, abstains from traditional mourning behavior, associates herself with clean and sweet-smelling things, and is not given over to strong emotion. A violation of these provisions renders her vulnerable to relapse. Yet the curing rite has opened communications between the two entities, and it is hoped that any future problems can be dealt with expeditiously. From the spirit's perspective, contracts with humans are infinitely renegotiable, so if the possessed wishes to allay further attack from her *zâr*, she must take scrupulous care to mollify it. If all goes well, what begins as an uneasy truce between a willful spirit and its initially reluctant host might graduate to positive symbiosis as their relationship stabilizes and matures. Alleviating the symptoms of possession illness is a matter of establishing reciprocal obligations between spirit and host; their relationship should become, like that between partners in a marriage, one of complementarity, exchange, and mutual accommodation.

Although the majority of men denounce the propitiation of *zayran*, this is not because they deny that such spirits exist. In Hofriyat, *zayran* comprise a distinct class of *jinn*,[17] mischievous invisible beings that populate a world that is parallel to our own and contiguous with it but imperceptible to humans most of the time. Typical of their exceptional attributes, jinn can transform themselves into animals, assume human form (but incompletely so, for their feet are always hooved), or take possession of live human bodies at will. *Jinn* are mentioned in the Quran (Suras 6, 17, 18, 34, 37, 46, 55, 72, and 114); they are a constant if often low-key part of both men's and women's daily lives.

Further, should a man become ill there is a chance that the diagnosis will be possession regardless of its feminine associations. Men recognize the powers of *zayran* and acknowledge that even the most pious among them occasionally succumbs to spirit attack. But this is where their public support for the cult stops: most insist that, despite a practiced resistance, *zayran*, like other jinn, must eventually capitulate to the powerful exorcistic techniques of Islamic medicine. In the company of their fellows they decry as un-Islamic women's ceremonial attempts to assuage and socialize the spirits.

In face of such weighty opposition the *zâr* cult thrives, and its rites are attended even by the most submissive and religious of wives. For women, *zâr* falls squarely within the purview of Islam. And when arguing their position with men (something I witnessed only twice), women said that Allah expects the afflicted to seek respite from their suffering—clearly, it is better to be healthy than "broken" by spirits or overzealous efforts to dislodge them. Perhaps men are right that involvement in the cult imperils one's prospect of a pleasurable afterlife, but then, is Allah not merciful?

Men, for their part, though publicly adamant that only exorcism is correct in the eyes of Islam, are privately not so intractable (cf. Barclay 1964: 206; Constantinides 1982). Often hesitant, concerned, uncertain that Islamic medications will effect a cure or fearing reprisals of a powerful spirit if it is put off, most do not interfere when their womenfolk conduct propitiatory ceremonies, and provide money to meet the spirits' demands. Here perhaps, as Lewis (1971: 88) suggests, men tacitly recognize the contradiction between the formal ideology of male supremacy and the social (and cultural) importance of women. Intriguing, too, in the light of the ethnographic situation in Hofriyat, is Lewis's more recent view that woman's participation in the *zâr* might offer men "the privilege of vicarious participation in what they ostensibly condemn as superstition and heresy. Thus, if there is a dual spiritual economy [male and female], its two branches are interdependent and complementary" (Lewis 1986: 106). It seems plausible that just as men's religious devotions count also for their womenfolk (1986: 106), so women's *zâr* devotions might count indirectly for their men. As noted earlier, several male informants confided in 1984 that they believe themselves incurably possessed by *zayran*. These men enjoy listening to spirit rituals from afar or watching *bi shubbak* ("through a window"), but do not openly attend for fear of ridicule. Such peripheral and vicarious participation echoes that of women at a *zikr*—the "dervish" rite of Islamic fraternities whose membership in Sudan is exclusively male.

## GLOSSARY

| | |
|---|---|
| dallûka | large pottery drum used in weddings and zâr ceremonies |
| hôsh | house yard and/or wall that encloses it |
| shabâl | woman's gesture of flicking her hair at an approaching man in the context of a wedding dance; said to confer luck |
| shaykha zâr | female curer of the zâr culta type of spirit, the illness it can cause, and the ritual by which the illness is assuaged; more generally, the "cult" that surrounds such spirits |
| zikr | remembrance: ceremony of the Islamic fraternities |
| zîr | large water jar |

*Acknowledgments.* I would like to thank Daphna Izraeli, Michael Harrison, and the *American Anthropologist* editor and reviewers for their help with this article. I am also grateful to the many superb anthropologists and historians of religion whose work I have cited here.

## NOTES

1. Hofriyat is a pseudonym for the Sudanese village where I began conducting field work in 1976. "Hofriyati" refers to the people of the village, all of whom speak Arabic and profess Islam. The village is located on the Nile, a little over 120 miles (200 km) north and east of Khartoum.
2. A woman's modesty garment, consisting of some nine meters of cloth wound around the body and covering the head.
3. A flick of the hair, a movement said to confer luck on the recipient.
4. I use an initial capital letter (e.g. He, She) when referring to a specific spirit in order to indicate its sex while distinguishing it from its human host.
5. Literally, mouth of the house.
6. For a discussion of the cult's possible origins, see Boddy (1989) and Constantinides (1991).
7. On northern Sudan, see Constantinides (1977, 1982, 1991); Kenyon (1991, 2000). On zar in Egypt, see Al-Guindi (1978); Kennedy (1978); Saunders (1977); in Ethiopia, Leiris (1958); Young (1975); in Somalia, where it is better known as *sar*, Lewis (1971, 1986); in Arabia, Trimingham (1965: 258); and in southern Iran, Modarressi (1968).
8. This term literally means "statute" or "constitutional law," and colloquially, "permission" (Wehr 1976: 281). In northern Sudan, however, the term also refers to a door jamb (Constantinides 1977: 65–66, n. 6) or a bolt (Hillelson 1930: 35). The reference to doorways is significant, and discussed in Boddy (1989).
9. See Barclay (1964: 196–206); Cloudsley (1983: 67–87); Constantinides (1972,1977);Trimingham (1965:174–77); Zenkovsky (1950).
10. For a discussion of the relationship between female fertility and possession, see Boddy (1989).
11. See Crapanzano (1977a). This point is more fully developed in Boddy (1989).
12. Although the fluctuating kinship networks of Hofriyati are individualistic, this is not to say that the individual is the focal social unit in Hofriya. Hofriyati women and men are always subordinate to a range of collective interests: family, lineage, village, religious group, etc.
13. Lewis (1971: 30) certainly does not consider other factors unimportant, yet they do not figure into his analysis to the same extent as does the question of cross-sex competition.
14. See Kapferer (1983: 100–110) for a similar view of the susceptibility of Sri Lankan women.
15. Interestingly, this is similar to the situations of men and women in a marriage: although men may divorce an unwanted wife at will, women must accommodate themselves to the marriage, however unhappy.
16. Spirits are hardly inanimate or genderless, as my use of the impersonal pronoun implies. But when not referring to specific spirits and possession episodes, I use the neuter form to avoid confusion between humans and *zayran*.
17. However, the classification of spirits varies somewhat from area to area in Sudan, and in some places (though not in Hofriyat or its environs) *zayran* and *jinn* are considered different forms of spirit being. On this issue, see Constantinides (1972: 102–4) and (Trimingham 1965: 177ff).

## REFERENCES

Al-Guindi, Fadwa. 1978. "The Angels of the Nile: A Theme in Nubian Ritual." In *Nubian Ceremonial Life*, edited by John Kennedy, pp. 104–113. Berkeley: University of California Press.

Barclay, Harold. 1964. *Buurri al-Lamaah: A Suburban Village in Sudan.* Ithaca, N.Y.: Cornell University Press.

Besmer, Fremont E. 1983. *Horses, Musicians, and Gods: The Hausa Cult of Possession-Trance.* South Hadley, Mass.: Bergin and Garvey.

Boddy, Janice. 1988. Spirits and Selves in Northern Sudan. The Cultural Therapeutics of Possession and Trance. *American Ethnologist* 15(1): 4–27.

_____. 1989. *Wombs and Alien Spirits: Women, Men and the Zâr Cult in Northern Sudan.* Madison: University of Wisconsin Press.

Bourguignon, Erika. 1973. "Introduction: A Framework for the Comparative Study of Altered States of Consciousness." In *Religion, Altered States of Consciousness, and Social Change*, edited by Erika Bourguignon, pp. 3–35. Columbus: Ohio State University Press.

_____. 1976. *Possession.* San Francisco: Chandler and Sharp.

Cloudsley, Ann. 1983. *Women of Omdurman: Life, Love, and the Cult of Virginity.* London: Ethnographica.

Constantinides, Pamela. 1972. Sickness and the Spirits: A Study of the "Zâr" Spirit Possession Cult in Northern Sudan. Ph.D. dissertation, University of London.

_____. 1977. "'Ill at Ease and Sick at Heart': Symbolic Behavior in a Sudanese Healing Cult." In *Symbols and Sentiments*, edited by Ian M. Lewis, pp. 185–205. Bloomington: Indiana University Press.

_____. 1982. "Women's Spirit Possession and Urban Adaptation in the Muslim Northern Sudan." In *Women United, Women Divided: Comparative Studies of Ten Contemporary Cultures*, edited by P. Caplan and D. Bujra, pp. 141–76. New York: John Wiley.

_____. 1991. "The History of Zâr in the Sudan." In *Women's Medicine: The Zâr-Bori Cult in Africa and Beyond*, edited by I. M. Lewis, Ahmed al-Safi, and Sayyid Hurreiz, pp. 83–99. Edinburgh: International African Institute, Edinburgh University Press.

Crapanzano, Vincent. 1973. *The Hamadsha: A Study in Moroccan Ethnopsychiatry*. Berkeley: University of California Press.

_____. 1977a. "Mohammed and Dawua: Possession in Morocco." In *Case Studies of Spirit Possession*, edited by Vincent Crapanzano and Vivian Garrison, pp. 141–76. New York: John Wiley.

_____. 1977b. *Introduction to Case Studies of Spirit Possession*, edited by Vincent Crapanzano and Vivian Garrison, pp. 1–39. New York: John Wiley.

_____. 1980. *Tuhami: Portrait of a Moroccan*. Chicago: University of Chicago Press.

Hillelson, S. 1930. *Sudan Arabic, English Arabic Vocabulary*. 2nd ed. London: Sudan Government.

Kapferer, Bruce. 1983. *A Celebration of Demons: Exorcism and the Aesthetics of Healing in Sri Lanka*. Bloomington: Indiana University Press.

_____. 1986. "Performance and the Structure of Meaning and Experience." In *The Anthropology of Experience*, edited by V. W. Turner and E. M. Bruner, pp. 188–206. Chicago: University of Illinois Press.

Kehoe, Alice B., and Dody H. Giletti. 1981. Women's Preponderance in Possession Cults: The Calcium Deficiency Hypothesis Extended. *American Anthropologist* 83(3): 549–61.

Kennedy, John G. 1978. *Nubian Ceremonial Life*, edited by John Kennedy. Berkeley: University of California Press.

Kenyon, Susan. 1991. *Five Women of Sennar*. New York: Oxford University Press.

_____. 2000. "The Case of the Butcher's Wife: Illness, Possession and Power in Central Sudan." In *Spirit Possession, Modernity, and Power in Africa*, edited by Heike Behrend and Ute Luig. Madison: University of Wisconsin Press.

Lambek, Michael. 1980. Spirits and Spouses: Possession as a System of Communication among the Malagasy Speakers of Mayotte. *American Ethnologist* 7(2): 318–31.

_____. 1981. *Human Spirits: A Cultural Account of Trance in Mayotte*. New York: Cambridge University Press.

Leiris, Michel. 1958. *La Possession et ses aspects théâtraux chez les Ethiopiens de Gondar*. L'Homme: Cahiers d'ethnologie, de géographie et de linguistique. Paris: Plon.

Lewis, I. M. 1971. *Ecstatic Religion: An Anthropological Study of Spirit Possession and Shamanism*. Baltimore, Md.: Penguin Books.

_____. 1986. *Religion in Context: Cults and Charisma*. Cambridge: University of Cambridge Press.

Modarressi, Tahgi. 1968. "The Zar Cult in South Iran." In *Trance and Possession States*, edited by Raymond Prince, pp. 149–55. Montreal: R. M. Bucke Memorial Society.

Morsy, Soheir. 1978. Sex Roles, Power, and Illness in an Egyptian Village. *American Ethnologist* 5: 137–50.

Nelson, Cynthia. 1971. Self, Spirit Possession, and World-View: An Illustration from Egypt. *International Journal of Psychiatry* 17: 194–209.

Obeyesekere, Gananath. 1970. The Idiom of Possession. *Social Science and Medicine* 4: 97–111.

_____. 1981. *Medusa's Hair: An Essay on Personal Symbols and Religious Experience*. Chicago: University of Chicago Press.

Saunders, Lucie Wood. 1977. "Variants in Zar Experience in an Egyptian Village." In *Case Studies in Spirit Possession*, edited by Vincent Crapanzano and Vivian Garrison, pp. 177–91. New York: John Wiley.

Trimingham, J. Spencer. 1965. *Islam in the Sudan*. 1949. Reprint. London: Oxford University.

Wehr, Hans. 1976. *A Dictionary of Modern Written Arabic*. 3rd ed. Edited by J. Milton Cowan. Ithaca, N.Y.: Spoken Language Services.

Wilson, Peter. 1967. Status Ambiguity and Spirit Possession. *Man*, n.s. 2: 366–78.

Young, Allan. 1975. Why Amhara Get Kureynya: Sickness and Possession in an Ethiopian Zar Cult. *American Ethnologist* 2(3): 567–84.

Zenkovsky, Sophie. 1950. Zar and Tambura as Practiced by the Women of Omdurman. *Sudan Notes and Records* 31(1): 65–81.

# *"Tradition" and Threat:*
## Women's Obscenity in Giriama Funerary Rituals

### Janet McIntosh

## INTRODUCTION

It is midday in the Giriama village outside the town of Malindi, Kenya, and women are gathering on one

Original material prepared for this text. Reprinted by permission of the author.

side of a well-swept clearing framed by mud and thatch huts. They sit with their legs stretched before them, comparing their finery—flamboyant *leso* cloths; clean, bright polyester blouses from town; and the customary bustles of grass and cotton that accentuate their hips. My black skirt and T-shirt seem dull by comparison, but as always the women greet me warmly, seating me on a woven mat on the earth next to them. We are assembling to mark the passing of a young woman who died in childbirth; her body lies in the center of the clearing, cradled by a bed of woven sisal ropes. Her mother and three elderly women flank the bed, waving small handkerchiefs in desultory motions to chase off the flies. They have not slept since the tragic night before, but some of them are capable of laughter as well as tears, and occasionally break into a low-key song and dance, swishing their handkerchiefs rhythmically. Other female kin are out of sight, gathered in a nearby hut where they will receive well-wishers during the next five days of ceremony. And at the other side of the homestead the men carry out their tasks: six or seven take turns digging a grave, while others decide where they will buy the planks to build a coffin. Most sit on mats, drinking from small gourds of palm wine, discussing local politics, and comparing the jobs they have lost and gained in town.

Word has gone out through the neighboring communities that a funeral has begun, and the crowd swells to about two hundred as the afternoon wears on. When a male song leader arrives and positions himself near the corpse, ten or fifteen enthusiastic women gather around him. At his cue, several of them begin to jangle winnowing trays laden with broken glass, creating a silvery percussive effect. The rest break into song and dance, shuffling in a circle, shimmying their hips emphatically, and punctuating their movement now and then by falling forward and catching themselves with a well placed step. Some of their songs speak to death and decay: "Fly away, housefly. You can't land on this body, because it's covered with rashes." But many of the lyrics are teasing and a little startling: "Mother's clothes are falling off," quips one song. As the singers warm to their task, the lyrics become graphic:

May I screw you? May I screw you?
An unmarried non-virgin will be screwed
A man's wife is maize meal and meat
I will die and stop screwing

One by one, women and girls from the surrounding crowd join in, and the circle widens to accommodate them. Soon they put aside the winnowing trays, clapping with enthusiasm as they sing and shuffle around the corpse and its tenders, who continue to whisk the flies away. From time to time the dancers stop in their tracks and face the center of the circle, clapping loudly. Several women leap into the middle and begin to gyrate their pelvises, inching up to the others to simulate sexual contact and intercourse. Normal decorum is abandoned; a seventy-year-old woman grinds against a thirty-year-old male song leader, while a young woman simulates sex with her mother-in-law. A woman with gray hair organizes a stunt, placing a giant wooden pestle upside down by the head of the corpse, climbing onto it and moving her pelvis in quick circles, barely keeping her balance. I turn to my neighbor, a married woman holding a baby, and remark: "I have talked to many people about your funerals, but I still wonder why the women perform these songs and dances."

"It's just our tradition," she says with a gentle smile, adding: "They are trying to distract the bereaved people from their pain." I ask why she doesn't join in. "My husband doesn't like me to," she replies, "He thinks the women who do the dances have no respect for their men." Another woman inside the circle, an unmarried forty-something, mimes a sex act with more zeal than most. A young man from the village passes me and whispers in my ear snidely: "That one is a prostitute; she keeps a lot of men happy." Another song begins:

Mr. Charo Baya knows how to screw
Finish fast; I want to get home and cook!
My husband doesn't screw me that way.
Charo Baya you've won me—Your penis is big;
my hips can't hold you.

As the dancing grows louder and more exuberant, three giggling teenagers pull me into the fray and prod me before them, daring me to perform the dance moves. An old woman glares at us from just outside the circle; like some other elders, she objects to the participation of young unmarried women, and I wonder if her ire is directed partly at me. I clap and step my way around the corpse until shyness gets the better of me and I withdraw to the margins, craning my neck to take in the scene. I can see the men still clustered on their side of the homestead, drinking, talking, and observing the grave-diggers, who sweat profusely as they struggle to complete their job before nightfall. A few young men stand on the edge of the dancing circle, looking on with small gourds of palm wine in their hands, ogling and occasionally lunging at the women they admire the most. One of the men plunges in and is set on by two women who gyrate against his side and back until he extricates himself, laughing. The circle closes again, a riot of stepping, clapping women, who seem to delight as each new song ups the ante of bawdy suggestion.

A Giriama funeral in the Malindi area is a momentous event, a protracted ritual far longer, more expensive, and better attended than any other rite in Giriama custom. Social life is magnified during these gatherings: men gain and lose prestige in displays of generosity; commerce in food, palm wine, and property quickens; old friends strike up new relations; and enemies settle their grudges, sometimes violently. Above all, women's funerary songs and dances escalate into lewd rebellions that, like the above scenario, far outstrip normal expectations for female behavior. What does this sexual performance by women signify? Is it considered mere "tradition," a benign ritual release, as the young woman above and many others wanted me to believe? Or do the currents of disapproval—her husband's denunciation of the dancing women, the passing young man's whisper, and the old woman's stare—suggest another level of interpretation, one that takes the rebellious overtones of the songs and dances more seriously?

These questions have a precedent in a broader literature that explores the relationship among gender, power, and ritual. Much of this literature emphasizes the unique opportunity that ritual offers subordinate groups, particularly women, to violate custom and express discontent. Ritual spirit possession, for example, has been heralded as a means of "[expressing] dissatisfaction with existing patterns" (Bourguignon 1973: 33), especially in cultures where other avenues of redress are not available (Lewis 1971). Possession can also open a space for violations of sexual protocol redolent of those in Giriama funerals; in Danforth's account of possession by St. Constantine among Anastenaridien Greeks, possessed women engage in "flamboyant, demonstrative, even flirtatious behavior that is considered more appropriate for men" (1989: 100). By becoming "symbolically male" through possession, Danforth says, such women garner publicity while enhancing their power and status beyond the domestic sphere (100). Whereas spirit possession partakes of its own special devices—including the appropriation of the agency and powers of the possessing spirit—other types of ritual offer women additional opportunities for misbehavior. In numerous sub-Saharan African rituals, for example, normative arrangements are turned upside-down and subordinate groups, women in particular, may temporarily take on the roles of their social superiors (Gluckman 1965). Ritual form, then, seems to lend itself to unruliness like that in Giriama women's funerary song and dance.

While it may provide a useful emotional outlet for women's frustrations, the enduring question is whether unruly ritual behavior poses a substantial threat to patriarchal orders. When there is no possessing spirit from which to borrow prestige, do the exceptional events within a ritual confer any new powers on the participants? Do ritual acts really challenge the tenets of social life once the ritual moment has passed? Social theorists have tended to address this issue in general terms. Mary Douglas, for example, sees ritual misbehavior as universally beguiling and potentially threatening to the status quo: "We seek to create order," she writes, "[yet] we do not simply condemn disorder. We recognise that it is destructive to

existing patterns; also that it has potentiality. It symbolizes both danger and power" (Douglas 1966: 94). In his analysis of medieval carnivals, Mikhael Bakhtin interprets ritual bawdiness as a moment of freedom that just might have enduring effects; a "true feast of becoming, change, and renewal" (Bakhtin 1962: 18). Although such readings credit unruly ritual with liberating potential, others doubt that it poses a genuine threat or challenge to the powers that be. According to Gluckman, a ritual of rebellion that takes place within a strong social structure is but an ineffectual gesture; a form of "instituted protest [that] in complex ways renews the unity of the system" (1954: 3).

In this essay, I approach the question of ritual power from a somewhat different angle. Rather than asking whether Giriama women's funerary songs and dances actually change the social system, I instead explore how Giriama themselves perceive them. And in a parallel to the tension between theorists like Douglas and Gluckman, I detect two conflicting interpretations of funerary obscenity among Giriama in the Malindi area. At one level, the women's performance is publicly couched as Gluckman might have predicted: a harmless "tradition" and a salubrious tool of emotional healing. Yet another, less formal discourse implies that the songs and dances threaten the sexual dignity of Giriama women. Although Douglas might locate this threat in some generic danger inherent to unruly ritual, "danger" is always construed in light of tensions specific to a given social moment. In fact, I argue, Giriama women's funerary songs have long been obscene, yet the current disapproval among Giriama in Malindi is distinctly colored by a development that is both modern and local: the arrival of Western lifestyles and tourism on the Kenya coast, and the corresponding emergence of a fraught sexual ethos in society-at-large.

## GIRIAMA, PAST AND PRESENT

The Giriama are the largest of nine related Bantu groups called the Mijikenda, who live in a 5,000-square-mile strip in the coastal hinterland of eastern Kenya. According to Mijikenda oral history, their people dwelled as subsistence farmers for centuries while based in fortified villages called *kaya* that were governed by male elders and organized by sacred spaces, age-set rituals, and semisecret societies termed *mwanza*. The *kaya* dispersed in the nineteenth century, and since then Mijikenda culture has been subject to forces that threaten older ways of life. But like all self-told histories, Mijikenda accounts are both reflections of the past and "statements of what informants feel it should be" (Willis 1993: 44). *Kaya* are often invoked as part of a nostalgic call for unity and "authenticity" in moments of social, economic, and political insecurity (Mazrui 1997; Parkin 1991), yet stories of isolated life in the *kayas* obscure the fact that for centuries, coastal Mijikenda have interacted with wealthier town-dwelling Arab and Swahili Muslims in fluid economic, religious, and even kin relations. And in the colonial and postcolonial eras, Mijikenda have endured difficult integration into a multicultural coastal economy of Europeans, Asians, Arabs, Swahili, and upcountry Kenyans. Today, cash is increasingly important for the essentials of life in and near Malindi, making wage labor a virtual necessity, yet many Giriama who seek jobs are hampered by lack of training and employer prejudice. Education is perceived as a key to wealth, but school fees are out of reach for many Giriama families. Now as then, few Mijikenda own land or large businesses, and other ethnic groups on the coast regard them as a low-status, "backward" people. Such economic and ideological pressures have resulted in numerous Giriama conversions to Islam or Christianity, yet aggressive assertions of Giriama "tradition" still play a role in local and governmental politics. And rituals such as funerals remain popular despite Muslim and Christian censure.[1]

## SEX AND DEATH IN FUNERARY RITUAL

The two major funerary song-and-dance types for Giriama women in the Malindi area, termed *kifudu* and *kihoma*, are considered "traditional," yet oral histories indicate that both originated outside of Giriama funerals. *Kifudu* songs are accompanied by the rhythmic shaking of shells or broken glass in a broad winnowing tray, and the dances involve much shimmying of the breasts and hips. According to Giriama elders, *kifudu* emerged from a women's fertility cult called *mwanza wa kifudu* that dates back to the *kaya* era. In the *mwanza wa kifudu*, women kept sacred clay pots that were named after their deceased former custodians and believed to have a life force of their own. Since *kifudu* pots could either protect or destroy women's health and reproductive capacities, they were supplicated at every new moon: removed from their shrines to be spoken to, sung and danced to, and "played" by blowing air over their openings. The supplicatory songs and dances were called *kifudu cha tsongo*, and, according to anthropologist Monica Udvardy, were characterized by "obscene or ludicrous" lyrics and correspondingly "suggestive movements" (Udvardy 1990b: 142). These songs were imported into the funerals of members of the *mwanza wa kifudu* but at some point, for unknown reasons, they were generalized to funerals at large. The propitiation of *kifudu* pots still takes place in some Giriama homesteads further

inland, but in many areas, including Malindi, the tradition has dwindled, and the *kifudu* fertility medicines have been dispersed among and reinterpreted by individual diviner/healers (Thompson 1990).[2] Yet *Kifudu* songs endure, and some women still compose new ones that address two major themes: death and grief, and bawdy sexual antics. *Kifudu* songs are customarily sung by postmenopausal women (Udvardy 1990a: 145), but in the Malindi area the sanctions for their performance have been blurred, and young women and even pubescent girls participate, to the dismay of some elders.

The second variety of funerary song, called *kihoma*, is said to be more obscene than *kifudu*. *Kihoma* involves a slightly different dance style accompanied by vigorous clapping and, unlike *kifudu*, is totally prohibited after the corpse has been buried. Men as well as women compose these songs, and the lyrics discuss graphic sexual themes from both male and female points of view.[3] In some Giriama groups, men occasionally dance to *kihoma* songs as well, but among Giriama close to Malindi, women and girls dominate the dancing almost exclusively. Giriama informants claim that *kihoma* songs originated with another Mijikenda group, the Chonyi, and some elders suggest they have been popularized in recent years by young funeral participants who are excessively zealous about their sexual content. But while elders distinguish between *kifudu* and *kihoma* and decry the changes in funerary performance, most youth are only dimly aware of the songs' histories, and are hard-pressed to categorize individual songs as either *kifudu* or *kihoma*. I will return to the subject of how elders regard changes in funerary songs below, for their disapproval signals more holistic changes in Giriama life.

Leaving these controversies aside for the moment, I want to explore Giriama explanations for why sexual songs should be performed at funerals in the first place. Anthropologists van Gennep (1960) and Victor Turner (1967) have written at length about the "liminal" phase in rites of passage, in which normal social rules are suspended and ritual participants behave in unorthodox ways. In many sub-Saharan funerals, liminality takes the specific form of inversion: a reversal of ordinary hierarchies and taboos.[4] In Giriama funerals, the visibility of the corpse defines the boundaries of the liminal phase; Giriama say that its uncanny presence opens behavioral possibilities that are curtained off from everyday experience.[5] And, in keeping with the sub-Saharan funerary theme of inversion, *kifudu* and *kihoma* song and dance upend customary expectations with implications of female promiscuity, female sexual aggression, incest, adultery, and homosexuality.[6] Yet funerary inversions in other African cultures include all kinds of reversals, including turning clothing inside out, moving in a counterclockwise direction, and slandering local rulers. So why should sexual license be the inversion of choice for Giriama? Giriama explain that sex has an antithetical relation to death, a tension that lends sexual imagery a special emotional charge. The funerary songs and dances, they say, "mock" death by confronting its power with defiant expressions of sexual pleasure. For those who remember that *kifudu* performances emerge from a fertility cult, the songs and dances also invoke reproductive capacity, the continuation of life even in the presence of its end. And the ecstatic and ridiculous elements of the songs and dances are said to "change the minds" of the bereaved, distracting them from their grief by presenting them with images pleasurable, extreme, and, sometimes, silly.[7] Witty double-entendres such as the line: "I'll bury something in you!" instantaneously defuse the miseries of death and burial by rhetorically transforming the death rite into a sexual encounter.

Yet there is another, more paradoxical relationship between death and sexual permissiveness at these funerals, in which they are not so much juxtaposed as aligned.[8] The dancing circle where the corpse lies is referred to as a "bad place" with negative supernatural overtones, and this "bad place," say informants, is a place in which "bad things can happen." The corpse, then, is both a signal that existential normalcy has vanished and a prompt to wreak further havoc, as the *kifudu* and *kihoma* songs and dances do with their dissolute symbolism. One Giriama man aligns the destruction of death with the disgrace of sexual abandon; when I asked him to explain *kifudu* and *kihoma* to me, he replied: "Someone has died! Things have already turned to shit, so why not let everything run to ruin?" Other informants assimilate grief and sexual expression on the emotional level, saying: "When someone has died, and your grief is so bad, what can you do but laugh and celebrate?" Such utterances surely have performative elements, as expressions of wishful thinking that might help to create the kind of celebration they describe and in so doing help the bereaved to forget their sorrow. But they also contain an implicit theory, a strange emotional geometry in which extreme grief passes beyond sorrow and travels full circle to the giddy version of joy seen in *kifudu* and *kihoma* performances. This paradox is echoed in the expression of some funeral participants: "A funeral is like a wedding; the last wedding of the deceased."

## GENDER, SEXUALITY, AND CHANGE IN GIRIAMA LIFE

The sexual content of *kifudu* and *kihoma* songs and dances appears to play an important role in processing and transforming the emotions that accompany

death, but it is also a pivotal site for complex and changing gender relationships among Giriama in the Malindi area. Before discussing local interpretations of women's funerary performances, I offer here a brief history of the shifting gender dynamics that underlie them. Since the nineteenth century, the patriarchal household arrangements of the *kaya* era have undergone considerable change in many Giriama communities, yet the theme of male dominance persists. Homesteads in the *kaya* model are made up of several polygynous households headed by a senior man who makes decisions about property allocation, conflicts, and patrilineal rituals. Parents and other elders oversee marital arrangements, including brideprice transactions, and women's rights to resources are severely constrained by a patrilineal inheritance system. These structures endure in some Giriama communities, but in others, economic changes and cultural contact have destabilized older ways of life. In the small villages flanking Malindi town, for example, household arrangements have an improvisational feel. Young men may split off from their father's homestead in search of economic opportunities closer to town, squatting on land owned by Muslims or upcountry Kenyans with other Mijikenda hopefuls, and building one or two huts for their wife or wives. In cases of divorce or abandonment, some women choose to live on their own, supporting themselves and their children rather than returning to their natal homestead. But shifting household arrangements have not greatly enhanced women's economic opportunities. Although men venture into town to seek wage labor, and may aspire to private investments and property ownership, women rarely accumulate capital or property of their own, tending to remain close to home as they raise children and till the family's small subsistence farm plot. For income they may sell domestic animals, firewood, thatch, deep-fried goods, and the surplus from their small farming plots, but such enterprises rarely yield a large profit. A significant number of women become professional diviner-healers, an increasingly popular choice that can lead to prestige and a limited degree of financial power (Thompson 1990). Yet even such creative pursuits do not weaken the pervasive gender ideology that limits girls' and women's prospects. Many parents prefer to spend their limited school fee money on their sons, a pattern that perpetuates both economic and ideological inequities. One man justifies the limitations on girls' education with the assertion that "our women are pure womanhood in its natural state." In Giriama discourse, this "natural state" is deemed servile, irresponsible, and capricious, while men, by contrast, are considered strong, brave, and more intellectual (McIntosh 1996; Thompson 1990).

The sexual customs that emerged from the *kaya* era have also changed in the Malindi area, yet a powerful residue of sanctions and proscriptions remains. According to *kaya* custom, sexual courtship and behavior should be highly discreet. Sex itself must be engaged in with care because it is believed to be linked to supernatural powers. Ritual sexual intercourse, for example, is said to bring prosperity and purification when performed at moments of significant social transition (Udvardy 1990a, 1990b). Termed "*mathumia*," these rites between spouses can mark the "coming out" ceremony of a newborn, the circumcision of a son, and the various training phases of a diviner-healer. They may sanction a child's marriage arrangement, or purify individuals in a compromised state (a widow, for example, should have ritual intercourse with another man if her husband dies an inauspicious death). Senior males are pivotal figures in *mathumia* rites; when an individual in a homestead dies, for example, or when a homestead relocates, the senior male must perform *mathumia* with his first wife before other homestead members can resume normal sexual relations. When a couple violates *mathumia* restrictions, their children are believed susceptible to illness and death. Udvardy suggests that *mathumia* rites underscore the "mutual dependence of the genders for the prosperous enactments of creation, recreation, and transformation" (Udvardy 1990a: 87), but, she adds, the rites often depend on the leadership of male homestead heads, and therefore re-inscribe their seniority. Meanwhile, the Giriama belief in women's "greater potential to cause disorder" (Thompson 1990) generates additional constraints for female sexuality. Unmarried girls are expected to protect their chastity, and married women (not men) who are unfaithful may inflict their children with a supernaturally borne illness termed *kirwa*.

With cultural contact and change, Giriama communities everywhere have altered some or all of these customs, yet women's sexuality is still policed by popular expectation. Christianity and Islam, of course, do not recognize *mathumia* or *kirwa* beliefs, but both portray premarital sex and overt expressions of sexuality as sinful, particularly among women. Among Giriama who do not consider themselves Muslim or Christian, *kirwa* beliefs and *mathumia* proscriptions are followed only erratically by members of the younger generation. In fact, popular expectations in Malindi operate primarily by means of secular ideologies. Whereas today's men are said to be more sexually aggressive than in the past, women are still expected to resist advances, defining their decency through modesty. In conversation this theme occasionally appears through trope of hunting: men play the role of predator, women of prey, and the ones with integrity elude capture until they can run no more. And while they may desire sex, women are constrained by an unwritten rule of silence: unlike men, women should not initiate sexual liaisons verbally. "A woman can say it [express desire] with her body," my informants tell me, "but not with her mouth." The female body's language, furthermore, should be subtle and indirect: a glance, a fleeting half-smile, or a slight, sinuous motion. The burden of sexual comportment, hence, has largely shifted from both sexes (as seen in *mathumia* proscriptions) to women and girls alone.

If sexual expectations continue their policing function, sexual behavior in Malindi town constantly threatens to violate these proscriptions. While Giriama communities everywhere are faced with sexual changes, Malindi's economic and cultural situation has created exceptional tensions. In recent decades, numerous upcountry Kenyans have moved to the coast for economic opportunities, bringing versions of modernity in tow, including nuclear family structure, consumerist aspirations, and "Western" sexual behavior with demonstrative premarital passion. The last twenty years have also brought a high volume of European and American tourists, who flock to the palm-lined beaches of the Indian Ocean in a display of wealth, hedonism, and exposed flesh. Malindi has become a popular "sex safari" destination, with visitors of both sexes searching for an exotic fling. This clientele has lured many young African men and women into hustling and prostitution in Malindi's casinos, hotels, and beaches. Even Giriama who rarely enter town are aware of the changing sexual habits in urban centers, reading about them in the newspapers, and noting the sexual lyrics of the urban-based music that pumps from young men's boom boxes. And the practice of exchanging sex for cash has filtered into the surrounding villages, where some women have begun to solicit local clients, often because of economic need. In one village on the outskirts of Malindi town, a sixty-year-old Giriama man was recently arrested for paying a thirteen-year-old girl for sex; she capitulated, she said, because her single mother had no source of income for food. Several elder women told me stories of schoolgirls selling their bodies to teachers and other students—narratives that entwine the elders' anxieties about the lures of prostitution and the perils of a Western-style education. Even Giriama women who do not sell sex are also said to be changing their sexual habits. One Giriama man in his late thirties, for example, told me that he had recently propositioned a woman for sexual relations, but was so shocked and revolted when she accepted on the spot (rather than putting him off time and again as he expected) that he withdrew the suggestion. Evidently, expectations of female modesty are alive in Giriama ideology in the Malindi area, but are constantly challenged and changed. This tension sets the stage for local interpretations of funerary songs.

## WOMEN'S RITUAL LICENSE: CONFLICTING INTERPRETATIONS

On the face of it, *kifudu* and *kihoma* performances offer Giriama women a unique opportunity to express their desires and decry male power while asserting their own self-worth. At a funeral, any woman—old, young, married or single—can intone a sexual invitation ("May I screw you?") and exult in the imagined pleasures of adultery ("Charo Baya knows how to screw!"). While they flout conventions verbally, the women enact further obscenities with their bodies by dancing suggestively and simulating sexual intercourse with partners normally forbidden to them. But *kifudu* and *kihoma* performances do not simply play with expressions of desire; they also enact women's rivalry with and resentment against men. Whereas Giriama men compete with other men during funerary "prestige competitions" (Parkin 1972: 81), women bond with one another in their funerary songs, directing antagonism and rivalry outward toward men and toward women from neighboring areas. Sexual derision is a popular weapon: "My husband doesn't know how to screw me," complains one lyric. Another song mocks jealous husbands while belittling their genitalia: "A jealous husband will not grow fat/He only has thin legs and long testicles." Still another song degrades women from a rival community, then berates an elderly man for being an inept provider: "You don't clothe me or feed me, grandfather. You know, you're just yoghurt." In a way, these songs are the symbolic antithesis of *mathumia*: they desacralize sex, they flout the order of sexual custom, they put a thumb in the eye of male elders, and they stress antagonism between genders rather than interdependence. In a culture where women's power, sexual autonomy, and general worth are constrained and demeaned, these full-throated testimonies of anger, sexual agency, and pride are surely emotionally significant gestures of resistance.

But can we assume that onlookers, and the singers themselves, understand the women's words and actions as an important and enduring statement of rebellion? *Kifudu* and *kihoma* take place within a ritual frame, and like all rituals, this one sets up an extraordinary and perplexing relationship between the ritual participants and what they are saying and doing. In his exploration of this relationship, Gluckman analyses numerous rituals of rebellion that flout the existing power structure through blasphemy, humor, and obscenity (Gluckman 1954, 1965). Using ethnographic

evidence from Zulu and other African cultures, he concludes that participation in such rituals does not constitute a threat to the status quo. In fact, he argues, such rituals often emerge from a strong social order, and further solidify it:

> The acceptance of the established order as right and good, and even sacred, seems to allow unbridled license, very rituals of rebellion, for the order itself keeps this rebellion within bounds. Hence to act the conflicts, whether directly or by inversion or in other symbolical forms, emphasizes the social cohesion within which the conflicts exist. (1965: 125)

The "ritual of rebellion," then, is a kind of cage for disorder, particularly in societies where social structure is already strong. If anything, Gluckman implies, rebellion is less likely after such rituals, for rebellious impulses are restricted to a socially sanctioned time and place, and thus reminded of their impotence.

At the same time that the ritual context brackets antisocial behavior, ritual form can also defuse subversive messages by virtue of the fact that most ritual behaviors are second-hand. Anthropologist Lila Abu-Lughod makes a related observation in her account of Egyptian Bedouin women's poetry (Abu-Lughod 1986). Bedouin women recite poetry to express feelings of grief and self-pity that would normally be unacceptable because in Bedouin culture, stoicism and emotional self-control are considered essential to social dignity. Abu-Lughod suggests that a poem is an acceptable medium of expression because it offers the woman who recites it a kind of alibi: if the woman reciting the poem did not author it, she cannot be fully credited with the sentiments in the text. As a result, a woman performing poetry is exempt from normal critiques of emotional expression, being evaluated instead by a "different set of standards regarding conformity to societal ideals" (207). While Abu-Lughod's analysis does not directly concern ritual, we can extrapolate her analysis to ritual form, in which participants' acts and utterances have a pre-scripted, second-hand quality similar to that of poetic recitation.

If we combine Gluckman's and Abu-Lughod's accounts, we can interpret ritual as doubly qualified to defuse potentially subversive messages. First, ritual is sharply bracketed from everyday life by a special space, time, and behavioral protocol; its boundaries might be likened to quotation marks that set it off from the continuous stream of ordinary happenings. Second, the content of ritual does not spring anew from the agency and opinions of ritual participants, but instead is derivative of rituals past, and as such, resembles reported speech more than first-hand utterance. If these devices are central to local interpretations of *kifudu* and *kihoma*, we might expect the performances to pose no threat to Giriama social order, and the singers themselves to be treated no differently for participating. And indeed, this is a common account of *kifudu* and *kihoma* among Giriama near Malindi. In interviews, I asked numerous informants whether women's funerary songs are permissible given the overarching expectation of female sexual modesty, and was repeatedly told that the songs are "just tradition," and hence do not constitute a genuine rebellion against social expectations. This reassurance was often delivered in a quick and patterned fashion, rather like a stock response designed to strip the performances of any significance beyond their generic status as "tradition," and, perhaps, to preclude further inquiry by this probing outsider.[9] These stock dismissals of *kifudu* and *kihoma* may have a protective function for the Giriama community at large, for they emphasize that such behaviors are restricted to the ritual frame and hence pre-empt accusations that their non-ritual social habits are primitive and debased. And women defend their performances as "just tradition" with special alacrity, guarding their most privileged moment of expression by denying that real expression is involved at all.

But are Giriama women's funerary utterances and actions completely absolved by the ritual context? Are women really free to say and do anything in ritual without consequence? Despite the public sanction for *kifudu* and *kihoma*, unofficial currents of ambivalence and disapproval run through the Giriama communities near Malindi town. In informal contexts such as casual conversations, gossip sessions, and whispered asides like that of the man who passed me during the funeral, men of all ages and elder women voice anxiety about *kifudu* and *kihoma* performances today. A number of young men say that although they might be tempted to sleep with a woman who enjoys performing the songs and dances, they would not marry her—implying that the free sexual expression in the performances is sexually attractive, but suggests inferior virtue. Still other men, like the husband of the woman I spoke to at the funeral above, forbid their wives to participate in the singing and dancing at all, seeming to fear either that stigma will attach to their wives, or that the performance might augur actual promiscuity. Meanwhile, older women complain that the young girls who participate in funerary songs and dances "don't respect their elders anymore" and are prone to promiscuity and prostitution. In such discussions, *kifudu* and *kihoma* are portrayed not as meaningless ritual behaviors, but instead as a kind of training ground for real sexual misconduct. Apparently, Giriama detect the seeds of genuine danger and resistance described by Douglas and Bakhtin, and fear that

these might escape the ritual boundary, putting down roots in ordinary life.

Where does this tension between stock approval of funerary obscenity and informal disapproval emerge from? The moralizing forces of Islam and Christianity doubtless contribute to the discourse of danger, since both religions construe Giriama rituals as heathenistic and corrupt. But those who regard the rituals with suspicion include numerous Giriama who do not call themselves converts—in fact some of them, including some elderly women, openly despise the influence of world religions on their milieu. Although Mary Douglas might ascribe their disapproval of funerary ritual to the inherent dangers of "disorder," she may undervalue the ways in which culturally specific anxieties define "disorder" as "dangerous." Interestingly, Gluckman anticipates the importance of context in construals of unruly ritual, though he deals with it only indirectly. Where there is little threat of misconduct outside of the ritual context, he says, ritual rebellion will not affect the extant social order. But, he predicts, "where the [social] relationships involved are weak, there cannot be license in ritual" (1965: 132). Gluckman does not explain the concept of "weak relationships" in great detail, but the fraught sexual issues in the Malindi area surely bring Giriama society under this rubric. While the homestead breaks apart, women and girls are loosed from the mast, and through a kind of *bricolage* of the examples that surround them, improvise new sexual identities. Male homestead heads in the Malindi area no longer orchestrate sexual conduct through *mathumia*, and as supernatural proscriptions for sexual transgression fade, fears of adultery mount. Women's potential promiscuity spells a drop in male control over female sexuality (and, by implication, paternity), giving men reason for discomfort.[10] Meanwhile, the elders' authority is shunted to the side, making both elder men and elder women uncomfortable as they watch old hierarchies of respect and resource distribution crumble.

As these social anxieties grow, the membrane surrounding the ritual becomes permeable in two directions. Sexual threats run from the outside in, as growing numbers of girls join the obscene dancing circles—a violation of previous ritual guidelines that the elders link to their exposure to promiscuity and prostitution in daily life. In turn, the portrayal of sexual dissolution in the ritual threatens, in the popular imagination, to spill beyond its bounds and influence daily behavior. Since the acts and utterances in funerary songs and dances have begun to speak of possible rather than unlikely behavior, the ritual content is no longer totally dismissed as a benign kind of reported speech. Instead, currents of suspicion frame the ritual content as a first-hand report of the unruly desires of women participants. Thus ritual participants are caught between two interpretations of their actions: although they are partially absolved by the protective cloak of tradition, they also risk the labels of promiscuity or unmarriageability. In funerary ritual today, an expressive space for women is offered with one hand and revoked with the other.

I would like to return briefly to a subject I mentioned earlier: the elder women's claim that funerary songs are now revoltingly obscene compared to the gentler, more graceful performances of their youth. Although this complaint may have an element of truth, I do not take it entirely at face value. First, I witnessed some of the same elderly women who complain about funerary obscenity participating in the lewdest songs and dances with delight; evidently, the style was not as alien to them as they suggested. Secondly, early missionary and colonial reports of *kifudu* song and dance suggest that it was obscene long before these women were young. Ludwig Krapf, the first missionary to East Africa, mentions "immoralities and abominations" practiced at a *mwanza wa kifudu* ceremony he witnessed in 1847, noting that "[these] are well known to every one" (Krapf 1968 [1860]: 162). The colonial officer Arthur Champion, writing around 1914, describes one *kifudu* dance as "demoniacal" and "frenz[ied]" (26), and relates that "[another] dance performed by two old women over the grave was of an extremely sensual character. This unseemly dance produced great mirth amongst the mourners" (Champion 1967: 28). Although these accounts are colored by an overarching colonialist horror toward African rites, and although they do not rule out the possibility that the rituals contain more brazen material now than then, they do suggest that overtly sexual material in funerary songs and dances is not new. It is possible, then, that the elder women's complaints are about something more than obscenity within ritual. Although the obscene signifiers within funerary ritual may not have changed significantly, the social context for their interpretation has changed, lending the sexual phenomena signified in the ritual a more real and threatening cast. The elder women's nostalgia, then, may not be for another kind of song, but for another way of life altogether.

## CONCLUSION

Sex is considered "appropriate" subject matter at a Giriama funeral for gender-neutral reasons. It symbolizes the extremity of life's borders, it distracts the mourners from their misery, and it mocks the despair and the finality of death. Yet in their songs and dances, women magnify these sexual elements and direct them at male targets, giving funerary rituals acute significance for Giriama gender politics. Through these ritual moments women assert female unity and pride,

vent their complaints about male power, and convey their joy in breaking through the sexual decorum normally expected of them.

Given all of this, what should we make of the original tension between Douglas' and Gluckman's accounts of ritual license? Gluckman's insistence that rituals of rebellion are benign is echoed by Giriama themselves when they attest that their funerals are "just tradition." But although the protective ritual frame may render their acts partially permissible, the women's fulminating grievances do not go unacknowledged. Douglas' suggestion that ritual disorder spells "danger" also circulates among Malindi-based Giriama as an interpretive possibility. Thus, for the ambivalent onlooker at a funeral, an archetypical expression of Giriama "tradition" threatens to encourage, if not serve as a catalyst for a transformation in the gendered order.

As I have suggested, the perceived "danger" in women's funerary songs stems not simply from the presence of disorder in the ritual, but largely from changes in the surrounding social context that influence the interpretation of that disorder. The new sexual options in Malindi both vex the patriarchal order and challenge the "official" notion that ritual can successfully contain its own subversive strains. But I don't mean to imply that Malindi is the only site of such contests over ritual meaning. Giriama everywhere interact with other cultures, creating local social tensions that could challenge the security of the ritual frame—a pattern that may reach into the past as well. Although elders idealize the virtuous sexual codes of their youth, their memories are shaped by nostalgia, raising the possibility that sexual behavior has long run up against customary expectations, and that a double discourse about women's funerary performances has obtained for some time. We might, in fact, expand this argument outward, into a general suggestion. Perhaps Gluckman idealizes the "official" discourses of social unity in the African societies he studies, and in so doing, overlooks the changes, tensions, and fault lines elemental to all societies. If this is the case, if no society is so intact, then disorderly ritual moments are potentially as uniformly "dangerous" as Mary Douglas posits—only the degree and shape of danger will be locally construed, and presumably construed differently by various groups within a given society. The mere presence of "danger" in ritual, then, should not encourage theoreticians to leap to a universally triumphant narrative of female ritual unruliness, for such a leap would overlook the nuance and force of local interpretations of the ritual and its relationship to everyday life. In the Giriama case, such interpretations limit the practical efficacy of women's ritual gestures, for either the ritual gestures are not taken seriously or they are taken seriously and met with the sort of redress we have seen (derision or prohibition). What women can accomplish through unruly ritual, then, remains an open question that can only be addressed case by case, with close attention to the local anxieties that define the perplexing relationship between the mundane social world and the exhilarating alternatives encoded in ritual.

## ACKNOWLEDGEMENTS

I would like to thank Jennifer Dickinson, Rachel Heiman, Larry Hirschfeld, Penelope Papailias, and Gaye Thompson for their valuable feedback on a draft of this essay. Gaye Thompson provided rich insights into Giriama society, as did Kainga Kalume Tinga. My research assistant, Maxwell Phares Kombe, supported me with astonishing patience and intelligence, for which I will always be grateful. The people who assisted me along the way are far too numerous to name, but they include many Giriama, Swahili, and Europeans who welcomed me, talked to me, and tolerated me, often with kindness and good humor. Thanks are also due to the Malindi Museum Society and Fort Jesus Museum, Mombasa for their interest and support. This research was carried out with a grant from the Fulbright-Hays Foundation.

## NOTES

1. Although Giriama have partially internalized the message that they are "backward," they counter it with themes of rebellion against the groups who have scorned them. A number of funerary songs, which I do not present here, are laced with expressions of defiance against Muslims, Christians, and upcountry tribes. The strategic use of a stigmatized "tradition" as a tool of vengeance has important implications for Giriama political ideology, but these are beyond the scope of this article.

2. Udvardy notes that despite their importance, the *kifudu* secret societies are "not much talked about" (1990b: 151) by comparison to men's cults, lending them a "muted" quality common to female-dominated institutions (Ardener 1977). Perhaps this relative silence has facilitated their rapid transformation and quick disappearance from memory. Most Giriama under thirty in Malindi know *kifudu* as funerary song and dance only, not as a secret society—despite the fact that the *kifudu* society is still active several kilometers west of the town.

3. The dual narrative perspective of funerary songs is important to their significance, but it introduces complexities beyond the scope of this article. Briefly, I think that the songs' narrative volatility helps to construct the "ritual alibi" I discuss later in this article, by making the songs seem more like reported speech than first person expression. Yet, clearly, this alibi is not sufficient to defuse all suspicion toward the women who participate.

4. A survey of texts on East Africa, conducted over forty years ago, found more than 600 sources describing inversions in connection with death rituals (Berglund 1957).

5. Kihoma songs must cease the instant the corpse has been buried, suggesting that the visibility of the corpse defines the boundaries of the liminal period. This seems a fitting criterion, given that a corpse appears to embody liminality itself: the dead person is neither here nor there, for breath and mind have vanished, yet the flesh, bafflingly, remains.

6. Despite the fact that women may dance against one another in a sexually suggestive way at funerals, I found no evidence that lesbian sex is a Giriama cultural category. While they are aware that female–female sexual relations can occur among their Swahili and Arab neighbors, they have no term for it in their mother tongue. Informants tell me that if a woman loves another woman, she will sexualize the relationship not through direct contact but by arranging an affair between her husband and the female object of her affection. Homosexual sex between men, on the other hand, is acknowledged and condemned.

7. In a village about fifty kilometers Southwest of Malindi, Udvardy reports that Giriama considered funerary songs "entertainment for the departing spirit . . . the songs must be sung to accompany the spirit, so that it knows it is not alone and need not be sad" (Udvardy 1990a: 145–146). In Malindi, however, the emphasis is entirely on the emotions of those still living. This discrepancy may reflect a gradual move away from customary ancestor propitiation in Malindi; those who decline to consider the departing spirit set a precedent for neglecting the ancestral spirit as well.

8. The alignment of sex and death has been suggested too by Western avant-garde theorists such as Georges Bataille (1897–1962), who posited a fundamental kinship between sex and death in the human psyche. According to Bataille (1962), sex and death are conceptually aligned for existential reasons: both can dissolve the social self, lifting the boundary between individual subjectivity and the rest of the world. Bataille's theory emerges from a particular moment in Western history—after Renaissance writers had construed orgasm as a "small death"; after de Sade made his mark with his sex- and violence-ridden fiction; and after Freud suggested that orgasm resolves both life and death instincts—so should be applied with caution to other cultural contexts. Yet it does seem that numerous cultures have drawn some kind of symbolic equivalence between sex and death, suggesting that their sign qualities lend them to symbolic interplay.

9. The category of "tradition" has strategic dimensions in numerous colonial and postcolonial contexts. It may, for example, be used to protect or decry a given cultural practice; to sanction new forms of authority; or to confer an aura of unquestionability upon an otherwise contentious act. For more on such processes, see Hobsbawm and Ranger (1983).

10. It is worth noting that male objections to funerary songs primarily address their obscene contents, and not the contents that articulate a female–male rivalry. I suggest this discrepancy emerges from the fact that at the economic and political levels, patriarchy among Giriama remains intact and so is not threatened by the songs that express rivalry per se. Male control over female sexuality, on the other hand, is under threat. Men's disapproval of funerary performances, then, is correspondingly focused on female sexual expression.

## REFERENCES

Abu-Lughod, Lila. 1986. *Veiled Sentiments: Honor and Poetry in a Bedouin Society.* Berkeley: University of California Press.

Ardener, Edwin. 1977. "Belief and the Problem of Women." In Shirley Ardener (ed.). *Perceiving Women,* pp. 1–27. New York: John Wiley and Sons.

Bakhtin, M. M. 1962. *Rabelais and His World.* Transl. Helene Iswolsky. Cambridge, MA: MIT Press.

Bataille, Georges. 1962. *Death and Sensuality: A Study of Eroticism and the Taboo.* New York: Walker and Company.

Berglund, A. I. 1957. *Some African Funerary Inversions.* Unpublished M.A. thesis. Uppsala, Sweden: Department of Cultural Anthropology, Library of the African Research Programme.

Bourguignon, Erika (ed.). 1973. *Religion, Altered States of Consciousness, and Social Change.* Columbus: Ohio State University Press.

Champion, A. M. 1967. *The Agiriama of Kenya.* London: Royal Anthropological Institute.

Danforth, Loring M. 1989. *Firewalking and Religious Healing: The Anastenaria of Greece and the American Firewalking Movement.* Princeton, NJ: Princeton University Press.

Douglas, Mary. 1966. *Purity and Danger: An Analysis of the Concepts of Pollution and Taboo.* London: Routledge.

Gluckman, Max. 1954. *Rituals of Rebellion in South-East Africa.* Manchester, UK: Manchester University Press.

_____. 1965. *Custom and Conflict in Africa.* Oxford, UK: Basil Blackwell.

Hobsbawm, Eric, and Terence Ranger. 1983. *The Invention of Tradition.* Cambridge, UK: Cambridge University Press.

Krapf, J. Lewis. 1968. *Travels, Researches, and Missionary Labors during an 18 Years' Residence in Eastern Africa.* Missionary Researches and Travels Nr. 2. London: Frank Cass and Co.

Lewis, I. M. 1971. *Ecstatic Religion: A Study of Shamanism and Spirit Possession.* London: Routledge.

Mazrui, Alamin M. 1997. *Kayas of Deprivation, Kayas of Blood: Violence, Ethnicity, and the State in Coastal Kenya.* Nairobi: Human Rights Commission.

McIntosh, Janet S. 1996. "Professed Disbelief and Gender Identity on the Kenya Coast." In Natasha Warner et al. (eds.). *Gender and Belief Systems,* pp. 481–490. Berkeley, CA: Berkeley Women and Language Group, University of California.

Parkin, David J. 1972. *Palms, Wine, and Witnesses: Public Spirit and Private Gain in an African Farming Community.* London: Intertext Books.

_____. 1991. *Sacred Void: Spatial Images of Work and Ritual among the Giriama of Kenya.* Cambridge, UK: Cambridge University Press.

Thompson, Sally Gaye. 1990. *Speaking "Truth" to Power: Divination as a Paradigm for Facilitating Change among Giriama in the Kenyan Hinterland.* Unpublished Doctoral dissertation in Anthropology, presented to the School of African and Oriental Studies, University of London.

Turner, Victor. 1967. *The Forest of Symbols.* Ithaca, NY: Cornell University Press.

Udvardy, Monica. 1990a. *Gender and the Culture of Fertility among the Giriama of Kenya.* Unpublished Doctoral dissertation in Anthropology, presented to the University of Uppsala, Sweden.

_____. 1990b. "Kifudu: A Female Fertility Cult among the Giriama." In Anita Jacobson-Widding and Walter van Beek (eds.). *The Creative Communion: African Folk Models of Fertility and the Regeneration of Life,* pp. 137–152. Uppsala: Academiae Ubsaliensis. Distributed by Almquist and Wiksell International, Stockholm, Sweden.

van Gennep, Arnold. 1960. *The Rites of Passage.* Transl. Monika B. Vizedom and Gabrielle L. Caffee. Chicago: University of Chicago Press.

Willis, Justin. 1993. *Mombasa, the Swahili, and the Making of the Mijikenda.* Oxford, UK: Clarendon Press.

# *Shamans, Bodies, and Sex:*
## Misreading a Korean Ritual

### *Laurel Kendall*

"But isn't it sexual?" This paper owes its genesis to the presentation of another—"Of Gods and Men: Performance, Possession, and Flirtation in Korean Shaman Ritual"—to the questions it raised, and to

Originally appeared in French in *Anthropologie et Sociétés*, vol. 22, n. 2, 1998 as "Mais n'est-ce pas sexuel, Le lapsus derrière le regard ethnographique," and in English as "But Isn't She Sexual? The Freudian Slip beneath the Ethnographic Gaze," in *Gender/Bodies/Religions,* edited by Sylvia Marcos, 2000. Reprinted here in English with the Permission of Anthropologie et Sociétés and Adler Publications.

my bemusement when more than one respondent, on more than one occasion, insisted that sexuality "explained" the activities of female Korean shamans.[1] Speaking of the modern, Western intellectual tradition, Michel Foucault describes sexuality as, "the general and disquieting meaning that pervades our conduct . . . a general signification, a universal secret, an omnipresent cause, a fear that never ends."[2] This chapter illustrates how this pervasive and common sense notion of sexuality gets in the way of ethnographic clarity.

The shamans who are the subjects of this chapter are women. Indeed, most Korean shamans are women and the minority of male shamans dress in traditional women's clothing before donning the spirits' robes for a ritual. Shamans are chosen by the spirits; women experience this calling as frighteningly vivid dreams and visions, manic behavior, and compulsions to wander. They also experience misfortunes, both personally, and within their families, which recur until they accept their calling and are initiated. The initiation enables the shaman to call on the spirits for inspiration and visions which she will use to prognosticate both during divination sessions and when speaking in the persona of the spirits during minor and major rituals. Through her ability to make this connection with the spirits, the Korean shaman secures their favor on behalf of her clients. Ill health, problematic personal relations, and increasingly, business reverses, cause clients to seek out shamans, obtain divinations, and sponsor rituals. In addition to performing divinations, newly-initiated shamans can, with a minimum of training, perform simple prayer ceremonies for the good fortune of a client's family or business. The client makes offerings to the spirits and the shaman makes a petition on behalf of the client, then briefly manifests the spirits, offering in the voices of household gods and ancestors advice and cautions for all members of the client's family. With more training and observation of experienced shamans, the initiate learns to perform more complicated rituals for healing, business success, success in finding a marriage partner, and conceiving a child.[3]

The most elaborate, potent, and expensive ritual that Korean shamans perform is called *kut*. In *kut*, shamans wear clothing associated with the gods and ancestors and through song and dance, summon these spirits, in proper sequence, to the ritual space, manifesting them in their own bodies. In the persona of demanding gods and tearful ancestors, they scold, banter and commiserate with the clients, offer advice and prognostications, and depart with promises to help the family move toward a more optimistic future. The *kut* satisfies the appetites and demands of household gods and the worldly cravings of ancestors so that the troubling emotions they have vented toward the living family are transformed into good will and promises of future blessing and protection. Ominous forces are expelled and the path to an auspicious fortune is opened wide. The work of successful shamanship, closely bound with the successful performance of *kut*, requires a range of skills: singing, dancing, miming, playing the drum and percussive instruments, arranging elaborate offerings, and above all, providing canny divinations and convincing spirit manifestations. How was sexuality read into my description of these activities?

## THE ETHNOGRAPHIC PROBLEM: "AMBIGUOUS SEXUALITY WAFTING"

The problem was of my own making. In my earlier ethnography, I had written that "an element of ambiguous sexuality wafts about the *mansin's* (shaman's) performance."[4] "Of Gods and Men" explored the sources of that ambiguity. The presentation began with a disturbing memory from the field of a male spectator pinching the breast of a dancing shaman while he secured a thousand-*won* bill under her chest band. I used this image to approach a nagging question: why is the Korean shaman profession constructed as both disreputable and a service to the gods? I located my answer in the domain of dance. Dance, a source of pleasure and play, becomes in shaman ritual an amusement for the gods as well as the spectators, all of whom are said "to play" (*nolda*). As a gateway for the release of playful impulses and powerful emotions and as a sign and instrument of healing, dance also carries the danger of emotional abandon and disgrace. In extreme cases, the gods seize the dancing woman and claim her as a shaman.

A colleague wrote to thank me for a copy of my paper on "erotic dance." Erotic dance? What had I said?

I had included dancers' descriptions of a sense of joy, mirth, or excitement rising from the belly to the chest[5] and noted that this rising of spirited feelings (*hung, sin-param*) mapped the same trajectory as that taken by the personal body-governing gods who rise up when clients borrow shamans' costumes to dance, and by choking, potentially fatal emotions of rage and frustration that rise to the chest in "fire sickness" (*hwabyong*) when they have been held too long inside. I had written that in shaman rituals, the dance becomes a gateway for the expression of strong emotion in the idiom of spirits who, when they "play" in the person of a shaman or a client, vent their desires and appetites and attain (temporary) satisfaction. Korean shaman rituals dramatize the obverse of the Buddhist ideal of transcendence and of the Confucian injunction to controlled moderation; they deal with the consequences of worldly craving, using the dance as one idiom of both symptom and cure. I suggested that these associations, and the attendant possibility of being possessed by either spirits or compulsions and consequently disgraced, vested both dancing and the women who dance for a living with an aura of moral ambivalence (Kendall 1991).

"It must be sexual."

One respondent to an oral presentation of my paper insisted that sexual cravings necessarily explained the sensations Koreans described as rising from the belly. In a dialogue that exhausted the question-and-answer period, I was equally stubborn in my insistence that dancing Koreans did not read these experiences as sexual, that sexual desire—expressed most explicitly in the dancing compulsion—was but one of several emotions that Koreans expressed through the dancing, possessed or otherwise. Was lust more profound than the other bundled appetites and cravings that even nominal Korean Buddhists would recognize as obstacles to enlightenment or, in popular religion, as burdens weighing upon the restless dead? Is sexuality the engine that propels the dancer and runs the dance? A classic Freudian reading would have it so. Is the power that shamans claim through their danced possession by (mostly but not exclusively) male gods the regenerative power of sexuality turned to ritual ends? This is what respondents to my paper seemed to insist upon. One discussant even delicately suggested that I should "not be afraid" to give my ethnography a sexual gloss. Why hadn't I seen it? Was I "hung up?" I was challenged, aware of corroborating examples elsewhere in the world, but I maintained an abiding unease with what seemed to be a reductionistic interpretation of the Korean material.

## WOMEN, BODIES, AND SEX

In the 1970s, anthropologists concerned with what were then called "sex roles" asked, "Is female to male as nature is to culture?" Sherry Ortner, who phrased the question, argued that while the symbolic relegation of women to a lower order of existence is necessarily a cultural construct, the near universality of such perceptions is grounded in "the body and the natural procreative functions specific to women alone."[6] Much subsequent anthropological writing echoed this assumption that disparate cultures constructed women within the biological "givens" of the female body.[7] While Sherry Ortner and Harriet Whitehead,[8] as well as Bryan Turner[9] all explicitly eschew a simple biological determinism, they nevertheless assume that much of the anxious life of a given society is constructed around women's bodies as instruments of sexuality and reproduction. This is the obverse and conscious rejection of an abiding but more simplistic assumption, sometimes encountered in the literature on women and spirit possession (see below) that sexual repression is a common female problem.

Michel Foucault speaks of the "hysterization of women's bodies," the notion that women's sexuality is "innately problematic and that women's problems are innately sexual," as a historical development of the early modern West.[10] The publication of Foucault's *The History of Sexuality* prompted a veritable cottage industry in social and historical writings about the body as a site through which social discipline is imposed and social power is affirmed.[11] These efforts have opened the question of gender to complex historical and cultural analyses—how are different notions of "masculinity" and "femininity" experienced through male

and female bodies that are made to act in socially prescribed ways? A few voices of caution have been raised against the ease with which such endeavors might slide into an older tendency to define "woman" through the body, sex, and reproduction to the exclusion of other dimensions of experience.[12]

In emphasizing that the men's and women's bodily experiences are redefined through history, Foucault offered liberation from, in Gayle Rubin's words, "the traditional understanding of sexuality as a natural libido yearning to break free of social constraint."[13] Sexualities could now be seen as multiple and both culturally and historically constituted, rather than simply "natural."[14] Eroticism is thus one dimension of a larger question posed by Clifford Geertz and restated by Nancy Scheper-Hughes and Margaret Lock as, ". . . whether any expression of human emotion and feeling—whether public or private, individual or collective, whether repressed or explosively expressed is ever free of cultural shaping and cultural meaning. The most extreme statement of Geertz's position, shared by many of the newer psychological and medical anthropologists, would be that without culture we would simply not know how to feel."[15]

What does this material bring to the question, "But isn't it sexual?" First, recognizing the importance of contemporary studies that regard women, and in particular the sexuality of women, as culturally and historically constituted, it simultaneously recognizes a deep-rooted impulse in Western social science writing to approach the question of women through sexuality and reproduction, an impulse that may obscure other possible readings.[16] Second, a plea for the recognition of culturally-constituted ideologies of eroticism, or any other expression of human feeling, is a plea for ethnographic precision and imagination and an honest recognition of the profound difficulty of interpreting human motivation in the absence of confident psychobiological "givens."

And now to Korea.

## IS POSSESSION EROTIC?

The idea that shamanic experience implies a sexual union between the female shaman and her guardian god does seem to lurk in some corners of the Korean popular imagination. In the film version of "Portrait of a Shaman" (*Munyodo*), released in the 1970s, but *not* in Kim Tongni's original novella, the seasoned shaman and her initiate periodically ingest a blood-red concoction of Chinese medicine, whereupon they emit orgasmic shrieks while painted images of brawny gods leer up in front of the camera. In fact, the use of hallucinogens is unknown in Korean shamanic practice. More recently, an initiate who came to the shaman profession after attending graduate school in the United States and reading Eliade, evolved a signature dance style that required her to kneel in front of the altar and bend her torso backward, gestures which Western observers readily interpreted as a sexual reception of the god. Her Korean shaman colleagues found these same movements strange and referred to her performance as the "vagina dance" (*poji chum*).[17] Both portrayals suggest the influence of foreign notions of an eroticized shamanism.

Shamans have told me that because *most* (but not all) of the gods are male, or *if* predominantly male gods possess a shaman (rather than female gods or divine couples), a shaman will have a troubled marital history. Some shamans claim that jealous gods prevent them from having marital relations with their husbands, but other *mansin* scoff at this.[18] Songjuk Mansin told me, "Male gods don't like what is between man and woman," a statement that suggested her own agreement. Similarly, Okkyong's Mother, who enjoys the most stable marriage of all of the shamans I know well, affirmed that she sleeps upstairs in her shrine while her husband sleeps on the ground floor. A shaman colleague, describing a similar arrangement, asserted that "men stink" (a literal translation).

Yongsu's Mother complained that her dead husband, installed as a guardian god in her shrine, had prevented her from marrying again after an early widowhood, but she made it clear that the god was no substitute for a flesh and blood husband, that she would have preferred not to live alone. An aged shaman, initiated while still a young woman, wept when she described her many long years without a mate. A young married shaman described the stress of periods of enforced abstinence before performing significant rituals. In sum, *mansin* may boast of their gods' jealousy as a measure of their gods' power, an attribute of the shaman's own professional success. The gods may drive living husbands away, but they do not, in most instances, replace absent husbands as sexual partners. If some shamans use the gods as a justification for avoiding sexual contact with their husbands, this seems more an expression of distaste than a divine cure for or sublimation of repressed sexuality. This material counters what Pat Caplan has dubbed "the so-called 'hydraulic' model of sexuality,"[19] the Freudian assumption that an innate and problematic sexual drive must necessarily find expression or sublimation, if not in men, then in gods. The Korean material contains only the thinnest and most idiosyncratic suggestion that these needs might ever find expression in some Korean shamans' experience of possession.

Among the many scholars who have published on the subject of Korean shamanism, to my knowledge only Jung Young Lee has attempted to make a case for "a fundamental motive in Korean shamanism through

a study of sexual repression."[20] Lee's study suffers from an excess of innuendo and inaccuracy—old men encountered in dreams are necessarily objects of sexual attraction, prayers for fertility are ultimately expressions of thwarted sexuality (rather than thwarted desires for sons), and the installation of guardian deities (who need not be male) in the initiate's shrine invariably establishes a sexual relationship between shaman and deity. The first two claims are unsubstantiated, either in the body of Lee's work or elsewhere in the literature on Korean shamanism. The third rests on the testimony of one shaman informant, possessed by a divine general, who "dreamed that she went to bed with the general."[21]

It is revealing that Lee utterly confuses the term "sexual repression"—the forcing of inexpressible sexual needs and desires into the subconscious mind—with "sexual oppression"—the systematic subjugation of women on the basis of gender.[22] This is an honest mistake insofar as psychological interpretations of female trance phenomena reveal an almost unconscious tendency to dissolve the social into the sexual. Consider, for example, psychiatrist and medical anthropologist Arthur Kleinman's field observation of a Taiwanese possession cult:

> Informants described it [possession] to me as one of the most exciting experiences they had ever witnessed or participated in. This must have been especially true for lower-class mothers and grandmothers, ordinarily trapped in the physical confines and daily routines of their homes. Cult members did not merely trance: they danced, jumped around, sang, exhibited glossolalia, gave voice to strong emotions, and sometimes engaged in activities with strong sexual overtones. For example, men and women touched and massaged each other; they jumped around together; women rubbed the inside of their thighs and men exhibited rapid thrusting movements of the pelvis; at times the ecstatic frenzy of the trances resembled orgasmic behavior.[23]

In this passage, "orgasmic behavior" and "sexual overtones" are the judgments of a clinical observer who deems the excitement of possession "especially true for lower-class mothers and grandmothers" as a release from "the physical confines and daily routines of their homes." The passage makes a reflex link between social constraints, sexual repression, and ritual release, and again, finds a locus in the problematic bodies of women, although pelvis-thrusting men were also present. Consider also Melford Spiro's well-known description of women in Burmese *nat* cults:

> Restricting this discussion to female shamans, it will be recalled that, typically, females are possessed by a *nat* [spirit], and/or decide to marry a *nat* who had previously possessed them, either in adolescence or in or near menopause. These are females, in short, who are either

first experiencing the mounting pressures of sexual desire and therefore—especially in Burma, where any physical contact with the opposite sex is prohibited—of sexual frustration, or they are females who, at menopause, are experiencing a heightening of their sex drives combined with the fear of losing their sexual attractiveness. The attendant frustration of the menopausal females is further intensified (in a large percentage of cases) by marriages with socially weak and sexually inadequate husbands. Add to this a previous observation, *viz.*, that the majority of those possessed, being of lower-class origin, are also suffering from status deprivation, and it then becomes at least plausible that one explanation for the differential effect of *nat* festivals is differential drive-intensity. That is, it is the women with the strongest frustrations (sexual, prestige, etc.) who are most susceptible to possession.[24]

By Spiro's logic, Burmese women respond to menarche and menopause with an emotional script that would not be out of place in an American women's magazine. And as in American women's magazines, "sexual attractiveness" is assumed to be at least as important to a woman's esteem as "prestige, etc." The contribution of Burmese culture to these constructions of self is that of a restrictive sluice gate, imposing sexual segregation upon the torrents of spring. The passage assumes a clinical familiarity with the subjects' "sexual frustration," "heightening of their sex drives," and "marriages with socially weak and sexually inadequate husbands," but elsewhere Spiro implies that these deductions must necessarily have been commonsensical, "When interviewed, these shamans describe the onset of possession as a highly pleasurable physical act, accompanied by deep and accelerated breathing, palpitations, and tingling of the flesh. The descriptions sounded very much like the description of sexual orgasm, but I could not pursue this line of inquiry because of *the near impossibility in Burma of discussing sexual matters with females*" (emphasis added).[25]

Spiro, at least, asked the shamans what the sensations of trance felt like. Gregory Bateson and Margaret Mead made inductive associations in their description of the Balinese trance dancer fallen backward onto the ground "writhing in some sort of orgasmic climax."[26] Perhaps possession behavior and erotic experience have so thoroughly bled together within the ethnographic gaze because, as Scheper-Hughes and Lock suggest, "It is sometimes during the experience of sickness, as in moments of deep trance or sexual transport, that mind and body, self and other become one."[27] For their part, Scheper-Hughes and Lock maintain a distinction between different kinds of experiences that may "sometimes" be equivalent in their consequences. They urge that such experiences be studied as part of an ambitious project to understand "the mindful body, as well as the self, social body, and body politic."[28] Such challenges are

foreclosed when one domain of experience, "deep trance," is subordinated to the explanatory power of another, "sexual transport." The association of possession and sexual experience is compounded when the subject is a woman who dances. The Western tradition has long associated dancing with sexual expression.[29] The Korean tradition also views the dancing woman as at least potentially sexually available but in very specific contexts.

To summarize, the question "But isn't it sexual?" seems to have been provoked by strong (Western) associations. In the literature, possession experiences have sometimes been described as "erotic" or equivalent to "orgasm," a particularly tempting association where those possessed are women, socially oppressed, and consequently (it is assumed) sexually repressed. Most Korean shamans are women and most (but not all) of the gods who claim any one shaman are male. Therefore (by the logic of a flawed deduction) shamans experience possession either sexually or as sublimation. The sex question is posed primarily because Korean shamans are women.

This path of association—women, possession, dance, sex—is at least loosely "Freudian;" ultimate causes are situated in the individual subconscious, in drives that find expression, satisfaction, or sublimation through ritual participation, dance, and the experience of possession. But "Isn't it sexual?" may also indicate a different and more subtle line of interpretation. Mikhail Bakhtin's characterized aspects of medieval and renaissance folk culture as a celebration of the regenerative power of the body and bodily life. "In carnivalistic portrayals of eating, drinking, copulation, and defecation, visions of a regenerated world were brought close to human experience through the body.[30] Bakhtin inverts the Freudian premise that all things come from psychobiological drives; rather, it is the body that takes the world into itself and reconstitutes it in performance."[31] Jean Comaroff describes the organizing sexual metaphors of a Tswana dance, performed to welcome male initiates after their return from the bush, as a regenerative replication of the Tswana social world. The different positions assumed by the dancing men and women and the different movements they assumed in the dance, the lateral rolling motions of the women and the vertical, or phallic movement of the upright sticks held by the men "implied not only the complementarily of male-female sexuality but the distinction between agnatic rank and matrilineality. . . . The map of the dance floor also replicated the spatial order of the social world, its organization of center and periphery, its opposed yet complementary relations between male and female."[32] Jean Comaroff postulates a widespread use of bodily metaphors in such world-defining dance forms, citing a similar emphasis on male "phallic" leaps and female lateral swaying in a fertility ritual of the Umeda people of the West Sepik District of New Guinea, described by Alfred Gell,[33] and Eric Ten Raa's description of mimed copulation in a ritual performed by the Sandawe of central Tanzania for the purpose of making the country fertile.[34] As Judith Lynn Hanna observes, dance is a particularly powerful medium for focusing awareness on the body and its associations.[35] Comaroff notes that danced celebrations of sexuality and Bakhtinean "bodily life" were precisely what provoked missionary ire in many parts of the world and, in some instances, resulted in local denials of prior practices.[36]

When an indigenous intelligentsia internalizes Western judgments, the result may be expurgated reinscriptions of custom. Frederique Marglin describes the nearly vanished devadasis of Puri, temple dancers and ritual specialists who celebrate the auspicious dimensions of female sexuality and fertility: "well-being and health or more generally . . . all that creates, promotes, and maintains life."[37] The devadasi's identity as a sexual being, as reflected in the link between temple dancing and prostitution, is central to Marglin's analysis of the devadasi's auspicious associations. To reach this understanding, Marglin first found it necessary to read through a process of historical reinterpretation. Indian reformers had attempted to retrieve Indian dance as an art form distinct from the onus of prostitution. It was claimed that the devadasi were originally chaste virgins, meant only for the gods, who were later debased by degenerate rulers and rich and powerful men, or that economic hardship had forced the devadasis into prostitution.[38]

We turn again to the Korean material with an awareness both of the expressive potential of the danced body, and of the likelihood of denials and redefinitions. Indeed, for the last twenty-five years, I have listened with amusement to emphatic denials of the existence of a living, vital, Korean shaman tradition. Over less than a decade in the 1970s, I saw elements of Bakhtinian body humor—mimed phallic display, defecation, and the unceremonious tossing away of a soiled baby—disappear from the performance of a rural masked dance tradition as it gained popularity among students and urbanites and was no longer performed as a celebration punctuating the agricultural cycle. Are the auspicious forces engendered by a Korean shaman's *kut* (her major ritual) in any sense generated by a danced and performed expression of positive sexual forces? Here, as elsewhere, the shamanic experience is realized in the performing body of the shaman.[39] Drumming and percussion inspire lively dancing and the inspiration to speak "the true words of the spirits." A successful *kut* resolves, in an atmosphere of play, the vexations (*soksanghada*) of the gods and ancestors and satisfies their tremendous appetites (*yoksim*). But are these "vexations" and

"appetites," expressed through the dancing, miming, and speaking body of the shaman, innately sexual? Is there any evidence at all that this should be the cause? This passage caused some of my readers to think so:

> The *mansin* (shaman) who performs the Official's play (the segment of a shaman ritual that appeases a particularly greedy god) is . . . encouraged to dance her way to the far sidelines and coax the men into accepting an empty wine cup which she fills to the brim. . . . Her gesture is suggestive. To fill a man's cup outside the intimacy of kinship suggests the behavior of a woman paid to serve men's pleasure, the hospitality offered in a wine house . . . [during the Official's play] the *mansin* who distributes the [Official's] . . . wine encourages a spectator of either sex to dance a few bars with her in the enthusiasm of the moment.[40]

The few bars of dance described here are distinct from the jumps, accompanied by percussive drum beats, that bring on possession.[41] When shamans dance a few steps while selling the Official's wine, and when they dance a slow and graceful prelude to the jumping dance of possession, they execute the basic steps performed at Korean country celebrations, arms stretched out from the shoulders and bent slightly at the elbows to gesture rhythmically as the dancer takes slow steps with slight bends of the knee. The grace of the dancer is in her arms, her strength and flexibility in her shoulders. Women dance this way with each other, and men with men. Indeed, the women with whom I danced at a village Mother's Day picnic told me that they could not imagine how Americans had any fun at parties where, as I had told them, men and women "played together."

Such dancing, in and of itself, is neither explicitly gendered nor erotically charged. To dance at a *kut* or a country party is to "play" (*nolda*), to amuse oneself in a relatively unrestrained and pleasurable moment. Sexual expression, danced or otherwise, is euphemized as "play," but certainly as a subset and not a generative form.[42] Between women and men, dancing takes on a flirtatious cast (but can we call it "erotic"?) when a woman—a *kisaeng* or a shaman—invites a man to dance and pours him a cup of wine. In the Official's play, the gesture is ambiguous, since the shaman acts in the persona of a masculine god, a "man" dancing with a man.[43]

In her *Dance, Sex and Gender*, Judith Hanna cites selections from my 1985 ethnography to present the interactions of Korean shamans and male spectators as one among many other examples of "aphrodisiac dancing . . . which conveys the gender role of sexual object or partner."[44] The reader might never realize that this material comes from an ethnography subtitled *Women in Korean Ritual Life*, that it is the men who are marginal at Korean shaman rituals. Taken as a whole, Hanna's ethnographic overview of sexual expression through dance unravels some of the many different contexts, stakes, and consequences of such expression: in courtship, in prostitution, as an expression of union with the sacred, as a means of coping with supernatural forces, as a sex-role script, or as a sublimation. Her interpretation of dance as the gendered body's mediation of an "instinctual sexual drive," however, leads her to appropriate decontextualized data in support of a universal psychobiological "truth." Hanna links "the sexuality of dance and its potential to excite" to her quantifiable, verifiable observation that "Dancing can lead to altered states of consciousness (with changed physiological patterns in brain wave frequency, adrenalin, and blood sugar) and hence to altered social action."[45]

My Korean data appears in Hanna's study under the heading "Seduction of Forces and Female Shamans," a section intended to illustrate that dance not only can be "performed to arouse the passion of a human lover, but it has sexual overtones in relationship to overcoming the forces of nature."[46] The selling of a cup of wine, a mildly nuanced flirtation, becomes, in this appropriation, an act of sexual arousal equivalent to a striptease. A marginal bit of business becomes the central encounter of a complex ritual process. What is assumed to happen between female shamans and male spectators "explains" what must then necessarily happen between shamans and gods.

Some representations in Korean popular culture—and, I suspect, many Korean men—assume that shamans are sexually promiscuous.[47] Recall that it was a male spectator's tweak of a shaman's breast that caused me to write about "performance, possession, and flirtation" in the first place. The stereotype is a function both of what shamans do—their public performance—and who they are (by virtue of what they do)—women who earn a livelihood outside the constraints and protections of respectable family life and who are simultaneously independent and vulnerable to harassment. Shamans whom I have known seem anxious to preserve their reputations and genuinely vexed by importunate men.[48] Is this flirtation/harassment a necessary part of the *kut*? From at least the turn of the century, some *kut* were always performed in shrines away from home, sometimes without the knowledge of the sponsor's husband, a tendency that may be even more pronounced today when *kut* are performed in commercial shrines rather than in cramped apartments where neighbors, particularly Christian neighbors, might complain about the noise of drum and symbols.[49] *Kut* were performed within the women's quarters of the palace and,[50] if we are to believe an old genre painting, in the segregated women's quarters of elite eighteenth-century homes. Thus, while shamans may, on the one hand, exploit the men's presence by selling lucky wine, and on the other, risk the men's harassment, the men's presence with its potential for play is not essential to the successful performance of a

Korean shaman ritual. An efficacious, auspicious ritual does not require the energies unleashed by a brief heterosexual danced encounter. Rather it is the gods and ancestors who must play and feast to their satisfaction while spectators, particularly the sponsoring woman, are encouraged to dance to satisfy their own body-governing spirits.

Korean shaman rituals do include some more general representations of Bakhtinian "bodily life," most notably in the final send-off of wandering ghosts (*yongsil*) in which the performing shaman mimics the manner of their death, clutching her throat and rolling her eyes for the hanged, pantomiming dysentery, or simulating childbirth by dropping a metal bowl with a clatter from under her skirts.[51] In this exorcistic sequence, the shaman's play suggests not so much the celebration of a regenerative life force as a comfortingly humorous acknowledgment of the terrors of the mortal body.

Manifestations of sexual appetite are mimed in a small bit of business when a shaman seizes a dried fish, drumstick, or gong mallet, thrusts it out from the vicinity of her well-clothed genitals, and draws it up, usually pointing in the direction of the ritual's female sponsor. Sometimes the phallus (I think we can safely call it a phallus) is manipulated under the shaman's costume to suggest an erection. This is a bit of improvisational business, not a requisite element of the formal structure of the *kut* as recorded by folklorists. (So far as I know, folklorists have not bothered to record it.) The gesture is sharp and quick, always too quick for my camera. However often performed, it is almost invariably met with giggles from the spectators and an exchange of smirks among the shaman team. When Songjuk Mansin wrapped the dried fish in her costume vest and proceeded to rub it, Yongsu's mother expressed humorously exaggerated disgust, swatting with her drumstick at Songjuk's hands and at the makeshift phallus. At another *kut*, Yongsu's mother complained to Songjuk Mansin that the Spirit Warrior, manifested by a third shaman, was making too many demands of the client. To underscore her point, she improvised a phallus with a length of twisted towel, held out taught, and muttered "too much of this" as she gave it a thrust and a jerk.

What does this body play signify? The gods who receive a phallus in passing are among the most stereotypically demanding (the Official and the Spirit Warrior), not the highest gods (the Mountain God, the Heavenly King, the House Lord) whose dignified portrayals in *kut* are briefer and far less amusing to the spectators. Gods of middling rank have less shame and are consequently more active in stirring up trouble in client households. When they appear in *kut* they level outrageous and comically executed demands for food, music, and cash, and are met with equally stubborn resistance from the female spectators. The shaman's humorous portrayals make it possible for shamans and clients to engage the gods in a bargaining, bantering process of reconciliation. In caricature, the god's phallus is less an instrument of domination, or object of desire, than one more comic sign of a demanding, overbearing appetite, "too much of this." Could the gesture and the remark just possibly be a shaman's comment upon the masculine gender? When I saw a shaman, in the persona of the Official, playfully tweak a client's breast, I began to wonder.

## CONCLUSION

Is it sexual? If so, then not in predictable ways. It would be difficult to read the phallic play described above as an expression of repressed sexual desire, or view these tumescent gods as idealized alternatives to mortal men. Indeed, they seem very much the opposite. If, as late twentieth century anthropological writing would have it, expressions of bodily life make statements about social relationships, then the gods' phallic exhibitionism underscores the general tenor of their dealings with mortals; they are, like lusty mortal men, bothersome and demanding. This is a measure of their power and of their obvious foibles. The "drag" act, Judith Butler suggests, is the "site of a certain ambivalence" against the order of things that can be both an expression of surrender and of insurrection,[52] but Rosalind Morris's cautions that this playful parody should not be over read as a serious act of resistance.[53]

Let us not, once again, mistake a part for the whole. That some shamans sometimes improvise phalluses adds a gloss to their portrayal of a particular category of masculine gods and gendered relationships more generally. These comic portrayals no more "explain" the sum of shamanic performance in sexual terms than does the shaman's occasional harassment by men or the selling of cups of wine. Such phenomena might, however, contribute to an analysis of gendered perceptions of a sexual Other. Performance offer a rich and subtle ground for such a project, as the work of Judith Butler, Linda Williams, Jennifer Robertson, and others suggests,[54] but this ground is also mined with booby traps. Ritual, myth, and art may, in Geertzian terms, show us "how people feel about things"[55] but interpretation comes through the reading eye, and there's the rub. The burden is on the anthropologist to provide the best and most valid reading possible, knowing that if it is worth considering, it is also worthy of contestation.

In other places, I have offered my own reading of the Korean shaman's relationship with her gods.[56] In this essay, I have been concerned with misreading, with how an observer, influenced by psychobiological interpretations of human—and particularly female—behavior could draw commonsensical but ultimately unfounded conclusions about sexual expression in Korean shaman rituals. I have also considered recent studies that regard social phenomena as "embodied," expressed by and through the body and its imagery. Specifically, I explored a possible interpretive link between those ritual dances observed elsewhere in the world that create and regenerate social worlds through their portrayal of heterosexual sexuality, encounters between female Korean shamans and male spectators, and instances of phallic play in shamanic ritual. I found this particular association weak as an overarching explanation but useful in one restricted case of performance business. A further consideration of the body and expressions of body life in Korean shaman ritual, in folk dramas, and in jokes and conversations, may offer other kinds of insights into the operation of gender and sexuality in Korean popular culture. But "Korean popular culture" is itself a moving target. The particular shamans who are the subjects of this chapter inhabit a very different world of experience from that of media-savvy young Korean women who, in the 1990s, have begun to articulate totally new and unabashedly explicit discourses of sexuality.[57] The argument is for more, better, and more varied fieldwork.

## NOTES

1. Laurel Kendall, "Of Gods and Men: Performance, Possession, and Flirtation in Korean Shaman Ritual," *Cahiers d'Extreme-Asie* (special issue on Korean Ritual, Alex Guillemoz, ed.), vol. 3 (1991/2), no. 2, pp. 185–202.
2. Michel Foucault, *The History of Sexuality, Volume I: An Introduction*, New York, Vintage Books, 1980, p. 69.
3. These are described in Laurel Kendall, *Shamans, Housewives, and Other Restless Spirits: Women in Korean Ritual Life*, Honolulu, University of Hawaii Press, 1985, p. 61.
4. Laurel Kendall, *Shamans, Housewives, and Other Restless Spirits: Women in Korean Ritual Life*, Honolulu, University of Hawaii Press, 1985, p. 61.
5. Cho Dongwha, cited in Alan C. Heyman, *Dances of the Three-Thousand-League Land*, Seoul, Dong-A Publishing Co, 1964, p. 5.
6. Sherry B. Ortner, "Is Female to Male as Nature Is to Culture?" in *Women, Culture, and Society*, M. Z. Rosaldo and L. Lamphere, eds., Stanford, Stanford University Press, 1974, pp. 67–87.
7. Judith Hock-Smith and Anita Spring, eds., *Women in Ritual and Symbolic Roles*, New York and London, Plenum Press, 1978, p. 3.
8. Sherry B. Ortner and Harriet Whitehead, eds., *Sexual Meanings: The Cultural Construction of Gender and Sexuality*, New York, Cambridge University Press, 1981, pp. 3, 19.
9. Sherry B. Ortner and Harriet Whitehead, eds., *Sexual Meanings: The Cultural Construction of Gender and Sexuality*, New York, Cambridge University Press, 1981, pp. 3, 19.
10. Foucault, *op. cit.*, especially pp. 104, 153. See also Pat Caplan, "Introduction," in *The Cultural Construction of Sexuality*, P. Caplan, ed., London and New York, Tavistock, 1987, pp. 1–30.

11. As a bellwether, in 1990 the American Ethnological Society took "the body" as the theme of its annual meeting. In this same year, the journal *History of Religions* devoted a theme issue to "the body." For a critical review of anthropological approaches to the body, see Nancy Scheper-Hughes and Margaret Lock, "The Mindful Body: A Prolegomenon to Future Work in Medical Anthropology," *Medical Anthropology Quarterly*, vol. 1, no. 1, 1987, pp. 6–41. For an overview of historical writing on sexuality and of anthropological thinking on this topic, see Caplan, *op. cit.*

12. See in particular Gesela Bock, "Women's History and Gender History: Aspects of an International Debate," *Gender and History*, vol. 1, no. 1, 1989, pp. 7–29; and Jane Flax, "Postmodernism and Gender Relations in Feminist Theory," *Signs: Journal of Women in Culture and Society*, vol. 12, no. 4, pp. 621–643.

13. Gayle Rubin, "Thinking Sex: Notes for a Radical Theory of the Politics of Sexuality," in *Pleasure and Danger: Exploring Female Sexuality*, C. Vance, ed., Boston, Routledge and Paul, 1984, pp. 287–319.

14. See Judith Butler, *Bodies that Matter: On the Discursive Limits of "Sex,"* New York, Routledge, 1993; Caplan, *op. cit.*, Teresa De Laruetis, ed., *Technologies of Gender*, Bloomington, University of Indiana Press, 1986; and Sherry B. Ortner, *Making Gender: The Politics and Erotics of Culture*, Boston, Beacon Press, 1996.

15. Scheper-Hughes and Lock, *op. cit.*, p. 28.

16. This tendency is not exclusively Western. Earlier generations of Japanese historians and folklorists regarded women as "mothers," a tendency that has lingering influence upon the historical study of Japanese women. See Helen Hardacre, "Sex and Gender in Women's History in Japan," paper presented to the Annual Meeting of the Association for Asian Studies, Chicago, April 8, 1990.

17. Chungmoo Choi, personal communication.

18. Youngsook Kim Harvey, *Six Korean Women: The Socialization of Shamans*, St. Paul, West Publishing Company, 1979, p. 200.

19. Caplan, *op. cit.*, p. 1.

20. Jung Young Lee, *Korean Shamanistic Rituals*, The Hague, Mouton, 1981.

21. Ibid., p. 174.

22. Ibid., pp. 167–170.

23. Arthur Kleinman, *Patients and Healers in the Context of Culture: An Exploration of the Borderland between Anthropology, Medicine, and Psychiatry*, Berkeley and Los Angeles, University of California Press, 1980, p. 315. "Sexual oppression" has been widely offered as an ultimate, and ultimately circular, explanation for the ethnographic predominance of women in spirit possession. For the most synthesized and intellectually provocative statement of this approach, see I. M. Lewis's, *Ecstatic Religion*, Harmondsworth, Penguin, 1969. The women are assumed to be manipulative, their possession a coercive strategy, although whether this is a conscious or a subconscious motivation is seldom made explicit. For a critique which, like much recent writing on religious activities, argues that possession activities should be understood through the meanings imparted to them by the participants, see Anita Spring, "Epidemiology of Spirit Possession among the Luvale of Zambia," in *Women in Ritual and Symbolic Roles*, J. Hock-Smith and A. Spring, eds., New York and London, Plenum Press, pp. 165–190. For a critique specific to the Korean material, see Kendall, 1985, *op. cit.*

24. Melford E. Spiro, *Burmese Supernaturalism*, Englewood Cliffs, New Jersey, Prentice-Hall, Inc., p. 223.

25. Ibid., p. 122.

26. Gregory Bateson and Margaret Mead, *Balinese Character: A Photographic Analysis*, Special Publications of the New York Academy of Sciences, vol. 2, 1942, p. 168.

27. Scheper-Hughes and Lock, *op. cit.*, p. 29.

28. Ibid.

29. Judith Lynne Hanna, *Dance, Sex, and Gender: Signs of Identity, Dominance, Defiance, and Desire*, Chicago and London, University of Chicago Press, 1988, p. 19.

30. Mikhail Bakhtin, *Rabelais and His World*, H. Isowolsky, trans., Cambridge, Mass., MIT Press, 1968 [1965], pp. 38–39.

31. Jean Comaroff, *Body of Power, Spirit of Resistance: The Culture and History of a South African People*, Chicago, University of Chicago Press, 1985, pp. 6–7.

32. Comaroff, *op. cit.*, p. 111.

33. Alfred Gell, *Metamorphosis of the Cassowaries: Umeda Society, Language, and Ritual*, New Jersey, Humanities Press Inc., 1975, p. 234.

34. Eric Ten Raa, "The Moon as a Symbol of Life and Fertility in Sandawe Throught," *Africa*, vol. 39, 1969, p. 38.

35. Hanna, 1988, *op. cit.*, p. 13.

36. Comaroff, *op. cit.*, p. 151.

37. Frederique Apffel Marglin, *Wives of the God-king: The Rituals of the Devadasis of Puri*, Delhi, Oxford University Press, 1985, p. 19.

38. Ibid., pp. 8–9. As in India, Korean dance has been recontextualized as an icon of "Korean tradition," taught to respectable young women in studios and university dance departments. Following Foucaultian logic, dancing could now be viewed as an instrument of discipline in the construction of Korean or Indian femininity.

39. Amanda Porterfield, "Shamanism: A Psychosocial Definition," *Journal of the American Academy of Religion*, vol. 55, no. 4, 1987, pp. 721–739.

40. Kendall, 1991, *op. cit.*

41. In summoning the gods, the shaman begins a slow and ordinary dance, broken by a sudden leap encouraged by a sudden burst of rapid drumbeats. The dancer continues to jump, rotating on the balls of her feet, pumping her arms up and down. When the dancer is a client who has borrowed the shaman's costume to entertain her personal spirits, this activity is sufficient. The client jumps to exhaustion, save on those rare occasions where her body-governing god chooses to gesture or speak. When the shaman stops jumping, however, she mimes, sings, and speaks in the persona of the god.

42. One can find explicit representations of sexual acts and possible erotic glosses in some more specialized Korean dances. Korean masked dance dramas seem to suggest sexual intercourse when two characters place their arms on each others' shoulders and rock from side to side, provoking humor rather than titillation. The multi-drum dance, performed as the grand finale of nearly every recital of "traditional Korean dance," has erotic overtones. The dance is said to express the Buddhist initiate's religious fervor but is also associated with the legend of a

famous courtesan who performed it to the distraction of a hypocritically lustful monk, as described by Alan C. Heyman, *op. cit.* It is almost invariably performed by a woman, but is taught now at dancing schools servicing the middle class and in university dance departments.

43. As the shaman Yongsu's Mother said, after knocking an importunate male customer against the wall, "Oh, that wasn't me, it was the honorable Official [the possessing spirit] who did that." See Kendall, 1985, *op. cit.*, p. 61.

44. Hanna, *op. cit.*, pp. 46, 71–72.

45. Ibid., p. 22.

46. Ibid., p. 70.

47. Ch'oe and Chang indicate that men used to gather and amuse themselves at the home of the *mansin*, Cho Yong-ja, until her son took up residence. The *mansin* recalls the village chief's proposition as a grievous insult. See Ch'oe Kil-sŬng and Chang Chu-gun, *KyŬnggido chiyŬk musok* (Regional shaman practices of KyŬnggi Province), Seoul, Ministry of Culture, 1967, pp. 32–33, 54. In folklore circles I have heard it said that shamans used also to serve as itinerant prostitutes, but I have no corroborating evidence. The novels of Kim Tongni portray the shaman as a woman who casually enters sexual liaisons.

48. See Kendall, 1985, *op. cit.*, pp. 61–62.

49. See "Korean Mudang and Pansu," *Korea Review*, vol. 3, 1903, p. 147.

50. For descriptions of shamanic practices in dynastic times, as gleaned from old records, see Yi Nung-hwa, *ChosŬn musok ko* (Reflections on Korean shamanism), translated into modern Korean by Yi Chae-gon, Seoul, Paengnŏk, 1976 [1927]. In historical references to shaman rituals on Cheju Island before the ChosŬn period (1392–1910), men and women together celebrated communal rituals "in the form of gregarious songs and dances." See Chang Chu-gun, *Kankoku no mingan sinko* (Korean Folk Beliefs), Tokyo, Kinkasha, 1973, English summary, p. 12. Chang

argues that the gendered dichotomy of Confucian rites for men and folk religious practices for women was a consequence of the Confucian transformation of Korean society during the ChosŬn period. If this local example can be expanded, and if these heterosexual songs and dances can be shown as fundamental to the ritual and not the sideline activities of more recent times, then perhaps one finds the Korean equivalent of a Bakhtinian carnival undermined by the imposition of a new moral hegemony. This would be an intriguing example, innocent of missionary influence and Western-derived values.

51. Watching one such performance, I realized that the shaman had borrowed some of the lines from the childbirth scene in the Yangju Masked Dance Drama which is still, despite self-censorship, a creditably Bakhtinian celebration of bodily life. In abbreviated contemporary *kut*, the final send-off of wandering ghosts is greeted with sighs of impatience from other members of the shaman team, anxious to finish up and get home.

52. Butler, *op. cit.*, p. 124.

53. Rosalind C. Morris, "All Made Up: Performance Theory and the New Anthropology of Sex and Gender," *Annual Review of Anthropology*, vol. 24, 1995, pp. 567–592.

54. Butler, *op. cit.*; and also Jennifer Robertson, "Doing and Undoing 'Female' and 'Male' in Japan: The Takarazuka Revue," in *Japanese Social Organization*, Takie Sugiyama Lebra, ed., Honolulu, University of Hawaii Press, 1992, pp. 79–107.

55. Clifford Geertz, *The Interpretation of Culture*, New York, Basic Books, 1973, p. 82.

56. Kendall, 1991/2, *op. cit.*

57. For the changing sexual discourses of young Korean women, see So-Hee Lee, "The Concept of Female Sexuality in Korean Popular Culture," in *Under Construction: The Gendering of Modernity, Class, and Consumption in the Republic of Korea*, L. Kendall, ed., Unpublished ms.

# How to Change a Man:
## Spiritual Transformation and Shifts in Gender Ideology in Evangelical El Salvador

### *José Leonardo Santos*

On a particularly sweaty day in 2006, I sat across from a man who told me about twenty years of alcoholism and infidelity, incidents of beating his wife and children, and sexually abusing his own daughter. I had, in fact, taken most of it in stride. Most of what I'd read

Santos, Jose Leonardo. 2001. How to Change a Man: Spiritual Transformation and Shifts in Gender Ideology in Evangelical El Salvador. *Gender in Cross-Cultural Perspective*, Third Edition. Ed. Brettell, Caroline B. & Sargent, Carolyn F.. Upper Saddle River, NJ: Prentice-Hall. pp. 409–422.

and seen had prepared me for stories of violence, substance abuse, and family dysfunction. At the mention of his daughter, however, I more or less lost composure. I leaned back in my chair, exhaled slowly, but forcefully, and muttered an obscenity in English. The man couldn't understand the specific word, but he understood my sentiment well enough.

It took me a few moments to calm myself. The incident he described had occurred years ago and I couldn't do anything about it at that specific moment. Further, he seemed absolutely filled with regret—

serene, calmly spoken, but terrible regret. He closed his eyes in weariness after he said it, wincing with the recognition of what he had done all those years ago, and the realization that nothing he could ever do would wipe away the harm he has wrought.

I knew this man. What mostly calmed me down was the fact that I knew this man well enough to be absolutely confused. He was, in my opinion up to (and eventually, after) that point, no rapist. He was kind, patient, warm, gentle, and loving. He did everything he could to help others, even me, an outsider and a stranger. I had trouble reconciling the man I knew with the things he was telling me about his past. Perhaps there was something to this Evangelical notion of conversion after all.

In the following months, I collected a number of such life histories from men like this in El Salvador. The stories were often similar. They involved a great deal of violence, alcoholism, drug abuse, promiscuity, misogyny, risk taking, and dominance seeking. Many of these men were simply trying to *be* men when they were doing these things, reaping the social benefits and hedonistic joy resulting from their behavior. They felt good, tough, and others respected or feared them.

Yet just as consistently as their descriptions of what it meant to be a man were, they also reported dramatic changes—shifts in their concept of masculinity that revolved around a spiritual awakening, a religious conversion. These men were fundamentalist Evangelical Christians, members of an expansive movement found throughout Latin America. A core concept in this movement is that participants must be "born again," become entirely new beings, and leave the old self behind. As their spiritual being is born again, so is the social self. Old concepts and practices, including those revolving around gender, are also transformed. As we will see, while there is indeed a shift in masculinity and femininity for the informants I worked with, it is not toward something absolutely foreign or unfamiliar, and it retains the gender hierarchy most informants were familiar with before.

Evangelical Christianity has rapidly grown in Latin America over the last half century or so. In El Salvador, Evangelicals were less than 1 percent of the population in 1940 (Coleman et al. 1993: 112), 12 percent by the 1980s (Peterson et al. 2001: 6), and were estimated around 20 percent at the end of the 1990s (ibid.). Local leaders in San Miguel, Catholic Priests and Evangelical Ministers, told me the current percentage is in the 25 to 30 percent range nationally. Much of this growth occurred during the period of the Salvadoran Civil War, from 1979 to 1992. This was a particularly traumatic civil war, extensively funded by the United States, which resulted in massive displacement, loss of life, and society-wide trauma. Triggered by deep historical inequalities, the periods before, during,

and after the civil war were characterized by religious revitalization among many Catholics as well. The Salvadoran folk hero, Archbishop Romero, was assassinated at the onset of the war, and the Jesuit faculties at the Central American University in San Salvador were also martyred. Simultaneously, however, the Catholic Church took great losses as more and more Salvadorans converted to Evangelicalism.

How to refer to the various groups that comprise the movement is often confusing. The term Protestant is technically correct, but they are generally not the mainline denominations (Methodist, Presbyterian, Lutheran, Baptist) of the United States. Most groups are Pentecostals, or like Pentecostals. They interpret the bible literally, seek to convert all others, and believe only those who accept Christ as their savior can go to heaven.

Many theories abound to explain this growth. Some say it is an intrusion from the north, as US Protestants supplant local culture and tradition. Others say that internal and external factors cause the changes, be it the pressure of modernization and development, social unrest, economic turmoil, or civil wars, which lead to a need for new identity, and the re-creation of social stability following its dissolution by change (Bastian 1993; Gomez 2001; Gomez and Vasquez 2001; Miguez-Bonino 1997; Patterson 2005; Peterson et al. 2001; Vasquez 1999). Social crises create a sense of anomie at the individual and social levels. Religious fundamentalism promotes an ordered worldview in the face of that turmoil, and is a common response. Others say that the demand for religion in Latin America has always been high, but now that people have new religious options, they are simply taking ones that suit them (Gill 1999).

Whatever factors account for their growth, Evangelicals possess a specific and distinct worldview. A dichotomy is apparent when they reflect on their environment. For them, the known universe can be divided into two basic categories: the world (*el mundo*) and the body of Christ (the Christian churches and individuals within them). For the Evangelical, the world is an inherently profane place. It is filled with sin and is the home of all the things an Evangelical is trying to avoid. In their cosmology, the world is destined for the fires of hell—it is the world of regular people, the unsaved, those who have not accepted Christ. The result is that all negative things are referred to as the "world," or as "worldly." Scholars distinguish between social realities such as globalization, economic distress, political instability, high crime rates, culture change, social prejudice, and the like. For the Evangelical, all these things are subsumed in the concept of "the world." Equally, the source of these things is also uniform. Unemployment, political corruption, modernization, and declining moral values are all the result of evil influences, such as the Judeo-Christian devil and the human proclivity toward sin. This dichotomy between Evangelicalism and the world, like any cosmology, provides the believer with a master trope, an explanatory model for their environment and experiences. While humility is a greatly espoused value among many Evangelicals, they often view themselves as necessarily apart from and morally superior to all nonbelievers.

Because they interpret the bible literally, most Evangelicals believe they should live by the ideology outlined within it. This has very concrete consequences in terms of gender relations and hierarchy. Paul outlines much of the gender ideology clearly in the New Testament. The man acts as Christ, and leads his family as a responsible patriarch. "Wives, submit to your husbands, as to the Lord. For the husband is the head of the family as also Christ is head of the church" (Ephesians 5:22–23; see also 1 Corinthians 11:2–10, 14:33–35). For fundamentalists, who take the bible literally, the gender ideology that God wants is clear, and hierarchical. Ultimately it means a simultaneous trend toward patriarchy within a region that is also influenced by a movement against it.

## CONTEMPORARY GENDER IDEOLOGIES IN LATIN AMERICA

The Evangelical shifts in gender ideology occur within a wider context of shifts in gender ideologies throughout Latin America. In many places, sex roles are moving from traditional patriarchal norms toward a somewhat more egalitarian, or at least less misogynistic, gender ideal. Essential in this is the wane of the hypermasculine ideal of manhood, commonly referred to as machismo, and the increased importance of women in domains such as social, economic, and political leadership, once restricted to them. Changes in popular notions of masculinity and femininity are reshaping the social landscape of Latin America.

Matthew Gutmann (1997) notes that the study of masculinity is compounded by the difficulty of defining precisely what it is. Some believe it is anything men think and do. Others say it is what men think and do when they are specifically trying to be manly. Another group of scholars sees masculinity as something that can be assessed by degrees, so that some men are manlier than others. Yet others view masculinity as part of a gendered polarity in terms of male/female relations, so that being a man implies anything done in order not to be a woman. Luckily, none of these perspectives seem mutually exclusive, and each appears to have some validity as far as men's self-perceptions is concerned. Although Gutmann somewhat problematizes their differences, it could simply be that there are fluid definitions of masculinity simply because masculinity itself is fluid. As Kimmel and Messner (2004) note, masculinity evolves over time, both at the social and individual level.

What it meant to be a man in the past does not necessarily hold in the present, as social conditions have changed. Equally, the experience of manhood is different for young, middle aged and elderly men. As men age, their priorities and ideas of what masculinity is evolve. Notions of manhood and womanhood are currently undergoing such an evolution at the social level in Latin America, and Evangelicalism provides many persons with models of manhood during this change.

One key issue here is the struggle against patriarchy, against "machismo." Leinstenschneider (2003), for example, describes a society-wide disintegration of the nuclear family in El Salvador, which he attributes to machismo, addiction, high rates of migration, religious differences, family dysfunction caused by absent fathers, and the media. Orellana (2003) also addresses the issue of Salvadoran machismo, and indicates it is being actively challenged by the women of the younger generations, resulting in a broader gender struggle.

But what is machismo? While many use the word to refer to a highly negative caricature of Latin males, it is an ambiguous term at best. Mirande (2004) asked Mexican and Mexican-American men in the United States to describe what is meant by the term "macho" and to list traits associated with the word. He then categorized responses by whether or not the term was viewed as negative, positive, or neutral by the respondent.

Mirande discovered two polarities in defining "macho." The first sees the macho as an exaggerated masculinity indicative of personal insecurity. This is a man obsessed with authority, particularly over the women in his life. He is violent and aggressive and, importantly, *self-centered.* Things must be done his way, and whatever he says goes. The second, positive, version of machismo is different. Such men are assertive, and stand up for their rights. They take their responsibilities seriously and are *selfless,* willing to make sacrifices for family, friends, and duties. They follow an unwritten code of ethics, and are sincere. While they demand respect, they are quite respectful in their dealings with others. They are confident and thus have nothing to prove.

Macho is obviously not a monolithic category, and is used by different people to refer to fairly contradictory things. In fact, one version of machismo seems to be inimical to the other. Competing ideals can be in tension with one another. Both can tug and pull on an individual and a society. Further, the conditions within a society will affect the interplay of masculinities.

While maintaining that Latin-American masculinities are variable, Gutmann (2003: 13) states: "With respect to employment, financially supporting one's family and work in general are without a doubt central defining features of masculinity for many men and women in various parts of the Americas." Altogether, this description of responsibility and duty appears to be similar to the positive version of machismo described by Mirande. The result for the "positive" macho in economic crisis is a challenge to his sense of manhood, a gap between ideology and reality. Likewise, for the negative macho, socioeconomic crisis is a challenge to his ability to demonstrate dominance through wealth and power. Latin-American masculinity thus carries a contradiction. The ideal is difficult to achieve, since historical factors make it difficult for most of the population to do so. Economic, social, and political crisis are nothing new for Latin-American men, and they have lived with this tension between wanting to be ideal men and being unable to do so for centuries.

Gutmann's (1996) work in Mexico reiterates that traditional notions of masculinity (being macho) are under increased pressure from social and economic factors. While such ideals still exist in popular imagination, men are increasingly forced to accept new realities—women in the workforce, shared household and public authority with women, and new domestic tasks like childrearing—that require a new sense of what it means to be a man. In Latin America, both economic necessity and new opportunities are driving more women into wage labor, a domain that had in some cases been restricted to men. Safa (1995: 33) notes that "[t]he increased economic importance of women . . . is challenging the myth of the man as the principle breadwinner" in Latin America. Lancaster (1992) notes a similar situation in Nicaragua, where traditional masculinity was under increasing challenge by new gender ideologies within the socialist state. The results in both cases are variable and multiple masculinities as men mediate between tradition and contemporary realities.

Conversion to Evangelicalism is one way of resolving this crisis, as men orient themselves toward an alternate value system and set of standards for proof of masculinity. Similar crises are noted among Chinese-American men who cannot achieve North American standards of manliness (Chen 2004), Filipino migrant workers confronted with contradictory standards of male behavior when living in the Middle East (Margold 1995), and even terrorists, whose inability to achieve culturally accepted standards of masculinity leads to frustration and violence (Kimmel 2004). Townsend (2002) notes a similar trend among North American males who, when they fail to achieve certain status markers in life (such as home ownership), feel tortured by a sense of inadequacy and failure. Many Latin Evangelical converts cope by transforming their masculinity, rejecting wider standards of manhood in favor of new, faith-based models. They approach what Chen (2004) refers to as "repudiation," whereby a man no longer judges himself by social standards he cannot achieve.

There is a clear preponderance of women in Latin-American churches, however. Faith promotes an appealing, benevolent masculinity for females confronted by a society filled with negative machismo. Brusco (1997: 15) contends that Colombian Evangelicalism is a strategic form of collective action on the part of women, in no small part because "[c]onversion takes its greatest toll on machismo." In short, traditional proofs of manhood (for elements of both the "negative" and "positive" machismo-wealth, drinking, fighting, promiscuity, etc.) do not apply for converts. "Success for men in the public sector in terms of jobs, education, and so forth becomes subsidiary to success in this revalued private realm. Status achievement is reinterpreted in terms of family-oriented values, fulfilling the role of the good provider" (Brusco, 1993: 149).

I contend that for the positive macho, economic provision was central, but is now replaced with attending to the spiritual/emotional needs of the family. One can be poor, but still be a good spiritual provider. For the negative macho, a far more drastic change occurs, and the initial masculine ideal is mostly rejected and negative behaviors are relinquished. One issue is that many of these men took the practices of the macho male to a great extreme. Very quickly, the behavioral traits associated with the negative macho can yield negative results, socially and emotionally. Both macho types, however, retain the notion of male dominance following conversion. Fundamentalist Christianity is almost always patriarchal, and in this sense, is a return to traditional values. It conflicts in many ways with the feminist movement in Latin America. What changes for Evangelicals is the meaning of male dominance. Whereas most Latin Americans see male dominance as a given, Evangelicals come to see that dominance as part of God's vision for men, women, family, and society.

## SALVADORAN EVANGELICAL MEN'S LIFE HISTORIES

In 2006 and 2007, I conducted fieldwork in and around San Miguel, El Salvador to examine the issue of conversion and masculinity. I worked with two Evangelical and two Catholic churches using interviews with leaders, married couples, network analysis, focus groups, and men's life history narratives. In total, I conducted twenty-six life histories with Evangelical men. I wished to explore why men would so drastically alter their sense of masculinity, going from stereotypically negative machos to god-fearing family men.

Evangelicals who talked about personal conversion in the context of this study seem to agree with the notion that crisis leads many men to Evangelicalism, that

**Table 9.1  Difficulties Reported by Evangelical Men**

| Life Difficulty | Frequency in Evangelical Life Histories (N = 26) |
|---|---|
| Poverty | 69% (18) |
| Absent/dead parent | 54% (14) |
| Childhood abuse | 27% (7) |
| Removed from nuclear family in childhood | 31% (8) |
| Substance abuse | 77% (20) |
| History of violence | 35% (9) |
| Prison time | 27% (7) |
| Failed marriages/ relationships | 31% (8) |
| Affected by war | 42% (11) |
| "Bumming around" | 38% (10) |

God is sought out by those in spiritual and material need. In the analysis of life histories, factors that might create such conditions of anomie were identified and are depicted in Table 9.1.

Many men reported growing up in poverty as a factor that made their lives more difficult. A large number of men also reported at least one absent or dead parent during their childhood and adolescence. The most common was an absent or dead father, although, some reported a combination that resulted in the absence of both parents, such as a dead father and absent mother, dead mother and absent father, or two absent parents. Slightly less than a third of respondents reported being displaced from their nuclear families at an early age.

Slightly more than a quarter of Evangelicals reported childhood abuse. Three Evangelical men reported physical beatings (well beyond the spankings that are fairly commonplace in El Salvador), three reported an alcoholic parent/guardian, and one reported sexual abuse.

Substance abuse was widely acknowledged as creating personal difficulties, and as a sin. Most Evangelical men mentioned such addictions. Most commonly, they abused a combination of drugs and alcohol, as reported by eleven men. Alcoholism (without other drugs) followed, and was found in eight Evangelical life histories. One other man claimed to have used drugs, but not alcohol.

Some men also report a history of violence, committed by themselves against other persons, ranging from domestic violence against a partner, to assaults, to drunken brawls, to mob style gang warfare. It was quite common for these acts to have been preceded by alcohol abuse. Seven individuals admitted to having been imprisoned. A number of Evangelicals also reported difficulties in romantic relationships, such as failed marriages.

Almost half of Evangelical men mentioned the war in their life histories. Five spoke of being witnesses to violence, two spoke of themselves as combatants, three others spoke of being affected without being witnesses, and one man confessed to killing others during the war.

Some men characterized their young lives using popular colloquialisms such as *andar por arriba y abajo* (literally—moving up and down), or *vagando* (literally—roaming, wandering). These terms often carry a connotation of guilt, or criticism when used. They are used to refer to idlers, miscreants, persons who not only wander around, but are up to no good, or up to absolutely nothing at all, like a lay about. (Indeed, *andar por arriba y abajo*, for a woman, can connote sexual promiscuity.) *Vagando* is often applied to the activities of the homeless (*vagos*). A number of men characterized their pasts this way, as street wanderers or miscreants, perhaps not homeless, but aimless.

Using the life histories as an index, the overall profile is of men in great difficulty, living through multiple crises, combining personal problems with a lack of stability.

## CHARACTERISTICS OF MANHOOD

At the end of life histories, all men were asked to list as many characteristics as they could that reflected the profile of a good man. They were asked what traits, ideas, and behaviors they felt that a man should possess. Once they had assembled this list, they were then asked if they had always believed that men should be this way—Would a younger version of themselves have made the same list? If not, they were then asked to construct another list of traits that, in the past, they believed should be possessed by the ideal man. The primary goal here was to have converts compare and contrast pre- and postconversion masculinities. Responses showed a tremendous amount of variability, yet demonstrate a number of underlying, unifying themes (Table 9.2).

**Table 9.2  Evangelical Life Histories, Traits from Past Masculinity**

| Past Masculine Ideal | Frequency in Evangelical Life Histories (N = 26) |
|---|---|
| Idolized violence | 62% (16) |
| Idolized pride/aggression | 58% (15) |
| Idolized substance abuse | 46% (12) |
| Idolized womanizing | 38% (10) |
| Demand respect of others | 23% (6) |

### Past Manhood

Among these Evangelicals, shifts in masculinity were almost universal, reported by 96 percent, all but one informant. In describing their past ideals, they above all idolized violence. A true man was a fighter, someone who could best others in physical confrontation. Violence is a way of exerting dominance, gaining social capital, and achieving one's goals. A variety of phrases were used to describe this, such as "[a man] solves things through punches"; "a man is [made] greater through violence"; "[a man] fights in a gang"; "[a man can] blow others away"; "[a man] hits her [his woman] if she rebels."

In second place for preconversion Evangelical ideals is the notion that a man should have a proud, aggressive character. A man should be "macho," daring, and unafraid in his dealings with others. He goes out of his way to improve his own standing by showing the faults in others. Phrases used include "[a man] won't let himself be ordered around"; "machismo, pride, and dominance"; "machismo, fearing no one"; "the angrier, the manlier"; "insolent, not timid"; and "[a man] offends, threatens people."

Almost half of Evangelicals used to equate substance abuse with manliness. This refers to any number of addictive substances, such as drugs and cigarettes. Among the possible inebriative substances available, however, most men named alcohol as the favorite. In addition to being associated with parties and good times, using high quantities of drugs and alcohol is also seen as a sign of stamina and strength. Phrases such as "[a man] can drink and use drugs more than others"; "more vices means more manly"; "you're not a man if you don't drink and smoke"; "[a man is] the one that drinks the most" were used.

The fourth most frequently listed characteristic for preconversion Evangelicals is that true men are womanizers, have relationships with multiple women, and/or have had many sexual partners, indicating that sexuality and masculinity are intertwined. Statements included "more women means more of a man"; "[a man] has two women"; "[a man] has three or four women"; "eight women is macho"; "finding girls and having girlfriends."

Some men listed respect, or being respected by others, as a masculine trait: "if you're disrespected, then you're not a man"; "[a man] gets respect"; "a man must be important to society." Five Evangelical men equated wealth, love of money, and materialism with their past masculine ideals: "[a man] wants cars and money"; "[a man] has a car and money"; "[a man] has money and things"; "[a man] lies about having cars and things." Four Evangelicals equated manhood with physical strength: "[a man] is big and strong"; "[a man] is stronger than the other guy"; "[a man] is the strongest."

Three Evangelicals equated masculinity with misogyny (in forms other than just the sexual exploitation mentioned above) and being "better than a woman": "[a man] is greater than a woman"; "[you are] not a man if a woman orders you around"; "man is more than woman." Two Evangelical men equated prior manhood with going to dances, nightclubs, bars, or parties.

### Present Manhood

Evangelical men overwhelmingly indicated that for them, at present, their masculinity, their notion of what a man should be, is closely tied to their faith. This includes a variety of answers, but all revolve around the notion that a good man is a Christian man and behaves as such (Table 9.3). Evangelicals said things such as "[a man] puts the Lord before everything"; "[a man] loves God"; "[a man] sees what God has given him"; "[a man] has Christ in his heart"; "[a man] is on the path of God"; "prayer makes a new man"; "[a man will] teach his children God's way"; "[a man] accepts Christ and preaches."

In terms of frequencies, this trait of godliness/religiosity/faith was most frequent on the lists of Evangelicals. As we will see, even the next most popular traits shows a significant drop in the number of Evangelicals. This indicates that for them, Christianity predominates in defining manhood. For Evangelicals, being Christian should connote everything good. Many feel that by saying "a man should be a good Christian," that is all that needs to be said, as it implies excellence in morality and behavior, as well as wisdom. That is, they clearly assumed that being Christian already implies a specific set of masculine traits; it follows its own gender ideology.

A great many men explained that they now conceive of a different, nonaggressive masculinity. In this case, the true man is not impulsive or domineering. Rather, he possesses self-control and restraint, and acts calmly to prove his points and achieve his goals. He does not offend, and gets along well with others: "[a man] controls his character and does not offend others"; "[a man is] humble, not self-exalting"; "[a man will]

**Table 9.3   Evangelical Life Histories, Traits from Present Masculinity**

| PRESENT MASCULINE IDEAL | FREQUENCY IN EVANGELICAL LIFE HISTORIES (N = 26) |
| --- | --- |
| Man has faith | 92% (24) |
| Man is not aggressive | 58% (15) |
| Man loves his family | 46% (12) |
| Man is decent/honest | 27% (7) |
| Man works hard | 23% (6) |

submit himself, not be *machista* [macho], and not mistreat others"; "[a man] is humble"; "[a man] lives in peace and does not get mad."

Another predominant theme for the respondents was the link between manhood and love of family. This can be demonstrated through responsible behavior, and by attempting to promulgate family values in one's children. The ideal image for these men is that of a loving father, caring husband, and devoted son. Some said: "[a man] obeys his parents and helps his family"; "[a man is] responsible and educates and clothes his children"; "[a man] submits to home and wife"; "[a man] maintains his home and doesn't let his family suffer"; "[a man is] faithful to his partner"; "[a man] loves his wife and children"; "[a man] is an example for his son."

A number of men listed specific character traits that they felt were positive in a man, and that reflect his decency and dignity. While it is difficult to construct a category that subsumes them all, most of these positive character traits revolve around the notion that a man should be honest, fair, and respectful of others. The most common terms used (and English approximations) are *recto* (straight), *sincero* (sincere), *honesto* (honest), *normal* (literally—normal, meaning well mannered). The general notion here is that the ideal man is decent. He is neither a liar, nor a betrayer. He is worthy of trust. Other terms included "well mannered"; "amiable"; "dependable."

Hard work is manly, according to about a quarter of respondents. Phrases used include "if you work, people see you as a man"; "[a man] is loyal in his work"; "[a man] works hard"; "[a man] can endure work"; "[a man] works, does not steal." Three Evangelical men felt that the ideal man should be brave. Interestingly, they appear to refer to spiritual bravery rather than bravery in the face of physical danger: "brave men are with God"; "bravery is to accept Christ." These men appear to refer to the bravery required to leave the world behind and become part of the church.

## MALE EVANGELICAL CONVERSION

What provokes radical change in men's identities? Why are men's lists of before and after masculinities so different? What does it take to turn a violent alcoholic into a loving father and husband? Let us examine a number of statements from Evangelical men's own conversion narratives:

I remember one time- I'll never forget this, either. I was drunk, falling asleep. I was trying to get back to my house. I was lying down. And I got up. And I looked and saw myself in a mirror. I looked at myself and saw my eyes all red. And I started thinking to myself- What am I doing with my life, you know? I don't know. I started thinking like- Why am I doing this for? [Sic] Like- What do I gain from this? You know, like . . . so many things going through my head . . . I guess it was like, spiritually speaking, it was the Lord already talking to me."

> Martin, 26 years old, a few months prior to conversion, on a binge

I couldn't think of anything. Neither anything good, nor anything bad. I was completely blank. I just felt the tears coming down, falling . . . I felt a hunger and a thirst . . . Now, I said in my mind, I want to return to those happy times.

> Oscar, 21 years old, describing the culto where he reconciled after years of crack use

I felt like I wanted to change myself. I didn't want to be in those things . . . I wanted to change so bad. I was like desperate to change, and do other things. And not be part of the gang anymore.

> Domingo, 31 years old, describing his conversion in prison

I didn't work anymore. I was just, only on drugs . . . little by little, taking money out of the bank. . . . I got close to the gospel when no one would give me anything. I had wasted everything. I no longer had anyone to tell me, "Look- this and this [is what you need] . . ."

> Marco, 42 years old, after a deportation from the United States, and on a drug binge

I ended up on the streets. I ended up without my children, without wife, without anything . . . The only thing holding my body together was the skin. I had no meat on me or anything . . . You end up without love for anybody, not even your mother . . . I was like dead. Like in a world where I didn't exist. I wasn't here.

> Jose, 36 years old, crack addict

I spent two years going to church . . . I would go to church . . . just thinking- Why? Why? Why? . . . On June 11th, 1984. It was a Saturday. I told the Lord (begins to weep)- I can't take it anymore. I told him . . . I want you to free me.

> Emilio, 66 years old, after two years of a crippling stomach illness

That's how we human beings are. Not until we're in trouble do we ask God for things . . . I had come to a costly ordeal, and I couldn't find a solution to the problem . . . In my problems, in my anguish, I received the Lord.

> Nando, 27 years old, while hiding from the law, pending trial

I felt, for my part, that I had to receive Christ as my only and sufficient Savior . . . I heard a voice, a voice that told me, "You must receive Christ." Then I felt an anguish to move up front and accept Christ. I felt that there was my answer. There was the solution to my problem.

> Miguel, 22 years old, after three years of drug use, homelessness, and on the run from gang troubles

In the first place, it wasn't so that God would get me out of there. And it wasn't out of fear, either. Because I wasn't afraid of anybody. On the inside in those first months, I carried around a knife like that, next to my ribs . . . There was a need in my heart. I felt alone . . . I felt alone and desperate . . . anguished, an anguish, and I felt something like fear. And I said, if these people feel joy here in prison because they are Christians, and I am suffering in my anguish and afflictions, I will try and see if it is true they are happy of heart. And just like I tried drugs out of curiosity, I tried Christ also to see what he was like. And when I tried him . . . I saw that it was not a passing happiness, but that it was permanent.

> Pedro, 24 years old, in answer to why he converted in prison

Peterson (2001), Brusco (1997), Gill (1990), and Vasquez (1999) all agree that Evangelical conversion causes a transformation in male priorities and behavior that is seen as highly advantageous to Latin-American women. Indeed, the life histories demonstrate that many men have exchanged aggression, violence, and addiction for serenity, love of family, and submission to Christ. Some, particularly Brusco (1993, 1995), have linked this desire for change with a "crisis" in masculinity. She correctly points out that many men cannot achieve the traditional status of provider, particularly when socioeconomic environments make it difficult to provide. Poor men face a dilemma of identity, unable to become what they wish to be.

The quoted statements above exemplify the crisis-driven conversion. These men are expressing an overwhelming anomie, pain coupled with solitude, a complete desperation.

The statements quoted above reveal that "crisis" is in no way limited to the inability to achieve the role of provider. There is a more general sense of anomie among these men, linked to a crisis, not just of economics, but of personality itself. Statements such as "What am I doing with my life?"; "I felt a hunger and a thirst"; "I wanted to change so bad"; "I got close to the gospel when no one would give me anything"; "I ended up without . . . anything"; "Why? Why? Why? I want you to free me"; "In my problems . . . I received the Lord"; "I felt an anguish to . . . accept Christ"; "There was a need in my heart. I felt alone"—all these and more, indicate a larger crisis. Some are crises of identity; some are crises of desperation and fear. Martin, Oscar, Marco, Jose, and Miguel were all wrestling with addictions, had hit rock bottom and were well aware of

it. This was made worse by Jose's loss of connection with his wife and children, and Miguel's homelessness. Domingo and Pedro were suffering in prison, and both sought a way to change their situation. Emilio endured a painful ailment, and asked for a miracle of deliverance. These are men who are at the end of their rope. They simply cannot continue to endure the life that has befallen them. These are men who *desire* transformation, who want their lives to change. Evangelical converts are often a self-selected group. In this context of individual crisis, Evangelicalism does not force change on people. Rather, people who want change become Evangelicals. Once presented with the option, those in crisis will choose to transform themselves.

We can thus broaden the notion of what drives men to conversion, beyond just a crisis in traditional roles. Many of these men were led to conversion because their lives were filled with pain (both physical and emotional), and because their way of living had led them to more suffering, rather than to solutions. Further, the masculine model they were following led many of them to this suffering. The substance abuse, violence, vying for dominance with other men and the women in their lives led to misery rather than fulfillment. For those who were following an extremely negative masculinity, it proved fruitless, an emotional dead end. These crises were about more than just gender, but masculinity played a central role in men's movement toward, and understanding of, their crisis.

Another caveat must be added, however, to the factors that lead to Evangelical conversion. It is not enough that a person suffers a personal crisis. The next necessary component is that they be exposed to Evangelicalism. Eighty percent of Evangelical life histories indicated *multiple* exposures to the Evangelical message. The role of family, friends, proselytizers, public preaching, all night vigils, neighborhood prayer meetings, and the like, all working in combination, should not be underestimated. Many authors note that (Coleman et al. 1993; Gomez 2001; Miguez-Bonino 1997; Stein 1999) one key to Evangelical success is that they have particularly targeted those in crisis in their efforts to proselytize—the disenfranchised, the marginalized, the displaced, criminals, and addicts. Such persons are in need of a life transformation, so Evangelicals go out of their way to make sure those in suffering are presented with the necessary message. Combining these two factors, personal crisis and multiple exposure to Evangelicals, seems most likely to lead to conversion.

As Miguez-Bonino (1997) and Peterson et al. (2001) suggest, conversion implies a re-creation of identity, an act of being "born again" that involves a rejection of the former self. Such a transformation is particularly attractive to those who wish a clean break with a troublesome, difficult, painful past. It provides a way out for those who feel trapped. It is the ultimate solution for the person at rope's end. The data here clearly corroborate this. To use the above examples, Martin had become sick of his own addictions, Domingo was desperate for a life change within his prison cell, Jose was in a constant state of physical pain, Nando was hiding from the law, and Miguel was homeless. That is, many of these men had already come to the conclusion that the masculine model they had been following was not only flawed, but damaging, even deadly.

These were men who no longer wanted to live the lives they were leading. When the opportunity for change, for healing, for a better life was promised, they took it.

Evangelical conversions have been greatly facilitated by the work of the Catholic Church over the last five hundred years. Because of the Catholic hegemony, most Salvadorans (and Latin Americans in general) are already familiar with Christian concepts and worldview. They already believe in (or at least are familiar with) the existence of heaven and hell, the notion of Jesus Christ as God-man, Satan, the status of the Bible as the word of God, a final judgment at the end of time, and the human tendency toward sin. An Evangelical proselytizer can ask Latin-American men, "Do you believe the bible is the word of God?" and anticipate many affirmative responses. Often, evangelizers begin with what they know their targets already believe and work from there. The preexisting notions supplied by Catholicism and Salvadoran culture have allowed Evangelicalism a foot in the door. They can then set about the process of teaching converts the "new" ideas, such as the sinfulness of the Catholic Church, the new standards in dress and behavior, new ways of praying, new social activities, and the like. Martin, mentioned above, felt that God was speaking to him even before his conversion—the existence of God was already established in his mind. Again, conversion requires some realignment of worldview, but this is facilitated because certain other elements remain the same. Spiritual transformation is often acceptable because it contradicts some, but not all, previous knowledge. The Catholic worldview has facilitated acceptance of the Evangelical worldview. Norris (2003) correctly notes that spiritual transformations combine preexisting notions with new terms, ideas, and practices. In gendered terms, male converts abandon a number of behaviors, but ultimately continue to believe in the authority men have over women. Part of what facilitates these drastic shifts is that the masculinity they are shifting toward is not something foreign. It is embodied in some aspects of what have here called the "positive" macho. In fact, I discovered it was very similar to the masculinity described by pious tra-

ditional Catholic men, some of whom also speak of a spiritual conversion. It is a masculine form familiar to the preconversion male, who may have feminized and derided it, but could certainly recognize it. They have known and dealt with men like this before, but simply had a different attitude toward them.

Yet Evangelicals must insist upon the differences between themselves and other men, even if they share traits. While those other men are in the "world," the Evangelical is in the world (he lives in it), but not of the world (because he is saved and has a stronger spiritual than physical nature). By definition, the Evangelical masculinity sees itself as set apart from all others. Evangelical masculinity, then, is constructed by these men in opposition to all other masculinities. It is necessarily a better masculinity, because they have been saved by Christ and other men have not.

While a number of issues have been elucidated here, a number of other questions remain. Since Evangelical men necessarily see themselves as distinct, to what degree did they overemphasize the differences between their past and present masculinity? A related issue is the role of intent in storytelling. Almost every narrative ended with an attempt by the informant to convert me. In fact, Evangelical conversion narratives all over the world tend to follow similar formats in their descriptions of how the individuals came to convert (Harding 1987; Kray 2002; Lawless 1983; Leavitt 1995; Saunders 1995; Stromberg 1990). This begs the question: Does the emphasis on crisis and transformation reflect Evangelical storytelling practices, stories constructed to facilitate the conversion of listeners, a common human tendency to seek personal transformation in distress, or all three? How do cultural variations in gender affect the story/plot line and what the individual is transforming from and into? The data from El Salvador suggests that the crisis of the individual is indeed heavily gendered. My informants demonstrated that the drives and attitudes of negative machismo often contributed to their crises, and it was a reformulated masculinity, now divinely legitimized, that helped restore their sense of self.

To answer the question of how to change a man, these informants gave one possible response. The man must reach a point where he desires change, where his previous model of masculinity is no longer useful, and then he must select a different model from available options that gives his life new meaning. Once he told me that he had assaulted his own daughter, the informant I mentioned at the beginning of this chapter explained why he had decided to share it with me. He wanted me to see that a man can change. Even the worst of us, the most despicable, the most horrible of men, can change, he said. He wanted me to believe, as he does, that there is hope for us all.

## REFERENCES

Bastian, Jean-Pierre. 1993. "The Metamorphosis of Latin American Protestant Groups: A Sociohistorical Perspective." *Latin American Research Review* 28(2): 33–61.

Brusco, Elizabeth. 1993. "The Reformation of Machismo: Asceticism and Masculinity among Columbian Evangelicals." In David Stoll (ed.). *Rethinking Protestantism in Latin America*. Philadelphia: Temple University Press.

_____. 1995. *The Reformation of Machismo: Evangelical Conversion and Gender in Colombia*. Austin: University of Texas Press.

_____. 1997. "The Peace That Passes All Understanding: Violence, the Family, and Fundamentalist Knowledge in Colombia." In Judy Brink and Joan Mencher (eds.). *Mixed Blessings: Gender and Religious Fundamentalism Cross Culturally*. New York: Routledge Press.

Chen, Anthony. 2004. "Lives at the Center of the Periphery, Lives at the Periphery of the Center: Chinese American Masculinities." In Michael Kimmel and Michael Messner (eds.). *Men's Lives*, pp. 48–65. Boston: Pearson Education.

Coleman, Kenneth, Edwin Aguilar, Jose Miguel Sandoval, and Timothy J. Steigenga. 1993. "Protestantism in El Salvador: Conventional Wisdom versus Survey Evidence." In David Stoll and Virginia Garrard-Burnett (eds.). *Rethinking Protestantism in Latin America*. Philadelphia: Temple University Press.

Gill, Anthony. 1999. "The Economics of Evangelization." In Paul E. Sigmund (ed.). *Religious Freedom and Evangelization in Latin America: The Challenge of Religious Pluralism*. Maryknoll: Orbis Books.

Gill, Lesley. 1990. "Like a Veil to Cover Them: Women and the Pentecostal Movement in La Paz." *American Ethnologist* 17(4): 708–719.

Gomez, Ileana. 2001. "Rebuilding Community in the Wake of War: Churches and Civil Society in Morazan." In Anna Peterson, Manuel Vazquez, and Phillip Williams (eds.). *Christianity, Social Change, and Globalization in the Americas*. New Brunswick, NJ: Rutgers University Press.

Gomez, Ileana, and Manuel Vasquez. 2001. "Youth Gangs and Religion among Slavadorans in Washington and El Salvador." In Anna Peterson, Manuel Vasquez, and Phillip Williams, eds. *Christianity, Social Change, and Globalization in the Americas*. New Brunswick: Rutgers University Press.

Gutmann, Matthew. 1996. *The Meanings of Macho: Being a Man in Mexico City*. Berkeley: University of California Press.

_____. 1997. "Trafficking in Men: The Anthropology of Masculinity." *Annual review of Anthropology* 26: 385–409.

_____ (ed.). 2003. *Changing Men and Masculinities in Latin America*. Durham: Duke University Press.

Harding, Susan F. 1987. "Convicted by the Holy Spirit: The Rhetoric of Fundamental Baptist Conversion." *American Ethnologist* 14(1): 167–181.

Kimmel, Michael. 2004. "Gender, Class, and Terrorism." In Michael Kimmel and Michael Messner (eds.). *Men's Lives*, pp. 79–86. Boston: Pearson Education.

Kimmel, Michael, and Michael Messner. 2004. "Introduction." In Michael Kimmel and Michael Messner (eds.). *Men's Lives*, pp. ix–xvii. Boston: Pearson Education.

Kray, Christine A. 2002. "The Pentecostal Re-Formation of Self: Opting for Orthodoxy in Yucatan." *Ethos* 29(4): 395–429.

Lancaster, Roger. 1992. *Life Is Hard: Machismo, Danger, and the Intimacy of Power in Nicaragua*. Berkeley: University of California Press.

Lawless, Elaine J. 1983. "Brothers' and Sisters: Pentecostals as a Religious Folk Group." *Western Folklore* 42(2): 85–104.

Leavitt, Stephen C. 1995. "Suppressed Meanings in Narratives about Suffering: A Case from Papua New Guinea." *Anthropology and Humanism* 20(2): 133–152.

Leinstenschneider, Freddy. 2003. "La Familia: Su Estructura Y Su Desintegracion." In Oscar Martinez Penate (ed.). *El Salvador: Sociologia General*. San Salvador: Nuevo Enfoque.

Margold, Jane. 1995. "Narratives of Masculinity and Transnational Migration: Filipino Workers in the Middle East." In A. Ong and M. Peletz (eds.). *Bewitching Women, Pious Men*, pp. 274–298. Durham, NC: Duke University Press.

Miguez-Bonino. 1997. *Faces of Latin American Protestantism*. Grand Rapids: William B. Eerdmans Publishing Co.

Mirande, Alfredo. 2004. "'Macho': Contemporary Conceptions." In Michael Kimmel and Michael Messner (eds.). *Men's Lives*, pp. 28–38. Boston: Pearson Education.

Norris, Rebecca Sachs. 2003. "Converting to What? Embodied Culture and the Adoption of New Beliefs." In Andrew Buckser and Stephen D. Glazier (eds.). *The Anthropology of Religious Conversion*. New York: Rowman and Littlefield Publishers, Inc.

Orellana, Nancy. 2003. "Machismo: Equidad de Genero Y Social." In Oscar Martinez Penate (ed.). *El Salvador: Sociologia General*. San Salvador: Nuevo Enfoque.

Patterson, Eric. 2005. *Latin America's Neo-Reformation*. New York: Routledge.

Peterson, Anna. 2001. "'The Only Way I Can Walk': Women, Christianity, and Everyday Life in El Salvador." In Anna Peterson, Manuel Vasquez, and Phillip Williams (eds.). *Christianity, Social Change, and Globalization in the Americas*. New Brunswick: Rutgers University Press.

Peterson, Anna, Manuel Vasquez, and Phillip William. 2001. "Introduction: Christianity and Social Change in the Shadow of Globalization." In Anna Peterson, Manuel Vasquez, and Phillip Williams (eds.). *Christianity, Social Change, and Globalization in the Americas*. New Brunswick: Rutgers University Press.

Safa, Helen I. 1995. "Economic Restructuring and Gender Subordination." *Latin American Perspectives* 22(2): 32–50.

Saunders, George R. 1995. "The Crisis of Presence in Pentecostal Conversion." *American Ethnologist* 22(2): 324–340.

Stein, Andrew J. 1999. "Nicaragua" In Paul E Sigmund, (ed.). *Religious Freedom and Evangelization in Latin America*. Maryknoll: Orbis Books.

Stromberg, Peter. 1990. "Ideological Language in the Transformation of Identity." *American Anthropologist*, New Series, 92(1): 42–56.

Townsend, Nicholas. 2002. *The Package Deal: Marriage, Work, and Fatherhood in Men's Lives*. Philadelphia: Temple University Press.

Vasquez, Manuel A. 1999. "Toward a New Agenda for the Study of Religion in the Americas." *Journal of Interamerican Studies and World Affairs* 41(4): 1–20.

# X

# *Gender, Politics, and Reproduction*

All human reproductive behavior is culturally patterned. This cultural patterning includes menstrual beliefs and practices; restrictions on the circumstances in which sexual activity may occur; representations and practices surrounding pregnancy, labor, and the postpartum period; understandings and management of infertility; and the significance of menopause. Although research on human biological reproduction has been dominated by medical concerns such as normal and abnormal physiological functioning, a now substantial anthropological literature emphasizes the centrality of reproduction to global social, political, and economic processes (Browner and Sargent 1990, 2011; Ginsburg and Rapp 1995; Sargent and Brettell 1996). Biological reproduction refers to the production of human beings, but this process is always a social activity, leading to the perpetuation of social systems and social relations. The ways in which societies structure human reproductive behavior reflect core social values and principles, informed by changing political and economic conditions (Browner and Sargent 1990: 215).

Much of the available anthropological data on reproduction prior to 1970 is to be found within ethnographies devoted to other subjects. For example, Montagu (1949) analyzed concepts of conception and fetal development among Australian aborigines, and Malinowski (1932) wrote about reproductive concepts and practices among the Trobriand Islanders. Several surveys of ethnographic data on reproduction were compiled, such as Ford's (1964) study of customs surrounding the reproductive cycle or Spencer's (1949–1950) list of reproductive practices around the world.

In the past forty years, anthropologists have sought to use cross-cultural data from preindustrial societies to help resolve women's health problems in the industrialized world (Davis-Floyd and Sargent 1997; Jordan 1978). For example, comparative research on birth practices has raised questions regarding the medicalization of childbirth in the United States. Anthropologists have also involved themselves in global initiatives to improve maternal and child health. These efforts include anthropological research that has helped clarify the relationship between population growth and poverty. While some analysts have held the view that overpopulation is a determinant of poverty and the poor must control their fertility to overcome impoverishment, others argue the reverse: people have many children because they are poor (Rubinstein and Lane 1991: 386).

Concern with population growth has often focused on women as the potential users of contraceptives, although women's personal desires to limit fertility may not be translated into action because of opposition from husbands, female relations, or others with influence or decision-making power. In this area of research, anthropologists have an important contribution to make in examining such factors as cultural concepts regarding fertility and family size, the value of children, dynamics of decision making within the family and community, and the relationship between women's reproductive and productive roles.

Since the 1970s, anthropological interest has turned to the linkages among cultural constructions of gender, the cultural shaping of motherhood, and reproductive beliefs and practices. In many societies throughout the world, the relationship between women's social positions and maternity is clear: a woman becomes adult by childbearing, and her prestige may be greatly enhanced by bearing numerous male children (Browner and Sargent 1990: 218; Sargent 1982). The conflation of woman/ mother, and the significance of son preference for women's social identities has been of particular note in parts of Asia, Africa, and the Middle East (Miller 2001).

In much of the world, infertility is dreaded by men and women alike but is a particular burden to women (Browner and Sargent 1990: 219; Inhorn and Van Balen 2002). Such pressure to reproduce is especially intense in agrarian societies, which have a high demand for labor. However, in many hunter–gatherer and horticultural societies, motherhood and reproduction are less emphasized. As Collier and Rosaldo observe, "Contrary to our expectation that motherhood provides women everywhere with a natural source of emotional satisfaction and cultural value, we found that neither women nor men in very simple societies celebrate women as nurturers or women's unique capacity to give life" (1981: 275).

Just as knowledge and practices regarding fertility are culturally patterned, birth itself is a cultural production (Jordan 1978). As Romalis notes, "The act of giving birth to a child is never simply a physio- logical act but rather a performance defined by and enacted within a cultural context" (1981: 6). Even in advanced industrial societies such as the United States, childbirth experiences are molded by cultural, political, and economic processes (Martin 1987; Michaelson et al. 1988; Oakley 1980). Studying the cultural patterning of birth practices can illuminate contested constructs of feminity and what it means to be female, the nature of domestic power relations and the roles of women as reproductive health specialists.

As Margaret MacDonald argues (in this book), feminist scholarship and midwifery have shared a common goal in studies of the gendered body—to retrieve the "natural" facts of pregnancy and birth. Her research on the changing meanings of "natural birth" in contemporary midwifery in Canada suggests a significant shift away from essentialized interpretations of the category "woman." In con- junction with second-wave feminism, "natural childbirth" emerged as an alternative that represented women as capable, strong, with competent bodies that do not require high-tech surveillance during pregnancy and birth. This representation of the empowered, self-sufficient female body contrasts markedly with that of the female body subject to technocratic birth (Davis-Floyd 2003).

Problematizing this dichotomy, MacDonald argues that the concept of natural birth has complex meanings for Canadian midwives and women themselves. Rather than emphasizing the "natural" as birth without technological interventions, contemporary midwifery complicates the construct, includ- ing within its meanings the possibility of interventions such as pain medication or cesarean births. Midwives emphasized the importance of informed choice; natural childbirth, then, is about educating women to validate their experiences of their bodies, and to foster personal responsibility. Resistance to medicalization is less central to the current Ontario midwifery paradigm, which in turn, is nuanced in its approach to medical technology. Ultimately, MacDonald contends that these shifts in ideology and practice are linked to modernity, and what is expected of the "modern woman."

Although reproduction is culturally patterned, not all individuals in a society share reproductive goals. As Browner (1986) points out, reproductive behavior is influenced by the interests of a woman's kin, neighbors, and other community members, and these interests may conflict. Government poli- cies regarding the size and distribution of population may differ from the interests of reproducing women. Women's goals in turn may not be shared by their partners or other individuals and groups in the society. Browner examines the ways in which access to power in a society determines how con- flicts concerning reproduction are carried out and dealt with by analyzing population practices in a Chinantec-Spanish-speaking township in Oaxaca, Mexico.

In this community, the government's policy to encourage fertility reduction was imposed on a preexisting conflict between the local community as a whole, which encouraged increased fertility, and women of the community, who sought to limit family size. Women and men manifested very different attitudes concerning fertility desires: women sought much smaller families than men. As children increasingly attended school, their economic benefits appeared slight to their mothers. Further, women viewed pregnancy as stressful and debilitating. Yet despite these negative views, women felt they could not ignore pressures to reproduce.

Such pressure came from community men, who valued a large population for the defense and well-being of the collectivity, and from women, who, while not desiring more children themselves, wanted other women to bear children in the interests of the group. In spite of the ease of obtain- ing government contraceptives, women rejected their use. In this cultural, political, and economic context, local women experienced conflict between personal desires to have few children, local pressures to be prolific, and national interests in reducing population growth.

State interests in shaping reproductive strategies are nowhere more evident than in the case of Romania during the Ceausescu regime, as Gail Kligman (in this book) documents in her powerful analysis of official pronatalist policies and citizens' everyday lived experiences. Romanian policy, from the mid-1960s, was one of extreme pronatalism, aimed at supporting a demographic trajectory that would build a strong socialist labor force. In this "political demography," the state engaged in coercive measures to underscore the significance of family and population growth.

As Kligman observes, the bodies of Romanian women became instruments used in the service of the state. According to state rhetoric, women occupied a position of singular value, as mothers (and thus as reproducers of the workforce) and as workers themselves. Mothers who gave birth to and raised many children were honored as socialist heroes. Yet in reality, officially obligatory childbearing in the absence of social supports (job security, childcare, maternity leaves) and in the context of a deteriorating economy generated overwhelming burdens for women and families.

State pronatalist strategies relied heavily on antiabortion legislation, penal sanctions for physicians and women, intrusive public health campaigns and required physical examinations for women of childbearing age, and lack of access to contraception. However, the surge in unwanted births led to abandonment of infants and children to the care of the state. Children institutionalized in state orphanages risked sickness, death, and generalized neglect; ultimately, such children generated an international adoption industry with mixed consequences. This period in Romania's demographic history effectively exemplifies "stratified reproduction" (Ginsburg and Rapp 1995), in which some categories of a population are encouraged to reproduce while others are not. In the Romanian case, the implications of state reproductive policies for women varied by social class, urban or rural residence, and ethnicity. Fundamentally, fertility control was the right of the state rather than that of women or families. However, personal and familial interests led to sometimes desperate measures of resistance in spite of this coercive state pronatalism.

Personal desires for children together with a pronatalist culture and advances in reproductive technologies have generated consumer interests of a very different sort in the United States—a demand for surrogate motherhood, as Heléna Ragoné's innovative research details (in this book). Ragoné explores surrogates' stated motivations for becoming surrogate mothers as well as the details of their actual experiences. She describes surrogates' explanations as a cultural script reflecting widely accepted ideas about reproduction, motherhood, and family. In contrast to popular opinion, surrogates deny being motivated by financial gain. Rather, they conceptualize surrogacy as a "gift," a priceless donation to the commissioning couple. The apparent "commodification" of women's bodies represented in surrogate motherhood remains a troubling issue, however. In addition, the recent shift from traditional surrogacy (in which the surrogate contributes an ovum) to gestational surrogacy, where the surrogate gestates the couples' embryos, raises important questions about what constitutes "real" parenthood. Surrogacy challenges the Euro-American emphasis on genetic relatedness and the biological basis of kinship and creates potential conflicts surrounding the claims of different kinds of biological and nonbiological mothers and fathers. Thus, surrogacy poses profound challenges to our understandings of kinship, family, and reproduction (see Teman 2010 for an important comparative perspective).

Advanced reproductive technologies, including fetal diagnostic testing and surveillance technologies such as amniocentesis and ultrasound imaging, continue to change values and expectations associated with conception, pregnancy, and birth (Rapp 1999). Critical feminist writings have questioned the excessive medicalization of women's reproductive processes, moving from the earlier focus on technocratic birth described by Davis-Floyd to the rapid developments in reproductive science and technology such as gestational surrogacy. These technologies, more widely available in industrialized societies, are increasingly accessible to populations in other countries as well, where they pose challenging ethical dilemmas as well as opportunities.

Women and men confronting infertility, for example, look to sophisticated medical interventions in the hope of a successful pregnancy outcome (Inhorn and Van Balen 2002; Layne 1999). Inhorn's (1994, 2006) rich accounts of Egyptian and Lebanese women's and men's attempts to overcome infertility have defined the expanding anthropological literature on infertility in societies with high-technology medical systems as well as in poorer countries where low-income populations have access principally to low-technology biomedical treatment. Globally, feminists have expressed concern at the gap between the growing availability of the technology and the public understanding of its social, legal, and moral implications. The low success rates of infertility technologies, the high expense, and the physical toll on women have prompted concerns that women's bodies are objectified as sites of medical experimentation.

Ginsburg (1987) also discusses reproduction as a domain of contested moral and medical meanings, using the example of abortion in American culture. She suggests that the focus of this conflict of interests is the relationship among reproduction, nurturance, sex, and gender. Using life histories of pro-life and pro-choice activists in Fargo, North Dakota, she reveals how different historical conditions affect reproductive decisions. The activist protesters in Fargo vie for the power to define womanhood in light of a basic American cultural script in which, in the context of marriage, pregnancy results in childbirth and motherhood. Ginsburg (1987) argues that the struggle over abortion rights is a contest for control over the meanings attached to reproduction in America and suggests that "female social activism in the American context operates to mediate the construction of self and gender with larger social, political, and cultural processes."

Similarly, Whitbeck argues that controversy over abortion rights in the United States must be understood in relation to a cultural context that neglects women's experiences and the status of women as "moral individuals." Rather, American culture regards women and women's bodies as "property to be bartered, bestowed, and used by men" (Whitbeck 1983: 259). Concern with restricting access to abortions derives from the interest of the state or others in power to control women's bodies and their reproductive capacity (Whitbeck 1983: 260).

Whereas Ginsburg discusses how abortion activists seek to define American womanhood in relation to cultural ideals of motherhood and nurturance, Ellen Gruenbaum (in this book) shows that cultural expectations of marriage and motherhood in Sudan form the context for the deeply embedded practice of female genital cutting (FGC). FGC is reported to exist in at least twenty-eight countries, and current estimates are that between 200,000 and 1 million girls experience some form of genital cutting annually. Other estimates suggest that as many as 5 million children are operated on each year (Kouba and Muasher 1985; Sargent 1991; Toubia 1994). The various forms of FGC present serious risks, such as infection and hemorrhage at the time of the procedure and future risks to childbearing; therefore, social scientists, feminists and other local activists, and public health organizations have opposed the practices. However, as Gruenbaum observes, FGC remains highly valued and continues to be most strongly defended by women who carry out the practice.

Women in Sudan derive status and security as wives and mothers. Virginity is a prerequisite for marriage, and in this context, clitoridectomy and infibulation, the major forms of FGC, are perceived as protecting morality. Thus, these practices persist because they are linked to the important goal of maintaining the reputation, marriageability, and long-term economic security of daughters. Decades of policy formulated by the Sudanese government and by global health organizations emphasizing the physically dangerous dimensions of FGC and prohibiting the most extensive forms of the practice have not resulted in its elimination, although conditions seem ripe for change. For anthropologists, FGC has tested the limits of cultural relativism and generated continuing debate about how to respect cultural difference while taking a stance in accord with one's own moral positions.

Miller's discussion of female infanticide and child neglect in North India (1987) is also set in a strongly patrilineal, patriarchal society and again dramatically illustrates ethical conflicts that emerge from prevailing gender ideologies that favor sons and the associated devaluation of daughters. In North India, family survival depends on the reproduction of sons for the rural labor force, and preference for male children is evident in substantial ethnographic data documenting discrimination against girls. In this region, preferences for male children result in celebrations at the birth of a boy, while a girl's birth goes unremarked. Sex-selective child care and female infanticide also indicate cultural favoring of male children.

Reports of female infanticide in India have occurred since the eighteenth century. There is evidence that a few villages in North India have never raised one daughter. In spite of legislation prohibiting female infanticide, the practice has not totally disappeared, although Miller argues that direct female infanticide has been replaced by indirect infanticide or neglect of female children. Indirect female infanticide is accomplished by nutritional and health care deprivation of female children, a phenomenon also discussed by Charlton (1984). Miller argues that the strong preference for sons in rural North India is related to their economic and social functions.

The preference for male children has important repercussions in the increasing demand for abortion of female fetuses following amniocentesis. For example, in one clinic in North India, 95 percent of female fetuses were aborted following prenatal sex determination. Thus, new reproductive technologies such as amniocentesis are seen to be manipulated by patriarchal interests. Miller suggests that, ultimately, understanding cultural constructs of masculinity in North India may help promote more effective health care and enhanced survival chances for female children.

The readings in this section illustrate the ways in which human reproductive behavior is socially constructed and influenced by global economic and political processes (Ginsburg and Rapp 1991). Rather than perceiving reproductive health in a narrow biological or purely personal framework, cross-cultural research suggests that women's health needs should be addressed in the context of their multifaceted productive, reproductive, and social roles. Consequently, decisions about such reproductive health issues as family size and composition are never left to the individual woman but are influenced by kin, community, and state interests. These interests are often contested with the introduction of new reproductive technologies enabling sophisticated prenatal testing, infertility interventions, and surrogate mothering. As these technologies increasingly spread throughout the world, their availability will raise important questions regarding cultural definitions of family, gender ideology, and reproductive health.

## REFERENCES

Browner, Carole. 1986. "The Politics of Reproduction in a Mexican Village." *Signs* 11(4): 710–724.

Browner, Carole, and Carolyn Sargent. 1990. "Anthropology and Studies of Human Reproduction." In Thomas M. Johnson and Carolyn Sargent (eds.). *Medical Anthropology: Contemporary Theory and Method*, pp. 215–229. New York: Praeger Publishers.

_____. 2007. "Engendering Medical Anthropology." In Serge Genest and Francine Saillant (eds.). *Medical Anthropology: Regional Perspectives and Shared Concerns*, pp. 233–251. Oxford: Blackwell Publishing, Ltd.

_____ (eds.). 2011. *Reproduction, Globalization and the State. New Ethnographic and Theoretical Perspectives*. Durham: Duke University Press.

Charlton, Sue Ellen M. 1984. *Women in Third World Development*. Boulder, CO: Westview Press.

Collier, Jane F., and Michelle Z. Rosaldo. 1981. "Politics and Gender in Simple Societies." In Sherry B. Ortner and Harriet Whitehead (eds.). *Sexual Meanings: The Cultural Construction of Gender and Sexuality*, pp. 275–329. Cambridge: Cambridge University Press.

Davis-Floyd, Robbie. 2003. *Birth as an American Rite of Passage*. Berkeley: University of California Press.

Davis-Floyd, Robbie, and Carolyn Sargent. 1997. "Introduction: The Anthropology of Birth." In Robbie Davis-Floyd and Carolyn Sargent (eds.). *Childbirth and Authoritative Knowledge*, pp. 1–51. Berkeley: University of California Press.

Ford, Clellan Stearns. 1964. *A Comparative Study of Human Reproduction. Yale University Publications in Anthropology* No. 32. New Haven, CT: Human Relations Area Files Press.

Ginsburg, Faye. 1987. "Procreation Stories: Reproduction, Nurturance, and Procreation in Life Narratives of Abortion Activists." *American Ethnologist* 14(4): 623–636.

Ginsburg, Faye, and Rayna Rapp. 1991. "The Politics of Reproduction." *Annual Review of Anthropology* 20: 311–343.

_____ (eds.). 1995. *Conceiving the New World Order: The Global Politics of Reproduction*. Berkeley: University of California Press.

Inhorn, Marcia. 1994. *Quest for Conception*. Philadelphia: University of Pennsylvania Press.

_____. 2006. "He Won't Be My Son." *MAQ* 20(1): 94–120.

Inhorn, Marcia, and Frank Van Balen. 2002. *Infertility Around the Globe*. Berkeley: University of California Press.

Jordan, Brigitte. 1978. *Birth in Four Cultures*. Montreal: Eden Press Women's Publications.

Kouba, Leonard J., and Judith Muasher. 1985. "Female Circumcision in Africa: An Overview." *African Studies Review* 28(1): 95–110.

Layne, Linda. 1999. "I Remember the Day I Shopped for Your Layette." In L. Morgan and M. Michaels (eds.). *Fetal Subjects, Feminist Positions*, pp. 251–278. Philadelphia: University of Pennsylvania Press.

Malinowski, Bronislaw. 1932. *The Sexual Life of Savages in Northwestern Melanesia*. London: Routledge and Kegan Paul.

Martin, Emily. 1987. *The Woman in the Body: A Cultural Analysis of Reproduction*. Boston: Beacon Press.

Michaelson, Karen et al. 1988. *Childbirth in America: Anthropological Perspectives*. South Hadley, MA: Bergin and Garvey.

Miller, Barbara. 1987. "Female Infanticide and Child Neglect in Rural India." In Nancy Scheper-Hughes (ed.). *Child Survival*, pp. 95–112. Dordrecht, Holland: D. Reidel Publishing.

_____. 2001. "Female-Selective Abortion in Asia: Patterns, Policies, and Debates." *American Anthropologist* 103: 1083–1095.

Montagu, M. F. Ashley. 1949. "Embryology from Antiquity to the End of the 18th Century." *Ciba Foundation Symposium* 10(4): 994–1008.

Oakley, Ann. 1980. *Women Confined: Towards a Sociology of Childbirth.* New York: Schocken Books.

Rapp, Rayna. 1999. *Testing Women, Testing the Fetus: The Social Impact of Amniocentesis in America.* New York: Routledge.

Romalis, Shelly (ed.). 1981. *Childbirth: Alternatives to Medical Control.* Austin: University of Texas Press.

Rubinstein, Robert A., and Sandra D. Lane. 1991. "International Health and Development." In Thomas M. Johnson and Carolyn Sargent (eds.). *Medical Anthropology: Contemporary Theory and Method*, pp. 367–391. New York: Praeger Publishers.

Sargent, Carolyn. 1982. *The Cultural Context of Therapeutic Choice.* Dordrecht, Holland: D. Reidel Publishing Company.

_____. 1991. "Confronting Patriarchy: The Potential for Advocacy in Medical Anthropology." *Medical Anthropology Quarterly* 5(1): 24–25.

Sargent, Carolyn F., and Caroline B. Brettell (eds.). 1996. *Gender and Health: An International Perspective.* Upper Saddle River, NJ: Prentice Hall.

Spencer, Robert. 1949–1950. "Introduction to Primitive Obstetrics." *Ciba Foundation Symposium* 11(3): 1158–1188.

Teman, Elly. 2010. *Birthing a Mother. The Surrogate Body and the Pregnant Self.* Berkeley: University of California Press.

Toubia, Nahid. 1994. "Female Circumcision as a Public Health Issue." *The New England Journal of Medicine* 331(11): 712–716.

Whitbeck, Caroline. 1983. "The Moral Implication of Regarding Women as People; New Perspectives on Pregnancy and Personhood." In William B. Bondeson et al. (eds.), *Abortion and the Status of the Fetus*, pp. 247–272. Dordrecht, Holland: D Reidel Publishing Co.

# *Natural Birth at the Turn of the Twenty-First Century:* Implications for Gender[1]

## *Margaret MacDonald*

The way I look at it is that we can make more decisions and we have more options, rather than in the hospital having somebody telling us how it's going to be. And that to me is natural. I'm not one that's into natural foods and all this kind of stuff. I'm not like that. But that's how I look at natural. It's natural in the hospital too, but what it means to me is making my own decisions.

*Claudine (32, mother of two children born at home with midwives)*

The notion of natural birth has long been used as a rhetorical strategy to counter the predominant biomedical or "technocratic" model of the pregnant and birthing body as inherently problematic and potentially dangerous to the fetus (Davis-Floyd 1994). Midwives, birthing women, and women's health writers and activists have

Margaret MacDonald. Chapter 4, *At Work in the Field of Birth.* 2007. Vanderbilt University Press.

often appealed to the authority of nature as a legitimizing basis for midwifery ideals and clinical practices. Natural birth at the turn of the twenty-first century, however, is not what it used to be. In this chapter, I explore the changing nature of natural birth in contemporary midwifery in Canada and argue that it is characterized by a fundamental shift away from essentialized understandings of female nature. I also discuss the implications of this shift for claims about gender.

Midwifery in Canada began as a radical social movement that grew out of the void left by the demise of traditional midwifery across the country in the nineteenth and early twentieth centuries. After a decades-long life in the margins, midwifery grew into an autonomous profession within the formal health care system, starting with the province of Ontario in 1994.[2] Ontario midwifery, on which the data for this chapter was gathered in the late 1990s, holds much in common ideologically and practically with radical midwifery in the United Kingdom and direct-entry and home birth midwifery in the United States in terms of its opposition to the medicalization of birth and model of low-tech, women-centered alternatives. Natural birth is an idiom for what midwives now clinically refer to as normal or physiological birth, but it bears a cultural and political legacy that goes beyond these latter terms. Indeed, midwifery has long shared a common goal with feminist scholarship on the gendered body: to expose the fictions of science and biomedicine built up about the female body to reveal its true nature—or, as one midwifery client said, "pregnancy and birth as it was meant to be"—underneath. Yet just as the universal female body as the basis for feminism has undergone a "destabilization," so has natural birth as a basis for midwifery. If we think of pregnancy and birth as gendered performances repeated within the "regulatory frames" of biomedical culture and institutions—rather than some prediscursive reality (Butler 1990; Lock and Scheper-Hughes 1990; Pasveer and Akrich 2001: 236)—then contemporary midwifery, I argue, is seeking to reconceive, rather than retrieve, the natural facts of pregnancy and birth. Natural birth, as a critical alternative, contains its own discursive intentions: to promote women as knowing, capable, and strong, their bodies perfectly designed to carry a fetus and to give birth successfully without the high-tech surveillance and interventions of physicians in a hospital setting. New expectations of pregnancy and birth in midwifery in turn give rise to new gender performances—deeply personal, highly political re-articulations—that are *naturalized* in the body and which positively inform their sense of self as physical beings, as women and mothers, and as persons.[3]

## NATURAL BIRTH IS A MATTER OF CHOICE

When asked directly about natural birth, midwives and the birthing women they attend respond in predictable ways: "It means drug free"; "It means no interventions"; "It means nonmedicalized, the opposite of a hospital birth." When probed, however, natural birth is often problematized by midwives and women themselves. Ada is a midwife who comes from rural Ontario. Her training began in the 1980s and was characterized by a mixture of formal education and apprenticeship. She worked for many years as a childbirth educator and a doula[4] before becoming a Registered Midwife. After offering me an initial definition of natural birth as the opposite of medical birth, Ada began to hedge.

> Well, I guess the obvious thing that comes to mind is non-intervention in the sense of augmentation, drugs, episiotomies, procedures, vacuum extractions—those kinds of

things. It's a hard one in terms of the medication issue because I would hate to say to a woman that she didn't have a natural birth because she required some pain medication. That's a hard one. On the one hand, she did have spontaneous vaginal delivery, and pain medication can be, in some cases, very positive for women. I guess I shy away from identifying what clearly is natural; maybe that's what got us into this trouble in the first place is that feeling we have to have some model of what natural is and we have to have techniques to obtain that natural birth.

Having a specific ideal of natural birth necessarily means that some women will fail to accomplish it. Indeed, a young woman in the prenatal classes that I attended (herself a midwifery student at the time) said she would feel "ashamed" in front of her classmates and her instructors if she ended up in the hospital, and especially if she had a C-section. Another woman I met several times at a midwifery clinic and interviewed at her home after the birth of her baby was apologetic about the fact that she "couldn't cope" and had "cried for an epidural" during labor and had asked to go to the hospital. "Next time it will be different" she told me. "Next time I will do it naturally." The inevitability that some women will fail in the goal to birth "naturally"—at home, without drugs, without interventions, without screaming in pain and feeling like they have lost control—is one reason that Ada, like many midwives, avoids offering an absolutely fixed definition of natural birth. Ada went on to discuss how midwifery can provide the context for women to feel a sense of control even when interventions do occur.

> By stressing that she's actively participating in a lot of the decisions; that there are still options—whether they are as simple as rolling from one side to the other. But [the important thing is] that she feels somehow empowered by exercising those limited options; that she has *some* choices, *some* decision making, and that those interventions occurred with her as the decision maker. . . . [E]ven in the event that a woman has a cesarean—it happens lots of times in this practice—they are usually not bad experiences because of that aspect that she still controlled—not controlled—but she had input into the process.

Another longtime midwife, Isobel, asserts that natural birth is a myth that says that, "if you are a together person you can squat in the corner and have your baby by candlelight (and) you have to have a vaginal birth to achieve some sort of womanhood." The myth of natural birth has served, however, to counter another myth: "that childbirth is so horrible that you need to be knocked out in the hospital." Isobel explains how her thinking about natural birth in the context of her work as a midwife developed.

I think that's really dangerous when you are making people try to fit into little boxes. But I started out thinking like that. My goal was to prevent cesareans. But I have seen so many women feel a sense of strength and dignity and satisfaction after a cesarean birth. And I think it's because they have given birth and they've worked really, really hard. Even like [when a woman has] an *abruptio placenta* and you have to have an immediate cesarean, it doesn't take away from it if you have that feeling that you are in control.[5] I hear this all the time. Women consistently say on our evaluation sheets or I hear directly, "I felt I was the one making the decisions. Even though I would have preferred not to have to make that decision, I made it, and I was ready for it, and it was great that you guys were there because I felt that I had a friend there, someone on my side to help me through that difficult time."

Making sure a woman has choices in labor may include where to labor, who to have with her, what to eat and drink, what position to labor in, how to manage pain and the progression of labor (including pharmaceuticals). Very occasionally, ensuring women have choices in childbirth means planning for an epidural early in labor—not exactly the kind of planning usually associated with natural childbirth. Even the midwives who think that natural birth *might* include epidurals are quick to elaborate how such preferences are negotiated in a prenatal visit and during labor. They don't want women making decisions based on fear of childbirth pain, peer pressure, or convenience. Midwives explain that if they do not have any pain medication, they are likely to have fewer interventions overall, feel better, and recover faster. Nevertheless, most midwives agree that when they have tried all the tricks in the book to relieve a woman's pain and exhaustion through physical and emotional support, an epidural can be "a blessed, wonderful thing." Other interventions too have their place in the realm of "natural." Isobel concludes, that "natural childbirth [is about] making sure the woman makes her own choices. That's my goal, not natural childbirth *per se.*"

The importance of informed choice in midwifery cannot be overstated. This inherently politicized notion is at the center of the philosophical and clinical practice of midwifery in Ontario; it is intended to foster a sense self-knowledge and personal responsibility among clients, and to create an egalitarian midwife–client relationship in which individualized, low-tech, even intuitive ways of knowing and doing are explored, valued, and acted upon. "The whole reason that midwifery arose in Ontario is because women wanted choice," one midwife asserts. Midwives explain informed choice as the act of conveying clinical knowledge to women and their partners in such a way that they can understand it and then make informed decisions about their own care. This may be something as simple as describing the importance of maternal nutrition on the developing fetus. Or it may involve citing the findings of a recent study on the effect of artificial rupture of membranes on fetal outcomes. Midwives also expect women to read on their own and generate their own questions. They stress that informed choice is about confirming and supporting women's own knowledge about their bodies and previous pregnancies. Trust in one's midwife as an expert is part of what makes women feel confident and helps them trust in their own bodies and what they can cope with or accomplish. Midwives do not offer informed choice on everything. Administering antihemorrhagic drugs for uterine bleeding after labor, for example, is not an informed-choice issue. Ada tells me this emphatically. "I wouldn't even ask her! If she was bleeding, I wouldn't ask her! It's not a choice. It's not a choice unless she wants to die. She's hired me to care for her. And that's my way of caring for her. And sometimes that means making decisions for her."

## NEGOTIATING MEDICAL TECHNOLOGY THROUGH INFORMED CHOICE

One of the most basic understandings in midwifery is that routine biomedical interventions disrupt the normal or natural process of birth, and moreover, that one intervention begets another. For example, if a woman has her labor artificially induced or augmented with intravenous oxytocin—commonly referred to by its trade name Pitocin or simply as a "Pit drip"—her contractions may come on so fast and strong that she is more likely to need pain medication, which in turn, makes her less likely to be able to push her baby out, which may result in prolonged third stage of labor, which may cause fetal distress and the need for an emergency C-section. A less extreme scenario is when a woman has an epidural, followed by an episiotomy, and then delivers a healthy baby vaginally, but her recovery time is much longer than if she had neither, and her baby is less alert and less likely to nurse right away. Evidence suggests that many of these interventions when used routinely are clinically unnecessary and do not change the health outcomes for either mother or baby; in some cases, these interventions are the source of measurable harm to mother and infant (Davis-Floyd 1992; Hartmann et al. 2005; Sleep, Roberts, and Chalmers 1989; Thacker and Stroup 1999). Midwives and women receiving midwifery care often state the belief that our tendency to rely on—or be subjected to—medical technology has destroyed our natural instincts about pregnancy and birth.

Midwives do, of course, use technology during prenatal care and delivery both in hospital and at home. They use Dopplers–handheld ultrasound devices—to listen to fetal heartbeats. They order routine blood tests. They order sonograms to confirm gestational age or check for fetal anomalies. At home births, they carry oxygen for mother and baby, if necessary, as well as intramuscular oxytocin injections to stop uterine bleeding. At hospital births, they may administer fluids and some medications, such as antibiotics, intravenously as ordered by a physician. (They can also do this at home births too, in some instances.) Some midwives are even seeking certification to manage laboring women with epidurals or to perform vacuum extractions (Kornelsen and Carty 2004: 5).

Giselle is a woman in her early thirties with two small children—the first born in a hospital with an obstetrician and the second born at home with midwives. After chatting several times at the midwifery clinic where I volunteered, I went to meet her at her home just after the birth of her second baby. She and her husband—both professionals—live in a three-storey Victorian house on a tree-lined residential street in a large city. Giselle sought out midwifery care for her second pregnancy because she was disappointed with the care she had received in the hospital with her first baby. She described being hooked up to a fetal monitor and recalled with frustration that everyone (including her husband) was focused on the monitor instead of her. She was unhappy with how her delivery was managed in other ways as well; she had delivered very quickly and sustained deep tears in her perineum. She felt her experience was typical of physician-attended hospital births and did not want to repeat it. When she became pregnant with her second baby, a good friend recommended midwifery. Giselle was very happy with her care throughout the pregnancy, delivery, and the postpartum period.

Giselle had maternal serum screening for both of her pregnancies, but she hinted to me that her midwife had discouraged her.[6]

In the doctor's office [maternal serum] is routine, so I had it. But with my second baby I was extremely well informed, and I chose to have it. There was no need for me to have further tests because my maternal serum came out fine. Had anything come up I could have had more tests and determined whether the child was Down syndrome or Spina Bifida, and we would have had to make a decision at that point. Thank God we never had to make that decision.

What is interesting here is that Giselle contextualized her decision to use prenatal diagnostic technology in terms of the midwifery principle of informed choice. The difference, according to Giselle, is that with midwifery care she was well informed and acted on the basis of what was right for her, rather than having the test as part of a routine at the doctor's office. Giselle also elected to have one ultrasound because they weren't sure about her dates, a detail that could affect the maternal serum. Again, she explained that the ultrasound was both necessary *and* her choice. She was satisfied with the ultrasound because it confirmed her dates. She was disappointed, however, with the image of the fifteen-week-old fetus—"We could hardly see her"—in contrast to the image of her seventeen-week-old fetus during her first pregnancy. Even so, because there was no reason for another ultrasound and her midwives, she knew, didn't like to do tests without a reason, she did not seek another one at a later gestational date, deciding she would just wait until the baby was born to see her again.

Clients like Giselle now make use of technology in a way that midwifery clients of the past seldom did—opting for maternal serum and longing for one more ultrasound yet planning a home birth and determined to avoid the alienating hospital experience of epidurals and fetal monitors. While it is clear that she prefers midwifery care generally, she is not beholden to it ideologically.

There is a perception there that if you are going to a midwife, you are going to refuse medical treatment and only go to a naturopath, that you must be an extremist. But you don't have to be an extremist to go to a midwife. There is a good way of giving birth. There is no hard line between delivering safely and delivering comfortably. But some people feel that if you are going to go with a midwife that you must be an extremist and you must be trying to make a statement. But I just learned from my first delivery, and from friends' stories who had midwives, that this is not right. It's not that I'm bucking the medical profession, but in my case, I don't think the medical profession knows how to handle a normal, uncomplicated birth. They want to complicate it . . . some people just can't get the idea, that [midwifery is] not a statement. It is just the natural way to go.

Giselle's "informed choice" use of technology might be seen to erode midwifery's political goal to resist the medicalization of birth and the social control of women's bodies by patriarchal institutions. Many midwives lament this trend and see it as a consequence of both their expanded scope of practice since being incorporated into the formal health care system, and the influx of clients who are, in their view, "less committed" to the low-tech ideals of the past. Part of the problem for women making choices like Giselle's at this time is that midwifery care in Ontario is still a relatively uncommon choice—and public knowledge about midwifery is still somewhat limited.[7] Also, there is tremendous pressure to use medical technology because it has become so routinized in mainstream maternity care and the social consequences of not using it can be severe (Mitchell 1994; Rapp 1990; Rothman 1986). Giselle's decisions around the use of medical routines and technologies in her maternity care might be best understood in terms of pragmatism (Lock and Kaufert 1998: 208). Steering away from essentialist explanations that women are inherently opposed to technology by virtue of their closeness to nature or wholly oppressed by technology and the systems in which it is embedded, pragmatism focuses on women's agency: what women do, rather than what is done to them.[8] The notion of pragmatism adds a level of nuance to our understanding of midwifery, paying attention to the subtleties of everyday usage not just the ideological basis encapsulated in such notions as medicalization versus natural birth.

## LABOR PAINS AND WOMEN'S POWER

It's like, who invented epidurals? The person should be shot. Because, you know, if they didn't exist, people would just shut up and grin and bear it. . . . And if there was nothing but the odd herb that would help you relax or something, then people would just do it.

(Anna Lisa, *mother of three children born at home with midwives*)

How midwives think about the pain of labor is key to their view of pregnant and birthing bodies as naturally capable and competent. The vast majority of midwives recognize pain medication as having its place, but in the case of normal labor and delivery, they generally take the view that pain can and should be managed in nonpharmaceutical ways. The pain of labor is one of the main fears that women express in prenatal classes and appointments. Midwives do not pretend that labor is not painful, and they shy away from offering magic solutions, but they do offer clients another way to think about and experience it. One woman in my study said that her midwives helped her prepare for labor and birth by teaching "almost another worldview . . . more of an attitude than anything else." In the midwifery model of pain, a number of things are emphasized. One, the pain of labor is not continuous like most other pain: contractions are intermittent and build slowly in intensity, so one can learn to cope. Two, the pain of labor is "pain with a purpose": you are pushing out your baby. Three, labor pain is universal: "Women have been doing this for centuries. Our bodies are designed to do it well." Midwives work hard to naturalize the pain of

birth even from the first minutes that a woman goes into labor. They advise women and their partners not to fuss too much in the early stages; they should do what they normally do—eat breakfast, do the dishes, go for a walk—so as to not give the woman the impression that she cannot cope. This kind of advice reflects an understanding that pregnancy is not an illness and labor and birth are not crises but, rather, normal physiological events.

Leigh's story is a good example of how midwifery works discursively to affect women's knowledge and experience of labor pain and how this becomes central (and desirable) to having a natural birth. When I met Leigh, a lawyer in her mid-thirties, she had just had her second baby with midwifery care. The first one occurred before midwifery was a recognized part of the formal health care system. It was a planned hospital delivery, with the shared care of a midwife and a physician. The second was a planned home birth several years later, with the same midwife as her primary care giver under the new regulated system. Leigh's experience of laboring without pain medication was a profoundly empowering for her. She attributes this to midwifery's unique "worldview" of birth, which "has everything to do" with her confidence in her body during pregnancy and birth.

One of the things that I was so fed up with was this stuff about how people in our society put a great deal of effort in making birth scary . . . Most of the women I know are terrified of birth. Terrified of the pain. Terrified of the difficulty. Really competent, interesting, smart women are terrified of birth. It is terrible that they look at birth that way; it is a difficult experience but it is also exhilarating . . . I felt really powerful after I had Martha. I felt really powerful after I had Zoe. I felt fantastic. I felt like it was my marathon. It was something that I had done, and I found it intensely interesting, too.

"Even in the moment? Even as you were laboring?" I asked her.

Yes, even in the moment. When you are in labor and you are trying to figure out how you can go with the labor, how you can help yourself dilate, how you can carry on through it, how you can let it happen—there is a long time in labor when you are dilating when you have to do all that work. And it's work that you can do. I mean your body helps you do it. And if you do it—at least for me—it is a very positive experience, and then at the end there is no more work because your body runs the show. But it's a very enriching experience because you end up thinking, "I did this! This was really hard and I did this!" And you can do it because your body will help you do it. You don't have to doubt that you can do it, if you believe that about yourself.

Leigh's determination to give birth without pain medication was for her, "a route to my power." She notes a clear difference between being in control of birth—something that she thinks is not totally possible on the physical level and something that midwives encourage women to give up—and being "in control of the circumstances of birth"—something that is possible to a great extent and something that Leigh and many other women cite as key to feelings of empowerment, strength, and even wisdom derived from midwifery care and birth. "The whole thing was a lesson to me. The pregnancy was a lesson to me, and the labor was a lesson to me. And it is a lesson in being almost someone not from our century," she concluded.

## NATURAL INTERVENTIONS

Leigh concluded that while in labor she was "guided by something very primitive, but I'm not just a primitive woman." When Leigh describes the situation during her second birth—the planned home birth that ended up in a hospital—her ambivalence about the definition of natural birth surfaces, and the line between nature and medical interventions becomes blurred. Because her first baby had meconium staining, Leigh was aware of the possibility of this happening again and refers to it in her description of how she labored at home with her second baby.[9]

> After six hours I got [my midwife] to break the waters—partly because I had that meconium thing in my head and partly because I didn't want six more hours of labor. Frederick Leboyer would hate me because he said that birth is violence and that breaking the waters would make birth more violent. I was worried about the meconium, and I didn't really care about Frederick Leboyer. And also [my baby] was seven days overdue. So that makes the risks higher. So it didn't seem to me to be a bad thing to do . . . So I don't think that breaking the waters is terribly unnatural—people have been doing that for a really long time, you know? And if I feel like I want to break the waters because that labor is long and something else is niggling at me—which is what was going on—then I guess that's not unnatural.

As it turns out, Leigh was right. Her baby was taken to hospital after the delivery at home, with meconium aspiration. Kelly's story echoes these sentiments. Kelly is in her early thirties living in a medium-sized city in Ontario. Her first child, Clara, was born at home under the care of midwives. I met Kelly at her spacious apartment on the third floor of a suburban low-rise building. She says that she has always known that birth was meant to be "totally natural and joyous, not frightening," and she grounds this faith in a kind of biological determinism. "As females—it seems very simple to me—we are born with these parts, with this purpose of our biology, and that's it. It's a process that happens, and it's supposed to happen. It's just biologically natural." During pregnancy she did not take any medication or undergo any prenatal tests. She was getting information from her midwife about nutrition, herbs, and natural remedies. She was thrilled. "For example," she tells me, "I was having heartburn and asked, 'What can I take?' and she said, 'You can eat almonds!'" During labor, she avoided interventions too. She explained that she did not have an episiotomy,

> [because] it is unnatural unless it's absolutely necessary. And there *are* a very small number of cases where that would be necessary. So, in that case, if everything else was dealt with without drugs or interventions—medical or technological types of interventions—then an episiotomy that is absolutely required would be—Now, for example, women who are dancers, their muscle tone and strength is so tight in that area of their body from dancing that they can't open up. Now they might need an episiotomy, and so if they went through the whole labor without any medicinal type things, then I would say that she had a natural birth, even if she had an episiotomy, because that was just part of her, of who she is, her physiology as a dancer. But it goes beyond the physical sphere of things. It includes your state of mind too. And if you stay at home to have your baby, you can add to the naturalness of it.

In Kelly's view, if an intervention is done because it is absolutely necessary, and not simply convenient or expedient, or done out of fear, then the birth could still be considered natural. Moreover, she is suggesting that there are degrees of naturalness.

One evening at the prenatal classes I attended at a local midwifery practice, a discussion arose about tears that can occur in the labia and vagina when a woman is pushing her baby out. Ingrid, the midwife instructor, reported that scientific research had recently confirmed what midwives knew all along: that routine episiotomies were unnecessary and that most women did not require them. She then made a surprising comment: that most women tear during the pushing stage of labor. I suppose we were expecting to hear that most women do not tear during the pushing stage, a piece of information that would confirm the routine use of episiotomy as brutally unnatural. Her point was that most tears are small and either repair themselves or require just a few stitches. Even deep tears, in her opinion, are preferable to large episiotomies because the tissue tears only as far as it needs to and then heals more efficiently. One woman in the class asked her, "Are tears, then, a natural thing?" to which Ingrid responded, "I would have to say yes."

The room was quiet for a moment after that. The discussion then turned to what midwives do to prevent tears. It starts with perineal massage in the prenatal period, something that pregnant women and their partners do at home, to stretch the tissues that will have to stretch during birth. During the birth itself, midwives use hot compresses and apply pressure to the perineum to support it as the baby's head descends, crowns, and is born. They massage and stretch the tissues with olive oil to ease the baby's head out of the vagina. Midwives will often ask a woman to stop pushing altogether for a moment so that the baby does not come out too quickly. Many women in my study described such moments with awe and appreciation for the esoteric skills of their midwives. The intervention of the midwife in preparing the tissues with massage and lubrication and then averting the woman's instinct to push are all part of a natural birth.

## NATURAL INTENTIONS

If some interventions are natural, they are nevertheless qualified. The case of artificial rupture of the membranes is a good example of how intention and context matter in the determination of the naturalness of birth. Although this intervention may be viewed as unnatural and recalled with anger or disappointment when experienced at the hands of a physician without being consulted, women in the care of midwives do not ordinarily regard it as a problem. In a clinic visit during my fieldwork, a couple—Marielle and Tom—came in with their newborn baby for a postpartum visit with their midwife, Isobel. The rapport between them was warm and sincere; Isobel had attended their first two babies' births and followed the pregnancy of their third, but she did not attend this newborn's birth.

As they discussed the birth, Marielle began to cry, recalling how, long into the labor, the alternate midwife had told her she was not working hard enough. "I know she just said it to inspire me, but it hurt my feelings, and it wasn't true." Marielle was even more upset that this midwife had insisted on breaking her waters to "get things moving." She described how different this was from the births of her first and second babies, when her waters had burst naturally in the pushing stage and the excitement of those moments inspired her and renewed her flagging energy. She felt that the alternate midwife had not respected her natural birth process. She was suspicious of her intentions, and this played a role in her evaluation of the artificial rupture of the membranes as an unnatural intervention. Thus, the exception to the trusting relationship between midwife and client reinforces the centrality of caring and trust in midwifery care itself as integral to natural pregnancy and birth.

## CONCLUSION

Midwives in Ontario and the women they attend are engaged in culturally productive strategies (both discursive and clinical) to redefine natural birth in ways that no longer strictly fix nature against culture, nature against medical and technological interventions, and, sometimes, nature against women themselves (in the case of the failure to birth "naturally"). Such flexibility reflects the growing comfort with the omnipresence of technology in our midst and, quite literally, in our bodies. The new professional context of midwifery and the influx of a more mainstream clientele have been factors as well. Yet this changing notion of natural birth still works to challenge the powerful discourses of science and medicine and the institutions of maternity care that have thus far shaped women's embodied subjectivity so much so that what midwives and their clients hope for and work for is often articulated in its terms. Natural birth seems to stand for midwifery itself and for a particular set of gender expectations inherent in these midwifery stories I have just relayed: that giving birth is hard but satisfying work that women are completely capable of performing; that with proper support women can handle the pain of labor and even find it empowering; and that women can trust their gut feelings in a context in which choice is paramount, interventions are negotiable, and trust characterizes the midwife–client relationship. This flexible rather than fixed construction and experience of natural birth strengthens rather than weakens its empowering potential.

The ideological foundation of such cultural work lies in modernity itself. Having choice is part of being a modern person and making choices about sexuality and reproduction—from contraception to method of birth—is expected of the modern woman (Paxson 2002: 216). Thus, the importance of having knowledge, having a sense of control, and having a choice during pregnancy and labor is fundamental to the definition and experience of natural birth in a fully modern sense. Overall, midwifery in Ontario seeks to replace the predominant cultural version of pregnant and birthing bodies with what is in their view a better—but equally cultural—version. For indeed, as Marilyn Strathern has said, "[n]ature cannot survive without cultural intervention" (1992: 174).

### NOTES

1. This chapter is based on material previously published by Vanderbilt University Press (VUP). The author gratefully acknowledges the permission of VUP to reproduce materials from Chapter Four of the book, *At Work in the Field of Birth*.

2. For detailed descriptions and analyses of this process, see Bourgeault (2006), Bourgeault, Benoit, and Davis-Floyd (2004), and MacDonald (2007).

3. Midwives argue that natural birth is empowering for families too, for example, by allowing fathers, other children, and even grandparents a greater role in the process.

4. Doula is the name given to the person who cares for the new mother after childbirth and who may also assist at the birth. It is a nonclinical but important role often taken on by close family members or friends who provide support for the new mother particularly with breastfeeding. Since the 1980s, the role has become professionalized with training programs in the United States and Canada and doulas charging fees for their services (Raphael 1993).

5. A condition that occurs during pregnancy or during labor in which the placenta pulls away from the uterus, causing bleeding and an emergency situation.

6. Maternal serum is a screening test performed at fifteen to eighteen weeks of pregnancy and is used to signal maternal risk for several fetal disabilities including neural tube disorders and Down syndrome. It is not a diagnostic test, and thus critics suggest that it creates anxiety and leads to increased use of other technologies (Blatt 1993: 237).

7. At the time I conducted the research for this work in the late 1990s, midwives attended approximately 6 percent of all births in the province; that figure has risen to 8 percent by 2007.

8. For more work on the relationship of women to technology, see also Haraway (1991), Riessman (1983), Sawicki (1991), Stabile (1994).

9. Meconium is the first stool excreted by the infant. Interuterine excretion (which can only be detected after the amniotic waters have broken) is associated with fetal distress. Meconium aspiration is a potentially dangerous situation for the baby and requires hospital-based intervention (Raines 1993: 244).

## REFERENCES

Blatt, R. J. 1993. "Maternal Serum Screening." In B. K. Rothman (ed.). *The Encyclopedia of Childbearing*, pp. 236–237. New York: Henry Holt.

Bourgeault, Ivy Lynn. 2006. *Push!* Toronto: McGill-Queen's University Press.

Bourgeault, I. L., C. Benoit, and R. Davis-Floyd (eds.). 2004. *Reconceiving Midwifery: The New Canadian Model*, pp. 46–66. Montreal: McGill-Queens University Press.

Butler, Judith. 1990. *Gender Trouble.* New York: Routledge.

Davis-Floyd, Robbie. 1992. *Birth as an American Rite of Passage.* Berkeley: University of California Press.

———. 1994. "The Technocratic Body: American Childbirth as Cultural Expression." *Social Science and Medicine* 38(8): 1125–1140.

Haraway, Donna. 1991. *Simians, Cyborgs, and Women.* New York: Routledge.

Hartmann, K., M. Viswanathan, R. Palmieri, G. Gartlehner, J. Thorp Jr., and K. L. Lohr. 2005. "Outcomes of Routine Episiotomy. A Systematic Review." *JAMA* 293: 2141–2148.

Kornelsen, Jude, and Elaine Carty. 2004. "Challenges to Midwifery Integration: Interprofessional relationships in British Columbia." In Ivy Lynn Bourgeault, Cecilia Benoit, and Robbie Davis-Floyd (eds.). *Reconceiving Midwifery*, pp. 111–130. Toronto: McGill-Queens University Press.

Lock, Margaret, and Patricia Kaufert (eds.). 1998. *Pragmatic Women and Body Politics.* Cambridge: Cambridge University Press.

Lock, Margaret, and Nancy Scheper-Hughes. 1990. "A Critical Interpretive Approach in Medical Anthropology: Rituals and Routines of Discipline and Dissent." In T. Johnson and C. Sargent (eds.). *Medical Anthropology: Contemporary Theory and Method*, pp. 47–72. New York: Greenwood Press.

MacDonald, Margaret. 2007. *At Work in the Field of Birth.* Nashville, TN: Vanderbilt University Press.

Mitchell, Lisa. 1994. "The Routinization of the Other: Ultrasound, Women, and the Fetus." In G. Basen, M. Eichler, and A. Lipman (eds.). *Misconceptions*, Vol. II, pp. 146–160. Hull: Voyageuer.

Pasveer, Bernike, and Madeleine Akrich. 2001. "Obstetrical Trajectories: On Training Women's Bodies for (Home) Birth." In R. DeVries, C. Benoit, E. R. Van Teijlingen, and S. Wrede (eds.). *Birth by Design*, pp. 229–242. New York: Routledge.

Paxson, Heather. 2002. "Rationalising Sex: Family Planning and the Making of Modern Lovers in Urban Greece." *American Ethnologist* 29(2): 307–334.

Raines, Deborah. 1993. "Meconium." In Barbara Katz Rothman (ed.). *The Encyclopedia of Childbearing*, pp. 243–244. New York: Henry Holt.

Raphael, Dana. 1993. "Doula." In Barbara Katz Rothman (ed.). *The Encyclopedia of Childbearing*, pp. 113–115. New York: Henry Holt.

Rapp, Rayna. 1990. "Constructing Amniocentesis: Maternal and Medical Discourses." In F. Ginsburg and A. L. Tsing (eds.). *Uncertain Terms: Negotiating Gender in American Culture*, pp. 28–42. Boston: Beacon Press.

Riessman, Catherine Kohler. 1983. "Women and Medicalization: A New Perspective." *Social Policy* 14: 3–18.

Rothman, Barbara Katz. 1986. *The Tentative Pregnancy: Prenatal Diagnosis and the Future of Motherhood.* New York: Viking Penguin.

Sawicki, Jana. 1991. *Disciplining Foucault.* New York: Routledge.

Sleep, J., J. Roberts, and I. Chalmers. 1989. "The Second Stage of Labour." In M. Enkin, M. J. N. C. Keirse, and I. Chalmers (eds.). *A Guide to Effective Care in Pregnancy and Childbirth*, pp. 1129–1144. Oxford: Oxford University Press.

Stabile, Carol. 1994. *Feminism and the Technological Fix.* Manchester: Manchester University Press.

Strathern, Marilyn. 1992. *After Nature: English Kinship in the Late 20th Century.* Cambridge: Cambridge University Press.

Thacker, S. B., and D. F. Stroup. 1999. *Continuous Electronic Fetal Heart Rate Monitoring versus Intermittent Auscultation for Assessment during Labor.* Cochrane Library. Issue 1. Oxford: Update Software.

# Political Demography:
## The Banning of Abortion in Ceausescu's Romania

### Gail Kligman

*Rumania . . . had anticipated Gilead in the eighties by banning all forms of birth control, imposing compulsory pregnancy tests on the female population, and linking promotion and wage increases to fertility.*

Margaret Atwood, *The Handmaid's Tale*

In Nicolae Ceausescu's Romania, the "marriage" between demographic concerns and nationalist politics turned women's bodies into instruments to be used in the service of the state. The paternalist state exercised its authority partially through the elaboration of a discourse and related set of practices centered on "the family." In that "traditional" Romanian family structure is patriarchal, the state's rhetoric about the family resonated with familiar cultural patterns (see Kligman 1988); the dependency relations created through patriarchal family organization were elevated to the level of the socialist state's "legitimate" rule over its citizens. In this chapter I explore the relationship between official rhetoric, policy, and everyday practice through an analysis of the politics of reproduction during Ceausescu's reign. Analysis of the politics of reproduction (or political demography, in regime parlance) serves partially as a focused case study of the relations between the state and its citizens. These policies brought the state directly into its citizens' bodies and their intimate relations. As such, the pronatalist policies may be viewed as indicative of the character of the polity, of how the state conceived of and represented itself. Analysis of the complex relationship between the official discourse about reproduction, the policies that translated this official rhetoric into state practices, and citizens' lived experiences of these policies in Ceausescu's Romania enables us to understand the means by which the regime was perpetuated and by which compliance and complicity were systemically structured. At the same time, analysis of this complex relationship underscores the increasing separation between the official rhetoric of the regime and the

Gail Kligman, "Political Demography: The Banning of Abortion in Ceausescu's Romania," in Faye D. Ginsberg and Rayna Rapp, eds., *Conceiving the New World Order: The Global Politics of Reproduction,* Berkeley: The University of California Press, 1995.

average citizen's experience; this growing disjunction ultimately contributed to the regime's downfall.

The former socialist states, driven by command economies, were actively engaged in social engineering. In theory, societal transformation incorporated all levels of life, and the population had to be mobilized accordingly. The "building of socialism" was predicated on a productionist mentality, the underlying rationale of which was the contribution of each citizen "according to his abilities." In recognition of one of women's "abilities"—childbearing—the socialist state intended to help women enter the economy by providing various forms of social assistance: guaranteed maternity leaves, job security, childcare facilities. These entitlements functioned as positive incentives and were progressive in intention if not in realization. Although gender equity was ideologically extolled in all of the formerly existing socialist states, the progressive legislation regarding women's rights as workers often came into conflict with their obligations as reproducers of the labor force—that is, with their roles as mothers. The resultant relation between state policy and demographic factors bore directly on issues of changing gender relations and underscored the often contradictory interests of the state and its citizens, especially women. Romanian policy was an "extreme case of the generalized pronatalism" (Teitelbaum and Winter 1985: 100) that, from the mid-1960s, typified the region. Pronatalist policies, aimed at securing an adequate work force to build socialism, formed part of the modernization strategies of these states.

Following a brief summary of key ideological tenets that contributed to the shaping and implementation of the Ceausescu regime's pronatalist policies, I present an overview of the development of these political demographic policies, concentrating on their full elaboration in the 1980s. I comment on the human dramas born of the pronatalist policies: illegal abortion, child abandonment, infant AIDS among abandoned "surplus" babies, and international adoption. I next discuss the politics of reproduction in post-Ceausescu Romania. Between 1989 and 1992, two phases of policy formulation related to reproduction may be distinguished. These phases reflect the gradual formation of effective institutional procedures meant to recognize and protect the rights of individuals in society. They are indicative of the fundamental changes taking place in Romania, however traumatically.

## THE PRONATALIST POLICIES

Under Ceausescu's rule, the Romanian state increasingly intruded into its citizens' intimate lives to ensure "normal demographic growth" of the labor force and the "triumph of socialism" (Resolution of the Executive Political Committee of the Central Committee of the Romanian Communist Party, March 1984). The Constitution and the Family Code laid the groundwork for active political-educational campaigns as well as for the implementation of positive incentives, augmented over the years by an increasing number of coercive measures. (See, for example, Trebici 1988). The Constitution of the Socialist Republic of Romania (SRR) granted all citizens the right to work as well as equal pay for equal work. Measures for protection and safety at work and special measures for the protection of women's and youth's work were also established by law.

The state assumed legal responsibility for the family as a way to underscore the family's significance in the development of the "new socialist person." The family's primary contributions to the building of socialism were in the realms of reproduction of the population (and, by implication, of the work force) and of education, with respect to the "spiritual reproduction of society" and the social integration of youth into society (See Liciu 1975: 10). Marriage into which partners entered on the basis of "free consent" was the legal foundation of the family. Law 4/1953, Article 1, of the Family Code read: "In the SRR, the state shall protect marriage and the family; it shall support the development and strengthening of the family through economic and social measures. The state shall defend the interests of mother and child and shall display a special care for the upbringing and education of the young generation."

In the state-controlled public sphere, women, like minorities, were represented in positions of authority. An operative quota system paid lip service to the participation of women and minorities (Hungarians, Germans, Gypsies, Jews) in leadership roles. Access to power was stratified. A few women entered the ranks of the Central Committee, such as Elena Ceausescu and Lina Ciobanu, who—as workers—respectively represented chemistry and the textile industry; most women, however, generally filled positions in cultural or educational institutions or in light industry—that is, positions deemed suitable for women. Women in the labor force tended to occupy lower-status, more poorly paid job niches. Moreover, the early emphasis on heavy industrialization as a modernizing strategy often led to the feminization of agriculture. Agricultural labor was more attractive to women because of flexible work schedules. They could both work and tend to families; they were not tied strictly to the clock of industrial production.

Women's participation in the national economy and society as workers and mothers created the classic double and triple burdens: working in the state sphere, doing housework, and raising children. (These burdens increased over the decades as the double burdens of the 1960s and 1970s became triple burdens in the 1980s when childbearing became officially obligatory.) Occupational "advances" were not coupled with the production of time-saving household devices or with any emphasis on changing gender roles within the family.

The initial pronatalist measures were instituted in 1966. The birthrate in Romania had fallen to 14.3 per 1,000 from a 1960 rate of 19.1 per 1,000 (*Anuarul statistic al Romaniei* 1990: 67). This decline was attributed, in part, to the liberal law that had legalized abortion and made it readily accessible. To remedy this situation, Law 770/1966 was introduced. This law prohibited abortions except if the pregnancy endangered the life of the woman and no other means could be taken to save it, a hereditary disease was involved, the pregnancy was the result of rape, the woman was forty-five years of age or over, or she had delivered and reared four children. The imposition of this law caught Romanians by surprise; in 1967 the birthrate dramatically shot up to 27.4. (There were 527,764 live births in 1967 compared with 273,678 in 1966; *Anuarul statistic al Romaniei* 1990: 66.) The antiabortion law was accompanied by a series of progressive measures meant to encourage women to bear children, including financial allowances for families and child-support benefits (Decree 410/1985),[1] maternity leaves and work protection (Decision 880/1965, Articles 13–17; maternity leaves were usually fifty-two days prior to delivery and sixty days thereafter, these being interchangeable), protection for working women and children (the Work Code, especially section VII), access to medical attention throughout all phases of pregnancy and to medical care for mother and child (Law 3/1978; Decree 246/1958), and access to childcare facilities (Decree 65/1982). Similar incentives existed throughout Eastern Europe, although their particulars varied. Romania followed the spirit of this progressive legislation but had the least adequate provisions. Ultimately, as shall be seen, Ceausescu added coercive measures unparalleled elsewhere.

As in other spheres of production, mothers who bore many children were honored as "heroes of socialist labor," for which they were awarded decorations and minor privileges. To this end, State Council Decree 190/1977, Article 13, announced that:

- Women who delivered and reared ten or more children were awarded the title of "Heroine Mother";
- Women who had delivered and reared nine children received the first-class "Order of Maternal Glory"; those with eight children, the second-class "Order of Maternal Glory"; those with seven, the third-class award in this category;
- Women who had delivered and reared six children were awarded the first-class "Medal of Maternity"; those with five, the second-class "Medal of Maternity."

The stipulations of this decree must be read carefully. A woman who bore ten children did not automatically qualify for the honor of Heroine Mother. She also had to have reared them. Given the high incidence of infant mortality, especially in rural areas, this honor was difficult to achieve. Wording is also significant in the 1966 abortion law, which states that women must have given birth to "four children and have them in her care." Children acquired through second marriages or adoption did not qualify women for medals or abortions.

The pronatalist policies introduced by Ceausescu in the 1960s were a mild version of what was later to become a draconian policy, and in the 1970s the minimum age for abortion was lowered to forty (Article 2, Instructions 27/1974). In these earlier years, Ceausescu emphasized the role of women in politics, the economy, and society. In 1971, he began promoting his wife, Elena. To legitimize this first step in the creation of "dynastic socialism,"[2] a political-educational campaign glorifying women in the labor force as workers and as mothers of future workers was inaugurated. Ceausescu opposed gender discrimination: "If we speak about the creation of conditions of full equality between the sexes, this means that we must treat all people not as men and women, but in their qualities as Party members, as citizens, for which they are exclusively judged according to their work contributions" (*Address to the Plenary Session of the Central Committee of the Romanian Communist Party* 1973). He also began stressing that "an obligation of national interest is the protection and consolidation of the family, the development of a corresponding consciousness about the growth of an increased number of children, and the formation of healthy and robust generations profoundly devoted to the cause of socialism; in this realm women have a distinguished role and a noble mission" (*Decisions of the Plenary Session of the Central Committee of the Romanian Communist Party* 1973).

Ceausescu superficially recognized the stress created for women by their roles as mothers and workers. In 1978 he urged that particular attention be paid to the solving of these problems through the construction of childcare facilities, the production and distribution of household appliances, the sale of semiprepared foods, so that women could use their time efficiently in their many pursuits. However these exhortations were not fulfilled and women experienced an inverse relationship between Ceausescu's official statements about their lives and the demands of their everyday reality.

Propaganda notwithstanding, by 1983, the birthrate had again declined to the 1966 level, although there had long been no prochoice law to which this decline could be attributed, as was the case in 1966. Romanians had managed as best they could in an environment in which contraceptives were unavailable through legal means;[3] pregnancies were avoided through illegal abortions, abstinence, and coitus interruptus. The decline in the birthrate coincided with a steady deterioration in the material conditions of everyday life. In the interest of national self-determination, Ceausescu had decided that Romania's outstanding foreign debts would be repaid—at enormous cost to the quality of life. Production was targeted for export. By 1984, winters were endured with little heat or electricity; food staples were rationed.

The Orwellian reproductive politics that inspired Margaret Atwood's novel *The Handmaid's Tale* and a Romanian national tragedy were unveiled on International Women's Day, March 8, 1984: Ceausescu saluted women's importance to the nation by again exhorting them to bear four or more children in order to fulfill the national goal of increasing the population from 22.6 to 25 million by 1990. As was inevitably the case, the popular response could be gauged by jokes. One noted that people were willing to agree to the four-child plan as long as it was applied consistently with state production policy: keep one child, and export the other three. This joke also referred to the unpublicized state trade in babies for hard currency. Also in 1984, Ana Blandiana, a revered poet (and now a fêted member of the Civic Alliance social movement), wrote a poem, "Children's Crusade," criticizing such brutal policies as the legal obligation of women to bear four (later five) children:

An entire population
as yet unborn
but condemned to birth
lined up in rows, before birth
fetus beside fetus
An entire population
which doesn't see, doesn't hear, doesn't understand
but develops
through the convulsed bodies of women
through the blood of mothers
Unasked.

*Amfiteatru*

Blandiana's poignant words presaged the death sentence unwanted children were later to face as a consequence of the AIDS-infected transfusions given routinely to children in orphanages. Statistics on this situation were deliberately suppressed. Nonetheless, pronatalist propaganda flourished. Demographers, doctors, and women's and youth organizations were solicited to participate in the propaganda campaign. Sex education was stepped up, including premarital health counseling and checkups, lectures, and films at work locales. Competitions about "health knowledge" were promoted in magazines such as *Sanatatea.* Ideological bombast was cemented by threats of punishment which ensured widespread complicity. The women's magazine *Femeia,* found in all of the cultural centers across the country, soon ceased being a typical magazine for women. By the 1980s, articles about household concerns were limited, while those about women in the work force had increased. The ads for clothing and household items characteristic of the 1960s had been replaced by pictures of the ruling couple, his speeches, and "patriotic" poems or stories from the national cultural festival, *Cintarea Romaniei,* the Singing of Romania. A new section on children, "the supreme joy, supreme responsibility," was introduced in 1987, in the interest again of increasing the birthrate. Motherhood— regardless of marital status—was the message.

Morality tales about good and bad mothers abounded. A young, single mother wanting to give her child up for adoption was chastised in the response to her letter of inquiry (of the "Dear Abby" sort). What kind of young woman was she? She had a job, was healthy with her whole future ahead of her. She herself had been left motherless at the age of thirteen. The thrust of the argument was that a "single mother is not to be condemned; a mother will always be respected. Perhaps for a while you won't be able to offer your child the maximum, but be certain that no one in this world can offer what you can [mother love]" (*Femeia* 12, 1988, p. 13).

Educators and activists received all manner of booklets about the relationship between health and demography, about marital harmony, care of infants and children, and the consequences of abortion. For example, one publication of the Health Ministry's Institute of Hygiene and Public Health included topics such as the methods and contents of health education in relation to the problems of demography; protection of mothers, children, and youth (including the topic of reproduction and problems related to it: fecundity, pregnancy, birth); elementary notions of infant and child care; and venereal diseases. A normal, regulated sexual life, with "normal relations of 3–4 weekly" was recommended.

The virtues of motherhood were extolled: "motherhood is itself the meaning of women's lives" was a ubiquitous formula. Articles in the state paper *Scinteia* instructed the population about the patriotic virtues of large families and the noble mission of mothers. For example, the headline for March 9, 1984, read: "Goals of extraordinary significance for the nation's future are contained in Comrade N. Ceausescu's address: Families with many children—a law of life and of human fulfillment, a noble patriotic duty." This theme was reiterated incessantly for the rest of the decade. A series of articles titled "A House with Many Children" (January to April 1986) highlighted individual families and whole villages as "heroes of socialist labor." Other headlines read: "Demographic growth—an exalted responsibility of the entire society" (April 3, 1984); "For the eternity of families, for the vigor of our people" (March 16, 1984); "The joy of being a mother" (June 4, 1987). Images of the happy maternal-child relation abounded.

Women were differentially affected by the pronatalist policies. Urban women with higher education managed to acquire black-market contraceptives or to arrange for illegal abortions performed by medical personnel. Others, such as factory workers, bore the costs, material and bodily, of these policies. It is assumed that rural women were less radically affected because of the influences of religion and local habits. Although these assumptions may generally be true, there was considerable regional variation. Many rural women participated in the seasonal migrant labor force and, as a consequence, were introduced to different practices. Some of them married outside their own region and had abortions that they might not have had in their natal villages. In an unsuccessful bid, the regime attempted to get rural women to sign contracts to produce four children in the same way that peasants signed contracts with the state to meet production quotas. "Women as cows" were castigated by village women, who questioned what would happen if they were unable to have a third or fourth child. Would they be sent to prison? What if a child died; would they be required to produce another? The "what ifs" were recounted with outrage. These same women, and their families, often expressed a desire to have more children although they were unable to support those they already had.

Also, and again undocumented by hard data, responses to these policies were differentiated by ethnicity as well as class. Physicians repeatedly pointed out that Hungarian Romanians, for example, had greater access to black-market contraceptives through their kin or ethnic networks. (Hungary was a source for contraceptives.) Moreover, many medical practitioners mentioned that Hungarian Romanians drew upon a different cultural and educational heritage, the relation between educational level and family planning being relevant. In 1983–84, as the pronatalist campaign intensified and in keeping with the ideological line, a Hungarian Romanian radio station offered a program on stimulating fertility. The editors of this show and of other Hungarian radio programs were informed that there was no need for them to offer this information. Although the pronatalist policies were formally applicable to all, there seems to have been an unstated preference to increase the birthrate of Romanians but not "hyphenated" Romanians such as Hungarians.[4]

Demographers also quietly called attention to the need to bring under control the birthrates of the Gypsy population. "Their exaggerated reproduction is determined especially by their lifestyle, the degree of their social and cultural backwardness."[5] The Gypsy natality rate created concern among Romanians, who pointed out derogatorily that Gypsies "multiply like rabbits," like people in the developing world, while the "European" birthrate—such as that of Romanians and Hungarian Romanians—mirrored West European trends (zero or declining population growth; this concern has been heightened throughout Europe). It is believed that most Gypsy women, in accordance with cultural beliefs, do not practice abortion, although this is not considered true for assimilated, urban middle-class Gypsies. It seems that, at the end of the 1970s, Gypsy women, regardless of their age or the number of children in their care, could get abortions in Arad, a city in Transylvania; whether this was a local initiative or a general policy remains unverified. In any event, the politics of reproduction in Romania had hidden dimensions to it: stringent measures could be more leniently applied in the case of ethnic "others."

When it became obvious in 1983 that the birthrate was not increasing despite the pronatalist policies already in effect, the regime resorted to a more determined strategy: coercion. On December 26, 1985, a stringent antiabortion law was passed. The age at which women became eligible for legal abortions was again raised to the 1966 limit of forty-five; the number of children "delivered and under her care" was increased to five. Also on this day, another pronatalist measure (originally signed into law in 1977) was modified, increasing the monthly "contributions of childless persons"— that is, all persons over the age of twenty-five, regardless of sex or marital status, who were childless. The sums subtracted from monthly wages varied, depending on the sector of the state economy in which one worked, those in agriculture being taxed somewhat less. To avoid this monthly fee, some quit their jobs in state enterprises to work as migrant laborers—a little-discussed adaptive strategy. One way or another, reproductive and abortion statistics had become political tools to discipline the population and were used accordingly.

The altered antiabortion law, and the "instructions" regarding its application, included provisions to punish both physicians and women. In an attempt to secure the obedience of the medical profession, medical practitioners were held responsible for rectifying the birthrate crisis, in part associated with alarming abortion and infant mortality statistics (discussed below). Health practitioners were assumed to assist in illegal abortions for personal gain. They became subject to imprisonment for any infraction of the abortion law, including failure to notify the prosecutor's office. Such notification alerted that office to cases for which doctors could be held responsible. Of course, prosecutors also had wives, sisters, and daughters who might need abortions, and so not all acted in strict accordance with the law. Others were paid off by concerned, and profit-interested, physicians. Given the penal sanctions for doctors, abortion costs were from 2,000 to 10,000 lei (then approximately $160 to $830, with basic salaries ranging between 1,500 and 2,400 lei per month).

Medical personnel were disciplined by various means, depending on their relations with legal authorities, co-workers, immediate superiors, as well as the nature of the legal infraction. Publications such as *Muncitorul Sanitar* (The Health Worker) regularly printed moralizing articles about professional responsibility. (These were similar in form to the articles in women's magazines about good and bad mothers, discussed above. Official rhetoric was disseminated homologously in all realms.) Such articles reported cases that had come before a Disciplinary Board for Health Personnel, which existed in each administrative region of the country. These boards functioned as public, institutionalized confessionals through which medical practitioners were disciplined.

From time to time, there were show trials of doctors, midwives, and backroom-abortion practitioners. In one case, several women were convicted of having performed illegal abortions or of having been involved in arranging them. The abortionist received 500 lei plus a package of coffee and dried soup for her efforts. Her sentence was lessened, however, because of her lack of prior convictions as well as her "sincerity" (cooperation with the police). Generally, those who informed on others were not sent to prison. Their sentences often made it possible for them to remain at work on carefully scrutinized probation. Those who did not cooperate, however, received prison sentences. If they were women, they frequently left children motherless at home—hardly the "ideal conditions" for their upbringing that the Romanian state claimed to have created.

The intrusion of the state into the intimacy of the body was inescapable. In 1986, Ceausescu introduced a campaign—unique in the history of Romanian medicine—to analyze the health of the population, particularly that of women between the ages of sixteen and forty-five, the years when most women are fertile. These exams, regardless of officially professed intentions, subjected women of childbearing age to state control of their reproductive lives. Women working in or attending state institutions were given at least annual, and in some places, trimesterly gynecological exams to verify that their reproductive health was satisfactory.[6] If, in such a routine exam, a woman was discovered to be pregnant, the development of her pregnancy could then be closely followed lest there be any untoward mishap. Women who had already had abortions (legal or not) were carefully watched for "preventive reasons" and, in some cases, were confined to a hospital. For women living in rural areas, local medical personnel were expected to follow up with home visits (a practice resented by all involved).

Much was written in the official press about these exams, and the language of these stories was telling. According to them, the intent of obtaining medical histories about women of childbearing age was to have "in evidence . . . all of the elements that might negatively influence the normal evolution of a pregnancy." While pre- and postnatal care may be commendable under normal circumstances, in the context of a coercive pronatalist policy, such prenatal care served to police the body, with doctors put in the position of aiding and abetting the interests of the state. Women were not always aware that they were deliberately being checked to see whether they were pregnant; annual exams were considered routine, another obligation. One doctor confided that among her staff, some took pleasure in "finding" a pregnant woman. Others, who were more compassionate, did not.

Despite the consequences for nonconformity with the law, many doctors—of all ranks in the party hierarchy (most doctors being party members)—became adept at manipulating both the official rhetoric and statistics. Strikingly, most people I queried offered praise for the attempts doctors made to assist women and families during these harsh years. Many doctors tried to "hide" a woman's pregnancy if she indicated that she, or she and her husband, did not want the child. As one doctor remarked: "If a woman adamantly was against having a child, there was nothing you could do about it. She would risk dying rather than bear the child. So we tried to help." Various ailments such as measles, recurrent fevers, hepatitis, tuberculosis, syphilis, malignant tumors, and diabetes qualified a woman for a legal abortion. Doctors took advantage of this rule as much as possible. Similarly, taking certain medications that are counterindicated during pregnancy (chemotherapy, antimalarial drugs, anticonvulsants) could be used as the excuse for an abortion.

Given the dearth of medications available in Romania, this excuse was not easily manufactured. Nonetheless, whenever possible, most doctors seem to have done what they could to accommodate a woman's "choice."

According to a document stamped *secret de serviciu* that circulated internally in the health ministry in 1988, the number of abortions increased between 1979 and 1988, with the exception of a decline in 1948–85 (Roznatovschi 1989). A similar drop in abortion rates occurred following the original 1966 antiabortion law. Citizens needed time to learn to adapt to the intensified pronatalist campaign. The increase in abortions coincided with the previously mentioned deterioration in the conditions of everyday life. Families were unable to feed the children they had, yet were required by law to have more.

In many cases, unwanted children were abandoned to the care of the paternalist state that had demanded them. That "care," best described as systematic neglect, resulted in institutionalization of the innocent, the rise of infant AIDS, and international trafficking in babies and children through adoption. Abandoning a child was the consequence of despair combined with dependence on the state for the basics of life. Centralized production and distribution limited what families had to eat. (The rise of the second economy paralleled that of illegal abortions; these were the means through which people managed their everyday lives.) These material and psychological conditions make it possible to understand why parents gave up their children. Traditionally, peasant families unable to support another child would ask a relative to raise one; others were adopted by childless couples. During the Ceausescu years, some mothers left their infants in the hospital; others left them at orphanages or in other places where they were likely to be found. (I have not heard of infanticide as a common practice, although punitive statutes exist in the legal code—for example, Article 177.) Some parents relied upon state institutions as a temporary residence for children; they then attempted to retrieve them later when they were able to support them at home. This "pawn-shop" strategy often succeeded; in other cases, parents were unable to locate the children they had given up. Only after the fall of the regime did they—and the rest of the world—learn why: institutionalized children often died of neglect or were put up for adoption.

Women who did not comply with the pronatalist law resorted to illegal abortions. Those privileged with connections and the means could bribe medical practitioners. Those without sought the assistance of less-qualified abortionists or used the varied remedies that abortion lore and popular practice offered them. When the state punished physicians who for humanistic or economic reasons performed illegal abortions, the increase in maternal deaths or deformities due to nonmedically performed abortions was assured. Between 1965 and 1989, 9,452 women died because of complications arising from illegal abortions. As Mezei notes: "The liberation of abortion in January 1990 proves yet again the positive dependent relation between delegalization of abortion and the rise of maternal mortality rates. If, following the chronology of events, 1989 represents the year with the most elevated maternal mortality figures [545] . . . for 1990, 181 cases of maternal deaths due to illegal abortions were registered, [numbers] that had not been seen since 1968" (1991: 4).

Among those who died were women who already had three or four children but who were unable to deal with yet another cold, hungry child. Thus, the population of orphaned or abandoned children necessarily increased.[7] So great were the traumas associated with the pronatalist policies that months after the legalization of abortion, the Ministry of Health still received files of mothers who had died as a result of illegal abortions; some of these were mothers of five children who would have been eligible for legal abortions even during the Ceausescu regime.

The heartbreaking and chilling irony of Ceausescu's pronatalist policies was that illegal abortion became the predominant contraceptive method. According to Ministry of Health statistics, the greatest number of abortions—60.1 percent—were "incomplete abortions" recorded upon the arrival of a woman at the hospital for emergency treatment.[8] The decision to abort (made by the woman alone or with her husband's consent) was a rational decision based on the real conditions of daily life. Insensitive to the realities of the lives of most Romanian citizens, the regime clung to its ideological visions of everyday productive—and reproductive—life. A stringent pronatalist policy was enforced through a series of coercive legal measures even as data on the rise of infant AIDS were suppressed and as the recording of births was delayed so that infant-mortality rates would not appear too large. The consequences of legislating reproduction without regard for the material conditions of daily life meant that many women, unable to fulfill their "patriotic duties" and "noble mission" in life, gave up their lives—and, frequently, those of their children—in the service of the state.

## POST-CEAUSESCU ABORTION AND INTERNATIONAL ADOPTION

The "revolution" of December 1989 liberated most women's bodies from the grip of the centralized state. The day after the execution of Ceausescu, abortion became fully legal in Romania. Legalization simultaneously kept abortion the preferred method of fertility control, other means being generally unavailable.[9] Urban and rural women alike expressed gratitude for the legalization of abortion. The fear of becoming pregnant had dramatically colored the sexual lives of women (especially), married or not. This fear compounded the basic culture of fear that had pervaded everyday life. The right to abortion granted women in Romania basic, if minimal, control over their lives again. Abortion, in this context, was understood as a fundamental aspect of the right to self-determination being articulated by republics and nationalities demanding their independence, as well as by ethnic groups clamoring for recognition and respect. Abortion was assumed to be an essential ingredient of democratic practice.

As a consequence of legalization, by the summer of 1990, the principal hospitals in Bucharest were each reporting 70 to 100 abortions daily. This rate seemed potentially problematic for women's health and future demographic trends. However, health officials and physicians (personal communications) pointed out that the legalization of abortion had quickly alleviated one of the problems from the past; they also suggested that there were more urgent concerns than these given that the country was in total disorder. In addition to finding ways to finance the development and distribution of contraceptives, the country desperately needed funds for AIDS research, treatment, and education.

By summer 1991, the skyrocketing number of abortions made attention to this issue imperative. The ratio of abortions to live births was reported at 3 to 1. (At the same time, the marked decrease in maternal mortality recorded for 1990 continued. The birthrate also declined.)[10] Doctors at one of the largest maternity wards in Bucharest stated that they had performed as many as three abortions for the same woman during the course of the year. In response, the government began to address the need for family planning and sex education. Several nongovernmental associations (NGOs) established soon after 1989 had already become active, although with limited means. NGOs hoped to maintain their politically independent identities. However, in the heightened political atmosphere in Romania, doing so has not been easy. One of the primary tasks for health workers is to educate the population. Because television remains essentially state-controlled, and the majority of newspapers have political agendas, access to and use of the mass media for education is fraught with problems that have subordinated health issues to political struggles. NGO workers have expressed concern that governmental institutions will coopt their efforts. At present, both governmental and nongovernmental organizations depend on international assistance, financial and instructional. As many of the doctors with whom I spoke noted, it is difficult for them to train specialists in family planning when they themselves are not trained. Obviously, in view of the former policies, physicians and others lacked access to such training.

Furthermore, years of propaganda against the use of contraceptives must be combatted. Thus far, the Ministry of Education—unlike the Ministry of Health—has not been overly receptive to governmental or nongovernmental proposals to introduce health and sex education into the high school curriculum. There has been more interest at the university level. The state-controlled media have also been reticent to engage in discussion of these issues, which are vital to the nation's health.

A similar mentality exists toward AIDS: ignore or downplay its importance. Some Romanian physicians insisted that AIDS was not a real problem in their country, claiming that the epidemic among children who received transfusions was contained within that population. By 1992, 1,557 cases of AIDS had been recorded. AIDS is likely to be on the rise because of poor hygiene in hospitals, increased drug traffic and usage, and increased prostitution without "safe sex" practices. Married women with children often become prostitutes with the full consent of their husbands so that they can obtain hard currency and increase household cash flow. One doctor interviewed who was concerned about the state of public health in Romania pointed out: "Here, people do not have respect for their own bodies." He attributed much of this attitude to the destructive effects of the former regime.

Without a concerted campaign to educate the population (including medical practitioners) about reproductive health, some physicians fear that women's health, in particular, will continue to be at risk. Most of the women factory workers I interviewed informally in 1990 mentioned often that their husbands would object to the use of contraceptives even if they were more readily available. In addition, although condoms are obtainable from tobacco shops, in general birth control devices and pills have to be obtained from pharmacies, hospital clinics, and some private medical practitioners. As several young gynecologists remarked, "People associate hospitals with illness. They will not come to the hospital to get contraceptives. It's impractical!" (This attitude also points to the problems of the medicalization of family planning. See Hord et al. 1991: 237–38.) Thus, for the immediate future, abortion will remain the primary method. Women of all ages wait in endless lines for abortions performed in factory-like conditions.

In an attempt to discourage women from having abortions, the hospital price was raised from 30 to 500 lei (500 lei was equivalent to about $2.50 in the summer of 1991). Obstetrician-gynecologists expressed concern that raising the price would encourage poor women to seek cheaper abortions done by nonmedically qualified persons, thereby repeating the problems of the past. Well-to-do women were already going to doctors in private practice, where prices are significantly higher, in exchange for privacy, personal attention, and more sterile conditions. At the same time, these physicians emphasized that the current situation has to be changed; raising the price of an abortion, increasing contraceptive availability, and introducing a multifaceted educational campaign were all considered necessary. Unfortunately, it is easier to adjust prices upward than to introduce family planning and sex education or to assure the production and distribution of contraceptives. Thus, women's health, especially among the poor and less educated, remains particularly vulnerable.

The vulnerability of women and children also emerged in another context that is only partially the direct result of Ceausescu's pronatalist policies: the international adoption of Romanian children.[11] During the later years of the regime, Ceausescu authorized limited foreign adoption of Romanian babies for hard currency. This little-publicized practice was a facet of the "commerce in human flesh" that usually enabled Jews and Germans to be "bought" out of Romania. (Hungarians wanting to emigrate to Hungary were not so fortunate, the *forint* not having been convertible to hard currency.) Children began to figure among Romania's export goods, in direct contradiction to the stated ideological goals of the pronatalist policies.

When the regime fell, and the plight of Romania's orphans surfaced, international humanitarian groups moved in to help. Many institutions and individuals contributed greatly to alleviating the pain of these children.[12] As it became known that not all of the children incarcerated in orphanages were "irrecoverable" or were the victims of the infant AIDS epidemic, foreigners journeyed to Romania with hopes of adopting children.

As word spread in the international community of persons wanting to adopt, Romania became the adoption hot spot. In early 1990, to deal with the growing number of adoptions, the Romanian government formed the National Adoption Commission. Among its tasks was coordination of data about available institutionalized children. However, lack of an adequate staff or a computerized information system led to bureaucratic inefficiency. Inadvertently, rather than facilitate the adoption process, creation of the commission encouraged expansion of the private market in adoptions, or "baby trading."

Gradually, as different channels for adoption developed, the emotional rhetoric about the humanitarian rescue of children from abysmal conditions in the orphanages lost its force. In its stead, a more generalized rhetoric emerged about saving children from the difficult living conditions in Romania and giving them the opportunity for a better life in the West. By July 1991 most children no longer came from the orphanages but were acquired through private connections, a fact usually overlooked in the numerous media accounts about the baby trade in Romania. According to U.S. consular representatives, most of these children were Gypsies, or Roma. Though they are notably dark-skinned by Romanian standards, Westerners do not generally consider them markedly different in appearance.[13] Given that prejudice against the Gypsies in Romania is unlikely to be eliminated in the near future, adoption was thought to provide a humanitarian road out for some of these children, whose chances for productive lives would otherwise be slim. Many Romanians viewed the exodus of adopted Gypsy children as a legitimate means to rid the country of them at the expense of foreigners; there are others who resented the squandering of Western altruism and resources on Gypsies.

For Westerners, opting for the private adoption process was faster than going through official bureaucratic procedures; it was also more expensive, arbitrary, and led to coercion and corruption. The victims of this process were not only, as is often implied in Western media coverage, foreign adoptive parents but rather poor or single (or both) Romanian mothers, many of whom were Gypsies. Some poor women considered their bearing of children to be little more than the means of production that yielded a valuable commodity. In these cases, private adoptions contributed to the exploitation of women's reproductive labor. Husbands, brothers, and parents found compensation for their "public shame" in the money so readily obtained. With it, they purchased refrigerators, video recorders, and the like, or finished building or furnishing their homes. Given the sharp rise in prices in Romania, increasing unemployment, and depressed wages, it is not difficult to explain why people were tempted to sell their own children, as well as those of other people. Dealing in babies is also a lucrative business for intermediaries, bureaucrats, and lawyers who may be bribed to falsify papers and speed up the process.

Hence, for all of the legitimate adoptions, there were many that were not legitimate. Coercion of Romanian mothers happened in various ways. By law, a mother had fifteen days in which to change her mind about consenting to the adoption of her child. When a mother had a change of heart (or conscience), her decision was not necessarily accepted graciously by the adoptive parents or their negotiators, regardless of the law. One Romanian woman was told by the translator that she would be responsible for the costs accrued during the stay of the American adoptive parents (personal communication from an official investigator of this case). No Romanian could conceivably have covered such expenses. Whether the Americans knew of the translator's methods is not known. That the translator had much to lose if the adoption fell through *is* known, as is the fact that the American woman intended to appeal to her Congressman. Most adoptive parents in such situations chose not to know about possible coercion, even though they may have intuited that something was amiss. Because of the language barrier, lack of knowledge was easy to rationalize. To have allowed themselves to know meant that they would have had to deal with their own emotional pain at the loss of a child with whom they might already have bonded. It was (and is) easier to believe, whatever the temporary experience, that adoption was simply for the good of the child, who would thereby escape from the hardships of Romania.

Since the fall of the Ceausescu regime, the Romanian government has embraced measures that suggest at least a minimal recognition of the fundamental significance of respecting citizens' rights. To be sure, these measures have been noticeably inadequate, particularly in the realm of ethnic rights. Nonetheless, in the midst of traumatic change, there has been some movement to redress certain of the dehumanizing policies of the past. Hence, the legalization of abortion in 1990 may be considered a necessary response to a dramatic situation fostered by the stringent political-demographic policies. At the same time, the legalization of abortion was not a policy decision made with socioeconomic and demographic aims, or long-term trends, in mind. The formation of the National Adoption Commission was similarly a practical response to circumstances—in this case, to the growing number of foreign adoptive parents. While the institutionalization of adoption procedures at that time may have been well-intentioned, it was not carefully planned, and it inadvertently contributed to the expansion of the private adoption market. Indeed, the systemic and societal confusion generated by the fall of the Ceausescu regime did not initially lead to effective policy formulation in the realm of family-related issues. This first phase of policy formulation was, in actuality, characterized by the lack of effective policy formulation and implementation.

On July 16, 1991, President Ion Iliescu signed a new adoption law meant to stop the Romanian baby trade; adoption would henceforth be done through institutional channels, thereby removing the private profit motives of all involved.[14] Among the law's provisions is the necessary institutionalization of orphaned children. This provision is meant to prevent the sale of children and to determine the legal status of children as orphans. (Children must be orphaned or abandoned; if they are under the care of a parent, then they are not legally adoptable.) Children must reside in an orphanage for six months, during which time the natal parents may change their minds or, if possible, adoptive parents may be found among Romanian citizens.[15] Only after that are foreigners legally able to adopt Romanian children.

The adoption law should be applauded for its attempt to apply the rule of law operative elsewhere in Europe. The politics of reproduction in Romania are now different from the situation in the Ceausescu period. Under Ceausescu's rule, the masses were forced to reproduce in the service of the state. Women's reproductive lives and human rights were blatantly exploited. Today, as Romania struggles with the "transition" and as Romanian society becomes more clearly class-differentiated, those who were most vulnerable—poor and single women—have often been forced to reproduce in the service of market demands. The adoption law has helped to diminish one source of abuse suffered by those women coerced into giving up their children.[16]

Moreover, this law was an important step toward the recognition and protection of citizens' rights, especially those of women and children. The political-demographic policies of the Ceausescu regime contributed significantly to the social atomization and dehumanization that remain a tragic legacy. Women's bodies were glorified as the machines that produced the future workers of the state. Celebrated in public political rhetoric, women were overwhelmed by the exigencies of daily life. Their identities as workers and mothers were ideologically dictated, but the conditions of everyday life did not make such identities attractive. The institutionalized violence of the state against its citizens resulted in the denial of women's rights in particular. The state's violence against its citizens was bolstered by a web of interdependent practices that engaged most people in the prescribed practices of the state: doctors were expected to perform gynecological exams; adults without children were taxed; those who had had an abortion were manipulated into becoming police informants. Men's and women's sexual relations were intimately affected, at great psychological cost to the population. Fertility control was proclaimed to be the right of the state, not of women or families. The loss of life (for women and children) due to illegal abortions was evidence of societal despair and increasing dehumanization. The abandonment of children to the "care" of the paternalist state's orphanages was yet another indicator of the extremely deteriorated conditions that made the upbringing of children next to impossible for most citizens of Romania.

By 1991, life in Romania had gradually acquired more routine; the government began to function somewhat more smoothly. The Ministries of Health, Labor, and Education—which were important for the concerns addressed here: reproduction, health, and welfare—each turned to the details of restructuring; what may be viewed as the second phase of policymaking began. Foreign agencies and individuals continued to offer needed and welcome assistance, particularly with respect to scientific exchange about AIDS (testing, research, education) and problems related to the orphanages. Diverse specialists came to train Romanians to care for the handicapped and to teach Romanian health professionals about family planning. All these efforts, combined with passage of the adoption law, have pointed to a recognition that the state must participate responsibly in the protection of its citizens' rights and well-being. To what extent it shall do so remains to be seen.

## IMPLICATIONS FOR REPRODUCTIVE POLICY

Romania's experience in the realm of reproductive health can guide policymakers, health administrators, and reproductive-health professionals throughout the world. "At a time when reproductive rights are increasingly threatened by conservative forces throughout central and eastern Europe and other parts of the world, the tragic elements of Romania's reproductive health experience under Ceausescu and the country's struggle to reverse that grim legacy can serve as a guide for health care professionals everywhere" (Hord et al. 1991: 238–39).

Restrictive reproductive legislation is on the agenda throughout Eastern Europe, with the notable—and understandable—exception of Romania. Similar legislation is being considered and contested in the United States, as well as elsewhere. Here, I wish to stress that the Romanian case must not be categorized as specific to the evils of the Ceausescu regime or of communism. This study enables us to focus on the social implications and human costs of restrictive reproductive legislation and policies, especially as they affect the lives of women and children.

The effects of banning abortion transcend political or religious interests. When abortion is criminalized, women resort to illegal abortions; that is a comparative as well as historical fact. Banning abortions does not stop women from having them; it simply makes abortion "invisible." Prohibiting abortion—as has always been the case—forces abortion underground and makes it the privilege of the wealthy, while further disenfranchising poor women, who generally bear the brunt of such policies. For poor women, illegal abortions are typically done by unqualified practitioners—the woman herself, backroom abortionists—and result in increased maternal deaths as well as maternal and fetal physical deformities. In Romania, the masses were poor. The tragic consequences have been detailed above.

Again, these consequences are specific neither to communism nor to Ceausescuism. Indeed, these consequences suggest that the Romanian case must be borne in mind by those who would ban abortion in the United States. If, as James Madison understood, a test of democracy lies in its treatment of society's most vulnerable members, among whom are women and children, then democracy in the late twentieth-century United States (and elsewhere) may fail.

## NOTES

This chapter is drawn from a final grant report (Kligman 1992c) submitted to the National Council for Soviet and East European Studies, which supported the final phase of a field research project. Additional funding was granted by the American Council of Learned Societies, the International Research and Exchanges Board, and the Rockefeller Foundation. Kligman (1992a) is based on the final section of the grant report and this chapter; Kligman (1992b) is an almost complete version of the grant report. Because of space constraints, notes have been kept to a minimum. For references and commentary, refer to the above-mentioned works.

1. These allowances were adjusted according to income level, number of children, and place of residence (urban or rural). They were lower in rural areas, the rationale being that rural families were able to provide some of their food from their personal plots, although these same citizens were required to provide "barter" to receive their ration cards for staples. Rural payments were erratic. As was typical, this system functioned well only in theory.

2. Ceausescu's consolidation of power involved securing key loyalties through appointment of extended-family members. Thus, his version of communist rule was variously described as *socialism in one family* or *dynastic socialism*. See, for example, Tismaneanu (1986). That so many members of the extended family were in key positions was captured in the play on the acronym for the Romanian Communist Party: PCR. Popularly, this also meant Petrescu (Elena Ceausescu's natal family), Ceausescu, and Rudele ("relatives"). Other plays on PCR underscore the importance of personal relations and influence in this regime.

3. Contraceptives were not forbidden by law; however, they were unavailable and thus could be obtained only through illegal, black-market connections. Abortion was illegal. The distinction is worth noting.

4. According to a study prepared by the Ministry of Health in 1986, the number of live births varied by nationality. For Romanian women, the median was 1.93 children; for Hungarians, 1.73; for Germans, 1.6; and for others, 2.56. The lower German birthrate is probably due to the older population of Germans; as conditions worsened under Ceausescu, many younger Germans with relatives abroad emigrated.

5. Mesaros (1990: 29). Dr. E. Mesaros was a member of the National Commission on Demography until 1985, when he resigned. The cited article was dated October 3, 1974. The distinction between a social and a national problem was meant partially to signal the class distinctions operative in reproductive behavior. The Gypsy birthrate was considered troublesome because of their low levels of education and presumed high degree of participation in delinquent behavior.

6. The Western press did exaggerate the extent and frequency of these exams. I could not obtain any verification from women that they had been subjected to the much-heralded monthly exams. The exams were ordered; how they were done is quite another matter. The Western press had little justification for sensationalism.

7. For 1989, the number of children left orphaned because of illegal abortions was reported to be 1,193; between 1981 and 1989, 8,004 children were orphaned as a consequence of illegal abortions. See Mezei (1991: 8).

8. These numbers do not include women who died from complications prior to arrival at a hospital. In 1989 at one of Bucharest's largest maternity clinics, 3,129 women were hospitalized for complications associated with illegally performed abortions. Of these 26.6 percent needed intensive treatment for raging infections, 3.9 percent had hysterectomies, and 1.1 percent died (See Mezei 1991). The second highest number of abortions were among women who had five or more children and had at least five in their care (22.8 percent), followed by those with legal medical reasons (16.6 percent) and those who were of legal age (0.5 percent forty-five years or older). See Roznatovschi (1989).

9. While international contributions of contraceptives began to pour into Romania in response to this tragic situation, problems associated with distribution and lack of contraceptive education meant that perceptions and behavior did not change significantly, even though Romanians were tired of "natural" methods and their uncertainty.

10. The maternal mortality figures for 1990 were 83 deaths per 100,000 live births, with maternal deaths from abortion decreasing to 69 percent of 249 maternal cases as compared with 87 percent of 588 maternal deaths attributable to abortions in 1989. Reported in Hord et al. (1991: 234).

11. It is beyond the scope of this chapter to discuss fully the adoption of Romanian children or the situation of children in Romanian orphanages. Refer to my grant report (Kligman 1992c) as well as to Kligman (1992b) for fuller discussions and references.

12. By the summer of 1992, almost all orphanages had a foreign agency (governmental or nongovernmental) working collaboratively with them.

13. Anti-Roma sentiment is widespread in Europe and, since 1989, has led to violence. Romania was the first of several countries with which Germany concluded agreements to deport illegal immigrants, among whom are many Roma.

14. Some Romanians accused the government of wanting to rob ordinary people of one of the few means by which

they could make money so that the government might profit instead. Some foreigners criticized the government for preventing them from taking Romanian children to a better life. In an update to a guide written by a woman who had adopted two Romanian children, the author summarized the consequences of the new law. (See Delvecchio 1991.) Her letter closed with: "God Bless You in your efforts to rescue a little one."

The new adoption law modified Law no. 11 signed in 1990. Another law, no. 47/1933, specifies the terms by which a court may declare a child legally abandoned. The adoption of Romanian children has been a prickly issue between the United States and Romania, and has been manipulated on both sides.

15. Infertility has reportedly been on the rise in Romania as a consequence of pollution, malnutrition, and deteriorated conditions. The preferential treatment accorded Romanian citizens in adopting Romanian orphans is meant to eliminate the demographic problems posed by a declining birthrate as well as the problems that may accompany intercultural adoptions as the children grow older.

16. Virtually no public attention is given to the physical abuse of women. Here, the government and its agencies, including research institutes that might well address such issues, are sorely negligent.

## REFERENCES

*Anuarul statistic al Romaniei.* 1990. Bucharest: Comisia Nationala Pentru Statistica.

*Decisions of the Plenary Session of the Central Committee of the Romanian Communist Party, July 18–19, 1973, with Attention to the Growth of the Role of Women in the Economic, Political, and Social Life of the Country.* 1973. Bucharest: Editura Politica.

Delvecchio, A.-M. 1991. "How to Adopt From Romania: A Comprehensive Step-by-Step Guide." Sebastopol, Calif.: Hearthstone Publishers.

Hord, C., H. P. David, F. Donnayi, and M. Wolf. 1991. "Reproductive Health in Romania: Reversing the Ceausescu Legacy." *Studies in Family Planning* 22(4): 231–40.

Kligman, G. 1988. *The Wedding of the Dead: Ritual, Poetics, and Popular Culture in Transylvania.* Berkeley: University of California Press.

_____. 1992a. "Abortion and International Adoption in Post-Ceausescu Romania." *Feminist Studies* 18(2): 405–20.

_____. 1992b. "The Politics of Reproduction in Ceausescu's Romania: A Case Study in Political Culture." *East European Politics and Society* 6(3): 364–418.

_____. 1992c. *When Abortion Is Banned: The Politics of Reproduction in Ceausescu's Romania.* Washington, D.C.: National Council for Soviet and East European Studies.

Liciu, V. 1975. *Pregatirea pedagogica a adolescentiilor pentru viata de familie: Cu privire speciala asupra educatiei afectivitatii si sexualitatii.* Bucharest: Editura didactica si Pedagogica.

Mesaros, E. 1990. "Consideratii asupra politicii demografice a Romaniei." *Alternative 90* 1(4): 29.

Mezei, S. 1991. "Une analyse démo-sociologique des consequences de la politique démographique roumaine." Unpublished manuscript.

Roznatovschi, L. 1989. *Aspecte ale intreruperilor de sarcina in R. S. Romania 1988.* Bucharest: Centrul de Calcul si Statistica Sanitara, Ministerul Sanatatii.

Teitelbaum, M., and J. Winter. 1985. *The Fear of Population Decline.* New York: Academic Press.

Tismaneanu, V. 1986. "Byzantine Rites, Stalinist Follies: The Twilight of Dynastic Socialism in Romania." *Orbis* (spring): 65–91.

Trebici. 1988. "Demografie intre stiinta si actiune sociala." *Viitorul Social* 81(1): 69–78.

# *Surrogate Motherhood:* Rethinking Biological Models, Kinship, and Family

*Heléna Ragoné*

In the wake of publicity created by the Baby M Case,[1] it seems unlikely that anyone in the United States can have remained unfamiliar with surrogate motherhood or can have failed to form an opinion. The Baby M Case raised, and ultimately left unanswered, many questions about what constitutes motherhood, fatherhood, family, reproduction, and kinship. When I began my field research in 1987, surrogate mother programs and directors had already become the subject of considerable media attention, a great deal of it sensationalized and negative in character. Much of what has been written about surrogate motherhood, has, however, been largely speculative or polemic in nature. Opinions have ranged from the view that surrogate motherhood is symptomatic of the dissolution

Original material prepared for this text. Reprinted by permission of the author.

of the American family[2] and the sanctity of motherhood, to charges that it reduces or assigns women to a breeder class structurally akin to prostitution (Dworkin 1978), or that it constitutes a form of commercial baby selling (Annas 1988; Neuhaus 1988).

Data for this chapter derive from nine years of ongoing ethnographic research. Twenty-eight formal interviews with traditional surrogates and twenty-six with gestational surrogates were conducted, as well as twenty-six interviews with individual members of couples (i.e., individuals who had enlisted the services of traditional as well as gestational surrogates) and five interviews with ovum donors. Aside from these formal interviews I also engaged in countless conversations with surrogates, observing them as they interacted with their families, testified before legislative committees, worked in surrogate programs, and socialized at program gatherings with directors and others. The opportunity to observe the daily workings of the surrogate mother programs provided me with invaluable data on the day-to-day operations of such programs. I attended the staff meetings of one such program on a regular basis and observed the consultations in which prospective couples and surrogates were interviewed singly by such members of the staff as the director, a psychologist, a medical coordinator, or the administrative coordinator.

In addition to these formal interviews I conducted thousands of hours of participant observation and was able to observe numerous consultations between program staff, intending couples, and prospective surrogate mothers. I have attempted, whenever possible, to select individuals from the various phases of the traditional and gestational surrogacy process: those individuals who have not yet been matched, those who are newly matched and are attempting "to get pregnant," those who have confirmed pregnancies, and those who have recently given birth, as well as those for whom several years have elapsed since the birth of their child. My decision to interview individuals in all stages of the process has been motivated by my wish to assess what, if any, shifts individuals might experience as they go through the process.

Historically there have been three profound shifts in the Western conceptualization of the categories of conception, reproduction, and parenthood. The first occurred in response to the separation of intercourse from reproduction through birth control methods (Snowden et al. 1983), a precedent that may have paved the way for surrogate motherhood in the 1980s (Andrews 1984: xiii). A second shift occurred in response to the emergence of assisted reproductive technologies (ARTs) and to the subsequent fragmentation of the unity of reproduction, when it became possible for pregnancy to occur without necessarily having

been "preceded by sexual intercourse" (Snowden et al. 1983: 5). The third shift occurred in response to further advances in reproductive medicine that called into question the "organic unity of fetus and mother" (Martin 1987: 20). It was not, however, until the emergence of reproductive medicine that the fragmentation of motherhood became a reality; with that historical change what was once the "single figure of the mother is dispersed among several potential figures, as the functions of maternal procreation—aspects of her physical parenthood—become dispersed" (Strathern 1991: 32).

## TRADITIONAL SURROGACY

There are two types of surrogate mother programs: "open" programs, in which surrogate and couple select one another and interact throughout the insemination and the pregnancy, and "closed" programs, in which couples select their surrogates from biographical and medical information and a photograph of the surrogate is provided to them by programs. After the child is born in a "closed" program, the couple and surrogate meet only to finalize the step-parent adoption. Due to advances in reproductive medicine and to consumer demand, there are now also two types of surrogacy: traditional surrogacy in which the surrogate contributes an ovum to the creation of the child, and gestational or in-vitro fertilization (IVF) surrogacy where the surrogate gestates the couple's embryos.

Studies of the surrogate population tend to focus, at times exclusively, on surrogates' stated motivations for becoming surrogate mothers (Parker 1983). Their stated reasons include the desire to help an infertile couple start a family, financial remuneration, and a love of pregnancy (Parker 1983: 140). Soon after I began my own research, I observed a remarkable degree of consistency or uniformity in surrogates' responses to questions about their initial motivations for becoming surrogates. It was as if they had all been given a script in which they espoused many of the motivations earlier catalogued by Parker: motivations that also, as I will show, reflect culturally accepted ideas about reproduction, motherhood, and family.

I also began to uncover several areas of conflict between professed motivations and actual experiences, discovering, for example, that although surrogates claim to experience "easy pregnancies" and "problem-free labor," it was not unusual for surrogates to have experienced miscarriages, ectopic pregnancies, and related difficulties. For example, Jeannie, age 36, divorced with one child, described the ectopic pregnancy she experienced while she was a traditional surrogate in this manner: "*I almost bled to death: I literally almost died for my couple.*" Nevertheless, she was again inseminated a second time for the same couple. As this and other cases demonstrate, even when their experiences are at odds with their stated motivations, surrogates tend not to acknowledge inconsistencies between their initially stated motivations and their subsequent experiences. This reformulation of motivations can be seen in the following instance. Fran, age 27, divorced with one child, described the difficulty of her delivery in this way: "*I had a rough delivery, a C-section, and my lung collapsed because I had the flu but it was worth every minute of it. If I were to die from childbirth, that's the best way to die. You died for a cause, a good one.*" As both these examples illustrate, some surrogates readily embrace the idea of meaningful suffering, heroism, or sacrifice, and although their stated motivations are of some interest they do not adequately account for the range of shifting motivations uncovered in my research.

One of the motivations most frequently assumed to be primary by the casual observer is remuneration and I took considerable pains in trying to evaluate the influence of monetary rewards on surrogates. In all programs, surrogates receive between $10,000 and $15,000 (for three to four months of insemination and nine months of pregnancy, on average), a fee that has changed only nominally since the early 1980s. As one program psychologist explained, the amount paid to surrogates is intentionally held at an artificially low rate so as to screen out women who might be motivated by monetary gain alone. One of the questions I sought to explore was whether surrogates were denying the significance of remuneration in order to cast their actions in the more culturally acceptable light of pure altruism, or whether they were motivated, at least in part, by remuneration and in part by other factors with the importance of remuneration decreasing as the pregnancy progressed, the version of events put forth by both program staff and surrogates.

The opinion popular among both scholars and the general population, that surrogates are motivated primarily by financial gain, has tended to result in oversimplified analyses of surrogate motivations. More typical of surrogate explanations for the connection between the initial decision to become a surrogate and the remuneration received are comments such as those expressed by Fran. "*It [surrogacy] sounded so interesting and fun. The money wasn't enough to be pregnant for nine months.*" Andrea, age 29, who was married with three children, said "*I'm not doing it for the money. Take the money: that wouldn't stop me. It wouldn't stop the majority.*" Sarah, age 27, who attended two years of college, and was married with two children, explained her feelings about remuneration in the following way: "*What's $10,000 bucks? You can't even buy a car. If it was just for the money you will want the baby. Money wasn't important.*"

*I possibly would have done it for expenses, especially for the people I did it for. My father would have given me the money not to do it.*"

The issue of remuneration proved to be of particular interest in that, although surrogates do accept monetary compensation for their reproductive work, its role is a multifaceted one. The surrogate pregnancy, unlike a traditional pregnancy, is viewed by the surrogate and her family as work; as such, it is informed by the belief that work is something that occurs only within the context of a paid occupation (Ferree 1984: 72). It is interesting to note that surrogates rarely spend the money they earn on themselves. The majority of surrogates I interviewed spent their earnings on home improvement, gifts for their husbands, a family vacation, or simply to pay off "family debts."

One of the primary reasons that most surrogates do not spend the money they earn on themselves alone appears to stem from the fact that the money serves as a buffer against and/or reward to their own families, particularly to their husbands who must make a number of compromises as a result of the surrogate arrangement. One of these compromises is obligatory abstention from sexual intercourse with their wives from the time insemination takes place until a pregnancy has been confirmed (a period that lasts on average from three to four months in length, but that may be extended for as long as one year).

The devaluation of the amount of the surrogate payment by the surrogates themselves as insufficient to compensate for "nine months of pregnancy" serves several important purposes. First, this view is representative of the cultural belief that children are "priceless" (Zelizer 1985); in this sense surrogates are merely reiterating a widely held cultural belief when they devalue the amount of remuneration they receive. For example, when the largest and one of the most well-established surrogate mother programs changed the wording of its advertising copy from "Help an Infertile Couple" to "Give the Gift of Life," the vastly increased volume of response revealed that the program had discovered a successful formula with which to reach the surrogate population. With surrogacy, the gift is conceptualized as a child, a formulation that is widely used in Euro-American culture—for example, in blood donation (Titmuss 1971) and organ donation (Fox and Swazey 1992).

The gift formulation holds particular appeal for surrogates because it reinforces the idea that having a child for someone is an act for which one cannot be compensated. As I have already mentioned, the gift of life narrative is further enhanced by some surrogates to include the near-sacrifice of their own lives in childbirth (Ragoné 1996, 1999). Fran, whose dismissal of the importance of payment I have already quoted, also offered another, even more revealing account of her decision to become a surrogate mother: "*I wanted to do the ultimate thing for somebody, to give them the ultimate gift. Nobody can beat that, nobody can do anything nicer for them.*" Stella, age 38, married with two children, noted that the commissioning couples "*consider it [the baby] a gift and I consider it a gift.*" Carolyn, age 33, married with two children, discussed her feelings about remuneration and having a surrogate child in these terms: "*It's a gift of love. I have always been a really giving person, and it's the ultimate way to give. I've always had babies so easily. It's the ultimate gift of love.*" For Euro-Americans it is "gift relations" rather than economic exchanges that characterize the family (Carrier 1990: 2). Thus, when surrogates minimize or dismiss the importance of money, they are on the one hand reiterating cultural beliefs about the pricelessness of children, and they are on the other hand suggesting that the exchange of a child for money is not a relationship of reciprocity but of kinship.

Once a surrogate enters a program, she also begins to recognize just how important having a child is to the commissioning couple. She sees with renewed clarity that no matter how much material success the couple has, their lives are emotionally impoverished because of their inability to have a child. In this way the surrogate's fertility serves as a leveling device for perceived, if unacknowledged, economic differences, and many surrogates begin to see themselves as altruistic or heroic figures who can rectify the imbalance in a couple's life. The surrogate's sense of place and her social network are greatly enlarged as she receives telephone calls from the program, rushes to keep doctor's appointments, meets with prospective couples (she may even be flown to other cities to meet couples), and later on attends (in the open programs) monthly or semimonthly surrogate support-group meetings. In some programs she may attend individual therapy sessions. She is often taken out socially by her couple, she may receive gifts from them for herself and her children, be telephoned regularly by them or receive cards and letters from them, and she attends holiday parties and other social events hosted by the program. Her sense of importance is also enhanced when she tells others about her new and unusual work. Once a surrogate meets, selects, and is selected by her couple and begins insemination—another rite of passage that confers additional status upon her—the couple becomes central to her life, adding an important steady source of social interaction and stimulation.

The entire surrogate experience serves to alter the balance of power in the surrogate's personal life, giving her entrée to a more public role and creating new and exciting demands upon her time. From the moment she places a telephone call to a surrogate mother program to the moment she delivers a child, the balance of power in a surrogate's personal life is altered radically. Her time can no longer be devoted exclusively to the care and nurture of her own family because she has entered into a legal and social contract to perform an important and economically rewarded task: helping an infertile couple to begin a family of their own. Unlike other types of employment, this activity cannot be regarded as unfeminine, selfish, or nonnurturant.

In this sense, we can see how surrogacy assists surrogates in their efforts to transcend the limitations of their domestic roles by highlighting "their differences from men . . . [b]y accepting and elaborating upon the symbols and expectations associated with their cultural definition" (Rosaldo 1974: 37), for example, motherhood. The gravity of the task provides the surrogate with an opportunity to do more than care for her family alone, and surrogates often report feeling that they are undertaking a task laden with importance, a project that fills them with a sense of pride and self-worth. Sally, age 33, married with two children and a full-time homemaker, discussed how surrogacy provided her with a feeling of unique accomplishment: "*Not everyone can do it. It's like the steelworkers who walk on beams ten floors up; not everyone can do it, not everyone can be a surrogate.*"

## GESTATIONAL SURROGATES

From 1987 to 1993, over 95 percent of all surrogacy arrangements were traditional. As of 1994, a profound shift occurred with 50 percent of all surrogacy arrangements gestational and as of 1999 that percentage continues to increase at the largest surrogate mother program (which is also the largest ovum donation program). With the advent of gestational surrogacy, however, reproduction is not only separated from sexual intercourse and motherhood but from pregnancy as well. In addition, gestational surrogacy creates three discernible categories of motherhood where there was previously only one: (1) the biological mother, the woman who contributes the ovum (traditionally assumed to be the "real mother"); (2) the gestational mother, the woman who gestates the embryos but who bears no genetic relationship to the child; and (3) the social mother, the woman who raises or nurtures the child.

The growing prevalence of gestational surrogacy is, in part, guided by recent legal precedents in which a surrogate who does not contribute an ovum toward the creation of a child has a significantly reduced possibility of being awarded custody in the event that she reneges on her contract and attempts to retain custody of the child. However, although legal factors have certainly contributed to the meteoric rise in the rates of gestational surrogacy, it should be remembered that for couples the ability to create a child genetically related to both parents is the primary reason that gestational surrogacy continues to grow in popularity.

But not all gestational surrogate arrangements involve the couple's embryos; numerous cases involve the combination of donor ova and the intending father's semen. Why then do couples pursue gestational surrogacy when traditional surrogacy provides them with the same degree of biogenetic linkage to the child, has a higher likelihood of being successful, and costs less? Several reasons are cited by the staff of the largest surrogate mother program. The primary reason is that many more women are willing to donate ova than are willing to serve as surrogate mothers. This surrogate program is now also the largest ovum donation program in the United States with over 300 screened donors on file. The second reason, as previously mentioned, is that the U.S. courts would, in theory, be less likely to award custody to a gestational surrogate than to a traditional surrogate who contributed her own ovum to the creation of the child.[3] But perhaps most importantly, when commissioning couples choose donor ova/gestational surrogacy, they sever the surrogate's genetic link to and/or claim to the child. By contrast, with traditional surrogacy the adoptive mother must emphasize the importance of nurturance and social parenthood, while the surrogate mother deemphasizes her biogenetic tie to the child.

An additional reason, and one of critical importance, is that couples from certain racial, ethnic and religious groups (e.g., Japanese, Taiwanese, and Jewish) could find women who were willing to donate their ova, but were rarely able to locate women who were willing to serve in the capacity of surrogate. Thus, couples from particular ethnic/racial/religious groups who are seeking donors from those groups often pursue ovum donation/gestational surrogacy.[4]

The gestational surrogate's articulated ideas about relatedness (or more accurately, the presumed lack thereof) also produce a shift in emphasis away from potentially problematic aspects of gestational surrogacy, such as race and ethnicity. Unlike traditional surrogate arrangements in which the majority of couples and surrogates are Euro-American, it is not unusual for gestational surrogates and commissioning couples to come from diverse racial, ethnic, religious and cultural backgrounds. In fact, approximately 30 percent of all gestational surrogate arrangements at the largest program now involve surrogates and couples matched from different racial, ethnic, and cultural backgrounds. I have, over the last four years, interviewed

a Mexican-American gestational surrogate who was carrying a child for a Japanese couple; an African-American gestational surrogate who had attempted several embryo transfers unsuccessfully for both a Japanese couple and a Euro-American couple; a Euro-American gestational surrogate who had delivered twins for a Japanese couple; and a Taiwanese couple looking for an Asian American ovum donor and gestational surrogate.

When I questioned Carole, an African-American gestational surrogate (who at twenty-nine was single, with one child, and had yet to sustain a gestational pregnancy) about the issue of racial difference (between herself and her couple), she stated: "*I had friends who had a problem because [they thought] I should help blacks. And I told them, Don't look at the color issue. If a white person offered to help you, you wouldn't turn them down.*" However, the following statement by Carole reveals that the issue of racial difference is further nuanced as a positive factor, one that actually facilitates the surrogate/child separation process: "*My mom is happy the couple is not black because she was worried I would want to keep it [the baby]. The first couple I was going to go with was black. I don't want to raise another kid.*"

When I questioned Linda, a thirty-year old Mexican-American woman pregnant with a child for a couple from Japan, about this issue, her reasoning illustrated how beliefs concerning racial difference can be used by surrogates (and couples) to resolve any conflicting feelings about the child being related to a surrogate by virtue of having been carried in her body: "*No, I haven't [thought of the child as mine], because she's not mine, she never has been. For one thing, she is totally Japanese. It's a little hard for me. In a way she will always be my Japanese girl; but she is theirs.*" In this quote, we can see how Linda recapitulates one of the initial motivations cited by gestational surrogates, the desire to bear a child for an infertile couple while highlighting the lack of physical and racial resemblance, or biogenetic tie. "*If I was to have a child, it would only be from my husband and me. With AI [traditional surrogacy], the baby would be a part of me. I don't know if I could let a part of me. . . . AI was never for me; I never considered it.*"

Carole and Linda are aware, of course, as are other gestational surrogates, that they do not share a genetic tie with the children they produce as gestational surrogates. But concerns such as Carole's about raising an African-American couple's child reveal how racial resemblance raises certain questions about relatedness even when there is no genetic tie.[5] Although she knows that the child is not genetically hers, certain boundaries become blurred for her when an African-American couple is involved whereas with a Euro-American couple the distinction between genetic/nongenetic or self/other is clear. Cultural conceptions such as this about the connection between race and genetics deserve further exploration.

Not surprisingly, the shift from traditional to gestational surrogacy has attracted a different population of women. Overall, women who elect to become gestational surrogates tend to articulate the belief that traditional surrogacy, even though less medically complicated[6] is not an acceptable option for them because they are uncomfortable with the prospect of contributing their own ovum to the creation of a child. They also cannot readily accept the idea that a child who is genetically related to them would be raised by someone else. In other words, they explicitly articulate the opinion in traditional surrogacy (where the surrogate contributes an ovum) that the surrogate is the mother of the child, whereas in gestational surrogacy (where she does not contribute an ovum) she is not. They are nonetheless interested in participating in gestational surrogacy because it provides them with access to the world of surrogacy.[7] This often includes, interestingly enough, women who have been voluntarily sterilized (tubal ligations). For example, Barbara, age 30, married with three children, a Mormon and a two-time gestational surrogate (now planning a third pregnancy) stated: "*The baby is never mine. I am providing a needed environment for it to be born and go back to mom and dad. It's the easy kind of babysitting.*"

Oddly enough, the beliefs of IVF surrogates run contrary to current legal opinion as expressed in the findings of both Britain's Warnock Report and the Australian Waller Commission's report that "when a child is born to a woman following the donation of another's egg the woman giving birth should, for all purposes, be regarded in law as the mother of that child" (Shalev 1989: 117). It should be noted that the opinion expressed in both the Warnock Report and the Waller Commission contradicts not only the views expressed by IVF surrogates but also by commissioning couples who choose gestational surrogacy precisely because it eliminates the issue of genetic relatedness for them. It also contradicts Euro-American kinship ideology, specifically the continued emphasis on the importance of biogenetic relatedness.[8] However, this effort to expand our definition of biological relatedness, which has until recently depended on a genetic component, runs contrary to the Euro-American emphasis on biogenetic relatedness, in which genetic parents are legally and socially considered the "real" parents. This fragmentation or dispersal of parenthood, a byproduct of reproductive technologies, has resulted in what Marilyn Strathern has describes as the "claims of one kind of biological mother against other kinds of biological and nonbiological mothers" (1992: 32) and fathers.

How then to account for the gestational surrogate's motivations? Should a gestational surrogate's maternal rights be "modeled on the law of paternity, where proof of genetic parentage establishes . . . parentage, or . . . on the nine month experience of pregnancy as establishing the preponderant interest of . . . parentage" (Hull 1990: 152). It is of fundamental importance to gestational surrogates to circumvent the biogenetic tie to the child, and they do so in spite of the greatly increased degree of physical discomfort and medical risk they face in IVF procedures (as compared to risks associated with traditional surrogacy, which are the same as those faced in traditional pregnancy).[9] Any effort, legal or ethical, to argue that pregnancy is a determining factor in parenthood not only fails to consider Euro-American kinship ideology but perhaps most importantly neglects to consider the position of the gestational surrogate and commissioning couple.

The medical procedures commonly encountered by gestational surrogates [the self-administration of hormonal medications] can cause considerable discomfort. In the following example, Barbara discussed her experience: "*After a while you dread having to do it; I had lumps from all those injections. Two times a day and twice a week, three injections a day. If you don't do it, the pregnancy would be lost. . . . You are just [as] concerned with the pregnancy as if it's your own, sometimes more.*" Vicky, age 33, Euro-American, married with three children, who had given birth three weeks earlier, explained how she was able to sustain her motivation and commitment throughout the difficult medical procedures: "*It was hard, but it needed to be done for the baby's sake. All the shots [were] on a daily basis. I didn't mind it at all, but it had to be at a certain time. It was like a curfew. Sure it was painful, but it does go away.*"

The sentiments expressed by Barbara and Vicky are similar to those expressed by traditional surrogates who have experienced difficult, sometimes life-threatening pregnancies and deliveries. Both cast these experiences in terms of meaningful or heroic suffering (Ragoné 1996). The vastly increased physical discomfort and scheduling difficulties are, however, a price that gestational surrogates are willing to endure in order to circumvent what they regard as the problematic biogenetic tie. Barbara expressed a belief shared by many gestational surrogates about their pregnancies when she stated: "*I separate AI [artificial insemination] and IVF completely, almost to the point I don't agree with AI. I feel like that person is entering into an agreement to produce a child to give to someone else. I feel it is her baby she is giving away.*" In a similar fashion, Lee, age 31, married with two children, Euro-American, who was waiting for an embryo transfer, discussed the differences between traditional (AI) and gestational surrogacy. "*Yes, it's [the fetus] inside my body, but as far as I am concerned, I don't have any biological tie. The other way [AI], I would feel that there is some part of me out there.*"

This view of surrogacy differs in several important ways from the one expressed by traditional surrogates, who advance the idea that the term "parent" should be applied only to individuals who actually choose to become engaged in the process of raising a child, regardless of the degree of relatedness. They achieve this perspective in part by separating motherhood into two components: biological motherhood and social motherhood. Only social motherhood is viewed by traditional surrogates as "real" motherhood; in other words, nurturance is held to be of greater importance than biological relatedness. In this respect, it is the gestational surrogate, not the traditional surrogate, who tends to subscribe to a decidedly more traditional rendering of relatedness.

It was perhaps impossible to predict with any degree of certainty that advances in reproductive medicine coupled with an increase in consumer demand would produce such a profound shift in the rates of traditional (AI) and gestational surrogacy. Assistive reproductive technologies (e.g., surrogate motherhood, ovum donation, and sperm donation), have called into question what was once understood to be the "natural" basis of parenthood. As we have seen, traditional surrogates underplay their own biological contribution in order to bring to the fore the importance of the social, nurturant role played by the adoptive mother. In this way motherhood is reinterpreted as primarily an important social role in order to sidestep problematic aspects of the surrogate's biogenetic relationship to the child and the adoptive mother's lack of a biogenetic link. For traditional surrogates nurture takes precedence and ascendancy over nature; motherhood is understood as a social construct rather than a biological phenomenon. Gestational surrogates however, interestingly remain committed to the genetic model of parenthood,[10] reasoning that "real" parenthood is in fact genetic.

Many of the early theories about the future of surrogacy focused, at times exclusively, upon its potential for exploitation, but they failed to take into consideration the fact that both fertility and infertility must be contextualized: both are embedded in a series of personal, social, historical, and cultural processes and practices. Within surrogates' statements, assessments, and questions is testimony to the plasticity and resilience of family, which in spite of these seemingly odd changes, persists.

## ACKNOWLEDGMENTS

I owe a very special thank you to Dr. Sydel Silverman of the Wenner Gren Foundation for Anthropological Research for her support. An additional thank you is also owed to the University of Massachusetts–Boston for ongoing support in the form of Faculty Development Grants. I am especially indebted to the women and men who have shared their experiences with me over the last ten years; their belief in and commitment to this research has made it an engaging and rewarding experience. I would also like to extend very special and heartfelt thanks to the directors, psychologists, and surrogate program staff who have over the years generously given of their time and their expertise.

## NOTES

1. A couple, Elizabeth and William Stern, contracted with a surrogate, Mary Beth Whitehead, to bear a child for them because Elizabeth Stern suffered from multiple sclerosis, a condition that can be exacerbated by pregnancy. Once the child was born, however, Whitehead refused to relinquish the child to the Sterns, and in 1987, William Stern, the biological father, filed suit against Whitehead in an effort to enforce the terms of the surrogate contract. The decision of the lower court to award custody to the biological father and to permit his wife to adopt the child was overturned by the New Jersey Supreme Court, which then awarded custody to William Stern, prohibiting Elizabeth Stern from adopting the child while granting visitation rights to Mary Beth Whitehead. These decisions mirrored public opinion about surrogacy (Hull 1990: 154).

2. See Rapp (1978: 279) and Gordon (1988: 3) for a historical analysis of the idea of the demise of the American family.

3. In June 1993, the California Supreme Court upheld the decisions of both the lower court and the court of appeals with respect to gestational surrogacy contracts. In *Anna Johnson v Mark and Crispina Calvert*, Case #SO 23721, a case involving an African-American gestational surrogate, a Filipina American mother and a Euro-American father, the gestational surrogate and commissioning couple both filed custody suits. Under California law, both of the women could, however, claim maternal rights: Johnson, by virtue of being the woman who gave birth to the child; and Calvert, who donated ovum, because she is the child's genetic mother. In rendering their decision, however, the court circumvented the issue of relatedness, instead emphasized the "intent" of the parties as the ultimate and decisive factor in any determination of parenthood. The court concluded that if the genetic and birth mother are not one and the same person then "she who intended to procreate the child—that is, she who intended to bring about the birth of a child that she intended to raise on her own—is the natural mother under California law."

4. Why women from certain cultural groups are willing to donate ova but not serve as surrogates is a subject of considerable interest. Since gestational surrogates reason that they (unlike traditional surrogates and ovum donors) do not part with any genetic material, they are

able to deny that the child(ren) they produce are related to them. Given the parameters of Euro-American kinship ideology, additional research will be required to ascertain why ovum donors do not perceive their donation of genetic material as problematic.

5. During the course of the interview, I specifically asked her what her feelings and ideas were about having a child for a couple from another racial background (I also asked this question of all the surrogates who were matched with couples from different racial backgrounds).

6. Gestational surrogates often complain about the discomfort they experience as a result of having to self-inject two or three times per day for as long as three to four months of the pregnancy. They report that progesterone is especially painful, since it is oil-based and has a tendency to pool and lump under the skin. Even though the largest of the surrogate programs claims to inform gestational surrogates about the need to self-administer shots, several gestational surrogates reported that they had not anticipated either the frequency or the discomfort of the injections.

7. I have discussed elsewhere in great detail the system of rewards that makes surrogate motherhood attractive to this group of women (Ragoné 1994, 1996, 1998, 1999, 2000).

8. While there are in fact observable differences in family patterns within the United States, most notably among poor and working poor African-Americans whose alternative models of mothering/parenting may stem from "West African cultural values" as well as "functional adaptations to race and gender oppression" (Collins 1988: 119; Stack 1974), we should not lose sight of the fact that such perceived differences in family patterns do not necessarily weaken Euro-American kinship ideology. They continue to privilege the biogenetic model of family.

9. Aside from studies of the increased rates of multiple births, there are few longitudinal studies on the effects of infertility treatments. Research does, however, suggest that infertility patients have an increased risk of ovarian cancer (Jensen et al. 1987). The question remains: Although an infertile woman knowingly accepts the risks associated with infertility treatments, do surrogacy and ovum donation programs provide their populations with adequate information about the possibility of long-term risk?

10. Once a gestational surrogate has begun to develop a relationship with her couple and has experienced several unsuccessful embryo transfers, she may begin to reformulate or revise her initial beliefs concerning relatedness and family. An unsuccessful gestational surrogate may, for example, opt to become what is referred to in surrogate-mother programs as a "cross-over," someone who chose initially to participate in gestational surrogacy but then decided to become a traditional surrogate.

## REFERENCES

Andrews, Lori. 1984. *New Conceptions: A Consumer's Guide to the Newest Infertility Treatments.* New York: Ballantine.

Annas, George. 1988. "Fairy Tales Surrogate Mothers Tell." In Larry Gostin (ed.). *Surrogate Motherhood: Politics and Privacy,* pp. 43–55. Bloomington: Indiana University Press.

Carrier, James. 1990. "Gifts in a World of Commodities: The Ideology of the Perfect Gift in American Society." *Social Analysis* 29: 19–37.

Collins, Patricia Hill. 1988. *Black Feminist Thought: Knowledge, Consciousness and the Politics of Empowerment.* New York: Routledge.

Dworkin, Andrea. 1978. *Right-Wing Women.* New York: Perigee Books.

Ferree, Myra. 1984. "Sacrifice, Satisfaction and Social Change: Employment and the Family." In Karen Sacks and Dorothy Remy (eds.). *My Troubles Are Going to Have Trouble with Me,* pp. 61–79. New Brunswick, NJ: Rutgers University Press.

Fox, Renee, and Judith Swazey. 1992. *Spare Parts: Organ Replacement in American Society.* New York and Oxford: Oxford University Press.

Gordon, Linda. 1988. *Heroes of Their Own Lives.* New York: Viking.

Hull, Richard. 1990. "Gestational Surrogacy and Surrogate Motherhood." In Richard Hull (ed.). *Ethical Issues in the New Reproductive Technologies,* pp. 150–155. Belmont, CA: Wadsworth Publishers.

Jensen, P., B. Riis, P. Rodbro, V. Stram, and C. Christiansen, 1987. "Climacteric Symptoms after Oral and Percutaneous Hormone Replacement Therapy." *Matvritas* 9: 207–215.

Martin, Emily. 1987. *The Woman in the Body: A Cultural Analysis of Reproduction.* Boston: Beacon Press.

Neuhaus, Robert. 1988. "Renting Women, Buying Babies and Class Struggles." *Society* 25 (3): 8–10.

Parker, Phillip. 1983. "Motivation of Surrogate Mothers: Initial Findings." *American Journal of Psychiatry* 140: 117–119.

Ragoné, Heléna. 1994. *Surrogate Motherhood: Conception in the Heart.* Boulder, CO, and Oxford, UK: Westview Press/Basic Books.

_____. 1996. "Chasing the Blood Tie: Surrogate Mothers, Adoptive Mothers and Fathers." *American Ethnologist* 23 (2): 352–365.

_____. 1998. "Incontestable Motivations." In Sarah Franklin and Heléna Ragoné (eds.). *Reproducing Reproduction: Kinship, Power, and Technological Innovation,* pp. 118–131. Philadelphia: University of Pennsylvania Press.

_____. 1999. "The Gift of Life: Surrogate Motherhood, Gamete Donations and Constructions of Altruism." In Linda Layne (ed.). *Transformative Mothering: On Giving and Getting, in a Consumer Culture,* pp. 132–176. New York: New York University Press.

_____. 2000. "Of Likeness and Difference: How Race Is Being Transfigured by Gestational Surrogacy." In Heléna Ragoné and France Winddance Twine (eds.). *Ideologies and Technologies of Motherhood: Race, Class, Sexuality and Nationalism.* New York and London: Routledge.

Rapp, Rayna. 1978. "Family and Class in Contemporary America: Notes Toward an Understanding of Ideology." *Science and Technology* 42 (3): 278–300.

Rosaldo, Michelle. 1974. "Woman, Culture and Society: A Theoretical Overview." In M. Rosaldo and L. Lamphere (eds.). *Woman, Culture and Society,* pp. 17–43. Stanford, CA: Stanford University Press.

Shalev, Carmel. 1989. *Birth Power: The Case for Surrogacy.* New Haven, CT: Yale University Press.

Snowden, R., G. Mitchell, and E. Snowden. 1983. *Artificial Reproduction: A Social Investigation.* London: Allen and Unwin.

Stack, Carol. 1974. *All Our Kin.* New York: HarperCollins.

Strathern, Marilyn. 1991. The Pursuit of Certainty: Investigating Kinship in the Late Twentieth Century. Distinguished Lecture. Society of the Anthropology of Europe.

_____. 1992. *Reproducing the Future: Anthropology, Kinship and the New Reproductive Technologies.* Manchester, UK: Manchester University Press.

Titmuss, Richard. 1971. *The Gift Relationship: From Human Blood to Social Policy.* New York: Pantheon Books.

Zelizer, Viviana. 1985. *Pricing the Priceless Child.* New York: Basic Books.

# *Female Genital Cutting:*
## Culture and Controversy

### *Ellen Gruenbaum*

"Get away! What's the matter with you? You kids are behaving like a bunch of animals!" an older Sudanese woman yelled from inside the adobe brick room where the circumcision was to take place. She slapped the wire netting that screened the window and stomped outside to chase the small throng of laughing, curious children away from the window where they were peeking inside. She rounded the corner of the well-built rectangular adobe house and accosted the boys and girls at the window in a high-pitched, agitated voice, "Move on! See this switch? Let's go!" She smacked the ground threateningly with her long, thin stick, the sort commonly used to prod a wayward donkey or goat.

The children scattered. An older, more sensible boy took up a position near the window where he could keep the others away. The woman adjusted her long *tobe*, the over garment that covers the hair and body but not the face, and returned to the other women inside, who were preparing for the circumcisions. They had already moved one bed, made of wood and woven rope, into the center of the room where the trained midwife would have good light. The cotton mattresses on three beds where the children would recuperate were covered with clean cotton sheets and pillows. The midwife directed them to cover the bed for the surgeries with a red oilcloth over a cotton pillow and a pile of clean cloth scraps that could support a girl gently, and wash it with soap and water. They boiled water in a kettle on the charcoal fire, and the midwife prepared her instruments to be sterilized in an enamel bowl: a hypodermic, two sharp new razors, a curved suture needle, suturing thread, and a small scissors.

"Come, sit right close to me so you can see everything!" the midwife urged, motioning me to a small, low stool beside her. I hesitated, wondering if I would be able to watch the little girls experience the cutting that awaited them, known locally as "Pharaonic circumcision." But as an anthropologist doing research on rural health services and women's roles in this Sudanese village, I wanted this opportunity to observe, to be better able to understand and describe this important experience in the lives of girls. What I was about to witness was the most severe form of female genital cutting and closure (infibulation) found anywhere in Africa.

## CLITORIDECTOMY, EXCISION, AND INFIBULATION

The term "female genital mutilation," or FGM, has been widely used in recent years, to describe various forms of "female circumcision" that are found in many countries. "Mutilation" is technically accurate for most variants of the practices since they entail damage to or removal of healthy tissues or organs. The provocative term, as well as the realities it conveys, has stimulated great international concern and action against the practices.

But since "mutilation" connotes intentional harm, its use is tantamount to accusing the women who do it of harmful intent. Some people, even those who favor stopping the practices, have been deeply offended by the term FGM, arguing that it is not women's intent to mutilate their daughters but to give them proper, socially expected treatment. Their intent is simply to "circumcise" or "purify." The words commonly used for female genital cutting in Arabic-speaking countries, *tahur* or *tahara*, means "purification," that is, the achievement of cleanliness through a ritual activity. "Female circumcision," however, echoes the term for the removal of the foreskin in the male, which has been considered non-mutilating (Toubia 1993:9)—at least until the recent movement to end that practice as well (see the work of the organization NOCIRC)—and is therefore rejected by many people, since it seems to trivialize the damage done and the huge scale of the practices. I prefer the term "Female Genital Cutting," or "FGC," which has become well established in international discourse: it avoids disparaging the practitioners yet does not minimize the seriousness of the issue.

There are several types of cutting and removal of tissues of genitalia of young girls and women, done to conform to social expectations in communities of many different religions and ethnicities. The form varies not only from one sociocultural context to another but even within a single village, such as the Sudanese village just described, where different ethnic groups do different types of cutting. Forms vary between families, too, with some preferring their ethnic group's traditional forms while other families seek less harmful forms. Also, trained midwives and other practitioners (including traditional birth attendants, other older women, barbers, and even medical doctors) have their own individual techniques of doing the procedures, resulting in varying amounts of tissue taken and various levels of hygiene. (In most countries, medical doctors are now strongly discouraged or forbidden by their professional organizations and governments from doing *any* form of FGC.)

In some cultural contexts, it is very young children who are cut, including infants or toddlers (Shandall 1967, Toubia 1993, 1994, Abdal Rahman 1997). Anne Jennings reported southern Egyptian girls undergoing genital cutting at age 1 or 2 (1995:48). Most commonly, it is done to young girls between the ages of 4 and 8. But in some cultural contexts (e.g. the Maasai of East Africa), cutting is delayed until a young woman is in her teens and about to be married (14–15 or even older).

In the past few years the World Health Organization has developed a comprehensive typology that technical experts use for the different types. People who practice female genital cutting have their own terms for different types in their many languages, of course, which may or may not fit well with the World Health Organization's four types. Researchers can, however, place the range of the practices into the following categories.

**Clitoridectomy.** The World Health Organization's Type I includes both the partial and total removal of the clitoris, called clitoridectomy, and also the less severe forms of the operations, such as the cutting away of part or all of the clitoral prepuce, or "hood," analogous to the foreskin removal of male circumcision. Removal of only the prepuce seems to be very rare, but partial removal of the clitoris is fairly common.

Clitoridectomy, whether partial or total, is often referred to by Muslims and others as "*sunna* circumcision" or "*sunna* purification." In my experience doing ethnographic research in Sudan, the term "*sunna* circumcision" was in fact applied to a wide variety of surgeries, perhaps because of the positive association between that word and Muslim religious values.

**Excision.** The World Health Organization's Type II is called "excision." In this type, the cutting goes further than clitoridectomy to include removal of the prepuce, the entire clitoris, and partial or total excision of the labia minora (the smaller inner lips of the vaginal opening). In Sudan this form is usually also called "*sunna*," even though it is more damaging than what some people mean by "*sunna*." They are grouped in common parlance because there are just two basic folk terms—*sunna* and pharaonic circumcision—and they use the "*sunna*" terminology for both clitoridectomy and excision. In fact, it is often applied to any circumcisions that are not "pharaonic." Imprecise terms (such as *nuss* for "half") are also used for some of the in-between forms that would be included in Type II.

Infibulation and reinfibulation. The most severe cutting occurs with Type III, or infibulation. It is the main type in Sudan, where it is commonly called "pharaonic circumcision." People think it dates back to the days of the Pharaohs. In Egypt, where this severe infibulation is rare, it is called "Sudanese circumcision." In this type, part or all of the external genitalia—prepuce, clitoris, labia minora, and all or part of the labia majora—are removed and the raw edges are infibulated (held together by stitching or thorns). When healed, infibulation leaves a perfectly smooth vulva of skin and scar tissue with only a single tiny opening for urination and menstrual flow, preserved during healing by the insertion of a small object such as a piece of straw. In a variation of infibulation that is slightly less severe, the trimmed labia minora are sewn shut but the labia majora are left alone. In either case, it is essential that a midwife be present for childbirth to make an incision in the tissue to allow the baby to be born. The new mother is then reinfibulated by the midwife, a practice that is repeated after each pregnancy. The new mother often asks the midwife to make the opening very small, "like a virgin," to enhance her husband's sexual pleasure. This is analogous to, although more severe than, what some North American obstetricians do: take an extra stitch, called "the husband's stitch," when doing an episiotomy, for the purpose of restoring tightness to the opening.

**Other variations.** Others that do not include tissue removal are grouped as Type IV. This includes practices such as pricking, piercing, incision, stretching of the clitoris or labia, cauterization, cuts or scrapes on the genitalia, or the use of harmful substances in the vagina. Labia stretching to pursue culturally preferred aesthetics of the body is not particularly harmful, but other variations can be painful or damaging. In some East African countries, some men's preference for "dry sex" has resulted in the introduction of dangerous or uncomfortable astringents into the vagina to dry it out before intercourse, which is included in Type IV. In Europe and North America, the fad of labia piercing could be included as a Type IV practice.

## HARMFUL EFFECTS

The harmful effects of these forms differ, but all forms—from clitoridectomy to infibulation—create risks for the girls at the time of cutting. Medical reports document cases of excess bleeding (hemorrhage), infections, blood poisoning (septicemia), retention of urine, or shock. Such complications can be life-threatening. Later on, the infibulated state sometimes results in retention of menses (if the vagina is blocked by scar tissue), difficulty in urination (if there is excess scar tissue around or over the urethra), and a high incidence of urinary tract and chronic pelvic infections. At first intercourse, the extremely small size of the opening created by infibulation presents a barrier which can make first sexual intercourse very difficult or impossible. Often the scar tissue around the opening must be painfully ruptured or is cut by the husband, a midwife, or a doctor. During childbirth, the inelastic scar tissue of infibulation must be cut by the birth attendant at the right time so labor will not be obstructed. Not only is obstructed labor dangerous to the baby, but also the mother's internal tissues can be damaged, creating a fistula (opening in the tissue separating the vagina from the urinary bladder), which can result in an embarrassing condition with constantly leaking urine (Shandall 1967, Toubia 1994, Shell-Duncan and Hernlund 2000b:14–18, Gruenbaum 2001).

The psychological effects are less well understood, not systematically researched, and no doubt differ a great deal from one situation to another. There is anecdotal evidence of adverse psychological effects, perhaps particularly if it comes without warning and seems a betrayal of trust. Yet many women simply accept the experience as just part of becoming a woman.

Damage to sexual responsiveness is suspected for many women, yet there is also data that suggests the frequency and extent of problems vary greatly. Many women do not lose sexual interest and retain the ability to achieve sexual satisfaction and orgasms, even among the infibulated (Gruenbaum 2001, chapter 5, and Lightfoot-Klein 1989). Sexual responsiveness could be affected differently depending on which tissues are cut and how, whether the surrounding or underlying tissues retain sensitivity, whether there is severe infibulation, and of course whether the emotional attachment of the partners is strong and the

relationship loving and supportive. Some midwives have been careful to avoid cutting too much of the sensitive tissue (clitoris and erectile tissue) hoping to preserve sensitivity, but still make the result look like an infibulation by joining the labia across the opening.

It is therefore erroneous to assume that all women who have been cut have lost their sexual responsiveness. Similarly, although many experience very harmful medical consequences, many do not, so one cannot generalize about the effects without reference to the specific practices and circumstances.

## BUT WHY?

Indeed, the world wonders how loving parents can allow their daughters to be held down and cut, usually causing fear, pain, and possible major damage to health and physical functions, immediate or long-term. It seems incongruous and shocking to imagine a six-year-old girl enduring such pain and indignity, particularly at the hands of those she trusts.

Yet current estimates are that somewhere between 200,000 and a million girls experience some form of female genital cutting each year (Yoder 2003), mostly in 28 countries in Africa, and many millions of women and girls are living with FGC's life-long effects. In addition, the practices are found in other countries where they have spread by immigration or due to adoption of genital cutting if they believe it is associated with their religion. Why do women continue to arrange for these practices to be done to their daughters?

Is it because of any particular religion? No. The practices are found in many countries and among people of widely different ethnic groups and religions, including Judaism, Christianity, Islam, and traditional African religions. Yet it often happens that people who follow circumcision traditions often *do* associate the practices with their own religious beliefs.

For example, although many learned religious scholars have declared that infibulation has no place in Islam, and others say that no form whatsoever should be permitted, other teachers consider female circumcision as an "ennobling" act that is very proper for Muslims, so long as they don't go beyond clitoridectomy, which is usually called "*sunna* circumcision." The basic meaning of the Arabic word "*sunna*" is "tradition," which usually connotes the traditions of the Prophet Mohammed, i.e., those things that he did or advocated during his lifetime (570–622 C.E.), handed down through oral tradition and the writings known as the *Hadith*. Muslims believe the Holy Qur'an to be God's direct revelation, and the first source of guidance for righteous living, and it is silent on female circumcision. But Muslims also respect the sayings and actions attributed to the Prophet Mohammed during his lifetime as a secondary source of guidance. Although disputes remain among Muslims about which stories and quotations offer the most reliable versions of the Prophet's advice and how the sayings and stories should be interpreted, many Muslims have concluded that the Prophet Mohammed's words on the subject— "Reduce but do not destroy"—mean that only the less severe cutting is acceptable, though not required. Others believe the Prophet actually advocated it, making it either an obligation or at least a blessing to do it. Others believe Muslims should avoid female circumcision completely, since it is not mentioned in the Qur'an as a duty of the faithful. Using the term *sunna*, then, seems to imply that it is expected of Muslims, and while the term may help convince Muslims to give up infibulation, it may reinforce their continuing clitoridectomy. No doubt there will be many lively discussions among Muslim scholars in the coming years!

How about male dominance—is that the cause of this practice? Many analysts have noted that female genital cutting forms a part of the subordination of women where it is found. While of course not all strongly patriarchal societies of the world utilize female genital cutting, where it is found it is indeed embedded in the patriarchal structures of male domination of the lives of women and girls ( Assaad 1980, El Saadawi 1980a, 1980b, Shell-Duncan and Hernlund 2000a, Gruenbaum 2001). That is not to say that women do not have any control or influence on the decisions, types, and timing of the cutting. And that does not mean it is always men who are pushing for it. Rather, the conditions of women's lives often encourage their participation in and celebration of the cutting, their advocacy or their tolerance of the rituals, and their willingness to endure or accept the health risks.

In analysis of several case examples, including my Sudanese research, the manifestation of male dominance is primarily in disparate economic and social circumstances of women and men. While women are usually economically productive (whether for the market economy or for subsistence), carry out important services in the domestic sphere, and have some distinctive rights in each of the different cultures of Africa, most societies nevertheless accord greater political and economic power to men, especially older and more dominant and successful men. Economic and social situations of women vary a great deal—traders/ market women have their own incomes to spend and farming women may have sources of income they use to help support their families or provide for their personal needs, but in many cultures, a woman's access to economic resources is mediated by men. In Islamic law, Muslim women are entitled to own and manage property, but the inheritance rules favor men—a

daughter receives half the share of a son, for example. Even then, local groups often expect daughters not to claim shares, so that their brothers can be more secure, arguing that women are entitled to rely on husbands and male kin for support and should not need separate holdings. In other cultures, women may be dependent on men for access to land, livestock, foodstuffs, a share of a husband's income, and old-age support by sons. But women are vulnerable to divorce or polygyny that might reduce their security. If economic security and socially-approved reproduction are mediated by the dominant roles of men, women clearly need to conform to whatever rules the culture requires, including varying expectations for virginity, excision, or infibulation in order to have successful marriages and child-bearing. Their enculturation process must prepare girls for their subordinate roles.

Women's consciousness regarding their positions may range from strong belief in the moral superiority of men, to wry acceptance of the role disparity, to willingness to challenge the status quo in favor of better futures. But given the power of social pressure and the rewards of acceptance of genital cutting— propriety, marriage, children, and financial support— it should not be surprising that most women have not yet jumped on the bandwagon of abandoning female genital cutting.

## CULTURAL CONTEXTS AND PEOPLE'S REASONS

The explicit reasons people give for circumcising their daughters are varied, depending on the cultural contexts in which FGC practices occur. For some, genital cutting is a rite of passage to marriageable womanhood. The Maasai of Kenya, for example, usually wait until a girl's marriage has been arranged, and she is then excised (Type II) and her head is shaved during the weeks of marriage preparations. After she has healed she goes to her husband and new home ready for womanhood.

Female genital cutting often plays a role in gender identity. Some even use terms like "male parts" for the clitoris and labia, saying removal of them results in a more feminine and aesthetically pleasing body. In many of the Nile Valley cultures of Egypt and Sudan, genital cutting helps to define feminine gender and is considered an essential prerequisite to marriage. Nile Valley girls are cut at earlier ages, so that they will be known to be virgins and ready for socially approved marriage when old enough.

The type of circumcision done sometimes defines ethnic identity. Even within a single village, such as the Sudanese village described above, different ethnic groups do different types of cutting. Thus, the Zabarma and Hausa minorities who have immigrated to Sudan anywhere from a century ago to more recent decades have usually resisted adopting infibulation, yet some have also adopted it along with other changes as part of their cultural and linguistic acculturation to the dominant Arab-Sudanese culture.

Some practitioners in Sudan advocated genital cutting as a way to preserve virginity. Not only is cutting expected to reduce some sexual sensitivity, thought to help girls and wives resist improper sexual relationships by taming what are thought to be overly powerful female sexual impulses, but also the infibulation is an actual barrier to penetration, preventing pre-marital pregnancy. People have even speculated, without any confirmation, that the practice may have developed in ancient times as a measure to prevent rape by strangers passing through on trade routes.

## THE BIG DAY

The morning cool was beginning to fade, and the day promised to be hot and dry, as usual. The midwife washed her hands thoroughly with soap and water, shook off the water, and let them dry. The two pretty little girls were guided through the door by their mother. Recently bathed, hair freshly plaited and dotted with some henna paste, the girls wore colorful new dresses and special ornaments known as *jirtig*, as protection against excessive blood loss or the harm that might be done by spirits (*jinn*). The family's gold jewelry was ready for them to put on during recovery. They looked proud, though a little anxious, about this first time to be treated as such special people.

Their male cousin, about 7, lay silently on a bed in the corner, his face to the wall. Earlier in the morning he had been taken by car to the small hospital in a town several kilometers away to be circumcised by a medical assistant. When he returned, he was greeted with celebratory ululations and helped into a bed in the corner of this room to recover.

As the dozen women present greeted the mother and girls with smiles and encouragement, the mother hesitated, reconsidering the wisdom of doing the younger, who looked to be only about four years old. The other was six, the best age to be able to complete healing before starting school. But there were many advantages to cutting three children the same day, since the families could share the expenses of the celebration and not have to do it again in two years for the younger one. The midwife and the others quickly overcame the mother's hesitation, urging her to do it right away. Don't worry, it will soon be over, she's already prepared, and, as the saying goes, "You grow up, you

forget" (*Tekbara, tensa*). Outside, other relatives and neighbors were cooking over charcoal fires, preparing a dried meat and yogurt stew, beans, bread, tea, and sweets for the well-wishers expected to begin arriving soon. The ceremony would not be easily delayed.

So, both girls were cut, the younger first. Thankfully the midwife's methods were fairly hygienic, not like the old methods, when the cutting was done using broken glass or an unsterilized knife with thorns for sutures. This midwife's better techniques were respected, as her patients usually avoided the worst complications. The first girl was washed carefully, held by loving but firm arms of the women, and injected—painfully—with the local anesthetic xylocaine into her clitoris, prepuce, and labia to deaden the feeling. A few minutes later, she was cut carefully, avoiding major arteries. She did not feel any pain when her prepuce, clitoris, and labia minora (inner lips) were cut off with one of the sterilized razor blades. Her labia majora (outer lips) were trimmed slightly and the two sides sutured together with the curved needle so they could heal with a smooth surface, leaving just one opening for urine and future menstrual flow. The second girl was done the same way, and after each cutting, the midwife rinsed the wound with an antiseptic, sprinkled the wound with antibiotic powder, and gave the girl some aspirin. Amid celebratory ululating, each girl was moved to a side bed to recover.

As soon as the work was completed, the bed cleaned up, and bowl with the discarded tissues carried out, adult well-wishers, both men and women, began arriving. They congratulated each child and tucked a little money under their pillows, then moved outside to share in the breakfast meal that the families had prepared. It was a joyful occasion of visiting and drinking tea. Meanwhile, as the local anesthetic wore off, the newly circumcised children endured their pain with aspirin and loving mothers.

## BUT WHAT ABOUT GIRLS' AND WOMEN'S HUMAN RIGHTS?

Did these young girls consent to this cutting? They appeared to be willing. Of course in other places where girls are not informed beforehand, the practice is to surprise the girl and circumcision is carried out by force (see for example El-Saadawi for Egypt) it is obvious that such girls did not consent. But it is also quite common in Sudan and other countries for older girls to make fun of younger uncircumcised girls, teasing them with peer pressure until the younger girls' enviousness of being a big girl (i.e., circumcised) leads them to nag their mothers to let them be cut. Or suppose you grow up simply knowing that it will happen, and when your mother prepares the new dress, fusses over getting you ready, and tells you the big day has arrived, you go willingly, trusting your mother that it is for the best? Have you given your informed consent?

People concerned about the human rights of children would say no. At 5 or 6 years of age, one is by no means fully informed about the risks and consequences. A girl probably has no idea about sexual pleasure or infections or childbirth. Similarly, if you live in a culture where arranged marriages are common, and at 13 your father and mother arrange for you to get married to a groom they have selected for you, would you be able to speak up for yourself? Like so many other girls, you would probably feel you had no choice, or you would trust that your parents know best and accept the situation.

Both are violations of what have come to be understood as human rights for girls—the right to bodily integrity (that is, not to have her body permanently altered) and the right to consent to or decline to marry. Both of these clearly have not always been accepted as rights and certainly are not yet accepted in many societies. But should they be rights? The international community increasingly agrees that they should be, although there is no general agreement on what the age of consent should be: 16? 18? Most of the world's countries are signatories to agreements like the Convention on Elimination of All Forms of Discrimination Against Women, the Convention on the Rights of the Child, and other international agreements that stand against violations of girls' and women's rights, but not all enforce them.

Bodily integrity is something an adult woman can decide for herself. In the United States or Europe, it is accepted that someone over 18 is free to get tattoos or consent to having her labia pierced if she wishes. But to impose a decision on a child that will permanently alter her body, even if she is passively acquiescing, is to deny her right to make that decision when she is old enough to understand the consequences.

## SO, WHAT'S BEING DONE ABOUT FEMALE GENITAL CUTTING?

As you might expect, many who learn about female genital cutting practices respond with outrage and take strong positions against the practices. Outsiders often have evoked horrible stereotypes of malicious intent, condemning the people who practice such genital cutting of girls as intending to "torture" females or "deprive women of their sexuality."

Local reformers sometimes engage in similar strongly worded condemnations in international discourse. But grassroots change agents realize that inflammatory rhetoric and "preaching" alone are not likely to change strongly held values and traditions. Reformers recognize that it may take some time to enlist local practitioners in the change process, so they have patiently promoted health education that they hope will lead people to voluntarily abandon female genital cutting. Others have introduced alternate rituals that contribute to the social goals, for example a rite of passage for maturing girls that substitutes for a traditional ritual of circumcision, but without the physical harm of cutting. Meanwhile, a large number of countries are also pursuing legal reforms and policy changes to criminalize or otherwise discourage the cutting of underage girls. (See Rahman and Toubia, 2000, for an international comparison of laws and policies on female genital cutting.)

But the first step in changing anything is to understand what it means to the people who do it. With more insight, we can better understand why people have resisted widespread change and why some are now pursuing change. Many writers, particularly social scientists and public health researchers, have tried to improve the understanding of people's reasons for genital cutting without condemning the people who have followed their traditional practices (El Dareer 1982, Gruenbaum 1982, 1996, 2001, Cloudsley 1983, Obermeyer 2003).

In the Sudanese villages I studied, female genital cutting still persists, but change is in progress. In one village in the Gezira area, over the past twenty years female circumcision has become an increasingly important topic for discussions. Some mothers have quietly arranged to have their daughters be cut less severely, moving from severe infibulation to preserving more of the tissue and not closing the opening as much. Others have gone further, dropping infibulation and doing only Type II or Type I, resisting the social pressure to conform.

A few years later, when I interviewed the midwife from the descriptions above on a return visit, she said she hoped to change over to doing only the milder *sunna*, but the vast majority of her clients still wanted infibulations. Her changing attitude was encouraged by the government trained medical assistant at their local clinic, who was taking an active role in persuading people to stop infibulating. The public health discussions that have been held separately among the women, among the men, among school boys, and among girls, have resulted in greater willingness to talk about modification, a moderate change, though not total abandonment. Throughout the country, doctors and other medical personnel have decided to actively oppose all forms of female genital cutting. A law against the severe form, dating back to 1946, had seldom been enforced, but recently, the government of Sudan is showing renewed interest in enforcement of the laws against all forms of female genital cutting.

Stated intentions, of course, are not always realized, especially when there is such opposition. Nevertheless it is encouraging that grassroots developments, education, and organized public health education are having an effect to reduce the incidence of new cases.

## SOCIAL MOVEMENTS FOR CHANGE

Successful social change requires widespread support, not merely written laws and policies. How will that support be won? Reformers need to endeavor to fully understand people's reasons. As Gerry Mackie has noted, "The followers of mutilation are good people who love their children; any campaign that insinuates otherwise is doomed to provoke defensive reaction" (Mackie 1996:1015).

But remaining detached and uninvolved with this serious problem tests the ethical limits of "cultural relativism" (the respect that anthropologists use to try to understand each culture in its own terms rather than to judge it ethnocentrically by the values of another culture). The World Health Organization, the United Nations Children's Fund (UNICEF) and United Nations Population Fund issued a joint statement in 1996:

> It is unacceptable that the international community remain passive in the name of a distorted vision of multiculturalism. Human behaviours and cultural values, however senseless or destructive they may appear from the personal and cultural standpoint of others, have meaning and fulfil a function for those who practise them. However, culture is not static but it is in constant flux, adapting and reforming. People will change their behaviour when they understand the hazards and indignity of harmful practices and when they realize that it is possible to give up harmful practices without giving up meaningful aspects of their culture.

Both elements are necessary to a successful change effort aimed at a cultural practice: a deep understanding of people's reasons and motivations for keeping a practice, yet recognition of the flexibility of culture. People have demonstrated many times that cultures can adapt, and people can make changes when convinced of the need without losing cultural identity and meaning. Ultimately, it is up to them to decide when the time is ripe, but can efforts within a cultural group and efforts from outside accelerate the process?

Opinion leaders and grassroots activists, working in different ways, are vital to social change. An outspoken critic of the Islamist government of Sudan and a long-time supporter of the leftist movement there, Fatima Ibrahim challenged the government's interpretation of Islam, and argued that the Islamic religion can be used to *support* women's rights and social justice. The Medical Assistant who holds discussions about FGC in the village where he works, the doctor who studies Islamic texts to help her clarify the limits of *sunna* circumcision to the medical establishment, the midwife who tries to convince her clients to do milder forms or none at all—all of these that I observed in Sudan are helping to prepare for change.

In the past two decades organized efforts for change throughout the African countries affected have accelerated dramatically, as international and non-governmental organizations have become involved and as African women have moved into leadership positions in speaking out about female genital cutting. International organizations, such as the Inter-African Committee Against Harmful Traditional Practices, have taken a lead role in conducting public health education by organizing discussion groups in towns and villages. The World Health Organization has taken on the anti-circumcision work, as have other international organizations. Can such a message be carried forward effectively, so that female circumcision might actually be ended soon?

## OBSTACLES TO CHANGE: RISK OF *NOT* CUTTING

The social conditions that act as barriers to parents taking the risk of leaving their daughters uncircumcised help to explain resistance to change (Gruenbaum 1996). No matter how clever the public health education message on the hazards of cutting or how authoritative the religious sources that say it is unnecessary, parents know that it *is* necessary if it is the prerequisite for their daughter's marriageability and long-term social and financial security. Even when the religious authorities speak against the practices and medical risks are known, these may not be sufficient reasons for parents to risk their daughters' marriageability and long-term security.

To counteract the social risks there are a number of possible directions for policy-makers and change agents to address. One is to reduce the economic dependency of women. Better educational opportunities and employment opportunities would allow young women and their families to see delayed marriage as something other than a disaster. Daughters could be encouraged more in their education and careers, secure in the knowledge that although marriage is desirable, failure to marry or loss of spouse will not necessarily result in penury and dependence on male relatives. Better support for inheritance rights of women might help.

This is indeed a part of the change process that I have observed in Sudan. The teachers, professors, public health workers, students and other activists now working on reform are, as a result of their awareness, literacy, and cosmopolitan outlook, better able to confidently state that female circumcision can be left behind, that it is both harmful to health and not Islamic. Such women are confident that they will have a say in the decision on the circumcision of daughters, and they endeavor to provide their daughters with the educational opportunities needed to be self-reliant.

But even educated and confident women cannot be certain their uncircumcised daughters will be marriageable. If the young men in the community remain committed to marrying infibulated brides, a daughter's education may preserve her from poverty, but it will not assure her of marriage and children. The risk is lessened if there are social and familial ties to progressive families where men prefer *sunna* or no circumcision.

But as this cultural debate unfolds (Gruenbaum 1996), it is encouraging that some young men do state their preference for uninfibulated brides. One educated young man I knew in Khartoum told me he had insisted that the family not infibulate his sister, and he swore he would not marry an infibulated woman, even if she were a cousin. But will he or others like him actually refuse to marry a cousin the family expects him to marry? Or would he refuse to marry the young woman who has caught his eye, simply because she is infibulated? And can young men effectively prevent their sisters' circumcisions? How do families cope with the risk that there may not be men like this for their daughters to marry?

Risk avoidance remains the most significant factor to explaining why otherwise well-informed families cling to female genital cutting practices. Gerry Mackie offered a provocative exploration of the risks involved in such social changes by comparing efforts to end infibulation and excision in Africa with the process of ending the painful, crippling footbinding of girls (i.e., tightly binding their small feet so they would not grow) practiced in China for centuries. Footbinding, which lasted until the early 20th century, was also related to making daughters marriageable (Mackie 1996).

While there had been efforts to change footbinding historically, parents were afraid to be the first to change, since men sought to marry women with tiny feet only. However, once a critical mass of people was persuaded of its harm through educational campaigns, they found they could take the risk of change when, with other parents, they pledged not to let their daughters' feet be bound nor let their sons marry women with bound feet. The movement led to wholesale abandonment of footbinding in a single generation (Mackie 1996:1001). Pledge groups do function in African societies for various purposes, so now that there is growing awareness of the risks of female genital cutting, perhaps people will develop this pledge idea for female genital cutting as well.

Thus, despite the spread of female genital cutting and its tenacity, there is no reason to conclude that it cannot change rapidly in the coming years, when people have learned enough about the issue and when they believe the risks of not doing it are not too high. The conditions are ripe for change in infibulation and excision practices in Africa. The international activism, the efforts at culturally appropriate approaches, and the emergence of, and a degree of support for, indigenous leaders of the movement make this an excellent time, if the additional resources can be mobilized, for rapid change to occur. Indeed, the World Health Organization, UNICEF, and the United Nations Population Fund have announced a joint plan to "significantly curb female genital mutilation over the next decade and completely eliminate the practice within three generations" (Reaves 1997).

To mobilize the Islamic religious arguments against infibulation—i.e., claiming only *sunna* is permitted for Muslims—often results in people favoring *sunna*, allowing them to continue to reject total abandonment of all forms. Reformers debate the wisdom of this: although abandoning infibulation constitutes a definite improvement in the health of women and girls, what public health officials have often advocated as "harm reduction," it might result in even stronger belief in the Islamic rightness of the remaining form, clitoridectomy, which might delay the demise of *all* forms.

## ALTERNATIVE RITES

Even where circumcisions continue in Sudan, the celebration of it has lessened. Whether that indicates a decline in importance of the event or is due to harsh economic conditions is not clear, but even wealthy families have curtailed the celebrations. Reduction in celebrations suggests that cutting is beginning to lose its symbolic power, and might in a few years decline.

An extremely positive development in the last few years has been even more explicit changes in the way circumcision is celebrated in several areas where activists have been at work. Recognizing that circumcision is a rite of passage in many of the places where it is practiced, reformers have begun to introduce alternative ways to mark these important life transitions without involving the usual genital cutting. One good example comes from Kenya, where rural families have been adopting an alternative rite to circumcision over the last few years, known as "Circumcision Through Words" (*Ntanira na Mugambo*). As described by Malik Stan Reaves (1997), groups of families have participated in bringing together their appropriate-aged daughters to spend a week of seclusion learning their traditions concerning women's roles as adults and as future parents. The Kenyan national women's group, Maendeleo ya Wanawake Organization, worked with international collaborators to develop this program to include self-esteem and dealing with peer pressure, along with traditional values, as well as messages on personal health and hygiene, reproductive issues, and communications skills. At the end of the week of seclusion, a community celebration of feasting, singing, and dancing affirms the girls' transition to their new status.

Such approaches recognize that female circumcision has deep cultural significance, and if that significance can be preserved while the actual cutting is discontinued, there is strong hope that change can be rapid. Indeed, Reaves quotes the Chair of the Maendeleo ya Wanawake Organization, Zipporah Kittony-said, as saying she was "overjoyed" to see the positive response and believes it was a critical achievement toward the eradication of female circumcision (Reaves 1997). This project serves as an excellent example of combining local initiative, international expertise, preparatory research and community discussion, and support from private foundations (including the Moriah Fund, Ford, Population Action International/Wallace Global Fund, and Save the Children–Canada) to accomplish a culturally sensitive alternative to female circumcision.

## PUBLIC HEALTH EDUCATION

Poster campaigns, teachers on lecture tours, training for health workers, and public health announcements in the media have all been used at various times and places for several decades to spread the word on the dangers of female genital cutting. In the past two decades, the movement has accelerated, with more respectful and effective teaching tools and methods available. The Inter-African Committee, for example, uses a technique that involves sending a woman health worker into a marketplace where women are found, and striking up a discussion. She asks questions like "What do you think, is female circumcision a good tradition?" Rather than preaching, she listens to what they have to say, what their beliefs are. "Are you aware of the hazards?" leads to a discussion of the short and long term complications.

The educator encourages women to bring up their beliefs and then discusses them respectfully. For example, there is an erroneous belief in some countries that if the clitoris touches the baby's head at birth the baby will die. An educator brought the idea up in one such discussion filmed by the Inter-African Committee for their film *Female Circumcision: Beliefs and Misbeliefs* (1992), and the health worker explained that that was not possible. She also discussed other potentially harmful traditional practices such as nutritional taboos and marrying too young, encouraging the women to offer opinions and discuss their ideas with each other.

The work of national women's organizations in the countries affiliated with the Inter-African Committee is having a positive effect. Through such means as community discussions, formal classes with anatomical teaching aids, and organizing in villages willing to undergo friendly "inspections" of their baby girls, to show the success of the message, each national committee is reporting progress. The Sudan National Committee for Traditional Harmful Practices, for example, has many rural branches now, and although their efforts were met with resistance initially, their work is now better received according to the Executive Secretary, Amna Abdel Rahman Hassan (2002). Rogaia Abusharaf noted that the Sudan National Committee consistently avoids making female circumcision a separate issue, but always discusses it as one among several reproductive health issues (1999). Discussing child spacing, contraceptive use, and maternal and child health first, women are better prepared to consider not only the anti-circumcision message but also their well-being and rights.

## TAKING A STANCE?

Regardless of the emotional or moral response one may feel about these situations, it is my opinion that those who are committed to improving the lives of women and girls must channel their responses into change efforts that are culturally informed and socially contextualized if they are to be effective. Anthropologists commonly advocate using cultural relativism to encourage people to overcome their prejudicial and ethnocentric tendencies and learn to understand cultures in their own terms. People who have been raised with the values and practices of their own culture, values and practices that have developed in adaptation to their own environment and social experiences, can be expected to have great faith in their own traditions. People are usually very unwilling to be judged according to, or expected to conform to, some other culture's values. So anthropologists rely on the mental exercise and teaching tool of cultural relativism to cultivate respect for cultural difference and enhance our ability to be analytical rather than ethnocentrically judgmental.

But that does not mean that we cannot discuss cultural practices in terms of their consequences, whether apparently neutral, helpful to some (e.g., to the preservation of identity), or harmful in certain respects (e.g., resulting in increased rates of infections). Indeed, most cultural practices are contested even within a cultural group: women and men may see things differently. Calm elders and testosterone-influenced youth may differ on when to fight. Men of a culture may like the "double standard" of sexual liberty for themselves but faithfulness for their wives, while the women have a different view of this.

As our human dialogs among cultures expand among societies and we humans try to agree on health protection measures or human rights protections, each culture must stretch a little as new information, experiences, and knowledge affect them. Once we have accepted that culture is dynamic and each of us is a citizen of a multi-cultural planet, it becomes easier to engage in respectful discussion, rather than the denunciation or preaching that often results from those who take a strong, absolute position in their interactions.

What feminist does not have respect for women's voices and their process of setting their own priorities, whether it be to end a war, get clean water, or change a traditional practice they have been questioning? What humanist can refuse to listen to the voices of women telling us of *their* priorities? And often anthropologists and public health workers, aware of possible harm from a practice, conduct a respectful dialog about it with people of another culture? Many anthropologists choose to advocate respectfully for change, and that is entirely in keeping with professional work in applied anthropology. But at other times an anthropologist steps back to observe, understand, and analyze in a non-interfering fashion, knowing that could be useful both for promoting mutual understanding and for assisting change agents.

As I see it, female genital cutting practices are changing and appear to be on their way to eventual abandonment as people become more knowledgeable, have alternative options that serve the same identity goals and promote values concerning morality, and become better able to resist the risks of change. Outsiders can help most effectively by offering understanding, respect, and support for grassroots and international change efforts, not only on female genital cutting but also on the *many* issues faced by the women and children of poor countries. It's fine to take a strong position ("I think people should stop doing this!"). But it's equally important to learn respectful dialog for those who do not see it your way.

My personal view is one of respectful challenge. As an anthropologist, my first commitment is to research and promote understanding, but as a humanist, I do not recoil from engagement in fostering improvements of the human condition. Female genital cutting practices vary so much that they clearly are not equally harmful. But because they are performed on non-consenting children, the human rights stance of total opposition to all forms, based on a right to bodily integrity, is ultimately hard to refute. [That principle would also prohibit male infant circumcision and ear-piercing of babies and toddlers, perhaps even extraction of a 12-year-old's teeth for orthodontia, so there are many ethical discussions to be had!] At the same time, my cultural relativism leads me to respect the values people choose to live by, recognizing that people themselves will make their future and choose when and how to change.

Thus, for outsiders, it has little practical consequence whether one is "for it" or "against it," since it is only the practitioners themselves who are in a position to abandon female genital cutting. What really matters is that we engender the respect and understanding for dialog to take place. That requires a respectful "cultural relativist" understanding on which to build the dialog for change, but anthropologists also recognize that "culture" is always contested and changing. Change is inevitable, and the world community should offer practitioners of female genital cutting not racist or ethnocentric condemnation, but understanding and listening. The international community can foster respectful dialog, help deliver information, and offer help with alternatives and improvement of underlying conditions that perpetuate the practices. Women and children living in poverty or marginal economic circumstances without the comforts of clean water, decent housing, adequate food resources, educational opportunities, job opportunities, electricity, or immunizations and basic health services may have social change agendas for their lives that do not list ending female genital cutting as their top priority. The international community would be wise to listen to African women and offer international assistance for their highest priorities as well.

While students, policy-makers, and the general public engage in disputes about female genital cutting, listening to the ideas of those affected and including attention to questions of context, motive, perspective, and the process of persuasion can only help. Change will need deep thinkers with passionate hearts and caring words.

# REFERENCES

Abdal Rahman, Awatif. 1997. Member of the Sudan National Committee on Harmful Traditional Practices, quoted in Reuter report, "Sudan Tackles 'Silent Issue' of Female Circumcision," Feb. 20.

Abusharaf, Rogaia. 1999. Personal communication, Nov. 18.

Assaad, Marie Bassili. 1980. "Female Circumcision in Egypt: Social Implications, Current Research, and Prospects for Change." *Studies in Family Planning* 11, no. 1:3–16.

Cloudsley, Anne. 1983. *Women of Omdurman: Life, Love, and the Cult of Virginity.* London: Ethnographia.

El Dareer, Asma. 1982. *Woman, Why Do You Weep? Circumcision and Its Consequences.* London: Zed Press.

El Saadawi, Nawal. 1980a. "Creative Women in Changing Societies: A Personal Reflection." *Race and Class* 22, no. 2:159–82.

_____. 1980b. *The Hidden Face of Eve: Women in the Arab World.* London: Zed Press.

Gruenbaum, Ellen. 1982. "The Movement Against Clitoridectomy and Infibulation in Sudan." *Medical Anthropology Newsletter* 13, no. 2:4–12. (Reissued in 1997 in *Gender in Cross-Cultural Perspective*, 2nd ed., ed. Caroline Brettell and Carolyn Sargent, pp. 441–53. Upper Saddle River, N.J.: Prentice Hall.)

_____. 1996. "The Cultural Debate Over Female Circumcision: The Sudanese Are Arguing This One Out for Themselves." *Medical Anthropology Quarterly* 10, no. 4:455–75.

_____. 2001. *The Female Circumcision Controversy: An Anthropological Perspective.* Philadelphia: University of Pennsylvania Press.

Hassan, Amna Abdal Rahman, Executive Secretary of the Sudan National Committee Against Harmful Traditional Practices. 2002. Personal communication.

Jennings, Anne. 1995. *The Nubians of West Aswan: Village Women in the Midst of Change.* Boulder, CO: Lynne Rienner.

Lightfoot-Klein, Hanny. 1989. *Prisoners of Ritual: An Odyssey into Female Genital Circumcis ion in Africa*, Binghamton, NY: Harrington Park Press.

Mackie, Gerry. 1996. "Ending Footbinding and Infibulation." *American Sociological Review* 61:991–1017.

Obermeyer, Carla Maklouf. 2003. "The Health Consequences of Female Circumcision: Science, Advocacy, and Standards of Evidence." *Medical Anthropology Quarterly* 17, no. 3:394–412.

Rahman, Anika, and Nahid Toubia. 2000. *Female Genital Mutilation: A Guide to Worldwide Laws and Policies.* London: Zed Press.

Reaves, Stanley. 1997. "Alternative Rite to Female Circumcision Spreading in Kenya." Africa News Services. Nov. 19.

Shandall, Ahmed Abu El Futuh. 1967. "Circumcision and Infibulation of Females." *Sudan Medical Journal* 5, no. 4:178–212.

Shell-Duncan, Bettina, and Ylva Hernlund, eds. 2000a. *Female "Circumcision" in Africa: Culture, Controversy, and Change.* Boulder, CO: Lynne Rienner.

Shell-Duncan, Bettina, and Ylva Hernlund. 2000b. "Female 'Circumcision' in Africa: Dimensions of the Practice and Debates." *In* Shell-Duncan and Hernlund, eds., 2000a:1–40.

Toubia, Nahid. 1993. *Female Genital Mutilation: A Call for Global Action.* New York: Women, Ink.

_____. 1994. "Female Circumcision as a Public Health Issue." *New England Journal of Medicine* 331, no. 11 (Sept. 15):712–16.

World Health Organization. 1996. *Female Genital Mutilation: A Joint WHO/UNICEF/UNFPA Statement.* Geneva: World Health Organization. www.unfpa.org/swp/1997/box16.htm.

Yoder, Stan. 2003. Personal communication, July 29.

# XI

# *Gender and the Global Economy*

We live today in a global world based on complex political and economic relationships. There are few places that remain untouched by international markets, the mass media, geopolitics, or economic aid. However, the global world, particularly the global economy, is not a new phenomenon. It has its roots in the sixteenth century, when the powerful countries of Western Europe began to colonize populations in Asia, Africa, and the Americas (Wolf 1982). Part of this process involved the extraction of raw materials such as gold, sugar, rubber, and coffee, and the exploitation of the labor of indigenous populations for the profit of the colonizing nations.

Although most of the colonized world achieved independence by the 1960s, the economic domination of the capitalist world system that was initiated during the colonial period has not been significantly altered. In the early twenty-first century, an imbalanced relationship between the countries of the industrial, or "developed," world and the developing, or Third World, remains. How have the men and women of the developing world experienced the continuing impact of the penetration of capitalism and the integration of their societies into the global economy?

This question has been addressed in particular with regard to women, and two opposing views have been formulated. Chaney and Schmink (1980), in a review of studies on women and modernization, describe a minority position suggesting that women in the Third World are downtrodden and that capitalist development can help them improve their situation. Those who hold this opinion emphasize that women's economic and social status can be enhanced by an increase in female labor-force participation. Another perspective, stimulated by Ester Boserup's argument that in the course of economic development women experience a decline in their relative status within agriculture (1970: 53), suggests that culture contact, colonialism, and development have introduced "a structure and ideology of male domination" (Leacock 1979: 131). In many parts of the world, originally egalitarian gender relationships have been replaced by more hierarchical ones, and women have consequently been marginalized and removed from the positions of economic and political decision making that they held in the precolonial period.

Researchers have demonstrated these negative effects of colonialism and capitalist penetration in a number of different historical contexts. Silverblatt (1980: 160), for example, portrays the Spanish conquest of the Andes as a "history of the struggle between colonial forces which attempted to break down indigenous social relations and reorient them toward a market economy and the resistance of the indigenous people to these disintegrating forces." The impact of this struggle on the lives of Andean women is particularly salient. In the pre-Inca periods, Andean women had status and power that were manifested in their customary usufruct rights to land and in their ability to organize labor. After the conquest, Spanish law came up against Andean custom with regard to the property rights of women. Patrilineal and patrilocal ties were strengthened at the expense of matrilineal and matrilocal ties, and women became both politically and religiously disenfranchised (see Covey in Section II).

In many historical contexts, however, women resisted colonization and acted to defend themselves (Etienne and Leacock 1980). This was true, for example, of Seneca women in Pennsylvania and New York who withstood the attempts of Quakers to put agricultural production in the hands of men, to individualize land tenure, and to deny them political participation (Rothenberg 1980). A similar resistance to change has been documented for several other North American Indian groups (Grumet 1980). According to Weiner (1980: 43), the colonial period did not diminish the economic power of women in the Trobriand Islands in Melanesia "because no one ever knew that banana leaves had economic value." Women's wealth withstood a number of Western incursions and, as a result, "served to integrate new kinds of Western wealth, as well as individual economic growth, into the traditional system."

Programs designed to stimulate economic development in Third World societies have often continued to perpetuate Western gender biases related to the division of labor, particularly the definition of men as breadwinners and women as homemakers (Charlton 1984; Scott 1995). Based on these assumptions, development planners, frequently with the support of local elites, have directed their efforts at providing new skills and technology to men, even when women are the ones involved in subsistence production and trade (Chaney and Schmink 1980; Escobar 1995). As Schrijvers (1979: 111–112) has observed, "If women got any attention, it was as mothers and housekeepers in family-planning projects and in training programs for home economics. . . . Male-centered development programs often resulted in new divisions of labor between the sexes, by which the dependency of women on men greatly increased." In other words, around the world, development programs have sometimes benefitted women and sometimes worked to their detriment. More recently, development planners have become more aware of the important economic contributions of women to rural economies around the world and have "set the stage for policy-changing arguments that aimed to protect and improve women's access to and control of economic resources as well as their right to participate in and benefit from increased economic opportunities in their communities" (Henderson 1995: 121).

This approach undergirds the myriad microcredit/microfinance programs that have emerged across the globe as part of economic development. Microcredit systems which are said to have originated with the Grameen Bank in Bangladesh, involve small loans that are made to support small industries and entrepreneurship, particularly among poor women (Armendariz 2005; Roy 2010). According to Cheston and Kuhn (2002: 5), the "microfinance industry has made great strides toward identifying barriers to women's access to financial services and developing ways to overcome those barriers." It has often been viewed as a mechanism for the empowerment of poor women. Moodie (in this book), drawing on her research in Rajasthan, India, offers a highly nuanced discussion of microcredit that moves us beyond the simply dichotomy of empowerment or disempowerment. She begins by reviewing some of the criticisms directed at such programs, noting the gap between rhetoric and reality. And yet, her data show that women continue to participate in these programs despite their shortcomings. In attempting to explain why this is the case, Moodie insists that we approach microcredit not only as an economic program but also as a social project. In Rajasthan, microcredit has become part of local ways in which resource distribution, caste relations, the meaning of daughters, and grassroots feminism are discussed.

Microfinance represents one form of capitalist integration with varying impacts on poor women around the world. Agribusiness and multinational industrial production are two additional forms that have brought mixed outcomes in developing countries (Henderson 1995). Arizpe and Aranda (1981), for example, have argued that strawberry agribusiness, although a major employer for women in Zamora, Mexico, has not enhanced women's status or create viable new opportunities for women. These researchers examine why women comprise such a high proportion of the employees in this business and cite cultural factors that constrain opportunities for women and continue to define women's work as temporary and supplementary. Employers take advantage of these constraints—they permit them to keep wages low and work schedules flexible. Arizpe and Aranda's conclusions support those of other researchers who point to a range of phenomena that make a female labor force attractive to multinational business and industry. "Women's socialization, training in needlework, embroidery and other domestic crafts, and supposedly 'natural' aptitude for detailed handiwork, gives them an advantage over men in tasks requiring high levels of manual dexterity and accuracy; women are also supposedly more passive—willing to accept authority and less likely to become involved in labor conflicts. Finally, women have the added advantage of 'natural disposability'—when they leave to get married or have children, a factory temporarily cutting back on production simply freezes their post" (Brydon and Chant 1988: 172).

As with agribusiness, the internationalization of capitalist production has led to the relocation in developing countries of many labor-intensive and export-oriented manufacturing and processing plants owned by multinational corporations. Many of these have provided new opportunities for employment, primarily for women. However, just as with the assessment of the impact of development schemes on the lives of women in the developing world, there are two opposing views about the impact of multinationals. Some emphasize the benefits of jobs that provide women with greater financial stability (Lim 1983), while others see multinationals perpetuating or even creating new forms of inequality as they introduce young women to a new set of individualist and consumerist values. The sexually segregated work force remains in place within paternalistic industrial contexts that encourage turnover and offer no opportunities for advancement (Nash and Fernandez-Kelly 1983; see also Gunewardena 2007; Kung 1994; Ong 1987).

Fernandez-Kelly (1984) has analyzed workers' responses to the international political and economic system at the levels of household and factory along the Mexican side of the US–Mexico border, where more than 100 assembly plants (*maquiladoras*) have been established. These industries primarily employ women. By working herself in the apparel industry, Fernandez-Kelly documented hiring practices and working conditions of factory women. Low wages, oppressive working conditions, lack of job mobility, and insecure job tenure make *maquiladoras* a precarious option, selected by women with few alternatives. Factory workers also suffer from the contradictions between idealized notions of women's roles and their actual involvement in wage labor, which causes conflict over mores and values.

M. Laetitia Cairoli (in this book) describes how young unmarried Moroccan women employed in the export garment industry in Fez, Morocco, reconcile some of the contradictions between the cultural values and role expectations for women and the reality of their industrial employment. Inspired by Aihwa Ong's (1991: 280) emphasis on the "experiential and interpretive dimensions of work relations," Cairoli discusses how these female laborers transform their workplace into an interior domestic space, operating in it as they would in their own household. "They model their position in the factory hierarchy on their role in the household and so are able not only to accept the domination of the factory, but to find in that domination their own sources of personal self-worth and power." Factory owners become like fathers who guard the virtue of their female workers. Fellow garment workers are like sisters and thus the authority of a female supervisor is akin to the authority of the eldest sister. As in the Moroccan home, female space in the factory is separated from male space.

Another result of globalization and the spread of capitalism is the movement of people, both men and women. In recent years, the literature focused on the impact of migration on gender roles and gender ideologies has grown significantly (Brettell 2003; Hondagneu-Sotelo 2003; Pessar 2003). This reflects the growing number of women involved in both internal and international population flows, a phenomenon that has led some scholars to speak of the "feminization of migration." These female migrants have become domestic workers in households as far afield as Washington, DC, Los Angeles, Italy, Kuwait, and Malaysia. They have become factory workers on the global assembly lines located along the US–Mexican border or throughout Asia and Southeast Asia—that is, working for multinational industries that are especially dependent on a mobile female labor force. They have become garment workers in the gateway cities of the United States. And migrant women, some of them very young, have become prostitutes in the cities of both the developed and developing world, part of the growing global sex industry.

Nicole Constable (in this book) outlines the case of Filipina domestic workers in Hong Kong. Women from the Philippines have been migrating to the United States to fill the demand for nurses (Ong and Azores 1994) and to Western Europe to serve as domestics (Parreñas 2001) since the 1970s when Ferdinand Marcos implemented a new labor export policy. Hong Kong became a major destination in the 1980s as the demand for domestic workers increased. As Constable notes, many of the Filipinas who responded to this demand had some advanced education, and this created problems for their Chinese employers who began to see these women as sexually threatening—morally loose and looking for men, and hence subject to discipline and restraint. Through the clothes they wear, Filipina immigrant women mediate and negotiate these stereotypes, often appropriating the self-discipline that is imposed on them by their employers.

Just as ideas of femininity are contested and negotiated in relation to migrant women, so too are ideas of masculinity. Drawing on rich ethnographic data, Osella and Osella (in this book) explore the relationship between migration, styles of masculinity, and male life cycle trajectories in Kerala in south India. In this region, masculine power and agency often depends on the display of substantial cash wealth. Wealth has come to the region through migration to the Gulf States. Migrants are typically young and unmarried men. When they return they typically marry and move into adult status. But to achieve full adult status they must continually demonstrate their competence in both masculinity and maturity and dominant masculinity requires more than competence. Osella and Osella outline four masculine identities that emerge in relation to Gulf migration: the *gulfan* (a returned migrant who is not fully mature and must be reintegrated into the life of the local community); the *pavam* (an unsuccessful man who squanders his wealth and hence his masculine prestige); the *kallan* (an antisocial individual who does not honor social obligations and remains unintegrated); and the classic householder, a successful and mature head of household. Their discussion demonstrates the fluidity of gendered identities and constructions of personhood (see Section V).

One additional form of capitalist integration is tourism, something that Lynn Bolles (2007: 215) has labeled as a "principal agent of globalization." Tourism has been linked with the sex trade and with sex trafficking (Farr 2004; Kara 2009). In her chapter in this book, Denise Brennan describes the encounters between Dominican sex workers and German sex tourists who meet in the transnational space of a tourist town (Sosúa) in the Dominican Republic as well as in Germany. Driven by an interest in how these men and women find out about one another, Brennan traces the relationship between the restructuring dimensions of global capitalism, the fantasies and desires that such restructuring produces both locally and globally, the impact of the Internet, the growing numbers of young, poor, single, and black mothers who turn to the sex trade to survive, and the demand for these women that is generated among foreign and white male tourists of various social class backgrounds. Many of the Dominican women who migrate to the town of Sosúa have a dream of marrying a foreign husband but for most that dream never materializes. By contrast, the foreign men succeed in getting what they want. The different outcomes serve to reinforce gender hierarchies within a global framework that facilitates encounters between sex workers and sex tourists.

The gendered approach to culture contact, colonialism, and development has demonstrated the close relationship among capitalist penetration, patriarchal gender ideologies, the sexual division of labor, and even sex trafficking and sexual tourism. This relationship has been present since the early days of colonialism and has been perpetuated by a global economy that has created an international division of labor often oppressing both men and women, but especially women. Global capitalism and international development programs have frequently resulted not only in environmental degradation, but also in the significant change, if not deterioration of the social environment because some people are either systematically excluded from or exploited by the processes of so-called modernization. And yet, in the context of capitalist integration, there are examples of agency and empowerment on the part of women who must negotiate the forces of globalization and do so in various ways (Gunewardena and Kingsolver 2007; Ong 1987). The impact of globalization on the lives of men and women is neither uniform nor, as Kingsolver (2007: 288) observes, is it "a unified experience of male dominance and female subordination and resistance in capitalist-organized milieu. National leaders implementing neoliberal policies that economically marginalize many in their nations are occasionally women . . . and some of the sex workers who are beaten or ostracized for providing the very services demanded in the global economy are men and boys. A full consideration of gendered globalization," she argues "requires an array of vantage points."

## REFERENCES

Arizpe, Lourdes, and Josefina Aranda. 1981. "The 'Comparative Advantages' of Women's Disadvantages: Women Workers in the Strawberry Export Agribusiness in Mexico." *Signs* 7: 453–473.

Armendariz, Beatrice. 2005. *The Economic of Microfinance.* Cambridge, MA: The MIT Press.

Bolles, A. Lynn. 2007. "The Caribbean Is on Sale: Globalization and Women Tourist Workers in Jamaica." In Nandini Gunewardena and Ann Kingsolver (eds.). *The Gender of Globalization: Women Navigating Cultural and Economic Marginalities*, pp. 215–231. Santa Fe, NM: School of Advanced Research Press.

Boserup, Ester. 1970. *Woman's Role in Economic Development.* New York: St. Martin's Press.

Brettell, Caroline B. 2003. "Gender and Migration." In Caroline B. Brettell (ed.). *Anthropology and Migration: Essays on Transnationalism, Ethnicity, and Identity*, pp. 139–151. Walnut Creek, CA: Altamira Press.

Brydon, Lynne, and Sylvia Chant. 1988. *Women in the Third World: Gender Issues in Rural and Urban Areas.* New Brunswick, NJ: Rutgers University Press.

Chaney, Elsa M., and Marianne Schmink. 1980. "Women and Modernization: Access to Tools." In June Nash and Helen I. Safa (eds.). *Sex and Class in Latin America*, pp. 160–182. South Hadley, MA: J. F. Bergin Publishers.

Charlton, Sue-Ellen M. 1984. *Women in Third World Development.* Boulder, CO: Westview Press.

Cheston, Susy, and Lisa Kuhn. 2002. *Empowering Women through Microfinance.* UNIFEM. www.microcreditsummit .org/papers/empowerment.pdf.

Escobar, Arturo. 1995. *Encountering Development: The Making and Unmaking of the Third World.* Princeton, NJ: Princeton University Press.

Etienne, Mona, and Eleanor Leacock. 1980. "Introduction." In Mona Etienne and Eleanor Leacock (eds.). *Women and Colonization: Anthropological Perspectives*, pp. 1–24. New York: Praeger.

Farr, Kathryn. 2004. *Sex Trafficking: The Global Market in Women and Children.* New York: W.W. Freedman.

Fernandez-Kelly, Maria Patricia. 1984. "Maquiladoras: The View from the Inside." In Karen Brodkin Sacks and Dorothy Remy (eds.). *My Troubles are Going to Have Trouble With Me*, pp. 229–246. New Brunswick, NJ: Rutgers University Press.

Grumet, Robert Steven. 1980. "Sunksquaws, Shamans, and Tradeswomen: Middle Atlantic Coastal Algonkian Women during the 17th and 18th Centuries." In Mona Etienne and Eleanor Leacock (eds.). *Women and Colonization: Anthropological Perspectives*, pp. 43–62. New York: Praeger.

Gunewardena, Nandini. 2007. "Disrupting Subordination and Negotiating Belonging: Women Workers in the Transnational Production Sites of Sri Lanka." In Nandini Gunewardena and Ann Kingsolver (eds.). *The Gender of Globalization: Women Navigating Cultural and Economic Marginalities*, pp. 35–60. Santa Fe, NM: School of Advanced Research Press.

Gunewardena, Nandini, and Ann Kingsolver. 2007. *The Gender of Globalization: Women Navigating Cultural and Economic Marginalities.* Santa Fe, NM: School of Advanced Research Press.

Henderson, Helen Kreider (ed.). 1995. *Gender and Agricultural Development: Surveying the Field.* Tucson: University of Arizona Press.

Hondagneu-Sotelo, Pierrette. 2003. *Gender and U.S. Immigration: Contemporary Trends.* Berkeley: University of California Press.

Kara, Siddharth. 2009. *Sex Trafficking: Inside the Business of Modern Slavery.* New York: Columbia University Press.

Kingsolver, Ann. 2007. "Navigating Paradoxical Globalizations." In Nandini Gunewardena and Ann Kingsolver (eds.). *The Gender of Globalization: Women Navigating Cultural and Economic Marginalities*, pp. 287–291. Santa Fe, NM: School of Advanced Research Press.

Kung, Lydia. 1994. *Factory Women in Taiwan.* New York: Columbia University Press.

Leacock, Eleanor. 1979. "Women, Development, and Anthropological Facts and Fictions." In Gerrit Huizer and Bruce Mannheim (eds.). *The Politics of Anthropology: From Colonialism and Sexism Toward a View from Below*, pp. 131–142. The Hague: Mouton.

Lim, Linda Y. C. 1983. "Capitalism, Imperialism, and Patriarchy: The Dilemma of Third-World Women Workers in Multinational Factories." In June Nash and Maria Patricia Fernandez-Kelly (eds.). *Women, Men and the International Division of Labor*, pp. 70–91. Albany: State University of New York.

Nash, June, and Maria Patricia Fernandez-Kelly (eds.). 1983. *Women, Men and the International Division of Labor.* Albany: State University of New York.

Ong, Aihwa. 1987. *Spirits of Resistance and Capitalist Discipline: Factory Women in Malaysia.* Albany: State University of New York Press.

_____. 1991. "The Gender and Labor Politics of Post-Modernity." *Annual Review of Anthropology* 20: 279–309.

Ong, Paul, and Tania Azores. 1994. "The Migration and Incorporation of Filipino Nurses." In Paul Ong, Edna Bonacich, and Lucie Cheng (eds.). *The New Asian Immigration in Los Angeles and Global Restructuring*, pp. 3–35. Philadelphia: Temple University Press.

Parreñas, Rhacel. 2001. *Servants of Globalization: Women, Migration, and Domestic Work.* Stanford, CA: Stanford University Press.

Pessar, Patricia. 2003. "Anthropology and the Engendering of Migration Studies." In Nancy Foner (ed.). *American Arrivals: Anthropology Engages the New Immigration*, pp. 75–98. Santa Fe, NM: School of American Research Press.

Rothenberg, Diane. 1980. "The Mothers of the Nation: Seneca Resistance to Quaker Intervention." In Mona Etienne and Eleanor Leacock (eds.). *Women and Colonization: Anthropological Perspectives*, pp. 63–87. New York: Praeger.

Roy, Ananya. 2010. *Poverty Capital: Microfinance and the Making of Development.* New York: Routledge.

Schrijvers, Joke. 1979. "Viricentrism and Anthropology." In Gerrit Huizer and Bruce Mannheim (eds.). *The Politics of Anthropology: From Colonialism and Sexism Toward a View from Below*, pp. 97–115. The Hague: Mouton.

Scott, Catherine V. 1995. *Gender and Development: Rethinking Modernization and Dependency Theory.* Boulder, CO: Lynne Rienner Publishers.

Silverblatt, Irene. 1980. "Andean Women Under Spanish Rule." In Mona Etienne and Eleanor Leacock (eds.). *Women and Colonization: Anthropological Perspectives*, pp. 149–185. New York: Praeger.

Weiner, Annette. 1980. "Stability in Banana Leaves: Colonization and Women in Kiriwina, Trobriand Islands." In Mona Etienne and Eleanor Leacock (eds.). *Women and Colonization: Anthropological Perspectives*, pp. 270–293. New York: Praeger.

Wolf, Eric. 1982. *Europe and the People without History*. Berkeley: University of California Press.

# *Enter Microcredit:*
# A New Culture of Women's Empowerment in Rajasthan?

## *Megan Moodie*

Despite its seeming out-of-the-wayness, rural Rajasthan has been a site of intense effort by the Indian state to empower women. Indeed, the idea that women are more oppressed in Rajasthan than anywhere else in India inspires a huge bureaucratic apparatus and a pervasive discourse about the need for women's uplift in the state.[1] Most of what I know about these efforts to improve the lives of women in rural Rajasthan I learned from Gangori Kanwar. My hostess in a small village at the southernmost reaches of Jaipur District, Gangori Kanwar is a *sathin* (lit. female accomplice–advocate) with Rajasthan's flagship women's empowerment initiative, the Women's Development Programme (WDP). This means that, since the late 1980s, she has participated in various training retreats to become a "change agent" in her home village, helping to spur and support efforts by her female peers to change cultural attitudes toward women, which are often characterized in Rajasthan as feudal and oppressive. Gangori Kanwar is also in charge of the village *anganwadi* (public preschool), runs an informal ayurvedic practice to treat infertility and gynecological problems, participates in local politics (she was once a candidate for village *sarpanch* [village headperson]), and is the wife of a Rajput *zamindar* (land owner). A truly compelling narrator of the woes of her poor village sisters and an undeniably dynamic figure, she has recently taken up a new role: conjuring microcredit loans for women in the village of Debaliya by enrolling groups, sometimes of multicaste–multiclass composition and sometimes socially uniform, with the various agencies that claim to work for women's empowerment in rural Rajasthan.

Microfinance has emerged as the main development model, especially for women in South Asia, over the last ten years. Recent case studies of microcredit initiatives, however, have been deeply skeptical of their problematic and sometimes violent outcomes. The picture the studies paint is grim: Many women simply hand over their loans to male relatives. Pressure to make timely payments is so strong that women often borrow money from moneylenders at exorbitant interest rates to do so, and they are subjected to violence and aggression when they cannot pay these additional loans (Rahman 1999). Even if they are able to start small-scale production enterprises, they have difficulty bringing goods to market (Mahmud 2003), and any increased contribution to household income they make may be met by a corresponding decrease from other household members (Mayoux 1999). Benefits, such as they are, seem to accrue to women who are already high status (Mayoux 1999). In other words, very few researchers find microcredit to be the sure route out of poverty it is claimed to be; the gap between the "rhetoric and reality" (Isserles 2003) of microcredit is wide.

In this chapter, I focus on the relationships between women within microcredit groups, rather than just on the relationship between borrowers and their male relatives, to better understand not why microcredit projects fail but why they seem to be so successful—not only on a global scale but on the ground as well. Despite the apparent failure of loans to increase anyone's household income significantly, all the women I knew in Debaliya wanted a loan. Although the desire for loans can be understood in very stark financial terms—on a particular day, more cash entered a household—local social factors cautioned against borrowing. Not everyone who joined microcredit groups trusted Gangori Kanwar, their main broker,

Adapted by author from "Enter microcredit: A new culture of women's empowerment in Rajasthan? *American Ethnologist* 35 (3), 2008, pp. 454–465.

representative, and beneficiary. The allegations that she stole loan monies from women, which I explore below, came out as soon as my research collaborator, Shally Vaish, and I started asking questions about loan groups. The question that continually bothered me during the several months that I conducted fieldwork in Debaliya, then, was why women continued to go along with Gangori Kanwar's plans to join an ever-growing number of nongovernmental and governmental microcredit schemes.[2] If women were not getting significant benefits or material gains from these programs, why did they continue to invest not only money but also considerable emotional energy in them? What was microcredit's magic that it compelled participation despite the perception by many group members that Gangori Kanwar swindled them?

To begin to answer this question, I have had to see microcredit not just as an "economic" arrangement but also, and maybe primarily, as a social project. This social project introduces new ideas and languages that interact with many others in the cultural terrain of rural Rajasthan. Microcredit is mixed up with various other local frameworks, from feminism to the evil eye, that women mobilize to make sense of the exchanges and transactions that characterize social life. This cobbling together of frameworks provides women in Debaliya with platforms for critiquing these very same exchanges and transactions; such a critique is one of the main activities within loan groups. Seen in this light, microcredit is attractive to the women in Debaliya because it provides them with another platform to discuss all kinds of issues that seemingly have nothing to do with microcredit: caste relations and the burdens of raising daughters, for example. It is not the only platform available but it is currently the one with the most "magic" behind it in terms of international acclaim and governmental funding.[3] As such, it is especially charged in contemporary village life, and critiques of and around loans have a special force. Rather than criticizing local microcredit initiatives for failing to empower women—although, to be clear, I believe they usually fail in this endeavor—I look at what is happening in loan groups. On the one hand, I believe that attention to the intragroup dynamics helps explain microcredit's success on the ground despite its inability to fulfill any of its own promises. On the other hand, looking at group-level struggles over loans illuminates an important part of how rural Rajasthani women, rather than being completely removed from or oppressed by economic relationships, engage in all kinds of negotiations and protests around local exchange despite the widely held view that they are among the least empowered women in India and perhaps, indeed, the world.

## A TERRAIN OF DIVERSE TRANSACTIONS

Feminist analyses of microcredit's ideology and operation have shown that it relies on discourses of natural individualism and entrepreneurialism. Linda Mayoux's (1999) well-known critique of the "virtuous spiral" underlying microcredit thinking forcefully questions the assumption that access to credit leads to economic empowerment and that economic gain in and of itself is enough to guarantee either familial well-being or wider social and political reform for women. In the absence of "alternative visions" of gender relations, microfinance does not lead to local critiques of women's subordination (Mayoux 1999). Robin Isserles, echoing Mayoux's critique, demonstrates the ways in which microcredit reproduces a U.S.-style "bootstrap" social program that, although appearing to center on efficiency and self-respect, in fact, "makes individual behavior central to overcoming poverty, avoiding structural analyses or critiques" (2003: 45). Both researchers draw attention to the ways in which microcredit seems to embody the values of what scholars refer to as neoliberalism and directly contravene the goal of women's empowerment as it might be imagined by development planners, including some feminists, in both the North and South.[4] In Rajasthan, their concerns are shared by recent analysts of the WDP, of which Gangori Kanwar is a part. As I discuss below, external reviewers looking at the WDP are concerned about the abandonment of efforts that promote cultural change in favor of lending activities.[5]

I suggest that both the construction of a one-to-one correspondence between income and empowerment implied by development planners and the critique of this perspective provided by recent authors provide few tools for understanding what poor women may be articulating or looking for in their embrace of microcredit. Both perspectives entail splitting the "economic" from the "social" to see how one does or does not contribute to the other. Following J. K. Gibson-Graham (2006: 1–23), I see this kind of thinking as hindering scholars' ability to perceive the economy—or society or gender, for that matter—as plural spaces, places of difference and struggle. It restricts us to the recognition of only certain kinds of transactions as being about empowerment. If, as I hope to show below, microcredit has become one of several platforms for articulation from which women in Debaliya can comment on many different kinds of local exchange, its real product is not economic or social but both and neither. In other words, microcredit produces cultural possibility. It is, therefore, most usefully evaluated not in terms of empowerment or disempowerment but in terms of the relationships and exchanges—the transactions—it does or does not make possible in a given setting.

I begin by contextualizing microcredit's entrance into the village within the larger history of efforts to empower Rajasthani women over the last 20 years. Despite the fears of WDP planners, microcredit groups have not so much supplanted an earlier feminist agenda as they have added another kind of platform for articulation. I then delve into the series of accusations and counteraccusations surrounding Gangori Kanwar and her abuse of loan monies. Although Gangori Kanwar seems to have occasionally taken advantage of her position, loan accusations against her were less about the specifics of money gained or lost and more about women's relationships to each other in the village. Caste relations, the burdens of daughters, and personal histories were all enacted and contested within the microcredit drama.

## MICROCREDIT AND THE WDP: A DOWNWARD SPIRAL

The WDP of Rajasthan began in 1984 as a joint venture between the Directorate of Women and Child Development and Nutrition; the Office of the District Collector; the Information and Development Resource Agency (IDARA); and the Institute of Development Studies, Jaipur (IDSJ).[6] Funded by UNICEF for the first six years of its existence, the project originally ran in six districts, Jaipur District among them, and was later expanded to all the districts of Rajasthan. The stated purpose was to "empower women through communication of information, education, and training to enable them to recognize their social and economic status" (Madhok 2003: ch. 3). The WDP, as an institution, represented the coming together of several historical streams. In the mid-1980s, "women's empowerment," as invoked by the UN platform for the Decade for Women, for example, offered an ideal means for the Indian state to move away from explicit family-planning agendas, which were highly unpopular after the excesses of the Emergency, but to continue to pursue its population-control project. This was also an important moment in the history of the Indian women's movement, when women from lower-status social groups began to make more vocal demands on the state, and academic feminism was forced to look at its urban, middle-class bias (John 1996; Mazumdar 1994). The WDP epitomizes the shift toward both empowerment and the greater participation of poor, rural, and tribal women in the project of the women's movement.

Its experimental design stressed communication, bureaucratic responsiveness, and structural flexibility, with the goal of enabling rural women to participate in their own development.[7] Rural women, the argument went, possessed great creativity and social force, which only needed to be harnessed to causes of gender and social justice. They could, in fact, become highly motivated to work for change within their own communities if given the kind of education that would couple their natural concern for their families with a sense of themselves and their rights and struggles as women. In the WDP model, solidarity could be built between women, across caste and class. A cadre of women, known as sathins, was recruited from rural villages to begin grassroots work toward gender equality and social empowerment. Gangori Kanwar and other sathins began intense training sessions with the urban organizers of the program, who were drawn from activist, academic, and bureaucratic circles, in which the values of self-determination, education, and gender equity were impressed on them.

The project, then, began as a locally inspired critique of feudal patriarchy (the organizers' terms). Monthly *jajams*, or meetings of sathins, encouraged women to articulate their concerns and reinforced a deep vertical connection between sathins in the villages and planners in the capital. A holistic empowerment approach was seen as especially important in Rajasthan, which vies with Bihar and Uttar Pradesh for the lowest rank in most assessments of women's status. High infant and maternal mortality, reports of infanticide and child marriage, the lowest literacy rates for women in all of India, and, most importantly, an intrinsically antifemale culture are all cited as proof of Rajasthan's singular oppressiveness. Such a characterization seemed confirmed when, just after the WDP's founding, in 1987, Roop Kanwar was immolated as a sati in Deorala village outside Jaipur.[8]

As Maya Unnithan and Kavita Srivastava (1997) note, much of the sathins' early work was directed toward matters of concern for "villagers as a whole," rather than those that development logics consider "women's issues." Records of early activities, recorded in the IDSJ report *Exploring Possibilities: A Review of the Women's Development Programme, Rajasthan* (WDP 1987), indicate that sathins were often most concerned about famine relief, access to wells and hand pumps, rules of the *panchayati raj* (local government), encroachment onto public lands by high-caste herders' cattle, rations, and reforestation. Family planning, reproductive health, child marriage, and male alcoholism also figured into early WDP activities, but as topics that affected village women's lives on a par with what might be thought of as broader livelihood and political issues. Further, the preferred method for communication and expression on these issues was to craft songs and plays in the Rajasthani dialect. In other words, WDP planners and the sathins with whom they worked took to heart lessons about the necessarily processual pursuit of a goal such as "women's empowerment," relying on local media to pursue concerns that were dictated by the sathins themselves.

Reports from the mid-1980s to early 1990s describe an unprecedented flow of people, resources, and ideas between the sathin villages and the program centers. Both program organizers and feminist activists outside Rajasthan widely believed that the program was both unique and successful, effecting real cultural changes to benefit women in Rajasthan; indeed, other states soon created their own programs based on the WDP model (see Gupta and Sharma 2006). In 1992, however, a sathin named Bhanwri Devi was gang raped by the male relatives of a small child whose marriage she was seeking to prevent. The subsequent acquittal of her attackers and the case's national visibility put a great deal of stress on the relationship between the sathins and the state.[9] The sathins, program participants argued, could not be expected to continue their culturally sensitive and often-dangerous work—Bhanwri Devi was not the only woman attacked in the line of duty—if they could not even count on the support of the state when they were assaulted. The controversy resulted in a scaling down of the program that accelerated from 1992 on. Since 1992, there has been a "silent shift" from the sathin model to the *samooh*, or self-help group, model. The group model not only undermined some of the local authority and notoriety of the sathins—some had become quite skilled at collective mobilization—but it was also compatible with new ideas within international circles about how women's empowerment programs should run. Notably, the existence of groups that are able to provide the "social collateral" (Isserles 2003) to ensure repayment was seen as essential to microcredit endeavors. The needs of the state government and this international microcredit trend dovetailed well so that, by the late 1990s, the sathin program was referred to as "defunct," even as some sathins were agitating for higher wages and recognition as real government employees.

In line with the microcredit vision, when I conducted fieldwork in 2002 and 2003, at least half a dozen government and nongovernment bodies required their field officers to start self-help groups for microcredit purposes in Jaipur District. These included, among others, the district and block officers; government-employed teachers; anganwadi workers[10]; and employees of the Center for Community Economics and Development Consultants Society (CECOEDECON),[11] Rotary International, the National Bank for Agriculture and Rural Development, and the WDP. Five different groups operated in the village where I conducted research, all under different programs, each named after a different goddess, such as Kali and Durga.

The result on the ground is a distracting confusion about who is loaning what to whom. Women may not even know what their loan money is supposed to be going toward. Women never cited specific banks or organizations as the sources of lending. In local ways of speaking, one "got" money from "Mahila Vikas," ("Women's Development," as it is locally known) whether or not the money came specifically from the WDP. My direct questions about funding sources were inevitably answered with such vague references, and any pertinent documentation that I was able to view contained only rupee amounts and lists of names. At the same time, there is a fierce and growing desire among Rajasthani women to forge ties to lending institutions or their officials.

The changes in the WDP's approach to empowerment have not gone unnoticed, and few think they have been for the best. Indeed, the sense is growing among project participants at all levels that the radical feminist component of the WDP has diminished over the past seven years. Whether this has been caused by microcredit is perhaps a matter of debate, but there is a clear parallel between the rise of the self-help group and the demise of the vocal sathin. Commenting on the new trend toward microfinance in the WDP, an independent review conducted in 2002 reported on these groups in general:

> We could not see evidence of these groups acting as a collective or as a conduit for spreading awareness amongst village women of their legal rights or as a problem or watchdog body which would have an outreach to the women. We found most of these groups rather pre-occupied with the nuts and bolts of borrowing, lending, and starting enterprises. (Sujaya et al. 2002: 18)

The report authors' skepticism echoes Mayoux's critique of "virtuous spirals" discussed above. Microcredit on its own, they suggest, is not enough to produce the kinds of changes initially sought by the WDP. It is not inherently mobilizing and does not work to further the interests of women's collective empowerment. Further, the report notes, women often did not have technical guidance in production or access to markets or marketing skills. Little evidence suggests that microcredit was making a noticeable difference in the economic lives of most rural Rajasthani women, and political gains, such as they were, reflected "the distinctive mark of the sathin . . . and the WDP" (Sujaya et al. 2002: 19), not microcredit itself.

This brief history makes clear the need to contemplate specific histories of microcredit in particular locations: Microcredit in Rajasthan has to be considered within the longer trajectory of projects, particularly of the WDP, for women's empowerment. On the ground, it is seen by planners and participants alike as part of larger efforts by the Rajasthani state to improve the lives of women, efforts that, with the publicity of the

Roop Kanwar and Bhanwri Devi cases, have largely been considered failures. The radical edge of the WDP, particularly its focus on land tenure and inheritance and on water and grazing rights, is thought to have been dulled as women have been brought together in groups for purposes that are often vague and overly individualistic. Clearly, there is great import to this analysis: Microcredit seems to enable few material or social changes as it operates in Rajasthan today.

But I propose that narratives of women's empowerment programs in India tend to stress profound paradigm shifts to the detriment of understanding how rural women think about and engage with the kinds of issues these programs attempt to affect in ways that often utilize many different platforms for articulation. At the level of the everyday, various constellations of ideas and languages interact when women are brought together in the name of empowerment. The sathin program, despite popular opinion and defunding, is not defunct. Feminist ideas and languages are not alien to Rajasthani culture. And critiques of social forces such as caste and gender discrimination emerge from inside and outside women's groups; such critiques may extend to the context of the women's group itself. The sociality of the group is not dictated by the project design through which it is convened, although the design may offer new possibilities for reflection, critique, manipulation, or magic.

## A DANGEROUS (IM)BALANCE: WOMEN, RESOURCES, AND EVIL EYE

Credit self-help groups may take two general forms, as programs currently operate in Rajasthan. In one, women get together in a group and each deposits a small amount of savings in an account. The group then provides loans to its members at fixed interest rates on the basis of the group's assessment of who most needs the money at a given moment. In the second, lenders give loans to groups of women to use as capital investment for microenterprise: to fund craft cooperatives or purchase animals, in theory. In the case of Debaliya, many women brought milk from goats and, sometimes, cows to sell in the neighboring village of Mosra, so the purchase of animals was a popular stated reason to seek a loan, whether or not an animal was ever actually purchased.

Most women among the higher-caste Brahmins, Rajputs, Jats, and Gujjars in Debaliya village practice some form of veiling, although it is not strictly maintained. They draw water from the one functional village hand pump, if they are veiled, and visit each other's homes; many participate in the labor of drought-relief works, moving heavy head loads of

mud to build rain storage tanks. Gangori Kanwar, undoubtedly the highest-status woman in the village as wife of the largest landowner, recounted with pride her personal transformation as a sathin, which taught her that the business of caste hierarchy was all wrong; now everyone was allowed to visit her home, in her telling.[12] On any given day, she might entertain or interact with Brahmin women, Nai (Barber) villagers, or Kumhars (Potters). Caste mixing, as reported by Gangori Kanwar, was an explicit goal of the WDP in its early days. Most sathins, unlike Gangori Kanwar, were drawn from lower castes. There is, then, a noticeable discourse within the village about the need for women to unite despite caste status; at the same time, lower-caste women told me that they were only permitted into Gangori Kanwar's home when I was present in the village. Otherwise, they were expected to maintain the social distance dictated by caste hierarchy.

A striking feature of women's social lives in the village is the low level of pooling of labor for mutual benefit. Women in Debaliya, even of the same caste, do not form work groups, although they may enlist daughters to help with chores. Women's separation, based on the separation of *chulhas*, or hearths, engenders a view that "each woman should be busy with her own work . . . rather than spending time with other women or contributing to the work of any other chulha" (Jeffrey et al. 1989: 48). Although Gangori Kanwar and her sister-in-law Roshan Kanwar lived next door to one another, they did not share in each other's domestic labors except on special occasions. Women across castes carry out the same daily tasks separately, but what they do together is talk. They may gossip about whose son's new wife brought in what dowry items, or about the price of fodder, but women's relationships are forged in conversation and social evaluation. The worst thing one can do to another woman is refuse to *avaz dena* (lit., give your voice) to her.

Women's daily tasks in Debaliya revolve around food: getting, storing, and preparing food. During my fieldwork in 2003, many families had at least one goat to provide milk and important by-products like yogurt and ghee (clarified butter)—an important source of calories—to the family. The goat had to be fed and looked after. In addition, some families managed to grow one crop of spinach for home consumption or a plot of cumin to sell, despite the drought that charred Rajasthan from 1999 to 2003. This kind of work too had to be rationed and negotiated. Another time-consuming job was managing wheat stores, which largely came to the village in the form of government-sponsored drought-relief rations. The wheat had to be processed on the grinding stone, turned into dough, and baked as thick *roti*s (flatbreads). The whole process was repeated twice a day.

Village norms say that one must share what one has but only if others know one has it. Village women were quite generous with me during my time at Gangori Kanwar's, often sending something from their gardens for my evening meal or inviting me to come and eat rotis with thick wads of ghee melting in their centers. These gifts entailed reciprocal obligations that I was happy to fulfill, carrying pounds of precious green vegetables from the city to the village on my back in a strange reversal of received notions about where food is produced and where it is consumed. Generosity is considered an important characteristic of a good woman.

Yet village architecture, storage technologies, and daily practices speak to the constant desire to hide what one possesses. Even the poorest households store their food out of sight, under lock and key. Other personal goods, like clothes, important papers, combs, and mirrors, are kept under tight control in large trunks, which are often the only pieces of furniture in a home besides string cots. Things used in food preparation, like ladles or cups, are tucked out of sight into roof eaves when not actually in use. The only household items that tend to sit in plain view are religious statues and offerings to the deities. Everything else is kept under strict watch. One of Gangori Kanwar's many tasks included managing her ring of keys, one key for each room of her four-room house. Each time a room had to be opened for some reason, she would take the proper key from her ring and unlock the door, only to relock the room and replace the key on a string around her neck as soon as the designated task was finished. More than once I had her open a room so that I could retrieve something or perform some task only to find after I had been called away momentarily that she had relocked the room in my brief absence.

The practices of hiding and secrecy lead to endless speculation about what women have and do not have. People often report that this or that poor woman really has a "trunk full of saris" hidden in her house. Hoarding food while one owes a debt of obligation to someone else is a grievous social injury. It is not hard to imagine why, then, in the context of group loans, when women know very little about how they are being funded or who is getting what, wild rumors circulate about large sums of money stashed away. It is also not surprising that the group form impelled by microcredit schemes poses serious difficulties in the face of norms of village sociality. Cooperative work among women is not the norm. There is no preexistent sisterhood to be harnessed by microcredit so much as there is a constantly shifting web of talk about and analysis of the possessions of others and relative neediness.

Food is charged with powerful force in Debaliya village, where one is always at risk of not having enough. Important rules govern how food is to be consumed and shared, rules that accord with general norms of generosity but are not immediately obvious to the outsider. One afternoon as I sat in the inner courtyard of Gangori Kanwar's home, she warned me not to eat my daily food in front of other women from the village, who often came to sit in the courtyard and visit. They were not "family" and their *nazar* (evil eye) could make me sick, which I often was during my stays in the village. Instead, I was to eat in the household *puja* room, behind closed doors, if possible.[13] Nazar-related illness, she explained, was caused when women felt envy about the food consumed by others. Children especially could be affected; there was also always the risk of *dakan*, or witches, killing them if a mother was not vigilant. She illustrated with an example:

> One day, [a woman] was feeding her child and a[nother] woman came to sell vegetables. That lady [selling vegetables] saw the child [of the potential customer]. The child had a lot of hair on his body. Only the face was clear—the rest was hairy. After she left, the child got very sick and died the next day. His mother grieved and cried a lot. . . . Now all the Rajputs asked how the child died. His mother told them the entire story. . . . Then four or five people took their swords and went to their graveyard. They understood the whole story. They climbed to the top of a tree and stayed there. They didn't whisper anything—it was nighttime. At twelve o'clock, the witch came and took off all her clothes and removed the mud [from the grave]. She took the child out and started playing with him [tossing him into the air]. So the child started crying . . . [and they] caught and tied her. Then they called Sati and said, "Look what a bad woman she is. She ate a child." [They let her go]. That child is still alive today . . . still today he has a lot of hair and a good, big family.

Many aspects of Gangori's story accord with previous studies of evil eye and witchcraft belief in South Asia. The curse begins with seemingly benign contact with a stranger who is secretly an ill wisher; in fact, in many cases an attack results from compliments delivered to children, who can hardly be said to have offended the bewitcher themselves. The stranger in this case is not of the same caste as the child or its mother and is presumably of a lower caste ("all the Rajputs asked how the child died"). And food figures in the story, another common feature of nazar tales. G. Morris Carstairs (1983) reports that many witchcraft accusations in Rajasthan seem to be made against poor, low-caste women who are widows or are barren. Women believe that individuals may harm others through their natural jealousy, and people are frequently described as "eating" children, emphasizing the consumptive aspects of evil-eye beliefs (Carstairs 1983). Evil eye resulting from food jealousy is perhaps the most common nazar there is, according to Gangori Kanwar. Further, Gangori Kanwar's story puts the figure of the dakan, or witch, into stark contrast with Sati Mata, the apotheosis of Rajput womanhood and thereby stresses the evil of her deed (see Gold 1988; Harlan 1991; see also Bharucha 2003).

Anything in excess—hair, food, money—is, in village norms of generosity, suspect. This is not a situation, however, as George Foster's (1965) "limited good" model would have it, in which any gain by an individual is seen as threatening (see Taussig 1980). In this case, excess itself is not the problem that provokes others but whether or not it is visible. If one is clever enough to gain and conceal, it is not one's *galati* (fault).

Excesses can also work as deficits. For instance, certain features of family life, such as the number of daughters a woman has borne, are considered socially appropriate markers of her neediness. In the karmic scheme of things, having too many daughters is both a disability and an entitlement to special sympathy from one's peers. In an often-confusing discursive play, women draw affinities between themselves and others on the basis of the number of girl children with which they have been burdened. The term *burdened* is apt because the birth of a girl child necessarily entails her family's responsibility to provide a proper dowry for her. In local family calculus, a daughter either has to be balanced out by a son, or the family has to find additional income.

The ideal, then, is an economy of goods and people in circulation so that some kind of just balance is reached. With the entrance of loans whose source and purpose is often unclear, a whole new set of charged possibilities opens up for generosity, greed, or fate. Women in Debaliya know that they are ignorant about much of what their relatives and neighbors possess. The possibility always exists that someone has both untapped resources and secret bad intentions. Women's folklore includes tales of the discovery of vast riches in mundane places, such as gold bangles in the belly of a fish. Despite the official ethics of microcredit and ideas about sharing, I heard the ubiquitous charge, "She has a whole trunk of saris hidden in her house." As in the story of the vegetable seller, appearances are not to be relied on, for they are often revealed as illusion. The gods are well known for disguising themselves in humble costumes only to reveal their true forms and reward those who have come to their aid and harm those who have not. Conversely, rumors about how seemingly poor women could be rich imply that just because you could not see something did not mean it was not there.

## THE SOCIAL LIFE OF LOANS

Undoubtedly one of the most burdened women in Debaliya was Saroj. Gangori Kanwar introduced me to Saroj—"poor thing"—early in my stay in Debaliya.

I admired Saroj from our first meeting. Despite obvious pain, this middle-aged Nai (Barber) woman and mother of four took great joy in sitting on the verandah of her low *kaccha* (unfinished; in this case, mud) house and talking with me or with my research collaborator, Shally. Her oldest child, and only son, lived in Jaipur, where he had a barber's stand; her three unmarried daughters still lived at home and clearly doted on their mother. Around six or seven years ago, Saroj had a *nasbandi* operation (a tubal ligation, the local term for which is the English *opration*) reportedly at the insistence of Gangori Kanwar, even though family planning was not considered the work of sathins. After this operation, she developed a serious kidney problem. Saroj had to visit doctors in Jaipur many times and was given medical treatment for three years before a diagnosis of "delayed excretion" convinced the doctors that she needed to have a kidney removed.[14] This operation was performed at great expense to the family, which was quite poor and lived on the edge of the village. When I met her five months later, Saroj continued to have a great deal of postoperative pain and was confused about what had happened to her. She cried as she told Shally and me about her struggles to obtain medicines, raise her daughters, and pull her weight in terms of household labor. She was certain that supernatural forces had entered her body during the first operation, causing her current malady.

Saroj was also angry. She claimed that her husband was given lowest priority at the drought-relief works, implying that it was run through upper-caste loyalties, a charge often made about relief work. The medicines that she continued to need were available with her medical ration card, which she could only use at the hospital in Jaipur and only to obtain two-weeks' supply at any one time. This meant that Saroj had to take the bus every two weeks to stay with her son in the city, at a cost of at least 60 rupees for each trip. Saroj felt that she was mistreated by the doctors in Jaipur. She was supposed to receive free care at the government hospital. Often, however, the doctor would call her to his home, where he felt justified in charging her hundreds of rupees for consultations. Her needs were, indeed, acute, and she was quite certain about what she deserved from the *panchayat* [village council] in terms of financial support as well as from other women in terms of sympathy: She had no money and could not work, her three daughters would all need to be married off, and she faced caste discrimination that, she seemed to imply, was worse because upper-caste people such as Gangori Kanwar hypocritically denied it existed.

Saroj's family had planted a plot of spinach to get them through the winter months and sent me some to have for dinner one evening. I tried to reciprocate their generosity, and, on my next trip to and from Jaipur,

I brought Saroj peas and cauliflower, a rare treat in rural areas in a drought winter. I wanted to further help the family with money for Saroj's trips to Jaipur and was in the process of figuring out how best to be of use in this regard when a series of conversations shifted my understanding of Saroj's predicament. Saroj had established a friendship with Gangori Kanwar's sister-in-law, Roshan Kanwar. Roshan Kanwar worked as Gangori Kanwar's assistant with the anganwadi program and sewed clothes for women and children in the village; she, like Gangori, was quite enterprising in her relationship with the WDP, although she was far more popular with other women in the village. Saroj clearly admired Roshan Kanwar and told Shally and me that Roshan Kanwar had gotten a loan by depositing ten rupees with Mahila Vikas. Saroj herself would not deposit money, because she was scared of Gangori Kanwar. Saroj told us,

> She [Gangori Kanwar] has gotten a loan. She will use it for herself. If she gets a loan in my name, she will also use it for herself. The day before yesterday, I met Gangori Kanwar in one of the Jat's house. The loan was sanctioned in the name of that Jat lady. She was left [without anything], and the loan is being used by Gangori Kanwar. When you came, the day before yesterday, the lady was saying [to Gangori Kanwar] "Please give two paisa."

When we asked why people did not try to stop Gangori Kanwar from taking their loan money, Saroj replied, "You can't say no. She is very *chaagti* [cunning or smart]. You can take me anywhere with you. If I am in Mahila Vikas and if I get a loan and if you tell me to give it [to you], I'll give it. Gangori Kanwar has her son's wedding [to pay for], so she is using it for that. This is Gangori Kanwar's galati [fault]."

These accusations against Gangori Kanwar were further explained by Roshan Kanwar on a separate occasion. She recounted a story in which a group of women had gotten together at Gangori Kanwar's suggestion and taken a group loan, which Gangori Kanwar had then kept in full. She effectively stole 10,000 rupees from Roshan Kanwar. "I would have given it to her if she had asked," Roshan Kanwar told me. "But she just took it."

Gangori Kanwar's role as a conjurer of resources came into stark relief as Saroj and Roshan Kanwar described further their reasons for not confronting her about the misuse of group loans: One could not go against her, a sathin, a zamindar's wife, and, they implied, a loose cannon. But this distrust was also clearly linked, at least for Saroj, to the prior deception on Gangori's part in convincing Saroj to have the tubal ligation. Gangori Kanwar was effectively the broker of the "prior operability" (Cohen 1999) that made Saroj vulnerable to her later illness and to what

was perhaps kidney theft. But Saroj was not a passive victim. She spoke out against Gangori Kanwar, at least to Roshan Kanwar and the foreign anthropologist, and was among the few women who did not join loan groups. Saroj's critique, then, was staged from various platforms for articulation: local ideas about magic, resources, and reproduction; feminist ethics; and discourses about caste equality.

The "facts" of history could not outweigh what Saroj experienced as a truer tale. Gangori Kanwar was only out for herself and had harmed others in the process; despite her WDP-inspired rhetoric of sisterhood and caste equality, she was manipulating people. Saroj never openly accused Gangori Kanwar of magical malfeasance in the case of her sterilization and later kidney troubles, but the possibility lurked that Gangori Kanwar had, like a dakan, eaten her kidney by benefiting from her role as motivator for the sterilization. It was not lost on Saroj that Gangori Kanwar effectively made a living by marketing the tribulations of her peers in the village to various officials, and her claims about Gangori Kanwar, are perhaps, partly true. Saroj could only articulate her suspicions in carefully chosen language. She told Shally, "I might have been cursed somehow" rather than "Gangori Kanwar put a curse on me" because the direction of witchcraft accusations, like the direction of family-planning and tubal-ligation motivation, loans, and other transactions, are already set on the basis of caste. Saroj could not accuse Gangori Kanwar in the local language of witchcraft because, ostensibly, there are no high-caste witches. But she could bring other ideas and languages, such as those espoused by the WDP or by microcredit groups, to bear on someone who seemed to be manipulating others.

Among Gangori Kanwar's skills was the ability to know, in an almost uncanny way, what was being said about her. On her return to the village after receiving a loan for her son's wedding, she seemed to want to disclose freely the terms of the loan. She told me she had taken a loan from the Durga group in the village to help her accumulate the 45–50,000 rupees she thought would be required for her son's wedding. Her loan payments would be 500–1,000 rupees per month. She did not pretend that the loan was going toward the purchase of fodder, which is what Gangori Kanwar claimed loans were supposed to fund. Then she threw in an unexpected twist: Her sister-in-law Roshan Kanwar had 50,000 rupees and would not share, a grave sin to Gangori Kanwar, who had five daughters to marry off and only one son. She seemed to imply that if Roshan Kanwar had shared, she would not have had to take out the loan at all.

Suddenly, it seemed possible that Roshan Kanwar was also conspiring against her peers. She was savvy about programs for women and was the woman closest to Gangori Kanwar—therefore, she was the most likely to understand loan structures. She had, by her own account, been going daily to the nearby regional rural development bank with another woman to try to qualify for a new loan. Or was this Gangori Kanwar's conjuring as well? Did Roshan Kanwar have 10,000 rupees or 50,000 rupees? How much did Gangori Kanwar have? Where did she get it? Gangori Kanwar's role was not easy to understand. Although she and Saroj clearly were engaged in an ongoing dispute, Gangori Kanwar had supported Saroj's petition for the renewal of her medical ration card with the panchayat, which was successful. Gangori Kanwar and Roshan Kanwar seemed to be friends, but were they cheating each other? Interestingly, Gangori Kanwar was willing to tell me openly about her betrayal of sathin values—she was not supposed to give or take dowry, of which she knew I was well aware—but she vehemently maintained that she was a victim in the loan groups because the burden of five daughters entitled her to more.

At moments, it seemed that Gangori Kanwar's power to conjure loan money and convince others to help her get it was, indeed, supernatural. It would be a mistake to see her simply as an agent of the state; however, her powers were limited and sometimes were completely thrown into question. On one particular morning, the ration *walla*, a civil servant in charge of managing villagers' ration cards and the local government-subsidized shop, approached Gangori Kanwar in her courtyard. He was angry and out of place in the insular female space. She met him at the doorway, where he promptly began questioning her. From my distant seat near the fire, Gangori Kanwar's responses were inaudible. The man's questions were loud, and he got progressively more adamant. "Where is the money?" he shouted. "I know you had a loan. The sarpanch also knows you had a loan!" His tone was threatening, and I felt nervous for Gangori Kanwar as he went on. She said nothing, and he stormed away. Ignoring my embarrassment and her own, Gangori Kanwar went back to work as if nothing had happened.

This encounter was unsettling to me, and, I think, to Gangori Kanwar, for it lends credence to the rumors of Gangori Kanwar's misdeeds (was she so bold as to try to steal from the ration walla?) and, at the same time, it exposed her real vulnerability in the face of the institutional structure that she usually managed like a virtuoso bureaucrat. For as much as Gangori Kanwar was able to create a world within a world, to build herself a space to maneuver in Debaliya, she did not set the terms that governed women's microcredit groups, or loans, or village politics. This woman, always filled with things to say, with curses for men who misbehaved, was, for once, silent.

## WHOSE MICROCREDIT CULTURE?

To ask of microcredit only whether it really empowers women is to take the institutions and discourses through which it is produced as the paradigm for women in the Global South at face value. The question begins from the joint premises that not only is something called the "empowerment of women" possible within microcredit's purview but also that those who study empowerment would know it if they saw it. As I hope I have shown, at least in rural Rajasthan the picture is rarely that clear, the subject positions rarely so neatly assigned. Who won and lost in Debaliya's loan groups? We might say that Gangori Kanwar won sometimes; we could point out that Roshan Kanwar got to keep a bit of money, whatever the amount, and the respect of her peers. Maybe it was Saroj who was empowered. Her criticism of Gangori Kanwar's loan misdeeds allowed her to launch a broader critique of drought-relief works and caste relations. Her publicly articulated refusal to join loan groups was a response to earlier personal conflicts and suspicions of magical malfeasance, and it also pointed to Gangori Kanwar's hypocrisy in the context of groups that were supposed to act for women's collective good.

If we, as scholars and feminists, ask our questions on microcredit's terms, we have to answer them on those terms, in ways that I have found unsatisfactory. We have to accept the gap between economic activities and social life that enables development planners' view that "culture" can be instrumentalized toward economic improvement. I have chosen, rather, to focus on what happened between the women who were brought together in new ways by the entrance of microcredit into daily life in rural Rajasthan to show that microcredit is not a preexistent economic logic that gets "culturized" but only ever happens in and through culture. A microcredit program that is not enmeshed in local ideas about generosity and sharing—about nazar—does not exist in Debaliya; microcredit does not interact with culture, with all of its unexpected convergences and disharmonies. Microcredit and the self-help-group form *are a part of* several cultural possibilities that women draw on in any given moment.

Part of the problem with both microcredit plans and their critics has to do with the assumption that the women involved share the same visions and positions. On both sides of the "is microcredit empowering?" issue lies that view that women recognize and reproduce themselves as a collectivity called "women" within the context of self-help groups (Berry 2003). It was this assumption that underlay my questions about why women would agree to go along with Gangori Kanwar. Surely they would recognize that her dealings were not always in their interests! But I was often surprised. Sometimes, the concerns of women in Debaliya were, in fact, collective: Everyone seemed to agree, for instance, on the karmic, moral, and economic weight of daughters. Women agreed that this weight should be counted when a particular woman's need was being calculated by her peers. But the next day, suspicions might run wild about this same woman: "She has a whole trunk of saris hidden in her house." Women neither wholly embraced nor completely rejected the relationship that microcredit groups attempted to create between them as "women." Which part of this complex social interplay is culture? Or, more to the point, to what extent should culture be recognized as including several different platforms for articulating critique and commentary in Debaliya: microcredit, WDP-styled feminism, nazar, and women's simple talk about one another? I hope to have given some sense of why microcredit is especially charged in rural Rajasthan—a glimpse of its magic—at the same time that I have refused to treat microcredit as if it were an isolated phenomenon in the world or a brand-new paradigm for women's empowerment that vacates all of the other ideas and languages that might be present.

The point, I think, is that there is a great deal at stake in refusing the instrumentalization of culture on which microcredit seems to rely by attending to its specificities, its ethnographic study; likewise, in light of the kinds of complex social interactions of which it is now a part, scholars should refuse to see microcredit as only, or even primarily, about the money it purports to make available to the poor. As Elyachar puts it, "Even if we hear the language of debt and finance, we should not assume that capitalist accumulation is underway" (2002: 511). I would add that just because microcredit can work as a disciplining apparatus does not mean it is always successful. Very little that happened in Debaliya's loan groups reproduced the microcredit vision of collectivities of women working together to create and sustain microenterprises for the good of rationalized families who no longer practice dowry.

Focusing on the instrumentalization of culture obscures all of those unwieldy cultural enactments that happen in and through the language of microcredit as it is joined to other, locally invoked ways of thinking about and evaluating the relationships that make up village social life. Focusing on the money obscures all the other kinds of transactions that happen in a particular location. Attending to the complexities of what happens in the intimate spaces of the loan groups themselves helps answer the question with which I

opened this article: What makes microcredit so attractive to women in rural Rajasthan? It is not that financial gains or the sisterhood born of the self-help group is dramatically altering women's lives. It is, rather, that microcredit has become part of local ways of discussing how resources should be distributed, caste relations, the meaning of daughters, and the possibility of grassroots feminism in this, the place where women are the "most oppressed."

## ACKNOWLEDGMENTS

Funding for the fieldwork on which this article is based was provided by the National Science Foundation's Graduate Student Fellowship (2001–03). In India, Sharada Nayak, Manindra Kapoor, Shail Mayaram, and the faculty at the Institute for Development Studies, Jaipur, have assisted me in important ways, both intellectually and logistically. Special thanks are owed to my research collaborator, Shally Vaish, for her patience during fieldwork and keen ear for the local dialect in Debaliya. Eunice Blavascunas, Anne-Maria Makhulu, K. B. Norwood, Triloki Pandey, Lisa Rofel, Bahiyyih Watson, and Sasha Welland all read this article in draft form and made extremely helpful suggestions and comments; it has also benefited tremendously from ongoing conversations with Anna Tsing, to whom I owe a debt of gratitude for her enduring spirit of collaboration. Additional input from the three anonymous reviewers at *American Ethnologist*, Donald Donham, and Linda Forman was invaluable. Finally, my heartfelt thanks to the women of Debaliya village in Jaipur District for generously allowing me to be a part of their lives as a sister and a daughter and for tolerating my intrusions as a researcher.

## NOTES

1. That women are more oppressed in Rajasthan than in other regions has a kind of commonsense currency in India. The state consistently scores among the bottom three states on most development indexes and has the lowest female literacy rate in India. During any given week, the national print media often include a story related to child marriage, sati, or dowry deaths that metonymically links this "backward" state with various forms of violence against women. Although I do not dispute that such violence does occur, I agree with the analysis of Gloria Goodwin Raheja and Ann Grodzins Gold that there is a "dominant mode in both academic and journalistic accounts depicting rural South Asian women as submissive if decorative, as kept in their subordinate place by a patriarchal economy and a religious tradition that devalues them" (1994: xiv); whereas Raheja and Gold are concerned with representations outside India, I would

argue that within India a version of this discourse surrounds women in Rajasthan specifically (Moodie 2006).

2. The ethnographic fieldwork on which this article is based was conducted during village stays of various duration from January to May of 2003, as part of my larger dissertation project, which examined and compared urban and rural schemes for women's empowerment in Jaipur District.

3. Microcredit's magic has a great deal to do with its international popularity, which has only increased with the emergence of "microcredit celebrities." Muhammed Yunus, founder of the Grameen Bank in Bangladesh, for instance, won the Novel Peace Prize in 2006, proclaiming credit a "human right." In the United States, Bill and Hillary Clinton have been vocal supporters of microcredit as the panacea for poor women in the developing world since their visit to a sathin village in Rajasthan in the late 1990s. I contend that a certain part of its success in interpellating women at the village level derives from this international magic.

4. I understand neoliberalism to refer to a set of political-economic practices that have been inaugurated around the globe since the 1970s, which include deregulation, liberalization, privatization, and the withdrawal of state support from social programs. I also understand neoliberalism as a value system that holds that "the social good will be maximized by maximizing the reach and frequency of market transactions" (Harvey 2005: 3) and therefore seeks to marketize human relations. Taking Lisa Rofel's argument that there is not "a universal set of principles from which derives, in a deterministic fashion, a singular type of neoliberal subject" (2007: 2) to heart, I see this set of practices and notion of value as powerful ideals that are rarely, if ever, enacted in practice. Indeed, part of my hope in this article is, following J. K. Gibson-Graham, to resist the allure of all-encompassing economic explanatory frameworks like neoliberalism.

5. These studies differ a bit in their discussion of the role of the women's loan groups themselves. Mayoux (1999: 963) seems to be critical of the assumption that membership in a women's group will produce the kinds of effects desired by gender-sensitive development agencies. Her skepticism is apt in light of accounts that demonstrate the extent to which "women" must be created as a category by development projects; indeed, in Kangra, Kim Berry (2003) has found that this is one of the primary results of development projects. Groups of women, they both maintain, cannot be seen as inevitably giving birth to feminist politics. Isserles (2003: 52), however, argues that any empowering results from microcredit are a result of the support network of women. Her informants, development planners in different parts of the world, report that loan meetings provide an important forum for women to talk about topics other than loans.

6. There is an extensive body of work around the WDP, in part because it included women's studies scholars in the original plan. In addition to the reports produced by project organizers and consultants from the IDSJ, including Jain et al. (1986), John (1996), and Mathur et al. (1997), see Mayaram (2002), Mathur (1999), Madhok (2003), Sunder Rajan (2003), and Unnithan and Srivastava (1997).

7. The sathin program is structured so that a group of ten sathins is under the supervision of one *pracheta*, often an educated, middle-class woman; however, Gangori Kanwar apparently had very little official supervision or on-the-ground assistance. The prachetas I knew were lively and dedicated to their work. However, one of their main tasks, which was going to visit each sathin in their area once a month, was given low priority—most likely because prachetas were not compensated for travel. C. P. Sujaya and colleagues (2002) found that out of a total of 237 pracheta posts, only 34 were filled.

8. The controversy over this well-known case sparked national and international outcry; in fact, some of its earliest investigators were from the WDP. For a full discussion of the case, see Sangari and Vaid (1996).

9. The accused, members of the Gujjar caste, are relatives of a prominent politician, Rajesh Pilot, now deceased. It is widely suspected that the men were given preferential treatment because of this relationship.

10. The anganwadi program of Integrated Child Development Services (ICDS) was started in 1975 to focus on the basic health and education of young children and child-bearing women. It was merged with the WDP in 2000, a move that continues to be extremely controversial and unpopular with the WDP core (see also Ferguson and Gupta 2002; Gupta and Sharma 2006 on ICDS).

11. CECOEDECON is an NGO that is active in and around Debaliya.

12. Lower-caste women reported that this was not really true; they were allowed into the front hall of Gangori Kanwar's home only when guests concerned with caste issues, such as a pracheta or myself, were present.

13. The puja room is a separate room reserved for the family's religious observances. It is indicative of Gangori Kanwar's status and wealth, as very few homes in the village had multiple rooms. She herself slept in the puja room at night.

14. This is the diagnosis as it appeared on her patient record from the main government hospital. A physician has since told me that this diagnosis is "ludicrous" and that it is possible that Saroj's ureter was severed accidentally during the sterilization procedure.

## REFERENCES

Berry, Kim
2003    Developing Women: The Traffic in Ideas about Women and Their Needs in Kangra, India. In *Regional Modernities: The Cultural Politics of Development in India*. K. Sivaramakrishnan and Arun Agarwal, eds. Pp. 75–98. Stanford: Stanford University Press.
Bharucha, Rustom
2003    *Rajasthan, an Oral History: Interviews with Komal Kothari*. New Delhi: Penguin Books.
Carstairs, G. Morris
1983    *Death of a Witch: A Village in North India 1950–1981*. London: Hutchinson.
Cohen, Lawrence
1999    Where It Hurts: Indian Material for an Ethics of Organ Transplantation. *Daedalus* 128(4):135–165.

Elyachar, Julia
2002   Empowerment Money: The World Bank, Non-Governmental Organizations, and the Value of Culture in Egypt. *Public Culture* 14(3):493–513.

Ferguson, James, and Akhil Gupta
2002   Spatializing States: Towards an Ethnography of Neoliberal Governmentality. *American Ethnologist* 29(4):981–1003.

Foster, George
1965   Peasant Society and the Image of Limited Good. *American Anthropologist* 67(2):293–315.

Gibson-Graham, J. K.
2006[1996]   *The End of Capitalism (As We Knew It): A Feminist Critique of Political Economy.* Minneapolis: University of Minnesota Press.

Gold, Ann Grodzins
1988   *Fruitful Journeys: The Ways of Rajasthani Pilgrims.* Prospect Heights, IL: Waveland Press.

Gupta, Akhil, and Aradhana Sharma
2006   Globalization and Postcolonial States. *Current Anthropology* 47(2):277–301.

Harlan, Lindsey
1991   *Religion and Rajput Women: The Ethic of Protection in Contemporary Narratives.* Berkeley: University of California Press.

Harvey, David
2005   *A Brief History of Neoliberalism.* Oxford: Oxford University Press.

Isserles, Robin G.
2003   Microcredit: The Rhetoric of Empowerment, the Reality of "Development as Usual." *Women's Studies Quarterly* 3–4:38–57.

Jain, Sharada, Kavita Srivastava, and Kanchan Mathur
1986   *Exploring Possibilities: A Review of the Women's Development Programme, Rajasthan.* Jaipur: Institute of Development Studies, Jaipur.

Jeffrey, Peter, Robin Jeffrey, and Andrew Lyon
1989   *Labour Pains and Labour Power: Women and Childbearing in India.* London: Zed.

John, Mary E.
1996   Gender and Development in India, 1970s–1990s. *Economic and Political Weekly* 31(47):3071–3077.

Madhok, Sumi
2003   *Autonomy, Subordination, and the "Social Woman": Examining Rights Narratives of Rural Rajasthani Women.* Ph.D. thesis, School of Oriental and African Studies, University of London.

Mahmud, Simeen
2003   Actually How Empowering Is Microcredit? *Development and Change* 34(4):577–605.

Mathur, Kanchan
1999   From Private to Public: The Emergence of Violence against Women as an Issue in the Women's Development Programme, Rajasthan. In *Institutions, Relations, and Outcomes: A Framework and Case Studies for Gender-Aware Planning.* Naila Kabeer and Ramya Subrahmanian, eds. Pp. 288–311. New Delhi: Kali for Women.

Mathur, Kanchan, Shobhita Rajagopal, and Varsha Joshi
1997   *Violence against Women: The WDP Perspective.* Jaipur: Institute of Development Studies, Jaipur.

Mayaram, Shail
2002   New Modes of Violence: The Backlash against Women in the Panchayat System. In *The Violence of Development: The Politics of Identity, Gender, and Social Inequalities in India.* Karin Kapadia, ed. Pp. 393–424. London: Zed.

Mayoux, Linda
1999   Questioning Virtuous Spirals: Micro-Finance and Women's Empowerment in Africa. Special issue, "The New Poverty Strategies, What Have They Achieved? What Have We Learned? Papers from the Inaugural DSA Policy Workshop 8–10 April 1999." *Journal of International Development* 11(7):957–984.

Mazumdar, Vina
1994   Women's Studies and the Women's Movement in India: An Overview. *Women's Studies Quarterly* 22(3–4):42–54.

Moodie, Megan C.
2006   *Culture or Freedom? The Gendered Intimacies of Modernization in Rajasthan.* Ph.D. dissertation, Department of Anthropology, University of California, Santa Cruz.

Raheja, Gloria Goodwin, and Ann Grodzins Gold
1994   *Listen to the Heron's Words: Reimagining Gender and Kinship in North India.* Berkeley: University of California Press.

Rahman, Aminur
1999   *Women and Microcredit in Rural Bangladesh: Anthropological Study of the Rhetoric and Realities of Grameen Bank Lending.* Boulder, CO: Westview.

Rofel, Lisa
2007   *Desiring China: Experiments in Neoliberalism, Sexuality, and Public Culture.* Durham and London: Duke University Press.

Sangari, Kumkum, and Sudesh Vaid
1996   Institutions, Beliefs and Ideologies: Widow Immolation in Contemporary Rajasthan. In *Embodied Violence: Communalising Women's Sexuality in South Asia.* Kumari Jayawardena and Malathi De Alwis, eds. Pp. 240–296. London: Zed.

Sujaya, C. P., Kumud Sharma, Lakshmi Murthy, and Uma Chakravarti
2002   *The Independent Review of the Women's Development Program, Rajasthan.* Jaipur: Government of Rajasthan.

Sunder Rajan, Rajeswari
2003   *The Scandal of the State: Women, Law, and Citizenship in Postcolonial India.* Durham, NC: Duke University Press.

Taussig, Michael
1980   *The Devil and Commodity Fetishism in South America.* Chapel Hill: University of North Carolina Press.

Unnithan, Maya, and Kavita Srivastava
1997   Gender Politics, Development and Women's Agency in Rajasthan. In *Discourses of Development: Anthropological Perspectives.* R. D. Grillo and R. L. Stirrat, eds. Pp. 157–181. Oxford: Berg.

Women's Development Program (WDP)
1987   *Exploring Possibilities: A Review of the Women's Development Programme.* Jaipur: Institute of Development Studies, Jaipur.

# Factory as Home and Family:
## Female Workers in the Moroccan Garment Industry

### M. Laetitia Cairoli

My factory is better . . . because every girl in it is like a daughter of the owner.

Thus, one Fez clothing factory worker explained why she had remained at her job for four years, despite the notoriously low pay and constant overtime demanded there. In the past two decades the Moroccan garment industry has developed into one of the country's most significant export trades and Moroccan females have become the labor power for clothing manufacture. Although their role in the garment factories is widely regarded as exploitative and demeaning, the workers themselves continue to use the idiom of family to describe their relationships to factory owners, administrators, supervisors, and their fellow workers. In the course of a year of ethnographic research in the city of Fez, I began an exploration of how garment factory workers make sense of their labor on the shop floor.

Inside one Fez garment factory, where I worked during a three-month period, I observed workers as they sought to impose their own assumptions and values upon the factory system and thereby render their labor meaningful. Nearly all of Morocco's garment factory workers are female and most are unmarried.[1] They confront the factory with a set of cultural values that order their social world, central to which is their identity as kinswoman, a self-perception workers believe to be ordained by Islam. Despite their engagement with the factory, workers continue to perceive themselves first and foremost as daughters, sisters, and perhaps wives and mothers in a patriarchal family. As such, they presume that their rightful place is in the private sphere of the home, which is the arena of their most noble efforts. Thus, they transform the workshop floor into an interior space, recast factory staff into family, and operate in the factory as they would in the household. In this way they retain their prized identity as kinswoman, even within the factory, and they convert factory labor into work that is significant to them.[2] In doing so, however, they render themselves more amenable to the factory's exploitation.

There are, of course, limits to the workers' re-creation of the factory: for Moroccan females, the garment factory is a new kind of public space with characteristics unlike the private arena of the home. In some instances, workers find that their efforts to impose the blueprint of home and family on the factory fall short, and they confront what they recognize to be foreign work regimes and excessive domination. When this occurs, workers resist. I do not see this behavior as contradictory; rather, I assert that the workers' ability to comply with factory domination (which occurs far more frequently than does resistance) is rooted in their conversion of factory into home. Here I explore how this transformation is enacted.

## THE "GLOBAL FACTORY"

Any study of Moroccan female garment workers must be set in the context of the recent literature on the phenomenon of women's participation in factory production. Over the past two decades, this scholarship has explored the effects of global capitalism on the definitions and meanings of gender. Two central questions have been posed: the first concerns the impact of women's participation in industrialization on the women themselves, on the men, on the family, and on the local culture. The second question is whether this impact—and the very participation of women in factories worldwide—is intrinsic to factory technology itself and/or capitalism, or if it results from local culture (Warren and Borque 1989). Researchers have sought to understand whether women's participation in these new forms of labor marks their liberation from local "patriarchy," or marks a new kind of enslavement to the demands of foreign capital. Those arguing the former possibility have pointed to ways in which factory work provided women an escape from the confines of home and new opportunities for personal autonomy (Lim 1983; Salaff 1981). Other researchers have emphasized, instead, the exploitation in modern production systems that is particularly detrimental to female status (Nash and Fernandez-Kelly 1983).

The literature on women and technology has demonstrated that women's entry into capitalist wage work affects the nature of gender roles and relations

Reproduced by permission of the Society for Applied Anthropology from *Human Organization* vol. 57, no. 2, 1998.

in complex and contradictory ways. As Nash (1981) notes, female participation in new forms of capitalist wage labor intensifies existing forms of gender subordination, while simultaneously decomposing and recomposing them. The roots of these transformations are found both in local patriarchies and in global capitalism. While the literature on women in the global factory has illuminated critical aspects of gender transformations which accompany the movement of global capital, much of the early research was limited in scope.

A particular weakness in the literature is its relative lack of detailed cultural analysis of what Ong (1991: 280) calls the "experiential and interpretive dimensions of work relations." Much of the earliest research overlooked the unique ways in which workers transform capitalist work regimes and formulate their own kinds of meanings. This limitation in the literature was partly a result of the analysts' perspective on the nature of capitalism. Characterizing the capitalist system as powerful and deterministic, theorists often assumed that the methods and relations of production associated with high-tech factories would occur wherever these factories were established (Blim 1992). Theorists would then analyze the new industrialization as an effect of a standard logic, or as the result of the intersection of capitalism and a local patriarchal system.

More recent conceptualizations of the global capitalist system stress the flexibility of capitalist processes and allow for a new interpretation of the effects of industrialization (Blim 1992; Ong 1991). Capitalism (including its associated technology) is no longer seen as a homogenizing agent that flattens local systems into replicas of each other. Instead, capitalism is now understood to merge with indigenous values and practices and thus to proliferate new kinds of labor processes and relations.

If this particular perspective on capitalism is adopted, the phenomenon of the factory, and the lives of its workers, can be studied as a cultural process linked to other local cultural forms, rather than as a consequence of capitalist production (Calagione and Nugent 1992). With this perspective, the local particulars in the worker's experience of industrialization become central; indeed, they become the focus of the study. Here, I follow this approach and discuss the Moroccan clothing factory as another expression of specifically Moroccan cultural values. Workers experience their labor according to Moroccan categories already familiar to them, and use their own cultural meanings to interpret the garment factory. The Fez garment factory is thoroughly "Moroccanized" despite imported technology and systems of production.

Inside the factory, the garment workers struggle to retain a notion of themselves as family members, specifically as daughters (or sometimes as wives) in patriarchal households. They have accepted a notion of themselves

as subservient and dutiful long before they enter the garment factory. They model their position in the factory hierarchy on their role in the household and so are able not only to accept the domination of the factory, but to find in that domination their own sources of personal self-worth and power. Thus, workers transform colleagues into loyal sisters and factory owners into concerned fathers. They are able to accept the constraints that the factory imposes by assimilating the owners' dominance into other, more acceptable forms of relationships. This re-molding of relationships formed inside the factory to fit the prototypes of ties formed outside ultimately makes the workers available for increased exploitation. Persons with authority in the factory capitalize on workers' interpretations of their roles to maximize production and ultimately increase profit.

## RESEARCH METHODS

I conducted the fieldwork for this study in the city of Fez from August 1994 to August 1995. The fieldwork involved intensive ethnography, which included formal interviews of Fez factory owners, formal and informal interviews of workers and their families, two random surveys carried out in separate garment factories in the city, and three months of participant observation inside one of those garment factories. The factory where I worked, which I call "Confection," employs some 150 workers and has been in operation for some six years. It is typical in size and operation of garment factories in Fez. At Confection I worked in the packaging department, where finished garments are tagged and prepared for shipment. This experience provided me a position from which to observe everyday work routines, the nature of the work process, staff hierarchies, and personal interactions inside the factory. It was through "acting like a worker" that I began to understand something of what factory work means to Moroccan factory girls.

## THE ECONOMIC CONTEXT OF GARMENT PRODUCTION

Today clothing manufacture is one of Morocco's chief export industries, and garments account for a quarter of the country's exports (Leymarie and Tripier 1992). Conservative estimates suggest that Morocco's garment factories employ close to a quarter of the country's factory workers: some 95,000 of the country's total 444,000 industrial workers produce garments. Virtually all of these workers are female (Ministère du Commerce 1994).[3]

The importance of the garment industry to the Moroccan economy is a recent phenomenon. Before the 1980s, garment manufacture was relatively insignificant. Between 1981 and 1991 the production of garments more than quadrupled (Leymarie and Tripier 1992) and, although males had formerly predominated in the garment factories, it was females who were hired, en masse, to staff the new enterprises.[4] The boom in the Moroccan garment business, and the concomitant employment of females, was fueled by several factors. These included the government economic readjustment program, trade agreements with the European Economic Community, and the movement of European production "off-shore."

The Moroccan government economic readjustment program, instituted in 1983, was a primary catalyst of the new trend (Leymarie and Tripier 1992). Before the institution of the readjustment program, Moroccan industry consisted largely of state-owned, high-tech enterprises with little capacity for generating employment. These included such industries as phosphate mining and production of thread and cloth. The program sought to replace such industries with private, low capital, labor-intensive ones. This change in Moroccan industry marked a shift in the gender of the country's work-force. As Morocco turned to light manufacturing for export, including garment production, food processing and electronics manufacturing, females flooded into factories. This employment of female factory workers is characteristic of export-oriented industries across the globe (Nash 1981; Nash and Fernandez-Kelly 1983; Ong 1987, 1991; Rothstein and Blim 1992).

European sub-contractors (predominantly French), motivated by favorable trade conditions and the desire for "off-shore" production sites, became involved in the industry in the late 1970s. They sought out Moroccan enterprises that could supply them with low cost labor, they sent in raw materials needed for production and exported the final products. These sub-contractors encouraged the wide scale employment of females, enjoying greater profits because women would accept far lower wages than the salaries men demanded (Joekes 1982a, 1982b, 1985). Thus, the nature and structure of the Moroccan garment industry is defined by the relationship between the European contractors and private Moroccan industrialists.

Moroccan garment factories are generally small, family-owned businesses with staffs of 50 employees or less, flexible enough to respond to a foreign, somewhat volatile, market. Because of their relatively small size they can, and often do, elude government regulation. The garment factories commonly do not heed Moroccan labor law, which in part accounts for their poor working conditions. The factories open and close rapidly and unexpectedly, with fluctuations in the external market. Thus, Moroccan females labor in an industry that provides them insecure positions and relatively poor conditions (Leymarie and Tripier 1992).

Originally, Morocco's garment factory workers, like all Moroccan factory hands, were predominantly male. Before the 1980s, female garment factory workers did unskilled work on the margins of production, but they did not operate sewing machines. Today, however, women and girls fill nearly all positions in the garment factories. The wide-scale employment of females as garment factory workers takes on new meanings in the Moroccan context.

## The Social Context of Garment Production

In my research I found that garment factory workers are, for the most part, unmarried young girls who live at home with their parents and unmarried siblings. This fact is widely recognized in Morocco. The workers are generally daughters of lower class households which, in comparison with others of their class, are relatively poor and suffer high rates of male unemployment. (I herein refer to the households where garment workers live as "factory households"). The vast majority of garment workers contribute all or at least part of their earnings to household support and are significant wage-earners.[5]

Despite their positions as breadwinners, factory workers retain a fierce hold on the value of the patriarchal family. Both in word and action, they revere the traditional hierarchy that establishes males as protectors and females as dependents. Garment workers speak of factory labor as a temporary aberration they must tolerate until a successful marriage places them in the position of non-working wife and mother (married workers, a minority, are often young and as yet childless; workers with children generally work because they are destitute).

In their homes, garment workers enact the rituals of subservience that confirm and reinforce their positions as daughters, or sometimes as wives, in either case female and junior members of the household. In spite of their engagement with the factory, workers strive to maintain their identity as kinswoman because this identity is more central to them than their self-perception as workers.[6]

Local ideologies of gender, to which workers adhere, reinforce the patriarchal structure of factory households. Male authority in the family is legitimized by an ideology that defines women as economically dependent, subservient, and in need of control. According to the Moroccan gender code, a woman's proper role is that of wife and mother, a position that is essentially non-economic and properly played out in the privacy of the domestic sphere. Men appropriately take the position of breadwinner and operate in the economic sphere outside the home. Thus, women are symbolically associated with the home and with private, interior domestic space. A family's honor is embedded in its ability to keep women inside and protected, thus maintaining the divide between male and female that is at once a separation between inside and outside, private and public, kin and non-kin, home and business.[7]

The favored portrayal of female activities as homebound, kin-related and non-economic obscures the fact that Moroccan women have always been active in the economy (Beneria 1984; Davis 1983). Today, the economic participation of Moroccan females represents 36% of national economic activity (Direction de la Statistique 1994), although it goes largely unrecognized. Still, the above-described gender code retains its position as an ideal, rooted in the popular understanding of Islam. The mass entry of Fez's women into the garment factories blatantly contradicts the pervasively held Moroccan notions of family and gender. In this article, I explore how factory workers live with this contradiction.

### The Factory in Fez

Fez is an ancient city, revered among Moroccans as a spiritual capital and regarded as a bulwark of Islam and Muslim society. Traditionally, Fez has been an important artisanal center. Today it is a textile town. At independence, the Moroccan government established its largest public cloth spinning and weaving factories in Fez, which were (and are today) staffed by men. During the 1980s garment manufacturing emerged as the city's principal industry and today the sewing factories of Fez employ more than a third of all Fez factory workers, nearly all of them women (Ministère du Commerce 1994). This is a vivid contrast to the situation that existed less than three decades ago, when the town's textile enterprises were the province of men.

Industrial enterprises are scattered throughout the city of Fez, although most industry is located in three industrial quarters. Small factories and artisanal workshops producing for the local market and the tourist trade are found in the ancient medina. Other modest-sized factories exist in the city's newer sections, including the Ville Nouvelle and the recently developed urban periphery. The bulk of Fez's industry, including the largest and most "modern" factories, many of which produce for export, is located in the city's industrial quarters. These include the oldest and largest, Quartier Industriel Sidi Brahim, the industrial quarter of Doukkarat, and the most recently created quarter in Ben Souda. Three-quarters of Fez's factory workers labor in these districts (Fejjal 1987).

The majority of Fez's garment factories are privately owned by a class of Moroccan elite, known as the Fassi. The term "*Fassi*" is used throughout the country to describe a group of influential families originally native to the city of Fez, who control much of Morocco's wealth and political power. The Fassi are at the top of the local class structure, which includes a middle level of educated bureaucrats and a lower level made up of the majority of city dwellers, who are relatively poor and uneducated. This lower class is the class with which garment workers identify.

## THE LABOR PROCESS AND FACTORY STAFF

The labor process in Fez garment factories involves six separate steps, which precede and follow upon the actual sewing of the garments. They include, in sequential order: the intake and inventory of fabric and supplies imported from Europe; the cutting of the fabric; the actual sewing of the garments, carried out by workers seated in rows ("sewing lines"); the ironing of finished products; the final inspection of completed garments; and packaging and shipment. This production sequence is carried out in the same manner, using the same kind of technology, in garment factories throughout the world.

These production tasks are carried out by factory staff who labor in a hierarchy of authority. At the top of this hierarchy are the factory owners, who are either upper-class Moroccans (generally the above-described Fassi) or Europeans; in both cases, those at the top of the factory hierarchy are most frequently men.[8] Owners generally leave the daily direction of the factory to be handled by administrators, the garment manufacturing technicians who plan and supervise production. Like the owners, these individuals are upper-class Moroccan men (often of the owner's family) or Europeans.[9] A workshop director, generally a Moroccan man, oversees the management of all factory staff on the workshop floor. Next in the hierarchy are the workshop supervisors, who manage each particular production process; there are, for instance, one or two line supervisors for each sewing line. These supervisors are generally Moroccan males or females, of the same class as the workers. Finally, at the bottom of the factory hierarchy, are the mass of factory workers, who are Moroccan females of the lower class.

On the margins of production are the factory mechanics, transport bus drivers, secretaries and maids. The mechanics and bus drivers are Moroccan lower-class men, the former considered relatively skilled. The secretaries are Moroccan females who, because they are literate and not engaged in manual work, hold relatively high status within the factory. The maids, unskilled and impoverished females in a demeaned occupation, occupy the lowest position in the hierarchy.

Factory staff relies on familiar and valued models of relationships to interact with each other and with those who control them. I will explore how local assumptions about home and family, assumptions that are themselves infused with ideas about gender, inform the workers' attempts to transform factory relations into meaningful intercourse.

## Factory as Home and Family

I like this factory very, very much. The people here are nice, it is like a family. There are hardly any men working here . . . so it is like being in your own house. . . . If I ever left this job, I would go straight back home.

The gendering of the workshop floor as female transforms what might have been a public and immoral space into a private and acceptable one. As Emen, a seven-year employee of the Confection expressed it above, the fact that garment factories hire (nearly) only females makes the work that goes on in them somewhat more respectable. The factory is a private space, like a house, because it is a female space, a space free from the threat of illicit sexuality. Whatever transpires inside the factory is less morally questionable because the shop floor is imagined to be a private rather than a public arena. As one worker explained with pride, "one girl passes her cloth to another girl, and we are at ease, because we are all girls."

Garment factory workers are generally demeaned by Fez inhabitants for their participation in factory labor. Factory labor is in itself poorly regarded because it is manual labor, neither autonomous nor artisanal, and participation in factory work connotes a low class status. But for females, it suggests as well a lack of family honor and the real or potential loss of personal virtue. Girls who engage in factory labor are assumed to be related to males who are unable to appropriately support and protect them. The glaring presence of factory girls on the streets of Fez is often cited as proof of the inability of families to control and monitor their daughters. In response to such deprecating images, garment workers take refuge in the fact that they work in a safe, protected, all-female environment.

The actual physical construction of the factories and the way workers approach and understand factory space expresses the notion of factory as home. The factories producing for export, situated in Fez's three industrial districts, are large, low-lying structures that look like warehouses. Rows of narrow windows parallel the factory roofs but are almost unnoticeable from outside. The windows are generally too high for a passerby to see inside and, unlike the male-staffed cement and construction factories (where metal doors are often left open and interior courtyards are visible to the outside), the garment factories in the same districts housing Moroccan girls are shut tight to the stranger's eye. They look at first glance as if they are unoccupied.

Large metal doors mark the entrance to the factories and a guardian sits directly behind these doors. The doors open into a courtyard where the trucks that transport materials to and from Europe load and unload. The factory men—the guardian, mechanics and drivers—often remain in this open, transitional space. On arrival workers file through the courtyard and directly into the workshop. This is an area separate from the courtyard, located behind it, or up a flight of stairs. Once they have arrived inside the factory, workers may not leave the building without permission (often written) from their supervisors. At the Confection factory, workers who became ill during the work day required written authorization to get past the guardian and walk out of the building. Even if a worker wished to quit the job permanently, she could not leave the premises with written permission. The factory is a private space, tightly enclosed and closely monitored.

Altogether, then, the garment factory is a concrete structure built around an open courtyard, monitored by a male guardian, in which women remain protected from view and separate from males present. This description of place is reminiscent of the traditional Fez household (Mernissi 1994), in which a male slave prevented the entrance of strangers, and where women remained protected inside, carrying out the labor specific to them. While such households may have existed only rarely and for the wealthy few, the notion of the home as a private, enclosed and specifically female space remains a Moroccan ideal. The female garment factory is modeled on this prototype.

Unlike Moroccan female bureaucrats who wear European business suits, or university students who wear western style skirts or jeans on campus,[10] garment factory workers do not don "professional" or western dress to go to work. They travel to and from the factory in the modest jellaba, a long, loose fitting robe worn in public spaces by traditional Moroccan women. Their retention of the jellaba signals identification with conventional Moroccan womanhood, as opposed to "modern" working women or with university girls (two other groups of women in transition). Inside the factories, workers are dressed in the informal clothing Moroccan women wear in the privacy of the home: baggy, pajama-like dresses or skirts or blue jeans in distinctive Moroccan combinations of style and color (in some factories workers must wear regulation smocks). Most wear plastic sandals on their bare feet, as they would at home. In summer the workshops can be stiflingly hot, and workers who take pains to dress modestly in the public arena of the streets labor in a minimum of clothing in the factory, as if confident that they are not exposed to a stranger's view.

Inside this production center imagined as domestic space, factory owners and workers alike assert that they work together "as a family"; owners claim to treat workers "as daughters." Workers identify the owners in a protective role that their fathers might hold, and assert that all fellow garment workers are "sisters."[11] Even where workers recognize the discontinuities between ties formed inside the factory and those formed at home, the analogy to family life is implicit. For example, one worker, who detested the factory, claimed she would prefer to stay at home because her mother, as she said, "would never yell at (her) the way this administrator does."

The factory is the home and family is the idiom through which factory personnel think about their relations to each other. The gendered dimension of family relationships is evident in the way female factory workers approach owners, co-workers and supervisors, male and female.

In using the metaphor of family, workers quite consciously help owners in their achievement of production goals. Despite a skill hierarchy among them, they treat each other as "sisters" and thus with relative equality. Workers vehemently assert that they support each other in the accomplishment of factory tasks. Repeatedly, I was told stories of lines of machine operators who had stayed late in order to help one of their slower members, or of individual machine operators who had fallen behind in their own tasks in order to assist an inexperienced newcomer. Workers emphasized their willingness to work well with each other, taking pride in their ability to behave in a sisterly fashion. At Confection (as at many other Fez factories) workers ate lunch together from communal plates, just as they would at home, making evident their attempts to replicate the atmosphere of the home inside the factory.

The sisterly relations among workers is perhaps most evident in the way they interact with their supervisors, particularly in their defiance of factory demands. Females are increasingly being placed in supervisory positions inside Fez factories and the majority of sewing line supervisors today are female. At Confection, workers were relatively free in directly challenging female supervisors; they seemed to fear these supervisors less than they feared supervisory males.

Disputes between workers and female supervisors were not uncommon and often took the form of loud and sudden outbursts of resistance from workers in response to unbearable production pressures. Before such exchanges became problematic, however, the defiant worker's co-workers would often intervene, attempting to assuage the stressed worker's feelings

and encourage her compliance. In one such case, I watched as a put-upon worker argued with her supervisor, refusing to complete a particular task. When the other workers tried to calm this worker and urge her compliance, the worker asked, "Why should she be allowed to boss me?" In response, her colleague asserted, "If Hakima cannot boss us, then who will?" The annoyed worker ultimately complied.

Co-workers had reminded the rebellious worker of the validity of the hierarchy among them, one not foreign to the mode of control used within the family. An age-hierarchy among siblings is accepted in traditional Moroccan homes, and it is recognized that the eldest sister has the authority to lead her younger sisters in the housework. Verbalization of defiance and argument is not uncommon among siblings in a household. Neither is the eventual cooperation attained through a common acknowledgement of, and respect for, a universally recognized hierarchy. The authority of the female supervisor gains validity because it is reminiscent of the authority of the eldest sister. This argument, like others between workers and their female supervisors, is reminiscent of arguments between sisters in a household. Arguments with male supervisors take on a different tone, as discussed below. First, however, it is necessary to discuss the position of males in the factory.

Workers and workshop-level supervisors are today nearly exclusively female. Still, there are some males present inside the factories and on the workshop floor. The men may be the factory owners, high level administrators, the workshop director, supervisors, or the male service workers (who include the factory transport drivers, guardians, and mechanics). It is now rare to find men on the sewing lines; three was the greatest number of male sewing machine operators I could identify in any Fez factory, and most have none.

In general, the factory men attempt to separate themselves from the females. Factory guardians and transport drivers generally remain in the courtyard, separate from the workshop floor and the females there. The mechanics' duties compel them to be present on the workshop floor amidst the females. At Confection, they did not dally on the floor and remained in a separate room when possible. The factory men took lunch together, eating only after the mass of workers had left the lunch room. Just as men in Moroccan homes often remove themselves after meals to retreat to the all-male public cafes and street corners, men in the factory did not linger with women in a space that was clearly female.

The men present on the workshop floor are most often the workshop director and the supervisors directing the labor of the female machine operators. As noted above, the majority of line supervisors in Fez factories today are female; still, most factories retain at least several men in the position of sewing line supervisor. Almost all factories have retained men in the position of cutting supervisor (a post requiring technical training largely unavailable to lower-class Moroccan females). All the Fez factories I visited retained a male as workshop director, the position of greatest authority on the workshop floor. Workshop directors are always men, one informant explained, because "a man can make the girls afraid, but a woman cannot."

This hierarchy of gender authority on the factory floor reflects the hierarchy within the domestic sphere, where women carry out the daily labor and men retain the authority. The organization and use of space inside the factory makes explicit a gender hierarchy taken for granted. The few men who are present on the workshop floor (either administrators, supervisors or mechanics) are free to move about the factory at will. The female workers, however, are not permitted to leave their positions without authorization; a pass is required even to use the restroom. Workers must remain in place until production quotas are met and often do not know when the workday will end. Officially, they are not permitted to speak while they work.[12]

Thus, the very few males present on the workshop floor are upright figures standing and moving with relative self-control across a space in which females are fixed. It appears that males control females in an otherwise all-female space. The apparent immobilization of women in fixed places inside the factory parallels the limits placed on their freedom of movement in the culture generally. It also reiterates the local gender ideology that defines women as subservient and men as in control.

Given this presumed hierarchy of authority between male and female, the female garment workers directly confront male supervisors less often than female supervisors. In one case I observed a young packaging worker carrying heavy boxes down a staircase while the male workshop supervisor stood by, watching her without assisting. When the task was done the worker complained to her colleagues that the supervisor had done nothing to help. One colleague responded, "What business does a man have working in this factory?" and the other coworkers agreed that a man has no compelling interest in factory work. The demeaned labor in the garment factory is not worthy of a man's time or energy. It is common in Moroccan households to watch females toil while males relax, and factory families invariably defend this as natural. Just as a girl would not expect her father, or even her brother, to help her carry out her household tasks, so a garment factory worker ought not to expect assistance from males on the workshop floor. Garment factory work is degraded work and it is the work of females.

Nonetheless, workers do occasionally resist the authority of men in the factory; they are, however, sanctioned for it. In one case at Confection, a sewing line operator asked her male supervisor for permission to use the restroom. When he refused her, she stood up to leave her seat nonetheless. He slapped her and she, in return, slapped him. She was fired for her deed. In explaining to me why the worker was forced to leave, one girl said, "In Morocco a man can hit a woman but a woman must never, ever, hit a man. Even if he hits her, she must not hit him back." These customs prevail on the shop floor.

Factory owners, almost always male, are removed from everyday interactions on the shop floor, and thus are not engaged in the quotidian labor process. According to the dominant metaphor, factory owners are fathers and the mass of females who toil on the workshop floor, daughters. Cast in the role of fathers, owners take their positions as guardians of female virtue seriously. They provide transportation so that workers can travel to and from the factory in the protected space of factory vans (which are frequently all-female spaces; male workers often travel separately). In this way, owners curb the workers' wanderings on the streets of Fez, like fathers protecting their chastity.[13] In many factories, owners required the workers to remain inside while awaiting the arrival of the company vans, thereby preventing their unnecessary exposure on the street. At Confection the owner instituted a rule forbidding workers from travelling to and from the factory on public transportation and requiring all workers to commute in the company vans. The rule was put in place when the owner discovered that young men were frequenting the local streets in the early evening, hoping to socialize with workers leaving the factory.

Thus, the owners' control of workers reaches beyond service inside the factory. The owners' efforts to monitor female comportment on the streets of Fez were approved by community members and workers as well. Owners themselves used the idiom of family to characterize their relations with workers. One owner described himself as the workers' "father, brother, uncle, friend." He reported that he gave extra money to the neediest workers, and he claimed to buy many of them the rams needed for the ritual annual sacrifice. Although it was impossible to corroborate his story, owners cultivated the loyalty of workers by presenting themselves as concerned and watchful fathers.

Typically, workers verbalized feelings of fondness and respect for the factory owners. Concerning the above-mentioned transportation regulations at Confection, many workers defended the restrictions placed on their movements outside the factory, claiming that such controls helped maintain their reputations and assure the community that they were honorable girls. In a similar way, I found that Moroccan girls who chafed at the restrictions their fathers and brothers placed upon them would nonetheless defend these men against criticism and readily portray their influence as a form of protection or an expression of concern. Thus, workers justified the owners' increased control just as they might justify the limits placed on them by male kin as the men's attempt to guard and shelter them. Workers, perceiving themselves as "daughters," were compelled by a sense of family obligation to comply with the limits imposed on them.

This rich and meaningful basis for relationship binds girls to the factory in a sort of moral obligation that many workers acknowledge. Work becomes a commitment to the father and, through fulfilling it, a worker demonstrates her high moral standing as a female, and as a member of the community. One worker at a Fez garment factory described the working of overtime as a kind of moral obligation, a burden necessary to bear. "If the boss needs us to stay and work till seven o'clock in the evening, we must stay. We have to help him keep his commitments with people overseas." She explained how a fellow worker got fired: one evening when they were working overtime, the girl just got up from her machine and said to the owner, "Just give me my money for my hours worked." She then left the factory without waiting to be certain the export truck was ready to go, unwilling to help the owner meet his deadlines. "One must not speak like that," the first worker said, criticizing the actions of her colleague. "It sounds hard, as if you do not trust that the boss will give you what he owes you." Although workers frequently see little of the factory owners, the relationship between worker and owner is phrased as highly personalized and based on trust.

Another worker described an incident that forced her to miss the seven-day naming ceremony for her sister's first-born child, which she sorely regretted. In recounting how this had come to pass, she emphasized the cooperative and dutiful quality of her own response:

> On the day of the naming ceremony, I went to the director and said, "Today is the seventh-day naming ceremony for my sister's first child, I want to leave early to attend." The director pleaded with me "Please, we cannot let you go early today. Please, don't go. You understand we need you, don't you?" I answered, "Yes, no problem."

In continuing, the worker explained that she could have feigned illness in order to be released from the factory that day, but she would not do so because she was an honest and trustworthy person. Although I prompted her, the worker would express no resentment or anger at this sequence of events. According to her interpretation, she was never forbidden to leave the factory but rather was begged to stay and help. And to this appeal she responded. She missed her sister's party because she was obliged to answer a higher duty.

This worker's description of loyalty to the factory is a familiar form of discourse among workers, and it precisely parallels the way in which relations with family are described. For instance, another worker described to me her premature departure from school, which came about when her father approached her and (by her account) said, "my little daughter . . . you can see the situation we are in. Please, can you leave school and try to get work to help us?" The worker emphasized that her father had never commanded her but rather had pleaded with her. As she recounted his words, the worker imitated her father's begging voice and placed her fingertips over her mouth and kissed them, mimicking the gesture her father had used to signal a request.

Within the family, workers do not experience authority simply as a gripping hold on their liberties and personal autonomy. Instead, in submitting to authority, they perceive themselves as providing a needed response to a call for service. The assistance they provide to the owners, and to their male kin as well, is in some ways a source of personal power, for it is these females alone who can answer the males' call for assistance. They interpret their own compliance as a moral obligation, and in cooperating they display their own good character and worthiness as daughters or wives.[14]

As the worker/owner relationship gets carried out in terms of the code associated with father/daughter, parent/child or possibly husband/wife, what might appear as domination or exploitation of workers by owners often gets reconfigured into something more acceptable. By thinking in terms of the family model, workers can experience owners and administrators not as dominating, but as begging or pleading for their cooperation and assistance. In cooperating with the owner, they assert their own moral rectitude as loyal, principled individuals who understand the importance of preserving the social tie above all else.

## CONCLUSION

It is young unmarried women who staff the garment factories of Morocco. Fez locals, and Moroccans generally, claim that the low pay, long hours, and unpaid overtime associated with garment factory labor are accepted by these young girls because they work "only for clothes and make-up." As daughters (or sometimes wives), workers are presumed to be supported by family males; they are believed to contribute minimally, at most, to household support. As noted above, contrary to public opinion, research indicates that garment factory workers are an important source of household support.

Nonetheless, the local understanding of women's participation in low-paid factory labor coincides with Marxist feminist explanations of female employment on the global assembly line (Elson and Pierson 1981). From both perspectives, it is women's role in reproduction, and their position as dependent daughters, wives, and/ or mothers, that explains their vulnerability to and acceptance of low-wage work.

Here, I have attempted to explore how Moroccan understandings of home, family and gender render females willing workers on the garment factory shop floor. Workers transform the public space of the factory into the private space of the home in an attempt to assuage the contradiction inherent in their presence inside the factory, outside the home, in a role ideologically reserved for men. They behave inside this "home" as kinswoman, using the assumptions and practices associated with family to regulate their comportment inside factory walls. They approach owners much like fathers, and supervisors like parents or elder sisters. They treat each other like siblings. They accept factory hierarchies based on their understanding of, and reverence for, the patriarchal family and the gender order it endorses.

Local meanings and values thus mediate the workers' approach to the factory. Their transformation of factory into a home allows them to accommodate the owners' power with little resistance. They willingly accept the factory administration's power as they would accept the authority of their own fathers, in their role as daughters, or that of their husbands in the role of wife. In this way, the owners are able to appropriate labor at a low cost without risking resistance. To some extent, workers and their families are willing accomplices in the factory's exploitation, because this exploitation gets phrased in terms that are not only accepted, but revered.

## NOTES

1. Here, the word "workers" refers to the female garment factory workers of Fez. I refer to the workers as "girls" rather than women because the vast majority of them are unmarried and thus defined, in Morocco, as girls, or *binet*. The residents of Fez, Moroccans generally, and the workers themselves refer to garment factory workers as girls.

2. Here I contrast the idea of "labor" with that of "work" as in Comaroff and Comaroff (1987) and Wallman (1979).

3. The accuracy of these numbers is questionable. The figures are based on government census materials and reflect only the factories officially registered with the government. It is widely understood in Morocco, however, that many industrial operations are unregistered and "hidden." Factory owners prefer to keep their operations unnoticed by the government to avoid the financial and legal implications that are inherent in official recognition. Even where the factory itself is recognized by the government, many of its workers may not be. Factory owners often regard even permanent, full-time employees as seasonal workers, temporary staff, or apprentices, and thus deny them the work papers that would ensure them the benefits prescribed by law. Obviously, government data cannot account for such employees. One economist in Morocco suggested that government figures be doubled to arrive at a more accurate count of industrial workers in Fez. During one year in Fez, I met few garment workers who held work registration papers. None of the 150 workers in the factory where I worked had working papers.

4. Moroccan men were slowly replaced by women in the garment industry. Throughout the 1980s females were hired to replace departing males in existing factories and most workers hired in new factories were female. Females were frequently hired to replace males involved in labor unrest. Fez factory owners recounted that males working in Fez garment factories before the general workers strike of 1990 were replaced by females. Morocco suffers high rates of unemployment, and male joblessness has not been alleviated by the boom in the garment industry.

5. According to my survey research, 76% of workers surveyed were never-married females, 16% were married, and 8% were divorced. Nearly all of the workers surveyed (92%) were between the ages of 13 and 25. Never-married and divorced workers (84% of the total) almost invariably lived as daughters in their natal households (divorced young women return to their natal homes when possible). Married workers lived either in their husband's natal home or in a separate conjugal home. The majority of married workers were newly married women who had worked in the factory before marriage. Most of the married workers who continued working after having children were destitute women whose husbands were unable to work. Workers earned anywhere from 300 to 800 dirhams per month, and 89% of workers reported contributing some or all of their salary to the family. These salaries were considered significant in lower class households in which men found difficulty securing steady work.

6. Although I am not in any way suggesting a privileged relationship between Islam and women's subjugation to factory labor, other researchers have investigated women's participation in wage labor with focus on the Muslim context (Hijab 1988; Ibrahim 1985; Macleod 1991; Ong 1987; White 1994).

7. Abu Lughod (1986) provides a complex exploration of the notion of honor, and an early, comprehensive collection on the notion of honor is found in Peristiany (1966). See Dwyer (1978), Mernissi (1987), Sabbah (1984), and Combs-Schilling (1989) for discussions of specifically Moroccan notions of honor as they pertain to gender and gender relations.

8. Related women—the wives and sometimes daughters of the owners—are prominent in the operation of a few Fez factories. But it is most frequently men who play the day-to-day role of factory owner and administrator.

9. It is interesting to note that many of the European technical directors are female while Moroccan technical directors are almost exclusively male.

10. There is a growing number of university students who today dress in distinctively Islamic robes, but I do not consider them here.

11. This situation is reinforced by the fact that many workers are related to each other through biological kinship. High level factory staff are often relatives of the factory owner (Fejjal 1987) so that there is a sense in each factory that this is a family enterprise. Personal ties are key in the recruitment of new workers: factory owners and administrators give the relatives and friends of trusted workers preference in hiring. It is common for sisters, cousins, even mother and daughter to work in the same factory, either at the same time or sequentially. At Confection, 10% of the workers had sisters or cousins working contemporaneously with them; others reported that their relatives had worked there previously. Nearly 20% of the workers surveyed had sisters who worked in other garment factories in Fez. Biological kin ties among the workers help contribute to making the idiom of family a reality.

12. Moroccans, men in particular, characterize women as "full of empty talk." Their propensity to be engaged in meaningless speech is prohibited on the factory floor.

13. There are economic reasons for providing transport as well: for many workers, the cost of public transportation to and from the factory would represent such a large percentage of the salary as to make working purposeless. The father of one former worker laughed wryly when he explained that his daughter's month of factory work had actually cost the family money; the girl's salary did not cover her bus fare to and from the factory. (She was considered an apprentice, which explains her absurdly low salary.)

14. Abu Lughod (1986) explores the dimensions of the authority relationship between Bedouin men and women.

## REFERENCES

Abu Lughod, Lila. 1986. *Veiled Sentiments*. Berkeley: University of California Press.

Beneria, Lourdes. 1984. Women and Rural Development: Morocco. *Cultural Survival Quarterly* 8(2): 30–32.

Blim, Michael L. 1992. Introduction: The Emerging Global Factory and Anthropology. In *Anthropology and the Global Factory: Studies of the New Industrialization in the Late Twentieth Century.* M. L. Blim and F. A. Rothstein, eds., pp. 1–30. New York: Bergin and Garvey.

Calagione, John and Daniel Nugent. 1992. Workers' Expressions: Beyond Accommodation and Resistance on the Margins of Capitalism. In *Worker's Expressions: Beyond Accommodation and Resistance.* J. Calagione and D. Nugent, eds., pp. 1–34. Albany: SUNY Press.

Comaroff, John L. and Jean Comaroff. 1987. The Madman and the Migrant: Work and Labor in the Historical Consciousness of a South African People. *American Ethnologist* 14(2): 191–209.

Combs-Schilling, M. Elaine. 1989. *Sacred Performances: Islam, Sexuality and Sacrifice.* New York: Columbia University Press.

Davis, Susan S. 1983. *Patience and Power: Women's Lives in a Moroccan Village.* New York: Schenkman.

Direction de la Statistique de Maroc. 1994. *Femme et Condition Feminine au Maroc.* Rabat: Les Editions Guessous.

Dwyer, Daisy H. 1978. *Images and Self-Images: Male and Female in Morocco.* New York: Columbia University Press.

Elson, Diane and Ruth Pierson. 1981. The Subordination of Women and the Internationalisation of Factory Production. In *Of Marriage and the Market: Women's Subordination in International Perspective.* Kate Yound, ed., pp. 144–166. London: CSE Books.

Fejjal, Ali. 1987. Industrie et Industrialisation à Fes. *Revenue de Geographie Marocaine Nouvelle Serie* 11(2): 55–70.

Hijab, Nadia. 1988. *Womanpower: The Arab Debate on Women at Work.* Cambridge: Cambridge University Press.

Ibrahim, Beth. 1985. Cairo's Factory Women. In *Women and the Family in the Middle East.* Elizabeth Fernea, ed., pp. 293–299. Austin: University of Texas Press.

Joekes, Susan. 1982a. The Multifibre Arrangement and Outward Processing: The Case of Morocco and Tunisia. In *EEC and the Third World.* C. Stevens, ed., pp. 102–112. London: Hodder and Soughton.

_____. 1982b. Female-led Industrialization and Women's Jobs in Third World Export Manufacturing: The Case of the Moroccan Clothing Industry. *Brighton: Institute of Development Studies Research Reports* No. 15.

_____. 1985. Working for Lipstick? Male and Female Labour in the Clothing Industry in Morocco. In *Women, Work and Ideology in the Third World.* H. Afshar, ed., pp. 183–214. London: Tavistock Publications.

Leymarie, Serge and Jean Tripier. 1992. *Maroc: Le Prochain Dragon?* Casablanoa: Editions Eddif Maroc.

Lim, Linda Y. C. 1983. Capitalism, Imperialism and Patriarchy: The Dilemma of Third-World Women Workers in Multinational Factories. In *Women, Men, and the International Division of Labor.* June Nash and M. P. Fernandez-Kelly, eds., pp. 205–223. Albany: State University of New York Press.

Macleod, Arlene E. 1991. *Accommodating Protest: Working Women, the New Veiling, and Change in Cairo.* New York: Columbia University Press.

Mernissi, Fatima. 1987. *Beyond the Veil: Male-Female Dynamics in a Modern Muslim Society.* Bloomington: Indiana University Press.

_____. 1994. *Dreams of Trespass: Tales of a Harem Girlhood.* New York: Addison-Wesley Publishing Company.

Ministère du Commerce de L'Industrie et de la Privatisation. 1994. *Situation des Industries de Transformation.* Rabat: Dèlegation de Commerce et de l'Industrie de la Wilaya de Fes.

Nash, June. 1981. Ethnographic Aspects of the World Capitalist System. *Annual Review of Anthropology* 10: 393–424.

Nash, June and Maria P. Fernandez-Kelly, eds. 1983. *Women, Men and the International Division of Labor.* Albany: State University of New York Press.

Ong, Aibwa. 1987. *Spirits of Resistance and Capitalist Discipline: Factory Women in Malaysia.* Albany: State University of New York Press.

_____. 1991. The Gender and Labor Politics of Postmodernity. *Annual Review of Anthropology* 20: 279–309.

Peristiany, J. G. 1966. *Honor and Shame: The Values of Mediterranean Society.* Chicago: University of Chicago Press.

Rothstein, Francis A. and Michael L. Blim, eds. 1992. *Anthropology and the Global Factory: Studies of the New Industrialization in the Late Twentieth Century.* New York: Bergen and Garvey.

Sabbah, Fatna. 1984. *Woman in the Muslim Unconscious.* New York: Oxford Pergamon Press.

Salaff, Janet. 1981. *Working Daughters of Hong Kong: Filial Piety or Power in the Family?* New York: Cambridge University Press.

Wallman, Sandra, ed. 1979. *The Social Anthropology of Work.* London: Academic Press.

Warren, Kay B. and Susan C. Bourque. 1989. Women, Technology and Development Ideologies: Frameworks and Findings. In *Gender and Anthropology.* S. Morgen, ed., pp. 382–411. Washington, DC: American Anthropological Association.

White, Jenny B. 1994. *Money Makes Us Relatives: Women's Labor in Urban Turkey.* Austin: University of Texas Press.

# Sexuality and Discipline among Filipina Domestic Workers in Hong Kong

## Nicole Constable

In January 1993 Christina, a 27-year-old unmarried Filipina, arrived in Hong Kong to begin work as a foreign domestic helper (or "FDH"). As she told me several months later, Mrs. Wong, her employer, met her at Kai Tak airport. In the car on the way home, Mrs. Wong began their conversation by reciting a list of rules: "On your day off you must be home by 8 P.M. You cannot wear dresses or skirts, only pants. You must keep your shoulders and upper arms covered at all times, and you cannot wear fingernail polish, jewelry, or perfume." Furthermore, she said that Christina's hair, which was thick and long at the time, had to be short. Mrs. Wong then proceeded directly to a barber shop where she instructed the barber to give Christina a "man's cut." Two days later Christina's contract was abruptly terminated.

I met Christina at the shelter for domestic workers where she was staying during the summer of 1993. As she described her ordeal, another Filipina interjected: "*Bruha* (witch) obviously didn't know you'd look even more beautiful with short hair!" I later described Christina's experiences to Mr. Chen, the owner and director of a successful employment agency that recruits women from the Philippines to work as "helpers" in Hong Kong. His comment was remarkably similar. He nonchalantly said, "Perhaps she was too pretty and the employer was worried about her husband."

In this article I argue that Mrs. Wong's treatment of Christina represents far more than the idiosyncratic behavior of a jealous and controlling employer. Instead, Mrs. Wong's attempt to reduce Christina to a less threatening, gender-neutral (or masculine) image is representative of general anxieties about the sexuality of foreign domestic workers in Hong Kong, and the threat that they are thought to pose to Chinese women employers in particular, the Chinese family in general, and Hong Kong society at large as it makes the transition from British colony to Special Administrative Region of the People's Republic of China. As I contend in this article, the public concern about Filipinas and their sexuality is linked to broader changes in women's roles in the home and the public workforce and in the social identities of foreign domestic workers.

Criticisms of Filipinas are partly a reflection of more private concerns writ large and superimposed on a rapidly changing and soon-to-be postcolonial city. On Sundays in Hong Kong's Central District, in what decades ago was an elite and largely male territory, young, nubile, foreign women gather in the thousands on their day off, "taking over," as the locals say, the core of the city's financial region. There, on the steps of such

*American Ethnologist* 24(3):539–558. Copyright © 1997, American Anthropological Association. Not for sale or further reproduction.

great monuments to capitalism as the Hong Kong and Shanghai Bank, foreign maids speak in languages that the locals cannot understand, and they conduct what is generally regarded as private (indoor) rituals or business—polishing nails, giving each other haircuts, and applying makeup—in public. Some dress up and others dress "like men"—both practices being cause for concern. In contrast to locals' images or memories of the Chinese "amahs" of the past, who are said to have "known their places" and to have posed no fundamental or moral challenge to existing patterns of authority (see Constable 1996; Gaw 1991; Ooi 1992), contemporary foreign domestic workers constitute a threat and are considered to be a symbol of a moral order turned inside out. This inversion in the public spaces of Hong Kong on Sundays is locally regarded as scandalous, immoral, provocative, and threatening because, for the other six days of the week, the discourse on sexuality is negotiated in a far more covert arena. The problematic integrity of the modern Chinese family, changing gender roles, and the rapidly changing social geography of Hong Kong is, in part, what the Sunday performance of foreign workers lays bare.

The concern of Hong Kong residents over the sexuality of foreign domestic workers—which is most clearly articulated through attempts by residents to control, discipline them, constrain their sexuality, and enforce their own morality on them—is not about the actual sexual licentiousness or lax morals of foreign domestic workers. As scholars recognize, allegations of promiscuity among the working class in Victorian England say more about the middle and upper classes who made the accusations, and about the wider socioeconomic conditions of the industrial revolution, than about those who stood accused of immorality and debauchery (see Barret-Ducrocq 1991; Gallagher 1987; Gilman 1985; Laqueur 1992). Similarly, the discourse on foreign domestic workers is inextricably linked, not to any actual disproportionate immorality on their part, but to broader social issues in modern, capitalist, international Hong Kong.[1]

Over the past decade and a half, the literature on histories and discourses of sexuality has grown exponentially to include entire journals devoted to the subject. This literature has emerged largely in response to Michael Foucault's *History of Sexuality* (1990[1976]) in the form of applications, refinements, and critiques of his work (see Parker and Gagnon 1995; Stanton 1992). Historians, literary critics, feminists, and scholars in the field of cultural studies are among those who have contributed most to this body of literature and, perhaps not surprisingly, the literature focuses almost exclusively on sexuality in western Europe and the United States. Anthropologists have also contributed to this field and have paid greater attention to discourses of sexuality in non-Western locales. Their studies of non-Western societies, however, are often grounded in, or proceed from, Western colonial ideas about sexuality as they were—and often continue to be—expressed in colonial and postcolonial settings (e.g., Hansen 1989, 1990; Kelly 1991; Stoler 1989).[2]

One of my objectives in this article is to move away from an analysis of sexuality that begins with Western notions of sexuality or focuses exclusively on the history of sexuality to one that is more ethnographically grounded in present day discourses. One could justifiably argue that the analysis of sexuality in contemporary, urban Hong Kong would benefit from greater attention to history and that Western and colonial—as well as Chinese—notions of appropriate sexuality are of relevance. This can be taken for granted. The purpose of my article, by contrast, is to begin with a critical focus on the present by describing the contemporary Hong Kong Chinese discourse on the sexuality of foreign domestic workers and by analyzing the modes of discipline that are deployed. In this article, an offshoot of my historical and ethnographic study of domestic workers in Hong Kong (Constable 1996, 1997), I focus specifically on the problematic relationships among work, discipline, and sexuality.[3]

In the following sections I look at the position of Filipina domestic workers in Hong Kong, the form and content of public images of domestic workers, the ways in which domestic workers are disciplined, and the ways in which workers experience or negotiate certain stereotypes in their day-to-day lives. I have chosen to examine distinct modes of dress among Filipina domestic workers because in this forum there is invaluable opportunity to examine the interface between employers' discipline of workers, domestic workers' self-discipline, and their contestation or appropriation of particular sexual images. As Barnes and Eicher contend, "social identity expressed in dress becomes not only an answer to *who* one is, but also *how* one is, and concerns the definition of the self in relation to a moral and religious value system" (1992:2; see also Broch-Due et al. 1993; Sandborg 1993). As such, modes of dress allow us to see how Filipina domestic workers simultaneously resist and embrace the existing system of power as it is inscribed in the discourse of sex and encoded in sexuality (Abu-Lughod 1990:47).

## GUEST WORKERS

Dramatic shifts in patterns of women's employment in Hong Kong are integrally related to the increasing numbers of foreign domestic workers. The proportion of women in Hong Kong's formal paid workforce rose from 21 percent in 1931 to 34 percent in 1971

(Salaff 1981:294), and stood at 49 percent in 1995 (Census and Statistics Department 1996).[4] The number of foreign domestic workers has also increased dramatically: there were a few hundred workers in the early 1970s, 38,000 in 1987, and almost four times that number—150,000—in late 1995. At that time approximately 130,000 of the domestic workers were from the Philippines and the remaining 20,000 came from Thailand, Indonesia, India, and Sri Lanka (Immigration Department, personal communication, June 1996). Currently over 90 percent of these workers are women; most are between the ages of 25 and 35; and at least three quarters of them are single. Restricted by Hong Kong immigration policies from bringing their families with them, even married foreign domestic workers are perceived as arriving in Hong Kong "unattached."

The rapid increase in the number of Filipina domestic workers is related to socioeconomic conditions in Hong Kong and to the Philippine labor export policy that was initiated by President Ferdinand Marcos during the 1970s. With the rapid growth of Hong Kong's manufacturing economy during the 1960s and 1970s, Chinese women domestic workers left their employers in favor of factory work, which they considered far less demeaning (Salaff 1981; Sankar 1978; cf. Armstrong 1990). The growth of industry was followed by an even greater boom in the service economy during the 1980s—linked in large part to the post-Mao economic liberalization on the mainland—and Hong Kong experienced a severe labor shortage. As a result many previously unemployed middle-class Chinese women were encouraged to take jobs in the service sector (Labour Department 1992). These factors, combined with the increase in numbers of nuclear households—which meant that households were less likely to have kin to share the household work and child care—led to an even greater need for alternative forms of household labor.[5] In response to this demand, the 1980s witnessed the establishment of hundreds of recruitment agencies in the Philippines and counterpart placement agencies in Hong Kong specializing in the international trade of "domestic helpers" (see Constable 1997). The Hong Kong government established special institutions and policies to control and regulate the rapidly growing number of foreign workers. Today almost ten percent of Hong Kong households—some 600,000 individuals—benefit directly from the labor of domestic workers.[6] Most employers, constituting the fastest growing group, come from the middle class. According to one government survey, the median monthly household income for employers of full-time domestic workers was $35,000 in Hong Kong dollars (U.S.$4,500) in 1993, and over 62 percent of households with a monthly income of $80,000 (U.S.$10,000) hired domestic workers (Census and Statistics Department 1995a:3).[7]

In contrast to Chinese amahs who might have stayed with the same family for decades or for life and who were reputed to uphold traditional Chinese familial values (Constable 1996; Gaw 1991; Sankar 1978), foreign domestic workers stay in Hong Kong for less than four years on average (i.e., generally two, back-to-back contracts of two years each), and are consequently less well-integrated into individual households. The class identity of Filipina domestic workers is also ambiguous. In contrast to uneducated Chinese domestic workers, Filipina domestic workers often have high levels of education and their previous "high status" occupations contradict their current identity as "servants." Indeed, surveys suggest that in 1989 almost two-thirds of Filipina domestic workers in Hong Kong had some postsecondary school education (Asian Migrant Centre 1991:15).[8] Many of the workers I interviewed were trained professionals who had previously worked in the Philippines as nurses or schoolteachers, while others had university degrees in such fields as agriculture and business. To employers, a number of whom have lower-level clerical occupations, or who have recently joined the ranks of the educated middle class, the education and class background of some of the new domestic workers come too close for comfort.[9] The ambiguous class identity of foreign domestic workers is one important factor that fuels anxiety, which is expressed in general terms as a concern over their morality and sexuality.

## SEXUAL THREATS: FAMILY AND ECONOMY

That women domestic workers are perceived as posing a sexual threat is not exceptional, either in Chinese society (Jaschok 1988; McMahon 1995; Watson 1991) or in other regions of the world (e.g., Hansen 1989, 1990; Rollins 1985, 1990). In a study of domestic workers and employers in Zambia, Karen Hansen shows how European women employers in colonial Northern Rhodesia resisted employing local women as household workers because of the threat posed by their sexuality. The preference for hiring "manservants" continues in postcolonial Zambia, where black women still view women servants as threatening. As Hansen notes, Zambian women explain in troubled voices how women workers are "insolent and cheeky . . . they steal; they go through your panties and toiletries. But worst of all, before you know it they move into the bedroom and take over the house" (1990:138). The concerns about women household workers in Hong Kong strike a similar chord, although the pattern of primarily employing women to cook, clean house, and care for children has been the norm among both Chinese and

Westerners in Hong Kong since at least the early 20th century (see Jaschok 1988; Sankar 1978; Watson 1991).

Foreign domestic workers are viewed as posing a challenge to the Chinese woman employer's role as both wife and mother. As Margery Wolf has argued, a woman's position within the extended Chinese household depended in large part on the creation of a "uterine family" and the maintenance of a close, affective bond with her sons (Wolf 1968, 1972; see also McMahon 1995:13). If a strong mother-child bond is still a source of women's power in the household, then a close relationship between a domestic worker and the children for whom she cares may threaten the mother's authority (see Constable 1996). In 1996 I learned of several cases of workers whose contracts were terminated because of the female employers' jealousy. In two cases, according to Chinese sources, the domestic worker was dismissed because her charge called her "mommy" and refused to address his "real" mother in this way. I heard of employers who hired workers for only one contract in order to prevent their children from becoming too attached to the workers.

Similarly, the domestic worker also poses a threat to a woman employer's role as wife and sexual partner. She is regarded as a potential seductress—as one who can both turn a man's attention away from family matters and also deplete his energy for productive and reproductive work. In Chinese literature and history, a man's sexual involvement with other women has been viewed as constituting a threat to the well-being of his wife, concubines, and other family members (Ebrey 1993; Jaschok 1988; McMahon 1995).[10] In contemporary Hong Kong, controlling a foreign domestic worker—and especially her sexuality—can be a wife's way of trying to control her husband and defend the integrity of her family unit against a potentially aggressive outsider.[11]

A connection between sexuality and work is made explicit in several studies of Victorian England. As Katherine Gallagher observes in the case of female Irish "costermongers" (street vendors) in London, their work was not viewed as "morally deleterious," yet they were still considered "fallen women" because they served as "a visible and audible emblem of the sexual and economic exploitation that . . . [went] on behind closed doors" (1987:101). If coster-mongers as a group were guilty of anything, it was "embodying and hence raising to the surface the consciousness of a ruthless struggle for marketplace advantage" (1987:101).

Like that of the Irish costermongers in Victorian London, the work of foreign domestic workers in Hong Kong is not itself considered immoral. It includes duties that once were, and in some cases still are, performed by a mother, wife, or daughter-in-law. Moreover, it would also be difficult to argue that bringing market relations into the household is in itself problematic for Hong Kong Chinese. Household work that is done for *another* family for a wage, however, is highly stigmatized compared with work done for no wage within one's own home; and paid household work is valued far less than most work that takes place outside the domestic sphere.[12] It is not that household work became debased in Hong Kong as it was transformed into wage labor: the status of unpaid bondservants was clearly below that of the lowliest paid servants in the past. But even today it remains true that Hong Kong women who are desperately in need of money hesitate to work as "maids" in other people's homes. Their reluctance has more to do with attitudes toward servants than with the work itself. Similarly, the sense of threat that foreign workers pose does not stem from the kind of work they do but from their reluctance to accept or enact the role of servant.

In an analysis of the ways in which sexuality and capitalism are intrinsically and inextricably linked in the discourses of the industrial revolution, Thomas Laqueur suggests that prostitutes in 19th-century England came to be viewed as "*the* social evil" (1992:212, 1990). They were deemed barren and sterile in an attempt to guard the social boundaries "between home and economy, between public and private, self and society" (1992:213). In a similar vein, following Mary Douglas, Aihwa Ong explains that "persons in an interstitial position are often symbolized as dangerous and filthy, since they suggest a poorly articulated social system" (Ong 1991:292; see also Douglas 1970[1966]). As young women, foreigners, and outsiders whose moral position in the social system is not clearly defined, foreign domestic workers have also come to be viewed as dangerous and filthy. Laqueur's argument hinges on the notion that home provided the safeguard "against the disintegrative forces of the market" (1990:230–233). In the Chinese case, it is not the market that people view as essentially disintegrative, but those individuals who lose sight of their familial role and obligations (Harrell 1985). Foreign domestic workers pose a threat, not simply because they work for wages or because a market economy is inherently evil, but because they are foreigners who work within the intimate realm of the household and refuse to accept their debased position. Foreign workers, moreover, reputedly maintain a primary commitment to their own families abroad, not to those of their employers.

Unlike Chinese domestic workers of the past, who allegedly accepted their lowly position in the household hierarchy, Filipinas are considered unwilling to accept their humble status. Many Filipinas proudly insist on being called "workers" rather than "helpers" and reject the idea that they are "servants" or "amahs." The "foreignness" of Filipina domestic workers, their cultural differences, their ambiguous class and social status, and their disinclination to accept such a role also make it more difficult to integrate them comfortably as fictive "members of the family" (Colen and Sanjek 1990:3–4; Gaw 1991; Watson 1991). The contractual nature of their position—linked to recruitment agencies, immigration policies, labor laws, and official contracts—is also more difficult to soften or disguise with familial metaphors and fictive kinship terms than were the market relations of Chinese servants of the past.

## PUBLIC IMAGES: FLIRTS, PROSTITUTES, AND MAIL-ORDER VIRGINS

Although foreign domestic workers usually labor in seclusion, the problem of their identity is far from private. An extensive public discourse on the topic of foreign domestic workers in Hong Kong generates and perpetuates certain notions and stereotypes that are openly expressed in both English- and Chinese-language newspaper editorials, in advertisements created by placement agencies, and in poems, stories, and jokes published in popular magazines. Much of this discourse is "public" in the sense that it is expressed and mediated in public spaces and fora. Local Chinese, Filipinos, and other foreigners all contribute to this discourse by espousing, contesting, or debating various aspects of the putative identity of domestic workers.

Despite the vital role that foreign domestic workers play in Hong Kong's economy, their presence has not—especially in recent years—evinced a public sense of gratitude and relief. Instead, some Chinese have characterized them as constituting an invasion, and concern and anxiety surround their presence. Among the stereotypes and popular images of foreign domestic workers are notions that they are lazy, demanding, lacking commitment to their work, or "only in it for the money." Hong Kong Chinese also label them as "apathetic" about Hong Kong, a "nuisance," "impolite guests," or ungrateful workers who make too much noise and leave litter in public places (Chan 1996; Chow 1987; Jaschok 1993; Lam 1996; Lee 1993). Many contradictory notions about domestic workers exist. They are at once criticized for acting "too much at home" and for not treating Hong Kong as home (Ong 1992). They are also characterized as poor, as being from "backward" countries, and as unsophisticated and uneducated (Chong 1985). Some view them as, on the whole, hard workers who contribute valuable labor to the colony, but others are far more critical. Filipinas are increasingly described

by Hong Kong Chinese as too smart, too savvy, and too assertive to make ideal workers.

Scholars have noted that young "nubile" women in the paid workforce are often represented as bearers of a rampant or "uncontained" sexuality (e.g., Enloe 1990; Ong 1991). As Aihwa Ong notes, the large number of Malay women in international manufacturing "has occasioned negative public commentary on the conduct of female workers. . . . As new workers, young women engage in activities that isolate traditional boundaries (spatial, economic, social, and political) in public life, forcing a redefinition of the social order" (1991:292). Filipina domestic workers in Hong Kong have evoked similar but even more volatile concerns than their industrial counterparts because they bring ambiguity and danger into a far more problematic domain: the archetypal, tightly knit, patriarchal Chinese home. Yet they are also highly visible in public places and much of the criticism of their behavior centers on the impropriety of their public behavior (see Constable 1997; Jaschok 1993).

On their Sundays off work, tens of thousands of foreign domestic workers gather in Statue Square and other areas of Central District. Their perceived flirtatiousness and friendliness in public contributes to an image that they are very different from Chinese women. Filipinas are not merely understood as friendlier or more outgoing than Chinese women—although this is certainly one part of the image. Filipinas are also characterized by local Hong Kong people as morally loose and on the lookout for men. They groom themselves in public and they drink, loiter, and gamble in public places. What Françoise Barret-Ducrocq writes of Victorian England could apply equally well to contemporary Hong Kong:

> As long as she was in a hurry, obviously busy, the woman . . . was playing her proper role; her brisk pace through the streets was the gauge of her honesty. Loitering in the street, on the other hand, hanging about for too long or without an obvious errand was seen as unnatural. . . . So any wandering about which could not be explained by shopping or some other necessary activity came to be perceived as a . . . factor or sign of doubtful morality. (1991:10)

Ideas about the sex trade in the Philippines and in Thailand also fuel stereotypes about promiscuous foreign domestic workers among the Hong Kong public. As one employment agency worker explained in 1994, the announcement of the closing of the U.S. bases in the Philippines caused numerous prospective Chinese employers to express concern that former Filipina prostitutes would come to Hong Kong in the guise of maids. One staff member said that her agency had recently stopped recruiting women from Thailand because prospective Chinese employers were even more fearful of Thai women becoming prostitutes. Hong Kong's mass media also fortify the association between foreign domestic workers and the sex trade. Both English and Chinese newspapers often carry sensational stories about prostitution in Hong Kong, and about Filipina and Thai women who are "lured" or coerced into prostitution after entering the colony—to work, presumably, as maids or entertainers (e.g., Bociurkiw 1992a, 1992b; Laxton 1993; Mendoza and Bociurkiw 1992; *South China Morning Post* 1992; Wallis 1992; Wong 1993). Domestic workers are viewed as poor and willing to leave their families (parents, siblings, husbands, and children) in order to earn money to send home. Prostitution, in the public imagination, is thought to be far more lucrative than domestic work. Although the "immoral" aspect of prostitution is an issue of public concern for many Hong Kong people, the notion of filial piety manifested in sacrificing oneself to such a dishonorable occupation for the sake of one's family's well-being is not unknown to the Chinese (Wolf 1968). But the family for whom the foreign domestic worker would be putatively making the sacrifice is not the Chinese family to whom she has sold her labor power, and for whom her public image and private behavior is of critical importance.

Ideas about Filipina "mail-order brides" fuel similar images. Despite protest from the Filipino community, the Australian-made film "Filipina Dream Girls" was aired on Hong Kong television in 1993. As an article in a Hong Kong Filipino migrant worker magazine describes it, the film gives viewers advice on "how to find a 'young, obedient and virgin' Filipina wife" (*Tinig Filipino* 1993a:25). According to Filipino critics, the film shows "an obese man playing the part of an agent . . . convincing sex-starved bachelors that 'Filipinas will do anything, *anything*'" (1993a:25). The Australian film maker is quoted as saying that the top export commodity of the Philippines is "Filipina virgins" and that they are "obedient . . . and do not complain even when they are maltreated" (1993a:25). More to the point, he says, "[Filipinas] would do anything to get a foreigner for a husband to attain economic security" (1993a:25). Although the impression of most Chinese women with whom I spoke was that Filipinas "prefer Western men," there is also a pervasive fear that they would take any man they could get, including Hong Kong Chinese.

## DISCIPLINE

A common view among Hong Kong Chinese is that Filipina domestic workers ought to be generally better disciplined and restrained. The perceived threat of rampant sexuality is one of several reasons for

employers and the Hong Kong public to increase the control and discipline they impose on domestic workers. Many employers, members of the Hong Kong Employers of Overseas Domestic Helpers Association, and the staff at employment agencies explained that strict forms of discipline were imposed for the workers' own good. Several Chinese employers commented that domestic workers could not be trusted to behave. Many employers considered themselves responsible for helping to assure that a domestic worker "won't get herself into trouble." As one woman employer explained, "even the most well-intentioned domestic workers need a bit of help resisting [sexual temptations]."

Thus employers use the potentially rampant sexuality of foreign workers to justify the imposition of strict curfews and rules. Typically these include eight or nine o'clock curfews on the worker's day off and strict dress codes. Sleeveless shirts, tight pants, skirts above the knee, perfume, jewelry, or makeup of any sort are forbidden. The following is an excerpt from a list of rules given to prospective domestic workers by one employment agency:

- Fingernails shall be kept short, clean and not polished. No makeup is allowed at home.
- Shorts, [and] nightgowns are not allowed except within servant's quarters.
- Personal hygiene is strictly emphasized.
- No smoking or drinking alcohol is allowed.
- All the clothes of the maid should separate to wash [from] the employer [*sic*].
- During holidays [the days off], you shall be back before curfew time as prescribed by the employer. Staying overnight elsewhere is strictly forbidden.

Numerous other lists I collected, or that were custom-made or tailored by employers, emphasize similar points. One list prohibits the domestic worker from closing her door or locking it except when undressing. Another warns her to "beware of the 'bad guys' when going in or out." Yet another stipulates that she "must not go out earlier than 10:00, . . . must be back home no later than 19:00 and . . . can never stay out overnight." Many employers require domestic workers to have a regular pregnancy test.[13]

As one official of the Hong Kong employers' association explained, employers are responsible for the well-being of their domestic workers and must insure that they not get into trouble. Regardless of domestic workers' age, they are often treated like children who might be tempted to stay out late, mix with bad company, and get into trouble. Time and time again, employers reiterated the idea that domestic workers must be controlled and disciplined. Some suggested that venues for good, clean fun should be provided for foreign workers so that they would not get into trouble or simply loiter and "waste time" in public places on their days off work.[14] As an employers' association official explained, "[Filipinas] are not all bad, but they are unfamiliar with Hong Kong. They can get into trouble, and then employers have to go to the trouble and the expense of finding and training a new one."

Some employers take it for granted that a Filipina domestic worker will be willing to provide sexual favors. Minda, 30 years old, married, and with two small children in the Philippines, had only worked for her new employers for two days when her male employer asked her to help him in the bathroom. When Minda arrived at the door of the bathroom, the 40-year-old man stood there completely naked and requested that she wash him and give him a massage. Minda was horrified, left, and began to look for a new job. Rosaria, aged 20, had a similar experience, and described how her employer's teenage son repeatedly appeared in the nude to greet her when his mother was not at home.

After several weeks of "stomach pain," Louisa, a 40-year-old with a husband and children in the Philippines, decided to go for a consultation at the local public hospital. She told the doctor that fried food seemed to irritate the problem. As she explained,

> the doctor, [a young Chinese man,] recommended that I have a pregnancy test. I told him "I'm having my period! And I'm married! My husband is in the Philippines." He winked at me and said "Don't worry, we won't tell anyone." He was joking with me. The worst thing was he also wanted to test for AIDS. I said "Doctor, I'm clean. Only with my husband." That tells you what they think about us Filipinas.

The issue of prostitution is important, not because domestic workers are likely to become prostitutes, but because it articulates with a number of other concerns regarding domestic workers that often have a more substantive basis. The relatively sudden appearance of a large number of "unattached" young foreign women creates anxiety among the host population for a variety of reasons. Foreign domestic workers, like other temporary migrants, are thought, regardless of particular circumstances and the uncertainty of the 1997 transition to Chinese rule, to want to remain in Hong Kong. Although the immigration figures for early 1996 suggest that the number of Filipinas may be starting to decrease, and although many expressed to me their intention of leaving Hong Kong before July 1997, some Hong Kong locals—echoing ideas from "Filipina Dream Girls"—fear that foreign domestic workers might be willing to do almost anything in order to stay. Their alleged tactics include seducing local married men with sex in the hopes of eventually marrying them to gain legal permanent residence. Very few

Filipinas intend to stay in Hong Kong permanently, and certainly not by these means. According to an Asian Migrant Centre survey, 85 percent of Filipina domestic workers would remain in the Philippines if they could earn as much there. Most go back to the Philippines after less than two contracts, citing the "discrimination" and "hostility" of the Hong Kong locals (Asian Migrant Centre 1991) and their concerns about 1997 as important factors in their decision to return home.

Yet domestic workers are still perceived as wanting to stay in Hong Kong. "Of course they would," one Chinese woman employer told me. "Why would anyone want to go back there [the Philippines], where it's so poor?" Foreign domestic workers who signed a contract in 1995 earn a monthly wage of $3,750 (U.S.$480) in addition to room and board. Most workers and employers consider this a good wage; it is more, I was told, than the workers could earn as doctors or lawyers in the Philippines. As another Chinese employer put it, her friends "are afraid that Filipinas are after whatever ugly old husband they have just to stay in Hong Kong." I had the opportunity to meet several current and former domestic workers who had married local men as a way to remain in Hong Kong. In some cases, I was told, it was "true love," but in others I learned that it was merely "convenient." Several Filipinas also joked with me, a white woman with a British passport, about whether I could introduce them to my brother. Yet far more women described their complete avoidance of local men, citing one example after another of women who had become involved with Chinese men or expatriates and were eventually deserted. This theme is especially common in poems and short stories by and about domestic workers (see Layosa and Luminarias 1992).

A Chinese social worker I interviewed offered a blunt explanation: Chinese women employers "may not feel comfortable having young attractive Filipinas living in their homes. . . . Although it would be very difficult for them to admit it, they may not entirely trust them with their husbands." As several domestic workers suggested, the mistrust that might be legitimately directed toward the husband is often directed instead at the domestic worker. The latter is in the awkward and powerless position of being a putative "seductress" in the home of the jilted wife. The domestic worker is the newcomer and in many cases has already been labeled as inherently promiscuous. Indeed, I met many women who came to the Mission for Filipino Domestic Workers (a nonprofit organization run mainly by Filipina volunteers) for legal or personal advice because male members of the household had made sexual advances and, in a few cases, had attempted rape.[15] In some instances, when domestic workers reported sexually aggressive behavior to their female employers, they were accused of having initiated the aggression. As one might expect, in cases of sexual assault reported in the local papers the employers' defense was usually that the domestic workers had initiated the sexual encounters. Many women who came to the mission for advice simply refused to speak to their female employers. They already feared the mistrust or jealousy of these women. Instead, they simply wanted advice on how to terminate their contracts.

A woman employer's jealousy is potentially dangerous. I was repeatedly told of women whose contracts were terminated on the first day, or immediately after arrival in Hong Kong, because the domestic worker was "too beautiful" and therefore posed a threat to her woman employer. A number of domestic workers told me that they thought their male employers were "much nicer" than their wives, but they went out of their way to avoid them lest they incur the woman employers' wrath and find their contracts terminated as a result.

Although the point may seem obvious, it is important to note that age, gender, menial status, and temporary legal residence place foreign domestic workers in a subordinate position. Although domestic workers are often viewed as the ones who pose a sexual threat, it is in fact they who are most vulnerable (Colen and Sanjek 1990:179). Unlike factory workers—who enjoy at least a degree of anonymity and strength in numbers— domestic workers not only work in the home, a moral and ethical crucible, but they live in separate households where they are isolated from the support of their coworkers and where they are usually outnumbered by their employers. In many cases domestic workers speak little or no Chinese and are economically vulnerable, often having acquired large debts in order to arrange to come to Hong Kong in the first place. As a result they are often unwilling to risk complaining or disobeying their employers.

## MEDIATING IMAGES

Domestic workers simultaneously resist and promote discipline. On one hand they attempt to counter certain negative public images. Some workers share their employers' enthusiasm for particular restrictions and forms of self-discipline, promoting sexual and other kinds of self-control among their compatriots. This they often do for the sake of Philippine national pride. Others actively espouse ways of remaining "feminine" without appearing too "sexy." On the other hand, domestic workers sometimes adopt or manipulate certain sexual images as a means of resisting controls placed on them by employers and the wider Hong Kong public.

Filipina domestic workers are well aware of their reputation as "loose" or willing to "do almost anything" to obtain permanent foreign residence, but most Filipinas would criticize this reputation as unfounded and as based on the bad image that a few women have created for all Filipinas. Some Filipinas, for example, opposed a family planning campaign aimed at Filipina domestic workers (Greenway 1986) and openly defended "Filipino people's lofty regard for chaste womanhood" (Nubla 1986). The campaign, Filipina critics claimed, "promoted the thinking and conclusion" that Filipinas in Hong Kong "mostly single and/or married women whose husbands are not here . . . need the services of the Family Planning Association" (Nubla 1986). Like African Americans who participated in the Social Hygiene Movement (1910–40) and promoted "sexual Victorianism" (Simmons 1993), some Filipinas actively promote "social improvements" and clean and healthy recreational activities aimed at keeping foreign workers off the streets.

Filipinas in Hong Kong use the terms *barracuda* or the acronym *AB* to refer to prostitutes, or women who are "sleeping around." Barracudas, I learned, are women associated with a Philippine gang whose members "wear barracuda tattoos." These women are reputed to work as prostitutes on ships and, like the barracuda (a "man-eating fish"), they "eat the flesh of drowning sailors." AB is slang that derives from the term *akyat barco* (literally "to enter a boat"). Akyat Barco, the name of a gang in the Philippines, is also slang for women who hustle sailors. In Hong Kong both terms are used by domestic workers to refer specifically to prostitutes, or, more commonly, as an epithet to chastise and insult women whose behavior appears to be loose or immoral. One worker used both terms to describe a woman who had slept with her husband in the Philippines.

Clothing is another vehicle through which critique and mediation are expressed and identity is negotiated (see Sandborg 1993). Advice Filipinas give one another reflects a strong concern for dressing appropriately and a notion that, if women dress in certain ways, they may be asking for trouble. In the domestic worker magazine, *Tinig Filipino*, Annabelle Basabica writes that some domestic workers "complain about their bosses because of sexual molestation but sometimes we forget that it is due to our own mistakes. Could you expect a man to act like a saint when you are garbed in sexy clothes? If you want to be respected, you should choose the right clothes [to] wear in various and specific occasions, so that everyone you meet will not frown" (1993:37). Basabica's article earned many accolades from fellow domestic workers. Marivic Dacilla (1993:25) and Thelma Ventenilla (1993:28) both agreed that Filipinas should be more moderate in their style—that they should not wear too much makeup or wear their "skirts too short or too [close-] fitting" (Ventenilla 1993:28). Another *Tinig Filipino* article, entitled "Protect Yourself From Sexual Molestation," makes an explicit connection between provocative clothing and sexual abuse, cautioning women, "Do not expose yourself to the possibility of abuse by the way you dress and conduct yourself" (1993b:45).

Acosta is one domestic worker who tries to steer clear of the barracuda image but who also tries "not to go too far toward the other extreme" in an attempt to create what she considers the "right" message about her sexuality. The way she dresses and acts in public is directly related to the particular conditions of her work. One reason for her concern is that much of the domestic work she does is illegal. She does "aerobics" (part-time work), which is not permitted according to the official domestic worker contract.[16] Acosta's contract is a scam that she created together with Mr. Woo ("the one who signed my contract"). While working for her previous full-time employer, Acosta also did some part-time work for Mr. Woo, a Hong Kong-born, Canadian-educated employee of the Hong Kong government. Mrs. Zee, the employer who had signed Acosta's previous contract, did not pay her the legal minimum wage stipulated in the official contract. Instead, she "allowed" Acosta to make up the difference by illegally working on a part-time basis. After the contract was terminated (i.e., when Mrs. Zee emigrated to Canada), Acosta asked Mr. Woo if he would hire her. As Acosta explained, Mr. Woo and his wife have a large apartment and their income was more than sufficient to enable them to employ a full-time domestic worker; Acosta suspected, however, that Mrs. Woo simply did not want her around. Acosta then suggested that Mr. Woo sign the contract and pay her half of a monthly salary in exchange for half a week's work. It was agreed that Acosta would arrange for her own housing and that she would use her free time as she liked. Although she feels she does more work for the Woos than a half-time worker should, she prefers this arrangement to one full-time job because she can earn more money. She also prefers the freedom it gives her to organize and manage her own time.[17]

Although it is illegal, at least a quarter of all foreign domestic workers have at one time or another done aerobics (Mission for Filipino Migrant Workers, personal communication, June 1994). Acosta's situation is somewhat extreme, however, and involves some risk. If discovered by immigration department officials, at best she could be deported; at worst she could be fined and imprisoned. Even though her employers are also legally at fault, employers are rarely, if ever, punished for hiring part-time workers.

Acosta works in as many as eight different households a week, some for as few as four hours a week.

This entails much commuting and traveling and many possibilities of encountering people who could potentially betray her to Labour or Immigration Department authorities for breach of contract. She is particularly concerned with the impression she makes on people like the Chinese building watchmen and elevator attendants, and is therefore extremely polite to them and often greets them in Cantonese.

Acosta's main objective is to dress in such a way that she is viewed as stylish and attractive enough to be mistaken for a local wife. She plays what she describes as the role of a "local Filipina lady" who, by virtue of the fact that she has a foreign (i.e., Anglo or expatriate) husband, would be legally permitted to work part-time. Although she has never become sexually or emotionally involved with a man in Hong Kong during the 15 years she has worked there (and she questioned whether something might be "wrong" with her because of her general lack of sexual desire), she wanted to project an appearance that would suggest to observers that she has a foreign husband.

Another concern, as she put it, "is that I look younger than I really am." In her early forties, she wears her hair longer and her skirts shorter than she otherwise would because she is afraid that employers may decide that she is getting too old for domestic work. But she does not want to dress so as to attract too much male attention or create the impression of being a barracuda. Thus, she wears skirts that reach above the knee, but are not too short; she wears some—but not too much—makeup; she wears nice shoes with heels but the heels that are not too high. Her jewelry and her blouses often introduce a South or Southeast Asian element such as batik or cotton print blouses and silver dangling earrings. Wearing such "ethnic clothing" was popular among both Filipina domestic workers and many Filipina "professionals" in 1993 and 1994 but was not generally associated with the style of barracudas—nor was it a style popular among Chinese women. Despite an awareness that her way of "dressing up" can be threatening to some employers, she prefers to take that risk than to wear what she calls the "DH uniform" of jeans, T-shirt, and tennis shoes that would undermine the image she wants to portray.

Because she works part-time, she must choose her employers carefully. She only works for people to whom she has been referred by friends or who are acquaintances of her current employers. In one case a new woman employer, Mrs. Cheung, reacted strongly to her appearance, asking on the first day whether she was "looking for a boyfriend" or "on the way to a disco." Acosta stood her ground and asserted her right to dress up and wear lipstick. She explained that she would change her shoes and clothes when she arrived but that she would not be seen "poorly dressed" in public. "Even in the Philippines I would not dress like that, so why should I do it here?" she recounted having told Mrs. Cheung. Eventually she stopped working for the Cheungs. Mr. Cheung made remarks about Acosta's attractiveness and teased his wife about her jealousy in Acosta's presence. Acosta decided it was better to resign than face the ultimate risk of possible deportation.

## BLUE JEANS, T-SHIRTS, AND T-BIRDS

The domestic worker "uniform" of blue jeans and T-shirts to which Acosta alluded is one of the most common outfits donned by domestic workers in Hong Kong and it is also a common style of dress among female workers in the Philippines. Most female employers approve—indeed encourage—this style of dress, as long as the blue jeans "are not too tight." Both Chinese employers and domestic workers agree that such clothes are cheap, comfortable, and easy for work (except in the sweltering summer months). This uniform fits the rules of many employers: the knees and shoulders are covered and the neckline is high. Domestic workers themselves usually much prefer the blue-jean uniform to the "real" uniform: the pastel pink, baby-blue, or pale green dress with a white apron, that many are required to wear in summer, or the heavier, black, long-sleeved dress with the white apron that many are required to wear in winter or on formal occasions in the household. Unlike the "playboy bunny" or "cocktail waitress" version of the maid's uniform, the real uniform is not short, fitted, and sexy, but is long, baggy, and matronly in appearance. As Maria explained, she is ashamed to be seen in public wearing a real uniform "because then everyone knows I'm a maid." The blue-jean uniform does not bear the same stigma as the formal uniform, which can, like other types of official uniforms, "negate the gender identity of the wearer" (Barnes and Eicher 1992:7; see also Young 1992); nor do blue jeans and T-shirts carry the connotation of sloppy clothing, as they are usually meticulously clean and carefully pressed. Like the official or formal uniform that some women must wear, however, the blue-jean uniform is nonetheless often striking for what employers and many workers regard as its asexual, "maidish" appearance. As domestic workers and agency staff explained, employers do not want to hire domestic workers who are "too attractive," nor do they want them to dress too enticingly (cf. Rollins 1990:84–85).

Mrs. Lee described how her friends and neighbors often commented on the attractiveness of her domestic worker and on the elegance of Sophia's clothes. Some of Sophia's clothes are in fact Mrs. Lee's fashionable, expensive, designer hand-me-downs. Mrs. Lee's friends disapprove of this practice. They ask her whether she is worried about having such a good-looking and well-dressed young woman around her husband. But Mrs. Lee feels secure—perhaps because, as she told me, Sophia is too fat to be really beautiful, is extremely religious, and has a boyfriend back home.

Sophia's situation is exceptional in the sense that Mrs. Lee allows her to wear whatever she wants at work and when she goes out in public. Many domestic workers must observe a strict dress code at all times. Even on their days off work they are not allowed to put on makeup or jewelry in their employers' homes, so many wait until they reach the destined park benches in Central District to do so. Others change in public lavatories or go to a friend's house to dress up each Sunday before going to town for the day.

On Sunday, the most common day off work for domestic workers, they reveal numerous styles of dress, but two patterns are especially striking. Many women take Sunday as an occasion to dress up in fancy dresses, heels, makeup, jewelry, and similar finery. Many others wear jeans and T-shirts. The first pattern—regardless of the details of the style—reflects the desire of domestic workers to escape the role of maid by which they feel confined during the rest of the work week. While dressing up follows different patterns, one concern is clearly expressed by Sophia and her churchgoing friends: they want to look "like ladies," not as though they were going to a bar.

The second pattern can be seen as a continuation of the workday style, but its variations carry a number of possible meanings. While most Hong Kong Chinese see T-shirts and blue jeans as simply a convenient—and sexually unthreatening—style for domestic workers, this style, taken to one extreme, can convey several other messages. One, as Acosta sees it, is that they are accommodating the demands of employers who want domestic workers to look and act like maids—that is, gender-neutral, submissive, and subordinate. Another meaning—of which domestic workers like Acosta are highly aware, but of which employers largely remained ignorant until early 1996—is the image of the "T-bird" or "tomboy."

Well before I had the opportunity to meet her, I heard Noel, an activist domestic worker, described as a T-bird. The terms *T-bird* (short for "thunderbird") or *tomboy* in Filipino slang refer to a lesbian; particularly one who adopts a masculine style of dress. A T-bird, I was told, is "a gay," but the term can also allude to a lesbian style of dress, common among Filipina workers. Noel sometimes wears jeans and T-shirts. In the summer she often wears a man's short-sleeved, button-down shirt, carefully ironed pleated pants, flat laced shoes, and a distinctive "flat top" haircut. Sometimes she also wears a baseball cap.

Several articles about lesbians and about the T-bird style were published in *Tinig Filipino* during the early 1990s (e.g., Corpuz 1993; Ferrer 1993; Saddi 1993; Torrefranca 1992). A striking feature of these articles is that while the T-bird or tomboy appears as a lesbian or as a member of a "third sex," the "Juliet," her partner, is not represented as lesbian or homosexual but as someone who is attracted to a T-bird in the same way she might be attracted to a man. In "The Modern Romeos in the Making," Lizby Eronico observes:

> If you happen to check the lesbian populace among Filipino migrant workers in Hong Kong, you will be amazed at their increasing number. Take for example Sundays and holidays. You can chop my head off if you can't find one with her "Juliet" by her side.
>
> And whether you like it or not, lesbians nowadays are going places. They have finally come out from their shells triumphant. Girls have started fighting over this new breed of "masculine women" who have become genuine lovers to the surprise of everyone. . . .
>
> In spite of being rejected by some segment of society at times, they enjoy playing a gentleman's game. Not to mention wearing men's accessories, perfumes and—hold your breath—men's underwear! With a haircut that will make Kevin Costner get envious and a perfume that makes everyone turn their heads . . . how can a very feminine woman resist?
>
> "*They're gorgeous, faithful, sympathetic, etc.* . . ." These are words from women who are too afraid of flushing their fetus down the toilet. "With a lesbian, I'm safe. . . ." Unlike men, lesbians don't regard women as their "sex objects." (1994:10)

During our first interview, Gina described her encounter in Statue Square one Sunday with Lorna, a friend from the Philippines whom she had not seen for several years. Lorna was very sad because she had just left her children and her husband back in the Philippines. When Gina ran into Lorna a few Sundays later, "the woman was transformed into a T-bird!" As Gina described, Lorna had cut off all her hair and had changed her name. She was wearing a white T-shirt with cigarettes rolled up her sleeve, blue jeans, and black leather boots and carried a leather jacket.

This T-bird style can be seen as one extreme of the blue-jean uniform. It is often considered acceptable by women employers, who usually interpret it as sexually neutral or at least as heterosexually neutral. Several Filipinas told me that this style conveys a clear message that women are not barracudas or after men. Yet many Filipinas consider dressing like a T-bird or even the milder version of the blue-jean uniform "not feminine enough." Several articles and editorials written by domestic workers in *Tinig Filipino* illustrate this

point. Veronica Gamboa (1993) and Nimfa Saddi (1993) both express frustration at the fact that they are mistaken for T-birds because of the way they dress. Saddi writes that "my hairstyle and my outfit look like that of a tomboy . . . [but] I feel more comfortable in this kind of attire" (1993:24). Gamboa says that like Saddi, she is "not a 'woman in disguise,' but some of my colleagues keep calling me a T-bird. According to them they haven't seen me yet wearing a lady's outfit. I'm used to wearing jeans or trousers with matching T-shirt and a baseball cap, too. Although I hate hearing those comments from them, I still keep my cool" (1993:24). Some women, Gamboa and Saddi suggest, don this style because it is comfortable, not because they are lesbians.

The disparagement of the T-shirt, blue-jean style among some Filipina domestic workers did not appear to emerge out of a general fear of being mistaken for a lesbian or out of a condemnation of lesbian sexuality, but out of a concern for appearing inelegant, unfeminine, and unrefined. Although several articles in *Tinig Filipino* (e.g., Corpuz 1993; Mommie Jingco 1991) criticized the immorality of lesbianism from a Christian or Catholic perspective, and one letter writer expressed the fear that "T-birds will lose their jobs if they are found out" (Sombrio 1996), these were not common themes. Like Acosta, most women to whom I spoke did not think lesbians were immoral but held that there were other, more appropriate feminine images for those who were not T-birds. As Maribel Mahusay implores T-birds and those who are mistaken for them: "Why don't you try wearing women's clothes? Show them all the feminine side of yourself. . . . This does not mean that you have to wear an inch-long skirt and heavy makeup. Just follow the appropriate and modest way of wearing women's clothes" (1993:25). The opposite of appearing like a loose or promiscuous woman is not to emulate men or to dress in a gender neutral style but to dress like "good" women.

In early 1996 employers became increasingly concerned about lesbianism when a television news documentary quoted a member of a domestic workers union who estimated that a quarter of all Filipina domestic workers were lesbians (Balagtas 1996; Wilde 1996). A hysterical letter in a local newspaper declared that employers should be alerted to the "threat posed to our children by Filipino T-birds or tomboys" (Ching 1996). According to Ching, "there are an alarming number of T-birds," and she wonders how she can explain women kissing other women to her children: "How can we explain the women the maid brings home. And how can we reason about the trousers, the rolled up sleeves, the hair cropped like a man, the men's clothes?" Ching fears, moreover, that "T-birds will bring to our homes and our children the danger of venereal and killer diseases."

## CONCLUSION

Broadly speaking, foreign domestic workers are faced with several options of clothing style and self-presentation. The complicated set of choices regarding self-presentation evokes different contradictions and dimensions of power within the Hong Kong context: the women can dress in a sexually unthreatening way, as their employers demand, and can submit to their control and class expectations; they can dress up and assert their femininity and be viewed as sexual competitors who threaten class boundaries, as do Acosta and Sophia; they can dress like, or be, T-birds like Noel, aligning themselves with masculine images of power, diffusing the heterosexual threat that they might pose but arousing homophobic reactions; or they can dress like barracudas, in a sexually provocative style, and "invite" abuse and perpetuate a stereotype.

Filipinas such as Sophia and Acosta reject the barracuda as well as the T-bird image in favor of what amounts to "feminine decorum." This decorum is more in keeping with their employers' notions of appropriate sexuality. Yet in many cases a significant difference emerges between the chaste femininity deemed appropriate by an employer and that espoused by domestic workers. While both groups are critical of appearing too cheap or too sexy, many domestic workers who accommodate themselves to this criticism are nevertheless viewed as attempting to dress more like elegant professional ladies than as the domestic helpers their employers would prefer.

Each of these examples suggest ways in which domestic workers may simultaneously contest, resist, and appropriate specific sexual images. Filipina domestic workers are not unlike the Bedouin women described by Lila Abu-Lughod, following Foucault, as both resisting and embracing the existing system of power (1990:47, 1986). In their attempts to dispel the widespread notion of Filipina rampant sexuality, Filipina domestic workers often find themselves arguing in favor of, or unintentionally supporting, the forms of self-discipline that their employers impose on them.

I have tried to show how domestic workers are both complicit in, and express resistance toward, various forms of control. I have also illustrated how the image of foreign domestic workers in Hong Kong is both molded by, and reflexive of, local social and cultural concerns. Although integral to the new economy, foreign domestic workers are commonly regarded as disruptive and dangerous. The sexuality of Filipina domestic workers in Hong Kong

is not an issue because they are highly sexed or lacking in self-control but because they are foreign-Asian others with an ambiguous class identity, highly visible, and intimately linked with changes occurring at the very core of Chinese households. In recent decades Chinese families in Hong Kong (as elsewhere) have seen a major shift in the role of mothers, a decrease in the importance of the extended household, and growing women's participation in wage employment. Changes in notions of romance and monogamy have also altered marital relations. In a situation where Chinese women appear to be losing the power they once derived from their role within the household, the discipline that women employers direct at controlling the sexuality of domestic workers offers them one way of continuing to exert authority. To control a domestic worker may be easier for a woman than to control her husband's fidelity, her children's affection, or the vicissitudes of her own workday experiences. Employers' discipline and control of domestic workers can also be seen as an attempt to reduce them to docile social bodies, to deprive them of full personhood, and to craft for them a less morally ambivalent—but sufficiently subordinate—position within the household.

An important lesson we may derive from the recent literature on Victorian sexuality is that the middle and upper classes were not as pious as they affected to be, nor were the working classes guilty of the sexual laxity and licentiousness attributed to them. The discovery of working-class testimonials and other historical documents (e.g., Barret-Ducrocq 1991; Peiss 1990; Peiss and Simmons 1989) suggests—and the ethnographic lesson of Hong Kong demonstrates—that the reputations of working-class women reveal more about upper-class anxieties than about working-class immorality and licentiousness (Gallagher 1987; Gilman 1985). Yet such an analysis cannot adequately account for some of the striking similarities between the images of Filipina domestic workers in Hong Kong in the 1990s and those of working-class women in 19th-century England. The underlying meanings are in all likelihood *not* the same. For one, it is foreign domestic workers who are depicted as promiscuous in Hong Kong, less so other young working women. Moreover, Hong Kong was industrialized long before the appearance of foreign domestic workers and their supposed debauchery. This suggests that foreign domestic workers are not considered dangerous because they render visible the evils of a market system—although the contractual nature of their employment is far more difficult to disguise than it was for Chinese amahs—but because they refuse to play the role of servants who willingly subordinate themselves to their employers' families. They therefore render visible broader changes in the family, gender roles, and political economy, and serve as a reminder of further changes yet to come as Hong Kong reverts to Chinese rule.

## ACKNOWLEDGMENTS

I presented an earlier version of this article at the 1994 American Anthropological Association meeting in Atlanta, GA, as part of a panel organized by Kathleen Adams and Sara Dickey. I am grateful to them, the members of the panel, and discussant Jane Atkinson, for their comments and suggestions. I also owe a debt of thanks to Nancy Abelmann, Joseph Alter, Jeanne Bergman, Corazon Canete, Mimi Chan, Michael Herzfeld, Richard Man-wui Ho, Jane Margold, Aihwa Ong, Elizabeth Sinn, Gabriele Stüzenhofecker, Maria Siu-mi Tam, Cynthia Tellez, Jun Tellez, Rubie Watson, the anonymous reviewers for *American Ethnologist*, the members of the Anthropology of Work seminar at the University of Pittsburgh, the staff and volunteers at the Mission for Filipino Migrant Workers, and numerous domestic workers and employers in Hong Kong. Research during the summer of 1993 was supported by a grant from the Western Michigan University Research and Creative Activities Support Fund, and in summer 1996 by grants from the Hewlett Foundation International Small Grants Program, and the Chinese Studies Program of the University of Pittsburgh.

## NOTES

1. Similar observations have been made about the sexual stereotypes of African Americans and Jews (e.g., Gilman 1994; JanMohamed 1992; Rollins 1985; Ware 1992).
2. There are exceptions; see, for example, Allison (1994), Alter (1994), Gladney (1994), Parker (1991), and the immense anthropological literature on the body. I am not, of course, alluding here to the vast anthropological literature on sex, which takes a less discursive approach to the subject.
3. I conducted research during the summer and fall of 1993, and the summers of 1994 and 1996. It included the collection of documentary materials including videotapes, newspaper and magazine articles, and editorials by and about domestic workers. Hundreds of hours of interviews were conducted with Filipina domestic workers, Chinese employers, employment agency staff, and representatives of various domestic worker and employer organizations.
4. The labor force participation rate in 1994 for women aged 25 to 29 was 81.7 percent; for those aged 30 to 34 it was 63.5 percent; and for those aged 35 to 44 it was 52.5 percent (Census and Statistics Department 1995b:18).
5. Between 1981 and 1991, nuclear households increased from 54 percent to 62 percent of the total (Census and Statistics Department 1995b:3).

6. In 1995 Hong Kong's population was 6.2 million (Census and Statistics Department 1996). Eighty percent of those with full-time, live-in domestic workers employed only one; and the average size of households employing domestic workers was 3.6 members (Census and Statistics Department 1995a:6, 8). Since many other employers hire part-time workers, this suggests that 550,000 to 600,000 people—about 150,000 households—employ domestic workers.
7. During the time of this research, $7.80 in Hong Kong dollars was worth approximately U.S.$1.00. In September 1994 a domestic worker's monthly income, on top of room and board, was officially raised from $3,500 to $3,750 (U.S.$480).
8. A 1984 study found that almost half of over 1,000 Filipina domestic workers surveyed attained a high school education, and that another 38 percent received university, college, or some sort of postsecondary education (French 1986). A 1989 study of 1,700 Filipinas found that 60 percent had a postsecondary education and that, of these, one third had obtained a college or university degree (Asian Migrant Centre 1991:15).
9. About 31 percent of the households employing full-time domestic workers in the 1993 government survey had a total household monthly income below $25,000 (U.S.$3,200) (Census and Statistics Department 1995a:7).
10. The competition and hostility felt by the spurned wife is graphically expressed in *Stories of the West Lake (Xihu erji)* where the wife has the maid, with whom her husband has had sexual relations, killed. She then has the maid's genitals cut off and forces her husband to wear them on his face (McMahon 1995:58).
11. Concerns about extramarital affairs may be heightened by the fact that polygyny has been illegal in Hong Kong since 1971. Although the law reinforces the exclusivity of the legal rights of the first wife, it also increases the risk that a man might divorce his wife in order to form a legal bond with another woman (see Jaschok 1988; Watson 1991).
12. Lisa Rofel explains that the distinction between "inside" and "outside" that traditionally marked appropriate activities for women in China "did not necessarily refer to the literal physical structure of the home" (1994:235). The inside/outside dichotomy did not necessarily oppose family to work. Inside work took place within a familial social sphere; outside work was done for or among strangers, outsiders, or non-kin. It was not, therefore, simply the wage that demeaned the housework of domestic workers, but the fact that it was done for people outside the familial social sphere. The same distinction does not seem to hold for the more prestigious outside work done by many women employers in Hong Kong today.
13. In Singapore foreign domestic workers are legally required to undergo pregnancy testing every six months.
14. The middle-class concern with providing "respectable" entertainment for working-class women was also an issue in the United States (Peiss 1990) and Victorian England (Barret-Ducrocq 1991).
15. As Colen and Sanjek write,
    Unlike concubines . . . female household workers do not provide sexual services as part of their role. Yet, in most

if not all places studied, sexual advances from males, harassment, and rape occur in some household workplaces, and this threat or danger is widely appreciated by women household workers. (1990:181)

16. "Aerobics" is sometimes also used to refer to "sexual encounters"—and is thus the topic of many jokes—but domestic workers more often use it to refer to illegal part-time jobs.

17. Chicana domestic workers express similar preferences for the greater freedom and control to be gained by working in several part-time jobs rather than one full-time one (Romero 1992).

## REFERENCES

Abu-Lughod, Lila
1986    *Veiled Sentiments: Honor and Poetry in a Bedouin Society.* Berkeley: University of California Press.
1990    The Romance of Resistance: Tracing Transformations of Power through Bedouin Women. *American Ethnologist* 17:41–55.

Allison, Anne
1994    *Nightwork: Sexuality, Pleasure, and Corporate Masculinity in a Tokyo Hostess Club.* Chicago: University of Chicago Press.

Alter, Joseph S.
1994    Celibacy, Sexuality, and the Transformation of Gender into Nationalism in North India. *Journal of Asian Studies* 53:45–65.

Armstrong, M. Jocelyn
1990    Female Household Workers in Industrializing Malaysia. In *At Work in Homes: Household Work in World Perspective.* Roger Sanjek and Shellee Colen, eds. Pp. 146–163. Washington, DC: American Anthropological Association.

Asian Migrant Centre
1991    *Foreign Domestic Workers in Hong Kong: A Baseline Study.* Hong Kong: Asian Migrant Worker's Centre.

Balagtas, B.
1996    Gay Report Is Irresponsible. *Eastern Express,* January 19.

Barnes, Ruth, and Joanne B. Eicher
1992    *Dress and Gender: Making and Meaning in Cultural Contexts.* Oxford: Berg.

Barret-Ducrocq, Françoise
1991    *Love in the Time of Victoria: Sexuality, Class and Gender in Nineteenth-Century London.* John Howe, trans. New York: Verso.

Basabica, Annabelle
1993    The Way We Wear in Summer. *Tinig Filipino,* May: 37.

Bociurkiw, Michael
1992a   Letters Home Give Vital Clues to Police on Mercy Mission. *Sunday Morning Post,* June 28.
1992b   Philippines Urged to Act Over "Sex Slaves" in HK. *Sunday Morning Post,* December 27.

Broch-Due, Vigdis, Ingrid Rudie, and Tone Bleie, eds.
1993    *Carved Flesh/Cast Selves: Gendered Symbols and Social Practices.* Oxford: Berg.

Census and Statistics Department
1995a   Domestic Helpers. In *Social Data Collected by the General Household Survey: Special Topics Report No. 12.* Pp. 3–10. Hong Kong: Government Printer.
1995b   *Hong Kong Social and Economic Trends.* 1995 Edition. Hong Kong: Government Printer.
1996    *Hong Kong in Figures.* 1996 Edition. Hong Kong: Government Printer.

Chan, Stephen
1996    Honest and Hard-Working. *South China Morning Post,* May 15.

Ching, Linda
1996    Motives for Defence of Lesbians Questioned. *Eastern Express,* January 22.

Chong, M. S.
1985    Filipina Maids Are Spoiled. *South China Morning Post,* June 18.

Chow, M. S.
1987    The Rising Tide against Domestics. *Hong Kong Standard,* May 11.

Colen, Shellee, and Roger Sanjek
1990    At Work in Homes I: Orientations and At Work in Homes II: Directions. In *At Work in Homes: Household Work in World Perspective.* Roger Sanjek and Shellee Colen, eds. Pp. 1–13, 176–188. American Ethnological Society Monograph Series, Number 3. Washington, DC: American Anthropological Association.

Constable, Nicole
1996    Jealousy, Chastity, and Abuse: Chinese Maids and Foreign Helpers in Hong Kong. *Modern China* 22:448–479.
1997    *Maid to Order in Hong Kong: Stories of Filipina Workers.* Ithaca, NY: Cornell University Press.

Corpuz, Daisy
1993    Is Homosexuality Already Accepted? *Tinig Filipino,* April: 25.

Dacilla, Marivic
1993    Cheers to "The Way We Wear. . . ." *Tinig Filipino,* June: 25.

Douglas, Mary
1970[1966]   *Purity and Danger.* Harmondsworth, UK: Penguin.

Ebrey, Patricia Buckley
1993    *The Inner Quarters: Marriage and the Lives of Chinese Women in the Sung Period.* Berkeley: University of California Press.

Enloe, Cynthia
1990    *Bananas, Beaches, and Bases: Making Feminist Sense of International Politics.* Berkeley: University of California Press.

Eronico, Lizby G.
1994    The Modern Romeos in the Making. *Tinig Filipino,* February: 10.

Ferrer, Babes
1993    Women in Disguise. *Tinig Filipino,* February: 8.

Foucault, Michel
1990[1976]   *The History of Sexuality: An Introduction,* Vol. 1. New York: Vintage Books.

French, Carolyn
1986    *Filipina Domestic Workers in Hong Kong.* Ph.D. dissertation, University of Surrey.

Gallagher, Catherine
1987    The Body versus the Social Body in the Works of Thomas Malthus and Henry Mayhew. In *The Making of the Modern Body: Sexuality and Society in the Nineteenth-Century.* Catherine Gallagher and Thomas Laqueur, eds. Pp. 83–106. Berkeley: University of California Press.

Gamboa, Veronica
1993    Misunderstood Me. *Tinig Filipino,* June: 24.

Gaw, Kenneth
1991    *Superior Servants: The Legendary Amahs of the Far East.* Singapore: Oxford University Press.

Gilman, Sander L.
1985    *Difference and Pathology: Stereotypes of Sexuality, Race, and Madness.* Ithaca, NY: Cornell University Press.
1994    Sigmund Freud and the Sexologists: A Second Reading. In *Sexual Knowledge, Sexual Science: The History of Attitudes to Sexuality.* Roy Porter and Kikulas Teich, eds. Pp. 323–349. New York: Cambridge University Press. Gladney, Dru
1994    Representing Nationality in China: Refiguring Majority/Minority Identities. *Journal of Asian Studies* 53:92–123.

Greenway, Alice
1986    Birth Campaign Aims at Filipinos. *South China Morning Post,* July 28.

Hansen, Karen Tranberg
1989    *Distant Companions: Servants and Employers in Zambia, 1900–1985.* Ithaca, NY: Cornell University Press.
1990    Part of the Household Inventory: Men Servants in Zambia. In *At Work in Homes: Household Work in World Perspective.* Roger Sanjek and Shellee Colen, eds. Pp. 119–145. Washington, DC: American Anthropological Association.

Harrell, Stevan
1985    Why Do the Chinese Work So Hard: Reflections on an Entrepreneurial Ethic. *Modern China* 13(1):90–109.

JanMohamed, Abdul R.
1992    Sexuality on/of the Racial Border: Foucault, Wright and the Articulation of "Racialized Sexuality." In *Discourses of Sexuality.* Domna Stanton, ed. Pp. 94–116. Ann Arbor: University of Michigan.

Jaschok, Maria
1988    *Concubines and Bondservants: A Social History.* London: Zed Books.
1993    "A Public Nuisance": Reflections on the Occupation of City Spaces by Filipina Domestic Helpers in Hong Kong. Paper Presented at the International Conference on Africa and Asia. Hong Kong, August 24, 1993.

Kelly, John D.
1991    *A Politics of Virtue: Hinduism, Sexuality, and Countercolonial Discourse in Fiji.* Chicago: University of Chicago Press.

Labour Department
1992    *Labour and Employment in Hong Kong.* Hong Kong: Government Printer.

Lam, Rowena
1996    Let Unhappy Maids Return to the Philippines. *South China Morning Post,* May 14.

Laqueur, Thomas W.
1990    *Making Sex: Body and Gender from the Greeks to Freud.* Cambridge, MA: Harvard University Press.
1992    Sexual Desire and the Market Economy during the Industrial Revolution. In *Discourses of Sexuality.* Domna Stanton, ed. Pp. 185–215. Ann Arbor: University of Michigan.

Laxton, Andrew
1993    Police Hunt "Asia's Biggest Pimp." *Sunday Morning Post,* September 19.

Layosa, Linda, and Laura P. Luminarias
1992    *Sa Pagyuko Ng Kawayan: A Collection of Short Stories by Overseas Workers.* Hong Kong: Asia Pacific Publishing Company.

Lee, P. K.
1993    Tax on Maids Is Workable. *South China Morning Post,* February 9.

Mahusay, Maribel
1993    Judge People by the Clothes They Wear. *Tinig Filipino,* August: 25.

McMahon, Keith
1995    *Misers, Shrews, and Polygamists: Sexuality and Male-Female Relations in Eighteenth-Century Chinese Fiction.* Durham, NC: Duke University Press.

Mendoza, Alice, and Michael Bociurkiw
1992    Thousands of Illegals Work in HK Brothels. *South China Morning Post,* July 5.

Mommie Jingco
1991    Shocking. *Tinig Filipino,* April: 24–25.

Nubla, M. G.
1986    Family Planning for Filipinas. *Hongkong Standard,* August 11.

Ong, Aihwa
1991    The Gender and Labor Politics of Postmodernity. *Annual Review of Anthropology* 20:279–309.

Ong, J.
1992    No Foreigner Can Stand above the Law. *South China Morning Post,* December 15.

Ooi, Keat Gin
1992    The Black and White Amahs of Malaya. *Journal of the Malaysian Branch of the Royal Asiatic Society* 65(2):69–84.

Parker, Richard G.
1991    *Bodies, Pleasures, and Passions: Sexual Culture in Contemporary Brazil.* Boston: Beacon Press.

Parker, Richard G., and John H. Gagnon, eds.
1995    *Conceiving Sexuality: Approaches to Sex Research in a Postmodern World.* New York: Routledge.

Peiss, Kathy
1990    "Charity Girls" and City Pleasures: Historical Notes on Working-Class Sexuality, 1880–1920. In *Unequal Sisters: A Multicultural Reader in U.S. Women's History.* Ellen Carol DuBois and Vicki L. Ruiz, eds. Pp. 157–166. New York: Routledge.

Peiss, Kathy, and Christina Simmons, eds., with Robert A. Padgug
1989    *Passion and Power: Sexuality in History.* Philadelphia: Temple University Press.

Rofel, Lisa
1994    Liberation Nostalgia and a Yearning for Modernity. In *Engendering China: Women, Culture and the State.*

Christina K. Gilmartin, Gail Hershatter, Lisa Rofel, and Tyrene White, eds. Pp. 226–249. Cambridge, MA: Harvard University Press.

Rollins, Judith
1985   *Between Women: Domestics and Their Employers.* Philadelphia: Temple University Press.
1990   Ideology and Servitude. In *At Work in Homes: Household Work in World Perspective.* Roger Sanjek and Shellee Colen, eds. Pp. 74–88. Washington, DC: American Anthropological Association.

Romero, Mary
1992   *Maid in the U.S.A.* New York: Routledge.

Saddi, Nimfa
1993   I Am Not a Woman in Disguise. *Tinig Filipino,* May: 24.

Salaff, Janet
1981   *Working Daughters of Hong Kong: Filial Piety or Power in the Family?* New York: Cambridge University Press.

Sandborg, Kirsten
1993   Malay Dress Symbolism. In *Carved Flesh/Cast Selves.* Vigdis Broch-Due, Ingrid Rudie, and Tone Bleie, eds. Pp. 195–206. Oxford: Berg.

Sankar, Andrea
1978   Female Domestic Service in Hong Kong. In *Female Servants and Economic Development.* Louise Tilly, Anna Rubbo, Michael Taussig, Susan Berkowitz Luton, and Andrea Sankar, eds. Pp. 51–62. Occasional Papers in Women's Studies, No. 1. Ann Arbor: University of Michigan.

Simmons, Christina
1993   African Americans and Sexual Victorianism in the Social Hygiene Movement, 1910–40. *Journal of the History of Sexuality* 4:51–75.

Sombrio, Rose
1996   Don't Just Cry for the T-Birds. *Eastern Express,* January 22.

*South China Morning Post*
1992   Sordid Truth of "Girlie Bars." October 29.

Stanton, Domna C.
1992   *Discourses of Sexuality: From Aristotle to AIDS.* Ann Arbor: University of Michigan.

Stoler, Ann
1989   Making Empire Respectable: The Politics of Race and Sexual Morality in 20th-Century Colonial Cultures. *American Ethnologist* 16:634–660.

*Tinig Filipino*
1993a   Filipina Virgins: Philippines' Top Export Commodity? June: 24.
1993b   Protect Yourself from Sexual Molestation. December: 45

Torrefranca, Ma. Shiela S.
1992   The Man Behind the Skirt. *Tinig Filipino,* April: 40.

Ventenilla, Thelma S.
1993   Hot Issue: The Way We Wear. *Tinig Filipino,* November: 28.

Wallis, Belinda
1992   Plea to Smash Sex Syndicates As Mercy Found. *South China Morning Post.* July 3.

Ware, Vron
1992   *Beyond the Pale: White Women, Racism and History.* New York: Verso.

Watson, Rubie S.
1991   Wives, Concubines and Maids: Servitude and Kinship in the Hong Kong Region, 1900–1940. In *Marriage and Inequality in Chinese Society.* Rubie S. Watson and Patricia Buckley Ebrey, eds. Pp. 231–255. Berkeley: University of California Press.

Wilde, Wally
1996   "Observation" Earns Contempt. *Eastern Express,* January 18.

Wolf, Margery
1968   *The House of Lim: A Study of a Chinese Farm Family.* Englewood Cliffs, NJ: Prentice Hall.
1972   *Women and the Family in Rural Taiwan.* Stanford, CA: Stanford University Press.

Wong, Joe
1993   Crackdown on Fake Weddings for Prostitutes. *Hongkong Standard,* December 11.

Young, Malcolm
1992   Dress and Modes of Address: Structural Forms for Policewomen. In *Dress and Gender.* Ruth Barnes and Joanne B. Eicher, eds. Pp. 266–284. Oxford: Berg.

# Migration, Money, and Masculinity in Kerala

## Caroline Osella and Filippo Osella

It has often been suggested that the experience of migration between different geographical localities, an experience which places people simultaneously 'inside' and 'outside' cultures and societies and exposes people to new ways of living, is a process which breaks up integrated 'whole persons', and re-makes them as fragmented and internally multiple persons, hybrid or split selves. Migrants have then often been used to represent a far wider general condition of contemporary life, in which clear-cut (modern) binary oppositions and essentialisms (here versus there, self versus other, insider versus outsider) get replaced by more fragmented (post-modern) understandings of and experiences of personhood. Migrant consciousness

Adapted by the authors from an article originally published in the *Journal of the Royal Anthropological Institute,* Volume 6, No 1, 2000, pp. 117–133.

becomes a wider metaphor for the ways in which we all, in our multi-cultural, globalized and media-saturated society, live with a generalized appreciation of hybridity, dislocation and multiplicity (Bhabha 1994; Chambers 1994; Clifford 1997; Gilroy 1993). Migration alerts us to the possibility that identities might not be exclusive, bounded and set once and for all (cf. Gupta & Ferguson 1992). As such, migrants have been used to think about and talk about the differences between essentialized identities (stable, clearly defined, firmly bounded, rooted back to something like territory or language, singular and whole and easily stereotyped) and fragmented identities (more complex forms which cannot easily be rooted in one single source and which display multiplicity at their heart). However, ethnographies of migrant communities have revealed that migrant identity entails not a simple process of fracture and change, but a more complex articulation between hybridity and essentialism, between the un-making of the self and re-making (cf. Baumann 1996; Frankenberg & Mani 1997; Friedman 1997; van der Veer 1997; Werbner & Modood 1997). Here, we will suggest some ways in which migration might not contribute to an outright fragmentation or destruction of an original identity, but may be folded back in to the self as experience, allowing migrants to become re-integrated persons. In the ethnography below, migration feeds into pre-existing local frameworks of self and subjectivity (in this case the life-cycle and longstanding recognized masculine statuses and identities). Our ethnography shows how migration may accelerate an individual's progress along a culturally idealized trajectory towards mature manhood; and how it may also accentuate characteristics already locally associated with essentialized categories of (i.e. corresponding roughly to stereotypes of) masculinity.

We also argue, however, that in contrast to literature placing Indian men neatly into easily identifiable and essentialized role-defined categories (e.g. householder, renouncer or priest, e.g. Madan 1982, 1987), or suggesting clear-cut projects of 'male dominance' (Derné 1995), we can identify even within the longstanding local identities many arenas and styles of masculinity, and we show that there are a series of subject positions available to South Indian men, as yet mostly still to be explored. We argue that male identities are continually negotiated between various positions as men pick their way through competing demands and maintain precarious balances (see e.g. Cornwall & Lindisfarne 1994; Loizos & Papataxiarchis 1991). At the same time, fragmented male identities are related to dominant essentialized notions of how successful mature men should be and behave in specific contexts and arenas. We are arguing, then, that where fragmentation exits, this is not the result of migration, but it is

because (gendered) identities are always anyway fragmented (Kondo 1990; Moore 1994). At the same time, identities become essentialized and de-fragmented in local projects of self-making, because the production of identity is all about hiding and damping down the reality of fragmentation and multiplicity in favor of making a more stable and comfortable simple clear-cut category which people can attach to and form groups around (Baumann 1996; Herzfeld 1997).

The prototypical Kerala migrant to the Gulf is successful and above all wealthy, and represents the aspirations of many Malayali *payyanmar* (young males). Four important local essentialized categories emerge. The first, the *Gulfan*, refers to the migrant during his periodic visits home and immediately upon return. A transitional and individualistic figure, defined largely through relationships to cash and consumption, he is typically an uprooted and not fully mature male who needs to be brought back into village life. During the period of re-integration and movement towards maturity following his return, the *Gulfan* must tread a balance between two local essentialized extremes. One is the *pavam*, the unsuccessful man who dissipates wealth by his over-scrupulous observance of social obligations and consequently lacks the means to support dependents and demonstrate personal masculine prestige. The other is the *kallan*, the anti-social individualist who, refusing to honor social obligations, remains asocial and not properly integrated into society. A fourth category is related to the classic Indian ethnographic figure of the householder and is the ideal goal, the widespread cross-community ideal of the successful, social, mature man: a head of a household holding substantial personal wealth, supporting many dependents and helping many clients. These styles connote time: *pavam*, *kallan*, and successful patron-householder are possible resolutions of the returning *Gulfan*'s dilemma. They also fit into the male life-cycle: first-time Gulf migrants are typically young and unmarried; return at the end of an initial (3–6 years) period of migration goes along with marriage, maturity and movement towards adult status. Attribution of full adult male status unfolds over time, and requires continual demonstrations of competence in both masculinity and also maturity; achievement of dominant masculinity requires more than mere competence. Displays of substantial cash wealth emerge as important displays of masculine power and agency which need to be expressed within a framework of maturity, specifically *buddhi* (intelligence or discernment, wisdom).

We based this chapter on a total of three years fieldwork done between 1989 and 1996 in Valiyagramam (pseudonym), a multi-community rural village in South Kerala, characterized by a rapidly expanding middle class, a small and declining elite, and a substantial and increasingly impoverished working-class sector, comprising many who work precariously as casual day laborers.

## GULF MIGRATION

Migration has been a significant feature of life in Valiyagramam, as in Kerala as a whole, for more than a century, a common response to slump and famine and chronic unemployment. The post-1970s economic boom within the Gulf countries gave international migration a considerable boost, reaching its peak in terms of both numbers and remittances between 1979 and1984 (Amjad 1989: 4; Nayyar 1989: 107). It is estimated that in 1983 half of Indians working in the Gulf states were from Kerala (Nair 1989: 343). In 1980–1, the height of Gulf migration, Gulf revenues were estimated to constitute over a quarter of Kerala's GDP, rising to a half in areas of high migration (Kurien 1994: 765). In one of Valiyagramam's neighbourhoods, typical of the village as a whole, migrants are 27 percent of the total male working population (461 men); while 36 percent of total migrants are working in the Gulf (and this is a low figure when compared to other regions of Kerala, where migration reaches even higher percentages). To these figures we need to add in an even greater number people who have resettled in the village after migration and are now either self-employed (as petty traders, money lenders, travel agents or lorry drivers) or live from the interest from their investments and bank accounts. Valiyagramam Gulf migration fits the Kerala profile: migrants are almost exclusively male, typically below 35, unmarried or recently married and with education at, or below, SSLC (Secondary School Leaving Certificate) level (Matthew & Nair 1978; Nair 1986: 72). Migration periods are limited because of contract and legal constraints in the Gulf states, and for those in unskilled or semi-skilled jobs – the majority – migration consists of a series of stretches in the Gulf, on average four to six years, alternating with periods in the village between contracts (Nair 1986: 87). Families are usually left behind. A substantial part of migrants' earnings are either remitted regularly or brought back as savings at the end of the period of migration. Unlike other migrations, Gulf migration offers to some the chance of rapid and vast accumulation of wealth by village standards. Gulf migrants cannot settle away but must, sooner or later, return home, where their newfound wealth and access to consumption may dramatically alter their status and their relationships with others, and offer them the chance to forge new identities.

Something we need to take into account is that migrants' life in the Gulf is, to a large extent, an extension of village life. Returning to Kerala only every two or three years, migrants in Dubai, Sharjah or Muscat join large Malayali communities, where they have access to food items imported daily from Kerala; they can watch Malayali satellite channels and the latest Malayali films; they can read daily Malayali newspapers and go to see performances of popular Malayali artists. Responding to questions about the assumed difficulties of dislocation, migrants pointed out that they live in the Gulf in fairly segregated zones, serviced by shops run by Malayalis which sell all conceivable Kerala produce. While migrants are physically separated from Kerala and their families, a sense of dislocation is mitigated and they are unlikely to be completely deracinated from the web of social relations and cultural practices they have left behind. The degree to which migration produces disruption must then not be over-estimated.

Gulf migration has begun to play a crucial role in movements along the male life-cycle. As most work available locally is temporary manual labor associated with poverty and untouchability, young men face either the unpalatable alternative of taking on a demeaning occupation, or the prospect of unemployment. Moreover, with no reliable source of income, a young man's marriage opportunities are limited and his chances of making a good match nil. A recent rise in marriage ages of both men and women reflects not only a rise in the number of young people staying in education to secondary and tertiary level, but also a problem posed by lack of ready employment among young men. Thus, migrating to the Gulf does not only spell an escape from unemployment, but is also a move away from *payyan*hood (young immature status) towards full adult status as a householder, defined by the combination of marriage, fatherhood and showing ability as a 'provider' (F. Osella & C. Osella 1999). The first step along this road is the accumulation and display of cash.

## MEN AND MONEY

Cash is prominent in many arenas of local life: at festivals, cash donations collected around the neighborhood go at the front of the procession, held aloft for all to see; celebrations are marked by giving cash gifts; a popular necklace design is the *pavan-mala*, a string of gold sovereigns; fake paper US$100 notes are available in local stationery shops. To policy-makers' and planners' dismay, there is no compulsion to convert cash or to invest in productive activity. Most commonly, Gulf migrants' money is re-invested in itself: those with large amounts operate private loan companies (locally known as *blades*; cf. Nair 1989: 348); money is invested in small amounts as life assurance policies, bonds or other forms of financial capital; the bulk of a family's cash assets are usually kept relatively liquid, in short-term fixed-deposit bank accounts. It is for its unique liquidity and ease of movement that cash is so valuable, making a large bank balance not only a sign of wealth but specifically a promise of cash richness (cf. Hindu kingly models of flowing wealth, Price 1996: 100 ff; Rao et al. 1992: 72 ff.). People commonly keep large amounts of cash in the house, and move it around in complex informal loans and transactions. Cash is an important sign of success and masculinity: a man is someone with liquidity, not just assets. Holding land and owning property is important, but so too is command over cash, and wealth is a central requirement in most styles of masculinity. In some styles, especially associated with younger men, the source of wealth, while not irrelevant, is of lesser importance than the amount. Money which is 'New', Gulf-earned, gained through running a blade, achieved by hard labor and saving, or even via semi-legal means, is all good money (cf. Parry & Bloch 1989: 23 ff.). Illegal money, such as comes from smuggling or cheating on a property deal, is at least better than no money at all. The very many young Hindus who are increasingly willing to make money in any way possible present a radical challenge to family and community insistence on the primacy of *manam* (dignity, status) and an orientation towards the symbolic capital of 'salaried government job' (cf. Heuzé 1992: 23). Migration helps maintain one's prestige by concealing one's occupation and by splitting the moment and site of wealth accumulation from its moment of consumption, enabling and encouraging a focus upon the result: cash earned.

Some ambivalences stem from attitudes towards consumption and display embedded in different styles of masculinity. Brahmin men disdain, at least publicly, accumulation of material wealth, focusing instead on possession of ritual knowledge and education. Among older men from communities which have since the 1920s been involved in long-term mobility strategies, such as 'small' Christians and Izhavas, a man is expected to enjoy his wealth but not to deplete it and should continue to work as long as he is able. Younger men dream of massive wealth as a means of resolving tensions between conformity to the older generation's accumulative impulse and the dominant Hindu prestige spending ethos. A common Christian criticism of Hindu Nayars, the older generation of which largely try to live up to the dominant 'spending' aesthetic, is that, 'They would sell all their properties and ruin themselves in order to celebrate Onam (new year) with show'. Amongst high-caste Hindus, assets may be sold if necessary to obtain hard cash. It is common practice to sell land to raise dowry money rather than giving the land itself as dowry. At the other end of the social spectrum, low-caste agricultural laborers display

a transient attitude towards wealth. When money is available, for example after the paddy harvest, laborers feel that it should not be accumulated but enjoyed, treating male friends to the toddy-shop, and buying presents of clothes and expensive food items for wife and children. In the mainstream, among men of all communities with an eye for local status and power games, the accumulation of wealth and its display and mobilization in (often expensive) prestige-enhancing spending activities go hand in hand. Importantly, this accumulation and spending set performance hierarchies of manliness, and the feminization of those who are not playing the game or, far worse, lose. In Kerala it is cash itself that carries the main functions of wealth that Ferguson (1985: 661) described for Lesotho pastoralists who convert cash to cattle and count cattle as male wealth: establishing a husband as household 'head' and providing tangible, visible support, even in his absence; acting as 'placeholder' for the migrant male, asserting symbolic presence in the face of absence; involving a man in relations of patronage and reciprocity which may enhance prestige. Following Taussig (1997: 129 ff.), we note that cash is particularly suited to act as a fetish and effect magical transformations. Cash is a magical substance. While cash, like gold, is of wide importance in Kerala, cash appears, like gold, to have a particular gendered angle: as gold is especially associated with women, cash appears especially linked with men. Wealthy men make large cash donations to temples and churches, the names and amounts recorded on noticeboards and in the printed festival calendar booklets distributed to houses. When a group of men go drinking together, Rs 100 notes will be flashed and masculine prestige gained by paying for rounds; men with money in their hands will subsidize an entire evening's drinking and eating. Male sociality demands generous spending, even excess. In this respect, it is not surprising that successful Gulf migrants, those who have access to and flaunt considerable amounts of cash, are commonly represented as hypermasculine, an effect magnified by rumors of their feminine conquests and drinking sessions in the Gulf, and often maintained to some extent by behavior on return trips home. Cash is then a signifier of masculine status, notes reckoning the worth of a man. This relation between men and money can be traced in several directions. A young man's value is calculated in monetary terms (how much dowry he can command) on the marriage market; a mature man's value is at least partly reckoned by his earning power, concretized in banknotes, which may be left raw or converted into other forms of objectified personhood. Money has no essential nature: life-cycle rites provide opportunities for self-enhancing public cash spending and gifting (Werbner 1990). At weddings, the bride's brother or cousin takes pride of place as he arrives with a black briefcase stuffed full of notes: the dowry. Since provision of dowry is officially a fraternal responsibility, the briefcase's contents speak directly of his status. Wedding gifts, presented during the ceremony are strictly gendered: women conventionally give cooking pots or (more lately) household items (ornaments, tea-sets) to the bride; men give cash gifts to the groom. Women's gifts link women, via other women, to the hearth and kitchen; men's cash gifts represent something more masculine – a flowing potency – passed from male guests to the groom.

## THE *GULFAN*

We are arguing that migration is a means of bridging a gap between *payyan*hood and manhood. The *Gulfan* is a figure spanning this transitional period: he belongs to an intermediate category, not yet fully adult but with a central characteristic of adult maleness, money. Focus on cash as the defining characteristic of failed or successful *Gulfan*s, and the focus on the consumer items brought and the expenditure while on visits at home, articulate with an idealized male lifecycle. Given that most *Gulfan*s begin their migration as young bachelors, leaving the village as immature youths (*payyan*mar), visits home are opportunities to demonstrate not only financial, but also age and gender-related progress. Consumer goods accumulated in the parental home will eventually form part of the *Gulfan*'s own household on marriage. Displays of substantial cash reassure onlookers that he is becoming a man of means, with resources to support a wife and children; marriage usually follows the second or third home visit. Perfect exemplars of the *Gulfan* exist only on the cinema screen and in books, not surprisingly in view of the impossible demands of inexhaustible wealth and never-ending spending sprees, but the ideal is the dominant aspiration for most young men. The Gulf migrant has joined the cast of stock characters in popular cinema, novels, magazine stories, travelling theatre and (vernacular) television serials (e.g. Nair & Mohamed 1993). He is something between a hero and a fool, glamourized and ridiculed. In popular films and plays, the returning *Gulfan* is invariably portrayed arriving by taxi from the airport, the car loaded with boxes and parcels. He wears a designer shirt, white trousers and the latest sports shoes. He smokes foreign cigarettes and wears Ray-Ban sunglasses. On one wrist he has a gold bracelet, on the other a gold watch and around his neck a weighty gold chain. When the boxes are opened, television sets, stereos, video-recorders, electrical kitchen gadgets, fridges and washing machines come out. His house is,

inevitably, new and concrete-made; inside, video, television and stereo are on full display. Every night he drinks with his friends the 'Johnny Walker Red Label' he brought from the Gulf; his stories, punctuated with English words, keep everyone with their mouths hanging open. He is a man about town, frequently to be seen in the air-conditioned bars of city hotels, treating his entourage to chilli chicken and whisky. He pays very large dowries for the marriage of his sisters, and, when he marries, receives a large dowry. The intriguing links here between cash and masculinity, spending and potency, draw us towards the work of Bataille, notably his insights into the logics of excess, found in consumption, violence and eroticism, all of which we identify as performance arenas especially inflected in Kerala by masculinity (see Bataille 1962, 1985: 116 ff.; Miller 1998: 84 ff). The *Gulfan* is the very image of Bataille's visions of excess, as far removed from Calvinist capitalism as could be.

### Baby Chacko

In Waliyagramam, Baby Chacko is the man who perhaps most closely lives up to the *Gulfan* stereotype. He started life poor; his father was a landless ploughman at the very bottom of the 'big' Christian Jacoba community. Baby and his father were huge and strong men and good agriculturalists, so landlords with no taste for farming passed land on to them to cultivate. Their lucky break came when land reforms gave them the land they were working, and hence the profits from it. Baby left his father in charge of the fields and, by judicious buying and selling of paddy, built up enough capital to get to Bahrain, where he worked as a mechanic for seven years. He now owns twelve acres of paddy land, a lorry, a car, a motorbike, two *blade*s (small money-lending businesses) and lives in a comfortable Gulf-architect-designed two-story house with garage and surrounding coconut garden, built on the main road near a large market center. When we arrived for our first visit, we could see through the open front door that Baby, his brother and a friend were in the front room playing cards for money and drinking good (imported) whisky. Baby leapt up to shake hands with and smack Filippo on the back, jokingly calling him 'Fillipachayan', using the suffix of affection and respect used towards mature Christian men. Baby wore a brightly colored and stylish synthetic lungi (waist-cloth), with a T-shirt. His friend and brother wore ready-made trousers and 'Vivaldi' (designer label) shirts. Baby had a gold watch, a long and heavy gold chain around his neck, a gold identity bracelet and a massive gold full-sovereign ring, all items bought in Bahrain.

Baby Chacko is often described as a *goonda* (villain). This is said by a few with contempt, but by the majority with grudging admiration or glee. Like many other *Gulfan*s, Baby Chacko is believed by many to have made his earnings abroad '*on the black*', by smuggling gold and dollars; several people told us in perfect seriousness that he had a printing press with which he turned out counterfeit notes. Other *Gulfan*s, especially those who have made substantial economic gains, are said to have become rich through deceiving business partners, running prostitution rings, marrying and then murdering wealthy widows, or by making use of *mandravadam* (sorcery). Such allegations suggest disbelief that the substantial fortunes accumulated by Gulf migrants can be accumulated in a short while through hard, honest work. They do not, however, express a negative moral judgment on the migrant: on the contrary they reinforce the clout, glamour and status surrounding the figure of the successful *Gulfan*. He shares the attributes of other heroic characters who, through outstanding individual qualities, such as wit, charisma, charm, initiative, trickery, courage and physical strength, manage to accumulate wealth without being tarnished by the indignity of labor. Nor do these allegations express a distinction between the 'inside' moral economy of the village and the tarnished 'outside' world of capitalist wage-labor: former landlords, whose profits were made through appropriation and hoarding of village lands and grain, are described, accused and grudgingly admired in exactly the same idioms (counterfeit, evil magic). Akin to the 'underworld king' popular in Hindi and Tamil films, the *Gulfan* is portrayed as enjoying access to an inexhaustible source of 'easy money' that enables him to conduct a life of luxury, ease and unlimited spending. What is central to the *Gulfan* is his mastery of large amounts of cash.

With his 'easy money' and conspicuous displays of wealth and consumption, the *Gulfan* strives to associate himself to a particularly powerful cultural prestige model, itself rooted in aesthetics of elite patronage. This is personified by the pre-land reform upper-caste landlord who, sitting on an easy-chair in the veranda, made money through other people's work rather than his own labor, and spent large amounts of money holding sumptuous religious celebrations. The fact that everybody knows that Gulf money is neither limitless nor 'easy', that most *Gulfan*mar work extremely hard, live in a harsh and difficult environment and save to the last Riyal, is, at this level, irrelevant. By colluding in the construction of an image of the successful *Gulfan* as a patron, endowed with the power and prestige of owning and displaying 'easy money', villagers can justify their demands for help and assistance. At the same time, the images of surplus and prodigality associated with foreign migration are too compelling and attractive to be let go (cf. Hansen 2001). This construction

is helped by the fact that the Gulf, the place where the wealth is accumulated, is far away from the village, the place where it is consumed and displayed. The other half of this ambivalent figure, antithesis to the successful *Gulfan*, is the failed *Gulfan*, who also commonly makes his appearance as stereotype. Just as the defining characteristic of the successful *Gulfan* is plenty of cash, this pathetic figure's main characteristic is lack of sufficient cash to sustain conspicuous consumption and display of wealth. According to local accounts of how to spot a failed *Gulfan*, following arrival from the airport in glory by taxi, after a few days in the village he starts using a rickshaw rather than a taxi and is soon reduced to the buses or an old, rusty bicycle. From drinking whisky and smoking foreign cigarettes, flashed around in packets, he reverts to visits to the local toddy shop and to buying single *bidi*s. Within a few weeks, the cash he brought back has all gone to pay off debts, and to provide dowries and loans to relatives and friends; slowly all the gold he initially displayed with pride is mortgaged to a *blade*. The short-lived flashiness and cautious use of cash of such *Gulfan*s show that what is being spent is not 'easy money', but hard earned, at the worst as a despised coolie worker on a building site. (To pre-empt this accusation, manual workers commonly send home a photograph of themselves in an office, posing at a desk with a pen or computer.)

## THE *GULFAN* PREDICAMENT: *KALLAN* OR *PAVAM?*

Returning migrants need to hold on to their personal wealth, but are under pressure to spend it. The extreme outcomes of these opposing forces are expressed via two categories, both ambivalently valued: that of the *kallan*, a self-interested maximizer cut off from and despised by local society, and the *pavam*, the innocent good-guy, generous to the point of self-destruction. Unlike Lesotho migrants, who are protected by the 'bovine mystique' from putting cattle wealth at others' disposal, Kerala migrants' wealth, expressed as cash, stands firmly in the 'domain of contestation' – wealth to be fought over (Ferguson 1985: 657). The prevalent but mistaken perception among villagers of the Gulf as a source of unlimited wealth and the *Gulfan* as beneficiary of quick and substantial profit puts great economic pressures on the migrant. He is under pressure to demonstrate success through being *jada* (lit. shiny, flashy) and *cettu* (lit. cutting, i.e. 'sharp', fashionable), and by spending lavishly. However, if he starts spending large amounts of money (typically to make major and public improvements to his house) regarded as going above immediate consumption needs, he will be under pressure not only to repay debts incurred to finance his migration but also to fulfill expensive obligations towards close kin and relatives, such as providing for dowries and lending large sums of money.

The *Gulfan* faces a dilemma. If he wants to reap full benefit from his newly earned wealth and concentrate on building up reserves of cash and goods for his future household, he must try to avoid social obligations (cf. Sagant 1996: 278 ff.) by claiming financial difficulties, arguing that he has not made enough money as yet, and trying to contain the pressures put on him by bringing back 'foreign items' for his relatives, especially to those from whom he had initially borrowed money. He can, of course, use such excuses only within limits, lest people begin to regard his migration as a failure, bringing shame upon him and his family. If demands come from affines (relatives related by marriage), default is less problematic, part of routine behavior in relation to them, but serious problems can occur when the close circle of direct kin is involved. In respect to them, a breach of the obligation to share one's fortunes might give rise to disputes, publicly aired, causing the *Gulfan* loss of face and reputation, breakdown of relationships and, eventually, social isolation.

Gopalakutty's sons benefited from positive discrimination policies and obtained degrees in engineering. One migrated to the Gulf, while the other went first to Bombay and then to the USA. Once the money started to pour in, their father back home began to distance himself from relatives and caste-fellows. In this way he tried to avoid both having to respond to demands for financial help and being too closely associated with his own (Scheduled Caste) low status group. As his isolation from his community grew, Gopalakutty tried to establish a new social position for the family by forming new relationships with higher-caste villagers. To prove his worth, he spent a considerable amount on buying the ancestral house of a local high status Nayar family forced to sell by partition. Gopalakutty's selfishness and transgression of social rules and expectations were subjects of continual disapproval and gossip among the community, including snubbed kin: behind his back he was called *kallan*. When Gopalakutty made a large public donation to a local temple during its annual festival, his fellow caste members and ex-neighbors spread the word that he was doing so because he needed and wanted to remove *dosham* (generic term for sins) accumulated by refusals to help relatives and friends. The behavior of Gopalakutty was widely compared to that of a local widow who combines the running of an illegal arrack shop with occasional prostitution: 'Every day she sells liquor and then once a month she pays for a reading of the Bhagavad Gita in her house. The next day she thinks all the *dosham* is gone and she starts selling again.'

Soman, an Izhava, second of ten brothers and sisters, has been working in Muscat (Oman) since 1982, where he has taken three four-year contracts in a *company* (this is the commonest, deliberately vague, description of employment volunteered by those who do non-prestigious jobs). For the last twelve years he has been working alongside two of his younger brothers, for whom he provided visas and jobs. Over this period, as well as sending regular remittances for family subsistence, the three have saved for the marriages of elder sisters, to pay for the education of younger siblings and to build a new concrete house for their parents. When Soman was thinking, in 1990, of returning permanently to Valiyagramam after eight years away, his cousin-brother (MZS), a medical representative, asked to borrow Rs 60,000 towards setting up a small medical shop. Soman willingly lent the money and the shop was opened, but after six months it closed for lack of business and profit. Soman lost more than a third of his savings and was forced to extend his contract in Muscat. Although villagers considered Soman as a shining example of moral behavior, they also said that he was a *pavam*, that his amenable character and good intentions led him to be taken advantage of by his relatives. Behind his back, villagers gossiped about him and mocked him as foolish and weak. In his inability to discriminate between sound and unsound loan requests, he failed to display the *buddhi* which distinguishes adults from children. In his unwillingness to refuse any request for help, he showed himself as lacking in masculine resolve and autonomy.

Here we see some delicate movements between different identity formations. While being a *kallan* is a positive attribute at the moment of accumulation of wealth in the Gulf, back in the village a migrant should behave like a social person, willingly prepared to utilize wealth to fulfill obligations and promote the well-being of relatives and close friends. Those *Gulfan*s who fail to do so, continuing to behave like self-interested, individualistic, immoral and anti-social *kallanmar* (thieves) towards their own people (*bandhukkar*, lit. the people you are tied to) become subject to condemnation, criticism and social boycott. They are able to stake claims for neither maturity nor adult masculinity. However, the behavior of those *Gulfan*s who, by dutifully discharging their obligations, end up dissipating their savings, is also subject to widespread condemnation: while publicly praised, they are privately ridiculed as *pavam*s, highly moral but also highly gullible people. While the descriptor *pavam* is widely used approvingly when speaking of women – brides, elder sisters, mothers-in-law – who should be amenable, kindly and free of intrigue, it is spoken maliciously of men. Spoken by one man of another, '*pavam*' is often accompanied by a smirk, implying that the speaker is more worldly-wise, more masculinely competent. When *pavam* comes as a judgment of a man spoken between women it is heavily ambivalent, implying a man who is at once kind, undemanding and easy to handle, but also – by virtue of failure to assert or dominate – somewhat feminized. The ambivalences and tensions expressed here find parallels in other societies: Yang's study of Chinese *guanxi* relationships of mutual help and patronage refers to the categories *you* – the 'oily' or 'greasy' person adept at manipulating *guanxi* relations, simultaneously distrusted and admired; and the *laoshi* – both 'honest' and 'reliable' but also 'malleable', 'obedient' and 'mindless' (Yang 1994: 64 ff.).

## MOVING TOWARDS BALANCE: THE *GULFAN* GIFT

Tensions between *kallan* and *pavam* modalities are ideally resolved by the migrant through finding a balance between ameliorating his own social and economic position and assisting the advancement of the larger group. A careful strategy of gift-giving can do this, while simultaneously offering the *Gulfan* an opportunity to move from immature, marginal *payyan* towards the decidedly mature and masculine status of man-at-the-centre (cf. Mines 1994; Mines & Gourishankar 1990; C. Osella & F. Osella 2007; Raheja 1988). By giving gifts and showing munificence, albeit at a controlled and calculated rate, the migrant can appear to live up to the stereotypical, prestigious image of the *Gulfan* as consumer and displayer of 'easy money', while gradually increasing his control and mastery of others. Whoever goes away to work is expected to bring back presents not only to the direct household, but also to a large number of relatives, neighbors and friends (cf. Addleton 1992: 139; Gardner 1993: 12; Werbner 1990: 203–4). These gifts hold multiple meanings for the migrant giver, which can be manipulated in different ways (cf. Werbner 1990: 229). By voluntary giving, migrants can partly pre-empt potentially limitless demands for large cash gifts and loans which threaten hard-earned savings and lead towards *pavam*-hood: prestige values attached to foreign items in some way compensates for lesser monetary values. Gifts are also given to avoid evil eye and ill feelings aroused by envy of migrants' alleged prosperity (cf. Ames 1966: 35; Good 1982: 27). Recipients of *Gulfan* gifts take them as tangible proof of relations with the donor, and as evidence of the continuity of affection (*sneham*) between parties in the face of temporary separation and reputed social advance.

As the metonymic embodiment of the migrant's *sneham*, love and care (F. Osella & C. Osella 1996), gifts reiterate kinship relations and friendships, proving that a *Gulfan* is not a ruthless, uncaring *kallan* and that he has the maturity and the substance necessary to recognize and to sustain important social relationships. At the same time, opportunities for gift-giving can be used instrumentally to create new, and transform existing, social relationships. Given to those of higher status, gifts establish relations of goodwill, said to soap the recipient. Non-reciprocal gifts can also be passed downwards, to create and maintain a network of clients; in this way, migrants can ensure some return for considerable outlays, becoming not *pavam* but patron, a big man at the center of a nexus of social relations, enjoying high status and wide reputation, and exemplifying the local working out of a more widespread style of dominant masculinity. That attempts towards resolution are tilted in the direction of *kallan*-ness is indicated by the tendency among successful migrants to extend patronage via strategic gift-giving to their close circle, representing kinship obligations as the voluntary open-hearted largesse of a patron. Recipients not in a financial position to resist being assimilated as clients will publicly continue to receive gifts as their just *sneham* dues. That the new relationship is tacitly understood is demonstrated by migrants' increased demands for assistance and services, going far beyond normal kinship obligations, by their non-reciprocation of such services, and by the meek compliance of the gift recipients.

## MONEY AND PATRONAGE

By exploring the figure of the Gulf migrant in its ideal pattern and in relation to the essentialized categories used locally as mooring points for otherwise precarious and fragmented selves doing continual identity work, we can see the unfolding of a particular approved trajectory and style of masculinity. A successful *Gulfan* is a man who enriches himself by circumventing rules which normally tie the accumulation of wealth to labor. Money is the basis of the migrant's success and he should display an almost careless attitude to it, suggesting both huge wealth and endless possibilities of making more. If he ceases to indulge in lavish consumption, he instantly puts his financial situation in doubt and hence loses his main claim to status. In this, he appears as hyper-masculine, a characteristic also suggested by his outshining others in displays of masculine competence undertaken in all-male performance arenas, such as card and drinking sessions with male friends, visits to prostitutes, paying for treats (cf. Colman 1990; e.g. Herzfeld 1985; Loizos & Papataxiarchis 1991). What helps make migration particularly relevant to masculinity is an enhanced relationship with money, a detachable form of masculine potency, and a means of exerting agency at a distance. As liquidity, as power, as flowing substance (*dravya*), as means to enjoyment (*bhoga*) and to support of dependents, cash holds an important place in South India as a central aspect of prestigious non-renunciatory styles of manhood.

The returning migrant's dilemma, that of striking the balance between becoming a *pavam* or a *kallan*, that of spending all his cash or selfishly holding on to it, is analogous to another 'dilemma of substance' faced by all adult men and much discussed in ethnographic literature. This is the difficult requirement to balance expenditure of semen, a flowing masculine substance which must also be accumulated, conserved carefully and channeled in socially (re)productive directions (for a discussion of the literatures on 'semen loss anxiety' or *dhat* syndrome, see C. Osella & F. Osella 2001). We are not suggesting that money acts as a metaphor for semen or that sexual exchange acts as source metaphor for all other types of exchange. Rather, we see correspondences between money and semen as rooted in metonymic principles of resemblance and based upon the aesthetics of patronage and leadership whereby 'abundant cash resources . . . [are used] in various playful and sensual modes' (Rao et al. 1992: 58). Connotations of lack, of promiscuous excess spending or of individualistic refusal to spend are similar with regard both to semen and to money: failure to demonstrate successful social mature male status, the mediation between manliness and *buddhi*, powers of discrimination. Successful negotiation of the idealized trajectory requires initial accumulation followed by controlled and judicious expenditure in which the element of containment is concealed, hidden beneath an adopted (elite) aesthetic of excess and ease (cf. Bourdieu and Bataille on contrasts between petty-bourgeois accumulation and aristocratic expenditure: Bataille 1997: 176; Bourdieu 1984). The process of transformation of the migrant into a patron runs concomitant with and shares similar predicaments with the growth-cycle into manhood. A moment of accumulation corresponds to youth (*payyan*-hood, celibacy) and to migration, in which a young man has few responsibilities or dependents. Return marks a period of reintegration, the *Gulfan* moving towards adult social status by marrying and taking a place within the community. During the moment of accumulation, the house and land unit (analogous to the self, Daniel 1984; F. Osella & C. Osella 1999) is built up and given substance, using remittances. When a satisfactory, reasonable level of individual-household improvement has been reached, the migrant's attention can and should turn outwards. At the dangerous

point of achieving hyper-masculinity (hyper-cash), but lack of maturity, the migrant must move forward if he is to reach manhood, a balanced combination of masculinity with maturity. The performance of the *Gulfan* who remains a complete *kallan*, failing to become a social man, will be judged a failure in so far as he remains asocial, immaturely individual, and not astute enough to take political advantage of the opportunities and expectations that his wealth generates: mere wealth maybe enough for a young man, but dominant masculinity demands far more. The *Gulfan* who does not retain control of his money, who gives in indiscriminately to those who have a moral claim upon his wealth, will also be considered unsuccessful. He displays weakness as well as lack of discernment and insight; people take advantage of his wealth without granting him prestige. As a result, like the anti-social *Gulfan*, the *kallan*-in-the-village, the *pavam* has neither dependents nor clients. Having depleted his resources for no return, he also loses the chance to use to their full extent the potentiality that spending and displaying wealth confers. Wealth alone suggests masculinity but not maturity, the other essential component of manhood; maturity demands *bhuddi* and the wise use of resources, a quality lacking in *kallan* and *pavam* alike. By fulfilling obligations in a way which places himself as a patron at the center of a web of dependents and clients, the migrant emerges a successful adult man who, having accumulated enough resources, manages to find a skillful balance between the pull of social obligations and the need to retain control of his resources, in other words between spending and saving.

## CONCLUSIONS

In recent years social scientists have used migration as a model for theorizing post-modern experiences of hybridity or dislocation, finding migration useful as a way to talk about multiple and fragmented subjects. Elsewhere, we have argued that in their consumption practices, Kerala people are constructing selves which are split: while externally seeking a relationship with the outside and with otherness (*vides*) via consumer goods, in their preference for locally produced food-items and in their specific relationships to the land, they are constructing internal, substantial selves that remain local and are felt to be rooted, stable (*nadan*) (F. Osella & C. Osella 1999; C. Osella & F. Osella 2008). We are arguing then that hybridization is partial, context-specific and external, and that it exists alongside – and can even reinforce – essentialized and interiorized senses of locality, belonging and stable continuity.

The ethnography we presented here suggests ways in which newly emerged experiences of fragmented and altered masculinity (the dilemmas faced by Gulf migrant returnees, the split between the tough labor conditions under which capital has been accumulated and its representation back in the village), articulate with and feed back into the older and local, essentialized masculine identities (*Gulfan*, *pavam*, *kallan* or patron-householder) against which male performance has long been gauged. Strauss argues that post-modern subjects enmeshed in complex relations of global capital do indeed experience the self as split and contradictory, but that partial integration of fragmented selves may be effected by means of reference to 'emotionally salient life experiences' (1997: 395–6). In Kerala, partial integration of (or, we would prefer, articulation between) different aspects of the self takes place by means of the movement over time from boyhood to manhood - a process involving labor, marriage and fatherhood and framed within a stereotyped ideal trajectory towards a strongly essentialized identity which draws upon colonial-modern notions of the bourgeois paterfamilias and householder, as well as upon older (and often kingly) ideas about landlordism, patronage and centrality. From this perspective, discussing whether or not migration may be experienced as a break or discontinuity in one's experience of self and others becomes secondary to understanding the ways that people make sense of migration and the ways that people's understandings are integrated into wider 'identity projects'.

## ACKNOWLEDGMENTS

We received generous financial support for various periods of fieldwork and writing up from the period June 1989 to September 1996 from: the Economic and Social Research Council of Great Britain; the London School of Economics; the Leverhulme Trust; the Nuffield Foundation; and the Wenner-Gren Foundation. We thank Penny Vera-Sanso for her comments on an early draft.

## REFERENCES

Addleton, J.S. 1992. *Undermining the centre: Gulf migration and Pakistan.* Karachi: Oxford University Press.

Ames, M. 1966. Ritual prestations and the nature of the Sinhalese pantheon. In *Anthropological studies in Theravada Buddhism (Southeast Asia Studies, Cultural Report Series 13)* (ed.) M. Nash, 27–50. New Haven: Yale University Press.

Amjad, R. 1989. An overview. In *To the Gulf and back: studies on the economic impact of Asian labour migration* (ed.) R. Amjad, 1–27. New Delhi: I.L.O.

Bataille, G. 1962 [1957]. *Eroticism.* London: John Calder.

Bataille, G. 1985. *Visions of excess: selected writings 1927–1939* (ed. and trans. A. Stoekl). Manchester: University Press.

Bataille, G. 1997. *The Bataille reader* (eds F. Botting & S. Wilson). Oxford: Blackwell.

Baumann, G. 1996. *Contesting culture: discourses of identity in multi-ethnic London.* Cambridge: University Press.

Bhabha, H. 1994. *The location of culture.* London: Routledge.

Bourdieu, P. 1984. *Distinction.* London: Routledge & Kegan Paul.

Chambers, I. 1994. *Migrancy, culture, identity.* London: Routledge.

Clifford, J. 1997. *Routes.* Cambridge, MA: Harvard University Press.

Colman, W. 1990. Doing masculinity/doing theory. In *Men, masculinities and social theory* (eds) J. Hearn & D. Morgan, 74–98. London: Unwin Hyman.

Cornwall, A. & N. Lindisfarne (eds) 1994. *Dislocating masculinity: comparative ethnographies.* London: Routledge.

Daniel, V. 1984. *Fluid signs: being a person the Tamil way.* Berkeley: University of California Press.

Derné, S. 1995. *Culture in action: family life, emotion, and male dominance in Banaras, India.* Albany: SUNY Press.

Ferguson, J. 1985. The bovine mystique: power, property and livestock in rural Lesotho. *Man* (N.S.) 20, 647–74.

Frankenberg, R. & L. Mani 1997. Crosscurrents, crosstalk: race, 'postcoloniality' and the politics of location. In *Contemporary postcolonial theory: a reader* (ed.) P. Mongia, 347–64. Delhi: Oxford University Press.

Friedman, J. 1997. Global crisis, the struggle for cultural identity and intellectual porkbarrelling: cosmopolitans versus locals, ethnics and nationals in an era of de-hegemonisation. In *Debating cultural hybridity: multicultural identities and the politics of anti-racism* (eds) P. Werbner & T. Modood, 70–89. London: Zed.

Gardner, K. 1993. Desh-bidesh: Sylethi images of home and away. *Man* (N.S.) 28, 1–16.

Gilroy, P. 1993. *The Black Atlantic: modernity and double consciousness.* London: Verso.

Good, A. 1982. The actor and the act: categories of prestation in South India. *Man* (N.S.) 17, 23–41.

Gupta, A. & J. Ferguson 1992. Beyond 'culture': space, identity and the politics of difference. *Cultural Anthropology* 7, 6–23.

Hansen, T.B. 2001. Bridging the Gulf: global horizons, mobility and local identity among Muslims in Mumbai. In *Community, empire and migration: South Asians in diaspora* (ed.) C. Bates, 261–85. London: Palgrave.

Herzfeld, M. 1985. *The poetics of manhood.* Princeton: University Press.

Herzfeld, M. 1997. *Cultural intimacy.* London: Routledge.

Heuzé, G. 1992. Les Indiens et le travail: une relation oublié. *Purusartha* 14, 9–30.

Kondo, D. 1990. *Crafting selves.* Chicago: University Press.

Kurien, P. 1994. Non-economic bases of economic behaviour: the comsumption, investment and exchange patterns of three emigrant communities in Kerala, India. *Development and Change* 25, 757–83.

Loizos, P. & E. Papataxiarchis (eds) 1991. *Contested identities: gender and kinship in modern Greece.* Princeton: University Press.

Madan, T.N. (ed.) 1982. *Way of life: king, householder, re-nouncer (essays in honour of Louis Dumont)*. New Delhi: Vikas Publishing.

Madan, T.N. 1987. *Non-renunciation: themes and interpretations in Hindu culture*. New Delhi: Oxford University Press.

Matthew, E.T. & G. Nair 1978. Socio-economic character-istics of emigrants and emigrants' households: a case study of two villages in Kerala. *Economic and Political Weekly* (July 15), 1141–53.

Miller, D. 1998. *A theory of shopping*. Cambridge: Polity Press.

Mines, M. 1994. *Public faces, private voices: community and in-dividuality in south India*. New Delhi: Oxford University Press.

Mines, M. & V. Gourishankar 1990. Leadership and indi-viduality in South Asia: the case of the South Indian big-man. *The Journal of Asian Studies* 49, 761–86.

Moore, H. 1994. *A passion for difference*. Cambridge: Polity Press.

Nair, P.R.G. 1986. India. In *Migration of Asian workers to the Arab world* (ed.) G. Gunatilleke, 66–109. Tokyo: United Nations University.

Nair, P.R.G. 1989. Incidence, impact and implications of migration to the Middle East from Kerala (India). In *To the Gulf and back* (ed.) R. Amjad, 343–64. New Delhi: I.L.O.

Nair, M.T.V. & N.P. Mohamed 1993. *Arab gold*. (novel trans. From Malayalam) New Delhi: Rupa.

Nayyar, D. 1989. International labour migration from India: a macro-economic analysis. In *To the Gulf and back* (ed.) R. Amjad, 95–141. New Delhi: I.L.O.

Osella, F. & C. Osella 1996. Articulation of physical and social bodies in Kerala. *Contributions to Indian Sociology* 30 (1), 37–68.

Osella, F. & C. Osella 1999. From transience to immanence: consumption, life-cycle and social mobility in Kerala, south India. *Modern Asian Studies* 33 (4), 989–1020.

Osella, Caroline & F. Osella 2001. Contextualising sexual-ity: young men in Kerala, south India. In *Coming of age in South and Southeast Asia: youth, courtship and sexuality* (eds) L. Manderson & P. L. Rice. London: Curzon Press.

Osella, Caroline & F. Osella 2007. *Men and Masculinities in South India*. London: Anthem Press.

Osella, Caroline & F. Osella 2008. Food, memory, commu-nity: Kerala as both 'Indian Ocean' zone and as agricul-tural homeland. *South Asia Journal of South Asian Studies* 31 (1), 170–98.

Parry, J. & M. Bloch 1989. Introduction. In *Money and the morality of exchange* (eds) J. Parry & M. Bloch, 1–32. Cam-bridge: University Press.

Price, P.G. 1996. *Kingship and political practice in colonial India*. Cambridge: University Press.

Raheja, G. 1988. *The poison in the gift*. Chicago: University Press.

Rao, V.N., D. Shulman & S. Subrahmanyam 1992. *Symbols of substance: court and state in Nayaka period Tamil Nadu*. Delhi: Oxford University Press.

Sagant, P. 1996. *The dozing shaman: the Limbus of eastern Ne-pal*. Delhi: Oxford University Press.

Strauss, C. 1997. Partly fragmented, partly integrated: an anthropological examination of 'postmodern frag-mented subjects'. *Cultural Anthropology* 12, 362–404.

Taussig, M. 1997. *The magic of the state*. London: Routledge.

van der Veer, P. 1997. 'The enigma of arrival': hybrid-ity and authenticity in the global space. In *Debating cultural hybridity: multi-cultural identities and the politics of anti-racism* (eds) P. Werbner & T. Modood, 90–115. London: Zed.

Werbner, P. 1990. *The migration process: capital, gifts and of-ferings among British Pakistanis*. Oxford: Berg.

Werbner, P. & T. Modood (eds) 1997. *Debating cultural hy-bridity: multi-cultural identities and the politics of anti-racism*. London: Zed.

Yang, M.M. 1994. *Gifts, favors and banquets: the art of social relationships in China*. Ithaca, NY: Cornell University Press.

# Sex Tourism, Globalization, and Transnational Imaginings

## Denise Brennan

### INTRODUCTION: "FANTASY"

This chapter explores how Dominican women and German men, who are unequal in power and wealth, imagine one another across national borders, and then examines what unfolds once they actually become

This piece is an abridged and adapted version of a previously pub-lished article, "Tourism in Transnational Places: Dominican Sex Workers and German Sex Tourists Imagine One Another," *Identities: Global Studies in Culture and Power* 7(4):621–663. 2001.

involved within the sex trade in Sosúa, a small town on the north coast of the Dominican Republic. Sosúa has become a popular vacation site for German male sex tourists. Poor Dominican women are drawn into Sosúa's sex trade and new migration patterns are set in motion. Dominican women migrate from through-out the Dominican Republic to work in Sosúa's sex trade where they hope to meet and to marry German men who will sponsor their migration to Germany. And, some German tourists and sex tourists fall in love with living in a Caribbean "paradise" and move to Sosúa permanently. With a large German population living in Sosúa, and a constant flow of European tourists, Sosúa has become a transnational sexual meeting ground, a "sexscape" of sorts, for two groups of individuals between whom there is a vast disparity in power.[1] One group consists of white, working class, and lower-middle and middle class males who have the resources to travel internationally or even to move permanently overseas if they want, while the other group consists predominantly of black, poor, single mothers who have limited resources and face innumerable constraints to legal migration off the island. A wide range of encounters mark their relationships. Some begin and end in less than an hour, while a few relationships become more long term as women migrate to Germany to live with their clients-turned-boyfriends/husbands.

In order to understand how Dominican sex workers and German tourists imagine each other, as well as their respective "home" countries, I explore the various cultural representations and gossip each group consumes and produces about the other. These depictions fuel their imaginations, and in some cases, initiate their migrations to one another's countries. Assumptions based on race, gender, class, and nationality are present in both sex tourists' and sex workers' descriptions of one another. By looking at the growth of transnational social fields that connect Sosúa and Germany, and the flights of imagination and fantasy that flourish in this transnational context, I hope to expand the current understanding of the concept of "transnational" and the ways in which gender, race, and nationality are mutually constituted within transnational contexts. We shall see that Afro-Caribbean Dominican women, both on the island and in Europe, increasingly are associated with the sex trade.

Fantasy clearly plays a large role in sex tourism. But the male sex tourists are not the only ones who travel to Sosúa to fulfill fantasies. Fantasy also plays a role in the experiences of Dominican women. Many women look to these relationships to provide not only much needed money but also possibly marriage, visas, and greater gender equity in the household. They might also hope for romance and love, but their fantasies are generally about resources and an easier life, rather than romantic bliss. However, even with these kinds of expectations, there are few "happy endings." Nanci,[2] for example, returned to Sosúa after living in Germany with her German husband, unhappy and empty-pocketed. She was living hand to mouth, yet this time supporting one more child, a little girl she had with her German husband. Nanci's story is a poignant example of the economic and emotional roller-coaster ride that many of these women experience. The few instances of migration of sex workers to

Germany as the girlfriends or wives of German tourists continue to propel the fantasy that anything can happen, even though the few cases of actual migration that were known to the sex work community ended in reversal of fortune.

## METHODOLOGY AND OVERVIEW OF SOCIO-ECONOMIC CHARACTERISTICS OF SEX WORKERS IN SOSÚA

This chapter draws from field research I conducted while living in Sosúa in the summer of 1993, 1994–1995, and the summers of 1999 and 2003, all of which form the basis of a book: *What's Love Got to Do with It? Transnational Desires and Sex Tourism in Sosúa, the Dominican Republic* (Brennan 2004). My first encounters with Sosúa's sex work community were through a Dominican nongovernmental organization, CEPROSH, which conducts peer to peer HIV-prevention workshops as well as other empowerment-based workshops on women's health. I accompanied *Mensajeras de Salud* (health messengers)—who were sex workers and former sex workers—when they gave presentations to women living in bars and boarding houses. While making the daily rounds with the health messengers, I had the opportunity to speak informally with hundreds of sex workers. I also closely followed the lives of fifty sex workers who lived in a variety of bars, boarding houses, and rented apartments, and I interviewed them, with a tape recorder rolling, as many times as possible. I selected these women to represent a range of living and working arrangements available to sex workers in Sosúa. I continue to keep in touch with some of these women through phone and e-mail.

Once women migrate to Sosúa to sell sex, they choose between working with foreign tourists or local Dominicans. This choice determines the amount of money they make, the number of hours they work, their degree of independence, and where they live. In fact, it is easy to identify sex workers' client base by their living arrangements. If women live at a bar, they work with Dominican clients and must follow the rules set by the bar owner. If they live on their own, either renting a room in a boarding house or renting an apartment or house (essentially shanties), they work with foreign clients. Because of the difference in the amount of independence each group exercises, particularly over their schedule, I call the two groups the "dependents" and the "independents." This chapter is about the "independents"—women who live either in boarding houses or rent private dwellings, and go to the tourist bars according to their own schedules to sell sex to foreign men. Also, I interviewed women whose rental apartments (and small houses) ranged in price.

Of the fifty women I interviewed, only two women were not mothers. (One of them was only fourteen years old, and the other woman was infertile.) The women ranged in skin color, but only a few identified themselves as *negra* (black), a term typically reserved for Haitians (del Castillo and Murphy 1986; Torres-Saillant 1995, 1999). Rather, they described themselves using a variety of terms, such as *morena, india,* and *india clara.*[3] Most were between 17 and 28 years old. The practice of consensual unions (of not marrying formally but of living together) that often organizes household dynamics for the poor in the Dominican Republic, also led to single motherhood and significant financial pressures for the women I met. Typically, these women receive no financial assistance from their children's fathers. I rarely met sex workers in Sosúa who had sold sex before migrating to Sosúa's sex trade, and, I believe their status as single mothers is the most decisive factor in their entrance into the sex trade. Often women migrated to Sosúa within days of their "husbands" (in consensual unions) departure from the household and their abandonment of their financial obligations to their children. Within a few months or maybe a year, most leave Sosúa as poor as when they first arrived, only to be replaced by another cohort of women.

Women who migrate to Sosúa to sell sex make the choice to try to earn more money—more quickly—than they can in any other legal job available to poor women with a limited education level (most have not finished school past their early teens), skill base, and social networks. These women come from *los pobres,* the poorest class in the Dominican Republic, and simply do not have the social networks to land work, such as office jobs, that offer security or mobility. Rather, they fall back on their own female-based social networks to find factory jobs, domestic work, or restaurant jobs. These same female-based social networks supply Sosúa's sex trade. Women often follow the advice of a cousin or neighbor that in Sosúa they can earn more money than in other jobs, and work fewer hours.

Also important for understanding these women's opportunities for economic and social mobility is the fact that they do not have immediate family members living abroad—particularly in New York, the primary migration destination for Dominicans. Without family members abroad, these women receive no support from remittances that sustain many families in the Dominican Republic. In addition, without relatives abroad, they cannot migrate legally through family sponsorship and have greater difficulty obtaining the visitor visas that would enable them to leave the country. Consequently, they turn to Germany as a new migration circuit and sex tourism as a way to enter it.

## SOSÚA AS A TRANSNATIONAL SPACE

The presence of "foreigners" in Sosúa and their ties off the island are not new. As a banana plantation for the United Fruit Company in the early part of the century, and as a safe haven for European Jews fleeing persecution in 1941, Sosúa for some time has been an economic, social, and cultural crossroads between the local and the foreign. The town has emerged not only as a place of fantasy for European male sex tourists, and Dominican female sex workers, but also for a variety of Dominicans who hope to find jobs in the tourist economy. Dominicans migrate from throughout the country to cash in on the tourist boom. They bank on the myth of endless opportunity in tourist spaces where vacationers spend their money. I suggest that Sosúa's "opportunity myth," which is tied up with its history as a transnational space, inspires a diverse group of individuals to believe that in this space they will realize their fantasies. The imagining of alternative lives, often fueled by the global circulation of media images (Appadurai 1991), spurs many Dominicans and foreigners to leave their current lives, either temporarily or permanently. While Dominicans come to Sosúa in search of money, often dreaming of striking it rich off the tourist trade, foreigners come for a beach vacation, to buy sex, or to start a new life in "paradise." Both groups are living out dreams they believe they can fulfill in Sosúa.

The intensity of transnational interactions has increased so dramatically with tourism that Dominicans envision the town as lying outside the authentic Dominican Republic. Time and time again I heard that Sosúa is not the "real" Dominican Republic, and Dominican friends urged me to visit towns in the countryside to see "true" Dominican culture. James Clifford could be describing Sosúa when he writes about "contact zones," those "transgressive intercultural frontiers," where "stasis and purity are asserted . . . against historical forces of movement and contamination" (Clifford 1997: 7). Therefore, when young women move to Sosúa to enter into sex work, they are able to see themselves as taking the first step toward entering another country with more and greater possibilities.

## AGENCY AND THE SEX TRADE

Sosúa's sex trade is not simply a story of women who use sex work as a survival strategy, but also of women who try to use sex work *in Sosúa* as an advancement strategy. Marriage and migration are the key components of this strategy. These women see Sosúa's sex trade and marriage to foreign tourists as a fast track to economic success—a way not just to solve short-term economic problems, but to change their lives, and their families' lives, through remittances, in the long term. These transnational relationships, sex workers candidly admit, are *por residencia* (for residence/for a green card), not *por amor* (for love). In this distinction, we see a highly strategic and rational element to these women's "fantasies." Without these transnational connections, Sosúa's sex trade would be no different than sex work in any other Dominican town. By migrating to Sosúa, these sex workers are engaged in an economic strategy that is both very familiar and something altogether new. In short, these women try to take advantage of the global linkages that exploit them.

Even though I distinguish between sex work as an advancement or a survival strategy, I do not want to romanticize Dominican women's experiences in the sex trade. Dominican women have limited room to maneuver within the tourist economy and the sex trade. However, I see a great deal of what Ortner calls "intentionality" in these women's use of the sex trade (Ortner 1996).[4] Sosúa's sex trade stands apart from many other sex-tourist destination and offers women a good deal of control over their working conditions. Working essentially as "free-lance" sex workers without paying any middle-men or women, they keep all their earnings, set their hours, and choose their clients. This is not to suggest that they do not risk rape, beatings, and arrest; engaging in sexual labor can be dangerous and Sosúa is no exception. Moreover, despite women's active strategizing to *progesar* (get ahead) through the sex trade, women rarely enjoy lasting economic gains. Through sex workers' accounts of their relationships with German men, which I provide in the next section, we get a sense of just how wildly unpredictable the course of these relationships can be, and find a wide range of instances of dependency and agency.

## DOMINICAN WOMEN'S MIGRATION TO SOSÚA: AS STEPPING STONE TO EUROPE AND A NEW TRANSNATIONAL FIELD

Since I claim that women's use of the sex trade for marriage is motivated primarily by hopes of migration, an economic strategy, it is important to understand the history of migration off the island. The past few decades of Dominican migration to New York and the transnational cultural flows between these two spaces have led many Dominicans to look *outside* the Dominican Republic for solutions to economic problems *inside* Dominican borders.[5] So adept are Dominicans at migrating off the island that Sørensen even calls them "natives" to transnational space (1998). The quest for

a visa, to Canada, the United States, or Europe is virtually a national pastime. Dominican musician, Juan Luis Guerra, captures this preoccupation with *fuera* and the visas necessary to get there, in his hit song "*Visa para un Sueño*" (Visa for a Dream). A variety of legitimate means to get *fuera*, as well as scams, abound. Some are so desperate to get off the island, that they willingly risk their lives in *yolas*, small boats or rafts used to travel to Puerto Rico.

The sex workers I interviewed have no immediate family members abroad, and have never had meaningful transnational resources available to them. Benefits of family members abroad can be considerable. One of Georges' (1990) informants summed up how class and opportunity, outside of the elite, are tied to migration networks to New York: "In the Dominican Republic there are three kinds of people: the rich, the poor, and those who travel to New York." Hanging out in the tourist bars in Sosúa is a better use of time than waiting in line at the US embassy in Santo Domingo.

In light of how difficult it is to migrate off the island, it becomes clear why Dominican migrants in Sosúa work so hard to establish transnational relationships with the tourist population. Their transnational romantic ties act as surrogate family migration networks. Consequently, migration to Sosúa from other parts of the Dominican Republic is both an internal and an international migration. As a transnational space, Sosúa represents a land of opportunity within the Dominican Republic, and a point of departure to other countries. Sex tourism links the two forms of migration in a powerfully gendered and racialized way.

From Sosúa's tourist and sex tourist trade, new "transnational social fields" and migrations emerge (Basch, Glick Schiller, Szanton-Blanc 1994). Even though most of these sex workers actually never will visit, let alone move to Germany, their links to German men through fax, phone, money wires, and return vacations to Sosúa, create new transnational social fields as German businesses, recreational, and personal networks tie Germany and Sosúa together. These networks encompass Dominican women. To understand the long-term implications of the incorporation of Dominican women within German transnational networks, scholars need to rethink their conceptualization of the scope of transnational relationships. First of all, we must acknowledge that persons who do not themselves move across borders can become incorporated within transnational social networks and live within a transnational social field. Second, we must address the issue of differential power held by the various actors within the transnational social field, a power delimited not just by differences in class, gender, and race, but also by the relative power of the states in which they hold citizenship rights.

Larger transnational processes and the globalization of capitalism have enabled the rapid growth of sex tourism in Sosúa. Also important are the differential privileges that citizenship in various states confers. German citizenship, and its accompanying benefits in the global economy, facilitate unimpeded travel and tourism, as well as migration and resettlement. Germans face no barriers in establishing homes or businesses in the Dominican Republic and moving back and forth between Germany and the Dominican Republic, if they resettle. And, German sex tourists travel with ease, since there are no visa requirements to enter the Dominican Republic. They hold much more economic power than the Dominican women from whom they buy sex.

To differentiate the freedom of persons from certain powerful states to travel and establish transnational social fields from the restrictive access to travel or migration of persons from weak impoverished states, I expand the use of the term transnationalism from above and below popularized by Smith and Guarnizo (1998).[6] I see Dominican women's creative use of the sex trade, with its intimate access to German citizens, as an example of transnational strategizing "from below."

## RELATIONSHIPS WITH GERMAN MEN

If the imagination of what "might be" plays an important role in how these women and men fantasize about one another, and one another's respective "home" countries, how do these relationships play out both in Sosúa and in Germany? Each group imagines the other as the opposite of the racialized sexual, romantic, or economic partners they meet in their home countries. Dominican sex workers try to establish ongoing transnational relationships with foreign men by exchanging phone numbers, and encouraging them to return again to Sosúa. They might mention that they need money for their children and remind them of the Western Union in town. And for those who have been dating over time, they may ask the men to put plans in motion for the women to visit Germany with a tourist visa.

All of these practices reveal sex workers' creative strategizing; but hinge on the men fulfilling their promises. These women labor try to take advantage (to the extent that they can) of the men—and their citizenship—who are in Sosúa to take advantage of them. The women are at once independent and dependent, and exploited and strategic. Here gender and race become central organizing factors of these women's migration to Germany. Keenly aware of German men's eroticization of Afro-Caribbean women (as indicated in sex workers'

narratives below), Dominican sex workers capitalize on their gender and race by using the sex trade as a way to the leave the island.

They also seek to establish relationships with these foreign men in reaction to Dominican machismo. They hope that German husbands will be more reliable financial providers than the Dominican men who have let them down. Yet, sex workers often assign characteristics to foreign men that are unmerited and unrealistic. For example, as I describe in the story below, it was only toward the end of Elena's relationship with a German man, Jürgen, when his drinking was so obviously out of control, that her friends finally admitted that, like the Dominican men they constantly criticized, Jürgen was trouble.

### Elena: Living with a German Man in Sosúa

Elena, a 22-year old sex worker, initially had migrated to Sosúa's sex trade after the father of her baby girl left her. She followed her older sister who, at the time, was working in the sex trade. Elena ended up being the main breadwinner for her extended family. She brought remittances back home to pay her parents' monthly *colmado* (small grocer) bill and she eventually became the surrogate mother for two younger sisters, a step-sister, and a younger sex worker who came to rely on Elena. All these girls, plus Elena and her daughter, lived in a one-room shack, rotating between sharing the bed and sleeping on the floor. Elena stood out in the community of sex workers because, along with being kind and generous, she was a leader to whom other women turned for all kinds of advice. It was little surprise to her friends, that she, literate and savvy, turned a long-distance relationship with a middle-aged German man, into, what many of them called a "marriage." After returning several times to Sosúa to spend time with Elena, Jürgen decided to move to Sosúa. He would return to Germany only several months out of the year to supervise his industrial construction company, and earn enough money to support him the rest of the year in his new Caribbean lifestyle.

To Elena and her friends, it appeared she was living out many sex workers' fantasy of quitting sex work and setting up house with a German man. Elena's older sisters and her friends envied the two-bedroom apartment with running water, electricity, and a full kitchen into which she, Jürgen, and all of her dependents (her daughter, and three younger sisters and step-sister) moved. But her actual relationship with Jürgen was far from ideal. Soon after Jürgen moved to town, Elena found out she was pregnant. At first, he was helpful around the house and doted on Elena. But, the novelty eventually wore off and he returned to his routine of spending most days drinking in the German-owned bar beneath their apartment. He also went out drinking every night with German friends. Most of the time he was drunk, and Elena saw him less and less frequently. What's more, their relationship reproduced traditional Dominican gender roles. He did not treat her any better than the previous Dominican men in her life. They constantly fought over money, which he tightly controlled. Since they were living together, and Jürgen was paying the bills (including tuition for her daughter to attend a private school), Elena considered them to be married. As her "husband" (in a consensual union), Elena saw Jürgen as financially responsible for the household, a role which she Elena perceived he was not fulfilling. She asked "Why isn't he giving me any money? He is my *esposo* (husband) and is supposed to give me money. I need to know if he is with me or someone else. He pays for this house and paid for everything here. I need to know what is going on."

They fought so regularly that Elena started sleeping permanently on the couch. One day, without warning, Jürgen packed his bags and left for Germany for business. He paid the rent for the apartment for a couple of months before he left. However, Elena had no cash flow into the household. In Jürgen's absence, Elena took her daughter out of the private school, and she started working at a small Dominican-owned restaurant. When Jürgen returned a couple of months later, they split up for good. She and her family returned to living in a shack without running water or electricity. She had not accumulated any savings or items she could pawn during her time with Jürgen and when they vacated their apartment, he took most of the furniture, and the TV, with him.

In many ways, Elena was better off—financially and emotionally—before she met Jürgen. Even though she was living out many sex workers' fantasies of "marrying" a foreign tourist, she now lives like many poor Dominicans, struggling day to day without access to the resources necessary to build long-term security. While she appeared to have all the trappings of many sex workers' fantasies of "marrying" a foreign tourist, she ended up living in the same conditions of poverty as before. Although sex workers take on great risks and occupy a stigmatized status in Dominican society, Elena's status as the "wife" of a German sex tourist-turned-resident brought no long-term gains. And, despite other sex workers' aspirations to achieve what Elena had, Elena's relationship with a foreign man replicated many of the failings of Dominican men that sex workers so often decry. Jürgen turned out to be a volatile alcoholic who slept with other women, thus putting Elena (since they did not use condoms), and possibly her baby, at risk for AIDS. And, soon after he returned to Sosúa, Jürgen set up house with another sex worker. He now lives, Elena hears, somewhere in Asia.

Underlying Elena's experience with Jürgen is another important question, the degree to which the sex workers' fantasies and realities of German men are shaped by the fact that the women are themselves migrants, having left their home to seek their future in Sosúa. The mobility strategy of the Dominican women who migrate to become sex workers in Sosúa changes their life, not only by bringing them into a transnational social field, but also through the experiences of migration and wage work. Both migration and wage work can have an impact on gender roles and on the expectations which women place upon men. Research on women-and-work questions whether wage labor increases women's authority in the household, while studies on women-and-migration reveal that the experience of living in a new country, combined with wage labor, often gives women greater social and economic independence and status (Hirsch 2003; Kibria 1993; Pessar 1984; Safa 1995). The lives of the Dominican women I studied highlight the complexities of these questions because these women often begin migration as heads of households, their migration spurred by the financial burden of supporting themselves and their children. Dominican women's internal migration for the sex trade is a complex social terrain in which gender roles are both reaffirmed and reconfigured (Hondagneu-Sotelo 1994; Mahler and Pessar 2001; Pessar 1999). Thus, the question arises, how do these women's experiences and responsibilities as female heads of household inform the way they seek authority in their future relationships—with foreign or Dominican men? Although the sex trade allows women to out-earn Dominican male migrants in Sosúa, they have little similar potential source of authority or independence in their relationships with foreign men.

### Nanci: Falling in Love

Whereas most sex workers explain their transnational relationships in terms of strategic economic imperatives, Nanci, recounted a love story. "This is completely for love," she gushed. Frank was a German man close to her age (she was 23 and he, 28). He spoke Spanish, and got along well with her three-year-old son. He bought her a plane ticket and helped her get a tourist visa so she could visit him in Germany for a month. When she returned, she showed me pictures of her visit to Germany, including pictures of Frank's parents and their middle-class home. Since Frank and Nanci agreed never to tell his family or friends that she had been a sex worker, the family did not know about her past. But since they decided to marry and made plans for Nanci to move to Germany with her son, she was fearful that they could find out. A former coworker of Nanci's, Rosa, lived thirty miles away from Frank's family with a German man she also met in Sosúa's sex trade. Nanci worried: "Rosa's mother-in-law knows what Rosa did in Sosúa. And she knows I'm a friend of Rosa's. What if she ever said anything to Frank's parents?" Nanci's ties to Sosúa put a new twist on the importance of social networks in the migration process. The nascent networks linking Sosúan sex workers to towns in Germany act as both sources of support and concern for sex workers-turned-migrants. In many instances, women believe that struggling in isolation in their new European settings is preferable to being found out.

After marrying and living in Germany for a year, the two of them moved to Sosúa, where they had a little girl together. But, soon after moving to Sosúa, Frank ran off with another sex worker. He stopped all financial support to Nanci and her children. Even though Nanci went to a lawyer and got Frank to pay child support for one month, there is little Nanci can do since Frank and this other woman are now living in Germany. Nanci simply does not have the resources to pursue child support from the Dominican Republic while Frank remains in Germany. Like Elena, Nanci has experienced a reversal of fortune. She and her two children are living in a two-room shack in Sosúa in much worse conditions than when I first met her, before she married Frank.

Because migrating to Germany is a relatively new phenomenon, not many former sex workers like Nanci have returned to Sosúa to dispel the myths and gossip of an easy and fantasy-filled life *allá* (over there). Instead, women imagine lives of material comfort—possibly excess—for themselves and their children. Stories of women who are living out this fantasy, circulate among sex workers like Dominicanized versions of the movie *Pretty Woman*. Sosúa and its tourists represent an escape. Sex workers, of course, hope for romance and love, and maybe even more help in the household than with Dominican partners, but none of this is truly expected and thus not prioritized. Rather, there is an expected trade-off of love and romance for financial security and mobility. After all, these relationships are for *residencia* (visas), not for *amor* (love). In Sosúa's economy of desire, why waste a marriage certificate on romantic love, when marriage can be parlayed into a visa?

## IMAGINING DOMINICAN WOMEN: DESIRING THE SEXUALIZED OTHER

Just as Dominican women look to German men to be better providers than Dominican men, German men, too, compare Dominican women to German women. They imagine Dominican women as more sexual, more compliant, and having fewer commodity needs and desires. In fact, as Dominican women hope (but do not expect) German men to break with traditional assumptions about gender roles, German men expect Dominican women to adhere to very traditional—and regressive—understandings of gender roles. And race plays a central role in how the white German sex tourists imagine Afro-Dominican sex workers.

In examining desire in colonial Southeast Asia, Stoler looks at the myths of the sexualized other in colonial texts, commenting that ". . . colonialism was that quintessential project in which desire was always about sex" and that "sex was always about racial power, and that both were contingent upon a particular representation of nonwhite women's bodies" (Stoler 1997: 43). In sex tourism, we are well familiar with first-world travelers/consumers seeking exoticized, racialized "native" bodies, in the developing world for cut-rate prices. These two components—race and its associated stereotypes and expectations, and the economic disparities between the developed and developing worlds—characterize sex-tourist destinations throughout the world.[7]

Through news articles and sex-tourism websites, there has been an ever-increasing association—both on the island and in Europe—between the sex trade and Dominican women. This association has worried Dominican women who *never have been* sex workers that the families and friends of their German boyfriends/spouses might wonder if they *had been* sex workers. And, since Dominican women's participation in the overseas sex trade has received so much press coverage in the Dominican Republic, women's experiences living or working in Europe are suspect. "I know when I tell people I was really with a folk dance group in Europe, they don't believe me," a former dancer worried. Often, in casual conversations with shop owners or friends (who were not sex workers), when Sosúans spoke of a woman working overseas as a domestic, waitress, or dancer, they inevitably would raise the possibility of sex work, or, explicitly rule it out, by vouching for the authenticity of a particular woman's version of events abroad. One Dominican café owner cynically explains why everyone assumes that Dominican women working overseas must be in, or have been in, the sex trade: "Dominican women have become known throughout the world as prostitutes. They are one of our biggest exports." Elena's German "husband," Jürgen, also comments on this association, "Everyone in Germany knows about the Dominican Republic, you know, like Thailand."

## CONCLUSION: TRANSNATIONALISM FROM ABOVE AND BELOW

Dominican women choose to migrate for sex work in Sosúa, as opposed to participating in sex work in other towns, based on their hopes of what "might be." Even though the imagination allows individuals throughout the world "to consider a wider set of 'possible' lives than they ever did before" (Appadurai 1991: 197), whether or not these fantasy lives are attainable depends on who is doing the imagining and where. The "local" becomes central to discussions about the "global." Transnational practices, such as e-mailing a German client or receiving money wires, are "embedded in specific social relations established between specific people, situated in unequivocal localities. . . ." (Smith and Guarnizo 1998: 11). Sex workers' experiences in Sosúa demonstrate that local social and economic realities inevitably override the power of the imagination. Fantasy images might draw a woman to Sosúa to sell sex, but her choices and experiences there depend on her class, gender, race, and nationality.

Transnational spaces not only are sites of new economic, cultural, and sexual possibilities but also are locations which can reproduce existing inequalities. In sites such as Sosúa, there is opportunity for transnational practices from "below," but they are often trumped by those from "above." Sex workers in Sosúa might exercise some control over their conditions of work, and might try to use the sex trade as a strategy of advancement, but their decisions and actions constantly collide with those of sex tourists. As one savvy sex worker, Ani, describes, sex workers (and other Dominican migrants hopeful of striking it rich off the tourist boom) who come to Sosúa often end up disillusioned. "They hear they can make money, and meet a gringo, so they come to Sosúa. Some of the women enter sex work, because they want it all so fast. They come with their big dreams. But then they find out it is all a lie."

Now that we have seen how both groups—tourists/ sex tourists and sex workers—imagine one another, I want to look beyond the obvious class and racial differences between these two groups of migrants. Connections are rarely made between these two kinds of migration—one by a group whose members have an opportunity to live well in their own country, and the other by a group whose members have limited opportunities. German men's and Dominican women's motivations to migrate to one another's countries are indeed quite distinct. However, both migrations result from global flows and rely upon specific transnational practices and technologies. German migration to the Dominican Republic, and Dominican sex workers' strategies to migrate to Germany, both epitomize globalized flows of people, culture, and most importantly in these cases, fantasy. The new migration circuits and cultural and economic loops that have emerged between Germany and Sosúa expand conceptualizations of transnationalism, while at the same time, they once again reveal the inequities—particularly those based

on race, gender, and nationality—that transnational processes rely on, reproduce, and challenge.

Yet there are also many clear differences between these two migrations. Whereas Dominican sex workers cannot travel or move to Germany without help securing visas or paying for airline tickets, German tourists/sex tourists are a privileged group that travels without visas, and can use vacations as a time to shop for girlfriends/brides. Clearly, this "bride shopping" as a transnational practice offers nothing liberating but rather grows out of an exploitative and regressive impulse to find women who might not try to negotiate for any kind of authority in the household. "Asymmetries of domination, inequality, racism, sexism, class conflict and uneven development in which transnational practices are embedded and which they sometimes even perpetuate" (Smith and Guarnizo 1998: 6) are clearly present in tourism, sex tourism, and the "bride shopping" that might develop while on vacation in Sosúa.

Ann Stoler asks how sex in both colonial and postcolonial contexts has been used as a "vehicle to master a practical world" (Stoler 1997: 43–44). Dominican women's strategizing within Sosúa's sex trade can result in German clients' paying for sex workers' children's education (as Jürgen did for Elena's daughter), or into helping sex workers get a fledgling business off the ground (such as a clothing store or hair salon). Yet, since any use of sex between black local women and white foreign men in a postcolonial context is a "crucial transfer point of power, tangled with racial exclusions in complicated ways" (Stoler 1997: 44 on Fanon 1967: 63), today's sex trade is inextricably linked with a violent colonial history for Hispaniola's women. In the relationships between sex tourists and sex workers, there are similarities to the relationships between the colonizer and the colonized. I do not mean to suggest that Dominican sex workers are simply "enslaved and colonized," but rather call attention to the fraught racialized components of women's sexual labor in the Caribbean.

Dominican sex workers use Sosúa's sex trade strategically as they actively try to transform their brief encounters with European clients into marriage proposals and visa sponsorships. However, despite their strategizing, a recurring story seems to unfold: most sex workers in Sosúa end up just getting by, rather than improving their children's futures as they hoped. They might see Sosúa and its tourists as a gateway to a better life, but they are still constrained by their status as poor women who engage in a highly dangerous and illegal profession. The failure of the majority of Dominican sex workers to leave Sosúa with foreign husbands or fattened bank accounts, underscores that within this economy of desire, some dreams are realized, while others prove hollow. White, middle-class and lower-middle class European visitors and residents are much better positioned to secure from "above" what they want in Sosúa than poor, Afro-Dominican sex workers and other Dominican migrants who are likely to be disillusioned by Sosúa, tourism, and tourists.

## NOTES

1. "Sexscape" builds on the five terms Arjun Appadurai coined to describe global cultural flows: ethnoscape, mediascape, technoscape, finanscape, and ideoscape (1990: 6–7). I use the term to refer to the spaces to which individuals travel to buy sex. These spaces depend on differences in power between the buyers (sex tourists) and the sellers (sex workers).
2. I have changed all names of sex workers and clients.
3. Torres-Saillant comments on Dominicans' downplaying of their African descent, even though, as he writes, "Blacks and mulattos make up nearly 90 percent of the contemporary Dominican population. . . . No other country in the hemisphere exhibits greater indeterminacy regarding the population's sense of racial identity . . . Some commentators would contend, in effect, that Dominicans have, for the most part, denied their blackness" (Torres-Saillant 1995: 126).
4. This sense of agency, of choice, presents an important counter-example to depictions of sex workers as powerless victims of violence and exploitation. McClintock warns against conflating agency with context in discussions about sex work, "Depicting all sex workers as slaves only travesties the myriad, different experiences of sex workers around the world. At the same time, it theoretically confuses social *agency* and identity with social *context*" (1993).
5. Two important studies document Dominican migration to New York, *Between Two Islands* (Grasmuck and Pessar 1991) and *The Making of a Transnational Community* (Georges* 1990). They shed light on Dominican migration strategies and transnational ties which link Dominican sending communities to New York as a "response and resistance" to the Dominican Republic's integration into the global economy (Basch, Glick Schiller, Szanton-Blanc 1994). This response is informed by ideologies that view New York, Germany, and other places off the island as spaces where individuals are more likely to make economic gains than within the Dominican Republic.
6. They distinguished between the transactional interactions and strategies of political leaders—transnationalism "from above"—and the mundane border crossing and personal and familial interactions of impoverished people. This latter set of processes Smith and Guarnizo dubbed transnationalism "from below."
7. O'Connell Davidson observes similar racialized fantasies in Cuba's sex trade. She describes the white-skinned sex tourists as "fascinated by black sexuality, which is

imagined to be 'untamed' and 'primitive' and therefore more uninhibited, exciting and abandoned than white sexuality" (1996: 46).

## REFERENCES

Appadurai, Arjun. 1990. "Disjuncture and Difference in the Global Cultural Economy." *Public Culture* 2(2): 1–24.

_____. 1991. "Global Ethnoscapes: Notes and Queries for a Transnational Anthropology." In Richard Fox (ed.). *Recapturing Anthropology: Working in the Present*, pp. 191–210. Santa Fe, NM: School of American Research Press.

Basch, Linda, Nina Glick Schiller, and Cristina Szanton-Blanc. 1994. *Nations Unbound: Transnational Projects, Postcolonial Predicaments and Deterritorialized Nation-States.* Langhorne, PA: Gordon and Breach Science Publishers.

Brennan, Denise. 2004. *What's Love Got to Do with It? Transnational Desires and Sex Tourism in Sosúa, the Dominican Republic.* Durham, NC: Duke University Press.

Clifford, James. 1997. *Routes: Travel and Translation in the Late Twentieth Century.* Cambridge, MA: Harvard University Press.

del Castillo, José, and Martin F. Murphy. 1986. "Migration, National Identity and Cultural Policy in the Dominican Republic." *Journal of Ethnic Studies* 15(3): 49–70.

Fanon, Frantz. 1967. *Black Skin, White Masks.* New York: Grove Press.

Georges, Eugenia. 1990. *The Making of a Transnational Community: Migration, Development and Cultural Change in the Dominican Republic.* New York: Columbia University Press.

Grasmuck, Sherri, and Patricia R. Pessar. 1991. *Between Two Islands: Dominican International Migration.* Berkeley: University of California Press.

Hirsch, Jennifer S. 2003. *A Courtship after Marriage: Sexuality and Love in Mexican Transnational Families.* Berkeley: University of California Press.

Hondagneu-Sotelo, Pierrette. 1994. *Gendered Transitions: Mexican Experiences of Immigration.* Berkeley: University of California Press.

Kibria, Nazli. 1993. *Family Tightrope: The Changing Lives of Vietnamese Americans.* Princeton, NJ: Princeton University Press.

Mahler, Sarah J., and Patricia R. Pessar. 2001. "Gendered Geographies of Power: Analyzing Gender across Transnational Spaces." *Identities* 7(4): 441–59.

McClintock, Anne. 1993. "Sex Workers and Sex Work: An Introduction." *Social Text* 11(4): 1–10.

O'Connell Davidson, Julia. 1996. "Sex Tourism in Cuba." *Race and Class* 38(1): 39–48.

Ortner, Sherry. 1996. *Making Gender: The Politics and Erotics of Culture.* Boston: Beacon Press.

Pessar, Patricia R. 1984. "The Linkage between the Household and Workplace of Dominican Women in the U.S." *International Migration Review* 18(4): 1188–1211.

_____. 1999. "The Role of Gender, Households and Social Networks in the Migration Process: A Review and Appraisal." In Charles Hirschman, Philip Kasinitz, and Josh DeWind (eds.). *The Handbook of International Migration:*

*The American Experience*, pp. 53–70. New York: Russell Sage Foundation.

Safa, Helen I. 1995. *The Myth of the Male Breadwinner: Women and Industrialization in the Caribbean.* Boulder, CO: Westview Press.

Smith, Michael P., and Luis Eduardo Guarnizo. 1998. "The Locations of Transnationalism." In Michael P. Smith and Luis E. Guarnizo (eds.). *Transnationalism from Below*, pp. 3–34. Vol. 6. Comparative Urban and Community Research series. New Brunswick, NJ: Transaction Publishers.

Sørensen, Ninna Nyberg. 1998. "Narrating Identity across Dominican Worlds." In Michael P. Smith and Luis E. Guarnizo (eds.). *Transnationalism from Below*, pp. 241–269. Vol. 6. Comparative Urban and Community Research series. New Brunswick, NJ: Transaction Publishers.

Stoler, Ann Laura. 1997. "Educating Desire in Colonial Southeast Asia: Foucault, Freud and Imperial Sexualities." In Lenore Manderson and Margaret Jolly (eds.). *Sites of Desire, Economies of Pleasure*, pp. 27–47. Chicago: University of Chicago Press.

Torres-Saillant, Silvio. 1995. "The Dominican Republic." In *No Longer Invisible: Afro-Latin Americans Today*, pp. 109–138. London: M. R. Group.

_____. 1999. *Introduction to Dominican Blackness.* New York: CUNY Dominican Studies Institute.

Torres-Saillant, Silvio, and Ramona Hernández. 1998. *The Dominican Americans.* Westport, CT: Greenwood Press.